Late in November 1987, the FASB issued its final pronouncement on the statement of cash flows (*Statement of Financial Accounting Standards No. 95*). The final pronouncement differs from the Exposure Draft in several ways. For example, in the final pronouncement the Board encourages use of the direct method, defines cash equivalents much more restrictively to exclude many short-term liquid investments, and requires that noncash investing and financing activities be excluded from the statement of cash flows.

We are pleased to report that Chapter 18 of this edition provides complete coverage of the final pronouncement.

Fundamental Accounting Principles

Fundamental Accounting Principles

Statement of Cash Flows Edition

Kermit D. Larson   The University of Texas at Austin

William W. Pyle

Eleventh Edition   1988

IRWIN Homewood, Illinois 60430

The Robert N. Anthony / Willard J. Graham Series in Accounting

ISBN 0-256-06823-2

Library of Congress Catalog Card No. 88–80215

Printed in the United States of America

2 3 4 5 6 7 8 9 0 **VHVH** 5 4 3 2 1 0 9 8

Acquisitions editor: Frank S. Burrows, Jr.
Project editor: Ethel Shiell
Production manager: Irene H. Sotiroff
Designer: James Buddenbaum
Compositor: Arcata Graphics/Kingsport
Typeface: 10/12 Baskerville
Printer: Arcata Graphics/Kingsport

Photo Credits

Cover
Woodfin Camp and Associates
Bill Ross, Houston

Part One
Woodfin Camp and Associates
Fred Mayer, Atlanta

Part Two
The Stock Market
Allen Lee Page

Part Three
West Light
Bill Ross, San Diego

Part Four
The Stock Market
Bob Shaw, Dallas

Part Five
West Light
Gene Stein

Part Six
Woodfin Camp and Associates
Robert Frerck, Chicago

Part Seven
West Light
Richard Fukuhara

Part Eight
The Image Bank
Cary Cralle, Toronto

Appendix A
Woodfin Camp and Associates
Bill Ross, Houston

Appendix B
Courtesy of CBS, Inc.

Preface

Fundamental Accounting Principles and its companion materials are intended to be a complete learning system for use in the first year-long accounting course at the college and university level. The students in this course have varied backgrounds and educational goals. In fact, this course provides many students with their first educational exposure to such business topics as alternative forms of business organization, typical business practices, financial statements, financial analysis, and legal instruments such as notes, bonds, and stocks. Objectives of this course generally include: (1) developing a general understanding of financial reports and analyses that students will be able to use in their personal affairs regardless of their fields of specialization, (2) introducing students to managerial decision processes and the use of accounting information by the managers of a business, (3) providing a strong foundation for subsequent courses in business and finance, and (4) initiating the coursework leading to a career in accounting. Fundamental Accounting Principles serves all of these objectives.

A hallmark of Fundamental Accounting Principles is the careful integration of conceptual principles and their applications to specific business situations. Throughout the book, the definitions and explanations of important concepts and principles are presented in close proximity to illustrations and practical applications of those concepts and principles. As a result, students do not need to hold abstract concepts in limbo before they see how the concepts are applied.

In studying the book, students learn how accounting data are accumulated, how the resulting reports and analyses are prepared, and how to interpret and use accounting information intelligently and effectively. The concepts and principles that guide the preparation of accounting information are persistently emphasized and explained so that students will be able to generalize and apply their knowledge to a variety of new situations.

New Features and Important Changes in the 11th Edition

In this revision, the broad objectives were to: (1) dramatically expand the range and quantity of assignment material; (2) make coverage more exciting, up-to-date, and rigorous while retaining the book's tradition of exceptional readability; (3) incorporate several important new areas of topical coverage; and (4) supplement the package with more examination material, more complete solutions to problems, and more computer-based learning aids for student use. Extraordinary measures have been taken to avoid errors in the text and in all supplementary materials. We believe students will find the book interesting to read and highly understandable. Instructors will find it rigorous, comprehensive, and flexible.

Many important new features have been introduced in the 11th edition. Some of the more significant include the following:

Many New Problem Assignments   One of the most noticeable changes is a dramatic increase in the number of exercises and problems at the end of each chapter. The number of exercises alone has been increased by more than 76 percent. In all, there are approximately 170 new and varied problem assignments. This greatly accelerates a trend that was initiated in the previous edition as a direct result of adopters' requests. The result is a much more diverse set of assignment materials.

Complete Revision of Assignment Materials   All of the exercises, problems, and provocative problems have been newly revised, and the number of questions for class discussion has been substantially increased.

Expanded Chapter Glossaries with Improved Definitions   Many adopters report that they are focusing increased attention on the definition of important concepts and terms. In response to this emphasis, over 50 important new terms have been added to the chapter glossaries, and a large number of the definitions have been carefully rewritten to clarify the conceptual essence of the terms. The glossaries now contain well over 500 definitions. As in the past, the glossaries are located at the end of each chapter so that students can easily locate the definitions that are relevant to their chapter-by-chapter review before examinations. Furthermore, in the index at the end of the book, each glossary term is listed and highlighted in color with appropriate page references.

More Supporting Calculations in the Solutions Manuals   The additional length of the Solutions Manuals for the 11th edition is only partially due to the expansion of assignment material. In response to adopters' requests, the solutions now include many more supporting calculations.

New, Real-World Illustrations and Problems   This edition reflects a substantially increased use of real company financial information in illustrations and particularly in the provocative problems. For example, factual data has been drawn from the annual reports of such companies as Adolph Coors, Black and Decker, CBS, Apple Computer, Chrysler, Time, and Crown Cork & Seal.

Expanded Coverage of Computers in Accounting   In at least six different chapters, greater attention is given to the role of computers in accounting. For example, (a) a new section discusses the effect of computers on internal control, (b) the discussion of cash controls explains the direct linkage of cash registers with computers, (c) the section on control of plant assets was rewritten to be consistent with computerized accounting systems, and (d) the effective use of computerized systems in obtaining departmental information is described.

New Computer Supplements for Students In addition to revised versions of the KC's Deals on Wheels and Lite Flight supplements, the 11th edition's computer-based supplements for students include a new corporate practice set (Kellogg Business Systems, Inc.) that may be assigned after Chapter 20, two examination review and study guides, and two software packages for solving selected problems from the text.

Examination Exercises on the Computer Test Bank The number of true/false and multiple choice questions in the computer bank of examination questions has been expanded. In addition, the bank now includes a large number of exercise-type problems.

Expanded Discussion of Internal Control In Chapter 7 the discussion of internal control principles and procedures has been expanded. Also, the importance of internal control is emphasized in several chapters.

New Illustrations of Modern Bank Statements The reconciliation of bank statements is now based on up-to-date, real-world bank statements. Also, an informal calculation or summary of petty cash payments has replaced the illustration of a Petty Cash Record.

A Clearer and More Complete Explanation of Bad Debts Chapter 8 includes a thoroughly new, more complete, and easier to understand discussion of bad debts. Both the income statement and balance sheet approaches to estimating bad debts are explained. Discussion of the balance sheet approach includes both a simplified version and an improved treatment of aging.

New Coverage of Credit Card Sales and Installment Accounts Receivable These timely topics are discussed in Chapter 8, which has been retitled "Credit Sales and Receivables."

Expanded Coverage of Perpetual Inventories The coverage of perpetual inventory systems has been rewritten and now includes journal entries comparing periodic and perpetual. LIFO under perpetual is discussed and illustrated, as is the difference between LIFO periodic and LIFO perpetual. The usefulness of the perpetual method in computerized accounting systems has also been clarified.

Easier to Understand Discussion of Lower of Cost or Market The discussion of inventory valuation under lower of cost or market has been completely rewritten. The new version has better illustrations, includes more descriptive headings, and is easier for students to understand.

New Coverage of Estimated Liabilities Chapter 12 contains a new section on the definition and classification of liabilities. In addition to distinguishing between current and long-term liabilities, it explains the difference between definite and estimated liabilities. New coverage of property taxes payable and product warranty liabilities is used to illustrate estimated liabilities.

Expanded Coverage of Contingent Liabilities A new section in Chapter 12 covers contingent liabilities and expands on the introduction to this topic in Chapter 8.

Improved Discussion of Mortgages The discussion of mortgages has been totally rewritten to more accurately describe mortgages as a form of security that may apply to both notes payable and bonds.

New Coverage of Installment Notes Payable A new section of Chapter 11 explains installment notes payable with two alternative payment patterns. This topical coverage corrects the typical failure of introductory accounting courses to explain this most popular form of long-term financing by businesses and individuals.

New Coverage of Discontinued Operations, Extraordinary Items, Accounting Changes, and Prior Period Adjustments Over half of the material in Chapter 19 is new. The first part of the chapter explains the income and retained earnings presentations of items that are unrelated to continuing operations. These items include discontinued operations, unusual, infrequent, and extraordinary items, changes in accounting principles, and prior period adjustments.

More Concise Coverage of Accounting for Price Changes The material on accounting for price changes has been compressed, simplified, and updated.

A Concise Introduction to International Accounting This edition introduces the special problems of companies that have transactions in foreign currencies or that have operations in more than one country—without excessive elaboration. This material and the coverage of price changes are conveniently located in separate sections at the end of Chapter 19 to facilitate variations in course design.

An Expanded Explanation of Earnings per Share A completely new discussion of earnings per share is presented in Chapter 20. This section illustrates calculations for companies with simple capital structures and explains the concepts of primary and fully diluted earnings per share without requiring complex calculations.

A New Discussion of Manufacturing Costs Several sections of Chapter 21 have been rewritten to clarify the differences between periodic and perpetual systems of accounting for manufacturing costs and to more clearly explain the flow of direct and indirect material costs. The discussions of inventory valuation and overhead allocation problems of manufacturing companies have been expanded and improved.

Improved Explanations of Job Order and Process Cost Systems New introductions have been written for each of these topics. Account titles have been modified to eliminate confusion about differences between the various types of cost accounting systems. This edition also includes an improved diagram of cost flows in process cost systems.

More Emphasis on Capital Budgeting Methods The Chapter 27 discussion of payback has been expanded to include instances where cash flows are not uniform from year to year. In addition, the chapter includes new discussions evaluating the strengths and weaknesses of different capital budgeting methods as a means of evaluating alternative investments.

Expanded Discussion of the Effect of Taxes on Business Decisions
Chapter 28 reflects the latest changes in tax laws. A new section discusses the changing nature of the tax laws and its effect on business planning. The expanded coverage also includes the topic of tax-free employee compensation.

Expanded Coverage of Present and Future Values   A new appendix at the end of the book provides an expanded analysis of present and future values. Instructors may choose to restrict the present value coverage to the material contained in Chapter 12. Or they may also assign the appendix and expand the coverage to include future values and a more detailed analysis of present values. The appendix concludes with large tables of present and future values and 19 exercises.

Additional Changes   Numerous additional changes and editorial refinements have been made to increase clarity and provide a thoroughly current work. Some examples include:

- New introductions to several chapters.
- An updated discussion of conservatism.
- A change in terminology from "premium on stock" to "contributed capital in excess of par value."
- An updated discussion of accelerated depreciation for tax purposes.
- More realistic interest rates and dollar amounts.
- Increased use of headings in selected areas.
- A new discussion of capital and revenue expenditures.
- A change in footnote citations to **Accounting Standards, Current Text**.
- An expanded number of problems in the Study Guide.
- Clearer discussions of employment taxes and of bond characteristics.

A Word about the Provocative Problems

Among the sharply expanded array of assignment material in **Fundamental Accounting Principles**, the 11th edition includes approximately 80 homework assignments that are described as *provocative problems*. This description stems from the fact that these problems are somewhat more thought-provoking than other problem assignments. Provocative problems are more like the real world, confronting students with somewhat more complexity and often requiring students to reach decisions about the illustrated situations. In this edition, many of the provocative problems are based on factual situations drawn from the financial reports of real companies. Provocative problems tend to be more challenging than other problem assignments. Although the Working Papers are plentiful enough to allow adaptation to the provocative problems, they have not been specifically designed to fit these problems. Students are therefore required to take greater responsibility for organizing their solutions.

We encourage instructors to include several provocative problems in their teaching plan as a means of enriching the diversity of assignment material and exposing students to the real-world applicability of accounting issues. Provocative problems can help instructors challenge their best students and demonstrate the contemporary relevance of the course to the entire class.

Computer-Based Supplements

A full complement of computer-based items support the teaching effectiveness of **Fundamental Accounting Principles**. Three items for student use were written by Christine Sprenger, Keith Weidkamp, and Clifford Burns. They are:

1. **Lite Flight—II**, a microcomputer practice set that may be assigned after Chapter 6.
2. **KC's Deals on Wheels—II**, a microcomputer practice set with expanded features that may be assigned after Chapter 11.
3. **Examination Review and Study Guide, Chapters 1–14** and **Chapters 15–28**, tutorials for student use in private study and review.

Leland Mansuetti joined the Sprenger, Weidkamp, and Burns team of authors to provide:

4. **Kellogg Business Systems, Inc.**, an extended corporate practice set that may be assigned after Chapter 20.
5. **Problem Solvers I** and **II**. These software packages allow students to use a microcomputer in solving selected problems from the text and introduce the use of spreadsheets.

For instructor use, the computer-based testing material includes:

6. **Computest**, a greatly enlarged bank of examination materials that now includes exercise-type problems as well as multiple-choice and true/false questions.
7. **Teletest**, a system whereby an adopter may obtain, via telephone request to the publisher, a laser-printed copy of examinations that consists of questions the adopter has selected from the computerized test bank.
8. **Compugrade**, a program for recording and weighting exam grades.

Other Supplements

The teaching package for **Fundamental Accounting Principles** also includes the following items:

- **Working Papers, Chapter 1–14** and **Chapters 14–28**. These are designed so that each volume can be used for assignments of problems or alternate problems.
- **Study Guides, Chapters 1–14** and **Chapters 14–28**. Each chapter presents learning objectives, an outline of the topical coverage in the chapter, and a series of self-examination questions with answers.
- **List of Check Figures** (available in quantity to adopters).
- **Hilltop Hardware Store**, a manual, single proprietorship practice set with business papers that may be assigned after Chapter 6.
- **Builders Supplies, Inc.**, a manual practice set that contains a narrative of transactions covering two accounting cycles; this set may be assigned after Chapter 8.
- **Kroy Manufacturing Company**, a manual practice set containing a narrative of transactions for a manufacturing corporation. The set may be assigned after Chapter 21.
- **Solutions Manual, Chapters 1–14** and **Chapters 15–28**.
- Transparencies of the solutions to all exercises and problems.

- **Instructor's Lecture Guide**, by Elliott S. Levy, Laurie W. Pant, and Michael Haselkorn. For each chapter, this guide includes a topical analysis of available assignment material, suggested lecture objectives and areas for emphasis, a detailed lecture outline, suggested assignments, sample syllabi, and selected enrichment materials.
- A special set of teaching transparencies.
- **Achievement Tests, Series A**, **B**, and **C**. Each series contains 10 examinations plus two final examinations: five examinations plus one final examination for Chapters 1–14, and five examinations plus one final examination for Chapters 15–28. They are available, free to adopters, in packages of 30 copies each.
- **Supplementary Examination Materials**, a book of examination questions that includes machine-gradable examinations, a variety of additional questions for each chapter, and the solutions to all of the printed examination materials. This book also includes a large number of short, exercise-type questions.

Acknowledgments

In preparing the 11th edition, the constructive input from numerous adopters has been the cornerstone of the revision plan. We are indebted to many individuals who have contributed comments, criticisms, and suggestions. At the risk of omitting many who have provided stimulation and guidance for the revision, several individuals should be recognized for their insightful contributions: Anna Fowler and Mary Christ, The University of Texas at Austin; Daniel J. Galvin, Diablo Valley College; L. L. Price, Ft. Steilacoom Community College, Bill Wells, Tulsa Junior College; Kenneth Miller, San Antonio College; Blanca M. Gonzalez, Miami-Dade Community College; Lee Baker, Alvin Community College; Court Huber, Trinity University; Jim Carr, New Hampshire College; Norman Sunderman, Texas A&I University; Ed Clanten, Solano Community College; James Gray, Robert LeRosen, and Lynn Pape, Northern Virginia Community College.

Extremely helpful reviews were provided by Marcella Y. Lecky, University of Southwestern Louisiana; Roy Smythers, Manatee Junior College; John R. Stewart, University of Northern Colorado; Wayne M. Schell, Christopher Newport College; Marjorie Lapham, Quinsigamond Community College; Charles V. Neal, Alfred State College; James S. Worthington, Auburn University; George Ihorn, El Paso County Community College; Eddy Birrer, Gonzaga University; O. Finley Graves, University of Mississippi; William T. Wrege, University of Wisconsin, Milwaukee; Joseph Milligan, College of DuPage; Jerry Van Os, Utah Technical College; Charles L. Vawter, Glendale Community College; Louis B. Lanzolotti, New Hampshire College; Jeanne E. Newhall, North Shore Community College; Donald P. Holman, Weber State College; Lana Bone, West Valley College; and Paul L. Donohue, Delaware County Community College. Once again for this edition, Patricia Kardash has provided invaluable assistance in all stages of preparing the manuscript.

Kermit D. Larson
William W. Pyle

Contents

Part One # Introduction

Part Two   Processing Accounting Data

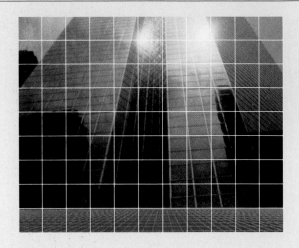

Part Three   # Accounting for Assets

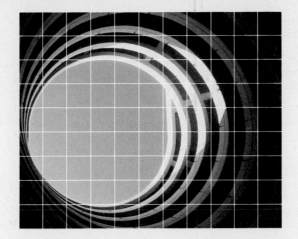

Computerized Accounting Simulation
KC's Deals on Wheels—II

Accounting for Equities: Liabilities and Partners' Equities

Part Four

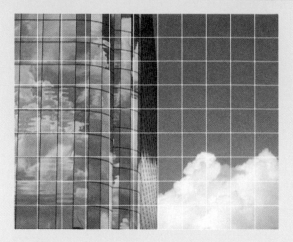

Part Five   Corporation Accounting

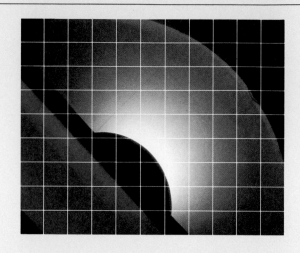

Financial Statements,
Part Six Interpretation and Modifications

Computerized Accounting Simulation
Kellogg Business Systems, Inc.

Part Seven # Managerial Accounting for Costs

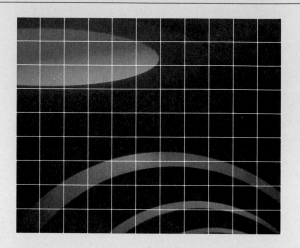

Planning and Controlling Business Operations

Part Eight

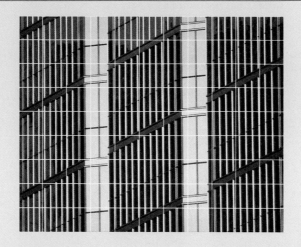

Appendix A

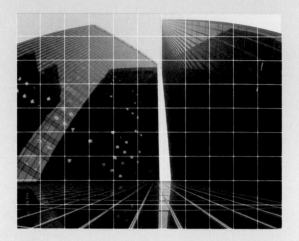

Present and Future Values: An Expansion   1023

Appendix B

Fundamental Accounting Principles

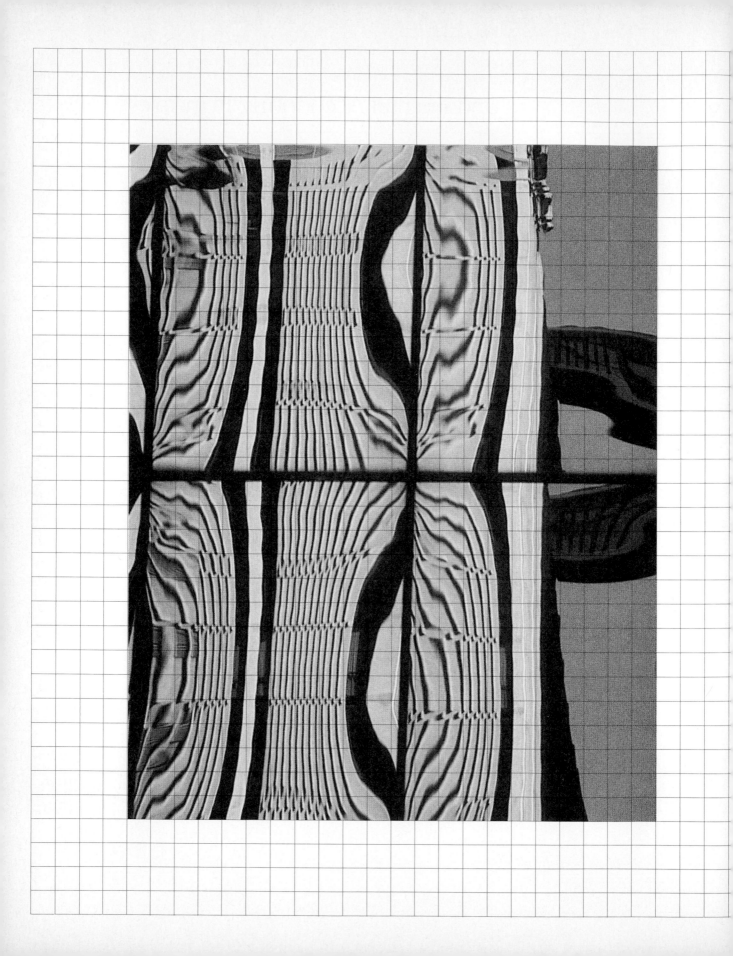

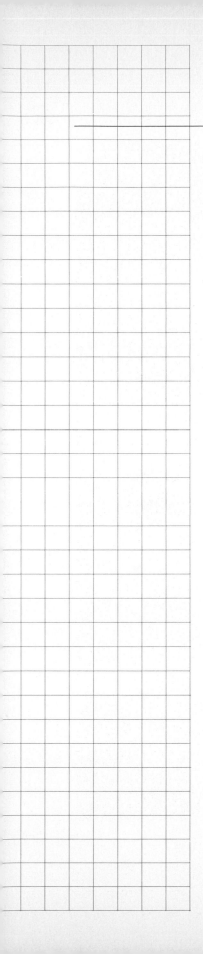

Part One

Introduction

1 Accounting, an Introduction to Its Concepts

After studying Chapter 1, you should be able to:

1. Tell the function of accounting and the nature and purpose of the information it provides.

2. List the main fields of accounting and tell the kinds of work carried on in each field.

3. List the accounting concepts and principles introduced and tell the effect of each on accounting records and statements.

4. Describe the purpose of a balance sheet and of an income statement and tell the kinds of information presented in each.

5. Recognize and be able to indicate the effects of transactions on the elements of an accounting equation.

6. Prepare simple financial statements.

7. Tell in each case the extent of the responsibility of a business owner for the debts of a business organized as a single proprietorship, as a partnership, or as a corporation.

8. Define or explain the words and phrases listed in the chapter Glossary.

Accounting is a service activity. Its function is to provide quantitative information about economic entities. The information is primarily financial in nature and is intended to be useful in making economic decisions.[1] If the entity for which the information is provided is a business, for example, the information is used by its management in answering questions such as: What are the resources of the business? What debts does it owe? Does it have earnings? Are expenses too large in relation to sales? Is too little or too much merchandise being kept? Are amounts owed by customers being collected rapidly? Will the business be able to meet its own debts as they mature? Should the plant be expanded? Should a new product be introduced? Should selling prices be increased?

In addition, grantors of credit such as banks, wholesale houses, and manufacturers use accounting information in answering such questions as: Are the customer's earning prospects good? What is its debt-paying ability? Has it paid its debts promptly in the past? Should it be granted additional credit? Likewise, governmental units use accounting information in regulating businesses and collecting taxes. Labor unions use it in negotiating working conditions and wage agreements, and investors make wide use of accounting data in investment decisions.

Why Study Accounting

Information for use in answering questions like the ones listed is conveyed in accounting reports. If a person is to use these reports effectively, he or she must have some understanding of how their data were gathered and the figures were put together. He or she must appreciate the limitations of the data and the extent to which portions are based on estimates rather than precise measurements. And, he or she must understand accounting terms and concepts. Needless to say, these understandings are gained in a study of accounting.

Another reason to study accounting to to make it one's lifework. A career in accounting can be very interesting and highly rewarding.

Accountancy as a Profession

Over the past half century, accountancy as a profession has attained a stature comparable with that of law or medicine. All states license **certified public accountants** or **CPAs** just as they license doctors and lawyers. The licensing helps ensure a high standard of professional service. Only individuals who have passed a rigorous examination of their accounting and related knowledge, met other education and experience requirements, and have received a license may designate themselves as certified public accountants.

The requirements for the CPA certificate or license vary with the states. In general, an applicant must be a citizen, 21 years of age, of unquestioned moral character, and a college graduate with a major concentration in accounting. Also, the applicant must pass a rigorous three-day examination in accounting theory, accounting practice, auditing, and business law. The three-day examination is uniform in all states and is given on the same days in all states. It is prepared by the American Institute of Certified

---

[1] Accounting Principles Board, "Basic Concepts and Accounting Principles Underlying Financial Statements of Business Enterprises," *APB Statement No. 4* (New York: AICPA, October 1970), par. 9.

Public Accountants (**AICPA**), which is the national professional organization of CPAs. In addition to the examination, many states require an applicant to have one or more years of work experience in the office of a CPA or the equivalent before the certificate is granted. However, some states do not require the work experience, and some states permit the applicant to substitute one or more years of experience for the college level education requirement. In 1969, the AICPA's Committee on Education and Experience Requirements for CPAs expressed the opinion that at least five years of college study are necessary to obtain the body of knowledge needed to be a CPA. For those meeting this standard, it recommended that no previous work experience be required.[2] A few states now require five years of college education. More will do so in the future. However, it will be several years before all states accept this recommendation. In the meantime, interested students can learn the requirements of any state in which they are interested by writing to its state board of accountancy.

■   ## The Work of an Accountant

Accountants are employed in three main fields: (1) in public accounting, (2) in private accounting, or (3) in government.

Public Accounting

Public accountants are individuals who offer their professional services and those of their employees to the public for a fee, in much the same manner as a lawyer or a consulting engineer.

Auditing The principal service offered by a public accountant is auditing. Banks commonly require an **audit** of the financial statements of a company applying for a sizable loan, with the audit being performed by a CPA who is not an employee of the audited concern but an independent professional person working for a fee. Companies whose securities are offered for sale to the public generally must also have such an audit before the securities may be sold. Thereafter, additional audits must be made periodically if the securities are to continue being traded.

The purpose of an audit is to lend credibility to a company's financial statements. In making the audit, the auditor carefully examines the company's statements and the accounting records from which they were prepared. In the examination, the auditor seeks to assure that the statements fairly reflect the company's financial position and operating results and were prepared in accordance with generally accepted accounting principles from records kept in accordance with such principles. Banks, investors, and others rely on the information in a company's financial statements in making loans, in granting credit, and in buying and selling securities. They depend on the auditor to verify the dependability of the information the statements contain.

Management Advisory Services In addition to auditing, accountants commonly offer **management advisory services**. An accountant gains from an audit an

[2] *Report of the Committee on Education and Experience Requirements for CPAs* (New York: AICPA, 1969), p. 11.

intimate knowledge of the audited company's accounting procedures and its financial position. Thus, the accountant is in an excellent position to offer constructive suggestions for improving the procedures and strengthening the position. Clients expect these suggestions as a useful audit by-product. They also commonly engage CPAs to conduct additional investigations for the purpose of determining ways in which their operations may be improved. Such investigations and the suggestions growing from them are known as management advisory services.

Management advisory services include the design, installation, and improvement of a client's general accounting system and any related information system it may have for determining and controlling costs. They also include the application of machine and computer methods to these systems, plus advice in financial planning, budgeting, forecasting, and inventory control. In fact, they include all phases of information systems and related matters.

Tax Services In this day of increasing complexity in income and other tax laws and continued high tax rates, few important business decisions are made without consideration being given to their tax effect. A CPA, through training and experience, is well qualified to render important service in this area. The service includes not only the preparation and filing of tax returns but also advice as to how transactions may be completed so as to incur the smallest tax.

Private Accounting

Accountants employed by a single enterprise are said to be in private accounting. A small business may employ only one accountant or it may depend upon the services of a public accountant and employ none. A large business, on the other hand, may have more than a hundred employees in its accounting department. They commonly work under the supervision of a chief accounting officer, commonly called the **controller,** who is often a CPA. The title controller results from the fact that one of the chief uses of accounting data is to control the operations of a business.

The one accountant of the small business and the accounting department of a large business do a variety of work, including general accounting, cost accounting, budgeting, and internal auditing.

General Accounting General accounting has to do primarily with recording transactions, processing the recorded data, and preparing financial and other reports for the use of management, owners, creditors, and governmental agencies. The private accountant may design or help the public accountant design the system used in recording the transactions. He or she will also supervise the clerical or data processing staff in recording the transactions and preparing the reports.

Cost Accounting The phase of accounting that has to do with collecting, determining, and controlling costs, particularly costs of producing a given product or service, is called **cost accounting.** A knowledge of costs and controlling costs is vital to good management. Therefore, a large company may have a number of accountants engaged in this activity.

Budgeting Planning business activities before they occur is called **budgeting.** The objective of budgeting is to provide management with an intelligent plan for future operations. Then, after the budget plan has been put into effect, it provides summaries and reports that can be used to compare actual accomplishments with the plan. Many large companies have a number of people who devote all their time to this phase of accounting.

Internal Auditing In addition to an annual audit by an independent firm of CPAs, many companies maintain a staff of internal auditors. The internal auditors constantly check the records prepared and maintained in each department or company branch. It is their responsibility to make sure that established accounting procedures and management directives are being followed throughout the company.

Governmental Accounting

Furnishing governmental services is a vast and complicated operation in which accounting is just as indispensable as in business. Elected and appointed officials must rely on data accumulated by means of accounting if they are to complete effectively their administrative duties. Accountants are responsible for the accumulation of these data. Accountants also check and audit the millions of income, payroll, and sales tax returns that accompany the tax payments upon which governmental units depend. And finally, federal and state agencies, such as the Interstate Commerce Commission, Securities and Exchange Commission, and so on, use accountants in many capacities in their regulation of business.

■ **Accounting and Bookkeeping**

Many people confuse **accounting** and **bookkeeping** and look upon them as one and the same. In effect, they identify the whole with one of its parts. Actually, bookkeeping is only part of accounting, the record-making part. To keep books is to record transactions, and a bookkeeper is one who records transactions either manually with pen and ink or with a bookkeeping machine. The work is often routine and primarily clerical in nature. The work of an accountant goes far beyond this, as a rereading of the previous section will show.

■ **Accounting and Computers**

Computers are used for many tasks in our modern society, including the processing of accounting data. A computer can accept and store accounting data, sort and rearrange it, perform arithmetic calculations on it, and prepare reports from the data. Furthermore, after accepting data, a computer can process it very rapidly and with little or no human intervention. However, before a computer can do this, a set of detailed instructions must be prepared and entered in the computer to tell it how to process the data. The person who prepares these instructions must have a thorough understanding of accounting procedures and accounting principles. A beginning on that understanding can be gained in the succeeding pages of this text.

■ **Accounting
    Statements**

Accounting statements are the end product of the accounting process, but a good place to begin the study of accounting. They are used to convey a concise picture of the profitability and financial position of a business. The two most important are the income statement and the balance sheet.

The Income Statement

A company's **income statement** (see Illustration 1-1) is perhaps more important than its balance sheet. It shows whether or not the business achieved or failed to achieve its primary objective—earning a "profit" or net income. A **net income** is earned when revenues exceed expenses, but a **net loss** is incurred if the expenses exceed the revenues. An income statement is prepared by listing the revenues earned during a period of time, listing the expenses incurred in earning the revenues, and subtracting the expenses from the revenues to determine if a net income or a net loss was incurred.

Revenues are inflows of cash or other properties received in exchange for goods or services provided to customers. Rents, dividends, and interest earned are also revenues. Coast Realty of Illustration 1-1 had revenue inflows from services that totaled $56,350.

Expenses are goods and services consumed in operating a business or other economic unit. Coast Realty consumed the services of its employees (salaries expense), the services of a telephone company, and so on.

The heading of an income statement tells the name of the business for which it is prepared and the time period covered by the statement. Both bits of information are important. However, the time covered is extremely significant, since the items on the statement must be interpreted in relation to the period of time. For example, the item "Commissions earned, $55,150" on the income statement of Illustration 1-1 has little significance until it is known that the amount represents one year's commissions and not the commissions of a week or a month.

Illustration 1-1

Coast Realty
Income Statement
For Year Ended December 31, 19—

Revenues:

Commissions earned	$55,150	
Property management fees	1,200	
Total revenues		$56,350
Operating expenses:		
Salaries expense	$12,800	
Rent expense	6,000	
Utilities expense	915	
Telephone expense	760	
Advertising expense.	4,310	
Total operating expenses		24,785
Net income		$31,565

[handwritten margin notes: balance sheet — Point in time; Resources | Sources; Ass. | Liab + Cap.; Ass - Liab = Net Assets O.E.]

The Balance Sheet

The purpose of a **balance sheet** is to show the financial position of a business on a specific date. It is often called a **position statement.** Financial position is shown by listing the **assets** of the business, its **liabilities** or debts, and the **equity of the owner or owners.** (An asset is a property or property right, and an equity is a right, claim, or interest in an asset or assets.) The name of the business and the date are given in the balance sheet heading. It is understood that the item amounts shown are as of the close of business on that date.

Before a business manager, investor, or other person can make effective judgments based on balance sheet information, he or she must understand balance sheet terminology and several accounting concepts and principles. For a beginning on these understandings, assume that on August 3, Joan Ball began a new business, called World Travel Agency. During the day, she completed these transactions in the name of the business:

Aug. 3 Invested $5,000 of her personal cash in the business.
   3 Rented suitable office space and paid the rent for three months in advance, $1,500. (In exchange for the $1,500 the business gained the right to occupy the office space for three months, an asset called prepaid rent.)
   3 Purchased for cash office equipment costing $2,500.
   3 Purchased on credit office supplies costing $100 and additional office equipment costing $500. (Purchased on credit means purchased with a promise to pay at a later date.)

A balance sheet reflecting the effects of these transactions appears in Illustration 1-2. It shows that after completing the transactions, the agency has four assets, a $600 debt, and its owner has a $5,000 equity in the business.

Observe that the two sides of the balance sheet are equal. This is where it gets its name. Its two sides must always be equal because one side shows the resources of the business and the other shows who supplied the resources. For example, World Travel Agency has $5,600 of resources (assets) of which $5,000 were supplied by its owner and $600 by its creditors.

Illustration 1-2

World Travel Agency
Balance Sheet
August 3, 19—

Assets		Liabilities	
Cash	$1,000	Accounts payable	$ 600
Office supplies	100		
Prepaid rent	1,500	**Owner's Equity**	
Office equipment	3,000	Joan Ball, capital	5,000
Total assets	$5,600	Total liabilities and owner's equity . . .	$5,600

(**Creditors** are individuals and organizations to whom the business owes debts.)

■ Assets, Liabilities, and Owner's Equity

The assets of a business are, in general, the properties or economic resources owned by the business. They include cash, amounts owed to the business by its customers for goods and services sold to them on credit (called **accounts receivable**), merchandise held for sale by the business, supplies, equipment, buildings, and land. Assets may also include such intangible rights as those granted by a patent or copyright.

The liabilities of a business are its debts. They include amounts owed to creditors for goods and services bought on credit (called **accounts payable**), salaries and wages owed employees, taxes payable, notes payable, and mortgages payable.

When a business is owned by one person, the owner's interest or equity in the assets of the business is shown on a balance sheet by listing the person's name, followed by the word **capital,** and then the amount of the equity. The use of the word capital comes from the idea that the owner has furnished the business with resources or "capital" equal to the amount of the equity.

A liability represents a claim or right to be paid. The law recognizes this right. If a business fails to pay its creditors, the law gives the creditors the right to force the sale of the assets of the business to secure money to meet creditor claims. Furthermore, if the assets are sold, the creditors are paid first, with any remainder going to the business owner. Obviously, then, by law creditor claims take precedence over those of a business owner.

Since creditor claims take precedence over those of an owner, an owner's equity in a business is always a residual amount. Creditors recognize this. When they examine the balance sheet of a business, they are always interested in the share of its assets furnished by creditors and the share furnished by its owner or owners. The creditors recognize that if the business must be liquidated and its assets sold, the shrinkage in converting the assets into cash must exceed the equity of the owner or owners before the creditors will lose.

■ Generally Accepted Accounting Principles

An understanding of financial statement information requires a knowledge of the generally accepted **accounting principles** that govern the accumulation and presentation of the data appearing on such statements. A common definition of the word *principle* is: "A broad general law or rule adopted or professed as a guide to action; a settled ground or basis of conduct or practice. . . ." Consequently, generally accepted accounting principles may be described as broad rules adopted by the accounting profession as guides in measuring, recording, and reporting the financial affairs and activities of a business. They consist of a number of concepts, principles, and procedures that are first discussed at the points shown in the following list. They also are referred to again and again throughout this text in order to increase your understanding of the information conveyed by accounting data.

	First Introduced	
	Chapter	Page
Generally accepted concepts:		
1. Business entity concept	1	14
2. Continuing-concern concept.	1	16
3. Stable-dollar concept	1	16
4. Time-period concept	3	80
Generally accepted principles:		
1. Cost principle	1	15
2. Objectivity principle	1	15
3. Realization principle	1	21
4. Matching principle	3	87
5. Materiality principle	8	296
6. Full-disclosure principle	8	303
7. Consistency principle	9	328
8. Conservatism principle	9	331

Generally accepted procedures:
These specify the ways data are processed and reported and are described and discussed throughout the text.

Source of Accounting Principles

Generally accepted accounting principles are not natural laws in the sense of the laws of physics and chemistry. They are man-made rules that depend for their authority upon their general acceptance by the accounting profession. They have evolved from the experience and thinking of members of the accounting profession, aided by such groups as the American Institute of Certified Public Accountants, the Financial Accounting Standards Board (**FASB**), the American Accounting Association, and the Securities and Exchange Commission.

The American Institute of Certified Public Accountants (AICPA) has long been influential in describing and defining generally accepted accounting principles. During the years from 1939 to 1959, it published a series of *Accounting Research Bulletins* that were recognized as expressions of generally accepted accounting principles. In 1959, it established an 18-member Accounting Principles Board (**APB**) composed of practicing accountants, educators, and representatives of industry, and gave the Board authority to issue opinions that were to be regarded by members of the AICPA as authoritative expressions of generally accepted accounting principles. During the years 1962 through 1973, the Board issued 31 such opinions. Added importance was given to these opinions beginning in 1964 when the AICPA ruled that its members must disclose in footnotes to published financial statements of the companies they audit any departure from generally accepted accounting principles as set forth in the *Opinions of the Accounting Principles Board.*

In 1973, after 11 years of activity, the APB was terminated. Its place was taken by a seven-member Financial Accounting Standards Board (FASB). The seven members serve full time, receive salaries, and must resign from accounting firms and other employment. They must have a knowledge of accounting, finance, and business, but are not required to be CPAs. This differs from the APB, all members of which were CPAs, who served part time, without pay, and continued their affiliations with accounting firms and other employment. The FASB issues *Statements of Financial Accounting Standards,* which, like the *Opinions of the Accounting Principles Board,* must be considered as authoritative expressions of generally accepted accounting principles. Both the *Statements* and *Opinions* are referred to again and again throughout this text.

The American Accounting Association (AAA), an organization with strong academic ties, has also been influential in describing and defining generally accepted accounting principles. It has sponsored a number of research studies and has published many articles dealing with accounting principles. However, its influence has not been as great as the AICPA, since it has no power to impose its views on the accounting profession but must depend upon the prestige of its authors and the logic of their arguments.

The Securities and Exchange Commission (SEC) plays a prominent role in financial reporting. The SEC is an independent quasi-judicial agency of the federal government. It was established to administer the provisions of various securities and exchange acts dealing with the distribution and sale of securities. Such securities, to be sold, must be registered with the SEC. This requires the filing of audited financial statements prepared in accordance with the rules of the SEC. Furthermore, the information contained in the statements must be kept current by filing additional audited annual reports. The SEC does not appraise the registered securities. However, it attempts to safeguard investors by requiring that all material facts affecting the worth of the securities be made public and that no important information be withheld. Its rules carry over into the annual reports of large companies and have contributed to the usefulness of these reports. In a real sense, the SEC should be viewed as the dominant authority in respect to the establishment of accounting principles. However, it has relied on the accounting profession, particularly the AICPA and the FASB, to determine and enforce accepted accounting principles. At the same time, it has pressured the accounting profession to reduce the number of acceptable accounting procedures.

■ Understanding Accounting Principles

Your authors believe that an understanding of **accounting principles** is best conveyed with examples illustrating the application of each principle. The examples must be such that a student can understand at his or her level of experience. Consequently, three **accounting concepts** and two accounting principles are introduced here. Discussions of the others are delayed until later in the text when meaningful examples of their application can be developed.

Business Entity Concept

Under the **business entity concept,** for accounting purposes, every business is conceived to be and is treated as a separate entity, separate and distinct from its owner or owners and from every other business. Businesses are so conceived and treated because, insofar as a specific business is concerned, the purpose of accounting is to record its transactions and periodically report its financial position and profitability. Consequently, the records and reports of a business should not include either the transactions or assets of another business or the personal assets and transactions of its owner or owners. To include either distorts the financial position and profitability of the business. For example, the personally owned automobile of a business owner should not be included among the assets of the owner's business. Likewise, its gas, oil, and repairs should not be treated as an expense of the business, for to do so distorts the reported financial position and profitability of the business.

Cost Principle

In addition to the **business entity concept,** an accounting principle called the **cost principle** should be borne in mind when reading financial statements. Under this principle, all goods and services purchased are recorded at cost and appear on the statements at cost. For example, if a business pays $50,000 for land to be used in carrying on its operations, the purchase should be recorded at $50,000. It makes no difference if the buyer and several competent outside appraisers thought the land "worth" at least $60,000. It cost $50,000 and should appear on the balance sheet at that amount. Furthermore, if five years later, due to booming real estate prices, the land's market value has doubled, this makes no difference either. The land cost $50,000 and should continue to appear on the balance sheet at $50,000 even though its estimated market value is twice that.

In applying the **cost principle,** costs are measured on a cash or cash-equivalent basis. If the consideration given for an asset or service is cash, cost is measured at the entire cash outlay made to secure the asset or service. If the consideration is something other than cash, cost is measured at the cash-equivalent value of the consideration given or the cash-equivalent value of the thing received, whichever is more clearly evident.[3]

Why are assets and services recorded at cost, and why are the balance sheet amounts for the assets not changed from time to time to reflect changing market values? The **objectivity principle** and the **continuing-concern concept** supply answers to these questions.

Objectivity Principle

The **objectivity principle** supplies the reason transactions are recorded at cost, since it requires that transaction amounts be objectively established. Whims and fancies plus, for example, something like an opinion of management that an asset is "worth more than it cost" have no place in accounting. To be fully useful, accounting information must be based on objective data. As a rule, costs are objective, since they normally are established by buyers and sellers, each striking the best possible bargain for himself or herself.

---

[3] FASB, *Accounting Standards—Current Text* (Stamford, Conn., 1984), sec. N35.105. First published as *APB Opinion No. 29,* par. 18.

Continuing-Concern Concept

Balance sheet amounts for assets used in carrying on the operations of a business are not changed from time to time to reflect changing market values. A balance sheet is prepared under the assumption that the business for which it is prepared will continue in operation, and as a continuing or going concern the assets used in carrying on its operations are not for sale. In fact, they cannot be sold without disrupting the business. Therefore, since the assets are for use in the business and are not for sale, their current market values are not particularly relevant and need not be shown. Also, without a sale, their current market values usually cannot be objectively established, as is required by the **objectivity principle.**

The **continuing-concern or going-concern concept** applies in most situations. However, if a business is about to be sold or liquidated, the **continuing-concern concept** and the **cost and objectivity principles** do not apply in the preparation of its statements. In such cases, amounts other than costs, such as estimated market values, become more useful and informative.

The Stable-Dollar Concept

In our country, accounting transactions are measured, recorded, and reported in terms of dollars. In the measuring, recording, and reporting process, the dollar has been treated as a stable unit of measure, like a gallon, an acre, or a mile. Unfortunately, however, the dollar, like other currencies, is not a stable unit of measure. When the general price level (the average of all prices) changes, the value of money (its purchasing power) also changes. For example, during the past 10 years, the general price level has approximately doubled, which means that over these years the purchasing power of the dollar has declined from 100 cents to approximately 50 cents.

Nevertheless, although the instability of the dollar is recognized, accountants in their reports continue to add and subtract items acquired in different years with dollars of different sizes. In effect, they ignore changes in the size of the measuring unit. For example, assume a company purchased land some years ago for $10,000 and sold it today for $20,000. If during this period the purchasing power of the dollar declined from 100 cents to 50 cents, it can be said that the company is no better off for having purchased the land for $10,000 and sold it for $20,000 because the $20,000 will buy no more goods and services today than the $10,000 at the time of the purchase. Yet, using the dollar to measure both transactions, the accountant reports a $10,000 gain from the purchase and sale.

The instability of the dollar as a unit of measure is recognized. Therefore, the question is should the amounts shown on financial statements be adjusted for changes in the purchasing power of the dollar. Techniques have been devised to convert the historical dollars of statement amounts into dollars of current purchasing power. Such statements are called **price-level-adjusted statements.** Also, by consulting catalogs and securing current prices from manufacturers and wholesalers, it is possible to determine replacement costs for various assets owned. As a result, such costs could be used in preparing financial statements. However, financial statements showing current replacement costs and also price-adjusted statements require subjective judgments in their preparation. Consequently, most accountants are of the opinion that the traditional statements based on the **stable-dollar concept** are best for general publication and use. Nevertheless, they also recognize that the information conveyed by traditional statements can be made more useful if accompanied by replacement cost and/or price-level-adjusted information. This is discussed in a later chapter.

From the discussions of the **cost principle,** the **continuing-concern concept,** and **stable-dollar concept,** it should be recognized that in most instances a balance sheet does not show the amounts at which the listed assets can be sold or replaced. Nor does it show the "worth" of the business for which it was prepared, since some of the listed assets may be salable for much more or much less than the dollar amounts at which they are shown.

■ Business Organizations

Accounting is applicable to all economic entities such as business concerns, schools, churches, fraternities, and so on. However, this text will focus on accounting for business concerns organized as single proprietorships, partnerships, and corporations.

Single Proprietorships

An unincorporated business owned by one person is called a **single proprietorship.** Small retail stores and service enterprises are commonly operated as single proprietorships. There are no legal requirements to be met in starting a single proprietorship business. Furthermore, single proprietorships are the most numerous of all business concerns.

In accounting for a single proprietorship, the **business entity concept** is applied, and the business is treated as a separate entity, separate and distinct from its owner. However, insofar as the debts of the business are concerned, no such legal distinction is made. The owner of a single proprietorship business is personally responsible for its debts. As a result, if the assets of such a business are not sufficient to pay its debts, the personal assets of the proprietor may be taken to satisfy the claims of the business creditors.

Partnerships

When a business is owned by two or more people as partners, it is called a **partnership.** Like a single proprietorship, there are no special legal requirements to be met in starting a partnership business. All that is required is for two or more people to enter into an agreement to operate a business as partners. The agreement becomes a contract and may be either oral or written, but to avoid disagreements, a written contract is preferred.

For accounting purposes, a partnership business is treated as a separate entity, separate and distinct from its owners. However, just as with a single proprietorship, insofar as the debts of the business are concerned, no such legal distinction is made. A partner is personally responsible for all the debts of the partnership, both his or her own share and the shares of any partners who are unable to pay. Furthermore, the personal assets of a partner may be taken to satisfy all the debts of a partnership if other partners cannot pay.

Corporations

A business incorporated under the laws of a state or the federal government is called a **corporation.** Unlike a single proprietorship or partnership, a corporation is a separate legal entity, separate and distinct from its owners. The owners are called **stockholders** or **shareholders** because their ownership is evidenced by shares of the corporation's **capital stock.** The stock may be sold and transferred from one shareholder to another without affecting the operation of the corporation.

Separate legal entity is the most important characteristic of a corporation. It makes a corporation responsible for its own acts and its own debts and relieves its stockholders of liability for either. It enables a corporation to buy, own, and sell property in its own name, to sue and be sued in its own name, and to enter into contracts for which it is solely responsible. In short, separate legal entity enables a corporation to conduct its business affairs as a legal person with all the rights, duties, and responsibilities of a person. However, unlike a person, it must act through agents.

A corporation is created by securing a charter from one of the 50 states or the federal government. The requirements for obtaining a charter vary; but in general, they call for filing an application with the proper governmental official and paying certain fees and taxes. If the application complies with the law and all fees and taxes have been paid, the charter is granted and the corporation comes into existence. At that point, the corporation's organizers and perhaps others buy the corporation's stock and become stockholders. Then, as stockholders they meet and elect a board of directors. The board then meets, appoints the corporation's president and other officers, and makes them responsible for managing the corporation's business affairs.

Lack of stockholder liability and the ease with which stock may be sold and transferred have enabled corporations to multiply, grow, and become the dominant form of business organization in our country. Nevertheless, because of its simplicity, it is best to begin the study of accounting with a single proprietorship.

■ The Balance Sheet Equation

As previously stated, a balance sheet is so called because its two sides must always balance. The sum of the assets shown on the balance sheet must equal liabilities plus the equity of the owner or owners of the business. This equality may be expressed in equation form for a single proprietorship business as follows:

$$\text{Assets} = \text{Liabilities} + \text{Owner's Equity}$$

When balance sheet equality is expressed in equation form, the resulting equation is called the **balance sheet equation.** It is also known as the **accounting equation,** since all double-entry accounting is based on it. Like any mathematical equation, its elements may be transposed and the equation expressed:

$$\text{Assets} - \text{Liabilities} = \text{Owner's Equity}$$

The equation in this form illustrates the residual nature of the owner's equity. An owner's claims are secondary to the creditors' claims.

Effects of Transactions on the Accounting Equation

A **business transaction** is an exchange of goods or services, and business transactions affect the elements of an accounting equation. However, regardless of what transactions a business completes, its accounting equation always remains in balance. Also, its assets always equal the combined claims of its creditors and its owner or owners. This may be demonstrated with the transactions of Larry Owen's law practice, a single proprietorship business, which follow.

On July 1, Larry Owen began a new law practice by investing $5,000 of his personal cash, which he deposited in a bank account opened in the name of the business, Larry Owen, Attorney. After the investment, the one asset of the new business and the equity of Owen in the business are shown in the following equation:

$$\text{Assets} \quad = \quad \text{Owner's Equity}$$

$$\underbrace{\text{Cash, \$5,000}} \quad \underbrace{\text{Larry Owen, Capital, \$5,000}}$$

Observe that after its first transaction, the new business has one asset, cash, $5,000. Therefore, since it has no liabilities, the equity of Owen in the business is $5,000.

To continue the illustration, after the investment (transaction 2), Owen used $900 of the business cash to pay the rent for three months in advance on suitable office space and (transaction 3) $3,700 to buy office equipment. These transactions were exchanges of cash for other assets. Their effects on the accounting equation are shown in color in Illustration 1-3. Observe that the equation remains in balance after each transaction.

Continuing the illustration, assume that Owen needed office supplies and additional equipment in the law office. However, he felt he should conserve the cash of the law practice. Consequently, he purchased on credit from Alpha Company office supplies costing $60 and office equipment that cost $300. The effects of these purchases (transaction 4) are shown in Illustration 1-4. Note that the assets were increased by the purchases. However, Owen's equity did not change because Alpha Company acquired a claim against the assets equal to the increase in the assets. The claim or amount owed Alpha Company is called an **account payable.**

A primary objective of a business is to increase the equity of its owner or owners by earning a profit or a net income. Owen's law practice will accomplish this objective by providing legal services to its clients on a

Illustration 1-3

		Assets			=	Owner's Equity
	Cash	+	Prepaid Rent	+	Office Equipment	=	Larry Owen, Capital
(1)	$5,000						$5,000
(2)	−900		+$900				
	$4,100		$900				$5,000
(3)	−3,700				+$3,700		
	$ 400	+	$900	+	$3,700	=	$5,000

Illustration 1-4

		Assets			= Liabilities +	Owner's Equity
	Cash +	Prepaid Rent +	Office Supplies +	Office Equipment =	Accounts Payable +	Larry Owen, Capital
(1)	$5,000					$5,000
(2)	−900	+$900				
	$4,100	$900				$5,000
(3)	−3,700			+$3,700		
	$ 400	$900		$3,700		$5,000
(4)			+**$60**	+**300**	+**$360**	
	$ 400 +	$900 +	$60 +	$4,000 =	$360 +	$5,000

fee basis. Of course, the practice will earn a net income only if legal fees earned are greater than the expenses incurred in earning the fees. Legal fees earned and expenses incurred affect the elements of an accounting equation. To illustrate their effects, assume that on July 12, Larry Owen completed legal work for a client (transaction 5) and immediately collected $500 in cash for the services rendered. Also, the same day (transaction 6) he paid the salary of the office secretary for the first two weeks of July, a $400 expense of the business. The effects of these transactions are shown in Illustration 1-5.

Observe first the effects of the legal fee. The $500 fee is a revenue, an inflow of assets from the sale of services. Note that the revenue not only increased the asset cash but also caused a $500 increase in Owen's equity. Owen's equity increased because total assets increased without an increase in liabilities.

Next observe the effects of paying the secretary's $400 salary, an expense. Note that the effects are opposite those of a revenue. Expenses are goods

Illustration 1-5

		Assets			= Liabilities +	Owner's Equity
	Cash +	Prepaid Rent +	Office Supplies +	Office Equipment =	Accounts Payable +	Larry Owen, Capital
(1)	$5,000					$5,000
(2)	−900	+$900				
	$4,100	$900				$5,000
(3)	−3,700			+$3,700		
	$ 400	$900		$3,700		$5,000
(4)			+$60	+300	+$360	
	$ 400	$900	$60	$4,000	$360	$5,000
(5)	+**500**					+**500**
	$ 900	$900	$60	$4,000	$360	$5,500
(6)	−**400**					−**400**
	$ 500 +	$900 +	$60 +	$4,000 =	$360 +	$5,100

and services consumed in the operation of a business. In this instance, the business consumed the secretary's services. When the services were paid for, both the assets and Owen's equity in the business decreased. Owen's equity decreased because cash decreased without an increase in other assets or a decrease in liabilities.

Note this about earning a net income: A business earns a net income when its revenues exceed its expenses, and the income increases both net assets and the equity of the owner or owners. (**Net assets** are the excess of assets over liabilities.) Net assets increase because more assets flow into the business from revenues than are consumed and flow out for expenses. The equity of the owner or owners increases because net assets increase. A net loss has opposite effects.

To simplify the material and emphasize the actual effects of revenues and expenses on owner's equity, in this first chapter revenues are added directly to and expenses are deducted from the owner's capital. However, this is not done in actual practice. In actual practice, revenues and expenses are first accumulated in separate categories. They are then combined; and their combined effect, the net income or loss, is added to or deducted from owner's capital. A further discussion of this is deferred to later chapters.

■   **Realization Principle**

In transaction 5, the revenue inflow was in the form of cash. However, revenue inflows are not always in cash because of the **realization principle** (also called the **recognition principle**), which governs the recognition of revenue. This principle (1) defines a revenue as an inflow of assets (not necessarily cash) in exchange for goods or services. (2) It requires that the revenue be recognized (entered in the accounting records as revenue) at the time, but not before, it is earned. (Generally, revenue is considered to be earned at the time title to goods sold is transferred or services are rendered and become billable.) (3) The principle also requires that the amount of revenue recognized be measured by the cash received plus the cash equivalent (fair value) of any other asset or assets received.

To demonstrate the recognition of a revenue inflow in a form other than cash, assume that (transaction 7) Larry Owen completed legal work for a client and billed the client $1,000 for the services rendered. Also assume that 10 days later, the client paid in full (transaction 8) for the services rendered. The effects of the two transactions are shown in Illustration 1-6.

Observe in transaction 7 that the asset flowing into the business was the right to collect $1,000 from the client, an account receivable. Compare transactions 5 and 7 and note that they differ only as to the type of asset received. Next observe that the receipt of cash (10 days after the services were rendered) is nothing more than an exchange of assets, cash for the right to collect from the client. Also note that the receipt of cash did not affect Owen's equity because the revenue was recognized in accordance with the **realization principle** and Owen's equity was increased upon completion of the services rendered.

As a final transaction assume that on July 30, Larry Owen paid Alpha

Illustration 1-6

		Assets					=	Liabilities	+	Owner's Equity
	Cash +	Accounts Receivable +	Prepaid Rent +	Office Supplies +	Office Equipment	=	Accounts Payable	+	Larry Owen, Capital
(1)	$5,000								$5,000
(2)	−900		+$900						
	$4,100		$900						$5,000
(3)	−3,700				+$3,700				
	$ 400		$900		$3,700				$5,000
(4)				+$60	+300		+$360		
	$ 400		$900	.$60	$4,000		$360		$5,000
(5)	+500								+500
	$ 900		$900	$60	$4,000		$360		$5,500
(6)	−400								−400
	$ 500		$900	$60	$4,000		$360		$5,100
(7)		**+$1,000**							**+1,000**
	$ 500	$1,000	$900	$60	$4,000		$360		$6,100
(8)	**+1,000**	**− 1,000**							
	$1,500 +	$ 0 +	$900 +	$60 +	$4,000	=	$360	+	$6,100

Company $100 of the $360 owed for the equipment and supplies purchased in transaction 4. This transaction reduced in equal amounts both assets and liabilities, and its effects are shown in Illustration 1-7.

■ **Important Transaction Effects**

Look again at Illustration 1-7 and observe that every transaction affected at least two items in the equation; and in each case, after the effects were entered in the columns, the equation remained in balance. The accounting system you are beginning to study is called a **double-entry system.** It is based on the fact that every transaction affects two or more items in an accounting equation such as that in Illustration 1-7 and requires a "double entry" or, in other words, entries in two or more places. Also, the fact that the equation remained in balance after each transaction is important, for this is a proof of the accuracy with which the transactions were recorded.

■ **Bases of Revenue Recognition**

Returning to the discussion of revenue recognition, the APB ruled that revenue is realized and in most cases should be recognized in the accounting records upon the completion of a sale or when services have been performed and are billable.[4] This is known as the **sales basis of revenue recognition.** Under it, a sale is considered to be completed when assets such as cash or the right to collect cash within a short period of time are received in exchange for goods sold or services rendered. Theoretically, revenue is earned throughout the entire performance of a service or throughout the whole process of securing goods for sale, taking a customer's order,

[4] Ibid., sec. R75.101. First published as *APB Opinion No. 10*, par. 12.

Illustration 1-7

		Cash	+	Accounts Receivable	+	Prepaid Rent	+	Office Supplies	+	Office Equipment	=	Accounts Payable	+	Larry Owen, Capital
						Assets					=	**Liabilities +**		**Owner's Equity**
(1)		$5,000												$5,000
(2)		−900				+$900								
		$4,100				$900								$5,000
(3)		−3,700								+$3,700				
		$ 400				$900				$3,700				$5,000
(4)								+$60		+300		+$360		
		$ 400				$900		$60		$4,000		$360		$5,000
(5)		+500												+500
		$ 900				$900		$60		$4,000		$360		$5,500
(6)		−400												−400
		$ 500				$900		$60		$4,000		$360		$5,100
(7)				+$1,000										+1,000
		$ 500		$1,000		$900		$60		$4,000		$360		$6,100
(8)		+1,000		−1,000										
		$1,500		$ 0		$900		$60		$4,000		$360		$6,100
(9)		**−100**										**−100**		
		$1,400 +				$900 +		$60 +		$4,000 −		$260 +		$6,100

and delivering the goods.[5] Yet, until all steps are completed, and there is a right to collect the sale price, the requirements of the **objectivity principle** are not fulfilled and revenue is not recognized.

An exception to the required use of the sales basis is made for installment sales when payments are to be made over a relatively long period of time and there is considerable doubt as to the amounts that ultimately will be collected. For such sales, when collection of the full sale price is in doubt, revenue may be recognized as it is collected in cash.[6] This is known as the **cash basis of revenue recognition.**

A second exception to the required use of the sales basis applies to construction firms. Large construction jobs often take two or more years to complete. Consequently, if a construction firm has only a few jobs in process at any time and it recognizes revenue on a sales basis (upon the completion of each job), it may have a year in which no jobs are completed and no revenue is recognized even though the year is one of heavy activity. As a result, construction firms may and do recognize revenue on a **percentage-of-completion basis.** Under this basis, for example, if a firm has incurred 40% of the estimated cost to complete a job, it may recognize 40% of the job's contract price as revenue.

Space does not permit a full discussion of the cash basis and the percentage-of-completion basis of revenue recognition. This must be reserved for a more advanced text.

[5] APB Statement No. 4, par. 149.
[6] FASB, Accounting Standards—Current Text, sec. R75.101. First published as APB Opinion No. 10, par. 12.

☐   **Glossary**   **Account payable** a debt owed to a creditor for goods or services purchased on credit.

Account receivable an amount receivable from a debtor for goods or services sold on credit.

Accounting the art of recording, classifying, reporting, and interpreting the financial data of an organization.

Accounting concept an abstract idea that serves as a basis in the interpretation of accounting information.

Accounting equation an expression in dollar amounts of the equivalency of the assets and equities of an enterprise, usually stated Assets = Liabilities + Owner's equity. Also called a **balance sheet equation.**

Accounting principle a broad rule adopted by the accounting profession as a guide in measuring, recording, and reporting the financial affairs and activities of a business.

AICPA American Institute of Certified Public Accountants, the professional association of certified public accountants in the United States.

APB Accounting Principles Board, a committee of the AICPA that was responsible for formulating accounting principles.

Asset a property or economic resource owned by an individual or enterprise.

Audit a critical exploratory review of the business methods and accounting records of an enterprise, made to enable the auditor to express an opinion as to whether the financial statements of the enterprise fairly reflect its financial position and operating results.

Balance sheet a financial report showing the assets, liabilities, and owner's equity of an enterprise on a specific date. Also called a **position statement.**

Balance sheet equation another name for the **accounting equation.**

Bookkeeping the record-making phase of accounting.

Budgeting the phase of accounting dealing with planning the activities of an enterprise and comparing its actual accomplishments with the plan.

Business entity concept the idea that a business is separate and distinct from its owner or owners and from every other business.

Business transaction an exchange of goods, services, money, and/or the right to collect money.

Capital stock ownership equity in a corporation represented by transferable certificates showing shares of ownership.

Continuing-concern concept the idea that a business is a going concern that will continue to operate, using its assets to carry on its operations and, with the exception of merchandise, not offering the assets for sale.

Controller the chief accounting officer of a large business.

Corporation a business incorporated under the laws of a state or other jurisdiction.

Cost accounting the phase of accounting that deals with collecting and controlling the costs of producing a given product or service.

Cost principle the accounting rule that requires assets and services plus any resulting liabilities to be taken into the accounting records at cost.

CPA certified public accountant, an accountant who has met legal requirements as to age, education, experience, residence, and moral character and is licensed to practice public accounting.

Creditor a person or enterprise to whom a debt is owed.

Debtor a person or enterprise that owes a debt.

Equity a right, claim, or interest in property.

Expense goods or services consumed in operating an enterprise.

FASB Financial Accounting Standards Board, the seven-member board that currently has the authority to formulate and issue pronouncements of generally accepted accounting principles.

General accounting that phase of accounting dealing primarily with recording transactions, processing the recorded data, and preparing financial statements.

Going-concern concept another name for the **continuing-concern concept.**

Income statement a financial statement showing revenues earned by a business, the expenses incurred in earning the revenues, and the resulting net income or net loss.

Internal auditing a continuing examination of the records and procedures of a business by its own internal audit staff to determine if established procedures and management directives are being followed.

Liability a debt owed.

Management advisory services the phase of public accounting dealing with the design, installation, and improvement of a client's accounting system, plus advice on planning, budgeting, forecasting, and all other phases of accounting.

Net assets assets minus liabilities.

Net income the excess of revenues over expenses.

Net loss the excess of expenses over revenues.

Objectivity principle the accounting rule requiring that wherever possible the amounts used in recording transactions be based on objective evidence rather than on subjective judgments.

Owner's equity the equity of the owner (or owners) of a business in the assets of the business.

Partnership an association of two or more persons to co-own and operate a business for profit.

Position statement another name for the balance sheet.

Price-level-adjusted statements financial statements showing item amounts adjusted for changes in the purchasing power of money.

Realization principle the accounting rule that defines a revenue as an inflow of assets, not necessarily cash, in exchange for goods or services and requires the revenue to be recognized at the time, but not before, it is earned.

Recognition principle another name for the **realization principle.**

Revenue an inflow of assets, not necessarily cash, in exchange for goods and services sold.

Shareholder a person or enterprise owning a share or shares of stock in a corporation. Also called a **stockholder.**

Single proprietorship a business owned by one individual.

Stable-dollar concept the idea that the purchasing power of the unit of measured used in accounting, the dollar, does not change.

Stockholder another name for a **shareholder.**

Tax services the phase of public accounting dealing with the preparation of tax returns and with advice as to how transactions may be completed in a way as to incur the smallest tax liability.

☐ **Questions for Class Discussion**

1. What is the nature of accounting and what is its function?
2. How does a business executive use accounting information?
3. Why do the states license certified public accountants?
4. What is the purpose of an audit? What do certified public accountants do when they make an audit?
5. A public accountant may provide management advisory services. Of what does this consist?
6. What do the tax services of a public accountant include beyond preparing tax returns?
7. Differentiate between accounting and bookkeeping.
8. What does an income statement show?
9. As the word is used in accounting, what is a revenue? An expense?
10. Why is the period of time covered by an income statement of extreme significance?
11. What does a balance sheet show?
12. Define *(a)* asset, *(b)* liability, *(c)* equity, and *(d)* owner's equity.
13. Why is a business treated as a separate entity for accounting purposes?
14. What is required by the cost principle? Why is such a principle necessary?
15. Why are not balance sheet amounts for the assets of a business changed from time to time to reflect changes in market values?
16. A business shows office stationery on its balance sheet at its $50 cost, although the stationery can be sold for not more than $0.25 as scrap paper. What accounting principles and concept justify this?
17. In accounting, transactions are measured, recorded, and reported in terms of dollars, and the dollar is assumed to be a stable unit of measure. Is the dollar a stable unit of measure?
18. What are generally accepted accounting principles?
19. Why are the *Statements* of the Financial Accounting Standards Board and the *Opinions* of the Accounting Principles Board of importance to accounting students?

20. How does separate legal entity affect the responsibility of a corporation's stockholders for the debts of the corporation? Does this responsibility or lack of responsibility for the debts of the business apply to the owner or owners of a single proprietorship or partnership business?
21. What is the balance sheet equation? What is its importance to accounting students?
22. Is it possible for a transaction to increase or decrease a single liability without affecting any other asset, liability, or owner's equity item?
23. In accounting, what does the realization principle require?

Class Exercises

Exercise 1-1

On May 31 of the current year, the balance sheet of Ski Shop, a single proprietorship, showed the following:

Cash	$ 1,500
Other assets	40,000
Accounts payable . .	15,000
Jack Hill, capital. . .	26,500

On that date, Jack Hill sold the "Other assets" for $20,000 in preparation for ending and liquidating the business of Ski Shop.

Required

1. Prepare a balance sheet for the shop as it would appear immediately after the sale of the assets.
2. Tell how the shop's cash should be distributed in ending the business and why.

Exercise 1-2

Determine the missing amount on each of the following lines:

	Assets	= Liabilities	+ Owner's Equity
a.	$32,600	$8,200	?
b.	28,800	?	$15,300
c.	?	7,200	21,500

Exercise 1-3

The effects of five transactions on the assets, liabilities, and owner's equity of Ted Lee in his law practice are shown in the following equation with each transaction identified by a letter. Write a short sentence or phrase telling the probable nature of each transaction.

	Cash +	Accounts Receivable +	Law Library +	Office Equipment =	Accounts Payable +	Ted Lee, Capital
	$800		$3,500	$8,600		$12,900
a.	−100		+100			
	$700		$3,600	$8,600		$12,900
b.				+300	+$300	
	$700		$3,600	$8,900	$300	$12,900
c.		+$500				+500
	$700	$500	$3,600	$8,900	$300	$13,400
d.	−300				−300	
	$400	$500	$3,600	$8,900	$ 0	$13,400
e.	+500	−500				
	$900 +	$ 0 +	$3,600 +	$8,900 =	$ 0 +	$13,400

Exercise 1-4

Determine:

a. The equity of the owner in a business having $96,800 of assets and $15,200 of liabilities.
b. The liabilities of a business having $72,800 of assets and in which the owner has a $51,400 equity.
c. The assets of a business having $6,300 of liabilities and in which the owner has a $31,600 equity.

Exercise 1-5

On October 1, Dale Beck began a new business, a real estate agency. The following accounting equation of the agency was prepared after it had completed four transactions. Analyze the equation and list the four transactions with their amounts.

Cash +	Office Supplies +	Office Furniture +	Land and Building =	Accounts Payable +	Mortgage Payable +	Dale Beck, Capital
$2,500	$250	$7,500	$100,000	$250	$75,000	$35,000

Exercise 1-6

A business had the following assets and liabilities at the beginning and at the end of a year:

	Assets	Liabilities
Beginning of the year . .	$65,000	$20,000
End of the year.	75,000	10,000

Determine the net income or net loss of the business during the year under each of the following unrelated assumptions:

a. The owner of the business made no additional investments in the business and no withdrawals of assets from the business during the year.
b. The owner made no additional investments in the business during the year but had withdrawn $1,500 per month to pay personal living expenses.

c. During the year, the owner had made no withdrawals but had made a $25,000 additional investment in the business.

d. The owner had withdrawn $2,000 from the business each month to pay personal living expenses and near the year-end had invested an additional $10,000 in the business.

Exercise 1-7

Jane Ball began the practice of dentistry and during a short period completed these transactions:

a. Invested $8,000 in cash and dental equipment having a $2,000 fair value in a dental practice.
b. Paid the rent on suitable office space for two months in advance, $1,500.
c. Purchased additional dental equipment on credit, $5,500.
d. Completed dental work for a patient and immediately collected $100 cash for the work.
e. Completed dental work for a patient on credit, $600.
f. Purchased additional dental equipment for cash, $400.
g. Paid the dental assistant's wages, $300.
h. Collected $200 of the amount owed by the patient of transaction (e).
i. Paid for the equipment purchased in transaction (c).

Required

Arrange the following asset, liability, and owner's equity titles in an equation form like Illustration 1-7: Cash; Accounts Receivable; Prepaid Rent; Dental Equipment; Accounts Payable; and Jane Ball, Capital. Then show by additions and subtractions the effects of the transactions on the elements of the equation. Show new totals after each transaction.

Exercise 1-8

On October 1 of the current year, Sue Davis began the practice of law. On October 31, her records showed the following asset, liability, and owner's equity items including revenue earned and expenses. From the information, prepare an October income statement and a month-end balance sheet like Illustration 1-2. Head the statements Sue Davis, Attorney. (The October 31 $3,500 amount of Sue's capital is the amount of her capital after it was increased and decreased by the October revenue and expenses.)

Cash	$ 400	Sue Davis, capital . . .	$3,500
Accounts receivable . .	200	Legal fees earned	2,300
Prepaid rent	500	Rent expense	500
Law library	2,500	Salaries expense . . .	800
Accounts payable . . .	100	Telephone expense . .	50

Exercise 1-9

List a transaction for each of the following that will:

a. Increase an asset and decrease an asset.
b. Increase an asset and increase a liability.
c. Decrease an asset and decrease a liability.

d. Decrease a liability and increase a liability.

e. Increase an asset and increase owner equity.

f. Decrease an asset and decrease owner equity.

□ **Problems**   **Problem 1-1**

June Cole, CPA, began a public accounting practice and during a short period completed these transactions:

a. Sold for $36,450 a personal investment in IBM stock and deposited $35,000 of the proceeds in a bank account opened in the name of the practice.

b. Purchased for $90,000 a small building to be used as an office. She paid $30,000 in cash and signed a mortgage contract promising to pay the balance over a period of years.

c. Took office equipment from home for use in the practice. The equipment had a $400 fair value.

d. Purchased office supplies for cash, $250.

e. Purchased office equipment on credit, $5,000.

f. Completed accounting work for a client and immediately collected $100 for the work done.

g. Paid a local newspaper $50 for a small notice of the opening of the practice.

h. Completed $750 of accounting work for a client on credit.

i. Made a $500 installment payment on the equipment purchased in transaction (e).

j. The client of transaction (h) paid $500 of the amount he owed.

k. Paid the office secretary's wages, $400.

l. June Cole withdrew $250 from the bank account of the practice to pay personal living expenses.

Required

1. Arrange the following asset, liability, and owner's equity titles in an equation like Illustration 1-7: Cash; Accounts Receivable; Office Supplies; Office Equipment; Building; Accounts Payable; Mortgage Payable; and June Cole, Capital.

2. Show by additions and subtractions the effects of each transaction on the elements of the equation. Show new totals after each addition or subtraction, as in Illustration 1-7.

Problem 1-2

Jed Hill began a new law practice and completed these transactions during June of the current year:

June 1 Transferred $5,000 from his personal savings account to a checking account opened in the name of the law practice, Jed Hill, Attorney.

  1 Rented the furnished office of a lawyer who was retiring, and paid cash for three months' rent in advance, $1,500.

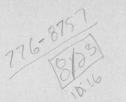

June 1 Purchased the law library of the retiring lawyer for $3,000, paying
$1,000 in cash and agreeing to pay the balance in one year.
2 Purchased office supplies for cash, $50.
8 Completed legal work for a client and immediately collected $150
in cash for the work done.
9 Purchased law books on credit, $300.
14 Completed legal work for Guaranty Bank on credit, $750.
18 Purchased office supplies on credit, $25.
19 Paid for the law books purchased on June 9.
22 Completed legal work for Apex Realty on credit, $1,000.
24 Received $750 from Guaranty Bank for the work completed on
June 14.
30 Paid the office secretary's salary, $950.
30 Paid the monthly utility bills, $80.
30 Recognized that one month's rent on the office had expired and
become an expense. (Reduce the prepaid rent and the owner's
equity.)
30 Took an inventory of unused office supplies and determined that
$25 of supplies had been used and had become an expense.

Required

1. Arrange the following asset, liability, and owner's equity titles in an
equation like Illustration 1-7: Cash; Accounts Receivable; Prepaid Rent;
Office Supplies; Law Library; Accounts Payable; and Jed Hill, Capital.

2. Show by additions and subtractions the effects of each transaction on
the items of the equation. Show new totals after each transaction.

3. Prepare for the law practice a June 30 balance sheet like Illustration
1-2.

4. Analyze the increases and decreases in the last column of the equation
and prepare a June income statement for the practice.

Problem 1-3

The records of Terry Blue, Realtor, show the following assets and liabilities
as of the ends of 1986 and 1987:

	December 31	
	1986	1987
Cash	$1,200	$ 600
Accounts receivable . .	800	400
Prepaid rent	600	
Office supplies	200	100
Prepaid insurance . . .	800	1,500
Office equipment . . .	5,200	6,800
Land.		25,000
Building		85,000
Accounts payable . . .	500	700
Note payable		10,000
Mortgage payable . . .		75,000

During the last week of December 1987, Mr. Blue purchased in the
name of the business, Terry Blue, Realtor, a small office building and

moved the business from rented quarters to the new building. The building and the land it occupied cost $110,000. The business paid $35,000 in cash and assumed a mortgage liability for the balance. Mr. Blue had to borrow $10,000 in the name of the business, signing a $10,000 note payable, and invest an additional $20,000 in the business to enable it to pay the $35,000. The business earned a satisfactory net income during 1987, which enabled Mr. Blue to withdraw $2,000 per month from the business to pay personal living expenses.

Required

1. Prepare balance sheets like Illustration 1-2 for the business as of the ends of 1986 and 1987.
2. Prepare a calculation to show the net income earned by the business during 1987.

Problem 1-4

Ned Hall graduated from college in June of the current year with a degree in architecture, and on July 1, Hall began the practice of his profession by investing $3,000 in a business he called Ned Hall, Architect. He then completed these transactions.

July 1 Rented the furnished office and equipment of an architect who was retiring, paying $1,800 cash for three months' rent in advance.

    1 Purchased drafting supplies for cash, $75.

    2 Purchased insurance protection for one year in advance for cash by paying the premium on two policies, $600.

    5 Completed architectural work for a client and immediately collected $250 cash for the work done.

    8 Completed architectural work for Valley Realty on credit, $750.

  15 Paid the salary of the draftsman, $500.

  18 Received payment in full for the work completed for Valley Realty on July 8.

  19 Completed architectural work for Western Contractors on credit, $800.

  20 Purchased additional drafting supplies on credit, $25.

  23 Completed architectural work for Dale West on credit, $600.

  27 Purchased additional drafting supplies on credit, $50.

  29 Received payment in full from Western Contractors for the work completed on July 19.

  30 Paid for the drafting supplies purchased on July 20.

  31 Paid the July telephone bill, $25.

  31 Paid the July utilities expense, $65.

  31 Paid the salary of the draftsman, $500.

  31 Recognized that one month's office rent had expired and become an expense. (Reduce the prepaid rent and owner's equity to record the expense.)

  31 Recognized that one month's prepaid insurance, $50, had expired.

  31 Took an inventory of drafting supplies and determined that $60 of drafting supplies had been used and had become an expense.

Required

1. Arrange the following asset, liability, and owner's equity titles in an equation like Illustration 1-7: Cash; Accounts Receivable; Prepaid Rent; Prepaid Insurance; Drafting Supplies; Accounts Payable; and Ned Hall, Capital.

2. Show the effects of the transactions on the elements of the equation by recording increases and decreases in the appropriate columns. Indicate an increase with a + and a decrease with a − before the amount. *Do not determine new totals for the items of the equation after each transaction.*

3. After recording the last transaction, determine and insert on the next line the final total for each item of the equation and determine if the equation is in balance.

4. Prepare a July 31 balance sheet for the practice like the one in Illustration 1-2. Head the statement Ned Hall, Architect.

5. Analyze the items in the last column of the equation and prepare a July income statement for the practice.

□ Alternate Problems

Problem 1-1A

June Cole secured her broker's license and opened a real estate office. During a short period she completed these transactions:

a. Sold for $31,250 a personal investment in General Electric stock, which she had inherited, and deposited $30,000 of the proceeds in a bank account opened in the name of the business, June Cole, Realtor.

b. Purchased for $80,000 a small building to be used as an office. She paid $25,000 in cash and signed a mortgage contract promising to pay the balance over a period of years.

c. Purchased office equipment for cash, $800.

d. Took from home for use in the business office equipment having a $350 fair value.

e. Purchased on credit office supplies, $50, and office equipment, $3,600.

f. Paid the local paper $110 for advertising.

g. Completed a real estate appraisal for a client on credit and billed the client $125 for the work done.

h. Sold a house and collected a $5,000 cash commission on completion of the sale.

i. June Cole withdrew $1,000 from the business to pay personal expenses.

j. The client paid for the appraisal of transaction (g).

k. Made a $2,000 installment payment on the amount owed from transaction (e).

l. Paid the office secretary's wages, $850.

Required

1. Arrange the following asset, liability, and owner's equity titles in an equation like Illustration 1-7: Cash; Accounts Receivable; Office Supplies; Office Equipment; Building; Accounts Payable; Mortgage Payable; and June Cole, Capital.

2. Show by additions and subtractions, as in Illustration 1-7, the effects of each transaction on the elements of the equation. Show new totals after each transaction.

Problem 1-2A

Jed Hill graduated from law school in June of the current year and on July 1 began a law practice by investing $3,000 in cash in the practice. He completed these additional transactions during July:

July 1   Rented the furnished office of a lawyer who was retiring and paid two month's rent in advance, $1,200.

       1   Moved from home to the law office law books acquired in college. (In other words, invested the books in the practice.) The books had a $400 fair value.

       2   Purchased office supplies for cash, $60.

       3   Purchased additional law books costing $1,000. Paid $500 in cash and promised to pay the balance within 90 days.

       6   Completed legal work for a client and immediately collected $250 for the work done.

    12   Completed legal work for Valley Bank on credit, $750.

    16   Purchased additional office supplies on credit, $25.

    22   Received $750 from Valley Bank for the work completed on July 12.

    26   Completed legal work for Vista Realty on credit, $650.

    30   Made $200 installment payment on the law books purchased on July 3.

    31   Paid the July telephone bill, $40.

    31   Paid the office secretary's wages, $950.

    31   Recognized that one month's rent on the office had expired and become an expense. (Reduce the prepaid rent and the owner's equity.)

    31   Took an inventory of unused office supplies and determined that $35 of supplies had been used and had become an expense.

Required

1. Arrange the following asset, liability, and owner's equity titles in an equation like Illustration 1-7: Cash; Accounts Receivable; Prepaid Rent; Office Supplies; Law Library; Accounts Payable, and Jed Hill, Capital.

2. Show by additions and subtractions the effects of each transaction on the elements of the equation. Show new totals after each transaction.

3. Prepare a July 31 balance sheet for the law practice. Head the statement Jed Hill, Attorney.

4. Analyze the items in the last column of the equation and prepare a July income statement for the practice.

Problem 1-3A

The accounting records of Maria Gomez's dental practice show the following assets and liabilities as of the ends of 1986 and 1987:

	December 31	
	1986	**1987**
Cash	$ 1,200	$ 700
Accounts receivable . .	2,900	3,500
Prepaid rent	900	
Office supplies	500	400
Prepaid insurance . . .	600	1,500
Office equipment . . .	12,200	14,100
Land.		40,000
Building		110,000
Accounts payable . . .	700	800
Note payable		10,000
Mortgage payable . . .		100,000

During the last week of December 1987, Dr. Gomez purchased a small office building in the name of the dental practice, Maria Gomez, DDS, and moved her practice from rented quarters to the new building. The building and the land it occupies cost $150,000; the practice paid $50,000 in cash and assumed a mortgage liability for the balance. Dr. Gomez had to borrow $10,000 in the name of the practice, signing a $10,000 note payable, and invest an additional $25,000 in the practice to enable it to pay the $50,000. The practice earned a satisfactory net income during 1987, which enabled Dr. Gomez to withdraw $2,000 per month from the practice to pay her personal living expenses.

Required

1. Prepare balance sheets like Illustration 1-2 for the practice as of the ends of 1986 and 1987.
2. Prepare a calculation to show the amount of net income earned by the practice during 1987.

Problem 1-4A

Ned Hall graduated from college, completed his internship, and on May 1 of the current year began an architectural practice by investing $3,000 in the practice. He then completed these additional transactions:

May 1   Rented the office and equipment of an architect who was retiring, paying $1,500 cash for two months' rent in advance.
     1   Purchased insurance protection for one year by paying the premium on two policies, $660.
     2   Purchased drafting supplies for cash, $60.
     5   Completed a short architectural assignment for a client and immediately collected $200 cash for the work done.
     8   Purchased additional drafting supplies on credit, $40.
   10   Completed architectural work for Ajax Contractors on credit, $700.
   15   Paid the salary of the draftsman, $600.
   18   Paid for the drafting supplies purchased on July 8.
   20   Received payment in full from Ajax Contractors for the work completed on May 10.

May 23   Completed architectural work for Valley Realtors on credit, $550.
    26   Purchased additional drafting supplies on credit, $30.
    30   Completed additional architectural work for Ajax Contractors on credit, $725.
    31   Paid the salary of the draftsman, $600.
    31   Paid the July telephone bill, $25.
    31   Paid the July electric bill, $70.
    31   Recognized that one month's office rent had expired and become an expense. (Reduce the prepaid rent and the owner's equity to record the expense.)
    31   Recognized that one month's prepaid insurance, $55, had expired.
    31   Took an inventory of the unused drafting supplies and determined that supplies costing $50 had been used and had become an expense.

Required

1. Arrange the following asset, liability, and owner's equity titles in an equation like Illustration 1-7: Cash; Accounts Receivable; Prepaid Rent; Prepaid Insurance; Drafting Supplies; Accounts Payable; and Ned Hall, Capital.

2. Show the effects of the transactions on the elements of the equation by recording increases and decreases in the appropriate columns. Indicate an increase with a + and a decrease with a − before the amount. *Do not determine new totals for the items after each transaction.*

3. After recording the last transaction, determine and enter on the next line the final total for each item and determine if the equation is in balance.

4. Prepare a May 31 balance sheet for the practice like the one in Illustration 1-2. Head the statement Ned Hall, Architect.

5. Analyze the items in the last column of the equation and prepare a May income statement for the practice.

Provocative Problems

Provocative Problem 1-1   County Fair Stand

Gary West invested $750 in a short-term enterprise, the sale of soft drinks during the county fair in his small rural town. He paid $150 for the right to sell soft drinks in the fair grounds. He constructed a stand from which to make the sales at a cost of $50 for lumber and crepe paper, none of which had any value at the end of the fair. He bought ice for which he paid $40 and purchased soft drinks costing $750. At this point, he had only $510 in cash and could not pay in full for the drinks, but since his credit rating was good, the soft drink company accepted $500 in cash and the promise that he would pay the balance the day after the fair ended. During the fair, he collected $1,540 in cash from sales, and at the end of the fair, he paid a young man $90 for helping with the sales. He had soft drinks left over that cost $35 and could be returned to the soft drink company.

Assemble the information in such a way that will enable you to prepare a balance sheet like Illustration 1-2 for Gary West as of the end of the fair. Also prepare an income statement showing the net income or loss of the enterprise. Assume the fair lasted three days, ending on July 15 of the current year.

Provocative Problem 1-2   Jack's Delivery Service

Jack Ives ran out of money at the end of the first semester of his sophomore year in college. He had to go to work, but he could not find a satisfactory job. However, since he had a motorcycle having a $2,400 fair value, he decided to go into business for himself. Consequently, he began Jack's Delivery Service with no assets other than the motorcycle. He kept no accounting records; and now, at the year-end, he has engaged you to determine the net income earned by the service during its first partial year of 42 weeks. You find that the service has a $700 year-end bank balance plus $50 of undeposited cash. Local stores owe the service $125 for delivering packages during the past month. The service still owns the motorcycle, but its fair value has declined by one fourth due to use in the business. In addition, the service has a new delivery truck that cost $6,800, but that has depreciated $400 through use since its purchase. The service still owes a finance company $4,000 as a result of the truck's purchase. Also, when the truck was purchased, Jack borrowed $1,500 from his father to help make the down payment. The loan was made to the delivery service, was interest free, and has not been repaid. Finally, since the service has been profitable from the beginning, Jack Ives has withdrawn $200 of its earnings each week for the 42 weeks of its existence to pay personal living expenses.

Determine and present a calculation to prove the net income earned by the business during the 42 weeks of its operations.

Part Two

Processing Accounting Data

2 Recording Transactions

After studying Chapter 2, you should be able to:

1. Explain the mechanics of double-entry accounting and tell why transactions are recorded with equal debits and credits.

2. State the rules of debit and credit and apply the rules in recording transactions.

3. Tell the normal balance of any asset, liability, or owner's equity account.

4. Record transactions in a General Journal, post to the ledger accounts, and prepare a trial balance to test the accuracy of the recording and posting.

5. Define or explain the words and phrases listed in the chapter Glossary.

Transactions are the raw material of the accounting process. The process consists of identifying transactions, recording them, and summarizing their effects in periodic reports for the use of management and other decision makers.

Some years ago, almost all companies used pen and ink to manually record and process the data resulting from transactions. Today, only very small companies use this method, companies small enough that their accounting can be done by one person working an hour or two each day. Larger, modern companies use electric bookkeeping machines and computers in recording transactions and in processing the recorded data.

Nevertheless, students normally begin their study of accounting by learning to process accounting data manually with a pen or pencil. By manually processing the data, students can more readily understand the data and the relationships between its parts. Also, almost everything learned through manual methods is applicable to machine and computer methods. Actually, the machines and computer equipment replace pen and ink in processing the data, speeding the work, and taking the drudgery out of the processing.

Business Papers

Business papers provide evidence of transactions completed and are the basis for accounting entries to record the transactions. For example, when goods are sold on credit, two or more copies of an invoice or sales ticket are prepared. One copy is enclosed with the goods or is delivered to the customer. The other is sent to the accounting department where it becomes the basis for an entry to record the sale. Also, when goods are sold for cash, the sales are commonly "rung up" on a cash register that prints the amount of each sale on a paper tape locked inside the register. At the end of the day, when the proper key is depressed, the register prints on the tape the total cash sales for the day. The tape is then removed and becomes the basis for an entry to record the sales. Also, when an established business purchases assets, it normally buys on credit and receives an invoice that becomes the basis for an entry to record the purchase. Likewise, when the invoice is paid, a check is issued and the check or a carbon copy becomes the basis for an entry to record the payment. Obviously, then, business papers are the starting point in the accounting process. Furthermore, verifiable business papers, particularly those originating outside the business, are also objective evidence of transactions completed and the amounts at which they should be recorded, as required by the **objectivity principle.**

Accounts

A company with an accounting system based on pen and ink or electric bookkeeping machines uses **accounts** in recording its transactions. A number of accounts are normally required. A separate account is used for summarizing the increases and decreases in each asset, liability, and owner's equity item appearing on the balance sheet and each revenue and expense appearing on the income statement.

In its most simple form, an account looks like the letter "T," is called a **T-account,** and appears as follows:

(Place for the Name of the Item Recorded in This Account)	
(Left side)	(Right side)

Note that the "T" gives the account a left side, a right side, and a place for the name of the item, the increases and decreases of which are recorded therein.

When a T-account is used in recording increases and decreases in an item, the increases are placed on one side of the account and the decreases on the other. For example, if the increases and decreases in the cash of Larry Owen's law practice of the previous chapter are recorded in a T-account, they appear as follows:

Cash

Investment	5,000	Prepayment of rent	900
Legal fee earned	500	Equipment purchase	3,700
Collection of account receivable	1,000	Salary payment	400
		Payment on account payable	100

The reason for putting the increases on one side and the decreases on the other is that this makes it easy to add the increases and then add the decreases. The sum of the decreases may then be subtracted from the sum of the increases to learn how much of the item recorded in the account the company has, owns, or owes. For example, the increases in the cash of the Owen law practice were:

Investment.	$5,000
Legal fee earned	500
Collection of an account receivable . .	1,000
Sum of the increases	$6,500

And the decreases were:

Prepayment of office rent	$ 900
Equipment purchase	3,700
Salary payment	400
Payment on account payable.	100
Sum of the decreases.	$5,100

And when the sum of the decreases is subtracted from the sum of the increases,

Sum of the increases	$6,500
Sum of the decreases.	5,100
Balance of cash remaining.	$1,400

The subtraction shows the law practice has $1,400 of cash remaining.

Balance of an Account

When the increases and decreases recorded in an account are separately added and the sum of the decreases is subtracted from the sum of the increases, the procedure is called determining the **account balance.** The balance of an account is the difference between its increases and decreases. It is also the amount of the item recorded in the account that the company has, owns, or owes at the time the balance is determined.

■ Accounts Commonly Used

A business uses a number of accounts in recording its transactions. However, the specific accounts used vary from one concern to another, depending upon the assets owned, the debts owed, and the information to be secured from the accounting records. Nevertheless, although the specific accounts vary, the following accounts are common.

Asset Accounts

If useful records of a company's assets are to be kept, an individual account is needed for each kind of asset owned. Some of the more common assets for which accounts are maintained are as follows:

Cash Increases and decreases in cash are recorded in an account called Cash. The cash of a business consists of money or any medium of exchange that a bank will accept at face value for deposit. It includes coins, currency, checks, and postal and bank money orders. The balance of the Cash account shows both the cash on hand in the store or office and that on deposit in the bank.

Notes Receivable A formal written promise to pay a definite sum of money at a fixed future date is called a **promissory note.** When amounts due from others are evidenced by promissory notes, the notes are known as notes receivable and are recorded in a Notes Receivable account.

Accounts Receivable Goods and services are commonly sold to customers on the basis of oral or implied promises of future payment. Such sales are known as sales on credit or sales on account; and the oral or implied promises to pay are known as accounts receivable. Accounts receivable are increased by sales on credit and are decreased by customer payments. Since it is necessary to know the amount currently owed by each customer, a separate record must be kept of each customer's purchases and payments. However, a discussion of this separate record is deferred until a later chapter. For the present, all increases and decreases in accounts receivable are recorded in a single account called Accounts Receivable.

Prepaid Insurance Fire, liability, and other types of insurance protection are normally paid for in advance. The amount paid is called a premium and may give protection from loss for one or more years. As a result, a large portion of each premium is an asset for a considerable time after payment.

When insurance premiums are paid, the asset prepaid insurance is increased by the amount paid. The increase is normally recorded in an account called Prepaid Insurance. Day by day, insurance premiums expire. Consequently, at intervals the insurance that has expired is calculated and the balance of the Prepaid Insurance account is reduced accordingly.

Office Supplies Stamps, stationery, paper, pencils, and like items are known as office supplies. They are assets when purchased, and continue to be assets until consumed. As they are consumed, the amounts consumed become expenses. Increases and decreases in the asset office supplies are commonly recorded in an account called Office Supplies.

Store Supplies Wrapping paper, cartons, bags, string, and similar items used by a store are known as store supplies. Increases and decreases in store supplies are recorded in an account of that name.

Other Prepaid Expenses Prepaid expenses are items that are assets at the time of purchase but become expenses as they are consumed or expire. Prepaid insurance, office supplies, and store supplies are examples. Other examples are prepaid rent and prepaid taxes. Each is accounted for in a separate account.

Equipment Increases and decreases in such things as typewriters, desks, chairs, and office machines are commonly recorded in an account called Office Equipment. Likewise, changes in the amount of counters, showcases, cash registers, and like items used by a store are recorded in an account called Store Equipment.

Buildings A building used by a business in carrying on its operations may be a store, garage, warehouse, or factory. However, regardless of use, an account called Buildings is commonly employed in recording the increases and decreases in the buildings owned by a business and used in carrying on its operations.

Land An account called Land is commonly used in recording increases and decreases in the land owned by a business. Land and the buildings placed upon it are inseparable in physical fact. Nevertheless, it is usually desirable to account for land and its buildings in separate accounts because buildings depreciate and wear out but the land on which they are placed is assumed not to do so.

Liability Accounts

Most companies do not have as many liability accounts as asset accounts; however, the following are common:

Notes Payable Increases and decreases in amounts owed because of promissory notes given to creditors are accounted for in an account called Notes Payable.

Accounts Payable An account payable is an amount owed to a creditor. Accounts payable result from the purchase of merchandise, supplies, equipment, and services on credit. Since it is necessary to know the amount owed each creditor, an individual record must be kept of the purchases from and the payments to each. However, a discussion of this individual record is deferred until a later chapter. For the present, all increases and decreases in accounts payable are recorded in a single Accounts Payable account.

Unearned Revenues The **realization principle** requires that revenue be earned before it is recognized in the accounts as revenue. Therefore, when payment is received for products or services before delivery, the amounts received are **unearned revenue.** An unearned revenue results in a liability that will be extinguished by delivering the product or service paid for in advance. Subscriptions collected in advance by a magazine publisher, rent collected in advance by a landlord, and legal fees collected in advance by a lawyer are examples. Upon receipt, the amounts collected are recorded in liability accounts such as Unearned Subscriptions, Unearned Rent, and Unearned Legal Fees. When earned by delivery, the amounts earned are transferred to the revenue accounts, Subscriptions Earned, Rent Earned, and Legal Fees Earned.

Other Short-Term Payables Wages payable, taxes payable, and interest payable are other short-term liabilities for which individual accounts must be kept.

Mortgage Payable A **mortgage payable** is a long-term debt for which the creditor has a secured prior claim against some one or more of the debtor's assets. The mortgage gives the creditor the right to force the sale of the mortgaged assets through a foreclosure if the mortgage debt is not paid when due. An account called Mortgage Payable is commonly used in recording the increases and decreases in the amount owed on a mortgage.

Owner's Equity Accounts

Several kinds of transactions affect the equity of a business owner. In a single proprietorship, these include the investment of the owner, his or her withdrawals of cash or other assets for personal use, revenues earned, and expenses incurred. In the previous chapter, the effects of all such transactions on owner's equity were entered in a column under the name of the owner. This simplified the material of the chapter but made it necessary to analyze the items entered in the column in order to prepare an income statement. Fortunately, such an analysis is not necessary. All that is required to avoid it is a number of accounts, a separate one for each owner's equity item appearing on the balance sheet and a separate one for each revenue and expense on the income statement. Then, as each transaction affecting owner's equity is completed, it is recorded in the proper account. Among the accounts required are the following:

Capital Account When a person invests in a business of his or her own, the investment is recorded in an account carrying the owner's name and the word **Capital.** For example, an account called Larry Owen, Capital is used in recording the investment of Larry Owen in his law practice. In addition to the original investment, the **capital account** is used for any permanent additional increases or decreases in owner's equity.

Withdrawals Account Usually a person invests in a business to earn income. However, income is earned over a period of time, say, a year. Often during this period, the business owner must withdraw a portion of the earnings to pay living expenses or for other personal uses. These withdrawals reduce both assets and owner's equity. To record them, an account carrying the name of the business owner and the word **Withdrawals** is used. For example, an account called Larry Owen, Withdrawals is used to record the withdrawals of cash by Larry Owen from his law practice. The **withdrawals account** is also known as the **personal account** or **drawing account.**

An owner of a small unincorporated business often withdraws a fixed amount each week or month to pay personal living expenses, and often thinks of these withdrawals as a salary. However, in a legal sense they are not a salary because the owner of an unincorporated business cannot enter into a legally binding contract with himself to hire himself and pay himself a salary. Consequently, in law and custom it is recognized that such withdrawals are neither a salary nor an expense of the business but are withdrawals in anticipation of earnings.

Revenue and Expense Accounts When an income statement is prepared, it is necessary to know the amount of each kind of revenue earned and each kind of expense incurred during the period covered by the statement. To accumulate this information, a number of revenue and expense accounts are needed. However, all concerns do not have the same revenues and expenses. Consequently, it is impossible to list all revenue and expense accounts to be encountered. Nevertheless, Revenue from Repairs, Commissions Earned, Legal Fees Earned, Rent Earned, and Interest Earned are common examples of revenue accounts. And Advertising Expense, Store Supplies Expense, Office Salaries Expense, Office Supplies Expense, Rent Expense, Utilities Expense, and Insurance Expense are common examples of expense accounts. It should be noted that the kind of revenue or expense recorded in each above-mentioned account is evident from its title. This is generally true of such accounts.

Real and Nominal Accounts

To add to your vocabulary, it may be said here that balance sheet accounts are commonly called **real accounts.** Presumably, this is because most of the items recorded in these accounts exist in objective form. Likewise, income statement accounts are called **nominal accounts** because items recorded in these accounts exist in name only.

■   **The Ledger**   A business may use from two dozen to several thousand accounts in recording its transactions. Each account is placed on a separate page in a bound or loose-leaf book, or on a separate card in a tray of cards. If the accounts are kept in a book, the book is called a **ledger.** If they are kept on cards in a file tray, the tray of cards is a ledger. Actually, as used in accounting, the word ledger means a group of accounts.

■ **Debit and Credit**

As previously stated, a T-account has a left side and a right side. However, in accounting, the left side is called the **debit** side, abbreviated "Dr."; and the right side is called the **credit** side, abbreviated "Cr." Furthermore, when amounts are entered on the left side of an account, they are called **debits,** and the account is said to be **debited.** When amounts are entered on the right side, they are called **credits,** and the account is said to be **credited.** The difference between the total debits and the total credits recorded in an account is the **balance of the account.** The balance may be either a **debit balance** or a **credit balance.** It is a debit balance when the sum of the debits exceeds the sum of the credits and a credit balance when the sum of the credits exceeds the sum of the debits. An account is said to be **in balance** when its debits and credits are equal.

The words **to debit** and **to credit** should not be confused with **to increase** and **to decrease.** To debit means simply to enter an amount on the left side of an account. To credit means to enter an amount on the right side. Either may be an increase or a decrease. This may readily be seen by examining the way in which the investment of Larry Owen is recorded in his Cash and capital accounts that follow:

Cash		Larry Owen, Capital	
Investment 5,000			Investment 5,000

When Owen invested $5,000 in his law practice, both the business cash and Owen's equity were increased. Observe in the accounts that the increase in cash is recorded on the left or debit side of the Cash account, while the increase in owner's equity is recorded on the right or credit side. The transaction is recorded in this manner because of the mechanics of **double-entry accounting.**

■ **Mechanics of Double-Entry Accounting**

The mechanics of double-entry accounting are such that every transaction affects and is recorded in two or more accounts with equal debits and credits. Transactions are so recorded because the equal debits and credits offer a means of proving the recording accuracy. The proof is, if every transaction is recorded with equal debits and credits, then the debits in the ledger must equal the credits.

The person who first devised double-entry accounting based the system on the accounting equation, $A = L + OE$. He assigned the recording of increases in assets to the debit side of asset accounts. He then recognized that equal debits and credits were possible only if increases in liabilities and owner's equity were recorded on the opposite or credit side of liability and owner's equity accounts. In other words, he recognized that if increases in assets were to be recorded as debits, then increases and decreases in all accounts would have to be recorded as follows:

Assets		=	Liabilities		+	Owner's Equity	
Debit for	**Credit for**		**Debit for**	**Credit for**		**Debit for**	**Credit for**
increases	decreases		decreases	increases		decreases	increases

From the T-accounts it is possible to formulate rules for recording transactions under a double-entry system. The rules are:

1. Increases in assets are debited to asset accounts; consequently, decreases must be credited.
2. Increases in liability and owner's equity items are credited to liability and owner's equity accounts; consequently, decreases must be debited.

At this stage, beginning students will find it helpful to memorize these rules. They should also note that in a single proprietorship there are four kinds of owner's equity accounts: (1) the capital account, (2) the withdrawals account, (3) revenue accounts, and (4) expense accounts. Furthermore, for transactions affecting these accounts, students should observe these additional points:

1. The original investment of the owner of a business plus any more or less permanent changes in the investment are recorded in the capital account.
2. Withdrawals of assets for personal use, including cash to pay personal expenses, decrease owner's equity and are debited to the owner's withdrawals account.
3. Revenues increase owner's equity and are credited in each case to a revenue account that shows the kind of revenue earned.
4. Expenses decrease owner's equity and are debited in each case to an expense account that shows the kind of expense incurred.

Transactions Illustrating the Rules of Debit and Credit

The following transactions of Larry Owen's law practice illustrate the application of debit and credit rules. They also show how transactions are recorded in the accounts. The number preceding each transaction is used throughout the illustration to identify the transaction in the accounts. Note that most of the transactions are the same ones used in Chapter 1 to illustrate the effects of transactions on the accounting equation.

To record a transaction, it must be analyzed to determine what items were increased or decreased. The rules of debit and credit are then applied to determine the debit and credit effects of the increases or decreases. An analysis of each of the following transactions is given in order to demonstrate the process.

1. On July 1, Larry Owen invested $5,000 in a new law practice.

Cash	
(1) 5,000	

Larry Owen, Capital	
	(1) 5,000

Analysis of the transaction: The transaction increased the cash of the practice and at the same time it increased the equity of Owen in the business. Increases in assets are debited, and increases in owner's equity are credited. Consequently, to record the transaction, Cash should be debited and Larry Owen, Capital should be credited for $5,000.

2. Paid the office rent for three months in advance, $900.

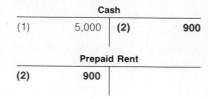

Analysis of the transaction: The asset prepaid rent, the right to occupy the office for three months, is increased; and the asset cash is decreased. Increases in assets are debited, and decreases are credited. Therefore, to record the transaction, debit Prepaid Rent and credit Cash for $900.

Cash			
(1)	5,000	(2)	900

Prepaid Rent			
(2)	900		

3. Purchased office equipment for cash, $3,700.

Analysis of the transaction: The asset office equipment is increased, and the asset cash is decreased. Debit Office Equipment and credit Cash for $3,700.

Cash			
(1)	5,000	(2)	900
		(3)	3,700

Office Equipment			
(3)	3,700		

4. Purchased on credit from Alpha Company office supplies, $60, and office equipment, $300.

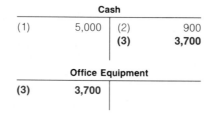

Analysis of the transaction: This transaction increased the assets office supplies and office equipment, but it also created a liability. Increases in assets are debits, and increases in liabilities are credits; therefore, debit Office Supplies for $60 and Office Equipment for $300 and credit Accounts Payable for $360.

Office Supplies			
(4)	60		

Office Equipment			
(3)	3,700		
(4)	300		

Accounts Payable			
		(4)	360

5. Completed legal work for a client and immediately collected a $500 fee.

Analysis of the transaction: This revenue transaction increased both assets and owner's equity. Increases in assets are debits, and increases in owner's equity are credits. Therefore, Cash is debited; and in order to show the nature of the increase in owner's equity and at the same time accumulate information for the income statement, the revenue account Legal Fees Earned is credited.

Cash			
(1)	5,000	(2)	900
(5)	500	(3)	3,700

Legal Fees Earned			
		(5)	500

6. Paid the secretary's salary for the first two weeks of July, $400.

Cash			
(1)	5,000	(2)	900
(5)	500	(3)	3,700
		(6)	**400**

Office Salaries Expense		
(6)	**400**	

Analysis of the transaction: The secretary's salary is an expense that decreased both assets and owner's equity. Debit Office Salaries Expense to decrease owner's equity and also to accumulate information for the income statement, and credit Cash to record the decrease in cash.

7. Signed a contract with Coast Realty to do its legal work on a fixed-fee basis for $300 per month. Received the fee for the first month and a half in advance, $450.

Cash			
(1)	5,000	(2)	900
(5)	500	(3)	3,700
(7)	**450**	(6)	400

Unearned Legal Fees		
	(7)	**450**

Analysis of the transaction: The $450 inflow increased cash, but the inflow is not a revenue until earned. Its acceptance before being earned created a liability, the obligation to do the client's legal work for the next month and a half. Consequently, debit Cash to record the increase in cash and credit Unearned Legal Fees to record the liability increase.

8. Completed legal work for a client on credit and billed the client $1,000 for the services rendered.

Accounts Receivable		
(8)	**1,000**	

Legal Fees Earned		
	(5)	500
	(8)	**1,000**

Analysis of the transaction: Completion of this revenue transaction gave the law practice the right to collect $1,000 from the client, and thus increased assets and owner's equity. Consequently, debit Accounts Receivable for the increase in assets and credit Legal Fees Earned to increase owner's equity and at the same time accumulate information for the income statement.

9. Paid the secretary's salary for the second two weeks of the month.

Cash			
(1)	1,000	(2)	900
(5)	500	(3)	3,700
(7)	450	(6)	400
		(9)	**400**

Office Salaries Expense		
(6)	400	
(9)	**400**	

Analysis of the transaction: An expense that decreased assets and owner's equity. Debit Office Salaries Expense to accumulate information for the income statement and credit Cash.

10. Larry Owen withdrew $200 from the law practice to pay personal expenses.

Cash

(1)	5,000	(2)	900
(5)	500	(3)	3,700
(7)	450	(6)	400
		(9)	400
		(10)	**200**

Analysis of the transaction: This transaction reduced in equal amounts both assets and owner's equity. Cash is credited to record the asset reduction; and the Larry Owen, Withdrawals account is debited for the reduction in owner's equity.

Larry Owen, Withdrawals

(10)	**200**

11. The client paid the $1,000 legal fee billed in transaction 8.

Cash

(1)	5,000	(2)	900
(5)	500	(3)	3,700
(7)	450	(6)	400
(11)	**1,000**	(9)	400
		(10)	200

Analysis of the transaction: One asset was increased, and the other decreased. Debit Cash to record the increase in cash, and credit Accounts Receivable to record the decrease in the account receivable, or the decrease in the right to collect from the client.

Accounts Receivable

(8)	1,000	**(11)**	**1,000**

12. Paid Alpha Company $100 of the $360 owed for the items purchased on credit in transaction 4.

Cash

(1)	5,000	(2)	900
(5)	500	(3)	3,700
(7)	450	(6)	400
(11)	1,000	(9)	400
		(10)	200
		(12)	**100**

Analysis of the transaction: Payments to creditors decrease in like amounts both assets and liabilities. Decreases in liabilities are debited, and decreases in assets are credited. Debit Accounts Payable and credit Cash.

Accounts Payable

(12)	**100**	(4)	360

13. Paid the July telephone bill, $30.
14. Paid the July electric bill, $35.

Cash

(1)	5,000	(2)	900
(5)	500	(3)	3,700
(7)	450	(6)	400
(11)	1,000	(9)	400
		(10)	200
		(12)	100
		(13)	**30**
		(14)	**35**

Analysis of the transactions: These expense transactions are alike in that each decreased cash; they differ in each case as to the kind of expense involved. Consequently, in recording them, Cash is credited; and to accumulate information for the income statement, a different expense account, one showing the nature of the expense in each case, is debited.

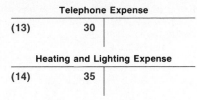

Telephone Expense

| (13) | 30 | |

Heating and Lighting Expense

| (14) | 35 | |

■ **The Accounts and the Equation**

In Illustration 2-1, the transactions of the Owen law practice are shown in the accounts, with the accounts brought together and classified under the elements of an accounting equation.

■ **Preparing a Trial Balance**

As previously stated, in a double-entry accounting system every transaction is recorded with equal debits and credits so that the equality of the debits and credits may be tested as a proof of the recording accuracy. This equality is tested at intervals by preparing a **trial balance**. A trial balance is prepared by (1) determining the balance of each account in the ledger; (2) listing the accounts having balances, with the debit balances in one column and the credit balances in another (as in Illustration 2-2); (3) adding the debit balances; (4) adding the credit balances; and then (5) comparing the sum of the debit balances with the sum of the credit balances.

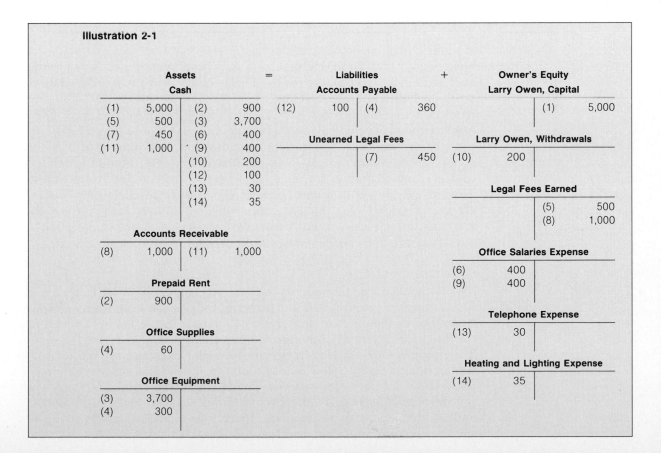

Illustration 2-1

| Assets | = | Liabilities | + | Owner's Equity |

Cash

(1)	5,000	(2)	900
(5)	500	(3)	3,700
(7)	450	(6)	400
(11)	1,000	(9)	400
		(10)	200
		(12)	100
		(13)	30
		(14)	35

Accounts Payable

| (12) | 100 | (4) | 360 |

Unearned Legal Fees

| | | (7) | 450 |

Larry Owen, Capital

| | | (1) | 5,000 |

Larry Owen, Withdrawals

| (10) | 200 | |

Accounts Receivable

| (8) | 1,000 | (11) | 1,000 |

Legal Fees Earned

| | | (5) | 500 |
| | | (8) | 1,000 |

Prepaid Rent

| (2) | 900 | |

Office Salaries Expense

| (6) | 400 | |
| (9) | 400 | |

Office Supplies

| (4) | 60 | |

Telephone Expense

| (13) | 30 | |

Office Equipment

| (3) | 3,700 | |
| (4) | 300 | |

Heating and Lighting Expense

| (14) | 35 | |

Illustration 2-2

Larry Owen, Attorney
Trial Balance
July 31, 19—

Cash	$1,185	
Prepaid rent	900	
Office supplies	60	
Office equipment	4,000	
Accounts payable		$ 260
Unearned legal fees		450
Larry Owen, capital		5,000
Larry Owen, withdrawals	200	
Legal fees earned		1,500
Office salaries expense	800	
Telephone expense	30	
Heating and lighting expense	35	
Totals	$7,210	$7,210

The illustrated trial balance was prepared from the accounts in Illustration 2-1. Note that its column totals are equal, or in other words, the trial balance is in balance. When a trial balance is in balance, debits equal credits in the ledger, and it is assumed that no errors were made in recording transactions.

■ **The Proof Offered by a Trial Balance**

If when a trial balance is prepared it does not balance, an error or errors have been made. The error or errors may have been either in recording transactions, in determining the account balances, in copying the balances on the trial balance, or in adding the trial balance columns. On the other hand, if a trial balance balances, it is assumed that no errors have been made. However, a trial balance that balances is not absolute proof of accuracy. Errors may have been made that did not affect the equality of its columns. For example, an error in which a correct debit amount is debited to the wrong account or a correct credit amount is credited to the wrong account will not cause a trial balance to be out of balance. Likewise, an error in which a wrong amount is both debited and credited to the right accounts will not cause a trial balance to be out of balance. Consequently, a trial balance in balance is only presumptive proof of recording accuracy.

■ **Balance Column Accounts**

T-accounts like the ones shown thus far are commonly used in textbook illustrations and also in accounting classes for blackboard demonstrations. In both cases, their use eliminates details and permits the student to concentrate on ideas. However, although widely used in textbooks and in teaching, T-accounts are not used in business for recording transactions. In recording transactions, accounts similar to the one in Illustration 2-3 are generally used. (Note the year in the date column of the illustrated account. Throughout the remainder of this text, years will be designated 198A, 198B, 198C, and so forth. In all such situations, 198A is the earliest year, 198B is the succeeding year, and so on through the series.)

Illustration 2-3

		Cash				Account No. 111	

Date		Explanation	PR	Debit	Credit	Balance
198A July	1		G1	5,000 00		5,000 00
	1		G1		900 00	4,100 00
	3		G1		3,700 00	400 00
	12		G1	500 00		900 00

The account of Illustration 2-3 is called a **balance column account**. It differs from a T-account in that it has columns for specific information about each debit and credit entered in the account. Also, its Debit and Credit columns are placed side by side, and it has a third or Balance column. In this Balance column, the account's new balance is entered each time the account is debited or credited. As a result, the last amount in the column is the account's current balance. For example, on July 1, the illustrated account was debited for the $5,000 investment of Larry Owen, which caused it to have a $5,000 debit balance. It was then credited for $900, and its new $4,100 balance was entered. On July 3, it was credited again for $3,700, which reduced its balance to $400. Then, on July 12, it was debited for $500, and its balance was increased to $900.

When a balance column account like that of Illustration 2-3 is used, the heading of the Balance column does not tell whether the balance is a debit balance or a credit balance. However, this does not create a problem because an account is assumed to have its normal kind of balance, unless the contrary is indicated. Furthermore, an accountant is expected to know the **normal balance of any account**. Fortunately, this too is not difficult because the balance of an account normally results from recording in it a larger sum of increases than decreases. Consequently, if increases are recorded as debits, the account normally has a debit balance. Likewise, if increases are recorded as credits, the account normally has a credit balance. Or, increases are recorded in an account in each of the following classifications as shown, and its normal balance is:

Account Classification	Increases Are Recorded as—	And the Normal Balance Is—
Asset	Debits	Debit
Contra asset*	Credits	Credit
Liability	Credits	Credit
Owner's equity:		
Capital	Credits	Credit
Withdrawals	Debits	Debit
Revenue	Credits	Credit
Expense	Debits	Debit

* Explained in the next chapter.

When an unusual transaction causes an account to have a balance opposite from its normal kind of balance, this opposite from normal kind of balance is indicated in the account by entering it in red or entering it in black and encircling the amount. Also, when a debit or credit entered in an account causes the account to have no balance, some bookkeepers place a –0– in the Balance column on the line of the entered amount. Other bookkeepers and bookkeeping machines write 0.00 in the column to indicate the account does not have a balance.

■ **Need for a Journal**

It is possible to record transactions by entering debits and credits directly in the accounts, as was done earlier in this chapter. However, when this is done and an error is made, the error is difficult to locate, because even with a transaction having only one debit and one credit, the debit is entered on one ledger page or card and the credit on another, and there is nothing to link the two together.

Consequently, to link together the debits and credits of each transaction and to provide in one place a complete record of each transaction, it is the universal practice in pen-and-ink systems to record all transactions in a **journal**. The debit and credit information about each transaction is then copied from the journal to the ledger accounts. These procedures are important when errors are made, since the journal record makes it possible to trace the debits and credits into the accounts and to see that they are equal and properly recorded.

The process of recording transactions in a journal is called **journalizing transactions.** Also, since transactions are first recorded in a journal and their debit and credit information is then copied from the journal to the ledger, a journal is called a **book of original entry** and a ledger a **book of final entry.**

■ **The General Journal**

The simplest and most flexible type of journal is a **General Journal.** For each transaction, it provides places for recording (1) the transaction date, (2) the names of the accounts involved, and (3) an explanation of the transaction. It also provides a place for (4) the account numbers of the accounts to which the transaction's debit and credit information is copied and (5) the transaction's debit and credit effect on the accounts named. A general journal page with two of the transactions of the Owen law practice recorded therein is shown in Illustration 2-4.

The first entry in Illustration 2-4 records the purchase of supplies and equipment on credit, and three accounts are involved. When a transaction involves three or more accounts and is recorded with a general journal entry, a compound entry is required. A **compound journal entry** is one involving three or more accounts. The second entry records a legal fee earned.

■ **Recording Transactions in a General Journal**

To record transactions in a General Journal:

1. The year is written in small figures at the top of the first column.
2. The month is written on the first line in the first column. The year

Illustration 2-4

	General Journal						Page 1		
Date	Account Titles and Explanation	PR	Debit			Credit			
198A									
July 5	Office Supplies		60	00					
	Office Equipment		300	00					
	Accounts Payable					360	00		
	Purchased supplies and equipment on credit.								
12	Cash		500	00					
	Legal Fees Earned					500	00		
	Collected a legal fee.								

and the month are not repeated except at the top of a new page or at the beginning of a new month or year.

3. The day of each transaction is written in the second column on the first line of the transaction.
4. The names of the accounts to be debited and credited and an explanation of the transaction are written in the Account Titles and Explanation column. The name of the account debited is written first, beginning at the left margin of the column. The name of the account credited is written on the following line, indented about one inch. The explanation is placed on the next line, indented about a half inch from the left margin. The explanation should be short but sufficient to explain the transaction and set it apart from every other transaction.
5. The debit amount is written in the Debit column opposite the name of the account to be debited. The credit amount is written in the Credit column opposite the account to be credited.
6. A single line is skipped between each journal entry to set the entries apart.

At the time transactions are recorded in the General Journal, nothing is entered in the **Posting Reference (Post. Ref. or PR) column.** However, when the debits and credits are copied from the journal to the ledger, the account numbers of the ledger accounts to which the debits and credits are copied are entered in this column. The Posting Reference column is sometimes called the **Folio column.**

■ **Posting Transaction Information**

The process of copying journal entry information from the journal to the ledger is called **posting.** Normally, near the end of a day, all transactions recorded in the journal that day are posted. In the posting procedure, journal debits are copied and become ledger account debits, and journal credits are copied and become ledger account credits.

The posting procedures for a journal entry are shown in Illustration 2-5, and they may be described as follows. To post a journal entry:

For the debit:

1. Find in the ledger the account named in the debit of the entry.
2. Enter in the account the date of the entry as shown in the journal, the **journal page number** from which the entry is being posted, and in the Debit column the debit amount. Note the letter "G" preceding the journal page number in the Posting Reference column of the account. The letter indicates that the amount was posted from the General Journal. Other journals are introduced in Chapter 6, and each is identified by a letter.
3. Determine the effect of the debit on the account balance and enter the new balance.
4. Enter in the Posting Reference column of the journal the account number of the account to which the amount was posted.

Illustration 2-5

General Journal   Page 1

Date	Account Titles and Explanation	PR	Debit	Credit
198A July 1	Cash	111	5,000 00	
	Larry Owen, Capital	311		5,000 00
	Invested in a law practice.			

Cash   Account No. 111

Date	Explanation	PR	Debit	Credit	Balance
198A July 1		G1	5,000 00		5,000 00

Larry Owen, Capital   Account No. 311

Date	Explanation	PR	Debit	Credit	Balance
198A July 1		G1		5,000 00	5,000 00

For the credit:

> Repeat the foregoing steps, with the exception that the credit amount is entered in the Credit column and has a credit effect on the account balance.

Observe that the last step (Step 4) in the posting procedure for either the debit or the credit of an entry is to insert the **account number** in the Posting Reference column of the journal. Inserting the account number in this column serves two purposes: (1) The account number in the journal and the journal page number in the account (called **posting reference numbers**) act as a cross-reference when it is desired to trace an amount from one record to the other. (2) Writing the account number in the journal as a last step in posting indicates that posting is completed. If posting is interrupted, the bookkeeper, by examining the journal's Posting Reference column, can easily see where posting stopped.

■ Account Numbers

Many companies use a three-digit system in assigning numbers to their accounts. In a system commonly used by service-type concerns, accounts are assigned numbers as follows:

Asset accounts, 111 through 199.
Liability accounts, 211 through 299.
Owner's equity accounts, 311 through 399.
Revenue accounts, 411 through 499.
Operating expense accounts, 511 through 599.

Observe that asset accounts are assigned numbers with first digits of 1, liability accounts are assigned numbers with first digits of 2, and so on. In each case, the first digit of an account's number tells its balance sheet or income statement classification. The second and third digits further identify the account. However, more about this in the next chapter.

■ Locating Errors

When a trial balance does not balance, an error or errors are indicated. To locate the error or errors, check the journalizing, posting, and trial balance preparation steps in their reverse order. First check the addition of the columns in the trial balance to see that no error in addition was made. Then check to see that the account balances were correctly copied from the ledger. Then recalculate the account balances. If at this stage the error or errors have not been found, check the posting and then the original journalizing of the transactions.

■ Correcting Errors

When an error is discovered in either the journal or the ledger, it must be corrected. Such an error is never erased, for this seems to indicate an effort to conceal something. However, the method of correction will vary with the nature of the error and the stage in the accounting procedures at which it is discovered.

If an error is discovered in a journal entry before the error is posted, it may be corrected by ruling a single line through the incorrect amount or account name and writing in above the correct amount or account name. Likewise, a posted error or an error in posting in which only the amount is wrong may be corrected in the same manner. However, when a posted error involves a wrong account, it is considered best to correct the error with a correcting journal entry. For example, the following journal entry to record the purchase of office supplies was made and posted:

Oct.	14	Office Furniture and Fixtures	15.00	
		Cash		15.00
		To record the purchase of office supplies.		

Obviously, the debit of the entry is to the wrong account; consequently, the following entry is needed to correct the error:

Oct.	17	Office Supplies	15.00	
		Office Furniture and Fixtures		15.00
		To correct the entry of October 14 in which the Office Furniture and Fixtures account was debited in error for the purchase of office supplies.		

The debit of the second entry correctly records the purchase of supplies, and the credit cancels the error of the first entry. Note the full explanation of the correcting entry. Such an explanation should always be full and complete so that anyone can see exactly what has occurred.

■ **Bookkeeping Techniques**

Commas and Decimal Points in Dollar Amounts

Preprinted journal and ledger paper has vertical rules to separate the digits of the recorded amounts. Consequently, when amounts are entered in a journal or a ledger, commas to indicate thousands of dollars and decimal points to separate dollars and cents are not necessary. The ruled lines accomplish this. However, when statements are prepared on unruled paper, the decimal points and commas are necessary.

Dollar Signs

Dollar signs are not used in journals or ledgers but are required on financial reports prepared on unruled paper. On such reports, a dollar sign is placed (1) before the first amount in each column of figures and (2) before the first amount appearing after a ruled line that indicates an addition or a subtraction. Examine Illustration 3-5, page 93, for examples of the use of dollar signs on a financial report.

Omission of Zeros in the Cents Columns

When an amount to be entered in a ledger or a journal is an amount of dollars and no cents, some bookkeepers will use a dash in the cents column in the place of two zeros to indicate that there are no cents. They feel that the dash is easier and more quickly made than the two zeros. This is a matter of choice in journal and ledger entries. However, on financial reports, the two zeros are preferred because they are neater in appearance.

Often in this text, where space is limited, exact dollar amounts are used in order to save space. Obviously, in such cases, neither zeros nor dashes are used to show that there are no cents involved.

□   **Glossary**

Account an accounting device used in recording and summarizing the increases and decreases in a revenue, an expense, asset, liability, or owner's equity item.

Account balance the difference between the increases and decreases recorded in an account.

Account number an identifying number assigned to an account.

Balance column account an account having a column for entering the new account balance after each debit or credit is posted to the account.

Book of final entry a ledger to which amounts are posted.

Book of original entry a journal in which transactions are first recorded.

Business paper a sales ticket, invoice, check, or other document arising in and evidence of a transaction.

Capital account an account used to record the more or less permanent changes in the equity of an owner in his or her business.

Compound journal entry a journal entry having more than one debit or more than one credit.

Credit the right-hand side of a T-account.

Debit the left-hand side of a T-account.

Double-entry accounting an accounting system in which each transaction affects and is recorded in two or more accounts with equal debits and credits.

Drawing account another name for the **withdrawals account.**

Folio column another name for the **Posting Reference column.**

General Journal a book of original entry in which any type of transaction can be recorded.

Journal a book of original entry in which transactions are first recorded and from which transaction amounts are posted to the ledger accounts.

Journal page number a posting reference number entered in the Posting Reference column of each account to which an amount is posted and which shows the page of the journal from which the amount was posted.

Ledger a group of accounts used by a business in recording its transactions.

Mortgage payable a debt, usually long term, that is secured by a special claim against one or more assets of the debtor.

Nominal accounts the income statement accounts.

Normal balance of an account the usual kind of balance, either debit or credit, that a given account has and that is a debit balance if increases are recorded in the account as debits and a credit balance if increases are recorded as credits.

Personal account another name for the **withdrawals account.**

Posting transcribing the debit and credit amounts from a journal to the ledger accounts.

Posting Reference (Post. Ref. or PR) column a column in a journal and in each account for entering posting reference numbers. Also called a **Folio column.**

Posting reference numbers journal page numbers and ledger account numbers used as a cross-reference between amounts entered in a journal and posted to the ledger accounts.

Prepaid expense an asset that will be consumed in the operation of a business; and as it is consumed, it will become an expense.

Promissory note an unconditional written promise to pay a definite sum of money on demand or at a fixed or determinable future date.

Real accounts the balance sheet accounts.

T-account an abbreviated account form, two or more of which are used in illustrating the debits and credits required in recording a transaction.

Trial balance a list of accounts having balances in the ledger, the debit or credit balance of each account, the total of the debit balances, and the total of credit balances.

Unearned revenue a liability that will be extinguished by delivering the product or service a customer has paid for in advance.

Withdrawals account the account used to record the withdrawals from a business by its owner of cash or other assets intended for personal use. Also known as **personal account** or **drawing account.**

□ **Questions for Class Discussion**

1. What is an account? What is a ledger?
2. What determines the number of accounts a business will use?
3. What are the meanings of the following words and terms: (a) debit, (b) to debit, (c) credit, and (d) to credit?
4. Does debit always mean increase and credit always mean decrease?
5. A transaction is to be entered in the accounts. How do you determine the accounts in which amounts are to be entered? How do you determine whether a particular account is to be debited or credited?
6. Why is a double-entry accounting system so called?
7. Give the rules of debit and credit for (a) asset accounts and (b) liability and owner's equity accounts.
8. Why are the rules of debit and credit the same for both liability and owner's equity accounts?
9. List the steps in the preparation of a trial balance.
10. Why is a trial balance prepared?
11. Why is a trial balance considered to be only presumptive proof of recording accuracy? What types of errors are not revealed by a trial balance?
12. What determines whether the normal balance of an account is a debit or a credit balance?
13. Can transaction debits and credits be recorded directly in the ledger accounts? What is gained by first recording transactions in a journal and then posting to the accounts?
14. In recording transactions in a journal, which is written first, the debit or the credit? How far is the name of the account credited indented? How far is the explanation indented?
15. What is a compound entry?
16. Are dollar signs used in journal entries? In the accounts?
17. If decimal points are not used in journal entries to separate dollars from cents, what accomplishes this purpose?

18. Define or describe each of the following:
    a. Journal.
    b. Ledger.
    c. Book of original entry.
    d. Book of final entry.
    e. Folio column.
    f. Posting.
    g. Posting Reference column.
    h. Posting reference numbers.

19. Entering in the Posting Reference column of the journal the account number to which an amount was posted is the last step in posting the amount. What is gained by making this the last step?

□   **Class Exercises**

Exercise 2-1

Prepare the following columnar form. Then (1) indicate the treatment for increases and decreases by entering the words *debited* and *credited* in the proper columns. (2) Indicate the normal balance of each kind of account by entering the word *debit* or *credit* in the last column of the form.

Kind of Account	Increases	Decreases	Normal Balance
Asset			
Liability			
Owner's capital			
Owner's withdrawals			
Revenue			
Expense			

Exercise 2-2

Place the following T-accounts on a sheet of notebook paper: Cash; Accounts Receivable; Office Supplies; Office Equipment; Accounts Payable; Ted Lee, Capital; Revenue from Services; and Utilities Expense. Then record these transactions by entering debits and credits directly in the accounts. Use the transaction letters to identify amounts in the accounts.

a. Ted Lee began a service business, called Quick Service, by investing $3,000 in the business.
b. Purchased office supplies for cash, $50.
c. Purchased office equipment on credit, $2,500.
d. Earned revenue by rendering services for a customer for cash, $200.
e. Paid for the office equipment purchased in transaction (c).
f. Earned revenue by rendering services for a customer on credit, $750.
g. Paid the monthly utility bills, $25.
h. Collected $250 of the amount owed by the customer of transaction (f).

Exercise 2-3

After recording the transactions of Exercise 2-2, prepare a trial balance for Quick Service. Use the current date.

Exercise 2-4

Ned East began a real estate agency, and after completing seven transactions, he prepared the trial balance that follows. Analyze the trial balance and prepare a list describing each transaction and its amount. (Hint: T-accounts will help.)

Ned East, Realtor
Trial Balance
October 5, 19—

Cash	$ 3,950	
Office supplies	150	
Prepaid rent	1,800	
Office equipment	4,000	
Accounts payable		$ 4,000
Ned East, capital		5,000
Ned East, withdrawals	2,000	
Commissions earned		3,000
Advertising expense	100	
Totals	$12,000	$12,000

Exercise 2-5

Prepare a form on notebook paper with the following three column headings: (1) Error, (2) Amount Out of Balance, and (3) Column Having Larger Total. Then for each of the following errors: (1) list the error by letter in the first column, (2) tell the amount it will cause the trial balance to be out of balance in the second column, and (3) tell in the third column which trial balance column will have the larger total as a result of the error. If the error does not affect the trial balance, write "none" in each of the last two columns.

a. A $70 debit to Office Supplies was debited to Office Equipment.
b. A $90 credit to Office Equipment was credited to Sales.
c. A $60 credit to Sales was credited to the Sales account twice.
d. A $40 debit to Office Supplies was posted as a $45 debit.
e. A $35 debit to Office Supplies was not posted.
f. An $11 credit to Sales was posted as a $110 credit.

Exercise 2-6

A trial balance did not balance. In looking for the error, the bookkeeper discovered that a transaction for the purchase of a calculator on credit for $350 had been recorded with a $350 debit to Office Equipment and a $350 debit to Accounts Payable. Answer each of the following questions, giving the dollar amount of the misstatement, if any.

a. Was the balance of the Office Equipment account overstated, understated, or correctly stated in the trial balance?
b. Was the balance of the Accounts Payable account overstated, understated, or correctly stated in the trial balance?
c. Was the debit column total of the trial balance overstated, understated, or correctly stated?
d. Was the credit column total of the trial balance overstated, understated, or correctly stated?
e. If the credit column total of the trial balance was $96,000 before the error was corrected, what was the total of the debit column?

Exercise 2-7

A careless bookkeeper prepared the following trial balance which does not balance, and you have been asked to prepare a corrected trial balance. In examining the records of the concern you discover the following: (1) The debits to the Cash account total $33,200, and the credits total $30,750. (2) A $75 receipt of cash from a customer in payment of the customer's account was not posted to Accounts Receivable. (3) A $25 purchase of shop supplies on credit was entered in the journal but was not posted to any account. (4) The 1 and the 2 in the balance of the Revenue from Services account, as shown on the bookkeeper's trial balance, were transposed in copying the balance from the ledger to the trial balance.

Joe's Fixit Shop
Trial Balance
December 31, 19—

Cash.	$ 2,550	
Accounts receivable		$ 3,175
Shop supplies.	3,300	
Shop equipment.	6,500	
Accounts payable	600	
Joe Sims, capital	8,175	
Joe Sims, withdrawals	18,000	
Revenue from services		31,200
Rent expense		7,200
Advertising expense	325	
Totals	$39,450	$41,575

Exercise 2-8

The following accounts contain seven transactions keyed together with letters. Write a short explanation of each transaction with the amount or amounts involved.

Cash			
(a)	5,000	(b)	1,650
(e)	300	(c)	50
		(f)	1,525
		(g)	60

Office Equipment		
(d)	7,500	

John Peal, Capital		
	(a)	8,000

Office Supplies		
(c)	50	
(d)	25	

Law Library		
(a)	3,000	

Legal Fees Earned		
	(e)	300

Prepaid Rent		
(b)	1,650	

Accounts Payable			
(f)	1,525	(d)	7,525

Utilities Expense		
(g)	60	

Exercise 2-9

Rule on note paper a general journal form like Illustration 2-4. Then prepare general journal entries to record the following transactions. Omit the year in the journal date column.

May 1   Dale Hall invested $2,000 in cash and an automobile having a
         $10,000 fair value in a real estate agency he called Valley Realty.
     1   Rented furnished office space and paid two months' rent in
         advance, $1,000.
     2   Purchased office supplies for cash, $60.
     14 Sold a building lot for a client and collected a $2,500 commission
         on the sale.
     31 Paid for gas and oil used in the agency car during May, $40.

Exercise 2-10

1. Open the following T-accounts on note paper: Cash; Prepaid Rent;
   Office Supplies; Automobile; Dale Hall, Capital; Commissions Earned;
   and Gas and Oil Expense.
2. Post the transactions of Exercise 2-9 to the T-accounts. Omit posting
   reference numbers.
3. Prepare a trial balance of the T-accounts.

□   **Problems**   **Problem 2-1**

Susan Kent began business as a real estate agent and during a short period
completed these transactions:

a. Invested $35,000 in cash and office equipment having a $5,000 fair
   value in a real estate agency she called Kona Realty.
b. Purchased land valued at $25,000 and a small office building valued
   at $85,000, paying $30,000 cash and signing a mortgage contract to
   pay the balance over a period of years.
c. Purchased office supplies on credit, $50.
d. Took her personal automobile, which had a $6,000 fair value, for
   exclusive use in the business.
e. Purchased additional office equipment on credit, $600.
f. Paid the office secretary's salary, $500.
g. Sold a house and collected a $6,600 cash commission on the sale.
h. Paid $125 for newspaper advertising that had appeared.
i. Paid for the supplies purchased on credit in transaction (c).
j. Gave a typewriter carried in the accounting records at $115 and $700
   cash for a new typewriter.
k. Completed a real estate appraisal on credit and billed the client $150
   for the appraisal.
l. Paid the secretary's salary, $500.
m. Received payment in full for the appraisal of transaction (k).
n. Susan Kent withdrew $1,000 from the business to pay personal
   expenses.

Required

1. Open the following T-accounts: Cash; Accounts Receivable; Office
   Supplies; Office Equipment; Automobile; Land; Building; Accounts
   Payable; Mortgage Payable; Susan Kent, Capital; Susan Kent,

Withdrawals; Commissions Earned; Appraisal Fees Earned; Office Salaries Expense; and Advertising Expense.

2. Record the transactions by entering debits and credits directly in the accounts. Use the transaction letters to identify each debit and credit amount.

3. Prepare a trial balance using the current date.

Problem 2-2

Dale Hall, CPA, completed these transactions during October of the current year:

Oct. 1 Began a public accounting practice by investing $3,500 in cash and office equipment having a $4,000 fair value.
1 Paid two months' rent in advance on suitable office space, $1,500.
2 Purchased on credit office equipment, $350, and office supplies, $65.
5 Completed accounting work for a client and immediately received $150 cash therefor.
9 Completed accounting work on credit for Guaranty Bank, $600.
11 Paid for the items purchased on credit on October 2.
12 Paid the $625 premium on an insurance policy.
19 Received payment in full from Guaranty Bank for the work completed on October 9.
25 Completed accounting work on credit for Hilltop Realty, $400.
29 Dale Hall withdrew $250 cash from the practice to pay personal expenses.
30 Purchased additional office supplies on credit, $40.
31 Paid the October utility bills, $135.

Required

1. Open the following accounts: Cash; Accounts Receivable; Prepaid Rent; Prepaid Insurance; Office Supplies; Office Equipment; Accounts Payable; Dale Hall, Capital; Dale Hall, Withdrawals; Accounting Revenue; and Utilities Expense.

2. Prepare general journal entries to record the transactions, post to the accounts, and prepare a trial balance. Head the trial balance Dale Hall, CPA.

Problem 2-3

Jerry Marsh began business as an excavating contractor and during a short period completed these transactions:

a. Began business by investing cash, $15,000; office equipment, $1,200; and machinery, $42,500.
b. Purchased land for an office site and for parking machinery, $17,500. Paid $5,500 in cash and signed a promissory note payable for the balance.
c. Purchased for cash a used prefabricated building and moved it onto the land for use as an office, $5,000.

d. Paid the premium on two insurance policies, $725.
e. Completed an excavating job and collected $875 cash in full payment.
f. Purchased additional machinery costing $6,800. Gave $1,800 in cash and signed a note payable for the balance.
g. Completed an excavating job on credit for Western Contractors, $1,200.
h. Purchased additional office equipment on credit, $350.
i. Completed an excavating job for Lakeside Contractors on credit, $950.
j. Received and recorded as an account payable a bill for rent on a special machine used on the Lakeside Contractors job, $150.
k. Received $1,200 from Western Contractors for the work of transaction (g).
l. Paid the wages of the machinery operator, $850.
m. Paid for the office equipment purchased in transaction (h).
n. Paid $125 cash for repairs to a machine.
o. Jerry Marsh wrote a $65 check on the bank account of the business to pay for repairs to his personal automobile. (The car is not used for business purposes.)
p. Paid the wages of the machinery operator, $900.
q. Paid for gas and oil consumed by the excavating machinery, $210.

Required

1. Open the following T-accounts: Cash; Accounts Receivable; Prepaid Insurance; Office Equipment; Machinery; Building; Land; Notes Payable; Accounts Payable; Jerry Marsh, Capital; Jerry Marsh, Withdrawals; Excavating Revenue; Machinery Repair Expense; Wages Expense; Machinery Rentals Expense; and Gas and Oil Expense.
2. Record the transactions by entering debits and credits directly in the accounts. Use the transaction letters to identify each debit and credit. Prepare a trial balance using the current date and headed Jerry Marsh, Contractor.

Problem 2-4

Nancy Ives completed these transactions during July of the current year:

July 1 Began an architectural practice by investing cash, $4,500; drafting supplies, $150; and office and drafting equipment, $3,750.
1 Paid two months' rent in advance on suitable office space, $1,200.
2 Paid the premium on an insurance policy taken out in the name of the practice, $560.
3 Purchased drafting equipment, $475, and drafting supplies, $35, on credit.
8 Delivered a set of plans to a contractor and collected $500 cash in full payment.
15 Completed and delivered a set of plans to Kemper Contractors on credit, $700.
15 Paid the draftsman's salary, $650.
17 Purchased drafting supplies on credit, $40.
18 Paid for the equipment and supplies purchased on July 3.

July 25   Received $700 from Kemper Contractors for the plans delivered on July 15.
26   Nancy Ives withdrew $200 from the practice for personal use.
27   Paid for the supplies purchased on July 17.
30   Completed architectural work for Kona Realty on credit, $500.
31   Paid the draftsman's salary, $650.
31   Paid the July utility bills, $115.
31   Paid the blueprinting expenses incurred in July, $85.

Required

1. Open the following accounts: Cash; Accounts Receivable; Prepaid Rent; Prepaid Insurance; Drafting Supplies; Office and Drafting Equipment; Accounts Payable; Nancy Ives, Capital; Nancy Ives, Withdrawals; Architectural Fees Earned; Salaries Expense; Blueprinting Expense; and Utilities Expense.
2. Prepare and post general journal entries to record the transactions. Prepare a trial balance, heading it Nancy Ives, Architect.

Problem 2-5

Ted Lee completed these transactions during May of the current year:

May   1   Began a new law practice by investing $2,500 in cash and law books having a $1,200 fair value.
1   Rented the furnished office of a lawyer who was retiring due to illness, and paid two months' rent in advance, $1,000.
1   Paid the premium on a liability insurance policy giving one year's protection, $420.
2   Purchased office supplies on credit, $40.
8   Completed legal work for a client and immediately collected $250 cash for the work.
12   Paid for the office supplies purchased on May 2.
15   Completed legal work for Evans Realty on credit, $850.
22   Completed legal work for Security Bank on credit, $750.
25   Received $850 from Evans Realty for the work completed on May 15.
27   Ted Lee wrote a $15 check on the bank account of the legal practice to pay his home telephone bill.
29   Purchased additional office supplies on credit, $45.
31   Paid the May telephone bill of the office, $25.
31   Paid the salary of the office secretary, $950.
31   Recognized that one month's rent on the office had expired and had become an expense. (Make a general journal entry to transfer the amount of the expense from the asset account to the Rent Expense account.)
31   Recognized that one month's insurance has expired and become an expense.
31   Took an inventory of unused office supplies and determined that supplies costing $30 had been used and had become an expense.

Required

1. Open the following accounts: Cash; Accounts Receivable; Prepaid Rent; Prepaid Insurance; Office Supplies; Law Library; Accounts Payable; Ted Lee, Capital; Ted Lee, Withdrawals; Legal Fees Earned; Rent Expense; Salaries Expense; Telephone Expense; Insurance Expense; and Office Supplies Expense.
2. Prepare general journal entries to record the transactions, post to the accounts, and prepare a trial balance headed Ted Lee, Attorney.
3. Analyze the transactions and prepare a May income statement and a May 31 balance sheet for the practice. (The $3,700 trial balance amount of capital for Ted Lee is his May 1 beginning-of-month capital. To determine the May 31 balance sheet amount of his capital, add the net income to his beginning capital and deduct the withdrawal. Show the ending capital as in Illustration 1-2.)

□ **Alternate Problems**   **Problem 2-1A**

Susan Kent completed these transactions during a short period:

a. Began a real estate agency by investing the following assets at their fair values: cash, $2,500; office equipment, $3,000; automobile, $5,300; land, $25,000; and building, $75,000. A bank holds a $60,000 mortgage on the land and building.
b. Purchased office supplies, $60, and additional office equipment, $350, on credit.
c. Collected a $6,600 commission from the sale of property for a client.
d. Purchased additional office equipment on credit, $425.
e. Paid for advertising that had appeared in the local paper, $125.
f. Traded the agency's automobile and $4,700 in cash for a new automobile.
g. Paid the office secretary's salary, $525.
h. Paid for the supplies and equipment purchased in transaction (b).
i. Completed a real estate appraisal for a client on credit, $175.
j. Collected a $2,500 commission from the sale of a building lot for a client.
k. The client of transaction (i) paid $75 of the amount owed.
l. Paid the secretary's salary, $525.
m. Paid $115 for newspaper advertising that had appeared.
n. Susan Kent withdrew $1,500 from the business for personal use.

Required

1. Open the following T-accounts: Cash; Accounts Receivable; Office Supplies; Office Equipment; Automobile; Land; Building; Accounts Payable; Mortgage Payable; Susan Kent, Capital; Susan Kent, Withdrawals; Commissions Earned; Appraisal Fees Earned; Office Salaries Expense; and Advertising Expense.
2. Record the transactions by entering debits and credits directly in the accounts. Use the transaction letters to identify the amounts in the accounts.

3. Prepare a trial balance headed Susan Kent, Realtor. Use the current date.

Problem 2-2A

Dale Hall began a public accounting practice and completed these transactions during August of the current year:

Aug. 1 Invested $4,500 in a public accounting practice begun this day.
1 Rented suitable office space and paid two months' rent in advance, $1,600.
2 Purchased office supplies, $65, and office equipment, $3,750, on credit.
3 Paid the premium on a liability insurance policy, $435.
8 Completed accounting work for a client and immediately collected $175 in cash for the work done.
13 Completed accounting work for Valley Bank on credit, $450.
15 Purchased additional office supplies on credit, $35.
23 Received $450 from Valley Bank for the work completed on August 13.
26 Dale Hall withdrew $250 from the accounting practice to pay personal expenses.
30 Completed accounting work for Kona Realty on credit, $350.
31 Made an $815 installment payment on the equipment and supplies purchased on August 2.
31 Paid the August utility bills of the accounting practice, $145.

Required

1. Open the following accounts: Cash; Accounts Receivable; Prepaid Rent; Prepaid Insurance; Office Supplies; Office Equipment; Accounts Payable; Dale Hall, Capital; Dale Hall, Withdrawals; Accounting Revenue; and Utilities Expense.
2. Prepare general journal entries to record the transactions, post to the accounts, and prepare a trial balance headed Dale Hall, CPA.

Problem 2-3A

Jerry Marsh completed these transactions during a short period:

a. Began business as an excavating contractor by investing cash, $25,000; office equipment, $1,500; and excavating machinery, $45,000.
b. Purchased for $25,000 land to be used as an office site and for parking equipment. Paid $10,000 in cash and signed a promissory note payable for the balance.
c. Purchased additional excavating machinery costing $21,750. Paid $6,750 in cash and signed a promissory note payable for the balance.
d. Paid $4,500 cash for a used prefabricated building and moved it on the land for use as an office.
e. Completed an excavating job and immediately collected $850 in cash for the work.
f. Paid the premium on an insurance policy giving one year's protection, $625.

g. Completed a $1,250 excavating job for Tri-City Contractors on credit.
h. Paid the wages of the equipment operator, $800.
i. Paid $160 cash for repairs to excavating machinery.
j. Received $1,250 from Tri-City Contractors for the work of transaction (g).
k. Completed an $800 excavating job for TVX Contractors on credit.
l. Received and recorded as an account payable a $110 bill for the rent of a special machine used on the TVX Contractors job.
m. Purchased additional office equipment on credit, $525.
n. Jerry Marsh withdrew $500 from the business for personal use.
o. Paid the wages of the equipment operator, $900.
p. Paid the $110 account payable resulting from renting the machine of transaction (l).
q. Paid for gas and oil consumed by the excavating machinery, $225.

Required

1. Open the following T-accounts: Cash; Accounts Receivable; Prepaid Insurance; Office Equipment; Machinery; Building; Land; Notes Payable; Accounts Payable; Jerry Marsh, Capital; Jerry Marsh, Withdrawals; Excavating Revenue; Machinery Repairs Expense; Wages Expense; Machinery Rentals Expense; and Gas and Oil Expense.

2. Record the transactions by entering debits and credits directly in the accounts. Use the transaction letters to identify each debit and credit. Prepare a trial balance using the current date and headed Jerry Marsh, Contractor.

Problem 2-4A

Nancy Ives completed these transactions during March of the current year:

Mar. 1 Began an architectural practice by opening a bank account in the name of the practice, Nancy Ives, Architect, and deposited $5,000 therein.

1 Rented suitable office space and paid two months' rent in advance, $1,000.

2 Purchased for $4,750 office and drafting equipment under an agreement calling for a $750 down payment and the balance in monthly installments. Paid the down payment and recorded the account payable.

3 Purchased drafting supplies for cash, $175.

9 Completed and delivered a set of plans to a contractor and immediately received $525 cash in full payment therefor.

11 Paid the premium on a liability insurance policy, $480.

12 Purchased on credit additional drafting supplies, $35, and drafting equipment, $115.

15 Paid the salary of the draftsman, $550.

18 Completed and delivered a set of plans to Lakeview Developers on credit, $1,200.

22 Paid in full for the supplies and equipment purchased on March 12.

26 Completed additional architectural work for Lakeview Developers on credit, $350.

Mar. 28   Received $1,200 from Lakeview Developers for the plans delivered on March 18.

   29   Nancy Ives withdrew $200 cash from the practice to pay personal expenses.

   31   Paid the salary of the draftsman, $550.

   31   Paid the March utility bills, $80.

   31   Paid $135 cash for blueprinting expense.

Required

1. Open the following accounts: Cash; Accounts Receivable; Prepaid Rent; Prepaid Insurance; Drafting Supplies; Office and Drafting Equipment; Accounts Payable; Nancy Ives, Capital; Nancy Ives, Withdrawals; Architectural Fees Earned; Salaries Expense; Blueprinting Expense; and Utilities Expense.

2. Prepare general journal entries to record the transactions, post to the accounts, and prepare a trial balance.

Problem 2-5A

Ted Lee graduated from college with a law degree in June of the current year, and during July, he completed these transactions:

July 1   Began the practice of law by investing $2,000 in cash and law books acquired in college and having an $800 fair value.

   1   Rented the furnished office of a lawyer who was retiring and paid two months' rent in advance, $950.

   2   Purchased law books costing $750 under an agreement calling for a $100 down payment and the balance in monthly installments. Paid the down payment and recorded the remaining $650 as an account payable.

   3   Purchased office supplies on credit, $45.

   5   Paid the premium on a liability insurance policy giving one year's protection, $360.

   9   Completed legal work for a client and immediately collected $300 for the work done.

   13   Paid for the office supplies purchased on credit on July 3.

   15   Completed legal work for Valley Bank on credit, $850.

   23   Ted Lee wrote a $20 check on the bank account of the legal practice to pay his home telephone bill.

   25   Received $850 from Valley Bank for the work completed July 15.

   27   Completed legal work for Hillside Realty on credit, $600.

   31   Paid the telephone bill of the legal practice, $30.

   31   Paid the salary of the office secretary, $900.

   31   Recognized that one month's rent on the office had expired and had become an expense. (Make a general journal entry to transfer the amount of the expense from the asset account to the Rent Expense account.)

   31   Recognized that one month's insurance had expired and had become an expense.

   31   Took an inventory of unused office supplies and determined that supplies costing $25 had been used and had become an expense.

Required

1. Open the following accounts: Cash; Accounts Receivable; Prepaid Rent; Prepaid Insurance; Office Supplies; Law Library; Accounts Payable; Ted Lee, Capital; Ted Lee, Withdrawals; Legal Fees Earned; Rent Expense; Salaries Expense; Telephone Expense; Insurance Expense; and Office Supplies Expense.

2. Prepare general journal entries to record the transactions, post to the accounts, and prepare a trial balance headed Ted Lee, Attorney.

3. Analyze the transactions and prepare a July income statement and a July 31 balance sheet. (The $2,800 trial balance amount of capital for Ted Lee is his July 1 beginning-of-month capital. To determine his July 31 balance sheet amount of capital, add the net income to his beginning capital and deduct the withdrawal. Show the ending capital as in Illustration 1-2.)

Provocative Problems

Provocative Problem 2-1   Summer Concession

Mary Cone, a school teacher, has just completed the first summer's operation of a concession on Blue Lake, at which she rents boats and sells sandwiches, soft drinks, and candy. She began the summer's operation with $3,000 in cash and a five-year lease on a boat dock and a small concession building on the lake. The lease requires a $1,200 annual rental, although the concession is open only from June 1 through August 31. On opening day, Mary paid the first year's rent in advance and purchased four boats at $350 each, paying cash. She estimated the boats would have a five-year life, after which she could sell them for $50 each.

During the summer, she purchased food, soft drinks, and candy costing $6,255, all of which was paid for by summer's end, excepting food costing $150 that was purchased during the last week's operation. By summer's end, she had paid electric bills, $235, and wages of a part-time helper, $880. She had also withdrawn $200 of earnings of the concession each week for 12 weeks for personal expenses.

She took in $1,510 in boat rentals during the summer and sold $12,870 of food and drinks, all of which was collected in cash, except $135 owed by Small Company for food and drinks for an employees' picnic.

On August 31, when she closed for the summer, Ms. Cone was able to return to the soft drink company several cases of soft drinks for which she received a $60 cash refund. However, she had to take home for personal consumption a number of candy bars and a few cans of soft drinks that cost $15 and could have been sold for $30.

Prepare an income statement showing the results of the summer's operations and an August 31 balance sheet. Head the statements Summer Concession. Determine Ms. Cone's ending equity by subtracting the liability from the assets. Then prepare a different calculation to prove the amount of the equity. (T-accounts will be helpful in organizing the data.)

Provocative Problem 2-2   Bright Glass Service

Ray Black began a window cleaning service by investing $750 in the business, Bright Glass Service. He made a $500 down payment and signed a promissory note payable to purchase a secondhand truck priced at $1,200. He then spent $150 for detergents, sponges, and other supplies to be used in the business. He also paid $60 for newspaper advertising through which he gained a number of customers, who together agreed to pay him approximately $300 per week for his services.

After six months, on June 30 of the current year, his records show he has collected $7,600 in cash from customers for his services and that other customers owe him $250 for washing windows. He has bought additional supplies for cash, $325, which brings the total supplies purchased during the six months to $475. However, supplies that cost $100 are on hand unused at the period end. He has spent $310 for gas and oil used in the truck. Through payments, he has reduced the balance owed on the truck to $350; but through use, the truck has worn out and depreciated an amount equal to one fourth of its cost. Also, he has withdrawn sufficient cash from the business each week to pay his personal living expenses.

Under the assumption that the business has a $225 balance of cash remaining at the period end, determine the amount of cash Ray has withdrawn from the business. Prepare an income statement for the six months and a balance sheet as of the period end. Determine Ray's end-of-period equity by subtracting the balance owed on the note payable from the total of the assets. Then prepare a calculation to prove in another way the amount of the ending equity. (T-accounts will be helpful in organizing the data.)

Provocative Problem 2-3   Ted's Lawn Service

Upon graduation from high school last summer, Ted Neal needed a job to earn a portion of his first-year college expenses. He was unable to find anything satisfactory and decided to go into the lawn-care business. He had $350 in a savings account that he used to buy a lawn mower and other lawn-care tools. However, to haul the tools from job to job, he needed a truck. Consequently, he borrowed $800 from a bank, agreeing to pay $1\frac{1}{4}\%$ interest per month, and used the entire amount to buy a secondhand truck.

From the beginning, he had as much work as he could do, and after two months, he repaid the bank loan plus two months' interest. On September 5, he ended the business after exactly three months' operations. Throughout the summer, he followed the practice of depositing in the bank all cash received from customers. An examination of his checkbook record showed he had deposited $3,550. He had written checks to pay $145 for gas, oil, and lubricants used in the truck and mower and a $35 check for mower repairs. A notebook in the truck contained copies of credit card tickets that showed the business owed $40 for additional gas and oil used in the truck and mower. The notebook also showed that customers owed Ted $125 for lawn-care services. He estimated that his lawn-care equipment had worn out and depreciated an amount equal to one half its cost, and the truck had worn out and depreciated an amount equal to one fourth its cost.

Under the assumption that Ted had withdrawn $525 from the business during the summer for spending money and to buy clothes, prepare an income statement showing the results of the summer's operations. Also prepare a September 5 balance sheet like Illustration 1-2. Head the statements Ted's Lawn Service. (T-accounts should be helpful in organizing the data. To determine the balance sheet amount of Ted's capital, add the net income to his beginning investment and deduct the withdrawals.)

3 Adjusting the Accounts and Preparing the Statements

After studying Chapter 3, you should be able to:

1. Explain why the life of a business is divided into accounting periods of equal length and why the accounts of a business must be adjusted at the end of each accounting period.

2. Prepare adjusting entries for prepaid expenses, accrued expenses, unearned revenues, accrued revenues, and depreciation.

3. Prepare entries to dispose of accrued revenue and expense items in the new accounting period.

4. Explain the difference between the cash and accrual bases of accounting.

5. Explain the importance of comparability in the financial statements of a business, period after period; and tell how the realization principle and the matching principle contribute to comparability.

6. Define each asset and liability classification appearing on a balance sheet, classify balance sheet items, and prepare a classified balance sheet.

7. Define or explain the words and phrases listed in the chapter Glossary.

The life of a business often spans many years, and its activities go on without interruption over the years. However, taxes based on annual income must be paid governmental units, and the owners and managers of a business must have periodic reports on its financial progress. Consequently, a **time-period concept** of the life of a business is required in accounting for its activities. This concept results in a division of the life of a business into time periods of equal length, called **accounting periods.** Accounting periods may be a month, three months, or a year in length. However, **annual accounting periods,** periods one year in length, are the norm.

An accounting period of any 12 consecutive months is known as a **fiscal year.** A fiscal year may coincide with the calendar year and end on December 31, or it may follow the **natural business year.** When accounting periods follow the natural business year, they end when inventories are at their lowest point and business activities are at their lowest ebb. For example, in department stores, the natural business year begins on February 1, after the Christmas and January sales, and ends the following January 31. Consequently, the annual accounting periods of department stores commonly begin on February 1 and end the following January 31.

■ Need for Adjustments at the End of an Accounting Period

As a rule, at the end of an accounting period, after all transactions are recorded, several of the accounts in a company's ledger do not show proper end-of-period balances for preparing the statements. This is true even though all transactions were correctly recorded. The balances are incorrect for statement purposes, not through error but because of the expiration of costs brought about by the passage of time. For example, the second item on the trial balance of Owen's law practice, as prepared in Chapter 2 and reproduced again as Illustration 3-1, is "Prepaid rent, $900." This $900 represents the rent for three months paid in advance on July 1. However, by July 31, $900 is not the balance sheet amount for this asset because one month's rent, $300, has expired and become an expense and only $600 remains as an asset. Likewise, a portion of the office supplies as represented by the $60 debit balance in the Office Supplies account has been used, and the office equipment has begun to wear out and depreciate. Obviously, then, the balances of the Prepaid Rent, Office Supplies, and Office Equipment accounts as they appear on the trial balance do not reflect the proper amounts for preparing the July 31 statements. The balance of each and the balances of the Office Salaries Expense and Legal Fees Earned accounts must be **adjusted** before they will show proper amounts for the July 31 statements.

■ Adjusting the Accounts

Prepaid Expenses

As previously stated, a prepaid expense is an expense that has been paid for in advance of its use. At the time of payment, an asset is acquired that will be used or consumed, and as it is used or consumed, it becomes an expense. For example:

On July 1, the Owen law practice paid three months' rent in advance and obtained the right to occupy a rented office for the following three months. On July 1, this right was an asset valued at its $900 cost. However,

Illustration 3-1

Larry Owen, Attorney
Trial Balance
July 31, 19—

Cash	$1,185	
Prepaid rent	900	
Office supplies	60	
Office equipment	4,000	
Accounts payable.		$ 260
Unearned legal fees.		450
Larry Owen, capital		5,000
Larry Owen, withdrawals. . . .	200	
Legal fees earned.		1,500
Office salaries expense	800	
Telephone expense	30	
Heating and lighting expense . .	35	
Totals	$7,210	$7,210

day by day the law practice occupied the office, and each day a portion of the prepaid rent expired and became an expense. On July 31, one month's rent, valued at one third of $900, or $300, had expired. Consequently, if Owen's July 31 accounts are to reflect proper asset and expense amounts, the following **adjusting entry** is required:

July	31	Rent Expense.	300.00	
		Prepaid Rent		300.00
		To record the expired rent.		

Posting the adjusting entry has the following effect on the accounts:

Prepaid Rent				Rent Expense	
July 1	900	**July 31**	300	**July 31**	300

After the entry is posted, the Prepaid Rent account with a $600 balance and the Rent Expense account with a $300 balance show proper statement amounts.

To continue, early in July, the Owen law practice purchased some office supplies and placed them in the office for use. Each day the secretary used a portion. The amount used or consumed each day was an expense that daily reduced the supplies on hand. However, the daily reductions were not recognized in the accounts because day-by-day information as to amounts used and remaining was not needed. Also, labor could be saved by recording only a single amount, the total of all supplies used during the month.

Consequently, if on July 31 the accounts are to reflect proper statement amounts, the dollar amount of office supplies used during the month must be determined and recorded. To learn the amount used, it is necessary to count or inventory the unused supplies remaining and to deduct their cost from the cost of the supplies purchased. If, for example, $35 of unused supplies remain, then $25 ($60 − $35 = $25) of supplies were used and have become an expense. The following adjusting entry is required to record this:

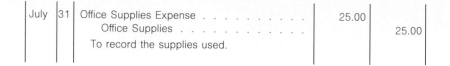

July	31	Office Supplies Expense	25.00	
		Office Supplies		25.00
		To record the supplies used.		

The effect of the adjusting entry on the accounts is:

Office Supplies			Office Supplies Expense	
July 5	60	July 31	25	July 31	25

Often, unlike in the two previous examples, items that are prepaid expenses at the time of purchase are both bought and fully consumed within a single accounting period. For example, a company pays its rent in advance on the first day of each month. Each month the amount paid results in a prepaid expense that is entirely consumed by the month's end and by the end of the accounting period. In such cases, it is best to ignore the fact that an asset results from each prepayment because an adjustment can be avoided if each prepayment is originally recorded as an expense.

Other prepaid expenses that are handled in the same manner as prepaid rent and office supplies are prepaid insurance, store supplies, and factory supplies.

Depreciation

An item of equipment used in carrying on the operations of a business in effect represent a "quantity of usefulness." Also, since the equipment will eventually wear out and be discarded, the cost of its "quantity of usefulness" must be charged off as an expense over the useful life of the equipment. This is accomplished by recording **depreciation.**

Depreciation is an expense just like the expiration of prepaid rent. For example, if a company purchases a machine for $4,500 that it expects to use for four years, after which it expects to receive $500 for the machine as a trade-in allowance on a new machine, the company has purchased a $4,000 quantity of usefulness ($4,500 − $500 = $4,000). Furthermore, this quantity of usefulness expires or the machine depreciates at the rate of $1,000 per year [($4,500 − $500) ÷ 4 years = $1,000]. Actually, when depreciation is compared to the expiration of a prepaid expense, the primary difference is that since it is often impossible to predict exactly how long an item of equipment will be used or how much will be received for it at the end of its useful life, the amount it depreciates each accounting period is only an estimate.

Estimating and apportioning depreciation can be simple, as in the foregoing example, or it can become complex. A discussion of more complex situations is unnecessary at this point and is deferred to Chapter 10. However, to illustrate the recording of depreciation, assume that on July 31, the Owen law practice estimated its office equipment had depreciated $40 during the month. The depreciation reduced the assets and increased expenses, and the following adjusting entry is required:

July	31	Depreciation Expense, Office Equipment . . .	40.00	
		Accumulated Depreciation, Office		
		Equipment		40.00
		To record the July depreciation.		

The effect of the entry on the accounts is:

Office Equipment				Depreciation Expense, Office Equipment	
July 3	3,700			July 31	40
5	300				

| Accumulated Depreciation, Office Equipment | | |
| | July 31 | 40 |

After the entry is posted, the Office Equipment account and its related Accumulated Depreciation, Office Equipment account together show the July 31 balance sheet amounts for this asset. The Depreciation Expense, Office Equipment account shows the amount of depreciation expense that should appear on the July income statement.

In most cases, a decrease in an asset is recorded with a credit to the account in which the asset is recorded. However, note in the illustrated accounts that this procedure is not followed in recording depreciation. Rather, depreciation is recorded in a **contra account,** the Accumulated Depreciation, Office Equipment account. (A contra account is an account the balance of which is subtracted from the balance of an associate account to show a more proper amount for the item recorded in the associated account.)

There are two good reasons for using contra accounts in recording depreciation. First, although based on objective evidence whenever possible, at its best depreciation is only an estimate. Second, the use of contra accounts better preserves the facts in the lives of items of equipment. For example, in this case, the Office Equipment account preserves a record of the equipment's cost, and the Accumulated Depreciation, Office Equipment account shows its depreciation to date.

A better understanding of the second reason for using contra accounts, along with an appreciation of why the word **accumulated** is used in the account name, can be gained when it is pointed out that depreciation is recorded at the end of each accounting period in a depreciating asset's life. As a result, at the end of the third month in the life of the law practice's office equipment, the Office Equipment and its related accumulated depreciation account will look like this:

Office Equipment			Accumulated Depreciation, Office Equipment	
July 3	3,700		July 31	40
5	300		Aug. 31	40
			Sept. 30	40

And the equipment's cost and three months' **accumulated depreciation** will be shown on its September 30 balance sheet thus:

Office equipment	$4,000	
Less accumulated depreciation	120	$3,880

Accumulated depreciation accounts are sometimes found in ledgers and on statements under titles such as Allowance for Depreciation, Store Equipment or the totally unacceptable caption, Reserve for Depreciation, Office Equipment. However, more appropriate terminology is Accumulated Depreciation, Store Equipment and Accumulated Depreciation, Office Equipment. The "Accumulated" terminology is better because it is more descriptive of the depreciation procedure.

Accrued Expenses

Most expenses are recorded during an accounting period at the time they are paid. However, when a period ends there may be expenses that have been incurred but have not been paid and recorded because payment is not due. These unpaid and unrecorded expenses for which payment is not due are called **accrued expenses.** Earned but unpaid wages are a common example. To illustrate:

The Owen law practice has a secretary who is paid $40 per day or $200 per week for a workweek that begins on Monday and ends on Friday. The secretary's wages are due and payable every two weeks on Friday; and during July, they were paid on the 12th and 26th and recorded as follows:

Cash			Office Salaries Expense	
July 12	400	July 12	400	
26	400	26	400	

If the calendar for July appears as illustrated and the secretary worked on July 29, 30, and 31, then at the close of business on Wednesday, July 31, the secretary has earned three days' wages that are not paid and recorded because payment is not due. However, this $120 of earned but unpaid wages is just as much a part of the July expenses as the $800 of wages that have been paid. Furthermore, on July 31, the unpaid wages are a liability. Consequently, if the accounts are to show the correct amount of wages for July and all liabilities owed on July 31, then an adjusting entry like the following must be made:

JULY						
S	**M**	**T**	**W**	**T**	**F**	**S**
	1	2	3	4	5	6
7	8	9	10	11	12	13
14	15	16	17	18	19	20
21	22	23	24	25	26	27
28	29	30	31			

July	31	Office Salaries Expense	120.00	
		Salaries Payable.		120.00
		To record the earned but unpaid wages.		

The effect of the entry on the accounts is:

Office Salaries Expense				Salaries Payable		
July 12	400				**July 31**	**120**
26	400					
31	**120**					

Unearned Revenues

An unearned revenue results when payment is received for goods or services in advance of their delivery. For instance, on July 15, Larry Owen entered into an agreement with Coast Realty to do its legal work on a fixed-fee basis for $300 per month. On that date, Owen received $450 in advance for services during the remainder of July and the month of August. The fee was recorded with this entry:

July	15	Cash	450.00	
		Unearned Legal Fees		450.00
		Received a legal fee in advance.		

Acceptance of the fee in advance increased the cash of the law practice and created a liability, the obligation to do Coast Realty's legal work for the next month and a half. However, by July 31, the law practice has discharged $150 of the liability and earned that much revenue, which according to the **realization principle** should appear on the July income statement. Consequently, on July 31, the following adjusting entry is required:

July	31	Unearned Legal Fees	150.00	
		Legal Fees Earned.		150.00
		To record a legal fee earned.		

Posting the entry has this effect on the accounts:

Unearned Legal Fees				Legal Fees Earned		
July 31	**150**	July 15	450		July 12	500
					19	1,000
					31	**150**

The effect of the entry is to transfer the $150 earned portion of the fee from the liability account to the revenue account. It reduces the liability and records as a revenue the $150 that has been earned.

Accrued Revenues

An **accrued revenue** is a revenue that has been earned but has not been collected because payment is not due. For example, assume that on July 20, Larry Owen also entered into an agreement with Guaranty Bank to do its legal work on a fixed-fee basis for $300 per month to be paid monthly. Under this assumption, by July 31, the law practice has earned one third of a month's fee, $100, which according to the **realization principle** should appear on its July income statement. Therefore, the following adjusting entry is required:

July	31	Accounts Receivable.	100.00	
		Legal Fees Earned.		100.00
		To record a legal fee earned.		

Posting the entry has this effect on the accounts:

Accounts Receivable					Legal Fees Earned	
July 19	1,000	July 29	1,000		July 12	500
31	**100**				19	1,000
					31	150
					31	**100**

■ **The Adjusted Trial Balance**

A trial balance prepared before adjustments is known as an **unadjusted trial balance,** or simply a trial balance. One prepared after adjustments is known as an **adjusted trial balance.** A July 31 adjusted trial balance for the law practice appears in Illustration 3-2.

■ **Preparing Statements from the Adjusted Trial Balance**

An adjusted trial balance shows proper balance sheet and income statement amounts. Consequently, it may be used in preparing the statements. When it is so used, the revenue and expense items are arranged into an income statement, as in Illustration 3-3. Likewise, the asset, liability, and owner's equity items are arranged into a balance sheet in Illustration 3-4.

When the statements are prepared, the income statement is normally prepared first because the net income, as calculated on the income statement, is needed in completing the balance sheet's owner's equity section. Observe in Illustration 3-4 how the net income is combined with the withdrawals and the excess is added to Owen's July 1 capital. The income increased Owen's equity, and the withdrawals reduced it. Consequently, when the excess of the income over the withdrawals is added to the beginning equity, the result is the ending equity.

■ **The Adjustment Process**

The **adjustment process** described in this chapter arises from recognition that the operation of a business results in a continuous stream of transactions. Some of the transactions affect several accounting periods. And,

Illustration 3-2

Larry Owen, Attorney
Adjusted Trial Balance
July 31, 19—

Cash	$1,185	
Accounts receivable	100	
Prepaid rent	600	
Office supplies	35	
Office equipment	4,000	
Accumulated depreciation, office equipment . .		$ 40
Accounts payable		260
Salaries payable		120
Unearned legal fees		300
Larry Owen, capital		5,000
Larry Owen, withdrawals	200	
Legal fees earned		1,750
Office salaries expense.	920	
Telephone expense	30	
Heating and lighting expense	35	
Rent expense.	300	
Office supplies expense	25	
Depreciation expense, office equipment. . . .	40	
Totals	$7,470	$7,470

the objective of the process is to allocate to each period that portion of a transaction's effects applicable to the period. For example, if a revenue is earned over several accounting periods, the adjustment process apportions and credits to each period its fair share. Likewise, if an expense benefits several periods, the adjustment process charges a fair share to each benefited period.

The adjustment process is based on two accounting principles, the **realization principle** and the **matching principle**. The **realization principle** requires that revenue be assigned to the accounting period in which it is earned, rather than to the period it is collected in cash. The **matching principle** requires that revenues and expenses be matched. As for matching revenues and expenses, it is recognized that a business incurs expenses in order to earn revenues. Consequently, it is only proper that expenses be matched with (deducted on the income statement from) the revenues they helped to produce.

The basic purpose behind the adjustment process, the **realization principle,** and the **matching principle** is to make the information on accounting statements comparable from period to period. For example, the Owen law practice paid its rent for three months in advance on July 1 and debited the $900 payment to Prepaid Rent. Then, at the end of July, it transferred $300 of this amount to its Rent Expense account, and the $300 appeared on its July income statement as the July rent expense. At the end of August, it will transfer another $300 to rent expense, and at the end of September, it will transfer the third $300. As a result, the amounts shown for rent expense on its July, August, and September income statements will be comparable.

Illustration 3-3

Larry Owen, Attorney
Adjusted Trial Balance
July 31, 19——

Cash	$1,185	
Accounts receivable	100	
Prepaid rent	600	
Office supplies	35	
Office equipment	4,000	
Accumulated depreciation, office equipment		$ 40
Accounts payable		260
Salaries payable		120
Unearned legal fees		300
Larry Owen, capital		5,000
Larry Owen, withdrawals	200	
Legal fees earned		**1,750**
Office salaries expense	**920**	
Telephone expense	**30**	
Heating and lighting expense	**35**	
Rent expense	**300**	
Office supplies expense	**25**	
Depreciation expense, office equipment	**40**	
Totals	$7,470	$7,470

Preparing the Income Statement
From the Adjusted Trial Balance

Larry Owen, Attorney
Income Statement
For Month Ended July 31, 19——

Revenue:		
Legal fees earned		$1,750
Operating expenses:		
Office salaries expense	$920	
Telephone expense	30	
Heating and lighting expense	35	
Rent expense	300	
Office supplies expense	25	
Depreciation expense, office equipment	40	
Total operating expenses		1,350
Net income		$ 400

Illustration 3-4

**Preparing the Balance Sheet
From the Adjusted Trial Balance**

Larry Owen, Attorney
Adjusted Trial Balance
July 31, 19—

Cash	**$1,185**	
Accounts receivable	**100**	
Prepaid rent	**600**	
Office supplies	**35**	
Office equipment	**4,000**	
Accumulated depreciation, office equipment		**$ 40**
Accounts payable		**260**
Salaries payable		**120**
Unearned legal fees		**300**
Larry Owen, capital		**5,000**
Larry Owen, withdrawals	**200**	
Legal fees earned		1,750
Office salaries expense	920	
Telephone expense	30	
Heating and lighting expense	35	
Rent expense	300	
Office supplies expense	25	
Depreciation expense, office equipment.	40	
Totals	$7,470	$7,470

Larry Owen, Attorney
Balance Sheet
July 31, 19—

Assets

Current assets:		
Cash	$1,185	
Accounts receivable.	100	
Prepaid rent	600	
Office supplies	35	
Total current assets		$1,920
Plant and equipment:		
Office equipment	$4,000	
Less accumulated depreciation	40	
Total plant and equipment		3,960
Total assets		$5,880

Liabilities

Current liabilities:		
Accounts payable.	$ 260	
Salaries payable	120	
Unearned legal fees.	300	
Total current liabilities		$ 680

Owner's Equity

Larry Owen, capital, July 1, 19—			$5,000
July net income	$400		
Less withdrawals	200		
Excess of income over withdrawals		200	
Larry Owen, capital, July 31, 19—			5,200
Total liabilities and owner's equity.			$5,880

**July net income
from the July
income statement**

An unsatisfactory alternate procedure would be to debit the entire $900 to Rent Expense at the time of payment and permit the entire amount to appear on the July income statement as rent expense for July. However, if this were done, the July income statement would show $900 of rent expense, and the August and September statements would show none. Thus, the income statements of the three months would not be comparable. In addition, the July net income would be understated $600 and the net incomes of August and September would be overstated $300 each. As a result, a person seeing only the fluctuations in net income might draw an incorrect conclusion.

■ Arrangement of the Accounts in the Ledger

Normally, the accounts of a business are classified and logically arranged in its ledger. This serves two purposes: (1) it aids in locating any account, and (2) it aids in preparing the statements. Obviously, statements can be prepared with the least difficulty if accounts are arranged in the ledger in the order of their statement appearance. This causes the accounts to appear on the adjusted trial balance in their statement order, which aids in rearranging the adjusted trial balance items into a balance sheet and an income statement. Consequently, the balance sheet accounts beginning with Cash and ending with the owner's equity accounts appear first in the ledger. These are followed by the revenue and expense accounts in the order of their income statement appearance.

■ Disposing of Accrued Items

Accrued Expenses

Several pages back, the July 29, 30, and 31 accrued wages of the secretary were recorded as follows:

July	31	Office Salaries Expense	120.00	
		Salaries Payable.		120.00
		To record the earned but unpaid wages.		

When these wages are paid on Friday, August 9, the following entry is required:

Aug.	9	Salaries Payable	120.00	
		Office Salaries Expense	280.00	
		Cash		400.00
		Paid two weeks' wages.		

The first debit in the August 9 entry cancels the liability for the three days' wages accrued on July 31. The second debit records the wages of August's first seven working days as an expense of the August accounting period. The credit records the amount paid the secretary.

Accrued Revenues

On July 20, Larry Owen entered into an agreement to do the legal work of Guaranty Bank on a fixed-fee basis for $300 per month. On July 31, the following adjusting entry was made to record one third of a month's revenue earned under this contract.

July	31	Accounts Receivable.	100.00	
		Legal Fees Earned.		100.00
		To record a legal fee earned.		

And when payment of the first month's fee is received on August 20, the following entry will be made:

Aug.	20	Cash	300.00	
		Accounts Receivable.		100.00
		Legal Fees Earned.		200.00
		Received a legal fee earned.		

The first credit in the August 20 entry records the collection of the fee accrued at the end of July. The second credit records as revenue the fee earned during the first 20 days of August.

■ **Cash and Accrual Bases of Accounting**

For income tax purposes, an individual or a business in which inventories of merchandise for sale are not a factor may report income on either a **cash basis** or an **accrual basis.** Under the cash basis, no adjustments are made for prepaid, unearned, and accrued items. Revenues are reported as being earned in the accounting period in which they are received in cash. Expenses are deducted from revenues in the accounting period in which cash is disbursed in their payment. As a result, under the cash basis, net income is the difference between revenue receipts and expense disbursements. Under the accrual basis, on the other hand, adjustments are made for accrued and deferred (prepaid and unearned) items. Under this basis, revenues are credited to the period in which earned, expenses are matched with revenues, and no consideration is given to when cash is received and disbursed. As a result, net income is the difference between revenues earned and the expenses incurred in earning the revenues.

The cash basis of accounting is satisfactory for individuals and a few concerns in which accrued and deferred items are not important. However, it is not satisfactory for most concerns since it results in accounting reports that are not comparable from period to period. Consequently, most businesses keep their records on an accrual basis.

■ **Classification of Balance Sheet Items**

The balance sheets in the first two chapters were simple ones, and no attempt was made to classify the items. However, a balance sheet becomes more useful when its assets and liabilities are classified into significant groups. A reader of such a **classified balance sheet** can better judge the adequacy of the different kinds of assets used in the business. The reader can also better estimate the probable availability of funds to meet the various liabilities as they become due.

Accountants are not in full agreement as to the best way in which to classify balance sheet items. As a result, they are classified in several ways. A common way classifies assets into (1) current assets, (2) long-term investments, (3) plant and equipment, and (4) intangible assets. It classifies liabilities into (1) current liabilities and (2) long-term liabilities.

Of the four asset classifications listed, only two, current assets and plant and equipment, appear on the balance sheet of Valley Store, Illustration 3-5. The store is small and has no long-term investments and intangible assets.

Current Assets

Current assets are primarily those to which current creditors (current liabilities) may look for payment. As presently defined, current assets consist of cash and assets that are reasonably expected to be realized in cash or be sold or consumed within one year or within one **operating cycle of the business,** whichever is longer. The accounts and notes receivable of Illustration 3-5 are expected to be realized in cash. The merchandise (merchandise inventory) is expected to be sold either for cash or accounts receivable that will be realized in cash. The prepaid insurance and supplies are to be consumed.

The operating cycle of a business is the average period of time between its acquisition of merchandise or raw materials and the realization of cash from the sale of the merchandise or the sale of the products manufactured from the raw materials. In many companies, this interval is less than one year; and as a result, these companies use a one-year period in classifying current assets. However, due to an aging process or other cause, some companies have an operating cycle longer than one year. For example, distilleries must age some products for several years before the products are ready for sale. Consequently, in such companies, inventories of raw materials, manufacturing supplies, and products being processed for sale are classified as current assets, although the products made from the inventories will not be ready for sale for more than a year.

Such things as prepaid insurance, office supplies, and store supplies are called prepaid expenses. Until consumed, they are classified as current assets. An AICPA committee said: "Prepaid expenses are not current assets in the sense that they will be converted into cash but in the sense that, if not paid in advance, they would require the use of current assets during the operating cycls."[1] This means that if the prepaid expense items were not already owned, current assets would be required for their purchase during the operating cycle.

The prepaid expenses of a business, as a total, are seldom a major item on its balance sheet. As a result, instead of listing them individually, as in Illustration 3-5, they are commonly totaled, and only the total is shown under the caption "Prepaid expenses."

---

[1] FASB, *Accounting Standards—Current Text* (Stamford, Conn., 1984), sec. B05.105. First published as *Accounting Research Bulletin No. 43,* ch3A, par. 4.

Illustration 3-5

Valley Store
Balance Sheet
December 31, 198A

Assets

Current assets:

Cash	$ 1,050	
Notes receivable	300	
Accounts receivable	3,961	
Merchandise inventory	20,248	
Prepaid insurance	109	
Office supplies	46	
Stores supplies	145	
Total current assets		$ 25,859

Plant and equipment:

Office equipment	$ 1,500		
Less accumulated depreciation	300	$ 1,200	
Store equipment	$ 3,200		
Less accumulated depreciation	800	2,400	
Buildings	$75,000		
Less accumulated depreciation	7,400	67,600	
Land		24,200	
Total plant and equipment			95,400
Total assets			$121,259

Liabilities

Current liabilities:

Notes payable	$ 3,000	
Accounts payable	2,715	
Wages payable	112	
Mortgage payable (current portion)	1,200	
Total current liabilities		$ 7,027

Long-term liabilities:

First mortgage payable, secured by a mortgage on land and buildings	78,800	
Total liabilities		$ 85,827

Owner's Equity

Samuel Jackson, capital, January 1, 198A		$33,721
Net income for the year	$19,711	
Less withdrawals	18,000	
Excess of income over withdrawals		1,711
Samual Jackson, capital, December 31, 198A		35,432
Total liabilities and owner's equity		$121,259

Long-Term Investments

The second balance sheet classification is long-term investments. Stocks, bonds, and promissory notes that will be held for more than one year or one cycle appear under this classification. Also, such things as land held for future expansion but not now being used in the business operations appear here.

Plant and Equipment

Plant assets are relatively long-lived assets of a tangible nature that are held for use in the production or sale of other assets or services. Examples are items of equipment, buildings, and land. The key words in the definition are **long-lived** and **held for use in the production or sale of other assets or services.** Land held for future expansion is not a plant asset. It is not being used to produce or sell other assets, goods, or services.

The words **Plant and equipment** are commonly used as a balance sheet caption. More complete captions are "Property, plant, and equipment" and "Land, buildings, and equipment." However, all three captions are long and unwieldy. As a result, items of plant and equipment will be called plant assets in this book.

The order in which plant assets are listed within the balance sheet classification is not uniform. However, they are often listed from the ones of least permanent nature to those of most permanent nature.

Intangible Assets

Intangible assets are assets having no physical nature. Their value is derived from the rights conferred upon their owner by possession. Goodwill, patents, and trademarks are examples.

Current Liabilities

Current liabilities are debts or other obligations that must be paid or liquidated within one year or one operating cycle, using presently listed current assets in their payment or liquidation. Common current liabilities are notes payable, accounts payable, wages payable, taxes payable, interest payable, and unearned revenues. Also, that portion of a long-term debt due within one year or one operating cycle, for example, the $1,200 portion of the mortgage debt shown in Illustration 3-5, is a current liability. The order of their listing within the classification is not uniform. Often notes payable are listed first because notes receivable are listed first after cash in the current asset section.

Unearned revenues are classified as current liabilities because current assets will normally be required in their liquidation. For example, payments for future delivery of merchandise will be earned and the obligation for delivery will be liquidated by delivering merchandise, a current asset.

Long-Term Liabilities

The second main liability classification is **long-term liabilities.** Liabilities that are not due and payable for a comparatively long period, usually more than one year, are listed under this classification. Common long-term liability items are mortgages payable, bonds payable, and notes payable due more than a year after the balance sheet date.

■ Owner's Equity on the Balance Sheet

Single Proprietorship

The equity of the owner of a single proprietorship business may be shown on a balance sheet as follows:

Owner's Equity

James Gibbs, capital, January 1, 198A.		$23,152
Net income for the year	$10,953	
Less withdrawals	12,000	
Excess of withdrawals over income		(1,047)
James Gibbs, capital, December 31, 198A . . .		$22,105

The withdrawals of James Gibbs exceeded his net income; and in the equity section, the excess is enclosed in parenthesis to indicate that it is a negative or subtracted amount. Negative amounts are commonly shown in this way on financial statements.

The illustrated equity section shows the increases and decreases in owner's equity resulting from earnings and withdrawals. Some accountants prefer to put these details on a supplementary schedule attached to the balance sheet and called a statement of owner's equity. When this is done, owner's equity is shown on the balance sheet as follows:

Owner's Equity

James Gibbs, capital (see schedule attached) $22,105

Partnerships

Changes in partnership equities resulting from earnings and withdrawals are commonly shown in a statement of partners' equities. Then, only the amount of each partner's equity and the total of the equities as of the statement date are shown on the balance sheet, as follows:

Partners' Equities

John Reed, capital	$16,534	
Robert Burns, capital	18,506	
Total equities of the partners.		$35,040

Corporations

Corporations are regulated by state corporation laws. These laws require that a distinction be made between amounts invested in a corporation by its stockholders and the increase or decrease in stockholders' equity due to earnings, losses, and dividends. Consequently, stockholders' equity is commonly shown on a corporation balance sheet as follows:

Stockholders' Equity

Common stock.	$500,000	
Retained earnings	64,450	
Total stockholders' equity		$564,450

If a corporation issues only one kind of stock (others are discussed later), it is called **common stock.** The $500,000 amount shown here for this item is the amount originally invested in this corporation by its stockholders through the purchase of the corporation's stock. The $64,450 of **retained earnings** represents the increase in the stockholders' equity resulting from earnings that exceeded any losses and any **dividends** paid to the stockholders. (A dividend is a distribution of assets made by a corporation to its stockholders. A dividend of cash reduces corporation assets and the equity of its stockholders in the same way a withdrawal reduces assets and owner's equity in a single proprietorship.)

Arrangement of Balance Sheet Items

The balance sheet of Illustration 1-2 in the first chapter, with the liabilities and owner's equity placed to the right of the assets, is called an **account form balance sheet.** Such an arrangement emphasizes that assets equal liabilities plus owner's equity. Account form balance sheets are often reproduced on a double page with the assets on the left-hand page and the liabilities and owner's equity on the right-hand page.

The balance sheet of Illustration 3-5 is called a **report form balance sheet.** Its items are arranged vertically and better fit a single page. Both forms are commonly used, and neither is preferred.

Account Numbers

A commonly used three-digit account numbering system was introduced in Chapter 2. In the system, the number assigned to an account not only identifies the account but also tells its balance sheet or income statement classification. In the system, the first digit in an account's number tells its main balance sheet or income statement classification. For example, account numbers with first digits of 1 are assigned to asset accounts. Liability accounts are assigned numbers with first digits of 2, and the accounts in each main balance sheet and income statement classification of a concern selling merchandise are assigned numbers as follows:

111 to 199 are assigned to asset accounts.
211 to 299 are assigned to liability accounts.
311 to 399 are assigned to owner's equity accounts.
411 to 499 are assigned to sales or revenue accounts.
511 to 599 are assigned to cost of goods sold accounts.
611 to 699 are assigned to operating expense accounts.
711 to 799 are assigned to other revenue and expense accounts.

In the system, the second digit further classifies an account. For example, the second digits under each of the following main classifications indicate the subclassification shown:

111 to 199.   Asset accounts
   111 to 119.   Current asset accounts (second digits of 1)
   121 to 129.   Long-term investment accounts (second digits of 2)
   131 to 139.   Plant asset accounts (second digits of 3)
   141 to 149.   Intangible asset accounts (second digits of 4)

211 to 299. Liability accounts
   211 to 219. Current liability accounts (second digits of 1)
   221 to 229. Long-term liability accounts (second digits of 2)

611 to 699. Operating expense accounts
   611 to 629. Selling expense accounts (second digits of 1 and 2)
   631 to 649. General and administrative expense accounts (second digits of 3 and 4)

The third digit of an account's number completes its identification. For example, third digits complete the identification of the following current asset accounts:

111 to 199. Asset accounts
   111 to 119. Current asset accounts
      111. Cash
      112. Petty Cash
      113. Notes Receivable
      114. Accounts Receivable

The sales and cost of goods sold accounts mentioned here are discussed in Chapter 5. The division of the operating expense accounts into selling expense accounts and general and administrative expense accounts is also discussed there. In a service-type business such as the ones described in this chapter, generally all expense accounts are classified as operating expense accounts without subdividing them.

□   **Glossary**   **Account form balance sheet** a balance sheet with the assets on the left and the liability and owner's equity items on the right.

Accounting period the time interval over which the transactions of a business are recorded and at the end of which its financial statements are prepared.

Accrual basis of accounting the accounting basis in which revenues are assigned to the accounting period in which earned regardless of whether or not received in cash and expenses incurred in earning the revenues are deducted from the revenues regardless of whether or not cash has been disbursed in their payment.

Accrued expense an expense that has been incurred during an accounting period but that has not been paid and recorded because payment is not due.

Accrued revenue a revenue that has been earned during an accounting period but has not been received and recorded because payment is not due.

Accumulated depreciation the cumulative amount of depreciation recorded against an asset or group of assets during the entire period of time the asset or assets have been owned.

Adjusted trial balance a trial balance showing account balances brought up-to-date by recording appropriate adjusting entries.

Adjusting entries journal entries made to assign revenues to the period in which earned and to match revenues and expenses.

Adjustment process the end-of-period process of recording appropriate adjusting entries to assign revenues to the period in which earned and to match revenues and expenses.

Cash basis of accounting the accounting basis in which revenues are reported as being earned in the accounting period received in cash and expenses are deducted from revenues in the accounting period in which cash is disbursed in their payment.

Classified balance sheet a balance sheet with assets and liabilities classified into significant groups.

Common stock the name given to a corporation's stock when it issues only one kind or class of stock.

Contra account an account the balance of which is subtracted from the balance of an associated account to show a more proper amount for the item recorded in the associated account.

Current asset cash or an asset that may reasonably be expected to be realized in cash or be consumed within one year or one operating cycle of the business, whichever is longer.

Current liability a debt or other obligation that must be paid or liquidated within one year or one operating cycle, and the payment or liquidation of which will require the use of presently classified current assets.

Depreciation the expiration of a plant asset's "quantity of usefulness."

Depreciation expense the expense resulting from the expiration of a plant asset's "quantity of usefulness."

Dividend a distribution of cash or other assets made by a corporation to its stockholders.

Fiscal year a period of any 12 consecutive months used as an accounting period.

Intangible asset an asset having no physical existence but having value because of the rights conferred as a result of its ownership and possession.

Long-term liability a debt that is not due and payable for a comparatively long period, usually more than one year.

Matching principle the accounting rule that all expenses incurred in earning a revenue be deducted from the revenue in determining net income.

Natural business year any 12 consecutive months used by a business as an accounting period, at the end of which the activities of the business are at their lowest point.

Operating cycle of a business the average period of time between the acquisition of merchandise or materials by a business and the realization of cash from the sale of the merchandise or product manufactured from the materials.

Plant and equipment tangible assets having relatively long lives that are used in the production or sale of other assets or services.

Report form balance sheet a balance sheet prepared on one page, at the top of which the assets are listed, followed down the page by the liabilities and owner's equity.

Retained earnings stockholders' equity in a corporation resulting from earnings in excess of losses and dividends declared.

Time-period concept the idea that the life of a business is divisible into time periods of equal length.

Unadjusted trial balance a trial balance prepared after transactions are recorded but before any adjustments are made.

☐ **Questions for Class Discussion**

1. Why are the balances of some of a concern's accounts normally incorrect for statement purposes at the end of an accounting period even though all transactions were correctly recorded?

2. Other than to make the accounts show proper statement amounts, what is the basic purpose behind the end-of-period adjustment process?

3. A prepaid expense is an asset at the time of its purchase or prepayment. When is it best to ignore this and record the prepayment as an expense? Why?

4. What is a contra account? Give an example.

5. What contra account is used in recording depreciation? Why is such an account used?

6. What is an accrued expense? Give an example.

7. How does an unearned revenue arise? Give an example of an unearned revenue.

8. What is the balance sheet classification of an unearned revenue?

9. What is an accrued revenue? Give an example.

10. When the statements are prepared from an adjusted trial balance, why should the income statement be prepared first?

11. The adjustment process results from recognizing that some transactions affect several accounting periods. What is the objective of the process?

12. When are a concern's revenues and expenses matched?

13. Why should the income statements of a concern be comparable from period to period?

14. What is the usual order in which accounts are arranged in the ledger?

15. Differentiate between the cash and the accrual bases of accounting?

16. What is a classified balance sheet?

17. What are the characteristics of a current asset? What are the characteristics of an asset classified as plant and equipment?

18. What are current liabilities? Long-term liabilities?

19. The equity section of a corporation balance sheet shows two items, common stock and retained earnings. What does the sum of the items represent? How did each item arise?

☐ **Class Exercises**

Exercise 3-1

A company has two shop employees who together earn a total of $150 per day for a five-day workweek that begins on Monday and ends on Friday. They were paid for the week ended Friday, December 26, and both worked full days on Monday, Tuesday, and Wednesday, December 29, 30, and 31. January 1 of the next year was an unpaid holiday and none of the employees worked, but all worked a full day on Friday, January 2. Give in general journal form the year-end adjusting entry to record the accrued wages and the entry to pay the employees on January 2.

Exercise 3-2

Give in general journal form the year-end adjusting entry for each of the following situations:

a. The Shop Supplies account had a $225 debit balance on January 1; $415 of supplies were purchased during the year; and a year-end inventory showed $120 of unconsumed supplies on hand.

b. The Prepaid Insurance account had a $765 debit balance at the end of the accounting period before adjustment for expired insurance. An examination of insurance policies showed $445 of insurance expired.

c. The Prepaid Insurance account had an $880 debit balance at the end of the accounting period before adjustment for expired insurance. An examination of insurance policies showed $265 of unexpired insurance.

d. Depreciation on shop equipment was estimated at $915 for the accounting period.

e. Four months' property taxes, estimated at $565, have accrued but are unrecorded and unpaid at the accounting period end.

Exercise 3-3

Assume that the required adjustments of Exercise 3-2 were not made at the end of the accounting period and tell for each adjustment the effect of its omission on the income statement and balance sheet prepared at that time.

Exercise 3-4

Determine the amounts indicated by the question marks in the columns below. The amounts in each column constitute a separate problem.

	(a)	(b)	(c)	(d)
Supplies on hand on January 1.	$235	$140	$375	?
Supplies purchased during the year	450	530	?	$630
Supplies remaining at the year-end	165	?	215	240
Supplies consumed during the year	?	480	670	560

Exercise 3-5

A company paid the $900 premium on a three-year insurance policy on May 1, 198A. The policy gave protection beginning on that date.

a. How many dollars of the premium should appear on the 198A income statement as an expense?
b. How many dollars of the premium should appear on the December 31, 198A, balance sheet as an asset?
c. Under the assumption that the Prepaid Insurance account was debited in recording the premium payment, give the December 31, 198A, adjusting entry to record the expired insurance.
d. Under the assumption that the bookkeeper incorrectly debited the Insurance Expense account for $900 in recording the premium payment, give the December 31, 198A, adjusting entry. (Hint: Did the bookkeeper's error change the answers to questions [a] and [b] of this exercise?)

Exercise 3-6

a. A tenant rented space in a building on October 1 at $300 per month, paying six months' rent in advance. The building owner credited Unearned Rent to record the $1,800 received. Give the year-end adjusting entry of the building owner.
b. Another tenant rented space in the building at $350 per month on October 1. The tenant paid the rent on the first day of October and again on the first day of November, but by December 31 the December rent had not yet been paid. Give the required adjusting entry of the building owner.
c. Assume the foregoing tenant paid the rent for December and January on January 2 of the new year. Give the entry to record the receipt of the $700.

Exercise 3-7

The adjusted trial balance that follows was taken from the ledger of Mary Luke, an attorney.

Mary Luke, Attorney
Adjusted Trial Balance
December 31, 19—

Cash	$ 1,500	
Accounts receivable.	3,200	
Prepaid insurance.	700	
Office supplies	100	
Office equipment	10,500	
Accumulated depreciation, office equipment . . .		$ 3,000
Building	110,000	
Accumulated depreciation, building		10,000
Land	40,000	
Salaries payable		200
Unearned legal fees.		800
Mortgage payable.		95,000
Mary Luke, capital		48,000
Mary Luke, withdrawals	36,000	
Legal fees earned.		85,000
Operating expenses (combined).	40,000	
Totals	$242,000	$242,000

Required

A subtraction of the combined operating expenses from the legal fees earned indicates that the law practice earned $45,000 during the year of the adjusted trial balance. A $5,000 payment on the mortgage is due within one year. Use this information and any relevant information from the adjusted trial balance to prepare a classified year-end balance sheet for the practice.

Exercise 3-8

An inexperienced bookkeeper prepared the first of the following income statements, but he forgot to adjust the accounts before its preparation. However, the oversight was discovered, and the second statement was prepared. Analyze the statements and prepare the adjusting journal entries that were made between the preparation of the two statements. Assume that one third of the additional property management fees resulted from recognizing accrued fees and two thirds resulted from previously recorded unearned fees that were earned by the date of the statements.

Hillside Realty
Income Statement
For Year Ended December 31, 19—

Revenues:		
Commissions earned		$54,750
Property management fees		3,000
Total revenues		$57,750
Operating expenses:		
Salaries expense	$11,500	
Rent expense.	9,000	
Advertising expense	2,500	
Gas, oil, and repairs expense.	500	
Total operating expenses.		23,500
Net income.		$34,250

Hillside Realty
Income Statement
For Year Ended December 31, 19—

Revenues:		
Commissions earned		$54,750
Property management fees		3,750
Total revenues		$58,500
Operating expenses:		
Salaries expense	$12,000	
Rent expense.	9,000	
Advertising expense	2,500	
Gas, oil, and repairs expense	500	
Office supplies expense	100	
Insurance expense	900	
Depreciation expense, office equipment	1,000	
Depreciation expense, automobile	2,000	
Total operating expenses.		28,000
Net income.		$30,500

Exercise 3-9

Following are data from the records of three single proprietorships. Prepare a year-end balance sheet equity section for each.

a. Frank Hall, capital, January 1, 19— $63,000
   Net income earned during the year 38,000
   Withdrawals during the year 30,000

b. Harry Beal, capital, January 1, 19— $36,000
   Net income earned during the year 15,000
   Withdrawals during the year 18,000

c. George Nash, capital, January 1, 19—. . . . $48,000
   Net loss incurred during the year 4,000
   Withdrawals during the year 12,000

Exercise 3-10

A corporation had $250,000 of common stock issued and outstanding during all of 198B. It began the year with $65,000 of retained earnings, and it declared and paid $20,000 of cash dividends to its stockholders. It also earned a $50,000 198B net income. Prepare the equity section of the corporation's year-end balance sheet. (Hint: Net income increases a corporation's assets and retained earnings, and dividends and losses reduce its assets and retained earnings. However, only the net amount of a corporation's retained earnings as of the statement date is shown on its balance sheet.)

☐ **Problems**   ### Problem 3-1

The following information for adjustments was available on December 31, the end of a yearly accounting period. Prepare an adjusting journal entry for each unit of information.

a. The Store Supplies account had a $125 debit balance at the beginning of the year, $560 of supplies were purchased during the year, and an inventory of unused store supplies at the year-end totaled $150.

b. An examination of insurance policies showed three policies, as follows:

Policy	Date of Purchase	Life of Policy	Cost
1	October 1 of previous year	3 years	$1,800
2	April 1 of current year	2 years	720
3	August 1 of current year	1 year	480

Prepaid Insurance was debited for the cost of each policy at the time of its purchase. Expired insurance was correctly recorded at the end of the previous year.

c. The company's two office employees earn $50 per day and $60 per day, respectively. They are paid each Friday for a five-day workweek that begins on Monday. This year December 31 fell on Tuesday, and the employees both worked on Monday and Tuesday.

d. The company owns a building that it completed and occupied for the first time on June 1 of the current year. The building cost $360,000, has an estimated 30-year life, and is not expected to have any salvage value at the end of that time.

e. The company occupies most of the space in its building, but it also rents space to two tenants. One tenant rented a small amount of space on September 1 at $400 per month. The tenant paid the rent on the first day of each month September through November, and the amounts paid were credited to Rent Earned. However, the tenant has not paid the rent for December, although on several occasions the tenant said the rent would be paid the next day. (f) The second tenant agreed on November 1 to rent a small amount of space at $450 per month, and on that date paid three months' rent in advance. The amount paid was credited to the Unearned Rent account.

Problem 3-2

A trial balance of the ledger of Apex Realty at the end of its annual accounting period carried the items shown on the following page.

Required

1. Open the accounts of the trial balance plus these additional ones: Accounts Receivable; Office Salaries Payable; Management Fees Earned; Insurance Expense; Office Supplies Expense; Depreciation Expense, Office Equipment; and Depreciation Expense, Automobile. Enter the trial balance amounts in the accounts.

2. Use the following information to prepare and post adjusting entries:
   a. An examination of insurance policies showed $645 of expired insurance.
   b. An inventory showed $65 of unused office supplies on hand.
   c. The year's depreciation on office equipment was estimated at $780 and (d) on the automobile at $1,800.

e. and (f) Apex Realty offers property management services and has two contracts with clients. In the first contract (e), it agreed to manage an office building beginning on November 1. The contract calls for a $150 monthly fee, and the client paid the first three months' fees in advance at the time the contract was signed. The amount paid was credited to the Unearned Management Fees account. In the second contract (f), Apex agreed to manage an apartment building for $100 per month payable at the end of each three-month period. The contract was signed on October 15, and two and a half months' fees have accrued.

g. The one office employee is paid weekly; and on December 31, three days' wages at $45 per day have accrued.

3. After posting the adjusting entries, prepare an adjusted trial balance, an income statement, and a classified balance sheet.

Apex Realty
Trial Balance
December 31, 19—

Cash	$ 1,940	
Prepaid insurance	915	
Office supplies	290	
Office equipment	6,250	
Accumulated depreciation, office equipment		$ 1,920
Automobile	12,780	
Accumulated depreciation, automobile		2,150
Accounts payable		225
Unearned management fees		450
Dale Pitts, capital		11,145
Dale Pitts, withdrawals	18,600	
Sales commissions earned		41,280
Office salaries expense	10,300	
Advertising expense	830	
Rent expense	4,800	
Telephone expense	465	
Totals	$57,170	$57,170

Problem 3-3

A year-end trial balance of the ledger of Lakeside Moving and Storage follows on page 106.

Required

1. Open the accounts of the trial balance plus these additional ones: Salaries and Wages Payable; Insurance Expense; Office Supplies Expense; Depreciation Expense, Office Equipment; Depreciation Expense, Trucks; and Depreciation Expense, Building. Enter the trial balance amounts in the accounts.

2. Prepare and post adjusting journal entries based on the information that follows:

a. An examination of insurance policies showed $2,350 of expired insurance.

b. An inventory showed $135 of unused office supplies on hand.

c. Estimated depreciation on the office equipment, $455; *(d)* on the trucks, $4,420; and *(e)* on the building, $5,600.

f. The company credits storage fees of customers who pay in advance to the Unearned Storage Fees account. Of the $1,730 credited to this account, $1,420 was earned by the year-end.

g. Accrued storage fees earned but unrecorded and uncollected at the year-end totaled $260.

h. There were $610 of earned but unrecorded drivers' and helpers' wages at the year-end.

3. Prepare an adjusted trial balance, an income statement for the year, and a classified year-end balance sheet. A $4,000 installment on the mortgage is due within one year.

Lakeside Moving and Storage
Trial Balance
December 31, 19—

Cash	$ 2,240	
Accounts receivable	545	
Prepaid insurance	3,580	
Office supplies	320	
Office equipment	3,650	
Accumulated depreciation, office equipment		$ 1,680
Trucks	44,200	
Accumulated depreciation, trucks		11,540
Building	168,000	
Accumulated depreciation, building		28,600
Land	17,500	
Unearned storage fees		1,730
Mortgage payable		120,000
John Hall, capital		54,110
John Hall, withdrawals	24,000	
Revenue from moving services		90,115
Storage fees earned		7,770
Office salaries expense	11,400	
Drivers' and helpers' wages expense	26,630	
Gas, oil, and repairs expense	2,680	
Mortgage interest expense	10,800	
Totals	$315,545	$315,545

Problem 3-4

After all transactions were recorded at the end of its annual accounting period, a trial balance of the ledger of Vista Trailer Park carried the items that follow on page 107.

Required

1. Open the accounts of the trial balance plus these additional ones: Accounts Receivable; Wages Payable; Property Taxes Payable; Interest Payable; Insurance Expense; Office Supplies Expense; Depreciation Expense, Office Equipment; and Depreciation Expense, Buildings and Improvements. Enter the trial balance amounts in the accounts.

2. Use the following information to prepare and post adjusting journal entries:

  a. An examination of insurance policies showed $1,180 of expired insurance.

  b. An office supplies inventory showed $115 of unused office supplies on hand.

  c. Estimated depreciation on office equipment, $290; and (d) on buildings and improvements, $4,600.

  e. The trailer park follows the practice of crediting the Unearned Rent account for rents paid in advance by tenants. An examination revealed that $580 of the balance of this account was earned by the year-end.

  f. A tenant is in arrears on rent payments, and this $85 of accrued revenue was unrecorded at the time the trial balance was prepared.

  g. The one employee of the trailer park works a five-day workweek at $40 per day. The employee was paid last week but has worked three days this week for which he has not been paid.

  h. Three months' property taxes, totaling $655, have accrued. This additional amount of property taxes expense has not been recorded.

  i. One month's interest on the mortgage, $885, has accrued but is unrecorded.

3. Post the adjusting entries and prepare an adjusted trial balance, an income statement for the year, and a classified balance sheet. A $6,000 installment on the mortgage is due within one year.

Vista Trailer Park
Trial Balance
December 31, 19—

Cash	$ 2,540	
Prepaid insurance	1,525	
Office supplies	260	
Office equipment	2,450	
Accumulated depreciation, office equipment		$ 815
Buildings and improvements	92,000	
Accumulated depreciation, buildings and improvements		21,350
Land	95,000	
Unearned rent		780
Mortgage payable		118,000
June Lake, capital		41,810
June Lake, withdrawals	18,200	
Rent earned		51,865
Wages expense	10,120	
Utilities expense	825	
Property taxes expense	1,965	
Interest expense	9,735	
Totals	$234,620	$234,620

Problem 3-5

Sue Hall purchased Vagabond Village, a mobile home park, last September 1, and she has operated it four months without keeping formal accounting records. However, she has deposited all receipts in the bank and has kept an accurate checkbook record of payments. An analysis of her cash receipts and payments follows.

	Receipts	Payments
Investment.	$42,000	
Purchased Vagabond Village:		
Office equipment . . . . $ 1,200		
Buildings and improvements 75,000		
Land 85,000		
Total $161,200		
Less mortgage assumed. 120,000		
Cash paid		$41,200
Insurance premium paid		960
Office supplies purchased		120
Wages paid		3,400
Utilities paid		370
Property taxes paid		1,260
Personal withdrawals of cash by owner . . .		4,000
Mobile home space rentals collected	16,150	
Totals	$58,150	$51,310
Cash balance, December 31		6,840
Totals	$58,150	$58,150

Ms. Hall wants you to prepare an accrual basis income statement for the village for the four-month period she has operated the business and a December 31 balance sheet. You ascertain the following. (T-accounts will be helpful in organizing the data.)

The buildings and improvements were estimated to have a 25-year remaining life when purchased and at the end of that time will be wrecked. It is estimated that the sale of salvaged materials will just pay the wrecking costs and the cost of clearing the site. The office equipment is in good condition. At the time of purchase, Ms. Hall estimated she would use the equipment for three years and would then trade it in on new equipment of like kind. She thought $120 a fair estimate of what she would receive for the old equipment when she traded it in at the end of three years.

The $960 payment for insurance was for a policy taken out on September 1. The policy's protection was for one year beginning on that date. Ms. Hall estimates that one third of the office supplies purchased have been used. She also says that the one employee of the village earns $40 per day for a five-day workweek that ends on Friday. The employee was paid last week but has worked Monday, Tuesday, Wednesday, and Thursday, December 28, 29, 30, and 31, for which he has not been paid.

Included in the $16,150 of mobile home rentals collected is $300 received from a tenant for three months' rent beginning on December 1. Also, a tenant has not paid his $100 rent for the month of December.

The mortgage requires the payment of 12% interest annually on the beginning principal balance and a $4,800 annual payment on the principal. The property tax payment was for one year's taxes that were paid on October 1 for the tax year beginning on September 1, the day Ms. Hall purchased the business.

☐ **Alternate Problems**   **Problem 3-1A**

The following information for preparing adjusting entries was available for the annual accounting period ended December 31 of the current year. Prepare the required adjusting entries.

a. The Store Supplies account had a $115 debit balance at the beginning of the year. Supplies costing $565 were purchased during the year, and an inventory of unused supplies at the year-end totaled $125.

b. An examination of insurance policies showed three policies, as follows:

Policy	Protection Began on	Life of Policy	Cost
1.	May 12 of the previous year	3 years	$840
2.	March 1 of current year	2 years	540
3.	August 1 of current year	1 year	420

Prepaid Insurance was debited for the cost of each policy at the time of purchase. Expired insurance was correctly recorded at the end of the previous year.

c. The company's two office employees earn $40 per day and $50 per day, respectively. They are paid each Friday for a five-day workweek that begins on Monday. December 31 fell on Wednesday, and the employees both worked on Monday, Tuesday, and Wednesday but have not been paid.

d. The company owns a building that it completed and occupied for the first time on June 1 of the current year. The building cost $450,000, has an estimated 25-year life, and is not expected to have any salvage value at the end of its life.

e. On September 1, the company received its property tax bill for the tax year beginning on October 1. The bill totaled $2,580 and was payable in two equal installments of $1,290 each. The company paid the first installment and debited the amount paid to the Property Taxes Expense account.

f. The company occupies most of the space in its building, but it also rents space to two tenants. One tenant rented a small amount of space on September 1 at $200 per month. The tenant paid the rent on the first day of each month, September through November, and the amounts paid were credited to the Rent Earned account. However, the tenant has not paid the rent for December, although on several occasions has said it would be paid the next day.

g. The second tenant agreed on November 1 to rent a small amount of space at $225 per month and on that date paid three months' rent in advance. The amount paid was credited to the Unearned Rent account.

Problem 3-2A

At the end of its annual accounting period, Pitts Realty prepared from its ledger the trial balance that follows on page 110.

Required

1. Open the accounts of the trial balance plus these additional ones: Accounts Receivable; Office Salaries Payable; Management Fees Earned;

Insurance Expense; Office Supplies Expense; Depreciation Expense, Office Equipment; and Depreciation Expense, Automobile. Enter the trial balance amounts in the accounts.

2. Use the information that follows to prepare and post adjusting entries:
   a. An examination of insurance policies showed $725 of expired insurance.
   b. An inventory showed $80 of unused office supplies on hand.
   c. The year's depreciation on office equipment was estimated at $815 and (d) on the automobile at $1,775.
   e. The December telephone bill arrived after the trial balance was prepared, and its $40 amount was not included in the trial balance amounts. Also, a bill for $110 of newspaper advertising that had appeared in December arrived after the trial balance was prepared and was not included in the trial balance amounts.
   f. A client who was taking a tour around the world signed a contract with Pitts Realty for the management of his apartment building. The contract calls for a $150 monthly fee, and management began on December 1. The client paid three months' fees in advance, and the amount paid was credited to the Unearned Management Fees account.
   g. Pitts Realty agreed to manage the small office building of a second client for $150 per month payable at the end of each three months. The contract was signed on November 15, and one and a half months' fees have accrued.
   h. The one office employee is paid weekly; and on December 31, four days' wages at $40 per day have accrued.

3. After posting the adjusting entries, prepare an adjusted trial balance, an income statement, and a classified balance sheet.

Pitts Realty
Trial Balance
December 31, 19—

Cash	$ 1,940	
Prepaid insurance.	915	
Office supplies	290	
Office equipment	6,250	
Accumulated depreciation, office equipment . .		$ 1,920
Automobile.	12,780	
Accumulated depreciation, automobile		2,150
Accounts payable.		225
Unearned management fees		450
Dale Pitts, capital		11,145
Dale Pitts, withdrawals.	18,600	
Sales commissions earned.		41,280
Office salaries expense	10,300	
Advertising expense.	830	
Rent expense	4,800	
Telephone expense	465	
Totals	$57,170	$57,170

Problem 3-3A

A year-end trial balance of the ledger of Corona Moving and Storage follows.

Corona Moving and Storage
Trial Balance
December 31, 19—

Cash.	$ 2,240	
Accounts receivable	545	
Prepaid insurance	3,580	
Office supplies.	320	
Office equipment.	3,650	
Accumulated depreciation, office equipment . . .		$ 1,680
Trucks	44,200	
Accumulated depreciation, trucks.		11,540
Building	168,000	
Accumulated depreciation, building.		28,600
Land.	17,500	
Unearned storage fees		1,730
Mortgage payable		120,000
John Hall, capital		54,110
John Hall, withdrawals	24,000	
Revenue from moving services.		90,115
Storage fees earned		7,770
Office salaries expense.	11,400	
Drivers' and helpers' wages expense.	26,630	
Gas, oil, and repairs expense	2,680	
Mortgage interest expense	10,800	
Totals	$315,545	$315,545

Required

1. Open the accounts of the trial balance plus these additional ones: Salaries and Wages Payable; Insurance Expense; Office Supplies Expense; Depreciation Expense, Office Equipment; Depreciation Expense, Trucks; and Depreciation Expense, Building. Enter the trial balance amounts in the accounts.

2. Use the information that follows to prepare and post adjusting entries:
   a. An examination of insurance policies showed $2,815 of expired insurance.
   b. An inventory showed $110 of unused office supplies on hand.
   c. Estimated depreciation on the office equipment, $515; *(d)* on the trucks, $5,220; and *(e)* on the building, $6,200.
   f. The company credits storage fees of customers who pay in advance to the Unearned Storage Fees account. Of the $1,730 credited to this account, $1,325 was earned by the year-end.
   g. Accrued storage fees earned but unrecorded and uncollected at the year-end totaled $345.
   h. There were $135 of earned but unrecorded office salaries and $755 of earned but unrecorded drivers' and helpers' wages at the year-end.

3. Prepare an adjusted trial balance, an income statement for the year, and a classified year-end balance sheet. A $6,000 installment on the mortgage is due within one year.

Problem 3-4A

At the end of its annual accounting period, after all transactions were recorded, a trial balance of the ledger of Lazy T Trailer Park carried the items that follow.

Lazy T Trailer Park
Trial Balance
December 31, 19—

Cash	$ 2,540	
Prepaid insurance	1,525	
Office supplies	260	
Office equipment	2,450	
Accumulated depreciation, office equipment		$ 815
Buildings and improvements	92,000	
Accumulated depreciation, buildings and improvements		21,350
Land	95,000	
Unearned rent		780
Mortgage payable		118,000
June Lake, capital		41,810
June Lake, withdrawals	18,200	
Rent earned		51,865
Wages expense	10,120	
Utilities expense	825	
Property taxes expense	1,965	
Interest expense	9,735	
Totals	$234,620	$234,620

Required

1. Open the accounts of the trial balance plus these additional ones: Accounts Receivable; Wages Payable; Property Taxes Payable; Interest Payable; Insurance Expense; Office Supplies Expense; Depreciation Expense, Office Equipment; and Depreciation Expense, Buildings and Improvements. Enter the trial balance amounts in the accounts.
2. Use the information that follows to prepare and post adjusting journal entries:
   a. An examination of insurance policies showed $1,235 of expired insurance.
   b. An inventory of office supplies showed $85 of unused supplies on hand.
   c. Estimated depreciation of office equipment, $310; and (d) of buildings and improvements, $5,250.
   e. The trailer park credits the Unearned Rent account for rents paid in advance. An examination revealed that $445 of the balance of this account was earned by the year-end.
   f. One tenant is in arrears on rent payments, and this $100 of accrued revenue was unrecorded at the time the trial balance was prepared.
   g. Four months' property taxes expense, estimated at $980, has accrued but was not recorded at the time the trial balance was prepared.

h. The one employee of the trailer park works a five-day workweek at $40 per day. He was paid last week but has worked four days this week for which he has not been paid.

i. Three months' interest on the mortgage, $3,245, has accrued but was unpaid and unrecorded on the trial balance date.

3. Post the adjusting entries and prepare an adjusted trial balance, an income statement for the year, and a classified balance sheet. A $5,500 payment on the mortgage is due within one year.

Problem 3-5A

Walter Swift, a lawyer, has always kept his records on a cash basis; at the end of 198B, he prepared the following cash basis income statement.

Walter Swift, Attorney
Income Statement
For Year Ended December 31, 198B

Revenues	$69,700
Expenses.	28,300
Net income	$41,400

In preparing the statement, the following amounts of accrued and deferred items were ignored at the ends of 198A and 198B.

	End of	
	198A	**198B**
Prepaid expenses . . .	$1,540	$1,215
Accrued expenses . . .	1,730	2,180
Unearned revenues. . .	2,210	3,620
Accrued revenues . . .	3,190	2,440

Required

Under the assumptions that the 198A prepaid expenses were consumed or expired in 198B, the 198A unearned revenues were earned in 198B, and the 198A accrued items were either paid or received in cash in 198B, prepare a 198B accrual basis income statement for Walter Swift. Attach to your statement calculations showing how you arrived at each 198B income statement amount.

Provocative Problems

□

Provocative Problem 3-1   Small Appliance Service

Ted Small began Small Appliance Service, a new business, on January 2. After one year's operations, Ted feels the business has done a lot of work during its first year. However, the bank has begun to dishonor its checks. Its creditors are dunning it for bills it is unable to pay, and Ted just cannot understand why. Consequently he has asked your help in determining the results of the first year's operations.

You find the service's accounting records, such as they are, have been kept by Ted's wife, who has no formal training in record-keeping. However, she has prepared for your inspection the statement of cash receipts and disbursements that follows.

Small Appliance Service
Cash Receipts and Disbursements
For Year Ended December 31,19—

Receipts:
Investment $12,000
Received from customers for services . . .   35,565 $47,565
Disbursements:
Rent expense . . . . $ 3,250
Repair equipment purchased.   5,400
Service truck expense   10,315
Wages expense   18,720
Insurance expense   1,270
Repair parts and supplies   8,650   47,605
Bank overdraft. . . . . $ (40)

There were no errors in the statement, and you learn these additional facts:

1. The lease contract for the shop space runs for five years and requires rent payments of $250 per month, with the first and last months' rent to be paid in advance. All required payments were made on time.

2. The repair equipment has an estimated six-year life, after which it will be valueless. It has been used a full year.

3. The service truck expense consists of $9,200 paid for the truck on January 2, plus $1,115 paid for gas and oil. Mr. Small expects to use the truck four years, after which he thinks he will get $1,200 for it as a trade-in on a new truck.

4. The wages expense consists of $3,120 paid the service's one employee who was hired on September 30, plus $15,600 of personal withdrawals by Mr. Small. Also, the one employee is owed $100 of earned but unpaid wages.

5. The $1,270 of insurance expense resulted from paying the premiums on two insurance policies on January 2. One policy cost $550 and gave protection for one year. The other policy cost $720 for two years' protection.

6. In addition to the $8,650 of repair parts and supplies paid for during the year, creditors are dunning the business for $485 for parts and supplies purchased and delivered, but not paid for. Also, an inventory shows $955 of unused parts and supplies on hand.

7. Mr. Small reports that the business does most of its work for cash, but customers owe $375 for repair work done on credit.

Prepare an accrual basis income statement showing the results of the first year's operations of the business and a classified balance sheet showing its year-end financial position.

Provocative Problem 3-2   The Fixit Shop

During the first week of January of the current year, Gary Blake began a small repair business he calls The Fixit Shop. He has kept no accounting records, but he does file any unpaid invoices for things purchased by impaling them on a nail in the wall over his workbench. He has kept a good record of the year's receipts and payments, which follows.

	Receipts	Payments
Investment	$ 5,000	
Shop equipment.		$ 4,000
Repair parts and supplies.		4,210
Rent payments		2,600
Insurance premiums paid		760
Newspaper advertising paid.		250
Utility bills paid		645
Part-time helper's wages paid		6,230
Gary Blake for personal use.		15,000
Revenue from repairs	29,955	
Subtotals.	$34,955	$33,695
Cash balance, December 31, 19—. . .		1,260
Totals	$34,955	$34,955

Gary would like to know how much the business actually earned during its first year. Therefore, he would like for you to prepare an accrual basis income statement and a year-end classified balance sheet for the shop.

You learn that the shop equipment has an estimated eight-year life, after which it will be worthless. There is a $315 unpaid invoice on the nail over Gary's workbench for supplies received, and an inventory shows $330 of unused supplies on hand. The shop space rents for $200 per month on a five-year lease. The lease contract requires payment of the first and last months' rents in advance, which were paid. The insurance premiums were for two policies taken out on January 2. The first is a one-year policy that cost $220. The second is a two-year policy that cost $540. There are $60 of earned but unpaid wages owed the helper, and customers owe the shop $385 for repair services they have received.

Provocative Problem 3-3   Tipton Realty

The 198A and 198B balance sheets of Tipton Realty show the following assets and liabilities at the end of each of the years:

	December 31	
	198A	198B
Prepaid insurance	$1,375	$1,010
Property management fees receivable. . .	300	575
Interest payable	415	360
Unearned property management fees . . .	725	850

The concern's records show the following amounts of cash disbursed and received for these items during 198B:

Cash disbursed to pay insurance premiums. . .	$2,320
Cash disbursed to pay interest	1,450
Cash received for managing property	6,280

Present calculations to show the amounts to be reported on Tipton Realty's 198B income statement for (a) insurance expense, (b) interest expense, and (c) property management fees earned.

4 The Work Sheet and Closing the Accounts of Proprietorships, Partnerships, and Corporations

After studying Chapter 4, you should be able to:

1. Explain why a work sheet is prepared and be able to prepare a work sheet for a service-type business.

2. Explain why it is necessary to close the revenue and expense accounts at the end of each accounting period.

3. Prepare entries to close the temporary accounts of a service business and prepare a post-closing trial balance to test the accuracy of the end-of-period adjusting and closing procedures.

4. Explain the nature of the retained earnings item on corporation balance sheets.

5. Explain why a corporation with a deficit cannot pay a legal dividend.

6. Prepare entries to close the Income Summary account of a corporation and to record the declaration and payment of a dividend.

7. List the steps in the accounting cycle in the order in which they are completed.

8. Define or explain the words and phrases listed in the chapter Glossary.

As an aid in their work, accountants prepare numerous memoranda, analyses, and informal papers that serve as a basis for the formal reports given to management or to their clients. These analyses and memoranda are called **working papers** and are invaluable tools of the accountant. The work sheet described in this chapter is such a working paper. It is prepared solely for the accountant's use. It is not given to the owner or manager of the business for which it is prepared but is retained by the accountant. Normally, it is prepared with a pencil, which makes changes and corrections easy as its preparation progresses.

Work Sheet in the Accounting Procedures

In the accounting procedures described in the previous chapter, at the end of an accounting period, as soon as all transactions were recorded, recall that adjusting entries were entered in the journal and posted to the accounts. Then, an adjusted trial balance was prepared and used in making an income statement and balance sheet. For a very small business, these are satisfactory procedures. However, if a company has more than a few accounts and adjustments, errors in adjusting the accounts and in preparing the statements are less apt to be made if an additional step is inserted in the procedures. The additional step is the preparation of a **work sheet.** A work sheet is a tool of accountants upon which they (1) achieve the effect of adjusting the accounts before entering the adjustments in the accounts, (2) sort the adjusted account balances into columns according to whether the accounts are used in preparing the income statement or balance sheet, and (3) calculate and prove the mathematical accuracy of the net income. Then, after the work sheet is completed, (4) accountants use it in preparing the income statement and balance sheet and in preparing adjusting and closing entries. (Closing entries are discussed later in this chapter.)

Preparing a Work Sheet

The Owen law practice of previous chapters does not have sufficient accounts or adjustments to warrant the preparation of a work sheet. Nevertheless, since its accounts and adjustments are familiar, they are used here to illustrate the procedures involved.

During July, the Owen law practice completed a number of transactions. On July 31, after these transactions were recorded but **before any adjusting entries were prepared and posted,** a trial balance of its ledger appeared as in Illustration 4-1.

Notice that the trial balance is an **unadjusted trial balance.** The accounts have not been adjusted for expired rent, supplies consumed, depreciation, and so forth. Nevertheless, this unadjusted trial balance is the starting point in preparing the work sheet for the law practice, which is shown in Illustration 4-2.

Note that the work sheet has five pairs of money columns and that the first pair is labeled Trial Balance. In this first pair of columns is copied the unadjusted trial balance of the law practice. Often when a work sheet is prepared, the trial balance is prepared for the first time in its first two money columns.

The second pair of work sheet columns is labeled Adjustments. The

Illustration 4-1

Larry Owen, Attorney
Trial Balance
July 31, 19—

Cash	$1,185	
Prepaid rent	900	
Office supplies	60	
Office equipment	4,000	
Accounts payable		$ 260
Unearned legal fees		450
Larry Owen, capital.		5,000
Larry Owen, withdrawals	200	
Legal fees earned		1,500
Office salaries expense	800	
Telephone expense.	30	
Heating and lighting expense . . .	35	
Totals.	$7,210	$7,210

adjustments are entered in these columns. Note they are, with one exception, the same adjustments for which adjusting journal entries were prepared and posted in the previous chapter. The one exception is the last one, *(e)* in which the two adjustments affecting the Legal Fees Earned account are combined into one compound adjustment. They were combined because both result in credits to the same account.

Note that the adjustments on the illustrated work sheet are keyed together with letters. When a work sheet is prepared, after it is completed, the adjusting entries still have to be entered in the journal and posted to the ledger. At that time, the key letters help identify each adjustment's related debits and credits. Explanations of the adjustments on the illustrated work sheet are as follows:

Adjustment *(a):* To adjust for the rent expired.
Adjustment *(b):* To adjust for the office supplies consumed.
Adjustment *(c):* To adjust for depreciation of the office equipment.
Adjustment *(d):* To adjust for the accrued secretary's salary.
Adjustment *(e):* To adjust for unearned and accrued revenue.

Each adjustment on the illustrated work sheet required one or two additional account names to be written in below the original trial balance. These accounts did not have balances when the trial balance was prepared. Consequently, they were not listed in the trial balance. Often, when a work sheet is prepared, the effects of the adjustments are anticipated and any additional accounts required are provided without amounts in the body of the trial balance.

When a work sheet is prepared, after the adjustments are entered in the Adjustments columns, the columns are totaled to prove the equality of the adjustments.

The third set of work sheet columns is labeled Adjusted Trial Balance. In preparing a work sheet, each amount in the Trial Balance columns is combined with its adjustment in the Adjustments columns, if any, and is

Illustration 4-2

Larry Owen, Attorney
Work Sheet for Month Ended July 31, 19—

Account Titles	Trial Balance Dr.	Trial Balance Cr.	Adjustments Dr.	Adjustments Cr.	Adjusted Trial Balance Dr.	Adjusted Trial Balance Cr.	Income Statement Dr.	Income Statement Cr.	Balance Sheet Dr.	Balance Sheet Cr.
Cash	1,185 00				1,185 00				1,185 00	
Prepaid rent	900 00			(a) 300 00	600 00				600 00	
Office supplies	60 00			(b) 25 00	35 00				35 00	
Office equipment	4,000 00				4,000 00				4,000 00	
Accounts payable		260 00				260 00				260 00
Unearned legal fees		450 00	(e) 150 00			300 00				300 00
Larry Owen, capital		5,000 00				5,000 00				5,000 00
Larry Owen, withdrawals	200 00				200 00				200 00	
Legal fees earned		1,500 00		(e) 250 00		1,750 00		1,750 00		
Office salaries expense	800 00		(d) 120 00		920 00		920 00			
Telephone expense	30 00				30 00		30 00			
Heating & lighting expense	35 00				35 00		35 00			
	7,210 00	7,210 00								
Rent expense			(a) 300 00		300 00		300 00			
Office supplies expense			(b) 25 00		25 00		25 00			
Depr. expense, office equip.			(c) 40 00		40 00		40 00			
Accum. depr., office equip.				(c) 40 00		40 00				40 00
Salaries payable				(d) 120 00		120 00				120 00
Accounts receivable			(e) 100 00		100 00				100 00	
			735 00	735 00	7,470 00	7,470 00	1,350 00	1,750 00	6,120 00	5,720 00
Net income							400 00			400 00
							1,750 00	1,750 00	6,120 00	6,120 00

entered in the Adjusted Trial Balance columns. For example, in Illustration 4-2, the Prepaid Rent account has a $900 debit balance in the Trial Balance columns. This $900 debit is combined with the $300 credit in the Adjustments columns to give Prepaid Rent a $600 debit in the Adjusted Trial Balance columns. Rent Expense has no balance in the Trial Balance columns, but it has a $300 debit in the Adjustments columns. Therefore, no balance combined with a $300 debit gives Rent Expense a $300 debit in the Adjusted Trial Balance columns. Cash, Office Equipment, and several other accounts have trial balance amounts but no adjustments. As a result, their trial balance amounts are carried unchanged into the Adjusted Trial Balance columns. Notice that the result of combining the amounts in the Trial Balance columns with the amounts in the Adjustments columns is an adjusted trial balance in the Adjusted Trial Balance columns.

After the combined amounts are carried to the Adjusted Trial Balance columns, the Adjusted Trial Balance columns are added to prove their equality. Then, the amounts in these columns are sorted to the proper Balance Sheet or Income Statement columns according to the statement on which they will appear. This is an easy task that requires answers to only two questions: (1) is the item to be sorted a debit or a credit, and (2) on which statement does it appear? As to the first question, an adjusted trial balance debit amount must be sorted to either the Income Statement debit column or the Balance Sheet debit column. Likewise, a credit amount must go into either the Income Statement credit or Balance Sheet credit column. In other words, debits remain debits and credits remain credits in the sorting process. As to the second question, it is only necessary in the sorting process to remember that revenues and expenses appear on the income statement and assets, liabilities, and owner's equity items go on the balance sheet.

After the amounts are sorted to the proper columns, the columns are totaled. At this point, the difference between the totals of the Income Statement columns is the net income or loss. The difference is the net income or loss because revenues are entered in the credit column and expenses in the debit column. If the credit column total exceeds the debit column total, the difference is a net income. If the debit column total exceeds the credit column total, the difference is a net loss. In the illustrated work sheet, the credit column total exceeds the debit column total, and the result is a $400 net income.

After the net income is determined in the Income Statement columns, it is added to the total of the Balance Sheet credit column. The reason for this is that with the exception of the balance of the capital account, the amounts appearing in the Balance Sheet columns are "end-of-period" amounts. Therefore, it is necessary to add the net income to the Balance Sheet credit column total to make the Balance Sheet columns equal. Also, adding the income to this column has the effect of adding it to the capital account.

Had there been a loss, it would have been necessary to add the loss to the debit column. This is because losses decrease owner's equity, and adding the loss to the debit column has the effect of subtracting it from the capital account.

Balancing the Balance Sheet columns by adding the net income or loss is a proof of the accuracy with which the work sheet was prepared. When the income or loss is added in the Balance Sheet columns and the addition makes these columns equal, it is assumed that no errors were made in preparing the work sheet. However, if the addition does not make the columns equal, it is proof that an error or errors were made. The error or errors may have been either mathematical or an amount may have been sorted to a wrong column.

Although balancing the Balance Sheet columns with the net income or loss is a proof of the accuracy with which a work sheet was prepared, it is not an absolute proof. These columns will balance even when errors have been made if the errors are of a certain type. For example, an expense amount carried into the Balance Sheet debit column or an asset amount carried into the debit column of the income statement section will cause both of these columns to have incorrect totals. Likewise, the net income will be incorrect. However, when such an error is made, the Balance Sheet columns will balance, but with the incorrect amount of income. Therefore, when a work sheet is prepared, care must be exercised in sorting the adjusted trial balance amounts into the correct Income Statement or Balance Sheet columns.

■ Work Sheet and the Financial Statements

As previously stated, the work sheet is a tool of the accountant and is not for management's use or publication. However, as soon as it is completed, the accountant uses it in preparing the income statement and balance sheet that are given to management. To do this, the accountant rearranges the items in the work sheet's Income Statement columns into a formal income statement and rearranges the items in the Balance Sheet columns into a formal balance sheet.

■ Work Sheet and Adjusting Entries

Entering the adjustments in the Adjustments columns of a work sheet does not get these adjustments into the ledger accounts. Consequently, after the work sheet and statements are completed, adjusting entries like the ones described in the previous chapter must still be entered in the General Journal and posted. The work sheet makes this easy, because its Adjustments columns provide the information for these entries. All that is needed is an entry for each adjustment appearing in the columns.

As for the adjusting entries for the illustrated work sheet, they are the same as the entries in the previous chapter, with the exception of the entry for adjustment *(e)*. Here a compound entry having a $150 debit to Unearned Legal Fees, a $100 debit to Accounts Receivable, and $250 credit to Legal Fees Earned is used.

■ Closing Entries

After the work sheet and statements are completed, in addition to adjusting entries, it is also necessary to prepare and post closing entries. Closing entries clear and close the revenue and expense accounts. The accounts are cleared in the sense that their balances are transferred to another account. They are closed in the sense that they have zero balances after closing entries are posted.

■ Why Closing Entries Are Made

The revenue and expense accounts are cleared and closed at the end of each accounting period by transferring their balances to a summary account called **Income Summary.** Their summarized amount, which is the net income or loss, is then tranferred in a single proprietorship to the owner's capital account. These transfers are necessary because—

a. Revenues actually increase the owner's equity, and expenses decrease it.
b. However, throughout an accounting period these increases and decreases are accumulated in revenue and expense accounts rather than in the owner's capital account.
c. As a result, closing entries are necessary at the end of each accounting period to transfer the net effect of these increases and decreases out of the revenue and expense accounts and on to the owner's capital account.

In addition, closing entries also cause the revenue and expense accounts to begin each new accounting period with zero balances. This too is necessary because—

a. An income statement reports the revenues and expenses incurred during just **one accounting period** and is prepared from information recorded in the revenue and expense accounts.
b. The revenue and expense accounts are not discarded at the end of each accounting period but are used in recording the revenues and expenses of succeeding periods.
c. Consequently, if at the end of a period the balances of these accounts are to reflect only a single period's revenues and expenses, the accounts must begin the period with zero balances.

■ Closing Entries Illustrated

At the end of July, after its adjusting entries were posted but before its accounts were cleared and closed, the owner's equity accounts of Owen's law practice had the balances shown in Illustration 4-3. (An account's Balance column heading as a rule does not tell the nature of an account's balance. However, in Illustration 4-3 and in the illustrations immediately following, the nature of each account's balance is shown as an aid to the student.)

Observe in Illustration 4-3 that Owen's capital account shows only its $5,000 July 1 balance. This is not the amount of Owen's equity on July 31. Closing entries are required to make this account show the July 31 equity.

Note also the third account in Illustration 4-3, the Income Summary account. This account is used only at the end of the accounting period in summarizing and clearing the revenue and expense accounts.

Closing Revenue Accounts

Before closing entries are posted, revenue accounts have credit balances. Consequently, to clear and close a revenue account, an entry debiting the account and crediting Income Summary is required.

Illustration 4-3

Credit

Larry Owen, Capital

Date		Explanation	Debit	Credit	Balance
July	1			5,000	**5,000**

Debit

Larry Owen, Withdrawals

Date		Explanation	Debit	Credit	Balance
July	26		200		**200**

Income Summary

Date		Explanation	Debit	Credit	Balance

Credit

Legal Fees Earned

Date		Explanation	Debit	Credit	Balance
July	12			500	500
	19			1,000	1,500
	31			250	**1,750**

Debit

Office Salaries Expense

Date		Explanation	Debit	Credit	Balance
July	12		400		400
	26		400		800
	31		120		**920**

Debit

Telephone Expense

Date		Explanation	Debit	Credit	Balance
July	31		30		**30**

Debit

Heating and Lighting Expense

Date		Explanation	Debit	Credit	Balance
July	31		35		**35**

Debit

Rent Expense

Date		Explanation	Debit	Credit	Balance
July	31		300		**300**

Debit

Office Supplies Expense

Date		Explanation	Debit	Credit	Balance
July	31		25		**25**

Debit

Depreciation Expense, Office Equipment

Date		Explanation	Debit	Credit	Balance
July	31		40		**40**

The Owen law practice has only one revenue account, and the entry to close and clear it is:

July	31	Legal Fees Earned.	1,750.00	
		Income Summary		1,750.00
		To clear and close the revenue account.		

Posting the entry has this effect on the accounts:

Credit

Legal Fees Earned

Date		Explanation	Debit	Credit	Balance
July	12			500	500
	19			1,000	1,500
	31			250	1,750
	31		**1,750**		**–0–**

Credit

Income Summary

Date		Explanation	Debit	Credit	Balance
July	**31**			**1,750**	**1,750**

Note that the entry clears the revenue account by transferring its balance as a credit to the Income Summary account. It also causes the revenue account to begin the new accounting period with a zero balance.

Closing Expense Accounts

Before closing entries are posted, expense accounts have debit balances. Consequently, to clear and close a concern's expense accounts, a compound entry debiting the Income Summary account and crediting each individual expense account is required. The Owen law practice has six expense accounts, and the compound entry to clear and close them is:

July	31	Income Summary	1,350.00	
		Office Salaries Expense		920.00
		Telephone Expense		30.00
		Heating and Lighting Expense		35.00
		Rent Expense		300.00
		Office Supplies Expense		25.00
		Depreciation Expense, Office Equipment		40.00
		To close and clear the expense accounts.		

Posting the entry has the effect shown in Illustration 4-4. Turn to Illustration 4-4 and observe that the entry clears the expense accounts of their balances by transferring the balances in a total as a debit to the Income Summary account. It also causes the expense accounts to begin the new period with zero balances.

Closing the Income Summary Account

After a concern's revenue and expense accounts are cleared and their balances transferred to the Income Summary account, the balance of the Income Summary account is equal to the net income or loss. When revenues exceed expenses, there is a net income, and the Income Summary account has a credit balance. On the other hand, when expenses exceed revenues, there is a loss, and the account has a debit balance. But, regardless of the nature of its balance, the Income Summary account is cleared, and its balance, the amount of net income or loss, is transferred to the capital account.

The Owen law practice earned $400 during July. Consequently, after its revenue and expense accounts are cleared, its Income Summary account has a $400 credit balance. This balance is transferred to the Larry Owen, Capital account with an entry like this:

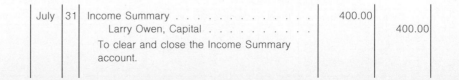

July	31	Income Summary	400.00	
		Larry Owen, Capital		400.00
		To clear and close the Income Summary account.		

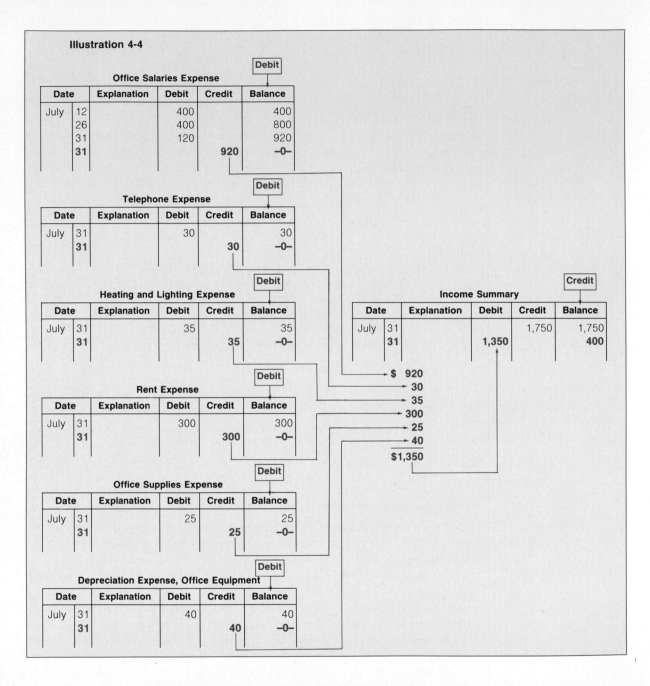

Illustration 4-4

Office Salaries Expense

Date		Explanation	Debit	Credit	Balance
July	12		400		400
	26		400		800
	31		120		920
	31			**920**	–0–

Telephone Expense

Date		Explanation	Debit	Credit	Balance
July	31		30		30
	31			**30**	–0–

Heating and Lighting Expense

Date		Explanation	Debit	Credit	Balance
July	31		35		35
	31			**35**	–0–

Rent Expense

Date		Explanation	Debit	Credit	Balance
July	31		300		300
	31			**300**	–0–

Office Supplies Expense

Date		Explanation	Debit	Credit	Balance
July	31		25		25
	31			**25**	–0–

Depreciation Expense, Office Equipment

Date		Explanation	Debit	Credit	Balance
July	31		40		40
	31			**40**	–0–

Income Summary

Date		Explanation	Debit	Credit	Balance
July	31			1,750	1,750
	31		**1,350**		**400**

$ 920
30
35
300
25
40
$1,350

Posting this entry has the following effect on the accounts:

Income Summary

Date		Explanation	Debit	Credit	Balance
July	31			1,750	1,750
	31		1,350		400
	31		**400**		–0–

Larry Owen, Capital

Date		Explanation	Debit	Credit	Balance
July	1			5,000	5,000
	31			**400**	**5,400**

Observe that the entry clears the Income Summary account, transferring its balance, the amount of the net income in this case, to the capital account.

Closing the Withdrawals Account

At the end of an accounting period, the withdrawals account shows the decrease in the owner's equity due to withdrawals. The account is closed, and its debit balance is transferred to the capital account with an entry like this:

July	31	Larry Owen, Capital	200.00	
		Larry Owen, Withdrawals		200.00
		To close and clear the withdrawals account.		

Posting the entry has this effect on the accounts:

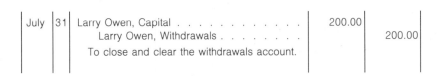

		Larry Owen, Withdrawals			**Debit**			Larry Owen, Capital			**Credit**
Date		**Explanation**	**Debit**	**Credit**	**Balance**	**Date**	**Explanation**	**Debit**	**Credit**	**Balance**
July	26		200		200	July	1			5,000	5,000
	31			**200**	**–0–**		31			400	5,400
							31		**200**		**5,200**

After the entry closing the withdrawals account is posted, observe that the two reasons for making closing entries are accomplished: (1) All revenue and expense accounts have zero balances. (2) The net effect of the period's revenue, expense, and withdrawal transactions on the owner's equity is shown in the capital account.

Temporary Accounts

Revenue and expense accounts plus the Income Summary and withdrawals accounts are often called **temporary accounts** because in a sense the items recorded in these accounts are only temporarily recorded therein. At the end of each accounting period, through closing entries, their debit and credit effects are transferred out and on to other accounts.

■ **Sources of Closing Entry Information**

Information for closing entries may be taken from the individual revenue and expense accounts. However, the work sheet provides this information in a more convenient form. Look at the work sheet on page 120. Every account having a balance in its Income Statement debit column has a debit balance in the ledger and must be credited in closing. Compare the amounts in the work sheet's Income Statement debit column with the credits in the compound closing entry on page 125. If the work sheet is used as the information source for the entry, it is not even necessary to add the entry's credits to learn the amount of the debit. The entry's debit to Income Summary is the column total.

The work sheet's Income Statement credit column is a convenient information source for the entry to close the revenue account.

■ The Accounts after Closing

At this stage, after both adjusting and closing entries have been posted, the Owen law practice accounts appear as in Illustration 4-5. Observe in the illustration that the asset, liability, and the owner's capital accounts show their end-of-period balances. Observe also that the revenue and ex-

Illustration 4-5

Cash   **Account No.** 111

Date		Explanation	PR	Debit		Credit		Balance	
198A									
July	1		G1	5,000	00			5,000	00
	1		G1			900	00	4,100	00
	3		G1			3,700	00	400	00
	12		G1	500	00			900	00
	12		G1			400	00	500	00
	15		G1	450	00			950	00
	26		G2			400	00	550	00
	26		G2			200	00	350	00
	29		G2	1,000	00			1,350	00
	30		G2			100	00	1,250	00
	31		G2			30	00	1,220	00
	31		G2			35	00	1,185	00

Accounts Receivable   **Account No.** 114

Date		Explanation	PR	Debit		Credit		Balance	
198A									
July	19		G2	1,000	00			1,000	00
	29		G2			1,000	00	–0	–
	31		G3	100	00			100	00

Prepaid Rent   **Account No.** 115

Date		Explanation	PR	Debit		Credit		Balance	
198A									
July	1		G1	900	00			900	00
	31		G3			300	00	600	00

Illustration 4-5
(continued)

Office Supplies   **Account No.** 116

Date		Explanation	PR	Debit		Credit		Balance	
198A									
July	5		G1	60	00			60	00
	31		G3			25	00	35	00

Office Equipment   **Account No.** 131

Date		Explanation	PR	Debit		Credit		Balance	
198A									
July	3		G1	3,700	00			3,700	00
	5		G1	300	00			4,00	00

Accumulated Depreciation, Office Equipment   **Account No.** 132

Date		Explanation	PR	Debit		Credit		Balance	
198A									
July	31		G3			40	00	40	00

Accounts Payable   **Account No.** 212

Date		Explanation	PR	Debit		Credit		Balance	
198A									
July	5		G1			360	00	360	00
	30		G2	100	00			260	00

Salaries Payable   **Account No.** 213

Date		Explanation	PR	Debit		Credit		Balance	
198A									
July	31		G3			120	00	120	00

Illustration 4-5
(continued)

Unearned Legal Fees   **Account No.** 214

Date		Explanation	PR	Debit		Credit		Balance	
198A									
July	15		G1			450	00	450	00
	31		G3	150	00			300	00

Larry Owen, Capital   **Account No.** 311

Date		Explanation	PR	Debit		Credit		Balance	
198A									
July	1		G1			5,000	00	5,000	00
	31		G3			400	00	5,400	00
	31		G3	200	00			5,200	00

Larry Owen, Withdrawals   **Account No.** 312

Date		Explanation	PR	Debit		Credit		Balance	
198A									
July	26		G2	200	00			200	00
	31		G3			200	00	−0	−

Income Summary   **Account No.** 313

Date		Explanation	PR	Debit		Credit		Balance	
198A									
July	31		G3			1,750	00	1,750	00
	31		G3	1,350	00			400	00
	31		G3	400	00			−0	−

Legal Fees Earned   **Account No.** 411

Date		Explanation	PR	Debit		Credit		Balance	
198A									
July	12		G1			500	00	500	00
	19		G2			1,000	00	1,500	00
	31		G3			250	00	1,750	00
	31		G3	1,750	00			−0	−

Illustration 4-5
(continued)

Office Salaries Expense — Account No. 511

Date		Explanation	PR	Debit		Credit		Balance	
198A July	12		G1	400	00			400	00
	26		G2	400	00			800	00
	31		G3	120	00			920	00
	31		G3			920	00	–0	–

Telephone Expense — Account No. 512

Date		Explanation	PR	Debit		Credit		Balance	
198A July	31		G2	30	00			30	00
	31		G3			30	00	–0	–

Heating and Lighting Expense — Account No. 513

Date		Explanation	PR	Debit		Credit		Balance	
198A July	31		G2	35	00			35	00
	31		G3			35	00	–0	–

Rent Expense — Account No. 514

Date		Explanation	PR	Debit		Credit		Balance	
198A July	31		G3	300	00			300	00
	31		G3			300	00	–0	–

Office Supplies Expense — Account No. 516

Date		Explanation	PR	Debit		Credit		Balance	
198A July	31		G3	25	00			25	00
	31		G3			25	00	–0	–

Illustration 4-5
(concluded)

Depreciation Expense, Office Equipment					Account No. 517		
Date	Explanation	PR	Debit		Credit		Balance
198A July 31		G3	40	00			40	00
31		G3			40	00	–0 –

pense accounts have zero balances and are ready for recording the new accounting period's revenues and expenses.

■ **The Post-Closing Trial Balance**

It is easy to make errors in adjusting and closing the accounts. Consequently, after all adjusting and closing entries are posted, a new trial balance is prepared to retest the equality of the accounts. This new, after-closing trial balance is called a **post-closing trial balance,** and for Owen's law practice appears as in Illustration 4-6.

Compare Illustration 4-6 with the accounts having balances in Illustration 4-5. Note that only asset, liability, and the owner's capital accounts have balances in Illustration 4-5. Note also that these are the only accounts that appear on the post-closing trial balance. The revenue and expense accounts have been cleared and have zero balances at this stage.

■ **Accounting for Partnerships and Corporations**

Partnership Accounting

Accounting for a partnership is like accounting for a single proprietorship except for transactions directly affecting the partners' capital and withdrawal accounts. For these transactions, there must be a capital account

Illustration 4-6

Larry Owen, Attorney
Post-Closing Trial Balance
July 31, 19—

Cash	$1,185	
Accounts receivable	100	
Prepaid rent	600	
Office supplies	35	
Office equipment	4,000	
Accumulated depreciation, office equipment		$ 40
Accounts payable		260
Salaries payable		120
Unearned legal fees		300
Larry Owen, capital		5,200
Totals	$5,920	$5,920

and a withdrawals account for each partner. Also, the Income Summary account is closed with a compound entry that allocates to each partner his or her share of the income or loss.

Corporation Accounting

A corporation's accounting also differs from that of a single proprietorship for transactions affecting the accounts that show the equity of the corporation's stockholders in the assets of the corporation. The difference results because accounting principles require a corporation to distinguish between stockholders' equity resulting from amounts invested in the corporation by its stockholders, called **contributed capital,** and stockholders' equity resulting from earnings. This distinction is important because in most states a corporation cannot pay a legal dividend unless it has stockholders' equity resulting from earnings. In making the distinction, two kinds of stockholders' equity accounts are kept: (1) contributed capital accounts and (2) retained earnings accounts. Amounts invested in a corporation (contributed) by its stockholders are shown in a contributed capital account such as the Common Stock account. Stockholders' equity resulting from earnings is shown in a retained earnings account.

To demonstrate corporation accounting, assume that five persons secured a charter for a new corporation. Each invested $10,000 in the corporation by buying 1,000 shares of its $10 par value common stock. The corporation's entry to record their investments is:

Jan.	5	Cash	50,000.00	
		Common Stock		50,000.00
		Sold and issued 5,000 shares of $10 par		
		value common stock.		

If during its first year the corporation earned $8,000, the entry to close its Income Summary account is:

Dec.	31	Income Summary	8,000.00	
		Retained Earnings		8,000.00
		To close the Income Summary account.		

If these were the only entries affecting the Common stock and Retained Earnings accounts during the first year, the corporation's year-end balance sheet will show the stockholders' equity as follows:

Stockholders' Equity

Common stock, $10 par value, 5,000 shares authorized	
and outstanding	$50,000
Retained earnings	8,000
Total stockholders' equity	$58,000

Since a corporation is a separate legal entity, the names of its stockholders are of little or no interest to a balance sheet reader and are not shown in the equity section. However, in this case, the section does show that the corporation's stockholders have a $58,000 equity in its assets, $50,000 of which resulted from their purchase of the corporation's stock and $8,000 from earnings. As to the equity from earnings, $8,000 more assets flowed into the corporation from revenues than flowed out for expenses. This not only increased the assets but also increased the stockholders' equity in the assets by $8,000.

Many beginning students have difficulty understanding the nature of the retained earnings item in the equity section of a corporation balance sheet. They would perhaps have less difficulty if the item were labeled "Stockholders' equity resulting from earnings." However, the retained earnings caption is common. Therefore, upon seeing it, a student must recognize that it represents nothing more than stockholders' equity resulting from earnings. Furthermore, it does not represent a specific amount of cash or any other asset, since these are shown in the asset section of the balance sheet.

To continue, assume that on January 10 of the corporation's second year its board of directors met and by vote declared a $1 per share dividend payable on February 1 to the January 25 **stockholders of record** (stockholders according to the corporation's records). The entries to record the declaration and payment are as follows:

Jan.	10	Retained Earnings	5,000.00	
		Common Dividend Payable		5,000.00
		Declared a $1 per share dividend.		
Feb.	1	Common Dividend Payable	5,000.00	
		Cash		5,000.00
		Paid the dividend declared on January 10.		

Note in the two entries that the dividend declaration and payment together reduced corporation assets and stockholders' equity just as a withdrawal of cash by the owner of a single proprietorship reduces assets and the owner's equity.

A cash dividend is normally paid by mailing checks to the stockholders. Also, as in this case, three dates are normally involved in a dividend declaration and payment: (1) the **date of declaration,** (2) the **date of record,** and (3) the **date of payment.** Since stockholders may sell their stock to new investors at will, the three dates give new stockholders an opportunity to have their ownership entered in the corporation's records in time to receive the dividend. Otherwise it would go to the old stockholders.

A dividend must be formally voted by a corporation's board of directors. Furthermore, courts have generally held that the board is the final judge of when if at all a dividend should be paid. Consequently, stockholders have no right to a dividend until declared. However, as soon as a cash dividend is declared, it becomes a liability of the corporation, normally a current liability, and must be paid. Furthermore, stockholders have the right to sue and force payment of a cash dividend once it is declared.

If during its second year the corporation of this illustration suffered a $7,000 net loss, the entry to close its Income Summary account is:

Dec.	31	Retained Earnings	7,000.00	
		Income Summary		7,000.00
		To close the Income Summary account.		

Posting the entry has the effect shown on the last line of the following Retained Earnings account.

Retained Earnings

Date		Explanation	PR	Debit	Credit	Balance
198A						
Dec.	31	Net income	G4		8,000.00	8,000.00
198B						
Jan.	10	Dividend declaration	G5	5,000.00		3,000.00
Dec.	31	Net loss	G9	7,000.00		⟨4,000.00⟩

After the entry was posted, due to the dividend and the net loss, the Retained Earnings account has a $4,000 debit balance. A debit balance in a Retained Earnings account indicates a negative amount of retained earnings, and a corporation with a negative amount of retained earnings is said to have a **deficit**. A deficit may be shown on a corporation's balance sheet as follows:

Stockholders' Equity

Common stock, $10 par value, 5,000 shares authorized		
and outstanding	$50,000	
Deduct retained earnings deficit	(4,000)	
Total stockholders' equity		$46,000

In most states, it is illegal for a corporation with a deficit to pay a cash dividend. Such dividends are made illegal because as a separate legal entity a corporation is responsible for its own debts. Consequently, if its creditors are to be paid, they must be paid from the corporation's assets. Therefore, making a dividend illegal when there is a deficit helps prevent a corporation in financial difficulties from paying out all of its assets in dividends and leaving nothing for payment of its creditors.

■   **The Accounting Cycle**   Each accounting period in the life of a business is a recurring **accounting cycle,** beginning with transactions recorded in a journal and ending with a post-closing trial balance. All steps in the cycle have now been discussed.

A knowledge of accounting requires that each step be understood and its relation to the others seen. The steps in the order of their occurrence are as follows:

1. **Journalizing** . . . . Analyzing and recording transactions in a journal.

2. **Posting** . . . . Copying the debits and credits of journal entries into the ledger accounts.

3. **Preparing a trial balance** . . . . . Summarizing the ledger accounts and testing the recording accuracy.

4. **Preparing a work sheet**. . . . . . Gaining the effects of the adjustments before entering the adjustments in the accounts. Then sorting the account balances into the Balance Sheet and Income Statement columns and finally determining and proving the income or loss.

5. **Preparing the statements** . . . . . Rearranging the work sheet information into a balance sheet and an income statement.

6. **Adjusting the ledger accounts**. . . . . Preparing adjusting journal entries from information in the Adjustments columns of the work sheet and posting the entries in order to bring the account balances up to date.

7. **Closing the temporary accounts**. . . . . Preparing and posting entries to close the temporary accounts and transfer the net income or loss to the capital account or accounts in a single proprietorship or partnership and to the Retained Earnings account in a corporation.

8. **Preparing a post-closing trial balance** . . . . Proving the accuracy of the adjusting and closing procedures.

Glossary

Accounting cycle the accounting steps that recur each accounting period in the life of a business and that begin with the recording of transactions and proceed through posting the recorded amounts, preparing a trial balance, preparing a work sheet, preparing the financial statements, preparing and posting adjusting and closing entries, and preparing a post-closing trial balance.

Closing entries entries made to close and clear the revenue and expense accounts and to transfer the amount of the net income or loss to a capital account or accounts or to the Retained Earnings account.

Closing procedures the preparation and posting of closing entries and the preparation of the post-closing trial balance.

Contributed capital stockholders' equity in a corporation resulting among other ways from amounts invested in the corporation by its stockholders.

Date of declaration date on which a dividend is declared.

Date of payment date for the payment of a dividend.

Date of record date on which the stockholders who are to receive a dividend is determined.

Deficit a negative amount of retained earnings.

Income Summary account the account used in the closing procedures to summarize the amounts of revenues and expenses, and from which the amount of the net income or loss is transferred to the owner's capital account in a single proprietorship, the partners' capital accounts in a partnership, or the Retained Earnings account in a corporation.

Post-closing trial balance a trial balance prepared after closing entries are posted.

Stockholders of record a corporation's stockholders according to its records.

Temporary accounts the revenue, expense, Income Summary, and withdrawals accounts.

Work sheet a working paper used by an accountant to bring together in an orderly manner the information used in preparing the financial statements and the adjusting and closing entries.

Working papers the memoranda, analyses, and other informal papers prepared by accountants and used as a basis for the more formal reports given to clients.

Questions for Class Discussion

1. A work sheet is a tool accountants use to accomplish three tasks. What are these tasks?
2. Is it possible to complete the statements and adjust and close the accounts without preparing a work sheet? What is gained by preparing a work sheet?
3. At what stage in the accounting process is a work sheet prepared?
4. From where are the amounts that are entered in the Trial Balance columns of a work sheet obtained?
5. Why are the adjustments in the Adjustments columns of a work sheet keyed together with letters?

6. What is the result of combining the amounts in the Trial Balance columns with the amounts in the Adjustments columns of a work sheet?

7. Why must care be exercised in sorting the items in the Adjusted Trial Balance columns to the proper Income Statement or Balance Sheet columns?

8. In extending the items in the Adjusted Trial Balance columns of a work sheet, what would be the effect on the net income of extending (*a*) an expense into the Balance Sheet debit column, (*b*) a liability into the Income Statement credit column, and (*c*) a revenue into the Balance Sheet debit column? Would each of these errors be automatically detected on the work sheet? Which would be automatically detected? Why?

9. Why are revenue and expense accounts called temporary accounts?

10. What two purposes are accomplished by recording closing entries?

11. What accounts are affected by closing entries? What accounts are not affected?

12. Explain the difference between adjusting and closing entries.

13. What is the purpose of the Income Summary account?

14. Why is a post-closing trial balance prepared?

15. An accounting student listed the item, "Depreciation expense, building, $1,800," on a post-closing trial balance. What did this indicate?

16. What two kinds of accounts are used in accounting for stockholders' equity in a corporation?

17. Explain how the retained earnings item found on corporation balance sheets arises.

18. What three dates are normally involved in the declaration and payment of a cash dividend?

19. Explain why the payment of a cash dividend by a corporation with a deficit is made illegal.

Class Exercises   Exercise 4-1

The balances of the following alphabetically arranged accounts appeared in the Adjusted Trial Balance columns of a work sheet. Copy the account numbers in a column on a sheet of note paper and beside each number indicate by letter the income statement or balance sheet column to which the account's balance would be sorted in completing the work sheet. Use the letter *a* to indicate the Income Statement debit column, *b* to indicate the Income Statement credit column, *c* to indicate the Balance Sheet debit column, and *d* to indicate the Balance Sheet credit column.

1. Accounts Payable.
2. Accounts Receivable.
3. Accumulated Depreciation, Repair Equipment.
4. Advertising Expense.
5. Cash.
6. Ed Lee, Capital.
7. Ed Lee, Withdrawals.
8. Prepaid Insurance.
9. Rent Expense.

10. Repair Equipment.

11. Repair Supplies.

12. Revenue from Repairs.

13. Wages Expense.

Exercise 4-2

The following item amounts are from the Adjustments columns of a work sheet. From the information prepare adjusting journal entries. Use December 31 as the date.

	Adjustments	
	Debit	Credit
Prepaid insurance		(a) 850
Office supplies		(b) 215
Accumulated depreciation, office equipment . .		(c) 540
Accumulated depreciation, shop equipment . .		(d) 3,345
Office salaries expense	(e) 50	
Shop wages expense	(e) 280	
Insurance expense, office equipment	(a) 85	
Insurance expense, shop equipment	(a) 765	
Office supplies expense	(b) 215	
Depreciation expense, office equipment . . .	(c) 540	
Depreciation expense, shop equipment	(d) 3,345	
Salaries and wages payable		(e) 330
Totals	5,280	5,280

Exercise 4-3

Copy the following T-accounts and their end-of-period balances on a sheet of note paper. Below the accounts prepare entries to close the accounts. Post to the T-accounts.

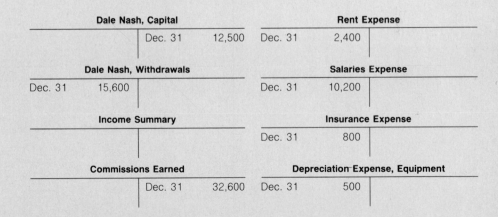

Dale Nash, Capital			Rent Expense	
	Dec. 31	12,500	Dec. 31 2,400	

Dale Nash, Withdrawals			Salaries Expense	
Dec. 31	15,600		Dec. 31 10,200	

Income Summary	Insurance Expense	
	Dec. 31 800	

Commissions Earned			Depreciation Expense, Equipment	
	Dec. 31	32,600	Dec. 31 500	

Exercise 4-4

The items that follow appeared in the Income Statement columns of a December 31 work sheet prepared for Walter Dole, an attorney. Under the assumption that Mr. Dole withdrew $24,000 from his law practice during the year, prepare entries to close the revenue, expense, Income Summary, and withdrawals accounts.

	Income Statement	
	Debit	Credit
Legal fees earned		54,000
Office salaries expense	13,000	
Rent expense	6,000	
Insurance expense	1,200	
Office supplies expense	300	
Depreciation expense, office equipment . .	2,400	
	22,900	54,000
Net income	31,100	
	54,000	54,000

Exercise 4-5

Open the following T-accounts on note paper for a corporation that does repair work for other companies. Below the T-accounts prepare entries to close the accounts. Post to the T-accounts.

Common Stock			Rent Expense		
	Dec. 31	50,000	Dec. 31	6,000	

Retained Earnings			Salaries Expense		
	Dec. 31	7,000	Dec. 31	25,000	

Income Summary			Insurance Expense		
			Dec. 31	1,000	

Revenue from Repairs			Depreciation Expense, Equipment		
	Dec. 31	50,000	Dec. 31	4,000	

Exercise 4-6

The items that follow appeared in the Income Statement columns of a December 31 work sheet prepared for a corporation that performs services for other concerns. Prepare closing journal entries for the corporation.

	Income Statement	
	Debit	Credit
Revenue from services		88,600
Office salaries expense	27,000	
Rent expense	12,000	
Insurance expense	1,800	
Office supplies expense	400	
Depreciation expense, office equipment . .	5,200	
	46,400	88,600
Net income	42,200	
	88,600	88,600

Exercise 4-7

1. On a sheet of note paper, open the following T-accounts: Cash, Accounts Receivable, Equipment, Notes Payable, Common Stock, Retained

Earnings, Income Summary, Revenue from Services, and Operating Expenses.

2. Record directly in the T-accounts these transactions of a corporation:
    a. Sold and issued $10,000 of common stock for cash.
    b. Purchased $9,000 of equipment for cash.
    c. Sold and delivered $25,000 of services on credit.
    d. Collected $22,000 of accounts receivable.
    e. Paid $20,000 of operating expenses.
    f. Purchased $5,000 of additional equipment, giving $3,000 in cash and a $2,000 promissory note.
    g. Closed the Revenue from Services, Operating Expenses, and Income Summary accounts.

3. Answer these questions:
    a. Does the corporation have retained earnings?
    b. Does it have any cash?
    c. If the corporation has retained earnings, why does it not also have cash?
    d. Can the corporation declare a legal cash dividend?
    e. Can it pay the dividend?
    f. In terms of assets, what does the balance of the Notes Payable account represent?
    g. In terms of assets, what does the balance of the Common Stock account represent?
    h. In terms of assets, what does the balance of the Retained Earnings account represent?

Exercise 4-8

A list of trial balance accounts and their balances follows. All are normal balances. To save time, the balances are in one- and two-digit numbers. However, to increase your skill in sorting adjusted trial balance amounts to the proper work sheet columns, the accounts are listed in alphabetical order.

Trial Balance Accounts and Balances

Accounts payable	$2	Rent expense	$ 2
Accounts receivable	3	Revenue from repairs	18
Accumulated depreciation,		Robert Ross, capital	11
shop equipment	2	Robert Ross, withdrawals	2
Cash	5	Shop equipment	7
Notes payable	1	Shop supplies	4
Prepaid insurance	3	Wages expense	8

Required

1. Prepare a work sheet form on notebook paper and enter the trial balance accounts and amounts on the work sheet in their alphabetical order.

2. Complete the work sheet using the following information:
    a. Estimated depreciation of shop equipment, $1.
    b. Expired insurance, $1
    c. Unused shop supplies per inventory, $1.
    d. Earned but unpaid wages, $2.

Exercise 4-9

The trial balance of Small Company, Inc., as of the end of its annual accounting period follows.

Small Company, Inc.
Trial Balance
December 31, 19—

Cash	$ 3,800	
Prepaid insurance	1,200	
Repair supplies	2,000	
Repair equipment	15,000	
Accumulated depreciation, repair equipment . .		$ 1,000
Common stock		10,000
Retained earnings		1,500
Revenue from repairs		40,000
Salaries expense	21,500	
Rent expense	9,000	
Totals	$52,500	$52,500

Required

1. Prepare a work sheet form on note paper and enter the trial balance.
2. Complete the work sheet using the information that follows:
   a. Expired insurance, $800.
   b. Unused repair supplies per inventory, $300.
   c. Estimated depreciation of repair equipment, $2,100.
   d. Earned but unpaid salaries, $500.

Exercise 4-10

Prepare adjusting and closing journal entries for the corporation of Exercise 4-9.

Problems

Problem 4-1

Dale Hall, John Nash, and Joel Teel began a business on January 5, 198A, in which each man invested $30,000. During 198A, the business lost $7,500; and during 198B, it earned $33,000. On January 3, 198C, the three men agreed to pay out to themselves $18,000 of the accumulated earnings of the business; and on January 8, the $18,000 was paid out.

Required

1. Under the assumption that the business is a partnership in which the partners share losses and gains equally, give the entries to record the investments and to close the Income Summary account at the end of 198A and again at the end of 198B. Under the further assumption that the partners shared equally in the $18,000 of earnings paid out, give the entry to record the withdrawals.
2. Under the assumption that the business is organized as a corporation and that each man invested in it by buying 3,000 shares of its $10 par value common stock, give the entry to record the investments. Also,

give the entries to close the Income Summary account at the end of 198A and again at the end of 198B and to record the declaration and payment of the $2 per share dividend. (Ignore corporation income taxes and assume that the three men are the corporation's board of directors.)

Problem 4-2

At the end of its annual accounting period, a trial balance from the ledger of Tim's Repair Service carried the items that follow.

Tim's Repair Service
Trial Balance
December 31, 19—

Cash	$ 1,215	
Prepaid insurance	865	
Repair supplies	2,925	
Repair equipment	5,240	
Accumulated depreciation, repair equipment		$ 1,280
Accounts payable		195
Tim Hill, capital		4,125
Tim Hill, withdrawals	18,800	
Revenue from repairs		37,230
Wages expense	10,140	
Rent expense	3,000	
Utilities expense	645	
Totals	$42,830	$42,830

Required

1. Enter the trial balance on a work sheet form and complete the work sheet using the information that follows:
   a. Expired insurance, $535.
   b. A repair supplies inventory showed $775 of unused supplies on hand.
   c. Estimated depreciation on repair equipment, $660.
   d. Wages earned by the one employee but unpaid and unrecorded, $80.
2. From the work sheet prepare an income statement and a classified balance sheet.
3. Prepare adjusting journal entries and compound closing entries.

Problem 4-3

(Covers two accounting cycles)
Sue Gage opened a real estate office she called Sue Gage Realty, and during May she completed these transactions:

May 2 Invested $2,000 in cash and an automobile having a $12,000 fair value in the real estate agency.
  2 Rented furnished office space and paid one month's rent, $500.
  2 Purchased office supplies for cash, $150.
  10 Paid the premium on a one-year insurance policy, $720.
  14 Paid the biweekly salary of the office secretary, $400.
  17 Sold a house and collected a $5,340 commission.

May 28   Paid the biweekly salary of the office secretary, $400.
      31   Paid the May telephone bill, $50.
      31   Paid for gas and oil used in the agency car during May, $60.

Required work for May

1. Open these accounts: Cash; Prepaid Insurance; Office Supplies; Automobile; Accumulated Depreciation, Automobile; Salaries Payable; Sue Gage, Capital; Sue Gage, Withdrawals; Income Summary; Commissions Earned; Rent Expense; Salaries Expense; Gas, Oil, and Repairs Expense; Telephone Expense; Insurance Expense; Office Supplies Expense; and Depreciation Expense, Automobile.

2. Prepare and post journal entries to record the transactions.

3. Prepare a trial balance in the Trial Balance columns of a work sheet form and complete the work sheet using the following information.
   a. Two thirds of a month's insurance has expired.
   b. An inventory shows $125 of unused office supplies remaining.
   c. Estimated depreciation on the automobile, $165.
   d. Earned but unpaid salary of the office secretary, $80.

4. Prepare a May income statement and a May 31 classified balance sheet.

5. Prepare and post adjusting and closing entries.

6. Prepare a post-closing trial balance.

During June, Sue Gage completed these transactions:

June 1   Paid the June rent on the office space, $500.
       5   Purchased additional office supplies for cash, $30.
      11   Paid the biweekly salary of the office secretary, $400.
      14   Sue Gage withdrew $2,000 cash from the business for personal uses.
      17   Sold a building lot and collected a $1,500 commission.
      25   Paid the biweekly salary of the office secretary, $400.
      30   Paid for gas and oil used in the agency car during June, $55.
      30   Paid the June telephone bill, $45.

Required work for June

1. Prepare and post journal entries to record the transactions.

2. Prepare a trial balance in the Trial Balance columns of a work sheet form and complete the work sheet using the following information:
   a. One month's insurance has expired.
   b. An office supplies inventory shows $125 of unused supplies.
   c. Estimated depreciation on the automobile, $165.
   d. Earned but unpaid secretary's salary, $160.

3. Prepare a June income statement and a June 30 classified balance sheet.

4. Prepare and post adjusting and closing entries.

5. Prepare a post-closing trial balance.

Problem 4-4

The accounts of Leisure Alleys, showing balances as of the end of its annual accounting period, appear in the booklet of working papers that accompanies this text, and a trial balance of its ledger is reproduced on a work sheet form provided there. The trial balance has the items that follow.

Leisure Alleys
Trial Balance
December 31, 19—

Cash	$ 775	
Bowling supplies	1,420	
Prepaid insurance	1,335	
Bowling equipment	19,565	
Accumulated depreciation, bowling equipment		$ 7,640
Accounts payable		135
Mortgage payable		10,000
Gary Berg, capital		21,200
Gary Berg, withdrawals	15,650	
Bowling revenue		54,500
Wages expense	16,255	
Equipment repairs expense	420	
Rent expense	4,800	
Utilities expense	2,135	
Taxes expense	520	
Interest expense	600	
Totals	$93,475	$93,475

Required

1. If the working papers are being used, complete the work sheet provided there for the solution of this problem, using the information that follows. If the working papers are not being used, enter the trial balance on a work sheet form and complete the work sheet.

    a. Bowling supplies inventory, $210.

    b. Expired insurance, $1,120.

    c. Estimated depreciation on bowling equipment, $4,750.

    d. The December electric bill for the bowling alley arrived in the mail after the trial balance was prepared. Its $220 amount was unrecorded.

    e. Wages earned but unpaid and unrecorded, $280.

    f. The lease contract on the building calls for an annual rental equal to 10% of the annual bowling revenue, with $400 payable each month on the first day of the month. The $400 was paid each month and debited to the Rent Expense account.

    g. Personal property taxes on the bowling equipment amounting to $190 have accrued but are unrecorded and unpaid.

    h. The mortgage debt was incurred on September 1, and interest on the debt is at a 12% annual rate or $100 per month. The mortgage contract calls for the payment of $300 interest each three months in advance. Interest payments were made on September 1 and December 1. A $1,000 payment on the mortgage principal is due next September 1.

2. Prepare an income statement and a classified balance sheet.

3. Prepare adjusting and closing entries.

4. Post the adjusting and closing entries and prepare a post-closing trial balance. (Omit this requirement if the working papers are not being used.)

Problem 4-5

The accounts of Ed's Delivery Service, showing balances as of the end of its annual accounting period, appear in the booklet of working papers that accompanies this text, and a trial balance of the accounts is reproduced on a work sheet form there. The trial balance has the items that follow.

Ed's Delivery Service
Trial Balance
December 31, 19—

Cash	$ 525	
Accounts receivable	670	
Prepaid insurance	2,275	
Office supplies	245	
Prepaid rent	250	
Office equipment	2,460	
Accumulated depreciation, office equipment		$ 570
Delivery equipment	14,790	
Accumulated depreciation, delivery equipment		3,150
Accounts payable		890
Unearned delivery service revenue		550
Edward Deal, capital		22,905
Edward Deal, withdrawals	12,000	
Delivery service revenue		41,555
Rent expense	2,500	
Telephone expense	345	
Office salaries expense	10,060	
Delivery wages expense	20,320	
Gas, oil, and repairs expense	3,180	
Totals	$69,620	$69,620

Required

1. If the working papers are being used, complete the work sheet provided there for the solution of this problem, using the information that follows. If the working papers are not being used, enter the trial balance on a work sheet form and complete the work sheet.
   a. Insurance expired on the office equipment, $100, and on the delivery equipment, $1,890.
   b. An inventory showed $110 of unused office supplies on hand.
   c. Estimated depreciation on the office equipment, $300, and *(d)* on the delivery equipment, $2,415.
   e. At the beginning of the year one month's rent was prepaid on the garage and office space occupied by the delivery service as shown by the balance of the Prepaid Rent account. Rents for February through November were paid each month and debited to the Rent Expense account. As of the trial balance date, the December rent had not been paid.

 f. Three stores signed contracts with the delivery service in which they agreed to pay a fixed fee for the delivery of packages. Two of the stores made advance payments on their contracts, and the amounts paid were credited to the Unearned Delivery Service Revenue account. An examination of their contracts shows $280 of the $550 paid was earned by the accounting period end. The third store's contract provides for a $200 monthly fee to be paid at the end of each month's service. It was signed on December 15, and one half of a month's revenue has accrued but is unrecorded.

 g. A $35 December telephone bill and a $60 bill for repairs to a motorcycle used in the business arrived in the mail on December 31. Neither bill was paid or recorded before the trial balance was prepared.

 h. Office salaries, $80, and delivery wages, $175, have accrued but are unpaid and unrecorded.

2. Prepare an income statement and a classified balance sheet.

3. Prepare adjusting and closing entries.

4. Post the adjusting and closing entries to the accounts and prepare a post-closing trial balance. (If the working papers are not being used, omit this requirement.)

Alternate Problems

Problem 4-1A

On January 3, 198A, Ted Hill, Jane Lee, and Carl Nye began a business in which Ted Hill invested $10,000, Jane Lee invested $20,000, and Carl Nye invested $30,000. During 198A, the business lost $3,000; and during 198B, it earned $18,000. On January 3, 198C, the three business owners agreed to pay out to themselves $12,000 of the accumulated earnings of the business; and on January 15, the $12,000 was paid out.

Required

1. Under the assumption that the business is a partnership in which the partners share losses and gains in proportion to their investments, give the entries to record the investments and to close the Income Summary account at the end of 198A and again at the end of 198B. Under the further assumption that the partners paid out the accumulated earnings in proportion to their investments, give the entry to record the withdrawals.

2. Under the assumption that the business is organized as a corporation and that the owners invested in the corporation by buying its $10 par value common stock, with Ted Hill buying 1,000 shares, Jane Lee buying 2,000 shares, and Carl Nye buying 3,000 shares, give the entry to record the investments. Also give the entries to close the Income Summary account at the end of 198A and again at the end of 198B. Then give the entries to record the declaration and payment of the $2 per share dividend. (Ignore corporation income taxes and assume the investors are the corporation's board of directors.)

Problem 4-2A

A trial balance of the ledger of Mr. Clean Janitorial Service at the end of its annual accounting period carried the items that follow.

Mr. Clean Janitorial Service
Trial Balance
December 31, 19—

Cash	$ 1,065	
Accounts receivable	215	
Prepaid insurance	1,320	
Cleaning supplies	815	
Prepaid rent	300	
Cleaning equipment	2,610	
Accumulated depreciation, cleaning equipment		$ 1,140
Trucks	16,560	
Accumulated depreciation, trucks		3,820
Accounts payable		645
Unearned janitorial revenue		400
Tom Reed, capital		11,745
Tom Reed, withdrawals	15,450	
Janitorial revenue earned		34,610
Wages expense	12,440	
Rent expense	800	
Gas, oil, and repairs expense	785	
Totals	$52,360	$52,360

Required

1. Enter the trial balance on a work sheet form and complete the work sheet using the information that follows:
   a. Expired insurance, $950.
   b. An inventory of cleaning supplies showed $125 of unused supplies on hand.
   c. The cleaning service rents garage and equipment storage space. At the beginning of the year, three months' rent was prepaid as shown by the debit balance of the Prepaid Rent account. Rents for April through November were paid on the first day of each month and debited to the Rent Expense account. The December rent was unpaid on the trial balance date.
   d. Estimated depreciation on the cleaning equipment, $365, and (e) on the trucks, $2,170.
   f. On November 15, the janitorial service contracted and began cleaning the office of Tops Realty for $200 per month. The realty company paid for two months' service in advance, and the amount paid was credited to the Unearned Janitorial Revenue account. The janitorial service also entered into a contract and began cleaning the office of Kona Insurance Agency on December 15. By the month's end, a half month's revenue, $120, had been earned on this contract but was unrecorded.
   g. Employee's wages amounting to $180 had accrued but were unrecorded on the trial balance date.

2. Prepare an income statement and a classified balance sheet for the business.

3. Prepare adjusting and closing entries.

Problem 4-3A

(Covers two accounting cycles)

Sue Gage began a business she called Sue Gage Realty, and during May she completed the transactions that follow:

May 1   Invested $2,500 in cash and an automobile having a $10,000 fair value in a real estate agency.

    1   Rented furnished office space and paid one month's rent, $400.

    1   Paid the premium on an insurance policy giving one year's protection, $660.

    2   Purchased office supplies for cash, $140.

  13   Paid the biweekly salary of the office secretary, $450.

  18   Sold a building lot and collected a $1,600 commission on the sale.

  27   Paid the biweekly salary of the office secretary, $450.

  31   Paid the May telephone bill, $45.

  31   Paid for gas and oil used in the agency car during May, $60.

Required work for May

1. Open these accounts: Cash; Prepaid Insurance; Office Supplies; Automobile; Accumulated Depreciation, Automobile; Salaries Payable; Sue Gage, Capital; Sue Gage, Withdrawals; Income Summary; Commissions Earned; Rent Expense; Salaries Expense; Gas, Oil, and Repairs Expense; Telephone Expense; Insurance Expense; Office Supplies Expense; and Depreciation Expense, Automobile.

2. Prepare and post journal entries to record the transactions.

3. Prepare a trial balance in the Trial Balance columns of a work sheet form and complete the work sheet using the information that follows:
   a. One month's insurance has expired.
   b. An inventory shows $110 of unused office supplies remaining.
   c. Estimated depreciation on the automobile, $160.
   d. Earned but unpaid wages of the secretary, $135.

4. Prepare a May income statement and a May 31 classified balance sheet.

5. Prepare and post adjusting and closing entries.

6. Prepare a post-closing trial balance.

These transactions were completed by Sue Gage during June:

June 1   Paid the June rent on the office space, $400.

   6   Sold a house and collected a $4,850 commission.

   8   Sue Gage withdrew $1,500 from the business to pay personal expenses.

   9   Paid the biweekly salary of the office secretary, $450.

  20   Purchased additional office supplies for cash, $35.

June 23   Paid the biweekly salary of the office secretary, $450.
   30   Paid the June telephone bill, $40.
   30   Paid for gas and oil used in the agency car, $50.

Required work for June

1. Prepare and post journal entries to record the transactions.
2. Prepare a trial balance in the Trial Balance columns of a work sheet form and complete the work sheet using the information that follows:
   a. One month's insurance has expired.
   b. An office supplies inventory shows $120 of unused office supplies.
   c. Estimated depreciation on the automobile, $160.
   d. Earned but unrecorded salary of the secretary, $225.
3. Prepare a June income statement and a June 30 classified balance sheet.
4. Prepare and post adjusting and closing entries.
5. Prepare a post-closing trial balance.

Problem 4-4A

The accounts of Leisure Alleys showing the end of its annual accounting period balances appear in the booklet of working papers that accompanies this text, and a trial balance of the accounts is reproduced on a work sheet form provided there. The trial balance has the items that follow.

Leisure Alleys
Trial Balance
December 31, 19—

Cash	$ 775	
Bowling supplies	1,420	
Prepaid insurance	1,335	
Bowling equipment	49,565	
Accumulated depreciation, bowling equipment		$ 7,640
Accounts payable		135
Mortgage payable		10,000
Gary Berg, capital		21,200
Gary Berg, withdrawals	15,650	
Bowling revenue		54,500
Wages expense	16,255	
Equipment repairs expense	420	
Rent expense	4,800	
Utilities expense	2,135	
Taxes expense	520	
Interest expense	600	
Totals	$93,475	$93,475

Required

1. If the working papers are being used, complete the work sheet provided there for the solution of this problem, using the information that follows. If the working papers are not being used, enter the trial balance on a work sheet form and complete the work sheet.
   a. Bowling supplies inventory, $180.
   b. Expired insurance, $1,195.

c. Estimated depreciation on the bowling equipment, $4,715.

d. A $165 bill for equipment repairs arrived in the mail after the trial balance was prepared. It is unrecorded and unpaid.

e. Wages earned but unpaid and unrecorded, $225.

f. The lease contract on the bowling alley space calls for an annual rental equal to 11% of the annual bowling revenue, with $400 payable each month on the first day of the month. The $400 was paid each month and debited to the Rent Expense account.

g. Personal property taxes on the bowling equipment amounting to $215 have accrued but are unrecorded and unpaid.

h. The mortgage debt was incurred on August 1. The interest on the debt is at a 12% annual rate or $100 per month. The mortgage contract requires the payment of $300 interest each three months in advance. Interest was paid on August 1 and November 1. A $2,000 payment on the mortgage principal is due next August 1.

2. Prepare an income statement and a classified balance sheet.

3. Prepare adjusting and closing entries.

4. Post the adjusting and closing entries and prepare a post-closing trial balance. (Omit this requirement if the working papers are not being used.)

Problem 4-5A

The accounts of Ed's Delivery Service showing balances as of the end of its annual accounting period appear in the booklet of working papers that accompanies this text, and a trial balance of the accounts is reproduced on a work sheet form there. The trial balance has the items that follow.

Ed's Delivery Service
Trial Balance
December 31, 19—

Cash	$ 525	
Accounts receivable	670	
Prepaid insurance	2,275	
Office supplies	245	
Prepaid rent	250	
Office equipment	2,460	
Accumulated depreciation, office equipment		$ 570
Delivery equipment	14,790	
Accumulated depreciation, delivery equipment		3,150
Accounts payable		890
Unearned delivery service revenue		550
Edward Deal, capital		22,905
Edward Deal, withdrawals	12,000	
Delivery service revenue		41,555
Rent expense	2,500	
Telephone expense	345	
Office salaries expense	10,060	
Delivery wages expense	20,320	
Gas, oil, and repairs expense	3,180	
Totals	$69,620	$69,620

Required

1. If the working papers are being used, complete the work sheet provided there for the solution of this problem, using the information that follows. If the working papers are not being used, enter the trial balance on a work sheet form and complete the work sheet.

   a. Expired insurance on the office equipment, $110, and on the delivery equipment, $1,775.

   b. An inventory showed $120 of unused office supplies on hand.

   c. Estimated depreciation on the office equipment, $290, and (d) on the delivery equipment, $2,330.

   e. At the beginning of the current year, one month's rent was prepaid on the garage and office space occupied by the delivery service as shown by the debit balance in the Prepaid Rent account. Rents for February through November were paid each month and debited to the Rent Expense account. As of the trial balance date, the December rent had not been paid.

   f. The delivery service has contracts with three stores for the delivery of packages on a fixed-fee basis. Two of the stores made advance payments on their contracts, and the amounts paid were credited to the Unearned Delivery Service Revenue account. An examination of the contracts shows that $320 of the $550 paid was earned by the accounting period end. The third store's contract provides for a $250 monthly fee to be paid at the end of each month's service. One half of a month's revenue has accrued on this contract, but it is unrecorded.

   g. An $85 bill for repairs to a delivery truck during December arrived in the mail after the trial balance was prepared. It is unpaid and unrecorded.

   h. Office salaries, $40, and delivery wages, $95, have accrued but are unpaid and unrecorded.

2. Prepare an income statement and a classified balance sheet.

3. Prepare adjusting and closing entries.

4. Post the adjusting and closing entries to the accounts and prepare a post-closing trial balance. (If the working papers are not being used, omit this requirement.)

□ **Provocative Problems**   **Provocative Problem 4-1 Statewide Moving Service**

During his second year in college, Dale West, as the only heir, inherited Statewide Moving Service upon the death of his father. He immediately dropped out of school and took over management of the business. At the time he took over, Dale recognized he knew little about accounting. However, he reasoned that since the business performed its services strictly for cash, if the cash of the business increased, the business was doing OK. Therefore, he was pleased as he watched the concern's cash balance grow from $1,250 when he took over to $11,975 at the year-end. Furthermore, at the year-end, he reasoned that since he had withdrawn

$25,000 from the business to buy a new car and to pay personal expenses, the business must have earned $35,725 during the year. He arrived at the $35,725 by adding the $10,725 increase in cash to the $25,000 he had withdrawn from the business. Consequently, he was shocked when he received the income statement that follows and learned that the business had earned less than the amounts withdrawn.

Statewide Moving Service
Income Statement
For Year Ended December 31, 19—

Revenue from moving services		$80,375
Operating expenses:		
Salaries and wages expense	$36,550	
Gas, oil, and repairs expense	3,225	
Telephone expense	350	
Taxes expense	2,475	
Insurance expense.	2,325	
Office supplies expense.	250	
Depreciation expense, office equipment . .	400	
Depreciation expense, trucks	6,250	
Depreciation expense, building	5,000	
Total operating expenses		56,825
Net income		$23,550

After mulling the statement over for several days, Dale has asked you to explain how, in a year in which the cash increased $10,725 and he had withdrawn $25,000, the business could have earned only $23,550. In examining the accounts of the business, you note that accrued salaries and wages payable at the beginning of the year were $125 but increased to $375 at the year's end. Likewise, the accrued taxes payable were $450 at the beginning of the year but had increased to $475 at the year-end. Also, the balance of the Prepaid Insurance account was $200 less and the balance of the Office Supplies account was $50 less at the end of the year than at the beginning. However, except for the changes in these accounts, the change in cash, and the changes in the balances of the accumulated depreciation accounts, there were no other changes in the balances of the concern's asset and liability accounts between the beginning of the year and the end. Back your explanation with a calculation accounting for the increase in the concern's cash.

Provocative Problem 4-2 Jane Otto, Attorney

During the first year-end closing of the accounts of Jane Otto's law practice, the office secretary became seriously ill and is in the hospital unable to have visitors. Ms. Otto is certain the secretary prepared a work sheet, income statement, and balance sheet, but she has only the income statement and cannot find either the work sheet or balance sheet. She does have a trial balance of the accounts of the law practice, and she wants you to prepare adjusting and closing entries from the trial balance and income statement that follows. She also wants you to prepare a classified balance sheet. She says the $1,200 of unearned legal fees on the trial balance represents a retainer fee paid by Security Bank. The bank retained Jane Otto on November 1 to do its legal work, agreeing to pay her $400 per month for her services. She says she has also entered into an agreement with Westside Realty to do its legal work on a fixed-fee basis. The agreement calls for a $300 monthly fee payable at the end of each three months. The agreement was signed on December 1, and one month's fee has accrued but has not been recorded.

Jane Otto, Attorney
Trial Balance
December 31, 19—

Cash	$ 1,225	
Legal fees receivable	1,500	
Office supplies	325	
Prepaid insurance	900	
Furniture and equipment	12,500	
Notes payable		$ 5,000
Accounts payable		350
Unearned legal fees		1,200
Jane Otto, capital		7,500
Jane Otto, withdrawals	18,000	
Legal fees earned		37,325
Salaries expense	11,750	
Rent expense	4,800	
Telephone expense	375	
Totals	$51,375	$51,375

Jane Otto, Attorney
Income Statement
For Year Ended December 31, 19—

Revenue:		
Legal fees earned		$38,425
Operating expenses:		
Salaries expense	$12,000	
Rent expense	4,800	
Telephone expense	375	
Office supplies expense	200	
Insurance expense	750	
Depreciation expense, furniture and equipment	1,200	
Interest expense	600	
Total operating expenses		19,925
Net income		$18,500

Provocative Problem 4-3   Hillside Realty

The balance sheet that follows was prepared for Hillside Realty at the end of its annual accounting period.

Hillside Realty
Balance Sheet
December 31, 19—

Assets

Current assets:

Cash.	$ 1,525	
Prepaid insurance	500	
Office supplies	110	
Total current assets		$ 2,135

Plant and equipment:

Office equipment.	$ 5,240		
Less accumulated depreciation	1,010	$ 4,230	
Automobile	$12,400		
Less accumulated depreciation	2,700	9,700	
Total plant and equipment			13,930
Total assets.			$16,065

Liabilities

Current liabilities:

Accounts payable	$ 210	
Unearned property management fees. . .	250	
Salaries payable.	180	
Total current liabilities		$ 640

Owner's Equity

Mary Hall, capital, January 1, 19—.	$10,565	
Net Income for the year	$28,860	
Less withdrawals	24,000	
Excess of income over withdrawals.	4,860	
Mary Hall, capital, December 31, 19— . . .		15,425
Total liabilities and owner's equity		$16,065

After completing the balance sheet, Hillside Realty's accountant prepared and posted the following adjusting and closing entries for the concern.

Dec.	31	Insurance Expense	1,150.00	
		Prepaid Insurance.		1,150.00
	31	Office Supplies Expense	210.00	
		Office Supplies		210.00
	31	Depreciation Expense, Office Equipment	640.00	
		Accumulated Depreciation, Office Equipment . .		640.00
	31	Depreciation Expense, Automobile.	2,100.00	
		Accumulated Depreciation, Automobile		2,100.00
	31	Unearned Property Management Fees	500.00	
		Property Management Fees Earned		500.00
	31	Salaries Expense	180.00	
		Salaries Payable		180.00

Dec.	31	Commissions Earned	49,600.00	
		Property Management Fees Earned	1,760.00	
		Income Summary		51,360.00
	31	Income Summary	22,500.00	
		Salaries Expense		11,000.00
		Rent Expense.		6,000.00
		Telephone Expense		460.00
		Gas, Oil, and Repairs Expense		940.00
		Insurance Expense		1,150.00
		Office Supplies Expense		210.00
		Depreciation Expense, Office Equipment		640.00
		Depreciation Expense, Automobile.		2,100.00
	31	Income Summary	28,860.00	
		Mary Hall, Capital		28,860.00
	31	Mary Hall, Capital	24,000.00	
		Mary Hall, Withdrawals.		24,000.00

Enter the relevant information from the balance sheet and the adjusting and closing entries on a work sheet form and complete the work sheet by working backward to the items that appeared in its Trial Balance columns.

5 Accounting for a Merchandising Concern

After studying Chapter 5, you should be able to:

1. Explain the nature of each item entering into the calculation of cost of goods sold and be able to calculate cost of goods sold and gross profit from sales.

2. Prepare a work sheet and the financial statements for a merchandising business using a periodic inventory system and organized as either a corporation or a single proprietorship.

3. Prepare adjusting and closing entries for a merchandising business organized as either a corporation or a single proprietorship.

4. Define or explain the words and phrases listed in the chapter Glossary.

The accounting records and reports of the Owen law practice, as described in previous chapters, are those of a service enterprise. Other service enterprises are laundries, taxicab companies, barber and beauty shops, theaters, and golf courses. Each performs a service for a commission or fee, and the net income of each is the difference between fees or commissions earned and operating expenses.

A merchandising company, on the other hand, whether a wholesaler or retailer, earns revenue by selling goods or merchandise. In such a company, a net income results when revenue from sales exceeds the cost of the goods sold plus operating expenses, as illustrated below:

XYZ Store
Condensed Income Statement

Revenue from sales	$100,000
Less cost of goods sold . . .	60,000
Gross profit from sales.	$ 40,000
Less operating expenses . . .	25,000
Net income.	$ 15,000

The store of the illustrated income statement sold for $100,000 goods that cost $60,000. It thereby earned a $40,000 gross profit from sales. From this it subtracted $25,000 of operating expenses to show a $15,000 net income.

Gross profit from sales, as shown on the illustrated income statement, is the "profit" before operating expenses are deducted. Accounting for the factors that enter into its calculation differentiates the accounting of a merchandising company from that of a service enterprise.

Gross profit from sales is determined by subtracting cost of goods sold from revenue from sales. However, before the subtraction can be made, both revenue from sales and cost of goods sold must be determined.

■ **Revenue from Sales**

Revenue from sales consists of gross proceeds from merchandise sales less returns, allowances, and discounts. It may be reported on an income statement as follows:

Kona Sales, Incorporated
Income Statement
For Year Ended December 31, 198B

Revenue from sales:		
Gross sales.		$306,200
Less: Sales returns and allowances . .	$1,900	
Sales discounts	4,300	6,200
Net sales.		$300,000

Gross Sales

The gross sales item on the partial income statement is the total cash and credit sales made by the company during the year. Cash sales were "rung up" on the cash register as each sale was completed. At the end of each day, the register total showed the amount of that day's cash sales, which was recorded with an entry like this:

Nov.	3	Cash	1,205.00	
		Sales		1,205.00
		To record the day's cash sales.		

In addition, an entry like this was used to record credit sales:

Nov.	3	Accounts Receivable.	45.00	
		Sales		45.00
		Sold merchandise on credit.		

Sales Returns and Allowances

In most stores, a customer is permitted to return any unsatisfactory merchandise purchased. Or the customer is sometimes allowed to keep the unsatisfactory goods and is given an allowance or an amount off its sales price. Either way, returns and allowances result from dissatisfied customers. Consequently, it is important for management to know the amount of such returns and allowances and their relation to sales. This information is supplied by the Sales Returns and Allowances account when each return or allowance is recorded as follows:

Nov.	4	Sales Returns and Allowances.	20.00	
		Accounts Receivable (or Cash)		20.00
		Customer returned unsatisfactory		
		merchandise.		

Sales Discounts

When goods are sold on credit, the terms of payment are always made definite so there will be no misunderstanding as to the amount and time of payment. The **credit terms** normally appear on the invoice or sales ticket and are part of the sales agreement. Exact terms granted usually depend upon the custom of the trade. In some trades, it is customary for invoices to become due and payable 10 days after the end of the month (**EOM**) in which the sale occurred. Invoices in these trades carry terms, "n/10 EOM." In other trades, invoices become due and payable 30 days after the invoice date and carry terms of "n/30." This means that the net amount of the invoice is due 30 days after the invoice date.

When credit periods are long, creditors commonly grant discounts, called **cash discounts,** for early payments. This reduces the amount invested in accounts receivable and thus the amount of money needed in carrying on the business operations. When discounts for early payment are granted, they are made part of the credit terms and appear on the invoice as, for example, "Terms: 2/10, n/60." Terms of 2/10, n/60 mean that the **credit period** is 60 days but that the debtor may deduct 2% from the invoice amount if payment is made within 10 days after the invoice date. The 10-day period is known as the **discount period.**

Since at the time of a sale it is not known if the customer will pay within the discount period and take advantage of a cash discount, normally a sales discount is not recorded until the customer pays. For example, on November 12, Kona Sales, Incorporated, sold $100 of merchandise to a customer on credit, terms 2/10, n/60, and recorded the sale as follows:

Nov.	12	Accounts Receivable.	100.00	
		Sales		100.00
		Sold merchandise, terms 2/10, n/60.		

At the time of the sale, the customer could choose either to receive credit for paying the full $100 by paying $98 any time on or before November 22. Or the customer could wait 60 days, until January 11, and pay the full $100. If the customer elected to pay by November 22 and take advantage of the cash discount, Kona Sales, Incorporated, would record the receipt of the $98 as follows:

Nov.	22	Cash	98.00	
		Sales Discounts.	2.00	
		Accounts Receivable.		100.00
		Received payment for the November 12 sale less the discount.		

Sales discounts are accumulated in the Sales Discounts account until the end of an accounting period. Their total is then deducted from gross sales in determining revenue from sales. This is logical. A sales discount is an "amount off" the regular price of goods that is granted for early payment. As a result, it reduces revenue from sales.

■ Cost of Goods Sold

Automobile dealers and appliance stores make a limited number of sales each day. Consequently, they can easily refer to their records at the time of each sale and record the cost of the car or appliance sold. A drugstore, on the other hand, would find this difficult. For instance, if a drugstore sells a customer a tube of toothpaste, a box of aspirin, and a magazine, it can easily record with a cash register the sale of these items at marked selling prices. However, it would be difficult to maintain records that would enable it to also "look up" and record as "cost of goods sold" the costs of the items sold. As a result, stores such as drug, grocery, and others selling a volume of low-priced items make no effort to record the cost of the goods sold at the time of each sale. Rather, they wait until the end of an accounting period, take a physical inventory, and from the inventory and their accounting records determine at that time the cost of all goods sold during the period.

The end-of-period inventories taken by drug, grocery, or like stores in order to learn the cost of the goods they have sold are called periodic inventories. Also, the system used by such stores in accounting for cost of goods sold is known as a **periodic inventory system.** Such a system is described and discussed in this chapter. The system used by a car or appliance dealer to record the cost of each car or appliance sold depends on a perpetual inventory record of cars or appliances in stock. As a result, it is known as a **perpetual inventory system** of accounting for goods on hand and sold. It is discussed in Chapter 9.

■ Cost of Goods Sold, Periodic Inventory System

As previously said, a store using a periodic inventory system does not record the cost of items sold as they are sold. Rather, it waits until the end of an accounting period and determines at one time the cost of all the goods sold during the period. And to do this, it must have information as to (1) the cost of the merchandise it had on hand at the beginning of the period, (2) the cost of the merchandise purchased during the period, and (3) the cost of the unsold goods remaining at the period end. With this information a store can, for example, determine the cost of the goods it sold during a period as follows:

Cost of goods on hand at beginning of period. . .	$ 19,000
Cost of goods purchased during the period	232,000
Goods available for sale during the period	$251,000
Less unsold goods on hand at the period end. . .	21,000
Cost of goods sold during the period.	$230,000

The store of the calculation had $19,000 of merchandise at the beginning of the accounting period. During the period, it purchased additional merchandise costing $232,000. Consequently, it had available and could have sold $251,000 of merchandise. However, $21,000 of this merchandise was on hand unsold at the period end. Therefore, the cost of the goods it sold during the period was $230,000.

The information needed in calculating cost of goods sold is accumulated as follows.

Merchandise Inventories

The merchandise on hand at the beginning of an accounting period is called the beginning inventory, and that on hand at the end is the ending inventory. Furthermore, since accounting periods follow one after another, the ending inventory of one period always becomes the beginning inventory of the next.

When a periodic inventory system is in use, the dollar amount of the ending inventory is determined by (1) counting the unsold items on the shelves in the store and in the stockroom, (2) multiplying the count for each kind of goods by its cost, and (3) adding the costs of the different kinds.

After the dollar cost of the ending inventory is determined in this manner, it is subtracted from the cost of the goods available for sale to determine cost of goods sold. Also, by means of a journal entry, the ending inventory amount is posted to an account called Merchandise Inventory. It remains there throughout the succeeding accounting period as a record of the inventory at the end of the period ended and the beginning of the succeeding period.

It should be emphasized at this point that, other than to correct errors, entries are made in the Merchandise Inventory account only at the end of each accounting period. Furthermore, since some goods are soon sold and the other goods purchased, the account does not long show the dollar amount of merchandise on hand. Rather, as soon as goods are sold or purchased, the account's balance becomes a historical record of the dollar amount of goods that were on hand at the end of the last period and the beginning of the current period.

Cost of Merchandise Purchased

Cost of merchandise purchased is determined by subtracting from purchases any discounts, returns, and allowances and then adding any freight or other transportation charges on the goods purchased. However, before examining this calculation it is best to see how the amounts involved are accumulated.

Under a periodic inventory system, when merchandise is bought for resale, its cost is debited to an account called Purchases, as follows:

Nov.	5	Purchases	1,000.00	
		Accounts Payable		1,000.00
		Purchased merchandise on credit, invoice		
		dated November 2, terms 2/10, n/30.		

The Purchases account has as its sole purpose the accumulation of the cost of all merchandise bought for resale during an accounting period. The account does not at any time show whether the merchandise is on hand or has been disposed of through sale or other means.

If a credit purchase is subject to a cash discount, payment within the discount period results in a credit to Purchases Discounts, as in the following entry:

Nov.	12	Accounts Payable	1,000.00	
		Purchases Discounts.		20.00
		Cash		980.00
		Paid for the purchase of November 5 less the		
		discount.		

When **purchases discounts** are involved, it is important that every invoice on which there is a discount be paid within the discount period, so that no discounts are lost. On the other hand, good cash management requires that no invoice be paid until the last day of its discount period. Consequently, to accomplish these objectives, every invoice must be filed in such a way that it automatically comes to the attention of the person responsible for its payment on the last day of its discount period. A simple way to do this is to provide a file with 31 folders, one for each day in a month. Then, after an invoice is recorded, it is placed in the file folder of the last day of its discount period. For example, if the last day of an invoice's discount period is November 12, it is filed in folder number 12. Then, on November 12, this invoice, together with any other invoices in the same folder, are removed and paid or refiled for payment without a discount on a later date.

Sometimes merchandise received from suppliers is not acceptable and must be returned. Or, if kept, it is kept only because the supplier grants an allowance or reduction in its price. When merchandise is returned, the purchaser "gets its money back"; but from a managerial point of view more is involved. Buying merchandise, receiving and inspecting it, deciding that the merchandise is unsatisfactory, and returning it is a costly procedure that should be held to a minimum. The first step in holding it to a minimum is to know the amount of returns and allowances. To make this information available, returns and allowances on purchases are commonly recorded in an account called Purchases Returns and Allowances, as follows:

Nov.	14	Accounts Payable	65.00	
		Purchases Returns and Allowances . . .		65.00
		Returned defective merchandise.		

When an invoice is subject to a cash discount and a portion of its goods is returned before the invoice is paid, the discount applies to just the goods kept. For example, if $500 of merchandise is purchased and $100 of the goods are returned before the invoice is paid, any discount applies only to the $400 of goods kept.

Sometimes a manufacturer or wholesaler pays transportation costs on merchandise it sells. The total cost of the goods to the purchaser then is the amount paid the manufacturer or wholesaler. Other times the purchaser must pay transportation costs. When this occurs, such charges are a proper addition to the cost of the goods purchased and may be recorded with a debit to the Purchases account. However, more complete information is obtained if such costs are debited to an account called **Transportation-In,** as follows:

Nov.	24	Transportation-In	22.00	
		Cash		22.00
		Paid express charges on merchandise purchased.		

When transportation charges are involved, it is important that the buyer and seller understand which party is responsible for the charges. Normally, in quoting a price, the seller makes this clear by quoting a price of, say, $300, **FOB** factory. FOB factory means free on board or loaded on board the means of transportation at the factory free of loading charges. The buyer then pays transportation costs from there. Likewise, FOB destination means the seller will pay transportation costs to the destination of the goods.

Sometimes, when terms are FOB factory, the seller will prepay the transportation costs as a service to the buyer, adding the amount onto the invoice. In such a case, if a cash discount is involved, the discount does not apply to the transportation charges.

When a classified income statement is prepared, the balances of the Purchases, Purchases Returns and Allowances, Purchases Discounts, and Transportation-In accounts are combined on it as follows to show the cost of the merchandise purchased during the period:

Purchases.		$235,800
Less: Purchases returns and allowances. . .	$1,200	
Purchases discounts.	4,100	5,300
Net purchases		$230,500
Add transportation-in		1,500
Cost of goods purchased		$232,000

Cost of Goods Sold

The last item in the foregoing calculation is the cost of the merchandise purchased during the accounting period. It is combined with the beginning and ending inventories to arrive at cost of goods sold as follows:

Cost of goods sold:			
Merchandise inventory, January 1, 198B. .			$ 19,000
Purchases.		$235,800	
Less: Purchases returns and			
allowances	$1,200		
Purchases discounts	4,100	5,300	
Net purchases		$230,500	
Add transportation-in		1,500	
Cost of goods purchased			232,000
Goods available for sale.			$251,000
Merchandise inventory, December			
31, 198B			21,000
Cost of goods sold			$230,000

Inventory Losses

Under a periodic inventory system, the cost of any merchandise lost through shrinkage, spoilage, or shoplifting is automatically included in cost of goods sold. For example, assume a store lost $500 of merchandise to shoplifters during a year. This caused its year-end inventory to be $500 less than it otherwise would have been, since these goods were not available for inclusion in the year-end count. Therefore, since the year-end inventory was $500 smaller because of the loss, the cost of the goods the store sold was $500 greater.

Many stores are troubled with shoplifting. Although under a periodic inventory system such losses are automatically included in cost of goods sold, it is often important to know their extent. Consequently, a way to estimate shoplifting losses is described in Chapter 9.

■ **Income Statement of a Merchandising Concern**

A classified income statement for a merchandising concern has (1) a revenue section, (2) a cost of goods sold section, and (3) an operating expenses section. The first two sections have been discussed, but note in Illustration 5-1 how they are brought together to show gross profit from sales.

Observe also in Illustration 5-1 how operating expenses are classified as either "Selling expenses" or "General and administrative expenses." **Selling expenses** include expenses of storing and preparing goods for sale, promoting sales, actually making sales, and delivering goods to customers. **General and administrative expenses** include the general office, accounting, personnel, and credit and collection expenses.

Sometimes an expenditure should be divided or prorated part to selling expenses and part to general and administrative expenses. Kona Sales, Incorporated, divided the rent on its store building in this manner, as an examination of Illustration 5-1 will reveal. However, it did not prorate its insurance expense because the amount involved was so small the company felt the extra exactness did not warrant the extra work.

The last item subtracted in Illustration 5-1 is income taxes expense. This income statement was prepared for Kona Sales, Incorporated, a corporation. Of the three kinds of business organizations, corporations alone are subject to the payment of state and federal income taxes. Often on a corporation income statement, as in Illustration 5-1, the operating expenses are subtracted from gross profit from sales to arrive at income from operations, after which income taxes are deducted to arrive at net income.

■ **Work Sheet of a Merchandising Concern**

A concern selling merchandise, like a service-type company, uses a work sheet in bringing together the end-of-period information needed in preparing its financial statements and adjusting and closing entries. Such a work sheet, that of Kona Sales, Incorporated, is shown in Illustration 5-2 on pages 168 and 169.

Illustration 5-2 differs from the work sheet in the previous chapter in several ways, the first of which is that it was prepared for a corporation. This is indicated by the word Incorporated in the company name. It is also indicated by the appearance on the work sheet of the Common Stock and Retained Earnings accounts. Note on lines 13 and 14 how the balances of these two accounts are carried unchanged from the Trial Balance credit column into the Balance Sheet credit column.

Illustration 5-2 also differs in that it does not have any Adjusted Trial Balance columns. The experienced accountant commonly omits these columns from a work sheet in order to reduce the time and effort required in its preparation. He or she enters the adjustments in the Adjustments

Illustration 5-1

Kona Sales, Incorporated
Income Statement
For Year Ended December 31, 198B

Revenue from sales:			
Gross sales			$306,200
Less: Sales returns and allowances		$ 1,900	
Sales discounts		4,300	6,200
Net sales			$300,000
Cost of goods sold:			
Merchandise inventory, January 1, 198B		$ 19,000	
Purchases	$235,800		
Less: Purchases returns and allowances	$1,200		
Purchases discounts	4,100	5,300	
Net purchases		$230,500	
Add transportation-in		1,500	
Cost of goods purchased		232,000	
Goods available for sale		$251,000	
Merchandise inventory, December 31, 198B		21,000	
Cost of goods sold			230,000
Gross profit from sales			$ 70,000
Operating expenses:			
Selling expenses:			
Sales salaries expense		$ 18,500	
Rent expense, selling space		8,100	
Advertising expense		700	
Store supplies expense		400	
Depreciation expense, store equipment		3,000	
Total selling expenses		$ 30,700	
General and administrative expenses:			
Office salaries expense		$ 25,800	
Rent expense, office space		900	
Insurance expense		600	
Office supplies expense		200	
Depreciation expense, office equipment		700	
Total general and administrative expenses		28,200	
Total operating expenses			58,900
Income from operations			$ 11,100
Less income taxes expense			1,700
Net income			$ 9,400

columns, combines the adjustments with the trial balance amounts, and sorts the combined amounts directly to the proper Income Statement or Balance Sheet columns in a single operation. In other words, the experienced accountant simply omits the adjusted trial balance in preparing a work sheet.

The remaining similarities and differences of Illustration 5-2 are best described column by column.

Account Titles Column

Several accounts that do not have trial balance amounts are listed in the Account Titles column, with each being listed in the order of its appearance on the financial statements. These accounts receive debits and credits in making the adjustments. Entering their names on the work sheet in statement order at the time the work sheet is begun makes later preparation of the statements somewhat easier. If required account names are anticipated and listed without balances, as in Illustration 5-2, but later it is discovered that a name not listed is needed, it may be entered below the trial balance totals as was done in Chapter 4.

Trial Balance Columns

The amounts in the Trial Balance columns of Illustration 5-2 are the unadjusted account balances of Kona Sales, Incorporated, as of the end of its annual accounting period. They were taken from the company's ledger after all transactions were recorded but before any end-of-period adjustments were made.

Note the $19,000 inventory amount appearing in the Trial Balance debit column on line 3. This is the amount of inventory the company had on January 1, at the beginning of the accounting period. The $19,000 was debited to the Merchandise Inventory account at the end of the previous period and remained in the account as its balance throughout the current accounting period.

Adjustments Columns

Of the adjustments appearing on the illustrated work sheet, only the adjustment for income taxes is new. A business organized as a corporation is subject to the payment of state and federal income taxes. As to the federal tax, near the beginning of each year a corporation must estimate the amount of income it expects to earn during the year. It must then pay in advance in installments an estimated tax on this income. The advance payments are debited to the Income Taxes Expense account as each installment is paid. Consequently, a corporation that expects to earn a profit normally reaches the end of the year with a debit balance in its Income Taxes Expense account. However, since the balance is an estimate and usually less than the full amount of the tax, an adjustment like that on lines 12 and 32 normally must be made to reflect the additional tax owed.

Combining and Sorting the Items   After all adjustments are entered on a work sheet like that of Illustration 5-2 and totaled, the amounts in the Trial Balance and Adjustments columns are combined and are sorted to the proper Income Statement and Balance Sheet columns. In sorting each item, answers to two questions are required. (1) Is the amount a debit or a credit and (2) on which statements does it appear? As to the first question, debit amounts must be sorted to a debit column and credit amounts must go into a credit column. As to the second question, asset, liability, and stockholders' (owners') equity items go on the balance sheet and are sorted to the Balance Sheet columns. Revenue, cost of goods sold, and expense items go on the income statement and are sorted to the Income Statement columns.

Income Statement Columns

Observe in Illustration 5-2 that revenue, cost of goods sold, and expense items maintain their debit and credit positions when sorted to the Income

Illustration 5-2

Kona Sales, Incorporated

Work Sheet for Year Ended December 31, 198B

	Trial Balance		Adjustments		Income Statement		Balance Sheet	
Account Titles	Dr.	Cr.	Dr.	Cr.	Dr.	Cr.	Dr.	Cr.
1 Cash	8,200 00						8,200 00	
2 Accounts receivable	11,200 00						11,200 00	
3 Merchandise inventory	19,000 00				19,000 00	21,000 00	21,000 00	
4 Prepaid insurance	900 00			(a) 600 00			300 00	
5 Store supplies	600 00			(b) 400 00			200 00	
6 Office supplies	300 00			(c) 200 00			100 00	
7 Store equipment	29,100 00						29,100 00	
8 Accumulated depreciation, store equipment		2,500 00		(d) 3,000 00				5,500 00
9 Office equipment	4,400 00						4,400 00	
10 Accumulated depreciation, office equipment		600 00		(e) 700 00				1,300 00
11 Accounts payable		3,600 00						3,600 00
12 Income taxes payable				(f) 100 00				100 00
13 Common stock		50,000 00						50,000 00
14 Retained earnings		4,600 00						4,600 00
15 Sales		306,200 00				306,200 00		
16 Sales returns and allowances	1,900 00				1,900 00			
17 Sales discounts	4,300 00				4,300 00			
18 Purchases	235,800 00				235,800 00			
19 Purchases returns and allowances		1,200 00				1,200 00		
20 Purchases discounts		4,100 00				4,100 00		
21 Transportation-In	1,500 00				1,500 00			
22 Sales salaries expense	18,500 00				18,500 00			
23 Rent expense, selling space	8,100 00				8,100 00			

	Account	Trial Balance Dr	Trial Balance Cr	Adjustments Dr	Adjustments Cr	Income Statement Dr	Income Statement Cr	Balance Sheet Dr	Balance Sheet Cr
24	Advertising expense	700 00				700 00			
25	Store supplies expense			(b) 400 00		400 00			
26	Depreciation expense, store equipment			(d) 3,000 00		3,000 00			
27	Office salaries expense	25,800 00				25,800 00			
28	Rent expense, office space	900 00				900 00			
29	Insurance expense			(a) 600 00		600 00			
30	Office supplies expense			(c) 200 00		200 00			
31	Depreciation expense, office equipment			(e) 700 00		700 00			
32	Income taxes expense	1,600 00		(f) 100 00		1,700 00			
33		372,800 00	372,800 00	5,000 00	5,000 00	323,100 00	332,500 00	74,500 00	65,100 00
34	Net income					9,400 00			9,400 00
35						332,500 00	332,500 00	74,500 00	74,500 00
36									
37									
38									
39									
40									
41									
42									
43									
44									
45									
46									
47									
48									

Statement columns. Note that sales returns and sales discounts in the debit column are in effect subtracted from sales in the credit column when the columns are totaled and the net income is determined.

Look at the beginning inventory amount on line 3. Note that the $19,000 trial balance amount is sorted to the Income Statement debit column. It is put in the Income Statement debt column because it is a debit amount and because it enters into the calculation of cost of goods sold and net income.

Entering the Ending Inventory on the Work Sheet Before beginning its work sheet, the company of Illustration 5-2 determined that it had a $21,000 ending inventory. The inventory amount was determined by counting the items of unsold merchandise and multiplying the count of each kind by its cost.

In preparing a work sheet like Illustration 5-2, after all items are sorted to the proper columns, the ending inventory amount is simply inserted or "plugged" into the Income Statement credit column and the Balance Sheet debit column. Observe the $21,000 ending inventory amounts that are "plugged" into these columns on line 3 of the work sheet.

In accounting, when an amount is "plugged" into a column of figures, it is simply put in the column to accomplish an objective. In this case, the ending inventory amount is "plugged" into the Income Statement credit column so that the difference between the two Income Statement columns will equal the net income. It is put in the Balance Sheet debit column because it is the amount of an end-of-period asset that must be added to the other asset amounts in completing the work sheet. (How the ending inventory amount gets into the accounts is explained later.)

■ **Cost of Goods Sold on the Work Sheet**

The item amounts that enter into the calculation of cost of goods sold are shown in color in the Income Statement columns of Illustration 5-2. The beginning inventory, purchases, and transportation-in amounts appear in the debit column. The amounts of the ending inventory, purchases returns and allowances, and purchases discounts appear in the credit column. Note in the following calculations that the sum of the three debit items minus the sum of the three credit items equals the $230,000 cost of goods sold shown in the income statement of Illustration 5-1.

Beginning inventory . . .	$ 19,000	Ending inventory	$21,000
Purchases	235,800	Purchases returns	1,200
Transportation-in.	1,500	Purchases discounts. . . .	4,100
Total debits	$256,300	Total credits	$26,300
Less total credits . . .	(26,300)		
Cost of goods sold. . . .	$230,000		

Therefore, the net effect of putting the six cost of goods sold amounts in the Income Statement columns is to put the $230,000 cost of the goods sold into the columns.

■ **Completing the
Work Sheet**

After all items are sorted to the proper columns and the ending inventory amount is "plugged" in, a work sheet like Illustration 5-2 is completed by adding the columns and determining and adding in the net income or loss, as was explained in the previous chapter.

■ **Preparing the
Statements**

After the work sheet is completed, the items in its Income Statement columns are arranged into a formal income statement. The items in its Balance Sheet columns are then arranged into a formal balance sheet. A classified income statement prepared from information in the Income Statement columns of Illustration 5-2 is shown in Illustration 5-1. The balance sheet appears in Illustration 5-3. Observe that since none of the company's prepaid items are material in amount, they are totaled and shown as a single item on the balance sheet. The $14,000 retained earnings amount on the balance sheet is the sum of the $4,600 of retained earnings appearing on line 14 of the work sheet plus the company's $9,400 net income.

Illustration 5-3

Kona Sales, Incorporated
Balance Sheet
December 31, 198B

Assets

Current assets:
Cash	$ 8,200	
Accounts receivable	11,200	
Merchandise inventory	21,000	
Prepaid expenses	600	
Total current assets		$41,000

Plant and equipment:
Store equipment	$29,100		
Less accumulated depreciation	5,500	$23,600	
Office equipment	$ 4,400		
Less accumulated depreciation	1,300	3,100	
Total plant and equipment			26,700
Total assets			$67,700

Liabilities

Current liabilities:
Accounts payable	$ 3,600	
Income taxes payable	100	
Total current liabilities		$ 3,700

Stockholders' Equity

Common stock, $5 par value, 10,000 shares authorized and outstanding	$50,000	
Retained earnings	14,000	
Total stockholders' equity.		64,000
Total liabilities and stockholders' equity. . .		$67,700

■ **Retained Earnings Statement**

In addition to an income statement and a balance sheet, a third financial statement called a **retained earnings statement** is commonly prepared for a corporation. It reports the changes that have occurred in the corporation's retained earnings during the period and accounts for the difference between the retained earnings reported on balance sheets of successive accounting periods.

The retained earnings statement of Kona Sales, Incorporated, appears in Illustration 5-4. It shows that the company began the year with $8,600 of retained earnings, which is also the amount of retained earnings it reported on its previous year-end balance sheet. Its retained earnings were reduced by the declaration of $4,000 of dividends and increased by the $9,400 net income to the $14,000 reported on its current year-end balance sheet. Information as to the beginning retained earnings and the dividends declared were taken from the company's Retained Earnings account.

Illustration 5-4

Kona Sales, Incorporated
Retained Earnings Statement
For Year Ended December 31, 198B

Retained earnings, January 1, 198B	$ 8,600
Add 198B net income	9,400
Total	$18,000
Deduct dividends declared	4,000
Retained earnings, December 31, 198B	$14,000

■ **Retained Earnings Account**

Illustration 5-5 shows the Retained Earnings account of Kona Sales, Incorporated. Compare the information in the account with the company's retained earnings statement. The account shows that the company began 198B with $8,600 of retained earnings. It declared and paid a $4,000 dividend in October, and it earned a $9,400 net income. The items are identified in the Explanation column of the account, but they need not be. The $9,400 net income reached the account when the closing entries, which are discussed in the next section, were posted.

Illustration 5-5

Retained Earnings   Account No. 312

Date		Explanation	PR	Debit	Credit	Balance
198A						
Dec.	31	198A net income	G10		8,600	8,600
198B						
Oct.	15	Dividend declared	G20	4,000		4,600
Dec.	31	198B net income	G23		9,400	14,000

■   **Adjusting and Closing Entries**

After the work sheet and statements are completed, adjusting and closing entries must be prepared and posted. The entries for Kona Sales, Incorporated, are shown in Illustration 5-6. They differ from previously illustrated adjusting and closing entries in that an explanation for each entry is not given. Individual explanations may be given, but are unnecessary. The words **Adjusting entries** before the first adjusting entry and **Closing entries** before the first closing entry are sufficient to explain the entries.

As previously explained, the Adjustments columns of its work sheet provide the information needed in preparing a concern's adjusting entries. Each adjustment in the Adjustments columns requires an adjusting entry that is journalized and posted. Compare the adjusting entries in Illustration 5-6 with the adjustments on the work sheet of Illustration 5-2.

When a work sheet like Illustration 5-2 is prepared, its Income Statement columns are a source of the information needed in preparing closing entries. Look at the first closing entry of Illustration 5-6 and the items in the Income Statement debit column of Illustration 5-2. Note that Income Summary is debited for the column total and each account having an amount in the column is credited. This entry removes the $19,000 beginning inventory amount from the Merchandise Inventory account. It also clears and closes all the revenue, cost of goods sold, and expense accounts that have debit balances.

Compare the second closing entry with the items in the Income Statement credit column of Illustration 5-2. Note that each account having an amount in the column is debited and the Income Summary account is credited for the column total. This entry clears and closes the revenue and cost of goods sold accounts having credit balances. It also enters the $21,000 ending inventory amount in the Merchandise Inventory account.

■   **Closing Entries and the Inventories**

There is nothing essentially new about the closing entries of a merchandising company. However, their effect on the Merchandise Inventory account should be understood.

Before its closing entries are posted, the Merchandise Inventory account of Kona Sales, Incorporated, shows in its $19,000 debit balance the amount of the company's beginning-of-period inventory as follows:

	Merchandise Inventory				**Account No.** 113
Date	**Explanation**	**PR**	**Debit**	**Credit**	**Balance**
198A Dec. 31		G10	19,000		19,000

Then when the first closing entry is posted, its $19,000 credit to Merchandise Inventory clears the beginning inventory amount from the inventory account as follows:

Illustration 5-6

Date		Account Titles and Explanation	PR	Debit		Credit	
198B		Adjusting Entries:					
Dec.	31	Insurance Expense	653	600	00		
		Prepaid Insurance	115			600	00
	31	Store Supplies Expense	614	400	00		
		Store Supplies	116			400	00
	31	Office Supplies Expense	651	200	00		
		Office Supplies	117			200	00
	31	Depreciation Expense, Store Equipment	615	3,000	00		
		Accumulated Depr., Store Equipment	132			3,000	00
	31	Depreciation Expense, Office Equipment	655	700	00		
		Accumulated Depr., Office Equipment	134			700	00
	31	Income Taxes Expense	711	100	00		
		Income Taxes Payable	213			100	00
		Closing Entries:					
	31	Income Summary	313	323,100	00		
		Merchandise Inventory	113			19,000	00
		Sales Returns and Allowances	412			1,900	00
		Sales Discounts	413			4,300	00
		Purchases	511			235,800	00
		Transportation-In	514			1,500	00
		Sales Salaries Expense	611			18,500	00
		Rent Expense, Selling Space	612			8,100	00
		Advertising Expense	613			700	00
		Store Supplies Expense	614			400	00
		Depreciation Expense, Store Equip.	615			3,000	00
		Office Salaries Expense	651			25,800	00
		Rent Expense, Office Space	652			900	00
		Insurance Expense	653			600	00
		Office Supplies Expense	654			200	00
		Depreciation Expense, Office Equip.	655			700	00
		Income Taxes Expense	711			1,700	00
	31	Merchandise Inventory	113	21,000	00		
		Sales	411	306,200	00		
		Purchases Returns and Allowances	512	1,200	00		
		Purchase Discounts	513	4,100	00		
		Income Summary	313			332,500	00
	31	Income Summary	313	9,400	00		
		Retained Earnings	312			9,400	00

Date		Explanation	PR	Debit	Credit	Balance
198A						
Dec.	31		G10	19,000		19,000
198B						
Dec.	31		G23		19,000	–0–

Merchandise Inventory — **Account No.** 113

When the second closing entry is posted, its $21,000 debit to Merchandise Inventory puts the amount of the ending inventory into the inventory account, as follows:

Date		Explanation	PR	Debit	Credit	Balance
198A						
Dec.	31		G10	19,000		19,000
198B						
Dec.	31		G23		19,000	–0–
	31		G23	21,000		21,000

Merchandise Inventory — **Account No.** 113

The $21,000 remains throughout the succeeding year as the debit balance of the inventory account and as a historical record of the amount of inventory at the end of 198B and the beginning of 198C.

■ **Other Inventory Methods**

There are several ways to handle the inventories in the end-of-period procedures. However, all have the same objectives. They are (1) to remove the beginning inventory amount from the inventory account and to charge (debit) it to Income Summary and (2) to enter the ending inventory amount in the inventory account and credit it to Income Summary. These objectives may be achieved with closing entries as explained in this chapter. Or, for example, adjusting entries to accomplish the same objectives may be used. Either method is satisfactory. However, most accountants prefer to use closing entries because less work is required than when adjusting entries are used.

■ **Income Statement Forms**

The income statement in Illustration 5–1 is called a classified income statement because its items are classified into significant groups. It is also a **multiple-step income statement** because cost of goods sold and the expenses are subtracted in steps to arrive at net income. Another income statement form, the **single-step form,** is shown in Illustration 5–7. This form is commonly used for published statements. Also, although it need not be, its information is commonly condensed as shown. Note how cost of goods sold and the expenses are added together in the illustration and are subtracted in "one step" from net sales to arrive at net income, thus the name of the form.

Illustration 5-7

Kona Sales, Incorporated
Income Statement
For Year Ended December 31, 198B

Revenue from sales		$300,000
Expenses:		
Cost of goods sold.	$230,000	
Selling expenses.	30,700	
General and administrative expenses	28,200	
Income taxes expense	1,700	
Total expenses		290,600
Net income		$ 9,400

Combined Income and Retained Earnings Statement

Many companies combine their income and retained earnings statements into a single statement. Such a statement may be prepared in either single-step or multiple-step form. A single-step statement is shown in Illustration 5-8.

Illustration 5-8

Kona Sales, Incorporated
Statement of Income and Retained Earnings
For Year Ended December 31, 198B

Revenue from sales		$300,000
Expenses:		
Cost of goods sold.	$230,000	
Selling expenses.	30,700	
General and administrative expenses	28,200	
Income taxes expenses.	1,700	
Total expenses		290,600
Net income		$ 9,400
Add retained earnings, January 1, 198B. . .		8,600
Total		$ 18,000
Deduct dividends declared		4,000
Retained earnings, December 31, 198B. . . .		$ 14,000

Statement of Changes in Financial Position

In addition to the retained earnings statement, another very important financial statement commonly prepared for a corporation is the **statement of changes in financial position.** It shows where the concern secured funds and where it applied or used the funds, such as in the purchase of plant assets or the payment of dividends. A discussion of this statement is deferred until Chapter 18, after further discussion of corporation accounting.

Debit and Credit Memoranda

Merchandise purchased that does not meet specifications, goods received that were not ordered, goods received short of the amount ordered and billed, and invoice errors are matters for adjustment between the buyer and seller. In some cases, the buyer can make the adjustment, for example, when there is an invoice error. If the buyer makes the adjustment, it must notify the seller of its action. It commonly does this by sending a **debit memorandum** or a **credit memorandum.**

A debit memorandum is a business form on which are spaces for the name and address of the concern to which it is directed and the printed words, "WE DEBIT YOUR ACCOUNT," followed by space for typing in the reason for the debit. A credit memorandum carries the words, "WE CREDIT YOUR ACCOUNT." To illustrate the use of a debit memorandum, assume a buyer discovers an invoice error that reduces the invoice total by $10. For such an error, the buyer notifies the seller with a debit memorandum reading: "WE DEBIT YOUR ACCOUNT to correct a $10 error on your November 17 invoice." A debit memorandum is sent because the correction reduces an account payable of the buyer, and to reduce an account payable requires a debit. In recording the purchase, the buyer normally marks the correction on the invoice and attaches a copy of the debit memorandum to show that the seller was notified. The buyer then debits Purchases and credits Account Payable for the corrected amount.

An adjustment, such as merchandise that does not meet specifications, normally requires negotiations between the buyer and the seller. In such a case, the buyer may debit Purchases for the full invoice amount and enter into negotiations with the seller for a return or a price adjustment. If the seller agrees to the return or adjustment, the seller notifies the buyer with a credit memorandum. A credit memorandum is used because the return or adjustment reduces an account receivable on the books of the seller, and to reduce an account receivable requires a credit. Upon receipt of the credit memorandum, the buyer records it by debiting Accounts Payable and crediting Purchases Returns and Allowances, if the purchase was originally recorded at the full invoice price.

From this discussion it can be seen that a debit or a credit memorandum may originate with either party to a transaction. The memorandum gets its name from the action of the originator. If the orginator debits, the originator sends a debit memorandum. If the originator credits, a credit memorandum is sent.

■ Trade Discounts

A **trade discount** is a deduction (often as much as 40% or more) from a **list price** (or catalog price) that is used in determining the actual price of the goods to which it applies. Trade discounts are commonly used by manufacturers and wholesalers to avoid republication of catalogs when selling prices change. If selling prices change, catalog prices can be adjusted by merely issuing a new list of discounts to be applied to the catalog prices. Such discounts are discussed here primarily to distinguish them from the cash discounts described earlier in this chapter.

Trade discounts are not entered in the accounts by either party to a sale. For example, if a manufacturer sells on credit an item listed in its catalog at $100, less a 40% trade discount, it will record the sale as follows:

Dec.	10	Accounts Receivable.	60.00	
		Sales		60.00
		Sold merchandise on credit.		

The buyer will also enter the purchase in its records at $60. Also, if a cash discount is involved, it applies only to the amount of the purchase, $60.

☐   **Glossary**   **Cash discount** a deduction from the invoice price of goods allowed if payment is made within a specified period of time.

Credit memorandum a memorandum sent to notify its recipient that the business sending the memorandum has in its records credited the account of the recipient.

Credit period the agreed period of time for which credit is granted and at the end of which payment is expected.

Credit terms the agreed terms upon which credit is granted in the sale of goods or services.

Debit memorandum a memorandum sent to notify its recipient that the business sending the memorandum has in its records debited the account of the recipient.

Discount period the period of time in which a cash discount may be taken.

EOM an abbreviation meaning "end-of-month."

FOB the abbreviation for "free on board," which is used to denote that goods purchased are placed on board the means of transportation at a specified geographic point free of any loading and transportation charges to that point.

General and administrative expenses the general office, accounting, personnel, and credit and collection expenses.

Gross profit from sales net sales minus cost of goods sold.

List price the catalog or other listed price from which a trade discount is deducted in arriving at the invoice price for goods.

Merchandise inventory the unsold merchandise on hand at a given time.

Multiple-step income statement an income statement on which cost of goods sold and the expenses are subtracted in steps to arrive at net income.

Periodic inventory system an inventory system in which periodically, at the end of each accounting period, the cost of the unsold goods on hand is determined by counting units of each product on hand, multiplying the count for each product by its cost, and adding the costs of the various products.

Perpetual inventory system an inventory system in which an individual record is kept for each product of the units on hand at the beginning, the units purchased, the units sold, and the new balance after each purchase or sale.

Purchases discounts discounts taken on merchandise purchased for resale.

Retained earnings statement a statement which reports changes in a corporation's retained earnings that occurred during an accounting period.

Sales discounts discounts given on sales of merchandise.

Selling expenses the expenses of preparing and storing goods for sale, promoting sales, making sales, and if a separate delivery department is not maintained, the expenses of delivering goods to customers.

Single-step income statement an income statement on which cost of goods sold and the expenses are added together and subtracted in one step from revenue to arrive at net income.

Trade discount the discount that may be deducted from a catalog list price to determine the invoice price of goods.

Transportation-in freight, express, or other transportation costs on merchandise purchased for resale.

□ **Questions for Class Discussion**

1. What is gross profit from sales?
2. May a concern earn a gross profit on its sales and still suffer a loss? How?
3. Why should a concern be interested in the amount of its sales returns and allowances?
4. Since sales returns and allowances are subtracted from sales on the income statement, why not save the effort of this subtraction by debiting all such returns and allowances directly to the Sales account?
5. What is a cash discount? If terms are 2/10, n/60, what is the length of the credit period? What is the length of the discount period?
6. How and when is cost of goods sold determined in a store using a periodic inventory system?
7. Which of the following are debited to the Purchases account of a grocery store: (a) the purchase of a cash register, (b) the purchase of a refrigerated display case, (c) the purchase of advertising space in a newspaper, and (d) the purchase of a case of tomato soup?
8. If a concern may return for full credit all unsatisfactory merchandise purchased, why should it be interested in controlling the amount of its returns?
9. When applied to transportation terms, what do the letters FOB mean? What does FOB destination mean?
10. At the end of an accounting period, which inventory, the beginning inventory or the ending, appears on the trial balance?
11. What is shown on a retained earnings statement? What is the purpose of the statement?
12. How does a single-step income statement differ from a multiple-step income statement?
13. During the year, a company purchased merchandise costing $220,000. What was the company's cost of goods sold if there were (a) no beginning or ending inventories? (b) a beginning inventory of $28,000 and no ending inventory? (c) a $25,000 beginning inventory and a $30,000 ending inventory? and (d) no beginning inventory and a $15,000 ending inventory?
14. In counting the merchandise on hand at the end of an accounting period, a clerk failed to count, and consequently omitted from the inventory, all the merchandise on one shelf. If the cost of the merchandise on the shelf was $100, what was the effect of the omission on (a) the balance sheet and (b) the income statement?
15. Suppose that the omission of the $100 from the inventory (Question 14) was not discovered. What would be the effect on the balance sheet and income statement prepared at the end of the next accounting period?

16. Distinguish between cash discounts and trade discounts. Is the amount of a trade discount on merchandise purchased credited to the Purchases Discounts account?

17. When a debit memorandum is issued, who debits, the originator of the memorandum or the company receiving it?

Class Exercises

Exercise 5-1

A store purchased merchandise having a $5,000 invoice price, terms 2/10, n/60, from a manufacturer and paid for the merchandise within the discount period. (a) Give without dates the journal entries made by the store to record the purchase and payment. (b) Give without dates the entries made by the manufacturer to record the sale and collection. (c) If the store borrowed sufficient money at a 12% annual rate of interest on the last day of the discount period to pay the invoice, how much did the store save by borrowing to take advantage of the discount?

Exercise 5-2

The following items, with the expenses condensed to conserve space, appeared in the Income Statement columns of a work sheet prepared for The Shop, a single proprietorship business, as of December 31, 198B, the end of its annual accounting period. From the information, prepare a 198B multiple-step income statement for The Shop.

	Income Statement	
	Debit	Credit
Merchandise inventory	36,000	40,000
Sales		200,000
Sales returns and allowances	1,000	
Sales discounts	1,500	
Purchases	120,000	
Purchases returns and allowances		600
Purchases discounts		2,400
Transportation-in	500	
Selling expenses	30,000	
General and administrative expenses	20,000	
	209,000	243,000
Net income	34,000	
	243,000	243,000

Exercise 5-3

Part 1. Assume that The Shop of Exercise 5-2 is owned by June Ellis and prepare entries to close the shop's revenue, expense, and Income Summary accounts.

Part 2. Rule a balance column Merchandise Inventory account on note paper, and under a December 31, 198A, date, enter the $36,000 beginning inventory of Exercise 5-2 as its balance. Then post to the account the portions of the shop's closing entries that affect the account. Post first the credit that removes the beginning inventory from the account.

Exercise 5-4

The following items, with expenses condensed to conserve space, appeared in the Income Statement columns of a work sheet prepared for Little Store, Incorporated, as of December 31, 198B, the end of its annual accounting period. From the information, prepare a 198B multiple-step income statement for the corporation.

	Income Statement	
	Debit	Credit
Merchandise inventory	40,000	50,000
Sales		300,000
Sales returns and allowances	1,500	
Sales discounts	3,000	
Purchases	180,000	
Purchases returns and allowances		1,000
Purchases discounts		2,500
Transportation-in	500	
Selling expenses	45,000	
General and administrative expenses	35,500	
Income taxes expense	8,000	
	313,500	353,500
Net income	40,000	
	353,500	353,500

Exercise 5-5

Part 1. Prepare entries to close the revenue, expense, and Income Summary accounts of Little Store, Incorporated (Exercise 5-4).

Part 2. Rule a balance column Merchandise Inventory account on note paper, and under a December 31, 198A, date, enter the $40,000 beginning inventory of Exercise 5-4 as its balance. Then post to the account the portions of the store's closing entries that affect the account. Post first the credit that removes the beginning inventory from the account.

Exercise 5-6

The information that follows was taken from an income statement.

Sales	$150,000	Purchases returns	$ 500
Sales returns	1,000	Purchases discounts	1,500
Sales discounts	2,000	Transportation-in	3,000
Beginning inventory	40,000	Gross profit from sales	47,000
Purchases	95,000	Net loss	4,000

Required

Prepare calculations to determine (*a*) total operating expenses, (*b*) cost of goods sold, and (*c*) ending inventory.

Exercise 5-7

The trial balance that follows was taken from the ledger of Beta, Incorporated, at the end of its annual accounting period. (To simplify the problem and to save you time, the account balances are in one- and two-digit numbers.)

Beta, Incorporated
Trial Balance
December 31, 19—

Cash.	$ 1	
Accounts receivable	2	
Merchandise inventory	5	
Store supplies.	3	
Store equipment	9	
Accumulated depreciation, store equipment		$ 2
Accounts payable		2
Salaries payable.	—	—
Common stock, $1 par value		10
Retained earnings		3
Sales.		40
Sales returns and allowances	1	
Purchases	18	
Purchases discounts		1
Transportation-in	1	
Salaries expense.	10	
Rent expense	6	
Advertising expense	2	
Depreciation expense, store equipment	—	—
Store supplies expense	—	—
Totals	$58	$58

Required

Prepare a work sheet form having no Adjusted Trial Balance columns on note paper, and copy the trial balance onto the work sheet. Then complete the work sheet using the information that follows:

a. Ending store supplies inventory, $1.

b. Estimated depreciation on the store equipment, $3.

c. Accrued salaries payable, $1.

d. Ending merchandise inventory, $6.

Exercise 5-8

Copy the following tabulation and fill in the missing amounts. Indicate a loss by placing parentheses around the amount. Each horizontal row of figures is a separate problem situation.

Sales	Begin-ning In-ventory	Pur-chases	Ending Inven-tory	Cost of Goods Sold	Gross Profit	Ex-penses	Net Income or Loss
$110,000	$ 80,000	$ 70,000	$?	$ 95,000	$?	$50,000	$?
185,000	65,000	?	75,000	80,000	?	55,000	50,000
150,000	50,000	?	30,000	?	85,000	45,000	40,000
?	75,000	110,000	60,000	?	100,000	40,000	?
160,000	60,000	95,000	?	105,000	?	70,000	?
50,000	15,000	?	25,000	30,000	?	?	5,000
?	115,000	220,000	130,000	?	140,000	?	50,000
80,000	?	50,000	35,000	?	30,000	?	10,000

Exercise 5-9

On January 6, 198A, X Company received $5,000 of merchandise and an invoice dated January 5, terms 2/10, n/30, FOB Y Company's factory.

On the day the goods were received, X Company paid Fast Freight Company $150 of shipping charges on the merchandise purchased. The next day X Company returned to Y Company $400 of the goods that were defective, and on January 15 it mailed Y Company a check for the amount owed. Prepare general journal entries to record the foregoing transactions (a) on the books of X Company and (b) on the books of Y Company. Assume that Y Company recorded the return and the check the next day after each was sent.

Exercise 5-10

The following two closing entries (with expenses combined to shorten the exercise) were made by Southwest Sales, a single proprietorship, at the end of its 198B annual accounting period.

Dec.	31	Income Summary	264,000.00	
		Merchandise Inventory		35,000.00
		Sales Returns and Allowances.		2,000.00
		Sales Discounts		3,000.00
		Purchases		150,000.00
		Transportation In.		4,000.00
		Selling Expenses		40,000.00
		General and Administrative Expenses. . .		30,000.00
	31	Merchandise Inventory	46,000.00	
		Sales	250,000.00	
		Purchases Returns and Allowances	1,000.00	
		Purchases Discounts.	2,000.00	
		Income Summary		299,000.00

Required

From the information in the closing entries, prepare an income statement for Southwest Sales.

Problems

Problem 5-1

Phoenix Sales, Inc., began 198B with $24,550 of retained earnings; and during the year, it declared and paid $20,000 of dividends on its outstanding common stock. At the year-end, the Income Statement columns of its work sheet carried the items that follow on page 184.

Required

1. Prepare a 198B, classified, multiple-step income statement for the corporation, showing the expenses and the items entering into cost of goods sold in detail.
2. Prepare a 198B retained earnings statement.
3. Prepare compound closing entries for the corporation.
4. Open a Merchandise Inventory account and enter the $22,510 beginning inventory under a December 31, 198A, date as its balance. Then post

the portions of the closing entries that affect the account. Post first the credit that clears the beginning inventory from the account.

| | Income Statement | |
	Debit	Credit
Merchandise inventory	22,510	23,860
Sales		220,340
Sales returns and allowances	1,315	
Purchases	144,510	
Purchases returns and allowances		520
Purchases discounts		2,170
Transportation-in	935	
Sales salaries expense	21,840	
Rent expense, selling space	10,800	
Advertising expense	790	
Store supplies expense	550	
Depreciation expense, store equipment . .	2,115	
Office salaries expense	10,650	
Rent expense, office space	1,200	
Telephone expense.	570	
Office supplies expense	215	
Insurance expense	1,440	
Depreciation expense, office equipment . .	530	
Income taxes expense	3,770	
	223,740	246,890
Net income	23,150	
	246,890	246,890

Problem 5-2

A December 31, 198B, year-end trial balance from the ledger of The Handy Store, a single proprietorship business, follows on page 185.

Required

1. Copy the trial balance on an eight-column work sheet form and complete the work sheet using the information that follows:
   a. Store supplies inventory, $135.
   b. Office supplies inventory, $85.
   c. Expired insurance, $1,490.
   d. Estimated depreciation of store equipment, $2,120.
   e. Estimated depreciation of office equipment, $385.
   f. Ending merchandise inventory, $34,880.
2. Prepare a multiple-step classified income statement showing the expenses and the items entering into cost of goods sold in detail.
3. Prepare compound closing entries for the store.
4. Open a balance-column Merchandise Inventory account and enter the beginning inventory under a December 31, 198A, date as its balance. Then post those portions of the closing entries that affect the account. Post first the entry that removes the beginning inventory from the account.

The Handy Store
Trial Balance
December 31, 198B

Cash	$ 1,335	
Merchandise inventory.	33,975	
Store supplies	785	
Office supplies	245	
Prepaid insurance	1,820	
Store equipment	21,210	
Accumulated depreciation, store equipment . . .		$ 8,540
Office equipment	5,915	
Accumulated depreciation, office equipment . . .		2,130
Accounts payable		4,870
Ned Handy, capital		40,300
Ned Handy, withdrawals.	18,000	
Sales.		190,430
Sales returns and allowances	1,165	
Sales discounts	2,120	
Purchases.	114,250	
Purchases returns and allowances		740
Purchases discounts		2,940
Transportation-in	645	
Sales salaries expense	21,280	
Rent expense, selling space	12,900	
Advertising expense.	385	
Store supplies expense	–0–	
Depreciation expense, store equipment	–0–	
Office salaries expense	12,420	
Rent expense, office space.	1,500	
Office supplies expense	–0–	
Insurance expense	–0–	
Depreciation expense, office equipment	–0–	
Totals.	$249,950	$249,950

Problem 5-3

(*If the working papers that accompany this text are not being used, omit this problem.*)
The unfinished work sheet of Western Store, Inc., is reproduced in the booklet of working papers. All adjustments have been made on the work sheet except for $550 of additional income taxes expense.

Required

1. Enter the income tax adjustment, sort the items to the proper work sheet columns, plug in the $23,430 ending inventory, and complete the work sheet.
2. Prepare a classified multiple-step income statement showing the details of cost of goods sold and the expenses.
3. Prepare a balance-column Merchandise Inventory account and enter the $25,220 beginning inventory under a December 31, 198A, date as its balance. Then prepare compound closing entries for Western Store, Inc., and post those portions of the entries that affect the account. Post first the entry that clears the beginning inventory from the account.

4. Prepare for the corporation a combined statement of income and retained earnings with the items condensed as in published statements. Western Store, Inc., began 198B with $12,160 of retained earnings, and it declared and paid $10,000 of dividends during the year.

Problem 5-4

The December 31, 198B, end of the annual accounting period trial balance of the ledger of Hobby Shop, Incorporated, follows.

Hobby Shop, Incorporated
Trial Balance
December 31, 198B

Cash	$ 3,650	
Merchandise inventory.	34,875	
Store supplies	615	
Office supplies	315	
Prepaid insurance	2,110	
Store equipment	37,195	
Accumulated depreciation, store equipment . .		$ 3,540
Office equipment	8,440	
Accumulated depreciation, office equipment . . .		925
Accounts payable		795
Salaries payable		–0–
Income taxes payable		–0–
Common stock, $10 par value		40,000
Retained earnings		4,550
Sales		274,820
Sales returns and allowances	1,860	
Purchases	167,810	
Purchases returns and allowances		745
Purchases discounts		2,925
Transportation-in	2,185	
Sales salaries expense	24,650	
Rent expense, selling space	10,500	
Advertising expense	3,435	
Store supplies expense	–0–	
Depreciation expense, store equipment	–0–	
Office salaries expense	25,160	
Rent expense, office space.	1,500	
Insurance expense	–0–	
Office supplies expense	–0–	
Depreciation expense, office equipment	–0–	
Income taxes expenses	4,000	
Totals	$328,300	$328,300

Required

1. Copy the trial balance on an eight-column work sheet form and complete the work sheet using the information that follows.
   a. Ending store supplies inventory, $165; and (*b*) ending office supplies inventory, $125.
   c. Expired insurance, $1,645.
   d. Estimated depreciation on the store equipment, $3,610; and (*e*) on the office equipment, $990.

    f. Accrued sales salaries payable, $225; and accrued office salaries payable, $160.

    g. Additional income taxes expense, $425.

    h. Ending merchandise inventory, $33,160.

2. Prepare a multiple-step classified income statement showing the expenses and the items entering into cost of goods sold in detail.

3. Prepare a retained earnings statement. Hobby Shop, Incorporated, began 198B with $14,550 of retained earnings, and it declared and paid $10,000 of dividends during the year.

4. Prepare compound closing entries for the corporation.

5. In addition to the foregoing, prepare a single-step statement of income and retained earnings with the items condensed as is commonly done in published statements.

Problem 5-5

The December 31, 198B, end of the annual accounting period trial balance of the ledger of Universal Sales, Inc., follows.

Universal Sales, Inc.
Trial Balance
December 31, 198B

Cash	$ 6,850	
Accounts receivable	15,110	
Merchandise inventory	34,565	
Store supplies	1,610	
Office supplies	515	
Prepaid insurance	2,170	
Store equipment	41,320	
Accumulated depreciation, store equipment		$ 7,220
Office equipment	8,340	
Accumulated depreciation, office equipment		1,885
Accounts payable		5,540
Salaries payable		–0–
Income taxes payable		–0–
Common stock, $5 par value		50,000
Retained earnings		10,675
Sales		374,760
Sales returns and allowances	3,380	
Purchases	256,725	
Purchases returns and allowances		1,215
Purchases discounts		3,140
Transportation-in	3,415	
Sales salaries expense	28,815	
Rent expense, selling space	13,500	
Store supplies expense	–0–	
Depreciation expense, store equipment	–0–	
Office salaries expense	32,220	
Rent expense, office space	1,500	
Office supplies expense	–0–	
Insurance expense	–0–	
Depreciation expense, office equipment	–0–	
Income taxes expense	4,400	
Totals	$454,435	$454,435

Required

1. Copy the trial balance on an eight-column work sheet form and complete the work sheet using the information that follows:
   a. Ending store supplies inventory, $295; and (b) ending office supplies inventory, $150.
   c. Expired insurance, $1,870.
   d. Estimated depreciation on the store equipment, $3,610; and (e) on the office equipment, $990.
   f. Accrued sales salaries payable, $295; and accrued office salaries payable, $140.
   g. Additional income taxes expense, $450.
   h. Ending merchandise inventory, $36,245.
2. Prepare a multiple-step income statement showing the expenses and cost of goods sold items in detail.
3. Prepare a year-end classified balance sheet with the prepaid expenses combined.
4. Prepare a retained earnings statement. Universal Sales, Inc., began 198B with $20,675 of retained earnings, and it declared and paid $10,000 of dividends during the year.
5. Prepare adjusting and compound closing entries.
6. Also prepare a single-step statement of income and retained earnings with the items condensed as is common in published statements.

Problem 5-6

Prepare general journal entries to record the following transactions:

Dec. 1 Purchased merchandise priced at $2,400 on credit, terms 1/15, n/30.
      2 A new computer for office use was purchased on credit for $6,000.
      2 Sold merchandise on credit, terms 2/10, 1/30, n/60, $1,200.
      3 Paid $75 cash for freight charges on the merchandise shipment of the December 1 transaction.
      8 Sold merchandise for cash, $240.
      9 Purchased merchandise on credit, terms 2/15, n/30, $1,000.
     11 Received a $200 credit memorandum for merchandise purchased on December 9 and returned for credit.
     18 Sold merchandise on credit, terms 2/10, n/30, $900.
     19 Issued a $150 credit memorandum to the customer of December 18 who returned a portion of the merchandise purchased.
     22 Purchased office supplies on credit, $125.
     23 Received a credit memorandum for unsatisfactory office supplies purchased on December 22 and returned for credit, $40.
     24 Paid for the merchandise purchased on December 9, less the return and the discount.
     27 The customer who purchased merchandise on December 2 paid for the purchase of that date less the applicable discount.
     28 Received payment for the merchandise sold on December 18, less the return and applicable discount.
     31 Paid for the merchandise purchased on December 1.

□ **Alternate Problems**　　**Problem 5-1A**

Dockside Sales, Inc., began 198B with $34,310 of retained earnings, and during the year it declared and paid $15,000 of dividends on its outstanding common stock. At the year-end, the Income Statement columns of its work sheet carried the items that follow.

	Income Statement	
	Debit	Credit
Merchandise inventory	46,220	44,365
Sales		642,480
Sales returns and allowances	3,810	
Sales discounts	9,720	
Purchases	434,490	
Purchases returns and allowances		1,820
Purchases discounts		5,980
Transportation-in	6,135	
Sales salaries expense	46,720	
Rent expense, selling space	22,000	
Store supplies expense	1,080	
Depreciation expense, store equipment . .	5,940	
Office salaries expense	37,880	
Rent expense, office space	2,000	
Office supplies expense	490	
Insurance expense	2,260	
Depreciation expense, office equipment . .	1,840	
Income taxes expense	12,750	
	633,335	694,645
Net income	61,310	
	694,645	694,645

Required

1. Prepare a 198B, classified, multiple-step income statement for the corporation, showing the expenses and items entering into cost of goods sold in detail.
2. Prepare a 198B retained earnings statement.
3. Prepare compound closing entries for the corporation.
4. Open a Merchandise Inventory account and enter the $46,220 beginning inventory under a December 31, 198A, date as its balance. Then post those portions of the closing entries that affect the account. Post first the credit that clears the beginning inventory from the account.

Problem 5-2A

The December 31, 198B, year-end trial balance of the ledger of Westgate Store, a single proprietorship business, follows on page 190.

Required

1. Copy the trial balance on an eight-column work sheet form and complete the work sheet using the information that follows:
   a. Store supplies inventory, $225; and (*b*) office supplies inventory, $120.
   c. Expired insurance, $1,845.

d. Estimated depreciation on the store equipment, $3,910; and (e) on the office equipment, $1,170.

f. Ending merchandise inventory, $32,655.

2. Prepare a multiple-step classified income statement showing the expenses and cost of goods sold items in detail.

3. Prepare compound closing entries for the store.

4. Open a balance column Merchandise Inventory account and enter the $31,335 beginning inventory under a December 31, 198A, date as its balance. Then post those portions of the closing entries that affect the account. Post first the credit that removes the beginning inventory from the account.

Westgate Store
Trial Balance
December 31, 198B

Cash	$ 4,870	
Merchandise inventory.	31,335	
Store supplies	1,145	
Office supplies	430	
Prepaid insurance	2,560	
Store equipment	38,490	
Accumulated depreciation, store equipment . .		$ 6,385
Office equipment	9,420	
Accumulated depreciation, office equipment . .		2,450
Accounts payable		3,120
Ned Handy, capital		62,390
Ned Handy, withdrawals	21,000	
Sales		319,235
Sales returns and allowances	2,125	
Sales discounts	3,460	
Purchases	220,875	
Purchases returns and allowances		1,230
Purchases discounts		3,150
Transportation-in	1,875	
Sales salaries expense	23,140	
Rent expense, selling space	16,000	
Advertising expense	815	
Store supplies expense	–0–	
Depreciation expense, store equipment	–0–	
Office salaries expense	18,420	
Rent expense, office space.	2,000	
Office supplies expense	–0–	
Insurance expense	–0–	
Depreciation expense, office equipment	–0–	
Totals	$397,960	$397,960

Problem 5-3A

The Corner Store, a single proprietorship business, had the items that follow in the Income Statement columns of its 198B year-end work sheet.

Required

1. Prepare a classified, multiple-step, 198B income statement for the store showing the expenses and cost of goods sold items in detail.

2. Under the assumption that Walter Evans, the owner of The Corner Store, withdrew $21,000 to pay personal expenses during 198B, prepare compound closing entries for the store.

3. Open a balance column Merchandise Inventory account and enter the store's $28,210 beginning inventory under a December 31, 198A, date as its balance. Then post the portions of the closing entries that affect this account. Post first the credit that removes the beginning inventory from the account.

	Income Statement	
	Debit	Credit
Merchandise inventory	28,210	27,770
Sales		319,255
Sales returns and allowances	2,820	
Sales discounts	1,460	
Purchases	219,915	
Purchases returns and allowances		1,045
Purchases discounts		2,950
Transportation in	3,125	
Sales salaries expense	27,135	
Rent expense, selling space	13,500	
Advertising expense	1,940	
Store supplies expense	715	
Depreciation expense, store equipment . .	2,950	
Office salaries expense	14,880	
Rent expense, office space	1,500	
Telephone expense	635	
Office supplies expense	210	
Insurance expense	1,890	
Depreciation expense, office equipment . .	765	
	321,650	351,020
Net income	29,370	
	351,020	351,020

Problem 5-4A

The December 31, 198B, end of the annual accounting period trial balance of the ledger of Nevada Sales, Inc., carried the items that follow on page 192.

Required

1. Copy the trial balance on an eight-column work sheet form and complete the work sheet using the information that follows.
   a. Ending store supplies inventory, $265; and (b) ending office supplies inventory, $125.
   c. Expired insurance, $2,475.
   d. Estimated depreciation on the store equipment, $4,260; and (e) on the office equipment, $1,145.
   f. Accrued sales salaries payable, $345; and accrued office salaries payable, $85.
   g. Additional income taxes expense, $525.
   h. Ending merchandise inventory, $42,870.

2. Prepare a multiple-step classified income statement showing the expenses and cost of goods sold items in detail.

3. Prepare a retained earnings statement. Nevada Sales, Inc., began 198B with $9,305 of retained earnings, and it declared and paid $5,000 of dividends during the year.
4. Prepare compound closing entries for the corporation.
5. In addition to the foregoing, prepare a single-step statement of income and retained earnings with the items condensed as is commonly done in published statements.

Nevada Sales, Inc.
Trial Balance
December 31, 198B

Cash	$ 5,890	
Merchandise inventory	44,540	
Store supplies	975	
Office supplies	440	
Prepaid insurance	2,895	
Store equipment	43,380	
Accumulated depreciation, store equipment		$ 6,235
Office equipment	9,670	
Accumulated depreciation, office equipment		1,525
Accounts payable		2,250
Salaries payable		–0–
Income taxes payable		–0–
Common stock, $10 par value		50,000
Retained earnings		4,305
Sales		356,540
Sales returns and allowances	2,120	
Purchases	234,895	
Purchases returns and allowances		1,445
Purchases discounts		3,280
Transportation-in	2,215	
Sales salaries expense	28,095	
Rent expense, selling space	13,000	
Advertising expense	3,665	
Store supplies expense	–0–	
Depreciation expense, store equipment	–0–	
Office salaries expense	26,200	
Rent expense, office space	2,000	
Insurance expense	–0–	
Office supplies expense	–0–	
Depreciation expense, office equipment	–0–	
Income taxes expense	5,600	
Totals	$425,580	$425,580

Problem 5-5A

The December 31, 198B, end of the annual accounting period trial balance of the ledger of Monroe Sales, Inc., follows.

Required

1. Copy the trial balance on an eight-column work sheet form and complete the work sheet using the information that follows.
   a. Ending store supplies inventory, $345; and (b) ending office supplies inventory, $185.

   c. Expired insurance, $1,970.

   d. Estimated depreciation on the store equipment, $3,310; and *(e)* on the office equipment, $945.

   f. Accrued sales salaries payable, $325; and accrued office salaries payable, $185.

   g. Additional income taxes expense, $450.

   h. Ending merchandise inventory, $35,890.

2. Prepare a multiple-step classified income statement showing the cost of goods sold and expense items in detail.

3. Prepare a year-end classified balance sheet with the prepaid expenses combined.

4. Prepare a retained earnings statement. Monroe Sales, Inc., began 198B with $18,560 of retained earnings, and it declared and paid $10,000 of dividends during the year.

5. Prepare adjusting and compound closing entries.

6. Also prepare a single-step statement of income and retained earnings with the items condensed as is common in published statements.

Monroe Sales, Inc.
Trial Balance
December 31, 198B

Cash	$ 6,780	
Accounts receivable	15,945	
Merchandise inventory	34,570	
Store supplies	1,485	
Office supplies	560	
Prepaid insurance	2,380	
Store equipment	37,520	
Accumulated depreciation, store equipment		$ 6,115
Office equipment	7,925	
Accumulated depreciation, office equipment		1,835
Accounts payable		2,560
Salaries payable		–0–
Income taxes payable		–0–
Common stock, $5 par value		50,000
Retained earnings		8,560
Sales		367,840
Sales returns and allowances	2,990	
Purchases	254,680	
Purchases returns and allowances		1,280
Purchases discounts		2,875
Transportation-in	2,950	
Sales salaries expense	26,350	
Rent expense, selling space	13,500	
Store supplies expense	–0–	
Depreciation expense, store equipment	–0–	
Office salaries expense	27,930	
Rent expense, office space	1,500	
Office supplies expense	–0–	
Insurance expense	–0–	
Depreciation expense, office equipment	–0–	
Income taxes expense	4,000	
Totals	$441,065	$441,065

Problem 5-6A

Prepare general journal entries to record the following transactions:

Oct. 1 Purchased merchandise on credit, terms 2/10, n/30, $4,800.
       2 Sold merchandise for cash, $500.
       6 Purchased merchandise on credit, terms 2/10, n/30, $3,500.
       6 Paid $150 cash for freight charges on the merchandise shipment
          of the previous transaction.
       7 Purchased delivery equipment on credit, $8,000.
      13 Sold merchandise on credit, terms 2/15, 1/30, n/60, $2,000.
      14 Received a $500 credit memorandum for merchandise purchased
          on October 6 and returned for credit.
      14 Purchased office supplies on credit, $160.
      16 Sold merchandise on credit, terms 2/10, 1/30, n/60, $1,400.
      16 Paid for the merchandise purchased on October 6, less the return
          and the discount.
      17 Received a credit memorandum for unsatisfactory office supplies
          purchased on October 14 and returned, $40.
      20 Issued a $140 credit memorandum to the customer who
          purchased merchandise on October 16 and returned a portion
          for credit.
      26 Received payment for the merchandise sold on October 16, less
          the return and applicable discount.
      28 The customer of October 13 paid for the purchase of that date,
          less the applicable discount.
      31 Paid for the merchandise purchased on October 1.

□ **Provocative Problems**

Provocative Problem 5-1   Jed's Nursery

Jed Larkin and Sam Reed were partners in a nursery. They disagreed,
closed the business, and ended their partnership. In settlement for his
partnership interest, Jed Larkin received an inventory of trees, plants, and
garden supplies having a $15,000 cost. Since there was nothing practical
he could do with the inventory, except to open a new nursery, he did so
by investing the inventory and $12,000 in cash. He used $10,000 of the
cash to buy equipment, and he opened for business on March 1. During
the succeeding 10 months, he paid out $42,500 to creditors for additional
trees, plants, and garden supplies and $14,000 in operating expenses. He
also withdrew $12,000 for personal expenses, and at the year-end, he
prepared the balance sheet that follows.

Jed's Nursery
Balance Sheet
December 31, 19—

Cash		$ 3,700	Accounts payable (all for		
Merchandise inventory		17,700	merchandise)		$ 2,200
Equipment	$10,000		Jed Larkin, capital		28,400
Less depreciation .	800	9,200			
			Total liabilities and		
Total assets		$30,600	owner's equity		$30,600

Based on the information given, prepare calculations to determine the net income earned by the business, the cost of goods sold, and the amount of its sales. Then prepare an income statement showing the result of the nursery's operations during its first 10 months.

Provocative Problem 5-2   Southgate Store

The 198B financial statements of Southgate Store were completed just before closing time yesterday. Ted Allen, the store's owner, took the statements home last night to examine but was unable to do so because of unexpected guests. This morning, he inadvertently left the 198B income statement at home when he came to work. However, he has the store's 198A and 198B balance sheets, which show the following in condensed form:

| | December 31 | |
	198A	198B
Cash	$ 2,500	$ 8,100
Accounts receivable	6,200	7,300
Merchandise inventory	30,400	20,500
Equipment (net after depreciation)	24,800	20,600
Total assets	$63,900	$64,500
Accounts payable	$ 9,300	$ 8,200
Accrued wages payable.	300	500
Ted Allen, capital.	54,300	55,800
Total liabilities and owner's equity	$63,900	$64,500

He also has the store's record of cash receipts and disbursements which shows:

Collection of accounts receivable. . . .	$268,400	
Payments for:		
Accounts payable		$166,200
Employees' wages		48,100
Other operating expenses		18,500
Ted Allen, withdrawals		30,000

Under the assumption that the store makes all purchases and sales on credit, prepare calculations to determine the 198B amounts of its accrual basis sales, purchases, and wages expense. Then prepare a 198B accrual basis income statement for the store.

Provocative Problem 5-3   Elmer's Paints

Elmer Wells worked in the bank in Hidden Valley for 20 years, until his aunt died, leaving him a comfortable estate. After sitting around for a year, doing little except being bored and watching his bank balance dwindle, he decided to open a retail paint store. At the time he began business, Hidden Valley had no such store, and it appeared to Elmer that such a business would be successful.

He began by depositing $35,000 in a bank account opened in the name of the business, Elmer's Paints. He then bought store equipment costing

$8,000, for which he paid cash. He expected the equipment to last 10 years, after which it would be valueless. He also bought a stock of merchandise costing $25,000, which he paid for with cash, and he paid the rent on the store space for six months in advance, $2,400.

He estimated that like stores in neighboring communities marked their goods for sale at prices averaging 35% above cost. In other words, an item that cost $10 was marked for sale at $13.50. In order to get his store off to a good start, he decided to mark his merchandise for sale at 30% above cost. Since his overhead would be low, he thought this would still leave a net income equal to 10% of sales.

Today, December 1, six months after opening his store, Elmer has come to you for advice. He thinks business has been good. He has replaced his inventory three times during the six months. He has paid his suppliers for all purchases when due and owes only for purchases, $7,900, made during the past 30 days and for which payment is not due. An income statement he has prepared for the six months ended November 30 shows a $22,500 gross profit and a $10,300 net income. However, you note that he has not charged any depreciation on his equipment. He says he has a full stock of merchandise that cost $25,000 and customers owe him $19,400. He explained that, since Hidden Valley is a small community and he personally knew all of his customers, he was generous in granting credit. In addition to the rent paid in advance, he has paid all his other expenses, $9,800, with cash.

Nevertheless, Elmer doubts the validity of his gross profit and net income figures, since he started business with $35,000 in cash, now has only $800 left, and owes $7,900 for merchandise purchased on credit.

Prepare an income statement for the business covering the six-month period ended November 30, a November 30 balance sheet, and a statement of cash receipts and disbursements accounting for the $800 ending cash balance of the business. (Hint: Begin by determining the various statement items. Then put the statements together.)

6 Accounting Systems

After studying Chapter 6, you should be able to:

1. Explain how columnar journals save posting labor.

2. State what type of transaction is recorded in each columnar journal described in the chapter.

3. Explain how a controlling account and its subsidiary ledger operate and give the rule for posting to a subsidiary ledger and its controlling account.

4. Record transactions in and post from the columnar journals described.

5. Explain how the accuracy of the account balances in the Accounts Receivable and Accounts Payable Ledgers is proved and be able to make such a proof.

6. Describe how data is processed in a large business.

7. Define or explain the words and phrases listed in the chapter Glossary.

An **accounting system** consists of the business papers, records, reports, and procedures that are used by a business in recording transactions and reporting their effects. Operation of an accounting system includes three important steps: (1) the quantities, dollar amounts, and other important data relating to business transactions must be captured on business papers or source documents; (2) the data contained in the source documents must be classified and recorded in the accounting records; and (3) the resulting information must be summarized in timely reports to management and other interested parties.

Even in relatively small businesses, the quantity of data that is processed through the accounting system is very large. As a result, the accounting system must be designed in a manner that allows the data to be processed efficiently.

The focus of Chapter 6 is to introduce some general procedures and techniques that are used in accounting systems to efficiently process data. The chapter begins with a discussion of techniques that are used primarily in manual, or pen-and-ink, accounting systems. Students should understand that the basic concepts introduced in this discussion are generally applicable to both manual and computerized accounting systems. Later in the chapter, the discussion turns specifically to electronic and computerized accounting systems.

■ Reducing Writing and Posting Labor

The General Journal used thus far is a flexible journal in which it is possible to record any transaction. However, each debit and credit entered in such a journal must be individually posted. Consequently, using a General Journal to record all the transactions of a business results in too much writing and too much labor in posting the individual debits and credits.

One way to reduce the writing and the posting labor is to divide the transactions of a business into groups of similar transactions and to provide a separate **special journal** for recording the transactions in each group. For example, if the transactions of a merchandising business are examined, the majority fall into four groups. They are sales on credit, purchases on credit, cash receipts, and cash disbursements. If a special journal is provided for each group, the journals are:

1. A Sales Journal for recording credit sales.
2. A Purchases Journal for recording credit purchases.
3. A Cash Receipts Journal for recording cash receipts.
4. A Cash Disbursements Journal for recording cash payments.

In addition, a General Journal must be provided for the few miscellaneous transactions that cannot be recorded in the special journals and also for adjusting, closing, and correcting entries.

Special journals require less writing in recording transactions than does a General Journal, as the following illustrations will show. In addition, they save posting labor by providing special columns for accumulating the debits and credits of similar transactions. The amounts entered in the special columns are then posted as column totals rather than as individual amounts. For example, if credit sales for a month are recorded in a Sales Journal like the one at the top of Illustration 6-1, posting labor is saved by waiting until the end of the month, totaling the sales recorded

Illustration 6-1

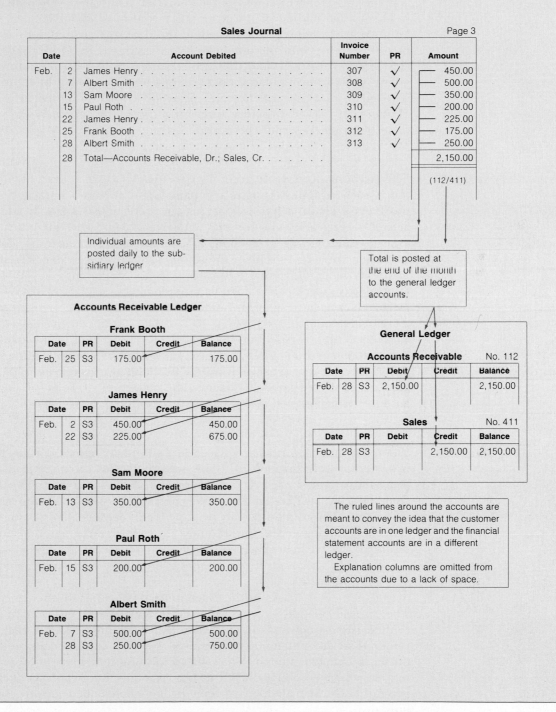

in the journal, and debiting Accounts Receivable and crediting Sales for the total.

Only seven sales are recorded in the illustrated journal. However, if the seven sales are assumed to represent 700 sales, a better appreciation is gained of the posting labor saved by the one debit to Accounts Receivable and the one credit to Sales, rather than 700 debits and 700 credits.

The special journal of Illustration 6-1 is also called a **columnar journal** because it has columns for recording the date, the customer's name, the invoice number, and the amount of each charge sale. Only charge sales can be recorded in it, and they are recorded daily, with the information about each sale being placed on a separate line. Normally, the information is taken from a copy of the sales ticket or invoice prepared at the time of the sale. However, before discussing the journal further, the subject of **subsidiary ledgers** must be introduced.

■ Subsidiary Ledgers

The Accounts Receivable account used thus far does not readily tell how much each customer bought and paid for or how much each customer owes. As a result, a business selling on credit must maintain additional accounts receivable, one for each customer, to provide this information. One possible means of keeping a separate account receivable for each customer would be to replace the single Accounts Receivable account with many accounts. However, this usually is not done. Instead, an account for each customer is maintained in a supplemental record called a **subsidiary ledger.** This collection of customer accounts may exist on tape or disk storage in a computerized system. In a manual system, the **Accounts Receivable Ledger** (subsidiary ledger) may take the form of a book or tray containing the customer accounts. In either case, the customer accounts in the subsidiary ledger are kept separate from the Accounts Receivable account, which appears in the financial statement. The collection of financial statement accounts is maintained in a separate record called the **General Ledger.**

■ Posting the Sales Journal

When customer accounts are placed in a subsidiary ledger, a Sales Journal is posted as in Illustration 6-1. The individual sales recorded in the Sales Journal are posted each day to the proper customer accounts in the Accounts Receivable Ledger. These daily postings keep the customer accounts up-to-date. This is important in granting credit because the person responsible for granting credit should know in each case the amount currently owed by the credit-seeking customer. The source of this information is the customer's account. If the account is not up-to-date, an incorrect decision may be made.

Note the check marks in the Sales Journal's Posting Reference column. They indicate that the sales recorded in the journal were individually posted to the customer accounts in the Accounts Receivable Ledger. Check marks rather than account numbers are used because customer accounts may not be numbered. Rather, as an aid in locating individual accounts, they may be alphabetically arranged in the Accounts Receivable Ledger, with new accounts being added in their proper alphabetical positions as required.

In addition to the daily postings to customer accounts, at the end of the month, the Sales Journal's Amount column is totaled and the total is debited to Accounts Receivable and credited to Sales. The credit records the month's revenue from charge sales. The debit records the resulting increase in accounts receivable.

Before going on, note again in Illustration 6-1 that the individual customer accounts in the subsidiary Accounts Receivable Ledger do not replace the Accounts Receivable account described in previous chapters but are in addition to it. The Accounts Receivable account must still be maintained in the General Ledger where it serves three functions: (1) It shows the total amount owed by all customers. (2) It allows the General Ledger to be a balancing ledger in which debits equal credits. (3) It offers a proof of the accuracy of the customer accounts in the subsidiary Accounts Receivable Ledger.

■ Identifying Posted Amounts

When several journals are posted to ledger accounts, it is necessary to indicate in the Posting Reference column before each posted amount the journal as well as the page number of the journal from which the amount was posted. The journal is indicated by using its initial. Thus, items posted from the Cash Disbursements Journal carry the initial "D" before their journal page numbers in the Posting Reference columns. Likewise, items from the Cash Receipts Journal carry the letter "R." Those from the Sales Journal carry the initial "S." Items from the Purchases Journal carry the initial "P," and from the General Journal, the letter "G."

■ Controlling Accounts

When a company maintains an Accounts Receivable account in its General Ledger and puts its customer accounts in a subsidiary ledger, the Accounts Receivable account is said to control the subsidiary ledger and is called a **controlling account.** The extent of the control is that after all posting is completed, if no errors were made, the sum of the customer account balances in the subsidiary ledger will equal the balance of the controlling account in the General Ledger. This equality is also a proof of the total of the customer account balances.

■ Cash Receipts Journal

A Cash Receipts Journal designed to save labor through posting column totals must be a multicolumn journal. A multicolumn journal is necessary because cash receipts differ as to sources and, consequently, as to the accounts credited when cash is received from different sources. For example, if the cash receipts of a store are classified as to sources, they normally fall into three groups: (1) cash from charge customers in payment of their accounts, (2) cash from cash sales, and (3) cash from miscellaneous sources. Note in Illustration 6-2 (on the next page) how a special column is provided for the credits resulting when cash is received from each of these sources.

Cash from Charge Customers

When a Cash Receipts Journal like Illustration 6-2 is used in recording cash received from a customer in payment of the customer's account, the customer's name is entered in the journal's Account Credited column. The amount credited to the customer's account is entered in the Accounts Receivable Credit column, and the debits to Sales Discounts and Cash are entered in the journal's last two columns.

Give close attention to the Accounts Receivable Credit column. Observe that (1) only credits to customer accounts are entered in this column. (2)

Illustration 6-2

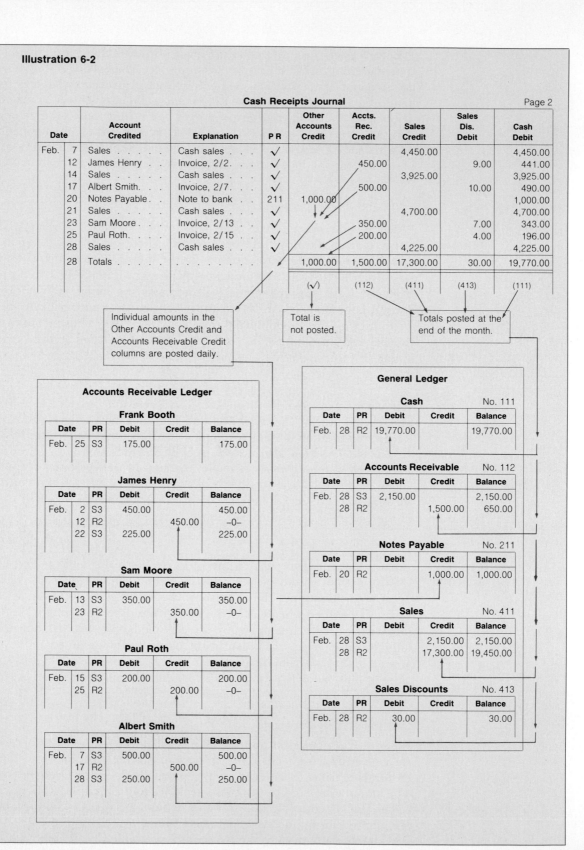

Cash Receipts Journal   Page 2

Date		Account Credited	Explanation	P R	Other Accounts Credit	Accts. Rec. Credit	Sales Credit	Sales Dis. Debit	Cash Debit
Feb.	7	Sales	Cash sales . . .	✓			4,450.00		4,450.00
	12	James Henry . .	Invoice, 2/2. . .	✓		450.00		9.00	441.00
	14	Sales	Cash sales . . .	✓			3,925.00		3,925.00
	17	Albert Smith. . .	Invoice, 2/7. . .	✓		500.00		10.00	490.00
	20	Notes Payable . .	Note to bank . .	211	1,000.00				1,000.00
	21	Sales	Cash sales . . .	✓			4,700.00		4,700.00
	23	Sam Moore . . .	Invoice, 2/13 . .	✓		350.00		7.00	343.00
	25	Paul Roth. . . .	Invoice, 2/15 . .	✓		200.00		4.00	196.00
	28	Sales	Cash sales . . .	✓			4,225.00		4,225.00
	28	Totals	. . . .		1,000.00	1,500.00	17,300.00	30.00	19,770.00
					(✓)	(112)	(411)	(413)	(111)

Individual amounts in the Other Accounts Credit and Accounts Receivable Credit columns are posted daily.

Total is not posted.

Totals posted at the end of the month.

Accounts Receivable Ledger

Frank Booth

Date		PR	Debit	Credit	Balance
Feb.	25	S3	175.00		175.00

James Henry

Date		PR	Debit	Credit	Balance
Feb.	2	S3	450.00		450.00
	12	R2		450.00	–0–
	22	S3	225.00		225.00

Sam Moore

Date		PR	Debit	Credit	Balance
Feb.	13	S3	350.00		350.00
	23	R2		350.00	–0–

Paul Roth

Date		PR	Debit	Credit	Balance
Feb.	15	S3	200.00		200.00
	25	R2		200.00	–0–

Albert Smith

Date		PR	Debit	Credit	Balance
Feb.	7	S3	500.00		500.00
	17	R2		500.00	–0–
	28	S3	250.00		250.00

General Ledger

Cash   No. 111

Date		PR	Debit	Credit	Balance
Feb.	28	R2	19,770.00		19,770.00

Accounts Receivable   No. 112

Date		PR	Debit	Credit	Balance
Feb.	28	S3	2,150.00		2,150.00
	28	R2		1,500.00	650.00

Notes Payable   No. 211

Date		PR	Debit	Credit	Balance
Feb.	20	R2		1,000.00	1,000.00

Sales   No. 411

Date		PR	Debit	Credit	Balance
Feb.	28	S3		2,150.00	2,150.00
	28	R2		17,300.00	19,450.00

Sales Discounts   No. 413

Date		PR	Debit	Credit	Balance
Feb.	28	R2	30.00		30.00

The individual credits are posted daily to the customer accounts in the subsidiary Accounts Receivable Ledger. (3) The column total is posted at the month-end to the credit of the Accounts Receivable controlling account. This is the normal recording and posting procedure when controlling accounts and subsidiary ledgers are used. When such accounts and ledgers are used, transactions are normally entered in a journal column. The individual amounts are then posted to the subsidiary ledger accounts, and the column total is posted to the controlling account.

Cash Sales

Cash sales are commonly "rung up" each day on one or more cash registers, and their total is recorded each day with an entry having a debit to Cash and a credit to Sales. When such sales are recorded in a Cash Receipts Journal like that of Illustration 6-2, the debits to Cash are entered in the Cash Debit column, and a special column headed "Sales Credit" is provided for the credits to Sales. By entering each day's cash sales in this column, the cash sales of a month may be posted at the month's end in a single amount, the column total. (Although cash sales are normally recorded daily from the cash register reading, the cash sales of Illustration 6-2 are recorded only once each week in order to shorten the illustration.)

At the time daily cash sales are recorded in the Cash Receipts Journal, some bookkeepers, as in Illustration 6-2, place a check mark in the Posting Reference (PR) column to indicate that no amount is individually posted from that line of the journal. Other bookkeepers use a double check (√√) to distinguish amounts not posted from amounts posted to customer accounts.

Miscellaneous Receipts of Cash

Most cash receipts are from collections of accounts receivable and from cash sales. However, other sources of cash include less frequent transactions such as borrowing money from a bank in exchange for a promissory note or selling unneeded assets for cash. For miscellaneous receipts such as these, the Other Accounts credit column is provided. In an average company, the items entered in this column are few and are posted to a variety of general ledger accounts. As a result, postings are less apt to be omitted if these items are also posted daily.

The Cash Receipts Journal's Posting Reference column is used only for daily postings from the Other Accounts and Accounts Receivable columns. The account numbers appearing in the column indicate items posted to general ledger accounts. The check marks indicate either that an item like a day's cash sales was not posted or that an item was posted to the subsidiary Accounts Receivable Ledger.

Month-End Postings

The amounts in the Accounts Receivable, Sales, Sales Discounts, and Cash columns of the Cash Receipts Journal are posted as column totals at the end of the month. However, the transactions recorded in any journal must result in equal debits and credits to general ledger accounts. Consequently, debit and credit equality in a columnar journal such as the Cash Receipts Journal is proved by **crossfooting** or cross adding the column totals before they are posted. To **foot** a column of numbers is to add it. To crossfoot the Cash Receipts Journal, the debit column totals are added together, the credit column totals are added together, and the two sums are compared for equality. For Illustration 6-2, the two sums appear as follows:

Debit Columns		Credit Columns	
Sales discounts debit	$ 30	Other accounts credit	$ 1,000
Cash debit	19,770	Accounts receivable credit . . .	1,500
		Sales credit	17,300
Total	$19,800	Total	$19,800

And since the sums are equal, the debits in the journal are assumed to equal the credits.

After the debit and credit equality is proved by crossfooting, the totals of the last four columns are posted as indicated in each column heading. As for the Other Accounts column, since the individual items in this column are posted daily, the column total is not posted. Note in Illustration 6-2 the check mark below the Other Accounts column. The check mark indicates that the column total was not posted. The account numbers of the accounts to which the remaining column totals were posted are indicated in parentheses below each column.

Posting items daily from the Other Accounts column with a delayed posting of the offsetting items in the Cash column (total) causes the General Ledger to be out of balance throughout the month. However, this is of no consequence because before the trial balance is prepared, the offsetting amounts reach the General Ledger in posting the Cash column total.

■ **Posting Rule**

Posting to a subsidiary ledger and its controlling account from two journals has been demonstrated, and a rule to cover all such postings can now be given. The rule is: **In posting to a subsidiary ledger and its controlling account, the controlling account must be debited periodically for an amount or amounts equal to the sum of the debits to the subsidiary ledger, and it must be credited periodically for an amount or amounts equal to the sum of the credits to the subsidiary ledger.**

■ **Creditor Accounts**

As with accounts receivable, the Accounts Payable account used thus far does not show how much is owed each creditor. As a result, to secure this information, an individual account, one for each creditor, must be maintained. These creditor accounts are commonly kept in an **Accounts Payable Ledger** that is controlled by an Accounts Payable controlling account in the General Ledger. Also, the controlling account, subsidiary ledger, and columnar journal techniques demonstrated thus far with accounts receivable apply to the creditor accounts. The only difference is that a Purchases Journal and a Cash Disbursements Journal are used in recording most of the transactions affecting these accounts.

■ **Purchases Journal**

A Purchases Journal having one money column may be used to record purchases of merchandise on credit. However, a multicolumn journal in which purchases of both merchandise and supplies can be recorded is commonly preferred. Such a journal may have the columns shown in Illustration 6-3. In the illustrated journal, the invoice date and terms together indicate the date on which payment for each purchase is due. The Accounts Payable credit column is used to record the amounts credited to each creditor's account. These amounts are posted daily to the individual creditor accounts in the Accounts Payable Ledger. The column total is posted to the Accounts Payable controlling account at the month-end. The items purchased are recorded in the debit columns and are posted in the column totals.

■ **The Cash Disbursements Journal and Its Posting**

The Cash Disbursements Journal, like the Cash Receipts Journal, has columns that make it possible to post repetitive debits and credits in column totals. The repetitive debits and credits of cash payments are debits to the Accounts Payable controlling account and credits to both Purchases Discounts and Cash. In most companies, the purchase of merchandise for cash is not common; therefore, a Purchases column is not needed and a cash purchase is recorded as on line 2 of Illustration 6-4.

Observe that the illustrated journal has a column headed Check Number (Ch. No.). In order to gain control over cash disbursements, all such disbursements, except petty cash disbursements, should be made by check. (Petty cash disbursements are discussed in the next chapter.) The checks should be prenumbered by the printer and should be entered in the journal in numerical order with each check's number in the column headed Ch. No. This makes it possible to scan the numbers in the column for omitted checks. When a Cash Disbursements Journal has a column for check numbers, it is often called a **Check Register.**

A Cash Disbursements Journal or Check Register like Illustration 6-4 is posted as follows. The individual amounts in the Other Accounts column are posted daily to the debit of the general ledger accounts named. The individual amounts in the Accounts Payable column are posted daily to the subsidiary Accounts Payable Ledger to the debit of the creditors named. At the end of the month, after the column totals are crossfooted to prove their equality, the Accounts Payable column total is posted to the debit of the Accounts Payable controlling account. The Purchases Discounts column total is credited to the Purchases Discounts account, and the Cash column total is credited to the Cash account. Since the items in the Other Accounts column are posted individually, the column total is not posted.

■ **Proving the Ledgers**

Periodically, after all posting is completed, the General Ledger and the subsidiary ledgers are proved. The General Ledger is normally proved first by preparing a trial balance. If the trial balance balances, the accounts

Illustration 6-3

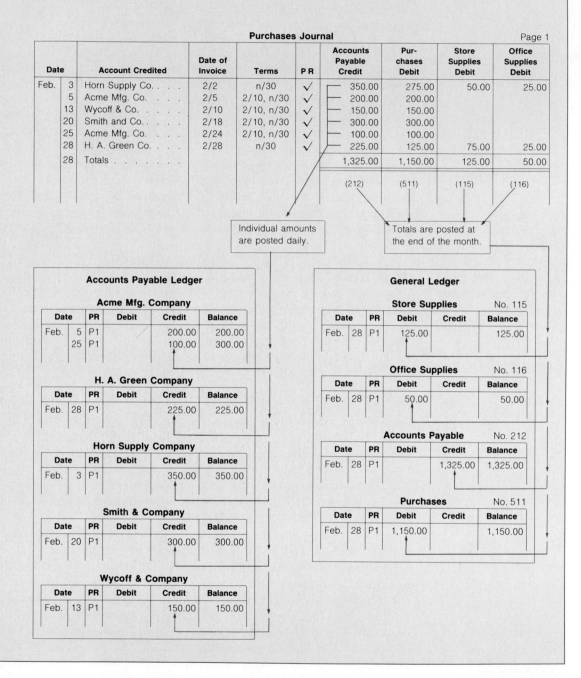

Purchases Journal — Page 1

Date		Account Credited	Date of Invoice	Terms	P R	Accounts Payable Credit	Purchases Debit	Store Supplies Debit	Office Supplies Debit
Feb.	3	Horn Supply Co. . . .	2/2	n/30	✓	350.00	275.00	50.00	25.00
	5	Acme Mfg. Co. . . .	2/5	2/10, n/30	✓	200.00	200.00		
	13	Wycoff & Co.	2/10	2/10, n/30	✓	150.00	150.00		
	20	Smith and Co.	2/18	2/10, n/30	✓	300.00	300.00		
	25	Acme Mfg. Co. . . .	2/24	2/10, n/30	✓	100.00	100.00		
	28	H. A. Green Co. . . .	2/28	n/30	✓	225.00	125.00	75.00	25.00
	28	Totals				1,325.00	1,150.00	125.00	50.00
						(212)	(511)	(115)	(116)

Individual amounts are posted daily.

Totals are posted at the end of the month.

Accounts Payable Ledger

Acme Mfg. Company

Date		PR	Debit	Credit	Balance
Feb.	5	P1		200.00	200.00
	25	P1		100.00	300.00

H. A. Green Company

Date		PR	Debit	Credit	Balance
Feb.	28	P1		225.00	225.00

Horn Supply Company

Date		PR	Debit	Credit	Balance
Feb.	3	P1		350.00	350.00

Smith & Company

Date		PR	Debit	Credit	Balance
Feb.	20	P1		300.00	300.00

Wycoff & Company

Date		PR	Debit	Credit	Balance
Feb.	13	P1		150.00	150.00

General Ledger

Store Supplies — No. 115

Date		PR	Debit	Credit	Balance
Feb.	28	P1	125.00		125.00

Office Supplies — No. 116

Date		PR	Debit	Credit	Balance
Feb.	28	P1	50.00		50.00

Accounts Payable — No. 212

Date		PR	Debit	Credit	Balance
Feb.	28	P1		1,325.00	1,325.00

Purchases — No. 511

Date		PR	Debit	Credit	Balance
Feb.	28	P1	1,150.00		1,150.00

in the General Ledger, including the controlling accounts, are assumed to be correct. The subsidiary ledgers are then proved, commonly by preparing schedules of accounts receivable and accounts payable. A **schedule of accounts payable,** for example, is prepared by listing with their balances the accounts in the Accounts Payable Ledger having balances. The balances

Illustration 6-4

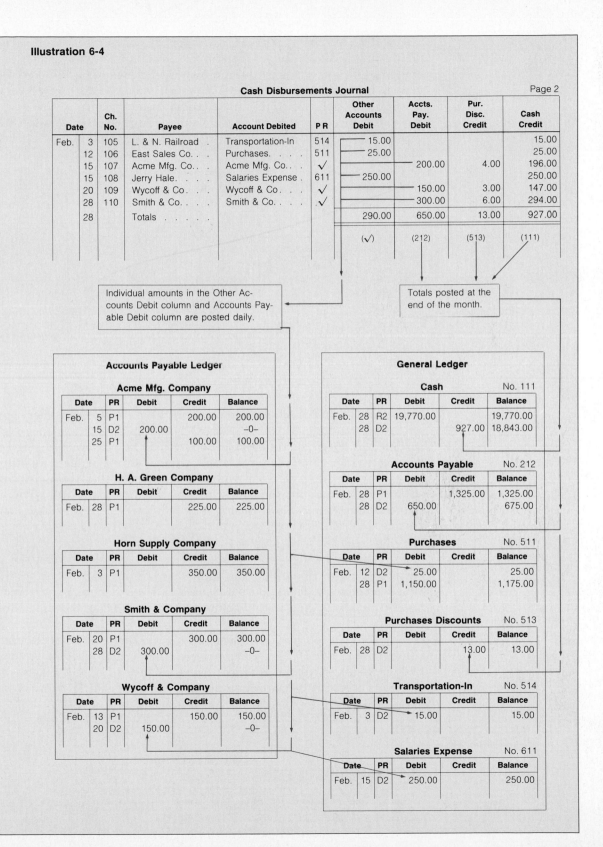

Cash Disbursements Journal   Page 2

Date	Ch. No.	Payee	Account Debited	P R	Other Accounts Debit	Accts. Pay. Debit	Pur. Disc. Credit	Cash Credit
Feb. 3	105	L. & N. Railroad .	Transportation-In	514	15.00			15.00
12	106	East Sales Co. . .	Purchases. . . .	511	25.00			25.00
15	107	Acme Mfg. Co. . .	Acme Mfg. Co. . .	✓		200.00	4.00	196.00
15	108	Jerry Hale. . . .	Salaries Expense .	611	250.00			250.00
20	109	Wycoff & Co. . .	Wycoff & Co. . .	✓		150.00	3.00	147.00
28	110	Smith & Co. . . .	Smith & Co. . . .	✓		300.00	6.00	294.00
28		Totals			290.00	650.00	13.00	927.00
					(✓)	(212)	(513)	(111)

Individual amounts in the Other Accounts Debit column and Accounts Payable Debit column are posted daily.

Totals posted at the end of the month.

Accounts Payable Ledger

Acme Mfg. Company

Date	PR	Debit	Credit	Balance
Feb. 5	P1		200.00	200.00
15	D2	200.00		–0–
25	P1		100.00	100.00

H. A. Green Company

Date	PR	Debit	Credit	Balance
Feb. 28	P1		225.00	225.00

Horn Supply Company

Date	PR	Debit	Credit	Balance
Feb. 3	P1		350.00	350.00

Smith & Company

Date	PR	Debit	Credit	Balance
Feb. 20	P1		300.00	300.00
28	D2	300.00		–0–

Wycoff & Company

Date	PR	Debit	Credit	Balance
Feb. 13	P1		150.00	150.00
20	D2	150.00		–0–

General Ledger

Cash   No. 111

Date	PR	Debit	Credit	Balance
Feb. 28	R2	19,770.00		19,770.00
28	D2		927.00	18,843.00

Accounts Payable   No. 212

Date	PR	Debit	Credit	Balance
Feb. 28	P1		1,325.00	1,325.00
28	D2	650.00		675.00

Purchases   No. 511

Date	PR	Debit	Credit	Balance
Feb. 12	D2	25.00		25.00
28	P1	1,150.00		1,175.00

Purchases Discounts   No. 513

Date	PR	Debit	Credit	Balance
Feb. 28	D2		13.00	13.00

Transportation-In   No. 514

Date	PR	Debit	Credit	Balance
Feb. 3	D2	15.00		15.00

Salaries Expense   No. 611

Date	PR	Debit	Credit	Balance
Feb. 15	D2	250.00		250.00

are totaled; and if the total is equal to the balance of the Accounts Payable controlling account, the accounts in the Accounts Payable Ledger are assumed to be correct. Illustration 6-5 shows a schedule of the creditor accounts having balances in the Accounts Payable Ledger of Illustration 6-4. Note that the schedule total is equal to the balance of the Accounts Payable controlling account in the General Ledger of Illustration 6-4. A **schedule of accounts receivable** is prepared in the same way as a schedule of accounts payable. Also, if its total is equal to the balance of the Accounts Receivable controlling account, the accounts in the Accounts Receivable Ledger are assumed to be correct.

Illustration 6-5

Hawaiian Sales Company
Schedule of Accounts Payable
December 31, 19—

Acme Mfg. Company	$100
H. A. Green Company	225
Horn Supply Company	350
Total accounts payable	$675

Instead of a formal schedule to prove the accounts in a subsidiary ledger, an adding machine list may be used. For example, the balances of the accounts in the Accounts Payable Ledger may be proved by listing on an adding machine the balance of each account in the ledger, totaling the list, and comparing the total with the balance of the Accounts Payable controlling account. A similar list may be used to prove the accounts in the Accounts Receivable Ledger.

Sales Taxes

Many cities and states require retailers to collect sales taxes from their customers and periodically remit these taxes to the city or state treasurer. When a columnar Sales Journal is used, a record of taxes collected can be obtained by adding special columns in the journal as shown in Illustration 6-6.

In posting the journal, the individual amounts in the Accounts Receivable column are posted daily to customer accounts in the Accounts Receivable Ledger, and the column total is posted at the end of the month to the Accounts Receivable controlling account. The individual amounts in the

Illustration 6-6

Sales Journal

Date		Account Debited	Invoice Number	P R	Accounts Receivable Debit	Sales Taxes Payable Credit	Sales Credit
Dec.	1	D. R. Horn . . .	7-1698		103.00	3.00	100.00

Sales Taxes Payable and Sales columns are not posted. However, at the end of the month the total of the Sales Taxes Payable column is credited to the Sales Taxes Payable account, and the total of the Sales column is credited to Sales.

A concern making cash sales upon which sales taxes are collected may add a special Sales Taxes Payable column in its Cash Receipts Journal.

■ Sales Invoices as a Sales Journal

To save labor, many companies do not enter charge sales in a Sales Journal. These companies post each sales invoice total directly to the customer's account in a subsidiary Accounts Receivable Ledger. Copies of the invoices are then bound in numerical order in a binder. At the end of the month, all the invoices of that month are totaled, and a general journal entry is made debiting Accounts Receivable and crediting Sales for the total. In effect, the bound invoice copies act as a Sales Journal. Such a procedure is known as direct posting of sales invoices.

■ Sales Returns

A company having only a few sales returns may record them in a General Journal with an entry like the following:

Oct.	17	Sales Returns and Allowances	412	17.50	
		Accounts Receivable—George Ball	112/√		17.50
		Customer returned merchandise.			

The debit of the entry is posted to the Sales Returns and Allowances account. The credit is posted to both the Accounts Receivable controlling account and to the customer's account. Note the account number and the check, 112/√, in the PR column on the credit line. This indicates that both the Accounts Receivable controlling account in the General Ledger and the George Ball account in the Accounts Receivable Ledger were credited for $17.50. Both were credited because the balance of the controlling account in the General Ledger will not equal the sum of the customer account balances in the subsidiary ledger unless both are credited.

Companies having sufficient sales returns can save posting labor by recording them in a special Sales Returns and Allowances Journal like that of Illustration 6-7. Note that this is in keeping with the generally recognized

Illustration 6-7

Sales Returns and Allowances Journal

Date		Account Credited	Explanation	Credit Memo No.	P R	Amount
Oct.	7	Robert Moore . . .	Defective mdse. . .	203	√	10.00
	14	James Warren . . .	Defective mdse. . .	204	√	12.00
	18	T. M. Jones	Not ordered	205	√	6.00
	23	Sam Smith	Defective mdse. . .	206	√	18.00
	31	Sales Returns and Allowances, Dr.; Accts. Receivable, Cr.				46.00
						412/112

idea that a company can design and use a special journal for any group of like transactions in which there are within the group sufficient transactions to warrant the journal. When a Sales Returns and Allowances Journal is used to record returns, the amounts entered in the journal are posted daily to the credit of each affected customer account. At the end of the month, the journal total is debited to Sales Returns and Allowances and credited to Accounts Receivable.

■ **General Journal Entries**

When columnar journals like the ones described are used, a General Journal must be provided for adjusting, closing, and correcting entries and for a few transactions that cannot be recorded in the special journals. Among these transactions, if a Sales Returns and Allowances Journal is not provided, are sales returns, purchases returns, and purchases of plant assets. Illustrative entries for the last two kinds of transactions follow:

Oct.	8	Accounts Payable—Medford Company	212/✓	32.00	
		Purchases Returns and			
		Allowances	512		32.00
		Returned defective merchandise.			
	11	Office Equipment	133	685.00	
		Accounts Payable—ABC Supply Co..	212/✓		685.00
		Purchased a typewriter.			

■ **Machine Methods**

Manual accounting systems like the ones described thus far are used only by small businesses, and an increasing number of these are switching to computerized accounting systems. However, even before computers became widely available, many businesses began to use electronic bookkeeping machines. While these machines are also being replaced by computers, a number of companies continue to use electronic bookkeeping machines.

An electronic bookkeeping machine usually has a typewriter-like keyboard and the keyboard of a 10-key calculator. It also has "function" keys that direct the machine's operation, instructing it to calculate, tabulate, and/or print out stored data. A bookkeeping machine can handle accounting for sales, cash receipts, purchases, cash payments, payroll, and other transactions, as well as posting to the General Ledger.

No attempt will be made here to describe a bookkeeping machine's operation in each of these applications. However, when used in accounting for credit sales, for example, the current page of the Sales Journal is placed in the machine. Then, for each charge sale, the operator puts the customer's account and month-end statement in the machine and depresses the proper keys to enter the information about the sale. The machine makes the entry in the Sales Journal, posts to the customer's account, updates the account balance, enters the sale on the customer's month-end statement, and updates the statement. At the same time, it accumulates the Sales Journal total for the month-end debit to Accounts Receivable and credit to Sales.

Furthermore, it does all of this in one operation from one entry into the machine of the proper data. And, it is equally efficient in handling other kinds of transactions.

Bookkeeping machines speed the processing of accounting data. They also reduce transposition errors by printing the same information on several different records in one operation. However, the speed of operation and the amount of work such a machine can do efficiently are limited. Consequently, many businesses turn to computerized data processing.

■ Computerized Data Processing

Computerized data processing involves the processing of data without human intervention through the use of a machine that is far more powerful and complex than is a bookkeeping machine, a **computer.** A computer is capable of—

1. Inputing and storing data.
2. Performing arithmetic calculations on the data.
3. Comparing units of the data to find which are larger or smaller.
4. Sorting or rearranging data.
5. Printing reports from the data stored in the machine.

Computers vary in size and in the speed with which they process data. They range from small desktop microcomputers to machines that with their peripheral equipment occupy a large room. Peripheral equipment includes devices to input or output data and to store data on reels of magnetic tapes or on magnetic disks.

Data may be entered into a computer by means of a computer terminal, a device that commonly has a typewriter-like keyboard, a 10-key numerical keyboard, and a TV-like screen. Data may also be entered with previously prepared punched cards, reels of magnetic tape, magnetic disks, and in other ways. For example, another means of entry uses a laser light that reads a bar code such as is found on many consumer products. Inside the computer each alphabetical letter or numerical digit of data becomes a combination of electrical or magnetic states that a computer can manipulate at very high rates of speed. Consequently, if of sufficient size, a computer can do 1 million or more additions, subtractions, multiplications, and divisions per second, all without error in a predetermined sequence according to instructions stored in the machine.

A computer can do nothing without a previously prepared set of instructions, called a **program,** that is entered and stored in the computer. However, with a properly prepared program, a computer will accept data, store and process the data, and produce the processed results, perhaps in the form of a report displayed on a TV-like screen, or typed out on an electric typewriter at the rate of approximately 10 characters per second, or printed by a line printer at up to 2,000 lines per minute.

The Program

A **computer program** is a set of instructions written in a language the computer "understands." Some of the widely used languages are COBOL, BASIC, RPG, and FORTRAN. The instructions specify each operation a computer is to perform and are entered into the computer before the data to be processed. The program may contain only a few or several thousand detailed instructions. For example, the following shows the steps that must be programmed to have a computer process customers' orders for merchandise.

Instructions to Be Programmed for Processing Customers' Orders

1. For the first item on the customer's order, compare the quantity ordered with the quantity on hand as shown by inventory data stored in the computer.
    a. If the quantity ordered is not on hand:
        (1) Prepare a back order notifying the customer that the goods are not available but will be shipped as soon as a new supply is received.
        (2) Go to the next item on the customer's order.
    b. If the quantity on hand is greater than the amount ordered:
        (1) Deduct the amount ordered from the amount on hand.
        (2) Prepare instructions to ship the goods.
        (3) Compare the amount of the item remaining after filling the customer's order with the reorder point for the item.
            (a) If the amount remaining is greater than the reorder point:
                1. Go to the next item on the customer's order.
            (b) If the amount remaining is less than the reorder point:
                1. Compute the amount to be purchased and prepare documents for the purchase.
                2. Go to the next item on the customer's order.

In addition to these instructions, a program for processing customer orders would have instructions for preparing invoices, recording sales, and updating customer accounts.

Designing the Program

Computers have the ability to compare two numbers and decide which is larger. This ability makes it possible for the computer to process data one way or another, depending on the result of the comparison. Note that this ability to compare numbers is essential if the computer is to follow instructions such as those for processing customer orders.

If a computer is to process data correctly, a person (the programmer) must first design a program for the computer to follow. In designing the program, the programmer determines in advance the alternative sets of calculations or processing steps to be made. Then, the programmer must devise the appropriate comparisons that will identify the circumstances under which each particular set of processing steps should be performed. Finally, the programmer must write specific instructions telling the computer how to process the data. A computer can follow through the program's maze of decisions and alternate instructions rapidly and accurately. However, if it encounters an exception not anticipated in the program, it is helpless and can only process the exception incorrectly or stop.

The ability to store a program and data and then to race through the maze of decisions and alternate instructions is what distinguishes a computer from an electronic bookkeeping machine. Some electronic bookkeeping machines can do an addition, a multiplication, or a division at the speed of a computer. Yet with all this speed, their operating rates are relatively slow, since they must depend on a person to push their function keys to tell them what to do.

Modes of Operation

Computers operate in one of two modes: either **batch processing** or **online processing.** In the batch mode, the program and data to be processed are inputed to the computer, processed, and then removed from the computer before another batch is begun. Then, the program for a new job and a new set of data are entered, and the new job is processed. Batch processing may result in customers' orders being processed daily, the payroll being run each week, financial statements being prepared monthly, and the processing of other jobs on a periodic basis. Because transactions are processed in groups or batches, this mode of operation may require less computer capacity, is usually less expensive than online operation, and is used when an immediate processing or an immediate computer response is not required.

In online processing, the program is kept in the computer along with any required data. As new data are entered, they are instantly processed by the computer. For example, in some department stores, the cash registers are connected directly into the store's computer. In addition to cash sales, the registers are used as follows in recording charge sales. After the customer selects merchandise for purchase, the salesperson uses the customer's plastic credit card to print the customer's name on a blank sales ticket. The sales ticket is then placed in the Forms Printer of the cash register, and the sale is recorded. The register prints all pertinent information on the sales ticket and totals it. In order to finalize the sale, controls within the register require that the salesperson depress the proper register keys to record the customer's account number. This, in effect, posts the sale to the customer's account. The salesperson does not actually post to the account. Rather, the data entered with the cash register's keys causes the store's computer to update the customer's account. The computer will also produce the customer's month-end statement, ready for mailing.

Another example of online operation is found in supermarkets, where each item of merchandise is imprinted with a machine-readable price tag similar to Illustration 6-8. At one of the store's checkout stands, each item of merchandise selected by a customer is passed over an optical scanner in the countertop, or an optical scanner in a wand is passed over each item's price tag. This actuates the cash register and eliminates the need for handkeying information into the register. It also transmits the sales information to a computer that updates the store's inventory records and prepares orders to a central warehouse to restock any item in low supply. At closing time, the computer prints out detailed summaries of the day's sales and item inventories. It thus provides management with up-to-the-minute information that could not otherwise be obtained.

Other examples of online operations are found in banks, airlines, and

Illustration 6-8

factories. However, all have the same results: they reduce human labor, create more accurate records, and provide management with both better and more up-to-date reports. Furthermore, when there are sufficient transactions, they do the work at less cost per transaction.

Time Sharing

Computer service companies provide computer service to many concerns on a time-sharing basis, using computers that are capable of working on many jobs simultaneously. In providing such service, the computer service company installs an input-output device on the premises of a subscriber to its service. The input-output device is connected to the service company's computer through wires leased from the phone company. The subscriber uses the input-output device to input data into the service company's computer. It is held in storage there until processing time is available, usually within a few seconds. The computer then processes the data and transmits the results to the subscriber. For this service the subscriber pays a monthly fee plus a charge for the computer time used.

Through **time sharing,** a growing number of concerns are using computers, even very small businesses. For example, a dentist or a physician practicing alone is a small business. Yet a significant number of such dentists and physicians have their accounts receivable and customer billing done by computer service companies.

Microcomputers

Another important factor leading to the expanded use of computers is the development of microcomputers. These very small computers have become less expensive in recent years and are now affordable by very small businesses and individuals. As more and more people become proficient in using these machines, manual accounting systems are being replaced by computerized systems.

■ **Recording Actual Transactions**

Transactions may be recorded in a pen-and-ink journal or with a bookkeeping machine or on a computer terminal, depending on the accounting system of the business completing the transactions. Nevertheless, in the remainder of this text, general journal entries will be used to illustrate the recording of most transactions. The general journal entries are intended to show the items increased and decreased by the transactions. The student should recognize that the entries actually would be made in a General Journal, or a columnar special journal, or with a bookkeeping machine or a computer terminal, depending on the accounting system of the business completing the transactions.

SJ — Sale of Mdse on A/c   — A/R —
                                    Sales
CR — Receipt of Cash — Debit to Cash
P — Purchase of Mdse — Off Sup, Stor Sup, on A/c   DR - P, SSOS
                                                     CR - A/P
CD — Payment of cash — Dr. to Cash

□   **Glossary**   **Accounting system** the business papers, records, reports, and procedures used by a business in recording transactions and reporting their effects.

Accounts Payable Ledger a subsidiary ledger having an account for each creditor.

Accounts Receivable Ledger a subsidiary ledger having an account for each customer.

Batch processing a mode of computer operation in which a program and data are entered in the computer, processed, and removed from the computer before the next program and data are entered.

Check Register a book of original entry for recording cash payments by check.

Columnar journal a book of original entry having columns, each of which is designated as the place for entering specific data about each transaction of a group of similar transactions.

Computer a complex electronic machine that has the capacity to store a program of instructions and data, process the data rapidly according to the instructions, and prepare reports showing the results of the processing operation.

Computer program a set of instructions that are entered in a computer and that specify the operations the computer is to perform.

Controlling account a general ledger account the balance of which (after posting) equals the sum of the balances of the accounts in a related subsidiary ledger, thereby proving the sum of those subsidiary account balances.

Crossfoot to add the debit column totals of a journal, add the credit column totals, and then compare the sums to prove that total debits equal total credits.

Foot to add a column of numbers.

General Ledger the ledger containing the financial statement accounts of a business.

Online processing a mode of computer operation in which the program and required data are maintained in the computer so that as new data are entered, they are processed instantly.

Schedule of accounts payable a list of the balances of all the accounts in the accounts payable ledger that is summed to show the total amount of accounts payable outstanding.

Schedule of accounts receivable a list of the balances of all the accounts in the accounts receivable ledger that is summed to show the total amount of accounts receivable outstanding.

Special journal a book of original entry that is designed and used for recording only a specified type of transaction.

Subsidiary ledger a group of accounts other than general ledger accounts which show the details underlying the balance of a controlling account in the General Ledger.

Time sharing a process by which several users of a computer, each having an input-output device, can input data into a single computer and, as processing time becomes available, have their data processed and transmitted back to their output device.

□ **Questions for Class Discussion**

1. What are three steps in the operation of an accounting system?
2. How does a columnar journal save posting labor?
3. Most transactions of a merchandising business fall into four groups. What are these four groups?
4. Why should sales to and receipts of cash from charge customers be recorded and posted daily?
5. What functions are served by the Accounts Receivable controlling account?
6. Both credits to customer accounts and credits to miscellaneous accounts are individually posted from a Cash Receipts Journal like that of Illustration 6-2. Why not put both kinds of credits in the same column and thus save journal space?
7. How is a multicolumn journal crossfooted? Why is such a journal crossfooted?
8. How is the equality of a controlling account and its subsidiary ledger accounts maintained?
9. Describe how copies of a company's sales invoices may be used as a Sales Journal.
10. When a general journal entry is used to record a returned charge sale, the credit of the entry must be posted twice. Does this cause the trial balance to be out of balance? Why or why not?
11. How does one tell from which journal a particular amount in a ledger account was posted?
12. How is a schedule of accounts payable prepared? How is it used to prove the balances of the creditor accounts in the Accounts Payable Ledger? What may be substituted for a formal schedule?
13. After all posting is completed, the balance of the Accounts Receivable controlling account does not agree with the sum of the balances in the Accounts Receivable Ledger. If the trial balance is in balance, where is the error apt to be?
14. Are computerized accounting systems used by small businesses?
15. What are some of the ways data can be entered into a computer?

□ **Class Exercises**

Exercise 6-1

A company that uses a Sales Journal, a Purchases Journal, a Cash Receipts Journal, a Cash Disbursements Journal, and a General Journal like the ones described in the chapter completed the following transactions. List the transactions by letter and opposite each letter give the name of the journal in which the transaction would be recorded.

a. A customer returned merchandise sold for cash; a check was issued.
b. Paid a creditor.
c. Sold merchandise for cash.
d. Sold merchandise on credit.
e. Purchased merchandise on credit.
f. Purchased office supplies on credit.
g. Gave a customer credit for merchandise purchased on credit and returned.

h. A customer paid for merchandise previously purchased on credit.
i. Purchased office equipment on credit.
j. Returned merchandise purchased on credit.
k. Recorded adjusting and closing entries.

Exercise 6-2

A company uses a Sales Journal, a Purchases Journal, a Cash Receipts Journal, a Cash Disbursements Journal, and a General Journal. The following transactions occurred during the month of May.

May 1 Purchased merchandise for $12 on credit from B Company.
  6 Sold merchandise to I. May for $25 cash, Invoice No. 11.
  8 Sold merchandise to J. Clay for $90, terms 2/15, n/60, Invoice No. 12.
  10 Borrowed $15 from the bank by giving a note to the bank.
  13 Sold merchandise to Z. Smith for $60, terms n/30, Invoice No. 13.
  21 Sold used store equipment to F Company for $100.
  23 Received $88.20 from J. Clay to pay for the purchase of May 8.
  30 Sold merchandise to W. Barley for $75, terms n/30, Invoice No. 14.

Required

On a sheet of notebook paper, draw a Sales Journal like the one that appears in Illustration 6-1. Journalize the transactions during May that should be recorded in the Sales Journal.

Exercise 6-3

A company uses a Sales Journal, a Purchases Journal, a Cash Receipts Journal, a Cash Disbursements Journal, and a General Journal. The following transactions occurred during the month of May.

May 1 J. Lay, the owner of the business, invested $20 in the business.
  5 Purchased merchandise for $12 on credit from B Company.
  8 Sold merchandise on credit to R. Dee for $8, subject to a $1 sales discount if paid by the end of the month.
  10 Borrowed $15 from the bank by giving a note to the bank.
  14 Sold merchandise to T. Barnes for $6 cash.
  28 Paid B Company $12 for the merchandise purchased on May 5.
  29 Received $7 from R. Dee to pay for the purchase of May 8.
  31 Paid salaries of $5.

Required

1. On a sheet of notebook paper, draw a multicolumn Cash Receipts Journal like the one that appears in Illustration 6-2. (Dollar amounts in this exercise are small so that you may use narrow columns.)
2. Journalize the transactions during May that should be recorded in the Cash Receipts Journal.

Exercise 6-4

A company uses a Sales Journal, a Purchases Journal, a Cash Receipts Journal, a Cash Disbursements Journal, and a General Journal. The following transactions occurred during the month of May.

May 1 N. Blake, the owner of the business, invested $30 in the business.
2 Purchased merchandise for $14 on credit from M Company, terms n/30.
7 Purchased store supplies from O Company for $3 cash.
9 Sold merchandise on credit to S. Dye for $10, subject to a $1 sales discount if paid by the end of the month.
12 Purchased on credit from C Company office supplies for $4 and store supplies for $7, terms n/30.
19 Sold merchandise to R. Tag for $16 cash.
30 Paid M Company $14 for the merchandise purchased on May 2.

Required

1. On a sheet of notebook paper, draw a multicolumn Purchases Journal like the one that appears in Illustration 6-3. (Dollar amounts in this exercise are small so that you may use narrow columns.)
2. Journalize the transactions during May that should be recorded in the Purchases Journal.

Exercise 6-5

A company uses a Sales Journal, a Purchases Journal, a Cash Receipts Journal, a Cash Disbursements Journal, and a General Journal. The following transactions occurred during the month of May.

May 1 Purchased merchandise for $40 on credit from G Company, terms 2/10, n/30.
3 Purchased merchandise for $50 on credit from K Company, terms 2/15, n/60.
6 Issued Check No. 4 to A Company to buy store supplies for $10.
14 Sold merchandise on credit to H. Fine for $80, terms n/30.
17 Issued Check No. 5 for $35 to repay a note payable to First Bank.
18 Issued Check No. 6 to K Company to pay the amount due for the purchase of May 3, less the discount.
31 Issued Check No. 7 to G Company to pay the amount due for the purchase of May 1.
31 Paid salary of $20 to J. Doaks by issuing Check No. 8.

Required

1. On a sheet of notebook paper, draw a multicolumn Cash Disbursements Journal like the one that appears in Illustration 6-4. (Dollar amounts in this exercise are small so that you may use narrow columns.)
2. Journalize the transactions during May that should be recorded in the Cash Disbursements Journal.

Exercise 6-6

A company uses a Sales Journal, a Purchases Journal, a Cash Receipts Journal, a Cash Disbursements Journal, and a General Journal. The following transactions occurred during the month of May.

May 1   F. Nifty, the owner of the business, invested $100 in the business.
   7   Purchased merchandise for $85 on credit from G Company, terms 2/10, n/30.
   10 F. Nifty, the owner of the business, contributed an automobile worth $500 to the business.
   12 Issued Check No. 4 to A Company to buy store supplies for $10.
   14 Sold merchandise on credit to H. Fine for $80, terms n/30.
   15 Returned $25 of defective merchandise to G Company from the purchase on May 7.
   18 Issued Check No. 6 to K Company to pay the $150 due for a purchase of April 19.
   25 H. Fine returned $30 of merchandise originally purchased on May 15.
   31 Accrued salaries payable of $20.

Required

Journalize the transactions during May that should be recorded in the General Journal.

Exercise 6-7

A company uses the following journals: Sales Journal, Purchases Journal, Cash Receipts Journal, Cash Disbursements Journal, and General Journal. On January 12, the company purchased merchandise priced at $10,000, subject to credit terms of 2/10, n/30. On January 22, the company paid the net amount due. However, in journalizing the payment, the bookkeeper debited the net amount to Accounts Payable and failed to record the cash discount. In what journals would the January 12 and the January 22 transactions have been recorded? What procedure is likely to disclose the error in journalizing the January 22 transaction?

Exercise 6-8

At the end of January, the Sales Journal of Comcraft Company appeared as follows:

Sales Journal

Date		Account Debited	Invoice Number	P R	Amount
Jan.	3	Jane Wilkins. . . .	253	✓	410.00
	8	Rafer Thomas . . .	254	✓	680.00
	14	Nancy Hall	255	✓	570.00
	23	Jane Wilkins. . . .	256	✓	190.00
	31	Total			1,850.00

The company had also recorded the return of merchandise with the following entry:

Jan.	20	Sales Returns and Allowances.	100.00	
		Accounts Receivable—Nancy Hall		100.00
		Customer returned merchandise.		

Required

1. On a sheet of notebook paper, open a subsidiary Accounts Receivable Ledger having a T-account for each customer listed in the Sales Journal. Post to the customer accounts the entries of the Sales Journal and also the portion of the general journal entry that affects a customer's account.

2. Open a General Ledger having T-accounts for Accounts Receivable, Sales, and Sales Returns and Allowances. Post the Sales Journal and the portions of the general journal entry that affect these accounts.

3. Prove the subsidiary ledger accounts with a schedule of accounts receivable.

Exercise 6-9

Drafter Company, a company that posts its sales invoices directly and then binds the invoices to make them into a Sales Journal, had the following sales during August.

Aug.	2	Jill Frantz	. . . .	$ 4,800
	7	Gil Blanken.	. . .	6,600
	15	James Easton	. .	9,600
	19	Gil Blanken.	. . .	13,200
	23	James Easton	. .	4,200
	29	George Dahl	. . .	9,000
		Total	. . . . . .	$47,400

Required

1. On a sheet of notebook paper, open a subsidiary Accounts Receivable Ledger having a T-account for each customer listed above. Post the invoices to the subsidiary ledger.

2. Give the general journal entry to record the end-of-month total of the Sales Journal.

3. Open an Accounts Receivable controlling account and a Sales account and post the general journal entry.

4. Prove the subsidiary Accounts Receivable Ledger with a schedule of accounts receivable.

Exercise 6-10

A company that records credit sales in a Sales Journal and records sales returns in its General Journal made the following errors. List each error by letter, and opposite each letter tell when the error should be discovered:

a. Posted a sales return recorded in the General Journal to the Sales Returns and Allowances account and to the Accounts Receivable account but did not post to the customer's account.

b. Made an addition error in determining the balance of a customer's account.

c. Made an addition error in totaling the Amount column of the Sales Journal.

d. Posted a sales return to the Accounts Receivable account and to the customer's account but did not post to the Sales Returns and Allowances account.

e. Correctly recorded a $200 sale in the Sales Journal but posted it to the customer's account as a $2,000 sale.

Exercise 6-11

Following are the condensed journals of a merchandising concern. The journal column headings are incomplete in that they do not indicate whether the columns are debit or credit columns.

Required

1. Prepare T-accounts on a sheet of ordinary notebook paper for the following general ledger and subsidiary ledger accounts. Separate the accounts of each ledger group as follows:

General Ledger Accounts	Accounts Receivable Ledger Accounts
Cash	Customer A
Accounts Receivable	Customer B
Prepaid Insurance	Customer C
Store Equipment	
Notes Payable	**Accounts Payable Ledger Accounts**
Accounts Payable	Company One
Sales	Company Two
Sales Returns	Company Three
Sales Discounts	
Purchases	
Purchases Returns	
Purchases Discounts	

2. Without referring to any of the illustrations showing complete column headings for the journals, post the following journals to the proper T-accounts.

Sales Journal

Account	Amount
Customer A. . .	3,500
Customer B. . .	5,250
Customer C. . .	7,000
Total.	15,750

Purchases Journal

Account	Amount
Company 1 . .	4,200
Company 2 . .	4,900
Company 3 . .	5,600
Total	14,700

General Journal

. . . .	Sales Returns.	700.00	
	Accounts Receivable—Customer C. . . .		700.00
. .	Accounts Payable—Company 3	1,050.00	
	Purchases Returns.		1,050.00

Cash Receipts Journal

Account	Other Accounts	Accounts Receivable	Sales	Sales Discounts	Cash
Customer A.	. . .	3,500	. . .	70	3,430
Cash Sales.	. . .	. . .	5,075	. . .	5,075
Notes Payable . . .	7,000	. . .	. . .	. . .	7,000
Cash Sales.	. . .	. . .	5,775	. . .	5,775
Customer B.	. . .	5,250	. . .	105	5,145
Store Equipment . . .	525	. . .	. . .	. . .	525
	7,525	8,750	10,850	175	26,950

Cash Disbursements Journal

Account	Other Accounts	Accounts Payable	Purchases Discounts	Cash
Prepaid Insurance . .	350	. . .	. . .	350
Company 2	. . .	4,900	98	4,802
Company 3	. . .	4,550	91	4,459
Store Equipment . . .	1,750	. . .	. . .	1,750
	2,100	9,450	189	11,361

Problems

Problem 6-1

Garfield Company completed these transactions during February of the current year:

Feb. 1 Purchased merchandise on credit from Seattle Company, invoice dated January 31, terms 2/10, n/60, $3,600.

1 Issued Check No. 770 to *The County Reporter* for advertising expense, $385.

2 Sold merchandise on credit to James Asner, Invoice No. 476, $6,450. (The terms of all credit sales are 2/10, n/60.)

3 Purchased on credit from Mason Company merchandise, $5,200; store supplies, $250; and office supplies, $200. Invoice dated February 2, terms n/10 EOM.

5 Received a $50 credit memorandum from Mason Company for unsatisfactory merchandise received on February 3 and returned for credit.

7 Sold merchandise on credit to Sharon Gable, Invoice No. 477, $5,850.

8 Purchased store equipment on credit from Casner Company, invoice dated February 8, terms n/10 EOM, $8,800.

10 Issued Check No. 771 to Seattle Company in payment of its January 31 invoice, less the discount.

11 Sold merchandise on credit to Darla Tilman, Invoice No. 478, $2,300.

12 Received payment from James Asner for the February 2 sale, less the discount.

13 Sold merchandise on credit to James Asner, Invoice No. 479, $3,200.

Feb. 15 Issued Check No. 772, payable to payroll, in payment of the sales salaries for the first half of the month, $2,230. Cashed the check and paid the employees.

15 Cash sales for the first half of the month, $14,870. (Cash sales are usually recorded daily from the cash register readings. However, they are recorded only twice in this problem to reduce the repetitive transactions.)

17 Received payment from Sharon Gable for the February 7 sale, less the discount.

18 Purchased merchandise on credit from Lang Company, invoice dated February 17, terms 2/10, n/60, $3,450.

19 Borrowed $12,000 from Dodge City Bank by giving a note payable.

20 Received payment from Darla Tilman for the February 11 sale, less the discount.

22 Purchased on credit from Casner Company merchandise, $1,400; store supplies, $180; and office supplies, $120. Invoice dated February 21, terms n/10 EOM.

23 Received payment from James Asner for the February 13 sale, less the discount.

23 Purchased merchandise on credit from Seattle Company, invoice dated February 22, terms 2/10, n/60, $2,100.

24 Received a $250 credit memorandum from Lang Company for defective merchandise received on February 18 and returned.

27 Issued Check No. 773 to Lang Company in payment of its February 17 invoice, less the return and the discount.

27 Sold merchandise on credit to Sharon Gable, Invoice No. 480, $2,840.

28 Sold merchandise on credit to Darla Tilman, Invoice No. 481, $1,650.

28 Issued Check No. 774, payable to Payroll, in payment of the sales salaries for the last half of the month, $2,230.

28 Cash sales for the last half of the month were $15,920.

Required

1. Open the following general ledger accounts: Cash, Accounts Receivable, Notes Payable, Sales, and Sales Discounts. Also open subsidiary accounts receivable ledger accounts for James Asner, Sharon Gable, and Darla Tilman.

2. Prepare a Sales Journal and a Cash Receipts Journal like the ones illustrated in this chapter.

3. Review the transactions of Garfield Company and enter those transactions that should be journalized in the Sales Journal and those that should be journalized in the Cash Receipts Journal. Ignore any transactions that should be posted in a Purchases Journal, a Cash Disbursements Journal, or a General Journal.

4. Post the items that should be posted as individual amounts from the journals. (Normally, such items are posted daily; but since they are few in number in this problem you are asked to post them only once.)

5. Foot and crossfoot the journals and make the month-end postings.
6. Prepare a trial balance of the General Ledger and prove the subsidiary ledger by preparing a schedule of accounts receivable.

Problem 6-2

On January 31, Garfield Company had a cash balance of $50,000 and a Notes Payable balance of $50,000. The February transactions of Garfield Company included those listed in Problem 6-1.

Required

1. Open the following general ledger accounts: Cash, Store Supplies, Office Supplies, Store Equipment, Notes Payable, Accounts Payable, Purchases, Purchases Returns and Allowances, Purchases Discounts, Advertising Expense, and Sales Salaries Expense. Enter the January 31 balances of Cash and Notes Payable ($50,000 each).
2. Open subsidiary accounts payable ledger accounts for Casner Company, Lang Company, Mason Company, and Seattle Company.
3. Prepare a General Journal, a Purchases Journal, and a Cash Disbursements Journal like the ones illustrated in this chapter.
4. Review the February transactions of Garfield Company and enter those transactions that should be journalized in the General Journal, the Purchases Journal, or the Cash Disbursements Journal. Ignore any transactions that should be posted in a Sales Journal or Cash Receipts Journal.
5. Post the items that should be posted as individual amounts from the journals. (Normally, such items are posted daily; but since they are few in number in this problem you are asked to post them only once.)
6. Foot and crossfoot the journals and make the month-end postings.
7. Prepare a trial balance and a schedule of accounts payable.

Problem 6-3

(If the working papers that accompany this text are not being used, omit this problem.)

It is July 20 and you have just taken over the accounting work of Nevada Company, a concern operating with annual accounting periods that end each June 30. The company's previous accountant journalized its transactions through July 19 and posted all items that required posting as individual amounts, as an examination of the journals and ledgers in the booklet of working papers will show.

The company completed these transactions beginning on July 20:

July 20   Purchased on credit from Taft Suppliers merchandise, $1,635; store supplies, $240; and office supplies, $165. Invoice dated July 20, terms n/10 EOM.

21   Received a $255 credit memorandum from Norton Company for merchandise received on July 16 and returned for credit.

22   Received a $60 credit memorandum from Taft Suppliers for office supplies received on July 20 and returned for credit.

July 23 Sold merchandise on credit to Sheila Barnes, Invoice No. 556, $1,845. (Terms of all credit sales are 2/10, n/60.)

24 Issued a credit memorandum to Jack Short for defective merchandise sold on July 19 and returned for credit, $195.

25 Purchased store equipment on credit from Taft Suppliers, invoice dated July 25, terms n/10 EOM, $2,205.

26 Issued Check No. 815 to Norton Company in payment of its July 16 invoice less the return and the discount.

26 Received payment from Sheila Barnes for the July 16 sale less the discount.

27 Issued Check No. 816 to Able Company in payment of its July 17 invoice less a 2% discount.

28 Sold merchandise on credit to Roger Nesland, Invoice No. 557, $2,475.

28 Sold a neighboring merchant a roll of wrapping paper (store supplies) for cash at cost, $90.

29 Received payment from Jack Short for the July 19 sale less the return and the discount.

30 Received merchandise and an invoice dated July 28, terms 2/10, n/60, from Able Company, $2,835.

30 Sally Fowler, the owner of Nevada Company, used Check No. 817 to withdraw $3,000 cash from the business for personal use.

31 Issued Check No. 818 to David Malone, the company's only sales employee, in payment of his salary for the last half of July, $960.

31 Issued Check No. 819 to City Power Company in payment of the July electric bill, $555.

31 Cash sales for the last half of the month, $29,985. (Cash sales are usually recorded daily but are recorded only twice in this problem in order to reduce the repetitive transactions.)

Required

1. Record the transactions in the journals provided.

2. Post to the customer and creditor accounts and also post any amounts that should be posted as individual amounts to the general ledger accounts. (Normally, these amounts are posted daily, but they are posted only once by you in this problem because they are few in number.)

3. Foot and crossfoot the journals and make the month-end postings.

4. Prepare a July 31 trial balance and prove the subsidiary ledgers by preparing schedules of accounts receivable and payable.

Problem 6-4

Motorcraft Company completed these transactions during March of the current year:

Mar. 1 Received merchandise and an invoice dated February 28, terms 2/10, n/60, from Slater Company, $5,250.

2 Sold merchandise on credit to Harry Ost, Invoice No. 425, $2,400. (Terms of all credit sales are 2/10, n/60.)

Mar. 3   Purchased on credit from Nagle Company merchandise, $5,565; store supplies, $225; and office supplies, $105. Invoice dated March 1, terms n/10 EOM.

5   Sold merchandise on credit to Shirley Tucker, Invoice No. 426, $3,750.

7   Borrowed $15,000 by giving Tempest National Bank a promissory note payable.

8   Purchased office equipment on credit from Intelcomp Company, invoice dated March 7, terms n/10 EOM, $1,875.

9   Sent Slater Company Check No. 341 in payment of its February 28 invoice less the discount.

11   Sold merchandise on credit to Kevin Stone, Invoice No. 427, $4,950.

12   Received payment from Harry Ost for the March 2 sale less the discount.

15   Received payment from Shirley Tucker for the March 5 sale less the discount.

15   Received merchandise and an invoice dated March 14, terms 2/10, n/60, from Newland Company, $5,955.

15   Issued Check No. 342, payable to Payroll, in payment of sales salaries for the first half of the month, $2,565. Cashed the check and paid the employees.

15   Cash sales for the first half of the month, $55,380. (Normally, cash sales are recorded daily; however, they are recorded only twice in this problem to reduce the number of repetitive entries.)

15   *Post to the customer and creditor accounts and also post any amounts that should be posted as individual amounts to the general ledger accounts. (Normally, such items are posted daily; but you are asked to post them on only two occasions in this problem because they are few in number.)*

17   Purchased on credit from Nagle Company merchandise, $1,230; store supplies, $135; and office supplies, $90. Invoice dated March 16, terms n/10 EOM.

17   Received a credit memorandum from Newland Company for unsatisfactory merchandise received on March 15 and returned for credit, $255.

18   Received a credit memorandum from Intelcomp Company for office equipment received on March 8 and returned for credit, $390.

21   Received payment from Kevin Stone for the sale of March 11 less the discount.

23   Issued Check No. 343 to Newland Company in payment of its invoice of March 14 less the return and the discount.

24   Sold merchandise on credit to Kevin Stone, Invoice No. 428, $2,505.

27   Sold merchandise on credit to Shirley Tucker, Invoice No. 429, $2,325.

29   Issued Check No. 344, payable to Payroll, in payment of sales salaries for the last half of the month, $2,565. Cashed the check and paid the employees.

Mar. 29 Cash sales for the last half of the month, $60,645.

29 *Post to the customer and creditor accounts and post any amounts that should be posted as individual amounts to general ledger accounts.*

29 *Foot and crossfoot the journals and make the month-end postings.*

Required

1. Open the following general ledger accounts: Cash, Accounts Receivable, Store Supplies, Office Supplies, Office Equipment, Notes Payable, Accounts Payable, Sales, Sales Discounts, Purchases, Purchases Returns and Allowances, Purchases Discounts, and Sales Salaries Expense.

2. Open the following accounts receivable ledger accounts: Harry Ost, Kevin Stone, and Shirley Tucker.

3. Open the following accounts payable ledger accounts: Intelcomp Company, Nagle Company, Newland Company, and Slater Company.

4. Enter the transactions in a Sales Journal, a Purchases Journal, a Cash Receipts Journal, a Cash Disbursements Journal, and a General Journal similar to the ones illustrated in this chapter. Post when instructed to do so.

5. Prepare a trial balance and prove the subsidiary ledgers by preparing schedules of accounts receivable and payable.

Problem 6-5

Eagle Grove Company completed these transactions during October of the current year:

Oct. 2 Received merchandise and an invoice dated September 29, terms 2/10, n/60, from Allen Company, $12,600.

2 Purchased store equipment on credit from Humboldt Company, invoice dated October 1, terms n/10 EOM, $4,700.

5 Sold merchandise on credit to Charles Beckwith, Invoice No. 388, $5,500. (Terms of all credit sales are 2/10, n/60.)

6 Sold merchandise on credit to Janis Shoop, Invoice No. 389, $7,100.

8 Cash sales for the week ended October 8, $14,800.

8 *Post to the customer and creditor accounts and also post any amounts that should be posted as individual items to the general ledger accounts. (Normally, such items are posted daily; but to simplify the problem, you are asked to post them only once each week.)*

8 Issued Check No. 490 to The Pink Sheets for advertising, $400.

9 Sold merchandise on credit to Bob Hodges, Invoice No. 390, $3,200.

9 Issued Check No. 491 to Allen Company in payment of its September 29 invoice less the discount.

11 Purchased on credit from Transfer Company merchandise, $3,900; store supplies, $370; and office supplies, $260. Invoice dated October 10, terms n/10 EOM.

13 Sold unneeded store equipment at cost for cash, $340.

15 Cash sales for the week ended October 15, $11,500.

Oct. 15   Received payment from Charles Beckwith for the sale of October 5 less the discount.

15   Issued Check No. 492, payable to Payroll, in payment of the sales salaries for the first half of the month, $2,600. Cashed the check and paid the employees.

15   *Post to the customer and creditor accounts and also post any amounts that should be posted as individual items to the general ledger accounts.*

16   Received payment from Janis Shoop for the sale of October 6 less the discount.

17   Sold merchandise on credit to Bob Hodges, Invoice No. 391, $4,350.

19   Sold merchandise on credit to Charles Beckwith, Invoice No. 392, $2,500.

19   Received merchandise and an invoice dated October 18, terms 2/10, n/60, from Lockhart Company, $6,300.

19   Received payment from Bob Hodges for the sale of October 9 less the discount.

20   Issued a credit memorandum to Bob Hodges for defective merchandise sold on October 17 and returned for credit, $450.

22   Cash sales for the week ended October 22, $13,800.

22   *Post to the customer and creditor accounts and also post any amounts that should be posted as individual items to the general ledger accounts.*

23   Received a $200 credit memorandum from Lockhart Company for defective merchandise received on October 19 and returned for credit.

24   Purchased on credit from Transfer Company merchandise, $2,700; store supplies, $300; and office supplies, $150. Invoice dated October 23, terms n/10 EOM.

25   Received merchandise and an invoice dated October 23, terms 2/10, n/60, from Allen Company, $5,700.

26   Received payment from Bob Hodges for the October 17 sale less the return and the discount.

27   Sold merchandise on credit to Janis Shoop, Invoice No. 393, $1,850.

27   Issued Check No. 493 to Lockhart Company in payment of its October 18 invoice, less the return and the discount.

29   Issued Check No. 494, payable to Payroll, in payment of the sales salaries for the last half of the month, $2,600.

29   Cash sales for the week ended October 29 were $12,750.

29   *Post to the customer and creditor accounts and also post any amounts that should be posted to the general ledger accounts as individual items.*

31   *Foot and crossfoot the journals and make the month-end postings.*

Required

1. Open the following general ledger accounts: Cash, Accounts Receivable, Store Supplies, Office Supplies, Store Equipment, Accounts Payable, Sales, Sales Returns and Allowances, Sales Discounts, Purchases, Purchases Returns and Allowances, Purchases Discounts, Sales Salaries Expense, and Advertising Expense.

2. Open the subsidiary accounts receivable ledger accounts: Charles Beckwith, Bob Hodges, and Janis Shoop.

3. Open these subsidiary accounts payable ledger accounts: Allen Company, Humboldt Company, Lockhart Company, and Transfer Company.

4. Prepare a Sales Journal, a Purchases Journal, a Cash Receipts Journal, a Cash Disbursements Journal, and a General Journal like the ones illustrated in this chapter. Enter the transactions in the journals and post when instructed to do so.

5. Prepare a trial balance and prove the subsidiary ledgers with schedules of accounts receivable and payable.

☐ Alternate Problems

Problem 6-1A

Hamilton Company completed these transactions during March of the current year:

Mar. 1 Issued Check No. 610 to *The Daily Review* for advertising expense, $720.

2 Purchased merchandise on credit from Roch Company, invoice dated March 1, terms 2/10, n/60, $4,350.

3 Sold merchandise on credit to Vickie Bedford, Invoice No. 570, $7,100. (The terms of all credit sales are 2/10, n/60.)

4 Purchased on credit from Nabors Company merchandise, $4,700; store supplies, $330; and office supplies, $170. Invoice dated March 4, terms n/10 EOM.

6 Sold merchandise on credit to Jerry Ingle, Invoice No. 571, $8,200.

7 Received a $350 credit memorandum from Nabors Company for unsatisfactory merchandise received on March 4 and returned for credit.

9 Purchased store equipment on credit from Bruhl Company, invoice dated March 9, terms n/10 EOM, $11,600.

10 Issued Check No. 611 to Roch Company in payment of its March 1 invoice, less the discount.

11 Sold merchandise on credit to Paul Tolo, Invoice No. 572, $3,100.

13 Received payment from Vickie Bedford for the March 3 sale, less the discount.

15 Issued Check No. 612, payable to Payroll, in payment of the sales salaries for the first half of the month, $3,250. Cashed the check and paid the employees.

15 Sold merchandise on credit to Vickie Bedford, Invoice No. 573, $4,900.

15 Cash sales for the first half of the month, $9,890. (Cash sales are usually recorded daily from the cash register readings. However, they are recorded only twice in this problem to reduce the repetitive transactions.)

16 Received payment from Jerry Ingle for the February 6 sale, less the discount.

Mar. 17 Purchased merchandise on credit from Liggett Company, invoice dated March 16, terms 2/10, n/60, $5,500.

19 Borrowed $10,000 from First State Bank by giving a note payable.

21 Received payment from Paul Tolo for the March 11 sale, less the discount.

22 Received a $200 credit memorandum from Liggett Company for defective merchandise received on March 17 and returned.

24 Purchased on credit from Bruhl Company merchandise, $2,940; store supplies, $230; and office supplies, $130. Invoice dated March 23, terms n/10 EOM.

25 Received payment from Vickie Bedford for the March 15 sale, less the discount.

26 Purchased merchandise on credit from Roch Company, invoice dated March 25, terms 2/10, n/60, $2,600.

26 Issued Check No. 613 to Liggett Company in payment of its March 16 invoice, less the return and the discount.

28 Sold merchandise on credit to Jerry Ingle, Invoice No. 574, $3,390.

30 Sold merchandise on credit to Paul Tolo, Invoice No. 575, $2,330.

31 Issued Check No. 614, payable to Payroll, in payment of the sales salaries for the last half of the month, $3,250.

31 Cash sales for the last half of the month were $13,880.

Required

1. Open the following general ledger accounts: Cash, Accounts Receivable, Notes Payable, Sales, and Sales Discounts. Also open subsidiary accounts receivable ledger accounts for Vickie Bedford, Jerry Ingle, and Paul Tolo.

2. Prepare a Sales Journal and a Cash Receipts Journal like the ones illustrated in this chapter.

3. Review the transactions of Hamilton Company and enter those transactions that should be journalized in the Sales Journal and those that should be journalized in the Cash Receipts Journal. Ignore any transactions that should be posted in a Purchases Journal, a Cash Disbursements Journal, or a General Journal.

4. Post the items that should be posted as individual amounts from the journals. (Normally, such items are posted daily; but since they are few in number in this problem you are asked to post them only once.)

5. Foot and crossfoot the journals and make the month-end postings.

6. Prepare a trial balance of the General Ledger and prove the subsidiary ledger by preparing a schedule of accounts receivable.

Problem 6-2A

On February 28, Hamilton Company had a cash balance of $20,000 and a Notes Payable balance of $20,000. The March transactions of Hamilton Company included those listed in Problem 6-1A.

Required

1. Open the following general ledger accounts: Cash, Store Supplies, Office Supplies, Store Equipment, Notes Payable, Accounts Payable, Purchases, Purchases Returns and Allowances, Purchases Discounts, Advertising Expense, and Sales Salaries Expense. Enter the February 28 balances of Cash and Notes Payable ($20,000 each).
2. Open subsidiary accounts payable ledger accounts for Bruhl Company, Liggett Company, Nabors Company, and Roch Company.
3. Prepare a General Journal, a Purchases Journal, and a Cash Disbursements Journal like the ones illustrated in this chapter.
4. Review the March transactions of Hamilton Company and enter those transactions that should be journalized in the General Journal, the Purchases Journal, or the Cash Disbursements Journal. Ignore any transactions that should be posted in a Sales Journal or Cash Receipts Journal.
5. Post the items that should be posted as individual amounts from the journals. (Normally, such items are posted daily; but since they are few in number in this problem you are asked to post them only once.)
6. Foot and crossfoot the journals and make the month-end postings.
7. Prepare a trial balance and a schedule of accounts payable.

Problem 6-3A

(If the working papers that accompany this text are not being used, omit this problem.)

It is July 20 and you have just taken over the accounting work of Branch Company, a concern operating with annual accounting periods that end each June 30. The company's previous accountant journalized its transactions through July 19 and posted all items that required posting as individual amounts, as an examination of the journals and ledgers in the booklet of working papers will show.

The company completed these transactions beginning on July 20:

July 20   Sold merchandise on credit to Shelia Barnes, Invoice No. 556, $5,535. (Terms of all credit sales are 2/10, n/60.)

21   Received a $455 credit memorandum from Norton Company for merchandise received on July 16 and returned for credit.

21   Purchased on credit from Taft Suppliers merchandise, $4,905; store supplies, $720; and office supplies, $495. Invoice dated July 20, terms n/10 EOM.

23   Issued a credit memorandum to Jack Short for defective merchandise sold on July 19 and returned for credit, $295.

24   Received a $180 credit memorandum from Taft Suppliers for office supplies received on July 21 and returned for credit.

24   Purchased store equipment on credit from Taft Suppliers, invoice dated July 23, terms n/10 EOM, $6,615.

25   Sold merchandise on credit to Roger Nesland, Invoice No. 557, $7,425.

26   Issued Check No. 815 to Norton Company in payment of its July 16 invoice less the return and the discount.

July 26   Received payment from Sheila Barnes for the July 16 sale less the discount.

     27   Issued Check No. 816 to Able Company in payment of its July 17 invoice less a 2% discount.

     29   Received merchandise and an invoice dated July 29, terms 2/10, n/60, from Able Company, $8,505.

     29   Received payment from Jack Short for the July 19 sale less the return and the discount.

     30   Sold a neighboring merchant a carton of computer ribbons (store supplies) for cash at cost, $270.

     31   Issued Check No. 817 to City Power Company in payment of the July electric bill, $1,665.

     31   Issued Check No. 818 to Lisa Dow, the company's only sales employee, in payment of her salary for the last half of July, $960.

     31   Cash sales for the last half of the month, $34,650. (Cash sales are usually recorded daily but are recorded only twice in this problem in order to reduce the repetitive transactions.)

     31   Sally Fowler, the owner of Branch Company, used Check No. 819 to withdraw $5,000 cash from the business for personal use.

Required

1. Record the transactions in the journals provided.

2. Post to the customer and creditor accounts and also post any amounts that should be posted as individual amounts to the general ledger accounts. (Normally, these amounts are posted daily, but they are posted only once by you in this problem because they are few in number.)

3. Foot and crossfoot the journals and make the month-end postings.

4. Prepare a July 31 trial balance and prove the subsidiary ledgers by preparing schedules of accounts receivable and payable.

Problem 6-4A

Washington Company completed these transactions during December of the current year:

Dec.   1   Borrowed $24,000 by giving World National Bank a promissory note payable.

     2   Received merchandise and an invoice dated November 30, terms 2/10, n/60, from Slater Company, $8,400.

     3   Purchased on credit from Nagle Company merchandise, $7,300; store supplies, $300; and office supplies, $150. Invoice dated December 2, terms n/10 EOM.

     4   Sold merchandise on credit to Harry Ost, Invoice No. 723, $6,200. (Terms of all credit sales are 2/10, n/60.)

     6   Purchased office equipment on credit from Intelcomp Company, invoice dated March 5, terms n/10 EOM, $9,700.

     8   Sold merchandise on credit to Shirley Tucker, Invoice No. 724, $5,900.

   10   Sent Slater Company Check No. 580 in payment of its November 30 invoice less the discount.

Dec. 13 Received merchandise and an invoice dated December 12, terms 2/10, n/60, from Newland Company, $8,600.

14 Received payment from Harry Ost for the December 4 sale less the discount.

15 Issued Check No. 581, payable to Payroll, in payment of sales salaries for the first half of the month, $4,800. Cashed the check and paid the employees.

15 Cash sales for the first half of the month, $29,800. (Normally, cash sales are recorded daily; however, they are recorded only twice in this problem to reduce the number of repetitive entries.)

15 *Post to the customer and creditor accounts and also post any amounts that should be posted as individual amounts to the general ledger accounts. (Normally, such items are posted daily; but you are asked to post them on only two occasions in this problem because they are few in number.)*

16 Sold merchandise on credit to Kevin Stone, Invoice No. 725, $7,250.

17 Purchased on credit from Nagle Company merchandise, $3,650; store supplies, $350; and office supplies, $280. Invoice dated March 16, terms n/10, EOM.

18 Received payment from Shirley Tucker for the December 8 sale less the discount.

20 Received a credit memorandum from Newland Company for unsatisfactory merchandise received on December 13 and returned for credit, $800.

21 Issued Check No. 582 to Newland Company in payment of its invoice of December 12 less the return and the discount.

24 Sold merchandise on credit to Kevin Stone, Invoice No. 726, $4,700.

26 Received payment from Kevin Stone for the sale of December 16 less the discount.

26 Received a credit memorandum from Intelcomp Company for office equipment received on December 6 and returned for credit, $500.

27 Sold merchandise on credit to Shirley Tucker, Invoice No. 727, $4,100.

31 Issued Check No. 583, payable to Payroll, in payment of sales salaries for the last half of the month, $4,800. Cashed the check and paid the employees.

31 Cash sales for the last half of the month, $33,700.

31 *Post to the customer and creditor accounts and post any amounts that should be posted as individual amounts to general ledger accounts.*

31 *Foot and crossfoot the journals and make the month-end postings.*

Required

1. Open the following general ledger accounts: Cash, Accounts Receivable, Store Supplies, Office Supplies, Office Equipment, Notes Payable, Accounts Payable, Sales, Sales Discounts, Purchases, Purchases Returns and Allowances, Purchases Discounts, and Sales Salaries Expense.

2. Open the following accounts receivable ledger accounts: Harry Ost, Kevin Stone, and Shirley Tucker.

3. Open the following accounts payable ledger accounts: Intelcomp Company, Nagle Company, Newland Company, and Slater Company.
4. Enter the transactions in a Sales Journal, a Purchases Journal, a Cash Receipts Journal, a Cash Disbursements Journal, and a General Journal similar to the ones illustrated in this chapter. Post when instructed to do so.
5. Prepare a trial balance and prove the subsidiary ledgers by preparing schedules of accounts receivable and payable.

Problem 6-5A

Dubuque Company completed these transactions during August of the current year:

Aug. 3   Received merchandise and an invoice dated August 2, terms 2/10, n/60, from Allen Company, $17,900.

4   Sold merchandise on credit to Charles Beckwith, Invoice No. 476, $8,100. (Terms of all credit sales are 2/10, n/60.)

5   Issued Check No. 520 to *The Daily Times* for advertising, $1,560.

7   Purchased store equipment on credit from Humboldt Company, invoice dated August 5, terms n/10 EOM, $24,200.

7   Sold merchandise on credit to Janis Shoop, Invoice No. 477, $9,300.

8   Cash sales for the week ended August 8, $16,400.

8   *Post to the customer and creditor accounts and also post any amounts that should be posted as individual items to the general ledger accounts. (Normally, such items are posted daily; but to simplify the problem, you are asked to post them only once each week.)*

10   Sold merchandise on credit to Bob Hodges, Invoice No. 478, $5,950.

11   Received a credit memorandum from Humboldt Company for the return of defective equipment originally purchased on August 7, $700.

12   Issued Check No. 521 to Allen Company in payment of its August 2 invoice less the discount.

12   Sold unneeded store equipment at cost for cash, $480.

14   Received payment from Charles Beckwith for the sale of August 4 less the discount.

15   Cash sales for the week ended August 15, $15,300.

15   Issued Check No. 522, payable to Payroll, in payment of the sales salaries for the first half of the month, $3,300. Cashed the check and paid the employees.

15   *Post to the customer and creditor accounts and also post any amounts that should be posted as individual items to the general ledger accounts.*

16   Purchased on credit from Transfer Company merchandise, $7,500; store supplies, $620; and office supplies, $380. Invoice dated August 15, terms n/10 EOM.

17   Received payment from Janis Shoop for the sale of August 7 less the discount.

18   Received merchandise and an invoice dated August 18, terms 2/10, n/60, from Lockhart Company, $11,100.

Aug. 18   Sold merchandise on credit to Bob Hodges, Invoice No. 479, $8,900.

19   Sold merchandise on credit to Charles Beckwith, Invoice No. 480, $7,850.

20   Received payment from Bob Hodges for the sale of October 10 less the discount.

21   Issued a credit memorandum to Bob Hodges for defective merchandise sold on August 18 and returned for credit, $100.

22   Cash sales for the week ended August 22, $18,300.

22   *Post to the customer and creditor accounts and also post any amounts that should be posted as individual items to the general ledger accounts.*

23   Received a $300 credit memorandum from Lockhart Company for defective merchandise received on August 18 and returned for credit.

24   Purchased on credit from Transfer Company merchandise, $6,800; store supplies, $220; and office supplies, $280. Invoice dated August 23, terms n/10 EOM.

25   Received merchandise and an invoice dated August 24, terms 2/10, n/60, from Allen Company, $10,200.

27   Received payment from Bob Hodges for the August 18 sale less the return and the discount.

27   Issued Check No. 523 to Lockhart Company in payment of its August 18 invoice, less the return and the discount.

28   Sold merchandise on credit to Janis Shoop, Invoice No. 481, $5,950.

29   Issued Check No. 524, payable to Payroll, in payment of the sales salaries for the last half of the month, $3,300.

29   Cash sales for the week ended August 29 were $9,750.

31   *Post to the customer and creditor accounts and also post any amounts that should be posted to the general ledger accounts as individual items.*

31   *Foot and crossfoot the journals and make the month-end postings.*

Required

1. Open the following general ledger accounts: Cash, Accounts Receivable, Store Supplies, Office Supplies, Store Equipment, Accounts Payable, Sales, Sales Returns and Allowances, Sales Discounts, Purchases, Purchases Returns and Allowances, Purchases Discounts, Sales Salaries Expense, and Advertising Expense.

2. Open the subsidiary accounts receivable ledger accounts: Charles Beckwith, Bob Hodges, and Janis Shoop.

3. Open these subsidiary accounts payable ledger accounts: Allen Company, Humboldt Company, Lockhart Company, and Transfer Company.

4. Prepare a Sales Journal, a Purchases Journal, a Cash Receipts Journal, a Cash Disbursements Journal, and a General Journal like the ones illustrated in this chapter. Enter the transactions in the journals and post when instructed to do so.

5. Prepare a trial balance and prove the subsidiary ledgers with schedules of accounts receivable and payable.

Bravo Company—A Minipractice Set

(If the working papers that accompany this text are not being used, omit this minipractice set.)

Assume it is Monday, June 3, the first business day of the month, and you have just been hired as accountant by Bravo Company, a company that operates with monthly accounting periods. All of the company's accounting work has been completed through the end of May, its ledgers show May 31 balances, and you are ready to begin work by recording the following transactions:

June 3   Purchased on credit from Easton Suppliers merchandise, $3,670; store supplies, $320; and office supplies, $110. Invoice dated June 3, terms n/10 EOM.

4   Sold merchandise on credit to Tisdale Company, Invoice No. 672, $3,700. (The terms of all credit sales are 2/10, n/60.)

4   Issued Check No. 812 to Commercial Realty in payment of the June rent, $1,950. (Use two lines to record the transaction. Charge 80% of the rent to Rent Expense, Selling Space and the balance to Rent Expense, Office Space.)

5   Received a $260 credit memorandum from Goodman Products for merchandise received on May 30 and returned for credit.

5   Issued a $150 credit memorandum to Berry Company for defective merchandise sold on May 31 and returned for credit.

6   Purchased office equipment on credit from Easton Suppliers, invoice dated June 5, terms n/10 EOM, $3,925.

7   Sold store supplies to the merchant next door at cost for cash, $25.

7   Issued Check No. 813 to Goodman Products to pay for the $2,360 of merchandise received on May 30 less the return and a 2% discount.

10   Received payment from Berry Company for the sale of May 31 less the return and the discount.

12   Received merchandise and an invoice dated June 11, terms 2/10, n/60, from Settle Brothers, $4,300.

13   Received a $175 credit memorandum from Easton Suppliers for defective office equipment received on June 6 and returned for credit.

14   Received payment from Tisdale Company for the June 4 sale less the discount.

15   Issued Check No. 814, payable to Payroll, in payment of sales salaries, $875, and office salaries, $750. Cashed the check and paid the employees.

15   Cash sales for the first half of the month, $14,290. (Such sales are normally recorded daily. They are recorded only twice in this problem in order to reduce the number of repetitive transactions.)

15   *Post to the customer and creditor accounts and post any amounts that should be posted to the general ledger accounts as individual amounts. (Such items are normally posted daily; but you are asked to post them only twice each month because they are few in number.)*

June 17   Received merchandise and an invoice dated June 17, terms 2/10, n/60, from Ulrich Materials, $5,300.

17   Sold merchandise on credit to Nate's Repairs, Invoice No. 673, $2,750.

19   Issued Check No. 815 to Settle Brothers in payment of its June 11 invoice less the discount.

19   Sold merchandise on credit to Berry Company, Invoice No. 674, $2,200.

21   Purchased on credit from Easton Suppliers merchandise, $3,330; store supplies, $110; and office supplies, $160. Invoice dated June 20, terms n/10 EOM.

24   Sold merchandise on credit to Mayfield Constructors, Invoice No. 675, $4,165.

25   Issued Check No. 816 to Ulrich Materials in payment of its June 17 invoice less the discount.

26   Received merchandise and an invoice dated June 26, terms 2/10, n/60, from Settle Brothers, $2,780.

27   Received payment from Nate's Repairs for the June 17 sale less the discount.

27   Ralph Weber, the owner of Bravo Company, used Check No. 817 to withdraw $1,800 from the business for personal use.

29   Issued Check No. 818, payable to Payroll, in payment of sales salaries, $875, and office salaries, $750. Cashed the check and paid the employees.

29   Issued Check No. 819 to City Utility in payment of the June electric bill, $495.

29   Cash sales for the last half of the month were $15,610.

29   *Post to the customer and creditor accounts and post any amounts that are posted as individual amounts to the general ledger accounts.*

29   *Foot and crossfoot the journals and make the month-end postings.*

Required

1. Enter the transactions in the journals and post when instructed to do so.

2. Prepare a trial balance in the Trial Balance columns of the work sheet form provided and complete the work sheet using the following information:
   a. Ending merchandise inventory, $32,440.
   b. Expired insurance, $340.
   c. Ending store suppplies inventory, $305; and office supplies inventory, $160.
   d. Estimated depreciation of store equipment, $300; and of office equipment, $200.

3. Prepare a multiple-step classified June income statement and a June 30 classified balance sheet.

4. Prepare and post adjusting and closing entries.

5. Prepare a post-closing trial balance and prove the subsidiary ledgers with schedules of accounts payable and accounts receivable.

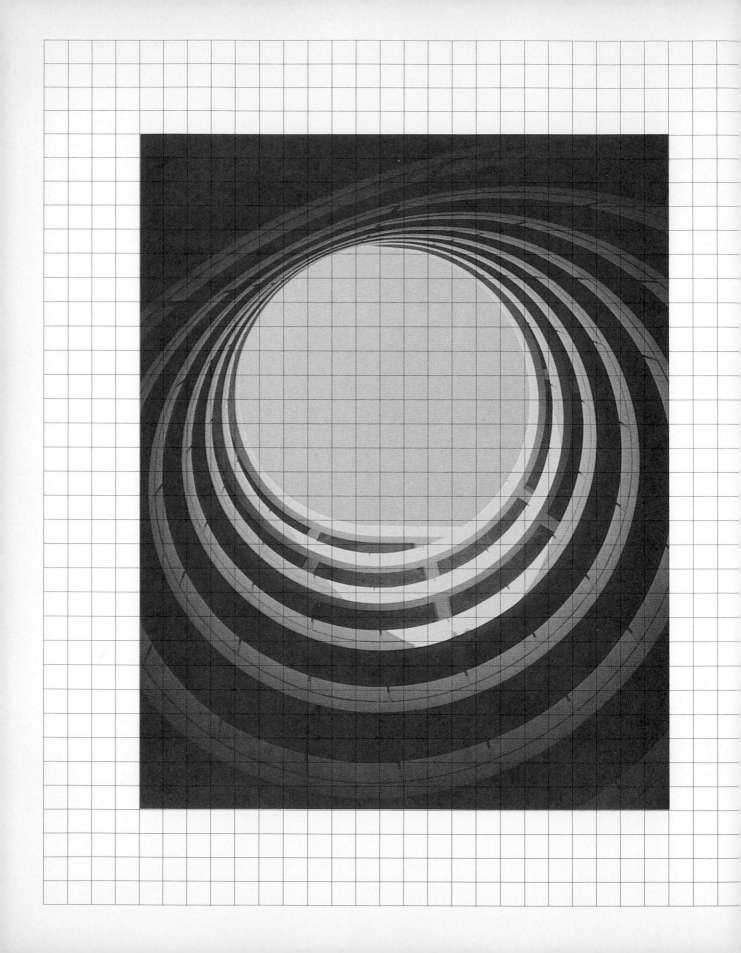

Part Three

Accounting for Assets

7 Accounting for Cash

After studying Chapter 7, you should be able to:

1. Explain why internal control procedures are needed in a large concern and state the broad principles of internal control.

2. Describe internal control procedures to protect cash received from cash sales, cash received through the mail, and cash disbursements.

3. Explain the operation of a petty cash fund and be able to make entries to establish and reimburse a petty cash fund.

4. Explain why the bank balance and the book balance of cash are reconciled and be able to prepare such a reconciliation.

5. Tell how recording invoices at net amounts helps gain control over cash discounts taken and be able to account for invoices recorded at net amounts.

6. Define or explain the words and phrases listed in the chapter Glossary.

Cash has universal usefulness, small bulk for high value, and no convenient identification marks by which ownership may be established. Consequently, in accounting for cash, the procedures for protecting it from fraud and theft are very important. They are called **internal control procedures** and apply to all assets owned by a business and to all phases of its operations.

■ **Internal Control**

In a small business, the owner-manager commonly controls the entire operation through personal supervision and direct participation in the activities of the business. For example, he or she commonly buys all the assets, goods, and services to be used in the business. Such a manager also hires and closely supervises all employees, negotiates all contracts, and signs all checks. As a result, in signing checks, for example, the manager knows from personal contact and observation that the assets, goods, and services for which the checks are in payment were received by the business. However, as a business grows, it becomes increasingly difficult to maintain this personal contact. Therefore, at some point it becomes necessary for the manager to delegate responsibilities and rely on internal control procedures rather than personal contact in controlling the operations of the business. A properly designed **internal control system** encourages adherence to prescribed managerial policies. It also promotes operational efficiencies; protects the business assets from waste, fraud, and theft; and ensures accurate and reliable accounting data.

Internal control procedures vary from company to company, depending on such factors as the nature of the business and its size. However, the same broad principles of internal control apply to all companies. These broad principles are described in the following paragraphs.

Responsibilities Should Be Clearly Established

Good internal control necessitates that responsibilities be clearly established and that one person be made responsible for each task. When responsibility is shared and something goes wrong, it is difficult to determine who is at fault. For example, when two salesclerks share the same cash drawer and there is a shortage, it is normally impossible to tell which clerk is at fault. Each will tend to blame the other. Neither can prove that he or she is not responsible. In such a situation, each clerk should be assigned a separate cash drawer, or one of the clerks should be given responsibility for making all change.

Adequate Records Should Be Maintained

Good records are an important means of protecting assets and assuring that employees follow prescribed procedures. They also give management reliable information to use in monitoring the operations of the business. For example, if detailed subsidiary records of manufacturing equipment and tools are not maintained, items may disappear without any discrepancy being noticed. And if a comprehensive chart of accounts is not documented carefully and followed precisely, some expenses may be debited to the wrong accounts. As a result, management may never discover that some expenses are excessive.

Numerous forms and internal business papers must be designed and properly used to maintain good internal control. For example, if sales slips are properly designed, sales personnel can record the proper information efficiently and without irritating delays to customers. And if all sales slips are prenumbered and controlled, each salesperson can be held responsible for the sales slips under his or her control. Thus, a salesperson is not apt to make a sale, destroy the sales slip, and pocket the cash.

Assets Should Be Insured and Employees Bonded

Assets should be covered by adequate casualty insurance, and employees who handle cash and negotiable assets should be bonded. Bonding provides a means for recovery if a loss occurs. It also tends to prevent losses, since a bonded employee is less apt to take assets if the employee knows a bonding company must be dealt with when the shortage is revealed.

Record-Keeping and Custody Should Be Separated

A fundamental principle of internal control requires that the person who has access to or is responsible for an asset should not maintain the accounting record for that asset. When this principle is observed, the custodian of an asset, knowing that a record of the asset is being kept by another person, is not apt to either misappropriate the asset or waste it; and the record-keeper, who does not have access to the asset, has no reason to falsify the record. Furthermore, if the asset is to be misappropriated and the theft concealed in the records, collusion is necessary.

Responsibility for Related Transactions Should Be Divided

Responsibility for a divisible transaction or a series of related transactions should be divided between individuals or departments in such a manner that the work of one acts as a check on that of another. This does not mean there should be duplication of work. Each employee or department should perform an unduplicated portion. For example, responsibility for placing orders, receiving the merchandise, and paying the vendors should not be given to one individual or department. To do so is to invite laxity in checking the quality and quantity of goods received, and carelessness in verifying the validity and accuracy of invoices. It also invites the purchase of goods for an employee's personal use and the payment of fictitious invoices.

Mechanical Devices Should Be Used Whenever Practicable

Cash registers, check protectors, time clocks, and mechanical counters are examples of control devices that should be used whenever practicable. A cash register with a locked-in tape makes a record of each cash sale. A check protector, by perforating the amount of a check into its face, makes it very difficult to change the amount. A time clock registers the exact time an employee arrived on the job and when the employee departed.

Regular and Independent Reviews

Regardless of how well designed the internal control system may be, there is a tendency for it to deteriorate over time. Changes in personnel and the stress of time pressures tend to bring about short cuts and omissions. Regular reviews of internal control procedures are necessary to be sure that the procedures are in fact being followed. These reviews should be performed by internal auditors who are not directly involved in operations. From this independent perspective, internal auditors can evaluate the overall efficiency of operations as well as the effectiveness of the internal control system.

Many companies also have audits by external CPAs. After testing the company's financial records, the CPAs give an opinion as to whether the company's financial statements are presented fairly in accordance with generally accepted accounting principles. However, before CPAs can decide on how much testing must be done, they first must evaluate the effectiveness of the internal control system.

Computers and Internal Control

The broad principles of internal control should be followed whether the accounting system is manual or computerized. However, computers have several important effects on internal control. Perhaps the most obvious is that computers provide much more rapid access to large quantities of information. As a result, management's ability to monitor and control business operations is greatly improved.

Computers Reduce Processing Errors

Computers reduce the number of errors in processing information. Once the data have been entered correctly, the human tendency to make mechanical and mathematical errors is largely eliminated. On the other hand, data entry errors may occur because the process of entering data sometimes appears less logical in a computerized system. Also, the lack of human involvement in later processing may cause data entry errors to go undiscovered.

Computers Allow More Extensive Testing of Records

The regular review and audit of records can include more extensive testing if a computerized system is used. To reduce the cost of testing when manual methods are used, only small samples of data might be tested. But when computers are used to process data, large samples or even complete data files can be reviewed and analyzed.

Computerized Systems May Limit Hard Evidence of Processing Steps

Because many data processing steps are performed by the computer, less hard evidence in the form of written forms and analyses may be available for review. Therefore, internal control may depend more on reviews of the design and operation of the computerized processing system and less on reviews of the documents left behind by the system.

Separation of Duties Must Be Maintained

A common risk with computerized systems is that the separation of critical responsibilities is not maintained. Companies that use computers must have employees with special skills to program and operate the computers. The duties of these employees must be carefully controlled to avoid the risk of fraud. The person who designs and programs the system generally should not also serve as the operator. Control over cash receipts and disbursements should be separated. And check-writing should not be controlled by the computer operator. This problem is particularly difficult in small companies.

■ Internal Control for Cash

A good system of internal control for cash should provide adequate procedures for protecting both cash receipts and cash disbursements. In the procedures, three basic principles should always be observed. First, there should be a separation of duties so that the people responsible for handling cash and for its custody are not the same people who keep the cash records. Second, all cash receipts should be deposited in the bank, intact, each day. Third, all payments should be made by check. The one exception to the last principle is that small disbursements may be made in cash from a petty cash fund. Petty cash funds are discussed later in this chapter.

The reason for the first principle is that a division of duties necessitates collusion between two or more people if cash is to be embezzled and the theft concealed in the accounting records. The second, requiring that all receipts be deposited intact each day, prevents an employee from making personal use of the money for a few days before depositing it. And if all receipts are deposited intact and all payments are made by check, the bank records provide a separate and external record of all cash transactions. These bank records are useful in proving the company's own records.

The exact procedures used to achieve control over cash vary from company to company. They depend upon such things as company size, number of employees, cash sources, and so on. Consequently, the following procedures are only illustrative of some that are in use.

Cash from Cash Sales

Cash sales should be rung up on a cash register at the time of each sale. To help ensure that correct amounts are rung up, each register should be placed so that customers can see the amounts rung up. Also, the clerks should be required to ring up each sale before wrapping the merchandise. Finally, each cash register should be designed to provide a permanent, locked-in record of each transaction. In some cases, this is accomplished by a direct connection between the register and a computer. The computer is programmed to accept cash register transactions and enter them in the accounting records. In other cases, the register prints a record of each transaction on a paper tape that is locked inside the register.

Good cash control, as previously stated, requires that custody over cash be separated from record-keeping for cash. For cash sales, this separation begins with the cash register. The salesclerk who has access to the cash in the register should not have access to its locked-in record. At the end of each day, the salesclerk is usually required to count the cash in the register and to turn the cash and its count over to an employee in the cashier's office. The employee in the cashier's office, like the salesclerk, has access to the cash and should not have access to the computerized accounting records (or the register tape if one is used). A third employee, commonly from the accounting department, examines the computerized record of register transactions (or the register tape) and compares its daily total with the total cash receipts reported by the cashier's office. If a register tape is used, it becomes the basis for the entry recording cash sales. The accounting department employee has access to the records for cash but does not have access to the actual cash. The salesclerk and the employee from the cashier's office do not have access to the accounting records and cannot take any cash without the shortage being revealed.

Cash Received through the Mail

Control of cash coming in through the mail begins with the person who opens the mail. Preferably, two people should be present when the mail is opened. One of those should make a list in triplicate of the money received. The list should give each sender's name, the purpose for which the money was sent, and the amount. One copy of the list is sent to the cashier with the money. The second copy goes to the bookkeeper. The third copy is kept by the mail clerk. The cashier deposits the money in the bank, and the bookkeeper records the amounts received in the accounting records. Then, if the bank balance is reconciled (discussed later) by a fourth person, errors or fraud by the mail clerk, the cashier, or bookkeeper will be detected. They will be detected because the cash deposited and the records of three people must agree. Furthermore, fraud is impossible, unless there is collusion. The mail clerk must report all receipts or customers will question their account balances. The cashier must deposit all receipts because the bank balance must agree with the bookkeeper's cash balance. The bookkeeper and the person reconciling the bank balance do not have access to cash and, therefore, have no opportunity to withhold any.

Cash Disbursements

It is important to gain control over cash from sales and cash received through the mail. However, most large embezzlements have not involved cash receipts but have been accomplished through the payment of fictitious invoices. Consequently, procedures for controlling cash disbursements are equally as important and sometimes more important than those for cash receipts.

To gain control over cash disbursements, all disbursements should be made by check, excepting those from petty cash. If authority to sign checks is delegated to some person other than the business owner, that person should not have access to the accounting records. This helps prevent a fraudulent disbursement being made and concealed in the accounting records.

In a small business, the owner-manager usually signs checks and normally knows from personal contact that the items to be paid for were received by the business. However, this is impossible in a large business. In a large business, internal control procedures must be substituted for personal contact. The procedures tell the person who signs checks that the obligations or which the checks were written are proper obligations, properly incurred, and should be paid. Often these procedures take the form of a **voucher system.**

A voucher system helps gain control over cash disbursements as follows: (1) It permits only authorized individuals to incur obligations that will result in cash disbursements. (2) It establishes procedures for incurring such obligations and for their verification, approval, and recording. (3) It permits checks to be issued only in payment of properly verified, approved, and recorded obligations. Finally (4), it requires that every obligation be recorded at the time it is incurred and every purchase be treated as an independent transaction, complete in itself. It requires this even though a number of purchases may be made from the same company during a month or other billing period.

When a voucher system is in use, control over cash disbursements begins with the incurrence of obligations that will result in cash disbursements. Only specified departments and individuals are authorized to incur such obligations, and the kind each may incur is limited. For example, in a large store, only the purchasing department may incur obligations by purchasing merchandise. However, to gain control, the purchasing-receiving-and-paying procedures are divided among several departments. They are the departments requesting that merchandise be purchased, the purchasing department, the receiving department, and the accounting department. To coordinate and control the responsibilities of these departments, business papers are used. A list of the papers follows, and an explanation of each will show how a large concern may gain control over cash disbursements resulting from the purchase of merchandise.

Business Paper	Prepared by the—	Sent to the—
1. Purchase requisition	Selling department manager desiring that merchandise be purchased	Purchasing department, with a copy to the accounting department
2. Purchase order	Purchasing department	Vendor, with a copy to the accounting and requisitioning departments
3. Invoice	Company selling the merchandise	Accounting department
4. Receiving report	Receiving department	Accounting department, with a copy to the purchasing and requisitioning departments
5. Invoice approval form	Accounting department	Attached to invoice in the accounting department
6. Voucher	Accounting department	Cashier's department with the foregoing business papers attached

Purchase Requisition

The department managers in a large store cannot be permitted to place orders directly with supply sources. If each manager were permitted to deal directly with wholesalers and manufacturers, the amount of merchandise purchased and the resulting liabilities could not be controlled. Therefore, to gain control over purchases and resulting liabilities, department managers are commonly required to place all orders through the purchasing department. In such cases, the function of the several department managers in the purchasing procedure is to inform the purchasing department of their needs. Each manager performs this function by preparing in triplicate and signing a business paper called a **purchase requisition.** On the requisition, the manager lists the merchandise needs of his or her department. The original and a duplicate copy of the purchase requisition are sent to the purchasing department. The third copy is retained by the requisitioning department as a check on the purchasing department.

Purchase Order

A **purchase order** is a business form used by the purchasing department in placing an order with a manufacturer or wholesaler. It authorizes the supplier to ship the merchandise ordered and takes the place of a typewritten letter placing the order. On receipt of a purchase requisition from a selling department, the purchasing department prepares four or more copies of the purchase order. The copies are distributed as follows:

Copy 1, the original copy, is sent to the supplier as a request to purchase and as authority to ship the merchandise listed.
Copy 2, with a copy of the purchase requisition attached, is sent to the accounting department where it will ultimately be used in approving the invoice of the purchase for payment.
Copy 3 is sent to the department issuing the requisition to acknowledge the requisition and tell the action taken.
Copy 4 is retained on file by the purchasing department.

Invoice

An **invoice** is an itemized statement of goods bought and sold. It is prepared by the seller or **vendor,** and to the seller it is a sales invoice. However, when the same invoice is received by the buyer or **vendee,** it becomes a purchase invoice to the buyer. Upon receipt of a purchase order, the manufacturer or wholesaler receiving the order ships the ordered merchandise to the buyer and mails a copy of the invoice covering the shipment. The goods are delivered to the buyer's receiving department. The invoice is sent directly to the buyer's accounting department.

Receiving Report

Most large companies maintain a special department assigned the duty of receiving all merchandise or other assets purchased. As each shipment is received, counted, and checked, the receiving department prepares four or more copies of a **receiving report.** On this report are listed the quantity, description, and condition of the items received. The original copy is sent to the accounting department. The second copy is sent to the department that requisitioned the merchandise. The third copy is sent to the purchasing department. The fourth copy is retained on file in the receiving department.

The copies sent to the purchasing and requisitioning departments act as notification of the arrival of the goods.

Invoice Approval Form

When the receiving report arrives in the accounting department, it has in its possession copies of the—

1. Requisition listing the items that were to be ordered.
2. Purchase order that lists the merchandise actually ordered.
3. Invoice showing quantity, description, unit price, and total of the goods shipped by the seller.
4. Receiving report that lists quantity and condition of the items received.

With the information on these papers, the accounting department is in a position to approve the invoice for entry on the books and ultimate payment. In approving the invoice, the accounting department checks and compares the information on all the papers. To facilitate the checking procedure and to ensure that no step is omitted, an **invoice approval form** is commonly used. This may be a separate business paper that is attached to the invoice, or the information shown in Illustration 7-1 may be stamped directly on the invoice with a rubber stamp.

As each step in the checking procedure is completed, the clerk making the check initials the invoice approval form. Initials in each space on the form indicate:

1. **Requisition check** . . . . . . The items on the invoice agree with the requisition and were requisitioned.
2. **Purchase order check** . . . . The items on the invoice agree with the purchase order and were ordered.
3. **Receiving report check** . . . . The items on the invoice agree with the receiving report and were received.
4. **Invoice check:**
    Price approval . . . . The invoice prices are the agreed prices.
    Calculations . . . . The invoice has no mathematical errors.
    Terms . . . . The terms are the agreed terms.

Illustration 7-1

```
                 Invoice Approval Form
        Purchase order number _____
        Requisition check _____
        Purchase order check _____
        Receiving report check _____
        Invoice check:
          Price approval _____
          Calculations _____
          Terms _____
        Approved for payment:

          _____
```

The Voucher

When a voucher system is in use, after the invoice is checked and approved, a **voucher** is prepared. A voucher is a business paper on which a transaction is summarized, its correctness certified, and its recording and payment approved. Vouchers vary somewhat from company to company. However, in general, they are so designed that the invoice, bill, or other documents from which they are prepared are attached to and folded inside the voucher. This makes for ease in filing. The inside of a voucher is shown in Illustration 7-2 and the outside in Illustration 7-3. The preparation of a voucher is a simple task requiring only that a clerk enter the required information in the proper blank spaces on a voucher form. The information is taken from the invoice and its supporting documents. After the voucher is completed, the invoice and its supporting documents are attached to and folded inside the voucher. The voucher is then sent to the desk of the chief clerk or auditor who makes an additional check, approves the accounting distribution (the accounts to be debited), and approves the voucher for recording.

After being approved and recorded, a voucher is filed until its due date, when it is sent to the office of the company cashier or other disbursing officer for payment. Here the person responsible for issuing checks depends upon the approved voucher and its signed supporting documents to verify that the obligation is a proper obligation, properly incurred, and should be paid. For example, the purchase requisition and purchase order attached

Illustration 7-2   Inside of a Voucher

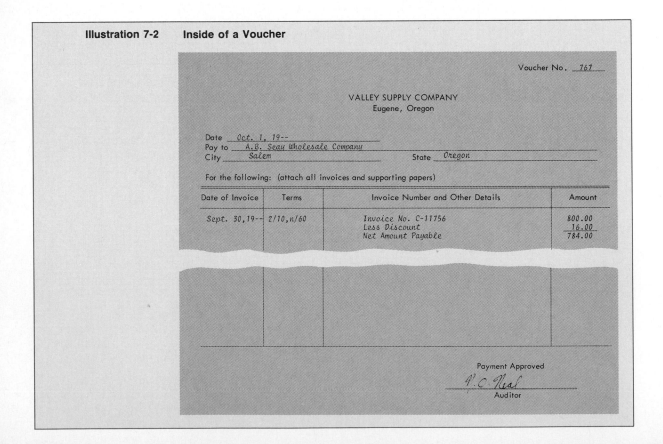

Illustration 7-3   Outside of a Voucher

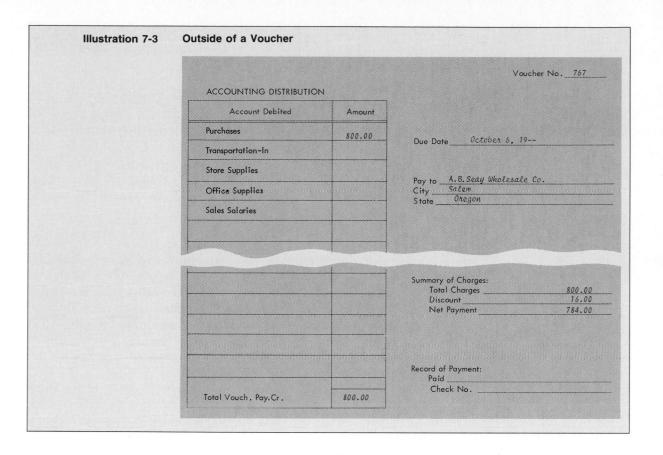

ACCOUNTING DISTRIBUTION

Voucher No. _767_

Account Debited	Amount
Purchases	800.00
Transportation-In	
Store Supplies	
Office Supplies	
Sales Salaries	

Due Date ____October 6, 19--____

Pay to ____A. B. Seay Wholesale Co.____
City ____Salem____
State ____Oregon____

Summary of Charges:
Total Charges _____ 800.00
Discount _____ 16.00
Net Payment _____ 784.00

Record of Payment:
Paid _____
Check No. _____

Total Vouch. Pay.Cr.	800.00

to the voucher confirm that the purchase was authorized. The receiving report shows that the items were received, and the invoice approval form verifies that the invoice was checked for errors. As a result, there is little chance for fraud, unless all the documents were stolen and the signatures forged, or there was collusion.

The Voucher System and Expenses

Under a voucher system, to gain control over disbursements, every obligation that will result in a cash disbursement must be approved for payment and recorded as a liability at the time it is incurred. This includes all expenses. As a result, for example, when the monthly telephone bill is received, it is verified and any long-distance calls are approved. A voucher is then prepared, and the telephone bill is attached to and folded inside the voucher. The voucher is then recorded, and a check is issued in its payment, or the voucher is filed for payment at a later date.

Requiring that an expense be approved for payment and recorded as an expense and a liability at the time it is incurred helps ensure that every expense payment is approved when information for its approval is available. Often invoices, bills, and statements for such things as equipment repairs are received weeks after the work is done. If no record of the repairs exists, it is difficult at that time to determine whether the invoice or bill is a correct statement of the amount owed. Also, if no records exist, it is possible for a dishonest employee to arrange with an outsider for more than one payment of an obligation, for payment of excessive amounts, and for payment for goods and services not received, all with kickbacks to the dishonest employee.

Recording Vouchers

Normally, a company large enough to use a voucher system will use a computer in recording its transactions. Consequently, for this reason and also because the primary purpose of this discussion is to describe the control techniques of a voucher system, a pen-and-ink system of recording vouchers is not described here. However, such a system is described in the Appendix at the end of this chapter.

The Petty Cash Fund

A basic principle in controlling cash disbursements is that all such disbursements be made by check. However, an exception to this rule is made for petty cash disbursements. Every business must make many small payments for items such as postage, express charges, telegrams, and small items of supplies. If each such payment is made by check, many checks for immaterial amounts are written. This is both time consuming and expensive. Therefore, to avoid writing checks for small amounts, a petty cash fund is established, and such payments are made from this fund.

When a petty cash fund is established, an estimate is made of the total small payments likely to be disbursed during a short period, usually not more than a month. A check is drawn and debited to the Petty Cash account for an amount slightly in excess of this estimate. The check is cashed, and the money is turned over to a member of the office staff who is designated **petty cashier** and who is responsible for the petty cash and for making payments therefrom.

The petty cashier usually keeps the petty cash in a locked box in the office safe. As each disbursement is made, a **petty cash receipt,** Illustration 7-4, is signed by the person receiving payment and is placed with the

Illustration 7-4

No _-1-_ $ _10.00_

RECEIVED OF PETTY CASH

DATE _Nov. 2_   19_--_

FOR _Washing windows_

CHARGE TO _Miscellaneous General Expense_
                                          ACCOUNT

APPROVED BY   RECEIVED BY
CdB.   _Bob Tone_
TOPS—FORM 3008

remaining money in the petty cashbox. Under this system, the petty cashbox should always contain paid petty cash receipts and money equal to the amount of the fund.

Each disbursement reduces the money and increases the sum of the receipts in the petty cashbox. When the money is nearly exhausted, the fund is reimbursed. To reimburse the fund, the petty cashier presents the receipts for petty cash payments to the company cashier. The company cashier stamps each receipt "paid" so that it may not be reused, retains the receipts, and gives the petty cashier a check for their sum. When this check is cashed and the proceeds returned to the petty cashbox, the money in the box is restored to its original amount, and the fund is ready to begin anew the cycle of its operations.

In making petty cash payments, some companies have the petty cashier enter each payment in a Petty Cash Record. This is a book in which the various petty cash payments are entered in columns according to the expense or other accounts to be debited when the fund is reimbursed. The columns have such headings as Postage, Transportation-In, Miscellaneous General Expense, Office Supplies, and so forth. The Petty Cash Record is not a book of original entry. It is only a supplementary record, the column totals of which provide information as to the amounts to be debited to the various accounts when the petty cash fund is reimbursed.

Although some companies use a Petty Cash Record, many companies are of the opinion that such a record is unnecessary. In the latter companies, when the petty cash fund is to be reimbursed, the petty cashier sorts the paid petty cash receipts into groups according to the expense or other accounts to be debited in recording payments from the fund. Each group is then totaled, and the totals are used in making the reimbursing entry. This method is assumed in the illustration that follows.

■ **Petty Cash Fund Illustrated**

To avoid writing numerous checks for small amounts, a company established a petty cash fund on November 1, designating one of its office clerks, Ned Fox, petty cashier. A $75 check was drawn, cashed, and the proceeds turned over to the clerk. The entry to record the check is shown in Illustration 7-5. The effect of the entry was to transfer $75 from the regular Cash account to the Petty Cash account.

Observe that the entry transfers $75 from the regular Cash account to the Petty Cash account. Also remember that the Petty Cash account is debited when the fund is established but is not debited or credited again unless the size of the fund is changed. If the fund is exhausted and reim-

Illustration 7-5

Cash Disbursements Journal

Date	Ch. No.	Payee	Account Debited	P R	Other Accts. Debit	Cash Credit
Nov. 1	58	Ned Fox, Petty Cashier	Petty Cash		75.00	75.00

Illustration 7-6

**Summary of Petty
Cash Payments**

Miscellaneous general expense:
Nov. 2, washing windows $10.00
Nov. 17, washing windows 10.00
Nov. 27, typewriter repairs 26.50 $46.50

Transportation-in:
Nov. 5, delivery of merchandise purchased . . . $ 6.75
Nov. 20, delivery of merchandise purchased. . . 8.30   15.05

Delivery expense:
Customer's package delivery 5.00

Office supplies:
Nov. 15, purchased paper clips 4.75
Total $71.30

bursements occur too often, the fund should be increased. This results in an additional debit to the Petty Cash account and a credit to the regular Cash account for the amount of the increase. If the fund is too large, part of its cash should be returned to general cash.

During November, the petty cashier of this illustration made several payments from the petty cash fund, each time taking a receipt from the person receiving payment. Then on November 27, the petty cashier made a $26.50 payment for repairs to an office typewriter and realized there was not sufficient cash in the fund for another payment. Consequently, the petty cash receipts were summarized and totaled as shown in Illustration 7-6. The summary and the petty cash receipts were then given to the company cashier in exchange for a $71.30 check to reimburse the fund. The petty cashier cashed the check, put the $71.30 proceeds in the petty cashbox, and was ready to begin again to make payments from the fund.

The reimbursing check was recorded in the Cash Disbursements Journal with the second entry of Illustration 7-7. Information for this entry came

Illustration 7-7

Cash Disbursements Journal

Date	Ch. No.	Payee	Account Debited	PR	Other Accts. Debit	Cash Credit
Nov. 1	58	Ned Fox, Petty Cashier	Petty Cash		75.00	75.00
Nov. 27	106	Ned Fox, Petty Cashier	Transportation-in. . .		15.05	
			Misc. General Expense		46.50	
			Office Supplies . . .		5.00	
			Delivery Expense . .		4.75	71.30

from the petty cashier's payments summary. Note that its debits record the petty cash payments. Such an entry is necessary to get the debits into the accounts. Consequently, petty cash must be reimbursed at the end of each accounting period, as well as at any time the money in the fund is low. If the fund is not reimbursed at the end of each accounting period, the asset petty cash is overstated, and the expenses and assets of the petty cash payments are understated on the financial statements.

Occasionally, at the time of a petty cash expenditure, a petty cashier will forget to secure a receipt, and by the time the fund is reimbursed, will have forgotten the expenditure. This causes the fund to be short. If for whatever reason the petty cash fund is short at reimbursement time, the shortage is recorded as an expense in the reimbursing entry with a debit to the **Cash Over and Short account** discussed in the next section.

Cash Over and Short

Regardless of care exercised in making change, customers are sometimes given too much change or are shortchanged. As a result, at the end of a day, the actual cash from a cash register is commonly not equal to the cash sales "rung up" on the register. For example, actual cash as counted is $557 but the register shows cash sales of $556, the entry in general journal form to record sales and the overage is:

Nov.	23	Cash	557.00	
		Cash Over and Short.		1.00
		Sales		556.00
		Day's cash sales and overage.		

If, on the other hand, cash is short, the entry in general journal form to record sales and the shortage would look like the following:

Nov.	24	Cash	621.00	
		Cash Over and Short	4.00	
		Sales		625.00
		Day's cash sales and shortage.		

Over a period of time, cash overages should about equal cash shortages. However, customers are more prone to report instances in which they are given too little change. Therefore, amounts of cash short are apt to be greater than amounts of cash over. Consequently, the Cash Over and Short account normally reaches the end of the accounting period with a debit balance. When it does so, the balance represents an expense. The expense may appear on the income statement as a separate item in the general and administrative expense section. Or if the amount is small, it may be combined with other miscellaneous expenses and appear as part of the item, miscellaneous expenses. When Cash Over and Short reaches the end of the period with a credit balance, the balance represents revenue and normally appears on the income statement as part of the item, miscellaneous revenues.

■ **Reconciling the Bank Balance**

Once every month banks provide each commercial depositor with a bank statement showing the activity in the depositor's account during the month. Different banks use a variety of different formats for their bank statements. However, all of them include in one place or another: (1) the balance of the depositor's account at the beginning of the month, (2) deposits and any other amounts added to the account, (3) checks and any other amounts deducted from the account, and (4) the account balance at the end of the month, according to the records of the bank. A typical bank statement is shown in Illustration 7-8.

Note that the changes in the account are summarized in part A of Illustration 7-8. Specific debits and credits to the account (other than canceled checks) are listed in part B. All canceled checks are listed in numerical order in part C. And the daily account balances are shown in part D.

Banks usually mail the bank statement to the depositor each month. Included in the envelope with the statement are the depositor's **canceled checks** and any debit or credit memoranda that have affected the account. The checks returned are the ones that the bank has paid during the month. They are called canceled checks because they have been stamped or punched to show that they have been paid. Other deductions that may appear on the bank statement include withdrawals through automatic teller machines (ATM withdrawals) and periodic payments arranged in advance by the depositor. In addition, the bank may deduct from the depositor's account amounts for service charges and fees, items deposited that are uncollectible, and amounts to correct previous errors. The bank notifies the depositor of each such deduction with a debit memorandum. A copy of each memorandum is included with the monthly statement.

In addition to deposits made by the depositor, the bank may add amounts to the depositor's account. Examples of additions would be amounts the bank has collected for the depositor and corrections of previous errors. A credit memorandum is used to notify the depositor of any such additions.

Another addition might be for interest the depositor has earned. Some checking accounts pay the depositor interest based on the average cash balance maintained in the account. The bank calculates the amount of interest earned and credits it to the depositor's account each month. Note in Illustration 7-8 that the bank has credited $8.42 of interest to the account of Valley Company. The methods used to calculate interest are discussed in the next chapter.

If all receipts are deposited intact and all payments, other than petty cash payments, are drawn from the checking account, the bank statement becomes a device for proving the depositor's cash records. The proof normally begins with the preparation of a **reconciliation of the bank balance.**

Need for Reconciling the Bank Balance

Normally, when the bank statement arrives, the balance of cash as shown by the statement does not agree with the balance in the depositor's accounting records. Consequently, in order to prove the accuracy of both the depositor's records and those of the bank, it is necessary to **reconcile** and account for any differences between the two balances.

Numerous factors may cause the bank statement balance to differ from the depositor's book balance of cash. Some are:

Illustration 7-8

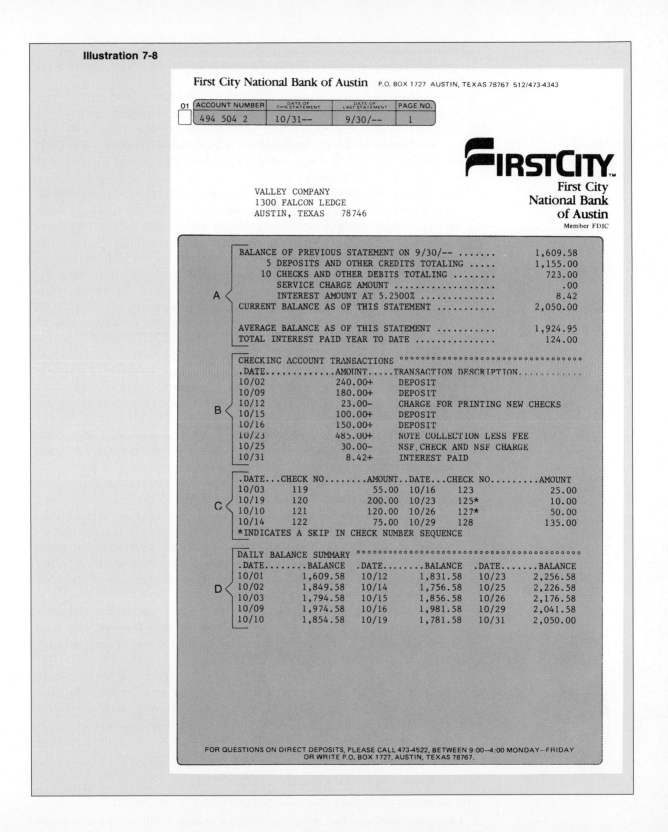

First City National Bank of Austin P.O. BOX 1727 AUSTIN, TEXAS 78767 512/473-4343

01	ACCOUNT NUMBER	DATE OF THIS STATEMENT	DATE OF LAST STATEMENT	PAGE NO.
	494 504 2	10/31--	9/30/--	1

FirstCity

First City National Bank of Austin
Member FDIC

VALLEY COMPANY
1300 FALCON LEDGE
AUSTIN, TEXAS   78746

A

```
BALANCE OF PREVIOUS STATEMENT ON 9/30/-- .......      1,609.58
     5 DEPOSITS AND OTHER CREDITS TOTALING .....      1,155.00
    10 CHECKS AND OTHER DEBITS TOTALING ........        723.00
       SERVICE CHARGE AMOUNT ...................           .00
       INTEREST AMOUNT AT 5.2500% ..............          8.42
CURRENT BALANCE AS OF THIS STATEMENT ..........      2,050.00

AVERAGE BALANCE AS OF THIS STATEMENT ..........      1,924.95
TOTAL INTEREST PAID YEAR TO DATE ..............        124.00
```

CHECKING ACCOUNT TRANSACTIONS °°°°°°°°°°°°°°°°°°°°°°°°°°°°°°°°°°°°°°

B

.DATE	AMOUNT	TRANSACTION DESCRIPTION
10/02	240.00+	DEPOSIT
10/09	180.00+	DEPOSIT
10/12	23.00-	CHARGE FOR PRINTING NEW CHECKS
10/15	100.00+	DEPOSIT
10/16	150.00+	DEPOSIT
10/23	485.00+	NOTE COLLECTION LESS FEE
10/25	30.00-	NSF CHECK AND NSF CHARGE
10/31	8.42+	INTEREST PAID

C

.DATE	CHECK NO	AMOUNT	.DATE	CHECK NO	AMOUNT
10/03	119	55.00	10/16	123	25.00
10/19	120	200.00	10/23	125*	10.00
10/10	121	120.00	10/26	127*	50.00
10/14	122	75.00	10/29	128	135.00

*INDICATES A SKIP IN CHECK NUMBER SEQUENCE

DAILY BALANCE SUMMARY °°°

D

.DATE	BALANCE	.DATE	BALANCE	.DATE	BALANCE
10/01	1,609.58	10/12	1,831.58	10/23	2,256.58
10/02	1,849.58	10/14	1,756.58	10/25	2,226.58
10/03	1,794.58	10/15	1,856.58	10/26	2,176.58
10/09	1,974.58	10/16	1,981.58	10/29	2,041.58
10/10	1,854.58	10/19	1,781.58	10/31	2,050.00

FOR QUESTIONS ON DIRECT DEPOSITS, PLEASE CALL 473-4522, BETWEEN 9:00—4:00 MONDAY--FRIDAY
OR WRITE P.O. BOX 1727, AUSTIN, TEXAS 78767.

1. **Outstanding checks.** These are checks that have been drawn by the depositor and deducted on the depositor's records but have not reached the bank for payment and deduction.

2. **Unrecorded deposits.** Concerns often make deposits at the end of each business day, after the bank has closed. These deposits are made in the bank's night depository and are not recorded by the bank until the next business day. Consequently, if a deposit is placed in the night depository the last day of the month, it does not appear on the bank statement for that month.

3. **Charges for uncollectible items and for service.** Sometimes, a company deposits a customer's check that is found to be uncollectible. Usually, the problem is nonsufficient funds in the customer's account to cover the check. Thus, the check is called a nonsufficient funds (NSF) check. The bank first credits the depositor's account for the full amount of the deposit. Then, when the bank learns that the check is uncollectible, it debits the depositor's account for the amount of the check. Also, the bank may charge the depositor a fee for processing the NSF check. The bank notifies the depositor of each such deduction with a debit memorandum. If the item is material in amount, the memorandum is mailed to the depositor on the day of the deduction. Although each deduction should be recorded on the day the memorandum is received, sometimes an entry is not made until the bank reconciliation is prepared. Also, memoranda for small amounts may not be sent to the depositor until the bank statement is mailed.

   Banks charge a depositor's account for other services such as the printing of new checks. And a monthly service charge may be made for general processing of checking account activity.

4. **Credits for collections and for interest.** Banks often act as collection agents for their depositors, collecting for a small fee promissory notes and other items. When an item such as a promissory note is collected, the bank usually deducts its fee and adds the net proceeds to the depositor's account. It then sends a credit memorandum as notification of the transaction. As soon as the memorandum is received, it should be recorded. Occasionally, these items remain unrecorded until the time of the bank reconciliation.

   Some bank accounts earn interest on the average cash balance in the account during the month. If an account earns interest, the bank statement will include a credit for the amount earned during the past month.

5. **Errors.** Regardless of care and systems of internal control for automatic error detection, both the bank and the depositor make errors that affect the bank balance. Occasionally, these errors are not discovered until the balance is reconciled. Also, the depositor may make errors in the accounting records. Such errors often are not discovered until the balance is reconciled.

Steps in Reconciling the Bank Balance

The steps in reconciling the bank balance are the following:

1. Compare deposits listed on the bank statement with deposits shown in the accounting records. Note any discrepancies and discover which is correct. List any errors or unrecorded items.

2. Examine all other credits to the account shown on the bank statement and determine whether each one has been recorded in the books. These items include collections by the bank, corrections of previous bank statement errors, and interest earned by the depositor. List any unrecorded items.

3. Compare the list of canceled checks on the bank statement with the actual checks returned with the statement. For each check, make sure that the correct amount was deducted by the bank and that the returned check was properly charged to the company's account. Note any discrepancies or errors.

4. Compare the outstanding checks listed on the previous month's bank reconciliation with the canceled checks listed on the bank statement. Prepare a list of any checks that remain outstanding at the end of the current month.

5. Compare the canceled checks listed on the bank statement with the checks recorded in the books since the last reconciliation. To make this process easier, the bank statement normally lists canceled checks in the same numerical order as the checks are numbered. List any outstanding checks. Although companies with reasonable internal controls would rarely if ever write a check without recording it, an individual may occasionally write a check and fail to record it in the books. List any canceled checks that are unrecorded in the books.

6. Examine all other debits to the account as shown on the bank statement and determine whether each one has been recorded in the books. These include bank charges for newly printed checks, NSF checks, stop payment orders, and monthly service charges.

7. Prepare a reconciliation of the bank statement balance with the book balance of cash. Such a reconciliation is shown in Illustration 7-9.

8. Determine if any debits or credits appearing on the bank statement are unrecorded in the books of account. Make journal entries to record them.

■ **Illustration of a Bank Reconciliation**

To illustrate a bank reconciliation, assume that Valley Company found the following when it attempted to reconcile its bank balance of October 31. The bank balance as shown by the bank statement was $2,050, and the cash balance according to the accounting records was $1,404.58. A $145 deposit, placed in the bank's night depository after banking hours on October 31, was unrecorded by the bank at the time the bank statement was mailed. Included with the bank statement was a credit memorandum showing the bank had collected a note receivable for the company on October 23. The note's proceeds of $500 less a $15 collection fee were credited to the company's account. The bank statement also showed a credit of $8.42 for interest earned on the average cash balance in the account. Neither the collection of the note nor the interest had been recorded on the company books.

A comparison of canceled checks with the company's books showed that two checks were outstanding. Check No. 124 for $150 and Check No. 126 for $200 were outstanding and unpaid by the bank. Other debits on the bank statement that had not been recorded on the books included: (1) a $23 debit memorandum for checks printed by the bank; and (2) an

Illustration 7-9

Valley Company
Bank Reconciliation
October 31, 19—

Book balance of cash . .		$1,404.58	Bank statement balance .	$2,050.00
Add:			Add:	
Proceeds of note less			Deposit of 10/31 . . .	145.00
collection fee	$485.00			
Interest earned	8.42	493.42		
		$1,898.00		$2,195.00
Deduct:			Deduct:	
NSF check plus			Outstanding checks:	
service charge . . .	$ 30.00		No. 124 . . . . . . $150.00	
Check printing charge .	23.00	53.00	No. 126 . . . . . . 200.00	350.00
		$1,845.00		$1,845.00

NSF (nonsufficient funds) check for $20 plus related processing fee of $10. The NSF check had been received from a customer, Frank Jones, on October 16, and had been included in that day's deposit.

The bank reconciliation that reflects the above items is shown in Illustration 7-9.

A bank reconciliation helps locate any errors made by either the bank or the depositor. It discloses any items that have been entered on the company books but have not come to the bank's attention. Also, it discloses items that should be recorded on the company books but are unrecorded on the date of the reconciliation. For example, in the reconciliation illustrated, the reconciled cash balance, $1,845, is the true cash balance. However, at the time the reconciliation is completed, Valley Company's accounting records show a $1,404.58 book balance. Consequently, entries must be made to adjust the book balance, increasing it to the true cash balance. This requires four entries. The first in general journal form is:

Nov.	2	Cash	485.00	
		Collection Expense	15.00	
		Notes Receivable		500.00
		To record the proceeds and collection fee of a note collected by the bank.		

This entry is self-explanatory. The bank collected a note receivable, deducted a collection fee, and deposited the difference to the Valley Company account. The entry increases the amount of cash on the books, records the collection expense, and reduces notes receivable.

The second entry records the interest credited to Valley Company's account by the bank. Interest earned is a revenue, and the entry recognizes both the revenue and the related increase in Cash. As mentioned earlier, interest calculations are discussed in the next chapter. The entry is:

Nov.	2	Cash	8.42	
		Interest Earned		8.42
		To record interest earned on the average		
		cash balance maintained in the checking		
		account.		

The third entry is:

Nov.	2	Accounts Receivable—Frank Jones	30.00	
		Cash		30.00
		To charge Frank Jones' account for his NSF		
		check and for the bank's fee.		

This entry records the NSF check returned as uncollectible. The $20 check was received from Jones in payment of his account and was deposited as cash. The bank, unable to collect the check, charged $10 for handling the NSF check and deducted $30 from the Valley Company account. This made it necessary for the company to reverse the entry made when the check was received and also record the $10 processing fee. Valley Company charged the $10 fee to Jones' account and will attempt to collect the entire $30 from Jones.

The fourth entry debits the check printing charge to Miscellaneous General Expenses and in general journal form is:

Nov.	2	Miscellaneous General Expense	23.00	
		Cash		23.00
		Check printing charge.		

■ **Other Internal Control Procedures**

Internal control procedures apply to every phase of a company's operations from purchases through sales, cash receipts, cash disbursements, and the control of plant assets. Many of these procedures are discussed in later chapters. However, the way in which a company can gain control over purchases discounts is discussed here, and the technique is illustrated below.

Recall that thus far the following entries in general journal form have been used in recording the receipt and payment of an invoice for merchandise purchased.

Oct.	2	Purchases	1,000.00	
		Accounts Payable		1,000.00
		Purchased merchandise, terms 2/10, n/60.		
	12	Accounts Payable	1,000.00	
		Purchases Discounts		20.00
		Cash		980.00
		Paid the invoice of October 2.		

The invoice of these entries was recorded at its **gross,** $1,000, amount. This is the way in which invoices are recorded in many companies. However, well-managed companies follow the practice of taking all offered cash discounts. In many of these companies, invoices are recorded at their **net** (after discount) amounts. To illustrate, a company that records invoices at net amounts purchased merchandise having a $1,000 invoice price, terms 2/10, n/60. On receipt of the goods, it deducted the offered $20 discount from the gross invoice amount and recorded the purchase with this debit and credit:

Oct.	2	Purchases	980.00	
		Accounts Payable		980.00
		Purchased merchandise on credit.		

If the invoice for this purchase is paid within the discount period, the cash disbursements entry to record the payment has a debit to Accounts Payable and a credit to Cash for $980. However, if payment is not made within the discount period and the discount is **lost,** an entry like the following must be made in the General Journal either before or when the invoice is paid:

Dec.	1	Discounts Lost	20.00	
		Accounts Payable		20.00
		To record the discount lost.		

A check for the full $1,000 invoice amount is then drawn, recorded, and mailed to the creditor.

Advantage of the Net Method

When invoices are recorded at gross amounts, the amount of discounts taken is deducted from the balance of the Purchases account on the income statement to arrive at the cost of merchandise purchased. However, when invoices are recorded at gross amounts, if through oversight or carelessness discounts are lost, the amount of **discounts lost** does not appear in any account or on the income statement and may not come to the attention of management. On the other hand, when purchases are recorded at net amounts, the amount of discounts taken does not appear on the income statement. However, the amount of discounts lost is called to management's attention through the appearance on the income statement of the expense account, Discounts Lost, as in the condensed income statement of Illustration 7-10.

Of the two methods, recording invoices at their net amounts probably supplies management with the more valuable information, the amount of discounts lost through oversight, carelessness, or other cause. It also gives management better control over the work of the people responsible for

---

Illustration 7-10

XYZ Company
Income Statement
For Year Ended December 31, 19—

Sales	$100,000
Cost of goods sold.	60,000
Gross profit from sales	$ 40,000
Operating expenses	28,000
Income from operations.	$ 12,000
Other revenues and expenses:	
Discounts lost	(150)
Net income	$ 11,850

---

taking cash discounts. If discounts are lost, someone must explain why. As a result, few discounts are lost through carelessness.

APPENDIX: RECORDING VOUCHERS, PEN-AND-INK SYSTEM

When a voucher system is in use, an account called Vouchers Payable replaces the Accounts Payable account described in previous chapters. And for every transaction that will result in a cash disbursement, a voucher is prepared and credited to this account. For example, when merchandise is purchased, the voucher covering the transaction is recorded with a debit to Purchases and a credit to Vouchers Payable. Likewise, when a plant asset is purchased or an expense is incurred, the voucher of the transaction is recorded with a debit to the proper plant asset or expense account and a credit to Vouchers Payable.

In a pen-and-ink system, vouchers are recorded in a **Voucher Register** similar to Illustration 7A-1. Such a register has a Vouchers Payable credit column and a number of debit columns. The exact debit columns vary from company to company, but merchandising concerns always provide a Purchases debit column. Also, as long as space is available, special debit columns are provided for transactions that occur frequently. In addition, an Other Accounts debit column is provided for transactions that do not occur often.

In recording vouchers in a register like that of Illustration 7A-1, all information about each voucher, other than information about its payment, is entered as soon as the voucher is approved for recording. The information as to payment date and the number of the paying check is entered later as each voucher is paid.

In posting a Voucher Register like that in Illustration 7A-1, the columns are first totaled and crossfooted to prove their equality. The Vouchers Payable column total is then credited to the Vouchers Payable account. The totals of the Purchases, Transportation-In, Sales Salaries Expense, Advertising Expense, Delivery Expense, and Office Salaries Expense are debited to these accounts. None of the individual amounts in these columns

Illustration 7A-1

Page 32 .... Voucher

Date 19—		Voucher No.	Payee	When and How Paid		Vouchers Payable Credit	Purchases Debit	Transportation-In Debit	
				Date	Check No.				
Oct.	1	767	A. B. Seay Co.	10/6	733	800.00	800.00		1
	1	768	Daily Sentinel	10/9	744	53.00			2
	2	769	Seaboard Supply Co.	10/12	747	235.00	155.00	10.00	3
	6	770	George Smith	10/6	734	85.00			4
	6	771	Frank Jones	10/6	735	95.00			5
	6	772	George Roth	10/6	736	95.00			6
	30	998	First National Bank	10/30	972	505.00			33
									34
	30	999	Pacific Telephone Co.	10/30	973	18.00			35
	31	1000	Tarbell Wholesale Co.			235.00	235.00		36
	31	1001	Office Equipment Co.	10/31	974	195.00			37
	31		Totals			5,079.00	2,435.00	156.00	38
						(213)	(511)	(514)	39
									40
									41

are posted. However, the individual amounts in the Other Accounts column are posted as individual amounts, and the column total is not posted.

The Unpaid Vouchers File

When a voucher system is in use, some vouchers are paid as soon as they are recorded. Others must be filed until payment is due. As an aid in taking cash discounts, vouchers for which payment is not due are generally filed in an unpaid vouchers file under the dates on which they are to be paid.

The file of unpaid vouchers takes the place of a subsidiary Accounts Payable Ledger. Actually, the file is a subsidiary ledger of amounts owed creditors. Likewise, the Vouchers Payable account is in effect a controlling account controlling the unpaid vouchers file. Consequently, after posting is completed at the end of a month, the balance of the Vouchers Payable account should equal the sum of the unpaid vouchers in the unpaid vouchers file. This is verified each month by preparing a schedule or an adding machine list of the unpaid vouchers in the file and comparing its total with the balance of the Vouchers Payable account. In addition, the unpaid vouchers in the file are compared with the unpaid vouchers shown in the Voucher Register's record of payments column. The number of each paying check and the payment date are entered in the Voucher Register's payments column as each voucher is paid. Consequently, the vouchers in the register without check numbers and payment dates should be the same as those in the unpaid vouchers file.

	Sales Salaries Expense Debit	Advertising Expense Debit	Delivery Expense Debit	Office Salaries Expense Debit	Other Accounts Debit		
Register							**Page 32**
					Account Name	P R	Amount Debit
1							
2		53.00					
3					Store Supplies	117	70.00
4				85.00			
5	95.00						
6	95.00						
33					Notes Payable	211	500.00
34					Interest Expense	721	5.00
35					Telephone Expense	655	18.00
36							
37					Office Equipment	134	195.00
38	740.00	115.00	358.00	340.00			935.00
39	(611)	(612)	(615)	(615)			(✓)
40							
41							

■ **The Voucher System Check Register**

In a voucher system, the Cash Disbursements Journal is replaced by a simpler Check Register. All checks drawn in payment of vouchers are recorded in the Check Register. No obligation is paid until a voucher covering the payment is prepared and recorded in the Voucher Register. Likewise, no check is drawn except in payment of a specific voucher. Consequently, all checks drawn result in debits to Vouchers Payable and credits to Cash, unless a discount must be recorded. Then, there are credits to both Purchases Discounts and to Cash. A Check Register is shown in Illustration 7A-2. Note that it has columns for debits to Vouchers Payable and credits to Purchases Discounts and to Cash. In posting, all amounts entered in these columns are posted in the column totals.

■ **Purchases Returns**

Occasionally, an item must be returned after the voucher recording its purchase has been prepared and entered in the Voucher Register. In such cases, the return may be recorded with a general journal entry similar to the following:

Nov.	5	Vouchers Payable	15.00	
		Purchases Returns and Allowances . . .		15.00
		Returned defective merchandise.		

Illustration 7A-2

Check Register

Date 19—		Payee	Voucher No.	Check No.	Vouchers Payable Debit	Purchases Discounts Credit	Cash Credit
Oct.	1	C. B. & Y. RR. Co.	765	728	14.00		14.00
	3	Frank Mills	766	729	73.00		73.00
	3	Ajax Wholesale Co.	753	730	250.00	5.00	245.00
	4	Normal Supply Co.	747	731	100.00	2.00	98.00
	5	Office Supply Co.	763	732	43.00		43.00
	6	A. B. Seay Co.	767	733	800.00	16.00	784.00
	6	George Smith	770	734	85.00		85.00
	6	Frank Jones	771	735	95.00		95.00
	30	First National Bank	998	972	505.00		505.00
	30	Pacific Telephone Co.	999	973	18.00		18.00
	31	Office Equipment Co.	1001	974	195.00		195.00
	31	Totals			6,468.00	28.00	6,440.00
					(213)	(512)	(111)

In addition to the entry, the amount of the return is deducted on the voucher, and the credit memorandum and other documents verifying the return are attached to the voucher. Then, when the voucher is paid, a check is drawn for its corrected amount.

☐

Glossary

Bank reconciliation an analysis explaining the difference between an enterprise's book balance of cash and its bank statement balance.

Canceled checks checks that have been punched or stamped by the bank to show they have been paid.

Cash Over and Short account an income statement account in which are recorded cash overages and cash shortages arising from making change.

Discounts lost cash discounts offered but not taken.

Gross method of recording purchases a method of recording purchases by which offered cash discounts are not deducted from the invoice price in determining the amount to be recorded.

Internal control system the procedures adopted by a business to encourage adherence to prescribed managerial policies; to protect its assets from waste, fraud, and theft; and to ensure accurate and reliable accounting data.

Invoice a document, prepared by a vendor, on which are listed the items sold, the sales prices, the customer's name, and the terms of sale.

Invoice approval form a document on which the accounting department notes that it has performed each step in the process of checking an invoice and approving it for recording and payment.

Net method of recording purchases a method of recording purchases by which offered cash discounts are deducted from the invoice price in determining the amount to be recorded.

Outstanding checks checks that have been written, recorded, and sent or given to payees but have not been received, paid, and canceled by the bank.

Purchase order a business form used in placing an order for the purchase of goods from a vendor.

Purchase requisition a business form used within a business to ask the purchasing department of the business to buy needed items.

Receiving report a form used within a business to notify the proper persons of the receipt of goods ordered and of the quantities and condition of the goods.

Reconcile to account for the difference between two amounts.

Vendee the purchaser of something.

Vendor the individual or enterprise selling something.

Voucher a business paper used in summarizing a transaction and approving it for recording and payment.

Voucher Register a book of original entry in which approved vouchers are recorded.

Voucher system an accounting system used to control the incurrence and payment of obligations requiring the disbursement of cash.

☐ **Questions for Class Discussion**

1. Name some of the broad principles of internal control.
2. Why should the person who keeps the record of an asset be a different person from the one responsible for custody of the asset?

3. Internal control procedures are important in every business, but at what stage in the development of a business do they become critical?

4. Why should responsibility for a sequence of related transactions be divided among different departments or individuals?

5. In a small business, it is sometimes impossible to separate the functions of record-keeping and asset custody, and it is sometimes impossible to divide responsibilities for related transactions. What should be substituted for these control procedures?

6. Are the principles of internal control for computerized accounting systems different from the principles of internal control for manual accounting systems?

7. What are some of the effects of computers on internal control?

8. What is meant by the phrase *all receipts should be deposited intact*? Why should all receipts be deposited intact on the day of receipt?

9. Why should a company's bookkeeper not be given responsibility for receiving cash for the company nor the responsibility for signing checks or making cash disbursements in any other way?

10. In purchasing merchandise in a large store, why are the department managers not permitted to deal directly with the sources of supply?

11. What are the duties of the selling department managers in the purchasing procedures of a large store?

12. Tell (a) who prepares, (b) who receives, and (c) the purpose of each of the following business papers:
   a. Purchase requisition.   d. Receiving report.
   b. Purchase order.   e. Invoice approval form.
   c. Invoice.   f. Voucher.

13. Do all companies need a voucher system? At what approximate point in a company's growth would you recommend the installation of such a system?

14. When a disbursing officer issues a check in a large business, he or she usually cannot know from personal contact that the assets, goods, or services for which the check pays were received by the business or that the purchase was properly authorized. However, if the company has an internal control system, the officer can depend on the system. Exactly what documents does the officer depend on to tell that the purchase was authorized and properly made and the goods were actually received?

15. Why are some cash payments made from a petty cash fund? Why are not all payments made by check?

16. What is a petty cash receipt? When a petty cash receipt is prepared, who signs it?

17. Explain how a petty cash fund operates.

18. Why must a petty cash fund be reimbursed at the end of each accounting period?

19. What are two results of reimbursing the petty cash fund?

20. What is a bank statement? What kind of information appears on a bank statement?

21. What is the meaning of the phrase *to reconcile a bank balance?*

22. Why are the bank statement balance of cash and the depositor's book balance of cash reconciled?

23. What valuable information becomes readily available to management when invoices are recorded at net amounts? Is this information readily available when invoices are recorded at gross amounts?

☐ **Class Exercises**

Exercise 7-1

A company established a $100 petty cash fund on March 15. Two weeks later, on March 29, there was $6.75 in cash in the fund and receipts for these expenditures: postage, $22.75; transportation-in, $18.25; miscellaneous general expenses, $28; and office supplies, $24.25. Give in general journal form *(a)* the entry to establish the fund and *(b)* the entry to reimburse it on March 29. *(c)* Assume that since the fund was exhausted so quickly, it was not only reimbursed on March 29 but also increased in size to $150. Give the entry to reimburse and increase the fund to $150.

Exercise 7-2

A company established a $125 petty cash fund on August 10. On August 31, there was $34.50 in cash in the fund and receipts for these expenditures: transportation-in, $14.75; miscellaneous general expenses, $27.50; and office supplies, $46.25. The petty cashier could not account for the $2 shortage in the fund. Give in general journal form *(a)* the entry to establish the fund and *(b)* the August 31 entry to reimburse the fund and reduce it to $100.

Exercise 7-3

Some of Trace Company's cash receipts from customers are sent to the company in the mail. Trace Company's bookkeeper opens the letters and deposits the cash received each day. What internal control problems are inherent in this arrangement? What changes would you recommend?

Exercise 7-4

Eastside Store deposits all receipts intact on the day received and makes all payments by check; and on December 31, after all posting was completed, its Cash account showed a $3,775 debit balance; but its December 31 bank statement showed only $3,256.50 on deposit in the bank on that day. Prepare a bank reconciliation for the store, using the following information:

a. Outstanding checks, $500.

b. Included with the December canceled checks returned by the bank was a $10 debit memorandum for bank services.

c. Check No. 642, returned with the canceled checks, was correctly drawn for $28 in payment of the telephone bill and was paid by the bank on December 8, but it had been recorded with a debit to Telephone Expense and a credit to Cash as though it were for $82.

d. The December 31 cash receipts, $1,062.50 were placed in the bank's night depository after banking hours on that date and were unrecorded by the bank at the time the December bank statement was prepared.

Exercise 7-5

Give in general journal form any entries that Eastside Store should make as a result of having prepared the bank reconciliation of the previous exercise.

Exercise 7-6

Barr Company incurred $28,000 of operating expenses in July, a month in which its sales were $100,000. The company began July with a $52,000 merchandise inventory and ended the month with a $56,000 inventory. During the month, it purchased merchandise having a $64,000 invoice price, all of which was subject to a 2% discount for prompt payment. The company took advantage of the discounts on $44,000 of the purchases; but through an error in filing it did not earn and could not take the discount on a $20,000 invoice paid on July 31.

Required

1. Prepare a July income statement for the company under the assumption that it records invoices at gross amounts.
2. Prepare a second income statement for the company under the assumption that it records invoices at net amounts.

Exercise 7-7

Complete the following bank reconciliation by filling in the missing amounts.

Eaton Company
Bank Reconciliation
May 31, 19—

Book balance of cash	$?	Bank statement balance	$3,634
Add: Collection of note	400	Add: Deposit of May 31.	?
Interest earned	12	Bank error	20
	$3,912		$?
Deduct: Service charge.	?	Deduct: Outstanding checks. . .	750
NSF check	200		
Reconciled balance	$?	Reconciled balanced.	$3,704

Problems   Problem 7-1

A concern completed the following petty cash transactions during January of the current year:

Jan. 1 Drew a $100 check, cashed it, and gave the proceeds and the petty cashbox to Tom Gray, an office clerk who was to act as petty cashier.

 5 Purchased computer paper with petty cash, $22.50.

 7 Paid $7.75 COD delivery charges on merchandise purchased for resale.

Jan. 10   Paid $6.25 parcel post charges on merchandise sold to a customer and delivered by mail.

12   Gave Mr. Bruce Hanson, husband of the business owner, $15 from petty cash for cab fare and other personal expenses.

19   Paid $7.50 COD delivery charges on merchandise purchased for resale.

23   Paid a service station attendant $6.50 for washing the personal car of Kay Hanson, the business owner.

24   Paid Speedy Delivery Service $5.50 from petty cash to deliver merchandise sold to a customer.

26   Paid $25.50 for minor repairs to an office typewriter.

29   Tom Gray sorted the petty cash receipts by accounts affected and exchanged them for a check to reimburse the fund for expenditures and, since there was only $1.50 in cash in the fund, for the shortage for which he could not account.

Required

1. Prepare a general journal entry to record the check establishing the petty cash fund.

2. Prepare a summary of petty cash payments that has these categories: Office supplies, Transportation-in, Delivery expense, Withdrawals, and Miscellaneous expenses. Sort the payments into the appropriate categories, total the expenses in each category, and prepare the general journal entry to reimburse the fund.

Problem 7-2

A business completed these transactions:

May 20   Drew a $75 check to establish a petty cash fund, cashed it, and delivered the proceeds and the petty cashbox to James Taft, an office secretary who was to act as petty cashier.

22   Paid Cy's Delivery Service $10 to deliver merchandise sold to a customer.

26   Purchased office supplies with petty cash, $17.75.

29   Paid $25 from petty cash to have the office windows washed.

31   Jay Speck, the owner of the business, signed a petty cash receipt and took $10 from petty cash for lunch money.

June 3   Paid $9.50 COD delivery charges on merchandise purchased for resale.

4   James Taft noted that there was only $2.75 cash remaining in the fund. Thus, he sorted the paid petty cash receipts by accounts affected and exchanged them for a check to reimburse the fund. However, since the fund had been so rapidly exhausted, the check was made for an amount large enough to increase the size of the fund to $150.

6   Paid Cy's Delivery Service $9.50 to deliver merchandise to a customer.

10   Paid the Westside Cleaner's delivery person $17.50 upon the delivery to the office of clothes Mr. Speck had dropped off at the cleaners.

June 12   Paid $21.50 COD delivery charges on merchandise purchased for resale.

18   Gave Mrs. Speck, the wife of the business owner, $25 from petty cash for cab fare and other personal expenditures.

21   Paid $38 for minor repairs to an office typewriter.

25   Purchased office supplies with petty cash, $8.50.

28   Paid $7.50 COD delivery charges on merchandise purchased for resale.

30   James Taft sorted the petty cash receipts by accounts affected and exchanged them for a check to reimburse the fund for expenditures and, since there was only $12.50 in cash in the fund, for the shortage which he could not explain.

Required

1. Prepare a general journal entry to record the check establishing the petty cash fund.

2. Prepare a summary of petty cash payments prior to June 4 that has these categories: Office supplies, Transportation-in, Delivery expense, Withdrawals, and Miscellaneous expenses. Sort the expenditures into the appropriate categories and total the expenses in each category. Prepare a similar summary of petty cash payments after June 4.

3. Prepare entries to reimburse the fund and increase its size on June 4 and to reimburse the fund on June 30.

Problem 7-3

The George Company has only one journal in its accounting system and records all transactions in that general journal. However, the company recently set up a petty cash fund to facilitate payments of small items. The following transactions involving the petty cash fund were noted by the petty cashier as occurring during March (the last month of the company's fiscal year).

Mar. 1   Received a company check for $150 to establish the petty cash fund.

11   Received a company check to replenish the fund for the following expenditures made since March 1 and to increase the fund to $450.

a.   Payment of $28.50 to Ace Trucking for freight on merchandise delivered to George Company.

b.   Purchased postage stamps for $35.

c.   Gave Katherine Jones, owner of the business, $25 for personal use.

d.   Paid $42.75 to Appliance Company for repairs of office equipment.

e.   Discovered that only $17.25 remained in the petty cash box.

31   Having decided that the March 11 increase in the fund was too large, received a company check to replenish the fund for the following expenditures made since March 11 but allowing the fund to be reduced in size to $350.

a. Payment of $67.50 for emergency repairs to the company's office computer printer.
b. Payment of $45 for janitorial service.
c. Purchased office supplies for $56.75.
d. Payment of $72.30 to Black Advertising for a space advertisement in a weekly newsletter.

Required

1. Prepare general journal entries to record the establishment of the fund on March 1 and its replenishments on March 11 and on March 31.
2. If George Company had failed to replenish the petty cash fund on March 31, what would have been the effect on net income for the fiscal year ended March 31 and on total assets on March 31? Explain your answer.

Problem 7-4

The following information was available to reconcile Prince Company's book balance of cash with its bank statement balance as of December 31:

a. The December 31 cash balance according to the accounting records was $8,340, and the bank statement balance for that date was $7,959.
b. Two checks, No. 722 for $309 and No. 726 for $279, were outstanding on November 30 when the book and bank statement balances were last reconciled. Check No. 726 was returned with the December canceled checks, but Check No. 722 was not.
c. Check No. 803 for $237 and Check No. 805 for $219, both written and entered in the accounting records in December, were not among the canceled checks returned.
d. When the December checks were compared with entries in the accounting records, it was found that Check No. 751 had been correctly drawn for $514 in payment for store supplies but was entered in the accounting records in error as though it were drawn for $415.
e. Two debit memoranda and a credit memorandum were included with the returned checks and were unrecorded at the time of the reconciliation. The credit memorandum indicated that the bank had collected a $1,500 note receivable for the company, deducted a $12 collection fee, and credited the balance to the company's account. One of the debit memoranda was for $132 and had attached to it an NSF check in that amount that had been received from a customer, Lee Branch, in payment of his account. The second debit memorandum was for a special printing of checks and was for $36.
f. The December 31 cash receipts, $2,367, had been placed in the bank's night depository after banking hours on that date and did not appear on the bank statement.

Required

Prepare a December 31 bank reconciliation for the company and the entries in general journal form required to bring the company's book balance of cash into conformity with the reconciled balance.

Problem 7-5

Bacon Company reconciled its book and bank statement balances of cash on October 31 and showed two checks outstanding at that time, No. 713 for $825 and No. 716 for $426. The following information was available for the November 30 reconciliation:

From the November 30 bank statement:

BALANCE OF PREVIOUS STATEMENT ON 10/31/—.	5,736.00
5 DEPOSITS AND OTHER CREDITS TOTALING	8,526.00
9 CHECKS AND OTHER DEBITS TOTALING.	7,227.00
SERVICE CHARGE AMOUNT	9.00
CURRENT BALANCE AS OF THIS STATEMENT	7,026.00

CHECKING ACCOUNT TRANSACTIONS°°°

.DATE	AMOUNT	TRANSACTION DESCRIPTION
11/ 3	936.00+	Deposit
11/14	1,653.00+	Deposit
11/21	1,536.00+	Deposit
11/28	1,416.00+	Deposit
11/29	129.00–	NSF check
11/30	9.00–	Service charge
11/30	2,985.00+	Credit memorandum

.DATE	CHECK NO	AMOUNT	DATE	CHECK NO	AMOUNT
11/ 2	713	825.00	11/ 9	721	2,211.00
11/ 3	718*	654.00	11/12	722	396.00
11/ 5	719	906.00	11/18	724*	852.00
11/12	720	225.00	11/28	725	1,029.00

* Indicates a skip in check sequence

From Bacon Company's accounting records:

Cash Receipts Deposited

Date			Cash Debit
Nov. 3			936.00
14			1,653.00
21			1,536.00
28			1,416.00
30			741.00
			6,282.00

Cash Disbursements

Check No.			Cash Credit
718			654.00
719			960.00
720			225.00
721			2,211.00
722			396.00
723			408.00
724			852.00
725			1,029.00
726			159.00
			6,894.00

Cash

Date		Explanation	PR	Debit	Credit	Balance
Oct.	31	Balance	√			4,485.00
Nov.	30	Total receipts	R-8	6,282.00		10,767.00
	30	Total disbursements	D-9		6,894.00	3,873.00

Check No. 719 was correctly drawn for $906 in payment for office equipment; however, the bookkeeper misread the amount and entered it in the accounting records with a debit to Office Equipment and a credit to Cash as though it were for $960.

The NSF check was received from a customer, Bob Burns, in payment of his account. Its return is unrecorded. The credit memorandum resulted from a $3,000 note collected for Bacon Company by the bank. The bank had deducted a $15 collection fee. The collection fee is not recorded.

Required

1. Prepare a November 30 bank reconciliation for the company.
2. Prepare in general journal form the entries needed to adjust the book balance of cash to the reconciled balance.

Problem 7-6

The March 31 credit balance in the Sales account of Austin Sales showed it had sold $97,000 of merchandise during the month. The concern began March with a $109,200 merchandise inventory and ended the month with a $90,200 inventory. It had incurred $33,000 of operating expenses during the month, and it had also recorded the following transactions:

Mar. 1   Received merchandise purchased at a $10,000 invoice price, invoice dated February 28, terms 2/10, n/30.

     5   Received a $1,000 credit memorandum (invoice price) for merchandise received on March 1 and returned for credit.

  11   Received merchandise purchased at a $16,000 invoice price, invoice dated March 9, terms 2/10, n/30.

  15   Received merchandise purchased at a $15,000 invoice price, invoice dated March 12, terms 2/10, n/30.

  19   Paid for the merchandise received on March 11, less the discount.

  22   Paid for the merchandise received on March 15, less the discount.

  27   The invoice received on March 1 had been refiled in error, after the credit memorandum was attached, for payment on this the last day of its credit period, causing the discount to be lost. Paid the invoice.

Required

1. Assume the concern records invoices at gross amounts and (*a*) prepare general journal entries to record the transactions. (*b*) Prepare a March income statement for the concern.
2. Assume the concern records invoices at net amounts and (*a*) prepare general journal entries to record the transactions. (*b*) Prepare a second income statement for the concern under this assumption.

Problem 7-7

(*This problem is based on information in the Appendix to this chapter.*)

Marney Company completed these transactions involving vouchers payable:

Mar. 3   Recorded Voucher No. 452 payable to Frost Company for merchandise having a $2,850 invoice price, invoice dated February 28, terms FOB factory, 2/10, n/30. The vendor had prepaid the freight, $135, adding the amount to the invoice and bringing its total to $2,985.

Mar. 5 Recorded Voucher No. 453 payable to *The Globe* for advertising expense, $330. Issued Check No. 838 in payment of the voucher.

6 Received a credit memorandum for merchandise having a $450 invoice price. The merchandise had been received from Frost Company on March 3, recorded on Voucher No. 452, and later returned for credit.

8 Recorded Voucher No. 454 payable to Central Realty for one month's rent on the space occupied by the store, $1,500. Issued Check No. 839 in payment of the voucher.

10 Recorded Voucher No. 455 payable to Over Supply Company for store supplies, $195, terms n/10 EOM.

12 Recorded Voucher No. 456 payable to San Marcos Company for merchandise having a $3,750 invoice price, invoice dated March 10, terms FOB factory, 2/10, n/60. The vendor had prepaid the freight charges, $150, adding the amount to the invoice and bringing its total to $3,900.

14 Recorded Voucher No. 457 payable to Payroll for sales salaries, $1,500, and office salaries, $1,125. Issued Check No. 840 in payment of the voucher. Cashed the check and paid the employees.

17 Recorded Voucher No. 458 payable to Bong Company for merchandise having a $2,250 invoice price, invoice dated March 15, terms 2/10, n/60, FOB factory. The vendor had prepaid the freight charges, $105, adding the amount to the invoice and bringing its total to $2,355.

20 Issued Check No. 841 in payment of Voucher No. 456.

24 Recorded Voucher No. 459 payable to San Marcos Company for merchandise having a $4,500 invoice price, invoice dated March 22, terms FOB factory, 2/10, n/60. The vendor had prepaid the freight charges, $210, adding the amount to the invoice and bringing its total to $4,710.

28 Discovered that Voucher No. 452 had been filed in error for payment on the last day of its credit period rather than on the last day of its discount period, causing the discount to be lost. Issued Check No. 842 in payment of the voucher, less the return.

31 Recorded Voucher No. 460 payable to Payroll for sales salaries, $1,500, and office salaries, $1,125. Issued Check No. 843 in payment of the voucher. Cashed the check and paid the employees.

Required

1. Assume that Marney Company records vouchers at gross amounts. Prepare a Voucher Register, a Check Register, and a General Journal, and record the transactions.

2. Prepare a Vouchers Payable account and post those entry portions that affect the account.

3. Prove the balance of the Vouchers Payable account by preparing a schedule of vouchers payable.

☐ **Alternate Problems**   **Problem 7-1A**

A concern completed the following petty cash transactions:

Apr. 1   Drew a $200 check, cashed it, and turned the proceeds and the
          petty cashbox over to Frank Smith, an office clerk who was to
          act as petty cashier.
      4   Paid $13.25 parcel post charges on merchandise sold to a
          customer and delivered by mail.
      7   Purchased computer paper with petty cash, $33.60.
      9   Paid $53.20 from petty cash for repairs to an office copier.
     11   Paid $14 COD delivery charges on merchandise purchased for
          resale.
     16   Paid Fastest Delivery Service $12.50 to deliver merchandise sold
          to a customer.
     20   Gave Fred Strayer, the owner of the business, $25 from petty
          cash for personal use.
     22   Paid $15.75 COD delivery charges on merchandise purchased
          for resale.
     26   Fred Strayer, owner of the business, signed a petty cash receipt
          and took $10 from petty cash for lunch money.
     29   Frank Smith exchanged his paid petty cash receipts for a check
          reimbursing the fund for expenditures and a shortage of cash
          in the fund that he could not account for. He reported a cash
          balance of $12.70 in the fund.

Required

1. Prepare a general journal entry to record the check establishing the
   petty cash fund.
2. Prepare a summary of petty cash payments that has these categories:
   Office supplies, Transportation-in, Delivery expense, Withdrawals, and
   Miscellaneous expenses. Sort the payments into the appropriate
   categories, total the expenses in each category, and prepare the general
   journal entry to reimburse the fund.

Problem 7-2A

A concern completed these petty cash transactions:

Feb. 2   Drew a $50 check to establish a petty cash fund, cashed it, and
          turned the proceeds and the petty cashbox over to June Eaton,
          an office worker who was appointed petty cashier.
      4   Paid $7.25 parcel post charges on merchandise sold to a customer
          and delivered by mail.
      8   Paid $12 to have the office windows washed.
     10   Purchased office supplies with petty cash, $14.50.
     12   Carol Rash, owner of the business, signed a petty cash receipt
          and took $5 from petty cash for coffee money.
     13   Paid $9.75 COD delivery charges on merchandise purchased for
          resale.

Feb. 15   June Eaton noted that only $1.50 remained in the petty cashbox. Thus, she sorted the petty cash receipts in terms of the accounts affected and exchanged the receipts for a check to reimburse the fund. However, since the fund had been exhausted so quickly, the check was made large enough to increase the size of the fund to $100.

16   Paid $22 from petty cash for minor repairs to an office machine.

19   Paid $7.50 COD delivery charges on merchandise purchased for resale.

21   Paid City Delivery Service $5 to deliver merchandise sold to a customer.

25   Purchased office supplies with petty cash, $10.50.

27   Carol Rash, owner of the business, signed a petty cash receipt and took $10 from petty cash for lunch money.

Mar. 2   Paid $14.50 COD delivery charges on merchandise purchased for resale.

6   Purchased paper clips and pencils with petty cash, $9.75.

11   Paid $16.75 COD delivery charges on merchandise purchased for resale.

12   June Eaton sorted the petty cash receipts and exchanged them for a check to replenish the fund for expenditures and, since there was only $1 in cash in the fund, for the unexplained shortage.

Required

1. Prepare a general journal entry to record the check establishing the petty cash fund.

2. Prepare a summary of petty cash payments prior to February 15 that has these categories: Delivery expense, Office supplies, Miscellaneous expenses, Withdrawals, and Transportation-in. Sort the payments into the appropriate categories and total the expenses in each category. Prepare a similar summary of petty cash payments after February 15.

3. Prepare entries to reimburse the fund and increase its size on February 15 and to reimburse the fund on March 12.

Problem 7-3A

The accounting system used by the Crawford Company requires that all entries be journalized in a general journal. To facilitate payments of small items Crawford Company recently established a petty cash fund. The following transactions involving the petty cash fund occurred during April (the last month of the company's fiscal year):

Apr. 1   A company check for $100 was drawn and made payable to the petty cashier to establish the petty cash fund.

12   A company check was drawn to replenish the fund for the following expenditures made since April 1 and to increase the fund to $250.

a. Purchased postage stamps for $25.

b. Payment of $38.25 to Smith Trucking for delivery of merchandise to customers.

      c. Gave Roger Banes, owner of the business, $20 for personal use.

      d. Paid $12.75 to Appliance Company for repairs of office equipment.

      e. Discovered that only $1 remained in the petty cash box.

Apr. 30 The petty cashier noted that $2.55 remained in the fund. Having decided that the April 12 increase in the fund was not large enough, a company check was drawn to replenish the fund for the following expenditures made since April 12 and to increase it to $350.

      a. Payment of $89.50 for office supplies to support the company's computer.

      b. Payment of $34.25 for items classified as miscellaneous general expense.

      c. Payment of $46 for janitorial service.

      d. Payment of $77.70 to Specialty Advertising Company for a space advertisement in a weekly newsletter.

Required

1. Prepare general journal entries to record the establishment of the fund on April 1 and its replenishments on April 12 and on April 30.

2. If Crawford Company had failed to replenish the petty cash fund on April 30, what would have been the effect on net income for the fiscal year ended April 30 and on total assets on April 30? Explain your answer. (Hint: The amount of Office Supplies to appear on a balance sheet is determined by a physical count of the supplies on hand.)

Problem 7-4A

The following information was available to reconcile Tango Company's book balance of cash with its bank statement balance as of July 31:

a. After all posting was completed on July 31, the company's Cash account had a $5,983 debit balance, but its bank statement showed a $7,845 balance.

b. Checks, No. 721 for $306 and No. 726 for $591, were outstanding on the June 30 bank reconciliation. Check No. 726 was returned with the July canceled checks, but Check No. 721 was not.

c. In comparing the canceled checks returned with the bank statement with the entries in the accounting records, it was found that Check No. 801 for the purchase of office equipment was correctly drawn for $619 but was entered in the accounting records as though it were for $691. It was also found that Check No. 835 for $375 and Check No. 837 for $150, both drawn in July, were not among the canceled checks returned with the statement.

d. A credit memorandum enclosed with the bank statement indicated that the bank had collected a $3,000 noninterest-bearing note for the concern, deducted a $30 collection fee, and had credited the remainder to the concern's account.

e. A debit memorandum for $370 listed a $360 NSF check plus a $10 NSF charge. The check had been received from a customer, Joe Schultz, and was among the canceled checks returned.

f. Also among the canceled checks was a $15 debit memorandum for bank services. None of the memoranda had been recorded.

g. The July 31 cash receipts, $1,626, were placed in the bank's night depository after banking hours on that date, and their amount did not appear on the bank statement.

Required

1. Prepare a bank reconciliation for the company.
2. Prepare entries in general journal form to bring the company's book balance of cash into conformity with the reconciled balance.

Problem 7-5A

Medusa Company reconciled its bank balance on May 31 and showed two checks outstanding at that time, No. 808 for $524 and No. 813 for $186. The following information is available for the June 30 reconciliation:

From the June 30 bank statement:

BALANCE OF PREVIOUS STATEMENT ON 5/31/—	3,668.00
5 DEPOSITS AND OTHER CREDITS TOTALING	6,120.00
8 CHECKS AND OTHER DEBITS TOTALING	4,736.00
SERVICE CHARGE AMOUNT	6.00
CURRENT BALANCE AS OF THIS STATEMENT	5,046.00

CHECKING ACCOUNT TRANSACTIONS°°°

.DATE	AMOUNT	TRANSACTION DESCRIPTION
6/ 3	446.00+	Deposit
6/12	1,890.00+	Deposit
6/22	1,298.00+	Deposit
6/28	1,496.00+	Deposit
6/29	480.00−	NSF check
6/30	6.00−	Service charge
6/30	990.00+	Credit memorandum

.DATE	CHECK NO	AMOUNT	DATE	CHECK NO	AMOUNT
5/25	808	524.00	6/15	817	102.00
6/ 5	814*	612.00	6/15	818	234.00
6/ 3	815	450.00	6/28	819	642.00
6/ 6	816	1,692.00			

* Indicates a skip in check sequence

From Medusa Company's accounting records:

Cash Receipts Deposited			Cash Disbursements	
Date		**Cash Debit**	**Check No.**	**Cash Credit**
June 3		446.00	814	612.00
12		1,890.00	815	450.00
22		1,298.00	816	1,692.00
28		1,496.00	817	102.00
30		638.00	818	234.00
		5,768.00	819	624.00
			820	258.00
			821	326.00
				4,298.00

Cash

Date		Explanation	PR	Debit	Credit	Balance
May	31	Balance				2,958.00
June	30	Total receipts	R-8	5,768.00		8,726.00
	30	Total disbursements	D-9		4,298.00	4,428.00

Check No. 819 was correctly drawn for $642 in payment for store equipment; however, the bookkeeper misread the amount and entered it in the accounting records with a debit to Store Equipment and a credit to Cash as though it were for $624. The bank paid and deducted the correct amount.

The NSF check was received from a customer, John Higgan, in payment of his account. Its return was unrecorded. The credit memorandum resulted from a $1,000 note which the bank had collected for the company, deducted a $10 collection fee, and deposited the balance in the company's account. The collection fee was not recorded.

Required

1. Prepare a bank reconciliation for Medusa Company.
2. Prepare in general journal form the entries needed to bring the company's book balance of cash into agreement with the reconciled balance.

Problem 7-6A

The August 31 credit balance in the Sales account of Bailey Sales showed it had sold $262,000 of merchandise during the month. The concern began August with a $229,000 merchandise inventory and ended the month with a $181,000 inventory. It had incurred $87,500 of operating expenses during the month, and it had also recorded the following transactions:

Aug. 3   Received merchandise purchased at a $30,000 invoice price, invoice dated July 30, terms 2/10, n/30.

7   Received a $5,000 credit memorandum (invoice price) for merchandise received on August 3 and returned for credit.

10   Received merchandise purchased at a $45,000 invoice price, invoice dated August 8, terms 2/10, n/30.

14   Received merchandise purchased at a $42,500 invoice price, invoice dated August 12, terms 2/10, n/30.

18   Paid for the merchandise received on August 10, less the discount.

22   Paid for the merchandise received on August 14, less the discount.

30   Discovered that the invoice received on August 3 had been refiled in error, after the credit memorandum was attached, for payment on this the last day of its credit period, causing the discount to be lost. Paid the invoice.

Required

1. Assume the concern records invoices at gross amounts and (a) prepare general journal entries to record the transactions. (b) Prepare an August income statement for the concern.

2. Assume the concern records invoices at net amounts and (a) prepare general journal entries to record the transactions. (b) Prepare a second income statement for the concern under this assumption.

Problem 7-7A

(This problem is based on information in the Appendix to this chapter.)

Neff Company completed these transactions involving vouchers payable:

June 1   Recorded Voucher No. 511 payable to Daggett Company for merchandise having a $1,500 invoice price, invoice dated May 28, terms FOB destination, 2/10, n/30.

5   Recorded Voucher No. 512 payable to Hanson Company for merchandise having a $2,300 invoice price, invoice dated June 3, terms FOB factory, 2/10, n/60. The vendor had prepaid the freight charges, $100, adding the amount to the invoice and bringing its total to $2,400.

6   Received a credit memorandum for merchandise having a $500 invoice price. The merchandise was received on June 1, Voucher No. 511, and returned for credit.

13   Issued Check No. 710 in payment of Voucher No. 512.

15   Recorded Voucher No. 513 payable to Payroll for sales salaries, $800, and office salaries, $600. Issued Check No. 711 in payment of the voucher. Cashed the check and paid the employees.

18   Recorded Voucher No. 514 payable to Office Designers for the purchase of office equipment having a $600 invoice price, terms n/10 EOM.

22   Recorded Voucher No. 515 payable to *The Chronicle* for advertising expense, $250. Issued Check No. 712 in payment of the voucher.

25   Recorded Voucher No. 516 payable to Gong Company for merchandise having a $1,700 invoice price, invoice dated June 22, terms FOB factory, 2/10, n/60. The vendor had prepaid the freight charges, $60, adding the amount to the invoice and bringing its total to $1,760.

27   Discovered that Voucher No. 511 had been filed in error for payment on the last day of its credit period rather than on the last day of its discount period, causing the discount to be lost. Issued Check No. 713 in payment of the voucher, less the return.

30   Recorded Voucher No. 517 payable to Payroll for sales salaries, $800, and office salaries, $600. Issued Check No. 714 in payment of the voucher. Cashed the check and paid the employees.

Required

Assume that Neff Company records vouchers at gross amounts. (a) Prepare a Voucher Register, a Check Register, and a General Journal and record the transactions. (b) Prepare a Vouchers Payable account and post those portions of the journal and register entries that affect the account. (c) Prove the balance of the Vouchers Payable account by preparing a schedule of unpaid vouchers.

☐   **Provocative**   **Provocative Problem 7-1   Magic Products Company**
           Problems

The Magic Products Company has enjoyed rapid growth since its beginning several years ago. Last year its sales were in excess of $10,000,000. However, its purchasing procedures may not have kept pace with its growth. When a plant supervisor or department head needs raw materials, plant assets, or supplies, he or she telephones a request to the purchasing department manager. The purchasing department manager prepares a purchase order in duplicate, sends one copy to the company selling the goods, and keeps the other copy in the files. When the seller's invoice is received, it is sent directly to the purchasing department. When the goods arrive, receiving department personnel count and inspect the items and prepare one copy of a receiving report which is sent to the purchasing department. The purchasing department manager attaches the receiving report and the retained copy of the purchase order to the invoice. If all is in order, the invoice is stamped "approved for payment" and signed by the purchasing department manager. The invoice and its supporting documents are then sent to the accounting department to be recorded and filed until due. On its due date, the invoice and its supporting documents are sent to the office of the company treasurer where a check is prepared and mailed. The number of the paying check is entered on the invoice, and the invoice is sent to the accounting department for an entry to record its payment.

Do the procedures of Magic Products Company make it fairly easy for someone in the company to institute the payment of fictitious invoices by the company? If so, who is most likely to commit the fraud, and what would that person have to do to receive payment of a fictitious invoice? What changes should be made in the company's purchasing procedures, and why should each change be made?

Provocative Problem 7-2   The Long-Term Employee

The bookkeeper at Old Time Company will retire next week after more than 40 years with the store, having been hired by the father of the store's present owner. He has always been a very dependable employee, and as a result has been given more and more responsibilities over the years. Actually, for the past 15 years, he has "run" the store's office, keeping books, verifying invoices, and issuing checks in their payment, which in the absence of the store's owner, Jay Jones, he could sign. In addition, at the end of each day, the store's salesclerks turn over their daily cash receipts to the bookkeeper. After counting the money and comparing the amounts with the cash register tapes, which he is responsbile for removing from the cash registers, he makes the journal entry to record cash sales and then deposits the money in the bank. He also reconciles the bank balance with the book balance of cash each month.

Mr. Jones, the store's owner, realizes he cannot expect a new bookkeeper to accomplish as much in a day as the old bookkeeper. And since the store is not large enough to warrant more than one office employee, he recognizes he must take over some of the old bookkeeper's duties when he retires. Mr. Jones already places all orders for merchandise and supplies and closely supervises all employees and does not want to add more to his duties than necessary.

Name the internal control principle violated here and tell which of the old bookkeeper's tasks should be taken over by Mr. Jones in order to improve the store's internal control over cash.

8 Credit Sales and Receivables

After studying Chapter 8, you should be able to:

1. Prepare entries to account for credit card sales.

2. Prepare entries accounting for bad debts both by the allowance method and the direct write-off method.

3. Explain the materiality principle and the full-disclosure principle.

4. Calculate the interest on promissory notes and the discount on notes receivable discounted.

5. Prepare entries to record the receipt of promissory notes and their payment or dishonor.

6. Prepare entries to record the discounting of notes receivable and, if dishonored, their dishonor.

7. Prepare reversing entries and explain the reasons for their use.

8. Define or explain the words and phrases listed in the chapter Glossary.

Several issues arise when accounting for transactions with customers, especially when sales are on credit. This chapter begins with a discussion of the procedures used to record credit card sales. It then focuses on accounting for the bad debts resulting from granting credit to customers and on accounting for notes receivable. Finally, the example of notes receivable is used to introduce the bookkeeping convenience of reversing entries.

■ Credit Card Sales

Many customers use credit cards such as VISA, MasterCard, or American Express to charge purchases from various businesses. This practice gives customers the ability to make purchases without carrying cash or writing checks. In addition, the customer usually obtains credit for a period of time and can defer payment to the credit card company. Having established credit with the credit card company, the customer also avoids having to establish credit with each store and having to make several monthly payments to a variety of creditors.

There are also good reasons why many businesses allow customers to use credit cards. First, the business does not have to evaluate the credit standing of each customer and make decisions about who should get credit and how much. Second, the business avoids the risk of extending credit to customers who cannot pay. Third, the business often receives cash from the credit card company quicker than it would if customers were granted credit.

With some credit cards, usually those issued by banks, the business deposits a copy of each credit card receipt in its bank account just as it would deposit a customer's check. Thus, the business receives a cash credit immediately upon deposit. In the case of other credit cards, the business sends the appropriate copy of each receipt to the credit card company and then is paid by the company. Until payment is received, the business has an account receivable from the credit card company. In return for the services provided to the business, credit card companies charge a fee ranging from 2 to 5 percent of credit card sales. This charge is deducted from the cash payment to the business.

Accounting for credit card sales depends on whether cash is received immediately upon deposit or is delayed until paid by the credit card company. If cash is received immediately, the entry (in general journal form) to record credit card sales would be as follows:

Jan.	25	Cash	96.00	
		Credit Card Expense	4.00	
		Sales		100.00
		To record credit card sales less a 4% credit card expense.		

If the business must send the receipts to the credit card company and wait for payment, the entry to record credit card sales would be:

Jan.	25	Accounts Receivable, Credit Card Co.	100.00	
		Sales		100.00
		To record credit card sales.		

When cash is received from the credit card company, the entry to record the receipt would be:

Feb.	10	Cash	96.00	
		Credit Card Expense	4.00	
		Accounts Receivable, Credit Card Co. . .		100.00
		To record cash receipt less 4% credit card expense.		

Observe in the above entries that the credit card expense was not recorded until cash was received from the credit card company. This is a matter of convenience. By following this procedure, the business avoids having to calculate the credit card expense each time a sale is recorded. Instead, the expense related to many sales can be calculated once and recorded when cash is received. However, the **matching principle** requires that credit card expense be reported in the same period as the sale. If the sales and the cash receipt occur in different periods, credit card expense should be accrued and reported in the period of sale.

Credit card expense is sometimes disclosed in the income statement as a type of discount that is deducted from sales to get net sales. Other companies classify it as a selling expense or even as an administrative expense. Arguments can be made for all three alternatives.

■ Bad Debts

When a company grants credit to its customers, there are almost always a few customers who do not pay. The accounts of such customers are called **bad debts** and are an expense of selling on credit.

It might be asked: Why do merchants sell on credit if bad debts result? The answer is, of course, that they sell on credit in order to increase sales and profits. They are willing to take a reasonable loss from bad debts in order to increase sales and profits. Therefore, bad debt losses are an expense of selling on credit, an expense incurred in order to increase sales. Consequently, if the requirements of the **matching principle** are met, bad debt losses must be matched against the sales they helped produce.

■ Matching Bad Debt Losses with Sales

Credit sales that result in bad debt losses are made in one accounting period, but final recognition that the customers will not pay commonly does not occur until a later period. Final recognition waits until every means of collecting has been exhausted, which may take a year or more. Therefore, if bad debt losses are matched with the sales they helped to produce, they must be matched on an estimated basis. The **allowance method of accounting for bad debts** does just that.

■ Allowance Method of Accounting for Bad Debts

Under the allowance method of accounting for bad debts, an estimate is made at the end of each accounting period of the total bad debts that are expected to result from the period's sales. An allowance is then provided for the loss. This has two advantages: (1) the estimated loss is charged to the period in which the revenue is recognized; and (2) the accounts receivable appear on the balance sheet at their estimated realizable value, a more informative balance sheet amount.

Recording the Estimated Bad Debts Expense

Under the allowance method of accounting for bad debts, the estimated bad debts expense is recorded at the end of each accounting period with a work sheet adjustment and an adjusting entry. For example, assume that Alpha Company had charge sales of $300,000 during the first year of its operations. At the end of the year, $20,000 remains uncollected in accounts receivable. Based on these facts, Alpha Company estimates that $1,500 of accounts receivable will prove to be uncollectible. This estimated expense is recorded with an adjusting entry like the following:

Dec.	31	Bad Debts Expense	1,500.00	
		Allowance for Doubtful Accounts.		1,500.00
		To record the estimated bad debts.		

The debit of this entry causes the estimated bad debts expense to appear on the income statement of the year in which the sales were made. As a result, the estimated $1,500 expense of selling on credit is matched with the $300,000 of revenue it helped to produce.

Note that the credit of the entry is to the contra account, Allowance for Doubtful Accounts. It is necessary to credit the contra account because at the time of the adjusting entry it is not known for certain which customers will fail to pay. (The total loss from bad debts can be estimated from past experience. However, the exact customers who will not pay cannot be known until every means of collecting from each has been exhausted.) Consequently, since the bad accounts are not identifiable at the time of the adjusting entry, they cannot be removed from the subsidiary Accounts Receivable Ledger. As a result, the Allowance for Doubtful Accounts account must be credited instead of the controlling account. The allowance account must be credited because to credit the controlling account without removing the bad accounts from the subsidiary ledger would cause the controlling account balance to differ from the sum of the balances in the subsidiary ledger.

Bad Debts in the Accounts and on the Balance Sheet

Bad debts expense normally appears on the income statement as an administrative expense rather than as a selling expense because granting credit is usually not a responsibility of the sales department. Therefore, since the sales department is not responsible for granting credit, it should not be held responsible for bad debts expenses. The sales department is usually not given responsibility for granting credit because it may at times be swayed in its judgment of a credit risk by its desire to increase sales.

Recall the assumption that Alpha Company has $20,000 of outstanding accounts receivable at the end of its first year of operations. Thus, after the bad debts adjusting entry is posted, the company's Accounts Receivable and Allowance for Doubtful Accounts accounts will show these balances:

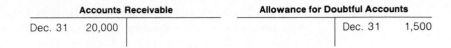

Accounts Receivable		Allowance for Doubtful Accounts	
Dec. 31 20,000			Dec. 31 1,500

The $1,500 credit balance in Allowance for Doubtful Accounts has the effect of reducing accounts receivable (net of the allowance) to their estimated **realizable value**. This term, realizable value, means the amount of cash that should be received as the assets are converted into cash in the ordinary course of business. Although $20,000 is legally owed to Alpha Company, only $18,500 is likely to be realized in cash.

When the balance sheet is prepared, the **allowance for doubtful accounts** is subtracted thereon from the accounts receivable to show the amount that is expected to be realized from the accounts, as follows:

Current assets:		
Cash		$11,300
Accounts receivable	$20,000	
Less allowance for doubtful accounts. . . .	(1,500)	18,500
Merchandise inventory		67,200
Prepaid expenses		1,100
Total current assets		$98,100

Writing off a Bad Debt

When an allowance for doubtful accounts is provided, accounts deemed uncollectible are written off against this allowance. For example, after spending a year trying to collect, Alpha Company finally concluded the $100 account of George Vale was uncollectible and made the following entry to write it off:

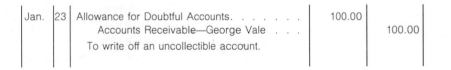

Jan.	23	Allowance for Doubtful Accounts.	100.00	
		Accounts Receivable—George Vale . . .		100.00
		To write off an uncollectible account.		

Posting the credit of the entry to the Accounts Receivable account removes the amount of the bad debt from the controlling account. Posting it to the George Vale account removes the amount of the bad debt from the subsidiary ledger. Posting the entry has this effect on the general ledger accounts:

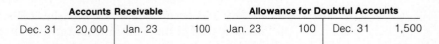

Accounts Receivable				Allowance for Doubtful Accounts			
Dec. 31	20,000	Jan. 23	100	Jan. 23	100	Dec. 31	1,500

Two points should be observed in the entry and accounts. First, although bad debts are an expense of selling on credit, the allowance account rather than an expense account is debited in the write-off. The allowance account is debited because the expense was recorded at the end of the period in which the sale occurred. At that time, the loss was foreseen, and the expense was recorded in the estimated bad debts adjusting entry.

Second, although the write-off removed the amount of the account receivable from the ledgers, it did not affect the estimated realizable amount of Alpha Company's accounts receivable, as the following tabulation shows:

	Before Write-Off	After Write-Off
Accounts receivable	$20,000	$19,900
Less allowance for doubtful accounts	1,500	1,400
Estimated realizable accounts receivable	$18,500	$18,500

Bad Debt Recoveries

Frequently, an error in judgment is made and accounts written off as uncollectible are later sometimes collected in full or in part. If an account is written off as uncollectible and later the customer pays part or all of the amount previously written off, the payment should be shown in the customer's account for future credit action. It should be shown because when a customer fails to pay and his or her account is written off, the customer's credit standing is impaired. Later when the customer pays, the payment helps restore the credit standing. When an account previously written off as a bad debt is collected, two entries are made. The first reinstates the customer's account and has the effect of reversing the original write-off. The second entry records the collection of the reinstated account.

For example, assume that George Vale, whose account was previously written off, pays in full on August 15. The entries in general journal form to record the bad debt recovery are:

Aug.	15	Accounts Receivable—George Vale	100.00	
		Allowance for Doubtful Accounts		100.00
		To reinstate the account of George Vale written off on January 23.		
	15	Cash	100.00	
		Accounts Receivable—George Vale . . .		100.00
		In full payment of account.		

In this case, George Vale paid the entire amount previously written off. Sometimes after an account is written off the customer will pay a portion of the amount owed. The question then arises, should the entire balance of the account be returned to accounts receivable or just the amount paid? The answer is a matter of judgment. If it is thought the customer will pay in full, the entire amount owed should be returned. However, only the amount paid should be returned if it is thought that no more will be collected.

Estimating the Amount of Bad Debts Expense

As previously discussed, the allowance method of accounting for doubtful accounts requires an adjusting entry at the end of each accounting period to estimate the bad debts expense for the period. That entry takes the following form:

What is the process by which a company estimates the amount to be recorded in this entry? There are two broad alternatives. One is to focus on the income statement relationship between bad debts expense and sales. The other is to focus on the balance sheet relationship between accounts receivable and allowance for doubtful accounts. Both alternatives involve a careful analysis of past experience.

Estimating Bad Debts by Focusing on the Income Statement

The income statement approach to estimating bad debts is based on the idea that some particular percentage of a company's credit sales will prove to be uncollectible. Hence, in the income statement, the amount of bad debts expense should be that same percentage of credit sales. Suppose, for example, that Baker Company's credit sales in 198A amounted to $400,000. Also suppose that according to past experience and knowledge of similar companies, 0.6% of credit sales are typically uncollectible. Using this information, Baker Company can expect $2,400 of bad debts expense to result from the year's sales ($400,000 × 0.006 = $2,400). Therefore, the adjusting entry to record bad debts expense would be as follows:

Importantly, this entry does not mean that the December 31, 198A, balance in Allowance for Doubtful Accounts will be $2,400. It will probably be some other amount. There are three reasons why this is true:

1. The bad debts percentage (0.6%) was only an estimate. The actual amount of accounts receivable that become uncollectible will likely be somewhat larger or smaller than this.
2. Some of the accounts arising from 198A credit sales may have been written off prior to December 31, 198A. If so, the entries to write them off involved debits to Allowance for Doubtful Accounts. Thus, the December 31 balance would be $2,400 less the amounts previously written off.
3. There probably was a credit balance in the account at the beginning of the year. In each past year, bad debts were estimated at year-end, and accounts that became uncollectible were written off. The balance in Allowance for Doubtful Accounts reflects these events from past years as well as those in the current year.

Often, when the addition to the Allowance for Doubtful Accounts account is based on a percentage of sales, the passage of several accounting periods is required before it becomes apparent that the percentage is either too large or too small. In such cases, when it becomes apparent the percentage is incorrect, a change in the percentage to be used in future periods should be made.

Estimating Bad Debts by Focusing on the Balance Sheet

The balance sheet approach to estimating bad debts is based on the idea that some portion of the outstanding accounts receivable as shown in the balance sheet will become uncollectible. Hence, after the bad debts adjusting entry is posted, the balance in Allowance for Doubtful Accounts should equal the portion of outstanding accounts receivable estimated to be uncollectible. The amount to be debited to Bad Debts Expense and credited to Allowance for Doubtful Accounts is whatever is necessary to result in the correct balance in Allowance for Doubtful Accounts. The balance sheet approach may take two forms: (1) a simplified approach and (2) aging of accounts receivable.

A Simplified Balance Sheet Approach Using the simplified balance sheet approach, a company observes the amount of outstanding accounts receivable at year-end. Based on past experience, some percentage of outstanding receivables is estimated to become uncollectible. This percentage is multiplied by the amount of outstanding receivables to determine the required ending balance in Allowance for Doubtful Accounts. Whatever balance exists in the account prior to the adjustment is then compared to the required balance to determine the amount of the adjustment.

For example, assume that Baker Company of the previous illustration has $50,000 of outstanding accounts receivable on December 31, 198A. Past experience indicates that 5% of outstanding receivables will become uncollectible. Thus, after the adjusting entry is posted, Allowance for Doubtful Accounts should have a $2,500 credit balance. Assume that before making the necessary adjustment, the account appears as follows:

Allowance for Doubtful Accounts

		Dec. 31 bal.	2,000
Feb. 6	800		
July 10	600		
Nov. 20	400		

Understand that the $2,000 beginning balance appeared on last year's balance sheet. Then, during 198A, accounts of specific customers were written off on February 6, July 10, and November 20. Consequently, the account has a $200 credit balance prior to the December 31, 198A, adjustment. The adjusting entry to give the account the required $2,500 balance is:

Dec.	31	Bad Debts Expense	2,300.00	
		Allowance for Doubtful Accounts.		2,300.00

Aging Accounts Receivable Both the income statement approach and the simplified balance sheet approach use the knowledge gained from past experience to estimate bad debts expense. However, neither method of analysis is as refined as is the balance sheet approach involving aging of accounts receivable.

Aging of accounts receivable requires that each outstanding account at the end of the period be classified in terms of how long it has been outstanding. In some cases, executives of the sales and credit departments may examine each account listed and by judgment decide which are probably uncollectible. More often, past experience is drawn upon to estimate a percentage of each category that will become uncollectible. This is done with a schedule like the one for Baker Company shown in Illustration 8-1.

The analysis of Illustration 8-1 indicates that the adjusted balance in Baker Company's Allowance for Doubtful Accounts should be $2,290 ($740 + $325 + $350 + $475 + $400 = $2,290). Since the account was previously assumed to have a pre-adjusted credit balance of $200, the aging of accounts receivable approach would require the following adjusting entry:

Dec.	31	Bad Debts Expense	2,090.00	
		Allowance for Doubtful Accounts.		2,090.00

Recall from page 293 that when the income statement approach was used, bad debts expense was estimated to be $2,400. When the simplified balance sheet approach was used (page 294), the estimate was $2,300. And when aging of accounts receivable was used, the estimate was $2,090. It should not be surprising that the amounts are different. After all, each approach is only an estimate. However, the aging of accounts receivable allows a more detailed examination of outstanding accounts and is usually most reliable.

■ **Direct Write-Off of Bad Debts**

The allowance method of accounting for bad debts is designed to satisfy the requirements of the **matching principle.** Consequently, it is the method that should be used in most cases. However, under certain circumstances

Illustration 8-1

Baker Company
Schedule of Accounts Receivable by Age

Customer's Name	Not Due	1 to 30 Days Past Due	31 to 60 Days Past Due	61 to 90 Days Past Due	Over 90 Days Past Due
Charles Abbot . . .	$ 450.00				
Frank Allen	710.00				
George Arden . . .		$ 200.00	$ 300.00		
Paul Baum.					$ 640.00
Totals	$37,000.00	$6,500.00	$3,500.00	$1,900.00	$1,000.00
	× 2%	× 5%	× 10%	× 25%	× 40%
Estimated uncollectible accounts.	$ 740.00	$ 325.00	$ 350.00	$ 475.00	$ 400.00

another method, called the **direct write-off method,** may be acceptable. Under this method, when it is decided that an account is uncollectible, it is written off directly to Bad Debts Expense with an entry like this:

Nov.	23	Bad Debts Expense	52.50	
		Accounts Receivable—Dale Hall		52.50
		To write off the uncollectible account.		

The debit of the entry charges the bad debt loss directly to the current year's Bad Debts Expense account. The credit removes the balance of the account from the subsidiary ledger and controlling account.

If an account previously written off directly to Bad Debts Expense is later collected in full, the following entries are used to record the recovery:

Mar.	11	Accounts Receivable—Dale Hall	52.50	
		Bad Debts Expense		52.50
		To reinstate the account of Dale Hall previously written off.		
	11	Cash	52.50	
		Accounts Receivable—Dale Hall		52.50
		In full payment of account.		

Sometimes a bad debt previously written off directly to the Bad Debts Expense account is recovered in the year following the write-off. If at that time the Bad Debts Expense account has no balance from other write-offs and no write-offs are expected, the credit of the entry recording the recovery can be to a revenue account called Bad Debt Recoveries.

Direct Write-Off Mismatches Revenues and Expenses

The direct write-off method commonly mismatches revenues and expenses. The mismatch results because the revenue from a bad debt sale appears on the income statement of one year while the expense of the loss may be deducted on the income statement of the following or a later year. Nevertheless, it may still be used in situations where its use does not materially affect reported net income. For example, it may be used in a concern where bad debt losses are immaterial in relation to total sales and net income. In such a concern, the use of direct write-off comes under the accounting principle of materiality.

The Materiality Principle

Under the **materiality principle,** it is held that a strict adherence to any accounting principle, in this case the **matching principle,** is not required when the lack of adherence does not materially affect the financial statements. Or in other words, failure to adhere is permissible when the failure does not produce an error or misstatement sufficiently large as to influence a financial statement reader's judgment of a given situation.

Installment Accounts and Notes Receivable

Many companies grant credit to customers and allow them to make periodic payments over several months. When this is done, the selling company's asset may be in the form of an installment account receivable or a note receivable. **Installment accounts receivable,** like any other accounts receivable, are typically evidenced by sales slips or invoices describing each sales transaction. A note receivable, on the other hand, is a written document promising payment and signed by the customer. In either case, when payments are to be made over several months or if the credit period is long, the customer is typically charged interest. Although the credit period of installment accounts and notes receivable often may be more than one year, they are normally classified as current assets if the company regularly offers customers such terms.

Notes receivable are generally preferred over accounts receivable when the credit period is long and the receivable relates to a single sale of fairly large amount. Notes are also used to replace accounts receivable when customers ask for additional time in which to pay their past-due accounts. In these situations, creditors prefer notes to accounts receivable because the notes may be converted into cash before becoming due by discounting (selling) them to a bank. Likewise, notes are preferred for legal reasons. If a lawsuit is needed to collect, a note represents written acknowledgment by the debtor of both the debt and its amount.

Promissory Notes

A promissory note is an unconditional promise in writing to pay on demand or at a fixed or determinable future date a definite sum of money. In the note shown in Illustration 8-2, Hugo Brown promises to pay Frank Black or his order a definite sum of money at a fixed future date. Hugo Brown is the **maker** of the note. Frank Black is the **payee.** To Hugo Brown, the illustrated note is a **note payable,** a liability. To Frank Black, the same note is a **note receivable,** an asset.

The illustrated Hugo Brown note bears interest at 12%. Interest is a charge for the use of money. To a borrower, interest is an expense. To a lender, it is a revenue. A note may be interest bearing or it may be

Illustration 8-2

$1,000.00   Eugene, Oregon   March 9, 19--

_____Thirty days_____ after date_____I_____ promise to pay to

the order of_____Frank Black_____

One thousand and no/100---dollars

for value received with interest at___12%___

payable at___First National Bank of Eugene, Oregon___

_____Hugo Brown_____

noninterest bearing. If a note bears interest, the rate or the amount of interest must be stated on the note.

■ Calculating Interest

Unless otherwise stated, the rate of interest on a note is the rate charged for the use of the principal for one year. The formula for calculating interest is:

$$\begin{matrix}\text{Principal} & & \text{Annual} & & \text{Time of the} & & \\ \text{of the} & \times & \text{rate of} & \times & \text{note expressed} & = & \text{Interest} \\ \text{note} & & \text{interest} & & \text{in years} & & \end{matrix}$$

For example, interest on a $1,000, 12%, one-year note is calculated:

$$\$1,000 \times \frac{12}{100} \times 1 = \$120$$

Most note transactions involve a period less than a full year, and this period is usually expressed in days. When the time of a note is expressed in days, the actual number of days elapsing, not including the day of the note's date but including the day on which it falls due, are counted. For example, a 90-day note, dated July 10, is due on October 8. This October 8 due date, called the **maturity date,** is calculated as follows:

Number of days in July.	31
Minus the date of the note	10
Gives the number of days the note runs in July	21
Add the number of days in August.	31
Add the number of days in September	30
Total through September 30	82
Days in October needed to equal the time of the note, 90 days, also the maturity date of the note—October	8
Total time the note runs in days	90

Occasionally, the time of a note is expressed in months. In such cases, the note matures and is payable in the month of its maturity on the same day of the month as its date. For example, a note dated July 10 and payable three months after that date is payable on October 10.

In calculating interest, it was once almost the universal practice to treat a year as having just 360 days. This simplified most interest calculations. However, the practice is no longer so common. Nevertheless, to simplify the calculation of interest in assigned problems and to be consistent in the illustrations and problems, the practice is continued in this text. It makes the interest calculation on a 90-day, 12%, $1,000 note as follows:

$$\text{Principal} \times \text{Rate} \times \frac{\text{Exact days}}{360} = \text{Interest}$$

or

$$\$1,000 \times \frac{12}{100} \times \frac{90}{360} = \text{Interest}$$

or

$$\$1{,}000 \times \frac{\overset{3}{\cancel{12}}}{\cancel{100}} \times \frac{\cancel{90}}{\underset{4}{\cancel{360}}} = \$30$$

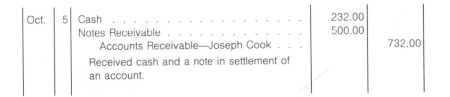

Recording the Receipt of a Note

Notes receivable are recorded in a single Notes Receivable account. Each note may be identified in the account by writing the name of the maker in the Explanation column on the line of the entry recording its receipt or payment. Only one account is needed because the individual notes are on hand. Consequently, the maker, rate of interest, due date, and other information may be learned by examining each note.

A note received at the time of a sale is recorded as follows:

Dec.	5	Notes Receivable	650.00	
		Sales		650.00
		Sold merchandise, terms six-month, 9% note.		

When a note is taken in granting a time extension on a past-due account receivable, the creditor usually attempts to collect part of the past-due account in cash. This reduces the debt and requires the acceptance of a note for a smaller amount. For example, Symplex Company agrees to accept $232 in cash and a $500, 60-day, 14% note from Joseph Cook in settlement of his $732 past-due account. When Symplex receives the cash and note, the following entry in general journal form is made:

Oct.	5	Cash	232.00	
		Notes Receivable	500.00	
		Accounts Receivable—Joseph Cook . . .		732.00
		Received cash and a note in settlement of		
		an account.		

Observe that this entry changes the form of $500 of the debt from an account receivable to a note receivable.

When Cook pays the note, this entry in general journal form is made:

Dec.	4	Cash	511.67	
		Notes Receivable		500.00
		Interest Earned		11.67
		Collected the Joseph Cook note.		

Look again at the last two entries. If Symplex Company uses columnar journals, the entry of December 4 would be recorded in its Cash Receipts Journal. Two lines would be required, one for the credit to Interest Earned and a second for the credit to Notes Receivable. Likewise, the October 5 transaction would be recorded with two entries, one in the Cash Receipts

Journal for the money received and a second entry in the General Journal for the note. Nevertheless, to simplify the illustrations, general journal entries are shown here and will be used through the remainder of this text. However, the student should realize that the entries would be made in a Cash Receipts Journal or other appropriate journal if in use.

■ **Dishonored Notes Receivable**

Occasionally, the maker of a note either cannot or will not pay the note at maturity. When a note's maker refuses to pay at maturity, the note is said to be **dishonored.** Dishonor does not relieve the maker of the obligation to pay. Furthermore, every legal means should be made to collect. However, collection may require lengthy legal proceedings.

The balance of the Notes Receivable account should show only the amount of notes that have not matured. Consequently, when a note is dishonored, its amount should be removed from the Notes Receivable account and charged back to the account of its maker. To illustrate, Symplex Company holds an $800, 14%, 60-day note of George Jones. At maturity, Jones dishonors the note. To remove the dishonored note from its Notes Receivable account, the company makes the following entry:

Oct.	14	Accounts Receivable—George Jones.	818.67	
		Interest Earned		18.67
		Notes Receivable		800.00
		To charge the account of George Jones for his dishonored note.		

Charging a dishonored note back to the account of its maker serves two purposes. It removes the amount of the note from the Notes Receivable account, leaving in the account only notes that have not matured. It also records the dishonored note in the maker's account. The second purpose is important. If in the future the maker of the dishonored note again applies for credit, his or her account will show all past dealings, including the dishonored note.

Observe in the entry that the Interest Earned account is credited for interest earned even though it was not collected. The reason for this is that Jones owes both the principal and the interest. Consequently, his account should reflect the full amount owed on the date of the entry.

■ **Discounting Notes Receivable**

As previously stated, a note receivable is preferred to an account receivable because the note can be turned into cash before maturity by discounting (selling) it to a bank. In **discounting a note receivable,** the owner endorses and delivers the note to the bank in exchange for cash. The bank holds the note to maturity and then collects its maturity value from the maker. To illustrate, assume that on May 28 Symplex Company received a $1,200, 60-day, 12% note dated May 27 from John Owen. It held the note until June 2 and then discounted it at its bank at 14%. Since the maturity date of this note is July 26, the bank must wait 54 days after discounting the note to collect from Owen. These 54 days are called the **discount period** and are calculated as follows:

Time of the note in days.	60
Less time held by Symplex Company:	
Number of days in May	31
Less the date of the note	27
Days held in May.	4
Days held in June	2
Total days held.	6
Discount period in days	54

At the end of the discount period, the bank expects to collect the **maturity value** of this note from Owen. Therefore, as is customary, it bases its discount on the maturity value of the note, which is calculated as follows:

Principal of the note	$1,200
Interest on $1,200 for 60 days at 12%	24
Maturity value.	$1,224

In this case, the bank's discount rate, or the rate of interest it charges for lending money, is 14%. Consequently, in discounting the note, it will deduct 54 days' interest at 14% from the note's maturity value and will give Symplex Company the remainder. The remainder is called the **proceeds of the note**. The amount of interest deducted is known as **bank discount**. The bank discount and the proceeds are calculated as follows:

Maturity value of the note	$1,224.00
Less interest on $1,224 for 54 days at 14% . . .	25.70
Proceeds	$1,198.30

Observe in this case that the proceeds, $1,198.30, are $1.70 less than the $1,200 principal amount of the note. Consequently, Symplex will make this entry in recording the discount transaction:

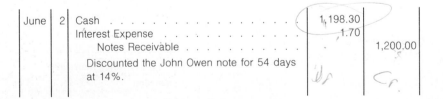

June	2	Cash	1,198.30	
		Interest Expense	1.70	
		Notes Receivable		1,200.00
		Discounted the John Owen note for 54 days at 14%.		

In recording the transaction, Symplex in effect offsets the $24 of interest it would have earned by holding the note to maturity against the $25.70 discount charged by the bank and records only the difference, the $1.70 excess of expense.

In the situation just described, the principal of the discounted note exceeded the proceeds. However, in many cases, the proceeds exceed the principal. When this happens, the difference is credited to Interest Earned. For example, suppose that instead of discounting the John Owen note on June 2, Symplex held the note and discounted it on June 26. If the note is discounted on June 26 at 14%, the discount period is 30 days, the discount is $14.28, and the proceeds of the note are $1,209.72, calculated as follows:

Maturity value of the note	$1,224.00
Less interest on $1,224 at 14% for 30 days . . .	14.28
Proceeds	$1,209.72

And since the proceeds exceed the principal, the transaction is recorded as follows:

June	26	Cash	1,209.72	
		Interest Earned		9.72
		Notes Receivable		1,200.00
		Discounted the John Owen note for 30 days at 14%.		

Contingent Liability

A person or company discounting a note is ordinarily required to endorse the note because an endorsement, unless it is qualified, makes the endorser contingently liable for payment of the note.[1] The **contingent liability** depends upon the note's dishonor by its maker. If the maker pays, the endorser has no liability. However, if the maker defaults, the endorser's contingent liability becomes an actual liability, and the endorser must pay the note for the maker.

A contingent liability, since it can become an actual liability, may affect the credit standing of the person or concern contingently liable. Consequently, a discounted note should be shown as such in the Notes Receivable account. Also, if a balance sheet is prepared before the discounted note's maturity date, the contingent liability should be indicated on the balance sheet. For example, if in addition to the John Owen note, Symplex Company holds $500 of other notes receivable, the record of the discounted John Owen note may appear in its Notes Receivable account as follows:

			Notes Receivable				
Date		**Explanation**	**PR**	**Debit**	**Credit**	**Balance**	
May	28	John Owen note	G6	1,200.00		1,200.00	
June	7	Earl Hill note	G6	500.00		1,700.00	
	26	Discounted the J. Owen note	G7		1,200.00	500.00	

[1] A qualified endorsement is one in which the endorser states in writing that he or she will not be liable for payment.

The contingent liability resulting from discounted notes receivable is commonly shown on a balance sheet by means of a footnote. If Symplex Company follows this practice, it will show the $500 of notes it has not discounted and the contingent liability resulting from discounting the John Owen note on its June 30 balance sheet as follows:

Current assets:	
Cash	$ 5,315
Notes receivable (Footnote 2)	500
Accounts receivable	21,475

Footnote 2: Symplex Company is contingently liable for $1,200 of notes receivable discounted.

Full-Disclosure Principle

The balance sheet disclosure of contingent liabilities is required under the **full-disclosure principle.** Under this principle, it is held that financial statements and their accompanying footnotes should disclose fully and completely all relevant data of a material nature relating to the financial position of the company for which they are prepared. This does not necessarily mean that the information should be detailed, for details can at times obscure. It simply means that all information necessary to an appreciation of the company's position be reported in a readily understandable manner and that nothing of a significant nature be withheld. For example, any of the following would be considered relevant and should be disclosed.

Contingent Liabilities In addition to discounted notes, a company that is contingently liable due to possible additional tax assessments, pending lawsuits, or product guarantees should disclose this on its statements.

Long-Term Commitments under a Contract If the company has signed a long-term lease requiring a material annual payment, this should be disclosed even though the liability does not appear in the accounts. Also, if the company has pledged certain of its assets as security for a loan, this should be revealed.

Accounting Methods Used Whenever there are several acceptable accounting methods that may be followed, a company should report in each case the method used, especially when a choice of methods can materially affect reported net income. For example, a company should report by means of footnotes accompanying its statements the inventory method or methods used, depreciation methods, method of recognizing revenue under long-term construction contracts, and the like.[2]

[2] APB, "Disclosure of Accounting Policies," *APB Opinion No. 22* (New York: AICPA, April 1972), pars. 12, 13.

■ **Dishonor of a Discounted Note**

A bank always tries to collect a discounted note directly from the maker. If it is able to do so, the one who discounted it will not hear from the bank and will need to do nothing more in regard to the note. However, according to law, if a discounted note is dishonored, the bank must before the end of the next business day notify each endorser of the note if it is to hold the endorsers liable on the note. To notify the endorsers, the bank will normally protest the dishonored note. To protest a note, the bank prepares and mails before the end of the next business day a **notice of protest** to each endorser. A notice of protest is a statement, usually attested by a notary public, that says the note was duly presented to the maker for payment and payment was refused. The cost of protesting a note is called a **protest fee,** and the bank will look to the one who discounted the note for payment of both the note's maturity value and the protest fee.

For example, suppose that instead of paying the $1,200 note previously illustrated, John Owen dishonored it. In such a situation, the bank would notify Symplex Company immediately of the dishonor by mailing a notice of protest and a letter asking payment of the note's maturity value plus the protest fee. If the protest fee is, say, $5, Symplex must pay the bank $1,229; and in recording the payment, Symplex will charge the $1,229 to the account of John Owen, as follows:

July	27	Accounts Receivable—John Owen	1,229.00	
		Cash		1,229.00
		To charge the account of Owen for the maturity value of his dishonored note plus the protest fee.		

Of course, upon receipt of the $1,229, the bank will deliver to Symplex the dishonored note. Symplex Company will then make every legal effort to collect from Owen, not only the maturity value of the note and protest fee but also interest on both from the date of dishonor until the date of final settlement. However, it may not be able to collect, and after exhausting every legal means to do so, it may have to write the account off as a bad debt. Normally, in such cases, no additional interest is taken onto the books before the write-off.

Although dishonored notes commonly have to be written off as bad debts, some are also eventually paid by their makers. For example, if 30 days after dishonor, John Owen pays the maturity value of his dishonored note, the protest fee, and interest at 12% on both for 30 days beyond maturity, he will pay the following:

Maturity value	$1,224.00
Protest fee	5.00
Interest on $1,229 at 12% for 30 days	12.29
Total	$1,241.29

And Symplex will record receipt of his money as follows:

Aug.	25	Cash	1,241.29	
		Interest Earned		12.29
		Accounts Receivable—John Owen		1,229.00
		Dishonored note and protest fee collected with interest.		

End-of-Period Adjustments

If any notes receivable are outstanding at the accounting period end, their accrued interest should be calculated and recorded. For example, on December 16, a company accepted a $3,000, 60-day, 12% note from a customer in granting an extension on a past-due account. If the company's accounting period ends on December 31, by then $15 interest has accrued on this note and should be recorded with this adjusting entry:

Dec.	31	Interest Receivable	15.00	
		Interest Earned		15.00
		To record accrued interest on a note receivable.		

The adjusting entry causes the interest earned to appear on the income statement of the period in which it was earned. It also causes the interest receivable to appear on the balance sheet as a current asset.

Collecting Interest Previously Accrued

When the note is collected, the transaction may be recorded as follows:

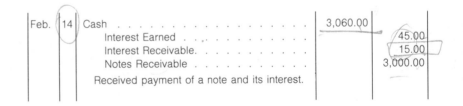

Feb.	14	Cash	3,060.00	
		Interest Earned		45.00
		Interest Receivable.		15.00
		Notes Receivable		3,000.00
		Received payment of a note and its interest.		

The entry's credit to Interest Receivable records collection of the interest accrued at the end of the previous period.

Reversing Entries

To correctly record a transaction like that of the February 14 entry just shown, a bookkeeper must remember the accrued interest recorded at the end of the previous year and divide the amount of interest received between the Interest Earned and Interest Receivable accounts. Many bookkeepers find this difficult, and they avoid "the need to remember" by preparing and posting entries to reverse any end-of-period adjustments of accrued items. These **reversing entries** are made after the adjusting and closing entries are posted and are normally dated the first day of the new accounting period.

To demonstrate reversing entries, assume that a company accepted a $3,000, 12%, 60-day note dated December 19, 12 days before the end of its annual accounting period. Sixty days' interest on this note is $60; and by December 31, $12 of the $60 has been earned. Consequently, the company's bookkeeper should make the following adjusting and closing entries to record the accrued interest on the note and to close the Interest Earned account.

Dec.	31	Interest Receivable		12.00	
		Interest Earned			12.00
		To record the accrued interest.			
	31	Interest Earned		12.00	
		Income Summary			12.00
		To close the Interest Earned account.			

In addition to the adjusting and closing entries, if the bookkeeper chooses to make reversing entries, he or she will make the following entry to reverse the accrued interest adjusting entry:

Jan.	1	Interest Earned		12.00	
		Interest Receivable.			12.00
		To reverse the accrued interest adjusting entry.			

Observe that the reversing entry is debit for credit and credit for debit, the reverse of the adjusting entry it reverses. After the adjusting, closing, and reversing entries are posted, the Interest Receivable and Interest Earned accounts appear as follows:

		Interest Receivable							Interest Earned			
Date		**Explanation**	**Dr.**	**Cr.**	**Bal.**		**Date**		**Explanation**	**Dr.**	**Cr.**	**Bal.**
Dec.	31	Adjusting	12		12		Dec.	31	Adjusting		12	12
Jan.	1	Reversing		12	–0–			31	Closing	12		–0–
							Jan.	1	Reversing	12		(12)

Notice that the reversing entry cancels the $12 of interest appearing in the Interest Receivable account. It also causes the accrued interest to appear in the Interest Earned account as a $12 debit. (Remember that an encircled balance means a balance opposite from normal.) Consequently, due to the reversing entry, when the note and interest are paid on February 17, the bookkeeper can record the transaction with this entry:

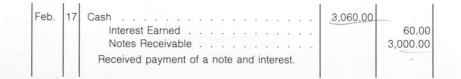

Feb.	17	Cash		3,060.00	
		Interest Earned			60.00
		Notes Receivable			3,000.00
		Received payment of a note and interest.			

The entry's $60 credit to Interest Earned includes both the $12 of interest earned during the previous period and the $48 of interest earned during the current period. However, when the entry is posted, because of the previously posted reversing entry, the balance of the Interest Earned account shows only the $48 of interest applicable to the current period, as follows:

Interest Earned

Date		Explanation	Dr.	Cr.	Bal.
Dec.	31	Adusting		12	12
	31	Closing	12		–0–
Jan.	1	Reversing	12		(12)
Feb.	17	Payment		60	48

Reversing entries are applicable to all accrued items, such as accrued interest earned, accrued interest expense, accrued taxes, and accrued salaries and wages. Nevertheless, they are not required but are a matter of convenience that enable a bookkeeper to forget an accrued item once its adjusting entry has been reversed.

☐   **Glossary**   **Aging accounts receivable** a process of classifying accounts receivable in terms of how long they have been outstanding.

Allowance for doubtful accounts the estimated amount of accounts receivable that will prove uncollectible.

Allowance method of accounting for bad debts an accounting procedure that (1) estimates the bad debts arising from credit sales and reports bad debt expense during the period of the sales, and (2) reports accounts receivable in the balance sheet net of estimated uncollectibles, which is their estimated realizable value.

Bad debt an uncollectible account receivable.

Bank discount the amount of interest charged by a bank when the interest is deducted in advance from money loaned.

Contingent liability a potential liability that will become an actual liability if and only if certain events occur.

Direct write-off method of accounting for bad debts the accounting procedure whereby uncollectible accounts are not estimated in advance and are not charged to expense until they prove to be uncollectible.

Discount period of a note the number of days following the date on which a note is discounted at the bank until the maturity date of the note.

Discounting a note receivable selling a note receivable to a bank or other concern.

Dishonoring a note refusal of a promissory note's maker to pay the amount due upon maturity of the note.

Full-disclosure principle the accounting requirement that financial statements and their accompanying notes disclose all information of a material nature relating to the financial position and operating results of the company for which they were prepared.

Installment accounts receivable accounts receivable that allow the customer to make periodic payments over several months and which typically earn interest.

Maker of a note one who signs a note and promises to pay it at maturity.

Materiality principle the accounting rule that strict adherence to any accounting principle is not required if lack of adherence will not produce an error sufficiently large as to influence the judgment of financial statement readers.

Maturity date of a note the date on which a note and any interest are due and payable.

Maturity value of a note principal of the note plus any interest due on the note's maturity date.

Notes receivable discounted notes receivable that have been discounted or sold by the payee and for which the payee is contingently liable.

Notice of protest a document informing each endorser of a promissory note that the note was presented for payment on its due date and payment was refused.

Payee of a note the one to whom a promissory note is made payable.

Proceeds of a discounted note the maturity value of a note minus any interest deducted because of its being discounted before maturity.

Protest fee the fee charged for preparing and issuing a notice of protest.

Realizable value the amount of cash that should be received from the conversion of an asset into cash in the ordinary course of business.

Reversing entry an entry, made as a bookkeeping convenience at the beginning of an accounting period, the debit and credit of which are opposite to an adjusting entry for an accrual that was made at the end of the previous period. As a result of the reversing entry, the subsequent receipt or payment of cash can be debited (or credited) entirely to the expense (or revenue) account.

☐ **Questions for Class Discussion**

1. Why do customers often prefer to charge their purchases to credit cards?
2. How do businesses benefit from allowing their customers to use credit cards?
3. Where is credit card expense disclosed on a classified income statement?
4. In meeting the requirements of the matching principle, why must bad debt expenses be matched with sales on an estimated basis?
5. What term describes the balance sheet valuation of accounts receivable less allowance for doubtful accounts?
6. What is a contra account? Why is estimated bad debt expense credited to a contra account rather than to the Accounts Receivable controlling account?
7. When bad debts are estimated by the income statement approach, what relationship is the focus of attention?
8. A company had $560,000 of charge sales in a year. How many dollars of bad debts expense may the company expect to experience from these sales if its past bad debts expense has averaged one fourth of 1% of charge sales?
9. Classify the following accounts: (*a*) Accounts Receivable, (*b*) Allowance for Doubtful Accounts, and (*c*) Bad Debts Expense.
10. Explain why writing off a bad debt against the allowance account does not reduce the estimated realizable value of a company's accounts receivable.
11. What are three reasons why Bad Debts Expense usually does not have the same adjusted balance as Allowance for Doubtful Accounts?
12. When bad debts are estimated by the simplified balance sheet approach, what relationship is the focus of attention?
13. Why does the direct write-off method of accounting for bad debts commonly fail in matching revenues and expenses?
14. What is the essence of the accounting principle of materiality?
15. Why might a business prefer a note receivable to an account receivable?
16. Define:
    - *a.* Promissory note.
    - *b.* Payee of a note.
    - *c.* Maturity date.
    - *d.* Dishonored note.
    - *e.* Notice of protest.
    - *f.* Discount period of a note.

g. Maker of a note.   *i.* Maturity value.

h. Principal of a note.   *j.* Contingent liability.

17. What are the due dates of the following notes: *(a)* a 90-day note dated July 10, *(b)* a 60-day note dated April 14, and *(c)* a 90-day note dated November 12?

18. Distinguish between bank discount and cash discount.

19. What does the full-disclosure principle require in a company's accounting statements?

□ **Class Exercises**   **Exercise 8-1**

Ackers Company allows customers to use two alternative credit cards in charging purchases. With the City State Bank Card, Ackers receives an immediate credit upon depositing sales receipts in its checking account. City State Bank makes a 3.5% service charge for credit card sales. The second credit card Ackers accepts is Western Card. Ackers sends the accumulated Western Card receipts to the Western Company on a weekly basis and is paid by Western Company approximately 10 days later. Western charges 3% of sales for using its card. Prepare entries in general journal form to record the following credit card transactions of Ackers Company:

Mar. 1   Sold merchandise for $2,300 on this day, accepting the customers' City State Bank Card. At the end of the day, the City State Bank Card receipts were deposited in the company's account at the bank.

2   Sold merchandise for $150, accepting the customer's Western Card.

6   Mailed $4,000 of credit card receipts to Western Company, requesting payment.

18   Received Western Company's check for the March 6 billing, less the normal service charge.

Exercise 8-2

On December 31, at the end of its annual accounting period, a company estimated it would lose as bad debts an amount equal to one half of 1% of its $450,000 of charge sales made during the year, and it made an addition to its Allowance for Doubtful Accounts equal to that amount. On the following April 7, it decided the $340 account of Ron Koplen was uncollectible and wrote it off as a bad debt. Two months later, on June 7, Mr. Koplen unexpectedly paid the amount previously written off. Give the required entries in general journal form to record these transactions.

Exercise 8-3

At the end of each year, a company uses the simplified balance sheet approach to estimate bad debts. On December 31, 198B, it has outstanding accounts receivable of $48,000 and estimates that 4% will prove to become uncollectible. *(a)* Give the entry to record bad debts expense for 198B under the assumption that Allowance for Doubtful Accounts had a $250 credit balance before the adjustment. (*b*) Give the entry under the assumption that Allowance for Doubtful Accounts has a $300 debit balance before the adjustment.

Exercise 8-4

Prepare general journal entries to record these transactions:

May   3   Accepted a $900, 60-day, 12% note dated this day from Ellen Doene in granting a time extension on her past-due account.

July   2   Ellen Doene dishonored her note when presented for payment.

Dec. 31   After exhausting all legal means of collecting, wrote off the account of Ellen Doene against the allowance for doubtful accounts.

Exercise 8-5

Prepare general journal entries to record these transactions:

Mar. 10   Sold merchandise to Jerry Dow, $1,800, terms 2/10, n/60.

May 10   Received $600 in cash and a $1,200, 90-day, 10% note dated May 9 in granting a time extension on the amount due from Jerry Dow.

June   8   Discounted the Jerry Dow note at the bank at 12%.

Aug.   7   Since notice protesting the Jerry Dow note had not been received, assumed that it has been paid.

Exercise 8-6

Prepare general journal entries to record these transactions:

June   5   Accepted a $3,000, 60-day, 12% noted dated June 3 from Donald Tucker granting a time extension on his past-due account.

8   Discounted the Donald Tucker note at the bank at 14%.

Aug.   4   Received notice protesting the Donald Tucker note. Paid the bank the maturity value of the note plus a $20 protest fee.

17   Received payment from Donald Tucker of the maturity value of his dishonored note, the protest fee, and interest at 12% on both for 15 days beyond maturity.

Exercise 8-7

On April 9, Mid-City Sales sold Larry Jones merchandise having a $5,625 catalog list price, less a 20% trade discount, 2/10, n/60. (Trade discounts were explained on page 177.) Jones was unable to pay and was granted a time extension on receipt of his 60-day, 11% note for the amount of the debt, dated June 8. Mid-City Sales held the note until June 23, when it discounted the note at its bank at 14%. The note was not protested. Answer these questions:

a. How many dollars of trade discount were granted on the sale?

b. How many dollars of cash discount could Jones have earned?

c. What was the maturity date of the note?

d. How many days were in the discount period?

e. How much bank discount was deducted by the bank?

f. What were the proceeds of the discounted note?

Exercise 8-8

Bradford Company accepted a $13,500, 12%, 60-day note date December 16, 15 days before the end of its annual accounting period, in granting a time extension on the past-due account of Frank Worst.

Required

1. Present general journal entries for Bradford Company *(a)* to record receipt of the note on December 16, *(b)* to record the accrued interest on the note of December 31, *(c)* to close the Interest Earned account, *(d)* to reverse the accrued interest adjusting entry, and *(e)* to record payment of the note and interest on February 14.

2. Open balance column accounts for Interest Receivable and Interest Earned and post the portions of the foregoing entries that affect these accounts.

Problems

Problem 8-1

Barrington Company allows a few customers to make sales on credit. Other customers may use either of two credit cards. The First State Bank makes a 4% service charge for sales on its credit card but immediately credits the checking account of its commercial customers when credit card receipts are deposited. Barrington deposits the First State Bank credit card receipts at the close of each business day.

When customers use the National Credit Card, Barrington Company accumulates the receipts for two or three days and then submits them to the National Credit Company for payment. National makes a 3% service charge and usually pays within one week of being billed.

Barrington Company completed the following transactions:

Nov. 2   Sold merchandise on credit to Tom Hall for $975. (Terms of all credit sales are 2/10, n/60.)

     3   Sold merchandise for $2,700 to customers who used their First State Bank credit cards. Sold merchandise for $2,000 to customers who used their National credit cards.

     4   Sold merchandise for $1,500 to customers who used their National credit cards.

     5   Wrote off the account of J. Marsh against the allowance for doubtful accounts. The $350 balance in Marsh's account stemmed from a credit sale in December of last year.

     5   The National credit card receipts accumulated since November 2 were submitted to the credit card company for payment.

   12   Received Tom Hall's check paying for the purchase of November 2.

   14   Received amount due from National Credit Company.

Required

Prepare general journal entries to record the above transactions.

Problem 8-2

On December 31, 198A, Conroe Company's unadjusted trial balance included the following items:

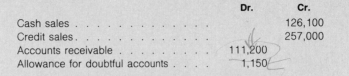

	Dr.	Cr.
Cash sales		126,100
Credit sales		257,000
Accounts receivable	111,200	
Allowance for doubtful accounts	1,150	

Required

1. Prepare the adjusting entry on the books of Conroe Company to estimate bad debts under each of the following independent assumptions:
   a. Bad debts are estimated to be 2% of total sales.
   b. Bad debts are estimated to be 3.5% of credit sales.
   c. An analysis suggests that 5% of outstanding accounts receivable on December 31, 198A, will become uncollectible.
2. Show how Accounts Receivable and Allowance for Doubtful Accounts would appear on the December 31, 198A, balance sheet given the facts in 1b above.
3. Show how Accounts Receivable and Allowance for Doubtful Accounts would appear on the December 31, 198A, balance sheet given the facts in 1c above.

Problem 8-3

Brandon Corporation had credit sales of $3,500,000 in 198A. On December 31, 198A, the company's Allowance for Doubtful Accounts had a credit balance of $4,000. The accountant for Brandon Corporation has prepared a schedule of the December 31, 198A, accounts receivable by age and on the basis of past experience has estimated the percentage of the receivables in each age category that will become uncollectible. This information is summarized as follows:

December 31, 198A Accounts Receivable	Age of Accounts Receivable	Uncollectible Percent Expected
$350,000	Not due (under 30 days)	2
180,000	1 to 30 days past due	3
55,000	31 to 60 days past due	15
35,000	61 to 90 days past due	40
20,000	Over 90 days past due	80

Required

1. Calculate the amount that should appear in the December 31, 198A, balance sheet as allowance for doubtful accounts.
2. Prepare the general journal entry to record bad debts expense for 198A.

3. On March 3, 198B, Brandon Corporation concluded that a customer's $6,500 accounts receivable was uncollectible and that the account should be written off. What effect will this action have on Brandon Corporation's 198B net income? Explain your answer.

Problem 8-4

Prepare entries in general journal form to record these transactions:

Jan.   6   Accepted a $3,825, 60-day, 12% note dated this day in granting a time extension on the past-due account of Gary White.

Mar.   7   Gary White paid the maturity value of his $3,825 note.

      10   Accepted a $1,500, 60-day, 10% note dated this day in granting a time extension on the past-due account of Bobbie Blaine.

May   9   Bobbie Blaine dishonored her note when presented for payment.

      13   Accepted a $2,500, 90-day, 14% note dated May 11 in granting a time extension on the past-due account of Jack Hobby.

      17   Discounted the Jack Hobby note at the bank at 16%.

Aug. 13   Since notice protesting the Jack Hobby note had not been received, assumed that it had been paid.

      15   Accepted a $2,000, 60-day, 12% note dated August 14 in granting a time extension on the past-due account of Bill Dame.

Sept. 7   Discounted the Bill Dame note at the bank at 14%.

Oct. 14   Received notice protesting the Bill Dame note. Paid the bank the maturity value of the note plus a $20 protest fee.

      15   Received a $3,000, 60-day, 11% note dated this day from Kay Whelan in granting a time extension on her past-due account.

Nov. 14   Discounted the Kay Whelan note at the bank at 14%.

Dec. 15   Received notice protesting the Kay Whelan note. Paid the bank the maturity value of the note plus a $20 protest fee.

      26   Received payment from Kay Whelan of the maturity value of her dishonored note, the protest fee, and interest on both for 12 days beyond maturity at 11%.

      31   Wrote off the accounts of Bobbie Blaine and Bill Dame against Allowance for Doubtful Accounts.

Problem 8-5

Prepare general journal entries to record these transactions:

Dec. 19   Accepted a $2,500, 60-day, 12% note dated this day in granting Dan Boggs a time extension on his past-due account.

      31   Made an adjusting entry to record the accrued interest on the Dan Boggs note.

      31   Closed the Interest Earned account.

Jan. 18   Discounted the Dan Boggs note at the bank at 14%.

Feb. 18   Received notice protesting the Dan Boggs note. Paid the bank the maturity value of the note plus a $20 protest fee.

Mar.   6   Accepted a $1,800, 11%, 60-day note dated this day in granting a time extension on the past-due account of Wallace Rogers.

      30   Discounted the Wallace Rogers note at the bank at 14%.

May   8   Since notice protesting the Wallace Rogers note had not been received, assumed that it had been paid.

June 11   Accepted a $2,000, 60-day, 10% note dated this day in granting a time extension on the past-due account of Mark Mangum.

Aug. 10   Received payment in full of the maturity value of the Mark Mangum note.

      13   Accepted a $1,500, 60-day, 10% note dated this day in granting Amy Searcy a time extension on her past-due account.

Sept. 2   Discounted the Amy Searcy note at the bank at 13%.

Oct. 14   Received notice protesting the Amy Searcy note. Paid the bank the maturity value of the note plus a $20 protest fee.

Nov. 11   Received payment from Amy Searcy of the maturity value of her dishonored note, the protest fee, and interest on both for 30 days beyond maturity at 10%.

Dec. 27   Wrote off the Dan Boggs account against Allowance for Doubtful Accounts.

Problem 8-6

A concern completed these transactions:

Dec. 16   Received $650 cash as partial payment of Jud Arrington's account and accepted a $2,200, 60-day, 12% note dated this day in granting a time extension on the remaining past-due balance.

      31   Aged the accounts receivable and estimated that $3,450 would prove uncollectible. Examined the Allowance for Doubtful Accounts account and determined that it had a $220 debit balance. Made adjusting entries to provide for the estimated bad debts and to record interest earned.

      31   Closed the Bad Debts Expense and Interest Earned accounts.

Feb. 14   Received payment of the maturity value of the Jud Arrington note.

      16   Learned of the bankruptcy of Mike Stewart and recorded a claim on his receiver in bankruptcy for the $975 owed by Mr. Stewart for merchandise purchased on credit.

Mar. 10   Learned that Glenn Reeves had gone out of business, leaving no assets to attach. Wrote off his $450 account as a bad debt.

Apr. 17   Accepted $300 in cash and a $1,200, 60-day, 12% note dated this day in granting a time extension on the past-due account of Bill Polkinghorn.

      23   Discounted the Bill Polkinghorn note at the bank at 14%.

June 19   Received notice protesting the Bill Polkinghorn note. Paid the bank the maturity value of the note plus a $15 protest fee.

July   7   Glenn Reeves paid $150 of the amount written off on March 10. In the letter accompanying the payment, he stated that his finances had improved and he expected to pay the balance owed within a short time.

Aug.   8   Received $150 from the receiver in bankruptcy of Mike Stewart. A letter accompanying the payment said that no more would be paid. Recorded the receipt of the $150 and wrote off the balance owed as a bad debt.

Oct. 4 Decided that the Bill Polkinghorn account was uncollectible and wrote it off as a bad debt.

Dec. 24 Made a compound entry to write off the accounts of H. C. Carnes, $595, and Frank Doan, $415.

31 Aged the accounts receivable and determined that $2,900 would probably prove uncollectible. Made the adjusting entry to provide for them.

31 Closed the Bad Debts Expense and Interest Earned accounts.

Required

1. Open Interest Receivable, Allowance for Doubtful Accounts, Interest Earned, and Bad Debts Expense accounts. Enter the $220 debit balance in the Allowance for Doubtful Accounts account.

2. Prepare general journal entries to record the transactions and post those portions of the entries that affect the accounts opened.

□ **Alternate Problems**

Problem 8-1A

A few of Bradford Company's customers are granted credit by the company. Other customers may use either of two credit cards. The Hilltop State Bank makes a 4% service charge for sales on its credit card but immediately credits the checking account of its commercial customers when credit card receipts are deposited. Bradford deposits the Hilltop State Bank credit card receipts at the close of each business day.

When customers use the World Credit Card, Bradford Company accumulates the receipts for two or three days and then submits them to the World Credit Company for payment. World makes a 3.2% service charge and usually pays within one week of being billed.

Bradford Company completed the following transactions:

Mar. 12 Sold merchandise on credit to Terry Bray for $650. (Terms of all credit sales are 2/10, n/60.)

13 Sold merchandise for $2,250 to customers who used their Hilltop State Bank credit cards. Sold merchandise for $2,500 to customers who used their World credit cards.

14 Sold merchandise for $1,800 to customers who used their World credit cards.

15 Wrote off the account of K. Britt against the allowance for doubtful accounts. The $475 balance in Britt's account stemmed from a credit sale in December of last year.

15 The World credit card receipts accumulated since March 12 were submitted to the credit card company for payment.

22 Received Terry Bray's check paying for the purchase of March 12.

24 Received amount due from World Credit Company.

Required

Prepare general journal entries to record the above transactions.

Problem 8-2A

On December 31, 198A, Bazley Corporation's unadjusted trial balance included the following items:

	Dr.	Cr.
Cash sales		302,000
Credit sales.		488,000
Accounts receivable	175,000	
Allowance for doubtful accounts		1,400

Required

1. Prepare the adjusting entry on the books of Bazley Corporation to estimate bad debts under each of the following independent assumptions:
   a. Bad debts are estimated to be 1.5% of total sales.
   b. Bad debts are estimated to be 3% of credit sales.
   c. An analysis suggests that 7% of outstanding accounts receivable on December 31, 198A, will become uncollectible.

2. Show how Accounts Receivable and Allowance for Doubtful Accounts would appear on the December 31, 198A, balance sheet given the facts in 1*b* above.

3. Show how Accounts Receivable and Allowance for Doubtful Accounts would appear on the December 31, 198A, balance sheet given the facts in 1*c* above.

Problem 8-3A

Diskette Corporation had credit sales of $5,600,000 in 198A. On December 31, 198A, the company's Allowance for Doubtful Accounts had a debit balance of $6,200. The accountant for Diskette Corporation has prepared a schedule of the December 31, 198A, accounts receivable by age and on the basis of past experience has estimated the percentage of the receivables in each age category that will become uncollectible. This information is summarized as follows:

December 31, 198A, Accounts Receivable	Age of Accounts Receivable	Uncollectible Percent Expected
$500,000	Not due (under 30 days)	1.75
200,000	1 to 30 days past due	3.25
60,000	31 to 60 days past due	18.00
30,000	61 to 90 days past due	45.00
24,000	Over 90 days past due	75.00

Required

1. Calculate the amount that should appear in the December 31, 198A, balance sheet as allowance for doubtful accounts.

2. Prepare the general journal entry to record bad debts expense for 198A.

3. On April 7, 198B, Diskette Corporation concluded that a customer's $7,800 accounts receivable was uncollectible and that the account should be written off. What effect will this action have on Diskette Corporation's 198B net income? Explain your answer.

Problem 8-4A

Prepare general journal entries to record these transactions:

Jan. 14   Accepted a $2,500, 60-day, 10% note dated this day in granting a time extension on the past-due account of Hank Williams.

Mar. 15   Hank Williams dishonored his note when presented for payment.

21   Accepted a $1,700, 90-day, 11% note dated this day in granting a time extension on the past-due account of Jane Rubin.

27   Discounted the Jane Rubin note at the bank at 14%.

June 25   Since notice protesting the Jane Rubin note had not been received, assumed the note had been paid.

27   Accepted $600 in cash and a $1,000, 60-day, 12% note dated this day in granting a time extension on the past-due account of Frank Dipprey.

July 21   Discounted the Frank Dipprey note at the bank at 15%.

Aug. 28   Received notice protesting the Frank Dipprey note. Paid the bank the maturity value of the note plus a $20 protest fee.

Sept. 6   Accepted a $1,300, 60-day, 13% note dated this day in granting a time extension on the past-due account of Barbara Gibb.

Oct. 12   Discounted the Barbara Gibb note at the bank at 16%.

Nov.   8   Received notice protesting the Barbara Gibb note. Paid the bank the maturity value of the note plus a $20 protest fee.

Dec.   5   Received payment from Barbara Gibb of the maturity value of her dishonored note, the protest fee, and interest at 13% on both for 30 days beyond maturity.

27   Decided the accounts of Hank Williams and Frank Dipprey were uncollectible and wrote them off against Allowance for Doubtful Accounts.

Problem 8-5A

Prepare general journal entries to record these transactions:

Dec. 11   Accepted a $2,800, 60-day, 12% note dated this day in granting a time extension on the past-due account of Lane Thompson.

31   Made an adjusting entry to record the accrued interest on the Lane Thompson note.

31   Closed the Interest Earned account.

Jan. 10   Discounted the Lane Thompson note at the bank at 15%.

Feb. 12   Since notice protesting the Lane Thompson note had not been received, assumed that it had been paid.

Mar. 1   Accepted a $1,600, 90-day, 11% note dated this day in granting a time extension on the past-due account of Jane Riddles.

7   Discounted the Jane Riddles note at the bank at 14%.

May 31   Received notice protesting the Jane Riddles note. Paid the bank the maturity value of the note plus a $25 protest fee.

June 29   Received payment from Jane Riddles of the maturity value of her dishonored note, the protest fee, and interest on both for 30 days beyond maturity at 11%.

July 2   Accepted a $1,250, 60-day, 11% note dated July 1 in granting a time extension on the past-due account of Gay Jackson.

Aug. 30 Gay Jackson dishonored her note when presented for payment.
    31 Accepted $500 in cash and a $1,000, 60-day, 10% note dated this day in granting a time extension on the past-due account of Tom Nixon.

Oct. 6 Discounted the Tom Nixon note at the bank at 13%.
    31 Received notice protesting the Tom Nixon note. Paid the bank its maturity value plus a $25 protest fee.

Dec. 27 Decided the Gay Jackson and Tom Nixon accounts were uncollectible and wrote them off against Allowance for Doubtful Accounts.

Problem 8-6A

A company completed these transactions:

Dec. 1 Accepted $400 in cash and a $1,200, 60-day, 12% note dated this day from Lanny Mingle in granting a time extension on his past-due account.
    31 Made an adjusting entry to record the accrued interest on the Lanny Mingle note.
    31 Examined the Allowance for Doubtful Accounts account and determined that it had a $380 credit balance. Made an adjusting entry to provide an addition to the allowance equal to one half of 1% of the $315,000 charge sales for the year.
    31 Closed the Interest Earned and Bad Debts Expense accounts.

Jan. 30 Received payment of the maturity value of the Lanny Mingle note.

Feb. 3 Learned of the bankruptcy of Grant Hester and made a claim on his receiver in bankruptcy for the $670 owed by Mr. Hester for merchandise purchased on credit.

Mar. 12 After making effort to collect, decided the $550 account of Candice Voth was uncollectible and wrote it off as a bad debt.

June 15 Received a letter from Candice Voth enclosing a $150 payment on the account written off on March 12. She stated in her letter that her finances had improved and that she expected to pay the balance owed within a short time.

Nov. 3 Received $195 from Grant Hester's receiver in bankruptcy. A letter accompanying the payment stated that no more would be paid. Made an entry to record the cash received and to write off the balance of Hester's account.

Dec. 22 Made a compound entry to write off the accounts of Ed Parsons, $840; Frank Daniels, $440; and Nancy Wilson, $1,365.
    31 Provided an addition to the allowance for doubtful accounts equal to one half of 1% of the $650,000 charge sales for the year.
    31 Closed the Interest Earned and Bad Debts Expense accounts.

Required

1. Open these accounts: Interest Receivable, Allowance for Doubtful Accounts, Interest Earned, and Bad Debts Expense. Enter the $380 credit balance in the Allowance for Doubtful Accounts account. Prepare

general journal entries to record the transactions and post those portions affecting the accounts opened.

2. Prepare an alternate bad debts adjusting entry for the second December 31 of the problem under the assumption that rather than providing an addition to the allowance account equal to one half of 1% of charge sales, the company aged its accounts receivable and estimated that $2,400 of accounts were probably uncollectible.

Provocative Problems

Provocative Problem 8-1   An Internal Control Failure

When his auditor arrived early in January to begin the annual audit, Greg Smith, the owner of Advanced Sales, asked that careful attention be given to accounts receivable. Two things caused this request: (1) During the previous week, Mr. Smith had met Jan Burr, a former customer, on the street and had asked her about her account which recently had been written off as uncollectible. Ms. Burr had indignantly replied that she had paid her $310 account in full, and she later produced canceled checks endorsed by Advanced Sales to prove it. (2) The income statement prepared for the quarter ended the previous December 31 showed an unusually large volume of sales returns. The bookkeeper who had prepared the statement was a new employee, having begun work on October 1, after being hired on the basis of out-of-town letters of reference. In addition to doing all the record-keeping, the bookkeeper also acts as cashier, receiving and depositing the cash from both cash sales and those received through the mail.

In the process of performing the audit, the auditor prepared from the company's records the following analysis of the accounts receivable for the period October 1 through December 31:

	Ashe	Burr	Cote	Duke	Eloe	Fout	Gage
Balance, October 1	$ 420	$ 250	$ 690	$ 500	$ 260	$1,090	$ 820
Sales	1,390	260	1,060		1,320	840	1,150
Totals	$ 1,810	$ 510	$1,750	$ 500	$1,580	$1,930	$ 1,970
Collections	(1,020)		(790)		(820)	(980)	(1,230)
Returns	(170)	(90)	(80)		(160)	(120)	(50)
Bad debts written off . . .		(420)		(500)			
Balance, December 31 . .	$ 620	–0–	$ 880	–0–	$ 600	$ 830	$ 690

The auditor communicated with all charge customers and learned that although their account balances as of December 31 agreed with the amounts shown in the company's records, the individual transactions did not. The customers reported credit purchases totaling $6,870 during the three-month period and $170 of returns for which credit had been granted. Correspondence with Mr. Duke, the customer whose $500 account had been written off, revealed that he had become bankrupt and his creditor claims had been settled by his receiver in bankruptcy at $0.22 on the dollar. The checks had been mailed by his receiver on October 30, and all had been paid and returned by the bank, properly endorsed by the recipients.

Under the assumption the bookkeeper has embezzled cash from the company, determine the total amount he has taken and attempted to conceal with false accounts receivable entries. Account for the deficiency by listing the concealment methods used and the amount he attempted to conceal with each method. Also outline an internal control system that will help protect the company's cash from future embezzlement. Assume the company will hire a new bookkeeper but that it is small and can have only one office employee who must do all the bookkeeping.

Provocative Problem 8-2   All-Parts Store

Kevin Barrows has operated All-Parts Store for five years. Three years ago he liberalized the store's credit policy in an effort to increase credit sales. Credit sales have increased, but now Kevin is concerned with the effects of the more liberalized credit policy. Bad debts written off (the store uses the direct write-off method) have increased materially in the last three years, and now Kevin wonders if the increase justifies the substantial bad debt losses which he is certain have resulted from the more liberal credit policy.

An examination of the shop's credit sales records, bad debt losses, and accounts receivable for the five years' operations reveal:

	1st Year	2nd Year	3rd Year	4th Year	5th Year
Credit sales	$150,000	$165,000	$225,000	$270,000	$300,000
Cost of goods sold.	90,000	99,300	134,850	162,450	180,150
Gross profit from credit sales .	$ 60,000	$ 65,700	$ 90,150	$107,550	$119,850
Expenses other than bad debts.	45,000	49,350	67,800	80,700	90,000
Income before bad debts . . .	$ 15,000	$ 16,350	$ 22,350	$ 26,850	$ 29,850
Bad debts written off	150	660	1,125	3,510	3,600
Income from credit sales . . .	$ 14,850	$ 15,690	$ 21,225	$ 23,340	$ 26,250
Bad debts by year of sales.	$ 600	$ 495	$ 2,925	$ 3,240	$ 4,200

The last line in the tabulation results from reclassifying bad debt losses by the years in which the sales that resulted in the losses were made. Consequently, the $4,200 of fifth-year losses includes $2,415 of estimated bad debts that are still in the accounts receivable.

Prepare a schedule showing in columns by years: income from credit sales before bad debt losses, bad debts incurred, and the resulting income from credit sales. Then below the income figures show for each year bad debts written off as a percentage of sales followed on the next line by bad debts incurred as percentage of sales. Also prepare a report for Mr. Barrows answering his concern about the new credit policy and recommending any changes you consider desirable in his accounting for bad debts.

9 Inventories and Cost of Goods Sold

After studying Chapter 9, you should be able to:

1. Calculate the cost of an inventory based on *(a)* specific invoice prices, *(b)* weighted-average cost, *(c)* FIFO, and *(d)* LIFO.

2. Explain the income tax effect of the use of LIFO.

3. Describe the requirements of the consistency principle.

4. Describe the requirements of the conservatism principle.

5. Calculate the lower-of-cost-or-market amount of an inventory.

6. Explain the effect of an inventory error on the income statements of the current and succeeding years.

7. Prepare entries to record merchandise transactions under a perpetual inventory system.

8. Estimate an inventory by the retail method and by the gross profit method.

9. Define or explain the words and phrases listed in the chapter Glossary.

A merchandising business earns revenue by selling merchandise. For such a concern, the phrase **merchandise inventory** is used to describe the tangible property it holds for sale. As a rule, the items held as merchandise inventory are sold within a year or one operating cycle. Consequently, merchandise inventory is a current asset, usually the largest current asset on the merchandising concern's balance sheet.

Matching Merchandise Costs with Revenues

Accounting for inventories affects both the balance sheet and the income statement. Nevertheless, "the major objective in accounting for the goods in the inventory is the matching of appropriate **costs** against revenues in order that there may be a proper determination of the realized income."[1] The matching process is already a familiar topic. For inventories, it consists of determining how much of the cost of the goods that were for sale during a period should be deducted from the period's revenue and how much should be carried forward as inventory to be matched against a future period's revenue.

When separating cost of goods available for sale into its components of cost of goods sold and cost of goods not sold, the key problem in a periodic inventory system is that of assigning a cost to the goods not sold or to the ending inventory. However, it should be borne in mind that the procedures for assigning a cost to the ending inventory are also the means of determining cost of goods sold because whatever portion of the cost of goods for sale is assigned to the ending inventory, the remainder goes into cost of goods sold.

Taking an Ending Inventory

As previously explained, when a **periodic inventory system** is in use, the dollar amount of the ending inventory is determined by counting the items of unsold merchandise remaining in the store, multiplying the count for each kind by its cost, and adding the costs for all the kinds. In making the count, items are less apt to be counted twice or omitted from the count if prenumbered **inventory tickets** like the one in Illustration 9-1 are used. Before beginning the inventory, a sufficient number of the tickets, at least one for each kind of product on hand, is issued to each department in the store. Next, a clerk counts the quantity of each product and from the count and the price tag attached to the merchandise fills in the information on the inventory ticket and attaches it to the counted items. After the count is completed, each department is examined for uncounted items. At this stage, inventory tickets are attached to all counted items. Consequently, any products without tickets attached are uncounted. After all items are counted and tickets attached, the tickets are removed and sent to the accounting department for completion of the inventory. To ensure that no ticket is lost or left attached to merchandise, all the prenumbered tickets issued are accounted for when the tickets arrive in the accounting department.

[1] FASB, *Accounting Standards—Current Text* (Stamford, Conn., 1984), sec. I78.104. Copyright © by the Financial Accounting Standards Board, High Ridge Park, Stamford, Conn. 06905. Quoted with permission. Copies of the complete document are available from the FASB.

Illustration 9-1

INVENTORY
TICKET no._____**786**_____

Item

Quantity counted

Sales price $

Cost price $

Purchase date

Counted by_____

Checked by_____

In the accounting department, the information on the tickets is copied on inventory summary sheets. The sheets are then completed by multiplying the number of units of each product by its unit cost. This gives the dollar amount of each product in the inventory, and the total for all the products is the dollar total of the inventory.

■ **Assigning Costs to Inventory Items**

In completing an inventory, it is necessary to assign costs to the inventory items. This offers no problem when costs remain fixed. However, when identical items were purchased during a period at different costs, a problem arises as to which costs apply to the ending inventory and which apply to the goods sold. There are four commonly used ways of assigning costs to goods in the ending inventory and to goods sold. They are (1) specific invoice prices; (2) weighted-average cost; (3) first-in, first-out; and (4) last-in, first-out. All four methods fall within **generally accepted accounting principles.**

To illustrate the four, assume that a company has on hand at the end of an accounting period 12 units of Product X. Also, assume that the company began the year and purchased Product X during the year as follows:

Jan. 1	Beginning inventory . .	10 units @ $100 =	$1,000
Mar. 13	Purchased	15 units @ $108 =	1,620
Aug. 17	Purchased	20 units @ $120 =	2,400
Nov. 10	Purchased	10 units @ $125 =	1,250
	Total	55 units	$6,270

Specific Invoice Prices

When it is possible to identify each item in an inventory with a specific purchase and its invoice, **specific invoice prices** may be used to assign costs. For example, assume that 6 of the 12 unsold units of Product X were from the November purchase and 6 were from the August purchase. Under this assumption, costs are assigned to the inventory and goods sold by means of specific invoice prices as follows:

Total cost of 55 units available for sale		$6,270
Less ending inventory priced by means of specific invoices:		
6 units from the November purchase at $125 each.	$750	
6 units from the August purchase at $120 each	720	
12 units in ending inventory		1,470
Cost of goods sold		$4,800

Weighted Average

Under this method, prices for the units in the beginning inventory and in each purchase are weighted by the number of units in the beginning inventory and in each purchase and are averaged to find the **weighted-average cost** per unit as follows:

10 units @ $100 =	$1,000
15 units @ $108 =	1,620
20 units @ $120 =	2,400
10 units @ $125 =	1,250
55	$6,270

$6,270 ÷ 55 = $114, weighted-average cost per unit

After the weighted-average cost per unit is determined, this average is used to assign costs to the inventory and the units sold as follows:

Total cost of 55 units available for sale	$6,270
Less ending inventory priced on a weighted-average	
cost basis: 12 units at $114 each.	1,368
Cost of goods sold	$4,902

First-In, First-Out

In a merchandising business, clerks may be instructed to sell the oldest merchandise first. When this instruction is followed, merchandise tends to flow out on a first-in, first-out basis. However, even if the physical flow of goods does not follow a first-in, first-out basis, this pattern may be assumed in pricing an inventory. When a first-in, first-out cost flow is assumed, the costs of the last items received are assigned to the ending inventory, and the remaining costs are assigned to goods sold. When first-in, first-out, or **FIFO** as it is often called, is used, costs are assigned to the inventory and goods sold as follows:

Total cost of 55 units available for sale		$6,270
Less ending inventory priced on a basis of FIFO:		
10 units from the November purchase at $125 each . .	$1,250	
2 units from the August purchase at $120 each	240	
12 units in the ending inventory		1,490
Cost of goods sold.		$4,780

Last-In, First-Out

Under this method of inventory pricing, commonly called **LIFO,** the cost of the last goods received are matched with revenue from sales. The theoretical justification for this is that a going concern must replace the inventory items it sells. When goods are sold, replacements are purchased. Thus, it is a sale that causes the replacement of goods. If costs and revenues are then matched, replacement costs should be matched with the sales that induced the acquisitions. Although the costs of the most recent purchases are not quite the same as the costs of the replacements, the costs of the most recent purchases are the most current costs. Thus, the costs of recent purchases closely approximate replacement costs.

Under LIFO, costs are assigned to the 12 remaining units of Product X and to the goods sold as follows:

Total cost of 55 units available for sale		$6,270
Less ending inventory priced on a basis of LIFO:		
10 units in the beginning inventory at $100 each. . . .	$1,000	
2 units from the first purchase at $108 each	216	
12 units in the ending inventory		1,216
Cost of goods sold		$5,054

Notice that this method of matching costs and revenue results in the final inventory being priced at the cost of the oldest 12 units.

Tax Effect of LIFO

During periods of rising prices, LIFO offers a tax advantage to its users. This advantage arises because when compared with other methods the application of LIFO results in assigning larger amounts of costs to goods sold. This in turn results in the smallest reported net incomes and income taxes.

The use of LIFO is not limited to concerns in which goods are actually sold on a last-in, first-out basis. A concern may choose LIFO even though it actually sells goods on a first-in, first-out or some other basis.

Comparison of Methods

In a stable market where prices remain unchanged, the inventory pricing method is of little importance. When prices are unchanged over a period of time, all methods give the same cost figures. However, in a changing market where prices are rising or falling, each method may give a different result. This may be seen by comparing the costs of the units in the ending inventory and the units of Product X sold as calculated by the several methods discussed. These costs are as follows:

	Ending Inventory	Cost of Units Sold
Based on specific invoice prices . . .	$1,470	$4,800
Based on weighted average	1,368	4,902
Based on FIFO	1,490	4,780
Based on LIFO.	1,216	5,054

Each of the four pricing methods is generally accepted, and arguments can be advanced for the use of each. In one sense, specific invoice prices may be said to exactly match cost and revenues. However, this method is of practical use only for relatively high-priced items of which only a few units are kept in stock and sold. Weighted-average costs tend to smooth out price fluctuations. FIFO causes the last costs incurred to be assigned to the ending inventory. It thus provides an inventory valuation for the balance sheet that most closely approximates current replacement cost. LIFO causes last costs incurred to be assigned to cost of goods sold. Therefore, it results in a better matching of current costs with revenues. However, the method used commonly affects the amounts of reported ending inventory, cost of goods sold, and net income. Consequently, the **full-disclosure principle** requires that a company show in its statements by means of footnotes or other manner the pricing method used.[2]

The Consistency Principle

Look again at the table of costs for Product X. Note that a company can change its reported net income for an accounting period simply by changing its inventory pricing method. However, the change would violate the accounting **principle of consistency.** Furthermore, it would make a comparison of the company's inventory and income with previous periods more or less meaningless.

As with inventory pricing, more than one generally accepted method or procedure has been derived in accounting practice to account for an item or an activity. In each case, one method may be considered better for one enterprise, while another may be considered more satisfactory for a concern operating under different circumstances. Nevertheless, the **consistency principle** requires a persistent application by a company of any selected accounting method or procedure, period after period. As a result, a reader of a company's financial statements may assume that in keeping

[2] Ibid., sec. A10.105, 106. First published as *APB Opinion No. 22*, pars. 12, 13.

its records and in preparing its statements the company used the same procedures employed in previous years. Only on the basis of this assumption can meaningful comparisons be made of the data in a company's statements year after year.

■ **Changing Accounting Procedures**

In achieving comparability, the **consistency principle** does not require that a method or procedure once chosen can never be changed. Rather, if a company decides that a different acceptable method or procedure from the one in use will better serve its needs, a change may be made. However, when such a change is made, the **full-disclosure principle** requires that the nature of the change, justification for the change, and the effect of the change on net income be disclosed in notes accompanying the statements.[3]

■ **Items Included on an Inventory**

A concern's inventory should include all goods owned by the business and held for sale, regardless of where the goods may be located at the time of the inventory. In the application of this rule, there are generally no problems with respect to most items. For most items all that is required is to see that they are counted, that nothing is omitted, and that nothing is counted more than once. However, goods in transit, goods sold but not delivered, goods on consignment, and obsolete and damaged goods are items that require special attention.

When goods are in transit on the inventory date, the purchase should be recorded, and the goods should appear on the purchaser's inventory if ownership has passed to the purchaser. Generally, if the buyer is responsible for paying the freight charges, ownership passes as soon as the goods are loaded aboard the means of transportation. Likewise, if the seller is to pay the freight charges, ownership passes when the goods arrive at their destination.

Goods on consignment are goods shipped by their owner (known as the **consignor**) to another person or firm (called the **consignee**) who is to sell the goods for the owner. Consigned goods belong to the consignor and should appear on the consignor's inventory.

Damaged goods and goods that have deteriorated or become obsolete should not be placed on the inventory if they are not salable. If such goods are salable but at a reduced price, they should be placed on the inventory at a conservative estimate of their **net realizable value** (sale price less the cost of making the sale). This causes the accounting period in which the goods were damaged, deteriorated, or became obsolete to suffer the resultant loss.

■ **Elements of Inventory Cost**

As applied to inventories, cost means the sum of the applicable expenditures and charges directly or indirectly incurred in bringing an article to its existing condition and location.[4] Therefore, the cost of an inventory item includes the invoice price, less the discount, plus any additional incidental costs necessary to put the goods into place and condition for sale.

[3] Ibid., sec. A06.113. First published as *APB Opinion No. 20,* par. 17.
[4] Ibid., sec. I78.402. Previously published as *Accounting Research Bulletin No. 43,* ch. 4, par. 5.

The additional incidental costs include import duties, transportation, storage, insurance, and any other applicable costs, such as those incurred during an aging process.

If incurred, any of the foregoing enter into the cost of an inventory. However, in pricing an inventory, most concerns do not take into consideration the incidental costs of acquiring merchandise. They price the inventory on the basis of invoice prices only and treat all incidental costs as expenses of the period in which incurred.

Although not correct in theory, treating incidental costs as expenses of the period in which incurred is commonly permissible and often best. In theory, a share of each incidental cost should be assigned to every unit purchased. This causes a portion of each to be carried forward in the inventory to be matched against the revenue of the period in which the inventory is sold. However, the expense of computing costs on such a precise basis usually outweighs any benefit from the extra accuracy. Consequently, when possible, most concerns take advantage of the **principle of materiality** and treat such costs as expenses of the period in which incurred.

■ **Lower of Cost or Market**

As previously explained, the **cost** of the ending inventory is determined by using one of the four pricing methods (FIFO, LIFO, weighted average, or specific invoice prices). However, the cost of the inventory is not necessarily the amount that is reported on the balance sheet. Generally accepted accounting principles require that the inventory be reported at market value whenever market is lower than cost. Thus, merchandise inventory is shown on the balance sheet at the **lower of cost or market.**

Market Normally Means Replacement Cost

What do accountants mean by the term **market?** For the purpose of assigning a value to merchandise inventory, market normally means **replacement cost.** That means the price a company would pay if it were to buy new items to replace those in its inventory. When the cost to replace merchandise drops below original cost, the sales price of the merchandise also is likely to fall. Therefore, the merchandise is worth less to the company and should be written down to replacement cost (or market).

Lower of cost or market may be applied to merchandise inventory in either of two ways. First, it may be applied to the inventory as a whole. Alternatively, it may be applied separately to each product in the inventory. To illustrate, assume that a company's year-end inventory contains three products (X, Y, and Z) with the following costs and replacement costs:

Product	Units on Hand	Per Unit Cost	Per Unit Market	Total Cost	Total Market	Lower of Cost or Market (by product)
X	20	$8	$7	$160	$140	$140
Y	10	5	6	50	60	50
Z	5	9	7	45	35	35
				$255		$225

Replacement cost (market)
of whole inventory. $235

Note that when the the whole inventory is priced at market, the total is $235, which is $20 lower than the $255 cost. Alternatively, when the lower of cost or market is applied separately to each product, the sum is only $225. A company may calculate lower of cost or market either way. However, whichever method is chosen, it should then be used consistently in future periods.

Inventory Should Never Be Valued at More than Its Net Realizable Value

The idea that **market** is defined as replacement cost is subject to an important exception. This exception is that inventory should never be valued at more than its net realizable value, which is the expected sales price less additional costs to sell. Understand that merchandise is written down to market because the value of the merchandise to the company has declined. Sometimes, the net realizable value is even less than replacement cost. In that case, the merchandise is worth no more than net realizable value and should be written down to that amount.

For example, assume that merchandise was purchased for $100 and was originally priced to sell for $125. By year-end, a general decline in prices resulted in a replacement cost of $90. However, the merchandise in question had been damaged. Management expects that the merchandise can be sold for $95, if it is first cleaned at a cost of $10. Therefore, net realizable value is $95 − $10, or $85. Since net realizable value ($85) is less than replacement cost ($90), the merchandise should be written down to net realizable value.

Inventory Should Never Be Valued at Less than Net Realizable Value Minus a Normal Profit Margin

A second exception to the idea that market means replacement cost is that merchandise should never be written down to an amount that is less than net realizable value minus a normal profit margin. To illustrate, suppose that a company normally buys merchandise for $80 and sells it for $100. The gross profit of $20 is 20% of the selling price. Now suppose the selling price falls from $100 to $90. A normal profit margin would be $90 × 20% = $18. Therefore, the inventory should not be written down below $90 − $18 = $72, even if replacement cost may have fallen below $72. If the inventory were written down below $72, the income statement of the current period would show an abnormally low profit margin. And when the merchandise is sold for $90 the next period, the income statement of that period would show an abnormally high gross margin.

■ **Principle of Conservatism**

Generally accepted accounting principles require that inventory be written down to market when market is less than cost. On the other hand, inventory generally cannot be written up to market when market exceeds cost. If writing inventory down to market is justified, why not also write inventory up to market? What is the reason for this apparent inconsistency?

Accountants often justify the lower-of-cost-or-market rule by citing the **principle of conservatism.** This principle is sometimes expressed simplistically as "recognize all losses but anticipate no profits." More realistically, the principle of conservatism attempts to give the accountant guidance in uncertain situations where amounts must be estimated. In general terms, it implies that when "two estimates of amounts to be received or paid in the future are about equally likely, . . . the less optimistic estimate"[5] should be used. Since the revenue to be received from selling inventory is usually uncertain, refusing to write the inventory up to market is clearly the less optimistic estimate.

■ **Inventory Errors— Periodic System**

When the **periodic inventory system** is used, special care must be exercised in taking the end-of-period inventory. An error in determining the end-of-period inventory will cause misstatements in cost of goods sold, gross profit, net income, current assets, and owner's equity. Also, the ending inventory of one period is the beginning inventory of the next. Therefore, the error will carry forward and cause misstatements in the succeeding period's cost of goods sold, gross profit, and net income. Furthermore, since the amount involved in an inventory is often large, the misstatements can be material without being readily apparent.

To illustrate the effects of an inventory error, assume that in each of the years 198A, 198B, and 198C, a company had $100,000 in sales. If the company maintained a $20,000 inventory throughout the period and made $60,000 in purchases in each of the years, its cost of goods sold each year was $60,000, and its annual gross profits were $40,000. However, assume the company incorrectly calculated its December 31, 198A, inventory at $18,000 rather than $20,000. The error would have the effects shown in Illustration 9-2.

Observe in Illustration 9-2 that the $2,000 understatement of the December 31, 198A, inventory caused a $2,000 overstatement in 198A cost of goods sold and a $2,000 understatement in gross profit and net income. Also, since the ending inventory of 198A became the beginning inventory of 198B, the error caused an understatement in the 198B cost of goods sold and a $2,000 overstatement in gross profit and net income. However, by 198C the error had no effect.

Illustration 9-2

	198A		198B		198C	
Sales		$100,000		$100,000		$100,000
Cost of goods sold:						
Beginning inventory	$20,000		$18,000*		$20,000	
Purchases	60,000		60,000		60,000	
Goods for sale	$80,000		$78,000		$80,000	
Ending inventory	18,000*		20,000		20,000	
Cost of goods sold		62,000		58,000		60,000
Gross profit		$ 38,000		$ 42,000		$ 40,000

* Should have been $20,000.

[5] FASB, *Statement of Financial Accounting Concepts No. 2* (1980), par. 95. Copyright © by the Financial Accounting Standards Board, High Ridge Park, Stamford, Conn., 06905. Quoted with permission. Copies of the complete document are available from the FASB.

In Illustration 9-2, the December 31, 198A, inventory is understated. Had it been overstated, it would have caused opposite results—the 198A net income would have been overstated, and the 198B income understated.

It has been argued that an inventory mistake is not too serious, since the error it causes in reported net income the first year is exactly offset by an opposite error in the second. However, such reasoning is unsound. It fails to consider that management, creditors, and owners base many important decisions on fluctuations in reported net income. Consequently, such mistakes should be avoided.

■ **Perpetual Inventory Systems**

The previous discussion of inventories was focused on the periodic inventory system. Under the periodic system, the Merchandise Inventory account is updated only once each accounting period. This occurs when the closing entries establish the ending amount of inventory in the Merchandise Inventory account. However, this account reflects the current balance of inventory only until the first purchase or sale in the following period. Thereafter, the Merchandise Inventory account no longer reflects the current balance.

By contrast, the **perpetual inventory system** updates the Merchandise Inventory account after each purchase and each sale. The account shows the current amount of inventory on hand whenever all of the entries have been posted. The system takes its name from the fact that the Merchandise Inventory account is "perpetually" up-to-date. When a perpetual inventory system is used, management is able to monitor the inventory on hand on a regular basis. This aids in planning future purchases.

Prior to the widespread use of computers in accounting, perpetual inventory systems were limited to companies that sold a limited number of products of relatively high value. The cost and effort of maintaining perpetual inventory records were simply too great for other types of companies. However, since computers have made the record-keeping chore much easier, an increasing number of companies are switching from periodic to perpetual.

■ **Comparing Journal Entries under Periodic and Perpetual Inventory Systems**

Illustration 9-3 shows in parallel columns the typical journal entries made under periodic and perpetual inventory systems. In Illustration 9-3, observe the entries for the purchase of transaction 1. The perpetual system does not use a Purchases account. Instead, the cost of the items purchased is debited directly to Merchandise Inventory. Similarly, in transaction 2, the perpetual system credits the cost of purchase returns directly to the Merchandise Inventory account instead of using a Purchases Returns and Allowances account.

Transaction 3 involves the sale of merchandise. Note that the perpetual system requires two entries to record the sale, one to record the revenue and another to record cost of goods sold. Thus, a Cost of Goods Sold account is used in the perpetual system, whereas in the periodic system the elements of cost of goods sold are not transferred to such an account. Instead, they are transferred to Income Summary in the process of recording the closing entries.

The closing entries under the two systems are shown as item 4 in Illustra-

Illustration 9-3

X Company purchases merchandise for $15 per unit and sells it for $25. The company begins the current period with 5 units of product on hand, which cost a total of $75.

Periodic			**Perpetual**		

1. Purchased on credit 10 units of merchandise for $15 per unit.

Purchases	150		Merchandise Inventory	150	
Accounts Payable		150	Accounts Payable		150

2. Returned 3 units of merchandise originally purchased in 1 above.

Accounts Payable	45		Accounts Payable	45	
Purc. Returns and Allow. .		45	Merchandise Inventory . . .		45

3. Sold 8 units for $200 cash.

Cash	200		Cash	200	
Sales		200	Sales		200
			Cost of Goods Sold	120	
			Merchandise Inventory . . .		120

4. Closing entries:

Income Summary	225		Income Summary	120	
Merchandise Inv. (Beg.) .		75	Cost of Goods Sold		120
Purchases		150			
Merchandise Inv. (Ending) . .	60		Sales	200	
Sales	200		Income Summary		200
Purc. Returns and Allow. . . .	45				
Income Summary		305			

	Units	**Cost**
Beginning inventory	5	$ 75
Purchases	10	150
Purchase returns	(3)	(45)
Goods available	12	$180
Goods sold	(8)	120
Ending inventory	4	$ 60

tion 9-3. Under the periodic system, all of the cost elements related to inventories are transferred to Income Summary. By comparison, under the perpetual system, those cost elements have already been recorded in a Cost of Goods Sold account. Thus, the closing entries simply transfer the balance in the Cost of Goods Sold account to Income Summary. Of course, Sales must be closed under both inventory systems.

In Illustration 9-3, both inventory systems result in the same amounts of sales, cost of goods sold, and end-of-period merchandise inventory.

■ **Subsidiary Inventory Records— Perpetual System**

When a company sells more than one product and uses the perpetual inventory system, the Merchandise Inventory account serves as a controlling account to a subsidiary Merchandise Inventory Ledger. This ledger contains a separate record for each product in stock. This ledger may be computerized or kept on a manual basis. In either case, the record for each product shows the number of units and cost of each purchase, the number of units and cost of each sale, and the resulting balance of product on hand.

An example of a subsidiary merchandise inventory record is shown in Illustration 9-4. This particular record is for Product Z, which is stored in Bin 8 of the stock room. In this case, the record also shows the company's policy of maintaining no more than 25 or no less than 5 units of Product Z on hand.

■ **First-In, First-Out—Perpetual Inventory System**

In Illustration 9-4, note that the beginning inventory consisted of 10 units that cost $10 each. The first transaction occurred on January 5 and was a sale of 5 units. Next, 20 units were purchased on January 8 at a cost of $10.50 per unit. And on January 10, 3 units were sold. Observe that these 3 units were "costed out" at $10 per unit. This indicates that a first-in, first-out basis is being assumed for this product. The entries to record the sale in the General Journal would have been the following:

Jan.	10	Cash (or Accounts Receivable)	xxx	
		Sales		xxx
	10	Cost of Goods Sold	30.00	
		Merchandise Inventory		30.00
		3 × $10.00.		

■ **Last-In, First-Out—Perpetual Inventory System**

Perpetual inventories may also be kept on a last-in, first-out basis. When this is done, each sale is recorded as being from the last units received, until these are exhausted, then sales are from the next to last, and so on. For example, if LIFO had been assumed for Product Z, the subsidiary merchandise inventory record would appear as in Illustration 9-5.

Illustration 9-4   First-In, First-Out Cost Flow

Item _Product Z_   Location in stock room _Bin 8_
Maximum _25_   Minimum _5_

Date	Received			Sold			Balance		
	Units	Cost	Total	Units	Cost	Total	Units	Cost	Balance
1/1							10	10.00	100.00
1/5				5	10.00	50.00	5	10.00	50.00
1/8	20	10.50	210.00				5	10.00	
							20	10.50	260.00
1/10				3	10.00	30.00	2	10.00	
							20	10.50	230.00

Illustration 9-5   Last-In, First-Out Cost Flow

Item _____ Product Z _____   Location in stock room _____ Bin 8 _____

Maximum _____ 25 _____   Minimum _____ 5 _____

Date	Received			Sold			Balance		
	Units	Cost	Total	Units	Cost	Total	Units	Cost	Balance
1/1							10	10.00	100.00
1/5				5	10.00	50.00	5	10.00	50.00
1/8	20	10.50	210.00				5	10.00	
							20	10.50	260.00
1/10				3	10.50	31.50	5	10.00	
							17	10.50	228.50

Compare Illustration 9-5 (LIFO) with Illustration 9-4 (FIFO). Observe that in both illustrations, the sale of 5 units on January 5 is recorded the same. The cost of these units came from the 10 units in the beginning inventory. However, the sale of 3 units on January 10 is recorded differently under LIFO than it is under FIFO. Assuming LIFO, as in Illustration 9-5, the January 10 sale is "costed out" at $10.50 per unit. This results in a balance of $228.50, which includes 5 units at $10.00 plus 17 units at $10.50.

The general journal entries to record the January 10 sale, assuming LIFO, are as follows:

Jan.	10	Cash (or Accounts Receivable)	xxx	
		Sales		xxx
	10	Cost of Goods Sold	31.50	
		Merchandise Inventory		31.50
		3 × $10.50.		

The Difference between LIFO (Perpetual) and LIFO (Periodic)

Look again at Illustration 9-5 (LIFO) and note the costs that were assigned to Cost of Goods Sold for the January 5 and January 10 sales. In each case, the costs were taken from the most recent purchase. Thus, the cost of the January 5 sale came from the units in the beginning inventory; they were the only units available on January 5. This means that, using LIFO, a perpetual inventory system and a periodic inventory system result in different amounts of Cost of Goods Sold (and ending inventory). With a periodic inventory system, the 8 units sold during the period would come from the last units purchased during the period.

The difference between LIFO (perpetual) and LIFO (periodic) in this case can be summarized as follows:

	LIFO (perpetual)	LIFO (periodic)
Cost of goods sold:		
January 5 sale	5 × $10.00 = $ 50.00	
January 10 sale.	3 × $10.50 = 31.50	
Total	$ 81.50	8 × $10.50 = $ 84.00
Ending inventory:		
From beginning inventory . .	5 × $10.00 = $ 50.00	10 × $10.00 = $100.00
From January 8 purchase . .	17 × $10.50 = 178.50	12 × $10.50 = 126.00
Total	$228.50	$226.00
Total goods available	$310.00	$310.00

In addition to FIFO and LIFO, perpetual inventory systems can also accommodate an average cost flow assumption. However, illustration of this alternative is deferred for a later course.

The Retail Method of Estimating Inventories

Good management requires that income statements be prepared more often than once each year, and inventory information is necessary in their preparation. However, taking a physical inventory in a retail store is both time-consuming and expensive. Consequently, many retailers use the so-called **retail inventory method** to estimate inventories without having to stop and take a physical count of inventory. Some companies use the retail inventory method to estimate monthly or quarterly statements and then take a physical inventory at the end of each year. These monthly or quarterly statements are called **interim statements,** since they are prepared in between the regular year-end statements. Other companies also use the retail inventory method to prepare the year-end statements. However, all companies must take a physical inventory at least once each year to correct for any errors or shortages.

Estimating an Ending Inventory by the Retail Method

When the retail method is used to estimate an inventory, a store's records must show the amount of inventory it had at the beginning of the period both **at cost** and **at retail.** At cost for an inventory means just that, while at retail means the dollar amount of the inventory at the marked selling prices of the inventory items.

In addition to the beginning inventory, the records must also show the amount of goods purchased during the period both at cost and at retail plus the net sales at retail. The last item is easy; it is the balance of the Sales account less returns and discounts. Then, with this information the interim inventory is estimated as follows: (Step 1) The amount of goods that were for sale during the period both at cost and at retail is first computed. Next (Step 2), "at cost" is divided by "at retail" to obtain a **cost ratio.** Then (Step 3), sales (at retail) are deducted from goods for sale (at retail) to arrive at the ending inventory (at retail). And finally (Step 4), the ending inventory at retail is multiplied by the cost ratio to reduce it to a cost basis. These calculations are shown in Illustration 9-6.

This is the essence of Illustration 9-6: (1) The store had $100,000 of goods (at marked selling prices) for sale during the period. (2) These goods cost 60% of the $100,000 total amount at which they were marked for sale. (3) The store's records (its Sales account) showed that $70,000 of these goods were sold, leaving $30,000 of merchandise unsold and presumably in the ending inventory. Therefore, (4) since cost in this store is 60% of retail, the estimated cost of this ending inventory is $18,000.

An ending inventory calculated as in Illustration 9-6 is an estimate arrived at by deducting sales (goods sold) from goods for sale. As previously stated, this method may be used for interim statements or even for year-end statements. However, at least once each year a physical inventory must be taken to correct for any errors or shortages.

Using the Retail Method to Reduce a Physical Inventory to Cost

Items for sale in a store normally have price tickets attached that show selling prices. Consequently, when a store takes a physical inventory, it commonly takes the inventory at the marked selling prices of the inventoried items. It then reduces the dollar total of this inventory to a cost basis by applying its cost ratio. It does this because the selling prices are readily available and the application of the cost ratio eliminates the need to look up the invoice price of each inventoried item.

For example, assume that the store of Illustration 9-6, in addition to estimating its inventory by the retail method, also takes a physical inventory at the marked selling prices of the inventoried goods. Assume further that the total of this physical inventory is $29,600. Under these assumptions, the store may arrive at a cost basis for this inventory, without having to look up the cost of each inventoried item, simply by applying its cost ratio to the $29,600 inventory total as follows:

$$\$29,600 \times 60\% = \$17,760$$

The $17,760 cost figure for this store's ending physical inventory is a satisfactory figure for year-end statement purposes. It is also acceptable to the Internal Revenue Service for tax purposes.

Illustration 9-6

		At Cost	At Retail
(Step 1)	Goods available for sale:		
	Beginning inventory	$20,500	$ 34,500
	Net purchases	39,500	65,500
	Goods available for sale	$60,000	$100,000
(Step 2)	Cost ratio: $60,000 ÷ $100,000 = 60%		
(Step 3)	Deduct sales at retail		70,000
	Ending inventory at retail		$ 30,000
(Step 4)	Ending inventory at cost ($30,000 × 60%)	$18,000	

Inventory Shortage

An inventory determined as in Illustration 9-6 is an estimate of the amount of goods that should be on hand. However, since it is arrived at by deducting sales from goods for sale, it does not reveal any actual shortages due to breakage, loss, or theft. Nevertheless, the amount of such shortages may be determined by first estimating an inventory as in Illustration 9-6 and then taking a physical inventory at marked selling prices.

For example, by means of the Illustration 9-6 calculations, it was estimated the store of this discussion had a $30,000 ending inventory at retail. However, in the previous section, it was assumed that this same store took a physical inventory and had only $29,600 of merchandise on hand. Therefore, if this store should have had $30,000 of goods in its ending inventory as determined in Illustration 9-6, but had only $29,600 when it took a physical inventory, it must have had a $400 inventory shortage at retail or a $240 shortage at cost ($400 × 60% = $240).

Markups and Markdowns

The calculation of a cost ratio is often not as simple as that shown in Illustration 9-6. It is not simple because many stores not only have a **normal markup** (often called a **markon**) that they apply to items purchased for sale but also make additional **markups** and **markdowns**. A normal markup or markon is the normal amount or percentage that is applied to the cost of an item to arrive at its selling price. For example, if a store's normal markup is 50% on cost and it applies this markup to an item that cost $10, it will mark the item for sale at $15. Normal markups appear in the calculation of a store's cost ratio as the difference between net purchases at cost and at retail.

Additional markups are markups made in addition to normal markups. Stores commonly give goods of outstanding style or quality such additional markups because they can get a higher than normal price for such goods. They also commonly mark down for a clearance sale any slow-moving merchandise.

When a store using the retail inventory method makes additional markups and markdowns, it must keep a record of them. It then uses the information in calculating its cost ratio and in estimating an interim inventory as in Illustration 9-7.

Observe in Illustration 9-7 that the store's $80,000 of goods for sale at retail were reduced $54,000 by sales and $2,000 by markdowns, a total of $56,000. (To understand the markdowns, visualize this effect of a markdown. The store had an item for sale during the period at $25. The item did not sell; and to move it, the manager marked its price down from $25 to $20. By this act the amount of goods for sale in the store at retail was reduced by $5. Likewise, by a number of such markdowns during the year, goods for sale at retail in the store of Illustration 9-7 were reduced $2,000). Now back to the calculations of Illustration 9-7. The store's $80,000 of goods for sale were reduced $54,000 by sales and $2,000 by markdowns, leaving an estimated $24,000 ending inventory at retail. Therefore, since "cost" is 65% of "retail," the ending inventory at "cost" is $15,600.

Illustration 9-7

	At Cost	At Retail
Goods available for sale:		
Beginning inventory	$18,000	$27,800
Net purchases	34,000	50,700
Additional markups		1,500
Goods available for sale	$52,000	$80,000
Cost ratio: $52,000 ÷ $80,000 = 65%		
Sales at retail		$54,000
Markdowns		2,000
Total sales and markdowns		$56,000
Ending inventory at retail ($80,000 less $56,000) . . .		$24,000
Ending inventory at cost ($24,000 × 65%)	$15,600	

Observe in Illustration 9-7 that markups enter into the calculation of the cost ratio but markdowns do not. It has long been customary in using the retail inventory method to add additional markups but to ignore markdowns in computing the percentage relation between goods for sale at cost and at retail. The justification for this was and is that a more conservative figure for the ending inventory results, a figure that approaches "cost of market, the lower." A further discussion of this phase of the retail inventory method is reserved for a more advanced text.

■ **Gross Profit Method of Estimating Inventories**

Often retail price information about beginning inventory, purchases, and markups is not kept. In such cases, the retail inventory method cannot be used. However, if a company knows its normal gross profit margin or rate; has information at cost in regard to its beginning inventory, net purchases, and transportation-in; and knows the amount of its sales and sales returns, the company can estimate its ending inventory by the **gross profit method.**

For example, on March 27, the inventory of a company was totally destroyed by a fire. The company's average gross profit rate during the past five years has been 30% of net sales. And on the date of the fire, the company's accounts showed the following balances:

Sales	$31,500
Sales returns	1,500
Inventory, January 1, 19—	12,000
Net purchases	20,000
Transportation-in	500

With this information, the gross profit method may be used to estimate the company's inventory loss for insurance purposes. The first step in applying the method is to recognize that whatever portion of each dollar of net sales was gross profit, the remaining portion was cost of goods

Illustration 9-8

Goods available for sale:		
Inventory, January 1, 19—		$ 12,000
Net purchases	$20,000	
Add transportation-in.	500	20,500
Goods available for sale		$ 32,500
Less estimated cost of goods sold:		
Sales	$31,500	
Less sales returns.	(1,500)	
Net sales	$30,000	
Estimated cost of goods sold (70% × $30,000)		(21,000)
Estimated March 27 inventory and inventory loss		$ 11,500

sold. Consequently, if the company's gross profit rate averaged 30%, then 30% of each dollar of net sales was gross profit, and 70% was cost of goods sold. The 70% is used in estimating the inventory and inventory loss as in Illustration 9-8.

To understand Illustration 9-8, recall that in a normal situation an ending inventory is subtracted from goods for sale to determine cost of goods sold. Then observe in Illustration 9-8 that the opposite subtraction is made. Estimated cost of goods sold is subtracted from goods for sale to arrive at the estimated ending inventory.

In addition to its use in insurance cases, as in this illustration, the gross profit method is also commonly used by accountants in checking on the probable accuracy of a physical inventory taken and priced in the normal way.

☐   **Glossary**   **Conservatism principle** the accounting principle that guides accountants to select the less optimistic estimate when two estimates of amounts to be received or paid are about equally likely.

Consignee one who receives and holds goods owned by another party for the purpose of selling the goods for the owner.

Consignor an owner of goods who ships them to another party who will then sell the goods for the owner.

Consistency principle the accounting rule requiring a persistent application of a selected accounting method or procedure, period after period.

FIFO inventory pricing the pricing of an inventory under the assumption that the first items received were the first items sold.

Gross profit inventory method a procedure for estimating an ending inventory in which an estimated cost of goods sold based on past gross profit rates is subtracted from the cost of goods available for sale to arrive at an estimated ending inventory.

Interim statements monthly or quarterly financial statements prepared in between the regular year-end statements.

Inventory cost ratio the ratio of goods available for sale at cost to goods available for sale at retail prices.

Inventory ticket a form attached to the counted items in the process of taking a physical inventory.

LIFO inventory pricing the pricing of an inventory under the assumption that the last items received were the first items sold.

Lower-of-cost-or-market pricing an accounting method whereby inventory is reported in the financial statements at the lower of what the inventory actually cost or market value, which normally is what it would cost to replace the inventory on the balance sheet date.

Markdown a reduction in the marked selling price of an item.

Markon the normal amount or percentage of cost that is added to the cost of an item to arrive at its selling price.

Markup an increase in the sales price of inventory above the normal markon given to an item.

Net realizable value the expected sales price of inventory items less additional costs to sell.

Normal markup a phrase meaning the same as markon.

Periodic inventory system an inventory system in which the Merchandise Inventory account is updated only once each accounting period, based on a physical count of the inventory.

Perpetual inventory system an inventory system in which cost of goods sold is recorded after each sale and the Merchandise Inventory account is updated after each purchase and each sale.

Retail inventory method a method for estimating an ending inventory based on the ratio of the cost of goods for sale at cost and cost of goods for sale at marked selling prices.

Specific invoice inventory pricing the pricing of an inventory where each inventory item can be associated with a specific invoice and be priced accordingly.

Weighted-average cost inventory pricing an inventory pricing system in which the units in the beginning inventory of a product and in each purchase of the product are weighted by the number of units in the beginning inventory and in each purchase to determine a weighted-average cost per unit of the product, and after which this weighted-average cost is used to price the ending inventory of the product.

□ **Questions for Class Discussion**

1. With respect to periodic inventory systems, it has been said that cost of goods sold and ending inventory are opposite sides of the same coin. What is meant by this?
2. Give the meanings of the following when applied to inventory: (a) first-in, first-out; (b) FIFO; (c) last-in, first-out; (d) LIFO; (e) cost; (f) market; (g) perpetual inventory; and (h) physical inventory.
3. If prices are rising, will the LIFO or the FIFO method of inventory valuation result in the higher gross profit?
4. May a company change its inventory pricing method each accounting period?
5. What is required by the accounting principle of consistency?
6. If a company changes one of its accounting procedures, what is required of it under the full-disclosure principle?
7. Of what does the cost of an inventory item consist?
8. Why are incidental costs commonly ignored in pricing an inventory? Under what accounting principle is this permitted?
9. What is meant when it is said that under a periodic inventory system, inventory errors "correct themselves"?
10. If inventory errors under a periodic inventory system "correct themselves," why be concerned when such errors are made?
11. What guidance for accountants is provided by the principle of conservatism?
12. What accounts are used in a periodic inventory system but not in a perpetual inventory system?
13. What account is used in a perpetual inventory system but not in a periodic inventory system?
14. Assuming a LIFO cost flow, why do perpetual inventory systems and periodic inventory systems result in different amounts of cost of goods sold and ending inventory?
15. Give the meanings of the following when applied in the retail method of estimating an inventory: (a) pricing inventory at retail, (b) cost ratio, (c) normal markup, (d) markon, (e) additional markup, and (f) markdown.
16. A company uses a periodic inventory system, records its merchandise purchases at cost, and assumes a FIFO cost flow. If a fire results in the loss of the company's inventory, what method might the company use to estimate the amount of inventory lost?

□ **Class Exercises**

Exercise 9-1

A concern began a year and purchased merchandise as follows:

Jan. 1	Beginning inventory	30 units @ $11.50 =	$ 345
Feb. 9	Purchased	120 units @ $12.50 =	1,500
June 16	Purchased	60 units @ $13.25 =	795
Aug. 22	Purchased	90 units @ $14.00 =	1,260
Dec. 15	Purchased	60 units @ $13.75 =	825
	Total	360 units	$4,725

Required

The company uses a periodic inventory system, and the ending inventory consisted of 90 units, 30 from each of the last three purchases. Determine the share of the $4,725 cost of the units for sale that should be assigned to the ending inventory and to goods sold under each of the following assumptions: (*a*) costs are assigned on the basis of specific invoice prices, (*b*) costs are assigned on a weighted-average cost basis, (*c*) costs are assigned on the basis of FIFO, and (*d*) costs are assigned on the basis of LIFO.

Exercise 9-2

A company's ending inventory includes the following items:

Product	Units on Hand	Cost per Unit	Replacement Cost per Unit
A	12	$ 8	$9
B	15	10	8
C	20	5	4
D	16	7	7

After evaluating each product's selling price and normal profit margin, replacement cost is found to be the best measure of market.

Required

1. Calculate lower of cost or market for the inventory as a whole.
2. Calculate lower of cost or market for the inventory, applied separately to each product.

Exercise 9-3

Calculate the lower of cost or market for the inventory in each of the following independent cases:

1. A company's inventory consists of 50 units of Product M, all of which have been damaged. The company bought the inventory for $10 per unit. Replacement cost is $9 per unit. Expected sales price is $11 per unit, but this can be realized only if $3 additional cost per unit is paid.
2. A company's inventory consists of 100 units of Product X which were purchased for $25 per unit. Replacement cost is $18 per unit. Expected sales price is $28 per unit, and a normal profit margin, based on this price, is $7.

Exercise 9-4

A company had $90,000 of sales during each of three consecutive years, and it purchased merchandise costing $65,000 during each of the years. It also maintained a $12,000 inventory from the beginning to the end of the three-year period. However, in accounting under a periodic inventory system, it made an error at the end of year 1 that caused its ending year 1 inventory to appear on its statements at $16,000, rather than the correct $12,000.

Required
1. State the actual amount of the company's gross profit in each of the years.
2. Prepare a comparative income statement like the one illustrated in this chapter to show the effect of this error on the shop's cost of goods sold and gross profit in year 1, year 2, and year 3.

Exercise 9-5

In its beginning inventory on January 1, 198A, X Company had 20 units of merchandise that had cost $2 per unit. Prepare general journal entries for X Company to record the following transactions during 198A, assuming a perpetual inventory system and a FIFO cost flow.

Feb. 11   Purchased on credit 100 units of merchandise at $2.25 per unit.
      14   Returned 10 defective units from the February 11 purchase to the supplier.
Aug. 21   Purchased for cash 60 units of merchandise at $2.50 per unit.
Nov. 5   Sold 75 units of merchandise for cash at $4.50 per unit.
Dec. 31   Prepare entries to close the revenue and expense accounts to Income Summary.

Exercise 9-6

In its January 1, 198A, inventory, Y Company had 40 units of merchandise that had cost $3 per unit. Prepare general journal entries for Y Company to record the following transactions during 198A, assuming a perpetual inventory system and a LIFO cost flow.

Feb. 15   Purchased on credit 80 units of merchandise at $3.25 per unit.
Apr. 20   Sold 50 units of merchandise for cash of $7.50 per unit.
July 18   Purchased for cash 70 units of merchandise at $3.50 per unit.
Nov. 25   Sold 75 units of merchandise for cash at a price of $7.50 per unit.
Dec. 31   Prepare entries to close the revenue and expense accounts to Income Summary.

Exercise 9-7

During an accounting period, a store sold $234,000 of merchandise at marked retail prices. At the period-end, the following information was available from its records:

	At Cost	At Retail
Beginning inventory	$ 45,000	$ 63,000
Net purchases	165,000	222,000
Additional markups		15,000
Markdowns.		6,000

Use the retail method to estimate the store's ending inventory at cost.

Exercise 9-8

Assume that in addition to estimating its ending inventory by the retail method, the store of Exercise 9-7 also took a physical inventory at the marked selling prices of the inventory items. Assume further that the total of this physical inventory at marked selling prices was $58,500. Then (*a*) determine the amount of this inventory at cost and (*b*) determine the store's inventory shrinkage from breakage, theft, or other cause at retail and at cost.

Exercise 9-9

On January 1, a store had a $42,500 inventory at cost. During the first quarter of the year, it purchased $162,500 of merchandise, returned $1,250, and paid freight charges on merchandise purchased totaling $8,750. During the past several years, the store's gross profit on sales has averaged 35%. Under the assumption the company had $240,000 of sales during the first quarter of the year, use the gross profit method to estimate its end of the first quarter inventory.

Problems

Problem 9-1

Cryer Company began a year with 750 units of Product X in its inventory that cost $75 each, and it made successive purchases of the product as follows:

Mar.	1	1,000 units @ $80 each
June	10	1,250 units @ $85 each
Aug.	29	1,000 units @ $95 each
Nov.	15	1,000 units @ $90 each

The company uses a periodic inventory system. On December 31, a physical count disclosed that 1,500 units of Product X remained in inventory.

Required

1. Prepare a calculation showing the number and total cost of the units that were for sale during the year.
2. Prepare calculations showing the amounts that should be assigned to the ending inventory and to cost of goods sold assuming: (*a*) a FIFO basis, (*b*) a LIFO basis, and (*c*) a weighted-average cost basis.

Problem 9-2

Blanchard Company sold 9,500 units of its product at $30 per unit during 198A. It incurred operating expenses of $6 per unit in selling the units, and it began the year and made successive purchases of the product as follows:

January 1 beginning inventory	900 units costing $17.00 per unit
Purchases:	
January 20	1,400 units costing $18.00 per unit
March 7	2,800 units costing $18.75 per unit
June 16	4,600 units costing $19.50 per unit
November 30	800 units costing $21.00 per unit

Required

Prepare a comparative income statement for the company showing in adjacent columns the net incomes earned from the sale of the product assuming the company uses a periodic inventory system and prices its ending inventory on the basis of: *(a)* FIFO, *(b)* LIFO, and *(c)* weighted-average cost.

Problem 9-3

Case 1: In this case, an evaluation of the expected selling price and normal profit margin for each product shows that replacement cost is the best measure of market. The inventory includes:

Product	Units on Hand	Cost	Replacement Cost
A	450	$13	$11
B	500	40	46
C	220	8	7

Case 2: In this case, the inventories of Products D and E have been damaged. If $6 additional cost per unit is paid to repackage the Product D units, they can be sold for $30 per unit. The Product E units can be sold for $50 per unit after paying additional cleaning costs of $5 per unit. The inventory includes:

Product	Units on Hand	Cost	Replacement Cost
D	150	$27	$28
E	350	48	44

Case 3: In this case, Product F normally is sold for $40 per unit and has a profit margin of 30%. However, the expected selling price has fallen to $30 per unit. Product G normally is sold for $80 per unit and has a profit margin of 25%. However, the expected selling price of Product G has fallen to $50 per unit. The inventory includes:

Product	Units on Hand	Cost	Replacement Cost
F	100	$28	$18
G	200	60	40

Required

In each of the above independent cases, calculate the lower of cost or market *(a)* for the inventory as a whole and *(b)* for the inventory applied separately to each product.

Problem 9-4

Sloppy Company keeps its inventory records on a periodic basis. The following amounts were reported in the company's financial statements:

	Financial Statements for Year Ended December 31		
	198A	**198B**	**198C**
Cost of goods sold	$40,000	$47,000	$42,000
Net income	13,000	18,000	10,000
Total current assets	75,000	80,000	68,000
Owners' equity	90,000	92,000	84,000

In making the physical counts of inventory, the following errors were made:

Inventory on December 31, 198A . . overstated $4,000
Inventory on December 31, 198B . . understated 7,000

Required

1. For each of the financial statement items listed above, prepare a schedule similar to the following and show the adjustments that would have been necessary to correct the reported amounts.

	198A	198B	198C
Cost of goods sold:			
Reported	___	___	___
Adjustments: 12/31/8A error. . .	___	___	___
12/31/8B error. . .	___	___	___
Corrected	___	___	___

2. What is the error in the aggregate net income for the three-year period that resulted from the inventory errors?

Problem 9-5

The VanSickle Company sells a product called Goodtool and uses a perpetual inventory system to account for its merchandise. The beginning balance of Goodtools and transactions during January of this year were as follows:

Jan. 1 Balance: 15 units costing $9 each.
      5 Purchased 25 units costing $10 each.
      8 Sold 10 units.
     13 Sold 14 units.
     20 Purchased 20 units costing $12 each.
     25 Sold 8 units.
     30 Sold 15 units.

Required

1. Under the assumption the concern keeps its records on a FIFO basis, enter the beginning balance and the transactions on a subsidiary inventory record like the one illustrated in this chapter.
2. Under the assumption the concern keeps its inventory records on a LIFO basis, enter the beginning inventory and the transactions on a second subsidiary inventory record.
3. Assume the 15 units sold on January 30 were sold on credit to Barry Dee at $17.50 each and prepare general journal entries to record the sale on a LIFO basis.

Problem 9-6

Golf Store takes a year-end physical inventory at marked selling prices and uses the retail method to reduce the inventory total to a cost basis for statement purposes. It also uses the retail method to estimate the amount of inventory it should have at the end of a year and by comparison determines any inventory shortage due to shoplifting or other cause. At the end of last year, its physical inventory at marked selling prices totaled $83,800, and the following information was available from its records:

	At Cost	At Retail
January 1 inventory	$ 48,840	$ 72,400
Purchases	333,540	479,600
Purchases returns	5,660	7,800
Additional markups		9,800
Markdowns		6,120
Sales		469,360
Sales returns		7,480

Required

1. Use the retail method to estimate the store's year-end inventory at cost.
2. Use the retail method to reduce the store's year-end physical inventory to a cost basis.
3. Prepare a schedule showing the inventory shortage at cost and at retail.

Problem 9-7

The records of MultiProducts Company provided the following information for the year ended December 31:

	At Cost	At Retail
January 1 beginning inventory . .	$ 47,660	$ 62,700
Purchases	324,232	459,180
Purchases returns	4,420	6,320
Additional markups		9,400
Markdowns		2,340
Sales		456,480
Sales returns		5,760

Required

1. Prepare an estimate of the company's year-end inventory by the retail method.
2. Under the assumption the company took a year-end physical inventory at marked selling prices that totaled $70,200, prepare a schedule showing the store's loss from theft or other cause at cost and at retail.

Problem 9-8

When the Eastside Store was opened for business on the morning of March 12, it was discovered that thieves had broken in and stolen the store's entire inventory. The following information for the period January 1 through March 11 was available to establish the amount of loss:

January 1 merchandise inventory at cost	$ 97,500
Purchases	276,930
Purchases returns	1,245
Transportation-in	1,680
Sales	419,625
Sales returns	4,125

Required

Under the assumption the store had earned an average 32% gross profit on sales during the past five years, prepare a statement showing the estimated loss.

Problem 9-9

Barker Supply wants to prepare interim financial statements for the first quarter of 198A. The company uses a periodic inventory system but would like to avoid making a physical count of inventory. During the last five years, the company's gross profit rate has averaged 34%; and the following information for the year's first quarter is available from its records:

January 1 beginning inventory	$ 96,875
Purchases	228,500
Purchases returns	2,125
Transportation-in	2,825
Sales.	361,600
Sales returns	5,350

Required

Use the gross profit method to prepare an estimate of the company's March 31 inventory.

☐ **Alternate Problems**

Problem 9-1A

Dangle Company began a year with 900 units of Product Y in its inventory that cost $30 each, and it made successive purchases of the product as follows:

Feb. 1	1,200 units @ $35 each
May 17	1,250 units @ $40 each
July 23	1,500 units @ $45 each
Oct. 16	1,500 units @ $42 each

The company uses a periodic inventory system. On December 31, a physical count disclosed that 1,800 units of Product Y remained in inventory.

Required

1. Prepare a calculation showing the number and total cost of the units that were for sale during the year.
2. Prepare calculations showing the amounts that should be assigned to the ending inventory and to cost of goods sold assuming: (*a*) a FIFO basis, (*b*) a LIFO basis, and (*c*) a weighted-average cost basis. Round the weighted-average cost per unit to four decimal places.

Problem 9-2A

Westlake Company sold 4,800 units of its product at $40 per unit during 198A. It incurred operating expenses of $9 per unit in selling the units, and it began the year and made successive purchases of the product as follows:

January 1 beginning inventory . .	500 units costing $14.00 per unit
Purchases:	
January 20.	1,000 units costing $15.00 per unit
March 7	1,500 units costing $16.00 per unit
June 16	2,000 units costing $18.00 per unit
November 30.	1,000 units costing $20.00 per unit

Required

Prepare a comparative income statement for the company showing in adjacent columns the net incomes earned from the sale of the product assuming the company uses a periodic inventory system and prices its ending inventory on the basis of: (*a*) FIFO, (*b*) LIFO, and (*c*) weighted-average cost.

Problem 9-3A

Case 1: In this case, an evaluation of the expected selling price and normal profit margin for each product shows that replacement cost is the best measure of market. The inventory includes:

Product	Units on Hand	Cost	Replacement Cost
A.	675	$16	$19
B.	750	27	24
C.	330	18	17

Case 2: In this case, the inventories of Products D and E have been damaged. If $10 additional cost per unit is paid to repackage the Product D units, they can be sold for $45 per unit. The Product E units can be sold for $60 per unit after paying additional cleaning costs of $12 per unit. The inventory includes:

Product	Units on Hand	Cost	Replacement Cost
D.	275	$37	$39
E.	420	50	45

Case 3: In this case, Product F normally is sold for $50 per unit and has a profit margin of 30%. However, the expected selling price has fallen to $40 per unit. Product G normally is sold for $72 per unit and has a profit margin of 25%. However, the expected selling price of Product G has fallen to $60 per unit. The inventory includes:

Product	Units on Hand	Cost	Replacement Cost
F.	280	$35	$25
G.	160	54	47

Required

In each of the above independent cases, calculate the lower of cost or market (*a*) for the inventory as a whole and (*b*) for the inventory, applied separately to each product.

Problem 9-4A

LessCare Company keeps its inventory records on a periodic basis. The following amounts were reported in the company's financial statements:

	Financial Statement for Year Ended December 31		
	198A	198B	198C
Cost of goods sold . . .	$ 56,000	$ 63,000	$ 54,000
Net income	20,000	33,000	18,000
Total current assets . . .	90,000	98,000	84,000
Owners' equity	120,000	131,000	135,000

In making the physical counts of inventory, the following errors were made:

Inventory on December 31, 198A . . .	understated	$ 8,000
Inventory on December 31, 198B . . .	overstated	12,000

Required

1. For each of the financial statement items listed above, prepare a schedule similar to the following and show the adjustments that would have been necessary to correct the reported amounts.

	198A	198B	198C
Cost of goods sold:			
Reported			
Adjustments: 12/31/8A error . .			
12/31/8B error . .			
Corrected			

2. What is the error in the aggregate net income for the three-year period that resulted from the inventory errors?

Problem 9-5A

The Shaefer Company sells a product called SquarePeg and uses a perpetual inventory system to account for its merchandise. The beginning balance of SquarePegs and transactions during January of this year were as follows:

Jan. 1 Balance: 22 units costing $7 each.
       4 Purchased 45 units costing $8 each.
       6 Sold 15 units.
      15 Sold 10 units.
      19 Purchased 25 units costing $10 each.
      23 Sold 12 units.
      28 Sold 27 units.

Required

1. Under the assumption the concern keeps its records on a FIFO basis, enter the beginning balance and the transactions on a subsidiary inventory record like the one illustrated in this chapter.
2. Under the assumption the concern keeps its inventory records on a

LIFO basis, enter the beginning inventory and the transactions on a second subsidiary inventory record.

3. Assume the 27 units sold on January 28 were sold on credit to Joey Linder at $20 each and prepare general journal entries to record the sale on a LIFO basis.

Problem 9-6A

Baytown Stores takes a year-end physical inventory at marked selling prices and uses the retail method to reduce the inventory total to a cost basis for statement purposes. It also uses the retail method to estimate the amount of inventory it should have at the end of a year, and by comparison determines any inventory shortage due to shoplifting or other cause. At the end of last year, its physical inventory at marked selling prices totaled $96,800, and the following information was available from its records:

	At Cost	At Retail
January 1 inventory . . .	$ 35,600	$ 53,500
Purchases	179,000	271,000
Purchases returns. . . .	3,740	5,600
Additional markups . . .		5,500
Markdowns		3,500
Sales		226,500
Sales returns		2,900

Required

1. Use the retail method to estimate the company's year-end inventory at cost.

2. Use the retail method to reduce the company's year-end physical inventory to a cost basis.

3. Prepare a schedule showing the inventory shortage at cost and at retail.

Problem 9-7A

The records of Data Products Company provided the following information for the year ended December 31:

	At Cost	At Retail
January 1 beginning inventory . . .	$ 66,100	$ 97,400
Purchases.	279,890	520,000
Purchases returns	5,980	11,400
Additional markups.		12,200
Markdowns		6,600
Sales.		567,000
Sales returns		8,700

Required

1. Prepare an estimate of the company's year-end inventory by the retail method.

2. Under the assumption the company took a year-end physical inventory at marked selling prices that totaled $51,400, prepare a schedule showing the store's loss from theft or other cause at cost and at retail.

Problem 9-8A

When the Fireplace Store was opened for business on the morning of March 20, it was discovered that thieves had broken in and stolen the store's entire inventory. The following information for the period January 1 through March 19 was available to establish the amount of loss:

January 1 merchandise inventory at cost . . .	$ 83,400
Purchases	247,800
Purchases returns	2,150
Transportation-in	10,500
Sales	479,600
Sales returns	8,800

Required

Under the assumption the store had earned an average 38% gross profit on sales during the past five years, prepare a statement showing the estimated loss.

Problem 9-9A

Chacon Fabrics wants to prepare interim financial statements for the first quarter of 198A. The company uses a periodic inventory system but would like to avoid making a physical count of inventory. During the last five years, the company's gross profit rate has averaged 29%, and the following information for the year's first quarter is available from its records:

January 1 beginning inventory	$ 58,800
Purchases	177,700
Purchases returns :	3,250
Transportation-in	7,850
Sales	285,000
Sales returns	4,200

Required

Use the gross profit method to prepare an estimate of the company's March 31 inventory.

Provocative Problems

Provocative Problem 9-1   Time Incorporated

The primary operations of Time Incorporated are in publishing and video. In the 1983 annual report of the company, the footnotes to the financial statements included the following item:

Summary of Significant Accounting Policies

Inventories. Cost of inventories amounting to $12,400,000 in 1983 and $11,900,000 in 1982 was determined by the last-in, first-out method (LIFO). The cost of the remaining inventories of $75,200,000 in 1983 and $107,-100,000 in 1982 was determined principally by the first-in, first-out method (FIFO).

If the FIFO method of inventory accounting had been applied to those inventories which were costed on the LIFO method, inventories would have been $13,100,000 and $14,000,000 higher than reported at December 31, 1983 and 1982, respectively.

Time Incorporated reported a net income of $168,934,000 in 1983. Retained earnings on December 31, 1983, was $667,866,000. If Time had used FIFO for all of its inventories and the average income tax rate applicable to the company was 40% in all past years, what would have been reported as total inventories on December 31, 1983, and December 31, 1982? What would have been reported as 1983 net income? What would have been the balance of retained earnings on December 31, 1983?

Comment on Time Incorporated's policy of using FIFO for some inventories and LIFO for other inventories. Is this practice acceptable in light of the consistency principle?

Provocative Problem 9–2   Western Footwear

The retail outlet of Western Footwear suffered extensive smoke and water damage and a small amount of fire damage on September 6. The company carried adequate insurance, and the insurance company's claims adjuster appeared the same day to inspect the damage. After completing his survey, the adjuster agreed with Becky Sewell, the store's owner, that the inventory could be sold to a company specializing in fire sales for about one fourth of its cost. The adjuster offered Ms. Sewell $37,500 in full settlement for the damage to the inventory. He suggested that the offer be accepted and said he had authority to deliver at once a check for that amount. He also pointed out that a prompt settlement would provide funds to replace the inventory in time for the store to participate in the Christmas shopping season.

Ms. Sewell felt the loss might exceed $37,500, but she recognized that a time-consuming count and inspection of each item in the inventory would be required to establish the loss more precisely. She was anxious to get back into business before the Christmas rush, the season making the largest contribution to annual net income, and was reluctant to take the time for the inventory count. Yet, she was also unwilling to take a substantial loss on the insurance settlement.

Ms. Sewell asked for and received a one-day period in which to consider the insurance company offer. She immediately went to her records for the following information:

		At Cost	At Retail
a.	January 1 inventory	$ 53,325	$ 83,400
	Purchases, January 1 through September 6. .	349,875	546,150
	Net sales, January 1 through September 6 . .		542,550

b. On February 15, the remaining inventory of winter footwear was marked down from $24,000 to $18,000 and placed on sale in the annual end-of-the-winter-season sale. Three fourths of the shoes were sold. The markdown on the remainder was canceled, and the shoes were returned to their regular retail prices. (A markdown cancelation is subtracted from a markdown, and a markup cancelation is subtracted from a markup.)

c. In June, a special line of imported Italian shoes proved popular, and 84 pairs were marked up from their normal $73.50 retail price to $81 per pair. Sixty pairs were sold at the higher price; and on July 20, the markup on the remaining 24 pairs was canceled, and they were returned to their regular $73.50 price.

d. Between January 1 and September 6, markdowns totaling $2,700 were taken on several odd lots of shoes. Recommend whether or not you think Ms. Sewell should accept the insurance company's offer. Back your recommendation with figures.

Provocative Problem 9-3   Crown Cork & Seal Company, Inc.

The operations of Crown Cork & Seal Company, Inc., include the manufacture of metal cans, crowns, and closures and the building of filling, packaging, and handling machinery. The 1983 annual report of the company included the following financial statement footnote concerning inventories:

NOTES TO CONSOLIDATED FINANCIAL STATEMENTS

B. INVENTORIES

Cost is determined for all U.S. can, crown, and closure inventories by the LIFO (last-in, first-out) method. These inventories represent 29% in 1983 and 27% in 1982 of worldwide consolidated inventories at December 31, 1983 and 1982. Cost of foreign inventories and machinery division inventories in the U.S. is determined on an average cost basis. If average cost for all U.S. can, crown, and closure inventories had been utilized, inventories would have been higher than reported by $34,908,000 at December 31, 1983, and $34,515,000 at December 31, 1982.

During 1983, 1982, and 1981, the company reduced inventory quantities resulting in a liquidation of LIFO inventory, the effect of which decreased cost of products sold by approximately $1,740,000 in 1983, $1,142,000 in 1982, and $5,897,000 in 1981 and increased net income by approximately $940,000 or $.07 per share in 1983, $617,000 or $.04 per share in 1982, and $2,949,000 or $.20 per share in 1981.

Courtesy of Crown, Cork & Seal Company, Inc.

Discuss the financial statement effects of experiencing a reduction in inventory when LIFO is used and explain how this applies to Crown Cork & Seal Company, Inc.

10 Plant and Equipment

After studying Chapter 10, you should be able to:

1. Tell what is included in the cost of a plant asset.

2. Allocate the cost of lump-sum purchases to the separate assets being purchased.

3. Describe the causes of depreciation and the reasons for depreciation accounting.

4. Calculate depreciation by the *(a)* straight-line, *(b)* units-of-production, *(c)* declining-balance, and *(d)* sum-of-the-years'-digits methods.

5. Explain how the original cost of a plant asset is recovered through the sale of the asset's product or service.

6. Explain how the accelerated cost recovery system defers income taxes.

7. Define or explain the words and phrases listed in the chapter Glossary.

Tangible assets that are used in the production or sale of other assets or services and that have a useful life longer than one accounting period are called **plant and equipment** or **plant assets.** The phrase fixed assets was used for many years. However, it is rapidly disappearing from published balance sheets. The more descriptive "plant and equipment" or perhaps "property, plant, and equipment" is now used more often.

Use in the production or sale of other assets or services is the characteristic that distinguishes a plant asset from an item of merchandise or an investment. An office or factory machine held for sale by a dealer is merchandise to the dealer. Likewise, land purchased and held for future expansion but presently unused is classified as a long-term investment. Only when the asset is put to use in the production or sale of other assets or services should it be classified as plant and equipment. However, standby equipment for use in case of a breakdown or for use during peak periods of production is a plant asset. Also, when equipment is removed from service and held for sale, it ceases to be a plant asset.

A productive or service life longer than one accounting period distinguishes an item of plant and equipment from an item of supplies. An item of supplies may be consumed in a single accounting period. If consumed, its cost is charged to the period of consumption. The productive life of a plant asset, on the other hand, is longer than one period. It contributes to production for several periods. Therefore, as a result of the **matching principle,** its cost must be allocated to these periods in a systematic and rational manner.[1]

Cost of a Plant Asset

Cost is the basis for recording the acquisition of a plant asset. The cost of a plant asset includes all normal and reasonable expenditures necessary to get the asset in place and ready to use. For example, the cost of a factory machine includes its invoice price, less any discount for cash, plus freight, unpacking, and assembling costs. Cost also includes any special concrete base or foundation, electrical or power connections, and adjustments needed to place the machine in operation. In short, the cost of a plant asset includes all normal, necessary, and reasonable costs incurred in getting the asset in place and ready to produce.

A cost must be normal and reasonable as well as necessary if it is to be properly included in the cost of a plant asset. For example, if a machine is damaged by being dropped in unpacking, repairs should not be added to its cost. They should be charged to an expense account. Likewise, a fine paid for moving a heavy machine on city streets without proper permits is not part of the cost of the machine. However, if secured, the cost of the permits would be.

After being purchased but before being put to use, a plant asset must sometimes be repaired or remodeled before it meets the needs of the purchaser. In such a case, the repairing or remodeling expenditures are part of its cost and should be charged to the asset account. Furthermore, depreciation charges should not begin until the asset is put in use.

[1] See FASB, *Statement of Financial Accounting Concepts No. 3,* "Elements of Financial Statements of Business Enterprises," (Stamford, Conn., 1980), par. 89.

When a plant asset is constructed by a business for its own use, cost includes material and labor costs plus a reasonable amount of overhead or indirect expenses such as heat, lights, power, and depreciation on the machinery used in constructing the asset. Cost also includes architectural and design fees, building permits, and insurance during construction. Needless to say, insurance on the same asset after it has been placed in production is an expense.

When land is purchased for a building site, its cost includes the amount paid for the land plus any real estate commissions. It also includes escrow and legal fees, fees for examining and insuring the title, and any accrued property taxes paid by the purchaser, as well as expenditures for surveying, clearing, grading, draining, and landscaping. All are part of the cost of the land. Furthermore, any assessments incurred at the time of purchase or later for such things as the installation of streets, sewers, and sidewalks should be debited to the Land account since they add a more or less permanent value to the land.

Land purchased as a building site sometimes has an old building that must be removed. In such cases, the entire purchase price, including the amount paid for the building, should be charged to the Land account. Also, the cost of removing the old building, less any amounts recovered through the sale of salvaged materials, should be charged to this account.

Since land has an unlimited life, it is not subject to depreciation. However, **land improvements** such as parking lot surfaces, fences, and lighting systems have limited useful lives. Such costs improve the value or usefulness of land but must be charged to separate Land Improvement accounts and subjected to depreciation. Finally, a separate Building account must be charged for the cost of purchasing or constructing a building to be used as a plant asset.

Often land, land improvements, and buildings are purchased together for one lump sum. When this occurs, the purchase price must be apportioned among the assets on some fair basis, since some of the assets depreciate and some do not. A fair basis may be tax-assessed values or appraised values. For example, assume that land independently appraised at $30,000, land improvements appraised at $10,000, and a building appraised at $60,000 are purchased together for $90,000. The cost may be apportioned on the basis of appraised values as follows:

	Appraised Value	Percent of Total	Apportioned Cost
Land	$ 30,000	30	$27,000
Land improvements . . .	10,000	10	9,000
Building	60,000	60	54,000
Totals	$100,000	100	$90,000

Nature of Depreciation

When a plant asset is purchased, in effect a quantity of usefulness that will contribute to production throughout the service life of the asset is acquired. However, since the life of any plant asset (other than land) is limited, this quantity of usefulness will in effect be consumed by the end of the asset's service life. Consequently, depreciation, as the term is used in accounting, is nothing more than the expiration of a plant asset's quantity of usefulness, and the recording of depreciation is a process of allocating and charging the cost of this usefulness to the accounting periods that benefit from the asset's use.

For example, when a company purchases an automobile to be used in the business, it in effect purchases a quantity of usefulness, a quantity of transportation. The cost of this quantity of usefulness is the cost of the car less whatever will be received for it when sold or traded in at the end of its service life. Recording depreciation on the car is a process of allocating the cost of this usefulness to the accounting periods that benefit from the car's use. Note that it is not the recording of physical deterioration nor the decline in the car's market value. Depreciation is a process of allocating cost.

The foregoing is in line with the current accounting standards approved by the FASB which describe depreciation as follows:

> The cost of an [asset] is one of the costs of the services it renders during its useful economic life. Generally accepted accounting principles require that this cost be spread over the expected useful life of the [asset] in such a way as to allocate it as equitably as possible to the periods during which services are obtained from the use of the [asset]. This procedure is known as **depreciation accounting,** a system of accounting that aims to distribute the cost or other basic value of tangible capital assets, less salvage (if any), over the estimated useful life of the unit . . . in a systematic and rational manner. It is a process of allocation, not of valuation.[2]

■ Service Life of a Plant Asset

The **service life** of a plant asset is the period of time it will be used in producing or selling other assets or services. This may not be the same as the asset's potential life. For example, typewriters have a potential six- or eight-year life. However, if a company finds that it is economically wise to trade in its old typewriters on new ones every three years, in this company typewriters have a three-year service life. Furthermore, in this business, the cost of new typewriters less their trade-in value should be charged to depreciation expense over this three-year period.

Predicting a plant asset's service life is sometimes difficult because several factors are often involved. Wear and tear from use determine the useful life of some assets. However, two additional factors, **inadequacy** and **obsolescence,** often need to be considered. When a business acquires plant assets, it should acquire assets of a size and capacity to take care of its foreseeable needs. However, a business often grows more rapidly than anticipated. In such cases, the capacity of the plant assets may become too small for the productive demands of the business long before they wear out. When this happens, inadequacy is said to have taken place. Inadequacy cannot easily be predicted. Obsolescence, like inadequacy, is also difficult to foresee

---

[2] FASB, *Accounting Standards—Current Text* (Stamford, Conn., 1984), sec. D40.101. Previously published in *Accounting Research Bulletin No. 43,* ch. 9C, par. 5.

because the exact occurrence of new inventions and improvements normally cannot be predicted. Yet, new inventions and improvements often cause an asset to become obsolete and make it wise to discard the obsolete asset long before it wears out.

A company that has previously used a particular type of asset may estimate the service life of a new asset of like kind from past experience. A company without previous experience with a particular asset must depend upon the experience of others or upon engineering studies and judgment.

■ **Salvage Value**

The total amount of depreciation that should be taken over an asset's service life is the asset's cost minus its **salvage value.** The salvage value of a plant asset is the portion of its cost that is recovered at the end of its service life. Some assets such as typewriters, trucks, and automobiles are traded in on similar new assets at the end of their service lives. The salvage values of such assets are their trade-in values. Other assets may have no trade-in value and little or no salvage value. For example, at the end of its service life, some machinery can be sold only as scrap metal.

When the disposal of a plant asset involves certain costs, as in the wrecking of a building, the salvage value is the net amount realized from the sale of the asset. The net amount realized is the amount received for the asset less its disposal cost. In the case of a machine, the cost to remove the machine often will equal the amount that can be realized from its sale. In such a case, the machine has no salvage value.

■ **Allocating Depreciation**

Many methods of allocating a plant asset's total depreciation to the several accounting periods in its service life have been suggested and are used. Four of the more common are the **straight-line method,** the **units-of-production method,** the **declining-balance method,** and the **sum-of-the-years'-digits method.** Each is acceptable and falls within the realm of **generally accepted accounting principles.**

Straight-Line Method

When **straight-line depreciation** is used, the cost of the asset minus its estimated salvage value is divided by the estimated number of accounting periods in the asset's service life. The result is the amount of depreciation to be taken each period. For example, if a machine costs $550, has an estimated service life of five years, and an estimated $50 salvage value, its depreciation per year by the straight-line method is $100 and is calculated as follows:

$$\frac{\text{Cost} - \text{Salvage}}{\text{Service life in years}} = \frac{\$550 - \$50}{5} = \$100$$

Note that the straight-line method allocates an equal share of an asset's total depreciation to each accounting period in its life.

Units-of-Production Method

The purpose of recording depreciation is to charge each accounting period in which an asset is used with a fair share of its cost. The straight-line method charges an equal share to each period; and when plant assets are used about the same amount in each accounting period, this method rather fairly allocates total depreciation. However, in some lines of business, the use of certain plant assets varies greatly from accounting period to accounting period. For example, a contractor may use a particular piece of construction equipment for a month and then not use it again for many months. For such an asset, since use and contribution to revenue may not be uniform from period to period, it is argued that **units-of-production depreciation** better meets the requirements of the **matching principle** than does the straight-line method.

When the units-of-production method is used in allocating depreciation, the cost of an asset minus its estimated salvage value is divided by the estimated units it will produce during its entire service life. This calculation gives depreciation per unit of production. Then, the amount the asset is depreciated in any one accounting period is determined by multiplying the units produced in that period by the depreciation per unit. Units of production may be expressed as units of product or in any other unit of measure such as hours of use or miles driven. For example, a truck costing $6,000 is estimated to have a $2,000 salvage value. If it is also estimated that during the truck's service life it will be driven 50,000 miles, the depreciation per mile, or the depreciation per unit of production is $0.08 and is calculated as follows:

$$\frac{\text{Cost} - \text{Salvage value}}{\text{Estimated units of production}} = \text{Depreciation per unit of production}$$

or

$$\frac{\$6,000 - \$2,000}{50,000 \text{ miles}} = \$0.08 \text{ per mile}$$

If these estimates are used and the truck is driven 20,000 miles during its first year, depreciation for the first year is $1,600. This is 20,000 miles at $0.08 per mile. If the truck is driven 15,000 miles in the second year, depreciation for the second year is 15,000 times $0.08, or $1,200.

Declining-Balance Method

Some depreciation methods result in larger depreciation charges during the early years of an asset's life and smaller charges in the later years. These methods are called **accelerated depreciation. Declining-balance depreciation** is one of these. Under this method, depreciation of up to twice the straight-line rate, without considering salvage value, may be applied each year to the declining book value of a new plant asset. If this method is followed and twice the straight-line rate is used, depreciation on an asset is determined as follows: (1) calculate a straight-line depreciation rate for the asset; (2) double this rate; and (3) at the end of each year in the asset's life, apply this doubled rate to the asset's remaining **book value.** (The book value of a plant asset is its cost less accumulated depreciation; it is the net amount shown for the asset on the books.)

If this method is used to charge depreciation on a $10,000 new asset that has an estimated five-year life and no salvage value, these steps are followed: (Step 1) A straight-line depreciation rate is calculated by dividing 100% by five (years) to determine the straight-line annual depreciation rate of 20%; (Step 2) this rate is doubled; and (Step 3) annual depreciation charges are calculated as in the following table:

Year	Annual Depreciation Calculation	Annual Depreciation Expense	Remaining Book Value
1st year . . .	40% of $10,000	$4,000.00	$6,000.00
2nd year . . .	40% of 6,000	2,400.00	3,600.00
3rd year . . .	40% of 3,600	1,440.00	2,160.00
4th year . . .	40% of 2,160	864.00	1,296.00
5th year . . .	40% of 1,296	518.40	777.60

Under the declining-balance method, the book value of a plant asset never reaches zero. Consequently, when the asset is sold, exchanged, or scrapped, any remaining book value is used in determining the gain or loss on the disposal. However, if an asset has a salvage value, the asset may not be depreciated beyond its salvage value. For example, if instead of no salvage value, the foregoing $10,000 asset has an estimated $1,000 salvage value, depreciation for its fifth year is limited to $296. This is the amount required to reduce the asset's book value to its salvage value.

Sum-of-the-Years'-Digits Method

Another frequently used method of accelerated depreciation is called **sum-of-the-years' digits.** Under the sum-of-the-years'-digits method, the years in an asset's service life are added. Their sum becomes the denominator of a series of fractions used in allocating total depreciation to the periods in the asset's service life. The numerators of the fractions are the years in the asset's life in their reverse order. For example, assume a machine is purchased that costs $7,000, has an estimated five-year life, and has an estimated $1,000 salvage value. The sum-of-the-years' digits in the asset's life are:

$$1 + 2 + 3 + 4 + 5 = 15$$

and annual depreciation charges are calculated as follows:

Year	Annual Depreciation Calculation	Annual Depreciation Expense
1st year	$\frac{5}{15}$ of $6,000	$2,000
2nd year	$\frac{4}{15}$ of 6,000	1,600
3rd year	$\frac{3}{15}$ of 6,000	1,200
4th year	$\frac{2}{15}$ of 6,000	800
5th year	$\frac{1}{15}$ of 6,000	400
Total depreciation . . .		$6,000

When a plant asset has a long life, the sum-of-the-years' digits in its life may be calculated by using the formula: $SYD = n[(n + 1)/2]$. For example, sum-of-the-years' digits for a five-year life is:

$$5\left(\frac{5 + 1}{2}\right) = 15$$

Accelerated depreciation methods are advocated by many accountants who claim that their use results in a more equitable "use charge" for long-lived plant assets than other methods. These accountants point out, for example, that as assets grow older, repairs and maintenance increase. Therefore, when smaller amounts of depreciation are added to increasing repair costs, a more equitable total expense charge to match against revenue results. Also, they point out that as an asset grows older, in some instances its ability to produce revenue is reduced. For example, rentals from an apartment building may be higher in the earlier years of its life but then decline as the building becomes less attractive. In such cases, many accountants argue that the requirements of the **matching principle** are better met with heavier depreciation charges in the earlier years and lighter charges in the later years of the asset's life.

Depreciation for Partial Years

Plant assets may be purchased or disposed of any time during the year. When an asset is purchased (or disposed of) at some time other than the beginning (or end) of an accounting period, depreciation must be recorded for part of a year. Otherwise, the year of purchase or the year of disposal is not charged with its share of the asset's depreciation. For example, assume a machine costing $4,600 and having an estimated five-year service life and a $600 salvage value is purchased on October 8 and the annual accounting period ends on December 31. Three months' depreciation on the machine must be recorded on the latter date. Three months are three twelfths of a year. Consequently, if straight-line depreciation is used, the three months' depreciation is calculated as follows:

$$\frac{\$4,600 - \$600}{5} \times \frac{3}{12} = \$200$$

Note that depreciation was calculated for a full three months, even though the asset was purchased on October 8. Depreciation is an estimate; therefore, calculation to the nearest full month is usually sufficiently accurate. This means that depreciation is usually calculated for a full month on assets purchased before the 15th of the month. Likewise, depreciation for the month of purchase is normally disregarded if the asset is purchased after the middle of the month.

The entry to record depreciation for three months on the machine purchased on October 8 is:

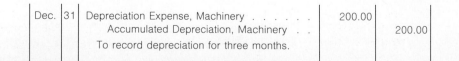

Dec.	31	Depreciation Expense, Machinery	200.00	
		Accumulated Depreciation, Machinery . .		200.00
		To record depreciation for three months.		

On December 31, 198B, and at the end of each of the following three years, a journal entry to record a full year's depreciation on this machine is required. The entry is:

Dec.	31	Depreciation Expense, Machinery	800.00	
		Accumulated Depreciation, Machinery . .		800.00
		To record depreciation for one year.		

After the December 31, 198E, depreciation entry is recorded, the accounts showing the history of this machine appear as follows:

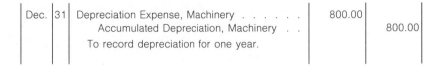

Machinery		Accumulated Depreciation, Machinery	
Oct. 8, '8A 4,600		Dec. 31, '8A 200	
		Dec. 31, '8B 800	
		Dec. 31, '8C 800	
		Dec. 31, '8D 800	
		Dec. 31, '8E 800	

If this machine is disposed of during 198F, two entries must be made to record the disposal. The first records 198F depreciation to the date of disposal, and the second records the actual disposal. For example, assume that the machine is sold for $800 on June 24, 198F. To record the disposal, depreciation for six months (depreciation to the nearest full month) must first be recorded. The entry for this is:

June	24	Depreciation Expense, Machinery	400.00	
		Accumulated Depreciation, Machinery . .		400.00
		To record depreciation for one-half year.		

After making the entry to record depreciation to the date of sale, a second entry to record the actual sale is made. This entry is:

June	24	Cash	800.00	
		Accumulated Deprecation, Machinery.	3,800.00	
		Machinery		4,600.00
		To record the sale of a machine at book value.		

In this instance, the machine was sold for its book value. Plant assets are commonly sold for either more or less than book value, and cases illustrating this are described in the next chapter.

■ **Apportioning Accelerated Depreciation**   When accelerated depreciation is used and accounting periods do not coincide with the years in an asset's life, depreciation must be apportioned between periods if it is to be properly charged. For example, the machine for which sum-of-the-years'-digits depreciation is calculated on page 363 is to be depreciated $2,000 during its first year, $1,600 during its second year, and so on for its five-year life. If this machine is placed in use on April 1 and the annual accounting periods of its owner end on December 31, the machine will be in use for three fourths of a year during the first accounting period in its life. Consequently, this period should be charged with $1,500 depreciation ($2,000 × ¾ = $1,500). Likewise, the second accounting period should be charged with $1,700 depreciation [(¼ × $2,000) + (¾ × $1,600) = $1,700]. Similar calculations should be used for the remaining periods in the asset's life.

■ Depreciation on the Balance Sheet

In presenting information about the plant assets of a business, the **full-disclosure principle** requires that both the cost of such assets and their accumulated depreciation be shown by major classes in the statements or in related footnotes. Also, a general description of the depreciation method or methods used must be given in a balance sheet footnote or other manner.[3] To comply, the plant assets of a business may be shown on its balance sheet or in a schedule accompanying the balance sheet as follows:

	Cost	Accumulated Depreciation	Book Value	
Plant assets:				
Store equipment . . .	$ 12,400	$1,500	$10,900	
Office equipment . . .	3,600	450	3,150	
Building.	72,300	7,800	64,500	
Land	15,000		15,000	
Totals	$103,300	$9,750		$93,550

When plant assets are thus shown and the depreciation methods described, a much better understanding can be gained by a balance sheet reader than if only information as to undepreciated cost is given. For example, $50,000 of assets with $40,000 of accumulated depreciation are quite different from $10,000 of new assets. Yet, the net undepreciated cost is the same in both cases. Likewise, the picture is different if the $40,000 of accumulated depreciation resulted from accelerated deprecation rather than straight-line depreciation.

■ Balance Sheet Plant Asset Values

From the discussion thus far, students should recognize that the recording of depreciation is not primarily a valuing process. Rather, it is a process of allocating the costs of plant assets to the several accounting periods that benefit from their use. Because the recording of depreciation is a cost allocation process rather than a valuing process, plant assets are reported on balance sheets at their remaining (undepreciated) costs, not at market values.

The fact that balance sheets show undepreciated costs rather than market

[3] Ibid., sec. D40.105. First published in *APB Opinion No. 12,* par. 5.

values seems to disturb many beginning accounting students. It should not. Normally, a company has no intention of selling its plant assets. Consequently, the market values of these assets may be of little significance to financial statement readers. Students should recognize that a balance sheet is prepared under the assumption the company is a going concern. This means the company is expected to continue in business long enough to recover the original costs of its plant assets through the sale of its products.

The assumption that a company will continue in business long enough to recover its plant asset costs through the sale of its products is known in accounting as the **continuing-** or **going-concern concept.** It provides the justification for carrying plant assets on the balance sheet at cost less accumulated depreciation; in other words, at the share of their cost applicable to future periods. It is also the justification for carrying at cost such things as stationery imprinted with the company name, though salable only as scrap paper. In all such instances, the intention is to use the assets in carrying on the business operations. They are not for sale, so it is pointless to place them on the balance sheet at market or realizable values, whether these values are greater or less than book values.

Uninformed financial statement readers sometimes mistakenly think that the accumulated depreciation shown on a balance sheet represents funds accumulated to buy new assets when present assets must be replaced. However, an informed reader recognizes that accumulated depreciation represents the portion of an asset's cost that has been charged off to depreciation expense during its life. Accumulated depreciation accounts are contra accounts having credit balances that cannot be used to buy anything. Furthermore, an informed reader knows that if a business has cash with which to buy assets, it is shown on the balance sheet as a current asset "Cash."

■   **Recovering the Costs of Plant Assets**

A company that earns a profit or breaks even (neither earns a profit nor suffers a loss) eventually recovers the original cost of its plant assets through the sale of its products. This is best explained with a condensed income statement like that of Illustration 10-1 which shows that Even Steven Company broke even during the year of the illustrated income statement. However, in breaking even it also recovered $5,000 of the cost of its plant assets through the sale of its products. It recovered the $5,000 because

Illustration 10-1

Even Steven Company
Income Statement
For Year Ended December 31, 198A

Sales		$100,000
Cost of goods sold	$60,000	
Rent expense	10,000	
Salaries expense	25,000	
Depreciation expense . . .	5,000	
Total		100,000
Net income		$ 0

$100,000 flowed into the company from sales and only $95,000 flowed out to pay for goods sold, rent, and salaries. No funds flowed out for depreciation expense. As a result, the company recovered this $5,000 portion of the cost of its plant assets through the sale of its products. Furthermore, if the company remains in business for the life of its plant assets, either breaking even or earning a profit, it will recover their entire cost in this manner.

At this point students commonly ask, "Where is the recovered $5,000?" The answer is that the company may have the $5,000 in the bank. However, the funds may also have been spent to increase merchandise inventory, to buy additional equipment, to pay off a debt, or they may have been withdrawn by the business owner. In short, the funds may still be in the bank or they may have been used for any purpose for which a business uses funds.

Accelerated Depreciation for Tax Purposes

The use of accelerated depreciation in preparing financial statements does *not* mean that the same methods must also be used for tax purposes. However, United States tax laws, as codified in the **Internal Revenue Code,** allow the use of accelerated methods in various circumstances. Depending on the year in which an asset was purchased and on the type of asset, several different kinds of accelerated depreciation methods have been allowed for tax purposes. The accelerated methods that have been allowed in past years include declining-balance, sum-of-the-years' digits, and other accelerated methods. Currently, the accelerated depreciation rules for tax purposes are called the **Accelerated Cost Recovery System (ACRS).**

As specified in the Tax Reform Act of 1986, depreciable personal property (property other than real estate) purchased after December 31, 1986, is classified into several classes ranging from a 3-year class to a 20-year class. Real property is classified into two classes: the 27½-year class for residential rental property and the 31½-year class for all other real estate. Both classes of real property must be depreciated on a straight-line basis. Personal property may be depreciated on a straight-line basis, but an accelerated method is also available for each class of personal property.

ACRS depreciation is accelerated for two reasons. First, the actual economic lives of the assets in any given class are usually longer than the arbitrary number of years assigned to the class. For example, the five-year class includes assets such as computer equipment, automobiles, light trucks, and over-the-road tractors. Normally, assets such as these would be expected to have useful lives longer than five years. Thus, even when straight-line depreciation is used for tax purposes, the assumed length of life (for tax purposes) may be shorter than the expected economic life of the asset (which should be used for financial accounting purposes).

The second reason why ACRS depreciation is accelerated is that ACRS involves using the declining-balance method with a switch to straight-line at the point where the switch serves to further accelerate the depreciation. The actual depreciation rates allowed for each class are shown in Illustration 10–2.

When calculating depreciation for tax purposes, salvage values on assets purchased after 1980 are ignored. Also, depreciation methods for personal

---

Illustration 10-2

Accelerated Cost Recovery System
For Assets Placed in Service after December 31, 1986

Class Life	Depreciation Rate
3–year	200% declining balance, switching to straight line
5–year	200% declining balance, switching to straight line
7–year	200% declining balance, switching to straight line
10–year	200% declining balance, switching to straight line
15–year	150% declining balance, switching to straight line
20–year	150% declining balance, switching to straight line
27½–year	straight line
31½–year	straight line

---

property are based on the assumption that the asset was purchased half-way through the year. This half-year convention is required regardless of when the asset was actually purchased. Depreciation methods for real property are based on a half-month convention.

To illustrate the ACRS method of switching from declining-balance to straight-line depreciation, assume an asset in the five-year class (for example, a light truck) is purchased at a cost of $10,000. For declining-balance, the depreciation rate is 200% of the straight-line rate. This is $(100\% \div 5) \times 2 = 40\%$. ACRS depreciation is calculated as follows:

Year	Depreciation for Year	Undepreciated Cost at End of Year	Method Used
1	20% × $10,000 = $2,000	$10,000–$2,000 = $8,000	Declining-balance
2	40% × 8,000 = 3,200	8,000– 3,200 = 4,800	Declining-balance
3	40% × 4,800 = 1,920	4,800– 1,920 = 2,880	Declining-balance
4	40% × 2,880 = 1,152	2,880– 1,152 = 1,728	Declining balance or straight line
5	($1,728/3) × 2 = 1,152	1,728– 1,152 = 576	Straight-line
6	($1,728/3) × 1 = 576	576– 576 = –0–	Straight-line

In this example, declining-balance depreciation for year 4 ($1,152) is exactly the same as straight-line depreciation. Remembering the half-year convention, the remaining life at the beginning of year 4 is 2½ years, or five 6-month periods. Thus, straight-line depreciation for year 4 would be $(\$2,880 \div 5) \times 2 = \$1,152$.

In year 5, a switch from declining-balance to straight-line depreciation has an accelerating effect. To prove this point, if declining-balance depreciation were continued in years 5 and 6, the depreciation would be as follows:

Year 5   Declining balance depreciation would be . . . . .   40% × $1,728 = $ 691.20
Year 6   Depreciate the remaining balance . . . . $1,728 – $691.20 = $1,036.80

By comparison, the switch to straight-line depreciation resulted in $1,152 depreciation in year 5 and $576 depreciation in year 6.

Students should understand that ACRS depreciation generally is not acceptable for use in preparing financial statements. ACRS is not acceptable because it allocates depreciation over a shorter period of time than the estimated useful life of the asset. However, using ACRS depreciation for tax purposes may have an important tax advantage.

The tax advantage of accelerated depreciation is that it **defers the payment of income taxes** from the early years of a plant asset's life until its later years. Taxes are deferred because accelerated depreciation causes larger amounts of depreciation to be charged to the early years. This results in smaller amounts of income and income taxes in these years. However, the taxes are only deferred; they are not avoided. The larger depreciation charges in earlier years are offset by smaller (or even zero) depreciation charges in later years. Thus, larger amounts of income and income taxes are reported and paid in the later years. Nevertheless, through accelerated depreciation a company gains the "interest-free" use of the deferred tax dollars until the later years of a plant asset's life.

Special problems in measuring net income may occur when a company uses one depreciation method for financial accounting purposes and another for tax purposes. These problems are discussed in Chapter 28.

Control of Plant Assets

Good internal control requires that each plant asset be separately identified, usually with a serial number that is etched or affixed to the asset. Periodically, an inventory of plant assets should be taken in which the existence and continued use of each asset are verified. Formal records of plant assets on hand should be maintained.

In keeping plant asset records, concerns usually divide their plant assets into functional groups and provide in the General Ledger a separate asset account and accumulated depreciation account for each group. The asset account and related accumulated depreciation account for each group serve as controlling accounts that control detailed subsidiary records. For example, in a store, the Store Equipment account and the Accumulated Depreciation, Store Equipment account control the **Store Equipment Ledger,** a subsidiary ledger having a separate record for each individual item of store equipment. The same is true for the Office Equipment account and the Accumulated Depreciation, Office Equipment account, which control the **Office Equipment Ledger.**

Whether plant asset records are computerized or handwritten, they provide the same basic information. To illustrate plant asset records, assume that a concern's office equipment consists of just one desk and a chair. The general ledger accounts for these assets are Office Equipment and Accumulated Depreciation, Office Equipment. Both are controlling accounts that control sections of the subsidiary record for the desk and chair. The general ledger and subsidiary ledger records of these assets are shown in Illustration 10-3 on pages 371 and 372.

At the top of each subsidiary record, observe the plant asset numbers assigned to these two items of office equipment. In each case, the assigned number consists of the number of the Office Equipment account, 132, followed by the asset's number. The remaining information on the subsidiary records is more or less self-evident. Note how the balance of the general ledger account, Office Equipment, is equal to the sum of the bal-

Illustration 10-3

Plant Asset
No. 132-1

SUBSIDIARY PLANT ASSET AND DEPRECIATION RECORD

Item Office chair

General Ledger
Account Office Equipment

Description Office chair

Mfg. Serial No.

Purchased
from   Office Equipment Co.

Where Located Office

Person Responsible for the Asset Office Manager

Estimated Life 6 years Estimated Salvage Value $10.00

Depreciation per Year $30.00 per Month $2.50

Date	Explanation	P R	Asset Record			Depreciation Record		
			Dr.	Cr.	Bal.	Dr.	Cr.	Bal.
July 2,198A		G1	190.00		190.00			
Dec. 31,198A		C23					15.00	15.00
Dec. 31,198B		G42					30.00	45.00
Dec. 31,198C		G65					30.00	75.00

Final Disposition of the Asset

Plant Asset
No. 132-2

SUBSIDIARY PLANT ASSET AND DEPRECIATION RECORD

Item Desk

General Ledger
Account Office Equipment

Description Office desk

Mfg. Serial No.

Purchased
from   Office Equipment Co.

Where Located Office

Person Responsible for the Asset Office Manager

Estimated Life 6 years Estimated Salvage Value $30.00

Depreciation per Year $120.00 per Month $10.00

Date	Explanation	P R	Asset Record			Depreciation Record		
			Dr.	Cr.	Bal.	Dr.	Cr.	Bal.
July 2,198A		G1	750.00		750.00			
Dec. 31,198A		G23					60.00	60.00
Dec. 31,198B		G42					120.00	180.00
Dec. 31,198C		G65					120.00	300.00

Final Disposition of the Asset

Illustration 10-3
(concluded)

		Office Equipment						Account No. 132	
Date		Explanation	PR	Debit		Credit		Balance	
198A July	2	Desk and chair	G1	940	00			940	00

		Accumulated Depreciation, Office Equipment						Account No. 132A	
Date		Explanation	PR	Debit		Credit		Balance	
198A Dec.	31		G23			75	00	75	00
198B Dec.	31		G42			150	00	225	00
198C Dec.	31		G65			150	00	375	00

ances in the asset record section of the two subsidiary records. The general ledger account controls this section of the subsidiary ledger. Observe also how the Accumulated Depreciation, Office Equipment account controls the depreciation record section of the subsidiary records. The disposition section at the bottom of the subsidiary records is used to record the final disposal of the asset. When the asset is discarded, sold, or exchanged, a notation telling of the final disposition is entered here. The record is then removed from the subsidiary ledger and filed for future reference.

■ **Plant Assets of Low Cost**

Individual plant asset records are expensive to keep. Consequently, many companies establish a minimum, say, $50 or $100, and do not keep such records for assets costing less than the minimum. Rather, they charge the cost of such assets directly to an expense account at the time of purchase. Furthermore, if about the same amount is expended for such assets each year, this is acceptable under the **materiality principle.**

Glossary

Accelerated cost recovery system (ACRS) a unique, accelerated depreciation method prescribed in the tax law.

Accelerated depreciation any depreciation method resulting in greater amounts of depreciation expense in the early years of a plant asset's life and lesser amounts in later years.

Book value the carrying amount for an item in the accounting records. When applied to a plant asset, it is the cost of the asset minus its accumulated depreciation.

Declining-balance depreciation a depreciation method in which up to twice the straight-line rate of depreciation, without considering salvage value, is applied to the remaining book value of a plant asset to arrive at the asset's annual depreciation charge.

Fixed asset a plant asset.

Inadequacy the situation where a plant asset does not produce enough product to meet current needs.

Internal Revenue Code the codification of the numerous tax laws passed by Congress.

Land improvements assets that improve or increase the value or usefulness of land but which have a limited useful life and are subject to depreciation.

Obsolescence the situation where because of new inventions and improvements, an old plant asset can no longer produce its product on a competitive basis.

Office Equipment Ledger a subsidiary ledger that contains a separate record for each item of office equipment owned.

Salvage value the share of a plant asset's cost recovered at the end of its service life through a sale or as a trade-in allowance on a new asset.

Service life the period of time a plant asset is used in the production and sale of other assets or services.

Store Equipment Ledger a subsidiary ledger that contains a separate record for each item of store equipment owned.

Straight-line depreciation a depreciation method that allocates an equal share of the total estimated amount a plant asset will be depreciated during its service life to each accounting period in that life.

Sum-of-the-years'-digits depreciation a depreciation method that allocates depreciation to each year in a plant asset's life on a fractional basis. The denominator of the fractions used is the sum-of-the-years' digits in the estimated service life of the asset, and the numerators are the years' digits in reverse order.

Units-of-production depreciation a depreciation method that allocates depreciation on a plant asset based on the relation of the units of product produced by the asset during a given period to the total units the asset is expected to produce during its entire life.

Questions for Class Discussion

1. What are the characteristics of an asset classified as plant and equipment?
2. What is the balance sheet classification of land held for future expansion? Why is such land not classified as a plant asset?

3. What is the difference between land and land improvements?

4. What in general is included in the cost of a plant asset?

5. A company asked for bids from several machine shops for the construction of a special machine. The lowest bid was $12,500. The company decided to build the machine itself and did so at a total cash outlay of $10,000. It then recorded the machine's construction with a debit to Machinery for $12,500, a credit to Cash for $10,000, and a credit to Gain on the Construction of Machinery for $2,500. Was this a proper entry? Discuss.

6. As used in accounting, what is the meaning of the term *depreciation?*

7. Is it possible to keep a plant asset in such an excellent state of repair that recording depreciation is unnecessary?

8. A machine that normally lasts 10 years is purchased even though management knows future growth of the company's operations will require that the machine be replaced in approximately 4 years. What factor in this situation tends to suggest that the machine be depreciated over four years?

9. A company purchases a machine that normally has a service life of 12 years. However, the company's management believes that the development of a more efficient machine will make it necessary to replace the machine in eight years. What period of useful life should be used in calculating depreciation on this machine?

10. A building estimated to have a useful life of 40 years was completed at a cost of $150,000. It was estimated that at the end of the building's life it would be wrecked at a cost of $12,000 and that materials salvaged from the wrecking operation would be sold for $20,000. How much straight-line depreciation should be charged on the building each year?

11. When straight-line depreciation is used, an equal share of the total amount a plant asset is to be depreciated during its life is assigned to each accounting period in that life. Describe a situation in which this may not be a fair basis of allocation. Name a depreciation method that might be fairer in the situation described.

12. Define the following terms as used in accounting for plant assets:
    a. Market value.   d. Inadequacy.
    b. Book value.   e. Obsolescence.
    c. Salvage value.

13. What is the sum-of-the-years' digits in the life of a plant asset that will be used for 15 years?

14. Does the recording of depreciation cause a plant asset to appear on the balance sheet at market value? What is accomplished by recording depreciation?

15. Does the balance of the account, Accumulated Depreciation, Machinery, represent funds accumulated to replace the machinery as it wears out? Describe in your own words what the balance of such an account represents.

16. Why is the accelerated cost recovery system not generally accepted for financial accounting purposes?

17. What is the purpose of periodically taking an inventory of plant assets?
18. What possible justification is there for charging to expense a plant asset that cost $75?
19. What is the implication of the going-concern concept on the valuation of plant assets in the accounting records?
20. Explain how a business that breaks even recovers the cost of its plant assets through the sale of its products. Where are the funds thus recovered?

□ **Class Exercises**

Exercise 10-1

A company purchased a machine for $16,000, terms 2/10, n/60, FOB shipping point. The seller prepaid the freight charges, $880, adding the amount to the invoice and bringing its total to $16,880. The machine required a special steel mounting and power connections costing $2,280, and another $2,160 was paid to assemble the machine and get it into operation. In moving the machine onto its steel mounting, it was dropped and damaged. The damages cost $560 to repair, and after being repaired, $240 of raw materials were consumed in adjusting the machine so it would produce a satisfactory product. The adjustments were normal for this type of machine and were not the result of its having been damaged. However, the product produced while the adjustments were being made was not salable. Prepare a calculation to show the cost of this machine for accounting purposes.

Exercise 10-2

A company paid $435,000 for real estate plus $9,000 in closing costs. The real estate included land appraised at $135,000; land improvements appraised at $54,000; and a building appraised at $351,000. The plan is to use the building as a factory. Prepare a calculation showing the allocation of cost to the assets purchased and present the journal entry to record the purchase.

Exercise 10-3

After planning to build a new manufacturing plant, a company purchased a large lot on which a small building was located. The negotiated purchase price of this real estate amounted to $250,000 for the lot plus $300,000 for the building. The company paid $40,000 to have the old building torn down and $50,000 for landscaping of the lot. Finally, it paid $1,800,000 construction costs for a new building, which included $80,000 for lighting and paving of a parking lot next to the building. Present a single general journal entry to record the costs incurred by the company, all of which were paid in cash.

Exercise 10-4

A company bought two pickup trucks and a forklift from a financially distressed supplier and had them shipped to the company's plant. The purchase price was $22,000, and $1,000 was paid for the shipping charge. The forklift was only half as large as a truck and weighed half as much. Appraised values of the trucks and forklift and costs of initial repairs to get them ready for service were as follows:

	Truck 1	Truck 2	Forklift
Appraised values	$12,000	$10,500	$7,500
Repair costs	750	500	375

Determine the cost of each asset for accounting purposes.

Exercise 10-5

A machine was installed in a factory at a $94,800 cost. Its useful life was estimated at five years or 30,000 units of product with a $4,800 trade-in value. During its second year, the machine produced 7,200 units of product. Determine the machine's second-year depreciation with depreciation calculated in each of the following ways: (a) straight-line basis, (b) units-of-production basis, (c) declining-balance basis at twice the straight-line rate, and (d) sum-of-the-years'-digits basis.

Exercise 10-6

A plant asset cost $20,000 installed and was estimated to have a four-year life and a $1,800 trade-in value. Use declining-balance depreciation at twice the straight-line rate to determine the amount of depreciation to be charged against the machine in each of the four years of its life.

Exercise 10-7

On September 1, 198A, a company purchased a machine for $450,000. The machine was expected to last six years and have a salvage value of $30,000. Calculate depreciation expense for 198B, assuming (a) straight-line depreciation, (b) sum-of-the-years'-digits depreciation, and (c) declining-balance depreciation at twice the straight-line rate.

Exercise 10-8

A machine was installed on January 2, 198A, at a total cost of $45,000. Straight-line depreciation was taken each year for four years, based on the assumption of a six-year life and no salvage value. The machine was disposed of on April 30, during its fifth year. Present the entries to record the partial year's depreciation on April 30 and to record the disposal under each of the following unrelated assumptions: (a) the machine was sold for $17,000; (b) the machine was sold for $7,000; and (c) the machine was totally destroyed in a fire and the insurance company settled the insurance claim for $10,600.

Exercise 10-9

A company recently paid $120,000 for equipment that will last four years and have a salvage value of $20,000. By using the machine in its operations for four years, the company expects to earn $40,000 annually, after deducting all expenses except depreciation. Present a schedule showing income before depreciation, depreciation expense, and net income for each year and the total amounts for the four-year period assuming (a) straight-line depreciation, (b) sum-of-the-years'-digits depreciation, and (c) declining-balance depreciation at twice the straight-line rate.

Exercise 10-10

In January 1987, an over-the-road tractor was purchased for $60,000. It will be used for eight years and then sold at an estimated salvage value of $12,000. The tractor is in the five-year class for tax purposes. Prepare a schedule showing each year's depreciation for tax purposes assuming (a) five-year straight-line depreciation and (b) ACRS depreciation rates.

Problems

Problem 10-1

In early 1987, Hoyle Company paid $805,000 for real estate that included a tract of land on which two buildings were located. The plan was to demolish Building One and build a new store in its place. Building Two was to be used as a company office and was appraised to have a value of $227,500, with a useful life of 15 years and a $17,500 salvage value. A lighted parking lot near Building Two had improvements valued at $91,000 that were expected to last another 10 years and have no salvage value. In its existing condition, the tract of land was estimated to have a value of $591,500.

Hoyle Company incurred the following additional costs:

Cost to demolish Building One.	$ 87,500
Cost to landscape new building site	28,000
Cost to build new building (Building Three), having a useful life of 30 years and a $105,000 salvage value . . .	1,050,000
Cost of new land improvements near Building Three, which have a 15-year useful life and no salvage value . .	122,500

Required

1. Prepare a form having the following column headings: Land, Building Two, Building Three, Land Improvements Two, and Land Improvements Three. Allocate the costs incurred by Hoyle Company to the appropriate columns and total each column.
2. Prepare a single journal entry dated April 1 to record all of the costs incurred, assuming they were all paid in cash.
3. Prepare December 31 adjusting entries to record depreciation for the nine months of 1987 during which the assets were in use. Use sum-of-the-years'-digits depreciation for the newly constructed Building Three and Land Improvements Three and straight-line depreciation for Building Two and Land Improvements Two.

Problem 10-2

Balsum Company recently negotiated a lump-sum purchase of several assets from a bus dealer who was planning to change locations. The purchase was completed on September 30, 198B, at a total cash price of $416,000 and included a garage with land and certain land improvements and a new light truck. The estimated market value of each asset was: garage, $286,000; land, $88,000; land improvements, $44,000; and truck, $22,000.

Required

1. Prepare a schedule to allocate the lump-sum purchase price to the separate assets that were purchased. Also present the general journal entry to record the purchase.
2. Calculate the 198C depreciation expense on the garage using the sum-of-the-years'-digits method and assuming a 12-year life and a $14,400 salvage value.
3. Calculate the 198B depreciation expense on the land improvements assuming a 10-year life and declining-balance depreciation at twice the straight-line rate.
4. The truck is in the five-year class for tax purposes but is expected to last six years and have a salvage value of $1,600. Prepare a schedule showing each year's depreciation on the truck for tax purposes, assuming (*a*) five-year straight-line, and (*b*) ACRS depreciation.

Problem 10-3

Part 1. A machine costing $50,000, having a five-year life, and an estimated $7,000 salvage value was installed in a factory. The factory management estimated the machine would produce 100,000 units of product during its life. It actually produced the following numbers of units: year 1, 14,000; year 2, 22,000; year 3, 20,000; year 4, 19,000; and year 5, 25,000.

Required

1. Prepare a calculation showing the number of dollars of this machine's cost that should be charged to depreciation over its five-year life.
2. Prepare a form with the following column headings:

Year	Straight Line	Units of Production	Declining Balance	Sum-of-the-Years' Digits

Then show the depreciation for each year and the total depreciation for the machine under each depreciation method. Use twice the straight-line rate for the declining-balance method.

Part 2. A used machine was purchased for $11,400 on January 2. The next day it was repaired at a cost of $1,350 and was installed on a new platform that cost $1,050. It was estimated the machine would be used for three years and would then have an $1,800 salvage value. Depreciation was to be charged on a straight-line basis. A full year's depreciation was charged on December 31, at the end of the first year of the machine's use; and on October 1, in its second year of use, the machine was retired from service.

Required

1. Prepare general journal entries to record the purchase of the machine, the cost of repairing it, and its installation. Assume cash was paid in each case.
2. Prepare entries to record depreciation on the machine on December 31 and on October 1.
3. Prepare entries to record the retirement of the machine under each of the following unrelated assumptions: *(a)* the machine was sold for $8,000; *(b)* it was sold for $4,600; and *(c)* it was destroyed in a fire and the insurance company paid $4,350 in full settlement of the loss claim.

Problem 10-4

On September 25, 198A, a company made a lump-sum purchase of two machines from another company that was going out of business. The machines cost $72,900 and were placed in use on October 2, 198A. This additional information about the machines is available:

Machine Number	Appraised Value	Salvage Value	Estimated Life	Installation Cost	Depreciation Method
1 . . .	$36,000	$1,800	4 years	$ 900	Sum-of-the-years' digits
2 . . .	45,000	3,000	4 years	1,500	Declining balance at twice the straight-line rate

Depreciation was taken on the machines at the end of 198A, 198B, and 198C; and during the first week in January 198D, the company decided to sell and replace them. Consequently, on January 7, 198D, it sold Machine 1 for $7,000, and on January 9 it sold Machine 2 for $13,500.

Required

1. Prepare a form with the following columnar headings:

Machine Number	198A Depreciation	198B Depreciation	198C Depreciation	198D Depreciation	198E Depreciation

Enter the machine numbers and the amounts of depreciation that would be taken each year if the machines had been used throughout their four-year useful lives.
2. Prepare general journal entries to record the purchase of the machines, their installation, the depreciation for each year they were in use, and their sale. Assume cash was paid and received in all transactions and the installation charges were paid for on the day the machines were put in use.

Problem 10-5

Morgan Salvage Company completed the following transactions involving plant assets:

198A

Jan. 4 Purchased on credit from Central Equipment an electronic scale priced at $2,650. The serial number of the scale was S-47752, its service life was estimated at five years with a trade-in value of $250, and it was assigned Plant Asset No. 445–1.

Apr. 2 Purchased on credit from Central Equipment a Sharr mixer priced at $4,094. The serial number of the mixer was M-11564, its service life was estimated at six years with a trade-in value of $350, and it was assigned Plant Asset No. 456–2.

Dec. 31 Recorded straight-line depreciation on the plant equipment for 198A.

198B

Nov. 3 Sold the Sharr mixer to Gainesville Steel for $2,500 cash.

3 Purchased a new Maxishaft mixer from Crawler Equipment for $3,600. The serial number of the mixer was TT-66887, its service life was estimated at eight years with a trade-in value of $480, and it was assigned Plant Asset No. 456–3.

Dec. 31 Recorded straight-line depreciation on the plant equipment for 198B.

Required

1. Open general ledger accounts for Plant Equipment and for Accumulated Depreciation, Plant Equipment. Prepare a subsidiary plant asset record card for each item of equipment purchased.

2. Prepare general journal entries to record the transactions and post to the proper general ledger and subsidiary ledger accounts.

3. Prove the December 31, 198B, balances of the Plant Equipment and Accumulated Depreciation, Plant Equipment accounts by preparing a list showing the cost and accumulated depreciation on each item of plant equipment owned by Morgan Salvage Company on that date.

☐ **Alternate Problems**   **Problem 10-1A**

In early 1987, Dawntreader Company paid $650,000 for real estate that included a tract of land on which two buildings were located. The plan was to demolish Building X and build a new store in its place. Building Y was to be used as a company office and was appraised to have a value of $210,000, with a useful life of 20 years and a $30,000 salvage value. A lighted parking lot near Building Y had improvements valued at $70,000 that were expected to last another five years and have no salvage value. In its existing condition, the tract of land was estimated to have a value of $420,000.

Dawntreader Company incurred the following additional costs:

Cost to demolish Building X	$ 47,500
Cost to landscape new building site	54,000
Cost to build new building (Building Z), having a useful life of 25 years and a $50,000 salvage value	750,000
Cost of new land improvements near Building Z, which have an eight-year useful life and no salvage value . .	125,000

Required

1. Prepare a form having the following column headings: Land, Building Y, Building Z, Land Improvements Y, and Land Improvements Z. Allocate the costs incurred by Dawntreader Company to the appropriate columns and total each column.

2. Prepare a single journal entry dated May 1 to record all of the costs incurred, assuming they were all paid in cash.

3. Prepare December 31 adjusting entries to record depreciation for the eight months of 1987 during which the assets were in use. Use declining-balance depreciation at twice the straight-line rate for the newly constructed Building Z and Land Improvements Z and straight-line depreciation for Building Y and Land Improvements Y.

Problem 10-2A

Hazelwood Company recently negotiated a lump-sum purchase of several assets from a road equipment dealer who was planning to change locations. The purchase was completed on August 31, 198B, at a total cash price of $580,000, and included a sales garage with land and certain land improvements and a new light truck. The estimated market value of each asset was: sales garage, $368,500; land, $221,100; land improvements, $67,000; and truck, $13,400.

Required

1. Prepare a schedule to allocate the lump-sum purchase price to the separate assets that were purchased. Also present the general journal entry to record the purchase.

2. Calculate the 198C depreciation expense on the sales garage using the sum-of-the-years'-digits method and assuming a 15-year life and a $25,000 salvage value.

3. Calculate the 198B depreciation expense on the land improvements assuming an eight-year life and declining-balance depreciation at twice the straight-line rate.

4. The truck is in the five-year class for tax purposes but is expected to last seven years and have a salvage value of $1,500. Prepare a schedule showing each year's depreciation on the truck for tax purposes, assuming (*a*) five-year straight-line, and (*b*) ACRS depreciation.

Problem 10-3A

Part 1. A company purchased and installed a new machine that cost $130,000, had a five-year life, and an estimated $18,200 salvage value. Management estimated that the machine would produce 80,000 units of product during its life. Actual production of units of product was as follows: year 1, 11,200; year 2, 17,600; year 3, 16,000; year 4, 15,200; and year 5, 20,000.

Required

1. Prepare a calculation showing the number of dollars of this machine's cost that should be charged to depreciation over its five-year life.

2. Prepare a form with the following column headings:

Year	Straight Line	Units of Production	Declining Balance	Sum-of-the-Years' Digits

Then show the depreciation for each year and the total depreciation for the machine under each depreciation method. Use twice the straight-line rate for the declining-balance method.

Part 2. On January 7, Baker Company purchased a used machine for $45,600. The next day it was repaired at a cost of $5,400 and was mounted on a new cradle that cost $4,200. It was estimated the machine would be used for three years and would then have a $7,200 salvage value. Depreciation was to be charged on a straight-line basis. A full year's depreciation was charged on December 31 of the first and the second years of the machine's use; and on March 28 of its third year of use, the machine was retired from service.

Required

1. Prepare general journal entries to record the purchase of the machine, the cost of repairing it, and its installation. Assume cash was paid in each case.
2. Prepare entries to record depreciation on the machine at the end of the first and second years and on March 28 of the third year.
3. Prepare entries to record the retirement of the machine under each of the following unrelated assumptions: (*a*) the machine was sold for $23,500; (*b*) it was sold for $16,100; and (*c*) it was destroyed in a fire and the insurance company paid $14,700 in full settlement of the loss claim.

Problem 10-4A

On April 2, 198A, Fastnet Company made a lump-sum purchase of two machines from another company that was going out of business. The machines cost $218,700 and were placed in use on April 5, 198A. This additional information about the machines is available:

Machine Number	Appraised Value	Salvage Value	Estimated Life	Installation Cost	Depreciation Method
1 . . .	$108,000	$5,400	4 years	$2,700	Sum-of-the-years' digits
2 . . .	135,000	9,000	4 years	4,500	Declining balance at twice the straight-line rate

Depreciation was taken on the machines at the end of 198A, 198B, and 198C; and during the first week in January 198D, the company decided to sell and replace them. Consequently, on January 4, 198D, it sold Machine 1 for $18,000, and on January 5 it sold Machine 2 for $40,500.

Required

1. Prepare a form with the following columnar headings:

Machine Number	198A Depreciation	198B Depreciation	198C Depreciation	198D Depreciation	198E Depreciation

Enter the machine numbers and the amounts of depreciation that would be taken each year if the machines had been used throughout their four-year useful lives.

2. Prepare general journal entries to record the purchase of the machines, their installation, the depreciation for each year they were in use, and their sale. Assume cash was paid and received in all transactions and the installation charges were paid for on the day the machines were put in use.

Problem 10-5A

Rafer Barnum Company completed the following transactions involving plant assets:

198A
Jan. 1 Purchased on credit from Northwest Equipment an electric packer priced at $13,250. The serial number of the packer was P-78861, its service life was estimated at five years with a trade-in value of $1,250, and it was assigned Plant Asset No. 360–1.

Apr. 7 Purchased on credit from Northwest Equipment a Blaum vibrator priced at $20,470. The serial number of the vibrator was V-44332, its service life was estimated at six years with a trade-in value of $1,750, and it was assigned Plant Asset No. 370–2.

Dec. 31 Recorded straight-line depreciation on the plant equipment for 198A.

198B
Nov. 2 Sold the Blaum vibrator to Concrete Products for $12,500 cash.
4 Purchased a new Supershake vibrator from Bigtime Equipment for $18,000. The serial number of the vibrator was SS-24686, its service life was estimated at eight years with a trade-in value of $2,400, and it was assigned Plant Asset No. 370–3.

Dec. 31 Recorded straight-line depreciation on the plant equipment for 198B.

Required

1. Open general ledger accounts for Plant Equipment and for Accumulated Depreciation, Plant Equipment. Prepare a subsidiary plant asset record card for each item of equipment purchased.

2. Prepare general journal entries to record the transactions and post to the proper general ledger and subsidiary ledger accounts.

3. Prove the December 31, 198B, balances of the Plant Equipment and Accumulated Depreciation, Plant Equipment accounts by preparing a list showing the cost and accumulated depreciation on each item of plant equipment owned by Rafer Barnum Company on that date.

☐   **Provocative Problems**

Provocative Problem 10-1   Chrysler Corporation

Chrysler Corporation's 1983 annual report to its stockholders included financial statements for the year ended December 31, 1983. Those statements showed that Chrysler had earned a $701 million dollar net income in 1983. That was the first profitable year for Chrysler since 1977. The footnotes to the 1983 financial statements contained the following item:

> **Note 1**
> *Summary of Significant Accounting Policies*
>
> *Depreciation and Tool Amortization*
>
> Property, plant, and equipment are carried at cost less accumulated depreciation. For assets placed in service beginning in 1980, depreciation is provided on a straight-line basis. For assets placed in service prior to 1980, depreciation is generally provided on an accelerated basis.
>
> The weighted-average service lives of assets are 30 years for buildings (including improvements and building equipment), 12 years for machinery and equipment, and 13 years for furniture. Certain assets relating to rear wheel-drive products are being depreciated over the remaining planned production periods.
>
> Courtesy of Chrysler Corporation.

Why might Chrysler have chosen to use straight-line depreciation for assets purchased in 1980 and subsequent years? Also, what might be the reason for the last sentence in the footnote?

Provocative Problem 10-2   Allocating Costs of a New Plant

Scientific Systems Company temporarily recorded the costs of a new plant in a summary account called Land and Buildings. Management has now asked you to examine this account and prepare any necessary entries to correct the account balances. In doing so, you find the following debits and credits to the account:

Debits

Jan.	5	Cost of land and buildings acquired for new plant site	$125,000
	11	Attorney's fee for title search	1,250
	24	Cost of wrecking old building on plant site	12,500
Feb.	2	Six months' liability and fire insurance on new building	3,750
June	29	Payment to building contractor on completion of building . . .	563,125
July	4	Architect's fee for new building	33,750
	6	City assessment for street improvements	8,750
	14	Cost of landscaping new plant site	5,000
			$753,125

Credits

Jan.	26	Proceeds from sale of salvaged materials from old building . .	$ 2,500
July	2	Refund of one month's insurance premium.	625
Dec.	31	Depreciation at 2½% per year.	9,375
	31	Balance.	740,625
			$753,125

Your investigation suggests that 40 years is a reasonable life expectancy for a building of the type involved and that an assumption of zero salvage value is reasonable. To summarize your analysis, you decide to prepare a schedule with columns headed Date, Description, Total Amount, Land, Buildings, and Other Accounts and to enter the items found in the Land and Buildings account on the schedule, distributing the amounts to the proper columns. You should show credits on the schedule by enclosing the amounts in parentheses. Realizing that the accounts have not been closed, you should also draft any required correcting entry or entries. Assume that an account called Depreciation Expense, Land and Buildings was debited in recording the $9,375 of depreciation.

Provocative Problem 10-3   Financial Statement Effects of Alternative Methods

Kemaro Company and Firedog Company are almost identical. Each began operations on January 1 of this year with $126,000 of equipment having an eight-year life and a $14,000 salvage value. Each purchased merchandise during the year as follows:

Jan. 1	280 units @ $300 per unit =	$ 84,000
Apr. 15	350 units @ $360 per unit =	126,000
June 25	525 units @ $375 per unit =	196,875
Nov. 5	295 units @ $400 per unit =	118,000
		$524,875

And now, on December 31 at the end of the first year, each has 340 units of merchandise in its ending inventory. However, Kemaro Company will use straight-line depreciation in arriving at its net income for the year, while Firedog Company will use declining-balance depreciation at twice the straight-line rate. Also, Kemaro Company will use FIFO in costing its ending inventory, and Firedog Company will use LIFO. The December 31 trial balances of the two concerns carried these amounts:

	Kemaro Company		Firedog Company	
Cash.	$ 12,250		$ 12,250	
Accounts receivable	28,000		28,000	
Equipment	126,000		126,000	
Accounts payable		$ 64,000		$ 64,000
J. Kemaro, capital		154,000		
T. Firedog, capital				154,000
Sales		595,000		595,000
Purchases	524,875		524,875	
Salaries expense	52,500		52,500	
Rent expense	42,700		42,700	
Other expenses	26,675		26,675	
Totals	$813,000	$813,000	$813,000	$813,000

Required

Prepare an income statement for each company and a schedule accounting for the difference in their reported net incomes. Write a short answer to this question: Which, if either, of the companies is the more profitable and why?

11 Plant and Equipment, Natural Resources, and Intangible Assets

After studying Chapter 11, you should be able to:

1. Prepare entries to record the purchase and sale or discarding of a plant asset.

2. Prepare entries to record the exchange of plant assets under accounting rules and under income tax rules and tell which rules should be applied in any given exchange.

3. Make the calculations and prepare the entries to account for revisions in depreciation rates.

4. Make the calculations and prepare the entries to account for plant asset repairs and betterments.

5. Prepare entries to account for wasting assets and for intangible assets.

6. Define or explain the words and phrases listed in the chapter Glossary.

Some of the problems met in accounting for property, plant, and equipment were discussed in the previous chapter. Additional problems involving plant assets and some of the accounting problems encountered with intangible assets are examined in this chapter.

■ Plant Asset Disposals

Sooner or later, a plant asset wears out, becomes obsolete, or becomes inadequate. When this occurs, the asset is discarded, sold, or traded in on a new asset. The entry to record the disposal depends on which action is taken.

Discarding a Plant Asset

When an asset's accumulated depreciation is equal to its cost, the asset is said to be fully depreciated; and if a fully depreciated asset is discarded, the entry to record the disposal is:

Jan.	7	Accumulated Depreciation, Machinery	1,500.00	
		Machinery		1,500.00
		Discarded a fully depreciated machine.		

Although often discarded, sometimes a fully depreciated asset is kept in use. In such situations, the asset's cost and accumulated depreciation should not be removed from the accounts; they should remain on the books until the asset is sold, traded, or discarded. Otherwise, the accounts do not show its continued existence. However, no additional depreciation should be recorded, since the reason for recording depreciation is to charge an asset's cost to depreciation expense. In no case should the expense exceed the asset's cost.

Sometimes an asset is discarded before being fully depreciated. For example, suppose an error was made in estimating the service life of a $1,000 machine and it becomes worthless and is discarded after having only $800 of depreciation recorded against it. In such a situation, there is a loss, and the entry to record the disposal is:

Jan.	10	Loss on Disposal of Machinery	200.00	
		Accumulated Depreciation, Machinery	800.00	
		Machinery		1,000.00
		Discarded a worthless machine.		

■ Discarding a Damaged Plant Asset

Occasionally, before the end of its service life, a plant asset is wrecked in an accident or destroyed by fire. For example, a machine that cost $900 and that had been depreciated $400 was totally destroyed in a fire. If the loss was partially covered by insurance and the insurance company paid $350 to settle the loss claim, the entry to record the machine's destruction is:

Jan.	12	Cash	350.00	
		Loss from Fire	150.00	
		Accumulated Depreciation, Machinery	400.00	
		Machinery		900.00
		To record the destruction of machinery and the receipt of insurance compensation.		

If the machine were uninsured, the entry to record its destruction would not have a debit to Cash, and the loss from fire would be $500.

Selling a Plant Asset

When a plant asset is sold, if the selling price exceeds the asset's book value, there is a gain. If the price is less than book value, there is a loss. For example, assume that a machine that cost $5,000 and had been depreciated $4,000 is sold for a price in excess of its book value, say, for $1,200. In this case, there is a gain, and the entry to record the sale is:

Jan	4	Cash	1,200.00	
		Accumulated Depreciation, Machinery	4,000.00	
		Machinery		5,000.00
		Gain on the Sale of Plant Assets		200.00
		Sold a machine at a price in excess of book value.		

However, if the machine is sold for $750, there is a $250 loss, and the entry to record the sale is:

Jan.	4	Cash	750.00	
		Loss on the Sale of Plant Assets	250.00	
		Accumulated Depreciation, Machinery	4,000.00	
		Machinery		5,000.00
		Sold a machine at a price below book value.		

■ **Exchanging Plant Assets**

Some plant assets are sold at the end of their useful lives. Others, such as machinery, automobiles, and office equipment, are commonly exchanged for new, up-to-date assets of like purpose. In such exchanges, a trade-in allowance is normally received on the old asset, with the balance being paid in cash. The APB ruled that in recording the exchanges, a material book loss should be recognized in the accounts but a book gain should not.[1] A book loss is experienced when the trade-in allowance is less than the book value of the traded asset. A book gain results from a trade-in allowance that exceeds the book value of the traded asset.

[1] FASB, *Accounting Standards—Current Text* (Stamford, Conn., 1984), sec. N35.109. First published in *APB Opinion No. 29*, par. 22.

Recognizing a Material Book Loss

To illustrate recognition of a material book loss on an exchange of plant assets, assume that a machine which cost $18,000 and had been depreciated $15,000 was traded in on a new machine having a $21,000 cash price. A $1,000 trade-in allowance was received, and the $20,000 balance was paid in cash. Under these assumptions, the book value of the old machine is $3,000, calculated as follows:

Cost of old machine.	$18,000
Less accumulated depreciation	15,000
Book value	$ 3,000

And since the $1,000 trade-in allowance resulted in a $2,000 loss on the exchange, the transaction should be recorded as follows:

Jan.	5	Machinery	21,000.00	
		Loss on Exchange of Machinery.	2,000.00	
		Accumulated Depreciation, Machinery	15,000.00	
		Machinery		18,000.00
		Cash		20,000.00
		Exchanged old machine and cash for a new machine of like purpose.		

The $21,000 debit to Machinery puts the new machine in the accounts at its cash price. The debit to Loss on Exchange of Machinery records the loss. The old machine is removed from the accounts with the $15,000 debit to Accumulated Depreciation and the $18,000 credit to Machinery.

Nonrecognition of a Book Gain

When there is a book gain on an exchange of plant assets, the APB ruled that the new asset should be taken into the accounts at an amount equal to the book value of the traded-in asset plus the cash given. This results in the nonrecognition of the gain. For example, assume that in acquiring the $21,000 machine of the previous section, a $4,500 trade-in allowance, rather than a $1,000 trade-in allowance, was received, and the $16,500 balance was paid in cash. A $4,500 trade-in allowance would result in a $1,500 gain on the exchange. However, in recording the exchange, the book gain should not be recognized in the accounts. Rather, it should be absorbed into the cost of the new machine by taking the new machine into the accounts at an amount equal to the sum of the book value of the old machine plus the cash given. This is $19,500 and is calculated as follows:

Book value of old machine	$ 3,000
Cash given in the exchange	16,500
Cost basis for the new machine . . .	$19,500

And the transaction should be recorded as follows:

Jan.	5	Machinery	19,500.00	
		Accumulated Depreciation, Machinery	15,000.00	
		Machinery		18,000.00
		Cash		16,500.00
		Exchanged old machine and cash for a new machine of like purpose.		

Observe that the $19,500 recorded amount for the new machine is equal to its cash price less the $1,500 book gain on the exchange ($21,000 − $1,500 = $19,500). In other words, the $1,500 book gain was absorbed into the amount at which the new machine was recorded. The $19,500 is called the **cost basis** of the new machine and is the amount used in recording depreciation on the machine or any gain or loss on its sale.

The APB based its ruling that gains on plant asset exchanges should not be recognized on the opinion that ". . . revenue should not be recognized merely because one productive asset is substituted for a similar productive asset but rather should be considered to flow from the production and sale of the goods or services to which the substituted productive asset is committed."[2] In other words, the APB's opinion was that any gain from a plant asset exchange should be taken in the form of increased net income resulting from smaller depreciation charges on the asset acquired. In this case, depreciation calculated on the recorded $19,500 cost basis of the new machine is less than if calculated on the machine's $21,000 cash price.

Tax Rules and Plant Asset Exchanges

Because depreciation methods for financial statement purposes are often different from those used for tax purposes, companies usually must keep two sets of depreciation records on each asset. Even where the depreciation methods and estimated lives are the same for tax and accounting purposes, two sets of records may be necessary. This is caused by the fact that **income tax rules** and accounting principles do not agree on the treatment of losses on plant asset exchanges. In the case of a gain, the tax rules and accounting principles agree.

According to the Internal Revenue Service, when an old asset is traded in on a new asset of like purpose, either a gain or a loss on the exchange must be absorbed into the cost of the new machine. This cost basis then becomes for tax purposes the amount that must be used in calculating depreciation on the new asset or any gain or loss on its sale or exchange. Consequently, for tax purposes, the cost basis of an asset acquired in an exchange is the sum of the book value of the old asset plus the cash given, and it makes no difference whether there is a gain or a loss on the exchange.

Since accounting principles and tax rules differ in their treatment of a loss on a plant asset exchange, two sets of depreciation records must be kept for the new asset even if the depreciation method and estimated life are the same for tax and accounting purposes. One set must be kept for

---

[2] APB, "Accounting for Nonmonetary Transactions," *APB Opinion No. 29* (New York: AICPA, May 1973), par. 16. Copyright © 1973 by the American Institute of Certified Public Accountants, Inc.

determining net income for accounting purposes and the other for deter-mining the depreciation deduction for tax purposes. Keeping two sets of records is obviously more costly than keeping one. Yet, when an exchange results in a material loss, the loss should be recorded and the two sets of records kept. On the other hand, when an exchange results in an imma-terial loss, it is permissible under the **principle of materiality** to avoid the two sets of records by putting the new asset on the books at its cost basis for tax purposes.

For example, an old typewriter that cost $500 was traded in at $50 on a new $600 typewriter, with the $550 difference being paid in cash. Depreci-ation on the old typewriter in the amount of $420 had been taken both for tax and accounting purposes. In this case, the old typewriter's book value is $80; and with the trade-in of $50, there was a $30 book loss on the exchange. However, the $30 loss is an immaterial amount; and the following method, called the income tax method, may be used in recording the exchange:

Jan.	7	Office Equipment	630.00	
		Accumulated Depreciation, Office Equipment .	420.00	
		Office Equipment		500.00
		Cash		550.00
		Traded an old typewriter and cash for a new typewriter.		

The $630 at which the new typewriter is taken into the accounts by the income tax method is its cost basis for tax purposes and is calculated as follows:

Book value of old typewriter ($500 less $420).	$ 80
Cash paid ($600 less the $50 trade-in allowance)	550
Income tax basis of the new typewriter.	$630

Not recording the loss on this exchange and taking the new typewriter into the accounts at its cost basis for income tax purposes violates the ruling of the APB that a loss on a plant asset exchange should be recorded. However, when there is an immaterial loss on an exchange, as in this case, the violation is permissible under the **principle of materiality**. Under this principle, an adherence to any accounting principle, including rulings of the APB and the FASB, is not required when the lack of adherence does not materially affect reported periodic net income. In this case, failing to record the $30 loss on the exchange would not materially affect the average company's statements.

■ **Revising Depreciation Rates**

An occasional error in estimating the useful life of a plant asset is to be expected. Furthermore, when such an error is discovered, it is corrected by spreading the remaining amount the asset is to be depreciated over its remaining useful life.[3] For example, seven years ago a machine was purchased at a cost of $10,500. At that time, the machine was estimated to have a 10-year life with a $500 salvage value. Therefore, it was depreciated at the rate of $1,000 per year [($10,500 − $500) ÷ 10 = $1,000]; and it began its eighth year with a $3,500 book value calculated as follows:

Cost	$10,500
Less seven years' accumulated depreciation	7,000
Book value	$ 3,500

Assume that at the beginning of its eighth year, the estimated number of years remaining in this machine's useful life is changed from three to five years with no change in salvage value. Under this assumption, depreciation for each of the machine's remaining years should be calculated as follows:

$$\frac{\text{Book value} - \text{Salvage value}}{\text{Remaining useful life}} = \frac{\$3,500 - \$500}{5 \text{ years}} = \$600 \text{ per year}$$

And $600 of depreciation should be recorded on the machine at the end of the eighth and each succeeding year in its life.

If depreciation is charged at the rate of $1,000 per year for the first seven years of this machine's life and $600 per year for the next five, depreciation expense is overstated during the first seven years and understated during the next five. However, if a business has many plant assets, the lives of some will be underestimated, and the lives of others will be overestimated at the time of purchase. Consequently, such errors will tend to cancel each other out with little or no effect on the income statement.

■ **Ordinary and Extraordinary Repairs**

Repairs made to keep an asset in its normal good state of repair are classified as **ordinary repairs.** A building must be repainted and its roof repaired. A machine must be cleaned, oiled, adjusted, and have any worn small parts replaced. Such repairs and maintenance are necessary, and their costs should appear on the current income statement as an expense.

Extraordinary repairs are major repairs made not to keep an asset in its normal good state of repair but to extend its service life beyond that originally estimated. As a rule, the cost of such repairs should be debited to the repaired asset's accumulated depreciation account under the assumption they make good past depreciation, add to the asset's useful life, and benefit future periods. For example, a machine was purchased for $8,000 and depreciated under the assumption it would last eight years and have no salvage value. As a result, at the end of the machine's sixth year, its book value is $2,000, calculated as follows:

[3] FASB, *Accounting Standards—Current Text,* sec. A06.130. First published in *APB Opinion No. 20,* par. 31.

Cost of machine.	$8,000
Less six years' accumulated depreciation . . .	6,000
Book value	$2,000

If, at the beginning of the machine's seventh year, a major overhaul extends its estimated useful life three years beyond the eight originally estimated, the $2,100 cost should be recorded as follows:

Jan.	12	Accumulated Depreciation, Machinery	2,100.00	
		Cash (or Accounts Payable).		2,100.00
		To record extraordinary repairs.		

In addition, depreciation for each of the five years remaining in the machine's life should be calculated as follows:

Book value before extraordinary repairs	$2,000
Extraordinary repairs	2,100
Total	$4,100
Annual depreciation expense for remaining years ($4,100 ÷ 5 years)	$ 820

And, if the machine remains in use for five years after the major overhaul, the five annual $820 depreciation charges will exactly write off its new book value, including the cost of the extraordinary repairs.

■   **Betterments**

A **betterment** involves modifying an existing plant asset to make it more efficient, usually by replacing part of the asset with an improved or superior part. The result of a betterment is a more efficient or more productive asset, but not necessarily one having a longer life. For example, if the manual controls on a machine are replaced with automatic controls, the cost of labor may be reduced. When a betterment is made, its cost should be debited to the improved asset's account, say, the Machinery account, and depreciated over the remaining service life of the asset. Also, the cost and applicable depreciation of the replaced asset portion should be removed from the accounts.

■   **Capital and Revenue Expenditures**

A **revenue expenditure** is one that should appear on the current income statement as an expense that is deducted from the period's revenues. Expenditures for ordinary repairs, rent, and salaries are examples. Expenditures for betterments and for extraordinary repairs, on the other hand, are examples of what are called **capital expenditures** or **balance sheet expenditures.** They should appear on the balance sheet as asset increases.

Obviously, care must be exercised to distinguish between capital and revenue expenditures when transactions are recorded because, if errors are made, such errors often affect a number of accounting periods. For instance, an expenditure for a betterment initially recorded in error as an expense overstates expenses in the year of the error and understates net income. Also, since the cost of a betterment should be depreciated over the remaining useful life of the bettered asset, depreciation expense of future periods is understated, and net income is overstated.

■ **Natural Resources**

Natural resources such as standing timber, mineral deposits, and oil reserves are known as wasting assets. In their natural state, they represent inventories that will be converted into a product by cutting, mining, or pumping. However, until cut, mined, or pumped, they are noncurrent assets and commonly appear on a balance sheet under such captions as "Timberlands," "Mineral deposits," or "Oil reserves."

Natural resources are accounted for at cost and appear on the balance sheet at cost less accumulated **depletion.** The amount such assets are depleted each year by cutting, mining, or pumping is commonly calculated on a "units-of-production" basis. For example, if a mineral deposit having an estimated 500,000 tons of available ore is purchased for $500,000, the depletion charge per ton of ore mined is $1. Furthermore, if 85,000 tons are mined during the first year, the depletion charge for the year is $85,000 and is recorded as follows:

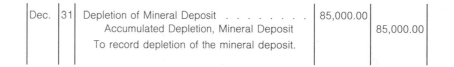

Dec.	31	Depletion of Mineral Deposit	85,000.00	
		Accumulated Depletion, Mineral Deposit		85,000.00
		To record depletion of the mineral deposit.		

On the balance sheet prepared at the end of the first year, the mineral deposit should appear at its $500,000 cost less $85,000 accumulated depletion. If the 85,000 tons of ore are sold by the end of the first year, the entire $85,000 depletion charge reaches the income statement as the depletion cost of the ore mined and sold. However, if a portion remains unsold at the year-end, the depletion cost of the unsold ore is carried forward on the balance sheet as part of the cost of the unsold ore inventory, a current asset.

Often, machinery must be installed or a building constructed in order to exploit a natural resource. The costs of such assets should be depreciated over the life of the natural resource with annual depreciation charges that are in proportion to the annual depletion charges. For example, if a machine is installed in a mine and one eighth of the mine's ore is removed during a year, one eighth of the amount the machine is to be depreciated should be recorded as a cost of the ore mined.

■ **Intangible Assets**

Intangible assets have no physical existence; rather, they represent certain legal rights and economic relationships that are beneficial to the owner. Patents, copyrights, leaseholds, goodwill, trademarks, and organization costs are examples. Notes and accounts receivable are also intangible in nature. However, these appear on the balance sheet as current assets rather than under the intangible assets classification.

Intangible assets are accounted for at cost and should appear on the balance sheet in the intangible asset section at cost or at that portion of cost not previously written off. Normally, the intangible asset section follows on the balance sheet immediately after the plant and equipment section. Intangibles should be systematically amortized or written off to expense accounts over their estimated useful lives, which in no case should exceed 40 years. Amortization is a process similar to the recording of depreciation. However, amortization of intangibles is limited to the straight-line method unless it can be demonstrated that another method is more appropriate.

Patents

Patents are granted by the federal government to encourage the invention of new machines and mechanical devices. A patent gives its owner the exclusive right to manufacture and sell a patented machine or device for a period of 17 years. When patent rights are purchased, all costs of acquiring the rights may be debited to an account called Patents. Also, the costs of a successful lawsuit in defense of a patent may be debited to this account.

A patent gives its owner exclusive rights to the patented device for 17 years. However, its cost should be **amortized** or written off over a shorter period if its useful or economic life is estimated to be less than 17 years. For example, if a patent costing $25,000 has an estimated useful life of only 10 years, the following adjusting entry is made at the end of each year in the patent's life to write off one tenth of its cost:

Dec.	31	Amortization of Patents.	2,500.00	
		Patents		2,500.00
		To write off one tenth of patent costs.		

The entry's debit causes $2,500 of patent costs to appear on the annual income statement as one of the costs of the patented product manufactured. The credit directly reduces the balance of the Patents account. Normally, patents are written off directly to the Patents account as in this entry.

Copyrights

A **copyright** is granted by the federal government and in most cases gives its owner the exclusive right to publish and sell a musical, literary, or artistic work during the life of the composer, author, or artist and for 50 years thereafter. Many copyrights have value for a much shorter time, and their costs should be amortized over the shorter period. Often, the only cost of a copyright is the fee paid the Copyright Office. If this fee is not material, it may be charged directly to an expense account. Otherwise, the copyright costs should be capitalized, and the periodic amortization of a copyright should be charged to Amortization Expense, Copyrights.

Leaseholds

Property is rented under a contract called a **lease.** The person or company owning the property and granting the lease is called the **lessor.** The person or company securing the right to possess and use the property is called the **lessee.** The rights granted the lessee under the lease are called a **leasehold.**

Some leases require no advance payment from the lessee but do require monthly rent payments. In such cases, a Leasehold account is not needed, and the monthly payments are debited to a Rent Expense account. Sometimes a long-term lease is so drawn that the last year's rent must be paid in advance at the time the lease is signed. When this occurs, the last year's advance payment is debited to the Leasehold account. It remains there until the last year of the lease, at which time it is transferred to Rent Expense.

Often, a long-term lease, one running 20 or 25 years, becomes very valuable after a few years because its required rent payments are much less than current rentals for identical property. In such cases, the increase in value of the lease should not be entered on the books since no extra cost was incurred in acquiring it. However, if the property is subleased and a cash payment is made for the rights under the old lease, the new tenant should debit the payment to a Leasehold account and write it off as additional rent expense over the remaining life of the lease.

Leasehold Improvements

Long-term leases often require the lessee to pay for any alterations or improvements to the leased property, such as new partitions and store fronts. Normally, the costs of **leasehold improvements** are debited to an account called Leasehold Improvements. Also, since the improvements become part of the property and revert to the lessor at the end of the lease, their cost should be amortized over the life of the lease or the life of the improvements, whichever is shorter. The amortization entry commonly debits Rent Expense and credits Leasehold Improvements.

Goodwill

The term **goodwill** has a special meaning in accounting. In accounting, **a business is said to have goodwill when its rate of expected future earnings is greater than the rate of earnings normally realized in its industry.** Above-average earnings and the existence of goodwill may be demonstrated as follows with Companies A and B, both of which are in the same industry:

	Company A	Company B
Net assets (other than goodwill)	$100,000	$100,000
Normal rate of return in this industry	10%	10%
Normal return on net assets	$ 10,000	$ 10,000
Expected net income	10,000	15,000
Expected earnings above average	$ 0	$ 5,000

Company B is expected to have an above-average earnings rate compared to its industry and is said to have goodwill. This goodwill may be the result of excellent customer relations, the location of the business, monopolistic privileges, superior management, or a combination of factors. Furthermore, a prospective investor would normally be willing to pay more for Company B than for Company A if the investor agreed the extra earnings rate should be expected. Thus, goodwill is an asset having value, and it can be sold.

Accountants are in agreement that goodwill should not be recorded unless it is bought or sold. This normally occurs only when a business is purchased and sold in its entirety. When this occurs, the goodwill of the business may be valued in several ways. Examples of three follow:

1. The buyer and seller may place an arbitrary value on the goodwill of a business being sold. For instance, a seller may be willing to sell a business having an above-average earnings rate for $115,000, and a buyer may be willing to pay that amount. If they both agree that the net assets of the business other than its goodwill have a $100,000 value, they are arbitrarily valuing the goodwill at $15,000.
2. Goodwill may be valued at some multiple of that portion of expected earnings which is above average. For example, if a company is expected to have $5,000 each year in above-average earnings, its goodwill may be valued at, say, four times that portion of its earnings which are above average, or at $20,000. In this case, it may also be said that the goodwill is valued at four years' above-average earnings. However, regardless of how it is said, this too is placing an arbitrary value on the goodwill.
3. The portion of a company's earnings that is above average may be capitalized in order to place a value on its goodwill. For example, if a business is expected to continue to have $5,000 each year in earnings that are above average and the normal rate of return on invested capital in its industry is 10%, the excess earnings may be capitalized at 10%, and a $50,000 value may be placed on its goodwill ($5,000 ÷ 10% = $50,000). Note that this values the goodwill at the amount that must be invested at the normal rate of return in order to earn the extra $5,000 each year ($50,000 × 10% = $5,000). It is a satisfactory method if the extra earnings are expected to continue indefinitely. However, this may not happen. Consequently, extra earnings are often capitalized at a rate higher than the normal rate of the industry, say, in this case, at twice the normal rate or at 20%. If the extra earnings are capitalized at 20%, the goodwill is valued at $25,000 ($5,000 ÷ 20% = $25,000).

There are other ways to value goodwill. Nevertheless, in the final analysis, goodwill is always valued at the price a seller is willing to accept and a buyer is willing to pay.

Trademarks and Trade Names

Proof of prior use of a trademark or trade name is sufficient under common law to prove ownership and right of use. However, both may be registered at the Patent Office at a nominal cost for the same purpose. The cost of developing, maintaining, or enhancing the value of a trademark or trade name, perhaps through advertising, should be charged to an expense account in the period or periods incurred. However, if a trademark or trade name is purchased, its cost should be amortized as explained in the next section.

Amortization of Intangibles

Some intangibles, such as patents, copyrights, and leaseholds, have determinable lives based on a law, contract, or the nature of the asset. The costs of such assets should be amortized over the shorter of their legal existence or the period expected to be benefited by their use. Other intangibles, such as goodwill, trademarks, and trade names, have indeterminable lives. However, the APB ruled that the value of any intangible will eventually disappear. As a result, a reasonable estimate of the period of usefulness of such assets should be made. Their costs should then be amortized over the periods estimated to be benefited by their use, which in no case should exceed 40 years.[4]

[4] Ibid., sec. I60.110. First published in *APB Opinion No. 17,* par. 29.

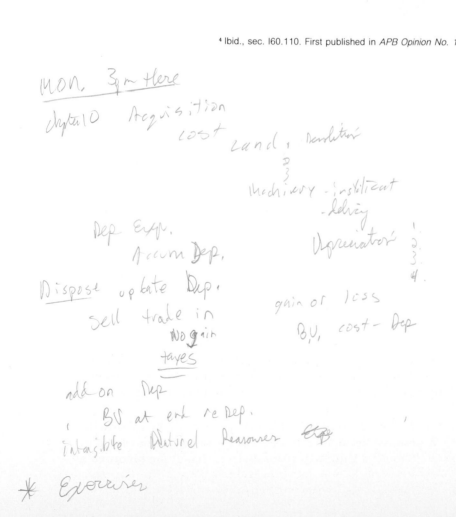

Glossary

Amortize to periodically write off as an expense a share of the cost of an asset, usually an intangible asset.

Balance sheet expenditure another name for **capital expenditure.**

Betterment the replacement of an existing asset portion with an improved or superior asset portion, the result of which is a more efficient or more productive asset.

Capital expenditure an expenditure that benefits future periods because the value or asset obtained by the expenditure does not fully expire by the end of the current period. Also called a **balance sheet expenditure.**

Copyright an exclusive right granted by the federal government to publish and sell a musical, literary, or artistic work for a period of years.

Depletion the amount a wasting asset is reduced through cutting, mining, or pumping.

Extraordinary repairs major repairs that extend the life of a plant asset beyond the number of years originally estimated.

Goodwill that portion of the value of a business due to its expected ability to earn a rate of return greater than the average in its industry.

Income tax rules rules governing how income for tax purposes and income taxes are to be calculated.

Intangible asset an asset having no physical existence but having value due to the rights resulting from its ownership and possession.

Lease a contract that grants the right to possess and use property.

Leasehold the rights granted to a lessee under the terms of a lease contract.

Leasehold improvements improvements to leased property made by the lessee.

Lessee an individual or enterprise that is given possession of property under the terms of a lease contract.

Lessor the individual or enterprise that gives up possession of property under the terms of a lease contract.

Ordinary repairs repairs made to keep a plant asset in its normal good operating condition.

Patent an exclusive right granted by the federal government to manufacture and sell a machine or mechanical device for a period of years.

Revenue expenditure an expenditure that benefits only the current period because the value or asset obtained by the expenditure will fully expire before the end of the current accounting period.

Questions for Class Discussion

1. If an asset that has been depreciated is sold for cash and the remaining book value of the asset is more than the cash proceeds from the sale, should the difference be debited to depreciation expense? How should the difference be recorded?

2. When should a loss on the exchange of a plant asset be recorded? When is it permissible to absorb a loss into the cost basis of the new plant asset? Should a gain on a plant asset exchange be recorded as such?

3. What is the essential meaning of the accounting principle of materiality?

4. When cash plus a plant asset is exchanged for another asset of like purpose, what determines the cost basis of the newly acquired asset for federal income tax purposes?

5. When the loss on an exchange of plant assets is immaterial in amount, why might it be convenient to take the newly acquired asset into the accounting records at the amount of its cost basis for tax purposes?

6. When an old plant asset is traded in at a book loss on a new asset of like purpose, the loss is not recognized for tax purposes. In the end, this normally does not reduce the aggregate tax deductions available to the taxpayer. Why?

7. If at the end of five years it is discovered that a machine that was expected to have a six-year life will actually have an eight-year life, how is this new information reflected in the accounts?

8. Distinguish between ordinary repairs and replacements and extraordinary repairs and replacements.

9. How should ordinary repairs to a machine be recorded? How should extraordinary repairs be recorded?

10. What is a betterment? How should a betterment to a machine be recorded?

11. Distinguish between revenue expenditures and capital expenditures and state the difference in how they should be recorded.

12. What is the difference between balance sheet expenditures and capital expenditures?

13. What is the name for the process of allocating the cost of natural resources to expense as the natural resources are used?

14. Is the declining-balance method an acceptable means of calculating depletion of natural resources?

15. What are the characteristics of an intangible asset?

16. What are the general procedures to be followed in accounting for an intangible asset?

17. Define (a) lease, (b) lessor, (c) leasehold, and (d) leasehold improvements.

18. In accounting, when is a business said to have goodwill?

19. X Company bought an established business and paid for goodwill. If X Company plans to incur substantial advertising and promotional costs each year to maintain the value of the goodwill, must the company also amortize the goodwill?

□   **Class Exercises**   **Exercise 11-1**

A machine with an expected service life of seven years and salvage value of $2,000 was purchased for $27,200. After taking straight-line depreciation for five years, the machine was sold. Present a general journal entry dated December 31 to record the sale assuming the cash proceeds from the sale were: (a) $9,200; (b) $12,300; (c) $8,500.

Exercise 11-2

A company traded in its old truck on a new truck, receiving a $11,100 trade-in allowance and paying the remaining $36,900 in cash. The old truck had cost $33,000, and straight-line depreciation of $18,000 had been recorded under the assumption it would last five years and have a $3,000 salvage value. Answer the following questions: (*a*) What was the book value of the old truck? (*b*) What is the loss on the exchange? (*c*) Assuming the loss is deemed to be material, what amount should be debited to the New Truck account? (*d*) Assuming the loss is not material and the income tax method is used to record the exchange, what amount should be debited to the New Truck account?

Exercise 11-3

A machine that cost $24,000 and that had been depreciated $15,000 was disposed of on January 3. Present without explanations the entries to record the disposal under each of the following unrelated assumptions:

a. The machine was sold for $3,600 cash.
b. The machine was traded in on a new machine of like purpose having a $27,000 cash price. A $10,500 trade-in allowance was received, and the balance was paid in cash.
c. A $3,600 trade-in allowance was received for the machine on a new machine of like purpose having a $27,000 cash price. The balance was paid in cash, and the loss was considered material.
d. Transaction (*c*) was recorded by the income tax method because the loss was considered immaterial.

Exercise 11-4

A machine that cost $68,000 was depreciated on a straight-line basis for five years under the assumption it would have an eight-year life and a $4,000 trade-in value. At that point it was recognized that the machine had five years of remaining useful life, after which it would have an estimated $3,000 trade-in value. (*a*) Determine the machine's book value at the end of its fifth year. (*b*) Determine the amount of depreciation to be charged against the machine during each of the remaining years in its life.

Exercise 11-5

A company owns a building that appeared on its balance sheet at the end of last year at its original $380,000 cost less $273,600 accumulated depreciation. The building has been depreciated on a straight-line basis under the assumption it would have a 25-year life and no salvage value. During the first week in January of the current year, major structural repairs were completed on the building at a $120,000 cost. The repairs did not improve the building's usefulness, but they did extend its expected life for 13 years beyond the 25 years originally estimated. (*a*) Determine the building's age on last year's balance sheet date. (*b*) Give the entry to record the cost of the repairs. (*c*) Determine the book value of the building after its repairs were recorded. (*d*) Give the entry to record the current year's depreciation.

Exercise 11-6

A company paid $45,000 for a machine that was expected to last six years and have a salvage value of $6,000. Present general journal entries dated December 31 to record the following costs related to the machine.

a. During the second year of the machine's life, $900 was paid for repairs necessary to keep the machine in good working order.

b. During the third year of the machine's life, $4,600 was paid for replacement parts that were expected to increase the machine's productivity by 15% each year.

c. During the fourth year of the machine's life, $6,200 was paid for repairs that were expected to increase the service life of the machine from six to eight years.

Exercise 11-7

On January 1, 198A, a company paid $135,000 for an ore body containing 600,000 tons of ore, and it installed machinery costing $120,000, having an estimated 12-year life and no salvage value, and capable of removing the entire ore body in 6 years. The company began mining operations on May 1, and it mined 48,000 tons of ore during the remaining nine months of the year. Give the entries to record the December 31, 198A, depletion of the ore body and the depreciation of the mining machinery.

Exercise 11-8

Farley Company purchased the copyright to a trade manual for $75,000 on January 1, 198A. The copyright legally protects its owner for 25 more years. However, management believes the trade manual can be successfully published and sold for only five more years. Prepare journal entires to record (a) the purchase of the copyright and (b) annual amortization of the copyright on December 31, 198A.

Exercise 11-9

K. Jones has devoted years to building a profitable business that earns an attractive return. Now Jones is considering the possibility of selling the business and is attempting to estimate the value of goodwill in the business. The recorded net assets of the business (excluding goodwill) amount to $150,000, and in a typical year, net income amounts to $27,000. Most businesses of this type are expected to earn a return of about 12% on net assets. Calculate goodwill assuming (a) the amount of goodwill is estimated to be six times the portion of earnings that are above average, and (b) the amount of goodwill is estimated by capitalizing above-average earnings at a rate of 15%.

☐   **Problems**   **Problem 11-1**

The Crutchfield Company completed these transactions involving the purchase and operation of delivery trucks.

198A

June 28   Paid cash for a new truck, $22,800 plus $1,140 state and city sales taxes. The truck was estimated to have a four-year life and a $6,000 salvage value.

July   6   Paid $1,260 for special racks and cleats installed in the truck. The racks and cleats did not increase the truck's estimated trade-in value.

Dec. 31   Recorded straight-line depreciation on the truck.

198B

June 28   Paid $1,640 to install an air-conditioning unit in the truck. The unit increased the truck's estimated trade-in value $200.

Dec. 31   Recorded straight-line depreciation on the truck.

198C

Mar. 19   Paid $220 for repairs to the truck's fender damaged when the driver backed into a loading dock.

Dec. 31   Recorded straight-line depreciation on the truck.

198D

Aug. 30   Traded the old truck and $19,540 in cash for a new truck. The new truck was estimated to have a three-year life and a $6,400 trade-in value, and the invoice for the exchange showed these items:

Price of the truck	$24,800
Trade-in allowance granted . . .	(6,000)
Balance	$18,800
State and city sales taxes . . .	740
Balance paid in cash	$19,540

The loss on the exchange was considered to be material.

Sept. 2   Paid $2,460 for special cleats and racks installed in the truck.

Dec. 31   Recorded straight-line depreciation on the new truck.

Required

Prepare general journal entries to record the transactions.

Problem 11-2

A company completed the following transactions involving machinery:

Machine No. 244-60 was purchased on April 1, 198A, at an installed cost of $32,400. Its useful life was estimated at four years with a $3,600 trade-in value. Straight-line depreciation was recorded on the machine at the end of 198A and 198B, and on July 7, 198C, it was traded in on Machine No. 244-61. An $18,000 trade-in allowance was received, and the balance was paid in cash.

Machine No. 244-61 was purchased on July 7, 198C, at an installed cash price of $42,000, less the trade-in allowance received on Machine 244-60. The new machine's life was estimated at five years with a $4,200 trade-in value. Sum-of-the-years'-digits depreciation was recorded on each December 31 of its life, and on January 5, 198H, it was sold for $6,000.

Machine No. 244-70 was purchased on January 6, 198C, at an installed cost of $30,000. Its useful life was estimated at five years, after which it would have a $3,000 trade-in value. Declining-balance depreciation at twice the straight-line rate was recorded on the machine at the end of 198C, 198D, and 198E; and on January 2, 198F, it was traded on Machine No. 244-72. A $5,400 trade-in allowance was received, the balance was paid in cash, the loss was considered immaterial, and the income tax method was used to record the transaction.

Machine No. 244-72 was purchased on January 2, 198F, at an installed cash price of $35,400, less the trade-in allowance received on Machine No. 244-70. It was estimated the new machine would produce 50,000 units of product during its useful life, after which it would have a $3,600 trade-in value. Units-of-production depreciation was recorded on the machine for 198F, a period in which it produced 5,000 units of product. Between January 1 and October 2, 198G, the machine produced 7,500 more units, and on the latter date, it was sold for $24,000.

Required

Prepare general journal entries to record: (a) the purchase of each machine, (b) the depreciation recorded on the first December 31 of each machine's life, and (c) the disposal of each machine. Treat the entries for the first two machines as one series of transactions and those of the next two machines as an unrelated second series. Only one entry is needed to record the exchange of one machine for another.

Problem 11-3

Part 1. On January 9, 1978, a company purchased and placed in operation a machine estimated to have a 10-year life and no salvage value. The machine cost $90,000 and was depreciated on a straight-line basis. On January 2, 1982, a $3,600 device that increased its output by one fourth was added to the machine. The device did not change the machine's estimated life nor its zero salvage value. During the first week of January 1985, the machine was completely overhauled at a $27,000 cost (paid for on January 8). The overhaul added three additional years to the machine's estimated life but did not change its zero salvage value. On June 30, 1986, the machine was destroyed in a fire, and the insurance company settled the loss claim for $30,000.

Required

Prepare general journal entries to record: (a) the purchase of the machine, (b) the 1978 depreciation, (c) the addition of the new device, (d) the 1982 depreciation, (e) the machine's overhaul, (f) the 1985 depreciation, and (g) the insurance settlement.

Part 2. A company purchased Machine 1 at a $37,200 installed cost on January 1, 1980, and depreciated it on a straight-line basis at the end of 1980, 1981, 1982, and 1983 under the assumption it would have a 10-year life and a $7,200 salvage value. After more experience and before recording 1984 depreciation, the company revised its estimate of the machine's remaining years downward from six years to four and revised the estimate of its salvage value downward to $6,000. On April 1, 1986, after recording 1984, 1985, and part of a year's depreciation for 1986, the company traded in Machine 1 on Machine 2, receiving a $15,000 trade-in allowance. The cash paid for Machine 2 was $48,900 less the trade-in allowance. Machine 2 was depreciated on a straight-line basis on December 31, 1986, under the assumption it would have a six-year life and $6,900 salvage value.

Required

Prepare entries to record: *(a)* the purchase of Machine 1, *(b)* its 1980 depreciation, *(c)* its 1984 depreciation, *(d)* the exchange of the machines, and *(e)* the 1986 depreciation on Machine 2.

Problem 11-4

Part 1. Ten years ago, Home Products Company leased space in a building for a period of 20 years. The lease contract calls for $45,000 annual rental payments on each January 1 throughout the life of the lease and also provides that the lessee must pay for all additions and improvements to the leased property. Recent construction nearby has made the location more valuable; and on December 28, Home Products Company subleased the space to Hightec, Inc., for the remaining 10 years of the lease, beginning on the next January 1. Hightec, Inc., paid $100,000 for the privilege of subleasing the property and in addition agreed to assume and pay the building owner the $45,000 annual rental charges. After taking possession of the leased space, Hightec, Inc., paid for remodeling the office portion of the leased space at a cost of $140,000. The remodeled office portion is estimated to have a life equal to the remaining life of the building, 20 years, and was paid for on January 8.

Required

Prepare entries in general journal form to record: *(a)* Hightec, Inc.'s payment to sublease the building space, *(b)* its payment of the annual rental charge to the building owner, and *(c)* payment for the new office portion. Also, prepare the adjusting entries required at the end of the first year of the sublease to amortize *(d)* a proper share of the $100,000 cost of the sublease and *(e)* a proper share of the office remodeling cost.

Part 2. On April 7 of the current year, Extract Company paid $816,000 for mineral land estimated to contain 5,000,000 tons of recoverable ore. It installed machinery costing $144,000, having a 12-year life and no salvage value, and capable of exhausting the mine in 10 years. The machinery was paid for on June 28, three days before mining operations began. During the first six months' operations the company mined 206,250 tons of ore.

Required

Prepare entries to record *(a)* the purchase of the mineral land, *(b)* the installation of the machinery, *(c)* the first six months' depletion under the assumption that the land will be valueless after the ore is mined, and *(d)* the first six months' depreciation on the machinery.

Problem 11-5

Blake Company's balance sheet on December 31, 198A, is as follows:

Cash	$ 63,000
Merchandise inventory.	91,000
Buildings	280,000
Accumulated depreciation	(73,500)
Land	157,500
Total assets	$518,000
Accounts payable.	$ 42,000
Long-term note payable	108,500
Common stock	262,500
Retained earnings.	105,000
Total liabilities and owners' equity . . .	$518,000

In Blake Company's industry, earnings average 12% of common stockholders' equity. Blake Company, however, is expected to earn $73,500 annually. The owners of Blake Company believe that the balance sheet amounts are reasonable estimates of fair market values except for goodwill. In discussing a plan to sell the company, they argue that goodwill should be recognized by capitalizing the amount of earnings above average at a rate of 15%. On the other hand, the prospective purchaser argues that goodwill should be valued at five times the earnings above average.

Required

1. Calculate the amount of goodwill claimed by Blake Company's owners.
2. Calculate the amount of goodwill according to the purchaser.
3. Suppose the purchaser finally agrees to pay the full price requested by Blake Company's owners. If the expected earnings level is obtained and the goodwill is amortized over the longest permissible time period, what will be the net income for the first year after the company is purchased?
4. If the purchaser pays the full price requested by Blake Company's owners, what percentage of the purchaser's investment will be earned as net income the first year?

□ **Alternate Problems**   ### Problem 11-1A

The Brothers Company completed these transactions involving the purchase and operation of delivery vans.

198A
July   1   Paid cash for a new van, $18,240 plus $912 state and city sales taxes. The van was estimated to have a four-year life and a $4,800 salvage value.
        5   Paid $1,008 for special racks and bins installed in the van. The racks and bins did not increase the van's estimated trade-in value.
Dec. 31   Recorded straight-line depreciation on the van.

198B

June 25   Paid $1,312 to install an air-conditioning unit in the van. The
          unit increased the van's estimated trade-in value $160.
Dec. 31   Recorded straight-line depreciation on the van.

198C

May 13   Paid $190 for repairs to the van's fender damaged when the
          driver backed into a loading dock.
Dec. 31   Recorded straight-line depreciation on the van.

198D

Aug. 26   Traded the old van and $15,632 in cash for a truck. The truck
          was estimated to have a three-year life and a $5,120 trade-in
          value, and the invoice for the exchange showed these items:

Price of the truck	$19,840
Trade-in allowance granted . . .	(4,800)
Balance	$15,040
State and city sales taxes	592
Balance paid in cash	$15,632

          The loss on the exchange was considered to be material.
Sept. 1   Paid $1,968 for special cleats and racks installed in the truck.
Dec. 31   Recorded straight-line depreciation on the truck.

Required

Prepare general journal entries to record the transactions.

Problem 11-2A

Doggett Company completed the following transactions involving
machinery:

Machine No. 156-80 was purchased on April 1, 198A, at an installed
cost of $51,840. Its useful life was estimated at four years with a $5,760
trade-in value. Straight-line depreciation was recorded on the machine at
the end of 198A and 198B, and on July 2, 198C, it was traded on Machine
No. 156-81. A $28,800 trade-in allowance was received, and the balance
was paid in cash.

Machine No. 156-81 was purchased on July 2, 198C, at an installed
cash price of $67,200, less the trade-in allowance received on Machine
No. 156-80. The new machine's life was estimated at five years with a
$6,720 trade-in value. Sum-of-the-years'-digits depreciation was recorded
on each December 31 of its life, and on January 6, 198H, it was sold for
$9,600.

Machine No. 156-85 was purchased on January 8, 198C, at an installed
cost of $48,000. Its useful life was estimated at five years, after which it
would have a $4,800 trade-in value. Declining-balance depreciation at twice
the straight-line rate was recorded on the machine at the end of 198C,
198D, and 198E; and on January 1, 198F, it was traded on Machine No.
156-86. A $8,640 trade-in allowance was received, the balance was paid

in cash, the loss was considered immaterial, and the income tax method was used to record the transaction.

Machine No. 156-86 was purchased on January 1, 198F, at an installed cash price of $56,640, less the trade-in allowance received on Machine No. 156-85. It was estimated the new machine would produce 40,000 units of product during its useful life, after which it would have a $5,760 trade-in value. Units-of-production depreciation was recorded on the machine for 198F, a period in which it produced 4,000 units of product. Between January 1 and October 1, 198G, the machine produced 6,000 more units, and on the latter date it was sold for $38,400.

Required

Prepare general journal entries to record: *(a)* the purchase of each machine, *(b)* the depreciation recorded on the first December 31 of each machine's life, and *(c)* the disposal of each machine. Treat the entries for the first two machines as one series of transactions and those of the next two machines as an unrelated second series. Only one entry is needed to record the exchange of one machine for another.

Problem 11-3A

Part 1. On January 5, 1978, Mingle Company purchased a machine estimated to have a 10-year life and no salvage value. The machine cost $144,000 and was depreciated on a straight-line basis. On January 3, 1982, a $5,760 improvement was added to the machine which had the effect of increasing its output by one fourth. The improvement did not change the machine's estimated life or its zero salvage value. On January 7, 1985, the machine was completely overhauled at a $43,200 cost. The overhaul added three additional years to the machine's estimated life but did not change its zero salvage value. On June 29, 1986, the machine was destroyed in a fire, and the insurance company settled the loss claim for $48,000.

Required

Prepare general journal entries to record: *(a)* the purchase of the machine, *(b)* the 1978 depreciation, *(c)* the addition of the new improvement, *(d)* the 1982 depreciation, *(e)* the machine's overhaul, *(f)* the 1985 depreciation, and *(g)* the insurance settlement.

Part 2. A company purchased Machine 1 at a $93,000 installed cost on January 10, 1980, and depreciated it on a straight-line basis at the end of 1980, 1981, 1982, and 1983 under the assumption it would have a 10-year life and a $18,000 salvage value. After more experience and before recording 1984 depreciation, the company revised its estimate of the machine's remaining years downward from six years to four and revised the estimate of its salvage value downward to $15,000. On April 10, 1986, after recording 1984, 1985, and part of a year's depreciation for 1986, the company traded in Machine 1 on Machine 2, receiving a $37,500 trade-in allowance. The cash paid for Machine 2 was $122,250 less the trade-in allowance. Machine 2 was depreciated on a straight-line basis on

December 31, 1986, under the assumption it would have a six-year life and $17,250 salvage value.

Required

Prepare entries to record: *(a)* the purchase of Machine 1, *(b)* its 1980 depreciation, *(c)* its 1984 depreciation, *(d)* the exchange of the machines, and *(e)* the 1986 depreciation on Machine 2.

Problem 11-4A

Part 1. Five years ago, Georgetown Company leased space in a building for a period of 20 years. The lease contract calls for $54,000 annual rental payments on each January 1 throughout the life of the lease and also provides that the lessee must pay for all additions and improvements to the leased property. Recent construction nearby has made the location more valuable, and on December 30 Georgetown Company subleased the space to Burnet, Inc., for the remaining 15 years of the lease, beginning on the next January 1. Burnet, Inc., paid $240,000 for the privilege of subleasing the property and in addition agreed to assume and pay the building owner the $54,000 annual rental charges. After taking possession of the leased space, Burnet, Inc., paid for remodeling the retail display area of the leased space at a cost of $180,000. The remodeled retail display area is estimated to have a life equal to the remaining life of the building, 25 years, and was paid for on January 9.

Required

Prepare entries in general journal form to record: *(a)* Burnet, Inc.'s payment to sublease the building space, *(b)* its payment of the annual rental charge to the building owner, and *(c)* payment for the remodeling. Also, prepare the adjusting entries required at the end of the first year of the sublease to amortize *(d)* a proper share of the $240,000 cost of the sublease and *(e)* a proper share of the remodeling cost.

Part 2. On May 10 of the current year, Digger Company paid $720,000 for mineral land estimated to contain 6,000,000 tons of recoverable ore. It installed machinery costing $125,000, having an eight-year life and no salvage value, and capable of exhausting the mine in five years. The machinery was paid for on June 26, four days before mining operations began. During the first six months' operations, the company mined 480,000 tons of ore.

Required

Prepare entries to record *(a)* the purchase of the mineral land, *(b)* the installation of the machinery, *(c)* the first six months' depletion under the assumption that the land will be valueless after the ore is mined, and *(d)* the first six months' depreciation on the machinery.

Problem 11-5A

Garrett Company's balance sheet on December 31, 198A, is as follows:

Cash	$ 113,400
Merchandise inventory	163,800
Buildings	504,000
Accumulated depreciation	(132,300)
Land	283,500
Total assets	$ 932,400
Accounts payable	$ 75,600
Long-term note payable	196,800
Common stock	471,000
Retained earnings	189,000
Total liabilities and owner's equity . . .	$ 932,400

In Garrett Company's industry, earnings average 11% of common stockholders' equity. Garrett Company, however, is expected to earn $132,600 annually. The owners of Garrett Company believe that the balance sheet amounts are reasonable estimates of fair market values except for goodwill. In discussing a plan to sell the company, they argue that goodwill should be recognized by capitalizing the amount of earnings above average at a rate of 20%. On the other hand, the prospective purchaser argues that goodwill should be valued at four times the earnings above average.

Required

1. Calculate the amount of goodwill claimed by Garrett Company's owners.
2. Calculate the amount of goodwill according to the purchaser.
3. Suppose the purchaser finally agrees to pay the full price requested by Garrett Company's owners. If the expected earnings level is obtained and the goodwill is amortized over the longest permissible time period, what will be the net income for the first year after the company is purchased?
4. If the purchaser pays the full price requested by Garrett Company's owners, what percentage of the purchaser's investment will be earned as net income the first year?

Provocative Problems

Provocative Problem 11-1   Goof Company's Bad Accounting

While investigating the accounting records of Goof Company, you discover two entries during 1986 that appear questionable. The first entry recorded the cash proceeds from an insurance settlement as follows:

Oct.	14	Cash	34,000.00	
		Loss from Fire	14,000.00	
		Accumulated Depreciation, Machinery	36,000.00	
		Machinery		84,000.00
		Received payment of fire loss claim.		

Your investigation shows that this entry was intended to record the receipt of an insurance company's $34,000 check to settle a claim resulting from the destruction of a machine in a small plant fire on October 3, 1986. The machine originally cost $72,000 and was put in operation on January 8, 1982. It was depreciated on a straight-line basis for four years under the assumption it would have an eight-year life and no salvage value. During the first week of January 1986, the machine had been overhauled at a cost of $12,000. The overhaul did not increase the machine's capacity or its salvage value. However, it was expected that the overhaul would lengthen the machine's service life two years beyond the eight originally expected.

The second entry that appears questionable was intended to record the receipt of a check from selling a portion of a tract of land. The tract was adjacent to the company's plant and had been purchased the year before. It cost $80,000, and $7,500 was paid for clearing and grading it. Both amounts had been debited to the Factory Land account. The land was to be used for storing finished product; but after the grading was completed, it was obvious the company did not need the entire tract. Goof Company had received an offer from a purchaser who was willing to pay $45,000 for the east half or $60,000 for the west half. The company decided to sell the west half, and it recorded receipt of the purchaser's check with the following entry:

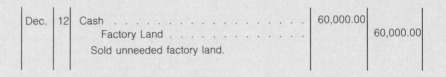

Dec.	12	Cash	60,000.00	
		Factory Land		60,000.00
		Sold unneeded factory land.		

Were any errors made in recording these transactions? If so, describe the errors and in each case give an entry or entries that will correct the account balances under the assumption the 1986 revenue and expense accounts have not been closed.

Provocative Problem 11-2 Comparing Apples and Oranges

Apple Company and Orange Company are similar businesses that sell competing products. Both companies began operations five years ago and are up for sale. Buyer Company is considering both Apple and Orange with the prospect of buying one of them.

In evaluating the two companies, the management of Buyer has observed that Apple Company has reported an average annual net income of $94,680. Orange Company, on the other hand, has reported an average of $114,000. However, the companies have not used the same accounting procedures, and Buyer Company management is concerned that the numbers are not comparable. The current balance sheets of the two companies show these items:

	Apple Company	Orange Company
Cash	$ 53,600	$ 65,600
Accounts receivable	412,800	468,000
Allowance for doubtful accounts	(25,600)	–0–
Merchandise inventory	570,400	688,800
Store equipment	230,400	204,800
Accumulated depreciation, store equipment . .	(192,000)	(128,000)
Total assets	$1,049,600	$1,299,200
Current liabilities	$ 499,200	$ 551,200
Owners' equity	550,400	748,000
Total liabilities and owners' equity	$1,049,600	$1,299,200

Apple Company has used the allowance method in accounting for bad debts and has added to its allowance each year an amount equal to 1% of sales. However, this seems excessive since an examination shows only $12,000 of its accounts that are probably uncollectible. Orange Company has used the direct write-off method but has been slow to write off bad debts. An examination of its accounts shows $24,000 of accounts that are probably uncollectible.

During the past five years, Apple Company has priced its inventories on a LIFO basis with the result that its current inventory appears on its balance sheet at an amount that is $96,000 below replacement cost. Orange Company has used FIFO, and its ending inventory appears at approximately its replacement cost.

Both companies have assumed eight-year lives and no salvage value in depreciating equipment; however, Apple Company has used sum-of-the-years'-digits depreciation, while Orange Company has used straight line. The management of Buyer Company is of the opinion that straight-line depreciation has resulted in Orange Company's equipment appearing on its balance sheet at approximately its fair market value and that straight line would have had the same result for Apple Company.

Buyer Company is willing to pay what its management considers fair market value for the assets of either business, not including cash but including goodwill measured at four times average annual earnings in excess of 15% on the fair market value of the net tangible assets. Buyer Company's management defines net tangible assets as all assets other than goodwill, including accounts receivable, minus liabilities. Buyer Company will also assume the liabilities of the purchased business, paying its owner the difference between total assets purchased and the liabilities assumed.

Required

Prepare the following schedules: (a) a schedule showing the net tangible assets of each company at their fair market values according to Buyer Company management, (b) a schedule showing the revised net incomes of the companies based on FIFO inventories and straight-line depreciation, (c) a schedule showing the calculation of each company's goodwill, and (d) a schedule showing the amount Buyer Company would pay for each business.

Provocative Problem 11-3   Metro Airlines, Inc.

Metro Airlines, Inc., with its two subsidiaries, Metroflight, Inc., and Metro Express, Inc., is one of the largest regional airlines in the United States. The company fleet of 27 aircraft serves 26 airports in eight southern states. The notes to the 1984 consolidated financial statements of Metro included the following comments regarding property and equipment:

Property and equipment, depreciation, and amortization:

Property and equipment are depreciated to residual values over their estimated service lives using the straight-line and declining-balance methods. Upon retirement or sale of property and equipment, the assets and reserve accounts are relieved of the cost and related accumulated depreciation, and the resulting gain or loss is recorded in income.

Maintenance:

Metroflight charges maintenance expense, on the basis of hours flown, for the estimated costs of Convair aircraft block overhauls. The provision rate per hour is adjusted periodically to reflect actual experience in hours between the block overhauls and in the costs of overhauls. The costs of block overhauls are charged to the reserve for block overhauls when incurred.

Required

1. If Metro uses both straight-line and declining-balance methods to depreciate property and equipment, isn't the company in violation of the consistency principle? Explain.
2. Are the maintenance expenses discussed in the footnote best classified as ordinary repairs or extraordinary repairs?
3. Metro's method of accounting for maintenance expense is different than the normal procedure as described in this chapter. Describe the difference.
4. Why do you think Metro accounts for maintenance expense in the manner described instead of following the procedure described in this chapter?

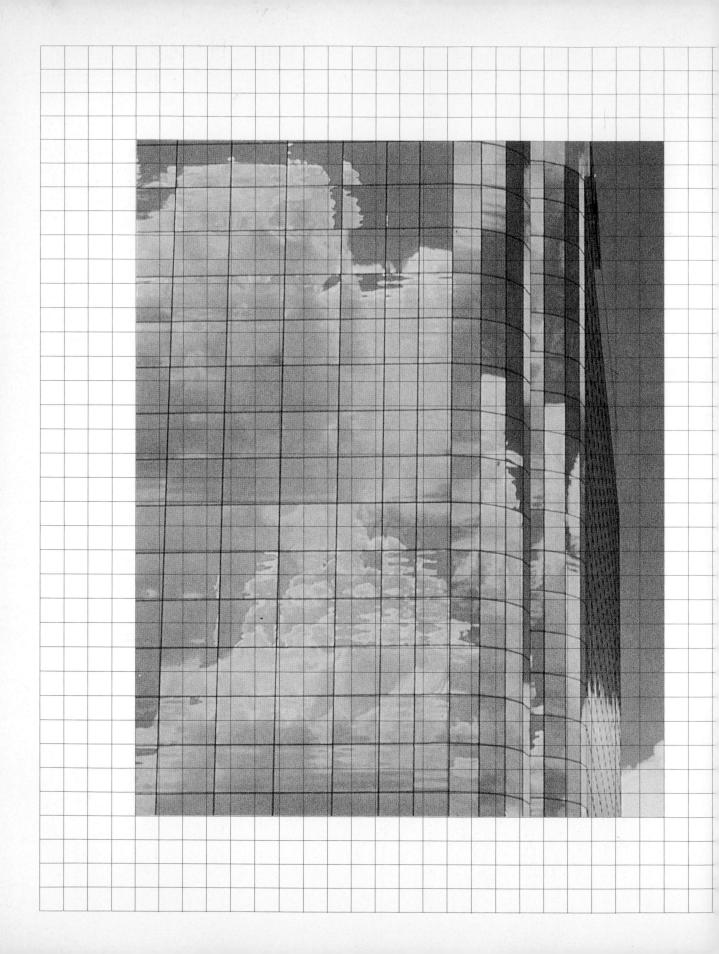

Part Four

Accounting for Equities: Liabilities and Partners' Equities

12   Current and Long-Term Liabilities

After studying Chapter 12, you should be able to:

1. Explain the difference between current and long-term liabilities.

2. Explain the meaning of definite and estimated liabilities.

3. Explain the difference between liabilities and contingent liabilities.

4. Record transactions involving liabilities such as property taxes payable, product warranties, and short-term notes payable.

5. Calculate the present value of a sum of money to be received a number of periods in the future or to be received periodically.

6. Account for long-term noninterest-bearing notes payable and for capital and operating leases.

7. Define or explain the words and phrases listed in the chapter Glossary.

Liabilities have been introduced in previous chapters as one of the three elements of the accounting equation (Assets = Liabilities + Owners' equity). Examples of liabilities that have been discussed include accounts payable, notes payable, wages payable, and unearned revenues.

Liabilities are examined more closely in this chapter, which explains how liabilities are defined, classified, and measured. Several types of liabilities are considered. They include property taxes payable, product warranties, single-payment notes payable, and leases. Contingent liabilities are also discussed. An important topic in this chapter is present value, which is a concept that is used in measuring many liabilities. Payroll liabilities are examined in Chapter 13, and in Chapter 17 installment notes payable and bonds payable are discussed.

■ The Definition and Classification of Liabilities

Liabilities are obligations that require the future payment of assets or performance of services. Not every expected future payment is a liability. To qualify as a liability, the obligation to make a future payment must have resulted from past transactions. Because liabilities result from past transactions, they normally are enforceable as legal claims against the enterprise.

Current and Long-Term Liabilities

Current Liabilities A business typically has several kinds of liabilities, which are classified as either current or long-term liabilities. **Current liabilities** are debts or other obligations the liquidation of which is expected to require the use of existing current assets or the creation of other current liabilities.[1] Current liabilities are due within one year of the balance sheet date or the operating cycle of the business, whichever is longer. Accounts payable, short-term notes payable, wages payable, dividends payable, product warranty liabilities, payroll and other taxes payable, and unearned revenues are common examples of current liabilities.

Long-Term Liabilities Obligations that will not require the use of existing current assets because they do not mature within one year (or one operating cycle, whichever is longer) are classifed as **long-term liabilities.** Examples of long-term liabilities include leases, long-term notes payable, product warranty liabilities, and bonds payable. Note that many liabilities may be either current or long term. The critical difference is the question of whether or not payment is to be made within one year or the current operating cycle of the business, whichever is longer.

Definite versus Estimated Liabilities

Three important questions concerning liabilities are: Who is to be paid? When is payment due? How much is to be paid? In many situations, the answers to these three questions are immediately determined at the time the liability is incurred. For example, an account payable may be for pre-

[1] FASB, *Accounting Standards—Current Text* (Stamford, Conn., 1984), sec. B05.402. First published as *Accounting Research Bulletin No. 43,* ch. 3A, par. 7.

cisely $100, payable to J. J. Dow, and due on August 15, 1988. This type of liability is definite with respect to all three questions.

When the Identity of the Creditor Is Uncertain Other types of liabilities may be indefinite with respect to one or more of the three questions. For example, in the case of dividends payable, the amount to be paid and the due date are definite. The question of who is to be paid, however, is not answerable until after the date of record. Even though the identity of the creditor may be uncertain, there is no doubt that the obligation is real and a liability should be recognized.

When the Due Date Is Uncertain An example of a liability with an uncertain due date is unearned legal fees that a lawyer accepts in return for the obligation to provide services to a client upon call. In this case, the amount of the liability is known. And the client for whom services are to be provided is also known. However, the question of when the services are to be performed is not definite. Usually, such arrangements are short-term and are classified as current liabilities.

When the Amount to Be Paid Is Uncertain When an obligation definitely exists but the amount to be paid is uncertain, the obligation is called an **estimated liability**. Two important examples of estimated liabilities are property taxes and product warranties.

■ Property Taxes Payable

A variety of governmental authorities such as counties, cities, and school districts levy taxes on property. However, the exact amount of the tax may not become known until the year is partially over. For example, the 198A tax to be paid on each item of property may not be fixed in amount until September 198A. And the tax may not be due perhaps until October 198A. Thus, if financial statements are prepared monthly, the tax expense must be estimated when statements are prepared for January through August.

For example, throughout 198B, a company owns property that has been assessed by the city as having a valuation of $400,000 for property tax purposes. The tax on the property during the previous year (198A) was $11,400. In preparing monthly financial statements during 198B, before the actual tax is known, the company estimates a monthly tax expense of $11,400/12 = $950. Until the 198B tax becomes definite, the company will make monthly adjusting entries as follows:

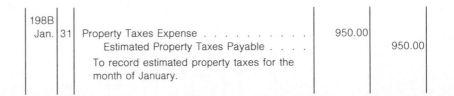

198B				
Jan.	31	Property Taxes Expense	950.00	
		Estimated Property Taxes Payable		950.00
		To record estimated property taxes for the month of January.		

In September 198B, the city announces that the tax levy for 198B will be $3 per $100 of assessed valuation. Now, the company calculates the actual 198B tax as (400,000/$100) × $3 = $12,000, which is $1,000 per month. For the first eight months (January through August), the estimated tax was less than the actual tax by $50 × 8 = $400. This may be recorded at the end of September along with the $1,000 monthly tax, as follows:

Sept.	31	Property Taxes Expense	1,400.00	
		Estimated Property Taxes Payable		1,400.00
		To record property taxes for the month of September and to correct for $50 estimate error during first eight months.		

When the annual tax is paid at the end of October 198B, the entry to record the payment is:

Oct.	31	Property Taxes Expense (Oct.)	1,000.00	
		Prepaid Property Taxes (Nov. and Dec.) . . .	2,000.00	
		Estimated Property Taxes Payable	9,000.00	
		Cash		12,000.00
		To pay property tax for 198B.		

■ **Product Warranty Liabilities**

Another example of an estimated liability is product warranty liability. Most companies provide warranties or guarantees for their products. A **product warranty** is a promise to the customer; the promise obligates the seller or manufacturer for a limited period of time to pay for items such as replacement parts or repair costs if the product breaks or fails to perform. For example, an automobile may be sold with a warranty that covers the mechanical parts for a period of one year or 12,000 miles, whichever comes first. The warranty may also include labor costs to install replacement parts.

When a product with a warranty is sold, the **matching principle** requires that all expenses to produce the sale be recorded in the same period as the sale. Therefore, the expense of the warranty must be recognized at the time of the sale. Since the exact amount of expense is not known at the time of the sale, the amount must be estimated based on past experience.

Consider the example of a used auto that is sold with a one-year or 12,000-mile warranty. The warranty covers mechanical parts, but the customer must pay for labor charges. Suppose the auto was sold on September 1, 198A, at a price of $16,000. Past experience shows that warranty expense runs 2% of the sales price. The entry to record the expense is:

Sept.	1	Warranty Expense	320.00	
		Estimated Warranty Liability		320.00
		$16,000 × 0.02 = $320.		

Now suppose the customer has a problem with the car and returns it for warranty repairs on January 9, 198B. The auto dealer performs the warranty work by replacing parts that cost $90 and charging the customer $110 for labor. The entry to record the warranty work and the customer's payment are as follows:

Jan.	9	Cash	110.00	
		Estimated Warranty Liability	90.00	
		Auto Parts Inventory		90.00
		Service Revenue		110.00
		To record warranty work and service revenue.		

What happens if the total warranty costs actually turn out to be different from the estimated $320 amount? On any given sale, some difference is very likely. Over the longer term, management must monitor warranty costs to be sure that 2% is the best estimate. When continued experience shows that warranty costs have changed, the percentage should be modified.

Contingent Liabilities

Contingent liabilities were discussed in Chapter 8 when discounted notes receivable were presented as an example of contingent liabilities. Contingent liabilities are not existing obligations and, therefore, are not recorded in the books as liabilities. However, the **full-disclosure principle** requires that contingent liabilities be disclosed in the financial statements or in footnotes.

What Distinguishes Liabilities from Contingent Liabilities?

Contingent liabilities become real liabilities only if some uncertain event takes place. For example, discounted notes receivable are contingent liabilities that become real liabilities only if the original signers of the notes fail to pay them.

Are product warranties a liability or contingent liability? A product warranty requires service or payment only if the product fails. That sounds like a contingent liability. However, the FASB has ruled that if a contingency is probable and if the liability can be reasonably estimated, it should be recorded in the books as a liability.[2] Most product warranties are real liabilities because the failure of some percentage of the products sold is probable and past experience allows a reasonable estimate of the amount of the liability.

What Are Other Examples of Contingent Liabilities?

Potential Legal Claims In today's legal environment, many companies may find themselves being sued for damages for a variety of reasons. Until such lawsuits are settled, the potential claims of the plaintiffs are contingent liabilities of the defendant.

Debt Guaranties Sometimes a company will guaranty the payment of a supplier, customer, or other company's debt, usually by cosigning the note

[2] Ibid., sec. C59.105. First published as *FASB Statement No. 5,* par. 8.

payable of the other company. When this is done, the guarantor is contingently liable for the debt of the other company.

■ **Short-Term Notes Payable**

Another current liability that requires further attention is short-term notes payable. Short-term notes payable sometimes arise in gaining an extension of time in which to pay an account payable. They frequently arise in borrowing from a bank.

Note Given to Secure a Time Extension on an Account

A note payable may be given to secure an extension of time in which to pay an account payable. For example, Brock Company cannot pay its past-due, $600 account with Ajax Company, and Ajax Company has agreed to accept Brock Company's 60-day, 12%, $600 note in granting an extension on the due date of the debt. Brock Company will record the issuance of the note as follows:

Aug.	23	Accounts Payable—Ajax Company	600.00	
		Notes Payable		600.00
		Gave a 60-day, 12% note to extend the due date on the amount owed.		

Observe that the note does not pay the debt. It merely changes it from an account payable to a note payable. Ajax Company should prefer the note to the account because in case of default and a lawsuit to collect, the note is written evidence of the debt and its amount.

When the note becomes due, Brock Company will give Ajax Company a check for $612 and record the payment of the note and its interest with an entry like this:

Oct.	22	Notes Payable	600.00	
		Interest Expense.	12.00	
		Cash		612.00
		Paid our note with interest.		

Borrowing from a Bank

In lending money, banks distinguish between **loans** and **discounts.** In case of a loan, the bank collects interest when the loan is repaid. In a **discount,** it deducts interest at the time the loan is made. To illustrate loans and discounts, assume that H. A. Green wishes to borrow approximately $2,000 for 60 days at the prevailing 15% rate of interest.

A Loan In a loan transaction, the bank will lend Green $2,000 in exchange for a signed promissory note. The note will read: "Sixty days after date I promise to pay $2,000 with interest at 15%." Green will record the transaction as follows:

Sept.	10	Cash	2,000.00	
		Notes Payable		2,000.00
		Gave the bank a 60-day, 15% note.		

When the note and interest are paid, Green makes this entry:

Nov.	9	Notes Payable	2,000.00	
		Interest Expense.	50.00	
		Cash		2,050.00
		Paid our 60-day, 15% note.		

Observe that in a loan transaction, the interest is paid at the time the loan is repaid.

A Discount If it is the practice of Green's bank to deduct interest at the time a loan is made, the bank will discount Green's $2,000 note. If it discounts the note at 15% for 60 days, it will deduct from the face amount of the note 60 days' interest at 15%, which is $50, and will give Green the difference, $1,950. The $50 of deducted interest is called **bank discount,** and the $1,950 are the **proceeds** of the discounted note. Green will record the transaction as follows:

Sept.	10	Cash	1,950.00	
		Interest Expense.	50.00	
		Notes Payable		2,000.00
		Discounted our $2,000 note payable at 15%.		

When the note matures, Green is required to pay the bank just the face amount of the note, $2,000, and Green will record the transaction like this:

Nov.	9	Notes Payable	2,000.00	
		Cash		2,000.00
		Paid our discounted note payable.		

Since interest is deducted in a discount transaction at the time the loan is made, the note used in such a transaction must state that only the principal amount is to be repaid at maturity. Such a note may read: "Sixty days after date I promise to pay $2,000 with no interest," and is commonly called a noninterest-bearing note. However, banks are not in business to lend money interest free. Interest is paid in a discount transaction. However, since it is deducted at the time the loan is made, the note must state that no additional interest is to be collected at maturity. Nevertheless, interest is collected in a discount transaction and at a rate slightly higher than in a loan transaction at the same stated interest rate. For example, in this instance, Green paid $50 for the use of $1,950 for 60 days, which was at an effective interest rate just a little in excess of 15% on the $1,950 received.

■ **End-of-Period Adjustments**

Accrued Interest Expense

Interest accrues daily on all interest-bearing notes. Consequently, if any notes payable are outstanding at the end of an accounting period, the accrued interest should be recorded. For example, a company gave its bank a $4,000, 60-day, 13.5% note on December 16 to borrow that amount of money. If the company's accounting period ends on December 31, by then 15 days' or $22.50 interest has accrued on this note. It may be recorded with this adjusting entry:

Dec.	31	Interest Expense	22.50	
		Interest Payable		22.50
		To record accrued interest on a note payable.		

The adjusting entry causes the $22.50 accrued interest to appear on the income statement as an expense of the period benefiting from 15 days' use of the money. It also causes the interest payable to appear on the balance sheet as a current liability.

When the note matures in the next accounting period, its payment may be recorded as follows:

Feb.	14	Notes Payable	4,000.00	
		Interest Payable	22.50	
		Interest Expense	67.50	
		Cash		4,090.00
		Paid a $4,000 note and its interest.		

Interest on this note for 60 days is $90. In the illustrated entry, the $90 is divided between the interest accrued at the end of the previous period, $22.50, and interest applicable to the current period, $67.50. Some accountants avoid the necessity of making this division by reversing the accrued interest adjusting entry as a last step in their end-of-period work.

Discount on Notes Payable

When a note payable is discounted at a bank, interest based on the principal of the note is deducted, and the interest is normally recorded as interest expense. Furthermore, since most such notes run for 30, 60, or 90 days, the interest is usually an expense of the period in which it is deducted. However, when the time of a note extends beyond a single accounting period, an adjusting entry is required. For example, on December 11, 198A, a company discounted at 15% its own $6,000, 60-day, noninterest-bearing note payable. It recorded the transaction as follows:

198A					
Dec.	11	Cash	5,850.00		
		Interest Expense	150.00		
		Notes Payable			6,000.00
		Discounted our noninterest-bearing, 60-day note at 15%.			

If this company operates with accounting periods that end each December 31, 20 days' interest on this note, or $50 of the $150 discount, is an expense of the 198A accounting period and 40 days' interest or $100 is an expense of 198B. Consequently, if revenues and expenses are matched, the company must make the following December 31, 198A, adjusting entry:

198A				
Dec.	31	Discount on Notes Payable	100.00	
		Interest Expense		100.00
		To set up as a contra liability the interest applicable to 198B.		

The adjusting entry removes from the Interest Expense account the $100 of interest that is applicable to 198B. It leaves in the account the $50 that is an expense of 198A. The $50 then appears on the 198A income statement as an expense, and the $100 appears on the December 31, 198A, balance sheet. If this is the only note the company has outstanding, the $100 is deducted on the balance sheet as follows:

Current liabilities:		
Notes payable	$6,000	
Less discount on notes payable . .	100	$5,900

When the adjusted discount on notes payable is subtracted as a contra liability, the net liability on the balance sheet shows the amount received in discounting the note plus the accrued interest on the note to the balance sheet date. In this example, $5,850 was received in discounting the note, and accrued interest on the note is $50. Together they total $5,900, which is the net liability to the bank on December 31.

Reversing Entries

The $100 interest set out as discount on notes payable in the previous paragraphs becomes an expense early in 198B. Consequently, sooner or later it must be taken from the Discount on Notes Payable account and returned to the Interest Expense account. Accountants commonly make this return with a **reversing entry.** The entry is made as the last step in the end-of-period work and is dated the first day of the new accounting period. Such a reversing entry appears as follows:

198B						
Jan.	1	Interest Expense			100.00	
		Discount on Notes Payable				100.00
		To reverse the adjusting entry that set out discount on notes payable.				

Observe that the reversing entry is debit for credit and credit for debit, the reverse of the adjusting entry it reverses. That is where it gets its name. Also, observe that it returns the $100 interest to the expense account so that it will appear on the 198B income statement as an expense without further ado.

The Concept of Present Value

The concept of present value enters into many financing and investing decisions and any resulting liabilities. Consequently, an understanding of present value is important for all students of business. The concept is based on the idea that the right to receive, say, $1 a year from today is worth somewhat less than $1 today. Or stated another way, $1 to be received a year hence has a **present value** of somewhat less than $1. How much less depends on how much can be earned on invested funds. If, say, a 10% annual return can be earned, the expectation of receiving $1 a year hence has a present value of $0.9091. This can be verified as follows: $0.9091 invested today to earn 10% annually will earn $0.09091 in one year, and when the $0.09091 earned is added to the $0.9091 invested—

Investment . .	$0.9091
Earnings . . .	0.09091
Total	$1.00001

the investment plus the earnings equal $1.00001, which rounds to the $1 expected.

Likewise, the present value of $1 to be received two years hence is $0.8264 if a 10% compound annual return is expected. This also can be verified as follows: $0.8264 invested to earn 10% compounded annually will earn $0.08264 the first year it is invested, and when the $0.08264 earned is added to the $0.8264 invested—

Investment	$0.8264
First year earnings	0.08264
End-of-year-1 amount . .	$0.90904

the investment plus the first year's earnings total $0.90904. And during the second year, this $0.90904 will earn $0.090904, which when added to the end-of-year-1 amount—

End-of-year-1 amount . .	$0.90904
Second year earnings . .	0.090904
End-of-year-2 amount . .	$0.999944

equals $0.999944, which rounds to the $1 expected at the end of the second year.

Present Value Tables

The **present value** of $1 to be received any number of years in the future can be calculated by using the formula, $1/(1+i)^n$. The i is the interest rate, and n is the number of years to the expected receipt. However, the formula need not be used, since tables showing present values computed with the formula at various interest rates are readily available. Table 12-1, with its amounts rounded to four decimal places, is such a table. (Four decimal places would not be sufficiently accurate for some uses but will suffice here.)

Observe in Table 12-1 that the first amount in the 10% column is the 0.9091 used in the previous section to introduce the concept of present value. The 0.9091 in the 10% column means that the expectation of receiving $1 a year hence when discounted for one period, in this case one year, at 10%, has a present value of $0.9091. Then, note that the second amount in the 10% column is the 0.8264 previously used, which means

Table 12-1		Present Value of $1 at Compound Interest								
Periods Hence	**4½%**	**5%**	**6%**	**7%**	**8%**	**9%**	**10%**	**12%**	**14%**	**16%**
1	0.9569	0.9524	0.9434	0.9346	0.9259	0.9174	0.9091	0.8929	0.8772	0.8621
2	0.9157	0.9070	0.8900	0.8734	0.8573	0.8417	0.8264	0.7972	0.7695	0.7432
3	0.8763	0.8638	0.8396	0.8163	0.7938	0.7722	0.7513	0.7118	0.6750	0.6407
4	0.8386	0.8227	0.7921	0.7629	0.7350	0.7084	0.6830	0.6355	0.5921	0.5523
5	0.8025	0.7835	0.7473	0.7130	0.6806	0.6499	0.6209	0.5674	0.5194	0.4761
6	0.7679	0.7462	0.7050	0.6663	0.6302	0.5963	0.5645	0.5066	0.4556	0.4104
7	0.7348	0.7107	0.6651	0.6228	0.5835	0.5470	0.5132	0.4524	0.3996	0.3538
8	0.7032	0.6768	0.6274	0.5820	0.5403	0.5019	0.4665	0.4039	0.3506	0.3050
9	0.6729	0.6446	0.5919	0.5439	0.5003	0.4604	0.4241	0.3606	0.3075	0.2630
10	0.6439	0.6139	0.5584	0.5084	0.4632	0.4224	0.3855	0.3220	0.2697	0.2267
11	0.6162	0.5847	0.5268	0.4751	0.4289	0.3875	0.3505	0.2875	0.2366	0.1954
12	0.5897	0.5568	0.4970	0.4440	0.3971	0.3555	0.3186	0.2567	0.2076	0.1685
13	0.5643	0.5303	0.4688	0.4150	0.3677	0.3262	0.2897	0.2292	0.1821	0.1452
14	0.5400	0.5051	0.4423	0.3878	0.3405	0.2993	0.2633	0.2046	0.1597	0.1252
15	0.5167	0.4810	0.4173	0.3625	0.3152	0.2745	0.2394	0.1827	0.1401	0.1079
16	0.4945	0.4581	0.3937	0.3387	0.2919	0.2519	0.2176	0.1631	0.1229	0.0930
17	0.4732	0.4363	0.3714	0.3166	0.2703	0.2311	0.1978	0.1456	0.1078	0.0802
18	0.4528	0.4155	0.3503	0.2959	0.2503	0.2120	0.1799	0.1300	0.0946	0.0691
19	0.4333	0.3957	0.3305	0.2765	0.2317	0.1945	0.1635	0.1161	0.0830	0.0596
20	0.4146	0.3769	0.3118	0.2584	0.2146	0.1784	0.1486	0.1037	0.0728	0.0514

that the expectation of receiving $1 two years hence, discounted at 10%, has a present value of $0.8264.

Using a Present Value Table

To demonstrate the use of the **present value table,** Table 12-1, assume that a company has an opportunity to invest $55,000 in a project, the risks of which it feels justify a 12% compound return. The investment will return $20,000 at the end of the first year, $25,000 at the end of the second year, $30,000 at the end of the third year, and nothing thereafter. Will the project return the original investment plus the 12% demanded? The calculations of Illustration 12-1, which use the first three amounts in the 12% column of the Table 12-1, indicate that it will. In Illustration 12-1, the expected returns in the second column are multiplied by the present value amounts in the third column to determine the present values in the last column. Since the total of the present values exceeds the required investment by $4,142, the project will return the $55,000 investment, plus a 12% return thereon, and $4,142 extra.

In Illustration 12-1, the present value of each year's return was separately calculated, after which the present values were added to determine their total. Separately calculating the present value of each of several returns from an investment is necessary when the returns are unequal, as in this example. However, in cases where the periodic returns are equal, there are shorter ways of calculating the sum of their present values. For instance, suppose a $17,500 investment will return $5,000 at the end of each year in its five-year life and an investor wants to know the present value of these returns, discounted at 12%. In this case, the periodic returns are equal, and a short way to determine their total present value at 12% is to add the present values of $1 at 12% for periods 1 through 5 (from Table 12-1) as follows—

0.8929
0.7972
0.7118
0.6355
0.5674
3.6048

Illustration 12-1

Years Hence	Expected Returns	Present Value of $1 at 12%	Present Value of Expected Returns
1	$20,000	0.8929	$17,858
2	25,000	0.7972	19,930
3	30,000	0.7118	21,354
Total present value of the returns			$59,142
Less investment required			55,000
Excess over 12% demanded			$ 4,142

and then to multiply $5,000 by the total. The $18,024 result ($5,000 × 3.6048 = $18,024) is the same as would be obtained by calculating the present value of each year's return and adding the present values. However, although the result is the same either way, the method demonstrated here requires four fewer multiplications.

Present Value of $1 Received Periodically for a Number of Periods

Table 12-2 is based on the idea demonstrated in the previous paragraph. To summarize, the present value of a series of equal returns to be received at periodic intervals is nothing more than the sum of the present values of the individual returns. Note the amount on the table's fifth line in the 12% column. It is the same 3.6048 amount arrived at in the previous section by adding the first five present values of $1 at 12%. All the amounts shown in Table 12-2 could be arrived at by adding amounts found in Table 12-1. However, there would be some slight variations due to rounding.

When available, Table 12-2 is used to determine the present value of a series of equal amounts to be received at periodic intervals. For example, what is the present value of a series of ten $1,000 amounts, with one $1,000 amount to be received at the end of each of 10 successive years, discounted at 8%? To determine the answer, go down the 8% column to the amount opposite 10 periods (years in this case). It is 6.7101, and $6.7101 is the present value of $1 to be received annually at the end of each of 10 years, discounted at 8%. Therefore, the present value of the ten $1,000 amounts is 1,000 × $6.7101, or $6,710.10.

Table 12-2		Present Value of $1 Received Periodically for a Number of Periods									

Periods Hence	4½%	5%	6%	7%	8%	9%	10%	12%	14%	16%
1	0.9569	0.9524	0.9434	0.9346	0.9259	0.9174	0.9091	0.8929	0.8772	0.8621
2	1.8727	1.8594	1.8334	1.8080	1.7833	1.7591	1.7355	1.6901	1.6467	1.6052
3	2.7490	2.7232	2.6730	2.6243	2.5771	2.5313	2.4869	2.4018	2.3216	2.2459
4	3.5875	3.5460	3.4651	3.3872	3.3121	3.2397	3.1699	3.0374	2.9137	2.7982
5	4.3900	4.3295	4.2124	4.1002	3.9927	3.8897	3.7908	3.6048	3.4331	3.2743
6	5.1579	5.0757	4.9173	4.7665	4.6229	4.4859	4.3553	4.1114	3.8887	3.6847
7	5.8927	5.7864	5.5824	5.3893	5.2064	5.0330	4.8684	4.5638	4.2883	4.0386
8	6.5959	6.4632	6.2098	5.9713	5.7466	5.5348	5.3349	4.9676	4.6389	4.3436
9	7.2688	7.1078	6.8017	6.5152	6.2469	5.9953	5.7590	5.3283	4.9464	4.6065
10	7.9127	7.7217	7.3601	7.0236	6.7101	6.4177	6.1446	5.6502	5.2161	4.8332
11	8.5289	8.3064	7.8869	7.4987	7.1390	6.8052	6.4951	5.9377	5.4527	5.0286
12	9.1186	8.8633	8.3838	7.9427	7.5361	7.1607	6.8137	6.1944	5.6603	5.1971
13	9.6829	9.3936	8.8527	8.3577	7.9038	7.4869	7.1034	6.4236	5.8424	5.3423
14	10.2228	9.8986	9.2950	8.7455	8.2442	7.7862	7.3667	6.6282	6.0021	5.4675
15	10.7395	10.3797	9.7123	9.1079	8.5595	8.0607	7.6061	6.8109	6.1422	5.5755
16	11.2340	10.8378	10.1059	9.4467	8.8514	8.3126	7.8237	6.9740	6.2651	5.6685
17	11.7072	11.2741	10.4773	9.7632	9.1216	8.5436	8.0216	7.1196	6.3729	5.7487
18	12.1600	11.6896	10.8276	10.0591	9.3719	8.7556	8.2014	7.2497	6.4674	5.8179
19	12.5933	12.0853	11.1581	10.3356	9.6036	8.9501	8.3649	7.3658	6.5504	5.8775
20	13.0079	12.4622	11.4699	10.5940	9.8182	9.1286	8.5136	7.4694	6.6231	5.9288

■ **Discount Periods Less than a Year in Length**

In the examples thus far, the discount periods have been measured in intervals one year in length. Often discount periods are based on intervals shorter than a year. For instance, although interest rates on corporation bonds are usually quoted on an annual basis, the interest on such bonds is normally paid semiannually. As a result, the present value of the interest to be received on such bonds must be based on interest periods six months in length.

To illustrate a calculation based on six-month interest periods, assume an investor wants to know the present value of the interest that will be received over a period of five years on some corporation bonds. The bonds have a $10,000 par value, and interest is paid on them every six months at a 14% annual rate. Although the interest rate is stated as an annual rate of 14%, it is actually a rate of 7% per six-month interest period. Consequently, the investor will receive $10,000 × 7% or $700 in interest on these bonds at the end of each six-month interest period. In five years, there are 10 such periods. Therefore, if these 10 receipts of $700 each are to be discounted at the interest rate of the bonds, to determine their present value, go down the 7% column of Table 12-2 to the amount opposite 10 periods. It is 7.0236, and the present value of the ten $700 semiannual receipts is 7.0236 × $700, or $4,916.52.

Students who want a more complete exposure to discounting should turn to Appendix A at the end of the book. Appendix A expands the discussion of how present value tables are developed and explains the development of future value tables. Large present value and future value tables are included in the Appendix, which closes with numerous exercises related to discounting.

■ **Exchanging a Note for a Plant Asset**

When a relatively high-cost plant asset is purchased, particularly if the credit period is long, a note is sometimes given in exchange for the purchased asset. If the amount of the note is approximately equal to the cash price for the asset and the interest on the note is at approximately the prevailing rate, the transaction is recorded as follows:

Feb.	12	Store Equipment	4,500.00	
		Notes Payable		4,500.00
		Exchanged a $4,500, three-year, 16% note payable for a refrigerated display case.		

A note given in exchange for a plant asset has two elements, which may or may not be stipulated in the note. They are (1) a dollar amount equivalent to the bargained cash price of the asset and (2) an interest factor to compensate the supplier for the use of the funds that otherwise would have been received in a cash sale. Consequently, when a note is exchanged for a plant asset and the face amount of the note approximately equals the cash price of the asset and the note's interest rate is at or near the prevailing rate, the asset may be recorded at the face amount of the note as in the previous illustration.

■ Notes that Have an Unreasonable or No Stated Interest Rate

Sometimes no interest rate is stated on a note, or the interest rate is unreasonable, or the face amount of the note materially differs from the cash price for the asset. In such cases, the asset should be recorded at its cash price or at the present value of the note, whichever is more clearly determinable.[3] In such a situation, to record the asset at the face amount of the note would cause the asset, the liability, and interest expense to be misstated. Furthermore, the misstatements could be material in case of a long-term note.

To illustrate a situation in which a note having no interest rate stated is exchanged for a plant asset, assume that on January 2, 198A, a noninterest-bearing, five-year, $10,000 note payable is exchanged for a factory machine, the cash price of which is not readily determinable. If the prevailing rate for interest on the day of the exchange is 14%, the present value of the note on that day is $5,194 [based on the fifth amount in the 14% column of Table 12-1 ($10,000 × 0.5194 = $5,194)], and the exchange should be recorded as follows:

198A					
Jan.	2	Factory Machinery.	5,194.00	
		Discount on Notes Payable	4,806.00	
		Long-Term Notes Payable		10,000.00
		Exchanged a five-year, noninterest-bearing note for a machine.		

The $5,194 debit amount in the entry is the present value of the note on the day of the exchange. It is also the cost of the machine and is the amount to be used in calculating depreciation and any future loss or gain on the machine's sale or exchange. The entry's notes payable and discount amounts together measure the liability resulting from the transaction. They should appear on a balance sheet prepared immediately after the exchange as follows:

Long-term liabilities:		
Long-term notes payable	$10,000	
Less unamortized discount based on the 14% interest rate prevailing on the date of issue	4,806	$5,194

Amortizing the Discount on a Note Payable

The $4,806 discount is a contra liability and also the interest element of the transaction. Column 3 of Illustration 12-2 shows the portions of the $4,806 that should be amortized and charged to Interest Expense at the end of each of the five years in the life of the note.

[3] Ibid., sec. 169.105. First published as *APB Opinion No. 21*, par. 12.

Illustration 12-2

Year	Beginning-of-Year Carrying Amount	Discount to Be Amortized Each Year	Unamortized Discount at the End of Year	End-of-Year Carrying Amount
198A	$5,194	$ 727	$4,079	$ 5,921
198B	5,921	829	3,250	6,750
198C	6,750	945	2,305	7,695
198D	7,695	1,077	1,228	8,772
198E	8,772	1,228	–0–	10,000

The first year's amortization entry is:

198A					
Dec.	31	Interest Expense		727.00	
		Discount on Notes Payable			727.00
		To amortize a portion of the discount on our long-term note.			

The $727 amortized is interest at 14% on the note's $5,194 value on the day it was exchanged for the machine. [The $727 is rounded to the nearest full dollar, as are all the Column 3 amounts ($5,194 × 14% = $727.16).]

Posting the amortization entry causes the note to appear on the December 31, 198A, balance sheet as follows:

Long-term liabilities:		
Long-term notes payable	$10,000	
Less unamortized discount based on the 14% interest rate prevailing on the date of issue	4,079	$5,921

Compare the net amount at which the note is carried on the December 31, 198A, balance sheet with the net amount shown for the note on the balance sheet prepared on its date of issue. Observe that the **carrying amount of the note** increased $727 between the two dates. The $727 is the amount of discount amortized and charged to Interest Expense at the end of 198A.

At the end of 198B and each succeeding year, the remaining amounts of discount shown in Column 3 of Illustration 12-2 should be amortized and charged to Interest Expense. This will cause the carrying amount of the note to increase each year by the amount of discount amortized that year and to reach $10,000, the note's maturity value, at the end of the fifth year. Payment of the note may then be recorded as follows:

198F					
Jan.	2	Long-Term Notes Payable		10,000.00	
		Cash			10,000.00
		Paid our long-term noninterest-bearing note.			

35010

Now return to Illustration 12-2. Each end-of-year carrying amount in the last column is determined by subtracting the end-of-year unamortized discount from the $10,000 face amount of the note. For example, $10,000 − $4,079 = $5,921. Each beginning-of-year carrying amount is the same as the previous year's end-of-year amount. The amount of discount to be amortized each year is determined by multiplying the beginning-of-year carrying amount by the 14% interest rate prevailing at the time of the exchange. For example, $5,921 × 14% = $829 (rounded). Each end-of-year amount of unamortized discount is the discount remaining after subtracting the discount amortized that year. For example, $4,806 − $727 = $4,079.

In the balance sheet at the end of each year, the carrying amount of a note payable must be divided into two parts. The portion to be paid during the next year must be shown as a current liability, with the remaining portion shown as a long-term liability.

64990

Liabilities from Leasing

How to Classify Leases

The leasing of plant assets, rather than purchasing them, has increased tremendously in recent years, primarily because leasing does not require a large cash outflow at the time the assets are acquired. Leasing has been called off-balance sheet financing because assets leased under certain conditions do not appear on the balance sheet of the lessee. However, some leases have essentially the same economic consequences as if the lessee secured a loan and purchased the leased asset. Such leases are called **capital leases** or **financing leases**. The FASB ruled that a lease meeting any one of the following criteria is a capital lease.[4]

1. Ownership of the leased asset is transferred to the lessee at the end of the lease period.
2. The lease gives the lessee the option of purchasing the leased asset at less than fair value at some point during or at the end of the lease period.
3. The period of the lease is 75% or more of the estimated service life of the leased asset.
4. The present value of the minimum lease payments is 90% or more of the fair value of the leased asset.

A lease that does not meet any one of the four criteria is classifed as an **operating lease.**

To illustrate accounting for leases, assume that Alpha Company plans to produce a product requiring the use of a new machine costing approximately $35,000 and having an estimated 10-year life and no salvage value. Alpha Company does not have $35,000 in available cash and is planning to lease the machine as of December 31, 198A. It will lease the machine under one of the following contracts, each of which requires Alpha Company to pay maintenance, taxes, and insurance on the machine: (1) lease the machine for five years, annual payments of $7,500 payable at the end

[4] Ibid., sec. L10.103. First published as *FASB Statement No. 13*, par. 7. Copyright © by the Financial Accounting Standards Board, High Ridge Park, Stamford, Conn. 06905, U.S.A. Quoted (or excerpted) with permission. Copies of the complete document are available from the FASB.

of each of the five years, the machine to be returned to the lessor at the end of the lease period; (2) lease the machine for five years, annual payments of $10,000 payable at the end of each of the five years, the machine to become the property of Alpha Company at the end of the lease period.

Accounting for an Operating Lease

If the interest rate available to Alpha Company is 16%, the first lease contract does not meet any of the four criteria of the FASB. Therefore, it is an operating lease. If Alpha Company chooses this contract, it should make no entry to record the lease contract. However, each annual rental payment should be recorded as follows:

198B Dec.	31	Machinery Rentals Expense.	7,500.00	
		Cash		7,500.00
		Paid the annual rent on a leased machine.		

Alpha Company should also charge to expense all payments for taxes, insurance, and any repairs to the machine. But since the leased machine was not recorded as an asset, depreciation expense is not recorded. Alpha should also append a footnote to its income statement giving a general description of the leasing arrangements.

Accounting for a Capital Lease

The second lease contract meets the first and fourth criteria of the FASB and is a capital lease. It is in effect a purchase transaction with the lessor company financing the purchase of the machine for Alpha Company. To charge each of the $10,000 lease payments to an expense account would overstate expenses during the first five years of the machine's life and understate expenses during the last five. It would also understate the company's assets and liabilities. Consequently, the FASB ruled that such a lease should be treated as a purchase transaction and be recorded on the lease date at the present value of the lease payments.

Recording the Lease Liability If Alpha Company chooses the second lease contract and the interest rate available to Alpha on such contracts is 16% annually, it should (based on the fifth amount in the 16% column of Table 12-2) multiply $10,000 by 3.2743 to arrive at a $32,743 present value for the five lease payments. It should then make this entry:

198A Dec.	31	Machinery	32,743.00	
		Discount on Lease Financing	17,257.00	
		Long-Term Lease Liability.		50,000.00
		Purchased a machine through a long-term lease contract.		

The $32,743 is the cost of the machine. As with any plant asset, it should be charged off to depreciation expense over the machine's expected service life. Note, however, that the expected service life of a leased asset may be limited to the term of the lease. If the lessee does not have the right to ownership at the end of the lease and the lease period is less than the asset's expected life, the lease period becomes the useful life of the asset.

Reporting a Long-Term Lease Liability on the Balance Sheet The $17,257 discount is the interest factor in the transaction. The long-term lease liability less the amount of the discount measures the net liability resulting from the purchase. The two items should appear on a balance sheet prepared immediately after the transaction as follows:

Long-term liabilities:		
Long-term lease liability[5]	$50,000	
Less unamortized discount based on the 16% interest		
rate available on the date of the contract	17,257	$32,743

Entries to Record Depreciation, Lease Payments, and Interest If Alpha Company plans to depreciate the machine on a straight-line basis over its 10-year life, it should make the following entries at the end of the first year in the life of the lease:

198B				
Dec.	31	Depreciation Expense, Machinery	3,274.30	
		Accumulated Depreciation, Machinery . .		3,274.30
		To record depreciation on the machine.		
	31	Long-Term Lease Liability.	10,000.00	
		Cash		10,000.00
		Made the annual payment on the lease.		
	31	Interest Expense	5,239.00	
		Discount on Lease Financing		5,239.00
		Amortized a portion of the discount on the lease financing.		

The first two entries need no comment. The $5,239 amortized in the third entry is interest at 16% for one year on the $32,743 beginning-of-year carrying amount of the lease liability ($32,743 × 16% = $5,239). The $5,239 is rounded to the nearest full dollar, as are all amounts in Column 5 of Illustration 12-3.

[5] To simplify the illustration, the fact that the first installment on the lease should probably be classified as a current liability is ignored here and should be ignored in the problems at the end of the chapter.

Illustration 12-3

Year	Beginning-of-Year Lease Liability	Beginning-of-Year Unamortized Discount	Beginning-of-Year Carrying Amount	Discount to Be Amortized	Unamortized Discount at End of Year	End-of-Year Lease Liability	End-of-Year Carrying Amount
198B . . .	$50,000	$17,257	$32,743	$5,239	$12,018	$40,000	$27,982
198C . . .	40,000	12,018	27,982	4,477	7,541	30,000	22,459
198D . . .	30,000	7,541	22,459	3,593	3,948	20,000	16,052
198E . . .	20,000	3,948	16,052	2,568	1,380	10,000	8,620
198F . . .	10,000	1,380	8,620	1,380*	–0–	–0–	–0–

* Adjusted for rounding.

Posting the entries recording the $10,000 payment and the amortization of the discount causes the **carrying amount of the lease** to appear on the December 31, 198B, balance sheet as follows:

Long-term liabilities:		
Long-term lease liability.	$40,000	
Less unamortized discount based on the 16% interest rate prevailing on the date of the contract	12,018	$27,982

At the end of 198C and each succeeding year thereafter, the remaining amounts in Column 5 of Illustration 12-3 should be amortized. This, together with $10,000 annual payments, will reduce the carrying amount of the lease liability to zero by the end of the fifth year.

Return again to Illustration 12-3, Column 5. Each year's amount of discount to be amortized is determined by multiplying the beginning-of-year carrying amount of the lease liability by 16%. For example, the 198C amount to be amortized is $4,477 ($27,982 × 16% = $4,477 rounded). Likewise, each end-of-year carrying amount is determined by subtracting the end-of-year unamortized discount from the remaining end-of-year lease liability. For example, the December 31, 198C, carrying amount is $30,000 − $7,541 = $22,459.

☐   **Glossary**   **Bank discount** interest charged and deducted by a bank at the time a loan is made.

Capital lease a lease having essentially the same economic consequences as if the lessee had secured a loan and purchased the leased asset.

Carrying amount of a lease the remaining lease liability minus the unamortized discount on the lease financing.

Carrying amount of a note the face amount of a note minus the unamortized discount on the note.

Estimated liability an obligation that definitely exists but for which the amount to be paid is uncertain.

Financing lease another name for a capital lease.

Long-term liabilities debts or obligations that will not require the use of existing current assets in their liquidation because they do not mature within one year or one operating cycle, whichever is longer.

Operating lease a lease not meeting any one of the criteria of the FASB that would make it a capital lease.

Present value the estimated worth today of an amount of money to be received at a future date.

Present value table a table showing the present values of one amount to be received at various future dates when discounted at various interest rates.

Product warranty a promise to a customer that obligates the seller or manufacturer for a limited period of time to pay for items such as replacement parts or repair costs if the product breaks or fails to perform.

☐   **Question for Class Discussion**

1. What is a liability?
2. Are all expected future payments liabilities?
3. Define (a) a current liability and (b) a long-term liability.
4. There are three important questions about which a liability may or may not be definite. What are those questions?
5. What is the nature of an estimated liability?
6. If a property tax liability is estimated at the end of year 1 and the actual payment of the liability in year 2 turns out to be more than the amount that was estimated, how is the excess accounted for in year 2?
7. Why are product warranties often recorded as liabilities instead of being disclosed as contingent liabilities?
8. The legal position of a company may be improved by its acceptance of a promissory note in exchange for granting a time extension on the due date of a customer's debt. Why?
9. What distinction do banks make between loans and discounts?
10. Which is to the advantage of a bank: (a) making a loan to a customer in exchange for the customer's $1,000, 60-day, 9% note, or (b) making a loan to the customer by discounting the customer's $1,000 noninterest-bearing note for 60 days at 9%? Why?
11. Distinguish between bank discount and cash discount.

12. What determines the present value of $1,000 to be received at some future date?

13. If a $5,000 noninterest-bearing, five-year note is exchanged for a machine, the face amount of the note equals the sum of two different economic costs. What are these two costs?

14. If the Machinery account is debited for $5,000 and Notes Payable is credited for $5,000 in recording the machine of Question 13, what effects will this have on the financial statements?

15. What is the advantage of leasing a plant asset instead of purchasing it?

16. Distinguish between a capital lease and an operating lease. Which causes an asset and a liability to appear on the balance sheet?

17. At what amount is a machine acquired through a capital lease recorded?

□   **Class Exercise**

Exercise 12-1

Throughout 198B, X Company owned property that was subject to county property taxes and had an assessed valuation for tax purposes of $600,000. The 198A tax levy was $0.50 per $100 of assessed valuation, and the company expected the 198B rate to remain unchanged. In early July, the county announced that the 198B tax levy would be $0.55 per $100 and that taxes would be due August 31, 198B. Prepare entries to record property tax expense for the months of June, July, and August (including the payment of the annual tax on August 31).

Exercise 12-2

A company manufactures one product for $8 per unit and sells it for $15 per unit. In November, the company sold 100,000 units subject to a one-year warranty. According to the warranty, customers must pay a $1.50 service charge to return a broken unit and have it replaced by a new unit. When a unit under warranty fails, the company simply discards the broken unit and replaces it with a new one. Past experience suggests a 1.5% failure rate of new products sold, and customers actually returned 1,200 broken units during the month of November. Prepare summary entries for the month of November to record product warranty expense and to record the replacement of 1,200 broken units.

Exercise 12-3

On December 1, 198A, a company borrowed $100,000 by giving a 90-day, 12% note payable. The company has an annual, calendar-year accounting period and does not make reversing entries. Prepare general journal entries to record: (a) the issuance of the note, (b) the required year-end adjusting entry, and (c) the entry to pay the note.

Exercise 12-4

On December 1, 198A, a company discounted its own $100,000, 90-day note payable at the bank. The discount rate was 12%. Prepare general journal entries to record: (a) the issuance of the note, (b) the required year-end adjusting entry, (c) the reversing entry on January 1, 198B, and (d) the entry to pay the note. (The company uses an annual, calendar-year accounting period.)

Exercise 12-5

Present calculations to show the following: (a) the present value of $20,000 to be received eight years hence, discounted at 14%; (b) the total present value of three payments consisting of $25,000 to be received one year hence, $30,000 to be received two years hence, and $40,000 to be received three years hence, all discounted at 12%; (c) the present value of seven payments of $6,000 each, with a payment to be received at the end of each of the next seven years, discounted at 9%.

Exercise 12-6

A company is offered a contract whereby it will be paid $8,000 every six months for the next 10 years. The first payment would be received six months from today. What will the company be willing to pay for this contract if it expects a 16% annual return on the investment? What if it expects an annual return of only 9%?

Exercise 12-7

A company is offered a contract whereby it will be paid $16,000 annually for the next 10 years. The first payment would be received one year from today. What will the company be willing to pay for this contract if it expects a 16% return on the investment? What if it expects an annual return of only 9%?

Exercise 12-8

An individual has offered to sell a machine for $9,000. A potential buyer has agreed to purchase the machine for the stated price but, as an alternative, has given the seller the option of receiving 10 annual payments of $1,500 each, the first payment to be one year from now. Assuming the seller expects an annual return of at least 8%, which of the two alternatives should the seller accept?

Exercise 12-9

Equipment was purchased on January 1 of the current year, with the terms of purchase including $14,000 cash plus a $25,000, noninterest-bearing, five-year note. The available interest rate on this date was 12%. (a) Prepare the entry to record the purchase of the machine. (b) Show how the liability will appear on a balance sheet prepared on the day of the purchase. (c) Prepare the entry to amortize a portion of the discount on the note at the end of its first year.

Exercise 12-10

On January 1, 198A, a day when the available interest rate was 14%, a company leased a machine for five years under a contract calling for a $30,000 annual lease payment at the end of each of the next five years, with the machine becoming the property of the lessee at the end of that period. The company decided to lease the machine. Prepare entries to record: *(a)* the leasing of the machine, *(b)* the amortization of the discount of the lease financing at the end of the first year, and *(c)* the first annual payment under the lease.

Problems

Problem 12-1

Part 1. Baffle Company sells a single product subject to a six-month warranty that covers replacement parts but not labor. The company uses a periodic inventory system to account for merchandise. Prepare journal entries to record the following transactions completed by the company during the month of May.

May   1   Purchased 1,000 units of merchandise for $22 per unit, paying cash.

        4   Purchased $2,600 of spare parts for making repairs to merchandise that is expected to be returned for warranty work.

        7   Sold 400 units of merchandise for $50 per unit, receiving cash.

      10   Repaired 20 units of merchandise that customers returned under the warranty. Replacement parts cost $344, and the customers paid $265 for labor.

      17   Sold 500 units of merchandise for $55 per unit.

      20   Repaired 14 units of merchandise under the product warranty. Replacement parts cost $210, and the customers paid $190 for labor.

      29   Recorded warranty expense for May. Past experience shows that 4.0% of the units sold require warranty work, and the average cost of replacement parts is $16 per unit returned. Average labor charges are $12.50.

Part 2. Superior Company expects to accrue 198B property taxes at the end of each month using recent experience as a means of estimating the tax. In January 198A, Superior's property was appraised at $800,000. The 198A tax levy was $1.50 per $100. In January 198B, Superior's property was reappraised at $880,000. (The reappraisal was not expected to affect the tax levy of $1.50 per $100.) Early in June 198B, the annual tax levy was set at $1.80 per $100. On November 30, 198B, Superior paid the 198B tax. Complete financial statements are prepared by the company on a monthly basis, and the company does not use reversing entries.

Required

Prepare entries at the end of January, June, November, and December, 198B, to record property tax expense for each of those months and to record the annual tax payment.

Problem 12-2

Prepare general journal entries to record these transactions:

Jan.   9   Purchased merchandise on credit from Foster Company, invoice dated January 8, terms 2/10, n/60, $10,400.

Feb.   6   Borrowed money at First City Bank by discounting our own $15,000 note payable for 60 days at 14%.

Mar.   9   Gave Foster Company $1,400 cash and a $9,000, 60-day, 14% note to secure an extension on our account that was due.

Apr.   7   Paid the note discounted at First City Bank on February 6.

May   8   Paid the note given Foster Company on March 9.

Nov.   1   Borrowed money at First City Bank by discounting our own $20,000 note payable for 90 days at 15%.

Dec. 16   Borrowed money at InterSecond Bank by giving a $15,000, 60-day, 15% note payable.

      31   Made an adjusting entry to remove from the Interest Expense account the interest applicable to next year on the note discounted at First City Bank on November 1.

      31   Made an adjusting entry to record the accrued interest on the note given InterSecond Bank on December 16.

Jan.   1   Made a reversing entry to return to the Interest Expense account the interest on the note discounted at First City Bank.

      30   Paid the note discounted at First City Bank on November 1.

Feb. 14   Paid the note given InterSecond Bank on December 16.

Problem 12-3

South Seas Adventures is negotiating with a naval architect and shipyard in planning the construction of a 70-foot, trimaran that South Seas expects to acquire and place in charter service. The yacht will be completed and ready for service four years hence. If Jordan pays for the yacht upon completion (Payment Plan A), it will cost $337,500. However, two alternative payment plans are available. Plan B would require an immediate payment of $243,750. Plan C would require four annual payments of $71,250, the first of which would be made one year hence. In evaluating the three alternatives, the management of South Seas has decided to assume an interest rate of 10%.

Required

Calculate the present value of each payment and indicate which plan South Seas should follow.

Problem 12-4

On January 2, 198A, a company gave its own $100,000 noninterest-bearing, five-year note payable in exchange for a machine, the cash price of which was not readily determinable. The market rate for interest on such notes on the day of the exchange was 9% annually.

Required
   (Round all amounts in your answers to the nearest whole dollar.)
1. Prepare a form with the following columnar headings and calculate and fill in the required amounts for the five years the note is outstanding.

Year	Beginning-of-Year Carrying Amount	Discount to Be Amortized Each Year	Unamortized Discount at End of Year	End-of-Year Carrying Amount

2. Prepare general journal entries to record: (a) the acquisition of the machine, (b) the discount amortized at the end of each year, and (c) the payment of the note on January 2, 198F.
3. Show how the note should appear on the December 31, 198C, balance sheet.

Problem 12-5

Hyden Production Company leased a machine on January 1, 198A, under a contract calling for annual payments of $32,000 on December 31 at the end of each of five years, with the machine becoming the property of the lessee company after the fifth $32,000 payment. The machine was estimated to have an eight-year life and no salvage value, and the interest rate available to Hyden for equipment loans on the day the lease was signed was 12%. The machine was delivered on January 4, 198A, and was immediately placed in operation. At the beginning of the eighth year in the machine's life, it was overhauled at a $2,040 total cost. The overhaul was paid for on January 10, and it did not increase the machine's efficiency but it did add an additional year to its expected service life. On March 31, during the ninth year in the machine's life, it was traded in on a new machine of like purpose having a $96,000 cash price. An $8,000 trade-in allowance was received, and the balance was paid in cash.

Required
(*Round all amounts in your answers to the nearest whole dollar.*)
1. Prepare a schedule with the columnar headings of Illustration 12-3. Enter the years 198A through 198E in the first column and complete the schedule by filling in the proper amounts.
2. Prepare the entry to record the leasing of the machine.
3. Prepare December 31, 198B, entries to record annual depreciation on a straight-line basis, to record the lease payment, and to amortize the discount in the life of the lease. Also show how the machine and the lease liability should appear on the December 31, 198B, balance sheet.
4. Prepare the entries to record the machine's overhaul and the depreciation on the machine at the end of its eighth year.
5. Prepare the March 31, 198I, entries to record the exchange of the machines.

Problem 12-6

The Bigtime Freight Company needs two new trucks, each of which has an estimated service life of nine years. The trucks could be purchased for $90,000 each, but Bigtime does not have enough cash to pay for them. Instead, Bigtime agrees to lease Truck 1 for six years, after which the truck remains the property of the lessor. In addition, Bigtime agrees to lease Truck 2 for eight years, after which the truck remains the property of the lessor. According to the lease contracts, Bigtime must pay $18,750 annually for each truck ($37,500 for two trucks), with the payments to be made at the end of each lease year. Both leases were signed on December 31, 198A, at which time the prevailing interest rate available to Bigtime for equipment loans was 12%.

Required
(*Round all amounts in your answers to the nearest whole dollar.*)
1. Prepare any required entries to record the lease of (*a*) Truck 1 and (*b*) Truck 2.
2. Prepare the required entries as of the end of the first year in (*a*) the life of Truck 1 and (*b*) the life of Truck 2. Use straight-line depreciation. (Hint: If the length of a capital lease is less than the asset's estimated service life and the asset remains the property of the lessor, depreciation must be taken over the length of the lease.)
3. Truck 1 was returned to the lessor on December 31, 198G, the end of the sixth year. Prepare the required entries as of the end of the sixth year in (*a*) the life of Truck 1 and (*b*) the life of Truck 2.
4. Show how Truck 2 and the lease liability for the truck should appear on the balance sheet as of the end of the sixth year in the life of the lease (after the year-end lease payment).

□ **Alternate Problems**   **Problem 12-1A**

Part 1. Terry Company sells a single product subject to a one-year warranty that covers replacement parts but not labor. The company uses a periodic inventory system to account for merchandise. Prepare journal entries to record the following transactions completed by the company during the month of August.

Aug. 1 Purchased 3,500 units of merchandise for $77 per unit, paying cash.
  3 Purchased $31,850 of spare parts for making repairs to merchandise that is expected to be returned for warranty work.
  6 Sold 1,400 units of merchandise for $175 per unit, receiving cash.
  12 Repaired 70 units of merchandise that customers returned under the warranty. Replacement parts cost $4,214, and the customers paid $3,246 for labor.
  19 Sold 1,750 units of merchandise for $193 per unit.
  24 Repaired 49 units of merchandise under the product warranty. Replacement parts cost $2,570, and the customers paid $2,328 for labor.
  30 Recorded warranty expense for August. Past experience shows that 4.0% of the units sold require warranty work, and the average cost of replacement parts is $56 per unit returned. Average labor charges are $44.

Part 2. Wimberley Company accrues property taxes at the end of each month and uses recent experience as a means of estimating the tax. In early 198A, Wimberley's property was appraised at $600,000. The 198A tax levy was $1.40 per $100. In January 198B, Wimberley's property was reappraised at $644,000. (The reappraisal was not expected to affect the tax levy of $1.40 per $100.) Early in July 198B, the annual tax levy was set at $1.65 per $100. On October 31, 198B, Wimberley paid the 198B tax. Complete financial statements are prepared by the company on a monthly basis, and the company does not use reversing entries.

Required

Prepare entries at the end of January, July, October, and November 198B, to record property tax expense for each of those months and to record the annual tax payment.

Problem 12-2A

Prepare general journal entries to record these transactions:

Jan. 28   Purchased merchandise on credit from Gaffey Company, invoice dated January 8, terms 2/10, n/60, $37,440.

Feb. 20   Borrowed money at Capital City Bank by discounting our own $54,000 note payable for 60 days at 10%.

Apr. 5   Gave Gaffey Company $2,440 cash and a $35,000, 60-day, 12% note to secure an extension on our past-due account.

21   Paid the note discounted at Capital City Bank on February 20.

June 4   Paid the note given Gaffey Company on April 5.

Nov. 16   Borrowed money at Capital City Bank by discounting our own $70,000 note payable for 90 days at 13%.

Dec. 1   Borrowed money at Farmers' First Bank by giving a $50,000, 60-day, 14% note payable.

31   Made an adjusting entry to remove from the Interest Expense account the interest applicable to next year on the note discounted at Capital City Bank on November 16.

31   Made an adjusting entry to record the accrued interest on the note given Farmers' First Bank on December 1.

Jan. 1   Made a reversing entry to return to the Interest Expense account the interest on the note discounted at Capital City Bank.

30   Paid the note given Farmers' First Bank on December 1.

Feb. 14   Paid the note discounted at Capital City Bank on November 16.

Problem 12-3A

High Sky Airways is negotiating with an airframe outfitter in planning the interior finishings of a nine-passenger turboprop that High Sky Airways expects to acquire and place in charter service. The airplane will be completed and ready for service four years hence. If High Sky pays for the airplane upon completion (Payment Plan A), it will cost $1,687,500. However, two alternative payment plans are available. Plan B would require an immediate payment of $1,218,750. Plan C would require four annual payments of $356,250, the first of which would be made one year hence.

In evaluating the three alternatives, the management of High Sky has decided to assume an interest rate of 9%.

Required

Calculate the present value of each payment and indicate which plan High Sky should follow.

Problem 12-4A

On January 1, 198A, Infomart Company gave its own $300,000 noninterest-bearing, six-year note payable in exchange for a machine, the cash price of which was not readily determinable. The market rate for interest on such notes on the day of the exchange was 8% annually.

Required
 (Round all amounts in your answers to the nearest whole dollar.)
1. Prepare a form with the following columnar headings and calculate and fill in the required amounts for the six years the note is outstanding.

Year	Beginning-of-Year Carrying Amount	Discount to Be Amortized Each Year	Unamortized Discount at End of Year	End-of-Year Carrying Amount

2. Prepare general journal entries to record. *(a)* the acquisition of the machine, *(b)* the discount amortized at the end of each of the first three years, and *(c)* the payment of the note on January 1, 198G.
3. Show how the note should appear on the December 31, 198C, balance sheet.

Problem 12-5A

Jetstar Production Company leased a machine on January 1, 198A, under a contract calling for annual payments of $57,600 on December 31 at the end of each of five years, with the machine becoming the property of the lessee company after the fifth $57,600 payment. The machine was estimated to have a six-year life and no salvage value, and the interest rate available to Jetstar for equipment loans on the day the lease was signed was 14%. The machine was delivered on January 3, 198A, and was immediately placed in operation. At the beginning of the sixth year in the machine's life, it was overhauled at a $6,800 total cost. The overhaul was paid for on January 6, and it did not increase the machine's efficiency but it did add an additional two years to its expected service life. On April 30, during the eighth year in the machine's life, it was traded in on a new machine of like purpose having a $172,000 cash price. A $12,000 trade-in allowance was received, and the balance was paid in cash.

Required
 (Round all amounts in your answers to the nearest whole dollar.)
1. Prepare a schedule with the columnar headings of Illustration 12-3. Enter the years 198A through 198E in the first column and complete the schedule by filling in the proper amounts.

2. Prepare the entry to record the leasing of the machine.

3. Prepare December 31, 198B, entries to record annual depreciation on a straight-line basis, to record the lease payment, and to amortize the discount in the life of the lease. Also show how the machine and the lease liability should appear on the December 31, 198B, balance sheet.

4. Prepare the entries to record the machine's overhaul and the depreciation on the machine at the end of its sixth year.

5. Prepare the April 30, 198H, entries to record the exchange of the machines.

Problem 12-6A

The Northwest News Company leased two new printing presses. Each of the presses has an estimated service life of seven years. Press 1 was leased for five years. Press 2 was leased for six years. Each lease agreement calls for $20,000 annual lease payments at the end of the year ($40,000 for both presses). When the period of each lease expires, each press will be returned to the lessor. Both leases were signed on December 31, 198A, at which time the prevailing interest rate available to Northwest News for equipment loans was 10%. Each of the presses could have been purchased for $90,000 cash.

Required
  (Round all amounts in your answers to the nearest whole dollar.)
1. Prepare any required entries to record the lease of (*a*) Press 1 and (*b*) Press 2.

2. Prepare the required entries as of the end of the first year in (*a*) the life of Press 1 and (*b*) the life of Press 2. Use straight-line depreciation. (Hint: If the length of a capital lease is less than the asset's estimated service life and the asset remains the property of the lessor, depreciation must be taken over the length of the lease.)

3. Press 1 was returned to the lessor on December 31, 198F, at the end of the fifth year. Prepare the required entries as of the end of the fifth year in (*a*) the life of Press 1 and (*b*) the life of Press 2.

4. Show how Press 2 and the lease liability for the press should appear on the balance sheet as of the end of the fifth year in the life of the lease (after the year-end lease payment).

☐ **Provocative Problems**

Provocative Problem 12-1   Rohr Industries, Inc.

Rohr Industries, Inc., is a manufacturing company with operations in California, Washington, Alabama, and France. The footnotes to the company's 1983 financial statements included the following comments:

In April 1983, the Grumman Corporation filed suit against the Company in a U.S. District Court of New York for $250 million in compensatory damages plus punitive damages for an equal amount. The suit alleges that at the time of the sale by the Company of a transit bus business to Grumman Corporation in January 1978, the Company materially misrepresented and concealed material facts relative to the development and testing of the Model 870 bus. The Company has engaged counsel, filed an answer to the complaint totally denying the allegations, and has commenced pretrial, discovery proceedings. The Company intends to vigorously defend this matter. It believes that it has numerous and substantial defenses, that it will ultimately prevail in the lawsuit, and that the resolution of this matter will not have a material adverse financial impact upon the Company.

Comment on the reasons why the management of Rohr Industries, Inc., decided to include the above statements among the footnotes to the company's financial statements. Based on the description in the footnote, would you expect fo find a loss reported in Rohr's 1983 income statement? Support your answer with reasons.

Provocative Problem 12-2   Financing Beckwith Corporation's New Equipment

Beckwith Corporation is planning to acquire some new equipment from Nelson Company and has asked you to assist in analyzing the situation. The equipment may be purchased for $275,000 and then will be leased by Beckwith under a 10-year lease contract to a customer for $50,000 payable at the end of each year. After the lease expires, Beckwith expects to sell the equipment for $75,000.

1. Suppose Beckwith has $275,000 cash available to buy the equipment and requires a 14% rate of return on its investments. Should the company buy the equipment and lease it to the customer?

2. As an alternative to paying cash, Beckwith can invest the $275,000 in other operations for five years and earn 14% annually on its investment. If this is done, the equipment may be purchased by signing a $500,000, five-year, noninterest-bearing note payable to Nelson Company. Should Beckwith pay $275,000 now or sign the $500,000 note?

3. Now suppose Beckwith does not have the option of signing a $500,000, five-year, noninterest-bearing note. Instead, the company may either pay $275,000 cash or lease the equipment from Nelson Company for eight years, after which the equipment would become the property of Beckwith. The lease contract would require $62,500 payments at the end of each year. If Beckwith leases the equipment, it will invest the $275,000 available cash in other operations and earn 14% on the investment. Should Beckwith pay cash or lease the equipment from Nelson?

13 Payroll Accounting

After studying Chapter 13, you should be able to:

1. List the taxes that are withheld from employees' wages and the payroll taxes that are levied on employers.

2. Calculate an employee's gross pay and the various deductions from the pay.

3. Prepare a Payroll Register and make the entries to record its information and to pay the employees.

4. Explain the operation of a payroll bank account.

5. Calculate and prepare the entries to record the payroll taxes levied on an employer and to record employee fringe benefit costs.

6. Define or explain the words and phrases listed in the chapter Glossary.

Wages or salaries generally amount to one of the largest expenses incurred by a business. Accounting for these items involves much more than simply recording liabilities and cash payments to employees. Payroll accounting also includes (1) amounts withheld from employees' wages, (2) payroll taxes levied on the employer, and (3) employee (fringe) benefits paid by the employer. Certain federal and state laws directly affect several aspects of payroll accounting. Thus, the discussion of this chapter begins with an overview of the more pertinent of these laws.

■ The Federal Social Security Act

The federal Social Security Act provides for a number of programs, two of which materially affect payroll accounting. These are (1) a federal old-age and survivors benefits program with medical care for the aged and (2) a joint federal-state unemployment insurance program.

Federal Old Age and Survivors Benefits Program

The Social Security Act provides that a qualified worker in a covered industry who reaches the age of 62 and retires shall receive monthly retirement benefits for the remainder of his or her life and certain medical benefits after reaching 65. It further provides benefits for the family of a worker covered by the act who dies either before or after reaching retirement age and benefits for covered workers who become disabled. The benefits in each case are based upon the earnings of the worker during the years of his or her employment in covered industries.

No attempt will be made here to list or discuss the requirements to be met by a worker or the worker's family to qualify for benefits. In general, any person who works for an employer covered by the act for a sufficient length of time qualifies himself or herself and family. All companies and individuals who employ one or more persons and are not specifically exempted are covered by the law.

Social Security (FICA) Taxes

Funds for the payment of old-age, survivors, and medical benefits under the Social Security Act come from payroll taxes. These taxes are imposed under a law called the Federal Insurance Contributions Act and are called **FICA taxes.** They are also commonly called social security taxes. These FICA taxes are imposed in equal amounts on covered employers and their employees. At this writing, the act imposes a 1985 tax on both employers and their employees amounting to 7.05% of the first $39,600 paid to each employee. Additional rate increases in the present laws are as follows:

	Tax on Employees	Tax on Employers
1986–87	7.15%	7.15%
1988–89	7.51	7.51
1990 and after.	7.65	7.65

The maximum amount of wages subject to FICA taxes is reviewed annually and often is increased (for 1986, the amount is $42,000). Also, Congress may change the rates listed above (probably increasing them) before they become effective. Consequently, since changes are almost certain, you generally are asked to use an assumed FICA tax rate of 7% on the first $39,600 of wages paid each employee each year in solving the problems at the end of this chapter. Although a few problems may specify some other rate, the 7% rate usually is assumed because it simplifies calculations. Also, no single rate is likely to be correct for the remaining years this text will be used.

The Federal Insurance Contributions Act in addition to setting rates requires that an employer—

1. Withhold from the wages of each employee each payday an amount of FICA tax calculated at the current rate. FICA taxes are withheld from each paycheck during the year until the tax-exempt point is reached.
2. Pay a payroll tax equal to the sum of the FICA taxes withheld from the wages of all employees.
3. Periodically deposit to the credit of the Internal Revenue Service in a bank authorized to receive such deposits (called a **federal depository bank**) both the amounts withheld from the employees' wages and the employer's tax.
4. Within one month after the end of each calendar quarter, file a tax information return known as Employer's Quarterly Federal Tax Return, Form 941. (See Illustration 13-1.)
5. Furnish each employee before January 31 following each year a Wage and Tax Statement, Form W-2, which tells the employee the amounts of his or her wages that were subject to FICA and federal income taxes and the amounts of such taxes withheld. (A W-2 Form is shown in Illustration 13-2.)
6. Send copies of the W-2 Forms to the Social Security Administration, which posts to each employee's social security account the amount of the employee's wages subject to FICA tax and the FICA tax withheld. These posted amounts become the basis for determining the employee's retirement and survivors benefits. In addition to the posting, the Social Security Administration transmits to the Internal Revenue Service the amount of each employee's wages subject to federal income tax and the amount of such tax withheld.
7. Keep a record for four years for each employee that shows among other things wages subject to FICA taxes and the taxes withheld. (The law does not specify the exact form of the record. However, most employers keep individual employee earnings records similar to the one shown later in this chapter.)

Observe that in addition to reporting its employees' and employer's FICA taxes on Form 941 (Illustration 13-1), an employer also reports the amount of its employees' wages that were subject to federal income taxes and the amount of such taxes that were withheld. (The withholding of employees' federal income taxes is discussed later in this chapter.) Employees' wages subject to federal income tax is shown on line 2 of Illustration

Illustration 13-1

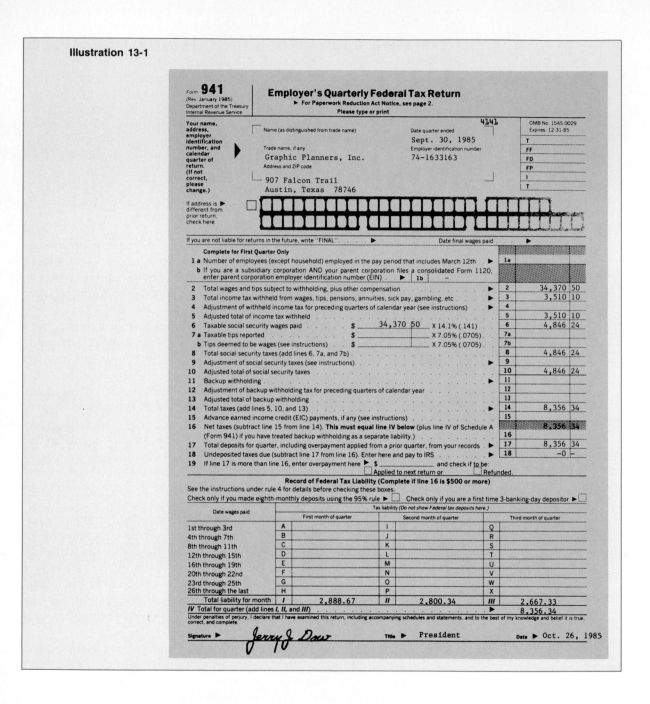

13-1, and the amount of tax withheld is reported on lines 3, 4, and 5. The combined amount of the employees' and employer's FICA taxes is reported on line 6 where it says, "Taxable social security wages paid . . . $34,370.50 multiplied by 14.1% = Tax, $4,846.24." The 14.1% is the sum of the (1985) 7.05% tax withheld from the employees' wages plus the 7.05% tax levied on the employer.

The frequency with which an employer must deposit to the credit of the Internal Revenue Service the FICA and employees' withheld income

Illustration 13-2

1 Control number	22222	For Paperwork Reduction Act Notice, see back of Copy D. OMB No. 1545-0008	For Official Use Only	
2 Employer's name, address, and ZIP code Graphic Planners, Inc. 907 Falcon Trail Austin, Texas 78746			3 Employer's identification number 74-1633163	4 Employer's State number 56-5678
			5 Statutory employee □ Deceased □ Legal rep. □ 942 emp □ Subtotal □ Void □	
			6 Allocated tips	7 Advance EIC payment
8 Employee's social security number 302-02-0222	9 Federal income tax withheld 2,487.20		10 Wages, tips, other compensation 24,560.60	11 Social security tax withheld 1,645.56
12 Employee's name (first, middle, last) Charles Robert Lusk			13 Social security wages 24,560.60	14 Social security tips
1310 East 5th Street Austin, Texas 78711 15 Employee's address and ZIP code			16 *	
			17 State income tax	18 State wages, tips, etc.	19 Name of State
			20 Local income tax	21 Local wages, tips, etc.	22 Name of locality

Form **W-2 Wage and Tax Statement** 1985   Copy A For Social Security Administration   Department of the Treasury
* See Instructions for Forms W-2 and W-2P   Internal Revenue Service

taxes depends on the amounts involved. If the sum of the FICA taxes plus the employees' income taxes is less than $500 for a quarter, the taxes may be paid when the employer files an Employer's Quarterly Tax Return, Form 941. This return is due on April 30, July 31, October 31, and January 31 following the end of each calendar quarter. A check for the taxes, if less than $500, may be attached to the return, or the taxes may be deposited in a federal depository bank at the time the return is filed. The check or the deposit is recorded in the same manner as a check paying any other liability.

If the taxes exceed $500 at the end of any month but are less than $3,000, payment must be made within 15 days after the end of the month. Companies with large payrolls may have to make tax payments as often as eight times each month. Note in Illustration 13-1 that each month is divided into eight periods. When the taxes exceed $3,000 at the end of any period, they must be paid within three banking days after the end of that period.

In the example shown in Illustration 13-1, the employer's tax liability exceeded $500 but was less than $3,000 at the end of each month during the quarter. It is assumed in the illustration that the employer paid the amounts due within 15 days after the end of each month.

Joint Federal-State Unemployment Insurance Program

The federal government participates with the states in a joint federal-state unemployment insurance program. Within this joint program each state has established and now administers its own unemployment insurance program under which it provides unemployment benefits to its insured workers. The federal government approves the state programs and pays a portion of their administrative expenses.

Federal Unemployment Tax Act The federal money for administering the state programs is raised by a tax imposed under a law called the Federal Unemployment Tax Act. This act levies a **payroll tax** on employers of one or more people. Note that the tax is imposed on employers only. Employees pay nothing. Also, the money from this tax is used for administrative purposes and not to pay benefits. In periods of high unemployment, however, these funds may also be loaned to states that have temporary fund deficits.

Historically, in 1935 when the Federal Unemployment Tax Act was first passed, only one state had an unemployment insurance program. At that time, Congress passed certain sections of the Social Security Act and the Federal Unemployment Tax Act with two purposes in view. The first was to induce the individual states to create satisfactory unemployment insurance programs of their own. The second was to provide funds to be distributed to the states for use in administering the state programs. These acts were successful in accomplishing their first purpose. All states immediately created unemployment benefit programs. Today, the acts remain in effect for their second purpose, to provide funds to be distributed to the states, and also to retain a measure of federal control over the state programs.

Federal Unemployment Tax   At this writing, the Federal Unemployment Tax Act requires employers of one or more employees to:

1. Pay an excise tax (FUTA tax) equal to 6.2% of the first $7,000 in wages paid each employee. However, the federal law grants a maximum credit of 5.4% to employers in a state that has an appropriately designed state unemployment tax program. Since all states have unemployment tax programs, the net federal tax normally is 0.8%.
2. On or before January 31 following the end of each year, file a tax return, called an Employer's Annual Federal Unemployment Tax Return, Form 940, reporting the amount of the tax. (Ten additional days are allowed for filing if all required tax deposits are made on a timely basis and the full amount of the tax is paid on or before January 31.)
3. Keep records to substantiate the information on the tax return. (In general, the records required by other payroll laws and the regular accounting records satisfy this requirement.)

An employer's federal unemployment tax for the first three quarters of a year must be deposited in a federal depository bank by the last day of the month following each quarter (i.e., on April 30, July 31, and October 31). However, no deposit is required if the tax for a quarter plus the undeposited tax for previous quarters is $100 or less. The tax for the last quarter of a year plus the undeposited tax for previous quarters must be deposited or paid on or before January 31 following the end of the tax year. If the Employer's Annual Federal Unemployment Tax Return is filed on or before that date, a check for the last quarter's tax and any undeposited tax for previous quarters may be attached to the form.

State Unemployment Insurance Programs   While the various state unemployment insurance programs differ in some respects, all have three common objectives. They are:

1. To pay unemployment benefits for limited periods to unemployed individuals. (To be eligible for benefits, an unemployed individual must

have worked for a tax-paying employer covered by the law. In general, the state laws cover employers of from one to four or more employees who are not specifically exempted.)
2. To encourage the stabilization of employment by covered employers. In all states this is accomplished by a so-called **merit rating** plan. Under a merit rating plan, the tax rate levied on an employer is adjusted to reflect the employer's past record in providing steady employment for employees.
3. To establish and operate employment facilities that assist unemployed individuals in finding suitable employment and assist employers in finding employees.

State Unemployment Tax All states support their unemployment insurance programs by placing a payroll tax on employers. The tax rate may range from 0% up to 9% or more and generally is applied to the first $7,000 paid each employee. The exact tax rate that must be paid by an employer depends on the employer's merit rating. An employer gains a favorable merit rating by not laying employees off during slack seasons, thereby avoiding their drawing of unemployment benefits. Clearly, a favorable merit rating offers an important tax savings. For example, if an employer can obtain a merit rating that reduces the tax rate from 5% to 1%, the annual savings is $280 for each employee who earns $7,000 or more per year (4% × $7,000 = $280). If the employer has 100 employees, the annual savings is $28,000.

The states vary as to required unemployment tax reports. Nevertheless, in general, all require a tax return and payment of the required tax within one month after the end of each calendar quarter. Also, since the benefits paid an eligible unemployed individual are based upon earnings, the tax return must usually name each employee and summarize the employee's wages.

In addition to reports and payment of taxes, all states require employers to maintain certain payroll records. These vary but in general require a payroll record for each pay period showing the pay period dates, hours worked, and taxable earnings of each employee. An individual earnings record for each employee is also commonly required. The earnings record generally must show about the same information that is required by social security laws. In addition, information is also commonly required as to (1) the date an employee was hired, rehired, or reinstated after a layoff; (2) the date the employee quit, was discharged, or laid off; and (3) the reason for termination.

■ **Withholding Employees' Federal Income Taxes**

With few exceptions, an employer of one or more persons is required to calculate, withhold, and remit to the Internal Revenue Service the federal income taxes of its employees. The amount of tax to be withheld from each employee's wages is determined by the amount of the wages earned and the number of the employee's personal exemptions, which for payroll purposes are called **withholding allowances.** At this writing (1985), each exemption or withholding allowance exempts $1,040 of the employee's yearly earnings from income tax. An employee is allowed one exemption for himself or herself, additional exemptions if the employee or the employee's spouse is blind or over 65, and an exemption for each dependent. Every covered employee is required to furnish his or her employer an employee's withholding allowance certificate, called a Form W-4, on which the employee indicates the number of exemptions claimed.

Most employers use a **wage bracket withholding table** similar to the one shown in Illustration 13-3 to determine the federal income taxes to be withheld from employees' **gross pay.** The illustrated table is for single employees and is applicable when a pay period is one week. Different tables are provided for married employees and for biweekly, semimonthly, and monthly pay periods. Somewhat similar tables are also available for determining FICA tax withholdings.

Determining the federal income tax to be withheld from an employee's gross wages is quite easy when a withholding table is used. First, the employee's wage bracket is located in the first two columns. Then, the amount to be withheld is found on the line of the wage bracket in the column showing the exemption allowances to which the employee is entitled. The column heading numbers refer to the number of exemption allowances claimed by an employee.

In addition to determining and withholding income tax from each employee's wages every payday, employers are required to—

1. Periodically deposit the withheld taxes to the credit of the Internal Revenue Service.
2. Within one month after the end of each calendar quarter, file a report showing the income taxes withheld. This report is the Employer's Quarterly Federal Tax Return, Form 941, discussed previously and shown in Illustration 13-1. It is the same report required for FICA taxes.
3. On or before January 31 following each year, give each employee a Wage and Tax Statement, Form W-2, which tells the employee (1) his

Illustration 13-3

SINGLE Persons—WEEKLY Payroll Period
(For Wages Paid After December 1984)

And the wages are—		And the number of withholding allowances claimed is—										
At least	But less than	0	1	2	3	4	5	6	7	8	9	10
		The amount of income tax to be withheld shall be—										
$380	$390	$65	$60	$55	$50	$46	$41	$37	$33	$29	$26	$22
390	400	68	63	58	53	48	43	39	35	31	27	24
400	410	71	65	60	55	50	46	41	37	33	29	26
410	420	73	68	63	58	53	48	43	39	35	31	27
420	430	76	71	65	60	55	50	46	41	37	33	29
430	440	78	73	68	63	58	53	48	43	39	35	31
440	450	81	76	71	65	60	55	50	46	41	37	33
450	460	84	78	73	68	63	58	53	48	43	39	35
460	470	87	81	76	71	65	60	55	50	46	41	37
470	480	90	84	78	73	68	63	58	53	48	43	39
480	490	93	87	81	76	71	65	60	55	50	46	41
490	500	96	90	84	78	73	68	63	58	53	48	43
500	510	99	93	87	81	76	71	65	60	55	50	46
510	520	102	96	90	84	78	73	68	63	58	53	48
520	530	105	99	93	87	81	76	71	65	60	55	50
530	540	108	102	96	90	84	78	73	68	63	58	53
540	550	111	105	99	93	87	81	76	71	65	60	55
550	560	114	108	102	96	90	84	78	73	68	63	58
560	570	117	111	105	99	93	87	81	76	71	65	60
570	580	121	114	108	102	96	90	84	78	73	68	63
580	590	124	117	111	105	99	93	87	81	76	71	65
590	600	127	121	114	108	102	96	90	84	78	73	68
600	610	131	124	117	111	105	99	93	87	81	76	71
610	620	134	127	121	114	108	102	96	90	84	78	73
620	630	138	131	124	117	111	105	99	93	87	81	76

or her total wages for the preceding year, (2) wages subject to FICA taxes, (3) income taxes withheld, and (4) FICA taxes withheld. A copy of this statement must also be given to each terminated employee within 30 days after his or her last wage payment.

4. On or before January 31 following the end of each year, send the Social Security Administration copies of all W-2 forms given employees. The Social Security Administration transmits the information as to employees' earnings and withheld taxes to the Internal Revenue Service.

■ **City and State Income Taxes**

In addition to deducting employees' federal income taxes, employers in many cities and in many states must also deduct employees' city and state income taxes. When levied, the city and state taxes are handled much the same as federal income taxes.

■ **Fair Labor Standards Act**

The Fair Labor Standards Act, often called the Wages and Hours Law, sets minimum hourly wages and maximum hours of work per week for employees, with certain exceptions, of employers engaged either directly or indirectly in interstate commerce. The law at this writing sets a $3.35 per hour minimum wage for employees in most occupations and a 40-hour workweek. It also provides that if an employee covered by the act works more than 40 hours in one week, he or she must be paid for the hours in excess of 40 at his or her regular pay rate plus an overtime premium of at least one half the regular rate. This gives an employee an overtime rate of at least one and one half times his or her regular hourly rate. The act also requires employers to maintain records for each covered employee similar to the employee's individual earnings record of Illustration 13-8.

■ **Union Contracts**

Employers commonly operate under contracts with their employees' union that provide even better terms than the Wages and Hours Law. For example, union contracts often provide for time and one half for work in excess of eight hours in any one day, time and one half for work on Saturdays, and double time for Sundays and holidays. When an employer is under such a union contract, since the contract terms are better than those of the Wages and Hours Law, the contract terms take precedence over the law.

In addition to specifying working hours and wage rates, union contracts often provide for the collection of employees' union dues by the employer. Such a requirement commonly provides that the employer deduct dues from the wages of each employee and remit the amounts deducted to the union. The employer is usually required to remit once each month and to report the name and amount deducted from each employee's pay.

■ **Other Payroll Deductions**

In addition to the payroll deductions discussed thus far, employees may individually authorize additional deductions, such as deductions for the purchase of U.S. savings bonds; to pay health, hospital, or life insurance premiums; to repay loans from the employer or the employees' credit union;

and to pay for merchandise purchased from the employer and for donations to charitable organizations.

■   **Timekeeping**   Compiling a record of the time worked by each employee is called **timekeeping.** In an individual company, the method of compiling such a record depends upon the nature of the business and the number of its employees. In a very small business, timekeeping may consist of no more than pencil notations of each employee's working time made in a memorandum book by the manager or owner. On the other hand, in larger companies, a time clock or several time clocks are often used to record on **clock cards** each employee's time of arrival and departure. When time clocks are used, they are usually placed near entrances to the office, store, or factory. At the beginning of each payroll period, a clock card for each employee similar to Illustration 13-4 is placed in a rack for use by the employee. Upon arriving at work, an employee takes his or her card from the rack and places it in a slot in the time clock. This actuates the clock to stamp the date and arrival time on the card. The employee then returns the card to the rack and proceeds to the employee's place of work. Upon leaving the plant, store, or office for lunch or at the end of the day, the procedure is repeated. The employee takes the card from the rack, places it in the clock, and the time of departure is automatically stamped. As a result, at the end of each pay period, the card shows the hours the employee was at work.

■ **The Payroll Register**   Each pay period the total hours worked as compiled on clock cards or otherwise is summarized in a Payroll Register. A typical example of such a register is shown in Illustration 13-5. The illustrated register is for a weekly pay period and shows the payroll data for each employee on a separate line. The column headings and the data recorded in the columns are, for the most part, self-explanatory.

The columns under the heading Daily Time shows the hours worked each day by each employee. The total of each employee's hours is entered in the column headed Total Hours. If hours worked include overtime hours, these are entered in the column headed O.T. Hours.

The column headed Reg. Pay Rate is for the hourly pay rate of each employee. Total hours worked multiplied by the regular pay rate equals regular pay. Overtime hours multiplied by the overtime premium rate equals overtime premium pay. And, regular pay plus overtime premium pay is the gross pay of each employee.

Under the heading Deductions, the amounts withheld from each employee's gross pay for FICA taxes are shown in the column marked FICA Taxes. These amounts are determined by multiplying the gross pay of each employee by the FICA tax rate in effect. In this and the remaining illustrations of this chapter, it is assumed that the rate is 7% on the first $39,600 paid each employee.

As previously stated, the income tax withheld from each employee depends upon his or her gross pay and exemptions. This amount is commonly determined by the use of a wage bracket withholding table; and when determined, it is entered in the column headed Federal Income Taxes.

Illustration 13-4

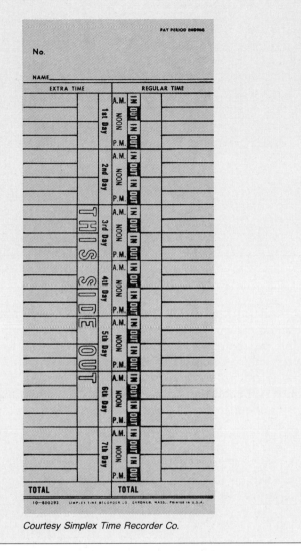

Courtesy Simplex Time Recorder Co.

The column headed Hosp. Ins. shows the amounts withheld to pay for hospital insurance for the employees and their families. The total withheld from all employees is a current liability of the employer until paid to the insurance company. Likewise, the total withheld for employees' union dues is a current liability until paid to the union. The column marked Union Dues in the illustrated Payroll Register is for this deduction.

Additional columns may be added to the Payroll Register for any other deductions that occur sufficiently often to warrant special columns. For example, a company that regularly deducts amounts from its employees' pay for U.S. savings bonds may add a special column for this deduction.

An employee's gross pay less total deductions is the employee's **net pay** and is entered in the column headed Net Pay. The total of this column

Illustration 13-5

											Earnings			
		Daily Time												
Employees	Clock Card No.	M	T	W	T	F	S	S	Total Hours	O.T. Hours	Reg. Pay Rate	Reg- ular Pay	O.T. Pre- mium Pay	Gross Pay
Robert Austin	114	8	8	8	8	8			40		10.00	400.00		400.00
Judy Cross	102	8	8	8	8	8			40		15.00	600.00		600.00
John Cruz	108	0	8	8	8	8	8		40		14.00	560.00		560.00
Kay Keife	109	8	8	8	8	8	8		48	8	14.00	672.00	56.00	728.00
Lee Miller	112	8	8	8	8	0			32		14.00	448.00		448.00
Dale Sears	103	8	8	8	8	8	4		44	4	15.00	660.00	30.00	690.00
Totals												3,340.00	86.00	3,426.00

Payroll
Week ended

is the amount to be paid the employees. The numbers of the checks used in paying the employees are entered in the column headed Check No.

The two columns under the heading Distribution are for sorting the various salaries into kinds of salary expense. Here each employee's gross salary is entered in the proper column according to the type of work performed. The column totals then indicate the amounts to be debited to the salary expense accounts.

Recording the Payroll

Generally, a Payroll Register such as the one shown is a supplementary memorandum record. As such, its information is not posted directly to the accounts but is first recorded with a general journal entry, which is then posted. The entry to record the payroll shown in Illustration 13-5 is:

Mar.	23	Sales Salaries Expense	2,336.00	
		Office Salaries Expense	1,090.00	
		FICA Taxes Payable		239.82
		Employees' Income Taxes Payable. . . .		558.00
		Employees' Hospital Insurance Payable. .		320.00
		Employees' Union Dues Payable.		40.00
		Accrued Payroll Payable		2,268.18
		To record the March 23 payroll.		

The debits of the entry were taken from the Payroll Register's distribution column totals. They charge the employee's gross earnings to the proper salary expense accounts. The credits to FICA Taxes Payable, Employees' Income Taxes Payable, Employees' Hospital Insurance Payable, and Employees' Union Dues Payable record these amounts as current liabilities.

	Deductions				Payment		Distribution	
FICA Taxes	Federal Income Taxes	Hosp. Ins.	Union Dues	Total Deduc- tions	Net Pay	Check No.	Sales Salaries	Office Salaries
28.00	50.00	40.00		118.00	282.00	893		400.00
42.00	117.00	56.00	10.00	225.00	375.00	894	600.00	
39.20	99.00	56.00	10.00	204.20	355.80	895	560.00	
50.96	120.00	56.00	10.00	236.96	491.04	896	728.00	
31.36	60.00	56.00	10.00	157.36	290.64	897	448.00	
48.30	112.00	56.00		216.30	473.70	898		690.00
239.82	558.00	320.00	40.00	1,157.82	2,268.18		2,336.00	1,090.00

Register
March 23, 19--

The credit to Accrued Payroll Payable records as a liability the net amount to be paid the employees.

Paying the Employees

Almost every business pays its employees with checks. In a company having few employees, these checks are often drawn on the regular bank account and entered in a Cash Disbursements Journal (or Check Register) like the one described in Chapter 6. Each check is debited to the Accrued Payroll Payable account. Therefore, posting labor can be saved by adding an Accrued Payroll Payable column in the journal. If such a column is added, entries to pay the employees of the Illustration 13-5 payroll will appear as in Illustration 13-6.

Illustration 13-6

Cash Disbursements Journal

Date		Check No.	Payee	Account Debited	PR	Other Ac- counts Debit	Accts. Pay. Debit	Accr. Payroll Pay Debit	Pur. Dis. Credit	Cash Credit
Mar.	23	893	Robert Austin	Accrued Payroll				282.00		282.00
	23	894	Judy Cross	"				375.00		375.00
	23	895	John Cruz	"				355.80		355.80
	23	896	Kay Keife	"				491.04		491.04
	23	897	Lee Miller	"				290.64		290.64
	23	898	Dale Sears	"				473.70		473.70

Although not required by law, most employers furnish each employee an earnings statement each payday. The objective of the statement is to inform the employee and give the employee a record of hours worked, gross pay, deductions, and net pay that may be retained. The statement usually takes the form of a detachable paycheck portion that is removed before the check is cashed. A paycheck with a detachable earnings statement is reproduced in Illustration 13-7.

Payroll Bank Account

A business with many employees normally makes use of a special **payroll bank account** in paying its employees. When such an account is used, one check for the total of the payroll is drawn on the regular bank account and deposited in the special payroll bank account. Then, individual payroll checks are drawn on this special account. Because only one check for the payroll total is drawn on the regular bank account each payday, use of a special payroll bank account simplifies reconciliation of the regular bank account. It may be reconciled without considering the payroll checks outstanding, and there may be many of these.

A company using a special payroll bank account completes the following steps in paying its employees:

1. First, it records the information shown on its Payroll Register in the usual manner with a general journal entry similar to the one previously illustrated. This entry causes the sum of the employees' net pay to be credited to the liability account Accrued Payroll Payable.
2. Next, a single check payable to Payroll Bank Account for the total of the payroll is drawn and entered in the Check Register. This results in a debit to Accrued Payroll Payable and a credit to Cash.
3. The check is then endorsed and deposited in the payroll bank account. This transfers an amount of money equal to the payroll total from the regular bank account to the special payroll bank account.

Illustration 13-7

Employee	Total Hours	O.T. Hours	Reg. Pay Rate	Regular Pay	O.T. Prem. Pay	Gross Pay	F.I.C.A. Taxes	Income Taxes	Union Dues	Hosp. Ins.	Total Deductions	Net Pay
Robert Austin	40		10.00	400.00		400.00	28.00	50.00		40.00	118.00	282.00

STATEMENT OF EARNINGS AND DEDUCTIONS FOR EMPLOYEE'S RECORDS—DETACH BEFORE CASHING CHECK

- -

VALLEY SALES COMPANY
2590 Chula Vista Street ● Eugene, Oregon

No. 893

PAY TO THE ORDER OF _____ Robert Austin _____ Date _March 23, 19--_ $ 282.00

Two hundred eighty two dollars and no cents -

VALLEY SALES COMPANY

James R. Morris

Merchants National Bank
Eugene, Oregon

4. Last, individual payroll checks are drawn on the special payroll bank account and delivered to the employees. These pay the employees and, as soon as all employees cash their checks, exhaust the funds in the special account.

A special Payroll Check Register may be used in connection with a payroll bank account. However, most companies do not use such a register but prefer to enter the payroll check numbers in their Payroll Register, making it act as a Check Register.

■ **Employee's Individual Earnings Record**

An **Employee's Individual Earnings Record,** Illustration 13-8, provides for each employee in one record a full year's summary of the employee's working time, gross earnings, deductions, and net pay. In addition, it accumulates information that—

1. Serves as a basis for the employer's state and federal payroll tax returns.
2. Indicates when an employee's earnings have reached the tax-exempt points for FICA and state and federal unemployment taxes.
3. Supplies data for the Wage and Tax Statement, Form W-2, which must be given to the employee at the end of the year.

Illustration 13-8

EMPLOYEE'S INDIVIDUAL EARNINGS RECORD

Employee's Name __Robert Austin__   S.S. Acct. No. __307-03-2195__   Employee No. __114__

Home Address __111 South Greenwood__   Notify in Case of Emergency __Margaret Austin__   Phone No. __964-9834__

Employed __June 7, 1980__   Date of Termination _____   Reason _____

Date of Birth __June 6, 1962__   Date Becomes 65 __June 6, 2027__   Male (X) Married (X)   Female ( ) Single ( )   Number of Exemptions __1__   Pay Rate __$10.00__

Occupation __Clerk__   Place __Office__

Date		Time Lost		Time Wk.		Reg. Pay	O.T. Prem. Pay	Gross Pay	F.I.C.A. Taxes	Federal Income Taxes	Hosp. Ins.	Union Dues	Total Deductions	Net Pay	Check No.	Cumulative Pay
Per. Ends	Paid	Hrs.	Reason	Total	O.T. Hours											
1/5	1/5			40		400.00		400.00	28.00	50.00	40.00		118.00	282.00	173	400.00
1/12	1/12			40		400.00		400.00	28.00	50.00	40.00		118.00	282.00	201	800.00
1/19	1/19			40		400.00		400.00	28.00	50.00	40.00		118.00	282.00	243	1,200.00
1/26	1/26	4	Sick	36		360.00		360.00	25.20	43.00	40.00		108.00	251.80	295	1,560.00
2/2	2/2			40		400.00		400.00	28.00	50.00	40.00		118.00	282.00	339	1,960.00
2/9	2/9			40		400.00		400.00	28.00	50.00	40.00		118.00	282.00	354	2,360.00
2/16	2/16			40		400.00		400.00	28.00	50.00	40.00		118.00	282.00	397	2,760.00
2/23	2/23			40		400.00		400.00	28.00	50.00	40.00		118.00	282.00	446	3,160.00
3/23	3/23			40		400.00		400.00	28.00	50.00	40.00		118.00	282.00	893	4,760.00

The payroll information on an Employee's Individual Earnings Record is taken from the Payroll Register. The information as to earnings, deductions, and net pay is first recorded on a single line in the Payroll Register. It is posted each pay period from there to the earnings record. Note the last column of the record. It shows an employee's cumulative earnings and is used to determine when the earnings reach the maximum amounts taxed and are no longer subject to the various payroll taxes.

Payroll Taxes Levied on the Employer

As previously explained, FICA taxes are levied in equal amounts on both covered employers and their employees. However, only employers are required to pay federal and, usually, state unemployment taxes. Each time a payroll is recorded, a general journal entry is also made to record the employer's FICA and state and federal unemployment taxes. For example, the entry to record the employer's payroll taxes on the payroll of Illustration 13-5 is:

Mar.	23	Payroll Taxes Expense	311.72	
		FICA Taxes Payable		239.82
		State Unemployment Taxes Payable . . .		56.76
		Federal Unemployment Taxes Payable . .		15.14
		To record the employer's payroll taxes.		

The $311.72 debit of the entry records as an expense the sum of the employer's payroll taxes. The $239.82 credit to FICA Taxes Payable is equal to and matches the FICA taxes deducted from the employees' pay and is credited to the same FICA Taxes Payable account. The $56.76 credit to State Unemployment Taxes Payable results from the assumptions that the employer's state unemployment tax rate is 3% on the first $7,000 paid each employee and that the employees have cumulative earnings prior to this pay period and earnings subject to the various taxes as shown in Illustration 13-9. Observe in the illustration that Dale Sears has earned more than $7,000, and his pay is assumed, as in most states, to be exempt from state unemployment tax. Judy Cross has previously earned $6,600, and only the first $400 of her pay is subject to tax. And since Kay Keife has previously earned $6,916, only $84 of her pay is subject to tax. The wages of the remaining employees are taxable in full. Consequently, the $56.76 credit to State Unemployment Taxes Payable in the entry recording the employer's payroll taxes resulted from multiplying the wages subject to tax ($1,892) by the assumed 3% rate.

As the law is presently amended, an employer's federal unemployment tax is also based on the first $7,000 in wages paid each employee. Therefore the $15.14 federal unemployment tax liability in the illustrated journal entry resulted from multiplying $1,892 by the 0.8% rate.

Accruing Taxes on Wages

Payroll taxes are levied on wages actually paid; consequently, there is no legal liability for taxes on accrued wages. Nevertheless, if the requirements of the **matching principle** are to be met, both accrued wages and the accrued

Illustration 13-9

Employees' Cumulative Earnings through the Last Pay Period and Earnings Subject to the Various Taxes

Employees	Earnings through Last Pay Period	Earnings This Pay Period	Earnings Subject to—	
			FICA Taxes	State and Federal Unemployment Taxes
Robert Austin. . .	$4,400.00	$ 400.00	$ 400.00	$ 400.00
Judy Cross. . . .	6,600.00	600.00	600.00	400.00
John Cruz	6,160.00	560.00	560.00	560.00
Kay Keite	6,916.00	728.00	728.00	84.00
Lee Miller	6,020.00	448.00	448.00	448.00
Dale Sears. . . .	7,050.00	690.00	690.00	
Totals		$3,426.00	$3,426.00	$1,892.00

taxes on the wages should be recorded at the end of an accounting period. However, since there is no legal liability and the amounts of such taxes vary little from one accounting period to the next, most employers apply the **materiality principle** and do not accrue payroll taxes.

■ **Employee (Fringe) Benefit Costs**

In addition to the wages earned by employees and the related payroll taxes paid by the employer, many companies provide their employees a variety of benefits. Since the costs of these benefits are paid by the employer, and the benefits are in addition to the amount of wages earned, they are often called fringe benefits. For example, an employer may pay for part (or all) of the employees' medical insurance, life insurance, and disability insurance. Another frequent employee benefit involves employer contributions to a retirement income plan. Perhaps the most typical employee benefit is vacation pay.

Employer Contributions to Employee Insurance and Retirement Plans

The entries to record employee benefit costs depend on the nature of the benefit. Some employee retirement plans are quite complicated and involve accounting procedures that are too complex for discussion in this introductory course. In other cases, however, the employer simply may be required to make periodic cash contributions to a retirement fund for each employee. Other employee benefits that require periodic cash payments by the employer include employer payments of insurance premiums for employees.

In the case of employee benefits that simply require the employer to make periodic cash payments, the entries to record the employer's obligations are similar to those used for payroll taxes.[1] For example, assume

[1] Many payments of employee benefits must be added to the gross salary of the employee for the purpose of calculating FICA taxes payable as well as federal and state unemployment taxes payable. However, in this chapter and in the problems at the end of the chapter, the possible effect of employee benefit costs on payroll taxes is ignored to avoid undue complexity in the introductory course.

an employer with five employees has agreed to pay medical insurance premiums of $100 per month for each employee. The employer also will contribute 10% of each employee's salary to a retirement program. If each employee earns $1,500 per month, the entry to record these employee benefits for the month of March is:

Mar.	31	Employees' Benefits Expense	1,250.00	
		Employees' Medical Insurance Payable . .		500.00
		Employees' Retirement Program Payable		750.00
		($1,500 × 5) × 10% = $750.		

Vacation Pay

Nearly all employers promise their employees paid vacation time as a benefit of employment. For example, many employees receive two weeks vacation in return for working 50 weeks each year. The effect of a two-week vacation is to increase the employer's payroll expenses by 4% (2/50 = .04). On the other hand, new employees often do not begin to accrue vacation time until after they've worked for a period of time, perhaps as much as a year. The employment contract may say that no vacation is granted until the employee works one year; but if the first year is completed, the employee receives the full two weeks. In this type of situation, the expense associated with vacation pay depends on the employee turnover rate. If the turnover experience of the employer suggests that only 90% of employees actually will be granted vacation time, the additional expense of a two-week vacation benefit would be 90% of 4%, or 3.6%.

To account for vacation pay, an employer should estimate and record the additional expense during the weeks the employees are working and earning the vacation time. For example, assume that a company with a weekly payroll of $20,000 grants two weeks vacation after one year's employment. Based on past turnover rates, the employer estimates that 90% of employees actually will be granted vacation time. The entry to record the estimated vacation pay is:

Date		Employees' Benefits Expense	720.00	
		Estimated Vacation Pay Liability		720.00
		$20,000 × .04 × .9 = $720.		

As employees take their vacations and receive their vacation pay, the entries to record the vacation payroll take the following general form:

Date		Estimated Vacation Pay Liability	xxx	
		FICA Taxes Payable		xxx
		Employees' Income Taxes Payable. . . .		xxx
		Other withholding liability accounts such as		
		Employees' Hospital insurance Insurance		
		Payable		xxx
		Accrued Payroll Payable		xxx

Payroll taxes and employee benefits costs are often a major catetory of expense incurred by a company. They may amount to well over 25% of the salaries earned by employees.

■   **Computerized Payroll Systems**   Manually prepared records like the ones described in this chapter are found in many small companies and very satisfactorily meet their needs. However, companies having many employees commonly use computers to process their payroll. The computer programs are designed to take advantage of the fact that each pay period the same calculations are performed and that much of the same information must be entered for each employee in the Payroll Register, on the employee's earnings record, and on the employees' paycheck. The computers simultaneously store or print the information in all three places.

test 12-13

Glossary terms. 12 + 13
objective
Problems - Exercises

□ **Glossary**

Clock card a card used by an employee to record his or her time of arrival and departure to and from work.

Employee's Individual Earnings Record a record of an employee's hours worked, gross pay, deductions, net pay, and certain personal information about the employee.

Federal depository bank a bank authorized to receive as deposits amounts of money payable to the federal government.

Federal unemployment tax a tax levied by the federal government and used to pay a portion of the costs of the joint federal-state unemployment programs.

FICA taxes Federal Insurance Contributions Act taxes, otherwise known as social security taxes.

Gross pay the amount an employee earns before any deductions such as FICA taxes and income tax withholdings.

Merit rating a rating granted to an employer by a state, based on whether or not the employer's employees have experienced periods of unemployment. A good rating reduces the employer's unemployment tax rate.

Net pay gross pay minus deductions; in other words, the portion of an employee's earnings that is paid to the employee.

Payroll bank account a special bank account into which at the end of each pay period the total amount of an employer's payroll is deposited and on which the employees' payroll checks are drawn.

Payroll tax a tax levied on the amount of a payroll or on the amount of an employee's gross pay.

State unemployment tax a tax levied by a state, the proceeds of which are used to pay benefits to unemployed workers.

Timekeeping making a record of the time each employee is at his or her place of work.

Wage bracket withholding table a table showing the amounts of income tax to be withheld from employees' wages at various levels of earnings.

Withholding allowance an amount of an employee's annual earnings not subject to income tax; also called a personal exemption.

□ **Questions for Class Discussion**

1. What are FICA taxes? Who pays these taxes, and for what purposes are the funds from FICA taxes used?

2. What are social security taxes?

3. X Company has one employee from whose pay it withholds $40.00 of federal income tax and $21.50 of FICA tax. The employee is paid twice each month. Y Company has six employees from whose pay it withholds each month a total of $750 of employee FICA taxes and $900 of federal income taxes. When must each of these companies remit these amounts to the Internal Revenue Service?

4. What benefits are paid to unemployed workers from funds raised by the Federal Unemployment Insurance Act? Why was this act passed?

5. Who pays federal unemployment insurance taxes? What is the typical tax rate, net of credits for contributions to state programs?

6. What are the objectives of state unemployment insurance laws? Who pays state unemployment insurance taxes?

7. What is a state unemployment merit rating? Why are such merit ratings granted?

8. What determines the amount that must be deducted from an employee's wages for federal income taxes?

9. What is a wage bracket withholding table?

10. What amount of income tax should be withheld from the salary of a single employee with three withholding allowances who earned $465 in a week? What if the employee earned $570 and had one withholding allowance? (Use the wage bracket withholding table in Illustration 13-3 to find the answers.)

11. What does the Fair Labor Standards Act require of a covered employer?

12. How is a clock card used in recording the time an employee is on the job?

13. How is a special payroll bank account used in paying the wages of employees?

14. At the end of an accounting period, a firm's special payroll bank account has a $685.50 balance because the payroll checks of two employees have not cleared the bank. Should this $685.50 appear on the firm's balance sheet? If so, where?

15. What information is accumulated on an employee's individual earnings record? Why must this information be accumulated? For what purposes is the information used?

16. What payroll taxes are levied on the employer? What taxes are deducted from the wages of an employee?

17. What are employee fringe benefits? Name some examples.

18. Should the salary of employees while they are on paid vacation be reported as an expense of the period during which they are on vacation? If not, when should the expense be reported?

□   **Class Exercises**   **Exercise 13-1**

Karen Tucker, an employee of a company subject to the Fair Labor Standards Act, worked 48 hours during the week ended January 7. Her pay rate is $12 per hour, and her wages are subject to no deductions other than FICA and federal income taxes. She claims three income tax exemptions. Calculate her regular pay, overtime premium pay, gross pay, FICA tax deduction at an assumed 7% rate, income tax deduction (use the wage bracket withholding table of Illustration 13-3), total deductions, and net pay.

Exercise 13-2

On January 6, at the end of its first weekly pay period in the year, the column totals of a company's Payroll Register showed that its sales employees had earned $2,280 and its office employees had earned $1,200. The employees were to have FICA taxes withheld at an assumed 7% rate plus $492 of federal income taxes, $80 of union dues, and $360 of hospital insurance premiums. Calculate the amount of FICA taxes to be withheld and give the general journal entry to record the Payroll Register.

Exercise 13-3

The following information as to earnings and deductions for the pay period ended April 10 was taken from a company's payroll records:

Employees	Gross Pay	Earnings to End of Previous Week	Federal Income Taxes	Health Insurance Deductions
Karen Bringol . . .	$ 530	$ 6,890	$ 70.00	$ 72.00
Tad Davison . . .	480	6,240	63.00	72.00
Bob Herzog . . .	400	5,200	39.00	44.50
Nancy Smith . . .	1,200	15,600	300.20	44.50
	$2,610		$472.20	$233.00

Required

1. Calculate the employees' FICA tax withholdings at an assumed 7% rate on the first $39,600 paid each employee. Also calculate total FICA taxes withheld, total deductions, and net pay.
2. Prepare a general journal entry to record the payroll. Assume all employees work in the office.

Exercise 13-4

Use the information provided in Exercise 13-3 to complete the following requirements:

1. Prepare a general journal entry to record the employer's payroll taxes resulting from the payroll. Assume a state unemployment tax rate of 1.9% and a federal unemployment tax of 0.8% on the first $7,000 paid each employee.
2. Prepare a general journal entry to record the following employee benefits incurred by the company: (1) health insurance costs equal to the amounts contributed by each employee and (2) contributions equal to 10% of gross pay for each employee's retirement income program.

Exercise 13-5

Barello Company's employees earn a gross pay of $15 per hour and work 40 hours each week. The FICA tax rate is 7%, the federal unemployment tax rate is 0.8%, and the state unemployment tax rate is 4.6%. In addition, Barello Company contributes 10% of gross pay to a retirement program for employees and pays medical insurance premiums of $30 per week per employee. What is Barello Company's total cost of employing a person for one hour? (Assume that individual wages are less than the $7,000 unemployment tax limit.)

Exercise 13-6

Hastings Corporation grants most of its employees two weeks vacation each year, providing they have worked for the company one complete year. After completing 10 years of service, employees receive four weeks of vacation. Hastings estimates that 95% of its employees with less than 10 years of service will be granted two weeks vacation this year, and 99% of those who will have completed 10 or more years of service during the year will be granted four weeks vacation (1% are expected to resign during their 10th year). The monthly payroll for January includes $150,000 to persons who will not complete 10 years of service this year, and $60,000 to persons who, if they do not resign, will have completed 10 years of service by year-end. On January 31, record the January expense arising from the vacation policy of the company.

Exercise 13-7

In an effort to reduce the federal government's annual deficit and provide more financial stability to the social security programs of the country, one proposal is to raise FICA tax rates from 7.15% to 10%, and to eliminate the $39,600 maximum limitation on the amount of earnings to which the rate applies. What effect would such a proposal have on the total payroll costs of a company with five employees whose salaries are as listed below?

A . . .	$32,500
B . . .	39,000
C . . .	48,000
D . . .	58,000
E . . .	75,000

Exercise 13-8

Eulich Company's payroll taxes and fringe benefit expenses include unemployment taxes of 0.8% (federal) and 5.0% (state) on the first $7,000 of each employee's salary, FICA taxes of 7% on the first $39,600, retirement fund contributions of 10% of total earnings, and health insurance premiums of $175 per employee per month. Given the following list of employee salaries, payroll taxes and fringe benefits constitute what percentage of salaries?

Barker . . .	$26,800
Day	45,500
Hanson . . .	53,300
Jones . . .	34,400
Kraft	40,000

Exercise 13-9

Ansel Parsons is single, claims four personal exemptions for income tax purposes, and earns a weekly salary of $610. In response to a city-wide effort to obtain charitable contributions to the local United Way programs, Parsons has requested that his employer withhold 1% of his salary (net of FICA and income taxes). Assume FICA taxes of 7% of the first $39,600 and use Illustration 13-3 to determine income tax withholdings. Under this program, what will be Parsons' annual contribution to the United Way?

Problems

Problem 13-1

On January 8, at the end of the first weekly pay period of the year, a company's Payroll Register showed that its employees had earned $11,250 of sales salaries and $2,750 of office salaries. Withholdings from the employees' salaries were to include FICA taxes at an assumed rate of 7%, $1,975 of federal income taxes, $560 of hospital insurance, and $185 of union dues.

Required

1. Calculate the total of the FICA Taxes Payable column in the Payroll Register, and prepare a general journal entry to record the register information.
2. Prepare a general journal entry to record the employer's payroll taxes resulting from the payroll. Assume the company has a merit rating that reduces its state unemployment tax rate to 3.8% of the first $7,000 paid each employee. The federal unemployment tax rate is 0.8%.
3. Under the assumption the company uses a payroll bank account and special payroll checks in paying its employees, give the check register entry (Check No. 678) to transfer funds equal to the payroll from the regular bank account to the payroll bank account.
4. Answer this question: After the check register entry is made and posted, are additional debit and credit entries required to record the payroll checks and pay the employees?

Problem 13-2

The payroll records of Service Corporation provided the following information for the weekly pay period ended December 24.

Employees	Clock Card No.	Daily Time							Pay Rate	Federal Income Taxes	Hospital Insur-ance	Union Dues	Earnings to End of Previous Week
		M	T	W	T	F	S	S					
Dick Hanson. . .	22	7	8	8	8	8	1	0	$18.00	$160.00	$ 38.00	$12.50	$35,000
Karen Dahl . . .	23	8	8	8	8	8	2	0	20.00	148.00	38.00	12.50	39,100
Bob Haines . . .	24	8	8	8	7	7	0	0	17.00	130.00	38.00	12.50	2,700
Jan Nichols . . .	25	8	8	7	8	8	3	0	15.00	104.00	32.00	12.50	29,500
Mike Smith . . .	26	8	7	8	8	8	4	0	22.00	184.00	38.00		41,200
Totals.										$726.00	$184.00	$50.00	

Required

1. Enter the relevant information in the proper columns of a Payroll Register and complete the register using a FICA tax rate of 7% on the first $39,600 paid each employee. Assume the company is subject

to the Fair Labor Standards Act. Charge the wages of Mike Smith to Office Salaries Expense and the wages of the remaining employees to Service Wages Expense.

2. Prepare a general journal entry to record the payroll register information.

3. Make the check register entry (Check No. 265) to transfer funds equal to the payroll from the regular bank account to the payroll bank account under the assumption the company uses special payroll checks and a payroll bank account in paying its employees. Assume the first payroll check is numbered 880 and enter the payroll check numbers in the Payroll Register.

4. Prepare a general journal entry to record the employer's payroll taxes resulting from the payroll. Assume the company has a merit rating that reduces its state unemployment tax rate to 4.4% of the first $7,000 paid each employee. The federal unemployment tax rate is 0.8%.

Problem 13-3

A company subject to the Fair Labor Standards Act accumulated the following payroll information for the weekly pay period ended December 22:

Employees	Clock Card No.	Daily Time							Pay Rate	Income Tax Exemp- tions	Medical Insur- ance	Union Dues	Earnings to End of Previous Week
		M	T	W	T	F	S	S					
Terry Dye . . .	18	8	6	8	8	8	4	0	$ 9.50	2	$25.00	$10.00	$19,000
Tom Jones . . .	19	8	8	8	7	8	4	0	11.00	1	25.00	10.00	6,100
Jay Tagg	20	8	8	8	8	8	0	0	14.00	4	35.00	10.00	27,800
Jane Weld . . .	21	8	8	8	9	9	0	0	12.50	3	35.00		3,200

Required

1. Enter the relevant information in the proper columns of a Payroll Register and complete the register. Assume a 7% FICA tax rate on the first $39,600 of each employee's wages. Use the wage bracket withholding table of Illustration 13-3 to determine the federal income tax to be withheld from the wages of each employee. Assume all employees are single and the first one is a salesperson, the second two work in the shop, and the last one works in the office.

2. Prepare a general journal entry to record the payroll register information.

3. Make the check register entry to transfer funds equal to the payroll from the regular bank account to the payroll bank account (Check No. 497) under the assumption the company uses special payroll checks and a payroll bank account in paying its employees. Assume the first payroll check is numbered 577 and enter the payroll check numbers in the Payroll Register.

4. Prepare a general journal entry to record the employer's payroll taxes

resulting from the payroll. Assume the company has a merit rating that reduces its state unemployment tax rate to 3.7%. The federal unemployment tax rate is 0.8%.

5. Prepare general journal entries to accrue employee fringe benefit costs for the week. Assume the company matches the employees' payments for medical insurance and contributes an amount equal to 10% of each employees' gross pay to a retirement program. Also, each employee accrues vacation pay at the rate of 4% of the wages and salaries earned. The company estimates that all employees eventually will be paid their vacation pay.

Problem 13-4

A company has four employees, each of whom earns $1,250 per month and is paid on the last day of each month. On June 1, the following accounts and balances appeared in its ledger:

a. FICA Taxes Payable, $700. (The balance of this account represents the liability for both the employer and employees' FICA taxes for the May 31 payroll only.)
b. Employees' Federal Income Taxes Payable, $592 (liability for May only).
c. Federal Unemployment Taxes Payable, $80 (liability for April and May only).
d. State Unemployment Taxes Payable, $290 (liability for April and May).
e. Employees' Medical Insurance Payable, $864 (liability for April and May).

During June and July, the company completed the following payroll-related transactions:

June 10 Issued Check No. 925 payable to First City Bank, a federal depository bank authorized to accept employers' payments of FICA taxes and employee income tax withholdings. The check was for $1,292 and was in payment of the May FICA and employee income taxes.

30 Prepared a general journal entry to record the June Payroll Record which had the following column totals:

FICA Taxes	Federal Income Taxes	Medical Insurance	Total Deductions	Net Pay	Office Salaries	Shop Wages
$350	$592	$216	$1,158	$3,842	$2,000	$3,000

30 Recorded the employer's $216 liability for its 50% contribution to the medical insurance plan of employees.

30 Issued Check No. 942 payable to Payroll Bank Account in payment of the June payroll. Endorsed the check, deposited it in the payroll bank account, and issued payroll checks to the employees.

June 30   Prepared a general journal entry to record the employer's payroll taxes resulting from the June payroll. The company has a merit rating that reduces its state unemployment tax rate to 2.9% of the first $7,000 paid each employee. The federal rate is 0.8%.

July 15   Issued Check No. 964 payable to First City Bank. The check was in payment of the June FICA and employee income taxes.

15   Issued Check No. 965 payable to Boston Insurance Company. The check was in payment of the April, May, and June employee medical insurance premiums.

15   Issued Check No. 966 to the State Tax Commission for the April, May, and June state unemployment taxes. Mailed the check along with the second quarter tax return to the State Tax Commission.

31   Issued Check No. 975 payable to First City Bank. The check was in payment of the employer's federal unemployment taxes for the second quarter of the year.

31   Mailed Form 941, reporting the FICA taxes and the employees' federal income tax withholdings for the second quarter.

Required

Prepare the necessary general journal entries to record the transactions.

□ Alternate Problems

Problem 13-1A

Brown Company's first weekly pay period of the year ended on January 6. On that date, the column totals of a company's Payroll Register indicated its sales employees had earned $13,250, its office employees had earned $6,250, and its delivery employees $1,500. The employees were to have FICA taxes withheld from their wages at an assumed 7% rate plus $2,100 federal income taxes, $950 medical insurance deductions, and $225 of union dues.

Required

1. Calculate the total of the FICA Taxes Payable column in the Payroll Register, and prepare a general journal entry to record the register information.

2. Prepare a general journal entry to record the employer's payroll taxes resulting from the payroll. Assume the company has a merit rating that reduces its state unemployment tax rate to 3.5% of the first $7,000 paid each employee.

3. Under the assumption the company uses special payroll checks and a payroll bank account in paying its employees, give the check register entry (Check No. 267) to transfer funds equal to the payroll from the regular bank account to the payroll bank account.

4. Answer this question: After the check register entry is made and posted, are additional debit and credit entries required to record the payroll checks and pay the employees?

Problem 13-2A

The following information was taken from the payroll records of Unlimited Computers Company for the weekly pay period ending December 20.

Employees	Clock Card No.	Daily Time							Pay Rate	Federal Income Taxes	Medical Insurance	Union Dues	Earnings to End of Previous Week
		M	T	W	T	F	S	S					
Mary Day	32	6	8	9	8	6	0	0	$22.00	$124.00	$ 24.00		$42,500
Ken Graff	33	7	8	8	8	8	6	0	16.00	104.00	30.00	$12.00	28,800
Mark Lang	34	8	9	9	9	9	0	0	15.00	87.00	36.00	12.00	4,500
Jane Thomas . . .	35	4	8	8	8	7	4	0	18.00	116.00	36.00	12.00	35,600
Jack Witt.	36	8	9	8	9	8	4	0	20.00	145.00	24.00		39,200
Totals										$576.00	$150.00	$36.00	

Required

1. Enter the relevant information in the proper columns of a Payroll Register and complete the register using a 7% FICA tax rate on the first $39,600 paid each employee. The company pays time and one half for hours in excess of 40 each week. Also, work on Saturdays is paid at time and one half whether the total for the week is over 40 or not. Charge the wages of Mary Day to Office Salaries Expense and the wages of the remaining employees to Plant Salaries Expense.

2. Prepare a general journal entry to record the payroll register information.

3. Assume the company uses special payroll checks drawn on a payroll bank account in paying its employees and make the check register entry (Check No. 375) to transfer funds equal to the payroll from the regular bank account to the payroll bank account. Also assume the first payroll check is No. 542 and enter the payroll check numbers in the Payroll Register.

4. Prepare a general journal entry to record the employer's payroll taxes resulting from the payroll. Assume the company has a merit rating that reduces its state unemployment tax rate to 2.5% of the first $7,000 paid each employee. The federal tax rate is 0.8%.

Problem 13-3A

The following information for the weekly pay period ended December 11 was taken from the records of a company subject to the Fair Labor Standards Act:

Employees	Clock Card No.	Daily Time							Pay Rate	Income Tax Exemptions	Medical Insurance	Union Dues	Earnings to End of Previous Week
		M	T	W	T	F	S	S					
Ray Ash	23	6	8	8	6	8	4	0	$13.00	1	$18.50		$23,800
Darwin Edds . .	24	7	8	8	8	8	4	0	9.00	0	12.00	$11.00	6,600
Jan Kirby	25	8	8	9	8	8	4	0	12.50	2	20.50		22,500
Betty Moxley . .	26	9	8	9	6	8	3	0	10.00	3	24.00	11.00	6,100

Required

1. Enter the relevant information in the proper columns of a Payroll Register and complete the register. Use a 7% FICA tax rate to calculate

the FICA tax of each employee. Use the wage bracket withholding table of Illustration 13-3 to determine the federal income taxes to be withheld from the wages of the employees. Assume that all employees are single and that the first employee works in the office, the second is a salesperson, and the last two work in the shop.

2. Prepare a general journal entry to record the payroll register information.

3. Make the check register entry (Check No. 278) to transfer funds equal to the payroll from the regular bank account to the payroll bank account. Assume the first payroll check is numbered 523 and enter the payroll check numbers in the Payroll Register.

4. Prepare a general journal entry to record the employer's payroll taxes resulting from the payroll. Assume the company has a merit rating that reduces its state unemployment tax rate to 4.0% of the first $7,000 paid each employee.

5. Prepare a general journal entry to accrue employee fringe benefit costs for the week. Assume the company matches the employees' payments for medical insurance and contributes an amount equal to 10% of each employees' gross pay to a retirement program. Also, Ash and Kirby accrue vacation pay at the rate of 6% of the wages and salaries earned. Edds and Moxley accrue vacation pay at the rate of 4%. The company estimates that all employees eventually will be paid their vacation pay.

Problem 13-4A

A company has three employees, each of whom earns $1,500 per month and is paid on the last day of each month. On March 1, the following accounts and balances appeared in its ledger:

a. FICA Taxes Payable, $630. (The balance of this account represents the liability for both the employer and employees' FICA taxes for the February 28 payroll only.)

b. Employees' Federal Income Taxes Payable, $680 (liability for February only).

c. Federal Unemployment Taxes Payable, $72 (liability for first two months of the year).

d. State Unemployment Taxes Payable, $360 (liability for January and February).

e. Employees' Medical Insurance Payable, $720 (liability for January and February).

During March and April, the company completed the following transactions related to payroll:

Mar. 10   Issued Check No. 615 payable to West Branch Bank, a federal depository bank authorized to accept employers' payments of FICA taxes and employee income tax withholdings. The $1,310 check was in payment of the February FICA and employee income taxes.

31   Prepared a general journal entry to record the March Payroll Record which had the following column totals:

FICA Taxes	Federal Income Taxes	Medical Insurance Deductions	Total Deductions	Net Pay	Office Salaries	Shop Wages
$315	$680	$180	$1,175	$3,325	$1,500	$3,000

Mar. 31   Recorded the employer's $180 liability for its 50% contribution to the medical insurance plan of employees.

31   Issued Check No. 655 payable to Payroll Bank Account in payment of the March payroll. Endorsed the check, deposited it in the payroll bank account, and issued payroll checks to the employees.

31   Prepared a general journal entry to record the employer's payroll taxes resulting from the March payroll. The company has a merit rating that reduces its state unemployment tax rate to 4.0% of the first $7,000 paid each employee. The federal rate is 0.8%.

Apr. 15   Issued Check No. 680 payable to West Branch Bank in payment of the March FICA and employee income taxes.

15   Issued Check No. 681 payable to National Insurance Company in payment of the employee medical insurance premiums for the first quarter.

15   Issued Check No. 682 to the State Tax Commission for the January, February, and March state unemployment taxes. Mailed the check along with a first quarter tax return to the State Tax Commission.

30   Issued Check No. 683 payable to West Branch Bank. The check was in payment of the employer's federal unemployment taxes for the first quarter of the year.

30   Mailed Form 941, reporting the FICA taxes and the employees' federal income tax withholdings for the second quarter.

Required

Prepare the necessary general journal entries to record the transactions.

Provocative Problems

Provocative Problem 13-1   Managing Payroll Costs

Runner's Universe Company has 100 regular employees, all earning in excess of $7,000 per year. The company's plant and office are located in a state in which the maximum unemployment tax rate is 5.4% of the first $7,000 paid each employee. However, the company has an excellent past unemployment record and a merit rating that reduces its state unemployment tax rate to 3.2% of the first $7,000 paid each employee.

The company has recently received an order for running shoes from a chain of department stores. The order should be very profitable and will probably be repeated each year. In filling the order, Runner's Universe Company can cut and form the parts for the shoes with present machines and employees. However, it will have to add 20 persons to its work force for 40 hours per week for 10 weeks to finish the shoes and pack them for shipment.

The company can hire these workers and add them to its own payroll, or it can secure the services of 20 people through Temporary Help, Inc. Runner's Universe will pay Temporary Help, Inc., $13 per hour for each hour worked by each person supplied. The people will be employees of Temporary Help, Inc., and it will pay their wages and all taxes on the wages. On the other hand, if Runner's Universe employs the workers and places them on its payroll, it will pay them $10 per hour and will also pay the following payroll taxes on their wages: FICA tax, 7.15% (assumed rate); federal unemployment tax, 0.8% on the first $7,000 paid each employee; state unemployment tax, 5.4% on the first $7,000 paid each employee. (The state unemployment tax rate will be 5.4% because if the company hires the temporary people and terminates them each year after 10 weeks, it will lose its merit rating.) The company will also have to pay medical insurance costs of $25 per employee per week.

Should Runner's Universe place the temporary help on its own payroll, or should it secure their services through Temporary Help, Inc.? Justify your answer.

Provocative Problem 13-2   Computer Services Company

Computer Services Company employs a highly skilled systems specialist at an annual salary of $54,000. The company pays federal unemployment taxes of 0.8% and state unemployment taxes of 3.7% on the first $7,000 of the specialist's wages. FICA taxes are 7.15% of the first $42,000. The company also pays $125 per month for the employee's medical insurance. Effective July 1, the company agreed to contribute 12% of the specialist's gross pay to a retirement program.

What was the total monthly cost of employing the specialist in January, March, August, and December? Assuming the employee works 170 hours each month, what is the cost per hour in January? If the annual gross salary is increased by $5,000, what will be the increase in the total annual costs of employing the specialist?

14 Partnership Accounting

After studying Chapter 14, you should be able to:

1. List the characteristics of a partnership and explain the importance of mutual agency and unlimited liability to a person about to become a partner.

2. Allocate partnership earnings to partners *(a)* on a stated fractional basis, *(b)* in the partners' capital ratio, and *(c)* through the use of salary and interest allowances.

3. Prepare entries for *(a)* the sale of a partnership interest, *(b)* the admission of a new partner by investment, and *(c)* the retirement of a partner by the withdrawal of partnership assets.

4. Prepare entries required in the liquidation of a partnership.

5. Define or explain the words and phrases listed in the chapter Glossary.

A majority of the states have adopted the Uniform Partnership Act to govern the formation and operation of partnerships. This act defines a **partnership** as "an association of two or more persons to carry on as co-owners a business for profit." A partnership has been further defined as "an association of two or more competent persons under a contract to combine some or all their property, labor, and skills in the operation of a business." Both of these definitions tell something of a partnership's legal nature. However, a better understanding of a partnership as a form of business organization may be gained by examining some of its characteristics.

■ Characteristics of a Partnership

A Voluntary Association

A partnership is a voluntary association into which a person cannot be forced against his or her will. This is because a partner is responsible for the business acts of his or her partners when the acts are within the scope of the partnership. Also, a partner is personally liable for all of the debts of his or her partnership. Consequently, partnership law recognizes it is only fair that a person be permitted to select the people he or she wishes to join in a partnership. Normally, a person will select only financially responsible people who have good judgment.

Based on a Contract

One advantage of a partnership as a form of business organization is the ease with which it may be begun. All that is required is that two or more legally competent people agree to be partners. Their agreement becomes a **partnership contract**. It should be in writing, with all anticipated points of future disagreement covered. However, it is binding if only orally expressed.

Limited Life

The life of a partnership is always limited. Death, bankruptcy, or anything that takes away the ability of one of the partners to contract automatically ends a partnership. In addition, since a partnership is based on a contract, if the contract is for a definite period, the partnership ends when that period expires. If the contract does not specify a time period, the partnership ends when the business for which it was created is completed. Or, if no time is stated and the business cannot be completed but goes on indefinitely, the partnership may be terminated at will by any one of the partners.

Mutual Agency

Normally, there is **mutual agency** in a partnership. This means that under normal circumstances, every partner is an agent of the partnership and can enter into and bind it to any contract within the apparent scope of its business. For example, a partner in a merchandising business can bind the partnership to contracts to buy merchandise, lease a store building, borrow money, or hire employees. These are all within the scope of a merchandising firm. On the other hand, a partner in a law firm, acting alone, cannot bind his or her partners to a contract to buy merchandise for resale or rent a store building. These are not within the normal scope of a law firm's business.

Partners among themselves may agree to limit the right of any one or more of the partners to negotiate certain contracts for the partnership. Such an agreement is binding on the partners and on outsiders who know of the agreement. However, it is not binding on outsiders who are unaware of its existence. Outsiders who are unaware of anything to the contrary have a right to assume that each partner has the normal agency rights of a partner.

Mutual agency offers an important reason for care in the selection of partners. Good partners benefit all; but a poor partner can do great damage. Mutual agency plus unlimited liability are the reasons most partnerships have only a few members.

Unlimited Liability

When a partnership business is unable to pay its debts, the creditors may satisfy their claims from the personal assets of the partners. Furthermore, if the property of a partner is insufficient to meet his or her share, the creditors may turn to the assets of the remaining partners who are able to pay. Thus, a partner may be called on to pay all the debts of his or her partnership and is said to have **unlimited liability** for its debts.

Unlimited liability may be illustrated as follows. Ned Albert and Carol Bates each invested $5,000 in a store to be operated as a partnership, under an agreement to share losses and gains equally. Albert has no property other than his $5,000 investment. Bates owns her own home, a farm, and has sizable savings in addition to her investment. The partners rented store space and bought merchandise and fixtures costing $30,000. They paid $10,000 in cash and promised to pay the balance at a later date. However, the night before the store opened the building in which it was located burned and the merchandise and fixtures were totally destroyed. There was no insurance, all the partnership assets were lost, and Albert has no other assets. Consequently, the partnership creditors may collect the full $20,000 of their claims from Bates. However, Bates may look to Albert for payment of half at a later date, if Albert ever becomes able to pay.

Limited Partnerships

In the business associations described thus far as partnerships, all of the partners have unlimited liability. Sometimes, however, a group of individuals want to invest in a partnership but are unwilling to accept the risk of unlimited liability. This can be accomplished by using a unique form of business called a **limited partnership.** A limited partnership has two classes of partners, general partners and limited partners. At least one of the partners, the **general partner(s),** must assume unlimited liability for the debts of the partnership. However, the remaining partners, the **limited partners,** have no personal liability beyond the amounts they invest in the business. Usually, a limited partnership is managed by the general partner(s). The limited partners have no active role except for certain major decisions as specified in the partnership agreement. To distinguish limited partnerships from others, partnerships in which all of the partners have unlimited liability are often called **general partnerships.**

■ **Advantages and Disadvantages of a Partnership**

Limited life, mutual agency, and unlimited liability are disadvantages of a partnership. Yet, a partnership has advantages over both the single proprietorship and corporation forms of organization. A partnership has the advantage of being able to bring together more money and skills than a single proprietorship. It is much easier to organize than a corporation. It does not have the corporation's governmental supervision nor its extra burden of taxation. And, partners may act freely and without the necessity of stockholders' and directors' meetings, as is required in a corporation.

■ **Partnership Accounting**

Partnership accounting is exactly like that of a single proprietorship except for transactions that directly affect the partners' equities. Because ownership rights in a partnership are divided between two or more partners, there must be (1) a capital account for each partner, (2) a withdrawals account for each partner, and (3) an accurate measurement and division of earnings.

Each partner's capital account is credited, and asset accounts showing the nature of the assets invested are debited in recording the investment of each partner. A partner's withdrawals are debited to his or her withdrawals account. And, in the end-of-period closing procedure, the capital account is credited for a partner's share of the net income. Obviously, these closing procedures are like those used for a single proprietorship. The only difference is that separate capital and withdrawals accounts are maintained for each partner. Thus, the closing procedures for a partnership require no further consideration. However, the matter of dividing earnings among partners requires additional discussion.

■ **Nature of Partnership Earnings**

Law and custom recognize that partners cannot enter into an employer-employee contractual relationship with themselves. Hence, partners cannot legally hire themselves and pay themselves a salary. Furthermore, law and custom recognize that a partner works for partnership profits and not a salary. Also, law and custom recognize that a partner invests in a partnership for earnings and not for interest. However, it should be recognized that partnership earnings may include a return for services, even though the return is contained within the earnings and is not a salary in a legal sense. Likewise, partnership earnings may include a return on invested capital, although the return is not interest in the legal sense of the term. Furthermore, if partnership earnings are to be fairly shared, it is often necessary to recognize this. For example, if one partner contributes five times as much capital as another, it is only fair that this be taken into consideration in the method of sharing. Likewise, if the services of one partner are much more valuable than those of another, some provision should be made for the unequal service contributions.

■ Division of Earnings

The law provides that in the absence of a contrary agreement, partnership income or loss is shared equally by the partners. However, partners may agree to any method of sharing. If they agree to a method of sharing income but say nothing of losses, losses are shared in the same way as income.

Several methods of sharing partnership earnings may be employed. All attempt in one way or another to recognize differences in service contributions or in investments, when such differences exist. Three frequently used methods to share earnings are: (1) on a stated fractional basis, (2) based on the ratio of capital investments, or (3) based on salary and interest allowances and the remainder in a fixed ratio.

■ Earnings Allocated on a Stated Fractional Basis

The easiest way to divide partnership earnings is to give each partner a stated fraction of the total. A division on a fractional basis may provide for an equal sharing if service and capital contributions are equal. An equal sharing may also be provided when the greater capital contribution of one partner is offset by a greater service contribution of another. Or, if the service and capital contributions are unequal, a fixed ratio may easily provide for an unequal sharing. All that is necessary in any case is for the partners to agree as to the fractional share to be given each.

For example, the partnership agreement of Morse and North may provide that each partner is to receive half the earnings. Or the agreement may provide for two thirds to Morse and one third to North. Or it may provide for three fourths to Morse and one fourth to North. Any fractional basis may be agreed upon as long as the partners feel earnings are fairly shared. For example, assume the agreement of Morse and North provides for a two-thirds and one-third sharing, and net income for a year is $30,000. After all revenue and expense accounts are closed, if net income is $30,000, the partnership Income Summary account has a $30,000 credit balance. It is closed, and the earnings are allocated to the partners with the following entry:

Dec.	31	Income Summary	30,000.00	
		A. P. Morse, Capital		20,000.00
		R. G. North, Capital		10,000.00
		To close the Income Summary account and allocate the earnings.		

■ Division of Earnings Based on the Ratio of Capital Investments

If the business of a partnership is of a nature that earnings are closely related to money invested, a division of earnings based on the ratio of partners' investments offers a fair sharing method. To illustrate this method, assume that Chase, Davis, and Fall have agreed to share earnings in the ratio of their investments. If these are Chase, $50,000, Davis, $30,000, and Fall, $40,000, and if net income for the year is $48,000, the respective shares of the partners are calculated as follows:

Step 1:   Chase, capital . . . . . $ 50,000
          Davis, capital   30,000
          Fall, capital   40,000
          Total invested $120,000

Step 2:   Share of earnings to Chase: $\dfrac{\$50,000}{\$120,000} \times \$48,000 = \$20,000$

          Share of earnings to Davis: $\dfrac{\$30,000}{\$120,000} \times \$48,000 = \$12,000$

          Share of earnings to Fall: $\dfrac{\$40,000}{\$120,000} \times \$48,000 = \$16,000$

The entry to allocate the earnings to the partners is then:

Dec.	31	Income Summary	48,000.00	
		T. S. Chase, Capital		20,000.00
		S. A. Davis, Capital		12,000.00
		R. R. Fall, Capital		16,000.00
		To close the Income Summary account and allocate the earnings.		

Salaries and Interest as Aids in Sharing

Sometimes partners' capital contributions are unequal. Also, the service contributions of the partners may not be equal. Even in partnerships in which all partners work full time, the services of one partner may be more valuable than the services of another. When these situations occur and, for example, the capital contributions are unequal, the partners may allocate a portion of their net income to themselves in the form of interest, so as to compensate for the unequal investments. Or, when service contributions are unequal, they may use salary allowances as a means of compensating for unequal service contributions. Or, when investment and service contributions are both unequal, they may use a combination of interest and salary allowances in an effort to share earnings fairly.

For example, Hill and Dale began a partnership business of a kind in which Hill has had experience and could command a $36,000 annual salary working for another firm of like nature. Dale is new to the business and could expect to earn not more than $24,000 working elsewhere. Furthermore, Hill invested $30,000 in the business and Dale invested $10,000. Consequently, the partners agreed that in order to compensate for the unequal service and capital contributions, they will share income or losses as follows:

1. A share of the profits equal to interest at 10% is to be allowed on the partners' initial investments.
2. Annual salary allowances of $36,000 per year to Hill and $24,000 per year to Dale are to be allowed.
3. The remaining balance of income or loss is to be shared equally.

Under this agreement, a first year $69,000 net income would be shared as in Illustration 14-1.

After the shares in the net income are determined, the following entry is used to close the Income Summary account. Observe in the entry that the credit amounts may be taken from the first two column totals of the computation of Illustration 14-1.

Dec.	31	Income Summary	69,000.00	
		Hill, Capital		41,500.00
		Dale, Capital		27,500.00
		To close the Income Summary account and allocate the earnings.		

In a legal sense, partners do not work for salaries, nor do they invest in a partnership to earn interest. They invest and work for earnings. Consequently, when a partnership agreement provides for salaries and interest, the partners should understand that the salaries and interest are not really expenses of the partnership. They are only a means of sharing income or losses.

In the illustration just completed, the $69,000 net income exceeded the salary and interest allowances of the partners. However, the partners would use the same method to share a net income smaller than their salary and interest allowances, or to share a loss. For example, assume that Hill and Dale earned only $45,000 in a year. A $45,000 net income would be shared by the partners as in Illustration 14-2.

Illustration 14-1	**Sharing Income When Income Exceeds Interest and Salary Allowances**		
	Share to Hill	**Share to Dale**	**Income Allocated**
Total net income			$69,000
Allocated as interest:			
Hill (10% on $30,000)	$ 3,000		
Dale (10% on $10,000)		$ 1,000	
Total allocated as interest.			4,000
Balance of income after interest allowances			$65,000
Allocated as salary allowances:			
Hill	36,000		
Dale		24,000	
Total allocated as salary allowances			60,000
Balance of income after interest and salary allowances			$ 5,000
Balance allocated equally:			
Hill	2,500		
Dale		2,500	
Total allocated equally			5,000
Balance of income.			–0–
Shares of the partners	$41,500	$27,500	

Illustration 14-2	Sharing Income When Interest and Salary Allowances Exceed Income			
		Share to Hill	Share to Dale	Income Allocated
Total net income				$ 45,000
Allocated as interest:				
Hill (10% on $30,000).		$ 3,000		
Dale (10% on $10,000)			$ 1,000	
Total allocated as interest				4,000
Balance of income after interest allowances				$ 41,000
Allocated as salary allowances:				
Hill		36,000		
Dale			24,000	
Total allocated as salary allowances.				60,000
Balance of income after interest and salary allowances (a negative amount).				$(19,000)
Balance allocated equally:				
Hill		(9,500)		
Dale			(9,500)	
Total allocated equally.				(19,000)
Balance of income				–0–
Shares of the partners.		$29,500	$15,500	

A net loss would be shared by Hill and Dale in the same manner as the foregoing $45,000 net income. The only difference is that the income-and-loss-sharing procedure would begin with a negative amount of income, in other words, a net loss. The amount allocated equally would then be a larger negative amount.

Partnership Financial Statements

In most respects, partnership financial statements are like those of a single proprietorship. However, one common difference is that the income allocation is often shown on the income statement following the reported net income. For example, an income statement prepared for Hill and Dale might show the allocation of the $45,000 net income of Illustration 14-2 as in Illustration 14-3.

Addition or Withdrawal of a Partner

A partnership is based on a contract between specific individuals. Consequently, an existing partnership is ended when a partner withdraws or a new partner is added. A partner may sell his or her partnership interest and withdraw from a partnership. Also, a partner may withdraw his or her equity, taking partnership cash or other assets. Likewise, a new partner may join an existing partnership by purchasing an interest from one or more of its partners or by investing cash or other assets in the business.

Sale of a Partnership Interest

Assume that Abbott, Burns, and Camp are partners in a partnership that has no liabilities and the following assets and owners' equity:

Assets		Owners' Equity	
Cash	$ 3,000	Abbott, capital	$ 5,000
Other assets	12,000	Burns, capital	5,000
		Camp, capital	5,000
Total assets	$15,000	Total owners' equity	$15,000

Camp's equity in this partnership is $5,000. If Camp sells this equity to Davis for $7,000, Camp is selling a $5,000 interest in the partnership assets. The entry on the partnership books to transfer the equity is:

Feb.	4	Camp, Capital	5,000.00	
		Davis, Capital		5,000.00
		To transfer Camp's equity in the partnership assets to Davis.		

After this entry is posted, the assets and owners' equity of the new partnership are:

Assets		Owners' Equity	
Cash	$ 3,000	Abbott, capital	$ 5,000
Other assets	12,000	Burns, capital	5,000
		Davis, capital	5,000
Total assets	$15,000	Total owners' equity	$15,000

Illustration 14-3

Hill and Dale
Income Statement
For Year Ended December 31, 19—

Sales		$332,400

~~~~~~

Net income		$ 45,000
Allocation of net income to the partners:		
To Hill:		
Interest at 10% on investment	$ 3,000	
Salary allowance	36,000	
Total	$39,000	
Less one half the remaining deficit	(9,500)	
Share of the net income		$ 29,500
To Dale:		
Interest at 10% on investment	$ 1,000	
Salary allowance	24,000	
Total	$25,000	
Less one half the remaining deficit	(9,500)	
Share of the net income		15,500
Net income allocated		$ 45,000

Two points should be noted in regard to this transaction. First, the $7,000 Davis paid Camp is not recorded in the partnership books. Camp sold and transferred a $5,000 equity in the partnership assets to Davis. The entry that records the transfer is a debit to Camp, Capital and a credit to Davis, Capital for $5,000. Furthermore, the entry is the same whether Davis pays Camp $7,000, or $70,000. The amount is paid directly to Camp. It is a side transaction between Camp and Davis and does not affect partnership assets.

The second point to be noted is that Abbott and Burns must agree to the sale and transfer if Davis is to become a partner. Abbott and Burns cannot prevent Camp from selling the interest to Davis. On the other hand, Camp cannot force Abbott and Burns to accept Davis as a partner. If Abbott and Burns agree to accept Davis, a new partnership is formed and a new contract with a new income-and-loss-sharing ratio must be drawn. If Camp sells to Davis and either Abbott or Burns refuses to accept Davis as a partner, under the Uniform Partnership Act Davis gets Camp's share of partnership income and losses and Camp's share of partnership assets if the firm is liquidated. However, Davis gets no voice in the management of the firm until admitted as a partner.

Investing in an Existing Partnership

Instead of purchasing the equity of an existing partner, an individual may gain an equity by investing assets in the business, with the invested assets becoming the property of the partnership. For example, assume that the partnership of Evans and Gage has assets and owners' equity as follows:

Assets		Owners' Equity	
Cash	$ 3,000	Evans, capital	$20,000
Other assets	37,000	Gage, capital	20,000
Total assets	$40,000	Total owners' equity	$40,000

Also, assume that Evans and Gage have agreed to accept Hart as a partner with a one-half interest in the business upon his investment of $40,000. The entry to record Hart's investment is:

Mar.	2	Cash	40,000.00	
		Hart, Capital		40,000.00
		To record the investment of Hart.		

After the entry is posted, the assets and owners' equity of the new partnership appear as follows:

Assets		Owners' Equity	
Cash	$43,000	Evans, capital	$20,000
Other assets	37,000	Gage, capital	20,000
		Hart, capital	40,000
Total assets	$80,000	Total owners' equity	$80,000

In this case, Hart has a 50% equity in the assets of the business. However, he does not necessarily have a right to one half of its net income. The sharing of income and losses is a separate matter on which the partners must agree. Furthermore, the agreed method may bear no relation to their capital ratio.

A Bonus to the Old Partners

Sometimes, when the equity of a partnership is worth more than the amounts of equity recorded in the accounting records, its partners may require an incoming partner to give a bonus for the privilege of joining the firm. For example, Judd and Kirk operate a partnership business, sharing its earnings equally. The partnership's accounting records show that Judd has a $38,000 equity in the business, and Kirk has a $32,000 equity. They have agreed to allow Lee a one-third equity and a one-third share of the partnership's earnings upon the investment of $50,000. Lee's equity is determined with a calculation like this:

Equities of the existing partners ($38,000 + $32,000) . . .	$ 70,000
Investment of the new partner	50,000
Total equities in the new partnership.	$120,000
Equity of Lee (⅓ of total).	$ 40,000

And the entry to record Lee's investment is:

May	15	Cash	50,000.00		
		Lee, Capital		40,000.00	
		Judd, Capital		5,000.00	
		Kirk, Capital		5,000.00	
		To record the investment of Lee.			

The $10,000 difference between the $50,000 invested by Lee and the $40,000 credited to his capital account is a bonus that is shared by Judd and Kirk in their income-and-loss-sharing ratio. Such a bonus is always shared by the old partners in their income-and-loss-sharing ratio. This is fair because the bonus compensates the old partners for increases in the worth of the partnership that have not yet been recorded as income.

Recording Goodwill Instead of allowing bonuses to the old partners, goodwill may be recorded in the admission of a new partner, with the amount of the goodwill being used to increase the equities of the old partners. This can be justified only if the old partnership has a sustained earnings rate in excess of the average for its industry. However, in practice, goodwill is seldom recognized upon the admission of a new partner. Instead, the bonus method is used.

Bonus to the New Partner

Sometimes the members of an existing partnership may be very anxious to bring a new partner into their firm. The business may need additional cash or the new partner may have exceptional abilities or business contacts that will increase profits. In such a situation, the old partners may be willing to give the new partner a larger equity in the business than the amount of his or her investment. For example, Moss and Owen are partners with capital account balances of $30,000 and $18,000, respectively, and sharing income and losses in a 2:1 ratio. The partners are anxious to have Pitt join their partnership and will allow him a one-fourth equity in the firm if he will invest $12,000. If Pitt accepts, his equity in the new firm is calculated as follows:

Equities of the existing partners ($30,000 + $18,000) . .	$48,000
Investment of the new partner	12,000
Total equities in the new partnership.	$60,000
Equity of Pitt (¼ of total).	$15,000

And the entry to record Pitt's investment is:

June	1	Cash	12,000.00	
		Moss, Capital	2,000.00	
		Owen, Capital	1,000.00	
		Pitt, Capital		15,000.00
		To record the investment of Pitt.		

Note that Pitt's bonus is contributed by the old partners in their income-and-loss-sharing ratio. Also remember that Pitt's one-fourth equity does not necessarily entitle him to one fourth of the earnings of the business, since the sharing of income and losses is a separate matter for agreement by the partners.

Withdrawal of a Partner

The best practice in regard to a partner's withdrawal from a partnership is for the partners to provide in advance in their partnership contract the procedures to be followed. Such procedures commonly provide for an audit of the accounting records and a revaluation of the partnership assets. The revaluation is very desirable since it places the assets on the books at current values. It also causes the retiring partner's capital account to reflect the current value of the partner's equity. Often in such cases the agreement also provides that the retiring partner is to withdraw assets equal to the book amount of the revalued equity.

For example, assume that Blue is retiring from the partnership of Smith, Blue, and Short. The partners have always shared income and losses in the ratio of Smith, one half; Blue, one fourth; and Short, one fourth. Their partnership agreement provides for an audit and asset revaluation upon the retirement of a partner. Just prior to the audit and revaluation, their balance sheet shows the following assets and owners' equity:

Assets			Owners' Equity	
Cash		$11,000	Smith, capital	$22,000
Merchandise inventory . .		16,000	Blue, capital	10,000
Equipment	$20,000		Short, capital	10,000
Less accum. depr.. . .	5,000	15,000		
Total assets		$42,000	Total owners' equity	$42,000

The audit and appraisal indicate the merchandise inventory is overvalued by $4,000. Also, due to market changes, the partnership equipment should be valued at $25,000 with accumulated depreciation of $8,000. The entries to record these revaluations are:

Oct.	31	Smith, Capital	2,000.00	
		Blue, Capital	1,000.00	
		Short, Capital	1,000.00	
		Merchandise Inventory		4,000.00
		To revalue the inventory.		
	31	Equipment	5,000.00	
		Accumulated Depreciation, Equipment . .		3,000.00
		Smith, Capital		1,000.00
		Blue, Capital		500.00
		Short, Capital		500.00
		To revalue the equipment.		

Note in the illustrated entries that income and losses are shared in the partners' income-and-loss-sharing ratio. Gains and losses from asset revaluations are always so shared. The fairness of this is easy to see when it is remembered that if the partnership did not terminate, such gains and losses would sooner or later be reflected on the income statement.

After the entries revaluing the partnership assets are recorded, a balance sheet will show these revalued assets and equities for Smith, Blue, and Short.

Assets			Owners' Equity	
Cash		$11,000	Smith, capital	$21,000
Merchandise inventory . .		12,000	Blue, capital	9,500
Equipment	$25,000		Short, capital	9,500
Less accum. depr. . .	8,000	17,000		
Total assets		$40,000	Total owners' equity	$40,000

After the revaluation, if Blue withdraws, taking assets equal to his revalued equity, the entry to record the withdrawal is:

Oct.	31	Blue, Capital	9,500.00	
		Cash		9,500.00
		To record the withdrawal of Blue.		

In withdrawing, Blue does not have to take cash in settlement of his equity. He may take any combination of assets to which the partners agree, or he may take the new partnership's promissory note. Also, the withdrawal of Blue generally creates a new partnership. Consequently, a new partnership contract and a new income-and-loss-sharing agreement may be required.

Partner Withdraws Taking Assets of Less Value than His Book Equity

Sometimes when a partner retires, the remaining partners may not wish to have the assets revalued and the new values recorded. In such cases, the partners may agree, for example, that the assets are overvalued. And, due to the overvalued assets, the retiring partner should in settlement of his equity take assets of less value than the book value of his equity. Sometimes, too, when assets are not overvalued, the retiring partner may be so anxious to retire that he is willing to take less than the current value of his equity just to get out of the partnership.

When a partner retires taking assets of less value than his equity, he is in effect leaving a portion of his book equity in the business. In such cases, the remaining partners share the unwithdrawn equity portion in their income-and-loss-sharing ratio. For example, assume that Black, Brown, and Green are partners sharing income and losses in a 2:2:1 ratio. Their assets and equities are:

Assets		Owners' Equity	
Cash	$ 5,000	Black, capital	$ 6,000
Merchandise	9,000	Brown, capital	6,000
Store equipment	4,000	Green, capital	6,000
Total assets	$18,000	Total owners' equity	$18,000

Brown is so anxious to withdraw from the partnership that he is willing to retire if permitted to take $4,500 in cash in settlement for his equity. Black and Green agree to the $4,500 withdrawal, and Brown retires. The entry to record the retirement is:

Mar.	4	Brown, Capital	6,000.00	
		Cash		4,500.00
		Black, Capital		1,000.00
		Green, Capital		500.00
		To record the withdrawal of Brown.		

In retiring, Brown did not withdraw $1,500 of his book equity. This is divided between Black and Green in their income-and-loss-sharing ratio. The income-and-loss-sharing ratio of the original partnership was Black, 2; Brown, 2; and Green, 1. Therefore in the original partnership, Black and Green shared in a 2:1 ratio. Consequently, the unwithdrawn book equity of Brown is shared by Black and Green in this ratio.

Partner Withdraws Taking Assets of Greater Value than His Book Equity

There are two common reasons for a partner receiving upon retirement assets of greater value than his book equity. First, certain of the partnership assets may be undervalued. Or, the partners continuing the business may be so anxious for the retiring partner to withdraw that they are willing to give him assets of greater value than his book equity.

When assets are undervalued and the partners do not wish to change the recorded values, the partners may agree to permit a retiring member to withdraw assets of greater value than his book equity. In such cases, the retiring partner is, in effect, withdrawing his own book equity and a portion of his partners' equities. For example, assume that Jones, Thomas, and Finch are partners sharing income and losses in a 3:2:1 ratio. Their assets and owners' equity are:

Assets		Owners' Equity	
Cash	$ 5,000	Jones, capital	$ 9,000
Merchandise	10,000	Thomas, capital	6,000
Equipment	3,000	Finch, capital	3,000
Total assets	$18,000	Total owners' equity	$18,000

Finch wishes to withdraw from the partnership. Jones and Thomas plan to continue the business. The partners agree that certain of their assets are undervalued, but they do not wish to increase the recorded values. They further agree that if current values were recorded, the asset total would be increased $6,000 and the equity of Finch would be increased $1,000. Therefore, the partners agree that $4,000 is the proper value for Finch's equity and that he may withdraw that amount in cash. The entry to record the withdrawal is:

May	7	Finch, Capital	3,000.00	
		Jones, Capital	600.00	
		Thomas, Capital	400.00	
		Cash		4,000.00
		To record the withdrawal of Finch.		

■ Death of a Partner

A partner's death automatically dissolves and ends a partnership, and the deceased partner's estate is entitled to receive the amount of his or her equity. The partnership contract should contain provisions for settlement in case a partner dies. Included should be provisions for (a) an immediate closing of the books to determine earnings since the end of the previous accounting period and (b) a method for determining and recording current values for the assets. After earnings are shared and the current value of the deceased partner's equity is determined, the remaining partners and the deceased partner's estate must agree to a disposition of the equity. They may agree to its sale to the remaining partners or to an outsider, or they may agree to the withdrawal of assets in settlement. Entries for both of these procedures have already been discussed.

■ Liquidations

When a partnership is liquidated, its business is ended. The assets are converted into cash, and the creditors are paid. The remaining cash is then distributed to the partners, and the partnership is dissolved. Although many combinations of circumstances occur in **liquidations,** only three are discussed here.

All Assets Realized before a Distribution; Assets Are Sold at a Profit

A partnership liquidation under this assumption may be illustrated with the following example. Ottis, Skinner, and Parr have operated a partnership for a number of years, sharing incomes and losses in a $3:2:1$ ratio. Due to several unsatisfactory conditions, the partners decide to liquidate as of December 31. On that date, the books are closed, the income from operations is transferred to the partners' capital accounts, and the following balance sheet is prepared:

Assets		Liabilities and Owners' Equity	
Cash	$10,000	Accounts payable	$ 5,000
Merchandise inventory	15,000	Ottis, capital	15,000
Other assets	25,000	Skinner, capital	15,000
		Parr, capital	15,000
		Total liabilities and	
Total assets	$50,000	owners' equity	$50,000

In a liquidation, either a gain or a loss normally results from the sale of each group of assets. These losses and gains are called "losses and gains from realization." They are shared by the partners in their income-and-loss-sharing ratio. If Ottis, Skinner, and Parr sell their inventory for $12,000 and their other assets for $34,000, the sales and the net gain allocation are recorded as follows:

Jan.	12	Cash	12,000.00	
		Loss or Gain from Realization	3,000.00	
		Merchandise Inventory		15,000.00
		Sold the inventory at a loss.		
	15	Cash	34,000.00	
		Other Assets		25,000.00
		Loss or Gain from Realization		9,000.00
		Sold the other assets at a profit.		
	15	Loss or Gain from Realization	6,000.00	
		Ottis, Capital		3,000.00
		Skinner, Capital		2,000.00
		Parr, Capital		1,000.00
		To allocate the net gain from realization to the partners in their $3:2:1$ income-and-loss-sharing ratio.		

Careful attention should be given to the last journal entry. In a partnership termination, when assets are sold at a loss or gain, the loss or gain is allocated to the partners in their income-and-loss-sharing ratio. In solving liquidation problems, students sometimes attempt to allocate the assets to the partners in their income-and-loss-sharing ratio. Obviously this is not correct. It is not assets but gains and losses that are shared in the income-and-loss-sharing ratio.

After the merchandise and other assets of Ottis, Skinner, and Parr are sold and the net gain is allocated, a new balance sheet shows the following:

Assets		Liabilities and Owners' Equity	
Cash	$56,000	Accounts payable	$ 5,000
		Ottis, capital	18,000
		Skinner, capital	17,000
		Parr, capital	16,000
		Total liabilities and	
Total assets	$56,000	owners' equity	$56,000

Observe that the one asset, cash, $56,000, exactly equals the sum of the liabilities and the equities of the partners.

After partnership assets are realized and the gain or loss shared, entries are made to distribute the realized cash to the proper parties. Since creditors have first claim, they are paid first. After the creditors are paid, the remaining cash is divided among the partners. Each partner has the right to cash equal to his equity or, in other words, cash equal to the balance of his capital account. The entries to distribute the cash of Ottis, Skinner, and Parr are:

Jan.	15	Accounts payable	5,000.00	
		Cash		5,000.00
		To pay the claims of the creditors.		
	15	Ottis, Capital	18,000.00	
		Skinner, Capital	17,000.00	
		Parr, Capital	16,000.00	
		Cash		51,000.00
		To distribute the remaining cash to the partners according to their capital account balances.		

Notice that after gains and losses are shared and the creditors are paid, each partner receives liquidation cash equal to the balance remaining in his capital account. The partners receive these amounts because a partner's capital account balance shows his equity in the one partnership asset, cash.

All Assets Realized before a Distribution; Assets Sold at a Loss; Each Partner's Capital Account Is Sufficient to Absorb His Share of the Loss

In a partnership liquidation, the assets are sometimes sold at a net loss. For example, if contrary to the previous assumptions the inventory of Ottis,

Skinner, and Parr is sold for $9,000 and the other assets for $13,000, the entries to record the sales and loss allocation are:

Jan.	12	Cash	9,000.00	
		Loss or Gain from Realization	6,000.00	
		Merchandise Inventory		15,000.00
		Sold the inventory at a loss.		
	15	Cash	13,000.00	
		Loss or Gain from Realization	12,000.00	
		Other Assets		25,000.00
		Sold the other assets at a loss.		
	15	Ottis, Capital	9,000.00	
		Skinner, Capital	6,000.00	
		Parr, Capital	3,000.00	
		Loss or Gain from Realization		18,000.00
		To allocate the loss from realization to the partners in their income-and-loss-sharing ratio.		

After the entries are posted, a balance sheet shows that the partnership cash exactly equals the liabilities and the equities of the partners, as follows:

Assets		Liabilities and Owners' Equity	
Cash	$32,000	Accounts payable	$ 5,000
		Ottis, capital	6,000
		Skinner, capital	9,000
		Parr, capital	12,000
		Total liabilities and	
Total assets	$32,000	owners' equity	$32,000

The following entries are required to distribute the cash to the proper parties:

Jan.	15	Accounts Payable	5,000.00	
		Cash		5,000.00
		To pay the partnership creditors.		
	15	Ottis, Capital	6,000.00	
		Skinner, Capital	9,000.00	
		Parr, Capital	12,000.00	
		Cash		27,000.00
		To distribute the remaining cash to the partners according to the balances of their capital accounts.		

Notice again that after losses are shared and creditors are paid, each partner receives cash equal to his capital account balance.

All Assets Realized before a Distribution; Assets Sold at a Loss; a Partner's Capital Account Is Not Sufficient to Cover His Share of the Loss

Sometimes, a partner's share of realization losses is greater than the balance of his capital account. In such cases, the partner must, if he can, cover the deficit by paying cash into the partnership. For example, assume contrary to the previous illustrations that Ottis, Skinner, and Parr sell their merchandise for $3,000 and the other assets for $4,000. The entries to record the sales and the loss allocation are:

Jan.	12	Cash		3,000.00	
		Loss or Gain from Realization		12,000.00	
		Merchandise Inventory			15,000.00
		Sold the inventory at a loss.			
	15	Cash		4,000.00	
		Loss or Gain from Realization		21,000.00	
		Other Assets			25,000.00
		Sold the other assets at a loss.			
	15	Ottis, Capital		16,500.00	
		Skinner, Capital		11,000.00	
		Parr, Capital		5,500.00	
		Loss or Gain from Realization			33,000.00
		To record the allocation of the loss from realization to the partners in their income-and-loss-sharing ratio.			

After the entry allocating the realization loss is posted, the capital account of Ottis has a $1,500 debit balance and appears as follows:

Ottis, Capital

Date		Explanation	Debit	Credit	Balance
Dec.	31	Balance			15,000.00
Jan.	15	Share of loss from realization	16,500.00		1,500.00

The partnership agreement provides that Ottis is allocated one half the losses or gains. Consequently, since his capital account balance is not large enough to absorb his loss share in this case, he must, if he can, pay $1,500 into the partnership to cover the **deficit**. If he is able to pay, the following entry is made:

Jan.	15	Cash		1,500.00	
		Ottis, Capital			1,500.00
		To record the additional investment of Ottis to cover his share of realization losses.			

After the $1,500 is received, the partnership has $18,500 in cash. The following entries are then made to distribute the cash to the proper parties:

Jan.	15	Accounts Payable	5,000.00	
		Cash		5,000.00
		To pay the partnership creditors.		
	15	Skinner, Capital	4,000.00	
		Parr, Capital	9,500.00	
		Cash		13,500.00
		To distribute the remaining cash to the partners according to the balances of their capital accounts.		

When a partner's share of partnership losses exceeds his capital account balance, he may be unable to make up the deficit. In such cases, since each partner has unlimited liability, the deficit must be borne by the remaining partner or partners. For example, assume that Ottis is unable to pay in the $1,500 necessary to cover the deficit in his capital account. If Ottis is unable to pay, his deficit must be shared by Skinner and Parr in their income-and-loss-sharing ratio. The partners share income and losses in the ratio of Ottis, 3; Skinner, 2; and Parr, 1. Therefore, Skinner and Parr share in a 2:1 ratio. Consequently, the $1,500 by which Ottis' share of the losses exceeded his capital account balance is apportioned between them in this ratio. Normally, the defaulting partner's deficit is transferred to the capital accounts of the remaining partners. This is accomplished for Ottis, Skinner, and Parr with the following entry:

Jan.	15	Skinner, Capital	1,000.00	
		Parr, Capital	500.00	
		Ottis, Capital		1,500.00
		To transfer the deficit of Ottis to the capital accounts of Skinner and Parr.		

After the deficit is transferred, the capital accounts of the partners appear as in Illustration 14–4.

After the deficit is transferred, the $17,000 of liquidation cash is distributed with the following entries:

Jan.	15	Accounts Payable	5,000.00	
		Cash		5,000.00
		To pay the partnership creditors.		
	15	Skinner, Capital	3,000.00	
		Parr, Capital	9,000.00	
		Cash		12,000.00
		To distribute the remaining cash to the partners according to their capital account balances.		

Illustration 14-4

Ottis, Capital

Date		Explanation	Debit	Credit	Balance
Dec.	31	Balance			15,000.00
Jan.	15	Share of loss from realization	16,500.00		1,500.00
	15	Deficit to Skinner and Parr		1,500.00	–0–

Skinner, Capital

Date		Explanation	Debit	Credit	Balance
Dec.	31	Balance			15,000.00
Jan.	15	Share of loss from realization	11,000.00		4,000.00
	15	Share of Ottis' deficit	1,000.00		3,000.00

Parr, Capital

Date		Explanation	Debit	Credit	Balance
Dec.	31	Balance			15,000.00
Jan.	15	Share of loss from realization	5,500.00		9,500.00
	15	Share of Ottis' deficit	500.00		9,000.00

It should be understood that the inability of Ottis to meet his loss share at this time does not relieve him of liability. If he becomes able to pay at some future time, Skinner and Parr may collect from him the full $1,500. Skinner may collect $1,000, and Parr, $500.

☐   **Glossary**

Deficit a negative balance in an account.

General partner a partner who assumes unlimited liability for the debts of the partnership.

General partnership a partnership in which all partners have unlimited liability for partnership debts.

Limited partners partners who have no personal liability for debts of the limited partnership beyond the amounts they have invested in the partnership.

Limited partnership a partnership that has two classes of partners, limited partners and one or more general partners.

Liquidation the winding up of a business by converting its assets to cash and distributing the cash to the proper parties.

Mutual agency the legal characteristic of a partnership whereby each partner is an agent of the partnership and is able to bind the partnership to contracts within the normal scope of the partnership business.

Partnership an association of two or more persons to carry on as co-owners a business for profit.

Partnership contract the document setting forth the agreed terms under which the members of a partnership will conduct the partnership business.

Unlimited liability of partners the legal characteristic of a partnership that makes each partner responsible for paying all the debts of the partnership if his or her partners are unable to pay their shares.

☐ **Questions for Class Discussion**

1. Hill and Dale are partners. Hill dies, and his son claims the right to take his father's place in the partnership. Does he have this right? Why?

2. If Ted Hall cannot legally enter into a contract, can he become a partner?

3. If a partnership contract does not state the period of time the partnership is to exist, when does the partnership end?

4. What is the meaning of the term *mutual agency* as applied to a partnership?

5. Karen and Frank are partners in the operation of a store. Without consulting Karen, Frank enters into a contract for the purchase of merchandise for resale by the store. Karen contends that she did not authorize the order and refuses to take delivery. The vendor sues the partners for the contract price of the merchandise. Will the firm have to pay? Why?

6. Would your answer to Question 5 differ if Karen and Frank were partners in a public accounting firm?

7. May partners limit the right of a member of their firm to bind their partnership to contracts? Is such an agreement binding (*a*) on the partners and (*b*) on outsiders?

8. What is the meaning of the term *unlimited liability* when it is applied to members of a partnership?

9. Jones organized a limited partnership and is the only general partner. Craven invested $10,000 in the partnership and was admitted as a limited partner with the understanding that he would receive 5% of the profits. After two unprofitable years, the partnership ceased doing business. At that point, partnership liabilities were $75,000 larger than partnership assets. How much money can the creditors of the partnership obtain from Craven in satisfaction of the unpaid partnership debts?

10. How does a limited partnership differ from a general partnership?

11. Brown, Dyckman, and Granger have been partners for three years. The partnership is dissolving. Brown is leaving the firm while Dyckman and Granger plan to carry on the business. In the final settlement, Brown places a $60,000 salary claim against the partnership. His contention is that since he devoted all of his time for three years to the affairs of the partnership, he has a claim for a salary of $20,000 for each year. Is his claim valid? Why?

12. The partnership agreement of Aimes and Bartlett provides for a two-thirds, one-third sharing of income but says nothing of losses. The first year of partnership operations resulted in a loss, and Aimes argues that the loss should be shared equally since the partnership agreement said nothing of sharing losses. Do you agree?

13. A, B, and C are partners with capital account balances of $6,000 each. D pays A $7,500 for his one-third interest and is admitted to the partnership. The bookkeeper debits A, Capital and credits D, Capital for $6,000. D objects. He wants his capital account to show a $7,500 balance, the amount he paid for his interest. Explain why D's capital account is credited for $6,000.

14. After all partnership assets are converted to cash and all liabilities have been paid, the remaining cash should equal the sum of the balances of the partners' capital accounts. Why?

15. Jim, Kathy, and Larry are partners. In a liquidation, Jim's share of partnership losses exceeds his capital account balance. He is unable to meet the deficit from his personal assets, and the excess losses are shared by his partners. Does this relieve Jim of liability?

16. A partner withdraws from a partnership and receives assets of greater value than the book value of his equity. Should the remaining partners share the resulting reduction in their equities in the ratio of their relative capital balances or in their income-and-loss-sharing ratio?

☐   **Class Exercises**   **Exercise 14-1**

On January 20, 198A, Freetag and Williamson formed a partnership in which Freetag contributed $50,000 and Williamson contributed land valued at $30,000 and a building valued at $70,000. They agree, to share profits as follows: Freetag is to receive an annual salary of $25,000, each partner is to receive 10% of his or her original capital investment, and any remaining profit or loss is to be shared equally. On November 12, 198A, Freetag withdrew cash of $20,000 and Williamson withdrew $10,000.

Present general journal entries to record the initial capital investments of the partners, the cash withdrawals of the partners, the December 31 closing of the withdrawals accounts and the Income Summary account, which had a credit balance of $48,000.

Exercise 14-2

Maybrey and Nickles began a partnership by investing $44,000 and $66,000, respectively; and during its first year, the partnership earned $168,000.

Required

Prepare calculations showing how the income should be allocated to the partners under each of the following plans for sharing income:

a. The partners failed to agree on a method of sharing income.
b. The partners had agreed to share income in their investment ratio.
c. The partners had agreed to share income by allowing 10% interest on investments, a $72,000 per year salary allowance to Maybrey, a $56,000 per year salary allowance to Nickles, and the balance equally.

Exercise 14-3

Assume the partners of Exercise 14-2 agreed to share incomes and losses by allowing 10% interest on their investments, yearly salary allowances of $72,000 to Maybrey and $56,000 to Nickles, and the balance equally. (*a*) Determine the shares of Maybrey and Nickles in a $131,200 first-year net income. (*b*) Determine the partners' shares in a first-year $20,800 net loss.

Exercise 14-4

The partners in Triple Y Partnership have agreed that partner Tavenor may sell his $60,000 equity in the partnership to Olsen, for which Olsen will pay Tavenor $45,000. Present the partnership's journal entry to record the sale on August 30.

Exercise 14-5

The Schnurr-Higgins Partnership has total partners' equity of $280,000, which is made up of Schnurr, Capital, $210,000, and Higgins, Capital, $70,000. The partners share incomes and losses in a ratio of 75% to Schnurr and 25% to Higgins. On January 1, Geer is admitted to the partnership and given a 20% interest in equity and in gains and losses. Prepare the journal entry to record the entry of Geer under each of the following unrelated assumptions. Geer invests cash of (*a*) $70,000; (*b*) $105,000; and (*c*) $42,000.

Exercise 14-6

Kent, Morris, and Nathan have been partners sharing incomes and losses in a 3:5:2 ratio. On November 30, the date Nathan retires from the partnership, the equities of the partners are Kent, $120,000; Morris, $180,000; and Nathan, $20,000.

Required

Present general journal entries to record Nathan's retirement under each of the following unrelated assumptions:

a. Nathan is paid $20,000 in partnership cash for his equity.
b. Nathan is paid $25,000 in partnership cash for his equity.
c. Nathan is paid $16,000 in partnership cash for his equity.

Exercise 14-7

The Bing, Bang, and Bong partnership was begun with investments by the partners as follows: Bing, $87,500; Bang, $52,500; and Bong, $70,000. The first year of operations did not go well, and the partners finally decided to liquidate the partnership, sharing all losses equally. On December 31, after all assets were converted to cash and all creditors were paid, only $21,000 in partnership cash remained.

Required

1. Calculate the capital account balances of the partners after the liquidation of assets and payment of creditors.
2. Assume that any partner with a deficit pays cash to the partnership to cover the deficit. Then, present the general journal entries on December 31 to record the cash receipt from the deficient partner(s) and the final disbursement of cash to the partners.
3. Now make the contrary assumption that any partner with a deficit is not able to reimburse the partnership. Present journal entries (*a*) to transfer the deficit of any deficient partners to the other partners and (*b*) to record the final disbursement of cash to the partners.

Exercise 14-8

Crosby, Davis, and Hill are partners sharing incomes and losses in a $1:3:4$ ratio. After lengthy disagreements among the partners and several unprofitable periods, the partners decided to liquidate the partnership. Before the liquidation, the partnership balance sheet showed total assets, $150,000; liabilities, $120,000; Crosby, Capital, $6,000; Davis, Capital, $9,000; and Hill, Capital, $15,000. The cash proceeds from selling the assets were sufficient to repay all of the creditors except $25,000. Calculate the loss from selling the assets, allocate the loss to the partners, and determine how much of the remaining liability should be paid by each partner.

Exercise 14-9

Assume that the Crosby, Davis, and Hill partnership of Exercise 14-8 is a limited partnership. Crosby and Davis are general partners, and Hill is a limited partner. How much of the remaining $25,000 liability should be paid by each partner?

Problems   **Problem 14-1**

Bruce Brown, Kay Craig, and Randal Gilpin invested $52,500, $42,000, and $31,500, respectively, in a partnership. During its first year, the firm earned $142,800.

Required

Prepare entries to close the firm's Income Summary account as of December 31 and to allocate the net income to the partners under each of the assumptions below. (Round your answers to the nearest whole dollar.)

a. The partners could not agree as to the method of sharing earnings.
b. The partners had agreed to share earnings in the ratio of their beginning investments.
c. The partners had agreed to share income by allowing a share of the income equal to 10% interest on the partners' investments; allowing annual salary allowances of $42,000 to Brown, $49,000 to Craig, and $35,000 to Gilpin; and sharing the remainder equally.

Problem 14-2

Barry Pingle and Shannon Hill are in the process of forming a partnership to which Pingle will devote one-third time and Hill will devote full time. They have discussed the following plans for sharing incomes and losses.

a. In the ratio of their investments which they have agreed to maintain at $25,000 for Pingle and $37,500 for Hill.
b. In proportion to the time devoted to the business.
c. A salary allowance of $2,500 per month to Hill, and the balance in their investment ratio.
d. A $2,500 per month salary allowance to Hill, 10% interest on their investments, and the balance equally.

The partners expect the business to generate income as follows: year 1, $15,000 net loss; year 2, $45,000 net income; and year 3, $90,000 net income.

Required

1. Prepare three schedules with the following columnar headings:

Income-Sharing Plan	Year _____		
	Calculations	Pingle	Hill

2. Complete a schedule for each of the first three years by showing how the partnership income for each year would be allocated to the partners under each of the four plans being considered.

Problem 14-3

Tom Boyd, Mike DeMoss, and Shirley Tucker formed the BDT Partnership by making capital contributions of $86,400, $96,000, and $105,600,

$\frac{1/3}{14/3}$

respectively. They anticipate annual net incomes of $150,000 and are considering the following alternative plans of sharing incomes and losses: (a) equally; (b) in the ratio of their initial investments; or (c) interest allowances of 10% on initial investments, salary allowances of $32,000 to Boyd, $17,000 to DeMoss, and $38,000 to Tucker, with any remaining balance shared equally.

Required

1. Prepare a schedule with the following columnar headings:

Income-Sharing Plan	Calculations	Share to Boyd	Share to DeMoss	Share to Tucker	Income Allo-cated

Use the schedule to show how a net income of $150,000 would be distributed under each of the alternative plans being considered.

2. Prepare the section of the partner's first year income statement showing the allocation of income to the partners' assuming they agree to use alternative (c) and the net income actually earned is $72,000.

3. Prepare the December 31 journal entry to close the Income Summary account assuming they agree to use alternative (c) and the net income is $72,000.

Problem 14-4

Part 1. Linder, Perry, and Wisner are partners with capital balances as follows: Linder, $122,500; Perry, $87,500; and Wisner, $210,000. The partners share losses and gains in a 1:2:3 ratio. Prepare general journal entries to record the April 1 withdrawal of Perry from the partnership under each of the following unrelated assumptions:

a. Perry sells his interest to Reed for $112,000 after Linder and Wisner approve the entry of Reed as a partner.
b. Perry gives his interest to a son-in-law, Bob McMeans. Linder and Wisner accept McMeans as a partner.
c. Perry is paid $87,500 in partnership cash for his equity.
d. Perry is paid $129,500 in partnership cash for his equity.
e. Perry is paid $17,500 in partnership cash plus delivery equipment recorded on the partnership books at $77,000 less accumulated depreciation of $42,000.

Part 2. Assume that Perry does not retire from the partnership described in Part 1. Instead, Baker is to be admitted to the partnership on April 1 and is to have a 25% equity. Prepare general journal entries to record the entry of Baker into the partnership under each of the following unrelated assumptions:

a. Baker invests $140,000.
b. Baker invests $105,000.
c. Baker invests $175,000.

Problem 14-5

Gilles, Halter, and Reeves plan to liquidate their partnership. They have always shared incomes and losses in a 1:4:5 ratio, and on the day of the liquidation their balance sheet appears as follows:

Gilles, Halter, and Reeves
Balance Sheet
May 31, 19—

Assets		Liabilities and Owners' Equity	
Cash.	$ 12,250	Accounts payable	$ 47,250
Other assets	157,500	Don Gilles, capital	17,500
		Eve Halter, capital	70,000
		Paula Reeves, capital.	35,000
		Total liabilities and	
Total assets.	$169,750	owners' equity.	$169,750

Required

Prepare general journal entries to record the sale of the other assets and the distribution of the cash to the proper parties under each of the following unrelated assumptions:

a. The other assets are sold for $176,750.
b. The other assets are sold for $105,000.
c. The other assets are sold for $77,000, and any partners with resulting deficits can and do pay in the amount of their deficits.
d. The other assets are sold for $70,000, and the partners have no assets other than those invested in the business.

Problem 14-6

Until June 17 of the current year, Fleck, Ham, and Moore were partners sharing incomes and losses in the ratio of their capital account balances (before closing their withdrawal accounts). On that date, Ham suffered a heart attack and died. Fleck and Moore immediately ended the business operations and prepared the adjusted trial balance on page 511.

Required

1. Prepare June 17 entries to close the revenue, expense, income summary, and withdrawals accounts of the partnership.
2. Assume the estate of Ham agreed to accept the land and building and assume the mortgage thereon in settlement of its claim against the partnership assets, and that Fleck and Moore planned to continue the business and rent the building from the estate. Give the June 29 entry to transfer the land, building, and mortgage and to settle with the estate.
3. Assume that in the place of the foregoing the estate of Ham demanded a cash settlement and the business had to be sold to a competitor who gave $238,000 for the noncash assets and assumed the mortgage but not the accounts payable. Give the June 29 entry to transfer the noncash

assets and mortgage to the competitor, and give the entries to allocate the loss to the partners and to distribute the partnership cash to the proper parties.

Fleck, Ham, and Moore
Adjusted Trial Balance
June 17, 19—

Cash	$ 15,750	
Accounts receivable	36,750	
Allowance for doubtful accounts		$ 1,750
Supplies inventory	80,500	
Equipment	47,250	
Accumulated depreciation, equipment . .		12,250
Land	15,750	
Building	175,000	
Accumulated depreciation, building		33,250
Accounts payable		10,500
Mortgage payable		35,000
Tom Fleck, capital		105,000
Donna Ham, capital		105,000
Ray Moore, capital		52,500
Tom Fleck, withdrawals	3,500	
Donna Ham, withdrawals	3,500	
Ray Moore, withdrawals	3,500	
Revenues		136,500
Expenses	110,250	
Totals	$491,750	$491,750

□ Alternate Problems

Problem 14-1A

Joan Crown, Bob Fogg, and Jan Hempel invested $78,750, $63,000, and $47,250, respectively, in a partnership. During its first year, the firm earned $214,200.

Required

Prepare entries to close the firm's Income Summary account as of December 31 and to allocate the net income to the partners under each of the assumptions below. (Round your answers to the nearest whole dollar.)

a. The partners could not agree as to the method of sharing earnings.
b. The partners had agreed to share earnings in the ratio of their beginning investments.
c. The partners had agreed to share income by allowing a share of the income equal to 10% interest on the partners' investments; allowing annual salary allowances of $63,000 to Crown, $73,500 to Fogg, and $52,500 to Hempel; and sharing the remainder equally.

Problem 14-2A

Katherine Shell and Henry Dock are in the process of forming a partnership to which Shell will devote one-fourth time and Dock will devote full time. They have discussed the following plans for sharing incomes and losses:

a. In the ratio of their investments which they have agreed to maintain at $42,500 for Shell and $63,750 for Dock.
b. In proportion to the time devoted to the business.
c. A salary allowance of $4,250 per month to Dock and the balance in their investment ratio.
d. A $4,250 per month salary allowance to Dock, 10% interest on their investments, and the balance equally.

The partners expect the business to generate income as follows: year 1, $25,500 net loss; year 2, $76,500 net income; and year 3, $153,000 net income.

Required

1. Prepare three schedules with the following columnar headings:

Income-Sharing Plan	Year _____		
	Calculations	Shell	Dock

2. Complete a schedule for each of the first three years by showing how the partnership income for each year would be allocated to the partners under each of the four plans being considered.

Problem 14-3A

Karen Bell, Dan Flint, and Joe Hallis formed the BFH Partnership by making capital contributions of $175,000, $200,000, and $125,000, respectively. They anticipate annual net incomes of $300,000 and are considering the following alternative plans of sharing incomes and losses: (*a*) equally; (*b*) in the ratio of their initial investments; or (*c*) interest allowances of 12% on initial investments, salary allowances of $75,000 to Bell, $25,000 to Flint, and $50,000 to Hallis, with any remaining balance shared equally.

Required

1. Prepare a schedule with the following columnar headings:

Income-Sharing Plan	Calculations	Share to Bell	Share to Flint	Share to Hallis	Income Allocated

Use the schedule to show how a net income of $300,000 would be distributed under each of the alternative plans being considered.

2. Prepare the section of the partner's first year income statement showing the allocation of income to the partners' assuming they agree to use alternative (*c*) and the net income actually earned is $75,000.

3. Prepare the December 31 journal entry to close the Income Summary account assuming they agree to use alternative (*c*) and the net income is $75,000.

Problem 14-4A

Part 1. Burns, Jacobs, and Kruse are partners with capital balances as follows: Burns, $127,500; Jacobs, $42,500; and Kruse, $85,000. The partners share incomes and losses in a 2:4:2 ratio. Prepare general journal entries to record the October 31 withdrawal of Kruse from the partnership under each of the following unrelated assumptions:

a. Kruse sells his interest to Legg for $35,700 after Burns and Jacobs approve the entry of Legg as a partner.
b. Kruse gives his interest to a son-in-law, S. Platt. Burns and Jacobs accept Platt as a partner.
c. Kruse is paid $85,000 in partnership cash for his equity.
d. Kruse is paid $49,000 in partnership cash for his equity.
e. Kruse is paid $39,000 in partnership cash plus delivery equipment recorded on the partnership books at $56,000 less accumulated depreciation of $37,000.

Part 2. Assume that Kruse does not retire from the partnership described in Part 1. Instead, Quick is to be admitted to the partnership on October 31 and is to have a 20% equity. Prepare general journal entries to record the entry of Quick under each of the following unrelated assumptions:

a. Quick invests $63,750.
b. Quick invests $45,000.
c. Quick invests $102,000.

Problem 14-5A

Forbes, Hofman, and Kasper, who have always shared incomes and losses in a 3:1:1 ratio, plan to liquidate their partnership. Just prior to the liquidation their balance sheet appeared as follows:

Forbes, Hofman, and Kasper
Balance Sheet
July 15, 19—

Assets		**Liabilities and Owners' Equity**	
Cash.	$ 11,250	Accounts payable	$ 47,250
Other assets	198,000	T. Forbes, capital	76,000
		J. Hofman, capital	50,000
		R. Kasper, capital	36,000
		Total liabilities and	
Total assets.	$209,250	owners' equity.	$209,250

Required

Under the assumption the other assets are sold and the cash is distributed to the proper parties on July 15, give the entries for the sales, the loss or gain allocations, and the distributions if—

a. The other assets are sold for $225,000.
b. The other assets are sold for $141,750.

c. The other assets are sold for $60,500, and any partners with resulting deficits can and do pay in the amount of their deficits.

d. The other assets are sold for $46,000, and the partners have no assets other than those invested in the business.

Problem 14-6A

Marcus, Newfeld and Price are partners. Marcus devotes full time to partnership affairs; Newfeld and Price devote very little time; and as a result, they share incomes and losses in a 4:1:1 ratio. Of late, the business has not been too profitable, and the partners have decided to liquidate. Just prior to the first realization sale, a partnership balance sheet appeared as follows:

Marcus, Newfeld, and Price
Balance Sheet
August 10, 19—

Assets			Liabilities and Owners' Equity	
Cash		$ 3,750	Accounts payable	$10,500
Accounts receivable . . .		14,250	Marcus, capital	9,000
Merchandise inventory . .		24,000	Newfeld, capital.	18,000
Equipment	$18,000		Price, capital	18,000
Less accum. depr. . . .	4,500	13,500		
			Total liabilities and	
Total assets		$55,500	owners' equity	$55,500

The assets were sold, the creditors were paid, and the remaining cash was distributed to the partners on the following dates:

Aug. 11   The accounts receivable were sold for $9,750.
     12   The merchandise inventory was sold for $16,500.
     14   The equipment was sold for $7,500.
     15   The creditors were paid.
     17   The remaining cash was distributed to the partners.

Required

1. Prepare general journal entries to record the asset sales, the allocation of the realization loss, and the payment of the creditors.

2. Under the assumption that any partners with capital deficits can and do pay in the amount of their deficits on July 17, give the entry to record the receipt of the cash and the distribution of partnership cash to the remaining partners.

3. Under the assumption that any partners with capital deficits cannot pay, give the entry to allocate the deficits to the remaining partners. Then give the entry to distribute the partnership cash to the remaining partners.

Provocative Problems

Provocative Problem 14-1   Which Partner Gets the Profits?

Haire and Kardash are partners who have agreed to share the annual profits or losses of their business as follows. If the partnership earns a net income, the first $40,000 is allocated 25% to Haire and 75% to Kardash so as to reflect the time devoted to the business by each partner. Incomes in excess of $40,000 are shared equally. However, if business operations result in a loss for the year, the partners have agreed to share the loss equally.

Required

1. Prepare a schedule showing how the 198A net income of $48,000 should be allocated to the partners.

2. Immediately after the closing entries for 198A were posted on December 31, 198A, the partners discovered unrecorded accounts payable amounting to $60,000. The accounts payable related to expenses incurred by the business. Kardash suggests that the $60,000 should be allocated equally between the partners as a loss. Haire disagrees and argues that an entry should be made to record the accounts payable and correct the capital accounts to reflect a $12,000 net loss for 198A. (*a*) Present the January 1, 198B, journal entry to record the accounts payable and allocate the loss to the partners according to Kardash's suggestion. (*b*) Now give the January 1, 198B, journal entry to record the accounts payable and correct the capital accounts according to Haire's argument. Show how you calculated the amounts in the entry.

3. Which partner do you think is right? Why?

Provocative Problem 14-2   Good Sounds

Janis Stern and Sally Tharp are partners that own and operate Good Sounds, a phonographic records and tapes store. Stern has a $63,000 equity in the business, and Tharp has a $38,250 equity. They share incomes and losses by allowing annual salary allowances of $22,500 to Stern and $18,000 to Tharp, with any remaining balance being shared 60% to Stern and 40% to Tharp.

Karen Stern, Janis Stern's daughter, has been working in the store on a salary basis. Prior to working in the store, Karen was a successful disk jockey and is well known among record and tape buyers in the community. As a result, Karen attracts a great deal of business to the store. The partners believe that at least one third of the past three years' sales can be traced directly to Karen's association with the store, and it is reasonable to assume she was instrumental in attracting even more.

Karen is paid $1,500 per month, but feels this is not sufficient to induce her to remain with the firm as an employee. However, she likes her work and would like to remain in the records and tapes business. What she really wants is to become a partner in the business.

Her mother is anxious for her to remain in the business and proposes the following:

a. That Karen be admitted to the partnership with a 20% equity in the partnership assets.

b. That she, Janis Stern, transfer from her capital account to that of Karen's one half the 20% interest; that Karen contribute to the firm's assets a noninterest-bearing note for the other half; and that she, Janis Stern, will guarantee payment of the note.

c. That incomes and losses be shared by continuing the $22,500 and $18,000 salary allowances of the original partners and that Karen be given an $18,000 annual salary allowance, after which any remaining income or loss would be shared 40% to Janis Stern, 40% to Sally Tharp, and 20% to Karen Stern.

Prepare a report to Ms. Tharp on the advisability of accepting Janis Stern's proposal. Under the assumption that net incomes for the past three years have been $55,500, $61,500, and $64,500, respectively, prepare schedules showing (a) how net income was allocated during the past three years and (b) how it would have been allocated had the proposed new agreement been in effect. Also, (c) prepare a schedule showing the partners' capital interests as they would be immediately after the admission of Karen.

Provocative Problem 14-3   Withdrawal of a Partner

The balance sheet of the Oldtime Partnership on December 31, 198A, is as follows:

Assets		Liabilities and Owners' Equity	
Cash	$30,000	Franks, capital	$15,000
Other assets	37,500	Maynard, capital	22,500
Land	22,500	Stone, capital	52,500
		Total liabilities and	
Total assets	$90,000	owners' equity	$90,000

The income-and-loss sharing percentages are: Franks, 20%; Maynard, 30% and Stone, 50%. Franks wishes to withdraw from the partnership, and the partners finally agree that the land owned by the partnership should be transferred to Franks in full payment for his equity. In reaching this decision, they recognize that the land has appreciated since it was purchased and is now worth $40,000. If Franks retires on January 1, 198B, what journal entries should be made on that date?

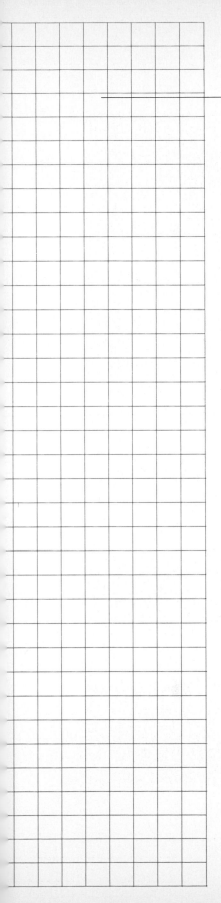

Part Five

Corporation Accounting

15 Organization and Operation of Corporations

After studying Chapter 15, you should be able to:

1. State the advantages and disadvantages of the corporate form of business organization and explain how a corporation is organized and managed.

2. Describe the differences in accounting for the owners' equity in a partnership and the stockholders' equity in a corporation.

3. Record the issuance of par value stock at par or at a premium in exchange for cash or other assets.

4. Record the issuance of no-par stock with or without a stated value.

5. Record transactions involving stock subscriptions and explain the effects of subscribed stock on corporation assets and stockholders' equity.

6. Explain the concept of minimum legal capital and explain why corporation laws governing minimum legal capital were written.

7. State the differences between common and preferred stocks and explain why preferred stock is issued.

8. Describe the meaning and significance of par, book, market, and redemption values of corporate stock.

9. Define or explain the words and phrases listed in the chapter Glossary.

The three common types of business organizations are single proprietorships, partnerships, and corporations. Of the three, corporations are fewer in number. In dollar volume, however, they transact more business than do the other two combined. In terms of their economic impact, corporations are clearly the most important form of business organization. Almost every student will at some time either work for or own an interest in a corporation. For these reasons, an understanding of corporations and corporation accounting is important to all students of business.

■ Advantages of the Corporate Form

Corporations have become the dominant type of business in our country because of the advantages offered by this form of business organization. Among the advantages are the following:

Separate Legal Entity

A corporation is a separate legal entity, separate and distinct from its stockholders who are its owners. Because it is a separate legal entity, a corporation, through its agents, may conduct its affairs with the same rights, duties, and responsibilities as a person.

Lack of Stockholders' Liability

As a separate legal entity a corporation is responsible for its own acts and its own debts, and its shareholders have no liability for either. From the viewpoint of an investor, this is perhaps the most important advantage of the corporate form.

Ease of Transferring Ownership Rights

Ownership rights in a corporation are represented by shares of stock that generally can be transferred and disposed of any time the owner wishes. Furthermore, the transfer has no effect on the corporation and its operations.

Continuity of Life

A corporation's life may continue for the time stated in its charter, which may be of any length permitted by the laws of the state of its incorporation. Furthermore, at the expiration of the stated time, the charter may normally be renewed and the period extended. Thus, a perpetual life is possible for a successful corporation.

No Mutual Agency

Mutual agency does not exist in a corporation. A corporation stockholder, acting as a stockholder, has no power to bind the corporation to contracts. Stockholders' participation in the affairs of the corporation is limited to the right to vote in the stockholders' meetings. Consequently, stockholders need not exercise the care of partners in selecting people with whom they associate themselves in the ownership of a corporation.

Ease of Capital Assembly

Lack of stockholders' liability, lack of mutual agency, and the ease with which an ownership interest may be transferred make it possible for a corporation to assemble large amounts of capital from the combined investments of many stockholders. Actually, a corporation's capital-raising ability is as a rule limited only by the profitableness with which it can employ the funds. This is very different from a partnership. In a partnership, capital-raising ability is always limited by the number of partners and their individual wealth. The number of partners is in turn usually limited because of mutual agency and unlimited liability.

■ Disadvantages of the Corporate Form

Governmental Regulation

Corporations are created by fulfilling the requirements of a state's corporation laws, and the laws subject a corporation to considerable state regulation and control. Single proprietorships and partnerships escape this regulation as well as the filing of many governmental reports required of corporations.

Taxation

Corporations as business units are subject to the same taxes as single proprietorships and partnerships. In addition, corporations are subject to several taxes not levied on either of the other two. The most burdensome of these are state and federal income taxes that together may take 50% of a corporation's pretax income. However, for the stockholders of a corporation, the burden does not end there. The income of a corporation is taxed twice, first as corporation income and again as personal income when distributed to the stockholders as dividends. This differs from single proprietorships and partnerships, which as business units are not subject to income taxes. Their income is normally taxed only as the personal income of their owners.

While the tax characteristics of a corporation are generally viewed as a disadvantage, in some instances they may work to the advantage of stockholders. If the stockholders have very large personal incomes and pay taxes at rates that exceed the corporate rate, the corporation may choose to avoid paying dividends. By not paying dividends, the income of the corporation is, at least temporarily, taxed only once at the lower corporate rate.

■ Organizing a Corporation

A corporation is created by securing a charter from one of the states. The requirements that must be met to secure a charter vary with the states. In general, however, a charter application must be signed by three or more subscribers to the prospective corporation's stock (who are called the incorporators). It must then be filed with the proper state official. If the application complies with the law and all fees are paid, the charter is issued and the corporation comes into existence. The subscribers then purchase the corporation's stock and become stockholders. After this, they meet and elect a board of directors who are made responsible for directing the corporation's affairs.

■ **Organization Costs**

The costs of organizing a corporation, such as legal fees, promoters' fees, and amounts paid the state to secure a charter, are called **organization costs** and are debited on incurrence to an asset account called Organization Costs. Theoretically, the sum of these costs represents an intangible asset from which the corporation will benefit throughout its life. However, this is an indeterminable period. Therefore, a corporation should make a reasonable estimate of the benefit period, which in no case should exceed 40 years, and write off its organization costs over the estimated period.[1] Although not necessarily related to the benefit period, income tax rules permit a corporation to write off organization costs as a tax-deductible expense over a period of not less than five years. Consequently, many corporations adopt five years as the period over which to write off such costs. There is no theoretical justification for this, but it is generally accepted in practice. Organization costs are usually immaterial in amount; and under the **principle of materiality,** the write-off eliminates an unnecessary balance sheet item.

■ **Management of a Corporation**

Although ultimate control of a corporation rests with its stockholders, this control is exercised indirectly through the election of the board of directors. The individual stockholder's right to participate in management begins and ends with a vote in the stockholders' meeting, where each stockholder has one vote for each share of stock owned.

Normally a corporation's stockholders meet once each year to elect directors and transact such other business as is provided in the corporation's bylaws. Theoretically, stockholders owning or controlling the votes of 50% plus one share of a corporation's stock can elect the board and control the corporation. Actually, because many stockholders do not attend the annual meeting, a much smaller percentage is frequently sufficient for control. Commonly, stockholders who do not attend the annual meeting delegate to an agent their voting rights. This is done by signing a legal document called a **proxy,** which gives the agent the right to vote the stock.

A corporation's board of directors is responsible and has final authority for the direction of corporation affairs. However, it may act only as a collective body. An individual director, as a director, has no power to transact corporation business. And, as a rule, although it has final authority, a board will limit itself to establishing policy. It will then delegate the day-by-day direction of corporation business to the corporation's administrative officers whom it selects and elects.

A corporation's administrative officers are commonly headed by a president who is directly responsible to the board for supervising the corporation's business. To aid the president, many corporations have one or more vice presidents who are vested with specific managerial powers and duties. In addition, the corporation secretary keeps the minutes of the meetings of the stockholders and directors. In a small corporation, the secretary may also be responsible for keeping a record of the stockholders and the changing amounts of their stock interest.

---

[1] FASB, *Accounting Standards—Current Text* (Stamford, Conn., 1984), sec. I60.110. First published in *APB Opinion No. 17,* par. 29.

■ **Stock Certificates and the Transfer of Stock**

When a person invests in a corporation by buying its stock, the person receives a stock certificate as evidence of the shares purchased. Usually, in a small corporation, only one certificate is issued for each block of stock purchased. The one certificate may be for any number of shares. For example, the certificate of Illustration 15–1 is for 50 shares. Large corporations commonly use preprinted 100-share denomination certificates in addition to blank certificates that may be made out for any number of shares.

An owner of stock may transfer at will either part or all of the shares represented by a stock certificate. To do so, the owner completes and signs the transfer endorsement on the reverse side of the certificate and sends the certificate to the corporation secretary in a small corporation or to the corporation's transfer agent in a large one. The old certificate is canceled and retained, and a new certificate is issued to the new stockholder.

Transfer Agent and Registrar

A large corporation whose stock is sold on a major stock exchange must have a registrar and a transfer agent who are assigned the responsibilities of transferring the corporation's stock. Also, the registrar is assigned the duty of keeping stockholder records and preparing official lists of stockholders for stockholders' meetings and for payment of dividends. Usually, registrars and transfer agents are large banks or trust companies.

Illustration 15-1

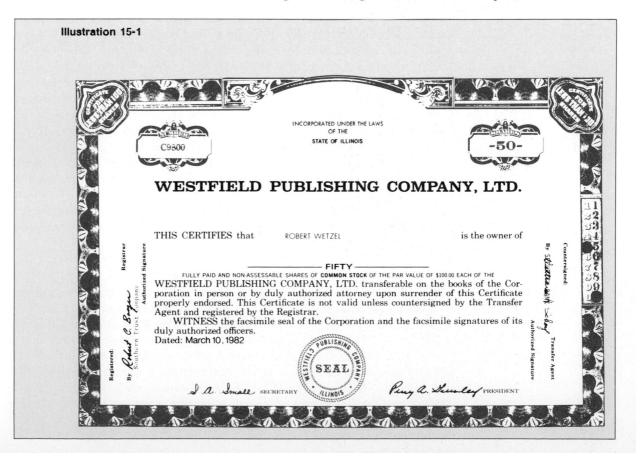

When the owner of stock in a corporation having a registrar and a transfer agent wishes to transfer the stock to a new owner, he or she completes the transfer endorsement on the back of the stock certificate and, usually through a stockholder, sends the certificate to the transfer agent. The transfer agent cancels the old certificate and issues one or more new certificates which the agent sends to the registrar. The registrar enters the transfer in the stockholder records and sends the new certificate or certificates to the proper owners.

■ **Corporation Accounting**

Corporation accounting was initially discussed in Chapter 4. In that discussion, entries were shown to record several basic transactions. An issue of common stock for cash was recorded. A net income (credit balance) was closed from Income Summary to Retained Earnings. The declaration and later payment of cash dividends were recorded. And, a net loss was closed from Income Summary to Retained Earnings. **At this point, students should review the discussion in Chapter 4 on pages 133 through 135 which explains these entries.** After completing that review, keep in mind that the stockholders' equity accounts of a corporation are divided into (1) contributed capital accounts and (2) retained earnings accounts. Also, remember that when a corporation's board of directors declares a cash dividend on the **date of declaration,** a legal liability of the corporation is incurred. The board of directors declares that on a specific future date, the **date of record,** the stockholders according to the corporation's records will be designated as those to receive the dividend. Finally, on the **date of payment,** the liability for the declared cash dividend is paid by the corporation.

The financial statements of a corporation were first illustrated in Chapter 5. The income statement was shown in Illustration 5-1 on page 166; the balance sheet was shown in Illustration 5-3 on page 172; and the retained earnings statement was shown in Illustration 5-4 on page 172. Reviewing these illustrations, students should note that income taxes were deducted on the income statement as an expense. Recall that a business that is organized as a corporation must pay income taxes, while a proprietorship or partnership does not pay income taxes. Also, cash dividends to stockholders are not an expense of the corporation; they are not deducted on the income statement. Instead, dividends are a distribution **of** net income, and are subtracted on the retained earnings statement. Finally, notice that the stockholders' equity in Illustration 5-3 is divided into common stock and retained earnings.

■ **Stockholders' Equity Accounts Compared to Partnership Accounts**

To demonstrate the use of separate accounts for contributed capital and retained earnings as found in corporation accounting and to contrast their use with the accounts used in partnership accounting, assume the following. On January 5, 198A, a partnership involving two equal partners and a corporation having five stockholders were formed. Assume further that $25,000 was invested in each. In the partnership, J. Olm invested $10,000 and A. Baker invested $15,000; in the corporation, each of the five stockholders bought 500 shares of its $10 par value common stock at $10 per share. Without dates and explanations, general journal entries to record the investments are:

Partnership				Corporation		
Cash.	10,000			Cash.	25,000	
J. Olm, Capital. . . .		10,000		Common Stock . . .		25,000
Cash.	15,000					
A. Baker, Capital. . .		15,000				

After the entries were posted, the owners' equity accounts of the two companies appeared as follows:

Partnership
J. Olm, Capital

Date	Dr.	Cr.	Bal.
Jan. 5, 198A		10,000	10,000

A. Baker, Capital

Date	Dr.	Cr.	Bal
Jan. 5, 198A		15,000	15,000

Corporation
Common Stock

Date	Dr.	Cr.	Bal.
Jan. 5, 198A		25,000	25,000

To continue the illustration, assume that during 198A, each company earned a net income of $8,000 and also distributed $5,000 to its owners. The partners share income equally, and the cash distribution was also divided equally. The corporation declared the dividends on December 20, 198A, and both companies made the cash payments to owners on December 25, 198A. The entries to record the distribution of cash to partners and the declaration and payments of dividends to stockholders are as follows:

Partnership				Corporation		
J. Olm, Withdrawals	2,500			Retained Earnings	5,000	
A. Baker, Withdrawals . . .	2,500			Dividends Payable . . .		5,000
Cash		5,000				
				Dividends Payable	5,000	
				Cash		5,000

At the end of the year, the entries to close the Income Summary accounts are as follows:

Partnership				Corporation		
Income Summary	8,000			Income Summary	8,000	
J. Olm, Capital		4,000		Retained Earnings . . .		8,000
A. Baker, Capital . . .		4,000				

Finally, the entry to close the withdrawals accounts is:

Partnership			Corporation
J. Olm, Capital	2,500		
A. Baker, Capital	2,500		
J. Olm, Withdrawals . .		2,500	
A. Baker, Withdrawals .		2,500	

After posting the above entries, the owners' equity accounts of the two companies are as follows:

Partnership
J. Olm, Capital

Date	Dr.	Cr.	Bal.
Jan. 5, 198A		10,000	10,000
Dec. 31, 198A		4,000	14,000
Dec. 31, 198A	2,500		11,500

Corporation
Common Stock

Date	Dr.	Cr.	Bal.
Jan. 5, 198A		25,000	25,000

A. Baker, Capital

Date	Dr.	Cr.	Bal.
Jan. 5, 198A		15,000	15,000
Dec. 31, 198A		4,000	19,000
Dec. 31, 198A	2,500		16,500

Retained Earnings

Date	Dr.	Cr.	Bal.
Dec. 20, 198A	5,000		(5,000)
Dec. 31, 198A		8,000	3,000

J. Olm, Withdrawals

Date	Dr.	Cr.	Bal.
Dec. 25, 198A	2,500		2,500
Dec. 31, 198A		2,500	–0–

A. Baker, Withdrawals

Date	Dr.	Cr.	Bal.
Dec. 25, 198A	2,500		2,500
Dec. 31, 198A		2,500	–0–

Observe that in the partnership, after all entries have been posted, the $28,000 equity of the owners appears in the capital accounts of the partners:

J. Olm, capital	$11,500
A. Baker, capital	16,500
Total owners' equity	$28,000

By comparison, the stockholders' equity of the corporation is divided between the contributed capital account and the Retained Earnings account, as follows:

Common stock	$25,000
Retained earnings	3,000
Total stockholders' equity	$28,000

■ **Authorization and Issuance of Stock**

When a corporation is organized, it is authorized in its charter to issue a certain amount of stock. The stock may be of one kind, **common stock,** or both common and preferred stock may be authorized. (Preferred stock is discussed later in this chapter.) However, regardless of whether one or two kinds of stock are authorized, the corporation may issue no more of each than the amount authorized by its charter.

Often a corporation will secure an authorization to issue more stock than it plans to sell at the time of its organization. This provides the means for future expansion through the sale of the additional stock, without means for future expansion through the sale of the additional stock, without the need of applying to the state for the right to issue more. When a balance sheet is prepared, both the amount of stock authorized and the amount issued are commonly shown in the equity section as on page 531.

Sale of Stock for Cash

When stock is sold for cash and immediately issued, an entry in general journal form like the following may be used to record the sale and issuance:

June	5	Cash	300,000.00	
		Common Stock		300,000.00
		Sold at par and issued 30,000 shares of $10 par value common stock.		

Exchanging Stock for Noncash Assets

A corporation may accept assets other than cash in exchange for its stock. When it does so, the transaction may be recorded like this:

Apr.	3	Machinery	10,000.00	
		Buildings	25,000.00	
		Land	5,000.00	
		Common Stock		40,000.00
		Exchanged 4,000 shares of $10 par value common stock for machinery, buildings, and land.		

A corporation may also give shares of its stock to its promoters in exchange for their services in organizing the corporation. In such a case, the corporation receives the intangible asset of being organized in exchange for its stock. The transaction is recorded as follows:

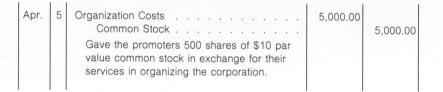

Apr.	5	Organization Costs	5,000.00	
		Common Stock		5,000.00
		Gave the promoters 500 shares of $10 par value common stock in exchange for their services in organizing the corporation.		

Par Value and Minimum Legal Capital

Many stocks have **par value**. The par value of a stock is an arbitrary value the issuing corporation chose for the stock at the time it sought authorization of the stock. A corporation may choose to issue stock having a par value of any amount, but par values of $100, $25, $10, $5, and $1 are common.

When a corporation issues par value stock, the par value is printed on each certificate and is used in accounting for the stock. Also, in many states when a corporation issues par value stock, it establishes for itself a **minimum legal capital** equal to the par value of the issued stock. For example, if a corporation issues 1,000 shares of $100 par value stock, it establishes for itself a minimum legal capital of $100,000.

Laws establishing minimum legal capital normally require stockholders in a corporation to invest assets equal in value to minimum legal capital or be liable to the corporation's creditors for the deficiency. In other words, these laws require stockholders to give a corporation par value for its stock or be liable for the difference. Minimum legal capital requirements also make illegal any payments to stockholders for dividends or their equivalent when these payments reduce stockholders' equity below minimum legal capital.

Corporation laws governing minimum legal capital were written in an effort to protect corporation creditors. The authors of these laws reasoned as follows: A corporation's creditors may look only to the assets of the corporation for satisfaction of their claims. Consequently, when a corporation is organized, its stockholders should provide it with a fund of assets equal to its minimum legal capital. Thereafter, this fund of assets should remain with the corporation and should not be returned to the stockholders in any form until all creditor claims are paid.

Par value helps establish minimum legal capital and is used in accounting for par value stock. However, it does not establish a stock's worth nor the price at which a corporation must issue the stock. If purchasers are willing to pay more than par, a corporation may sell and issue its stock at a price above par. If purchasers will not pay par, it may be possible in some states for a corporation to issue its stock at a price below par.

Stock Premiums and Discounts

Premiums on Stock

When a corporation sells and issues stock at a price above the stock's par value, the stock is said to be issued at a **premium**. For example, if a corporation sells and issues its $10 par value common stock at $12 per share, the stock is sold at a $2 per share premium. Although a premium is an amount in excess of par paid by purchasers of newly issued stock, it is not considered a profit to the issuing corporation. Rather, a premium is part of the investment of stockholders who pay more than par for their stock.

In accounting for stock sold at a premium, the premium is recorded separately from the par value and is typically called contributed capital in excess of par value. For example, if a corporation sells and issues 10,000 shares of its $10 par value common stock for cash at $12 per share, the sale is recorded as follows:

Dec.	1	Cash	120,000.00	
		Common Stock		100,000.00
		Contributed Capital in Excess of		
		Par Value, Common Stock		20,000.00
		Sold and issued 10,000 shares of $10 par		
		value common stock at $12 per share.		

When stock is issued in exchange for assets other than cash and the fair value of the assets exceeds the par value of the stock, a premium is recorded as contributed capital in excess of par value. If fair value for the assets cannot be determined within reasonable limits, a price established by recent sales of the stock may be used in recording the exchange. This too may require that a premium be recorded.

When a balance sheet is prepared, any contributed capital in excess of par value is added in the equity section to the par value of the stock to which it applies, as follows:

Stockholders' Equity

Common stock, $10 par value, 25,000 shares authorized, 20,000 shares issued.	$200,000
Contributed capital in excess of par value, common stock	30,000
Total contributed capital.	$230,000
Retained earnings	82,400
Total stockholders' equity	$312,400

Discounts on Stock

Stock issued at a price below par is said to be issued at a **discount.** Many states prohibit the issuance of stock at a discount because the stockholders would be investing less than minimum legal capital. In states where stock may be issued at a discount, purchasers of the stock usually become contingently liable to the issuing corporation's creditors for the amount of the discount. Consequently, stock is seldom issued at a discount, and a discussion of stock discounts is of little practical importance. However, if stock were issued at less than par, the discount would be debited to a discount account and subtracted on the balance sheet from the par value of the stock to which it applies.

■   **No-Par Stock**   At one time, all stocks were required to have a par value. Today, all jurisdictions permit the issuance of **no-par stocks** or stocks without a par value. The primary advantage claimed for no-par stock is that since it does not have a par value, it may be issued at any price without having a discount liability attached. Also, printing a par value, say, $100, on a stock certificate may cause a person lacking in knowledge to believe a share of the stock to be worth $100, when it actually may be worthless. Therefore, eliminating the par value helps force such a person to examine the factors that give a stock value, which are earnings, dividends, and future prospects.

In some states, the entire proceeds from the sale of no-par stock becomes minimum legal capital and must be credited to a no-par stock account. In these states, if a corporation issues 1,000 shares of no-par stock at $42 per share, the transaction is recorded like this:

Oct.	20	Cash	42,000.00	
		No-Par Common Stock		42,000.00
		Sold and issued 1,000 shares of no-par common stock at $42 per share.		

In other states, a corporation may place a **stated value** on its no-par stock. The stated value then becomes minimum legal capital and is credited to the no-par stock account. If the stock is issued at an amount in excess of stated value, the excess is credited to a paid-in capital account called Contributed Capital in Excess of Stated Value, No-Par Common Stock. In these states, if a corporation issues at $42 per share 1,000 shares of no-par common stock on which it has placed a $25 per share stated value, the transaction is recorded as follows:

Oct.	20	Cash	42,000.00	
		No-Par Common Stock		25,000.00
		Contributed Capital in Excess of Stated Value, No-Par Common Stock		17,000.00
		Sold at $42 per share 1,000 shares of no-par stock having a $25 per share stated value.		

In still other states, a corporation may place a stated value on its no-par stock and record the transaction as in the preceding entry, but the entire proceeds from the sale of the stock becomes minimum legal capital.

■   **Sale of Stock through Subscriptions**   Often stock is sold for cash and immediately issued. Often, too, especially in organizing a new corporation, stock is sold by means of **stock subscriptions**. In the latter instance, a person wishing to become a stockholder signs a subscription blank or a subscription list, agreeing to buy a certain number of the shares at a specified price. When the subscription is accepted by the corporation, it becomes a contract; and the corporation acquires an asset, the right to receive payment from the subscriber. At the same time, the subscriber gains an equity in the corporation equal to the amount the subscriber agrees to pay. Payment may be in one amount or in installments.

To illustrate the sale of stock through subscriptions, assume that on June 6, Northgate Corporation accepted subscriptions to 5,000 shares of its $10 par value common stock at $12 per share. The subscription contracts called for a 10% down payment to accompany the subscriptions and the balance in two equal installments due in 30 and 60 days.

The subscriptions are recorded with the following entry:

June	6	Subscriptions Receivable, Common Stock. . .	60,000.00		
		Contributed Capital in Excess of Par			
		Value, Common Stock		10,000.00	
		Common Stock Subscribed		50,000.00	
		Accepted subscriptions to 5,000 shares of $10 par value common stock at $12 per share.			

Notice that, at the time the subscriptions are accepted, the subscriptions receivable account is debited for the sum of the stock's par value and premium. This is the amount the subscribers agree to pay. Notice, too, that the **Common Stock Subscribed** account is credited for par value and that the premium is credited to Contributed Capital in Excess of Par Value at the time the subscriptions are accepted. The subscriptions receivable and stock subscribed accounts are of temporary nature. The subscriptions receivable will be turned into cash when the subscribers pay for their stock. Likewise, when payment is completed, the subscribed stock will be issued and will become outstanding stock. Normally, subscribed stock is not issued until completely paid for.

Receipt of the down payments and the two installment payments may be recorded with these entries:

June	6	Cash	6,000.00	
		Subscriptions Receivable, Common Stock		6,000.00
		Collected 10% down payments on the common stock subscribed.		
July	6	Cash	27,000.00	
		Subscriptions Receivable, Common Stock		27,000.00
		Collected the first installment payments on the common stock subscribed.		
Aug.	5	Cash	27,000.00	
		Subscriptions Receivable, Common Stock		27,000.00
		Collected the second installment payments on the common stock subscribed.		

In this case, the down payments accompanied the subscriptions. Consequently, the entry to record the receipt of the subscriptions and the entry to record the down payments may be combined.

When stock is sold through subscriptions, the stock is usually not issued until the subscriptions are paid in full. However, as soon as the subscriptions are paid, the stock is issued. The entry to record the issuance of the Northgate common stock appears as follows:

Aug.	5	Common Stock Subscribed	50,000.00	
		Common Stock		50,000.00
		Issued 5,000 shares of common stock sold through subscriptions.		

Most subscriptions are collected in full, although not always. Sometimes a subscriber fails to pay. If this happens, the subscription contract must be canceled. In such a case, if the subscriber has made a partial payment on the contract, the amount paid may be returned. Or, a smaller amount of stock than that subscribed, an amount equal to the partial payment, may be issued. Or, in some states the subscriber's partial payment may be kept by the corporation to compensate for any damages suffered.

Subscriptions Receivable and Stock Subscribed on the Balance Sheet

Subscriptions receivable are normally to be collected within a relatively short time. Consequently, they appear on the balance sheet as a current asset. If a corporation prepares a balance sheet after accepting subscriptions to its stock but before the stock is issued, it should show both its issued stock and its subscribed stock on the balance sheet as follows:

Common stock, $10 par value, 25,000 shares authorized, 20,000 shares issued	$200,000	
Common stock subscribed, 5,000 shares	50,000	
Total common stock issued and subscribed	$250,000	
Contributed capital in excess of par value, common stock	40,000	
Total contributed capital		$290,000

■ **Rights of Common Stockholders**

When investors buy a corporation's common stock, they acquire all the specific rights granted by the corporation's charter to its common stockholders. They also acquire the general rights granted stockholders by the laws of the state in which the company is incorporated. The laws vary, but common stockholders generally have the following rights:

1. The right to vote in the stockholders' meetings.
2. The right to sell or otherwise dispose of their stock.
3. The right of first opportunity to purchase any additional shares of common stock issued by the corporation. (This is called the common stockholders' **preemptive right.** It gives common stockholders the opportunity to protect their proportionate interest in the corporation. For example, a stockholder who owns one fourth of a corporation's common stock

has the first opportunity to buy one fourth of any new common stock issued. This enables the stockholder to maintain a one-fourth interest.)

4. The right to share pro rata with other common stockholders in any dividends distributed to common stockholders.
5. The right to share in any assets remaining after creditors are paid if the corporation is liquidated.

■ Preferred Stock

A corporation may issue more than one kind or class of stock. If two classes are issued, one is generally known as common stock and the other as **preferred stock.** Preferred stock generally has a par value and, like common stock, may be sold at a price that is greater than par (or perhaps less than par). Separate paid-in capital accounts are used to record the issuance of preferred stock. For example, if 50 shares of $100 par, preferred stock are issued for $6,000 cash, the entry to record the issue is:

June	1	Cash	6,000.00	
		Preferred Stock		5,000.00
		Contributed Capital in Excess of Par Value,		
		Preferred Stock		1,000.00

Preferred stock is so called because of the preferences granted to its owners. These commonly include a preference as to payment of **dividends,** and may include a preference in the distribution of assets if the corporation is liquidated.

Preferred Dividends

A preference as to dividends does not grant an absolute right to dividends. Rather, if dividends are declared, it gives the preferred stockholders the right to receive their preferred dividends before the common stockholders are paid a dividend. In other words, if dividends are declared, a dividend must be paid the preferred stockholders before a dividend may be paid to the common stockholders. However, if the directors are of the opinion that no dividends should be paid, then neither the preferred nor the common stockholders receive a dividend.

Participating and Nonparticipating Preferred Stock

Dividends to common stockholders are limited only by the earning power of the corporation and the judgment of its board of directors. Dividends to preferred stock, however, are generally limited to a fixed maximum amount. When preferred stock is so limited, it is called **nonparticipating preferred stock.** For example, a corporation has outstanding 1,000 shares of $100 par, 9%, nonparticipating, preferred stock and 4,000 shares of $50 par, common stock. If the corporation's board of directors declares cash dividends of $42,000 in a year, this amount would be allocated as follows:

	To Preferred	To Common
First, to preferred [9% × (1,000 × $100)]	$9,000	
Remainder to common		$33,000

While most preferred stock is nonparticipating, some preferred stock may be paid additional dividends in excess of the stated percentage or amount that is preferred. Such preferred stock is called **participating preferred stock.** Participating preferred stock may be fully participating or partially participating.

To illustrate fully participating preferred stock, assume that the 1,000 shares of $100 par, 9% preferred stock in the previous example are fully participating. Now the allocation of $42,000 cash dividends in a year would be as follows:

	To Preferred	To Common
First, to preferred [9% × (1,000 × $100)]	$ 9,000	
Next, to common [9% × (4,000 × $50)]		$18,000
Remainder maintains equal percentage to preferred and common:		
($42,000 − $9,000 − $18,000 = $15,000)		
$15,000 × ($100,000 ÷ $300,000)	5,000	
$15,000 × ($200,000 ÷ $300,000)		10,000
Totals	$14,000	$28,000

Observe that the first step satisfies the preferred stock's right to 9% before any dividends are paid to common. Next, the common shares receive 9%. Finally, any additional dividends are allocated on the basis of the relative par value amounts outstanding. As a consequence, both preferred and common shares are paid the same percentage (14% in this case). This is confirmed by the following calculation:

	Par Value	Total Dividend	Percent of Par
Preferred (1,000 × $100)	$100,000	$14,000	14
Common (4,000 × $50).	200,000	28,000	14
Totals	$300,000	$42,000	14

No matter how much larger the dividend declaration might be, fully participating preferred stock has the right to participate with common on an equal percentage basis.

As mentioned before, participating preferred stock may be fully participating or partially participating. With partially participating preferred stock, the right to receive additional dividends beyond the basic preferred percentage is limited to a stated amount or percentage. Continuing with the previous example, the 1,000 shares of 9%, preferred stock might be participating up to an additional 3%. If so, the preferred shares would have received no more than 12% × $100,000, or $12,000. Of the $42,000 dividends declared, the remaining $30,000 would be paid entirely to common.

Cumulative and Noncumulative Preferred Stock

In addition to being participating or nonparticipating, preferred stock is either **cumulative** or **noncumulative.** If stock is cumulative, any undeclared dividends accumulate each year until paid. If preferred stock is noncumulative, the right to receive dividends is forfeited in any year that dividends are not declared.

The accumulation of dividends on cumulative preferred stocks does not guarantee payment. Dividends cannot be guaranteed because earnings from which they are paid cannot be guaranteed. However, when a corporation issues cumulative preferred stock, it does agree to pay its cumulative preferred stockholders both their current dividends and any unpaid back dividends, called **dividends in arrears,** before it pays a dividend to its common stockholders.

In addition to the preferences it receives, preferred stock carries with it all the rights of common stock, unless such rights are specifically denied in the corporation charter. Preferred stock often is denied the right to vote in the stockholders' meetings.

Preferred Dividends in Arrears on the Balance Sheet Date

A liability for a dividend does not come into existence until the dividend is declared by the board of directors; and unlike interest, dividends do not accrue. Consequently, if on the dividend date a corporation's board fails to declare a dividend on its cumulative preferred stock, the dividend in arrears is not a liability and does not appear on the balance sheet as such. However, if there are preferred dividends in arrears, the **full-disclosure principle** requires that this information appear on the balance sheet. Normally, such information is given in a balance sheet footnote. When a balance sheet does not carry such a footnote, a balance sheet reader has the right to assume that there are no dividends in arrears.

■ **Why Preferred Stock Is Issued**

Two common reasons why preferred stock is issued can best be shown by means of an example. Suppose that three persons with a total of $100,000 to invest wish to organize a corporation requiring $200,000 capital. If they sell and issue $200,000 of common stock, they will have to share control with other stockholders. However, if they sell and issue $100,000 of common stock to themselves and sell to outsiders $100,000 of 8%, cumulative preferred stock having no voting rights, they can retain control of the corporation for themselves.

Also, suppose the three promoters expect their new corporation to earn an annual after-tax return of $24,000. If they sell and issue $200,000 of common stock, this will mean a 12% return. However, if they sell and issue $100,000 of each kind of stock, retaining the common for themselves, they can increase their own return to 16%, as follows:

Net after-tax income.	$24,000
Less preferred dividends at 8%.	(8,000)
Balance to common stockholders (equal to 16% on	
their $100,000 investment)	$16,000

In this case, the common stockholders earn 16% because the dividends on the preferred stock are less than the amount that can be earned on the preferred stockholders' investment.

■   **Stock Values**   In addition to a par value, stocks may have a redemption value, a market value, and a book value.

Redemption Value

Redemption values apply to preferred stocks. Corporations that issue preferred stock often reserve the right to redeem or retire the stock by paying a specified amount to the preferred stockholders. The amount a corporation agrees to pay to redeem a share of its preferred stock is set at the time the stock is issued and is called the redemption value of the stock. Normally, the redemption value includes the par value of the stock plus a premium. To this amount must be added any dividends in arrears.

Market Value

The market value of a share of stock is the price at which a share can be bought or sold. Market values are influenced by earnings, dividends, future prospects, and general market conditions.

Book Value

The **book value of a share of stock** measures the equity of the owner of one share of the stock in the net assets of the issuing corporation. If a corporation has issued only common stock, its book value per share is determined by dividing total stockholders' equity by the number of shares outstanding. For example, if total stockholders' equity is $285,000 and there are 10,000 shares outstanding, the book value per share is $28.50 ($285,000 ÷ 10,000 = $28.50).

To compute book values when both common and preferred stock are outstanding, the preferred stock is assigned a portion of the total stockholders' equity equal to its redemption value (or par value if there is no redemption value) plus any cumulative dividends in arrears. The remaining stockholders' equity is then assigned to the common shares outstanding. After this, the book value of each class is determined by dividing its share of stockholders' equity by the number of shares of that class outstanding. For instance, assume a corporation has the stockholders' equity as shown in Illustration 15-2.

If the preferred stock is redeemable at $103 per share and two years

Illustration 15-2

Stockholders' Equity

Preferred stock, $100 par value, 7% cumulative and nonparticipating, 2,000 shares authorized, 1,000 shares issued and outstanding	$100,000	
Contributed capital in excess of par value, preferred stock	5,000	
Total capital contributed by preferred stockholders . .		$105,000
Common stock, $25 par value, 12,000 shares authorized, 10,000 shares issued and outstanding	$250,000	
Contributed capital in excess of par value, common stock	10,000	
Total capital contributed by common stockholders . . .		260,000
Total contributed capital		$365,000
Retained earnings		82,000
Total stockholders' equity		$447,000

of cumulative preferred dividends are in arrears, the book values of the corporation's shares are calculated as follows:

Total stockholders' equity			$ 447,000
Less equity applicable to preferred shares:			
Redemption value	$103,000		
Cumulative dividends in arrears	14,000	(117,000)	
Equity applicable to common shares			$330,000
Book value of preferred shares ($117,000 ÷ 1,000)		$117	
Book value of common shares ($330,000 ÷ 10,000)		33	

Corporations in their annual reports to their shareholders often highlight the increase that has occurred in the book value of the corporation's shares during a year. Book value may also be of significance in a contract. For example, a stockholder may enter into a contract to sell shares at their book value at some future date. However, book value should not be confused with **liquidation value** because if a corporation is liquidated, its assets will probably sell at prices quite different from the amounts at which they are carried on the books. Also, book value generally has little bearing upon the market value of stock. Dividends, earning capacity, and future prospects are usually of much more importance. For instance, a common stock having an $11 book value may sell for $25 per share if its earnings, dividends, and prospects are good. However, it may sell for $5 per share if these factors are unfavorable.

□   **Glossary**

Book value of a share of stock the equity represented by one share of stock in the issuing corporation's net assets.

Common stock stock of a corporation that has only one class of stock; if there is more than one class, the class that has no preferences relative to the corporation's other classes of stock.

Common stock subscribed unissued common stock for which the issuing corporation has a subscription contract to issue.

Cumulative preferred stock preferred stock on which undeclared dividends accumulate annually until paid.

Discount on stock the difference between the par value of stock and the amount below par value contributed by stockholders.

Dividend a distribution made by a corporation to its stockholders of cash, other assets, or additional shares of the corporation's own stock.

Dividends in arrears unpaid prior period dividends on preferred stock which must be paid before dividends are paid to common stockholders.

Minimum legal capital an amount, as defined by state law, that stockholders must invest in a corporation or be contingently liable to its creditors.

Noncumulative preferred stock a preferred stock for which the right to receive dividends is forfeited in any year in which dividends are not declared.

No-par stock a class of stock that does not have an arbitrary (par) value placed on the stock at the time the stock is first authorized.

Organization costs costs of bringing a corporation into existence, such as legal fees, promoters' fees, and amounts paid the state to secure a charter.

Participating preferred stock preferred stock that has the right to share in dividends above the fixed amount or percentage which is preferred.

Par value an arbitrary value placed on a share of stock at the time the stock is authorized.

Preemptive right the right of common stockholders to protect their proportionate interests in a corporation by having the first opportunity to purchase additional shares of common stock issued by the corporation.

Preferred stock stock the owners of which are granted certain preferences over common stockholders, such as a preference to payment of dividends or in the distribution of assets in a liquidation.

Premium on stock the amount of capital contributed by stockholders above the stock's par value.

Proxy a legal document that gives an agent of a stockholder the right to vote the stockholder's shares.

Redemption value of stock the amount a corporation must pay if and when it exercises its right to require the return of a share of preferred stock previously issued by the corporation.

Stated value of no-par stock an amount, established by a corporation's board of directors, that is credited to the no-par stock account at the time the stock is issued.

Stock subscription a contractual commitment to purchase unissued shares of stock and become a stockholder.

1. What are the advantages and disadvantages of the corporate form of business organization?
2. Why is the income of a corporation said to be taxed twice?
3. Who is responsible for directing the affairs of a corporation?
4. What is a proxy?
5. What are organization costs? List several.
6. How are organization costs classified on the balance sheet?
7. What are the duties and responsibilities of a corporation's registrar and transfer agent?
8. Why is a corporation the stock of which is sold on a stock exchange required to have a registrar and transfer agent? Why is such a corporation required to have both a registrar and a transfer agent?
9. List the general rights of common stockholders.
10. What is the preemptive right of common stockholders?
11. Laws place no limit on the amounts partners may withdraw from a partnership. On the other hand, laws regulating corporations place definite limits on the amounts stockholders may withdraw from a corporation in dividends. Why is there a difference?
12. What is a stock premium? What is a stock discount?
13. Does a corporation earn a profit by selling its stock at a premium? Does it incur a loss by selling its stock at a discount?
14. Why do corporation laws make purchasers of stock at a discount contingently liable for the discount? To whom are such purchasers contingently liable?
15. What is the main advantage of no-par stock?
16. What are the meanings of the following when applied to preferred stock: (a) preferred, (b) participating, (c) nonparticipating, (d) cumulative, and (e) noncumulative?
17. What are the balance sheet classifications of the accounts: (a) Subscriptions Receivable, Common Stock and (b) Common Stock Subscribed?
18. What are the meanings of the following terms when applied to a share of stock: (a) par value, (b) book value, (c) market value, and (d) redemption value?

Exercise 15-1

Prepare general journal entries on October 10 to record the following issuances of stock by various corporations:

1. Fifty shares of $100 par value common stock are issued for $800 cash.
2. One hundred shares of no-par common stock are issued to promoters in exchange for their efforts in organizing the corporation. The promoters' efforts are estimated to be worth $15,000, and the stock has no stated value.
3. Assume the same facts as in 2 above, except that the stock has a $10 stated value.

Exercise 15-2

Barry Dow and Jane Harwood begin a new business on January 5 by investing $75,000 each in the company. Assume that on December 25 it is decided that $12,000 of the company's cash will be distributed equally between the owners. Checks for $6,000 are prepared and given to the owners on December 30. On December 31, the company reports a $21,000 net income. Prepare journal entries to record the investments by the owners, the distribution of cash to the owners, and the closing of the Income Summary account assuming: (a) the business is a partnership and (b) the business is a corporation that issued 1,000 shares of $10 par value, common stock to each owner.

Exercise 15-3

A corporation sold and issued 5,000 shares of its common stock for $157,500 on May 25. (a) Give the entry to record the sale under the assumption the stock is no-par stock and the board of directors did not place a stated value on the stock. (b) Give the entry to record the sale under the assumption the stock is no-par stock and the board placed a $5 per share stated value on the stock. (c) Give the entry to record the sale under the assumption the stock is $10 par stock.

Exercise 15-4

On June 23, Expando Corporation accepted subscriptions to 20,000 shares of its $10 par value common stock at $12.50 per share. The subscription contracts called for one fourth of the subscription price to accompany each contract as a down payment and the balance to be paid on August 15. Give the entries to record: (a) the subscriptions, (b) the down payments, (c) receipt of the remaining amounts due on the subscriptions, and (d) issuance of the stock.

Exercise 15-5

A corporation has outstanding 10,000 shares of $100 par value, 8% cumulative and nonparticipating preferred stock and 45,000 shares of $25 par value common stock. During the first four years in its life, the corporation paid out the following amounts in dividends: first year, $–0–; second year, $95,000; third year, $200,000; and fourth year, $125,000. Determine the total dividends paid to each class of stockholders each year.

Exercise 15-6

Determine the total dividends paid each class of stockholders of the previous exercise under the assumption that rather than being cumulative and nonparticipating, the preferred stock is noncumulative and nonparticipating.

Exercise 15-7

A corporation has outstanding 10,000 shares of $100 par value, 9% cumulative and fully participating preferred stock and 60,000 shares of $10 par value common stock. It has regularly paid all dividends on the preferred stock. This year the board of directors voted to pay out a total of $200,000 in dividends to the two classes of stockholders. Determine the percent of par to be paid each class of stockholders and the dividend per share to be paid each class.

Exercise 15-8

Three individuals have agreed to begin a new business that will require a total investment of $1,000,000. Each of the three will contribute $150,000, and the remaining $550,000 will be raised from other investors. Two alternative plans for raising the money are being considered: (1) issue $100 par, common stock to all investors, or (2) issue $100 par, common stock to the three founders and $100 par, 9%, preferred stock to the remaining investors. In either case, all of the shares will be issued at par. If the business is expected to earn an after-tax net income of $120,000, which of the two plans will provide the highest return to the three founders? What rate of return will the founders earn under each alternative?

Exercise 15-9

What would be your answer to Exercise 15-8 if the business is expected to earn an annual, after-tax net income of only $80,000?

Exercise 15-10

The stockholders' equity section from a corporation's balance sheet appeared as follows:

Stockholders' Equity

Preferred stock, 10% cumulative and nonparticipating, $100 par value, $108 redemption value, 4,000 shares issued and outstanding	$ 400,000
Common stock, $10 par value, 80,000 shares issued and outstanding	800,000
Retained earnings.	300,000
Total stockholders' equity	$1,500,000

Required

1. Determine the book value per share of the preferred stock and of the common stock under the assumption there are no dividends in arrears on the preferred stock.
2. Determine the book value per share for each kind of stock under the assumption that two years' dividends are in arrears on the preferred stock.

Problems

Problem 15-1

When Airride Company was organized, it was authorized to issue 10,000 shares of $100 par value, 9% cumulative and nonparticipating, preferred stock and 225,000 shares of $10 par value common stock. It then completed these transactions:

June 3 Accepted subscriptions to 75,000 shares of common stock at $18 per share. Down payments equal to 20% of the subscription price accompanied each subscription.

14 Gave the corporation's promoters 2,000 shares of common stock for their services in getting the corporation organized. The board valued the services at $35,000.

July 5 Accepted subscriptions to 5,000 shares of preferred stock at $120 per share. The subscriptions were accompanied by 50% down payments.

20 Collected the balance due on the June 3 common stock subscriptions and issued the stock.

31 Accepted subscriptions to 2,500 shares of preferred stock at $110 per share. The subscriptions were accompanied by 50% down payments.

Aug. 5 Collected the balance due on the July 5 preferred stock subscriptions and issued the stock.

Required

1. Prepare general journal entries to record the transactions.
2. Prepare the stockholders' equity section of the corporation's balance sheet as of the close of business on August 5.

Problem 15-2

Polansky Company's corporate charter authorizes the company to issue 600,000 shares of $1 par value common stock and 30,000 shares of 12%, cumulative and nonparticipating, $50 par value preferred stock. The company completed the following transactions:

198A

Apr. 7 Issued 135,000 shares of common stock at par for cash.

30 Gave the corporation's promoters 90,000 shares of common stock for their services in getting the corporation organized. The directors valued the services at $150,000.

May 2 Exchanged 300,000 shares of common stock for the following assets at fair market values: land, $75,000; buildings, $300,000; and machinery, $375,000.

Dec. 31 Closed the Income Summary account. A $75,000 loss was incurred.

198B

Jan. 12 Issued 3,000 shares of preferred stock at par.

Mar. 15 Accepted subscriptions to 30,000 shares of common stock at $1.80 per share. Down payments of 25% accompanied the subscription contracts.

Dec. 31 Closed the Income Summary account. A $207,000 net income was earned.

198C

Jan. 18 The board of directors declared a 12% dividend to preferred shares and $0.10 per share to outstanding common shares, payable on February 8 to the January 26 stockholders of record.

Feb. 8 Paid the previously declared dividends.

Mar. 10 Polansky Company's $30,000 note payable (plus interest of $1,500) was due and payable on this date. The interest had already been credited to Interest Payable. The lender accepted 21,000 shares of Polansky's common stock in payment of this note and accrued interest.

Dec. 31 Closed the Income Summary account. A $240,000 net income was earned.

Required

1. Prepare general journal entries to record the transactions.
2. Prepare the stockholders' equity section of a balance sheet as of the close of business on December 31, 198C.

Problem 15-3

Part 1. The balance sheet of Exotic Boat Charters Corporation includes the following information:

Stockholders' Equity

Preferred stock, 9% cumulative and nonparticipating, $100 par value, authorized and issued 1,500 shares	$150,000
Common stock, no-par value, 60,000 shares authorized and issued	600,000
Retained earnings	90,000
Total stockholders' equity	$840,000

Required

Assume that the preferred stock has a redemption value of $105 plus any dividends in arrears. Calculate the book value per share of the preferred and common stocks under each of the following assumptions:

a. There are no dividends in arrears on the preferred stock.
b. One year's dividends are in arrears on the preferred stock.
c. Three years' dividends are in arrears on the preferred stock.

Part 2. Since its organization, Singleton Corporation has had outstanding 3,000 shares of $100 par value, 11%, preferred stock and 45,000 shares of $10 par value common stock. No dividends have been paid this year, and two prior years' dividends are in arrears on the preferred stock. However, the company has recently prospered and the board of directors wants to know how much cash will be required for dividends if a $1.60 per share dividend is paid on the common stock.

Required

Prepare a schedule showing the amounts of cash required for dividends to each class of stockholders under each of the following assumptions:

a. The preferred stock is noncumulative and nonparticipating.
b. The preferred stock is cumulative and nonparticipating.
c. The preferred stock is cumulative and fully participating.
d. The preferred stock is cumulative and participating to 14%.

Problem 15-4

Wide Ranch Company has outstanding 1,200 shares of $100 par value, 10%, preferred stock and 25,000 shares of $10 par value common stock. During a seven-year period, the company paid out the following amounts in dividends: 198A, $–0–; 198B, $35,000; 198C, $–0–; 198D, $20,000; 198E, $26,000; 198F, $32,000; and 198G, $74,000.

Required

1. Prepare three schedules with columnar headings as follows:

Year	Calculations	Preferred Dividend per Share	Common Dividend per Share

2. Complete a schedule under each of the following assumptions. There were no dividends in arrears for the years prior to 198A.
   a. The preferred stock is noncumulative and nonparticipating.
   b. The preferred stock is cumulative and nonparticipating.
   c. The preferred stock is cumulative and fully participating.

Problem 15-5

Crenshaw Corporation's common stock is selling on a stock exchange today at $21.75 per share, and a just-published balance sheet shows the stockholders' equity in the corporation as follows:

Stockholders' Equity

Preferred stock, 9.5% cumulative and nonparticipating, $100 par value, 3,000 shares authorized and outstanding	$ 300,000
Common stock, $10 par value, 75,000 shares authorized and outstanding . .	750,000
Retained earnings.	252,000
Total stockholders' equity	$1,302,000

Required

Answer these questions: (1) What is the market value of the corporation's common stock? (2) What are the par values of its (a) preferred stock and (b) common stock? (3) If there are no dividends in arrears, what are the book values of the (a) preferred stock and (b) common stock? (4) If two years' dividends are in arrears on the preferred stock, what are the book values of the (a) preferred stock and (b) common stock? (Assume the corporation does not have the right to redeem the preferred stock, which therefore has no redemption value.)

☐ **Alternate Problems**   **Problem 15-1A**

Overdrive Corporation is authorized to issue 18,000 shares of $100 par value, 10% cumulative and nonparticipating, preferred stock and 400,000 shares of no-par value common stock. The board of directors established a $10 stated value for the no-par common stock. Overdrive Corporation then completed these transactions:

Sept. 7 Accepted subscriptions to 135,000 shares of common stock at $16 per share. Down payments equal to 30% of the subscription price accompanied each subscription.

16 Gave the corporation's promoters 3,600 shares of common stock for their services in getting the corporation organized. The board valued the services at $63,000.

Oct. 3 Accepted subscriptions to 9,000 shares of preferred stock at $115 per share. The subscriptions were accompanied by 40% down payments.

7 Collected the balance due on the September 7 common stock subscriptions and issued the stock.

31 Accepted subscriptions to 4,500 shares of preferred stock at $109 per share. The subscriptions were accompanied by 40% down payments.

Nov. 10 Collected the balance due on the October 3 preferred stock subscriptions and issued the stock.

Required

1. Prepare general journal entries to record the transactions.
2. Prepare the stockholders' equity section of the corporation's balance sheet as of the close of business on November 10.

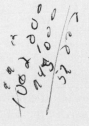

Problem 15-2A

Rathgaber Company is authorized by its charter to issue 500,000 shares of $10 par value common stock and 25,000 shares of 11% cumulative and nonparticipating, $100 par value preferred stock. The company completed the following transactions:

198A

May 8 Issued 26,000 shares of common stock at par for cash.

27 Gave the corporation's promoters 1,800 shares of common stock for their services in getting the corporation organized. The directors valued the services at $20,000.

June 6 Exchanged 80,000 shares of common stock for the following assets at fair market values: land, $185,000; buildings, $380,000; and machinery, $270,000.

Dec. 31 Closed the Income Summary account. A $47,000 loss was incurred.

198B

Jan. 26 Issued 2,000 shares of preferred stock at par.

Feb. 22 Accepted subscriptions to 6,000 shares of common stock at $12.50 per share. Down payments of 30% accompanied the subscription contracts.

Dec. 31 Closed the Income Summary account. A $166,000 net income was earned.

198C

Mar. 14 The board of directors declared an 11% dividend to preferred shares and $0.50 per share to outstanding common shares, payable on April 2 to the March 23 stockholders of record.

Apr. 2 Paid the previously declared dividends.

May 19 Rathgaber Company's $90,000 note payable (plus interest of $5,900) was due and payable on this date. The interest had already been credited to Interest Payable. The lender accepted 9,500 shares of Rathgaber's common stock in payment of this note and accrued interest.

Dec. 31 Closed the Income Summary account. A $198,000 net income was earned.

Required

1. Prepare general journal entries to record the transactions.
2. Prepare the stockholders' equity section of a balance sheet as of the close of business on December 31, 198C.

Problem 15-3A

Part 1. The balance sheet of Crumley Services Corporation includes the following information:

Stockholders' Equity

Preferred stock, 10% cumulative and nonparticipating, $100 par value, preferred stock, authorized and issued 1,000 shares	$100,000
Common stock, no-par value, 40,000 shares authorized and issued	400,000
Retained earnings	60,000
Total stockholders' equity	$560,000

Required

Assume that the preferred stock has a redemption value of $106 plus any dividends in arrears. Calculate the book value per share of the preferred and common stocks under each of the following assumptions:

a. There are no dividends in arrears on the preferred stock.
b. One year's dividends are in arrears on the preferred stock.
c. Three years' dividends are in arrears on the preferred stock.

Part 2. Since its organization, Triple Corporation has had outstanding 4,000 shares of $100 par value, 12%, preferred stock and 60,000 shares of $10 par value common stock. No dividends have been paid this year, and two prior years' dividends are in arrears on the preferred stock. However, the company has recently prospered and the board of directors wants to know how much cash will be required for dividends if a $1.75 per share dividend is paid on the common stock.

Required

Prepare a schedule showing the amounts of cash required for dividends to each class of stockholders under each of the following assumptions:

a. The preferred stock is noncumulative and nonparticipating.
b. The preferred stock is cumulative and nonparticipating.
c. The preferred stock is cumulative and fully participating.
d. The preferred stock is cumulative and participating to 14%.

Problem 15-4A

Farm Finance Company has outstanding 2,000 shares of $100 par value, 11%, preferred stock and 60,000 shares of $10 par value common stock. During a seven-year period, the company paid out the following amounts in dividends: 198A, $–0–; 198B, $46,000; 198C, $–0–; 198D, $25,000; 198E, $52,000; 198F, $60,000; and 198G, $140,000.

Required

1. Prepare three schedules with columnar headings as follows:

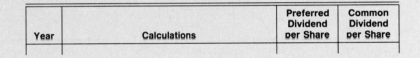

Year	Calculations	Preferred Dividend per Share	Common Dividend per Share

2. Complete a schedule under each of the following assumptions. Round your calculations of dividends per share to the nearest penny. There were no dividends in arrears for the years prior to 198A.
   a. The preferred stock is noncumulative and nonparticipating.
   b. The preferred stock is cumulative and nonparticipating.
   c. The preferred stock is cumulative and fully participating.

Problem 15-5A

Daley Corporation's common stock is selling on a stock exchange today at $26.25 per share, and a just-published balance sheet shows the stockholders' equity in the corporation as follows:

Stockholders' Equity

Preferred stock, 8.8% cumulative and nonparticipating, $100 par value, 2,100 shares authorized and outstanding	$ 210,000
Common stock, $100 par value, 9,200 shares authorized and outstanding . .	920,000
Retained earnings	336,000
Total stockholders' equity	$1,466,000

Required

Answer these questions: (1) What is the market value of the corporation's common stock? (2) What are the par values of its (a) preferred stock and (b) common stock? (3) If there are no dividends in arrears, what are the book values of the (a) preferred stock and (b) common stock? (4) If two years' dividends are in arrears on the preferred stock, what are the book values of the (a) preferred stock and (b) common stock? (Assume the corporation does not have the right to redeem the preferred stock, which therefore has no redemption value.)

□

Provocative Problems

Provocative Problem 15-1   MEL's Sports, Inc.

Mark Mangum and Mike Linder have operated a sports equipment company, M & M's Sports, for a number of years as partners sharing losses and gains in a 3:2 ratio. Because the business is growing, the two partners entered into an agreement with Tim Ewing to reorganize their firm into a corporation. The charter of the new corporation, MEL's Sports, Inc., authorizes the corporation to issue 50,000 shares of $10 par value common stock. On the date of the reorganization, November 13 of the current year, a trial balance of the partnership ledger appears as follows:

M & M's Sports
Trial Balance
November 13, 19—

Cash	$ 25,500	
Accounts receivable	46,500	
Allowance for doubtful accounts		$ 1,750
Merchandise inventory	211,250	
Store equipment	49,000	
Accumulated depreciation, store equipment		10,500
Buildings	250,000	
Accumulated depreciation, buildings		50,000
Land	62,500	
Accounts payable		27,750
Mortgage payable		175,000
Mark Mangum, capital		226,250
Mike Linder, capital		153,500
Totals	$644,750	$644,750

The agreement between the partners and Ewing carries these provisions:

1. The partnership assets are to be revalued as follows:
   a. The $1,500 account receivable of Lost Cagers is known to be uncollectible and is to be written off as a bad debt.
   b. The allowance for doubtful accounts is to be increased to 5% of the remaining accounts receivable.
   c. The merchandise inventory is to be written down to $190,000 to allow for damaged and shopworn goods.
   d. Insufficient depreciation has been taken on the store equipment; consequently, its book value is to be decreased to $32,500 by increasing the balance of the accumulated depreciation account.
   e. The building is to be written up to its replacement cost, $325,000, and the balance of the accumulated depreciation account is to be increased to show the building to be one fifth depreciated.
2. After the partnership assets are revalued, the assets and liabilities are to be transferred to the corporation in exchange for its stock, with each partner accepting stock at par value for his equity in the partnership.
3. Tim Ewing is to buy any remaining stock for cash at par value.

After reaching the agreement outlined, the three men hired you as accountant for the new corporation. Your first task is to determine the amount of stock each person should receive, and to prepare entries on the corporation's books to record the issuance of stock in exchange for the partnership assets and liabilities and the issuance of stock to Ewing for cash. In addition, prepare a balance sheet for the corporation as it should appear after all its stock is issued.

Provocative Problem 15-2   Harkins Company

The management of Harkins Company is considering the expansion of its business operations to a new and exciting line of business in which newly invested assets can be expected to earn 15% per year. At the present time Harkins Company has only 16,000 shares of $50 par, common stock outstanding, no other contributed capital accounts, and retained earnings of $160,000. Existing operations consistently earn approximately $120,000 each year. To finance the new expansion, management is considering three alternatives: (a) Issuing 4,000 shares of $100 par, 10% cumulative, nonparticipating, nonvoting, preferred stock. Investment advisers of the company have concluded that these shares could be issued at par. (b) Issuing 2,000 shares of $100 par, 10% cumulative, fully participating, nonvoting, preferred stock. The investment advisers conclude that these shares could be sold for $200 per share. (c) Issuing 5,000 shares of common stock at $80 per share.

In evaluating these three alternatives, Harkins Company management has asked you to calculate the dividends that would be distributed to each class of stockholder based on the assumption that each year the board of directors will declare dividends equal to the total net income earned by the corporation. Your calculations should show the distribution of dividends to preferred and common stockholders under each of the three alternative financing plans. You should also calculate dividends per share of preferred and dividends per share of common.

As a second part of your analysis assume that you own 1,000 of the common shares outstanding prior to the expansion and that you will not acquire or purchase any of the newly issued shares. Based on your whole analysis, would you prefer that the proposed expansion in operations be rejected? If not, comment on the relative merits of each alternative from your point of view as a common stockholder.

Provocative Problem 15-3   A Comparison of Alternative Investments

Having recently inherited $50,000, Ross Barnett is thinking about investing the money in one of two securities. They are: Barnhold Corporation common stock or the preferred stock issued by Blazertype Company. The companies manufacture and sell competing products, and both have been in business about the same length of time—four years in the case of Barnhold Corporation and five years for Blazertype Company. Also, the two companies have about the same amounts of stockholders' equity, as the following equity sections from their latest balance sheets show:

Barnhold Corporation

Common stock, $1 par value, 5,000,000 shares authorized, 2,000,000 shares issued	$2,000,000
Retained earnings	1,000,000
Total stockholders' equity	$3,000,000

Blazertype Company

Preferred stock, $100 par value, 7% cumulative and nonparticipating, 10,000 shares authorized and issued	$1,000,000*
Common stock, $10 par value, 200,000 shares authorized and issued. . . .	2,000,000
Retained earnings	75,000
Total stockholders' equity	$3,075,000

* The current and one prior year's dividends are in arrears on the preferred stock.

Barnhold Corporation did not pay a dividend on its common stock during its first year's operations; however, since then, for the past three years, it has paid a $0.10 per share annual dividend on the stock. The stock is currently selling for $1.59 per share. The preferred stock of Blazertype Company, on the other hand, is selling for $92 per share. Mr. Barnett favors this stock as an investment. He feels the stock is a real bargain since it is not only selling below its par value but also $22 below book value, and as he says, "Since it is a preferred stock, the dividends are guaranteed." Too, he feels the common stock of Barnhold Corporation, selling at 6% above book value and 59% above par value while paying only a $0.10 per share dividend, is overpriced.

a. Is the preferred stock of Blazertype Company selling at a price $22 below its book value, and is the common stock of Barnhold Corporation selling at a price 6% above book value and 59% above par value?

b. From an analysis of the stockholders' equity sections, express your opinion of the two stocks as investments and describe some of the factors Mr. Barnett should consider in choosing between the two securities.

16 Additional Corporation Transactions and Stock Investments

After studying Chapter 16, you should be able to:

1. Record stock dividends and compare them with stock splits.

2. Record purchases and sales of treasury stock and describe their effects on stockholders' equity.

3. Describe restrictions and appropriations of retained earnings and the disclosure of such items in the financial statements.

4. State the criteria for classifying stock investments as current assets or as long-term investments.

5. Describe the circumstances under which the cost method of accounting for stock investments is used and the circumstances under which the equity method is used.

6. Record and maintain the accounts for stock investments according to the cost method and the equity method.

7. Prepare consolidated financial statements that include such matters as excess of investment cost over book value and minority interests.

8. Define or explain the words and phrases listed in the chapter Glossary.

When a corporation earns a net income, more assets flow into the business from revenues than flow out for expenses. As a result, a net income increases both assets and stockholders' equity. The increase in stockholders' equity appears on the corporation's balance sheet as retained earnings. Once retained earnings were commonly called **earned surplus**. However, since the word **surplus** is subject to misinterpretation, the AICPA's Committee on Terminology recommended that its use be discontinued. Consequently, the term **surplus** has all but disappeared from published balance sheets.

■ **Retained Earnings and Dividends**

In most states, a corporation must have retained earnings in order to pay a cash dividend. However, the payment of a cash dividend reduces in equal amounts both cash and stockholders' equity. Consequently, in order to pay a cash dividend, a corporation must have not only a credit balance in its Retained Earnings account but also cash with which to pay the dividend. If cash or assets that will shortly become cash are not available, a board of directors may think it wise to forgo the declaration of a dividend, even though retained earnings exist. Often, the directors of a corporation with a large retained earnings balance will not declare a dividend because all current assets will be needed in the operation of the business.

In considering the wisdom of a dividend, a board of directors must recognize that earnings are a source of assets. Perhaps some assets from earnings should be paid out in dividends and some should be retained for emergencies and to pay dividends in years when earnings are not sufficient to pay normal dividends. Also, if a corporation is to expand, management may wish to finance the expansion by using assets acquired through earnings rather than by borrowing or selling equity.

Entries for the declaration and distribution of a cash dividend were presented on page 134 and need not be repeated here.

■ **Distributions from Contributed Capital**

Generally, contributed capital may not be returned to stockholders as dividends. However, in some states, dividends may be debited or charged to certain contributed capital accounts. Seldom may dividends be deducted from the par or stated value of the outstanding stock. However, the exact contributed capital accounts to which a corporation may charge dividends depend upon the laws of the state of its incorporation. For this reason, it is usually wise for a board of directors to secure competent legal advice before voting to charge dividends to any contributed capital account.

■ **Stock Dividends**

A **stock dividend** is a distribution by a corporation of shares of its own stock to its stockholders without any consideration being received in return from its stockholders. Usually, the distribution is prompted by a desire to give the stockholders some evidence of their interest in retained earnings without distributing cash or other assets that the board of directors wants to retain in the business. A clear distinction should be made between a cash dividend and a stock dividend. A cash dividend reduces both assets and stockholders' equity. A stock dividend differs in that shares of the corporation's own stock rather than cash are distributed. Such a dividend has no effect on assets, total capital, or the amount of a stockholder's equity.

A stock dividend has no effect on corporation assets, total capital, and the amount of a stockholder's equity because it involves nothing more than a transfer of retained earnings to contributed capital. To illustrate this, assume that Northwest Corporation has the following stockholders' equity:

Stockholder's Equity

Common stock, $10 par value, authorized 15,000 shares issued and outstanding 10,000 shares	$100,000
Contributed capital in excess of par value, common stock	8,000
Total contributed capital	$108,000
Retained earnings.	35,000
Total stockholders' equity	$143,000

Assume further than on December 28, the directors of Northwest Corporation declared a 10% or 1,000-share stock dividend distributable on January 20 to the stockholders of record on January 15.

If the market value of Northwest Corporation's stock on December 28 is $15 per share, the following entries would record the dividend declaration and distribution:

Dec.	28	Retained Earnings	15,000.00	
		Common Stock Dividend Distributable . .		10,000.00
		Contributed Capital in Excess of Par Value, Common Stock		5,000.00
		To record the declaration of a 1,000-share common stock dividend.		
Jan.	20	Common Stock Dividend Distributable	10,000.00	
		Common Stock		10,000.00
		To record the distribution of a 1,000-share common stock dividend.		

Note that the entries shift $15,000 of the stockholders' equity from retained earnings to contributed capital, or as it is said, $15,000 of retained earnings are **capitalized.** Note also that the amount of retained earnings capitalized is equal to the market value of the 1,000 shares issued ($15 × 1,000 shares = $15,000).

As previously pointed out, a stock dividend does not distribute assets to the stockholders; it does not affect in any way the corporation assets. Likewise, it has no effect on total capital and on the equities of the individual stockholders. To illustrate these last points, assume that Johnson owned 100 shares of Northwest Corporation's stock prior to the stock dividend. The corporation's total contributed and retained capital before the dividend and the book value of Johnson's 100 shares were as follows:

Common stock (10,000 shares)	$100,000
Contributed capital in excess of par value, common stock	8,000
Retained earnings	35,000
Total contributed and retained capital	$143,000

$143,000 ÷ 10,000 shares outstanding = $14.30 per share book value.
$14.30 × 100 = $1,430 for the book value of Johnson's 100 shares.

A 10% stock dividend gives a stockholder one new share for each 10 shares previously held. Consequently, Johnson received 10 new shares. After the dividend, the contributed capital and retained earnings of the corporation and the book value of Johnson's holdings are as follows:

Common stock (11,000 shares)	$110,000
Contributed capital in excess of par value, common stock	13,000
Retained earnings	20,000
Total contributed and retained capital	$143,000

$143,000 ÷ 11,000 shares outstanding = $13 per share book value.
$13 × 110 = $1,430 for the book value of Johnson's 110 shares.

Before the stock dividend, Johnson owned 100/10,000 or 1/100 of the Northwest Corporation stock, and his holdings had a $1,430 book value. After the dividend, he owned 110/11,000 or 1/100 of the corporation, and his holdings still had a $1,430 book value. In other words, there was no effect on his equity other than that it was repackaged from 100 units into 110. Likewise, the only effect on corporation capital was a permanent transfer to contributed capital of $15,000 from retained earnings. Consequently, insofar as both the corporation and Johnson are concerned, there was no shift in equities or corporation assets.

Why Stock Dividends Are Distributed

If a stock dividend has no effect on corporation assets and stockholders' equities other than to repackage the equities into more units, why are such dividends declared and distributed? One of the reasons for the declaration of stock dividends is directly related to the market price of a corporation's common stock. For example, if a profitable corporation grows by retaining earnings, the price of its common stock also tends to grow. Eventually, the price of a share may become high enough to prevent some investors from considering a purchase of the stock. Thus, the corporation may declare stock dividends to keep the price of its shares from growing too high. For this reason, some corporations declare small stock dividends each year.

Some stockholders may desire stock dividends for another reason. Often, corporations declaring stock dividends continue to pay the same cash dividend per share after a stock dividend as before, with the result that stockholders receive more cash each time dividends are declared.

Amount of Retained Earnings Capitalized

Some stockholders may incorrectly believe that earnings are distributed in a stock dividend. Consequently, it was decided that the amount of retained earnings capitalized in a small stock dividend and made unavailable for future dividends should equal the market value of the shares to be distributed.[1] A **small stock dividend** was defined as one of 25% or less of the previously outstanding shares.

A small stock dividend is likely to have only a small impact on the price of the stock. On the other hand, a large stock dividend normally has a pronounced impact, and for this reason is not apt to be perceived as a distribution of earnings. Therefore, in recording a large stock dividend (over 25%), it is necessary to capitalize retained earnings only to the extent required by law. As a result, in most states, a corporation may record a large stock dividend by debiting Retained Earnings and crediting the stock account for the par value of the shares issued.[2]

Stock Dividends on the Balance Sheet

Since a stock dividend is "payable" in stock rather than in assets, it is not a liability of its issuing corporation. Therefore, if a balance sheet is prepared between the declaration and distribution dates of a stock dividend, the amount of the dividend distributable should appear on the balance sheet in the stockholders' equity section as follows:

Common stock, $10 par value, 50,000 shares authorized, 20,000 shares issued	$200,000
Common stock subscribed, 5,000 shares	50,000
Common stock dividend distributable, 1,900 shares	19,000
Total common stock issued and to be issued	$269,000
Contributed capital in excess of par value, common stock	46,000
Total capital contributed and subscribed by common stockholders	$315,000

Stock Splits

Sometimes, when a corporation's stock is selling at a high price, the corporation will call it in and issue two, three, or more new shares in the place of each previously outstanding share. For example, a corporation having outstanding $100 par value stock selling for $375 a share may call in the old shares and issue to the stockholders four shares of $25 par, or 10 shares of $10 par, or any number of shares of no-par stock in exchange for each $100 share formerly held. This is known as a **stock split.** The usual purpose of a stock split is to reduce the market price of the stock and, consequently, to facilitate trading in the stock.

A stock split has no effect on total stockholders' equity, the equities of the individual stockholders, or on the balances of any of the contributed

---

[1] FASB, *Accounting Standards—Current Text* (Stamford, Conn., 1984), sec. C20.103, 106. Previously published in *Accounting Research Bulletin No. 43*, ch. 7, sec. B, pars. 10,13.
[2] Ibid., sec. C20.104.

capital or retained earnings accounts. Consequently, all that is required in recording a stock split is a memorandum entry in the stock account reciting the facts of the split. For example, such a memorandum might read, "Called in the outstanding $100 par value common stock and issued 10 shares of $10 par value common stock for each old share previously outstanding." Also, there would be a change in the description of the stock on the balance sheet.

■   **Treasury Stock**

Corporations often reacquire shares of their own stock. Sometimes a corporation will purchase its own stock on the open market to be given to employees as a bonus or to be used in acquiring other corporations. Occasionally, shares are bought in order to maintain a favorable market for the stock. Regardless of the reason, if a corporation reacquires shares of its own stock, such stock is known as **treasury stock**. Treasury stock is a corporation's own stock that has been issued and then reacquired either by purchase or gift. Notice that the stock must be the corporation's own stock. The acquisition of stock of another corporation does not create treasury stock. Furthermore, treasury stock must have been issued and then reacquired. This distinguishes treasury stock from unissued stock. The distinction is important because stock once issued at par or above and then reacquired as treasury stock may be legally reissued at a discount without discount liability. Although treasury stock differs from unissued stock in that it may be sold at a discount without discount liability, in other respects it has the same status as unissued stock. Neither of the two is an asset. Both are subtracted from authorized stock to determine outstanding stock when such things as book values are calculated. Neither receives cash dividends nor has a vote in the stockholders' meetings.

■   **Purchase of Treasury Stock[3]**

When a corporation purchases its own stock, it reduces in equal amounts both its assets and its stockholders' equity. To illustrate this, assume that on May 1 of the current year, the condensed balance sheet of Curry Corporation appears as in Illustration 16-1.

If on May 1, Curry Corporation purchases 1,000 shares of its outstanding stock at $11.50 per share, the transaction is recorded as follows:

May	1	Treasury Stock, Common.	11,500.00	
		Cash		11,500.00
		Purchased 1,000 shares of treasury stock at $11.50 per share.		

The debit of the entry records a reduction in the equity of the stockholders. The credit records a reduction in assets. Both are equal to the cost of the treasury stock. After the entry is posted, a new balance sheet will show the reductions as in Illustration 16-2.

---

[3] There are several ways of accounting for treasury stock transactions. This text discusses the so-called cost basis, which seems to be the most widely used. Other methods are left for a more advanced course.

Illustration 16-1

Curry Corporation
Balance Sheet
May 1, 19—

Assets		Capital	
Cash.	$ 30,000	Common stock, $10 par value, autho-	
Other assets	95,000	rized and issued 10,000 shares . . .	$100,000
		Retained earnings	25,000
Total assets.	$125,000	Total capital.	$125,000

Notice in the second balance sheet that the cost of the treasury stock appears in the stockholders' equity section as a deduction from common stock and retained earnings. In comparing the two balance sheets, notice that the treasury stock purchase reduces both assets and stockholders' equity by the $11,500 cost of the stock. Also, observe that the dollar amount of issued stock remains at $100,000 and is unchanged from the first balance sheet. The amount of **issued stock** is not changed by the purchase of treasury stock. However, the purchase does reduce **outstanding stock.** In Curry Corporation, the purchase reduced the outstanding stock from 10,000 to 9,000 shares.

There is a distinction between issued stock and outstanding stock. Issued stock may or may not be outstanding. Outstanding stock has been issued and remains currently outstanding. Only outstanding stock is effective stock, receives cash dividends, and is given a vote in the meetings of stockholders.

Restricting Retained Earnings by the Purchase of Treasury Stock

The purchase of treasury stock by a corporation has the same effect on its assets and stockholders' equity as the payment of a cash dividend. Both

---

Illustration 16-2

Curry Corporation
Balance Sheet
May 1, 19—

Assets		Capital	
Cash.	$ 18,500	Common stock, $10 par value, autho-	
Other assets	95,000	rized and issued 10,000 shares of	
		which 1,000 are in the treasury . . .	$100,000
		Retained earnings of which $11,500 is	
		restricted by the purchase of	
		treasury stock	25,000
		Total.	$125,000
		Less cost of treasury stock	11,500
Total assets.	$113,500	Total capital.	$113,500

transfer corporation assets to stockholders and thereby reduce assets and stockholders' equity. Consequently, in most states, a corporation may purchase treasury stock or it may pay cash dividends, but the sum of both cannot exceed the amount of its retained earnings available for dividends.

Unlike the payment of a cash dividend, the purchase of treasury stock does not reduce the balance of the Retained Earnings account. However, the purchase does place a restriction on the amount of retained earnings available for dividends. Note how the restriction is shown in Illustration 16-2. It is also commonly shown by means of a balance sheet footnote.

The restriction of retained earnings because of treasury stock purchases is a matter of state law. Other types of legal restrictions on retained earnings may be imposed by law or by contract.

■ Reissuing Treasury Stock

When treasury stock is reissued, it may be reissued at cost, above cost, or below cost. If reissued at cost, the entry to record the transaction is the reverse of the entry used to record the purchase.

Although treasury stock may be sold at cost, it is commonly sold at a price either above or below cost. When sold above cost, the amount received in excess of cost is credited to a contributed capital account called Contributed Capital, Treasury Stock Transactions. For example, if Curry Corporation sells for $12 per share 500 of the treasury shares purchased at $11.50 per share, the entry to record the transaction appears as follows:

June	3	Cash	6,000.00	
		Contributed Capital, Treasury Stock		
		Transactions		250.00
		Treasury Stock		5,750.00
		Sold at $12 per share 500 treasury shares		
		that cost $11.50 per share.		

When treasury stock is reissued at a price below cost, the entry to record the sale depends upon whether or not there is contributed capital from previous treasury stock transactions. If there is no such contributed capital, the "loss" is debited to Retained Earnings. However, if there is such contributed capital, the "loss" is debited to the account of this contributed capital, the "loss" is debited to the account of this contributed capital to the extent of its balance. Any remainder is then debited to Retained Earnings. For example, if Curry Corporation sells its remaining 500 shares of treasury stock at $10 per share, the entry to record the sale is:

July	10	Cash	5,000.00	
		Contributed Capital, Treasury Stock		
		Transactions	250.00	
		Retained Earnings	500.00	
		Treasury Stock		5,750.00
		Sold at $10 per share 500 treasury shares		
		that cost $11.50 per share.		

■ **Retirement of Stock**

A corporation may purchase shares of its own stock with the intent of retiring the stock rather than holding it as treasury stock. Such shares are permanently canceled upon receipt. The purchase and retirement of stock is permissible if the interests of creditors and other stockholders are not jeopardized.

When stock is purchased for retirement, all capital items related to the shares being retired are removed from the accounts. If there is a "gain" on the transaction, it should be credited to contributed capital. On the other hand, a loss should be debited to Retained Earnings.

For example, assume a corporation originally issued its $10 par value common stock at $12 per share, with the premium being credited to Contributed Capital in Excess of Par Value, Common Stock. If the corporation later purchased for retirement 1,000 shares of this stock at the price for which it was issued, the entry to record the retirement is:

Apr.	12	Common Stock	10,000.00	
		Contributed Capital in Excess of Par Value,		
		Common Stock	2,000.00	
		Cash		12,000.00
		Purchased and retired 1,000 shares of		
		common stock at $12 per share.		

If on the other hand the corporation paid $11 per share instead of $12, the entry for the retirement is:

Apr.	12	Common Stock	10,000.00	
		Contributed Capital in Excess of Par Value,		
		Common Stock	2,000.00	
		Cash		11,000.00
		Contributed Capital from the Retirement of		
		Common Stock		1,000.00
		Purchased and retired 1,000 shares of		
		common stock at $11 per share.		

Or, if the corporation paid $15 per share, the entry for the purchase and retirement is:

Apr.	12	Common Stock	10,000.00	
		Contributed Capital in Excess of Par Value,		
		Common Stock	2,000.00	
		Retained Earnings	3,000.00	
		Cash		15,000.00
		Purchased and retired 1,000 shares of		
		common stock at $15 per share.		

■ **Appropriations of Retained Earnings**

A corporation may **appropriate retained earnings** for some special purpose or purposes and show the amounts appropriated as separate items in the equity section of its balance sheet. In contrast to **retained earnings restrictions** which are binding by law or by contract, appropriations of retained earnings are voluntarily made by the board of directors. Such appropriations may be recorded by transferring portions of retained earnings from the Retained Earnings account to accounts such as Retained Earnings Appropriated for Contingencies or Retained Earnings Appropriated for Plant Expansion.

The appropriations do not reduce total retained earnings. Rather, their purpose is to inform balance sheet readers that portions of retained earnings are not available for the declaration of cash dividends. When the contingency or other reason for an appropriation has passed, the appropriation account is eliminated by returning its balance to the Retained Earnings account.

Appropriations of retained earnings were once common, but such appropriations are seldom seen on balance sheets today. Today, the same information is conveyed with less chance of misunderstanding by means of footnotes accompanying the financial statements.

Stocks as Investments

The stock transactions illustrated thus far have been transactions in which a corporation sold and issued its own stock. Such transactions represent only a small portion of the daily transactions in stocks. Most stock sales involve transactions between investors which are arranged through brokers who charge a commission for their services.

Brokers acting as agents for their customers buy and sell stocks and bonds on exchanges such as the New York Stock Exchange. Some securities are not listed or traded on an organized stock exchange, and brokers act for their customers to buy and sell such securities in the "over-the-counter" market. Each security in this market is handled by one or more brokers who receive from other brokers offers to buy or sell the security at specific "bid" or "ask" prices. Stock prices are quoted on the basis of dollars and ⅛ dollars per share. For example, a stock quoted at 46⅛ means $46.125 per share, and a stock quoted at 25½ means $25.50 per share.

Classifying Investments

Equity securities generally include common and preferred stocks. Many equity securities are actively traded, so that "sales prices or bid and ask prices are currently available on a national securities exchange or in the over-the-counter market." Such securities are called **marketable equity securities**.[4] If, in addition to being marketable, a stock investment is held as "an investment of cash available for current operations," it is classified as a current asset.[5]

Investments that are not intended as a ready source of cash in case of need are classified as **long-term investments.** They include funds earmarked for a special purpose, such as bond sinking funds, as well as land or other assets owned but not employed in the regular operations of the business. They also include investments in stocks that are not marketable or that, although marketable, are not intended to serve as a ready source of cash.

[4] FASB, *Accounting Standards—Current Text,* sec. I89.404. First published in *Statement of Financial Accounting Standards No. 12,* par. 7.

[5] Ibid., sec. B05.105. Previously published in *Accounting Research Bulletin No. 43,* ch. 3, sec. A, par. 4.

Long-term investments appear on the balance sheet in a classification of their own titled "Long-term investments."

■ **Accounting for Investments in Stock**

Most investments in a corporation's stock represent a small percentage of the total amount of stock outstanding. As a consequence, the investor does not exercise a significant influence over the financial or operating policies of the corporation. However, in some cases, an investor will buy a large portion of the outstanding stock of a corporation in order to influence or control its operations. For example, corporations frequently buy a large share of another corporation's stock in order to influence its activities as well as to receive part of its income.

The method of accounting for stock investments on the books of the investor depends upon whether the investor has the ability to significantly influence the operating and financial policies of the corporation. If the investor can exercise a significant influence, the accounting method used is called the **equity method.** If the investor does not have a significant influence, the accounting method used is called the **cost method.** In general, ownership of 20% or more of the voting stock of a corporation is presumptive evidence of the ability to significantly influence its operations.[6] Thus, common stock investments of 20% or more of the voting stock usually are accounted for according to the equity method while investments of less than 20% usually are accounted for according to the cost method. There may be instances, however, where the accountant concludes that the 20% test of significant influence should be overruled by other, more persuasive, evidence.[7]

The Cost Method of Accounting for Stock Investments

When stock is purchased as either a short- or long-term investment, the purchase is recorded at total cost, which includes any commission paid to the broker. For example, 1,000 (10%) of Dot Corporation's 10,000 outstanding common shares were purchased as an investment at 23¼ plus a $300 broker's commission. The entry to record the transaction is:

Sept.	10	Investment in Dot Corporation Stock	23,550.00	
		Cash		23,550.00
		Purchased 1,000 shares of stock for $23,250		
		plus a $300 broker's commission.		

Observe that nothing is said about a premium or a discount on the Dot Corporation stock. Premiums and discounts are normally recorded only by the corporation that issues the stock. An investor records the entire cost as a debit to the investment account, even though the cost may be above or below par value.

When the cost method is used to account for either a short- or long-

---

[6] Ibid., sec. I82.104. First published in *APB Opinion No. 18,* par. 17.
[7] Ibid., sec. I82.107–108. First published in *FASB Interpretation No. 35,* pars. 3–4.

term investment and a dividend is received on the stock, an entry similar to the following is made:

Oct.	5	Cash	1,000.00	
		Dividends Earned		1,000.00
		Received a $1 per share dividend on the stock.		

Dividends on stocks do not accrue; consequently, an end-of-period entry to record accrued dividends is never made. However, if a balance sheet is prepared after a dividend is declared but before it is paid, an entry debiting Dividends Receivable and crediting Dividends Earned would be appropriate.

A dividend in shares of stock is not income, and a debit and credit entry recording it should not be made. However, a memorandum entry or a notation as to the additional shares should be made in the investment account. Also, receipt of a stock dividend does affect the per share cost of the old shares. For example, if a 20-share dividend is received on 100 shares originally purchased for $1,500 or at $15 per share, the cost of all 120 shares is $1,500 and the cost per share is $12.50 ($1,500 ÷ 120 shares = $12.50 per share).

Under the cost method, when an investment in stock is sold and the proceeds net of any sales commission differ from cost, a gain or loss must be recorded. For example, consider the 1,000 shares of Dot Corporation common stock that were purchased at a cost of $23,550. If these shares are sold at 25¾ less a sales commission of $315, there is a $1,885 gain, and the transaction is recorded:

Jan.	7	Cash	25,435.00	
		Investment in Dot Corporation Stock . . .		23,550.00
		Gain on Sale of Investments		1,885.00
		Sold 1,000 shares of stock for $25,750 less a $315 commission.		

If the net amount received for these shares had been less than their $23,550 cost, there would have been a loss on the transaction.

Lower of Cost or Market

For balance sheet presentation, an investment in stock that is not marketable is accounted for at cost. However, investments in marketable equity securities are divided into two portfolios: (1) those to be shown as current assets and (2) those to be shown as long-term investments. Then the total current market value of each portfolio is calculated and compared to the total cost of each portfolio. Each portfolio is reported at the lower of cost or market.[8]

[8] Ibid., sec. I89.102–103. First published in *Statement of Financial Accounting Standards No. 12,* pars. 8–9.

In the case of the current asset portfolio, a decline in total market value below the previous balance sheet valuation (or cost) is reported in the income statement as a loss. Subsequent recoveries of market value are reported in the income statement as gains, but market value increases above original cost are not recorded.[9]

In the case of long-term investment portfolios of marketable equity securities, market value declines are reported in the income statement **only** if they appear to be permanent. Usually, they are not assumed to be permanent, in which case the market value decline is disclosed as a separate item in the stockholders' equity section of the balance sheet.[10]

The Equity Method of Accounting for Common Stock Investments

If a common stock investor has a significant influence over or even controls the investee, the equity method of accounting for the investment must be used. When the stock is acquired, the purchase is recorded at cost just as it is under the cost method. For example, on January 1, 198A, James, Inc., purchased 3,000 shares (30%) of RMS, Inc., common stock for a total cost of $70,650. The entry to record the purchase on the books of James, Inc., is as follows:

Jan.	1	Investment in RMS, Inc.	70,650.00	
		Cash		70,650.00
		Purchased 3,000 shares of common stock.		

Under the equity method, it is recognized that the earnings of the investee corporation not only increase the net assets of the investee corporation but also increase the investor's equity in the assets. Consequently, when the investee closes its books and reports the amount of its earnings, the investor takes up its share of those earnings in its investment account. For example, RMS, Inc., reported net income of $20,000. James, Inc.'s entry to record its share of these earnings is:

Dec.	31	Investment in RMS, Inc.	6,000.00	
		Earnings from Investment in RMS, Inc. . .		6,000.00
		To record 30% equity in investee's earnings of $20,000.		

The debit records the increase in James, Inc.'s equity in RMS, Inc. The credit causes 30% of RMS, Inc.'s net income to appear on James, Inc.'s income statement as earnings from the investment, and James, Inc., closes the earnings to its Income Summary account and on to its Retained Earnings account just as it would close earnings from any investment.

If, instead of a net income, the investee corporation incurs a loss, the investor debits the loss to an account called Loss from Investment and credits and reduces its Investment in Stock account. It then transfers the

[9] Ibid., I89.105.
[10] Ibid., I89.105, 115.

loss to its Income Summary account and on to its Retained Earnings account.

Dividends paid by an investee corporation decrease the investee's assets and retained earnings, and also decrease the investor's equity in the investee. Since, under the equity method, the investor records its equity in the full amount of earnings reported by an investee, the receipt of dividends does not constitute income; instead, dividend receipts from the investee represent a decrease in the equity. For example, RMS, Inc., declared and paid $10,000 in dividends on its common stock. The entry to record James, Inc.'s share of these dividends, which it received on January 9, 198B, is:

Jan.	9	Cash	3,000.00	
		Investment in RMS, Inc.		3,000.00
		To record receipt of 30% of the $10,000		
		dividend paid by RMS, Inc.		

Notice that the carrying value of a common stock investment, accounted for by the equity method, changes in reflection of the investor's equity in the undistributed earnings of the investee. For example, after the above transactions have been recorded on the books of James, Inc., the investment account would appear as follows:

Investment in RMS, Inc.

Date		Explanation	Debit	Credit	Balance
198A					
Jan.	1	Investment	70,650.00		70,650.00
Dec.	31	Share of earnings	6,000.00		76,650.00
198B					
Jan.	9	Share of dividend		3,000.00	73,650.00

When common stock, accounted for by the equity method, is sold, the gain or loss on the sale is determined by comparing the proceeds from the sale with the carrying value of the stock on the date of sale. For example, on January 10, 198B, James, Inc., sold its RMS, Inc., stock for $80,000. The entry to record the sale is as follows:

Jan.	10	Cash	80,000.00	
		Investment in RMS, Inc.		73,650.00
		Gain on Sale of Investments		6,350.00
		Sold 3,000 shares of stock for $80,000.		

Parent and Subsidiary Corporations

Corporations commonly own stock in and may even control other corporations. For example, if Corporation A owns more than 50% of the voting stock of Corporation B, Corporation A can elect Corporation B's board of directors and thus control its activities and resources. In such a situation, the controlling corporation, Corporation A, is known as the **parent company** and Corporation B is called a **subsidiary.**

When a corporation owns all the outstanding stock of a subsidiary, it can take over the subsidiary's assets, cancel its stock, and fuse the subsidiary into the parent company. However, instead of operating the business as a single corporation, there are often financial, legal, and tax advantages if a large business is operated as a parent company that controls one or more subsidiaries. Actually, most large companies are parent corporations owning one or more subsidiaries.

When a business is operated as a parent company with subsidiaries, separate accounting records are kept for each corporation. Also, from a legal viewpoint, the parent and each subsidiary are separate entities with all the rights, duties, and responsibilities of a separate corporation. However, investors in the parent company depend on the parent to present a set of **consolidated statements** that show the results of all operations under the parent's control, including those of any subsidiaries. In these statements, the assets and liabilities of all affiliated companies are combined on a single balance sheet and their revenues and expenses are combined on a single income statement, as though the business were in fact a single company.

Consolidated Balance Sheets

When parent and subsidiary balance sheets are consolidated, duplications in items are eliminated so that the combined figures do not show more assets and equities than actually exist. For example, a parent's investment in a subsidiary is evidenced by shares of stock that are carried as an asset in the parent company's records. However, these shares actually represent an equity in the subsidiary's assets. Consequently, if the parent's investment in a subsidiary and the subsidiary's assets were both shown on the consolidated balance sheet, the same resources would be counted twice. To prevent this, the parent's investment and the subsidiary's capital accounts are offset and eliminated in preparing a consolidated balance sheet.

Likewise, a single enterprise cannot owe a debt to itself. This would be analogous to a student borrowing $20 for a date from funds saved for next semester's expenses and then preparing a balance sheet showing the $20 as both a receivable from himself and a payable to himself. To prevent such double counting, intercompany debts and receivables are also eliminated in preparing a consolidated balance sheet.

Balance Sheets Consolidated at Time of Acquisition

When a parent's and a subsidiary's assets are combined in the preparation of a consolidated balance sheet, a work sheet is normally used to effect the consolidation. Illustration 16-3 shows such a work sheet. It was prepared to consolidate the accounts of Parent Company and its subsidiary, called Subsidiary Company, on January 1, 198A, the day Parent Company acquired Subsidiary Company through the cash purchase of all its outstanding $10 par value common stock. The stock had a book value of $115,000, or $11.50 per share, which in this first illustration is the amount Parent Company is assumed to have paid for it. Explanation of the work sheet's two eliminating entries follows.

Illustration 16-3

Parent Company and Subsidiary Company
Work Sheet for a Consolidated Balance Sheet
January 1, 198A

	Parent Company	Subsidiary Company	Eliminations Debit	Eliminations Credit	Consolidated Amounts
Assets					
Cash.	5,000	15,000			20,000
Notes receivable. . . .	10,000			(a) 10,000	
Investment in Subsidiary Company.	115,000			(b) 115,000	
Other assets	190,000	117,000			307,000
	320,000	132,000			327,000
Liabilities and Equities					
Accounts payable . . .	15,000	7,000			22,000
Notes payable.		10,000	(a) 10,000		
Common stock	250,000	100,000	(b) 100,000		250,000
Retained earnings . . .	55,000	15,000	(b) 15,000		55,000
	320,000	132,000	125,000	125,000	327,000

Entry (a) On the day it acquired Subsidiary Company, Parent Company lent Subsidiary Company $10,000 for use in the subsidiary's operations. It took the subsidiary's note as evidence of the transaction. This intercompany debt was in reality a transfer of funds within the organization. Consequently, since it did not increase the total assets and total liabilities of the affiliated companies, it is eliminated by means of entry (a). To understand this entry, recall that the subsidiary's promissory note is represented by a $10,000 debit in Parent Company's Notes Receivable account. Then, observe that the first credit in the Eliminations column exactly offsets and eliminates this item. Next, recall that the subsidiary's note appears as a credit in its Notes Payable account. Then, observe that the $10,000 debit in the Eliminations column completes the elimination of this intercompany debt.

Entry (b) When a parent company buys a subsidiary's stock, the investment appears on the parent's balance sheet as an asset, "Investment in Subsidiary." The investment represents an equity in the subsidiary's net assets. Consequently, to show both the subsidiary's (net) assets and the parent company's investment in the subsidiary on a consolidated balance sheet would be to double count those resources. As a result, on the work sheet the amount of the parent's investment (an equity in the subsidiary's assets) is offset against the subsidiary's stockholder equity accounts, which also represent an equity in the assets, and both are eliminated.

After the intercompany items are eliminated on a work sheet like Illustration 16-3, the assets of the parent and the subsidiary and the remaining equities in these assets are combined and carried into the work sheet's last column. The combined amounts are then used to prepare a consolidated balance sheet showing all the assets and equities of the parent and its subsidiary.

Parent Company Does Not Buy All of Subsidiary's Stock and Does Not Pay Book Value

In the situation just described, Parent Company purchased all of its subsidiary's stock, paying book value for it. Often, a parent company purchases less than 100% of a subsidiary's stock, and commonly pays a price either above or below book value. To illustrate such a situation, assume Parent Company purchased for cash only 80% of its subsidiary's stock rather than 100%, and that it paid $13 per share, a price $1.50 above the stock's book value.

These new assumptions result in a more complicated work sheet entry to eliminate the parent's investment and the subsidiary's stockholders' equity accounts. The entry is complicated by (1) the minority interest in the subsidiary and (2) the excess over book value paid by the parent company for the subsidiary's stock.

Minority Interest When a parent buys a controlling interest in a subsidiary, the parent company is the subsidiary's majority stockholder. However, when the parent owns less than 100% of the subsidiary's stock, the subsidiary has other stockholders who own a **minority interest** in its assets and share its earnings. Consequently, when there is a minority interest, the minority interest must be set out as on the last line of Illustration 16-4 in making the work sheet entry to eliminate the stockholders' equity accounts of the subsidiary. In this case, the minority stockholders have a 20% interest in the subsidiary. Consequently, 20% of the subsidiary's common stock and retained earnings accounts [($100,000 + $15,000) × 20% = $23,000] is set out on the work sheet as the minority interest.

Excess of Investment Cost over Book Value Parent Company paid $13 per share for its 8,000 shares of Subsidiary Company's stock. Consequently, the cost of these shares exceeded their book value by $12,000, calculated as follows:

Cost of stock (8,000 shares at $13 per share) . . .	$104,000
Book value (8,000 shares at $11.50 per share) . . .	92,000
Excess of cost over book value.	$ 12,000

Now observe how this excess of cost over book value is set out on the work sheet in eliminating the parent's investment in the subsidiary. Then, it is carried into the Consolidated Amounts column as an asset.

After the work sheet of Illustration 16-4 was completed, the consolidated amounts in the last column were used to prepare the consolidated balance sheet of Illustration 16-5. Note the treatment of the minority interest in the balance sheet. The minority stockholders have a $23,000 equity in

Illustration 16-4

Parent Company and Subsidiary Company
Work Sheet for a Consolidated Balance Sheet
January 1, 198A

	Parent Company	Subsidiary Company	Eliminations Debit	Eliminations Credit	Consolidated Amounts
Assets					
Cash	16,000	15,000			31,000
Notes receivable . . .	10,000			(a) 10,000	
Investment in Subsidiary Company . .	104,000			(b) 104,000	
Other assets	190,000	117,000			307,000
Excess of cost over book value			(b) 12,000		12,000
	320,000	132,000			350,000
Liabilities and Equities					
Accounts payable . .	15,000	7,000			22,000
Notes payable		10,000	(a) 10,000		
Common stock . . .	250,000	100,000	(b) 100,000		250,000
Retained earnings . .	55,000	15,000	(b) 15,000		55,000
Minority interest . . .				(b) 23,000	23,000
	320,000	132,000	137,000	137,000	350,000

the consolidated assets of the affiliated companies. Many have argued that this item should be disclosed in the stockholders' equity section. Others believe it should be shown in the long-term liabilities section. However, a more common alternative is to disclose the minority interest as a separate item between the liabilities and stockholders' equity sections, as is shown in Illustration 16-5.

Next, observe that the $12,000 excess over book value paid by the parent company for the subsidiary's stock appears on the consolidated balance sheet as the asset described as "Goodwill from consolidation." When a parent company purchases an interest in a subsidiary, it may pay more than book value for its equity because (1) certain of the subsidiary's assets are carried on the subsidiary's books at less than fair value. It also may pay more because (2) certain of the subsidiary's liabilities are carried at book values which are greater than fair values, or (3) the subsidiary's earnings prospects are good enough to justify paying more than the net fair (market) value of its assets and liabilities. In this illustration, it is assumed that the book values of Subsidiary Company's assets and liabilities are their fair values. However, Subsidiary Company's expected earnings justified paying $104,000 for an 80% equity in the subsidiary's net assets (assets less liabilities).

The APB ruled that where a company pays more than book value because the subsidiary's assets are undervalued or its liabilities are overvalued, the cost in excess of book value should be allocated to those assets and

Illustration 16-5

Parent Company and Subsidiary
Consolidated Balance Sheet
January 1, 198A

Assets

Cash	$ 31,000	
Other assets	307,000	
Goodwill from consolidation.	12,000	
Total assets		$350,000

Liabilities and Stockholders' Equity

Liabilities:		
Accounts payable	$ 22,000	
Minority interest	23,000	
Stockholders' equity:		
Common stock	$250,000	
Retained earnings	55,000	
Total stockholders' equity.		305,000
Total liabilities and stockholders' equity. . .		$350,000

liabilities so that they are restated at fair values. After the subsidiary's assets and liabilities have been restated to reflect fair values, any remaining cost in excess of book value should be reported on the consolidated balance sheet as "Goodwill from consolidation."[11]

Occasionally, a parent company pays less than book value for its interest in a subsidiary. In such a case, since a "bargain" purchase is very unlikely, the logical reason for a price below book value is that certain of the subsidiary's assets are carried on its books at amounts in excess of fair value. In such a situation, the APB ruled that the amounts at which the overvalued assets are placed on the consolidated balance sheet should be reduced accordingly.[12]

Earnings and Dividends of a Subsidiary

As previously discussed, a parent accounts for its investment in a subsidiary according to the equity method. As a consequence, the parent's recorded net income and Retained Earnings account include the parent's equity in the net income earned by the subsidiary since the date of acquisition. Also, the balance of the parent's Investment in Subsidiary account increases (or decreases) each year by an amount equal to the parent's equity in the subsidiary's earnings (or loss) less the parent's share of any dividends paid by the subsidiary.

For example, assume that Subsidiary Company of this illustration earned $12,500 during its first year as a subsidiary and at year-end paid out $7,500 in dividends. Parent Company recorded its 80% equity in these earnings and dividends as follows:

[11] Ibid., sec. B50.403. First published in *APB Opinion No. 16,* par. 87.
[12] Ibid., B50.160.

Dec.	31	Investment in Subsidiary Company	10,000.00	
		Earnings from Investment in Subsidiary . .		10,000.00
		To record 80% of the net income reported by Subsidiary Company.		
Dec.	31	Cash	6,000.00	
		Investment in Subsidiary Company		6,000.00
		To record the receipt of 80% of the $7,500 dividend paid by Subsidiary Company.		

■ Consolidated Balance Sheets at a Date after Acquisition

Illustration 16-6 shows the December 31, 198B, work sheet to consolidate the balance sheets of Parent Company and Subsidiary Company. To simplify the illustration, it is assumed that Parent Company had no transactions during the year other than to record its equity in Subsidiary Company's earnings and dividends. Also, the other assets and liabilities of Subsidiary Company did not change, and the subsidiary has not paid the note given Parent Company.

Compare Illustration 16-6 with 16-4 and note the changes in Parent Company's balance sheet (the first column). Parent Company's Cash increased from $16,000 to $22,000 as a result of the dividends received

Illustration 16-6

Parent Company and Subsidiary Company
Work Sheet for a Consolidated Balance Sheet
December 31, 198B

	Parent Company	Subsidiary Company	Eliminations Debit	Eliminations Credit	Consolidated Amounts
Assets					
Cash	22,000	20,000			42,000
Notes receivable . . .	10,000			(a) 10,000	
Investment in Subsidiary Company.	108,000			(b) 108,000	
Other assets	190,000	117,000			307,000
Excess of cost over book value			(b) 12,000		12,000
	330,000	137,000			361,000
Liabilities and Equities					
Accounts payable . . .	15,000	7,000			22,000
Notes payable		10,000	(a) 10,000		
Common stock	250,000	100,000	(b) 100,000		250,000
Retained earnings . . .	65,000	20,000	(b) 20,000		65,000
Minority interest				(b) 24,000	24,000
	330,000	137,000	142,000	142,000	361,000

from the subsidiary. The Investment in Subsidiary Company account increased from $104,000 to $108,000 as a result of the equity method entries during the year. Finally, Parent Company's Retained Earnings increased by $10,000, which was the parent's equity in the subsidiary's earnings.

In the second column of Illustration 16-6, note only two changes: (1) Subsidiary Company's Cash balance increased by $5,000, which is the difference between its $12,500 net income and $7,500 payment of dividends. (2) Retained Earnings also increased from $15,000 to $20,000, which is the amount eliminated on the work sheet.

Two additional items in Illustration 16-6 require explanation. First, the minority interest set out on the year-end work sheet is greater than on the beginning-of-year work sheet (Illustration 16-4). The minority stockholders have a 20% equity in Subsidiary Company, and the $24,000 shown on the year-end work sheet is 20% of the year-end balances of the Subsidiary's Common Stock and Retained Earnings accounts. This $24,000 is $1,000 greater than the beginning-of-year minority interest because the subsidiary's retained earnings increased $5,000 during the year and the minority stockholder's share of this increase is 20% or $1,000. Second, the $12,000 amount set out as the excess cost of Parent Company's investment over its book value is, in this illustration, the same on the end-of-year work sheet as on the work sheet at the beginning. The APB ruled that such excess cost or "goodwill" should be amortized by systematic charges to income over the accounting periods estimated to be benefited.[13] An explanation of the amortization entries is left to a more advanced text.

■ **Other Consolidated Statements**

Consolidated income statements and consolidated retained earnings statements are also prepared for affiliated companies. However, a discussion of the procedures to prepare these statements is deferred to an advanced accounting course. Knowledge of the procedures is not necessary for a general understanding of such statements. At this point, the reader need only recognize that all duplications in items and all profit arising from intercompany transactions are eliminated in their preparation. Also, the amounts of net income and retained earnings that are reported in consolidated statements are equal to the amounts recorded by the parent under the equity method.

■ **The Corporation Balance Sheet**

A number of balance sheet sections have been illustrated in this and previous chapters. To bring together as much of the information from all these sections as space allows, the balance sheet of Betco Corporation is shown in Illustration 16-7.

Betco Corporation's balance sheet is a consolidated balance sheet, as indicated in the title and by the items "Goodwill from consolidation" and "Minority interest." In preparing the balance sheet, Betco Corporation's investment in its subsidiary was eliminated. Consequently, the Toledo Corporation stock shown on the consolidated balance sheet represents an investment in an unconsolidated (outside) company that is not a subsidiary of either Betco or Betco's subsidiary.

---

[13] Ibid., sec. I60.108–112. First published in *APB Opinion No. 17*, pars. 27–31.

Illustration 16-7

Betco Corporation
Consolidated Balance Sheet
December 31, 198A

Assets

Current assets:

Cash.		$ 15,000
Marketable securities.		5,000
Accounts receivable	$ 50,000	
Less allowance for doubtful accounts	1,000	49,000
Merchandise inventory		115,000
Subscriptions receivable, common stock		15,000
Prepaid expenses		1,000
Total current assets		$200,000

Long-term investments:

Bond sinking fund		$ 15,000
Toledo Corporation common stock		5,000
Total long-term investments		20,000

Plant assets:

Land		$ 50,000
Buildings	$285,000	
Less accumulated depreciation	30,000	255,000
Store equipment	$ 85,000	
Less accumulated depreciation	20,000	65,000
Total plant assets		370,000

Intangible assets:

Goodwill from consolidation		10,000
Total assets		$600,000

Liabilities

Current liabilities:

Notes payable.	$ 10,000	
Accounts payable	14,000	
State and federal income taxes payable.	16,000	
Total current liabilities		$ 40,000

Long-term liabilities:

First 8% real estate mortgage bonds, due in 199E	$100,000	
Less unamortized discount based on the 8¼% market rate for bond interest prevailing on the date of issue	2,000	98,000
Total liabilities		$138,000
Minority interest		15,000

Stockholders' Equity

Contributed capital:

Common stock, $10 par value, authorized 50,000 shares, issued 30,000 shares of which 1,000 are in the treasury.	$300,000	
Unissued common stock subscribed, 2,500 shares	25,000	
Contributed capital in excess of par value, common stock	33,000	
Total contributed capital	$358,000	
Retained earnings (Note 1)	105,000	
Total contributed and retained capital	$463,000	
Less cost of treasury stock	16,000	
Total stockholders' equity		447,000
Total liabilities and stockholders' equity		$600,000

Note 1: Retained earnings in the amount of $31,000 is restricted under an agreement with the corporation's bondholders and because of the purchase of treasury stock, leaving $74,000 of retained earnings not so restricted.

☐   **Glossary**   **Appropriated retained earnings**   retained earnings voluntarily earmarked for a special use as a means of informing stockholders that assets from earnings equal to the appropriations are unavailable for dividends.

Consolidated statements   financial statements that show the results of all operations under the parent's control, including those of any subsidiaries. Assets and liabilities of all affiliated companies are combined on a single balance sheet and their revenues and expenses are combined on a single income statement as though the business were in fact a single company.

Cost method of accounting for stock investments   an accounting method whereby the investment is recorded at total cost and maintained at that amount; subsequent investee earnings and dividends do not affect the investment account.

Earned surplus   a synonym for retained earnings, no longer in general use.

Equity method of accounting for stock investments   an accounting method whereby the investment is recorded at total cost, and the investment account balance is subsequently increased to reflect the investor's equity in earnings of the investee, and decreased to reflect the investor's equity in dividends of the investee.

Long-term investments   investments, not intended as a ready source of cash in case of need, such as bond sinking funds, land, and marketable securities that are not held as a temporary investment of cash available for current operations.

Marketable equity securities   common and preferred stocks that are actively traded so that sales prices or bid and ask prices are currently available on a national securities exchange or in the over-the-counter market.

Minority interest   the portion of a subsidiary company's stockholders' equity that is not owned by the parent corporation.

Parent company   a corporation that owns a controlling interest (more than 50% of the voting stock is required) in another corporation.

Restricted retained earnings   retained earnings that are unavailable for dividends as a result of law or binding contract.

Small stock dividend   a stock dividend that amounts to 25% or less of the issuing corporation's previously outstanding shares.

Stock dividend   a distribution by a corporation of shares of its own stock to its stockholders without any consideration being received in return.

Stock split   the act of a corporation of calling in its stock and issuing more than one new share in the place of each share previously outstanding.

Subsidiary   a corporation that is controlled by another (parent) corporation because the parent owns more than 50% of the subsidiary's voting stock.

Treasury stock   issued stock that has been reacquired by the issuing corporation.

☐ **Questions for Class Discussion**   1. What effect does the declaration of a cash dividend have on the assets, liabilities, and stockholders' equity of the corporation that declares the dividend? What is the effect of the subsequent payment of the cash dividend?

2. What effect does the declaration of a stock dividend have on the assets, liabilities, and total stockholders' equity of the corporation that declares the dividend. What is the effect of the subsequent distribution of the stock dividend?

3. In accounting for a stock dividend, what criterion is used to distinguish between a small stock dividend and a large stock dividend?

4. What amount of retained earnings should be capitalized in accounting for a small stock dividend?

5. What is the difference between a stock dividend and a stock split?

6. Courts have held that a dividend in the stock of the distributing corporation is not taxable income to its recipients. Why?

7. If a balance sheet is prepared between the date of declaration and the date of payment or distribution of a dividend, how should the dividend be shown if it is (a) a cash dividend or (b) a stock dividend?

8. What is treasury stock? How is it like unissued stock? How does it differ from unissued stock? What is the legal significance of this difference?

9. Western Products Corporation bought 10,000 shares of National Iron Corporation stock and turned it over to the treasurer of Western Products for safekeeping. Is this treasury stock? Why or why not?

10. What effect does the purchase of treasury stock have on assets and total stockholders' equity?

11. Distinguish between issued stock and outstanding stock.

12. Why do state laws place limitations on the purchase of treasury stock?

13. What is meant by "marketable securities"?

14. Under what conditions should a stock investment be classified as a current asset?

15. In accounting for common stock investments, when should the cost method be used? When should the equity method be used?

16. When a parent corporation uses the equity method to account for its investment in a subsidiary, what recognition is given by the parent corporation to the income or loss reported by the subsidiary? What recognition is given to dividends declared by the subsidiary?

17. What are consolidated financial statements?

18. What account balances must be eliminated in preparing a consolidated balance sheet? Why are they eliminated?

19. Why would a parent corporation pay more than book value for the stock of a subsidiary?

20. When a parent pays more than book value for the stock of a subsidiary, how should this additional cost be reported in the consolidated balance sheet?

21. What is meant by "minority interest"? Where is this item disclosed on a consolidated balance sheet?

□   **Class Exercises**   **Exercise 16-1**

Stockholders' equity in a corporation appeared as follows on May 15:

Common stock, $10 par value, 200,000 shares authorized,	
36,000 shares issued	$360,000
Contributed capital in excess of par value, common stock . . .	28,800
Total contributed capital	$388,800
Retained earnings	50,000
Total stockholders' equity.	$438,800

On May 15, when the stock was selling at $12.50 per share, the corporation's directors voted a 5% stock dividend distributable on June 10 to the May 25 stockholders of record. The stock was selling at $12.00 per share at the close of business on June 11.

Required

1. Prepare general journal entries to record the declaration and distribution of the dividend.
2. Under the assumption that Patricia Kelley owned 900 of the shares on May 15 and received her dividend shares on June 10, prepare a schedule showing the numbers of shares she held on May 15 and June 11, with their total book values and total market values. Assume no change in total stockholders' equity from May 15 to June 11.

Exercise 16-2

On June 30, 198A, the stock of a corporation was selling for $150 per share and the stockholders' equity section of the corporation's balance sheet appeared as follows:

Common stock, $50 par value, 300,000 shares authorized,	
5,000 shares issued.	$250,000
Contributed capital in excess of par value, common stock . . .	50,000
Total contributed capital	$300,000
Retained earnings	400,000
Total stockholders' equity	$700,000

Required

1. Assume the corporation declares and immediately issues a 100% stock dividend and capitalizes the minimum required amount of retained earnings. Answer the following questions about the stockholders' equity of the corporation after the new shares are issued:
   a. What will be the retained earnings balance?
   b. What will be the total amount of stockholders' equity?
   c. How many shares will be outstanding?
2. Assume that instead of declaring a 100% stock dividend, the corporation changes the par value of the stock to $5 and immediately effects a 2 for 1 stock split. Answer the following questions about the stockholders' equity of the corporation after the stock split takes place:
   a. What will be the retained earnings balance?
   b. What will be the total amount of stockholders' equity?
   c. How many shares will be outstanding?

Exercise 16-3

On April 30, the stockholders' equity section of a corporation's balance sheet appeared as follows:

Stockholders' Equity

Common stock, $25 par value, 17,500 shares authorized and issued	$437,500
Retained earnings	148,750
Total stockholders' equity.	$586,250

On April 30, the corporation purchased 500 shares of treasury stock at $40 per share. Give the entry to record the purchase and prepare a stockholders' equity section as it would appear immediately after the purchase.

Exercise 16-4

On May 29, the corporation of Exercise 13-3 sold at $44 per share 200 of the treasury shares purchased on April 30, and on October 12 it sold the remaining treasury shares at $34 per share. Prepare general journal entries to record the sales.

Exercise 16-5

The stockholders' equity section of Kratovil Company's December 31, 198A, balance sheet is as follows:

Common stock, $1 par value, 150,000 shares authorized, 60,000 shares issued	$ 60,000
Contributed capital in excess of par value, common stock . . .	420,000
Total contributed capital	$480,000
Retained earnings	120,000
Total stockholders' equity	$600,000

On the date of the balance sheet, the company purchased and retired 1,000 shares of its common stock. Prepare general journal entries to record the purchase and retirement under each of the following independent assumptions: (a) the stock was purchased for $6 per share, (b) the stock was purchased for $8 per share, (c) the stock was purchased for $12 per share.

Exercise 16-6

Prepare general journal entries to record the following events on the books of X Company:

198A

Jan. 3 Purchased 5,000 shares of Y Company common stock for $62,500 plus broker's fee of $1,750. Y Company has 100,000 shares of common stock outstanding, and X Company does not have a significant influence on Y Company policies.

May 11 Y Company declared and paid a cash dividend of $0.60 per share.

Dec. 31 Y Company announced that net income for the year amounted to $75,000.

198B
May 20   Y Company declared and paid a cash dividend of $0.30 per share.
Aug. 18   Y Company declared and issued a stock dividend of one additional share for each 10 shares already outstanding.
Dec. 29   X Company sold 2,750 shares of Y Company for $35,000.
      31   Y Company announced that net income for the year amounted to $40,000.

Exercise 16-7

Prepare general journal entries to record the following events on the books of Echo Company:

198A
Jan.   2   Purchased 5,000 shares of Hotel Company for $62,500 plus broker's fee of $1,750. Hotel Company has 25,000 shares of common stock outstanding and has acknowledged the fact that its policies will be significantly influenced by Echo Company.
May   16   Hotel Company declared and paid a cash dividend of $0.60 per share.
Dec. 31   Hotel Company announced that net income for the year amounted to $64,000.

198B
May   28   Hotel Company declared and paid a cash dividend of $1.20 per share.
Aug. 21   Hotel Company declared and issued a stock dividend of one additional share for each 10 shares already outstanding.
Dec. 31   Hotel Company announced that net income for the year amounted to $44,000.
      31   Echo Company sold 2,750 shares of Hotel Company for $35,000.

Exercise 16-8

On December 31, 198A, X Company and Y Company each purchased 6,000 shares of N Company stock at a cost of $15 per share. On that date, the stockholders' equity of N Company appeared as follows:

Common stock ($10 par)	$300,000
Retained earnings.	150,000
Total	$450,000

Because of certain legal agreements, Y Company does not have a significant influence over N Company. However, X Company is presumed to have a significant influence over N Company.

During 198B and 198C, N Company earned an annual net income of $50,000 and paid cash dividends of $20,000 each year. On December 31, 198C, calculate the carrying value of (a) X Company's investment in N Company and (b) Y Company's investment in N Company.

Exercise 16-9

On December 31, S Company had the following stockholders' equity:

Common stock, $1 par value, 75,000
    shares issued and outstanding . . . . . $ 75,000
Retained earnings   45,000
Total stockholders' equity $120,000

On the same day (December 31), P Company purchased 50,000 of S Company's outstanding shares, paying $2 per share, and a work sheet to consolidate the balance sheets of the two companies was prepared. In general journal form, give the entry made on this work sheet to eliminate P Company's investment and the related stockholders' equity accounts of S Company.

Exercise 16-10

During the year following its acquisition by P Company (see Exercise 16-9), S Company earned $15,000, paid out $9,000 in dividends, and retained the balance for use in its operations. In general journal form, give the entry under these assumptions to eliminate P Company's investment and S Company's stockholders' equity account balances as of the end of the year.

Problems

Problem 16-1

Riviera Corporation's stockholders' equity at the beginning of the current year consisted of the following:

Common stock, $25 par value, 20,000 shares authorized,
    9,600 shares issued $240,000
Contributed capital in excess of par value, common stock . . .   36,000
Retained earnings   92,000
Total stockholders' equity $368,000

During the year, the company completed these transactions:

Apr. 9   Purchased 800 shares of treasury stock at $38 per share.

     29   The directors voted a $0.40 per share cash dividend payable on May 28 to the May 14 stockholders of record.

May 28   Paid the dividend declared on April 29.

July 18   Sold 400 of the treasury shares at $43 per share.

Oct. 11   Sold 400 of the treasury shares at $35 per share.

Dec. 20   The directors voted a $0.40 per share cash dividend payable on January 27 to the January 15 stockholders of record, and they voted a 2% stock dividend distributable on February 16 to the February 1 stockholders of record. The market value of the stock was $39 per share.

     31   Closed the Income Summary account and carried the company's $24,500 net income to Retained Earnings.

Required

1. Prepare general journal entries to record the transactions.
2. Prepare a retained earnings statement for the year and the stockholders' equity section of the company's year-end balance sheet.

Problem 16-2

Last September 30, Tortolla Corporation had a $540,000 credit balance in its retained earnings account. On that date, the corporation's contributed capital consisted of 50,000 authorized shares of $100 par, common stock, of which 6,000 shares had been issued at $110 and were outstanding. It then completed the following transactions:

Oct.   1   The board of directors declared a $24 per share dividend on the common stock, payable on November 3 to the October 20 stockholders of record.

Nov.   3   Paid the dividend declared on October 1.

      10   The board declared a 10% stock dividend, distributable on December 5 to the November 24 stockholders of record. The stock was selling at $120 per share, and the directors voted to use this amount in recording the dividend.

Dec.   5   Distributed the stock dividend declared on November 10.

      31   On this day the company earned $165,000, and then closed the Income Summary account.

Jan.   9   The board of directors voted to split the corporation's stock 5 for 1 by calling in the old stock and issuing five $20 par value shares for each $100 share held. The stockholders voted approval of the split and authorization of 100,000 new $20 par value shares to replace the $100 shares; all legal requirements were met; and the split was completed on February 8.

Required

1. Prepare general journal entries to record these transactions and to close the Income Summary account at year-end. (No entry is required for the split; however, a memorandum reciting the facts would be entered in the Common Stock account.)

2. Under the assumption Jay Evans owned 500 of the $100 par value shares on September 30 and neither bought nor sold any shares during the period of the transactions, prepare a schedule with columns for the date, supporting calculations, book value per share, and book value of Evans' shares. Then complete the schedule by calculating the book value per share of the corporation's stock and the book value of Evans' shares at the close of business on September 30, October 1, November 3, December 5, December 31, and February 8.

3. Prepare three stockholders' equity sections for the corporation, the first showing the stockholders' equity on September 30, the second on December 31, and the third on February 8. Assume that the only income earned by the company during these periods was the $165,000 earned and closed on December 31.

Problem 16-3

The equity sections from the 198A and 198B balance sheets of Moran Industries, Inc., appeared as follows:

Stockholders' Equity
(As of December 31, 198A)

Common stock, $10 par value, 500,000 shares authorized, 60,000 shares issued	$ 600,000
Contributed capital in excess of par value, common stock	120,000
Total contributed capital	$ 720,000
Retained earnings	585,480
Total stockholders' equity	$1,305,480

Stockholders' Equity
(As of December 31, 198B)

Common stock, $10 par value, 500,000 shares authorized, 65,940 shares issued of which 600 are in the treasury	$ 659,400
Contributed capital in excess of par value, common stock	203,160
Total contributed capital	$ 862,560
Retained earnings	471,180
Total	$1,333,740
Less: Cost of treasury stock	12,600
Total stockholders' equity	$1,321,140

On March 9, June 3, August 27, and again on November 14, 198B, the board of directors declared $0.30 per share dividends on the outstanding stock. The treasury stock was purchased on June 26. On August 27, while the stock was selling for $24 per share, the corporation declared a 10% stock dividend on the outstanding shares. The new shares were issued on September 18.

Required

Under the assumption that there were no transactions affecting retained earnings other than the ones given, determine the 198B net income of Moran Industries, Inc. Show your calculations.

Problem 16-4

Holder Company was organized on January 1, 198A, for the purpose of investing in the shares of other companies. Holder Company immediately issued 30,000 shares of $5 par, common stock for which it received $150,000 cash. On January 6, 198A, Holder Company purchased 8,000 shares (20%) of Tarton Company's outstanding stock at a cost of $150,000. The following transactions and events subsequently occurred:

198A

May   31   Tarton Company declared and paid a cash dividend of $1.50 per share.

Dec.   31   Tarton Company announced that its net income for the year was $90,000.

198B

July   14   Tarton Company declared and issued a stock dividend of one share for each two shares already outstanding.

Sept.   9   Tarton Company declared and paid a cash dividend of $1.00 per share.

Dec. 31   Tarton Company announced that its net income for the year
           was $75,000.

198C
Jan.   2   Holder Company sold all of its investment in Tarton Company
           for $168,000 cash.

Part 1. Because Holder Company owns 20% of Tarton Company's
outstanding stock, Holder Company is presumed to have a significant
influence over Tarton Company.

Required

1. Give the entries on the books of Holder Company to record the above
   events regarding its investment in Tarton Company.
2. Calculate the cost per share of Holder Company's investment, as
   reflected in the investment account on January 1, 198C.
3. Calculate Holder Company's retained earnings balance on January 3,
   198C, after a closing of the books.

Part 2. Although Holder Company owns 20% of Tarton Company's
outstanding stock, a thorough investigation of the surrounding
circumstances indicates that Holder Company does not have a significant
influence over Tarton Company, and the cost method is the appropriate
method of accounting for the investment.

Required

1. Give the entries on the books of Holder Company to record the above
   events regarding its investment in Tarton Company.
2. Calculate the cost per share of Holder Company's investment, as
   reflected in the investment account on January 1, 198C.
3. Calculate Holder Company's retained earnings balance on January 3,
   198C, after a closing of the books.

Problem 16-5

On January 1, 198A, Brownwood Company purchased 80% of Mondak
Company's outstanding stock at $32 per share. On that date, Brownwood
Company had retained earnings of $345,000. Mondak Company had
retained earnings of $90,000, and had outstanding 15,000 shares of $10
par, common stock, originally issued at par.

Part 1.

Required

1. Give the elimination entry to be used on a work sheet for a consolidated
   balance sheet dated January 1, 198A.
2. Determine the amount of consolidated retained earnings that should
   be shown on a consolidated balance sheet dated January 1, 198A.

Part 2. During the year ended December 31, 198A, Brownwood Company
paid cash dividends of $45,000 and earned net income of $85,000 excluding
earnings from its investment in Mondak Company. Mondak Company

earned net income of $42,000 and paid dividends of $20,000. Except for Brownwood Company's Retained Earnings account and the Investment in Mondak Company account, the balance sheet accounts for the two companies on December 31, 198A, are as follows:

	Brownwood Company	Mondak Company
Cash.	$105,200	$ 82,800
Notes receivable.	36,000	
Merchandise	244,800	118,800
Building, net	232,000	144,000
Land.	140,000	126,000
Investment in Mondak Company	?	
Total assets.	$?	$471,600
Accounts payable	$293,000	$173,600
Note payable		36,000
Common stock	448,000	150,000
Retained earnings	?	112,000
Total liabilities and stockholders' equity	$?	$471,600

Brownwood Company loaned $36,000 to Mondak Company during 198A, for which Mondak Company signed a note. On December 31, 198A, the note had not been repaid.

Required

1. Calculate the December 31, 198A, balances in Brownwood Company's Investment in Mondak Company account and Retained Earnings account.
2. Complete a work sheet to consolidate the balance sheets of the two companies.

Problem 16-6

The following items appeared in the first two columns of a work sheet prepared to consolidate the balance sheets of Parent Company and Subsidiary Company on the day Parent Company gained control of Subsidiary Company by purchasing 21,250 shares of its $10 par value common stock at $13 per share.

At the time Parent Company acquired control of Subsidiary Company, it took Subsidiary Company's note in exchange for $25,000 in cash and it sold and delivered $5,000 of equipment at cost to Subsidiary Company on open account (account receivable). Both transactions are reflected in the accounts on page 585.

Required

1. Prepare a work sheet to consolidate the balance sheets of the two companies and prepare a consolidated balance sheet.
2. Under the assumption that Subsidiary Company earned $25,000 during the first year after it was acquired by Parent Company, paid out $15,000 in dividends, and retained the balance of its earnings in its operations, give the entry to eliminate Parent Company's investment in the

subsidiary and Subsidiary Company's stockholders' equity accounts at the year's end.

	Parent Company	Subsidiary Company
Assets		
Cash	$ 18,750	$ 27,500
Note receivable, Subsidiary Company	25,000	
Accounts receivable, net	70,000	60,000
Inventories	105,000	87,500
Investment in Subsidiary Company	276,250	
Equipment, net	200,000	175,000
Buildings, net	212,500	
Land	50,000	
Total assets	$957,500	$350,000
Liabilities and Stockholders Equity		
Accounts payable	$ 52,500	$ 25,000
Note payable, Parent Company		25,000
Common stock	625,000	250,000
Retained earnings	280,000	50,000
Total liabilities and stockholders' equity . . .	$957,500	$350,000

□ Alternate Problems

Problem 16-1A

Dapper Corporation's stockholders' equity at the beginning of the current year consisted of the following:

Common stock, $1 par value, 800,000 shares authorized, 408,000 shares issued	$408,000
Contributed capital in excess of par value, common stock . . .	61,200
Retained earnings	156,400
Total stockholders' equity	$625,600

During the year, the company completed these transactions:

Feb. 12 Purchased 20,000 shares of treasury stock at $1.20 per share.

Mar. 26 The directors voted a $0.05 per share cash dividend payable on April 21 to the April 10 stockholders of record.

Apr. 21 Paid the dividend declared on March 26.

June 9 Sold 8,000 of the treasury shares at $1.40 per share.

Nov. 6 Sold 12,000 of the treasury shares at $0.90 per share.

Dec. 22 The directors voted a $0.05 per share cash dividend payable on January 14 to the January 1 stockholders of record, and they voted a 3% stock dividend distributable on February 1 to the January 15 stockholders of record. The market value of the stock was $1.10 per share.

31 Closed the Income Summary account and carried the company's $56,000 net income to Retained Earnings.

Required

1. Prepare general journal entries to record the transactions.

2. Prepare a retained earnings statement for the year and the stockholders' equity section of the company's year-end balance sheet.

Problem 16-2A

Last March 31, St. Thomas Corporation had a $2,500,000 credit balance in its Retained Earnings account. On that date, the corporation's contributed capital consisted of 500,000 authorized shares of $10 par, common stock of which 100,000 shares had been issued at $15 and were outstanding. It then completed the following transactions:

Apr. 1   The board of directors declared a $4 per share dividend on the common stock, payable on May 5 to the April 18 stockholders of record.

May 5   Paid the dividend declared on April 1.

      10   The board declared a 20% stock dividend, distributable on June 12 to the May 26 stockholders of record. The stock was selling at $45 per share, and the directors voted to use this amount in recording the dividend.

June 12   Distributed the stock dividend declared on May 10.

      30   On this day, the corporation earned $600,000 which was closed from Income Summary to Retained Earnings.

July 15   The board of directors voted to split the corporation's stock 5 for 1 by calling in the old stock and issuing five $2 par value shares for each $10 share held. The stockholders voted approval of the split and authorization of 1,000,000 new $2 par value shares to replace the $10 shares; all legal requirements were met; and the split was completed on August 4.

Required

1. Prepare general journal entries to record these transactions and to close the Income Summary account at year-end. (No entry is required for the split; however, a memorandum reciting the facts would be entered in the Common Stock account.)

2. Under the assumption Karen Froh owned 2,500 of the $10 par value shares on March 31 and neither bought nor sold any shares during the period of the transactions, prepare a schedule with columns for the date, supporting calculations, book value per share, and book value of Froh's shares. Then complete the schedule by calculating the book value per share of the corporation's stock and the book value of Froh's shares at the close of business on March 31, April 1, May 5, June 12, June 30, and July 15.

3. Prepare three stockholders' equity sections for the corporation, the first showing the stockholders' equity on March 31, the second on June 30, and the third on July 15. Assume that the only income earned by the company during these periods was the $600,000 carned and closed on June 30.

Problem 16-3A

The equity sections from the 198A and 198B balance sheets of Berry Island Corporation appeared as follows:

Stockholders' Equity
(As of December 31, 198A)

Common stock, no-par, $10 stated value, 400,000 shares authorized, 75,000 shares issued	$ 750,000
Contributed capital in excess of stated value	150,000
Total contributed capital	$ 900,000
Retained earnings.	731,850
Total stockholders' equity	$1,631,850

Stockholders' Equity
(As of December 31, 198B)

Common stock, no-par, $10 stated value, 400,000 shares authorized, 78,650 shares issued of which 2,000 are in the treasury	$ 786,500
Contributed capital in excess of stated value	223,000
Total contributed capital	$1,009,500
Retained earnings.	588,975
Total	$1,598,475
Less: Cost of treasury stock	44,000
Total stockholders' equity	$1,554,475

On March 1, May 28, August 30, and again on November 20, 198B, the board of directors declared $0.40 per share dividends on the outstanding stock. The treasury stock was purchased on June 15. On August 30, while the stock was selling for $30 per share, the corporation declared a 5% stock dividend on the outstanding shares. The new shares were issued on September 27.

Required

Under the assumption that there were no transactions affecting retained earnings other than the ones given, determine the 198B net income of Berry Island Corporation. Show your calculations.

Problem 16-4A

Buyer Company was organized on January 1, 198A, for the purpose of investing in the shares of other companies. Buyer Company immediately issued 36,000 shares of $5 par, common stock for which it received $180,000 cash. On January 6, 198A, Buyer Company purchased 16,000 shares (20%) of Hunter Company's outstanding stock at a cost of $180,000. The following transactions and events subsequently occurred:

198A

Apr. 30   Hunter Company declared and paid a cash dividend of $0.80 per share.

Dec. 31   Hunter Company announced that its net income for the year was $130,000.

198B

July 1   Hunter Company declared and issued a stock dividend of one share for each four shares already outstanding.

Oct. 15   Hunter Company declared and paid a cash dividend of $0.75 per share.

Dec. 31   Hunter Company announced that its net income for the year was $140,000.

198C

Jan.   3   Buyer Company sold all of its investment in Hunter Company for $200,000 cash.

Part 1. Because Buyer Company owns 20% of Hunter Company's outstanding stock, Buyer Company is presumed to have a significant influence over Hunter Company.

Required

1. Give the entries on the books of Buyer Company to record the above events regarding its investment in Hunter Company.
2. Calculate the cost per share of Buyer Company's investment, as reflected in the investment account on January 2, 198C.
3. Calculate Buyer Company's retained earnings balance on January 4, 198C, after a closing of the books.

Part 2. Although Buyer Company owns 20% of Hunter Company's outstanding stock, a thorough investigation of the surrounding circumstances indicates that Buyer Company does not have a significant influence over Hunter Company, and the cost method is the appropriate method of accounting for the investment.

Required

1. Give the entries on the books of Buyer Company to record the above events regarding its investment in Hunter Company.
2. Calculate the cost per share of Buyer Company's investment, as reflected in the investment account on January 2, 198C.
3. Calculate Buyer Company's retained earnings balance on January 4, 198C, after a closing of the books.

Problem 16-5A

On January 1, 198A, Bigtime Company purchased 90% of Littletime Company's outstanding stock at $48 per share. On that date, Bigtime Company had retained earnings of $517,500. Littletime Company had retained earnings of $210,000, and had outstanding 15,000 shares of $10 par, common stock, originally issued at par.

Part 1.

Required

1. Give the elimination entry to be used on a work sheet for a consolidated balance sheet dated January 1, 198A.
2. Determine the amount of consolidated retained earnings that should be shown on a consolidated balance sheet dated January 1, 198A.

Part 2. During the year ended December 31, 198A, Bigtime Company paid cash dividends of $67,500 and earned net income of $127,500 excluding earnings from its investment in Littletime Company. Littletime Company earned net income of $63,000 and paid dividends of $30,000. Except for Bigtime Company's Retained Earnings account and the Investment in

Littletime Company account, the balance sheet accounts for the two companies on December 31, 198A, are as follows:

	Bigtime Company	Littletime Company
Cash	$160,800	$124,200
Notes receivable	54,000	
Merchandise	295,200	178,200
Building, net	348,000	216,000
Land	210,000	189,000
Investment in Littletime Company	?	
Total assets	$?	$707,400
Accounts payable	$439,500	$260,400
Note payable		54,000
Common stock	672,000	150,000
Retained earnings	?	243,000
Total liabilities and stockholders' equity	$?	$707,400

Bigtime Company loaned $54,000 to Littletime Company during 198A, for which Littletime Company signed a note. On December 31, 198A, the note had not been repaid.

Required

1. Calculate the December 31, 198A, balances in Bigtime Company's Investment in Littletime Company account and Retained Earnings account.

2. Complete a work sheet to consolidate the balance sheets of the two companies.

Problem 16-6A

The following items appeared in the first two columns of a work sheet prepared to consolidate the balance sheets of Top Company and Bottom Company on the day Top Company gained control of Bottom Company by purchasing 12,750 shares of its $50 par value common stock at $65 per share.

	Top Company	Bottom Company
Assets		
Cash	$ 67,250	$ 82,500
Note receivable, Bottom Company	64,000	
Accounts receivable, net	210,000	180,000
Inventories	315,000	262,500
Investment in Bottom Company	828,750	
Equipment, net	600,000	525,000
Buildings, net	637,500	
Land	150,000	
Total assets	$2,872,500	$1,050,000
Liabilities and Stockholders' Equity		
Accounts payable	$ 157,500	$ 86,000
Note payable, Top Company		64,000
Common stock	1,875,000	750,000
Retained earnings	840,000	150,000
Total liabilities and stockholders' equity	$2,872,500	$1,050,000

At the time Top Company acquired control of Bottom Company, it took Bottom Company's note in exchange for $64,000 in cash and it sold and delivered $25,000 of equipment at cost to Bottom Company on open account (account receivable). Both transactions are reflected in the foregoing accounts.

Required

1. Prepare a work sheet to consolidate the balance sheets of the two companies and prepare a consolidated balance sheet.

2. Under the assumption that Bottom Company earned $75,000 during the first year after it was acquired by Top Company, paid out $45,000 in dividends, and retained the balance of its earnings in its operations, give the entry to eliminate Top Company's investment in the subsidiary and Bottom Company's stockholders' equity accounts at the year's end.

Provocative Problems

Provocative Problem 16-1   Farmtree Corporation

On January 1, 198A, Bob Algoe purchased 500 shares of Farmtree Corporation stock at $37.50 per share. On that date, the corporation had the following stockholders' equity:

Common stock, $25 par value, 400,000 shares authorized, 200,000 shares issued and outstanding	$5,000,000
Contributed capital in excess of par value, common stock . .	625,000
Retained earnings	1,400,000
Total stockholders' equity	$7,025,000

Since purchasing the 500 shares, Mr. Algoe has neither purchased nor sold any additional shares of the company's stock; and on December 31 of each year, he has received dividends on the shares held as follows: 198A, $825; 198B, $1,031.25; and 198C, $1,375.

On May 15, 198A, at a time when its stock was selling for $43.75 per share, Farmtree Corporation declared a 10% stock dividend which was distributed one month later. On September 22, 198B, the corporation doubled the number of its authorized shares and split its stock 2 for 1; and on April 7, 198C, it purchased 10,000 shares of treasury stock at $22.50 per share. The shares were still in its treasury at year-end.

Required

Under the assumption that Farmtree Corporation's stock had a book value of $33.75 per share on December 31, 198A, a book value of $18.00 per share on December 31, 198B, and a book value of $19.25 on December 31, 198C, do the following:

1. Prepare statements showing the nature of the stockholders' equity in the corporation at the end of 198A, 198B, and 198C.

2. Prepare a schedule showing the amount of the corporation's net income for each of 198A, 198B, and 198C, under the assumption that the changes in the company's retained earnings during the three-year period resulted solely from earnings and dividends.

Provocative Problem 16-2   MoCity Company

MoCity Company's stockholders' equity on October 14 consisted of the following amounts:

Common stock, $50 par value, 300,000 shares authorized, 70,000 shares issued and outstanding	$3,500,000
Contributed capital in excess of par value, common stock . .	525,000
Retained earnings	2,275,000
Total stockholders' equity	$6,300,000

On October 15, when the stock was selling at $100 per share, the corporation's directors voted a 20% stock dividend, distributable on November 5 to the October 22 stockholders of record. The directors also voted a $4.25 per share annual cash dividend, payable on December 25 to the December 12 stockholders of record. The amount of the latter dividend was a disappointment to some stockholders, since the company had for a number of years paid a $5.00 per share annual cash dividend.

Julie Stewart owned 1,000 shares of MoCity Company stock on October 22, which she had purchased a number of years ago, and as a result she received her dividend shares. She continued to hold all of her shares until after she received the December 25 cash dividend. However, she did note that her stock had a $100 per share market value on October 15, a market value it held until the close of business on October 22, when the market value declined to $87.50 per share.

Give the entries to record the declaration and payment of the dividends involved here, and answer these questions:

a. What was the book value of Stewart's total shares on October 15 (after taking into consideration the actions of the Board of Directors on that day), and what was the book value on November 5, after she received the dividend shares?
b. What fraction of the corporation did Stewart own on October 15, and what fraction did she own on November 5?
c. What was the market value of Stewart's total shares on October 15, and what was the market value at the close of business on October 22?
d. What did Stewart gain from the stock dividend?

Provocative Problem 16-3   Questions from Stockholders

When corporations have their annual meetings with stockholders, the managements often have to deal with difficult questions from stockholders. For example, at the recent stockholders' meeting of Tekcon, Inc., one of the stockholders made the following statements. "I have owned shares of Tekcon for several years, but am now questioning whether management is telling the truth in the annual financial statements. At the end of 1983, you announced that Tekcon had just acquired a 30% interest in the outstanding stock of Fibercrete Corporation. You also stated that the 112,000 shares had cost Tekcon about $11,200,000. In the financial statements for 1984, you told us that the investments of Tekcon were proving to be very profitable, and reported that earnings from all investments had amounted to more than $3.22 million. In the financial statements for 1985, you explained that Tekcon had sold the Fibercrete shares during the first week of the year, receiving $12,740,000 cash proceeds from the sale. Nevertheless, the income statement for 1985 reports only a $280,000 gain on the sale (before taxes). I realize that Fibercrete did not pay any dividends during 1984, but it was very profitable. As I recall, it reported net income of $4,200,000 for 1984. Personally, I do not think you should have sold the shares. But, much more importantly, you reported to us that our company gained only $280,000 from the sale. How can that be true if the shares were purchased for $11,200,000 and were sold for $12,740,000?''

Explain to this stockholder why the $280,000 gain is correctly reported.

Provocative Problem 16-4   American Motor Inns, Incorporated

American Motor Inns (AMI) is engaged in the business of operating hotels and restaurants. In 1983, the company operated hotels in nine states and in St. Thomas in the U.S. Virgin Islands. The 1983 annual report of AMI included the following footnote to its financial statements:

(7) MINORITY INTEREST IN SUBSIDIARY

In December, 1980, the Company's previously wholly owned subsidiary, Universal Communication Systems, Inc. sold 750,000 shares of its common stock to the public resulting in net proceeds of $8,725,000. This reduced the Company's holding in that subsidiary to approximately 84% of the outstanding common stock.

Given this information, would you expect the 1980 (and years thereafter) consolidated financial statements of American Motor Inns to report its investment in Universal Communication Systems according to the equity method? Why or why not? Also, assume that American Motor Inns prepared a consolidated balance sheet immediately after the subsidiary's sale of stock to the public. Did the sale of stock have any effects on that balance sheet? If so, explain the effects.

17 Installment Notes Payable and Bonds

After studying Chapter 17, you should be able to:

1. Calculate and record the payments on an installment note.

2. Explain the differences between an installment note payable, a bond, and a share of stock.

3. Describe the advantages and disadvantages of securing capital by issuing bonds.

4. Explain how bond interest rates are established.

5. Use present value tables to calculate the premium or the discount on a bond issue.

6. Prepare entries to account for bonds issued between interest dates at par.

7. Prepare entries to account for bonds sold at par, at a discount, or at a premium.

8. Explain the purpose and operation of a bond sinking fund and prepare entries for its operation.

9. Describe the procedures used to account for investments in bonds.

10. Define or explain the words and phrases listed in the chapter Glossary.

When a business borrows money by signing a promissory note, the terms of the note may require a single lump-sum payment of the amount borrowed plus interest. Notes that require a single payment of the amount due were discussed in the previous chapter. Many notes, however, require a series of payments that consist of interest plus a portion of the original amount borrowed. Notes payable of this type are called **installment notes.** This chapter begins with a discussion of installment notes payable. The discussion then turns to bonds payable. By issuing bonds, a company may be able to borrow money from a large number of investors.

■ **Installment Notes Payable**

When an installment note is used to borrow money, the borrower records the note in the same manner as any other note. For example, suppose a company borrows $60,000 by signing a 12% installment note that is to be repaid with six annual payments. The entry to record the loan is as follows:

198A Dec.	31	Cash	60,000.00	
		Notes Payable		60,000.00
		Borrowed by signing a 12% note.		

An installment note payable requires the borrower to pay back the debt in a series of periodic payments. Usually, each payment includes all of the interest that has accrued to the date of the payment plus some portion of the original amount that was borrowed. The terms of installment notes commonly call for one of two alternative payment patterns.

Installment Payments of Accrued Interest plus Equal Amounts of Principal

Some installment notes require payments that consist of accrued interest to date plus equal amounts of principal. Since each periodic payment reduces the amount borrowed, the next period's interest is reduced and the total amount of each payment becomes smaller period after period. For example, suppose that the $60,000, 12% note recorded above requires that $10,000 of principal plus accrued interest be paid at the end of each year. The entries to record the first and the second annual payments are as follows:

198B Dec.	31	Notes Payable ($60,000/6)	10,000.00	
		Interest Expense ($60,000 × 0.12).	7,200.00	
		Cash		17,200.00
		To record first installment payment.		
198C Dec.	31	Notes Payable ($60,000/6)	10,000.00	
		Interest Expense ($50,000 × 0.12).	6,000.00	
		Cash		16,000.00
		To record second installment payment.		

Illustration 17-1

Period Ending	(a) Beginning-of-Period Principal Balance	(b) Periodic Payment	(c) Interest Expense for the Period (a) × 12%	(d) Portion of Payment that Is Principal (b) − (c)	(e) End-of-Period Principal Balance (a) − (d)
12/31/8B . .	$60,000	$14,594	$7,200	$ 7,394	$52,606
12/31/8C . .	52,606	14,594	6,313	8,281	44,325
12/31/8D . .	44,325	14,594	5,319	9,275	35,050
12/31/8E . .	35,050	14,594	4,206	10,388	24,662
12/31/8F. . .	24,662	14,594	2,959	11,635	13,027
12/31/8G . .	13,027	14,590*	1,563	13,027	–0–

* Note that the final payment is $4 smaller than the first five payments due to rounding. Although the note called for equal payments, a minor adjustment to the final payment is commonly necessary to repay the exact amount of debt.

Note that the balance of the debt at the beginning of each interest period is used to calculate the interest expense for the period. As a result, each payment is smaller than the previous payment.

Installment Payments that Are Equal in Total Amount

At this point students who are not sure of their understanding of the concept of present value should turn back to Chapter 12 and review this concept before going further into this chapter. For additional study of discounting, an expanded analysis of present and future values is presented in Appendix A at the end of this book.

Many installment notes require a series of equal payments. In other words, the payments are equal in total amount and consist of changing amounts of interest and principal. For example, assume that the $60,000, 12% note does not require six principal payments of $10,000 each plus accrued interest. Instead, assume that the note simply requires a series of six equal payments to be made at the end of each year. Each payment is to be $14,594.

Allocating Each Payment between Interest and Principal Each payment of $14,594 includes both principal and interest. To determine the amounts of interest and principal that are included in each payment, understand that $60,000 is the present value of $14,594 to be paid annually for six years, discounted at 12%. (In this chapter, all dollar amounts are rounded to the nearest whole dollar.) The allocation of each payment between interest and principal is shown in Illustration 17-1.

In Illustration 17-1, observe that interest expense is calculated each period as 12% multiplied by the beginning-of-period principal balance. Then, the interest expense is subtracted from the periodic payment to determine the portion of the payment that is a repayment of principal. Each number in the table has been rounded to the nearest whole dollar.

The journal entry to record the first periodic payment is:

198B					
Dec.	31	Notes Payable	7,394.00		
		Interest Expense.	7,200.00		
		Cash		14,594.00	
		To record first installment payment.			

Similar entries are used to record each of the remaining payments.

How to Calculate the Periodic Payments In the example, the $60,000, 12% loan required six annual payments of $14,594. Illustration 17-1 proves that these payments are just what is necessary to repay the loan. But, how was the $14,594 calculated?

The correct amount of the periodic payments may be calculated with the help of a table for the present value of $1 received (or paid) periodically for a number of periods. (See Table 12-2 on page 431.) In Table 12-2, the present value of $1 paid at the end of each year for six years, discounted at 12%, is $4.1114. This relationship between the periodic payments of $1 and the present value of $4.1114 may be expressed as a ratio, as follows:

$$\frac{\text{Periodic payment}}{\text{Present value}} = \frac{\$1}{\$4.1114}$$

This ratio of periodic payments to present value is the same for all situations in which six payments ($n = 6$) are discounted at an interest rate of 12% ($i = 12\%$). In other words, when the present value is $60,000, the periodic payments can be calculated as follows:

$$\frac{\text{Periodic payment}}{\$60,000} = \frac{1}{4.1114}$$

$$\text{Periodic payment} = \frac{\$60,000 \times 1}{4.1114} = \$14,593.57, \text{ or } \$14,594$$

Borrowing by Issuing Bonds

Business corporations often borrow money by issuing **bonds.**[1] Like notes payable, bonds involve a written promise to pay interest and principal or **par value.** The par value, also called the **face amount,** is printed on the bond. The interest rate stated on the bond is applied to the par value in determining the annual interest to be paid. Also, the par value is the amount that is repaid when the bond matures. Bonds usually require that interest be paid semiannually, and that the par value be repaid at a fixed future date (the maturity date).

Difference between Notes Payable and Bonds

When a business (or an individual) borrows money by signing a note payable, the money is generally borrowed from a single creditor such as a bank. In contrast to a note payable, a bond issue typically includes a large number of bonds, usually in denominations of $1,000, that are sold to

---

[1] The federal government and other governmental units such as cities, states, and school districts, also issue bonds. However, the examples and discussion of this chapter are limited to the bonds of business corporations.

many different lenders. After they are originally issued, bonds are frequently bought and sold by investors and may be owned by a number of people before they mature.

Difference between Stocks and Bonds

The phrase **stocks and bonds** commonly appears on the financial pages of newspapers and is often heard in conversations. However, the difference between stocks and bonds should be clearly understood. A share of stock represents an equity or ownership right in a corporation. For example, if a person owns 1,000 of the 10,000 shares of common stock a corporation has outstanding, the person has an equity in the corporation measured at one tenth of the corporation's total stockholders' equity and has an equity in one tenth of the corporation's earnings. On the other hand, if a person owns a $1,000, 11%, 20-year bond issued by a corporation, the bond represents a debt or a liability of the corporation. Its owner has two rights: (1) the right to receive 11% or $110 interest each year the bond is outstanding, and (2) the right to be paid $1,000 when the bond matures 20 years after its date of issue.

■ **Why Issue Bonds Instead of Stock?**

A corporation in need of long-term funds may consider issuing additional shares of stock or issuing bonds. Each has its advantages and disadvantages. Since stockholders are owners, additional stock spreads ownership, control of management, and earnings over more shares. Bondholders, on the other hand, are creditors and do not share in either management or earnings. However, bond interest must be paid whether there are any earnings or not.

The issuance of bonds instead of stock often results in increased earnings for the common stockholders of the issuing corporation. For example, assume a corporation with 200,000 shares of common stock outstanding needs $1,000,000 to expand its operations. Management estimates that after the expansion, the company can earn $900,000 annually before bond interest, if any, and before corporation income taxes. Two plans for securing the needed funds are proposed. Plan A calls for issuing 100,000 additional shares of the corporation's common stock at $10 per share. This will increase the total outstanding shares to 300,000. Plan B calls for the sale at par of $1,000,000 of 10% bonds. Illustration 17-2 shows how the plans will affect the corporation's earnings.

Illustration 17-2

	Plan A	Plan B
Earnings before bond interest and income taxes . . .	$ 900,000	$ 900,000
Deduct bond interest expense		(100,000)
Income before corporation income taxes	$ 900,000	$ 800,000
Deduct income taxes (assumed 50% rate).	(450,000)	(400,000)
Net income	$ 450,000	$ 400,000
Plan A income per share (300,000 shares)	$1.50	
Plan B income per share (200,000 shares)		$2.00

Corporations are subject to state and federal income taxes, which together may take as much as 50% of the corporation's before-tax income. However, interest expense is a deductible expense in arriving at income subject to taxes. Consequently, when the combined state and federal tax rate is 50%, as in Illustration 17-2, the tax reduction from issuing bonds equals one half the annual interest on the bonds. In other words, the tax savings in effect pays one half the interest cost of the bonds.

■ Characteristics of Bonds

Over the years, corporation lawyers and financiers have created a wide variety of bonds, each with different combinations of characteristics. Some of the more common characteristics of different bond issues are discussed in the following paragraphs.

Serial Bonds

Some bond issues include bonds that mature at different points in time so that the entire bond issue is repaid gradually over a period of years. Bonds of this type are called **serial bonds.** For example, a $1,000,000 issue of serial bonds may include $100,000 of bonds that mature each year from year 6 through year 15.

Sinking Fund Bonds

In contrast to serial bonds, **sinking fund bonds** all mature on the same date and are paid in one lump sum from a separate pool of assets (a sinking fund) that was established specifically for that purpose. Sinking funds are discussed later in this chapter.

Registered Bonds and Bearer Bonds

Most bonds are registered. The name and address of the owner of a **registered bond** are recorded with the issuing corporation. This offers some protection from loss or theft. If bonds are not registered, they are made payable to bearer and are called **bearer bonds.**

Coupon Bonds

Interest payments on registered bonds are usually made by checks mailed to the registered owners. If interest is not paid in this manner, the bonds are called **coupon bonds.** Coupon bonds obtain their name from the interest coupons attached to each bond. Each coupon calls for payment on the interest payment date of the interest due on the bond. The coupons are detached as they become due and are deposited with a bank for collection.

Secured Bonds and Debentures

When bonds are secured, specific assets of the issuing corporation are pledged or mortgaged to be used, if necessary, to repay the bonds. Mortgages are discussed later in this chapter. Unsecured bonds that depend upon the general credit standing of the issuing corporation for security are called **debentures.** A company generally must be financially strong if it is to successfully issue unsecured bonds.

■ **The Process of Issuing Bonds**

When a corporation issues bonds, it normally sells the bonds to an invest-ment firm known as the **underwriter.** The underwriter in turn resells the bonds to the public. The legal document that states the rights and obliga-tions of the company and the bondholders is called the **bond indenture.** In other words, the bond indenture is the written, legal contract between the issuing company and the bondholders. Each bondholder receives a **bond certificate** which is evidence of the corporation's debt to the bond-holder.

Since there may be many bondholders, they are represented by a **trustee.** The trustee has the responsibility of monitoring the corporation's actions to be sure that it fulfills its obligations as stated in the bond indenture. In most cases, the trustee is a large bank or trust company that is selected by the issuing company.

Accounting for the Issuance of Bonds

When a corporation issues bonds, the bond certificates are printed and the indenture is drawn and deposited with the trustee of the bondholders. At that point, a memorandum describing the bond issue is commonly en-tered in the Bonds Payable account. Such a memorandum might read, "Authorized to issue $8,000,000 of 9%, 20-year bonds dated January 1, 19—, and with interest payable semiannually on each July 1 and January 1." As in this case, bond interest is usually payable semiannually.

After the bond indenture is deposited with the trustee of the bondholders, all or a portion of the bonds may be sold. If all are sold at their par value, an entry like the following is made to record the sale:

Jan.	1	Cash	8,000,000.00	
		Bonds Payable		8,000,000.00
		Sold 9%, 20-year bonds at par on their interest date.		

When the semiannual interest is paid on these bonds, the transaction is recorded as follows:

July	1	Bond Interest Expense.	360,000.00	
		Cash		360,000.00
		Paid the semiannual interest on the bonds.		

And when the bonds are paid at maturity, an entry like the following is made:

Jan.	1	Bonds Payable	8,000,000.00	
		Cash		8,000,000.00
		Paid bonds at maturity.		

■ **Bonds Sold between Interest Dates**

Sometimes bonds are sold on their date of issue, which is also their interest date, as in the previous illustration. More often they are sold after their date of issue and between interest dates. In such cases, it is customary to charge and collect from the purchasers the interest that has accrued on the bonds since the previous interest payment and to return this accrued interest to the purchasers on the next interest date. For example, assume that on March 1, a corporation sold at par $100,000 of 9% bonds on which interest is payable semiannually on each January 1 and July 1. (Small dollar amounts are used to conserve space.) The entry to record the sale between interest dates is:

Mar.	1	Cash	101,500.00	
		Bond Interest Expense.		1,500.00
		Bonds Payable		100,000.00
		Sold $100,000 of 9%, 20-year bonds on which two months' interest has accrued.		

At the end of four months, on the July 1 semiannual interest date, the purchasers of these bonds are paid a full six months' interest. This payment includes four months' interest earned by the bondholders after March 1 and the two months' accrued interest collected from them at the time the bonds were sold. The entry to record the payment is:

July	1	Bond Interest Expense.	4,500.00	
		Cash		4,500.00
		Paid the semiannual interest on the bonds.		

After both of these entries are posted, the Bond Interest Expense account has a $3,000 debit balance and appears as follows:

Bond Interest Expense

July 1 (Payment)	4,500.00	Mar. 1 (Accrued interest)	1,500.00

The $3,000 debit balance represents the interest on the $100,000 of bonds at 9% for the four months from March 1 to July 1.

It may seem strange to charge bond purchasers for accrued interest when bonds are sold between interest dates, and to return this accrued interest in the next interest payment. However, this is the custom. All bond transactions are "plus accrued interest," and there is a good reason for the practice. For instance, if a corporation sells portions of a bond issue on different dates during an interest period without collecting the accrued interest, it must keep records of the purchasers and the dates on which they bought bonds. Otherwise, it cannot pay the correct amount of interest to each. However, if it charges each buyer for accrued interest at the time of the purchase, it need not keep records of the purchasers and their purchase dates. It can pay a full period's interest to all purchasers for the period in which they bought their bonds; each receives the interest earned and gets back the accrued interest paid at the time of the purchase.

■ **Bond Interest Rates**

A corporation issuing bonds specifies in the bond indenture and on each bond certificate the interest rate it will pay. This rate is called the **contract rate.** It is usually stated on an annual basis, although bond interest is normally paid semiannually. Also, it is applied to the par value of the bonds to determine the dollars of interest the corporation will pay. For example, if a corporation issues a $1,000, 8% bond on which interest is paid semiannually, $80 will be paid each year in two semiannual installments of $40 each.

Although the contract rate establishes the interest a corporation will pay, it is not necessarily the interest the corporation will incur in issuing bonds. The interest it will incur depends upon what lenders consider their risks to be in lending to the corporation and upon the current **market rate for bond interest.** The market rate for bond interest is the rate borrowers are willing to pay and lenders are willing to take for the use of money at the level of risk involved. It fluctuates from day to day as the supply and demand for loanable funds fluctuate. It goes up when the demand for bond money increases and the supply decreases, and it goes down when the supply increases and the demand decreases.

Also, note that on any single day, the market rate for bond interest is not the same for all corporations. The rate for a specific corporation's bonds depends on the level of risk investors attach to those bonds. As the perceived level of risk increases, the rate increases.

A corporation issuing bonds usually offers a contract rate of interest equal to what it estimates the market will demand on the day the bonds are to be issued. If its estimate is correct, and the contract rate and market rate coincide on the day the bonds are issued, the bonds will sell at par, their face amount. However, when bonds are sold, their contract rate seldom coincides with the market rate. As a result, bonds usually sell either at a premium or at a discount.

■   **Bonds Sold at a Discount**

When a corporation offers to sell bonds carrying a contract rate below the prevailing market rate, the bonds will sell at a **discount.** Given the level of risk, investors can get the market rate of interest elsewhere for the use of their money, so they will buy the bonds only at a price that will yield the prevailing market rate on the investment. What price will they pay and how is it determined? The price they will pay is the **present value** of the expected returns from the investment. It is determined by discounting the returns at the current market rate for bond interest.

To illustrate how bond prices are determined, assume that on a day when the market rate for bond interest is 9%, a corporation offers to sell and issue bonds having a $100,000 par value, a 10-year life, and on which interest is to be paid semiannually at an 8% annual rate.[2] In exchange for current dollars, the buyers of these bonds will gain two monetary rights:

---

[2] The spread between the contract rate and the market rate of interest on a new bond issue is seldom more than a fraction of a percent. However, a spread of a full percent is used here to simplify the illustrations.

1. The right to receive $100,000 at the end of the bond issue's 10-year life.
2. The right to receive $4,000 in interest at the end of each 6-month interest period throughout the 10-year life of the bonds.

Since both are rights to receive money in the future, to determine their present value, the amounts to be received are discounted at the market rate of interest. If the market rate is 9% annually, it is 4½% semiannually; and in 10 years, there are 20 semiannual periods. Consequently, using the last number in the 4½% column of Table 12-1, page 429, to discount the first amount and the last number in the 4½% column of Table 12-2, page 431, to discount the series of $4,000 amounts, the present value of the rights and the price informed buyers will offer for the bonds is:

Present value of $100,000 to be received 20 periods hence, discounted at 4½% per period ($100,000 × 0.4146)	$41,460
Present value of $4,000 to be received periodically for 20 periods, discounted at 4½% ($4,000 × 13.0079)	52,032
Present value of the bonds	$93,492

If the corporation accepts the $93,492 offered for its bonds and sells them on their date of issue, the sale will be recorded with an entry like this:

Jan.	1	Cash	93,492.00	
		Discount on Bonds Payable	6,508.00	
		Bonds Payable		100,000.00
		Sold 8%, 10-year bonds at a discount on their date of issue.		

If the corporation prepares a balance sheet on the day the bonds are sold, it may show the bonds in the long-term liability section as follows:

Long-term liabilities:		
First-mortgage, 8% bonds payable, due January 1, 199A	$100,000	
Less unamortized discount based on the 9% market rate for bond interest prevailing on the date of issue	6,508	$93,492

On a balance sheet, any unamortized discount on a bond issue is deducted from the par value of the bonds to show the amount at which the bonds are carried on the books, called the **carrying amount.**

Amortizing the Discount

The corporation of this discussion received $93,492 for its bonds, but in 10 years it must pay the bondholders $100,000. The difference, the $6,508 discount, is a cost of using the $93,492 that is incurred because the contract rate of interest on the bonds was below the prevailing market rate. It is a cost that must be paid when the bonds mature. However, each semiannual interest period in the life of the bond issue benefits from the use of the $93,492. Consequently, it is only fair that each should bear a fair share of this cost.

Straight-Line Method The procedure for dividing a discount and charging a share to each period in the life of the applicable bond issue is called **amortizing** a discount. A simple method of amortizing a discount is the **straight-line method,** a method in which an equal portion of the discount is amortized each interest period. If this method is used to amortize the $6,508 discount of this discussion, the $6,508 is divided by 20, the number of interest periods in the life of the bond issue, and $325 ($6,508 ÷ 20 = $325.40, or $325)[3] of the discount is amortized at the end of each interest period with an entry like this:

July	1	Bond Interest Expense	4,325.00	
		Discount on Bonds Payable		325.00
		Cash		4,000.00
		To record payment of six months' interest and amortization of one twentieth of the discount.		

Illustration 17-3, with amounts rounded to full dollars, shows the interest expense to be recorded, the discount to be amortized, and so forth, when the straight-line method of amortizing a discount is applied to the bonds in this discussion. In examining Illustration 17-3, note these points:

1. The bonds were sold at a $6,508 discount, which when subtracted from their face amount gives a beginning-of-Period-1 carrying amount of $93,492.
2. The semiannual $4,325 interest expense amounts equal $4,000 paid to bondholders plus $325 amortization of discount.
3. Interest to be paid bondholders each period is determined by multiplying the par value of the bonds by the contract rate of interest ($100,000 × 4% = $4,000).
4. The discount to be amortized each period is $6,508 ÷ 20 = $325.40, or $325.
5. The unamortized discount at the end of each period is determined by subtracting the discount amortized that period from the unamortized discount at the beginning of the period.
6. The end-of-period carrying amount for the bonds is determined by subtracting the end-of-period amount of unamortized discount from the face amount of the bonds. For example, at the end of Period 1: $100,000 − $6,183 = $93,817.

Straight-line amortization once was commonly used. However, the APB ruled that it may now be used only in situations where the results do not materially differ from those obtained through use of the so-called interest method.[4]

---

[3] In this chapter and in the problems at the end of the chapter, all calculations involving bonds have been rounded to the nearest whole dollar.

[4] FASB, *Accounting Standards—Current Text* (Stamford, Conn., 1984), sec. I69.108. First published in *APB Opinion No. 21,* par. 15.

Illustration 17-3

Period	Beginning-of-Period Carrying Amount	Interest Expense to Be Recorded	Interest to Be Paid the Bondholders	Discount to Be Amortized	Unamortized Discount at End of Period	End-of-Period Carrying Amount
1 . . .	$93,492	$4,325	$4,000	$325	$6,183	$ 93,817
2 . . .	93,817	4,325	4,000	325	5,858	94,142
3 . . .	94,142	4,325	4,000	325	5,533	94,467
4 . . .	94,467	4,325	4,000	325	5,208	94,792
5 . . .	94,792	4,325	4,000	325	4,883	95,117
6 . . .	95,117	4,325	4,000	325	4,558	95,442
7 . . .	95,442	4,325	4,000	325	4,233	95,767
8 . . .	95,767	4,325	4,000	325	3,908	96,092
9 . . .	96,092	4,325	4,000	325	3,583	96,417
10 . . .	96,417	4,325	4,000	325	3,258	96,742
11 . . .	96,742	4,325	4,000	325	2,933	97,067
12 . . .	97,067	4,325	4,000	325	2,608	97,392
13 . . .	97,392	4,325	4,000	325	2,283	97,717
14 . . .	97,717	4,325	4,000	325	1,958	98,042
15 . . .	98,042	4,325	4,000	325	1,633	98,367
16 . . .	98,367	4,325	4,000	325	1,308	98,692
17 . . .	98,692	4,325	4,000	325	983	99,017
18 . . .	99,017	4,325	4,000	325	658	99,342
19 . . .	99,342	4,325	4,000	325	333	99,667
20 . . .	99,667	4,333*	4,000	333*	–0–	100,000

* Adjusted to compensate for accumulated rounding of amounts.

Interest Method   When the interest method is used, the interest expense to be recorded each period is determined by applying a constant rate of interest to the beginning-of-period carrying amount of the bonds. The constant rate applied is the market rate for the bonds at the time the bonds were issued. The discount amortized each period is then determined by subtracting the interest to be paid the bondholders from the interest expense to be recorded. Illustration 17-4 shows the interest expense to be recorded, the discount to be amortized, and so forth, when the interest method is applied to the bonds in this discussion.

Compare Illustration 17-4 with 17-3 and note these unique aspects of the interest method as shown in Illustration 17-4.

1. The interest expense amounts result from multiplying each beginning-of-period carrying amount by the 4½% semiannual market rate that prevailed when the bonds were issued. For example, $93,492 × 4½% = $4,207 and $93,699 × 4½% = $4,216.
2. The discount to be amortized each period is determined by subtracting the amount of interest to be paid the bondholders from the amount of interest expense.

When the interest method is used in amortizing a discount, the periodic amortizing entries are like the entries used with the straight-line method; only the dollar amounts are different. For example, the entry to pay the

Illustration 17-4

Period	Beginning-of-Period Carrying Amount	Interest Expense to Be Recorded	Interest to Be Paid the Bondholders	Discount to Be Amortized	Unamortized Discount at End of Period	End-of-Period Carrying Amount
1 . . .	$93,492	$4,207	$4,000	$207	$6,301	$ 93,699
2 . . .	93,699	4,216	4,000	216	6,085	93,915
3 . . .	93,915	4,226	4,000	226	5,859	94,141
4 . . .	94,141	4,236	4,000	236	5,623	94,377
5 . . .	94,377	4,247	4,000	247	5,376	94,624
6 . . .	94,624	4,258	4,000	258	5,118	94,882
7 . . .	94,882	4,270	4,000	270	4,848	95,152
8 . . .	95,152	4,282	4,000	282	4,566	95,434
9 . . .	95,434	4,295	4,000	295	4,271	95,729
10 . . .	95,729	4,308	4,000	308	3,963	96,037
11 . . .	96,037	4,322	4,000	322	3,641	96,359
12 . . .	96,359	4,336	4,000	336	3,305	96,695
13 . . .	96,695	4,351	4,000	351	2,954	97,046
14 . . .	97,046	4,367	4,000	367	2,587	97,413
15 . . .	97,413	4,384	4,000	304	2,203	97,797
16 . . .	97,797	4,401	4,000	401	1,802	98,198
17 . . .	98,198	4,419	4,000	419	1,383	98,617
18 . . .	98,617	4,438	4,000	438	945	99,055
19 . . .	99,055	4,457	4,000	457	488	99,512
20 . . .	99,512	4,488*	4,000	488	–0–	100,000

* Adjusted to compensate for accumulated rounding of amounts.

bondholders and amortize a portion of the discount at the end of the first semiannual interest period of the bond issue in Illustration 17-4 is:

July	1	Bond Interest Expense	4,207.00	
		Discount on Bonds Payable		207.00
		Cash		4,000.00
		To record payment to the bondholders and amortization of a portion of the discount.		

Similar entries, differing only in the amount of interest expense recorded and discount amortized, are made at the end of each semiannual interest period in the life of the bond issue.

Consider the differences between the interest method of amortizing a discount and the straight-line method (previously discussed). The following table shows these financial statement differences:

Period	Interest-Method Amortization			Straight-Line Amortization		
	Beginning-of-Period Carrying Amount	Interest Expense to Be Recorded	Interest Expense as a Percent of Carrying Amount	Beginning-of-Period Carrying Amount	Interest Expense to Be Recorded	Interest Expense as a Percent of Carrying Amount
1 . . .	$93,492	$4,207	4.5	$93,492	$4,325	4.63
11 . . .	96,037	4,322	4.5	96,742	4,325	4.47
19 . . .	99,055	4,457	4.5	99,342	4,325	4.35

The table shows the beginning-of-period carrying amount of the bond liability and the interest expense for each of three six-month periods during the life of the bonds. The first three columns of the table show that in each and every six-month period, the interest method provides an interest expense amount that is 4.5% of the beginning-of-period carrying amount. The last three columns show the amounts that would result from using the straight-line method. Observe that when the straight-line method is used, the percentage changes each period. Recall that the bonds were issued at a price that reflected a discounting of cash flows at 4.5% per six-month period. The interest method is most consistent with this fact; and it is the preferred method.

Because the above example involves a bond discount, the straight-line method results in a declining percentage. When a premium is amortized, the straight-line method results in an increasing percentage. In either case, however, the straight-line method can be used only where the results do not differ materially from those obtained through use of the interest method.

Bonds Sold at a Premium

When a corporation offers to sell bonds carrying a contract rate of interest above the prevailing market rate for the risks involved, the bonds will sell at a **premium.** Buyers will bid up the price of the bonds, going as high, but no higher, than a price that will return the current market rate of interest on the investment. What price will they pay? They will pay the present value of the expected returns from the investment, determined by discounting these returns at the market rate of interest for the bonds. For example, assume that on a given day a corporation offers to sell bonds having a $100,000 par value and a 10-year life with interest to be paid semiannually at an 11% annual rate. On that day, the market rate of interest for the corporation's bonds is 10%. Buyers of these bonds will discount the expectation of receiving $100,000 in 10 years and the expectation of receiving $5,500 semiannually for 20 periods at the current 10% market rate as follows:

Present value of $100,000 to be received 20 periods hence, discounted at 5% per period ($100,000 × 0.3769)	$ 37,690
Present value of $5,500 to be received periodically for 20 periods, discounted at 5% ($5,500 × 12.4622).	68,542
Present value of the bonds.	$106,232

Investors will offer the corporation a total of $106,232 for its bonds. If the corporation accepts and sells the bonds on their date of issue, say, May 1, 198A, it will record the sale as follows:

198A					
May	1	Cash	106,232.00		
		Premium on Bonds Payable		6,232 00	
		Bonds Payable		100,000.00	
		Sold bonds at a premium on their date of issue.			

It may then show the bonds on a balance sheet prepared on the day of the sale as follows:

Long-term liabilities:
  First-mortgage, 11% bonds payable, due May 1, 199A $100,000
  Add unamortized premium based on the 10% market rate for
    bond interest prevailing on the date of issue. 6,232 $106,232

On a balance sheet, any unamortized premium on bonds payable is added to the par value of the bonds to show the carrying amount of the bonds, as illustrated.

Amortizing the Premium

Although the corporation discussed here received $106,232 for its bonds, it will have to repay only $100,000 to the bondholders at maturity. The difference, the $6,232 premium, represents a reduction in the cost of using the $106,232. It should be amortized over the life of the bond issue in such a manner as to lower the recorded bond interest expense. If the $6,232 premium is amortized by the interest method, Illustration 17-5 shows the amounts of interest expense to be recorded each period, the premium to be amortized, and so forth.

Illustration 17-5

Period	Beginning-of-Period Carrying Amount	Interest Expense to Be Recorded	Interest to Be Paid the Bondholders	Premium to Be Amortized	Unamortized Premium at End of Period	End-of-Period Carrying Amount
1. .	$106,232	$5,312	$5,500	$188	$6,044	$106,044
2. .	106,044	5,302	5,500	198	5,846	105,846
3. .	105,846	5,292	5,500	208	5,638	105,638
4. .	105,638	5,282	5,500	218	5,420	105,420
5. .	105,420	5,271	5,500	229	5,191	105,191
6. .	105,191	5,260	5,500	240	4,951	104,951
7. .	104,951	5,248	5,500	252	4,699	104,699
8. .	104,699	5,235	5,500	265	4,434	104,434
9. .	104,434	5,222	5,500	278	4,156	104,156
10. .	104,156	5,208	5,500	292	3,864	103,864
11. .	103,864	5,193	5,500	307	3,557	103,557
12. .	103,557	5,178	5,500	322	3,235	103,235
13. .	103,235	5,162	5,500	338	2,897	102,897
14. .	102,897	5,145	5,500	355	2,542	102,542
15. .	102,542	5,127	5,500	373	2,169	102,169
16. .	102,169	5,108	5,500	392	1,777	101,777
17. .	101,777	5,089	5,500	411	1,366	101,366
18. .	101,366	5,068	5,500	432	934	100,934
19. .	100,934	5,047	5,500	453	481	100,481
20. .	100,481	5,019*	5,500	481	–0–	100,000

* Adjusted to compensate for accumulated rounding of amounts.

Observe in Illustration 17-5 that the premium to be amortized each period is determined by subtracting the interest to be recorded from the interest to be paid the bondholders.

Based on Illustration 17-5, the entry to record the first semiannual interest payment and premium amortization is:

198A				
Nov.	1	Bond Interest Expense	5,312.00	
		Premium on Bonds Payable.	188.00	
		Cash		5,500.00
		To record payment of the bondholders and amortization of a portion of the premium.		

Note how the amortization of the premium results in a reduction in the amount of interest expense recorded. Similar entries having decreasing amounts of interest expense and increasing amounts of premium amortized are made at the ends of the remaining periods in the life of the bond issue.

Accrued Bond Interest Expense

Often when bonds are sold, the bond interest periods do not coincide with the issuing company's accounting periods. In such cases, it is necessary at the end of each accounting period to make an adjustment for accrued interest. For example, it was assumed that the bonds of Illustration 17-5 were issued on May 1, 198A, and interest was paid on these bonds on November 1 of that year. If the accounting periods of the corporation end each December 31, on December 31, 198A, two months' interest has accrued on these bonds, and the following adjusting entry is required:

198A				
Dec.	31	Bond Interest Expense	1,767.00	
		Premium on Bonds Payable.	66.00	
		Bond Interest Payable		1,833.00
		To record two months' accrued interest and amortize one third of the premium applicable to the interest period.		

Two months are one third of a semiannual interest period. Consequently, the amounts in the entry are one third of the amounts applicable to the second interest period in the life of the bond issue. Similar entries will be made on each December 31 throughout the life of the issue. However, the amounts will differ, since in each case they will apply to a different interest period.

When the interest is paid on these bonds on May 1, 198B, an entry like this is required:

198B					
May	1	Bond Interest Expense	3,535.00	
		Bond Interest Payable	1,833.00	
		Premium on Bonds Payable.	132.00	
		Cash		5,500.00
		Paid the interest on the bonds, a portion of which was previously accrued, and amortized four months' premium.		

■ **Sale of Bonds by Investors**

A purchaser of a bond may not hold it to maturity but may sell it after a period of months or years to another investor at a price determined by the market rate for bond interest on the day of the sale. The market rate for bond interest on the day of the sale determines the price because the new investor could get this current rate elsewhere. Therefore, the investor will discount the right to receive the bond's face amount at maturity and the right to receive its interest for the remaining periods of life at the current market rate to determine the price to pay for the bond. As a result, since bond interest rates may vary greatly over a period of months or years, a bond that originally sold at a premium may later sell at a discount, and vice versa.

■ **Redemption of Bonds**

Bonds are commonly issued with the provision that they may be redeemed at the issuing corporation's option, usually upon the payment of a redemption premium. Such bonds are known as **callable bonds.** Corporations commonly insert redemption clauses in deeds of trust because if interest rates decline, it may be advantageous to call and redeem outstanding bonds and issue in their place new bonds paying a lower interest rate.

Not all bonds have a provision giving their issuing company the right to call. However, even though the right is not provided, a company, may secure the same effect by purchasing its bonds on the open market and retiring them. Often such action is wise when a company has funds available and its bonds are selling at a price below their carrying amount. For example, assume that a company has outstanding on their interest date $1,000,000 of bonds on which there is $12,000 unamortized premium. The bonds are selling at 98½ (98½% of par value), and the company decides to buy and retire one tenth of the issue. The entry to record the purchase and retirement is:

Apr.	1	Bonds Payable	100,000.00	
		Premium on Bonds Payable	1,200.00	
		Gain on the Retirement of Bonds		2,700.00
		Cash		98,500.00
		To record the retirement of bonds.		

The retirement resulted in a $2,700 gain in this instance because the bonds were purchased at a price $2,700 below their carrying amount.

In the last paragraph, the statement was made that the bonds were selling at 98½. Bond quotations are commonly made in this manner. For example, a bond may be quoted for sale at 101¼. This means the bond is for sale at 101¼% of its par value, plus accrued interest, of course, if applicable.

■ **Bond Sinking Fund**

Bonds appeal to some investors because bonds usually provide greater security than stocks. Often a corporation will give additional security by agreeing in the bond indenture to create a **bond sinking fund.** This is a fund of assets accumulated during the life of the bonds to repay the bondholders at maturity.

When a corporation agrees to create a bond sinking fund, it normally agrees to create the fund by making periodic cash deposits with a sinking fund trustee. It is the duty of the trustee to safeguard the cash, to invest it in securities of reasonably low risk, and to add the interest or dividends earned to the sinking fund. Generally, when the bonds become due, it is also the duty of the sinking fund trustee to sell the sinking fund securities and to use the proceeds to pay the bondholders.

When a sinking fund is created, the amount that must be deposited periodically in order to provide enough money to retire a bond issue at maturity will depend upon the net rate of compound interest that can be earned on the invested funds. The rate is a compound rate because earnings are continually reinvested by the sinking fund trustee to earn an additional return. It is a net rate because the fee for the trustee's services commonly is deducted from the earnings.

To illustrate the operation of a sinking fund, assume a corporation issues $1,000,000 par value, 10-year bonds and agrees to deposit with a sinking fund trustee at the end of each year in the bond issue's life sufficient cash to create a fund large enough to retire the bonds at maturity. If the trustee is able to invest the funds in such a manner as to earn an 8% net return, $69,029[5] must be deposited each year, and the fund will grow to maturity (in rounded dollars) as shown in Illustration 17-6.

Illustration 17-6			
End of Year	**Amount Deposited**	**Interest Earned on Fund Balance**	**Balance in Fund after Deposit and Interest**
1. . . .	$69,029	$ –0–	$ 69,029
2. . . .	69,029	5,522	143,580
3. . . .	69,029	11,486	224,095
4. . . .	69,029	17,928	311,052
5. . . .	69,029	24,884	404,965
6. . . .	69,029	32,397	506,391
7. . . .	69,029	40,511	615,931
8. . . .	69,029	49,274	734,234
9. . . .	69,029	58,739	862,002
10. . . .	69,029	68,969	1,000,000

[5] An understanding of how this number is calculated may be gained by studying Appendix A at the end of the book.

When a sinking fund is created by periodic deposits, the entry to record the amount deposited each year appears as follows:

Dec.	31	Bond Sinking Fund	69,029.00	
		Cash		69,029.00
		To record the annual sinking fund deposit.		

Each year the sinking fund trustee invests the amount deposited, and each year it collects and reports the earnings on the investments. The earnings report results in an entry to record the sinking fund income. For example, if $69,029 is deposited at the end of the first year in the sinking fund, the accumulation of which is shown in Illustration 17-6, and 8% is earned, the entry to record the sinking fund earnings of the second year is:

Dec.	31	Bond Sinking Fund	5,522.00	
		Sinking Fund Earnings		5,522.00
		To record the sinking fund earnings.		

Sinking fund earnings appear on the income statement as financial revenue in a section titled "Other revenues and expenses." A sinking fund is the property of the company creating the fund and should appear on its balance sheet in the long-term investments section.

When bonds mature, it is usually the duty of the sinking fund trustee to convert the fund's investments into cash and pay the bondholders. Normally the sinking fund securities, when sold, produce either a little more or a little less cash than is needed to pay the bondholders. If more cash than needed is produced, the extra cash is returned to the corporation; and if less cash is produced than needed, the corporation must make up the deficiency. For example, if the securities in the sinking fund of a $1,000,000 bond issue produce $1,001,325 when converted to cash, the trustee will use $1,000,000 to pay the bondholders and will return the extra $1,325 to the corporation. The corporation will then record the payment of its bonds and the return of the extra cash with an entry like the following:

Jan.	3	Cash	1,325.00	
		Bonds Payable	1,000,000.00	
		Bond Sinking Fund		1,001,325.00
		To record payment of our bonds and the return of extra cash from the sinking fund.		

Restriction on Dividends Due to Outstanding Bonds

To protect a corporation's financial position and the interests of its bondholders, a bond indenture may restrict the dividends the corporation may pay while its bonds are outstanding. Commonly, the restriction provides that the corporation may pay dividends in any year only to the extent that the year's earnings exceed sinking fund requirements.

Converting Bonds to Stock

To make a bond issue more attractive, bondholders may be given the right to exchange their bonds for a fixed number of shares of the issuing company's common stock. Such **convertible bonds** offer investors initial investment security, and if the issuing company prospers and its stock increases in price, an opportunity to share in the prosperity by converting their bonds to the more valuable stock. Conversion is always at the bondholders' option and therefore does not take place unless it is to their advantage.

When bonds are converted into stock, the conversion changes a liability into owners' equity. The generally accepted rule for measuring the contribution for the issued shares is that the carrying amount of the converted bonds becomes the book value of the capital contributed for the new shares. For example, assume the following: (1) A company has outstanding $1,000,000 of bonds upon which there is $8,000 unamortized discount. (2) The bonds are convertible at the rate of a $1,000 bond for 90 shares of the company's $10 par value common stock. And (3) $100,000 in bonds have been presented on their interest date for conversion. The entry to record the conversion is:

May	1	Bonds Payable.	100,000.00	
		Discount on Bonds Payable		800.00
		Common Stock.		90,000.00
		Contributed Capital in Excess of Par		
		Value, Common Stock.		9,200.00
		To record the conversion of bonds.		

Note in this entry that the bonds' $99,200 carrying amount sets the accounting value for the capital contributed. Usually, when bonds have a conversion privilege, it is not exercised until the stock's market value and normal dividend payments are sufficiently high to make the conversion profitable to the bondholders.

Investments in Bonds

The discussion of bonds has thus far focused on the issuing corporation. Attention is now shifted to the purchasers of bonds. When bonds are purchased as an investment, they are recorded at cost, including any brokerage fees. If interest has accrued at the date of purchase, it is also paid for by the purchaser and is recorded with a debit to Bond Interest Receivable. The entry to record a bond purchase is as follows:

May	1	Investment in X Corporation Bonds.	46,400.00	
		Bond Interest Receivable	1,500.00	
		Cash		47,900.00
		Purchased 50 $1,000, 9%, 10-year bonds dated December 31, 198A, at a price of 92 plus a $400 brokerage fee and accrued interest.		

Note that the $46,400 cost of the bonds was 92% × $50,000 par value plus the $400 brokerage fee, which leaves a discount of $3,600. Most companies do not record the discount (or premium) in a separate account. The investment account is simply debited for the net cost. The accrued interest on May 1 was 4/12 × 9% × $50,000, or $1,500.

Assuming interest is paid semiannually on June 30 and December 31, the entry to record the receipt of interest on June 30 would be as follows:

June	30	Cash	2,250.00	
		Bond Interest Receivable		1,500.00
		Bond Interest Earned.		750.00

This entry correctly reflects the fact that the purchaser owned the bonds for two months during which time interest amounted to 2/12 × 9% × $50,000, or $750. However, recall that the bonds were purchased at a discount and observe that the June 30 entry does not include any amortization of the discount. This is acceptable only if the bonds are held as a short-term, temporary investment. Under these conditions, the bond investment is shown as a current asset at cost. The market value of the bonds on the date of the balance sheet should also be reported parenthetically, as follows:

Current assets:
   Investment in X Corp. Bonds (market value is $xx,xxx) $46,400

When the bonds are sold, the gain or loss on the sale is calculated as the difference between the sale proceeds and cost.

What if the bonds are held as a long-term investment? In this case, one should expect the market value of the bonds to move generally toward par value as the maturity date approaches. Therefore, any discount (or premium) should be amortized so that each interest period includes some amortization in the calculation of interest earned. The procedures for amortizing discount or premium on bond investments parallel those that were discussed and applied previously to bonds payable. The only difference is that the amount of discount (premium) to be amortized is debited (credited) directly to the investment account. As a consequence, on the maturity date, the investment account balance will equal the par value on the bonds.

Mortgages as Security for Notes Payable and Bonds

Earlier in this chapter, bonds were said to be either secured or unsecured. This is also true of notes payable. When bonds or notes are unsecured, the obligation to pay interest and par or principal is equal in standing with other unsecured liabilities of the issuing company. If the company becomes financially troubled and is unable to pay, none of the unsecured creditors is given preference over any other.

The ability of a company to borrow money by signing an unsecured note or issuing unsecured bonds depends on the company's general credit standing. In many cases, a company simply cannot obtain debt financing without providing security to the creditors. In other cases, the rate of interest that creditors would charge to provide unsecured debt is very high. As a result, many notes payable and bond issues are secured by a mortgage.

A **mortgage** is a legal agreement that helps protect a lender if a borrower fails to make the payments required by a note payable or bond indenture. A mortgage gives the lender the right to be paid from the cash proceeds from the sale of the borrower's mortgaged assets.

The terms of a mortgage are written in a separate legal document, the **mortgage contract.** The mortgage contract is given to the trustee of the bond issue or to the lender along with the note payable. A mortgage contract commonly requires the borrower to keep the mortgaged property in a good state of repair and adequately insured. In addition, it normally grants the mortgage holder (the lender) the right to foreclose if the borrower fails to pay. In a foreclosure, a court either sells the property or grants possession of the mortgaged property to the lender who sells it. When the property is sold, the proceeds go first to pay court costs and the claims of the mortgage holder. Any money remaining is then paid to the former owner of the property.

□   **Glossary**   **Bearer bond** a bond that is not registered and is made payable to whoever holds the bond (the bearer).

Bond a long-term liability of a corporation or governmental unit, usually issued in denominations of $1,000, that requires periodic payments of interest and final payment of par value when it matures.

Bond discount the difference between the par value of a bond and the price at which it is issued when issued at a price below par.

Bond indenture the contract between the issuing corporation and the bondholders that states the rights and obligations of both parties.

Bond premium the difference between the par value of a bond and the price at which it is issued when issued at a price above par.

Bond sinking fund a fund of assets accumulated to repay a bond issue at maturity.

Callable bond a bond that may be redeemed or repaid before its maturity date at the option of the issuing corporation.

Carrying amount of a bond issue the par value of a bond issue less any unamortized discount or plus any unamortized premium.

Contract rate of bond interest the rate of interest that is applied to the par value of bonds to determine the annual cash payment to the bondholders.

Convertible bond a bond that may be exchanged for shares of its issuing corporation's stock at the option of the bondholder.

Coupon bond a bond that has interest coupons attached to the bond certificate, which are detached and submitted to the issuing corporation for payment.

Debenture an unsecured bond.

Face amount of a bond the bond's par value.

Installment notes notes that require a series of payments consisting of interest plus a portion of the original amount borrowed.

Market rate for bond interest the interest rate that a corporation is willing to pay and investors are willing to take for the use of their money to buy that corporation's bonds.

Mortgage a legal agreement that helps protect a lender by giving the lender the right to be paid from the cash proceeds from the sale of the borrower's mortgaged assets.

Mortgage contract a legal document setting forth the rights of the lender and the obligations of the borrower with respect to mortgaged assets.

Par value of a bond the face amount of the bond, which is the amount the borrower agrees to repay at maturity and the amount on which interest payments are based.

Registered bond a bond for which the name and address of the owner are recorded with the issuing corporation.

Serial bonds an issue of bonds that mature at different points in time so that the entire bond issue is repaid gradually over a period of years.

Sinking fund bonds bonds that require the issuing corporation to accumulate a separate fund of assets during the life of the bonds for the purpose of repaying the bondholders at maturity.

□ **Questions for Class Discussion**

1. What are two commonly used payment patterns on installment notes?
2. How is the interest portion of an installment note payment calculated?
3. What is the difference between a note payable and a bond issue?
4. What is the primary difference between a share of stock and a bond?
5. Why may bonds be preferred to stock as a means of long-term financing?
6. What is a bond indenture? What are some of the provisions commonly contained in an indenture?
7. What role is played by the underwriter when bonds are issued?
8. What is the function of the trustee on a bond issue?
9. Define or describe: (a) registered bonds, (b) coupon bonds, (c) serial bonds, (d) sinking fund bonds, (e) callable bonds, (f) convertible bonds, and (g) debenture bonds.
10. Why does a corporation that issues bonds between interest dates charge and collect accrued interest from the purchasers of the bonds?
11. As it relates to a bond issue, what is the meaning of "contract rate of interest"? What is the meaning of "market rate for bond interest"?
12. What determines bond interest rates?
13. When the straight-line method is used to amortize bond discount, how is the interest expense for each period calculated?
14. When the interest method is used to amortize bond discount or premium, how is the interest expense for each period calculated?
15. If a $1,000 bond is sold at 98¼, at what price is it sold? If a $1,000 bond is sold at 101½, at what price is it sold?
16. If the quoted price for a bond is 97¾, does this include accrued interest?
17. What purpose is served by creating a bond sinking fund?
18. How are bond sinking funds classified for balance sheet purposes?
19. Why are convertible bonds attractive to investors?
20. What two legal documents are involved when a company signs a note payable that is secured by a mortgage? What is the purpose of each?

□ **Class Exercises**

In solving the exercises and problems at the end of Chapter 17, round all dollar amounts to the nearest whole dollar.

Exercise 17-1

On December 31, 198A, a company borrowed $75,000 by signing a five-year, 14% installment note. The note requires annual payments on December 31 of accrued interest plus equal amounts of principal. Prepare journal entries to record the first payment on December 31, 198B, and the last payment on December 31, 198F.

Exercise 17-2

On December 31, 198A, a company borrowed $75,000 by signing a five-year, 14% installment note. The note requires annual payments of $21,846 to be made on December 31. Prepare journal entries to record the first payment on December 31, 198B, and the second payment on December 31, 198C.

Exercise 17-3

A company borrowed $80,000 by signing an eight-year, 12% installment note. The terms of the note require eight annual payments of an equal amount, the first of which is due one year after the date of the note. Calculate the amount of the installment payments, based on the present values contained in Table 12-2.

Exercise 17-4

On May 31 of the current year, a corporation sold at par plus accrued interest $1,000,000 of its 10.2% bonds. The bonds were dated January 1 of the current year, with interest payable on each July 1 and January 1. (*a*) Give the entry to record the sale. (*b*) Give the entry to record the first interest payment. (*c*) Set up a T-account for bond Interest Expense and post the portions of the entries that affect the account. Answer these questions: (*d*) How many months' interest were accrued on these bonds when they were sold? (*e*) How many months' interest were paid on July 1? (*f*) What is the balance of the Bond Interest Expense account after the entry recording the first interest payment is posted? (*g*) How many months' interest does this balance represent? (*h*) How many months' interest did the bondholders earn during the first interest period?

Exercise 17-5

On March 1 of the current year, a corporation sold $3,000,000 of its 10.8%, 20-year bonds. The bonds were dated March 1 of the current year, with interest payable on each September 1 and March 1. Give the entries to record the sale at 98¾ and the first semiannual interest payment under the assumption that the straight-line method is used to amortize the discount.

Exercise 17-6

On December 31 of the current year, a corporation sold $2,000,000 of its 9.8%, 10-year bonds at a price that reflected a 12% market rate for bond interest. Interest is payable each June 30 and December 31. Calculate the sales price of the bonds and prepare a general journal entry to record the sale of the bonds. (Use the present value tables, Tables 12-1 and 12-2, pages 429 and 431.)

Exercise 17-7

The corporation of Exercise 17-6 uses the interest method of amortizing bond discount or premium. Under the assumption the corporation of Exercise 17-6 sold its bonds for $1,747,650, prepare a schedule with the columnar headings of Illustration 17-4 and present the amounts in the schedule for the first two interest periods. Also, prepare general journal entries to record the first and second payments of interest to bondholders.

Exercise 17-8

A corporation sold $800,000 of its own 11%, eight-year bonds on November 1, 198A, at a price that reflected a 10% market rate of bond interest. The bonds pay interest each May 1 and November 1. (a) Calculate the price at which the bonds sold, and (b) prepare a general journal entry to record the sale. (Use the present value tables, Tables 12-1 and 12-2, pages 429 and 431.)

Exercise 17-9

Assume the bonds of Exercise 17-8 sold for $843,343 and that the corporation uses the interest method to amortize bond discount or premium. Prepare general journal entries to accrue interest on December 31, 198A, and to record the first payment of interest on May 1, 198B.

Exercise 17-10

A corporation sold $700,000 of its 9.2%, 20-year bonds at 95½ on their date of issue, January 1, 19—. Five years later, on January 1, after the bond interest for the period had been paid and 25% of the total discount on the issue had been amortized, the corporation purchased $100,000 par value of the bonds on the open market at 101¼ and retired them. Give the entry to record the retirement.

Exercise 17-11

On January 1, 198A, a corporation sold $1,500,000 of 15-year sinking fund bonds. The corporation expects to earn 8% on assets deposited with the sinking fund trustee and is required to deposit $55,244 with the trustee at the end of each year in the life of the bonds. (a) Prepare a general journal entry to record the first deposit of $55,244 with the trustee on January 1, 198B. (b) Prepare a general journal entry on December 31, 198B, to record the $4,380 earnings for 198B reported to the corporation by the trustee. (c) After the final payment to the trustee, the sinking fund had an accumulated balance of $1,506,780. Prepare the general journal entry to record the payment to the bondholders on January 1, 199F.

Exercise 17-12

A corporation has outstanding $10,000,000 of 8%, 20-year bonds on which there is $225,000 of unamortized bond premium. The bonds are convertible into the corporation's $1 par value common stock at the rate of one $1,000 bond for 200 shares of the stock, and $500,000 of the bonds have been presented for conversion. Give the entry to record the conversion as of July 12.

Exercise 17-13

On October 1, 198B, Nickle Company purchased 50 $1,000 par value, 12%, 10-year Blanco Corporation bonds dated December 31, 198A. The bonds pay interest semiannually on June 30 and December 31. Nickle Company bought the bonds at 96 plus accrued interest and a $900 brokerage fee. Nickle intends to hold the bonds as a temporary investment.

Prepare journal entries for Nickle Company to record the purchase and to record the receipt of interest on December 31, 198B.

□   **Problems**   *In solving the problems at the end of this chapter, round all dollar amounts to the nearest whole dollar.*

Problem 17-1

Kramer Company financed a major expansion of its production capacity by borrowing money and signing an installment note at the bank. The four-year, 14%, $300,000 note is dated June 30, 198A, and requires equal semiannual payments beginning December 31, 198A.

Required

1. Calculate the amount of the installment payments. (Use Table 12-2 on page 431.)
2. Prepare a table with columnar headings like the table in Illustration 17-1. Complete the table for the Kramer Company note.
3. Prepare general journal entries to record the first and the last payments on the note.
4. Assume that the note does not require equal payments. Instead, assume the note requires payments of accrued interest plus equal amounts of principal. Prepare general journal entries to record the first and the last payments on the note.

Problem 17-2

A corporation sold $1,000,000 of its own 9.3%, 10-year bonds on their date of issue, January 1, 198A. Interest was payable on the bonds on each June 30 and December 31, and they were sold at a price to yield the buyers a 10% annual return. The corporation uses the straight-line method of amortizing discount or premium.

Required

1. Prepare a calculation to show the price at which the bonds were sold. (Use the present value tables, Tables 12-1 and 12-2, pages 429 and 431.)
2. Prepare a form with the columnar headings of Illustration 17-3 and fill in the amounts for the first two interest periods of the bond issue. Round all amounts to the nearest whole dollar.
3. Prepare entries in general journal form to record the sale of the bonds and the first two payments of interest.

Problem 17-3

On January 1, 198A, a corporation sold $1,500,000 of its own 12.9%, 10-year bonds. The bonds were dated January 1, 198A, with interest payable on each June 30 and December 31, and were sold to yield the buyers a 12% annual return. The corporation uses the interest method of amortizing premium or discount.

Required

1. Prepare a calculation to show the price at which the bonds were sold. (Use the present value tables, Tables 12-1 and 12-2, pages 429 and 431.)
2. Prepare a form with the columnar headings of Illustration 17-5 and fill in the amounts for the first two interest periods of the bond issue. Round all amounts to the nearest whole dollar.
3. Prepare entries in general journal form to record the sale of the bonds and the first two payments of interest.

Problem 17-4

Prepare general journal entries to record the following transactions of Dazzle Corporation. Use the present value tables, Tables 12-1 and 12-2, pages 429 and 431, as necessary, to calculate the amounts in your entries. Remember to round all amounts to the nearest whole dollar.

198A
Jan.   1   Sold $700,000 of its own 13.3%, 10-year bonds dated January 1, 198A, with interest payable on each June 30 and December 31. The bonds sold for a price that reflected a 14% market rate of bond interest.
June 30   Paid the semiannual interest on the bonds and amortized a portion of the discount calculated by the straight-line method.
Dec. 31   Paid the semiannual interest on the bonds and amortized a portion of the discount calculated by the straight-line method.
       31   Deposited $43,925 with the sinking fund trustee to establish the sinking fund to repay the bonds.

198B
Dec. 30   Received the report of the sinking fund trustee that the sinking fund had earned $4,350.

199A
Jan.   1   Received a report from the sinking fund trustee which noted that the bondholders had been paid $700,000 on that day. Included was a $2,160 check for the extra cash accumulated in the sinking fund.

Problem 17-5

Prepare general journal entries to record the following bond transactions of McAdams Corporation.

198A
Oct.   1   Sold $5,000,000 par value of its own 9.7%, 10-year bonds at a price to yield the buyers a 9% annual return. The bonds were dated October 1, 198A, with interest payable on each April 1 and October 1.
Dec. 31   Made an adjusting entry to record the accrued interest on the bonds and to amortize the premium applicable to 198A. The interest method was used in calculating the premium amortized.

198B

Apr. 1 Paid the semiannual interest on the bonds and amortized the remainder of the premium applicable to the first interest period.

Oct. 1 Paid the semiannual interest on the bonds and amortized the premium applicable to the second interest period of the issue.

198C

Oct. 1 After recording the entry paying the semiannual interest on the bonds on this date and amortizing a portion of the premium, the carrying amount of the bonds on McAdams Corporation's books was $5,196,330. McAdams then purchased one tenth of the bonds at 101¼ and retired them. Record the purchase and retirement of the bonds.

Problem 17-6

On December 31, 198A, Wimberly Corporation sold $2,500,000 of 10-year, 9.3% bonds payable at a price that reflected a 10% market rate of bond interest. The bonds pay interest on June 30 and December 31. Use the present value tables, Tables 12-1 and 12-2, pages 429 and 431, as necessary, in calculating the amounts in your answers.

Required

1. Present a general journal entry to record the sale of the bonds.

2. Present general journal entries to record the first and second payments of interest on June 30, 198B, and on December 31, 198B, assuming straight-line amortization of premium or discount.

3. Present general journal entries to record the first and second payments of interest on June 30, 198B, and on December 31, 198B, assuming the use of the interest method to amortize premium or discount.

4. Prepare a schedule like the one on page 605 that has columns for the beginning-of-period carrying amount, interest expense to be recorded, and interest expense as a percentage of carrying amount, assuming use of the (1) interest method, and (2) straight-line method. In completing the schedule, present the amounts for Period 1 and Period 2.

□ **Alternate Problems**   *In solving the following alternate and provocative problems, round all dollar amounts to the nearest whole dollar.*

Problem 17-1A

On June 30, 198A, Mandel Company borrowed $180,000 at the bank by signing a five-year, 12% installment note. The terms of the note require equal semiannual payments beginning December 31, 198A.

Required

1. Calculate the amount of the installment payments. (Use Table 12-2 on page 431.)

2. Prepare a table with column headings like the table in Illustration 17-1. Complete the table for the Mandel Company note.

3. Prepare general journal entries to record the first and the last payments on the note.

4. Assume that the note does not require equal payments. Instead, assume the note requires payments of accrued interest plus equal amounts of principal. Prepare general journal entries to record the first and the last payments on the note.

Problem 17-2A

Armen Corporation sold $500,000 of its own 8.5%, 10-year bonds on their date of issue, January 1, 198A. Interest was payable on the bonds on each June 30 and December 31, and they were sold at a price to yield the buyers a 9% annual return. The corporation uses the straight-line method of amortizing discount or premium.

Required

1. Prepare a calculation to show the price at which the bonds were sold. (Use the present value tables, Tables 12-1 and 12-2, pages 429 and 431.)

2. Prepare a form with the columnar headings of Illustration 17-3 and fill in the amounts for the first two interest periods of the bond issue. Round all amounts to the nearest whole dollar.

3. Prepare entries in general journal form to record the sale of the bonds and the first two payments of interest.

Problem 17-3A

Nifty Corporation sold $1,200,000 of its own 14.8%, 10-year bonds on January 1, 198A. The bonds were dated January 1, 198A, with interest payable on each June 30 and December 31, and were sold to yield the buyers a 14% annual return. The corporation uses the interest method of amortizing premium or discount.

Required

1. Prepare a calculation to show the price at which the bonds were sold. (Use the present value tables, Tables 12-1 and 12-2, pages 429 and 431.)

2. Prepare a form with the columnar headings of Illustration 17-5 and fill in the amounts for the first two interest periods of the bond issue. Round all amounts to the nearest whole dollar.

3. Prepare entries in general journal form to record the sale of the bonds and the first two payments of interest.

Problem 17-4A

Prepare general journal entries to record the following transactions of Westlink Corporation. Use the present value tables, Tables 12-1 and 12-2, pages 429 and 431, as necessary, to calculate the amounts in your entries. Remember to round all amounts to the nearest whole dollar.

198A

Jan.   1   Sold $1,600,000 of its own 11.1%, 10-year bonds dated January 1, 198A, with interest payable on each June 30 and December 31. The bonds sold for a price that reflected a 12% market rate of bond interest.

June 30   Paid the semiannual interest on the bonds and amortized a portion of the discount calculated by the straight-line method.

Dec. 31   Paid the semiannual interest on the bonds and amortized a portion of the discount calculated by the straight-line method.

      31   Deposited $91,175 with the sinking fund trustee to establish the sinking fund to repay the bonds.

198B

Dec. 30   Received the report of the sinking fund trustee that the sinking fund had earned $10,950.

199A

Jan.   1   Received a report from the sinking fund trustee which noted that the bondholders had been paid $1,600,000 on that day. Included was a $4,780 check for the extra cash accumulated in the sinking fund.

Problem 17-5A

Prepare general journal entries to record the following bond transactions of Reister Corporation.

198A

Nov.   1   Sold $3,000,000 par value of its own 9.5%, 10-year bonds at a price to yield the buyers a 9% annual return. The bonds were dated November 1, 198A, with interest payable on each May 1 and November 1.

Dec. 31   Made an adjusting entry to record the accrued interest on the bonds and to amortize the premium applicable to 198A. The interest method was used in calculating the premium amortized.

198B

May   1   Paid the semiannual interest on the bonds and amortized the remainder of the premium applicable to the first interest period.

Nov.   1   Paid the semiannual interest on the bonds and amortized the premium applicable to the second interest period of the issue.

198C

Nov.   1   After recording the entry paying the semiannual interest on the bonds on this date and amortizing a portion of the premium, the carrying amount of the bonds on Reister Corporation's books was $3,076,663. Reister then purchased one tenth of the bonds at 100¾ and retired them. Record the purchase and retirement of the bonds.

Problem 17-6A

On December 31, 198A, Raindeer Corporation sold $2,400,000 of 10-year, 11.3% bonds payable at a price that reflected at 12% market rate of bond interest. The bonds pay interest on June 30 and December 31. Use the present value tables, Tables 12-1 and 12-2, pages 429 and 431, as necessary, in calculating the amounts in your answers.

Required

1. Present a general journal entry to record the sale of the bonds.
2. Present general journal entries to record the first and second payments of interest on June 30, 198B, and on December 31, 198B, assuming straight-line amortization of premium or discount.
3. Present general journal entries to record the first and second payments of interest on June 30, 198B, and on December 31, 198B, assuming the use of the interest method to amortize premium or discount.
4. Prepare a schedule like the one on page 605 that has columns for the beginning-of-period carrying amount, interest expense to be recorded, and interest expense as a percentage of carrying amount, assuming use of the (1) interest method, and (2) straight-line method. In completing the schedule, present the amounts for Period 1 and Period 2.

Provocative Problems

Provocative Problem 17-1   A Comparison of Alternative Bond Issues

Ticket Sales Company is planning a major expansion of its operations and needs $1,000,000 to finance the expansion. The company has been presented with three alternative financing proposals. Each involves issuing bonds that pay interest semiannually. The alternatives are:

Plan A: Issue at par $1,000,000 of 10-year, 12% bonds.
Plan B: Issue $1,130,000 of 10-year, 10% bonds.
Plan C: Issue $897,000 of 10-year, 14% bonds.

Regardless of which plan is followed, the market rate of interest for the bonds is expected to be 12%.

For each bond issue, calculate the cash proceeds of the issue, the interest expense for the first six-month period, and the expected cash outflow each six-month period for interest. Use the interest method of amortizing bond premium or discount. Which plan has the smallest cash demands on the company prior to the final payment at maturity? Which requires the largest payment upon maturity?

Provocative Problem 17-2   Financing with Stock or Bonds

The stockholders' equity of Raider Corporation consists of 500,000 shares of outstanding common stock on which the corporation has earned an average of $0.45 per share during each of the last three years. In an effort to increase earnings, management is planning an expansion that will require the investment of an additional $2,500,000 in the business. The $2,500,000 is to be acquired either by selling an additional 250,000 shares of the company's common stock at $10 per share or selling at par $2,500,000 of 8%, 20-year bonds. Management estimates that the expansion will double the company's before-tax earnings the first year after it is completed and will increase before-tax earnings an additional 25% over that level in the years that follow.

Raider Corporation's management wants to finance the expansion in the manner that will serve the best interests of present stockholders and has asked you to evaluate the two alternatives from this perspective. In your report express an opinion as to the relative merits and disadvantages of each of the proposed ways of securing the funds needed for the expansion. Attach to your report a schedule showing expected earnings per share of the common stockholders under each method of financing. In preparing your schedule, assume the company presently pays out in state and federal income taxes 50% of its before-tax earnings and that it will continue to pay out the same share after the expansion.

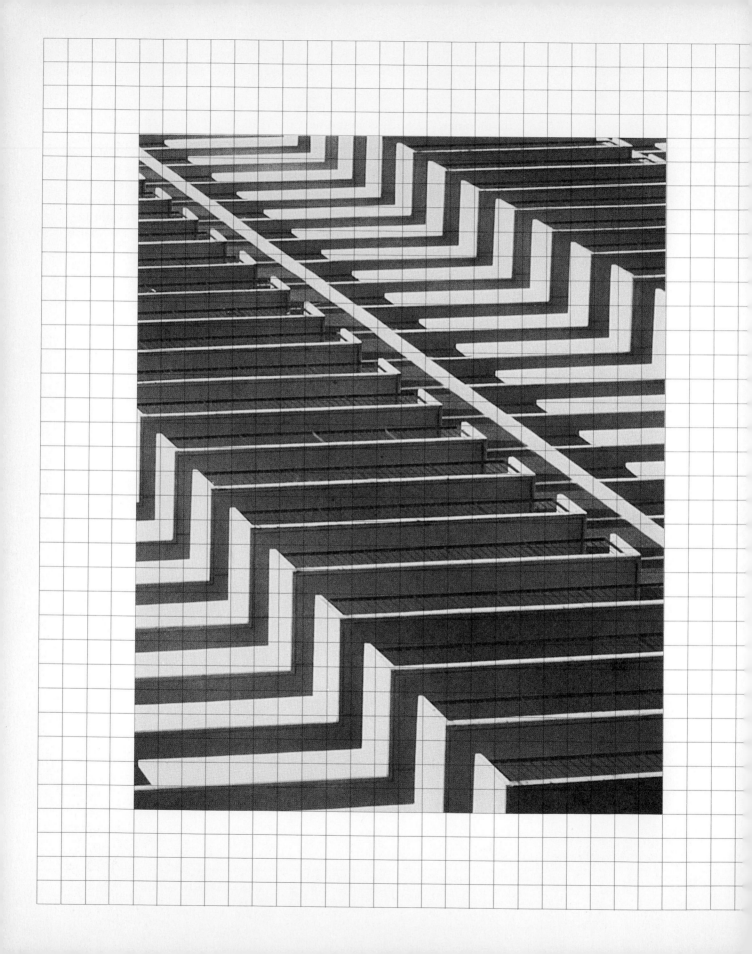

Part Six

Financial Statements, Interpretation and Modifications

18   Statement of Cash Flows

After studying Chapter 18, you should be able to:

1. Explain the differences between operating, investing, and financing activities, and assign a company's cash inflows and outflows to these categories.

2. Calculate cash inflows and outflows by inspecting the noncash account balances of a company and related information about its transactions.

3. Prepare a working paper for a statement of cash flows in which cash flows from operating activities are reported according to the direct method.

4. Prepare a statement of cash flows in which cash flows from operating activities are reported according to the direct method, and prepare a schedule of noncash investing and financing activities.

After studying the appendix at the end of this chapter, you should be able to:

5. Calculate the net cash provided or used by operating activities according to the indirect method and prepare the statement of cash flows.

6. Prepare a working paper for a statement of cash flows in which the net cash flows from operating activities are calculated by the indirect method.

Cash is the lifeblood of a business enterprise. It is the fuel that keeps a business alive. Without cash, employees and suppliers cannot be paid, loans cannot be repaid, and owners cannot receive dividends. In other words, a business must have an adequate amount of cash to operate. For reasons such as these, decision makers typically pay close attention to a company's cash position and the events and transactions that cause that position to change. Information about the events and transactions that affect the cash position of a company is reported in a financial statement called the **statement of cash flows.** By studying this chapter, you will learn how to prepare and interpret a statement of cash flows.

Why Cash Information Is Important

Information about cash flows can influence decision makers in many ways. For example, if a company's regular operations bring in more cash than it uses, investors will value the company higher than if property and equipment must be sold in order to finance operations. Information about cash flows can help creditors decide whether a company will have enough cash to pay its debts as they mature. Management and investors use cash flow information to evaluate a company's ability to meet unexpected obligations. Cash flow information is also used to evaluate a company's ability to take advantage of new business opportunities that may arise. These are just a few of the many ways in which cash flow information is useful to a variety of different people.

The importance of cash flow information to decision makers has directly influenced the thinking of accounting authorities. For example, the FASB's stated objectives of financial reporting clearly reflect the importance of cash flow information. The FASB stated that financial statements should include information:

> About how a business obtains and spends cash.
> About its borrowing and repayment activities.
> About the sale and repurchase of its ownership securities.
> About dividend payments and other distributions to its owners.
> About other factors that affect a company's liquidity or solvency.[1]

To accomplish these objectives, a financial statement is needed to summarize, classify, and report the periodic cash inflows and outflows of a business. This is achieved by preparing a statement of cash flows.

Statement of Cash Flows

In November 1987, the FASB issued *Statement of Financial Accounting Standards No. 95,* "Statement of Cash Flows." This standard requires businesses to include a statement of cash flows in all financial reports that contain both a balance sheet and an income statement. The primary purpose of this statement is to present information about a company's cash receipts and disbursements during the reporting period.

The content of the statement of cash flows is shown graphically in Illustration 18-1. In the illustration, note that cash flows are grouped in three

---

[1] FASB, *Statement of Financial Accounting Concepts No. 1,* "Objectives of Financial Reporting by Business Enterprises" (Stamford, Conn., 1978), par. 49. Copyright © by the Financial Accounting Standards Board, High Ridge Park, Stamford, Conn. 06905, U.S.A. Quoted (or excerpted) with permission. Copies of the complete document are available from the FASB.

Illustration 18-1   Categories of Information in the Statement of Cash Flows

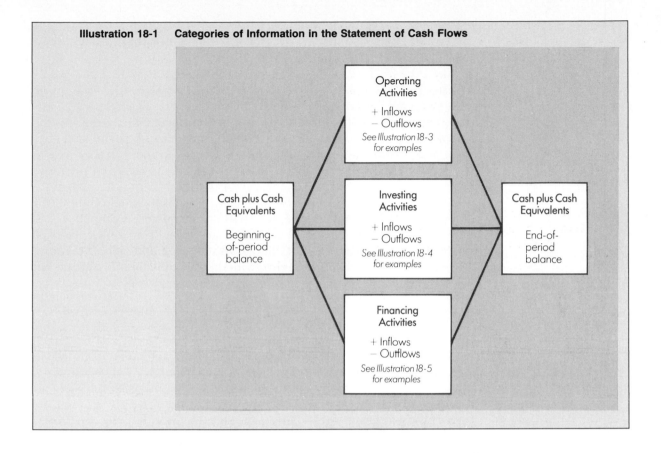

categories: cash flows from operating activities, cash flows from investing activities, and cash flows from financing activities. Within each category, there may be both inflows and outflows. Because all cash inflows and outflows are reported, the statement reconciles the beginning-of-period and end-of-period balances of cash plus cash equivalents.

Direct Method of Presenting Cash Flows from Operating Activities

When you prepare a statement of cash flows, the net cash provided (or used) by operating activities can be calculated two different ways. One is called the **direct method of calculating net cash provided (or used) by operating activities.** The other is the indirect method. When the direct method is used, you list separately each major class of operating cash receipts (e.g., cash received from customers) and each major class of cash payments (such as payments for merchandise). Then, the payments are subtracted from the receipts to determine the net cash provided (or used) by operating activities. The FASB encourages companies to use the direct method.

Indirect Method of Presenting Cash Flows from Operating Activities

The **indirect method of calculating net cash provided (or used) by operating activities** is less informative than the direct method. The indirect method is less informative because it does not disclose the individual cash inflows and outflows from operating activities. Instead, the only cash flow from operating activities that is disclosed by the indirect method is the **net** cash provided (or used) by operating activities.

When the indirect method is used, net income is listed first and then is adjusted for items that are necessary to reconcile net income to the net cash provided (or used) by operating activities. For example, you know that depreciation expense is subtracted in the calculation of net income. But, depreciation expense does not involve a current cash payment. Therefore, depreciation expense is added back to net income in the process of reconciling net income to the net cash provided (or used) by operating activities.

Since the direct method is most informative and is the method the FASB recommends, the remainder of this chapter is focused on that approach. However, the indirect method is allowed and some companies are likely to use that method in spite of the FASB's recommendation. Therefore, we explain and illustrate the indirect method in the appendix at the end of this chapter.

Designing the Statement of Cash Flows (Direct Method)

Illustration 18-2 contains the statement of cash flows for Grover Company. Notice that in the operating activities section of the statement, major classes of cash inflows and cash outflows are listed separately. This is the direct method. Within the operating activities category, the cash outflows are subtracted from the cash inflows to determine the net cash provided (or used) by operating activities. Also, in each of the other two categories,

---

Illustration 18-2

Grover Company
Statement of Cash Flows
For Year Ended December 31, 1988

Cash flows from operating activities:		
Cash received from customers	$570,000	
Cash payments for merchandise	(319,000)	
Payments for wages and other operating expenses	(218,000)	
Payments for interest	(8,000)	
Payments for taxes	(5,000)	
Net cash provided by operating activities		$ 20,000
Cash flows from investing activities:		
Cash paid for purchase of plant assets	$ (10,000)	
Cash received from sale of plant assets	12,000	
Net cash provided by investing activities		2,000
Cash flows from financing activities:		
Cash received from issuance of stock	$ 15,000	
Cash paid to retire bonds	(18,000)	
Cash paid for dividends	(14,000)	
Net cash used in financing activities		(17,000)
Net increase in cash		$ 5,000
Cash balance at beginning of 1988		12,000
Cash balance at end of 1988		$ 17,000

the cash outflows are subtracted from the cash inflows to determine the cash provided (or used) by those categories of transactions.

Compare Illustration 18-2 with Illustration 18-1. Notice that in Illustration 18-1, the beginning and ending balances are called *cash plus cash equivalents.* However, in Illustration 18-2, the beginning and ending balances refer only to cash. The balances in Illustration 18-2 are called *cash* simply because Grover Company does not own any **cash equivalents.** However, this difference between the two illustrations raises the question: What are cash equivalents?

Cash and Cash Equivalents

In *Statement of Financial Accounting Standards No. 95,* the FASB concluded that a statement of cash flows should explain the differences between the beginning and ending balances of cash and cash equivalents. Prior to this new standard, cash equivalents were generally understood to be short-term, temporary investments of cash. However, not all short-term investments meet the FASB's definition of cash equivalents. To qualify as a cash equivalent, an investment must satisfy two criteria. They are:

1. The investment must be readily convertible to a **known** amount of cash.
2. The investment must be sufficiently close to its maturity date so that its market value is relatively insensitive to interest rate changes.

In general, these criteria are satisfied only by investments that are purchased within three months of their maturity dates.[2] Examples of cash equivalents include short-term investments in U.S. Treasury bills, commercial paper, and money market funds.

The idea of classifying short-term, highly liquid investments as cash equivalents is based on the assumption that the reason companies make these investments is to earn a return on idle cash balances. However, some companies have other reasons for investing in items that meet the criteria of cash equivalents. For example, an investment company that specializes in the purchase and sale of securities may buy such items as part of its investing activities.

When items that meet the criteria of cash equivalents are not held as temporary investments of idle cash balances, the FASB allows companies to exclude them from the cash equivalents classification. Companies must develop a clear policy for determining which items are included and which are excluded. This policy must be disclosed in the footnotes to the financial statements and must be followed consistently from period to period.

■   **Classifying Cash Transactions**

Since a statement of cash flows describes the change in cash plus cash equivalents, cash payments to purchase cash equivalents and cash receipts from selling cash equivalents are not reported on the statement. All other cash receipts and payments are classified as operating, investing, or financing activities. Within each category, individual cash receipts and payments

[2] FASB, *Statement of Financial Accounting Standards No. 95,* "Statement of Cash Flows" (Stamford, Conn., 1987), par. 8. Copyright © by the Financial Accounting Standards Board, High Ridge Park, Stamford, Conn. 06905, U.S.A. Quoted (or excerpted) with permission. Copies of the complete document are available from the FASB.

are summarized and described in a manner that clearly presents the general nature of the company's cash transactions. Then, the summarized cash receipts and payments within each category are netted against each other. A category provides a net cash flow if the receipts in the category exceed the payments. And if the payments in a category exceed the receipts, the category is a net user of cash during the period.

Operating Activities

In Illustration 18-2, look at the types of cash flows that are reported as **operating activities.** You should recognize that operating activities generally include only transactions that relate to the calculation of net income. However, some income statement items are not related to operating activities. These items will be discussed later.

As disclosed in a statement of cash flows, operating activities are understood to involve the production or purchase of merchandise and the sale of goods and services to customers. Operating activities also include the expenditures related to administering the business. In fact, cash flows from operating activities include all cash flows from transactions that are not defined as investing or financing activities. Typical cash inflows and outflows from operating activities are shown in Illustration 18-3.

Investing Activities

Transactions that involve making and collecting loans or that involve purchasing and selling plant assets, other productive assets, and investments (other than cash equivalents) are called **investing activities.** Usually, investing activities involve the purchase or sale of assets that are classified on the balance sheet as plant and equipment, intangible assets, or long-term investments. However, the purchase and sale of short-term investments other than cash equivalents are also investing activities. Examples of cash flows from investing activities are shown in Illustration 18-4.

The second type of receipt listed in Illustration 18-4 involves proceeds from collecting the principal amount of loans. Regarding this item, cash receipts that relate to notes receivable must be examined carefully. If the notes resulted from sales to customers, the cash receipts are classified as

Illustration 18-3	Cash Flows from Operating Activities

Cash Inflows	**Cash Outflows**
Cash sales to customers.	Payments to employees for salaries and wages.
Cash collections from credit customers.	Payments to suppliers of goods and services.
Receipts of cash dividends from stock investments in other entities.	Payments to government agencies for taxes, fines, and penalties.
Receipts of interest payments.	Interest payments, net of amounts capitalized.
Refunds from suppliers.	Contributions to charities.
Cash collected from a lawsuit.	Cash refunds to customers.

Illustration 18-4   **Cash Flows from Investing Activities**

Cash Inflows	**Cash Outflows**
Proceeds from selling productive assets (e.g., land, buildings, equipment, natural resources, and intangible assets).	Payments to purchase property, plant and equipment or other productive assets (excluding merchandise inventory).
Proceeds from collecting the principal amount of loans.	Payments to acquire equity securities of other companies.
Proceeds from selling investments in the equity securities of other companies.	Payments to acquire debt securities of other entities, except cash equivalents.
Proceeds from selling investments in the debt securities of other entities, except cash equivalents.	Payments in the form of loans made to other parties.
Proceeds from the sale (discounting) of loans made by the enterprise.	

---

operating activities. This is true even if the notes are long-term notes. But, if a company loans money to other parties, the cash receipts from collecting the loans are classified as investing activities. Nevertheless, the FASB concluded that collections of **interest** are not investing activities; they are reported as operating activities.

Financing Activities

A company's transactions with its owners and long-term creditors are typically described as **financing activities.** Also, financing activities include borrowing cash on a short-term basis. However, cash payments to settle credit purchases of merchandise, whether on account or by note, are operating activities. Examples of cash flows from financing activities are shown in Illustration 18-5.

■ **Noncash Investing and Financing Activities**

Some important investing and financing activities do not involve cash receipts or payments during the current period. For example, a company might purchase land and buildings and finance 100 percent of the purchase by giving a long-term note payable. Although this transaction clearly in-

---

Illustration 18-5   **Cash Flows from Financing Activities**

Cash Inflows	**Cash Outflows**
Proceeds from the issuance of equity securities (e.g., common and preferred stock).	Payments of dividends and other distributions to owners.
Proceeds from the issuance of bonds and notes payable.	Payments to purchase treasury stock.
Proceeds from other short- or long-term borrowing transactions.	Repayments of cash loans.
	Payments of the principal amounts involved in long-term credit arrangements.

volves both investing and financing activities, it is not reported in the current period's statement of cash flows because no cash was received or paid.

Other investing and financing activities may involve some cash receipt or payment but also involve giving or receiving other types of consideration. An example would be the purchase of machinery valued at $12,000 by paying cash of $5,000 and trading in old machinery that has a market value of $7,000. In this case, the statement of cash flows reports only the $5,000 cash outflow for the purchase of machinery. As a result, this $12,000 investing transaction is only partially described in the statement of cash flows.

In its 1987 pronouncement, the FASB concluded that the noncash portions of investing and financing activities should **not** be reported in the statement of cash flows. However, the Board recognized that noncash investing and financing activities are important events that should be disclosed. To accomplish this, you must prepare a separate schedule of noncash investing and financing activities or provide a narrative description of these activities. Illustration 18-6 shows an example of how a company might disclose its noncash investing and financing activities.

In Illustration 18-6, notice the last item which describes an exchange of machinery. Following the requirements of the FASB, the schedule describes **both** the cash and noncash aspects of this transaction. The $5,000 cash payment is reported in Decco Company's statement of cash flows as an investing activity. Nevertheless, the schedule of noncash investing and financing activities includes both the cash and noncash aspects of the transaction.

Examples of transactions that must be disclosed as noncash investing and financing activities include the following:

The conversion of debt securities to equity securities.
The conversion of preferred stock into common stock.
The leasing of assets in a transaction that qualifies as a capital lease.
The purchase of long-term assets financed by a note payable to the seller.
The exchange of a noncash asset for other noncash assets.
The purchase of noncash assets in exchange for equity or debt securities.

■ **Preparing a Statement of Cash Flows**

The information needed to prepare a statement of cash flows comes from a variety of sources. They include comparative balance sheets at the beginning and the end of the accounting period, an income statement for the period, and a careful analysis of each noncash balance sheet account. How-

Illustration 18-6	**Decco Company—Schedule of Noncash Investing and Financing Activities**

The company issued 1,000 shares of common stock for the purchase of land and buildings with fair values of $5,000 and $15,000, respectively.

The company entered into a capital lease obligation of $12,000 for new computer equipment.

The company exchanged old machinery with a fair value of $7,000 and a book value of $8,000 for new machinery valued at $12,000. The balance of $5,000 was paid in cash.

ever, since our goal is to report cash inflows and cash outflows, we might begin our investigation by looking at the transactions recorded in the Cash account.

Analyzing the Cash Account

All of a company's cash receipts and cash payments are recorded in the Cash account in the general ledger. Therefore, the Cash account would seem to be the logical place to look for information about cash flows from operating, investing, and financing activities. To demonstrate, review the summarized Cash account of Grover Company presented below.

Summarized Cash Account, Grover Company

Balance, 1/1/88	12,000	Payments for mechandise	319,000
Receipts from customers	570,000	Payments for wages and other	
Proceeds from sale of plant		operating expenses	218,000
assets	12,000	Interest payments	8,000
Proceeds from stock issuance	15,000	Tax payments	5,000
		Payments for purchase of plant	
		assets	10,000
		Payments to retire bonds	18,000
		Dividend payments	14,000
Balance, 12/31/88	17,000		

In this account, the individual cash transactions have already been summarized in terms of major types of receipts and payments. For example, individual receipts from customers have been totaled and listed in the account as a single debit. All that remains is to determine whether each type of cash inflow or outflow is an operating, investing, or financing activity and to place it in its proper category on the statement of cash flows. The completed statement of cash flows appears in Illustration 18-2.

While an analysis of the Cash account may appear to be an easy way to prepare a statement of cash flows, it has two serious drawbacks. First, most companies have so many individual cash receipts and disbursements it is not practical to review them all. Imagine what a problem this would be for IBM, General Motors, Kodak, or Exxon, or even for a relatively small business. Second, the Cash account usually does not contain a description of each cash transaction. As a result, while you can determine the amount of each cash receipt and payment by looking at the Cash account, you generally cannot discover the nature of each transaction. Thus, the Cash account does not provide the information that you need to prepare a statement of cash flows. To obtain the necessary information, you must analyze the changes in the noncash accounts.

Analyzing Noncash Accounts to Determine Cash Flows

When a company records cash inflows and outflows with debits and credits to the Cash account, it also records credits and debits in other accounts. Some of these accounts are balance sheet accounts. Others are revenue and expense accounts which are closed to Retained Earnings, a balance sheet account. As a result, all cash transactions eventually affect the noncash balance sheet accounts. Therefore, the nature of the cash inflows and outflows can be determined by examining the changes in the noncash balance sheet accounts. This important relationship between the Cash account and the noncash balance sheet accounts is shown in Illustration 18-7.

In Illustration 18-7, notice that the balance sheet equation labeled (1) is expanded in (2) so that cash is separated from the other assets. Then, the equation is rearranged in (3) so that cash is set equal to the sum of the liability and equity accounts less the noncash asset accounts. The illustration then points out in (4) that changes in one side of the equation (cash) must be equal to the changes in the other side (noncash accounts). Part (4) makes the important point that if you discover the changes in liabilities, owners' equity, and noncash assets, it is possible to fully explain the changes in cash. This information is all that is necessary to prepare a statement of cash flows.

This overall process has one added advantage. The examination of each noncash account also identifies any noncash investing and financing activities that occurred during the period. As we mentioned earlier, these noncash items must also be disclosed, but not on the statement of cash flows.

When you begin to analyze the changes in the noncash balance sheet accounts, recall that Retained Earnings is affected by revenues, expenses, and dividend declarations. Therefore, you need to look at the income statement accounts to help explain the change in Retained Earnings. In fact, the income statement accounts provide important information that relates to the changes in several balance sheet accounts.

Some of these relationships between income statement accounts, balance sheet accounts, and possible cash flows are summarized in Illustration 18-8. For example, to determine the cash receipts from customers during a period, you must adjust the amount of sales revenue for the increase or

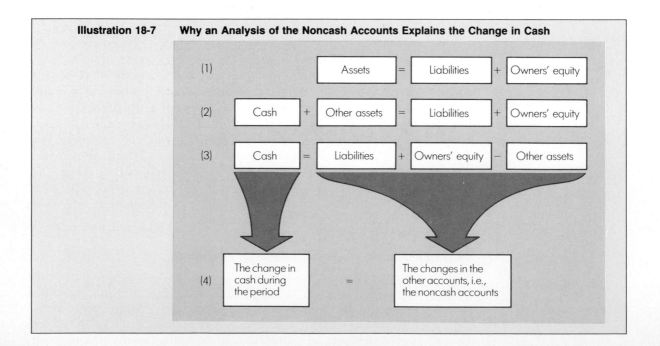

Illustration 18-7   Why an Analysis of the Noncash Accounts Explains the Change in Cash

(1)   Assets = Liabilities + Owners' equity

(2)   Cash + Other assets = Liabilities + Owners' equity

(3)   Cash = Liabilities + Owners' equity − Other assets

(4)   The change in cash during the period = The changes in the other accounts, i.e., the noncash accounts

---

Illustration 18-8   **Key Relationships between Income Statement Items and Balance Sheet Accounts**

Income Statement Items	Related Balance Sheet Accounts	Possible Cash Flow Effects
Sales	Accounts receivable	Cash receipts from customers
Cost of goods sold	Merchandise inventory, accounts payable	Cash payments to suppliers
Depreciation expense	Accumulated depreciation	None
Operating expenses	Prepaid expenses, accrued liabilities	Cash payments for operating expenses
Gain or loss on sale of plant assets	Plant assets, accumulated depreciation, notes receivable	Cash receipts from sale of plant assets
Gain or loss on retirement of bonds payable	Bonds payable, premium or discount on bonds payable	Cash payments for retirement of bonds

---

decrease in Accounts Receivable.[3] If the Accounts Receivable balance was unchanged, you may infer that the cash collected from customers is equal to sales revenue. On the other hand, if the Accounts Receivable balance decreased, cash collections must have been equal to sales revenue plus the reduction in Accounts Receivable. And if the Accounts Receivable balance increased, the cash collected from customers must have been equal to Sales less the increase in Accounts Receivable.

If you analyze all of the noncash balance sheet accounts and the related income statement accounts in this fashion, you will obtain the information you need for a statement of cash flows. So that you will clearly understand this process, we will illustrate this process by examining the accounts of Grover Company.

■ **Grover Company— A Comprehensive Example**

Grover Company's December 31, 1987 and 1988, balance sheets and its 1988 income statement are presented in Illustration 18-9. Our objective is to prepare a statement of cash flows that explains the $5,000 increase in Cash, based on these financial statements and the additional information about 1988 transactions that follows:

a. Accounts payable balances resulted from merchandise purchases.
b. Plant assets that cost $70,000 were purchased by paying $10,000 cash and issuing $60,000 of bonds payable to the seller.
c. Plant assets with an original cost of $30,000 and accumulated depreciation of $12,000 were sold for $12,000 cash. The result was a $6,000 loss.

---

[3] This introductory explanation assumes there is no bad debts expense. However, if bad debts occur and are written off directly to Accounts Receivable, the change in the Accounts Receivable balance will be due in part to the write-off. The remaining change results from credit sales and from cash receipts. This chapter does not discuss the allowance method of accounting for bad debts since it would make the analysis unnecessarily complex at this time.

d. The proceeds from issuing 3,000 shares of common stock was $15,000.
e. The $16,000 gain on retirement of bonds resulted from paying $18,000 to retire bonds with a book value of $34,000.
f. Cash dividends of $14,000 were declared and paid.

Operating Activities

We begin the analysis by calculating the cash flows from operating activities. In general, this involves adjusting the income statement items related to operating activities for changes in their related balance sheet accounts.

Cash Received from Customers The calculation of cash receipts from customers begins with sales revenue. If all sales are for cash, the amount of cash received from customers is equal to sales. However, when sales are on account, you must adjust the amount of sales revenue for the change in Accounts Receivable to determine the cash received.

In Illustration 18-9, look at the Accounts Receivable balances on December 31, 1987 and 1988. The beginning balance was $40,000 and the ending balance was $60,000. And the income statement shows that sales revenue was $590,000. With this information, we can reconstruct the Accounts Receivable account and determine the amount of cash received from customers, as follows:

Accounts Receivable

12/31/87 Bal.	40,000		
1988 Sales	590,000	**Collections =**	**570,000**
12/31/88 Bal.	60,000		

This account shows that since the balance of Accounts Receivable increased from $40,000 to $60,000, cash receipts from customers are equal to sales of $590,000 plus the $40,000 beginning balance less the $60,000 ending balance, or $570,000. To state the calculation in more general terms:

Cash received from customers = Sales − Increase in accounts receivable

And if the balance of Accounts Receivable decreases, the calculation is:

Cash received from customers = Sales + Decrease in accounts receivable

Now turn back to Illustration 18-2 and note that the $570,000 of cash Grover Company received from customers is shown on the statement of cash flows as a cash inflow from operating activities.

Cash Payments for Merchandise The calculation of cash payments for merchandise begins with cost of goods sold and merchandise inventory. Suppose for a moment that all merchandise purchases are for cash and that the ending balance of Merchandise Inventory is unchanged from the beginning balance. In this case, the total cash payments for merchandise is equal to cost of goods sold. However, this is not a typical case. Usually, you would expect some amount of change in a company's Merchandise Inventory balance during a period. Also, purchases of merchandise usually are made

Illustration 18-9

Grover Company
Balance Sheet
December 31, 1988 and 1987

	1988		**1987**	
Assets				
Current assets:				
Cash		$ 17,000		$ 12,000
Accounts receivable		60,000		40,000
Merchandise inventory		84,000		70,000
Prepaid expenses		6,000		4,000
Total current assets		$167,000		$126,000
Long-term assets:				
Plant assets	$250,000		$210,000	
Less accumulated depreciation	60,000	190,000	48,000	162,000
Total assets		$357,000		$288,000
Liabilities				
Current liabilities:				
Accounts payable		$ 35,000		$ 40,000
Interest payable		3,000		4,000
Income taxes payable		22,000		12,000
Total current liabilities		$ 60,000		$ 56,000
Long-term liabilities:				
Bonds payable		90,000		64,000
Total liabilities		$150,000		$120,000
Stockholders' Equity				
Contributed capital:				
Common stock, $10 par value	$ 95,000		$ 80,000	
Retained earnings	112,000		88,000	
Total stockholders' equity		207,000		168,000
Total liabilities and stockholders' equity		$357,000		$288,000

Income Statement
For Year Ended December 31, 1988

Sales		$590,000
Cost of goods sold	$300,000	
Wages and other operating expenses	216,000	
Interest expense	7,000	
Income taxes expense	15,000	
Depreciation expense	24,000	(562,000)
Loss on sale of plant assets		(6,000)
Gain on retirement of debt		16,000
Net income		$ 38,000

on account, and you would expect some amount of change in the Accounts Payable balance.

When the balances of Merchandise Inventory and Accounts Payable change, you must adjust cost of goods sold for the changes in these accounts to determine the cash payments for merchandise. This involves two steps.

First, the change in the balance of Merchandise Inventory is combined with cost of goods sold to determine the cost of purchases during the period. Second, the change in the balance of Accounts Payable is combined with the cost of purchases to determine the total cash payments to suppliers of merchandise.

Consider the example of Grover Company. First, the reported amount of cost of goods sold ($300,000) is combined with the Merchandise Inventory beginning balance ($70,000) and with the ending balance ($84,000) to determine the amount that was purchased during the period. This can be accomplished by reconstructing the Merchandise Inventory account, as follows:

Merchandise Inventory

12/31/87 Bal.	70,000		
Purchases =	**314,000**	Cost of goods sold	300,000
12/31/88 Bal.	84,000		

This account shows that the $14,000 increase in merchandise inventory must be added to cost of goods sold of $300,000 to get purchases of $314,000.

To determine the cash paid for merchandise, you must adjust purchases for the change in accounts payable. This can be done by reconstructing the Accounts Payable account, as follows:

Accounts Payable

		12/31/87 Bal.	40,000
Payments =	**319,000**	Purchases	314,000
		12/31/88 Bal.	35,000

In this account, you can see that purchases of $314,000 plus a beginning balance of $40,000, less the ending balance of $35,000, equals cash payments of $319,000. In other words, purchases of $314,000 plus the $5,000 decrease in accounts payable equals cash payments of $319,000.

To summarize the adjustments to cost of goods sold that are necessary to calculate cash payments for merchandise:

$$\text{Purchases} = \text{Cost of goods sold} \begin{bmatrix} + \text{ Increase in merchandise inventory} \\ or \\ - \text{ Decrease in merchandise inventory} \end{bmatrix}$$

And,

$$\begin{matrix} \text{Cash payments} \\ \text{for merchandise} \end{matrix} = \text{Purchases} \begin{bmatrix} + \text{ Decrease in accounts payable} \\ or \\ - \text{ Increase in accounts payable} \end{bmatrix}$$

For Grover Company, look at Illustration 18-2 and notice that payments for merchandise of $319,000 are reported on the statement of cash flows as a cash outflow from operating activities.

Cash Payments for Wages and Other Operating Expenses Grover Company's income statement shows wages and other operating expenses of $216,000 (see Illustration 18-9). To determine the amount of cash paid during the period for wages and other operating expenses, you must combine this amount with the changes in any related balance sheet accounts. In Grover Company's beginning and ending balance sheets (Illustration 18-9), you must look for prepaid expenses and any accrued liabilities that relate to wages and other operating expenses. In this example, the balance sheets show that Grover Company has prepaid expenses but does not have any accrued liabilities. Thus, the adjustment to the expense item is limited to the change in prepaid expenses. The amount of the adjustment can be determined by assuming that all cash payments of wages and other operating expenses were originally debited to Prepaid Expenses. With this assumption, we can reconstruct the Prepaid Expenses account as follows:

	Prepaid Expenses		
12/31/87 Bal.	4,000		
Payments	**218,000**	Wages and other	
		operating expenses	216,000
12/31/88 Bal.	6,000		

This account shows that because prepaid expenses increased by $2,000 during the period, the cash payments for wages and other operating expenses were $2,000 more than the reported expense. Thus, the amount paid for wages and other operating expenses is $216,000 plus $2,000, or $218,000.

In reconstructing the Prepaid Expenses account, we assumed that all cash payments for wages and operating expenses were debited to Prepaid Expenses. However, this assumption does not have to be true. If cash payments were debited directly to the expense account, the total amount of cash payments would be the same. In other words, the cash paid for operating expenses still equals the $216,000 expense plus the $2,000 increase in prepaid expenses.

If Grover Company's balance sheets had shown accrued liabilities, the expense would also have had to be adjusted for the change in accrued liabilities. In general terms, the calculation is as follows:

$$
\begin{array}{c}\text{Cash paid for}\\\text{wages and}\\\text{other operating}\\\text{expenses}\end{array} = \begin{array}{c}\text{Wages}\\\text{and other}\\\text{operating}\\\text{expenses}\end{array} \begin{bmatrix}+\text{ Increase in prepaid expenses}\\or\\-\text{ Decrease in prepaid expenses}\end{bmatrix} \begin{bmatrix}+\text{ Decrease in accrued liabilities}\\or\\-\text{ Increase in accrued liabilities}\end{bmatrix}
$$

Payments for Interest and Taxes Grover Company's remaining operating cash flows involve cash payments for interest and for taxes. The analysis of these items is similar because both require adjustments for changes in related liability accounts. Grover Company's income statement shows interest expense of $7,000 and income taxes expense of $15,000. To calculate the related cash payments, interest expense must be adjusted for the change in interest payable and income taxes expense must be adjusted for the change in income taxes payable. These calculations are accomplished by reconstructing the liability accounts, as follows:

Interest Payable				**Income Taxes Payable**		
		12/31/87 Bal.	4,000		12/31/87 Bal.	12,000
Interest paid =	8,000	Interest exp.	7,000	Income taxes paid = 5,000	Income tax exp.	15,000
		12/31/88 Bal.	3,000		12/31/88 Bal.	22,000

These reconstructed accounts show that interest payments were $8,000 and income tax payments were $5,000. The general form of each calculation is:

$$\text{Cash payment} = \text{Expense} \begin{bmatrix} + \text{ Decrease in related payable} \\ or \\ - \text{ Increase in related payable} \end{bmatrix}$$

Both of these cash payments appear as operating items on Grover Company's statement of cash flows in Illustration 18-2.

Investing Activities

Investing activities usually refer to transactions that affect long-term assets. Recall from the information that was provided about Grover Company's transactions that the company purchased plant assets and also sold plant assets. Both of these transactions are investing activities.

Purchase of Plant Assets Grover Company purchased plant assets that cost $70,000 by issuing $60,000 of bonds payable to the seller and paying the $10,000 balance in cash. The $10,000 payment is reported as a cash outflow on the statement of cash flows (see Illustration 18-2). Also, since $60,000 of the purchase was financed by issuing bonds payable, this transaction involves noncash investing and financing activities. Therefore, it must be described in a schedule of noncash investing and financing activities or described narratively in the financial statement footnotes. This description might appear as follows:

Schedule of Noncash Investing and Financing Activities:
Purchased plant assets	$70,000
Issued bonds payable to finance purchase	60,000
Balance paid in cash	$10,000

Sale of Plant Assets Grover Company sold plant assets that cost $30,000 and had been depreciated $12,000. The sale resulted in a loss of $6,000 and a cash receipt of $12,000. This cash receipt is reported in the statement of cash flows as a cash inflow from investing activities (see Illustration 18-2).

Recall from Grover Company's income statement that depreciation expense was $24,000. Depreciation does not use or provide cash. However, we should notice the effects of depreciation expense, the plant asset purchase, and the plant asset sale on the Plant Assets and Accumulated Depreciation accounts. These accounts are reconstructed, as follows:

Plant Assets				Accumulated Depreciation		
12/31/87 Bal.	210,000				12/31/87 Bal.	48,000
Purchase	70,000	Sale	30,000	Sale 12,000		24,000
12/31/88 Bal.	250,000				12/31/88 Bal.	60,000

The beginning and ending balances of these accounts were taken from Grover Company's balance sheets (Illustration 18-9). Reconstructing the accounts shows that the beginning and ending balances of both accounts are completely reconciled by the purchase, the sale, and the depreciation expense. As a result, you can conclude that you have not omitted any of the investing activities related to plant assets.

Financing Activities

Financing activities usually relate to a company's long-term debt and stockholders' equity accounts. The information about Grover Company indicated that four transactions had occurred that involved financing activities. One of these, the $60,000 issuance of bonds payable to purchase plant assets, was discussed previously as a noncash investing and financing activity. The remaining three transactions were the retirement of bonds, the issuance of common stock, and the payment of cash dividends.

Payment to Retire Bonds Payable Grover Company's December 31, 1987, balance sheet showed bonds payable of $34,000 which were retired in 1988 by paying $18,000 cash. The income statement reports the $16,000 difference as a gain. The statement of cash flows shows the $18,000 payment as a cash outflow from financing activities (see Illustration 18-2).

Notice that the beginning and ending balances of Bonds Payable are reconciled by the $60,000 issuance of new bonds and the retirement of $34,000 of old bonds. This is shown in the reconstructed Bonds Payable account that follows:

Bonds Payable			
		12/31/87 Bal.	64,000
Retired bonds	34,000	Issued bonds	60,000
		12/31/88 Bal.	90,000

Receipt from Common Stock Issuance During 1988, Grover Company issued 3,000 shares of common stock for $5 per share. This $15,000 cash receipt is reported on the statement of cash flows as a financing activity. Look at the beginning and ending balance sheets in Illustration 18-9, and notice that the Common Stock account balance increased from $80,000 at the beginning of the year to $95,000 at the end of the year. Thus, the $15,000 stock issue reconciles the change in the Common Stock account.

Payment of Cash Dividends According to the facts provided about Grover Company's transactions, cash dividends of $14,000 were paid during 1988. This payment is reported as a cash outflow from financing activities. Also, note that the effects of this $14,000 payment and the reported net income of $38,000 fully reconcile the beginning and ending balances of Retained Earnings. This is shown in the reconstructed Retained Earnings account that follows:

<table>
<tr><td colspan="4" align="center">**Retained Earnings**</td></tr>
<tr><td></td><td></td><td>12/31/87 Bal.</td><td>88,000</td></tr>
<tr><td>Cash dividend</td><td>14,000</td><td>Net income</td><td>38,000</td></tr>
<tr><td></td><td></td><td>12/31/88 Bal.</td><td>112,000</td></tr>
</table>

All of Grover Company's cash inflows and outflows have been described in the previous paragraphs. We also described one noncash investing and financing transaction. In the process of making these analyses, we reconciled the changes in all of the noncash balance sheet accounts. The change in the Cash account is reconciled by the statement of cash flows, as shown in Illustration 18-2.

■ Preparing a Working Paper for a Statement of Cash Flows (Direct Method)

When a company has a large number of accounts and many operating, investing, and financing transactions, the analysis of noncash accounts can be difficult and confusing. In these situations, a working paper can help you organize the information needed for a statement of cash flows. A working paper also makes it easier for you to check the accuracy of your work.

Designing the Working Paper

Examine the working paper for Grover Company presented in Illustration 18-10. Observe that the balance sheet account balances at the beginning and end of the period have been entered in the first and fourth money columns, respectively. The middle two columns are for reconciling the differences in these balances and for the development of the statement of cash flows.

The process of reconciling the changes in the balance sheet accounts begins with the income statement. The income statement is recorded below the balance sheet in the Analysis of Changes columns, and the statement of cash flows is developed below the income statement. As noncash investing and financing activities are identified during the analysis, they are recorded at the bottom of the working paper.

In Illustration 18-10, note that the beginning and ending balances of each noncash balance sheet account have been reconciled by the amounts shown in the Analysis of Changes columns. Look at the Cash account

Illustration 18-10

Grover Corporation
Working Paper for Statement of Cash Flows (Direct Method)
For Year Ended December 31, 1988

	December 31, 1987	Analysis of Changes		December 31, 1988
		Debit	**Credit**	
Balance sheet—Debits:				
Cash	12,000			17,000
Accounts receivable	40,000	(a1) 590,000	(a2) 570,000	60,000
Merchandise inventory	70,000	(b2) 314,000	(b1) 300,000	84,000
Prepaid expenses	4,000	(c2) 2,000		6,000
Plant assets	210,000	(j1) 70,000	(g) 30,000	250,000
	336,000			417,000
Balance sheet—Credits:				
Accumulated depreciation	48,000	(g) 12,000	(f) 24,000	60,000
Accounts payable	40,000	(b3) 319,000	(b2) 314,000	35,000
Interest payable	4,000	(d2) 8,000	(d1) 7,000	3,000
Income taxes payable	12,000	(e2) 5,000	(e1) 15,000	22,000
Bonds payable	64,000	(h) 34,000	(j2) 60,000	90,000
Common stock, $5 par value	80,000		(k) 15,000	95,000
Retained earnings	88,000	(l) 14,000	(l) 38,000	112,000
	336,000			417,000
Income statement:				
Sales			(a1) 590,000	
Cost of goods sold		(b1) 300,000		
Wages and other operating expenses . . .		(c1) 216,000		
Interest expense		(d1) 7,000		
Income taxes expense		(e1) 15,000		
Depreciation expense		(f) 24,000		
Loss on sale of plant assets		(g) 6,000		
Gain on retirement of bonds			(h) 16,000	
Net income		(i) 38,000		
Statement of cash flows:				
Operating activities:				
Receipts from customers		(a2) 570,000		
Payments for merchandise			(b3) 319,000	
Payments for wages and other			(c1) 216,000	
operating expenses			(c2) 2,000	
Payments for interest			(d2) 8,000	
Payments for taxes			(e2) 5,000	
Investing activities:				
Receipt from sale of plant assets		(g) 12,000		
Payment to purchase plant assets			(j1) 10,000	
Financing activities:				
Payment to retire bonds			(h) 18,000	
Receipts from issuance of stock		(k) 15,000		
Payments of dividends			(l) 14,000	
Noncash investing and financing activities:				
Purchase of plant assets financed				
by bonds		(j2) 60,000	(j1) 60,000	
		2,631,000	2,631,000	

and note that the Analysis of Changes columns are empty. The reconciliation of the Cash account is not done on the Cash account row. Instead, the Cash account is reconciled by all of the items shown in the statement of cash flows section of the working paper.

Three characteristics of the working paper in Illustration 18-10 are particularly important. First, it is designed to provide the information you need to report cash flows from operating activities by the direct method. Second, it provides all the information necessary to prepare the statement of cash flows. You can see this if you compare the statement of cash flows section of the working paper with the formal statement of cash flows shown in Illustration 18-2. Third, the working paper also provides the information necessary to disclose the noncash investing and operating activities.

Basic Steps to Prepare a Working Paper (Direct Method)

The information you need to prepare the working paper includes an income statement, the beginning and ending balance sheets, and other information about the activities of the period. There are six basic steps to prepare a working paper that includes enough information to report cash flows from operating activities by the direct method. They are:

1. List the beginning balance sheet in the first column and the ending balance sheet in the fourth column. Debit balance accounts are listed first and credit balance accounts second. Total and prove the equality of the debits and credits in each balance sheet.
2. List each income statement item below the balance sheets and enter its amount in the Analysis of Changes columns (debit for expense, credit for revenue). As you record each income statement credit, also record the corresponding debit next to the appropriate noncash balance sheet account. And as you record each income statement debit, record the corresponding credit next to the related noncash balance sheet account.

    After an income statement item is entered, analyze the changes in the noncash balance sheet accounts related to that income statement item. Examples of these relationships are listed in Illustration 18-8. In the process of entering these changes, any cash flow effect is entered in the statement of cash flows section of the working paper.

    If an expense (or revenue) was paid (or received) in cash, it had no effect on any of the noncash balance sheet accounts. Therefore, when you record the expense (or revenue) in the income statement section of the working paper, the corresponding credit (or debit) should be entered as a cash outflow in the statement of cash flows section of the working paper.
3. As you enter income statement gains and losses, reconstruct the entries that created the gains or losses. These entries help reconcile the balance sheet accounts. The cash effects of gain and loss transactions are recorded as inflows or outflows in the investing or financing categories of the statement of cash flows.
4. Cross-reference the debits and credits of each entry by assigning them a letter (and number if more than one entry is needed to determine a specific cash flow). As your analyses of changes begin to fill out the income statement and statement of cash flows sections of the working

paper, leave some blank lines in each category to allow room for the rest of your analyses.

5. Review each balance sheet account to determine whether any differences between beginning and ending balances remain unreconciled. If any remain, examine the additional information about the activities of the company and enter the necessary reconciling amounts in the Analysis of Changes columns.

6. To prove the arithmetic accuracy of your work, total the two middle columns and note that they are equal.

Entering the Analysis of Changes on the Working Paper

To help you understand the relationship between the items entered in the Analysis of Changes columns of the working paper and the facts of the Grover Company example, the information about the income statement and other transactions is restated below. Each item of information is identified with a letter (and sometimes a number) that corresponds to the entries on the working paper.

As you study the information below and the working paper in Illustration 18-10, you can clarify any items that appear confusing by reviewing the previous section of the chapter. Recall that each cash flow was calculated and explained by reconstructing the related noncash accounts.

Items *(a1)* and *(a2)* provide the facts and the analysis of changes that relate to **receipts from customers.**

(a1) Sales revenue was $590,000. On the working paper, the analysis of change labeled *(a1)* enters the sales revenue as a credit in the income statement section and as a debit to Accounts Receivable. This starts the reconciliation of the change in Accounts Receivable.

(a2) Receipts from customers were the only source of decreases in Accounts Receivable. On the working paper, the analysis of change labeled *(a2)* enters the receipts from customers as an operating activity and as a decrease in Accounts Receivable. This completes the reconciliation of the change in Accounts Receivable.

Notice that the analysis of *(a1)* and *(a2)* assumes that all sales were on account. However, even if some sales had been for cash, the analysis would correctly determine cash receipts from customers. Whether sales are for cash or on account, total cash receipts from customers equals sales revenue minus the increase (or plus the decrease) in Accounts Receivable.

Items *(b1)*, *(b2)*, and *(b3)* provide the facts and the analysis of changes that relate to **cash payments for merchandise.**

(b1) Cost of goods sold was $300,000. On the working paper, the analysis of change entry enters cost of goods sold in the income statement section and reduces Merchandise Inventory.

(b2) Purchases of merchandise were on credit. This entry on the working paper increases Merchandise Inventory and increases Accounts Payable. Note that Merchandise Inventory is now reconciled.

(b3) The only decreases in Accounts Payable involved payments to creditors. The entry labeled *(b3)* reconciles the Accounts Payable account and records the cash payment for merchandise as an operating activity.

Items *(c1)* and *(c2)* provide the facts and the analysis of changes related to **cash payments for wages and other operating expenses.**

(c1) Wages and other operating expenses were $216,000 and were paid in cash. On the working paper, entry *(c1)* records these expenses and shows them as a cash outflow from operating activities.

(c2) Prepaid expenses increased. Entry *(c2)* reconciles the Prepaid Expense account and increases the amount of cash paid for wages and other operating expenses.

Items *(d1)* and *(d2)* provide the facts and the analysis of changes related to **payments for interest.**

(d1) Interest expense was $7,000. Entry *(d1),* which assumes that all interest was accrued before being paid, records interest expense and credits Interest Payable.

(d2) Decreases in Interest Payable involved payments of interest. Entry *(d2)* reconciles the Interest Payable account and classifies the cash payment of interest as an operating activity.

Items *(e1)* and *(e2)* provide the facts and the analysis of changes related to **payments for taxes.**

(e1) Income taxes expense was $15,000. Entry *(e1),* which assumes that taxes were accrued before being paid, records the expense and credits Income Taxes Payable.

(e2) Payments of taxes were debited to Income Taxes Payable. Entry *(e2)* reconciles the Income Taxes Payable account and classifies the cash payments of taxes as an operating activity.

(f) Depreciation expense was $24,000. Entry *(f)* records the expense and credits the Accumulated Depreciation account. This begins the reconciliation of Accumulated Depreciation.

(g) Plant assets with an original cost of $30,000 and accumulated depreciation of $12,000 were sold for $12,000 cash. The result was a $6,000 loss. Entry *(g)* decreases Plant Assets, completes the reconciliation of Accumulated Depreciation, enters the loss in the income statement section, and classifies the cash **receipt from sale of plant assets** as an investing activity.

(h) A $16,000 gain on retirement of bonds resulted from paying $18,000 to retire bonds with a book value of $34,000. Entry *(h)* decreases bonds payable, enters the gain in the income statement section, and classifies the cash **payment to retire bonds** as a financing activity.

(i) Net income amounted to $38,000. Entry *(i)* completes the income statement section and helps start the reconciliation of Retained Earnings.

Items *(j1)* and *(j2)* provide the facts and the analysis of changes related to the purchase of plant assets, the issuance of bonds payable to finance part of the purchase, and the remaining cash **payment to purchase plant assets.**

(j1) Plant assets that cost $70,000 were purchased by paying $10,000 cash and issuing $60,000 of bonds payable. Entry *(j1)* completes the reconciliation of Plant Assets, classifies the cash payment as an investing

activity, and shows the bond issue to be part of a noncash investing and financing transaction.

(j2) The issuance of bonds to purchase plant assets was recorded by increasing Bonds Payable. Entry *(j2)* completes the reconciliation of Bonds Payable and classifies this portion of the purchase to be part of a noncash investing and financing transaction.

(k) The proceeds from issuing 3,000 shares of common stock were $15,000. Entry *(k)* reconciles the Common Stock account and classifies the **receipt from issuing stock** as a financing activity.

(l) Cash dividends of $14,000 were declared and paid. Entry *(l)* completes the reconciliation of Retained Earnings and classifies the **payment of dividends** as a financing activity.

After all the above analyses have been performed, note that the balances of each noncash balance sheet account have been completely reconciled. The Analysis of Changes columns are now totaled and shown to be equal.

■ **Reconciling Net Income to Net Cash Provided (or Used) by Operating Activities**

As we explained earlier, the FASB recommends that the statement of cash flows be prepared according to the direct method. This means the statement discloses each major class of cash inflows and outflows from operating activities. However, when the direct method is used, the FASB also requires that companies disclose a reconciliation of net income to the net cash provided (or used) by operating activities. This reconciliation is precisely what is meant by the indirect method of calculating the net cash provided (or used) by operating activities. The indirect method is explained in the following appendix.

APPENDIX: THE INDIRECT METHOD OF CALCULATING NET CASH PROVIDED (OR USED) BY OPERATING ACTIVITIES

When the indirect method is used, net income is listed first and then is adjusted for items that are necessary to reconcile the net income amount to the net cash provided (or used) by operating activities. To see the results of the indirect method, look at Illustration 18–11. This illustration shows the reconciliation of Grover Company's net income to the net cash provided by operating activities.

In Illustration 18-11, notice that the net cash provided by operating activities is $20,000. This is the same amount that was reported on the statement of cash flows (direct method) in Illustration 18-2. However, these illustrations show entirely different ways to calculate the $20,000 net cash inflow. In Illustration 18-2 (the direct method), major classes of operating cash outflows were subtracted from major classes of cash inflows. By comparison, none of the individual cash inflows or cash outflows are reported in Illustration 18-11 (the indirect method). Instead, net income is adjusted to exclude amounts that were included in the determination of net income but which did not provide operating cash inflows or outflows during the period.

There are three types of adjustments shown in Illustration 18-11. The adjustments grouped under (1) are for changes in noncash current assets

Illustration 18-11   **Grover Company—Reconciliation of Net Income to Net Cash Provided by Operating Activities**

Net income		$ 38,000
Adjustments to reconcile net income to net cash provided by operating activities:		
1 Increase in accounts receivable	$(20,000)	
Increase in merchandise inventory	(14,000)	
Increase in prepaid expenses	(2,000)	
Decrease in accounts payable	(5,000)	
Decrease in interest payable	(1,000)	
Increase in income taxes payable	10,000	
2 Depreciation expense	24,000	
3 Loss on sale of plant assets	6,000	
Gain on retirement of bonds	(16,000)	
Total adjustments		(18,000)
Net cash provided by operating activities		$ 20,000

and current liabilities that relate to operating activities. The adjustments identified as (2) are for other items that relate to operating activities but which did not provide cash inflows or cash outflows during the period. The adjustments grouped under (3) eliminate gains and losses that do not relate to operating activities. These gains and losses resulted from investing and financing activities.

■ **Adjustments for Changes in Current Assets and Current Liabilities**

To help you understand why adjustments for changes in noncash current assets and current liabilities are necessary, we will use as an example the transactions of a very simple company. Assume that Simple Company's income statement shows only two items, as follows:

Sales	$20,000
Operating expenses . . .	12,000
Net income	$ 8,000

For a moment, assume that all of Simple Company's sales and operating expenses are for cash. The company has no current assets other than cash and has no current liabilities. Given these assumptions, the net cash provided by operating activities during the period is $8,000, which is the cash received from customers less the cash paid for operating expenses. The net cash provided by operating activities also equals net income.

Adjustments for Changes in Noncash Current Assets

Now assume that Simple Company's sales are on account. Also assume that its Accounts Receivable balance was $2,000 at the beginning of the year and $2,500 at the end of the year. Under these assumptions, cash receipts from customers equal sales of $20,000 minus the $500 increase in Accounts Receivable, or $19,500. Therefore, using the direct method, the net cash provided by operating activities is $19,500 − $12,000 = $7,500.

When the indirect method is used to calculate the net cash flow, net income of $8,000 is adjusted for the $500 increase in Accounts Receivable to get a net cash provided by operating activities of $7,500. Both calculations are as follows:

Direct Method:

Receipts from customers ($20,000 − $500) . .	$ 19,500
Payments for operating expenses	−12,000
Cash provided by operating activities	$ 7,500

Indirect Method:

Net income	$ 8,000
Less the increase in Accounts Receivable . .	−500
Cash provided by operating activities	$ 7,500

Notice that the increase in Accounts Receivable is **subtracted** from net income in the indirect method calculation.

As an alternative example, assume that the Accounts Receivable balance decreased from $2,000 to $1,200. Under this assumption, cash receipts from customers equal sales of $20,000 plus the $800 decrease in Accounts Receivable, or $20,800. By the direct method, the net cash provided by operating activities is $20,800 − $12,000 = $8,800. And when the indirect method is used, the $800 decrease in Accounts Receivable is **added** to the $8,000 net income to get $8,800 net cash provided by operating activities.

When the indirect method is used, adjustments like those for Accounts Receivable are required for all noncash current assets related to operating activities. When a noncash current asset increases, part of the assets derived from operating activities are allocated to the increase, leaving a smaller amount as a net cash inflow. Therefore, when you calculate the net cash inflow using the indirect method, the noncash current asset increase must be **subtracted** from net income. But when a noncash current asset decreases, the opposite adjustment is necessary. These adjustments for changes in current assets related to operating activities are as follows:

Net income
Add: Decreases in current assets
Subtract: Increases in current assets
Net cash provided (or used) by operating activities

Adjustments for Changes in Current Liabilities

To illustrate the adjustments for changes in current liabilities, we return to the original assumptions about Simple Company. Sales of $20,000 are for cash, and operating expenses are $12,000. However, assume now that

Simple Company has one current liability, Interest Payable, that relates to operating expenses. Also assume that the beginning-of-year balance in Interest Payable was $500 and the end-of-year balance was $900. This increase means that the operating expenses of $12,000 include $400 of interest that was not paid in cash during the period. Therefore, the cash payments for operating expenses were $11,600, or ($12,000 − $400). Under these assumptions, the direct method calculation of net cash provided by operating activities is $8,400, or $20,000 receipts from customers less $11,600 payments for expenses. The indirect method calculation of $8,400 is net income of $8,000 plus the $400 increase in Interest Payable.

Alternatively, if the Interest Payable balance had decreased, say by $600, the cash outflow for operating expenses would have been the $12,000 expense plus the $600 liability decrease, or $12,600. Then, the direct calculation of net cash flow is $20,000 − $12,600 = $7,400. The indirect calculation is $8,000 − $600 = $7,400. In other words, when the indirect method is used, a **decrease** in Interest Payable is **subtracted** from net income.

When the indirect method is used, adjustments like those for Interest Payable are required for all current liabilities related to operating activities. When a current liability decreases, part of assets derived from operating activities are allocated to pay for the decrease. Therefore, the decrease is subtracted from net income to determine the remaining net cash inflow. And when a current liability increases, the opposite adjustment is necessary. These adjustments for changes in current liabilities related to operating activities are:

Net income
Add: Increase in current liabilities
Subtract: Decrease in current liabilities

Net cash provided by operating activities

Adjustments for Other Operating Items that Do Not Provide or Use Cash

Some operating items that appear on an income statement do not provide or use cash during the current period. An obvious example is depreciation. Other examples are amortization of intangible assets, depletion of natural resources, and bad debts expense.

These expenses are recorded with debits to expense accounts and credits to noncash accounts. They reduce net income but do not require cash outflows during the period. Therefore, when adjustments to net income are made according to the indirect method, these noncash expenses must be added back to net income.

In addition to noncash expenses such as depreciation, net income may include some revenues that do not provide cash inflows during the current period. An example is equity method earnings from a stock investment in another entity. If net income includes revenues that do not provide cash inflows, the revenues must be subtracted from net income in the process of reconciling net income to the net cash provided by operating activities.

The (indirect method) adjustments for expenses and revenues that do not provide or use cash during the current period are:

Net income
Add: Expenses that do not use cash
Subtract: Revenues that do not provide cash
Net cash flows provided by operating activities

Adjustments for Nonoperating Items

Some income statement items are not related to the operating activities of the company. These are gains and losses that result from investing and financing activities. Examples are gains or losses on the sale of plant assets and gains or losses on the retirement of bonds payable.

Remember that the indirect method reconciles net income to the net cash provided (or used) by **operating** activities. Therefore, net income must be adjusted to exclude gains and losses from investing and financing activities. In making the adjustments under the indirect method, gains from financing and investing activities are subtracted from net income and losses are added back to net income.

Net income
Add: Losses from investing or financing activities
Subtract: Gains from investing or financing activities
Net cash provided by operating activities

■ **Applying the Indirect Method to Grover Company**

To determine the net cash flows provided (or used) by operating activities according to the indirect method, you need balance sheets at the beginning and end of the period, the current period's income statement, and other information about selected transactions. The income statement and balance sheet information for Grover Company is shown in Illustration 18-9. Based upon this information, the indirect method reconciliation of net income to net cash provided by operating activities is presented in Illustration 18-11.

Preparing the Indirect Method Working Paper

In addition to Grover Company's comparative balance sheets and income statement presented in Illustration 18-9, the information that is needed to prepare the working paper is restated below. The letter that identifies each item of information is also used in the working paper to cross-reference related debits and credits.

(a) Net income was $38,000.
(b) Accounts receivable increased by $20,000.
(c) Merchandise inventory increased by $14,000.
(d) Prepaid expenses increased by $2,000.

(e) Accounts payable decreased by $5,000.

(f) Interest payable decreased by $1,000.

(g) Income taxes payable increased by $10,000.

(h) Depreciation expense was $24,000.

(i) Loss on sale of plant assets was $6,000; assets costing $30,000 with accumulated depreciation of $12,000 were sold for $12,000 cash.

(j) Gain on retirement of bonds was $16,000; bonds with a book value of $34,000 were retired with a cash payment of $18,000.

(k) Plant assets costing $70,000 were purchased; the payment consisted of $10,000 cash and the issuance of a $60,000 note payable.

(l) Sold 3,000 shares of common stock for $15,000.

(m) Paid cash dividends of $14,000.

The indirect method working paper for Grover Company is shown in Illustration 18-12. Notice that the beginning and ending balance sheets are recorded on the working paper in the same manner as when the direct method is used. Following the balance sheets, information is entered in the Analysis of Changes columns about cash flows from operating, investing, and financing activities and about noncash investing and financing activities. Note that the working paper does not include a reconstruction of the income statement. Instead, net income is entered as the first source of cash flows from operating activities.

Entering the Analysis of Changes on the Working Paper

After the balance sheets have been entered, we recommend that you use the following sequence of procedures to complete the working paper:

1. Enter net income as an operating cash inflow (a debit) and as a credit to Retained Earnings.

2. In the statement of cash flows section, adjustments to net income are entered as debits if their effects are to increase cash inflows and as credits if their effects are to decrease cash inflows. Following this rule, adjust net income for the change in each noncash current asset and current liability related to operating activities. For each adjustment to net income, the offsetting debit or credit should reconcile the beginning and ending balances of a current asset or current liability.

3. Enter the adjustments to net income for income statement items such as depreciation that did not provide or use cash during the period. For each adjustment, the offsetting debit or credit should help reconcile a noncash balance sheet account.

4. Adjust net income to eliminate any gains or losses from investing and financing activities. Since the cash inflow of a gain is being excluded from operating activities, it is entered as a credit. On the other hand, losses are entered with debits. For each of these adjustments, the related debits and/or credits help reconcile balance sheet accounts and also involve entries to show the cash flow from investing or financing activities.

5. After reviewing any unreconciled balance sheet accounts and related information, enter the reconciling entries for all remaining investing and financing activities. These include items such as purchases of plant assets, issuance of long-term debt, sale of capital stock, and dividend

Illustration 18-12

Grover Corporation
Working Paper for Statement of Cash Flows (Indirect Method)
For Year Ended December 31, 1988

	December 31, 1987	Analysis of Changes Debit	Analysis of Changes Credit	December 31, 1988
Balance sheet—Debits:				
Cash	12,000			17,000
Accounts receivable	40,000	(b) 20,000		60,000
Merchandise inventory	70,000	(c) 14,000		84,000
Prepaid expenses	4,000	(d) 2,000		6,000
Plant assets	210,000	(k1) 70,000	(i) 30,000	250,000
	336,000			417,000
Balance sheet—Credits:				
Accumulated depreciation	48,000	(i) 12,000	(h) 24,000	60,000
Accounts payable	40,000	(e) 5,000		35,000
Interest payable	4,000	(f) 1,000		3,000
Income taxes payable	12,000		(g) 10,000	22,000
Bonds payable	64,000	(j) 34,000	(k2) 60,000	90,000
Common stock, $5 par value	80,000		(l) 15,000	95,000
Retained earnings	88,000	(m) 14,000	(a) 38,000	112,000
	336,000			417,000
Statement of cash flows:				
Operating activities:				
Net income		(a) 38,000		
Increase in accounts receivable . . .			(b) 20,000	
Increase in merchandise inventory . .			(c) 14,000	
Increase in prepaid expenses			(d) 2,000	
Decrease in accounts payable			(e) 5,000	
Decrease in interest payable			(f) 1,000	
Increase in income taxes payable. . .		(g) 10,000		
Depreciation expense		(h) 24,000		
Loss on sale of plant assets		(i) 6,000		
Gain on retirement of bonds			(j) 16,000	
Investing activities:				
Receipts from sale of plant assets . .		(i) 12,000		
Payment for purchase of plant assets .			(k1) 10,000	
Financing activities:				
Payments to retire bonds			(j) 18,000	
Receipts from issuance of stock . . .		(l) 15,000		
Payments of dividends			(m) 14,000	
Noncash investing and financing activities:				
Purchase of plant assets financed by bonds		(k2) 60,000	(k1) 60,000	
		337,000	337,000	

payments. Some of these may require entries in the noncash investing and financing activities section of the working paper.

6. Confirm the accuracy of your work by totaling the Analysis of Changes columns and by determining that the change in each balance sheet account has been explained.

For Grover Company, these steps have been performed in Illustration 18-12. Step 1 is reflected in entry *(a);* step 2 in entries *(b) – (g);* step 3 in entry *(h);* step 4 in entries *(i) – (j);* and step 5 in entries *(k) – (m).* These adjustments correspond with the individual items of information presented earlier in the appendix. Because adjustments *(i), (j),* and *(k)* are somewhat more complex, they are shown below in debit and credit form.

(i)	Loss from Sale of Plant Assets	6,000.00	
	Accumulated Depreciation	12,000.00	
	Receipt from Sale of Plant Assets	12,000.00	
	Plant Assets		30,000.00
	To reconstruct the sale of plant assets.		
(j)	Bonds Payable	34,000.00	
	Payments to Retire Bonds		18,000.00
	Gain on Retirement of Bonds		16,000.00
	To reconstruct the retirement of bonds.		
(k1)	Plant Assets	70,000.00	
	Payment to Purchase Plant Assets		10,000.00
	Purchase of Plant Assets Financed by		
	Bonds		60,000.00
	To show purchase of plant assets, the cash		
	payment and the use of noncash financing.		
(k2)	Purchase of Plant Assets Financed by Bonds .	60,000.00	
	Bonds Payable		60,000.00
	To show the issuance of bonds payable to		
	finance purchase of plant assets.		

□   **Glossary**   **Cash equivalent** an investment that is readily convertible to a known amount
of cash and that is sufficiently close to its maturity date so that its market
value is relatively insensitive to interest rate changes.

Direct method of calculating net cash provided or used by operating activities a
calculation of the net cash provided or used by operating activities that
lists the major classes of operating cash receipts, such as receipts from
customers, and subtracts the major classes of operating cash
disbursements, such as cash paid for merchandise.

Financing activities transactions of a business that involve borrowing cash
on a short-term basis or that are with the owners or long-term creditors
of the business.

Indirect method of calculating net cash provided or used by operating activities a
calculation that begins with net income and then adjusts the net income
amount by adding and subtracting items that are necessary to reconcile
net income to the net cash provided or used by operating activities.

Investing activities transactions that involve making and collecting loans
or that involve purchasing and selling plant assets, other productive
assets, or investments (other than cash equivalents).

Operating activities activities that involve the production or purchase of
merchandise and the sale of goods and services to customers, including
expenditures to administer the business.

Statement of cash flows a financial statement that reports the cash inflows
and outflows for an accounting period, and that classifies those cash
flows as operating activities, investing activities, and financing activities.

*Among the following questions, exercises, and problems, those that are based on
the appendix at the end of the chapter are identified with an asterisk (*).*

□ **Questions for Class**
Discussion
1. What information is shown on a statement of cash flows?
2. What are the three categories of cash flows shown on a statement of
cash flows?
3. What are some examples of items that are reported on a statement
of cash flows as investing activities?
4. What are some examples of items that are reported on a statement
of cash flows as financing activities?
5. When a statement of cash flows is prepared by the direct method,
what are some examples of items that are reported as cash flows
from operating activities?
6. A machine that was held as a long-term asset for use in business
operations is sold for cash. Where should this cash flow appear on
the statement of cash flows?
7. A business purchases merchandise inventory for cash. Where should
this cash flow appear on the statement of cash flows?
8. If a corporation pays cash dividends, where on the corporation's
statement of cash flows should the payment be reported?
9. A company purchases land for $200,000, and finances 100 percent
of the purchase with a long-term note payable. Should this transaction

be reported on a statement of cash flows? If so, where on the statement should it be reported?

10. A company purchases land for $100,000, paying $20,000 cash and borrowing the remainder on a long-term note payable. How should this transaction be reported on a statement of cash flows?

11. What is meant by the direct method of reporting cash flows from operating activities?

12. What is meant by the indirect method of reporting cash flows from operating activities?

13. Do the direct and indirect methods of calculating cash flows from operating activities lead to the same net amount?

14. Is depreciation a source of cash?

15. On June 3, a company borrowed $50,000 by giving its bank a 60-day, interest-bearing note. On the statement of cash flows, where should this item be reported?

16. A company borrowed $50,000 by giving its bank a 60-day, 12 percent interest-bearing note. When the note was repaid, the company also paid interest of $1,000. On the statement of cash flows, where should the $1,000 interest payment be reported?

17. When a working paper for the preparation of a statement of cash flows is prepared, all changes in noncash balance sheet accounts are accounted for on the working paper. Why?

18. A company retired a long-term note payable by issuing, at par, shares of common stock. How is this event analyzed on the statement of cash flows working paper?

*19. If a company reports a net income for the year, is it possible for the company to show a net cash outflow from operating activities? Explain your answer.

*20. Why are expenses such as depreciation and amortization of goodwill added to net income when cash flow from operations is calculated by the indirect method?

*21. A company had $70,000 of merchandise inventory at the beginning of a period and $40,000 of merchandise inventory at the end of the same period. If the net cash flow from operating activities is calculated by the indirect method, how should this decrease in inventory be treated in the calculation?

*22. A company reports a net income of $15,000 that includes a $3,000 gain on sale of plant assets. Why is this gain subtracted from net income in the process of reconciling net income to the net cash provided or used by operating activities?

☐ **Class Exercises**   **Exercise 18-1**

Examine each of the following items to determine (a) where on the statement of cash flows the item should be included, or (b) if it should be included in the schedule of noncash investing and financing activities, or (c) if it should not be included in either the statement of cash flows or the schedule of noncash investing and financing activities. Prepare a table for your answers and record your answers with checks in the appropriate columns.

	Statement of Cash Flows			Schedule of Noncash Investing & Financing Activities	Not Reported on Statement or Schedule
	Operating Activities	Investing Activities	Financing Activities		
a. A six-month note receivable was accepted in exchange for a building that had been used in operations.	_____	_____	_____	_____	_____
b. A cash dividend that had been declared in a previous period was paid in the current period.	_____	_____	_____	_____	_____
c. Surplus merchandise inventory was sold for cash.	_____	_____	_____	_____	_____
d. Paid cash to purchase a trademark.	_____	_____	_____	_____	_____
e. Long-term bonds payable were retired by issuing common stock.	_____	_____	_____	_____	_____
f. Borrowed cash from the bank by signing a six-month note payable.	_____	_____	_____	_____	_____

Exercise 18-2

Use the following information about the 1988 cash flows of Techniboard Company to prepare a statement of cash flows and a schedule of noncash investing and financing activities.

Cash and cash equivalents balance, December 31, 1987	$24,000
Cash and cash equivalents balance, December 31, 1988	17,000
Cash paid to retire long-term notes payable	150,000
Cash received from sale of building	85,000
Cash payments for merchandise	72,000
Cash paid for store equipment	15,000
Cash borrowed on six-month note payable	22,000
Cash dividends paid	12,000
Bonds payable retired by issuing common stock	100,000
Cash paid for salaries	37,000
Cash payments for other expenses	46,000
Land purchased and financed by long-term note payable	60,000
Cash received from customers	210,000
Cash received as interest	8,000

Exercise 18-3

In each of the following cases, use the information provided about the 1988 operations of Barney Company to calculate the indicated cash flow:

Case A: Calculate cash paid for rent:

Rent expense	$19,000
Prepaid rent, January 1	4,500
Prepaid rent, December 31	3,000

Case B: Calculate cash paid to employees:

Salaries expense	$14,000
Salaries payable, January 1	5,000
Salaries payable, December 31	8,000

Case C: Calculate cash received from customers:

Sales revenue	$60,000
Accounts receivable, January 1	12,000
Accounts receivable, December 31	9,000

Exercise 18-4

In each of the following cases, use the information provided about the 1988 operations of Lehman Company to calculate the indicated cash flow.

Case A: Calculate cash received from interest:

Interest revenue	$34,000
Interest receivable, January 1	2,500
Interest receivable, December 31	1,800

Case B: Calculate cash paid for utilities:

Utilities expense	$16,800
Utilities payable, January 1	7,500
Utilities payable, December 31	4,700

Case C: Calculate cash paid for merchandise:

Cost of goods sold	$59,000
Merchandise inventory, January 1	18,600
Accounts payable, January 1	14,300
Merchandise inventory, December 31	19,200
Accounts Payable, December 31	11,700

Exercise 18-5

Given the following income statement and information about changes in noncash current assets and current liabilities, present the cash flows from operating activities using the direct method:

Ecosystems Company
Income Statement
For Year Ended December 31, 1988

Sales		$225,000
Cost of goods sold		130,000
Gross profit from sales		$ 95,000
Operating expenses:		
Salaries and wages	$31,250	
Depreciation expense	3,750	
Rent expense	9,000	
Amortization of goodwill	1,750	
Interest expense	2,375	48,125
Total		$ 46,875
Gain on sale of machinery		1,000
Net income		$ 47,875

Changes in current asset and current liability accounts during the year, all of which related to operating activities, were as follows:

Accounts receivable	$4,000 decrease
Merchandise inventory	5,000 increase
Accounts payable	7,000 increase
Salaries and wages payable . . .	3,000 decrease

*Exercise 18-6

Refer to the information about Ecosystems Company presented in Exercise 18-5. Use the indirect method and calculate the cash provided (or used) by operating activities.

*Exercise 18-7

Megan Corporation's 1988 income statement showed the following: net income, $42,000; depreciation expense, $7,000; amortization expense, $3,500; and loss on sale of plant assets, $4,000. An examination of the company's current assets and current liabilities showed the following changes as a result of operating activities: accounts receivable increased $5,600; merchandise inventory decreased $7,000; prepaid expenses increased $2,800; accounts payable decreased $4,200; other payables increased $1,900. Use the indirect method to calculate the cash flow from operating activities.

Exercise 18-8

Use the following information to prepare a schedule of noncash investing and financing activities for Digit Corp.

a. The income statement shows a $5,000 loss on exchange of machinery. The loss related to an old machine that had a book value of $25,000 when it was exchanged for a new machine that had a cash price of $20,000.

b. Outstanding bonds payable carried on the books at $100,000 were retired by issuing 800 shares of $100 par, common stock.

c. Land valued at $250,000 was purchased by paying cash of $50,000 and signing a long-term note payable for the balance.

d. The income statement shows a $30,000 gain on the sale of a building. The building had a book value of $90,000 and was sold for $120,000. Digit Corp. received $50,000 cash and accepted a long-term promissory note for the balance of the sales price.

Exercise 18-9

Gail Company's 1988 and 1987 balance sheets carried the following items:

	December 31	
	1988	**1987**
Debits		
Cash	$ 15,000	$ 12,000
Accounts receivable	24,000	27,000
Merchandise inventory	63,000	54,000
Equipment	53,000	45,000
Totals	$155,000	$138,000
Credits		
Accumulated depreciation, equipment . . .	$ 14,000	$ 9,000
Common stock, $10 par value	75,000	75,000
Retained earnings	66,000	54,000
Totals	$155,000	$138,000

An examination of the company's activities during 1988, including the income statement, reveals the following:

a. Sales (all on credit) $190,000
b. The only decreases in Accounts Receivable
   involved receipts from customers.
c. Cost of goods sold $103,000
d. All merchandise purchases were for cash.
e. Depreciation expense.   5,000
f. Other operating expenses   60,000   168,000
   Net income . . . . $ 22,000

g. Equipment was purchased for $8,000 cash.
h. The company declared and paid $10,000 of cash dividends during the
   year.

Required

Prepare a statement of cash flows that follows the direct method to calculate the net cash provided (or used) by operating activities. Do not prepare a working paper but show any supporting calculations.

*Exercise 18-10

Refer to the facts presented in Exercise 18-9 about Gail Company and prepare a statement of cash flows that follows the indirect method of calculating the net cash provided (or used) by operating activities. Do not prepare a working paper but show any supporting calculations.

Problems   **Problem 18-1**

Mason Corporation's 1988 and 1987 balance sheets carried the following items:

	December 31	
	1988	1987
Debits		
Cash	$ 63,000	$ 24,000
Accounts receivable	48,000	54,000
Merchandise inventory	126,000	108,000
Equipment.	111,000	90,000
Totals	$348,000	$276,000
Credits		
Accumulated depreciation, equipment . . .	$ 27,000	$ 18,000
Accounts payable	51,000	30,000
Income taxes payable.	6,000	12,000
Common stock, $10 par value	165,000	150,000
Contributed capital in excess of		
par value, common stock	33,000	30,000
Retained earnings	66,000	36,000
Totals	$348,000	$276,000

An examination of the company's activities during 1988, including the income statement, shows the following:

a1.	Sales (all on credit)		$750,000
a2.	Credits to Accounts Receivable during the period involved receipts from customers.		
b1.	Cost of goods sold	$400,000	
b2.	Purchases of merchandise were on credit.		
b3.	Debits to Accounts Payable during the period resulted from payments for merchandise.		
c.	Depreciation expense	9,000	
d.	Other operating expenses	241,000	
e1.	Income taxes expense	40,000	690,000
e2.	The only decreases in Income Taxes Payable involved payments of taxes.		
f.	Net income		$ 60,000

g. Equipment was purchased for $21,000 cash.
h. Fifteen hundred shares of stock were issued for cash at $12 per share.
i. The company declared and paid $30,000 of cash dividends during the year.

Required

Prepare a statement of cash flows that reports the cash inflows and outflows from operating activities according to the direct method. Do not prepare a working paper. Instead, prepare the statement directly from your examination of the balance sheets and the additional information provided about the income statement and other transactions of the company. Show your supporting calculations.

Problem 18-2

Refer to the information about Mason Corporation presented in Problem 18-1. Prepare a working paper for a statement of cash flows according to the direct method.

*Problem 18-3

Refer to Mason Corporation's balance sheets presented in Problem 18-1. The additional information about the company's activities during 1988 is restated as follows:

a. Net income was $60,000.
b. Accounts receivable decreased.
c. Merchandise inventory increased.
d. Accounts payable increased.
e. Income taxes payable decreased.
f. Depreciation expense was $9,000.
g. Equipment was purchased for $21,000 cash.
h. Fifteen hundred shares of stock were issued for cash at $12 per share.
i. The company declared and paid $30,000 of cash dividends during the year.

Required

Prepare a schedule that reconciles net income to the net cash provided or used by operating activities.

*Problem 18-4

Refer to the facts about Mason Corporation presented in Problem 18-1 and Problem 18-3. Prepare a statement of cash flows working paper that follows the indirect method of calculating cash flows from operating activities. Identify the debits and credits in the Analysis of Changes columns with letters that correspond to the list of information about the company presented in Problem 18-3.

Problem 18-5

Skipper Corporation's 1988 and 1987 balance sheets included the following items:

	December 31	
	1988	**1987**
Debits		
Cash	$ 97,800	$ 25,800
Accounts receivable	48,000	60,000
Merchandise inventory	189,000	192,000
Prepaid expenses	6,000	7,200
Equipment	220,600	154,000
Totals	$561,400	$439,000
Credits		
Accumulated depreciation, equipment . . .	$ 36,600	$ 32,800
Accounts payable	129,000	107,400
Short-term notes payable	15,000	9,000
Long-term notes payable	76,000	60,000
Common stock, $10 par value	155,000	150,000
Contributed capital in excess of		
par value, common stock	40,000	
Retained earnings	109,800	79,800
Totals	$561,400	$439,000

Additional information about the 1988 activities of the company is as follows:

a1.	Sales revenue, all on credit		$425,000
a2.	Credits to Accounts Receivable during the period involved receipts from customers.		
b1.	Cost of goods sold	$260,000	
b2.	All merchandise purchases were on credit.		
b3.	Debits to Accounts Payable during the period resulted from payments to creditors.		
c.	Depreciation expense	12,600	
d1.	Other expenses	90,150	
d2.	The decrease in prepaid expenses was charged to Other Expenses.		
e.	Income taxes expense	12,450	
f.	Loss on sale of equipment	1,800	377,000
	The equipment cost $14,800, had been depreciated $8,800, and was sold for $4,200.		
g.	Net income		$ 48,000

h1. Equipment that cost $81,400 was purchased by paying cash of $41,400 and *(h2)* by signing a long-term note payable for the balance.

i. Borrowed $6,000 by signing a short-term note payable.

j. Paid $24,000 to reduce a long-term note payable.

k. Issued 500 shares of common stock for cash at $90 per share.

l. Declared and paid cash dividends of $18,000.

Required

Prepare a statement of cash flows that reports the cash inflows and outflows from operating activities according to the direct method. Do not prepare a working paper. Instead, prepare the statement directly from your examination of the balance sheets and the additional information provided about the income statement and other transactions of the company. Show your supporting calculations.

Also prepare a schedule of noncash investing and financing activities.

Problem 18-6

Refer to the information about Skipper Corporation presented in Problem 18-5. Prepare a working paper for a statement of cash flows according to the direct method.

*Problem 18-7

Refer to Skipper Corporation's balance sheets presented in Problem 18-5. The additional information about the company's activities during 1988 is restated as follows:

a. Net income was $48,000.

b. Accounts receivable decreased.

c. Merchandise inventory decreased.

d. Prepaid expenses decreased.

e. Accounts payable increased.

f. Depreciation expense was $12,600.

g. Equipment that cost $14,800 and had been depreciated $8,800 was sold for $4,200 cash, which resulted in a loss of $1,800.

h. Equipment that cost $81,400 was purchased by paying cash of $41,400 and (i) by signing a long-term note payable for the balance.

j. Borrowed $6,000 by signing a short-term note payable.

k. Paid $24,000 to reduce a long-term note payable.

l. Issued 500 shares of common stock for cash at $90 per share.

m. Declared and paid cash dividends of $18,000.

Required

Prepare a schedule that reconciles net income to the net cash provided or used by operating activities.

*Problem 18-8

Refer to the facts about Skipper Corporation presented in Problems 18-5 and 18-7. Prepare a statement of cash flows working paper that follows the indirect method of calculating cash flows from operating activities. Identify the debits and credits in the Analysis of Changes columns with letters that correspond to the list of information about the company presented in Problem 18-7.

□ **Alternate Problems**   **Problem 18-1A**

Cemco Corporation's 1988 and 1987 balance sheets carried the following items:

	December 31	
	1988	**1987**
Debits		
Cash	$ 50,400	$ 19,200
Accounts receivable	38,400	43,200
Merchandise inventory	100,800	86,400
Equipment.	88,800	72,000
Totals	$278,400	$220,800
Credits		
Accumulated depreciation, equipment . . .	$ 21,600	$ 14,400
Accounts payable	40,800	24,000
Income taxes payable.	4,800	9,600
Common stock, $10 par value	132,000	120,000
Contributed capital in excess of		
par value, common stock	26,400	24,000
Retained earnings	52,800	28,800
Totals	$278,400	$220,800

An examination of the company's activities during 1988, including the income statement, shows the following:

a1. Sales (all on credit)		$600,000
a2. The only decreases in Accounts Receivable involved receipts from customers.		
b1. Cost of goods sold	$320,000	
b2. Purchases of merchandise were on credit.		
b3. Credits to Accounts Payable during the period resulted from payments for merchandise.		
c. Depreciation expense	7,200	
d. Other operating expenses	192,800	
e1. Income taxes expense	32,000	552,000
e2. The only decreases in Income Taxes Payable involved payments of taxes.		
f. Net income		$ 48,000

g. Equipment was purchased for $16,800 cash.

h. Twelve hundred shares of stock were issued for cash at $12 per share.

i. The company declared and paid $24,000 of cash dividends during the year.

Required

Prepare a statement of cash flows that reports the cash inflows and outflows from operating activities according to the direct method. Do not prepare a working paper. Instead, prepare the statement directly from your examination of the balance sheets and the additional information provided about the income statement and other transactions of the company. Show your supporting calculations.

Problem 18-2A

Refer to the information about Cemco Corporation presented in Problem 18-1A. Prepare a working paper for a statement of cash flows according to the direct method.

*Problem 18-3A

Refer to Cemco Corporation's balance sheets presented in Problem 18-1A. The additional information about the company's activities during 1988 is identified as follows:

a. Net income was $48,000.

b. Accounts receivable decreased.

c. Merchandise inventory increased.

d. Accounts payable increased.

e. Income taxes payable decreased.

f. Depreciation expense was $7,200.

g. Equipment was purchased for $16,800 cash.

h. Twelve hundred shares of stock were issued for cash at $12 per share.

i. The company declared and paid $24,000 of cash dividends during the year.

Required

Prepare a schedule that reconciles net income to the net cash provided or used by operating activities.

*Problem 18-4A

Refer to the facts about Cemco Corporation presented in Problems 18-1A and 18-3A. Prepare a statement of cash flows working paper that follows the indirect method of calculating cash flows from operating activities. Identify the debits and credits in the Analysis of Changes columns with letters that correspond to the above list of information about the company.

Problem 18-5A

Columbus Corporation's 1988 and 1987 balance sheets included the following items:

	December 31	
	1988	**1987**
Debits		
Cash	$146,700	$ 38,700
Accounts receivable	72,000	90,000
Merchandise inventory	283,500	288,000
Prepaid expenses	9,000	10,800
Equipment	330,900	231,000
Totals	$842,100	$658,500
Credits		
Accumulated depreciation, equipment . . .	$ 54,900	$ 49,200
Accounts payable	193,500	161,100
Short-term notes payable	22,500	13,500
Long-term notes payable	114,000	90,000
Common stock, $15 par value	232,500	225,000
Contributed capital in excess of		
par value, common stock	60,000	
Retained earnings	164,700	119,700
Totals	$842,100	$658,500

Additional information about the 1988 activities of the company is as follows:

a1.	Sales revenue, all on credit		$637,500
a2.	Decreases in accounts receivable resulted only from receipts from customers.		
b1.	Cost of goods sold	$390,000	
b2.	All merchandise purchases were on credit.		
b3.	Credits to Accounts Payable during the period resulted from payments for merchandise.		
c.	Depreciation expense	18,900	
d1.	Other expenses	135,225	
d2.	The decrease in prepaid expenses was charged to Other Expenses.		
e.	Income taxes expense	18,675	
f.	Loss on sale of equipment	2,700	565,500
	The equipment cost $22,200, had been depreciated $13,200, and was sold for $6,300.		
g.	Net income		$ 72,000

h1. Equipment that cost $122,100 was purchased by paying cash of $62,100 and *(h2)* signing a long-term note payable for the balance.
i. Borrowed $9,000 by signing a short-term note payable.
j. Paid $36,000 to reduce a long-term note payable.
k. Issued 500 shares of common stock for cash at $135 per share.
l. Declared and paid cash dividends of $27,000.

Required

Prepare a statement of cash flows that reports the cash inflows and outflows from operating activities according to the direct method. Do not prepare a working paper. Instead, prepare the statement directly from your examination of the balance sheets and the additional information provided about the income statement and other transactions of the company. Show your supporting calculations.

Also prepare a schedule of noncash investing and financing activities.

Problem 18-6A

Refer to the information about Columbus Corporation presented in Problem 18-5A. Prepare a working paper for a statement of cash flows according to the direct method.

*Problem 18-7A

Refer to Columbus Corporation's balance sheets presented in Problem 18-5A. The additional information about the company's activities during 1988 is restated as follows:

a. Net income was $72,000.
b. Accounts receivable decreased.
c. Merchandise inventory decreased.
d. Prepaid expenses decreased.
e. Accounts payable increased.
f. Depreciation expense was $18,900.
g. Equipment that cost $22,200 and had been depreciated $13,200 was sold for $6,300 cash, which resulted in a loss of $2,700.
h. Equipment that cost $122,100 was purchased by paying cash of $62,100 and signing a long-term note payable for the balance.
i. Borrowed $9,000 by signing a short-term note payable.
j. Paid $36,000 to reduce a long-term note payable.
k. Issued 500 shares of common stock for cash at $135 per share.
l. Declared and paid cash dividends of $27,000.

Required

Prepare a schedule that reconciles net income to the net cash provided or used by operating activities.

*Problem 18-8A

Refer to the facts about Columbus Corporation presented in Problems 18-5A and 18-7A. Prepare a statement of cash flows working paper that follows the indirect method of calculating cash flows from operating activities. Identify the debits and credits in the Analysis of Changes columns with letters that correspond to the above list of information about the company.

Provocative Problems

Provocative Problem 18-1Yaupon, Inc.

Yaupon, Inc.'s 1988 statement of cash flows appeared as follows:

Cash flows from operating activities:
Cash receipts from customers	$ 772,800	
Cash payments for merchandise	(425,400)	
Payments for other operating expenses	(169,800)	
Payments of income taxes	(32,400)	
Net cash provided by operating activities		$145,200

Cash flows from investing activities:
Receipt from sale of office equipment	$ 5,100	
Purchase of store equipment	(33,000)	
Net cash used by investing activities		(27,900)

Cash flows from financing activities:
Payment to retire bonds payable	$ (42,300)	
Payment of dividends	(30,000)	
Net cash used by financing activities		(72,300)
Net increase in cash		$ 45,000
Cash balance at beginning of year		45,400
Cash balance at end of year		$ 90,400

Yaupon, Inc.'s beginning and ending balance sheets were as follows:

	December 31	
	1988	1987
Debits		
Cash	$ 90,400	$ 45,400
Accounts receivable	114,900	100,200
Merchandise inventory	212,700	260,300
Prepaid expenses	9,000	4,400
Equipment	99,100	108,600
Totals	$526,100	$518,900
Credits		
Accumulated depreciation, equipment	$ 18,200	$ 30,200
Accounts payable	58,500	74,800
Income taxes payable	10,900	6,500
Dividends payable	–0–	7,500
Bonds payable	–0–	50,000
Common stock, $5 par value	300,000	300,000
Retained earnings	138,500	49,900
Totals	$526,100	$518,900

An examination of the company's statements and accounts showed:

a. All sales were made on credit.

b. All merchandise purchases were on credit.

c. Accounts Payable balances resulted from merchandise purchases.
d. Prepaid expenses relate to other operating expenses.
e. Equipment that cost $42,500 and had been depreciated $24,000 was sold for cash.
f. Equipment was purchased for cash.
g. The change in the balance of Accumulated Depreciation resulted from depreciation expense and from the sale of equipment.
h. The change in the balance of Retained Earnings resulted from dividend declarations and net income.

Required

Present Yaupon, Inc.'s income statement for 1988. Show your supporting calculations.

Provocative Problem 18–2   James Company

The following items include the 1989 income statement and the 1989 and 1988 balance sheets of the James Company. Additional information about the company's 1989 transactions is presented after the financial statements.

James Company
Income Statement
For Year Ended December 31, 1989

Revenues:		
Sales	$120,000	
Gain on sale of stock investment	3,000	
Dividend income	500	
Interest income	400	$123,900
Expenses and losses:		
Cost of goods sold	$ 50,000	
Other expenses	54,800	
Interest expense	2,000	
Income tax expense	2,500	
Depreciation expense, buildings	2,000	
Depreciation expense, equipment	4,000	
Loss on sale of equipment	600	
Total expenses and losses		115,900
Net income		$ 8,000

James Company
Balance Sheet
December 31, 1989 and 1988

	1989		1988	
Assets				
Current assets:				
Cash and cash equivalents	$ 1,000		$ 800	
Accounts receivable	4,500		3,100	
Merchandise inventory	19,000		16,000	
Prepaid expenses	700		600	
Total current assets		$25,200		$20,500
Long-term investments:				
Icahn Corporation common stock		10,000		12,000
Plant assets:				
Land		9,000		4,000
Buildings	$60,000		$60,000	
Less accumulated depreciation	38,000	22,000	36,000	24,000
Equipment	$21,000		$16,000	
Less accumulated depreciation	6,000	15,000	4,000	12,000
Total assets		$81,200		$72,500
Liabilities				
Current liabilities:				
Notes payable	$ 5,000		$ 3,500	
Accounts payable	9,000		10,000	
Other accrued liabilities	5,300		4,200	
Interest payable	400		300	
Taxes payable	300		500	
Total current liabilities		$20,000		$18,500
Long-term liabilities:				
Bonds payable, due in 1998		25,000		22,000
Total liabilities		$45,000		$40,500
Stockholders' Equity				
Contributed capital:				
Common stock, $1 par value	$11,000		$10,000	
Contributed capital in excess of par value .	5,000		4,000	
Retained earnings	22,000		18,000	
Total	$38,000		$32,000	
Less cost of Treasury stock	1,800		–0–	
Total stockholders' equity		36,200		32,000
Total liabilities and stockholders' equity		$81,200		$72,500

Additional information:

1. Received $5,000 from the sale of Icahn Corporation common stock that originally cost $2,000.
2. Received a cash dividend of $500 from the Icahn Corporation.
3. Received $400 cash from the First National Bank on December 31, 1989, as interest income.
4. Sold old equipment for $1,400. The old equipment originally cost $4,000 and had accumulated depreciation of $2,000.
5. Purchased land costing $5,000 on December 31, 1989, in exchange for a note payable. Both principal and interest are due on June 30, 1990.
6. Purchased new equipment for $9,000 cash.
7. Purchased Treasury stock for $1,800.
8. Paid off the notes payable of $3,500.
9. Sold additional bonds payable at par of $3,000 on January 1, 1989.
10. Issued 1,000 shares of common stock for cash at $2 per share.
11. Declared and paid a $4,000 cash dividend on October 1, 1989.

(The working papers that accompany the text include forms for this problem.)

Required

a. Prepare a direct method working paper for James Company's 1989 statement of cash flows.
b. Prepare the statement of cash flows for 1989.
c. Prepare a schedule that reconciles net income to the company's net cash provided (or used) by operating activities for 1989.

19 Additional Financial Reporting Issues

After studying Chapter 19, you should be able to:

1. Describe the income statement sections that follow "Income from continuing operations."

2. Explain the general requirements for reporting the income effects of a discontinued operation, an extraordinary item, a change in accounting principles, and a prior period adjustment.

3. State the reasons why conventional financial statements fail to adequately account for price changes.

4. Explain how price changes should be measured and how to construct a price index.

5. Restate historical cost/nominal dollar costs into constant dollar amounts and calculate purchasing power gains and losses.

6. Explain the difference between current costs and historical costs stated in constant dollars.

7. Describe the FASB requirements for disclosing financial information adjusted for price changes.

8. Describe the primary problems of accounting for international operations and prepare entries to account for sales to foreign customers.

9. Define or explain the words and phrases listed in the chapter Glossary.

Chapter 19 is divided into three sections. The first section explains special reporting requirements for income and loss items that are not directly related to continuing operations. These include: (1) income or losses relating to business operations that are being discontinued, (2) items that are defined as extraordinary, (3) income effects of changes in accounting principles, and (4) corrections of income in prior periods. The second section examines the accounting problem of changing prices. And the third section exposes students to the problems of accounting for international operations.

INCOME AND LOSS ITEMS NOT DIRECTLY RELATED TO CONTINUING OPERATIONS

When the revenue and expense transactions of a company are made up entirely of routine operating activities, the company's single-step income statement will show revenues followed by a listing of operating expenses and finally by net income. However, if the company's activities include operations that are being discontinued, the income or loss effects of the discontinued operations are reported separately from continuing operations. For example, consider the income statement shown in Illustration 19-1.

In Illustration 19-1, observe that the income statement has been separated into five sections labeled 1 through 5. The first portion of the income statement (the portion labeled as 1) shows the revenues, expenses, and income generated by the company's continuing operations. This portion appears just like the single-step income statement first discussed in Chapter 5. The next income statement section, labeled 2, pertains to discontinued operations.

■ **Discontinued Operations**

Separating Discontinued Operations on the Income Statement

Large companies often operate in several different lines of business or have several different classes of customers. A company's operations that involve a particular line of business or class of customers may qualify as a segment of the business. To qualify as a **segment of a business,** the assets, activities, and financial results of operations involving a particular line of business or class of customers must be distinguished from other parts of the business.

Normally, the revenues and expenses of all business segments are added together and reported as the continuing operations of the business (as in section 1 of Illustration 19-1). However, when a business makes a definite commitment to sell or dispose of a business segment, the results of that segment's operations should be separated and reported as shown in section 2 of Illustration 19-1.[1] In the illustration, the results of the discontinued operations are completely separated from the results of other activities. This separation allows statement readers to better evaluate and judge the continuing operations of the business.

[1] FASB, *Accounting Standards—Current Text* (Stamford, Conn., 1984), sec. I13.105. Originally published as *APB Opinion No. 30*, par. 8.

Illustration 19-1

Connelly Corporation
Income Statement
For Year Ended December 31, 198A

Net sales		$ 8,443,000
Gain on sale of old equipment		30,000
Total		$ 8,473,000
Costs and expenses:		
Cost of goods sold	$5,950,000	
Depreciation expense	35,000	
Other selling, general, and administrative expenses . . .	515,000	
Interest expense	20,000	
Income taxes.	990,000	(7,510,000)
Unusual loss on sale of surplus land.		(45,000)
Infrequent gain on relocation of a plant.		72,000
Income from continuing operations		$ 990,000

Discontinued operations:

Income from operations of discontinued Division A		
(net of $350,000 income taxes)	$ 100,000	
Loss on disposal of Division A (net of $60,000 tax		
benefit)	(150,000)	250,000
Income before extraordinary items and cumulative		
effect of a change in accounting principle		$ 1,240,000

Extraordinary items:

Gain on sale of unused land expropriated by the		
state for a highway interchange (net of $35,000		
income taxes)	$ 142,500	
Loss from earthquake damage (net of $310,000		
income taxes)	(670,000)	

Cumulative effect of a change in accounting principle:

Effect on prior years' income (to December 31, 198A)		
of changing to a different depreciation method		
(net of $22,500 income taxes)	22,500	(505,000)
Net income		$ 735,000

Earnings per common share (250,000 shares outstanding):

Income from continuing operations	$ 3.96
Discontinued operations	1.00
Extraordinary items	(2.11)
Cumulative effect of a change in accounting principle . .	.09
Net income	$ 2.94

Separating the Results of Operating a Segment That Is Being Discontinued from the Gain or Loss on Disposal

Within section 2 of Illustration 19-1, note that the income or loss from **operating** Division A (the operation that is being discontinued) during the period is reported separately from the gain or loss on the final **disposal** of Division A. Finally, note that the income tax effects of the discontinued operations are separated from the income tax expense shown in section 1 of Illustration 19-1. As a result, the results of the discontinued operations are reported net of tax. Also, the amount of tax related to each item is disclosed.

This discussion summarizes the method of **reporting** the results of discontinued operations on the income statement. Further discussion of the detailed requirements for **measuring** the income or losses of discontinued operations is left for a more advanced course.

■ **Extraordinary Items**   Section 3 of the income statement in Illustration 19-1 discloses gains and losses that are defined as extraordinary. To qualify as an **extraordinary gain or loss,** an item must be both unusual and infrequent of occurrence. An **unusual gain or loss** is abnormal and unrelated or only incidentally related to the ordinary activities and environment of the business. An **infrequent gain or loss** is not expected to occur again, given the operating environment of the business.[2]

Given these definitions of unusual and infrequent, very few items meet both criteria; in other words, very few items qualify as extraordinary gains or losses. For example, none of the following generally qualify as being extraordinary:

a. Write-down or write-off of assets unless caused by a major casualty, an expropriation, or prohibition under a newly enacted law.
b. Gains or losses from exchange or translation of foreign currencies.
c. Gains and losses on disposal of a segment of a business.
d. Other gains and losses from sale or abandonment of property, plant, or equipment unless caused by a major casualty, an expropriation, or prohibition under a newly enacted law.
e. Effects of a strike, including those against competitors and major suppliers.
f. Adjustment of accruals on long-term contracts.[3]

Some gains or losses are **neither** unusual **nor** infrequent. They are reported among the revenues or costs and expenses of continuing operations. Other gains or losses may be unusual **or** infrequent but not both. Such gains or losses are **not** extraordinary items. On the income statement, items that are unusual or infrequent but not both are listed below the costs and expenses of continuing operations. Section 1 of Illustration 19-1 displays a "Gain on sale of old equipment" that is neither unusual nor infrequent. The illustration also shows an unusual loss and an infrequent gain. Note that the correct classification of these items is not obvious from their descriptions. Instead, a careful examination of the circumstances surrounding the gain or loss is necessary to determine the correct classification.

■ **Changes in Accounting Principles**

The Consistency Principle Does Not Preclude Changes in Accounting Principles

After a company chooses to use particular accounting principles, it must continue to use the same principles period after period. This is required by the **consistency principle.** (In this discussion, methods such as FIFO and straight-line depreciation are called accounting principles.) Nevertheless, the **consistency principle** does not mean that a company may never make

---

[2] Ibid., sec. I17.107. Originally published as *APB Opinion No. 30*, par. 20.
[3] Ibid., sec. I17.110. Originally published as *APB Opinion No. 30*, par. 23.

changes. A company may change from one accounting principle to another if the company justifies the change as an improvement in financial reporting.

When a company changes from one accounting principle to another, the change often affects the amount of income to be reported. For example, assume a company has only one asset that cost $210,000, has no salvage value, and is being depreciated on a sum-of-the-years'-digits basis over six years. Also, assume a 50% income tax rate. Early in year 4, the company decides to switch to straight-line depreciation and justifies the change as an improvement in financial reporting. A comparison of the two depreciation methods during the six-year life of the asset is shown in Illustration 19-2.

Illustration 19-2

Year		Sum-of-the-Years'-Digits Depreciation	Straight-Line Depreciation	After-Tax Difference in Methods
		a	b	(a − b) × 50%
Prior years:				
1	(6/21)	$ 60,000	$ 35,000	$ 25,000 × 50% = $ 12,500
2	(5/21)	50,000	35,000	15,000 × 50% = 7,500
3	(4/21)	40,000	35,000	5,000 × 50% = 2,500
Totals				$ 45,000 $ 22,500*
Year of change:				
4	(3/21)	30,000	**35,000***	(5,000) × 50% = (2,500)
Future years:				
5	(2/21)	20,000	35,000	(15,000) × 50% = (7,500)
6	(1/21)	10,000	35,000	(25,000) × 50% = (12,500)
Totals		$210,000	$210,000	$ −0−

* These two numbers are reported on the income statement in Illustration 19-1.

Reporting Requirements for Changes in Accounting Principles

How should the change in depreciation methods be reported on the income statement? The correct method of disclosure is shown in Illustration 19-1. In section 1 of Illustration 19-1, note that depreciation expense for the current year is $35,000. That is the straight-line amount in the year of change as calculated in Illustration 19-2. In section 4 of Illustration 19-1, the effect of the change on prior years' income is reported (net of $22,500 income taxes) as $22,500. Compare this with the calculations in Illustration 19-2. The total after-tax difference between the two depreciation methods in prior years is shown to be $22,500.

To summarize, a company that wants to make a change in accounting principles must justify that change. The information that must be reported by the company generally includes the following:[4]

a. The nature and justification for the change should be described in the footnotes to the financial statements.
b. The cumulative effect of the change on prior periods should be shown on the income statement below extraordinary items. Also, the effect

[4] Ibid., sec. A06.113–116. Originally published as *APB Opinion No. 20,* pars. 17–20.

on earnings per share must be shown separately. (See section 5 of Illustration 19-1.)

c. In the year of the change, the footnotes should also state the effect of the change on income before extraordinary items and on net income.

Correct reporting of changes in accounting principles also includes more detailed disclosure requirements. However, further study of these topics is left for an advanced course.

■ Earnings per Share on the Income Statement

The procedures for calculating earnings per share are discussed in Chapter 20. However, observe in section 5 of Illustration 19-1 that earnings per share information is presented on the face of the income statement. Also note that separate earnings per share numbers are presented for each of the income statement categories previously discussed in this chapter.

■ Prior Period Adjustments

In preparing the annual financial statements of a corporation, the income effect of one type of item is excluded entirely from the current income statement. This type of item is called a **prior period adjustment** and is limited primarily to corrections of errors made in past years. Prior period adjustments are reported in the current statement of retained earnings as corrections to the beginning retained earnings balance. They are reported net of any related tax effect, the amount of which is also disclosed. For example, a partial statement of retained earnings with a prior period adjustment might appear as follows:

Retained earnings, January 1, 198A	$160,000
Prior period adjustment:	
Cost of land that was incorrectly charged to expense	
($30,000, net of $20,000 income taxes)	30,000
Retained earnings, January 1, 198A, as adjusted . . .	$190,000

■ Changes in Accounting Estimates

Errors of past periods that qualify as prior period adjustments must be distinguished from revisions or **changes in accounting estimates.** Errors are represented by mathematical mistakes or failure to take known facts into consideration. On the other hand, the preparation of financial statements requires many estimates about the future such as salvage values and estimated useful lives of buildings and equipment. As new information becomes available, it may become necessary to change such estimates. Changes in accounting estimates are not allowed to affect the income of prior periods. Instead, the revised estimate is applied in calculating the appropriate revenue or expense of the current and future periods. One example of a change in an accounting estimate, the revision of depreciation rates, was discussed on pages 392 and 393 in Chapter 11.

DISCLOSING THE EFFECTS OF CHANGING PRICES

The problem of accounting for changing prices has been discussed for many years. Sometimes, when prices are changing very rapidly, the discussion is heated and attempts are made to improve accounting practices. Other times, when prices are changing at a slower rate, the problem of accounting for price changes gets less attention. In any case, frequent changes in the prices paid for economic goods and services present a major problem in accounting.

■ **Conventional Financial Statements Fail to Account for Price Changes**

Perhaps all accountants agree that conventional financial statements provide useful information for making economic decisions. However, many accountants also agree that conventional financial statements fail to adequately account for the impact of changing prices. This failure of conventional financial statements may sometimes even make the statements misleading. That is, the statements may imply certain facts that are inconsistent with the real state of affairs. As a result, decision makers may be inclined to make decisions that are inconsistent with their objectives.

Failure to Account for Price Changes on the Balance Sheet

In what ways do conventional financial statements fail to account for changing prices? The general problem is that transactions are recorded in terms of the historical number of dollars paid. These amounts are not adjusted even though subsequent price changes may dramatically change the value of the items that were purchased. For example, Old Company purchased 10 acres of land for $25,000. At the end of each accounting period thereafter, Old Company presented a balance sheet showing "Land, $25,000." Six years later, after price increases of 97%, New Company purchased 10 acres of land that was adjacent and nearly identical to Old Company's land. New Company paid $49,250 for the land. In comparing the conventional balance sheets of the two companies, which own identical pieces of property, the following balances are observed:

Balance Sheets

	Old Company	New Company
Land.	$25,000	$49,250

Without knowing the details that underlie these balances, a statement reader is likely to conclude that New Company either has more land than does Old Company or that New Company's land is more valuable. But, both companies own 10 acres that are of equal value. The entire difference between the prices paid by the two companies is explained by the 97% price increase between the two purchase dates. That is, $25,000 × 1.97 = $49,250.

Failure to Account for Price Changes on the Income Statement

The failure of conventional financial statements to adequately account for changing prices also shows up in the income statement. For example, assume that in the previous example, machinery was purchased instead of land. Also, assume that the machinery of Old Company and New Company is identical except for age; it is being depreciated on a straight-line basis over a 10-year period, with no salvage value. As a result, the annual income statements of the two companies show the following:

Income Statements

	Old Company	New Company
Depreciation expense, machinery	$2,500	$4,925

Although assets of equal value are being depreciated, the income statements show that New Company's depreciation expense is 97% higher than is Old Company's. This is inconsistent with the fact that both companies own the same machines that are subject to the same depreciation factors. Furthermore, although Old Company will appear more profitable, it must pay more income taxes due to the apparent extra profits. Old Company also may not recover the full replacement cost of its machinery through the sale of its product.

Understanding Price-Level Changes

In one way or another, all readers of this book have experienced the effects of **inflation,** which is a general increase in the prices paid for goods and services. A general decrease in prices is called **deflation.** Of course, the prices of specific items do not all change at the same rate. Even when most prices are rising, the prices of some goods or services may be falling. For example, consider the following prices of four different items:

Item	Price/Unit in 1986	Price/Unit in 1987	Percent Change
A	$1.00	$1.30	+30
B	2.00	2.20	+10
C	1.50	1.80	+20
D	3.00	2.70	−10
Totals . . .	$7.50	$8.00	

The Problem of Describing Price Changes What can be said to describe these price changes? One possibility is to state the percentage change in the price per unit of each item (see above). This information is very useful for some purposes. But, it does not show the average effect or impact of the price changes that occurred.

The Average Change in Unit Prices A better indication of the average effect would be to determine the average increase in the per unit prices of the four items. Thus: $8.00/$7.50 − 1.00 = 6.7% average increase in per unit prices.[5] However, even this average probably fails to show the impact of the price changes on most individuals or businesses. It is a good indicator only if the typical buyer purchased an equal number of units of each item.

The Weighted-Average Change in Prices What if the four items are typically purchased in unequal amounts? For example, assume that for each unit of A purchased, 2 units of B, 5 units of C, and 1 unit of D are purchased. With a different number of each item being purchased, the impact of changing prices must take into account the typical quantity of each item purchased. Hence, the average change in the price of the A, B, C, D "market basket" would be calculated as follows:

Item	Units Purchased		1986 Prices			Units Purchased		1987 Prices		
A	1 unit	×	$1.00	=	$ 1.00	1 unit	×	$1.30	=	$ 1.30
B	2 units	×	$2.00	=	4.00	2 units	×	$2.20	=	4.40
C	5 units	×	$1.50	=	7.50	5 units	×	$1.80	=	9.00
D	1 unit	×	$3.00	=	3.00	1 unit	×	$2.70	=	2.70
Totals					$15.50					$17.40

Weighted-average price change = $17.40/$15.50 − 1.00 = 12.3%

It may now be said that the annual rate of inflation in the prices of these four items was 12.3%. Of course, not every individual and business will purchase these four items in exactly the same proportion of 1 unit of A, 2 units of B, 5 units of C, and 1 unit of D. As a consequence, the stated inflation rate is only an approximation of the impact of price changes on each buyer. But if these proportions represent the typical buying pattern, the stated 12.3% inflation rate fairly reflects the inflationary impact on the average buyer.

■ Construction of a Price Index

When the cost of purchasing a given market basket is determined for each of several periods, the results can be expressed as a **price index.** In constructing a price index, one year is arbitrarily selected as the "base" year. The cost of purchasing the market basket in that year is then assigned a value of 100. For example, suppose the cost of purchasing the A, B, C, D market basket in each year is:

1981	$ 9.00
1982	11.00
1983	10.25
1984	12.00
1985	13.00
1986	15.50
1987	17.40

[5] Throughout this chaper, only final answers are rounded. Percentages or index numbers are rounded to the nearest 1/10% and dollar amounts to the nearest whole dollar.

If 1984 is selected as the base year, then the $12 cost for 1984 is assigned a value of 100. The index number for each of the other years is then calculated and expressed as a percent of the base year's cost. For example, the index number for 1983 is 85.4, or ($10.25/$12.00 × 100 = 85.4). The index numbers for the remaining years are calculated in the same way. The entire price index for the years 1981 through 1987 is presented in Illustration 19-3.

Illustration 19-3

Year	Calculations of Price Level			Price Index
1981 . . .	($ 9.00/$12.00)	×	100 =	75.0
1982 . . .	($11.00/$12.00)	×	100 =	91.7
1983 . . .	($10.25/$12.00)	×	100 =	85.4
1984 . . .	($12.00/$12.00)	×	100 =	100.0
1985 . . .	($13.00/$12.00)	×	100 =	108.3
1986 . . .	($15.50/$12.00)	×	100 =	129.2
1987 . . .	($17.40/$12.00)	×	100 =	145.0

Having constructed a price index for the A, B, C, D market basket, it is possible to make comparative statements about the cost of purchasing these items in various years. For example, it may be said that the price level in 1987 was 45.0% (145/100) higher than it was in 1984; the price level in 1987 was 34.3% (145/108) higher than it was in 1985; and 12.4% (145/129) higher than it was in 1986. Stated another way, it may be said that $1 in 1987 would purchase the same amount of A, B, C, D as would $0.69 in 1984 (100/145 = 0.68966). Also, $1 in 1987 would purchase the same amount of A, B, C, D as would $0.52 in 1981 (75/145 = 0.51724).

Specific versus General Price-Level Indexes

Price changes and price-level indexes can be calculated for narrow groups of commodities or services, such as housing construction material costs; or for broader groups of items, such as all construction costs; or for very broad groups of items, such as all items produced in the economy. A **specific price-level index,** as for housing construction materials, indicates the changing purchasing power of a dollar spent for items in that specific category; that is, to pay for housing construction materials. A **general price-level index,** such as the Consumer Price Index for All Urban Consumers, indicates the changing purchasing power of a dollar, spent for a very broad range of items.

Using Price Index Numbers in Accounting

In accounting, one use of a general price index is to restate dollar amounts of cost that were paid in earlier years into the current price level. In other words, a specific dollar amount of cost in a previous year can be restated in terms of the comparable number of dollars that would have been incurred if the cost had been paid with dollars of the current amount of purchasing power.

For example, suppose that $1,000 was paid in 1983 to purchase items

A, B, C, D. Stated in terms of 1987 prices, that 1983 cost is $1,000 $\times$ (145/85) = $1,706. As another example, if $1,500 were paid for A, B, C, D in 1984, that 1984 cost, restated in terms of 1987 prices, is $1,500 $\times$ (145/100) = $2,175.

Note that the 1984 cost of $1,500 correctly states the number of monetary units (dollars) expended for items A, B, C, D in 1984. Also, the 1983 cost of $1,000 correctly states the units of money expended in 1983. However, in a very important way, the 1983 monetary units do not mean the same thing as do the 1984 monetary units. A dollar (one monetary) unit in 1983 represented a different amount of purchasing power than did a dollar in 1984. Both of these dollars represent different amounts of purchasing power than a dollar in 1987.

To communicate the amount of purchasing power expended or incurred, the historical number of monetary units must be restated in terms of dollars with the same amount of purchasing power. For example, the total amount of cost incurred during 1983 and 1984 could be stated in terms of the purchasing power of 1984 dollars, or stated in terms of the purchasing power of 1987 dollars. These calculations are presented in Illustration 19-4.

Illustration 19-4

Year Cost Was Incurred	Monetary Units Expended (a)	Price Index Factor for Adjustment to 1984 Dollars (b)	Historical Cost Stated in 1984 Dollars (a × b = c)	Price Index Factor for Adjustment to 1987 Dollars (d)	Historical Cost Stated in 1987 Dollars (c × d)
1983	$1,000	100/85 = 1.17647	$1,176	145/100 = 1.45000	$1,706*
1984	1,500	—	1,500	145/100 = 1.45000	2,175
Total cost . . .	$2,500		$2,676		$3,881

* Raised $1 to correct for rounding. An alternative calculation is $1,000 $\times$ (145/85) = $1,706.

Accounting Systems that Make Adjustments for Price Changes

There are at least two important accounting systems that use price indexes to develop comprehensive financial statements. Both are alternatives to the conventional accounting system in general use in the United States. One alternative, called **current cost accounting,** is discussed later in the chapter. Current cost accounting uses specific price-level indexes (along with appraisals and other means) to develop statements that report assets and expenses in terms of the current costs to acquire those assets or services. The other alternative is called historical cost/constant dollar accounting.

Historical Cost/ Constant Dollar Accounting

Conventional financial statements disclose revenues, expenses, assets, liabilities, and owners' equity in terms of the historical monetary units exchanged when the transactions occurred. As such, they are sometimes referred to as **historical cost/nominal dollar financial statements.** This is intended to emphasize the difference between conventional statements and historical cost/constant dollar statements. **Historical cost/constant dollar accounting** uses a general price-level index to restate the conventional, nominal dollar financial statements into dollar amounts that represent current, general purchasing power.

Students should understand clearly that the same principles for determining depreciation expense, cost of goods sold, accruals of revenue, and so forth, apply to both historical cost/nominal dollar statements and historical cost/constant dollar statements. The same generally accepted accounting principles apply to both. The only difference between the two is that constant dollar statements reflect adjustments for general price-level changes; nominal dollar statements do not.

The Impact of General Price Changes on Assets

Monetary Assets The effect of general price-level changes on investments in assets depends on the nature of the assets. Some assets, called **monetary assets,** represent money or claims to receive a fixed amount of money. The number of dollars owned or to be received does not change, regardless of changes that may occur in the purchasing power of the dollar. Examples of monetary assets are cash, accounts receivable, notes receivable, and investments in bonds.

Because the amount of money to be received from a monetary asset is fixed, a monetary asset is not adjusted for general price-level changes on an historical cost/constant dollar balance sheet. For example, assume that $800 in cash was owned at the end of 1987. Regardless of how the price level has changed since the cash was acquired, the amount to be reported on the December 31, 1987, historical cost/constant dollar balance sheet is $800.

General Purchasing Power Gains or Losses Result from Owning Monetary Assets Because the amount of money to be received from monetary assets does not change with price-level changes, there is a special risk associated with owning such assets. An investment in monetary assets held during a period of inflation results in a loss of purchasing power. During a period of deflation, an investment in monetary assets results in a gain of purchasing power.

For example, assume that the $800 cash balance on December 31, 1987, resulted from the following:

Cash balance, December 31, 1986	$ 200
Cash receipts, assumed to have been received uniformly throughout the year	1,500
Cash disbursements, assumed to have been made uniformly throughout the year	(900)
Cash balance, December 31, 1987	$ 800

Also assume that the general price index was 150.0 at the end of 1986, that it averaged 160.0 throughout 1987, and was 168.0 at the end of that year. In this example, the beginning cash balance of $200 and the net receipts less disbursements of $600 lost purchasing power as the price level rose during 1987. This reduction in purchasing power constitutes a loss. To calculate the loss during the year, the beginning cash balance and each receipt or disbursement must be adjusted for price changes to the end of the year. Then, the adjusted balance is compared with the actual balance to determine the loss.

The amount of the loss is calculated as follows:

	Nominal Dollar Amounts	Price Index Factor for Restatement to December 31, 1987	Restated to December 31, 1987	Gain or (Loss)
Beginning balance.	$ 200	168.0/150.0 = 1.12000	$ 224	
Receipts	1,500	168.0/160.0 = 1.05000	1,575	
Disbursements	(900)	168.0/160.0 = 1.05000	(945)	
Ending balance, adjusted. .			$ 854	
Ending balance, actual . . .	$ 800		(800)	
Purchasing power loss . . .				$(54)

In the calculation, note that the receipts and disbursements were adjusted from the **average** price level during the year (**160.0**) to the ending price level (168.0). Because the receipts and disbursements were assumed to have occurred uniformly throughout the year, the average price level was used to approximate the price level at the time each receipt and disbursement took place. If receipts and disbursements do not occur uniformly, then each receipt and each disbursement must be adjusted separately from the price index at the time of the receipt or disbursement to the price index at year-end.

Nonmonetary Assets Assets that have fluctuating prices are called **nonmonetary assets.** In other words, nonmonetary assets include all assets other than monetary assets. The prices at which nonmonetary assets may be bought and sold tend to increase or decrease over time as the general price-level increases or decreases. Consequently, as the general price-level changes, investments in nonmonetary assets tend to retain the amounts of purchasing power originally invested. As a result, the reported amounts of nonmonetary assets on historical cost/constant dollar balance sheets are adjusted to reflect changes in the price level that have occurred since the nonmonetary assets were acquired.

For example, assume $500 was invested in land (a nonmonetary asset) at the end of 1979, and the investment was held throughout 1987. During this time, the general price index increased from 96.0 to 168.0. The historical cost/constant dollar balance sheets would disclose the following amounts:

Asset	December 31, 1979 Historical Cost/Constant Dollar Balance Sheet (a)	Price Index Factor for Adjustment to December 31, 1987 (b)	December 31, 1987 Historical Cost/Constant Dollar Balance Sheet (a × b)
Land	$500	168.0/96.0 = 1.75000	$875

The $875 shown as the investment in land at the end of 1987 has the same amount of general purchasing power as did $500 at the end of 1979. Thus, no change in general purchasing power was recognized from holding the land.

The Impact of General Price Changes on Liabilities and Stockholders' Equity

The effect of general price-level changes on liabilities depends on the nature of the liability. Most liabilities are monetary items, but stockholders' equity and a few liabilities are nonmonetary items.[6]

Monetary Liabilities Obligations that are fixed in terms of the amount owed are called **monetary liabilities.** The number of dollars to be paid does not change regardless of changes in the general price level. Since monetary liabilities are unchanged in amounts owed even when price levels change, monetary liabilities are not adjusted for price-level changes.

General Purchasing Power Gains and Losses Result from Owing Monetary Liabilities

A company with monetary liabilities outstanding during a period of general price-level change will experience a **general purchasing power gain or loss.** Assume, for example, that a note payable for $300 was outstanding on December 31, 1986, when the price index was 150.0. On April 5, 1987, when the price index was 157.0, a $700 increase in the note resulted in a $1,000 balance that remained outstanding throughout the remainder of 1987. On December 31, 1987, the price index was 168.0. On the historical cost/constant dollar balance sheet for December 31, 1987, the note payable would be reported at $1,000. The general purchasing power gain or loss during 1987 is calculated as follows:

	Nominal Dollar Amounts	Price Index Factor for Restatement to December 31, 1987	Restated to December 31, 1987	Gain or (Loss)
Beginning balance	$ 300	168.0/150.0 = 1.12000	$ 336	
April 5 increase	700	168.0/157.0 = 1.07006	749	
Ending balance, adjusted . .			$ 1,085	
Ending balance, actual . . .	$1,000		(1,000)	
Purchasing power gain . . .				$85

Stated in terms of general purchasing power at year-end, the amount that was borrowed was $1,085. Since the company can pay the note with $1,000, the $85 difference is a gain in general purchasing power earned by the firm. Alternatively, if the general price index had decreased during 1987, the monetary liability would have resulted in a general purchasing power loss.

---

[6] Depending on its nature, preferred stock may be treated as a monetary item. If so, it is an exception to the general rule that stockholders' equity items are nonmonetary items.

To determine a company's total purchasing power gain or loss during a year, the accountant must analyze each monetary asset and each monetary liability. The final gain or loss may then be described as **the purchasing power gain (or loss) on net monetary items owned or owed.**

Nonmonetary Liabilities and Stockholders' Equity Obligations that are not fixed in amount are called **nonmonetary liabilities.** They therefore tend to change with changes in the general price level. For example, product warranties may require that a manufacturer pay for repairs and replacements for a specified period of time after the product is sold. The amount of money required to make the repairs or replacements tends to change with changes in the general price level. Consequently, there is no purchasing power gain or loss associated with such warranties. Further, the historical cost/constant dollar balance sheet amount of such a nonmonetary liability must be adjusted to reflect changes in the general price index that occur after the liability comes into existence. Stockholders' equity items, with the possible exception of preferred stock, are also nonmonetary items. Hence, they also must be adjusted for changes in the general price index.

Illustration 19-5 summarizes the impact of general price-level changes on monetary items and nonmonetary items. The illustration indicates what adjustments must be made in preparing an historical cost/constant dollar balance sheet and what purchasing power gains and losses must be recognized on a constant dollar income statement.

Illustration 19-5

Financial Statement Item	When the General Price Level Rises (inflation)		When the General Price Level Falls (deflation)	
	Balance Sheet Adjustment Required	Income Statement Gain or Loss	Balance Sheet Adjustment Required	Income Statement Gain or Loss
Monetary assets	No	Loss	No	Gain
Nonmonetary assets	Yes	None	Yes	None
Monetary liabilites	No	Gain	No	Loss
Nonmonetary equities and liabilities.	Yes	None	Yes	None

---

■ **Historical Cost/ Constant Dollar Accounting Fails to Report Current Values**

As discussed previously, prices do not all change at the same rate. Indeed, when the general price level is rising, some specific prices may be falling. If this were not so, if prices all changed at the same rate, then historical cost/constant dollar accounting would report current values on the financial statements.

For example, suppose that a company purchased land for $50,000 on January 1, 1986, when the general price index was 130.0. Then the price level increased until December 1987, when the price index was 168.0. An historical cost/constant dollar balance sheet for this company on December 31, 1987, would report the land at $50,000 × 168.0/130.0 = $64,615. If all prices increased at the same rate during that period, the price of the land would have increased from $50,000 to $64,615, and the company's historical cost/constant dollar balance sheet would coincidentally disclose the land at its current value.

However, since all prices do not change at the same rate, the current value of the land may differ substantially from the historical cost/constant dollar amount of $64,615. For example, assume that the company obtained an appraisal of the land and determined that its current value on December 31, 1987, was $80,000. The difference between the original purchase price of $50,000 and the current value of $80,000 can be explained as follows:

Unrealized holding gain	$80,000 − $64,615 = $15,385
Adjustment for general price-level	
increase	$64,615 − $50,000 = 14,615
	$30,000

In that case, the historical cost/constant dollar balance sheet would report land at $64,615, which is $15,385 ($80,000 − $64,615) less than its current value. This illustrates a very important fact concerning historical cost/constant dollar accounting; it does not attempt to report current values. Rather, historical cost/constant dollar accounting restates original transaction prices into equivalent amounts of current, **general** purchasing power. Only if current, **specific** purchasing power were the basis of valuation would the balance sheet display current values.

■ **Current Cost Accounting**

Current Costs on the Income Statement

In the current cost approach to accounting, the reported amount of each expense should be the number of dollars that would be required, at the time the expense is incurred, to acquire the resources consumed. For example, assume that the annual sales of a company included an item that was sold in May for $1,500 and the item had been acquired on January 1 for $500. Also, suppose that in May, at the time of the sale, the cost to replace this item was $700. Then the annual current cost income statement would show sales of $1,500 less cost of goods sold of $700. To state this idea more generally, when an asset is acquired and then held for a time before it expires, the historical cost of the asset likely will differ from its current cost at the time it expires. **Current cost accounting** requires that the reported amount of expense be measured at the time the asset expires.

The result of measuring expenses in terms of current costs is that revenue is matched with the current (at the time of the sale) cost of the resources that were used to earn the revenue. Thus, operating profit is not greater than zero unless revenues are sufficient to replace all of the resources that were consumed in the process of producing those revenues. The operating profit figure is therefore thought to be an important (and improved) basis for evaluating the effectiveness of operating activities.

Current Costs on the Balance Sheet

On the balance sheet, current cost accounting requires that assets be reported at the amounts that would have to be paid to purchase them as of the balance sheet date. Similarly, liabilities should be reported at the amounts that would have to be paid to satisfy the liabilities as of the balance sheet date. Note that this valuation basis is similar to historical cost/constant dollar accounting in that a distinction exists between monetary and non-monetary assets and liabilities. Monetary assets and liabilities are fixed in amount regardless of price changes. Therefore, monetary assets need not be adjusted in amount. But all of the nonmonetary items must be evaluated at each balance sheet date to determine the best approximation of current cost.

A little reflection on the variety of assets reported on balance sheets will confirm the presence of many difficulties in obtaining reliable estimates of current costs. In some cases, specific price indexes may provide the most reliable source of current cost information. In other cases, where an asset is not new and has been partially depreciated, its current cost may be estimated by determining the cost to acquire a new asset of like nature. Depreciation on the old asset is then based on the current cost of the new asset. Clearly, the accountant's professional judgment is an important factor in developing current cost data.

Disclosing the Effects of Changing Prices: FASB Requirements

The FASB requirements for disclosing the effects of changing prices are limited in two important ways. First, the requirements apply only to large companies. They apply only to companies with assets of more than $1 billion or inventories plus property, plant, and equipment (before deducting depreciation) of more than $125 million. Second, the requirements do not affect the conventional financial statements. Only supplemental information is required.

The supplemental information to be presented includes:[7]

a. The general purchasing power gain or loss on net monetary items for the current fiscal year.
b. Income from continuing operations on a current cost basis.
c. Current cost of inventory, property, plant, and equipment at the end of the year.
d. Increases or decreases for the current fiscal year in the current cost amounts of inventory, property, plant, and equipment, net of inflation.
e. A five-year summary of selected financial data.

Examples of the required disclosures are presented in Illustrations 19-6 and 19-7. Compare the requirements listed above as items (a) through (d) with the information shown in Illustration 19-6. Each of the required items is disclosed.

Observe in Illustration 19-6 that the only restated income statement items are "Cost of goods sold" and "Depreciation and amortization expense." These are the only income statement items (plus depletion expense, if any) that must be restated to meet the minimum FASB requirements. Net sales, other operating expense, interest expense, and provision for income taxes do not have to be restated. These latter items may well have

---

[7] FASB, *Accounting Standards—Current Text,* sec. C27.107–113, as revised by *FASB Statement of Financial Accounting Standards No. 82,* November 1984. Copyright © by the Financial Accounting Standards Board, High Ridge Park, Stamford, Conn. 06905, U.S.A. Quoted (or excerpted) with permission. Copies of the complete documents are available from the FASB.

Illustration 19-6

Statement of Income from Continuing Operations
Adjusted for Changing Prices
For the Year Ended December 31, 198E
($000)

	As Reported in the Primary Statements	Adjusted for Changes in Specific Prices (current costs)
Net sales and other operating revenues . .	$253,000	$253,000
Cost of goods sold	$197,000	$205,408
Depreciation and amortization expense . .	10,000	19,500
Other operating expense.	20,835	20,835
Interest expense	7,165	7,165
Provision for income taxes	9,000	9,000
	$244,000	$261,908
Income (loss) from continuing operations. .	$ 9,000	$ (8,908)
Gain from decline in purchasing power of net amounts owed		$ 7,729
Increase in specific prices (current cost) of inventories and property, plant, and equipment held during the year*		$ 24,608
Effect of increase in general price level . .		18,959
Excess of increase in specific prices over increase in the general price level. . . .		$ 5,649

* At December 31, 198E, current cost of inventory was $65,700 and current cost of property, plant and equipment, net of accumulated depreciation was $85,100.

Adapted from FASB, *Statement of Financial Accounting Standards No. 33,* Appendix A, Schedule B, p. 33, as revised by *Statement of Financial Accounting Standards No. 82.*

been affected by inflation. And the FASB would **permit** companies to adjust such items. But the Board does not require it.

Note that the general purchasing power gain or loss is called "Gain from decline in purchasing power of net amounts owed." In this case, total monetary liabilities owed were in excess of monetary assets owned. The net amount was owed during a period of inflation and the result was a gain. Since a general purchasing power gain or loss of some amount is to be expected each year, it would have seemed reasonable to include this item in the calculation of income (loss) from continuing operations. However, the FASB decided against this approach and concluded that the purchasing power gain or loss should be listed separately.

The five-year summary of financial data is shown in Illustration 19-7. Observe that current cost information is shown for the years 198A through 198E.

■ **Using Recoverable Amounts that Are Lower than Current Cost**

In general, **current cost** is the cost that would be required to currently acquire (or replace) an asset or service. However, the FASB recognized an important exception to this general description of current cost accounting. That exception involves the use of recoverable amounts.

In the case of an asset about to be sold, the recoverable amount is its net realizable value. In other words, the recoverable amount is the asset's

Illustration 19–7

Five-Year Comparison of Selected
Supplementary Financial Data Adjusted for Effects of Changing Prices
($000 of average 198E dollars)

	Years Ended December 31				
	198A	**198B**	**198C**	**198D**	**198E**
Net sales and other operating revenues	$265,000	$235,000	$240,000	$237,063	$253,000
Current Cost Information					
Income (loss) from continuing operations	(3,650)	(4,039)	(5,100)	(4,125)	(8,908)
Income (loss) from continuing operations per common share	(2.52)	(2.79)	(3.53)	(2.75)	(5.94)
Excess of increase in specific prices over increase in the general price level	1,892	1,659	140	2,292	5,649
Net assets at year-end	68,050	73,100	77,170	70,006	81,466
Gain from decline in purchasing power of net amounts owed	7,950	6,080	6,420	7,027	7,729
Cash dividends declared per common share	2.59	2.43	2.26	2.16	2.00
Market price per common share at year-end	32	31	43	39	35
Average consumer price index	170.5	181.5	195.4	205.0	220.9

Adapted from *FASB Statement of Financial Accounting Standards No. 33*, Appendix A, Schedule B, p. 34, as revised by *Statement of Financial Accounting Standards No. 82*.

expected sales price less related costs to sell. If an asset is to be used rather than sold, the recoverable amount is the present value of future cash flows expected from using the asset. A recoverable amount is reported instead of current cost whenever the recoverable amount appears to be materially and permanently lower than current cost. Both the asset and the expense associated with using it (or selling it) should be measured in terms of the recoverable amount.[8]

The reason for using recoverable amounts is that an asset should not be reported at an amount that is larger than its value to its owner. If the recoverable amount of an asset is less than its current cost, a business is not likely to replace it. A business would not be willing to pay more for an asset than it could expect to recover from using or selling the asset. Hence, the value of the asset to the business can be no higher than the recoverable amount. When value to the business is less than current cost, it is believed that current cost is not relevant to an analysis of the business.

ACCOUNTING FOR INTERNATIONAL OPERATIONS

Many companies, particularly large corporations, engage in business activities in more than one country. In fact, the operations of some companies

[8] Ibid., sec. C27.143–144.

involve so many different countries that they are described as being **multinational businesses.** The problems of managing and accounting for a company that has international operations can be very complex, and detailed study of these issues should be reserved for advanced courses in business.

However, there are two accounting problems that warrant a general introduction. Both of these problems stem from the fact that businesses with transactions in more than one country generally have to deal with more than one currency. To aid understanding, the discussion of these problems takes the perspective of companies that have a base of operations in the United States and therefore prepare their financial statements in terms of the United States dollar. Hence, the **reporting currency** of such firms is the U.S. dollar.

Exchange Rates between Currencies

Students should understand that an active market exists for the purchase and sale of foreign currencies. U.S. dollars may be exchanged for Canadian dollars, British pounds, French francs, and so forth. The price of one currency is stated in terms of another currency and is called a **foreign exchange rate.** For example, on May 7, 1985, the current exchange rate for British pounds and U.S. dollars was expressed as $1.18, which means that one pound could have been exchanged for $1.18. On the same day, the exchange rate between West German marks and U.S. dollars was $0.303. These foreign exchange rates fluctuate on a daily basis based on the changing supply and demand for each currency.

Sales (or Purchases) Denominated in a Foreign Currency

When a U.S. company makes a sale to a foreign customer, a special problem may arise in accounting for the sale and account receivable. If the foreign customer is required, by the terms of the sale, to make payment in the form of U.S. dollars, no special problem arises. But if the terms of the sale state that payment is to be in a foreign currency, the U.S. company must go through special steps in accounting for the sale and account receivable.

For example, suppose a United States company, the Boston Company, makes a credit sale to London Outfitters, a British company. The sale occurs on December 12, 198A, and the price is 10,000 pounds due February 10, 198B. To record the sale in its accounting records (which are, of course, kept in terms of U.S. dollars), Boston Company must translate the sales price from pounds to dollars. This should be done using the current exchange rate available on the date of the sale. Assuming the current exchange rate on December 12 is $1.22, the sale would be recorded as follows:

Dec.	12	Accounts Receivable—London Outfitters . . .	12,200.00	
		Sales		12,200.00
		10,000 × $1.22 = $12,200.		

Now assume that Boston Company prepares annual financial statements on December 31 and the current exchange rate on that date has risen to $1.24. Generally accepted accounting principles require that the receivable be translated at the current exchange rate. This change in valuation of the receivable is recorded as follows:

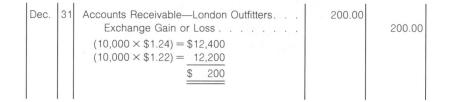

Dec.	31	Accounts Receivable—London Outfitters. . . .	200.00	
		Exchange Gain or Loss		200.00
		(10,000 × $1.24) = $12,400		
		(10,000 × $1.22) = 12,200		
		$ 200		

The Exchange Gain or Loss is closed to Income Summary and included on the income statement.[9]

On February 10, when Boston Company receives London Outfitters' payment of 10,000 pounds, the foreign exchange rate is $1.19. The receipt and the loss associated with the decline in the exchange rate is recorded as follows:

Feb.	10	Cash (10,000 × $1.19)	11,900.00	
		Exchange Gain or Loss	500.00	
		Accounts Receivable—London Outfitters		12,400.00

■ Consolidated Statements with Foreign Subsidiaries

A second problem of accounting for international operations involves the preparation of consolidated financial statements when the parent company has a foreign subsidiary. For example, suppose a U.S. company owns a controlling interest in a Mexico City subsidiary. The reporting currency of the U.S. parent is, of course, the dollar. However, the Mexican subsidiary maintains its financial records in pesos. Before a consolidated working paper can be prepared, the financial statements of the Mexican company must be translated into U.S. dollars. After the translation is completed, the preparation of consolidated statements is no different than for any other subsidiary.

The procedures for accomplishing the translation of a foreign subsidiary's account balances depend on the nature of the subsidiary's operations. However, the general process is one of selecting appropriate foreign exchange rates and applying those rates to the account balances of the foreign subsidiary. Students in business generally need not be concerned with any more detailed discussion of these procedures. For those who will major in accounting, a thorough analysis of these procedures typically is included in a senior level course in advanced accounting.

[9] FASB, *Accounting Standards—Current Text,* sec. F60.122. First published as *FASB Statement of Financial Accounting Standards No. 52,* par. 15.

Glossary

Changes in accounting estimates adjustments to previously made assumptions about the future such as salvage values and the length of useful lives of buildings and equipment.

Current cost in general, the cost that would be required to acquire (or replace) an asset or service at the present time. On the income statement, the numbers of dollars that would be required, at the time the expense is incurred, to acquire the resources consumed. On the balance sheet, the amounts that would have to be paid to replace the assets or satisfy the liabilities as of the balance sheet date.

Current cost accounting an accounting system that uses specific price-level indexes (and other means) to develop financial statements that report items such as assets and expenses in terms of the current costs to acquire or replace those assets or services.

Deflation a general decrease in the prices paid for goods and services.

Extraordinary gain or loss a gain or loss that is both unusual and infrequent of occurrence.

Foreign exchange rate the price of one currency stated in terms of another currency.

General price-level index a measure of the changing purchasing power of a dollar, spent for a very broad range of items; for example, the Consumer Price Index for All Urban Consumers.

General purchasing power gain or loss the gain or loss that results from holding monetary assets and/or owing monetary liabilities during a period in which the general price level changes.

Historical cost/constant dollar accounting an accounting system that adjusts historical cost/nominal dollar financial statements for changes in the general purchasing power of the dollar.

Historical cost/nominal dollar financial statements conventional financial statements that disclose revenues, expenses, assets, liabilities, and owners' equity in terms of the historical monetary units exchanged at the time the transactions occurred.

Inflation a general increase in the prices paid for goods and services.

Infrequent gain or loss a gain or loss that is not expected to occur again, given the operating environment of the business.

Monetary assets money or claims to receive a fixed amount of money; the number of dollars to be received does not change regardless of changes in the purchasing power of the dollar.

Monetary liabilities fixed amounts that are owed; the number of dollars to be paid does not change regardless of changes in the general price level.

Multinational business a company that operates in a large number of different countries.

Nonmonetary assets assets that have fluctuating prices.

Nonmonetary liabilities obligations that are not fixed in amount.

Price index a measure of the changes in prices of a particular market basket of goods and/or services.

Prior period adjustment items that are reported in the current statement of retained earnings as corrections to the beginning retained earnings balance; limited primarily to corrections of errors made in past years.

Reporting currency the currency in which a company presents its financial statements.

Segment of a business operations of a company involving a particular line of business or class of customer, providing the assets, activities, and financial results of the operations can be distinguished from other parts of the business.

Specific price-level index an indicator of the changing purchasing power of a dollar spent for items in a specific category; includes a much narrower range of goods and services than does a general price index.

Unusual gain or loss a gain or loss that is abnormal and unrelated or only incidentally related to the ordinary activities and environment of the business.

□ Questions for Class Discussion

1. In the annual income statement of a corporation, what are four major sections of the statement that might appear below "Income from continuing operations"?

2. If a company has business operations in several different lines of business, what criteria must be met if the operations in a particular line of business are to qualify as a business segment?

3. If a company makes a definite plan to sell one of its business segments early in January of 198A, and the disposal of the segment is completed in November of that year, what two items concerning that segment should appear on the company's 198A income statement?

4. Where on the income statement should a company disclose a gain that is abnormal and unrelated to the ordinary activities of the business and that is expected to recur no more often than once every five years?

5. Which of the following items would qualify as an extraordinary gain or loss: (*a*) operating losses resulting from a strike against a major supplier, (*b*) a gain from the sale of surplus equipment, (*c*) a loss from damage to a building caused by a tornado (a type of storm that rarely occurs in the geographical region of the company's operations).

6. In past years, a company paid its sales personnel annual salaries without additional incentive payments. This year, a new policy is being instituted whereby they will receive sales commissions rather than annual salaries. Does this new policy require a prior period adjustment? Explain why or why not.

7. After taking five years straight-line depreciation on an asset that was expected to have an eight-year life, a company concluded that the asset would last another six years. Does this decision involve a change in accounting principles? If not, how would you describe this change?

8. Some people argue that conventional financial statements fail to adequately account for inflation. What is the general problem with conventional financial statements that generates this argument?

9. During a period of inflation, is it possible for the prices of specific items to fall? Why or why not?

10. Explain the difference between an "average change in per unit prices" and a "weighted-average change in per unit prices."

11. What is the significance of the "base" year in constructing a price index? How is the base year chosen?

12. What is the difference between a specific price-level index and a general price-level index?

13. What is the fundamental difference in the price-level adjustments made under current cost accounting and under historical cost/constant dollar accounting?

14. What is meant by "historical cost/nominal dollar" financial statements?

15. Define *monetary assets.*

16. Explain the meaning of *nonmonetary assets.*

17. Define *monetary liabilities* and *nonmonetary liabilities.* Give examples of both.

18. If the monetary assets held by a firm exceed its monetary liabilities throughout a period in which prices are rising, which should be recorded on a historical cost/constant dollar income statement—a purchasing power gain or loss? What if monetary liabilities exceed monetary assets during a period in which prices are falling?

19. If accountants preferred to display current values in the financial statements, would they use historical cost/constant dollar accounting or current cost accounting?

20. Describe the meaning of *operating profit* under a current cost accounting system.

21. "The distinction between monetary assets and nonmonetary assets is just as important for current cost accounting as it is for historical cost/constant dollar accounting." Is this statement true? Why?

22. The FASB has required several specific disclosures of information concerning price changes. List the general disclosure requirements of the FASB.

23. According to the FASB, when should recoverable amounts be reported instead of current costs?

24. What are two basic problems of accounting for international operations?

25. In preparing its December 31, 198B, financial statements a U.S. company had to report an account receivable that was denominated in a foreign currency. The receivable stemmed from a sale made on November 14, 198A. In translating the receivable into dollars, should the accountant use the foreign exchange rate on November 14 or on December 31?

□ **Class Exercises**   **Exercise 19-1**

The following list of items was extracted from the December 31, 198A, trial balance of X Company. Using the information contained in this listing, prepare X Company's income statement for 198A. You need not complete the earnings per share calculations.

	Debit	Credit
Salaries expense	$14,000	
Income tax expense	15,000	
Loss from operating segment B (net of $18,000 tax)	42,000	
Sales		$93,500
Cumulative effect on prior years' income of change from declining-balance to straight-line depreciation (net of $3,000 tax)	7,200	
Extraordinary gain on state's condemnation of land owned by X Company (net of $10,000 tax)		26,000
Depreciation expense	13,200	
Gain on sale of segment B (net of $8,000 tax)		20,000
Cost of goods sold	29,000	

Exercise 19-2

A company with one depreciable asset that cost $540,000 has decided to switch from straight-line depreciation to sum-of-the-years'-digits depreciation. In prior years, the company depreciated the asset for two years based on straight-line depreciation, no salvage value, and an eight-year life. The company is subject to a 40% income tax rate. Calculate the amount of depreciation expense to be reported in the current year and the cumulative effect of the change on prior years' incomes. Indicate whether the cumulative effect of the change on prior years' incomes should be added or subtracted when calculating the current year's net income.

Exercise 19-3

In preparing the annual financial statements for a company, the correct manner of reporting the following items was not clear to the company's employees. Explain where each of the following items should appear in the financial statements.

a. The company keeps its delivery equipment for several years before disposing of the old equipment and buying new equipment. This year, for the first time in seven years, it sold old equipment for a gain of $6,500 and then purchased new equipment.
b. After amortizing a trademark for three years based on an expected life of five years, the company decided this year that the value of the trademark would last four more years. As a result, the amortization for the current year is $4,000 instead of $8,000.
c. This year the accounting department of the company discovered that two years ago, a cost had been charged to maintenance expense when it should have been charged to land. The after-tax effect of the charge to maintenance expense was $25,000.

Exercise 19-4

Market basket No. 1 consists of 1 unit of A, 4 units of B, and 2 units of D. Market basket No. 2 consists of 2 units of B, 5 units of C, and 2 units of D. The per unit prices of each item during 198A and during 198B were as follows:

Item	198A Price per Unit	198B Price per Unit
A	$2.00	$1.80
B	4.00	4.60
C	5.00	6.00
D	3.00	2.70

Required

Compute the annual rate of inflation for market basket No. 1 and for market basket No. 2. Round your answers to the nearest 1/10%.

Exercise 19-5

The following total prices of a specified market basket were calculated for each of the years 198A through 198E:

Year	Total Price
198A	$19,200
198B	26,000
198C	32,400
198D	35,600
198E	48,400

Required

1. Using 198C as the base year, prepare a price index for the five-year period. Round your answers to the nearest 1/10%.
2. Convert the index from a 198C base year to a 198E base year.

Exercise 19-6

A company's plant and equipment consisted of land purchased in late 198A for $270,000, a building purchased in late 198C for $468,000, and equipment purchased in late 198E for $72,000. The general price index for December of the years 198A through 198G is as follows:

198A	100.0
198B	108.0
198C	116.0
198D	120.0
198E	125.0
198F	145.0
198G	159.5

Required

1. Assuming the above price index adequately represents end-of-year price levels, calculate the amount of each cost that would be shown on an historical cost/constant dollar balance sheet for (*a*) December 31, 198F, and (*b*) December 31, 198G. Ignore any accumulated depreciation.
2. Would the historical cost/constant dollar income statement for 198G disclose any purchasing power gain or loss as a consequence of holding the above assets? If so, how much?

Exercise 19-7

Determine whether the following items are monetary or nonmonetary items.

1. Merchandise.
2. Common stock.
3. Prepaid rent.
4. Goodwill.
5. Salaries payable.
6. Retained earnings.
7. Prepaid insurance.
8. Product warranties liability.
9. Trademarks.
10. Accounts payable.
11. Furniture and fixtures.
12. Contributed capital in excess of par value, common stock.
13. Savings accounts.
14. Notes receivable.

Exercise 19-8

A company made the following purchases of land: in 198A, at a cost of $40,000 and in 198B at a cost of $15,000. What is the current cost of the land purchases in (a) 198C and (b) 198D, given the following specific price index for land costs? (Round your answers to the nearest whole dollar.)

198A	84.0
198B	100.0
198C	96.0
198D	105.0

Exercise 19-9

Calculate the general purchasing power gain or loss in 198B given the following information:

Time Period	Price Index
December 198A.	120.0
Average during 198B	144.0
December 198B.	180.0

a. The Cash balance on December 31, 198A, was $1,200. During 198B, cash sales occurred uniformly throughout the year and amounted to $18,400. Payments of expenses also occurred evenly throughout the year and amounted to $12,500. Accounts payable of $4,100 were paid in December.

b. Accounts payable amounted to $2,000 on December 31, 198A. Additional accounts payable amounting to $3,800 were recorded evenly throughout 198B. The only payment of accounts during the year was $4,100 in late December.

Exercise 19-10

Nickles Company, of El Paso, Texas, sells its products to customers in the United States and in Mexico. On November 15, 198A, Nickles Company sold merchandise on credit to the Mexico Products Company at a price of 945,000 pesos. The exchange rate on that day was 1 peso equals $0.0040. On December 31, 198A, when Nickles Company prepared its financial statements, the exchange rate was 1 peso for $0.0050. Mexico Products paid its bill in full on March 15, 198B, at which time the exchange rate was 1 peso for $0.0046 pesos. Prepare journal entries on November 15, December 31, and March 15, to account for the sale and account receivable on the books of Nickles Company.

Problems

Problem 19-1

Radford Company had several unusual transactions during 198A and has prepared the following list of trial balance items from which the appropriate items should be selected and used in constructing the 198A income statement for the company.

	Debit	Credit
Depreciation expense	$ 14,600	
Income from operations of Fox Division (net of $6,000 income taxes).		$ 15,000
Sales		292,000
Cost of goods sold	87,400	
Gain on sale of artwork in company offices (an unusual transaction for the company that occurs only when major redecorations are required and expensive new artwork is purchased, which happens about every four to six years)		32,500
Loss on a patent infringement suit (This patent is essential to the operations of the business, and it is not unusual for companies in this industry to be involved in patent infringement suits. However, the lawsuit appears to have settled the matter in this case and the problem is not expected to arise in the foreseeable future)	140,000	
Income tax expense	36,600	
Gain on payment from supplier to compensate for loss of customers who had been sold products containing inferior materials purchased from the supplier (In this industry, such settlements with suppliers occur quite frequently.)		24,000
Maintenance expense costs (net of $5,000 income taxes) incurred in late December of last year and incorrectly charged to building	12,100	
Gain on sale of investment in stock (net of $7,000 income taxes) The stock was originally donated to Radford by an elderly stockholder and was held out of courtesy until that stockholder's death. Radford has never held stock investments before and has no intention of doing so in the future		43,800
Accumulated depreciation, buildings		36,000
Loss on sale of Fox Division (net of $8,800 income taxes)	21,000	
Interest earned		3,500
Other operating expenses	72,300	

	Debit	Credit
Effect on prior years' income of switching from accelerated depreciation to straight-line depreciation (net of $42,000 income taxes)		47,000
Estimated product warranty liability.		23,000

Required

Prepare Radford Company's income statement for 198A, excluding the earnings per share statistics.

Problem 19-2

On January 1, 198A, the Chris Company purchased a major item of machinery for use in its operations. The machine cost $450,000 and was expected to have a salvage value of $50,000. Depreciation was taken through 198D on a declining-balance method at twice the straight-line rate assuming an eight-year life. Early in 198E, the company concluded that given the economic conditions in the industry, a straight-line method would result in more meaningful financial statements. They argue that straight-line depreciation would allow better comparisons with the financial results of other firms in the industry.

Required

1. Is Chris Company allowed to change depreciation methods in 198E?
2. Prepare a table that shows the depreciation expense to be reported each year of the asset's life under both depreciation methods and the cumulative effect of the change on prior years' incomes. Assume an income tax rate of 40%, and round your answers to the nearest whole dollar.
3. State the amount of depreciation expense to be reported in 198E and the cumulative effect of the change on prior years' incomes. How should the cumulative effect be reported? Is the cumulative effect on 198E net income positive or negative?
4. Now assume that Chris Company had used straight-line depreciation through 198D and justified a change to declining-balance depreciation in 198E. What amount of depreciation expense should be reported in 198E? How does the reporting of the cumulative effect of the change differ from your answer to Requirement 3?

Problem 19-3

The costs of purchasing a common "market basket" in each of several years are as follows:

Year	Cost of Market Basket
198A	$ 81,000
198B	85,860
198C	91,800
198D	91,260
198E	108,000
198F	113,400
198G	111,240
198H	121,500

Required

1. Construct a price index using 198B as the base year. Round each index number to 1/10%.

2. Using the index constructed in Requirement 1, what was the percent increase in prices from 198D to 198H?

3. Using the index constructed in Requirement 1, how many dollars in 198H does it take to have the same purchasing power as $1 in 198A?

4. Using the index constructed in Requirement 1, if $75,000 were invested in land during 198C and $90,000 were invested in land during 198F, what would be reported as the total land investment on a constant dollar balance sheet prepared in 198G? What would your answer be if the investments were in U.S. long-term bonds rather than in land?

Problem 19-4

Martin Company purchased machinery for $576,000 on January 2, 198B. The equipment was expected to last nine years and have no salvage value; straight-line depreciation was to be used. The equipment was sold on December 31, 198E, for $425,000. End-of-year general price index numbers during this period of time were as follows:

198A	98.0
198B	127.4
198C	137.2
198D	156.8
198E	166.6

Required

(Round all answers to the nearest whole dollar.)

1. What should be presented for the equipment and accumulated depreciation on an historical cost/constant dollar balance sheet dated December 31, 198C? Hint: Depreciation is the total amount of cost that has been allocated to expense. Therefore, the price index numbers that are used to adjust the nominal dollar cost of the asset should also be used to adjust the nominal dollar amount of depreciation.

2. How much depreciation expense should be shown on the historical cost/constant dollar income statement for 198D?

3. How much depreciation expense should be shown on the historical cost/constant dollar income statement for 198E?

4. How much gain on the sale of equipment would be reported on the historical cost/nominal dollar income statement for 198E?

5. After adjusting the equipment's cost and accumulated depreciation to the end-of-198E price level, how much gain in (loss of) general purchasing power was realized by the sale of the equipment?

Problem 19-5

Bancroft Express had three monetary items during 198B: cash, accounts receivable, and accounts payable. The changes in these items during the year were as follows:

Cash:

Beginning balance	$ 8,000
Cash proceeds from sale of surplus equipment (in mid-January 198B)	12,800
Cash receipts from customers (spread evenly throughout the year)	87,400
Payments of accounts payable (spread evenly throughout the year)	(49,200)
Payments of other cash expenses during March 198B	(19,600)
Dividends declared and paid in mid-September 198B	(15,000)
Ending balance	$ 24,400

Accounts receivable:

Beginning balance	$ 14,500
Sales to customers (spread evenly throughout the year)	96,100
Cash receipts from customers (spread evenly throughout the year)	(87,400)
Ending balance	$ 23,200

Accounts payable:

Beginning balance	$ 16,900
Merchandise purchases (spread evenly throughout the year)	38,500
Special purchase near end of December 198B	11,000
Payments of accounts payable (spread evenly throughout the year)	(49,200)
Ending balance	$ 17,200

General price index numbers at the end of 198A and during 198B are as follows:

December 198A	175.0
January 198B	178.0
March 198B	182.7
September 198B	189.7
December 198B	193.0
Average for 198B	186.0

Required

Calculate the general purchasing power gain or loss experienced by Bancroft Express in 198B. Round all amounts to the nearest whole dollar.

Problem 19-6

Roberson, Incorporated purchased a tract of land for $120,000 in 198A, when the general price index was 83.7. At the same time, a price index for land values in the area of Roberson's tract was 91.5. In 198B, when the general price index was 89.2 and the specific price index for land was 103.0, Roberson bought another tract of land for $180,000. In late 198H, the general price index is 162.4 and the price index for land values is 247.3.

Required

1. In preparing a balance sheet at the end of 198H, what amount should be shown for land on:
   a. An historical cost/nominal dollar balance sheet.
   b. An historical cost/constant dollar balance sheet.
   c. A current cost balance sheet.
   Round all amounts to the nearest whole dollar.

2. In Roberson, Incorporated's December 198H meeting of the board of directors, one director insists that Roberson has earned a gain in general purchasing power as a result of owning the land. A second director argues that there could not have been a purchasing power gain or loss since land is a nonmonetary asset. Which director do you think is correct? Explain your answer.

Problem 19-7

Worldwide Sales Corporation, a United States company that has customers in several foreign countries, had the following transactions in 198A and 198B:

July   7   Sold merchandise for 33,500 francs to LePanache of Paris, payment in full to be received in 60 days. On this day, the foreign exchange rate for francs into dollars was quoted as $0.1061.

Aug.   20   Sold merchandise to San Miguel Distributers of Mexico for $2,300 cash. The exchange rate for pesos into dollars was $0.0039.

Sept.   5   Received LePanache's payment for its purchase of July 7. Noted the current foreign exchange rate for francs into dollars was $0.1073.

Oct.   12   Sold merchandise on credit to Scandia Imports, Inc., a company located in Oslo, Norway. The price of 147,000 kroner was to be paid 90 days from the date of sale. On October 12, the foreign exchange rate for kroner into dollars was $0.1125.

Nov.   25   Sold merchandise for 16,900 punts to Callahan Company of Ireland, payment in full to be in 60 days. The exchange rate for punts into dollars was $1.0110.

Dec.   31   Prepared adjusting entries to recognize exchange gains or losses on the annual financial statements. Rates of exchanging foreign currencies into dollars on this day included the following:

Francs (France)	$0.1068
Kroner (Norway). . . .	0.1082
Pesos (Mexico)	0.0048
Punts (Ireland)	1.0190

Jan.   10   Received Scandia Imports, Inc.'s full payment for the sale of October 12. The exchange rate for kroner into dollars was $0.1090.

       24   Received full payment from Callahan Company for the sale of Nov. 25. The exchange rate for punts into dollars was $0.9670.

Required

1. Prepare general journal entries to account for these transactions of Worldwide Sales Corporation. Round all amounts to the nearest whole dollar.

2. Calculate the exchange gain or loss to be reported on Worldwide Sales Corporation's 198A income statement.

☐ **Alternate Problems**   **Problem 19-1A**

Tisdale Corporation had several unusual transactions during 198A and has prepared the following list of trial balance items from which the appropriate items should be selected and used in constructing the 198A income statement for the company:

	Debit	Credit
Loss on sale of antique automobile displayed in company showroom (an unusual transaction for the company that occurs about once every four years when a new customer attraction is obtained).	$ 18,600	
Cost of goods sold	113,600	
Gain on settlement with supplier to compensate for negative customer reaction to receipt of products with faulty materials Tisdale had purchased from the supplier (In this industry, attempts to obtain such settlements with suppliers are not unusual but occur infrequently.)		$ 31,200
Income tax expense	47,500	
Loss from operating Sucker Division (net of $7,800 income tax benefit)	19,500	
Revenue received in advance late last year and incorrectly credited to a revenue account instead of a liability account (net of $6,500 income taxes)	15,700	
Depreciation expense	18,900	
Gain on sale of investment in stock (Tisdale regularly maintains a large portfolio of stock investments as part of its business activities, expecting to enhance the earnings of the company through purchases and sales of such securities.).		56,900
Accumulated depreciation, buildings	51,000	
Effect on prior years' income of switching from straight-line depreciation to declining-balance depreciation, justified in this case as an improvement in financial reporting (net of $54,000 income taxes).	61,100	
Other operating expenses	93,900	
Loss on sale of Sucker Division (net of $11,400 income taxes)	27,300	
Interest earned		7,200
Gain on condemnation of land by city (net of $26,000 income taxes). This is probably the only time in the company's past or future that it will have land condemned by a government. The event is highly unusual		91,000
Sales		379,600
Accrued liabilities		32,000

Required

Prepare Tisdale Corporation's income statement for 198A, excluding the earnings per share statistics.

Problem 19-2A

On January 1, 198A, Boxwell Corporation purchased a large item of machinery for use in its manufacturing operations. The machine cost $600,000 and was expected to have a salvage value of $50,000. Depreciation was taken through 198E on a sum-of-the-years'-digits method assuming a 10-year life. Early in 198F, the company concluded that given the economic conditions in the industry, a straight-line method would result in more meaningful financial statements. They argue that straight-line depreciation would allow better comparisons with the financial results of other firms in the industry.

Required

1. Is Boxwell Corporation allowed to change depreciation methods in 198F?
2. Prepare a table that shows the depreciation expense to be reported each year of the asset's life under both depreciation methods and the cumulative effect of the change on prior years' incomes. Assume an income tax rate of 30%, and round your answers to the nearest whole dollar.
3. State the amount of depreciation expense to be reported in 198F and the cumulative effect of the change on prior years' incomes. How should the cumulative effect be reported? Is the cumulative effects on 198F net income positive or negative?
4. Now assume that Boxwell Corporation had used straight-line depreciation through 198E and justified a change to sum-of-the-years'-digits depreciation in 198F. What amount of depreciation expense should be reported in 198F? How does the reporting of the cumulative effect of the change differ from your answer to Requirement 3?

Problem 19-3A

The costs of purchasing a common "market basket" in each of several years are as follows:

Year	Cost of Market Basket
198A	$ 72,000
198B	79,500
198C	84,700
198D	93,400
198E	105,400
198F	102,700
198G	110,300
198H	124,100

Required

1. Construct a price index using 198D as the base year. Round each index number to 1/10%.
2. Using the index constructed in Requirement 1, what was the percent increase in prices from 198A to 198G?
3. Using the index constructed in Requirement 1, how many dollars in 198H does it take to have the same purchasing power as $1 in 198C?
4. Using the index constructed in Requirement 1, if $80,000 were invested in land during 198B and $50,000 were invested in land during 198D, what would be reported as the total land investment on a constant dollar balance sheet prepared in 198H? What would your answer be if the investments were in U.S. long-term bonds rather than in land?

Problem 19-4A

Senchak Corporation purchased machinery for $668,000 on December 30, 198A. The equipment was expected to last eight years and have no salvage value; straight-line depreciation was to be used. The equipment was sold on December 31, 198E, for $500,000. End-of-year general price index numbers during this period of time were as follows:

198A	197.0
198B	254.8
198C	274.4
198D	313.6
198E	333.2

Required
  (Round all answers to the nearest whole dollar.)
1. What should be presented for the equipment and accumulated depreciation on an historical cost/constant dollar balance sheet dated December 31, 198C? Hint. Depreciation is the total amount of cost that has been allocated to expense. Therefore, the price index numbers that are used to adjust the nominal dollar cost of the asset should also be used to adjust the nominal dollar amount of depreciation.
2. How much depreciation expense should be shown on the historical cost/constant dollar income statement for 198D?
3. How much depreciation expense should be shown on the historical cost/constant dollar income statement for 198E?
4. How much gain on the sale of equipment would be reported on the historical cost/nominal dollar income statement for 198E?
5. After adjusting the equipment's cost and accumulated depreciation to the end-of-198E price level, how much gain in (loss of) general purchasing power was realized by the sale of the equipment?

Problem 19-5A

Westlake Drafters had three monetary items during 198B, cash, accounts receivable, and accounts payable. The changes in these accounts during the year were as follows:

Cash:
  Beginning balance. . . . . $ 19,200
  Cash proceeds from sale of land (in mid-January 198B)   30,720
  Cash receipts from customers (spread evenly throughout the year)   209,760
  Payments of accounts payable (spread evenly throughout the year). . . . .   (118,080)
  Dividends declared and paid during March 198B . . . .   (47,040)
  Payments of other cash expenses in mid-September 198B . . . .   (36,000)
  Ending balance . . . . $ 58,560

Accounts receivable:
  Beginning balance. . . . . $ 34,800
  Sales to customers (spread evenly throughout the year).   230,640
  Cash receipts from customers (spread evenly throughout the year) . . . . .   (209,760)
  Ending balance . . . . $ 55,680

Accounts payable:
Beginning balance.	$ 40,560
Merchandise purchases (spread evenly throughout the year).	92,400
Special purchase near end of December 198B	26,400
Payments of accounts payable (spread evenly throughout the year).	(118,080)
Ending balance	$ 41,280

General price index numbers at the end of 198A and during 198B are as follows:

December 198A	105.0
January 198B.	106.8
March 198B	109.6
September 198B	113.8
December 198B	115.8
Average for 198B	111.6

Required

Calculate the general purchasing power gain or loss experienced by Westlake Drafters in 198B. Round all amounts to the nearest whole dollar.

Problem 19-6A

Olson Company purchased a tract of land for $140,000 in 198A, when the general price index was 86.5. At the same time, a price index for land values in the area of Olson's tract was 81.4. In 198B, when the general price index was 97.3 and the specific price index for land was 98.2, Olson bought another tract of land for $200,000. In late 198I, the general price index is 185.3 and the price index for land values is 160.7.

Required

1. In preparing a balance sheet at the end of 198I, what amount should be shown for land on:
   a. An historical cost/nominal dollar balance sheet.
   b. An historical cost/constant dollar balance sheet.
   c. A current cost balance sheet.
   Round all amounts to the nearest whole dollar.
2. In Olson Company's December 198I meeting of the board of directors, one director insists that Olson has incurred a loss of general purchasing power as a result of owning the land. A second director argues that there could not have been a purchasing power gain or loss since land is a nonmonetary asset. Which director do you think is correct? Explain your answer.

Problem 19-7A

Universal Sales Company, a United States corporation that has customers in several foreign countries, had the following transactions in 198A and 198B:

June 27   Sold merchandise for 24,500 punts to O'Riley Company of Ireland, payment in full to be received in 60 days. On this day, the foreign exchange rate for punts into dollars was quoted as $1.0230.

July   14   Sold merchandise to Fyord Retailers of Norway for $8,700 cash. The exchange rate for kroner into dollars was $0.1124.

Aug. 26   Received O'Riley Company's payment for its purchase of June 27. Noted the current foreign exchange rate for punts into dollars was $1.0100.

Oct. 20   Sold merchandise on credit to Rio Distributers, Inc., a company located in Mexico City. The price of 800,000 pesos was to be paid 90 days from the date of sale. On October 20, the foreign exchange rate for pesos into dollars was $0.0044.

Nov. 28   Sold merchandise for 53,200 francs to Le Bistrot Suppliers of Paris, France, payment in full to be in 60 days. The exchange rate for francs into dollars was $0.1077.

Dec. 31   Prepared adjusting entries to recognize exchange gains or losses on the annual financial statements. Rates of exchanging foreign currencies into dollars on this day included the following:

Francs (France).	$0.1095
Kroner (Norway)	0.1086
Pesos (Mexico).	0.0040
Punts (Ireland)	1.0190

Jan.   18   Received Rio Distributers, Inc.'s full payment for the sale of October 20. The exchange rate for pesos into dollars was $0.0049.

        27   Received full payment from Le Bistrot Suppliers for the sale of November 28. The exchange rate for francs into dollars was $0.1086.

Required

1. Prepare general journal entries to account for these transactions of Universal Sales Company. Round all amounts to the nearest whole dollar.

2. Calculate the exchange gain or loss to be reported on Universal Sales Company's 198A income statement.

☐   **Provocative Problems**   **Provocative Problem 19-1   Classifying Mather Corporation's Special Transactions**

Mather Corporation had several rather special transactions and events in 198A, each of which is described below:

a. Mather Corporation's continuing operations involve a high technology production process. Technical developments in this area occur regularly and the production machinery is subject to becoming obsolete surprisingly often. Because such developments had occurred recently,

Mather decided that it was forced to sell certain items of machinery at a significant loss and replace those items with a different type of machinery. The problem is how to report the loss.

b. Early last year, Mather purchased a new type of equipment for use in its production process. Although much of the production equipment is depreciated over 5 years, a careful analysis of the situation led the company to decide that the new equipment should be depreciated over 10 years. Nevertheless, in the rush of year-end activities, the new equipment was included with the older equipment and depreciated on a five-year basis. In preparing adjustments at the end of 198A, the accountant discovered that $70,000 depreciation was taken on the new equipment last year, when only $35,000 should have been taken. The company is subject to a 50% income tax rate.

c. Mather has a mining operation in several foreign countries, one of which has been subject to political unrest. After a sudden change in governments, the new ruling body resolved that the amount of foreign investment in the country was excessive. As a result, Mather was forced to transfer ownership in its mines in that country to the new government. Mather was able to continue its mining operation in a neighboring country and was allowed to transfer much of its mining equipment to the neighboring country. Nevertheless, the price paid to Mather for its mines resulted in a significant loss.

d. Two years previously, Mather Corporation purchased some highly specialized equipment that was to be used in the operations of a new division that Mather intended to acquire. The new division was in a separate line of business and would have constituted a separate segment of the business. After lengthy negotiations, the acquisition of the division was not accomplished and the company abandoned any hope of entering that line of business. Although the equipment had never been used, it was sold in 198A at a significant loss. Mather Corporation does not have a history of expanding into new lines of business and has no plans of doing so in the future.

Required

Examine Mather Company's special transactions and events and describe how each one should be reported on the income statement or statement of retained earnings. Also state the particular characteristics of the item that support your decision.

Provocative Problem 19-2   Helmsman Corporation

Although Helmsman Corporation is not required to present financial information adjusted for price changes, the company has often been willing to consider new, innovative ways of reporting to its stockholders. For example, it has presented supplemental historical cost/constant dollar financial statements in its annual reports. The constant dollar balance sheets of Helmsman Corporation for December 31, 198A, and 198B, were as follows:

Helmsman Corporation
Historical Cost/Constant Dollar Balance Sheets

	As Presented on December 31, 198B	As Presented on December 31, 198A
Assets		
Cash	$ 35,000	$ 10,000
Accounts receivable	93,000	50,000
Notes receivable	20,000	—
Inventory	25,761	12,960
Equipment.	198,545	171,818
Accumulated depreciation	(56,727)	(24,545)
Land	156,391	98,182
Total assets	$471,970	$318,415
Liabilities and Stockholders' Equity		
Accounts payable	$ 61,000	$ 11,000
Notes payable	43,000	13,000
Common stock.	283,636	245,455
Retained earnings	84,334	48,960
Total liabilities and stockholders' equity	$471,970	$318,415

A new member of Helmsman Corporation's board of directors has expressed interest in the relationship between historical cost/constant dollar statements and historical cost/nominal dollar statements. The board member understands that constant dollar statements are derived from nominal dollar statements, but wonders if the process can be reversed. Specifically, you are asked to show how the historical cost/constant dollar balance sheets for December 31, 198A, and 198B, could be restated back into nominal dollar statements.

Additional Information

1. The outstanding stock was issued in January 198A, and the company's equipment was purchased at that time. The equipment has no salvage value and is being depreciated over seven years.

2. The note receivable was acquired on June 30, 198B.

3. Notes payable consists of two notes, one for $13,000 which was issued on January 1, 198A, and the other for $30,000 which was issued on January 1, 198B.

4. The land account includes two parcels, one of which was acquired for $80,000 on January 1, 198A. The remaining parcel was acquired in June 198B.

5. Selected numbers from a general price-level index are:

January 198A	165.0
June 198A (also average for 198A)	187.5
December 198A	202.5
June 198B (also average for 198B)	218.0
December 198B	234.0

6. The inventory at the end of each year was acquired evenly throughout that year.

7. Hint: If all other accounts are properly adjusted from constant dollars back to nominal dollars, the correct retained earnings balance can be determined simply by "plugging" the amount necessary to make the balance sheet balance.

Provocative Problem 19-3   Adolph Coors Company

The Adolph Coors Company is an increasingly diversified business with its primary operations in the brewing industry. In its 1984 annual reports, the company included the following information concerning the effects of price changes:

	Historical cost (as reported in the consolidated financial statements)	Current cost (adjusted for changes in specific prices)
	(In millions, except per share data)	
Net sales	$1,132.6	$1,132.6
Cost of goods sold	804.8	834.3
Other costs and expenses	270.4	275.6
	1,075.2	1,109.9
Income before taxes	57.4	22.7
Income taxes	12.7	12.7
Net income	$ 44.7	$ 10.0
Net income per share of common stock	$1.28	$0.29
Unrealized purchasing power gain		$ 1.3
Depreciation, depletion and amortization	$ 76.9	$ 109.0
Increase in current cost of inventories and properties held during the year (based upon specific price changes)		$ 40.7
Effect of increase in general price level		52.9
Decrease in current cost of inventories and properties held during the year, net of changes in the general price level (holding loss)		$ 12.2

Required

1. Given that 1984 was a year of inflation, were the monetary assets owned by the Adolph Coors Company more than or less than monetary liabilities owed?

2. Adolph Coors Company reported a $12.2 million "holding loss" during 1984. Explain how this could have occurred given the fact that 1984 was a period of inflation.

3. Based on the information presented, did price changes appear to have positive or negative effects on the financial operations and position of the Adolph Coors Company? Explain the basis for your answer.

4. To what extent did price changes effect the importance of income taxes incurred by Coors?

20 Analyzing Financial Statements

After studying Chapter 20, you should be able to:

1. List the three broad objectives of financial reporting by business enterprises.

2. Describe comparative financial statements, how they are prepared, and the limitations associated with interpreting them.

3. Prepare common-size comparative statements and interpret them.

4. Explain the importance of working capital in the analysis of financial statements and list the typical ratios used to analyze working capital.

5. Calculate the common ratios used in analyzing the balance sheet and income statement and state what each ratio is intended to measure.

6. State the limitations associated with using financial statement ratios and the sources from which standards for comparison may be obtained.

7. Calculate earnings per share for companies with simple capital structures. Explain the difference between primary and fully diluted earnings per share.

8. Define or explain the words and phrases listed in the chapter Glossary.

A large variety of persons are interested in receiving and analyzing financial information about business firms. They range from managers, employees, directors, customers, suppliers, owners, lenders, and potential investors to brokers, regulatory authorities, lawyers, economists, labor unions, financial advisors, and the financial press. Some of these groups, such as managers and some regulatory agencies, have the ability to require a company to prepare specialized financial reports designed to meet their specific interests. Many other groups must rely on the **general-purpose financial statements** that are periodically published by the companies. General-purpose financial statements usually include the income statement, balance sheet, statement of retained earnings, and statement of changes in financial position. These statements are typically accompanied by a variety of additional financial information such as that contained in the footnotes to the financial statements. See, for example, the financial statements and related footnotes of CBS Inc. shown in Appendix B at the end of the book. Financial information about companies may also be obtained from a variety of news announcements issued from time to time by management.

The process of preparing and issuing financial information about a company is called **financial reporting.** While financial reporting includes more than general-purpose financial statements, the objectives of those statements are essentially the same as are the objectives of financial reporting.

Objectives of Financial Reporting

The great variety of persons who use financial information about a business undoubtedly differ widely in their reasons for analyzing that information. Nevertheless, the FASB suggests that such users are "generally interested in [the business'] ability to generate favorable cash flows because their decisions relate to amounts, timing, and uncertainties of expected cash flows."[1] Based on this general assumption about the interests of financial information users, the FASB has prescribed three broad objectives of financial reporting. Those objectives are as follows:

1. Financial reporting should provide information that is useful to present and potential investors and creditors and other users in making rational investment, credit, and similar decisions. The information should be comprehensible to those who have a reasonable understanding of business and economic activities and are willing to study the information with reasonable diligence.
2. Financial reporting should provide information to help present and potential investors and creditors and other users in assessing the amounts, timing, and uncertainty of prospective cash receipts from dividends or interest and the proceeds from the sale, redemption, or maturity of securities or loans. Since investors' and creditors' cash flows are related to enterprise cash flows, financial reporting should provide information to help investors, creditors, and others assess the amounts, timing, and uncertainty of prospective net cash inflows to the related enterprise.

[1] FASB, *Statement of Financial Accounting Concepts No. 1,* "Objectives of Financial Reporting by Business Enterprises" (Stamford, Conn., 1978), par. 25. Copyright © by the Financial Accounting Standards Board, High Ridge Park, Stamford, Conn. 06905, U.S.A. Quoted (or excerpted) with permission. Copies of the complete document are available from the FASB.

3. Financial reporting should provide information about the economic resources of an enterprise, the claims to those resources (obligations of the enterprise to transfer resources to other entities and owners' equity), and the effects of transactions, events, and circumstances that change its resources and claims to those resources.[2]

These three objectives of financial reporting were published by the FASB as the first part of its new conceptual framework for financial accounting.[3] The conceptual framework is intended to assist accountants in resolving questions about how accounting problems should be solved. In addition, however, the objectives provide important background information for the person who is beginning to learn how to analyze financial statements.

Although users of financial information may have other reasons for analyzing financial statements, they should understand that the authoritative body for establishing accounting principles (the FASB) intends for financial reporting (and financial statements) to be focused on these basic objectives. The primary idea is that financial reporting should help the information user predict the amounts, timing, and uncertainty of future net cash inflows to the business. The methods of analysis and techniques explained in this chapter should contribute to this process.

When the financial statements of a business are analyzed, individual statement items are in themselves generally not too significant. However, relationships between items and groups of items plus changes that have occurred are significant. As a result, financial statement analysis requires that relationships between items and groups of items and changes in items and groups be described.

Comparative Statements

Changes in statement items can be seen most clearly when item amounts for two or more successive accounting periods are placed side by side in columns on a single statement. Such a statement is called a **comparative statement.** Each of the financial statements, or portions thereof, may be presented in the form of a comparative statement.

In its most simple form, a comparative balance sheet consists of the item amounts from two or more of a company's successive balance sheets arranged side by side so that changes in amounts may be seen. However, such a statement can be improved by also showing in both dollar amounts and in percentages the changes that have occurred. When this is done, as in Illustration 20-1, large dollar and large percentage changes become more readily apparent.

A comparative income statement is prepared in the same manner as a comparative balance sheet. Income statement amounts for two or more successive periods are placed side by side, with dollar and percentage

[2] Ibid., p. viii.

[3] Other major sections of the FASB's conceptual framework project published to date include *Statement of Financial Accounting Concepts No. 2,* "Qualitative Characteristics of Accounting Information" (May 1980); *Statement of Financial Accounting Concepts No. 4,* "Objectives of Financial Reporting by Nonbusiness Organizations" (December 1980); *Statement of Financial Accounting Concepts No. 5,* "Recognition and Measurement in Financial Statements of Business Enterprises" (December 1984); and *Statement of Financial Accounting Concepts No. 6,* "Elements of Financial Statements" (December 1985). *Statement No. 6* replaced an earlier version *(Statement No. 3)* that was also titled "Elements of Financial Statements."

Illustration 20-1

Anchor Supply Company
Comparative Balance Sheet
December 31, 198B, and December 31, 198A

	Years Ended December 31		Amount of Increase or (Decrease) during 198B	Percent of Increase or (Decrease) during 198B
	198B	198A		
Assets				
Current assets:				
Cash	$ 15,000	$ 20,500	$ (5,500)	(26.8)
Temporary investments	3,000	70,000	(67,000)	(95.7)
Accounts receivable, net.	68,000	64,000	4,000	6.3
Merchandise inventory	90,000	84,000	6,000	7.1
Prepaid expenses	5,800	6,000	(200)	(3.3)
Total current assets.	$181,800	$244,500	$ (62,700)	(25.6)
Long-term investments:				
Real estate	–0–	$ 30,000	$ (30,000)	(100.0)
Apex Company common stock	–0–	50,000	(50,000)	(100.0)
Total long-term investments	–0–	$ 80,000	$ (80,000)	(100.0)
Plant and equipment:				
Office equipment, net	$ 3,500	$ 3,700	$ (200)	(5.4)
Store equipment, net	17,900	6,800	11,100	163.2
Buildings, net	176,800	28,000	148,800	531.4
Land	50,000	20,000	30,000	150.0
Total plant and equipment	$248,200	$ 58,500	$189,700	324.3
Total assets	$430,000	$383,000	$ 47,000	12.3
Liabilities				
Current liabilities:				
Notes payable	$ 5,000	–0–	$ 5,000	
Accounts payable.	43,600	$ 55,000	(11,400)	(20.7)
Taxes payable	4,800	5,000	(200)	(4.0)
Wages payable.	800	1,200	(400)	(33.3)
Total current liabilities	$ 54,200	$ 61,200	$ (7,000)	(11.4)
Long-term liabilities:				
Notes payable (secured by mortgage) . .	$ 60,000	$ 10,000	$ 50,000	500.0
Total liabilities	$114,200	$ 71,200	$ 43,000	60.4
Capital				
Common stock, $10 par value	$250,000	$250,000	–0–	–0–
Retained earnings	65,800	61,800	$ 4,000	6.5
Total capital	$315,800	$311,800	$ 4,000	1.3
Total liabilities and capital	$430,000	$383,000	$ 47,000	12.3

changes in additional columns. Such a statement is shown in Illustration 20-2.

Analyzing and Interpreting Comparative Statements

In analyzing and interpreting comparative data, it is necessary for the analyst to select for study any items showing significant dollar or percentage changes. The analyst then tries to determine the reasons for each change and if possible whether they are favorable or unfavorable. For example, in Illustration 20-1, the first item, "Cash," shows a decrease of $5,500.

Illustration 20-2

Anchor Supply Company
Comparative Income Statement
Years Ended December 31, 198B, and 198A

	Years Ended December 31		Amount of Increase or (Decrease) during 198B	Percent of Increase or (Decrease) during 198B
	198B	198A		
Gross sales.	$973,500	$853,000	$120,500	14.1
Sales returns and allowances	13,500	10,200	3,300	32.4
Net sales.	$960,000	$842,800	$117,200	13.9
Cost of goods sold	715,000	622,500	92,500	14.9
Gross profit from sales	$245,000	$220,300	$ 24,700	11.2
Operating expenses:				
Selling expenses:				
Advertising expense	$ 7,500	$ 5,000	$ 2,500	50.0
Sales salaries expense.	113,500	98,000	15,500	15.8
Store supplies expense.	3,200	2,800	400	14.3
Depreciation expense, store equipment . .	2,400	1,700	700	41.2
Delivery expense	14,800	14,000	800	5.7
Total selling expenses	$141,400	$121,500	$ 19,900	16.4
General and administrative expenses:				
Office salaries expense.	$ 41,000	$ 40,050	$ 950	2.4
Office supplies expense	1,300	1,250	50	4.0
Insurance expense.	1,600	1,200	400	33.3
Depreciation expense, office equipment. .	300	300	–0–	–0–
Depreciation expense, buildings	2,850	1,500	1,350	90.0
Bad debts expense	2,250	2,200	50	2.3
Total general and admin. expenses . . .	$ 49,300	$ 46,500	$ 2,800	6.0
Total operating expenses	$190,700	$168,000	$ 22,700	13.5
Operating income	$ 54,300	$ 52,300	$ 2,000	3.8
Less interest expense	2,300	1,000	1,300	130.0
Income before taxes	$ 52,000	$ 51,300	$ 700	1.4
Income taxes	19,000	18,700	300	1.6
Net income.	$ 33,000	$ 32,600	$ 400	1.2
Earnings per share	$1.32	$1.30	$0.02	0.2

Furthermore, the next item, "Temporary investments," shows an extremely large decrease. At first glance these changes appear very unfavorable. However, when the decreases in "Cash" and "Temporary investments" are considered with the decrease in "Long-term investments" and the increase in "Store equipment," "Buildings," and "Land," plus the increase in "Note payable (secured by mortgage)," it becomes apparent the company has materially increased its plant assets between the two balance sheet dates. Further study reveals the company has apparently constructed a new building on land it has held as an investment until needed in this expansion. Also, it seems the company paid for its new plant assets by reducing cash, selling its Apex Company common stock, and issuing a $50,000 mortgage.

As an aid in controlling operations, a comparative income statement is usually more valuable than a comparative balance sheet. For example, in Illustration 20-2, "Gross sales" increased 14.1% and "Net sales" increased 13.9%. At the same time, "Sales returns" increased 32.4%, or at a rate more than twice that of gross sales. Returned sales represent wasted sales effort and indicate dissatisfied customers. Consequently, such an increase in returns should be investigated, and the reason for the increase determined if at all possible. Also, in addition to the large increase in the "Sales returns," it is significant that the rate of increase in "Cost of goods sold" is greater than that of "Net sales." This is an unfavorable trend and should be remedied if at all possible.

In attempting to find reasons for Anchor Supply Company's increase in sales, the increases in advertising and in plant assets must be considered. It is reasonable to expect an increase in advertising to increase sales. It is also reasonable to expect an increase in plant assets to result in a sales increase.

Calculating Percentage Increases and Decreases

When percentage increases and decreases are calculated for comparative statements, the increase or decrease in an item is divided by the amount shown for the item in the base year. No problems arise in these calculations when positive amounts are shown in the base year. However, when no amount is shown or a negative amount is shown in the base year, a percentage increase or decrease cannot be calculated. For example, in Illustration 20-1, there were no notes payable at the end of 198A, and a percentage change for this item cannot be calculated.

In this text, percentages and ratios are typically rounded to one or two decimal places. However, there is no uniform agreement on this matter. In general, percentages should be carried out to the point of assuring that meaningful information is conveyed. However, they should not be carried so far that the significance of relationships tends to become "lost" in the length of the numbers.

Trend Percentages

Trend percentages or index numbers emphasize changes that have occurred from period to period and are useful in comparing data covering a number of years. Trend percentages are calculated as follows:

1. A base year is selected, and each item amount on the base year statement is assigned a weight of 100%.
2. Then, each item from the statements for the years after the base year is expressed as a percentage of its base year amount. To determine these percentages, the item amounts in the years after the base year are divided by the amount of the item in the base year.

For example, if 198A is made the base year for the following data, the trend percentages for "Sales" are calculated by dividing by $210,000 the amount shown for "Sales" in each year after the first. The trend percentages for "Cost of goods sold" are found by dividing by $145,000 the amount shown for "Cost of goods sold" in each year after the first. And, the trend percentages for "Gross profit" are found by dividing the amounts shown for "Gross profit" by $65,000.

	198A	198B	198C	198D	198E	198F
Sales.	$210,000	$204,000	$292,000	$284,000	$310,000	$324,000
Cost of goods sold. . .	145,000	139,000	204,000	198,000	218,000	229,000
Gross profit	$ 65,000	$ 65,000	$ 88,000	$ 86,000	$ 92,000	$ 95,000

When these divisions are made, the trends for these three items appear as follows:

	198A	198B	198C	198D	198E	198F
Sales.	100%	97%	139%	135%	148%	154%
Cost of goods sold. . .	100	96	141	137	150	158
Gross profit	100	100	135	132	142	146

It is interesting to note in the illustrated trends that while after the second year the sales trend is upward, the cost of goods sold trend is upward at a slightly more rapid rate. This indicates a contracting gross profit rate and should receive attention.

It should be pointed out in a discussion of trends that the trend for a single balance sheet or income statement item is seldom very informative. However, a comparison of trends for related items often tells the analyst a great deal. For example, a downward sales trend with an upward trend for merchandise inventory, accounts receivable, and loss on bad debts would generally indicate an unfavorable situation. On the other hand, an upward sales trend with a downward trend or a slower upward trend for accounts receivable, merchandise inventory, and selling expenses would indicate an increase in operating efficiency.

Common-Size Comparative Statements

The comparative statements illustrated thus far do not show proportional changes in items except in a general way. Changes in proportions are often shown and emphasized by **common-size comparative statements.**

A common-size statement is so called because its items are shown in common-size figures, figures that are fractions of 100%. For example, on a common-size balance sheet (1) the asset total is assigned a value of 100%. (2) The total of the liabilities and owner's equity is also assigned a value of 100%. Then (3), each asset, liability, and owners' equity item is shown as a percentage of total assets (or total equities). When a company's successive balance sheets are shown in this manner (see Illustration 20-3), proportional changes are emphasized.

A common-size income statement is prepared by assigning net sales a 100% value and then expressing each statement item as a percent of net sales. Such a statement is an informative and useful tool. If the 100% sales amount on the statement is assumed to represent one sales dollar, then the remaining items show how each sales dollar was distributed to costs, expenses, and profit. For example, on the comparative income statement shown in Illustration 20-4, the 198A cost of goods sold consumed 73.86 cents of each sales dollar. In 198B, cost of goods sold consumed 74.48 cents of each sales dollar. While this increase is small, if in 198B the proportion of cost of goods sold had remained at the 198A level, almost $6,000 of additional gross profit would have been earned.

Common-size percentages point out efficiencies and inefficiencies that are otherwise difficult to see. For this reason, they are a valuable management tool. To illustrate, sales salaries of Anchor Supply Company took a higher percentage of each sales dollar in 198B than in 198A. On the other hand, office salaries took a smaller percentage. Furthermore, although the loss from bad debts is greater in 198B than in 198A, loss from bad debts took a smaller proportion of each sales dollar in 198B than in 198A.

Analysis of Working Capital

When balance sheets are analyzed, working capital always receives close attention because an adequate amount of working capital enables a company to meet current debts, carry sufficient inventories, and take advantage of cash discounts. However, the amount of working capital a company has is not a measure of these abilities. This may be demonstrated as follows with Companies A and B:

	Company A	Company B
Current assets	$100,000	$20,000
Current liabilities . . .	90,000	10,000
Working capital. . . .	$ 10,000	$10,000

Companies A and B have the same amounts of working capital. However, Company A's current liabilities are nine times its working capital, while Company B's current liabilities and working capital are equal. As a result, if liabilities are to be paid on time, Company A must experience much less shrinkage and delay in converting its current assets to cash than Company B. Thus, the amount of a company's working capital is not a measure of its working capital position. However, the relation of its current assets to its current liabilities is such a measure.

Illustration 20-3

Anchor Supply Company
Common-Size Comparative Balance Sheet
December 31, 198B, and December 31, 198A

	Years Ended December 31		Common-Size Percentages	
	198B	**198A**	**198B**	**198A**
Assets				
Current assets:				
Cash	$ 15,000	$ 20,500	3.49	5.35
Temporary investments	3,000	70,000	0.70	18.28
Accounts receivable, net	68,000	64,000	15.81	16.71
Merchandise inventory	90,000	84,000	20.93	21.93
Prepaid expenses	5,800	6,000	1.35	1.57
Total current assets	$181,800	$244,500	42.28	63.84
Long-term investments:				
Real estate	–0–	$ 30,000		7.83
Apex Company common stock	–0–	50,000		13.05
Total long-term investments	–0–	$ 80,000		20.88
Plant and equipment:				
Office equipment, net	$ 3,500	$ 3,700	0.81	0.97
Store equipment, net	17,900	6,800	4.16	1.78
Buildings, net	176,800	28,000	41.12	7.31
Land	50,000	20,000	11.63	5.22
Total plant and equipment	$248,200	$ 58,500	57.72	15.28
Total assets	$430,000	$383,000	100.00	100.00
Liabilities				
Current liabilities:				
Notes payable	$ 5,000	–0–	1.16	
Accounts payable	43,600	$ 55,000	10.14	14.36
Taxes payable	4,800	5,000	1.12	1.31
Wages payable	800	1,200	0.19	0.31
Total current liabilities	$ 54,200	$ 61,200	12.61	15.98
Long-term liabilities:				
Notes payable (secured by mortgage)	$ 60,000	$ 10,000	13.95	2.61
Total liabilities	$114,200	$ 71,200	26.56	18.59
Capital				
Common stock, $10 par value	$250,000	$250,000	58.14	65.27
Retained earnings	65,800	61,800	15.30	16.14
Total capital	$315,800	$311,800	73.44	81.44
Total liabilities and capital	$430,000	$383,000	100.00	100.00

Current Ratio

The relation of a company's current assets to its current liabilities is known as its **current ratio**. A current ratio is calculated by dividing current assets by current liabilities. The current ratio of the foregoing Company B is calculated as follows:

$$\frac{\text{Current assets, \$20,000}}{\text{Current liabilities, \$10,000}} = 2$$

After the division is made, the relation can be described by saying that Company B's current assets are two times its current liabilities, or simply Company B's current ratio is 2 to 1.

The current ratio is the relation of current assets and current liabilities expressed mathematically. A high current ratio indicates a large proportion of current assets to current liabilities. The higher the ratio, the better is a company's current position, and normally the more capable it is of meeting its current obligations.

Illustration 20-4

Anchor Supply Company
Common-Size Comparative Income Statement
Years Ended December 31, 198B, and 198A

	Years Ended December 31		Common-Size Percentages	
	198B	198A	198B	198A
Gross sales	$973,500	$853,000	101.41	101.21
Sales returns and allowances	13,500	10,200	1.41	1.21
Net sales	$960,000	$842,800	100.00	100.00
Cost of goods sold	715,000	622,500	74.48	73.86
Gross profit from sales	$245,000	$220,300	25.52	26.14
Operating expenses:				
Selling expenses:				
Advertising expense.	$ 7,500	$ 5,000	0.78	0.59
Sales salaries expense	113,500	98,000	11.82	11.63
Store supplies expense	3,200	2,800	0.33	0.33
Depreciation expense, store equipment	2,400	1,700	0.25	0.20
Delivery expense	14,800	14,000	1.54	1.66
Total selling expenses.	$141,400	$121,500	14.72	14.41
General and administrative expenses:				
Office salaries expense	$ 41,000	$ 40,050	4.27	4.75
Office supplies expense	1,300	1,250	0.14	0.15
Insurance expense	1,600	1,200	0.17	0.14
Depreciation expense, office equipment	300	300	0.03	0.04
Depreciation expense, buildings	2,850	1,500	0.30	0.18
Bad debts expense	2,250	2,200	0.23	0.26
Total general and administrative expenses	$ 49,300	$ 46,500	5.14	5.52
Total operating expenses	$190,700	$168,000	19.86	19.93
Operating income.	$ 54,300	$ 52,300	5.66	6.21
Less interest expense	2,300	1,000	0.24	0.12
Income before taxes	$ 52,000	$ 51,300	5.42	6.09
Income taxes	19,000	18,700	1.98	2.22
Net income	$ 33,000	$ 32,600	3.44	3.87
Earnings per share	$1.32	$1.30	—	—

For years, bankers and other credit grantors measured a credit-seeking company's debt-paying ability by whether or not it had a 2 to 1 current ratio. Today, most credit grantors realize that the 2 to 1 rule of thumb is not an adequate test of debt-paying ability. They realize that whether or not a company's current ratio is good or bad depends upon at least three factors:

1. The nature of the company's business.
2. The composition of its current assets.
3. The turnover of certain of its current assets.

The nature of a company's business has much to do with whether or not its current ratio is adequate. A public utility that has no inventories other than supplies and grants little or no credit can operate on a current ratio of less than 1 to 1. On the other hand, because a misjudgment of style can make an inventory of goods for sale almost worthless, a company in which style is the important sales factor may find a current ratio of much more than 2 to 1 to be inadequate. Consequently, when the adequacy of working capital is studied, consideration must be given to the type of business under review.

Also, in an analysis of a company's working capital, the composition of its current assets should be considered. Normally, a company with a high proportion of cash to accounts receivable and merchandise is in a better position to meet quickly its current obligations than is a company with most of its current assets tied up in accounts receivable and merchandise. The company with cash can pay its current debts at once. The company with accounts receivable and merchandise must often turn these items into cash before it can pay.

Acid-Test Ratio

An easily calculated check on current asset composition is the **acid-test ratio,** also called the **quick ratio** because it is the ratio of "quick assets" to current liabilities. "Quick assets" are cash, temporary investments, accounts receivable, and notes receivable. They are the current assets that can quickly be turned into cash. An acid-test ratio of 1 to 1 is normally considered satisfactory. However, this is a rule of thumb and should be applied with care. The acid-test ratio of Anchor Supply Company as of the end of 198B is calculated as follows:

Quick assets:		Current liabilities:	
Cash.	$15,000	Notes payable.	$ 5,000
Temporary investments	3,000	Accounts payable	43,600
Accounts receivable	68,000	Taxes payable	4,800
		Wages payable	800
Total	$86,000	Total.	$54,200

Acid-test ratio is $86,000/$54,200 = 1.59, or 1.6 to 1

Certain current asset turnovers affect working capital requirements. For example, assume Companies A and B sell the same amounts of merchandise on credit each month. However, Company A grants 30-day terms to its customers, while Company B grants 60 days. Both collect their accounts at the end of the credit periods granted. But as a result of the difference in terms, Company A turns over or collects its accounts twice as rapidly as does Company B. Also, as a result of the more rapid turnover, Company A requires only one half the investment in accounts receivable that is required of Company B and can operate with a smaller current ratio.

Accounts Receivable Turnover

Accounts receivable turnover is calculated by dividing net sales for a year by the average accounts receivable balance during the year. The average balance is usually approximated by averaging the beginning and ending balances. For example, Anchor Supply Company's accounts receivable turnover for 198B is calculated as follows:

a.	December 31, 198A, accounts receivable	$ 64,000
b.	December 31, 198B, accounts receivable	68,000
c.	Average balance (a + b)/2	66,000
d.	Net sales for year	960,000
e.	Times accounts receivable were turned over ($960,000/$66,000)	14.5

If accounts receivable are collected rapidly, the accounts receivable turnover will be high. In general, this is considered to be favorable. However, an accounts receivable turnover may be too high, if it means that credit terms are so limited that they are having a negative effect on sales volume.

Sometimes the ending accounts receivable balance is used as a substitute for the average balance in calculating accounts receivable turnover. This is acceptable if the effect is not significant. Also, credit sales should be used rather than the sum of cash and credit sales; and accounts receivable before subtracting the allowance for doubtful accounts should be used. However, information as to credit sales is seldom available in a published balance sheet. Likewise, many published balance sheets report accounts receivable at their net amount. Consequently, total sales and net accounts receivable must often be used.

Days' Sales Uncollected

Accounts receivable turnover is one indication of the speed with which a company collects its accounts. **Days' sales uncollected** is another indication of the same thing. To illustrate the calculation of days' sales uncollected, assume a company had charge sales during a year of $250,000, and that it has $25,000 of accounts receivable at the year-end. In other words, one tenth of its charge sales, or the charge sales made during one tenth of a year, or the charge sales of 36.5 days ($\frac{1}{10} \times$ 365 days in a year = 36.5 days) are uncollected. This calculation of days' sales uncollected in equation form appears as follows:

$$\frac{\text{Accounts receivable, \$25,000}}{\text{Charge sales, \$250,000}} \times 365 = 36.5 \text{ days' sales uncollected}$$

Days' sales uncollected takes on more meaning when credit terms are known. According to a rule of thumb, a company's days' sales uncollected should not exceed one and one-third times the days in its credit period when it does not offer discounts and one and one-third times the days in its discount period when it does. If the company, whose days' sales uncollected is calculated in the illustration just given, offers 30-day terms, then 36.5 days is within the rule-of-thumb amount. However, if its terms are 2/10, n/30, its days' sales uncollected seem excessive.

Turnover of Merchandise Inventory

A company's **merchandise turnover** is the number of times its average inventory is sold during an accounting period. A high turnover is considered an indication of good merchandising. Also, from a working capital point of view, a company with a high turnover requires a smaller investment in inventory than one producing the same sales with a low turnover. Merchandise turnover is calculated by dividing cost of goods sold by average inventory. Cost of goods sold is the amount of merchandise at cost that was sold during an accounting period. Average inventory is the average amount of merchandise at cost on hand during the period. The 198B merchandise turnover of Anchor Supply Company is calculated as follows:

$$\frac{\text{Cost of goods sold, \$715,000}}{\text{Average merchandise inventory, \$87,000}} = \frac{\text{Merchandise turnover}}{\text{of 8.2 times}}$$

The cost of goods sold is taken from the company's 198B income statement. The average inventory is found by dividing by two the sum of the $84,000, January 1, 198B, inventory and the $90,000, December 31, 198B, inventory. In a company in which beginning and ending inventories are not representative of the inventory normally on hand, a more accurate turnover may be secured by using the average of all the 12 month-end inventories.

Standards of Comparison

When financial statements are analyzed by computing ratios and turnovers, the analyst must determine whether the ratios and turnovers obtained are good, bad, or just average. Furthermore, in making the decision, the analyst must have some basis for comparison. The following are available:

1. A trained analyst may compare the ratios and turnovers of the company under review with mental standards acquired from past experiences.
2. An analyst may calculate for purposes of comparison the ratios and turnovers of a selected group of competitive companies in the same industry as the one whose statements are under review.
3. Published ratios and turnovers such as those published by Dun & Bradstreet may be used for comparison.
4. Some local and national trade associations gather data from their members and publish standard or average ratios for their trade or industry. These offer the analyst a very good basis of comparison when available.
5. Rule-of-thumb standards may be used as a basis for comparison.

Of these five standards, the ratios and turnovers of a selected group of competitive companies normally offer the best basis for comparison.

Rule-of-thumb standards should be applied with care if erroneous conclusions are to be avoided.

Other Balance Sheet and Income Statement Relations

Several balance sheet and income statement relationships in addition to those dealing with working capital are important to the analyst. Some of the more important are discussed below.

Capital Contributions of Owners and Creditors

The share of a company's assets contributed by its owners and the share contributed by creditors are always of interest to the analyst. The owners' and creditors' contributions of Anchor Supply Company are calculated as follows:

	198B	198A
a. Total liabilities	$114,200	$ 71,200
b. Total owners' equity.	315,800	311,800
c. Total liabilities and owners' equity	$430,000	$383,000
Creditors' equity (a ÷ c).	26.6%	18.6%
Owners' equity (b ÷ c)	73.4%	81.4%

Creditors like to see a high proportion of owners' equity because owners' equity acts as a cushion that absorbs losses. The greater the equity of the owners in relation to liabilities, the greater the losses that can be absorbed by the owners before the creditors begin to lose.

From the creditors' standpoint, a high percentage of owners' equity is desirable. However, if an enterprise can earn a return on borrowed capital that is in excess of the capital's cost, then a reasonable amount of creditors' equity is desirable from the owners' viewpoint.

Pledged Plant Assets to Secured Liabilities

Companies commonly borrow by issuing a note or bonds secured by a mortgage on certain of their plant assets. The ratio of pledged plant assets to secured liabilities is often calculated to measure the protection provided to the secured creditors by the pledge of assets. This ratio is calculated by dividing the pledged assets' book value by the liabilities for which the assets are pledged. It is calculated for Anchor Supply Company as of the end of 198B and 198A as follows:

	198B	198A
Buildings, net	$176,800	$28,000
Land	50,000	20,000
a. Book value of pledged plant assets.	$226,800	$48,000
b. Notes payable (secured by mortgage) . . .	$ 60,000	$10,000
Ratio of pledged assets to secured liabilities (a ÷ b).	3.8 to 1	4.8 to 1

The usual rule-of-thumb minimum for this ratio is 2 to 1. However, the ratio needs careful interpretation because it is based on the **book value** of the pledged assets. Book values often bear little or no relation to the amount that would be received for the assets in a foreclosure or a liquidation. As a result, estimated liquidation values or foreclosure values are normally a better measure of the protection provided by pledged assets. Also, the long-term earning ability of the company whose assets are pledged is usually more important to secured creditors than the pledged assets' book value.

Times Fixed Interest Charges Earned

The number of **times fixed interest charges were earned** is often calculated to measure the security of the return offered to bondholders or a mortgage holder. The amount of income before the deduction of fixed interest charges and income taxes is the amount available to pay the fixed interest charges. Consequently, the calculation is made by dividing income before fixed interest charges and income taxes by fixed interest charges. The result is the number of times fixed interest charges were earned. Often, fixed interest charges are considered secure if the company consistently earns its fixed interest charges two or more times each year.

Rate of Return on Total Assets Employed

The **return earned on total assets employed** is a measure of management's performance. Assets are used to earn a profit, and management is responsible for the way in which they are used. Consequently, the return on assets employed is a measure of how efficient management has been in the use of assets.

The return figure used in this calculation should be income before interest and income taxes are deducted. Interest and income taxes are included because they are affected by items other than the efficient use of assets. If the amount of assets has fluctuated during the year, an average of the beginning- and end-of-year assets employed should be used in the calculation.

The rates of return earned on the average total assets employed by Anchor Supply Company during 198B and 198A are calculated as follows:

	198B	198A
a. Income before interest and taxes (operating income)	$ 54,300	$ 52,300
b. Average total assets employed	406,500	380,000
Rate of return on total assets employed (a ÷ b).	13.4%	13.8%

In the case of Anchor Supply Company, the change in the rates is not too significant. It is also impossible to tell whether the returns are good or bad without some basis of comparison. The best comparison would be the returns earned by similar-size companies engaged in the same kind of business. A comparison could also be made with the returns earned by this company in previous years. Neither of these is available in this case.

Rate of Return on Common Stockholders' Equity

A primary reason for the operation of a corporation is to earn a net income for its common stockholders. The **rate of return on the common stockholders' equity** is a measure of the success achieved in this area. Usually an average of the beginning- and end-of-year equities is used in calculating the return. For Anchor Supply Company, the 198B and 198A calculations are as follows:

	198B	198A
a. Net income after taxes.	$ 33,000	$ 32,600
b. Average stockholders' equity	313,800	309,000
Rate of return on stockholders' equity *(a ÷ b)*	10.5%	10.6%

Compare Anchor Supply Company's returns on stockholders' equity with its returns on total assets employed and note that the return on the stockholders' equity is greater in both years. The greater returns resulted from using borrowed money.

When there is preferred stock outstanding, the preferred dividend requirements must be subtracted from net income to arrive at the common stockholders' share of income to be used in this calculation.

■ Earnings per Share

Earnings per share of common stock are among the most commonly quoted statistics on the financial pages of daily newspapers. Such data are used by investors in evaluating the past performance of a business, in projecting its future earnings, and in weighing investment opportunities.

Companies with Simple Capital Structures

Earnings per share calculations may be quite simple or very complex. The calculations are less difficult for companies that have simple capital structures. A company is said to have a **simple capital structure** if it has only common stock and perhaps nonconvertible preferred stock outstanding.

Calculating Earnings per Share When the Number of Common Shares Outstanding Does Not Change Consider a company that has only common stock and nonconvertible preferred stock outstanding. If the number of common shares outstanding does not change during the period, earnings per share is calculated as follows:

$$\text{Earnings per share} = \frac{\text{Net income} - \text{Preferred dividends}}{\text{Common shares outstanding}}$$

For example, assume that in 198A, Blackwell Company's net income was $40,000 and preferred dividends of $7,500 were declared. On January 1,

198A, the company had 5,000 common shares outstanding and this number did not change during the year. Earnings per share for 198A is:

$$\text{Earnings per share} = \frac{\$40,000 - \$7,500}{5,000} = \$6.50$$

However, the calculation is more complex if the number of common shares outstanding changed during the period. The number of common shares outstanding may change (1) because the company sells additional shares or buys treasury shares, or (2) because of stock dividends and stock splits.

Adjusting the Denominator for Sales or Purchases of Common Shares   If additional shares are sold or treasury shares are purchased during the year, earnings per share must be based on the weighted-average number of shares outstanding during the year. For example, suppose that in 198B, Blackwell Company again earned $40,000 and preferred dividends were $7,500. However, on July 1, 198B, Blackwell sold 4,000 additional common shares. Also, on November 1, 198B, Blackwell purchased 3,000 treasury shares. In other words, 5,000 shares were outstanding for six months, then 9,000 shares were outstanding for four months, then 6,000 shares were outstanding for two months. The weighted-average number of shares outstanding during 198B is calculated as follows:

Time Period	Shares Outstanding	Weighted by Portion of Year Outstanding		
January–June	5,000	× (6/12)	=	2,500
July–October	(5,000 + 4,000)	× (4/12)	=	3,000
November–December . .	(9,000 − 3,000)	× (2/12)	=	1,000
Weighted-average common shares outstanding				6,500

And the calculation of earnings per share for 198B is:

$$\text{Earnings per share} = \frac{\$40,000 - \$7,500}{6,500} = \$5.00$$

Adjusting the Denominator for Stock Splits and Stock Dividends   A stock split or stock dividend is quite different from a stock sale. When stock is sold, the company receives new assets that can be used to generate additional earnings in the future. On the other hand, stock splits and stock dividends do not provide additional assets for the company. Instead, a stock split or stock dividend simply means that the company's earnings must be allocated to a larger number of outstanding shares.

Because of the nature of stock splits and stock dividends, they must be treated differently from stock sales when calculating the weighted-average number of shares outstanding. When a stock split or stock dividend occurs, all **previous** sales or purchases of stock must be retroactively adjusted to reflect the stock split or dividend. For example, consider the previous example of Blackwell Company. However, assume that the stock transactions in 198B included a stock split, as follows:

Jan. 1:	5,000 common shares were outstanding.
July 1:	Blackwell sold 4,000 additional shares of common stock.
Nov. 1:	Blackwell purchased 3,000 common shares as treasury stock.
Dec. 1:	**Outstanding common shares were split 2 for 1.**

The weighted-average number of shares outstanding during 198B is calculated as follows:

Time Period	Shares Outstanding	Adjusted for Stock Split	Weighted by Portion of Year Outstanding
January–June . .	5,000	× 2	× (6/12) = 5,000
July–October . . .	(5,000 + 4,000)	× 2	× (4/12) = 6,000
November	(9,000 − 3,000)	× 2	× (1/12) = 1,000
December	12,000	—	× (1/12) = 1,000
Weighted-average common shares outstanding			13,000

Note that every time stock was sold or purchased, the resulting number of outstanding shares was adjusted for the subsequent stock split. The same type of adjustment is required for stock dividends. If, for example, the 2 for 1 stock split on December 1 had been a 10% stock dividend, the previous amounts of outstanding shares would have been adjusted by a multiplier of 1.10 instead of 2.

The calculation of Blackwell Company's earnings per share for 198B is:

$$\text{Earnings per share} = \frac{\$40,000 - \$7,500}{13,000} = \$2.50$$

Companies with Complex Capital Structures

Companies with **complex capital structures** have outstanding securities such as bonds or preferred stock that are convertible into common stock. Earnings per share calculations for companies with complex capital structures tend to be complicated. Often, such companies must present two types of earnings per share calculations. One is called **primary earnings per share,** and the other is called **fully diluted earnings per share.**

For a moment, assume that an outstanding security such as preferred stock had been converted into common stock at the beginning of the current period. The result of this assumed conversion would have been to increase the number of common shares outstanding and to reduce preferred dividends. The net result may have been to reduce earnings per share, or to increase earnings per share. When the assumed conversion of a security reduces earnings per share, the security is said to be **dilutive;** those that increase earnings per share are **antidilutive.**

Primary Earnings per Share Based on detailed rules, convertible securities are evaluated at the time they are issued.[4] If eventual conversion appears highly probable, the convertible security is called a **common stock equivalent.** Primary earnings per share is calculated as if dilutive, common stock equivalents had already been converted at the beginning of the period.

Fully Diluted Earnings per Share Common stock equivalents have terms that make their eventual conversion very probable. Other convertible securities are less apt to be converted. Nevertheless, an assumed conversion of those securities may have the effect of reducing earnings per share—in other words, a dilutive effect. Fully diluted earnings per share is calculated as if **all** dilutive securities had already been converted.

Presentations of Earnings per Share on the Income Statement

Because of the importance attached to earnings per share data, generally accepted accounting principles require that this information be shown on the face of published income statements. Separate earnings per share calculations must be presented for (1) income from continuing operations, (2) gains or losses from discontinued operations, (3) extraordinary items, (4) the cumulative effect of changes in accounting principles, and (5) net income. A good example of these presentations is provided by the 1984 financial statements of Uniroyal, Inc. The bottom portion of Uniroyal's comparative income statement for 1984, 1983, and 1982, appeared as shown in Illustration 20-5.

Illustration 20-5

| | | | *Uniroyal, Inc.* |
In thousands, except per share amounts	**1984**	1983	1982
Net Income	**$77,146**	66,998	25,598
Per Common Share			
Primary			
Income from continuing operations	**$ 2.81**	2.16	1.01
Loss from discontinued operations	**(1.34)**	(.61)	(.23)
Extraordinary credits	**2.34**	.48	—
Cumulative effect of accounting change	**(1.68)**	—	—
Net income	**$ 2.13**	2.03	.78
Fully diluted			
Income from continuing operations	**$ 2.65**	2.02	.96
Loss from discontinued operations	**(1.24)**	(.56)	(.20)
Extraordinary credits	**2.16**	.43	—
Cumulative effect of accounting change	**(1.55)**	—	—
Net income	**$ 2.02**	1.89	.76

Courtesy of Uniroyal, Inc.

---

[4] FASB, *Accounting Standards—Current Text* (Stamford, Conn., 1984), sec. E09.122–127. First published as *APB Opinion No. 15,* par. 31, 33, 35–37. Also see FASB, *Statement of Financial Accounting Standards No. 85* (March 1985), par. 2.

Price-Earnings Ratios

Price-earnings ratios are commonly used in comparing investment opportunities. A price-earnings ratio is calculated by dividing market price per share by earnings per share. For example, if Anchor Supply Company's common stock sold at $12 per share at the end of 198B, the stock's end-of-year price-earnings ratio is calculated as:

$$\frac{\text{Market price per share, \$12}}{\text{Earnings per share, \$1.32}} = 9.09$$

After the calculation is made, it may be said that the stock had a 9.1 price-earnings ratio at the end of 198B, or it may be said that approximately $9.10 was required at that time to buy $1 of the company's 198B earnings.

In comparing price-earnings ratios, it must be remembered that such ratios vary from industry to industry. For example, in the steel industry, a price-earnings ratio of 8 to 10 is normal, while in a growth industry, such as high-technology electronics, a price-earnings ratio of 20 to 25 might be expected.

18 14, + 20

Homework no objective

☐   **Glossary**   **Accounts receivable turnover** an indication of how long it takes a company
to collect its accounts, calculated by dividing net sales or credit sales
by the average accounts receivable balance.

Acid-test ratio the relation of quick assets, such as cash, temporary
investments, accounts receivable, and notes receivable, to current
liabilities, calculated as quick assets divided by current liabilities.

Antidilutive securities convertible securities that would increase earnings
per share if they had been converted at the beginning of the period.

Common-size comparative statements comparative financial statements in
which each amount is expressed as a percentage of a base amount. In
the balance sheet, total assets is usually selected as the base amount
and is expressed as 100%. In the income statement, net sales is usually
selected as the base amount.

Common stock equivalent a convertible security the eventual conversion
of which appears, at the time of issuance, to be very probable.

Comparative statement a financial statement with data for two or more
successive accounting periods placed in columns side by side in order
to better illustrate changes in the data.

Complex capital structure a capital structure that includes securities that
are convertible into common stock.

Current ratio the relation of a company's current assets to its current
liabilities, that is, current assets divided by current liabilities.

Dilutive securities convertible securities that would reduce earnings per
share if they had been converted at the beginning of the period.

Earnings per share the amount of net income (or components of income)
that accrues to common shares divided by the weighted-average number
of common shares outstanding.

Financial reporting the process of preparing and issuing financial
information about a company.

Fully diluted earnings per share earnings per share statistics that are
calculated as if all dilutive securities had already been converted.

General-purpose financial statements financial statements (usually including
the income statement, balance sheet, statement of retained earnings,
and statement of changes in financial position) published by a company
for use by persons who do not have the ability to obtain specialized
financial reports designed to meet their interests.

Merchandise turnover the number of times a company's average inventory
is sold during an accounting period, calculated by dividing cost of goods
sold by the average merchandise inventory balance.

Price-earnings ratio market price per share of common stock divided by
earnings per share.

Primary earnings per share earnings per share statistics that are calculated
as if dilutive, common stock equivalents had already been converted at
the beginning of the period.

Quick ratio a synonym for acid-test ratio.

Rate of return on common stockholders' equity net income after taxes and
dividends on preferred stock divided by average common stockholders'
equity.

Rate of return on total assets employed income before interest and income taxes, expressed as a percentage of the average amount of total assets employed during the period.

Simple capital structure a capital structure that includes only common stock and perhaps nonconvertible preferred stock.

Times fixed interest charges earned an indicator of a company's ability to satisfy fixed interest charges, calculated as net income before fixed interest charges and income taxes divided by fixed interest charges.

□ **Questions for Class Discussion**

1. Who are the intended readers of general-purpose financial statements?

2. What are the three broad objectives of financial reporting prescribed by the FASB?

3. Comparative balance sheets may be prepared with columns showing increases and decreases in both dollar amounts and percentages. Why is this so?

4. When trends are calculated and compared, it is often informative to compare the trend of sales with the trends of several other financial statement items. What are some of the items that should be compared to sales in this fashion?

5. What is meant by *common-size* financial statements?

6. What items are assigned a value of 100% (*a*) on a common-size balance sheet and (*b*) on a common-size income statement?

7. Why is working capital given special attention in the process of analyzing balance sheets?

8. Indicate which of the following transactions increase working capital, which decrease working capital, and which have no effect on working capital:
   a. Collected accounts receivable.
   b. Borrowed money by giving a 90-day interest-bearing note.
   c. Declared a cash dividend.
   d. Paid a cash dividend previously declared.
   e. Sold plant assets at their book value.
   f. Sold merchandise at a profit.

9. List several factors that have an effect on working capital requirements.

10. What are several reasons why a 2 to 1 current ratio may not be adequate for a particular company?

11. State the significance of each of the following ratios and turnovers and tell how each is calculated.
   a. Current ratio.
   b. Acid-test ratio.
   c. Turnover of accounts receivable.
   d. Turnover of merchandise inventory.
   e. Rate of return on common stockholders' equity.
   f. Ratio of pledged plant assets to secured long-term liabilities.

12. How are days' sales uncollected calculated? What is the significance of the number of days' sales uncollected?

13. Why do creditors like to see a high proportion of total assets being financed by owners' equity?

14. Why must the ratio of pledged plant assets to secured liabilities be interpreted with care?

15. What does the rate of return on total assets employed tell about management?

16. How are earnings per share calculated for a corporation with a simple capital structure?

17. In calculating the weighted-average number of common shares outstanding, how are stock splits and stock dividends treated?

18. Why are not all convertible securities considered to be common stock equivalents?

19. What is the difference between primary earnings per share and fully diluted earnings per share?

20. What is the difference between simple capital structures and complex capital structures?

21. How is a price-earnings ratio calculated?

☐ **Class Exercises**

Exercise 20-1

Calculate trend percentages for the following items using 198A as the base year. Then state whether the situation shown by the trends appears to be favorable or unfavorable:

	198E	198D	198C	198B	198A
Sales.	$429,000	$409,500	$390,000	$377,000	$325,000
Cost of goods sold. . .	266,400	246,050	229,400	218,300	185,000
Accounts receivable . .	45,440	43,520	40,320	37,440	32,000

Exercise 20-2

Where possible, calculate percentages of increase and decrease for the following unrelated items. The parentheses indicate deficit items.

	198B	198A
Equipment, net	$136,300	$94,000
Notes receivable	–0–	11,000
Notes payable.	26,000	–0–
Retained earnings	(3,400)	17,000
Cash.	6,600	(800)

Exercise 20-3

Express the following income statement information in common-size percentages and evaluate the situation shown as favorable or unfavorable.

Crown Corporation
Comparative Income Statement
For Years Ended December 31, 198B, and 198A

	198B	198A
Sales	$160,000	$135,000
Cost of goods sold	106,400	83,700
Gross profit from sales	$ 53,600	$ 51,300
Operating expenses.	38,880	20,520
Net income	$ 14,720	$ 30,780

Exercise 20-4

Western Products Company's financial statements are presented below:

Western Products Company
Income Statement
For the Year Ended December 31, 198B

Sales.		$450,000
Cost of goods sold:		
Merchandise inventory, January 1, 198A.	$ 22,000	
Purchases.	296,000	
Goods available for sale	$318,000	
Merchandise inventory, December 31, 198A	32,000	
Cost of goods sold		286,000
Gross profit on sales		$164,000
Operating expenses		123,000
Operating income		$ 41,000
Interest expense on long-term notes		10,000
Income before taxes		$ 31,000
Income taxes		12,400
Net income		$ 18,600

Western Products Company
Balance Sheet
December 31, 198B

Assets		Liabilities and Stockholders' Equity	
Cash	$ 19,800	Accounts payable	$ 47,600
Accounts receivable, net . . .	60,000	Long-term note payable,	
Merchandise inventory	32,000	secured by mortgage on	
Prepaid expenses	5,800	the plant assets	95,000
Plant assets, net	180,000	Common stock, $10 par	
		value	85,000
		Retained earnings	70,000
		Total liabilities and	
Total assets	$297,600	stockholders' equity	$297,600

Required

Calculate the following: (*a*) current ratio, (*b*) acid-test ratio, (*c*) days' sales uncollected, (*d*) percentage of capital contributed by owners, (*e*) ratio of pledged plant assets to secured liabilities, and (*f*) times fixed interest charges earned. (Assume all sales were on credit.)

Exercise 20-5

Refer to the 198B financial statements of Western Products Company presented in Exercise 20-4. Additional information from the 198A financial statements is as follows:

Accounts receivable	$ 52,000
Merchandise inventory	22,000
Total assets.	268,000
Common stock, $10 par . . .	85,000
Retained earnings	60,000

Required

Calculate the following for 198B: *(a)* accounts receivable turnover, *(b)* merchandise turnover, *(c)* return on total assets employed, and *(d)* return on stockholders' equity.

Exercise 20-6

Common-size and trend percentages for a company's sales, cost of goods sold, and expenses follow:

	Common-Size Percentages				Trend Percentages		
	198C	**198B**	**198A**		**198C**	**198B**	**198A**
Sales	100.0	100.0	100.0	Sales	93.5	96.7	100.0
Cost of goods sold	56.5	59.9	62.0	Cost of goods sold	85.2	93.4	100.0
Expenses	28.4	27.8	28.0	Expenses	94.8	96.0	100.0

Required

Present statistics to prove whether the company's net income increased, decreased, or remained unchanged during the three-year period represented above.

Exercise 20-7

A company reported $153,375 net income in 198A and declared preferred dividends of $12,000. The following changes in common shares outstanding occurred during the year:

> Jan. 1: 20,000 common shares were outstanding.
> Mar. 1: Sold 15,000 common shares for par.
> July 1: Declared and issued a 50% common stock dividend, or
> $(35,000 \times 50\%) = 17,500$ additional shares.

Calculate the weighted-average number of common shares outstanding during the year and earnings per share.

Exercise 20-8

A company reported $315,000 net income in 198A and declared preferred dividends of $25,000. The following changes in common shares outstanding occurred during the year.

> Jan. 1: 30,000 common shares were outstanding.
> Apr. 1: Sold 50,000 common shares for par plus a $10 premium.
> Aug. 1: Purchased 2,000 shares to be held as treasury stock.
> Nov. 1: Declared and issued a 3 for 1 stock split.

Calculate the weighted-average number of common shares outstanding during the year and earnings per share.

Exercise 20-9

A company's 198A income statement, excluding the earnings per share portion of the statement, was as follows:

Sales		$150,000
Costs and expenses:		
Depreciation	$ 8,000	
Income taxes	12,000	
Other expenses	88,000	108,000
Income from continuing operations		$ 42,000
Loss from operating discontinued business segment		
(net of $7,600 taxes)	$20,000	
Loss on sale of business segment		
(net of $9,000 tax)	26,000	(46,000)
Loss before extraordinary items and change in		
accounting principle		$ (4,000)
Extraordinary gain (net of $16,000 taxes)	$54,000	
Cumulative effect of a change in accounting principle		
(net of $8,800 taxes)	33,000	87,000
Net income		$ 83,000

Assuming that dilutive, common stock equivalents were converted at the beginning of the year, the weighted-average number of common shares outstanding during the year was 90,000. Assuming that all dilutive securities had been converted at the beginning of the year, the weighted-average number of common shares outstanding during the year was 106,000.

Required

Present the earnings per share portion of the 198A income statement.

Problems   Problem 20-1

The condensed statements of Eagle Grove Company follow:

Eagle Grove Company
Comparative Income Statement
For Years Ended December 31, 198C, 198B, and 198A
(in $000)

	198C	198B	198A
Sales	$52,000	$47,000	$42,000
Cost of goods sold	38,064	33,370	29,190
Gross profit from sales	$13,936	$13,630	$12,810
Selling expenses	$ 6,916	$ 6,392	$ 5,880
Administrative expenses	4,992	4,747	4,410
Total expenses	$11,908	$11,139	$10,290
Income before taxes	$ 2,028	$ 2,491	$ 2,520
State and federal income taxes	528	697	756
Net income	$ 1,500	$ 1,794	$ 1,764

Eagle Grove Company
Comparative Balance Sheet
December 31, 198C, 198B, and 198A
(in $000)

	198C	198B	198A
Assets			
Current assets	$ 3,500	$ 3,200	$ 3,900
Long-term investments	–0–	50	500
Plant and equipment	14,600	15,000	12,600
Total assets	$18,100	$18,250	$17,000

Liabilities and Capital	198C	198B	198A
Current liabilities	$ 1,700	$ 1,600	$ 1,400
Common stock	9,000	9,000	8,500
Other contributed capital	300	300	250
Retained earnings	7,100	7,350	6,850
Total liabilities and capital	$18,100	$18,250	$17,000

Required

1. Calculate each year's current ratio.
2. Express the income statement data in common-size percentages.
3. Express the balance sheet data in trend percentages.
4. Comment on any significant relationships revealed by the ratios and percentages.

Problem 20-2

The condensed comparative statements of Branding Iron Corporation follow:

Branding Iron Corporation
Comparative Income Statement
For Years Ended December 31, 198G–198A
(in $000)

	198G	198F	198E	198D	198C	198B	198A
Sales	$975	$900	$800	$740	$650	$590	$500
Cost of goods sold	540	480	420	379	321	292	240
Gross profit from sales	$435	$420	$380	$361	$329	$298	$260
Operating expenses	376	332	275	225	200	174	140
Income before taxes	$ 59	$ 88	$105	$136	$129	$124	$120

Branding Iron Corporation
Comparative Balance Sheet
December 31, 198G–198A
($000)

	198G	198F	198E	198D	198C	198B	198A
Assets							
Cash	$ 10	$ 16	$ 18	$ 21	$ 23	$ 20	$ 26
Accounts receivable, net	100	98	96	70	62	60	48
Merchandise inventory	243	235	221	182	158	135	117
Other current assets	6	8	5	10	8	8	5
Long-term investments	–0–	–0–	–0–	49	49	49	49
Plant and equipment, net	464	474	450	226	228	222	224
Total assets	$823	$831	$790	$558	$528	$494	$469
Liabilities and Capital							
Current liabilities	$145	$150	$135	$110	$ 97	$ 74	$ 62
Long-term liabilities	200	225	230	91	94	97	100
Common stock	200	200	200	150	150	150	150
Other contributed capital	75	75	75	60	60	60	60
Retained earnings	203	181	150	147	127	113	97
Total liabilities and capital	$823	$831	$790	$558	$528	$494	$469

Required

1. Calculate trend percentages for the items of the statements.
2. Analyze and comment on the situation shown in the statements.

Problem 20-3

The year-end statements of Crankcase Corporation follow:

Crankcase Corporation
Income Statement
For the Year Ended December 31, 198B

Sales		$795,600
Cost of goods sold:		
Merchandise inventory, January 1, 198B	$ 58,900	
Purchases	495,800	
Goods available for sale	$554,700	
Merchandise inventory, December 31, 198B . .	46,300	
Cost of goods sold		508,400
Gross profit from sales		$287,200
Operating expenses		225,900
Operating income		$ 61,300
Interest expense		9,800
Income before taxes		$ 51,500
Income taxes		15,450
Net income		$ 36,050

Crankcase Corporation
Balance Sheet
December 31, 198B

Assets		Liabilities and Stockholders' Equity	
Cash	$ 15,600	Accounts payable	$ 37,800
Temporary investments	17,500	Accrued wages payable	4,700
Notes receivable	4,200	Income taxes payable	5,700
Accounts receivable, net . . .	40,400	Long-term note payable,	
Merchandise inventory	46,300	secured by mortgage on	
Prepaid expenses	1,900	assets	96,000
Plant assets, net	269,200	Common stock, $5 par value .	150,000
		Retained earnings	100,900
		Total liabilities and	
Total assets	$395,100	stockholders' equity	$395,100

Assume all sales were on credit. On the December 31, 198A, balance sheet, the assets totaled $339,500, common stock was $150,000, and retained earnings was $80,100.

Required

Calculate the following: (*a*) current ratio, (*b*) acid-test ratio, (*c*) days' sales uncollected, (*d*) merchandise turnover, (*e*) ratio of pledged plant assets to secured liabilities, (*f*) times fixed interest charges earned, (*g*) return on total assets employed, and (*h*) return on stockholders' equity.

Problem 20-4

Two companies that operate in the same industry as competitors are being evaluated by a bank that may lend money to each one. Summary information from the financial statements of the two companies is provided below:

Data from the Current Year-End Balance Sheets

	Quanto Company	Judgo Company
Cash	$ 17,100	$ 24,500
Notes receivable	6,000	4,800
Accounts receivable	51,800	84,200
Merchandise inventory	64,200	99,900
Prepaid expenses	4,600	6,800
Plant and equipment, net	297,300	305,500
Total assets	$441,000	$525,700
Current liabilities	$ 77,700	$106,300
Long-term notes payable	85,000	100,000
Common stock, $10 par value	150,000	180,000
Retained earnings	128,300	139,400
Total liabilities and capital	$441,000	$525,700

Data from the Current Year's Income Statements

	Quanto Company	Judgo Company
Sales	$742,000	$966,000
Cost of goods sold	547,000	715,000
Interest expense	5,500	11,800
Income tax expense	8,400	12,400
Net income	33,600	41,400

Beginning-of-Year Data

	Quanto Company	Judgo Company
Merchandise inventory	$ 50,600	$ 85,100
Total assets	389,000	465,300
Common stock, $10 par value	150,000	180,000
Retained earnings	91,700	110,600

Required

1. Calculate current ratios, acid-test ratios, merchandise turnovers, and days' sales uncollected for the two companies. Then state which company you think is the better short-term credit risk and why.

2. Calculate earnings per share, rate of return on total assets employed, and rate of return on stockholders' equity. Assuming that each company's stock can be purchased at $18 per share, which company's stock would you recommend as the better investment? Why?

Problem 20-5

Metro Sales Corporation began the month of April with $380,000 of current assets, a current ratio of 2.5 to 1, and an acid-test ratio of 1.5 to 1. During the month, it completed the following transactions:

Apr. 2   Bought $50,000 of merchandise on account. (The company uses a perpetual inventory system.)

5   Sold for $60,000 merchandise that cost $28,000.

Apr. 8   Collected a $16,000 account receivable.
      11 Paid a $23,000 account payable.
      18 Wrote off a $7,500 bad debt against the Allowance for Doubtful Accounts account.
      20 Declared a $1 per share cash dividend on the 20,000 shares of outstanding common stock.
      24 Paid the dividend declared on April 20.
      28 Borrowed $70,000 by giving the bank a 60-day, 12% note.
      29 Borrowed $100,000 by signing a long-term secured note.
      30 Used the $170,000 proceeds of the notes to buy additional machinery.

Required

Prepare a schedule showing the company's current ratio, acid-test ratio, and working capital after each of the foregoing transactions. Round to two decimal places.

Problem 20-6

Except for the earnings per share statistics, the 198C, 198B, and 198A income statements of Foxbat Company were originally presented as follows:

	198C	198B	198A
Sales.	$480,000	$ 435,000	$398,000
Costs and expenses	415,000	390,000	320,000
Income from continuing operations	$ 65,000	$ 45,000	$ 78,000
Loss on discontinued operations	—	(120,000)	—
Income (loss) before extraordinary items and changes in accounting principles	$ 65,000	$ (75,000)	$ 78,000
Extraordinary gains (losses)	112,000	—	(27,000)
Cumulative effect of change in accounting principle	—	—	33,000
Net income (loss)	$177,000	$ (75,000)	$ 84,000

Information on common stock:

Shares outstanding on January 1, 198A	20,000
Sale of shares on April 1, 198A	+8,000
Purchase of treasury shares on May 1, 198A	−4,000
Stock dividend of 12.5% on September 1, 198A	+3,000
Shares outstanding on December 31, 198A.	27,000
Sale of shares on April 1, 198B.	+6,000
Sale of shares on July 1, 198B	+9,000
Shares outstanding on December 31, 198B.	42,000
Purchase of treasury shares on April 1, 198C.	−3,000
Sale of shares on June 1, 198C.	+15,000
Stock split of 2 for 1 on November 1, 198C	+54,000
Shares outstanding on December 31, 198C.	108,000

Required

1. Calculate the weighted-average number of common shares outstanding during (*a*) 198A, (*b*) 198B, and (*c*) 198C.

2. Present the earnings per share portions of (a) the 198A income statement, (b) the 198B income statement, and (c) the 198C income statement.

□ **Alternate Problems**   **Problem 20-1A**

The condensed statements of Kingman Corporation follow:

Kingman Corporation
Comparative Income Statement
For Years Ended December 31, 198C, 198B, and 198A
(in $000)

	198C	198B	198A
Sales	$95,000	$79,500	$68,000
Cost of goods sold	52,400	40,800	31,300
Gross profit from sales	$42,600	$38,700	$36,700
Selling expenses	$10,350	$ 7,100	$ 7,500
Administrative expenses	6,450	7,800	6,900
Total expenses	$16,800	$14,900	$14,400
Income before taxes	$25,800	$23,800	$22,300
State and federal income taxes	9,030	7,860	6,630
Net income.	$16,770	$15,940	$15,670

Kingman Corporation
Comparative Balance Sheet
December 31, 198C, 198B, and 198A
(in $000)

	198C	198B	198A
Assets			
Current assets	$18,500	$ 7,600	$10,700
Long-term investments	–0–	500	2,900
Plant and equipment	48,000	50,000	36,400
Total assets.	$66,500	$58,100	$50,000
Liabilities and Capital			
Current liabilities.	$ 8,000	$ 6,700	$ 4,200
Common stock	13,000	13,000	10,000
Other contributed capital	1,500	1,500	1,000
Retained earnings	44,000	36,900	34,800
Total liabilities and capital.	$66,500	$58,100	$50,000

Required

1. Calculate each year's current ratio.
2. Express the income statement data in common-size percentages.
3. Express the balance sheet data in trend percentages.

4. Comment on any significant relationships revealed by the ratios and percentages.

Problem 20-2A

The condensed comparative statements of Barton River Company follow:

Barton River Company
Comparative Income Statement
For Years Ended December 31, 198G–198A
(in $000)

	198G	198F	198E	198D	198C	198B	198A
Sales	$340	$360	$350	$380	$420	$410	$450
Cost of goods sold.	166	173	170	184	195	188	190
Gross profit from sales	$174	$187	$180	$196	$225	$222	$260
Operating expenses	145	152	150	169	176	180	200
Income before taxes	$ 29	$ 35	$ 30	$ 27	$ 49	$ 42	$ 60

Barton River Company
Comparative Balance Sheet
December 31, 198G–198A
($000)

	198G	198F	198E	198D	198C	198B	198A
Assets							
Cash	$ 14	$ 17	$ 16	$ 20	$ 29	$ 26	$ 30
Accounts receivable, net . . .	68	79	73	75	86	84	92
Merchandise inventory	124	130	128	137	140	150	143
Other current assets	12	13	14	16	15	18	20
Long-term investments	60	40	20	67	67	67	80
Plant and equipment, net . . .	338	344	350	255	260	265	270
Total assets	$616	$623	$601	$570	$597	$610	$635
Liabilities and Capital							
Current liabilities	$131	$138	$121	$ 90	$112	$140	$185
Long-term liabilities	110	125	140	155	170	185	200
Common stock	125	125	125	125	125	125	125
Other contributed capital . . .	40	40	40	40	40	40	40
Retained earnings	210	195	175	160	150	120	85
Total liabilities and capital . . .	$616	$623	$601	$570	$597	$610	$635

Required

1. Calculate trend percentages for the items of the statements.
2. Analyze and comment on the situation shown in the statements.

Problem 20-3A

The year-end statements of Clearlake Corporation follow:

Clearlake Corporation
Income Statement
For the Year Ended December 31, 198B

Sales		$576,000
Cost of goods sold:		
Merchandise inventory, January 1, 198B	$ 49,700	
Purchases	342,600	
Goods available for sale	$392,300	
Merchandise inventory, December 31, 198B. . .	37,800	
Cost of goods sold.		354,500
Gross profit from sales		$221,500
Operating expenses		173,300
Operating income		$ 48,200
Interest expense.		8,100
Income before taxes		$ 40,100
Income taxes		12,300
Net income		$ 27,800

Clearlake Corporation
Balance Sheet
December 31, 198B

Assets		Liabilities and Stockholders' Equity	
Cash	$ 10,100	Accounts payable	$ 30,600
Temporary investments	5,500	Accrued wages payable. . . .	5,900
Notes receivable	3,000	Income taxes payable.	3,100
Accounts receivable, net . . .	36,600	Long-term note payable,	
Merchandise inventory	37,800	secured by mortgage on	
Prepaid expenses	2,800	assets	82,000
Plant assets, net	257,400	Common stock, $1 par value .	120,000
		Retained earnings	111,600
		Total liabilities and	
Total assets	$353,200	stockholders' equity	$353,200

Assume all sales were on credit. On the December 31, 198A, balance sheet, the assets totaled $310,600, common stock was $120,000, and retained earnings was $90,800.

Required

Calculate the following: (*a*) current ratio, (*b*) acid-test ratio, (*c*) days' sales uncollected, (*d*) merchandise turnover, (*e*) ratio of pledged plant assets to secured liabilities, (*f*) times fixed interest charges earned, (*g*) return on total assets employed, and (*h*) return on stockholders' equity.

Problem 20-4A

Two companies that operate in the same industry as competitors are being evaluated by a bank that may lend money to each one. Summary information from the financial statements of the two companies follows:

Data from the Current Year-End Balance Sheets

	Stone Company	Rock Company
Cash	$ 29,300	$ 56,200
Notes receivable	16,000	14,500
Accounts receivable	103,500	116,500
Merchandise inventory	96,300	131,700
Prepaid expenses	14,900	16,700
Plant and equipment, net	329,100	337,900
Total assets	$589,100	$673,500
Current liabilities	$109,800	$138,400
Long-term notes payable	117,400	132,000
Common stock, $20 par value	180,000	210,000
Retained earnings	181,900	193,100
Total liabilities and capital	$589,100	$673,500

Data from the Current Year's Income Statements

Sales	$701,100	$989,500
Cost of goods sold	515,800	706,600
Interest expense	12,800	15,100
Income tax expense	20,700	41,500
Net income	52,700	72,200

Beginning-of-Year Data

Merchandise inventory	$116,900	$ 91,200
Total assets	512,000	598,300
Common stock, $20 par value	180,000	210,000
Retained earnings	156,800	150,300

Required

1. Calculate current ratios, acid-test ratios, merchandise turnovers, and days' sales uncollected for the two companies. Then state which company you think is the better short-term credit risk and why.

2. Calculate earnings per share, rate of return on total assets employed, and rate of return on stockholders' equity. Assuming that each company's stock can be purchased at $40 per share, which company's stock would you recommend as the better investment? Why?

Problem 20-5A

Ft. Meyers Corporation began the month of February with $264,000 of current assets, a current ratio of 2.2 to 1, and an acid-test ratio of 0.9 to 1. During the month, it completed the following transactions:

Feb. 2   Sold for $45,000 merchandise that cost $26,000.
  3   Collected a $27,000 account receivable.
  9   Bought $48,000 of merchandise on account. (The company uses a perpetual inventory system.)
  13   Borrowed $50,000 by giving the bank a 60-day, 12% note.
  16   Borrowed $80,000 by signing a long-term secured note.

Feb. 21   Used the $130,000 proceeds of the notes to buy additional machinery.

22   Declared a $1.50 per share cash dividend on the 30,000 shares of outstanding common stock.

24   Wrote off an $11,000 bad debt against the Allowance for Doubtful Accounts account.

25   Paid a $37,000 account payable.

28   Paid the dividend declared on February 21.

Required

Prepare a schedule showing the company's current ratio, acid-test ratio, and working capital after each of the foregoing transactions. Round to two decimal places.

Problem 20-6A

Except for the earnings per share statistics, the 198C, 198B, and 198A income statements of Fireside Corporation were originally presented as follows:

	198C	198B	198A
Sales	$765,000	$577,000	$645,000
Costs and expenses	664,000	448,000	469,000
Income from continuing operations	$101,000	$129,000	$176,000
Loss on discontinued operations	—	(83,000)	(55,000)
Income (loss) before extraordinary items and changes in accounting principles	$101,000	$ 46,000	$121,000
Extraordinary gains (losses)		(68,000)	(38,000)
Cumulative effect of change in accounting principle	29,500	—	—
Net income (loss)	$130,500	$ (22,000)	$ 83,000

Information on common stock:	
Shares outstanding on January 1, 198A	24,000
Sale of shares on June 1, 198A	+3,000
Purchase of treasury shares on October 1, 198A	−1,500
Shares outstanding on December 31, 198A	25,500
Sale of shares on March 1, 198B	+5,100
Sale of shares on April 1, 198B	+8,100
Stock split of 2 for 1 on September 1, 198B	+38,700
Shares outstanding on December 31, 198B	+77,400
Purchase of treasury shares on March 1, 198C	−3,000
Sale of shares on June 1, 198C	+14,100
Stock dividend of 20% on November 1, 198C	+17,700
Shares outstanding on December 31, 198C	106,200

Required

1. Calculate the weighted-average number of common shares outstanding during (*a*) 198A, (*b*) 198B, and (*c*) 198C.

2. Present the earnings per share portions of (*a*) the 198C income statement, (*b*) the 198B income statement, and (*c*) the 198A income statement.

Provocative Problem 20-1   The Black and Decker Manufacturing Company

Black and Decker is the world's largest producer of power tools. The company began operations over 75 years ago as a small machine shop and has grown to the point of having worldwide manufacturing facilities and sales volume in excess of $1.5 billion. The 1984 annual report of Black and Decker included an 11-year financial summary, from which the following information has been extracted:

(thousands of dollars except per share data)	1984	1983	1982	1981
Summary of Operations				
Net sales	$1,532,883	$1,167,752	$1,160,233	$1,244,510
% change	31.3	.6	(6.8)	2.0
Earnings from continuing				
operations	95,404	28,151	40,681	72,998
% of net sales	6.2	2.4	3.5	5.9
% change	238.9	(30.8)	(44.3)	(8.6)
Per Share Data				
Earnings (loss):				
Continuing operations	1.95	.65	.97	1.74
Discontinued operations	—	.37	(2.79)	(.15)
Total	1.95	1.02	(1.82)	1.59
Cash dividends	.58	.52	.76	.76
Stockholders' equity	13.58	11.79	10.70	13.68
Other Data				
Working capital	461,545	423,809	406,542	420,123
Current ratio	2.2	2.8	2.8	2.8
Net sales to average total assets	1.25	1.18	1.09	1.07
% return on average stockholders'				
equity	15.4	5.2	8.1	14.5

Courtesy of The Black and Decker Manufacturing Company.

Discuss the format of Black and Decker's presentation relative to the illustrations in the chapter. Then evaluate the company's performance over the four-year period as it is disclosed by the above data.

Provocative Problem 20-2   Storm Gear Company

In your position as controller of Storm Gear Company, you have the responsibility of keeping the board of directors informed about the financial activities and status of the company. In preparation for the next meeting of the board, you have calculated the following ratios, turnovers, and percentages to enable you to answer questions:

	198C	198B	198A
Current ratio	2.4 to 1	2.3 to 1	1.9 to 1
Acid-test ratio	0.9 to 1	1.1 to 1	1.2 to 1
Merchandise turnover	8.6 times	9.4 times	10.5 times
Accounts receivable turnover	7.4 times	7.9 times	8.3 times
Return on stockholders' equity	10.30%	11.75%	12.24%
Return on total assets	9.88%	10.35%	10.97%
Sales to plant assets	4.2 to 1	4.1 to 1	3.7 to 1
Sales trend	128.00	119.00	100.00
Selling expenses to net sales	9.16%	14.65%	15.35%

Required

Using the statistics given, answer each of the following questions and explain how you arrived at your answer.

1. Is it becoming easier for the company to meet its current debts on time and to take advantage of cash discounts?
2. Is the company collecting its accounts receivable more rapidly?
3. Is the company's investment in accounts receivable decreasing?
4. Are dollars invested in inventory increasing?
5. Is the company's investment in plant assets increasing?
6. Is the stockholders' investment becoming more profitable?
7. Is the company using its assets efficiently?
8. Did the dollar amount of selling expenses decrease during the three-year period?

Provocative Problem 20-3   Z-Ray versus Skybolt

Z-Ray, Inc., and Skybolt, Inc., are competing companies with similar backgrounds. The stock of both companies is traded locally, and each stock can be purchased at its book value. Jim Grey has an opportunity to invest in either company but is undecided as to which is the better managed company and which is the better investment. Prepare a report to Mr. Grey stating which company you think is the better managed and which company's stock you think may be the better investment. Back your report with any ratios, turnovers, and other analyses you think pertinent.

Balance Sheets
December 31, 198A

	Z-Ray, Inc.	Skybolt, Inc.
Cash.	$ 39,500	$ 40,100
Accounts receivable, net	95,400	102,700
Merchandise inventory	132,800	139,400
Prepaid expenses	2,900	4,200
Plant and equipment, net	480,400	462,000
Total assets.	$751,000	$748,400
Current liabilities.	$114,000	$130,200
Long-term notes payable	164,000	150,800
Common stock, $10 par value . . .	305,000	272,000
Retained earnings	168,000	195,400
Total liabilities and capital.	$751,000	$748,400

Income Statements
For the Year Ended December 31, 198A

	Z-Ray, Inc.	Skybolt, Inc.
Sales	$1,744,000	$1,850,000
Cost of goods sold.	1,247,000	1,350,400
Gross profit on sales	$ 497,000	$ 499,600
Operating expenses	420,600	456,000
Operating income	$ 76,400	$ 43,600
Interest expense.	15,600	14,900
Income before taxes	$ 60,800	$ 28,700
Income taxes	18,500	7,400
Net income	$ 42,300	$ 21,300

January 1, 198A, Data

Accounts receivable	$ 80,300	$ 125,300
Merchandise inventory	100,800	119,000
Total assets	739,000	700,800
Common stock	305,000	272,000
Retained earnings	164,300	177,600

Provocative Problem 20-4   CBS Inc.

Use the financial statements and related footnotes of CBS Inc. shown in Appendix B at the end of the book to complete the following requirements:

Required

1. Calculate the following ratios and turnovers for 1985 and 1984: *(a)* current ratio, *(b)* acid-test ratio, *(c)* days' sales uncollected, *(d)* rate of return on total assets employed, and *(e)* rate of return on common stockholders' equity.

2. Prepare common-size statements for the portions of the 1985 and 1984 income statements that relate to continuing operations. These should be prepared in the following manner. The total of net broadcasting sales plus net product sales should be expressed as 100%. All items other than costs of sales should be expressed as percentages of net broadcasting sales plus net product sales. The cost of broadcasting sales should be expressed as a percent of net broadcasting sales, and the cost of product sales should be expressed as a percent of net product sales.

3. After reviewing your answers to Requirements 1 and 2, and reviewing the financial statements and related footnotes of CBS Inc., write a brief summary and evaluation of the results of 1985 compared to 1984.

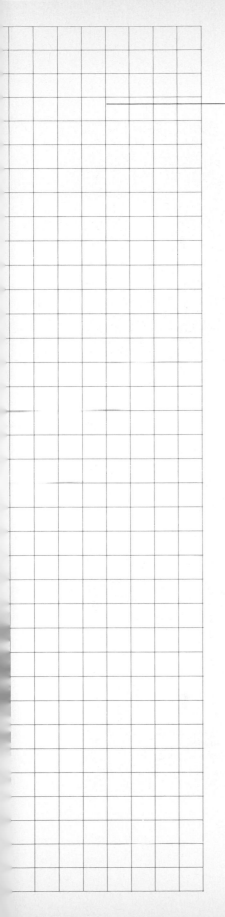

Part Seven

Managerial Accounting for Costs

21 Accounting for Manufacturing Companies

After studying Chapter 21, you should be able to:

1. Describe the basic differences in the financial statements of manufacturing companies and merchandising companies.

2. Describe the procedures inherent in a general accounting system for a manufacturing company.

3. List the different accounts that appear on a manufacturing company's books and state what the accounts represent.

4. Explain the purpose of a manufacturing statement, how one is composed, and how the statement is integrated with the primary financial statements.

5. Prepare financial statements for a manufacturing company from a work sheet.

6. Prepare the adjusting and closing entries for a manufacturing company.

7. Explain the procedures for assigning costs to the different manufacturing inventories.

8. Define or explain the words and phrases listed in the chapter Glossary.

Manufacturing and merchandising companies are alike in that both depend upon the sale of one or more commodities or products for revenue. However, they differ in one important way. A merchandising company buys the goods it sells in the same condition in which they are sold. A manufacturing company, on the other hand, buys raw materials that it manufacturers into the finished products it sells. For example, a shoe store buys shoes and sells them in the same form in which they are purchased; but a manufacturer of shoes buys leather, cloth, glue, nails, and dye and turns these items into salable shoes.

Most of the topics that have been discussed in previous chapters apply equally well to service companies, merchandising companies, and manufacturing companies. However, whenever inventories and cost of goods sold have been discussed, the examples and illustrations have been limited to merchandising companies. In this chapter (and in Chapter 22), we shift our attention to the unique problems of accounting for manufacturing companies.

Alternative Systems of Accounting for Manufacturing Companies

Some manufacturing companies use accounting systems that are based on periodic inventories. In keeping records on raw materials that are purchased for use in production, goods that are in the process of being produced, and finished goods that are ready for sale, periodic physical counts of the goods on hand are taken for the purpose of determining ending inventories as well as the amounts used or sold during the period. When a manufacturing company uses periodic inventories to determine the total cost of all goods manufactured during each accounting period, the accounting system is called a **general accounting system.** General accounting systems are explained in the remainder of this chapter.

Many manufacturing companies use accounting systems that are based on perpetual inventories. Systems of accounting for manufacturing operations that incorporate perpetual inventories are usually called **cost accounting systems.** These systems provide information about the unit cost of manufacturing a product and are designed to assist management's efforts to control costs. Chapter 22 is devoted to explaining cost accounting systems.

What Is the Basic Difference between Accounting for Merchandisers and Manufacturers?

The basic difference in accounting for merchandising and manufacturing companies stems from the fact that a merchandising company buys the goods it sells in their finished ready-for-sale state. A manufacturer must create what it sells from raw materials. As a result, the merchandising company can easily determine the cost of the goods it has bought for sale by examining the debit balance of its Purchases account. In contrast, the manufacturer must combine the balances of a number of material, labor, and overhead accounts to determine the cost of the goods it has manufactured for sale.

To emphasize this difference, the cost of goods sold section from a merchandising company's income statement is condensed and presented below alongside the cost of goods sold section of a manufacturing company.

Notice in the cost of goods sold section from the manufacturing company's income statement that the inventories of goods for sale are called

	Merchandising Company			**Manufacturing Company**	
Cost of goods sold:			Cost of goods sold:		
Beginning merchandise inventory		$14,200	Beginning finished goods inventory		$ 11,200
Cost of goods purchased. . .		34,150	Cost of goods manufactured (see Manufacturing Statement)		170,500
Goods available for sale . . .		$48,350	Goods available for sale. . .		$181,700
Ending merchandise inventory		12,100	Ending finished goods inventory		10,300
Cost of goods sold		$36,250	Cost of goods sold		$171,400

finished goods inventories rather than merchandise inventories. Notice too that the "Cost of goods purchased" element of the merchandising company becomes "Cost of goods manufactured (see Manufacturing Statement)" on the manufacturer's income statement. These differences exist because the merchandising company buys its goods ready for sale, while the manufacturer creates its salable products from raw materials.

The words **see Manufacturing Statement** refer the income statement reader to a separate schedule. A **manufacturing statement** (see page 757) shows the costs of manufacturing the products produced by a manufacturing company. The records and techniques used in accounting for these costs are the distinguishing characteristics of manufacturing accounting.

■   **Elements of Manufacturing Costs**

A manufacturing company usually incurs a large variety of costs in the process of manufacturing its products. There are, however, only three different types or classes of manufacturing costs. They are: direct materials, direct labor, and factory overhead.

Direct Materials

Direct materials are the commodities that enter into and become a part of a finished product. Such items as leather, dye, cloth, nails, and glue are direct materials used by shoe manufacturers. Since **direct materials** physically become part of the finished product, the cost of direct materials is easily traced to units of product or batches of production. As a result, the direct materials cost of production can be directly charged to units of product or batches of production without the use of arbitrary or highly judgmental cost allocation procedures.

Direct materials must be distinguished from **indirect materials** which include factory supplies such as grease and oil for machinery, cleaning fluids, and so on. Indirect materials are used in the manufacturing process but are not easily traced to specific units or batches of production and are accounted for as factory overhead. Generally, indirect materials do not enter into or become a part of the finished product.

The commodities that a company buys for use in the manufacturing process are sometimes called **raw materials.** Usually, raw materials are intended for use in the production process as **direct** materials. Purchases of materials that are intended for use as **indirect** materials are debited to a Factory Supplies account. Occasionally, however, some raw materials may be used as factory supplies (indirect materials). When this is done, a special adjusting entry is required to transfer the cost of those materials from Raw Material Purchases to an account called Factory Supplies Used.

Direct Labor

The labor of those people who work, either with machines or hand tools, specifically on the materials being converted into finished products is described as **direct labor.** The cost of direct labor can be easily associated with and charged to the units or batches of production to which the labor was applied.

In accounting for manufacturing operations, direct labor must be distinguished from indirect labor. **Indirect labor** is used in the manufacturing process but is not applied specifically to the finished product. Therefore, indirect labor is not easily associated with or charged to units or batches of production. Examples of indirect labor include the labor of superintendents, foremen, millwrights, engineers, janitors, and others who do not work specifically on the manufactured products but do aid in production. The labor provided by these workers makes production possible, but it is not applied specifically to the finished product. Indirect labor is accounted for as a factory overhead cost.

In a general accounting system, an account called Direct Labor is debited each payday for the wages of those workers who work directly on the product. Likewise, each payday, the wages of indirect workers are debited to one or more indirect labor accounts. Also, at the end of each period, the amounts of accrued direct and indirect labor are recorded in the direct and indirect labor accounts by means of adjusting entries. From this you can see that a manufacturing company's payroll accounting is similar to that of a merchandising company. When a cost accounting system is not involved, no new techniques are required and only the new direct and indirect labor accounts distinguish the payroll accounting of a manufacturer from that of a merchant.

Factory Overhead

Factory overhead is also called **manufacturing overhead** or **factory burden.** **Factory overhead** includes all manufacturing costs other than direct materials and direct labor costs. Examples of factory overhead are:

Indirect labor	Heat, lights, and power
Factory supplies	Depreciation of plant and equipment
Repairs to buildings and equipment	ment
Insurance on plant and equipment	Amortization of patents
Taxes on plant and equipment	Small tools written off
Taxes on raw materials and work in process	Workmen's compensation insurance
	Payroll taxes on the wages of the factory workers

Factory overhead does not include selling and administrative expenses. Selling and administrative expenses are not factory overhead because they are not incurred in the manufacturing process. These costs could be called selling and administrative overhead, but not factory overhead.

All factory overhead costs are accumulated in overhead cost accounts that vary in number and description from company to company. The exact accounts used in each case depend upon the nature of the company and the information desired. For example, one account called Expired Insurance on Plant Equipment may be maintained, or separate expired insurance accounts for buildings and the different kinds of equipment may be used. Regardless of the accounts used, overhead costs are recorded in the same way as are selling and administrative expenses. Some, such as indirect labor and light and power, are recorded in registers or journals as they are paid and are then posted to the accounts. Other costs, such as depreciation and expired insurance, are recorded in the accounts through adjusting entries.

■ **Product Costs and Period Costs**

A manufacturing company is said to incur both product costs and period expenses. All manufacturing costs (direct materials, direct labor, and factory overhead) are **product costs.** Product costs are assigned to units of product rather than to expense accounts. Product costs are reported in the balance sheet as inventories. They do not show up in the income statement until the units of product are sold; then product costs appear as cost of goods sold. **Period costs** include all selling expenses and administrative expenses, which are not part of the manufacturing operation. Period costs are closely related to the periods of time in which they are incurred; they are not closely related to the manufacture of products. Thus, period costs are charged to expense in the period they are incurred.

■ **Comparing the Flow of Product Costs for Merchandising and Manufacturing Companies**

Illustration 21-1 displays the flow of product costs (or cost of merchandise) for merchandising companies and manufacturing companies that use periodic inventory systems. On the left side of the illustration, the cost flow of merchandising companies is seen to be a simple, end-of-period allocation of purchases between cost of goods sold and ending inventory. The cost flows of manufacturing companies are shown on the right side of the illustration. Note that the costs of raw materials, direct labor, and overhead are recorded as they are incurred throughout the period. Then, in the end-of-period closing process, these costs are allocated between raw materials inventory, goods in process inventory, finished goods inventory, and cost of goods sold.

■ **Accounts Unique to a Manufacturing Company**

Because of the nature of its operations, a manufacturing company's ledger normally contains more accounts than that of a merchandising company. However, some of the same accounts are found in the ledgers of both, for example, Cash, Accounts Receivable, Sales, and many selling and administrative expenses. Nevertheless, many accounts are unique to a manufacturing company. For instance, accounts such as Machinery and Equipment, Accumulated Depreciation of Machinery and Equipment, Factory Supplies, Factory Supplies Used, Raw Materials Inventory, Raw Material Purchases,

Illustration 21-1   **Flow of Merchandise or Product Costs—Periodic Inventory System (assumes no beginning inventories)**

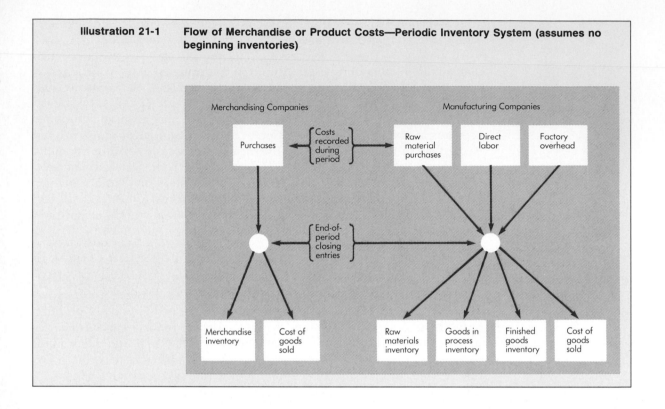

Goods in Process Inventory, Finished Goods Inventory, and Manufacturing Summary are normally found only in the ledgers of manufacturing companies. Some of these accounts merit special attention.

Raw Material Purchases Account

When a general accounting system is in use, the cost of all raw materials purchased is debited to an account called Raw Material Purchases. Often a special column is provided in the Voucher Register or other special journal for the debits of the individual purchases. Thus, it is possible to periodically post these debits in one amount, the column total.

Raw Materials Inventory Account

When a general accounting system is in use, the raw materials on hand at the end of each accounting period are determined by a physical inventory count; and through a closing entry, the cost of this inventory is debited to Raw Materials Inventory. That account becomes a record of the materials on hand at the end of one period and the beginning of the next.

Goods in Process Inventory Account

Most manufacturing companies have on hand at all times partially processed products called **goods in process** or **work in process.** These are products in the process of being manufactured, products that have received a portion or all of their materials and have had some labor and overhead applied but that are not completed.

When a general manufacturing accounting system is used, the amount of goods in process at the end of each accounting period is determined by a physical inventory count; and through a closing entry, the cost of this inventory is debited to Goods in Process Inventory. This account then becomes a record of the goods in process at the end of one period and the beginning of the next.

Finished Goods Inventory Account

The **finished goods** of a manufacturer are the equivalent of a store's merchandise; they are products in their completed state ready for sale. Actually, the only difference is that a manufacturing company creates its finished goods from raw materials, while a store buys its merchandise in a finished, ready-for-sale state.

In a general accounting system, the amount of finished goods on hand at the end of each period is determined by a physical inventory; and through a closing entry, the cost of this inventory is debited to Finished Goods Inventory. That account provides a record of the finished goods at the end of one period and the beginning of the next.

The three inventories—raw materials, goods in process, and finished goods—are classified as current assets for balance sheet purposes. Factory supplies is also a current asset.

■ **Income Statement of a Manufacturing Company**

The income statement of a manufacturing company is similar to that of a merchandising company. To see this, compare the income statement of Kona Sales Incorporated, Illustration 5-1 on page 166, with that of Excel Manufacturing Company, Illustration 21-2. Notice that the revenue, selling, and general and administrative expense sections are very similar. However, when the cost of goods sold sections are compared, a difference is apparent. Here the item "Cost of goods manufactured" replaces the "Purchases" element, and finished goods inventories take the place of merchandise inventories.

Observe the cost of goods sold section of Excel Manufacturing Company's income statement. Only the **total** cost of goods manufactured is shown. It would be possible to expand this section to show the detailed costs of the materials, direct labor, and factory overhead entering into the cost of goods manufactured. However, this would make the income statement long and unwieldy. Consequently, the common practice is to show only the total cost of goods manufactured on the income statement and to attach a supporting schedule showing the details. This supporting schedule is called a **schedule of the cost of goods manufactured** or a **manufacturing statement.**

■ **Manufacturing Statement**

The cost elements of manufacturing are direct materials, direct labor, and factory overhead; and a manufacturing statement is normally constructed in such a manner as to emphasize these elements. Notice in Illustration 21-3 that the first section of the statement shows the cost of direct materials used. Also observe the manner of presentation is the same as that used on the income statement of a merchandising company to show cost of goods purchased and sold.

Illustration 21-2

The Excel Manufacturing Company
Income Statement
For the Year Ended December 31, 198A

Revenue:		
Sales		$310,000
Cost of goods sold:		
Finished goods inventory, January 1, 198A	$ 11,200	
Cost of goods manufactured (see		
Manufacturing Statement)	170,500	
Goods available for sale	$181,700	
Finished goods inventory, December 31, 198A . .	10,300	
Cost of goods sold		171,400
Gross profit		$138,600
Operating expenses:		
Selling expenses:		
Sales salaries expense.	$18,000	
Advertising expense	5,500	
Delivery wages expense	12,000	
Shipping supplies expense	250	
Delivery equipment insurance expense	300	
Depreciation expense, delivery equipment	2,100	
Total selling expenses	$ 38,150	
General and administrative expenses:		
Office salaries expense	$15,700	
Miscellaneous general expense	200	
Bad debts expense	1,550	
Office supplies expense	100	
Depreciation expense, office equipment	200	
Mortgage interest expense	4,000	
Total general and administrative expenses . . .	21,750	
Total operating expenses.		59,900
Income before state and federal income taxes		$ 78,700
Less state and federal income taxes		32,600
Net income		$ 46,100
Net income per common share		
(20,000 shares outstanding)		$ 2.31

The second section shows the cost of direct labor used in production, and the third section shows factory overhead costs. If overhead accounts are not too numerous, the balance of each is often listed in this third section, as in Illustration 21-3. However, if overhead accounts are numerous, only the total of all may be shown. In such cases, the total is supported by a separate schedule showing each cost.

In the fourth section, the calculation of costs of goods manufactured is completed. Here the cost of the beginning goods in process inventory is added to the sum of the manufacturing costs to show the total cost of all goods in process during the period. From this total, the cost of the goods still in process at the end of the period is subtracted to show cost of the goods manufactured.

The manufacturing statement is prepared from the Manufacturing Statement columns of a work sheet. The items that appear on the statement are summarized in these columns, and all that is required in constructing

Illustration 21-3

Excel Manufacturing Company
Manufacturing Statement
For the Year Ended December 31, 198A

Direct materials:			
1 Raw materials inventory, January 1, 198A . . .		$ 8,000	
Raw material purchases.	$85,000		
Freight on raw materials purchased	1,500		
Delivered cost of raw materials purchased . . .		86,500	
Raw materials available for use.		$94,500	
Raw materials inventory, December 31, 198A .		9,000	
Direct materials used			$ 85,500
2 Direct labor			60,000
Factory overhead costs:			
Indirect labor		$ 9,000	
Supervision		6,000	
Power		2,600	
Repairs and maintenance		2,500	
3 Factory taxes		1,900	
Factory supplies used.		600	
Factory insurance expired		1,100	
Small tools written off		200	
Depreciation of machinery and equipment . . .		3,500	
Depreciation of building		1,800	
Amortization of patents		800	
Total factory overhead costs			30,000
Total manufacturing costs			$175,500
Add goods in process inventory, January 1, 198A			2,500
4 Total goods in process during the year			$178,000
Deduct goods in process inventory,			
December 31, 198A			7,500
Cost of goods manufactured			$170,500

the statement is a rearrangement of the items into the proper statement order. Illustration 21-4 shows the manufacturing work sheet.

■ **Work Sheet for a Manufacturing Company**

In examining Illustration 21-4, note first that there are no Adjusted Trial Balance columns. The experienced accountant commonly omits such columns to save time and effort. How a work sheet without Adjusted Trial Balance columns is prepared and how this saves time and effort were explained in Chapter 5.

To understand the work sheet of Illustration 21-4, recall that a work sheet is a tool with which the accountant—

1. Achieves the effect of adjusting the accounts before entering the adjustments in a journal and posting them to the accounts.
2. Sorts the adjusted account balances into columns according to the financial statement upon which they appear.
3. Calculates and confirms the mathematical accuracy of the net income.

Work Sheet of a Manufacturing Company Compared to a Merchandising Company

A primary difference between the work sheet of a manufacturing company and that of a merchandising company is an additional set of columns.

Illustration 21-4

The Excel Manufacturing Company
Manufacturing Work Sheet for the Year Ended December 31, 198A

Account Titles	Trial Balance Dr.	Trial Balance Cr.	Adjustments Dr.	Adjustments Cr.	Mfg. Statement Dr.	Mfg. Statement Cr.	Income Statement Dr.	Income Statement Cr.	Balance Sheet Dr.	Balance Sheet Cr.
Cash	11,000								11,000	
Accounts receivable	32,000								32,000	
Allowance for doubtful accounts		300		(a) 1,550						1,850
Raw materials inventory	8,000				8,000	9,000			9,000	
Goods in process inventory	2,500				2,500	7,500			7,500	
Finished goods inventory	11,200						11,200	10,300	10,300	
Office supplies	150			(b) 100					50	
Shipping supplies	300			(c) 250					50	
Factory supplies	750			(d) 500					250	
Prepaid insurance	1,700			(e) 1,400					300	
Small tools	1,300			(f) 200					1,100	
Delivery equipment	9,000								9,000	
Accumulated depreciation of delivery equipment		1,900		(g) 2,100						4,000
Office equipment	1,700								1,700	
Accumulated depreciation of office equipment		200		(h) 200						400
Machinery and equipment	72,000								72,000	
Accumulated depreciation of machinery and equipment		3,000		(i) 3,500						6,500
Factory building	90,000								90,000	
Accumulated depreciation of factory building		1,500		(j) 1,800						3,300
Land	9,500								9,500	
Patents	12,000			(k) 800					11,200	
Accounts payable		14,000								14,000
Mortgage payable		50,000								50,000
Common stock, $5 par value		100,000								100,000
Retained earnings		3,660								3,660
Sales		310,000						310,000		
Raw material purchases	85,100			(d) 100	85,000					
Freight on raw materials	1,500				1,500					
Direct labor	59,600		(l) 400		60,000					
Indirect labor	8,940		(l) 60		9,000					

Account	Trial Balance Dr	Adjustments Dr	Adjustments Cr	Manufacturing Dr	Manufacturing Cr	Income Statement Dr	Income Statement Cr	Balance Sheet Dr	Balance Sheet Cr
Supervision	6,000			6,000					
Power expense	2,600			2,600					
Repairs and maintenance	2,500			2,500					
Factory taxes	1,900			1,900					
Sales salaries expense	18,000					18,000			
Advertising expense	5,500					5,500			
Delivery wages expense	11,920	(l) 80				12,000			
Office salaries expense	15,700					15,700			
Miscellaneous general expense	200					200			
Mortgage interest expense	2,000	(m) 2,000				4,000			
	484,560								
Bad debts expense		(a) 1,550				1,550			
Office supplies expense		(b) 100				100			
Shipping supplies expense		(c) 250				250			
Factory supplies used		(d) 600		600					
Factory insurance expired		(e) 1,100		1,100					
Delivery equipment insurance expense		(e) 300				300			
Small tools written off		(f) 200		200					
Depreciation expense, delivery equipment		(g) 2,100				2,100			
Depreciation expense, office equipment		(h) 200				200			
Depreciation of machinery and equipment		(i) 3,500		3,500					
Depreciation of building		(j) 1,800		1,800					
Amortization of patents		(k) 800		800					
Accrued wages payable			(l) 540						540
Mortgage interest payable			(m) 2,000						2,000
State and federal income taxes expense		(n) 32,600				32,600			
State and federal income taxes payable			(n) 32,600						32,600
		47,640	47,640	187,000	16,500	187,000			
Cost of goods manufactured to Income Statement columns					170,500	170,500			
				187,000	187,000	274,200	320,300	264,950	218,850
Net income						46,100			46,100
						320,300	320,300	264,950	264,950

Insofar as the adjustments are concerned, they are made in the same way on both kinds of work sheets. Also, the mathematical accuracy of the net income is confirmed in the same way. However, since an additional accounting statement, the manufacturing statement, is prepared for a manufacturing company, the work sheet of such a company has an additional set of columns, the Manufacturing Statement columns, into which are sorted the items appearing on the manufacturing statement.

Preparing a Manufacturing Company's Work Sheet

A manufacturing company's work sheet is prepared in the same manner as that of a merchandising company. First, a trial balance of the ledger is entered in the Trial Balance columns.

Entering the Adjustments After the trial balance is entered, information for the adjustments is assembled, and the adjustments are entered in the Adjustments columns. The adjustments information for the work sheet shown in Illustration 21-4 is as follows:

a. Bad debt expense estimated to be ½% of sales, or $1,550.
b. Office supplies used, $100.
c. Shipping supplies used, $250.
d. Factory supplies used, $500. In addition, raw materials costing $100 were used as factory supplies.
e. Expired insurance on factory, $1,100; and expired insurance on the delivery equipment, $300.
f. The small tools inventory shows $1,100 of usable small tools on hand. As is frequently done, small hand tools are in this case accounted for in the same manner as are supplies.
g. Depreciation of delivery equipment, $2,100.
h. Depreciation of office equipment, $200.
i. Depreciation of factory machinery and equipment, $3,500.
j. Depreciation of factory building, $1,800.
k. Yearly amortization of ¹⁄₁₇ of the cost of patents, $800.
l. Accrued wages: direct labor, $400; indirect labor, $60; delivery wages, $80. All other employees paid monthly on the last day of each month.
m. One-half year's interest accrued on the mortgage, $2,000.
n. State and federal income taxes expense, $32,600.

Sorting Adjusted Amounts to the Proper Financial Statement Columns After the adjustments are completed, the amounts in the Trial Balance columns are combined with the amounts in the Adjustments columns and are sorted to the proper Manufacturing Statement, Income Statement, or Balance Sheet columns, according to the statement on which they appear.

In the sorting process, just two decisions are required for each item: First, does the item have a debit balance or a credit balance; and second, on which statement does it appear? The first decision is necessary because a debit item must be sorted to a debit column and a credit item to a credit column. As for the second, a work sheet is a tool for sorting items according to their statement appearance. Asset, liability, and owners' equity items are sorted to the Balance Sheet columns. The beginning finished goods inventory plus the revenue, selling, general and administrative, and financial expense items are sorted to the Income Statement columns. And finally, the raw material, goods in process, direct labor, and factory overhead items are sorted to the Manufacturing Statement columns.

Entering the Ending Inventory Amounts   After the trial balance items with their adjustments are sorted to the proper statement columns, the ending inventory amounts are entered on the work sheet. Since the ending raw materials and goods in process inventories appear on the manufacturing statement, they are entered in the Manufacturing Statement credit and Balance Sheet debit columns. They must be entered in the Manufacturing Statement credit column in order to make the difference between the two columns equal cost of goods manufactured. Likewise, since these inventory amounts represent end-of-period assets, they must be entered in the Balance Sheet debit column with the other assets.

Note in Illustration 21-4 that the ending raw materials inventory is assumed to be $9,000 and the ending work in process inventory is assumed to be $7,500. These amounts were determined on the basis of a physical inventory taken at the end of the year.

The ending finished goods inventory is also determined on the basis of a physical inventory taken at the end of the year. In Illustration 21-4, Excel Manufacturing Company's ending finished goods inventory of $10,300 is entered in the Income Statement credit column and the Balance Sheet debit column.

The ending finished goods inventory is the equivalent of an ending merchandise inventory and receives the same work sheet treatment. It is entered in the Income Statement credit column so that the net income may be determined; and since it is a current asset, it must also be entered in the Balance Sheet debit column.

After the ending inventories are entered on the work sheet, the Manufacturing Statement columns are added and their difference determined. This difference is the cost of the goods manufactured; and after it is determined, it is entered in the Manufacturing Statement credit column to make the two columns equal. Also, it is entered in the Income Statement debit column, the same column in which the balance of the Purchases account of a merchant is entered. After this, the work sheet is completed in the usual manner.

■ **Preparing the Financial Statements**

After completion, the manufacturing work sheet is used in preparing the statements and in making adjusting and closing entries. The manufacturing statement is prepared from the information in the work sheet's Manufacturing Statement columns, the income statement from the information in the Income Statement columns, and the balance sheet from information in the Balance Sheet columns. After this, the adjusting and closing entries are entered in the journal and posted.

■ **Adjusting Entries**

The adjusting entries of a manufacturing company are prepared in the same way as those of a merchandising company. An adjusting entry is entered in the General Journal for each adjustment appearing in the work sheet Adjustments columns.

In the case of Excel Manufacturing Company, the only adjustment that may require further attention is adjustment *d* as described on page 760 (see also Illustration 21-4). When purchased, most of the factory supplies were debited to a Factory Supplies account. The information for adjustment *d* states that $500 of these supplies were used. However, the factory also used $100 of its raw materials as factory supplies. Therefore, the adjusting entry to record all of the factory supplies used is:

Dec.	31	Factory Supplies Used	600.00	
		Factory Supplies		500.00
		Raw Material Purchases		100.00
		To record factory supplies used.		

After Raw Material Purchases is credited for $100, the remaining $85,000 is correctly shown on the manufacturing statement in the calculation of direct materials cost (see Illustration 21-3).

■   Closing Entries

The account balances that enter into the calculation of cost of goods manufactured reflect the manufacturing costs for a particular accounting period and must be closed at the end of each period. Normally they are closed to a Manufacturing Summary account, which is in turn closed to the Income Summary account.

The entries to close the manufacturing accounts of Excel Manufacturing Company are as follows:

Dec.	31	Manufacturing Summary.	187,000.00	
		Raw Materials Inventory		8,000.00
		Goods in Process Inventory		2,500.00
		Raw Material Purchases		85,000.00
		Freight on Raw Materials		1,500.00
		Direct Labor		60,000.00
		Indirect Labor		9,000.00
		Supervision		6,000.00
		Power Expense.		2,600.00
		Repairs and Maintenance		2,500.00
		Factory Taxes		1,900.00
		Factory Supplies Used		600.00
		Factory Insurance Expired		1,100.00
		Small Tools Written Off		200.00
		Depreciation of Machinery and Equipment		3,500.00
		Depreciation of Building		1,800.00
		Amortization of Patents		800.00
		To close those manufacturing accounts having debit balances.		
	31	Raw Materials Inventory	9,000.00	
		Goods in Process Inventory	7,500.00	
		Manufacturing Summary.		16,500.00
		To set up the ending raw materials and goods in process inventories and to remove their balances from the Manufacturing Summary account.		

The entries are taken from the information in the Manufacturing Statement columns of the Illustration 21-4 work sheet. Compare the first entry with the information shown in the Manufacturing Statement debit column. Note how the debit to the Manufacturing Summary account is taken from the column total, and how each account having a balance in the column is credited to close it. Also observe that the second entry has the effect of subtracting the ending raw materials and goods in process inventories from the manufacturing costs shown in the work sheet's debit column.

The effect of the two entries is to cause the Manufacturing Summary account to have a debit balance equal to the $170,500 cost of goods manufactured. This $170,500 balance is closed to the Income Summary account along with the other cost and expense accounts having balances in the Income Statement debit column. Observe the following entry which is used to close the accounts having balances in the Income Statement debit column of the Illustration 21-4 work sheet and especially note its last credit.

Dec.	31	Income Summary.	274,200.00	
		Finished Goods Inventory		11,200.00
		Sales Salaries Expense		18,000.00
		Advertising Expense		5,500.00
		Delivery Wages Expense.		12,000.00
		Office Salaries Expense		15,700.00
		Miscellaneous General Expense		200.00
		Mortgage Interest Expense.		4,000.00
		Bad Debts Expense.		1,550.00
		Office Supplies Expense		100.00
		Shipping Supplies Expense		250.00
		Delivery Equipment Insurance Expense .		300.00
		Depreciation Expense, Delivery Equipment		2,100.00
		Depreciation Expense, Office Equipment .		200.00
		State and Federal Income Taxes Expense		32,600.00
		Manufacturing Summary.		170,500.00
		To close the income statement accounts having debit balances.		

After the foregoing entry, the remainder of the income statement accounts of Illustration 21-4 are closed as follows:

Dec.	31	Finished Goods Inventory	10,300.00	
		Sales.	310,000.00	
		Income Summary.		320,300.00
		To close the Sales account and to bring the ending finished goods inventory on the books.		
	31	Income Summary.	46,100.00	
		Retained Earnings		46,100.00
		To close the Income Summary account.		

Inventory Valuation Problems of a Manufacturer

In a manufacturing company using periodic inventories (a general accounting system), an accounting value must be placed on the inventories of raw materials, goods in process, and finished goods at the end of each period. No particular problems are encountered in valuing raw materials because the items are in the same form in which they were purchased. However, placing a valuation on goods in process and finished goods is generally not as easy. These goods consist of direct materials to which certain amounts of labor and overhead have been added. They are not in the same form in which they were purchased. Consequently, a price paid a previous producer cannot be used to measure their inventory value. Instead, their inventory value must be built up by adding together estimates of the direct materials, direct labor, and factory overhead costs applicable to each item.

Estimating Direct Material Costs in the Ending Inventories

Estimating direct material costs applicable to a goods in process or finished goods item is usually not too difficult. After the partially finished units of product in the work in process inventory are counted, a responsible plant official normally can estimate how much direct material has been used in each unit and then calculate the cost of direct material in the inventory. The same process is used to calculate the cost of direct material in the finished goods inventory.

Estimating Direct Labor Costs in the Ending Inventories

The process of estimating the direct labor costs in the ending goods in process and finished goods inventories is essentially the same as for direct materials. A responsible plant official must estimate the percentage of completion of the units in the goods in process inventory and then calculate the direct labor cost that has been applied to those units. A similar estimate must be made of the direct labor cost that has been applied to the units in the finished goods inventory.

Estimating Factory Overhead Costs in the Ending Inventories

Factory overhead consists of many items, none of which is directly associated with specific units or batches of production. As a result, estimating factory overhead costs in the ending inventories presents a difficult problem. This problem is often solved by assuming that factory overhead costs are closely related to direct labor costs. Usually, this is a reasonable approach. There is often a close relation between direct labor costs and such indirect costs as supervision, power, repairs, and so forth. Furthermore, when this relation is used to apply overhead costs, it is assumed that the relation of overhead costs to the direct labor costs in each goods in process and finished goods item is the same as the relation between total factory overhead costs and total direct labor costs for the accounting period.

Estimating the Ending Inventory Costs of Excel Manufacturing Company

For example, an examination of the manufacturing statement in Illustration 21-3 shows that Excel Manufacturing Company's total direct labor costs were $60,000 and its overhead costs were $30,000. Or, in other words, during the year the company incurred in the production of all its products $2 of direct labor for each $1 of factory overhead costs; overhead costs were 50% of direct labor cost.

$$\frac{\text{Overhead costs, }\$30,000}{\text{Direct labor, }\$60,000} \times 100 = 50\%$$

Consequently, in estimating the overhead applicable to a goods in process or finished goods item, Excel Manufacturing Company may assume that this 50% overhead rate is applicable. Since total overhead costs were 50% of total labor costs, it would appear reasonable to assume that this relationship applies to each goods in process and finished goods item.

Recall from Illustration 21-4 that the ending goods in process inventory was $7,500 and the ending finished goods inventory was $10,300. To see how these amounts might have been determined, assume that a physical count of the ending inventories showed that there were 1,000 partially finished units in the goods in process inventory and 800 units in the finished goods inventory. The costs of the ending inventories were determined as follows:

	Goods in Process			Finished Goods		
	Cost per Unit	Units of Product	Total Cost	Cost per Unit	Units of Product	Total Cost
Direct materials	$3.75	1,000	$3,750	$5.00	800	$ 4,000
Direct labor	2.50	1,000	2,500	5.25	800	4,200
Factory overhead—50% of direct labor	1.25	1,000	1,250	2.625	800	2,100
			$7,500			$10,300

To summarize, the per unit costs for direct materials and direct labor were estimated by appropriate plant officials. The factory overhead cost per unit was calculated as 50% of the direct labor cost. And the number of units of product in each inventory was determined by physically counting the units on hand.

Glossary

Cost accounting system an accounting system that uses perpetual inventories in accounting for manufacturing operations and is designed to assist management's efforts to control costs.

Direct labor the labor of those people who work specifically on the conversion of raw materials into finished products; in other words, labor that can be easily associated with and charged to units or batches of production.

Direct materials commodities that enter into and become a part of a finished product; therefore, commodities the cost of which is easily traced to units of product or batches of production.

Factory burden a synonym for factory overhead or manufacturing overhead.

Factory overhead all manufacturing costs other than for direct materials and direct labor.

Finished goods manufactured products that have been completed and are ready for sale; the equivalent of a store's merchandise.

General accounting system for manufacturers an accounting system that uses periodic inventories to determine the total cost of all goods manufactured during each accounting period.

Goods in process products in the process of being manufactured that have received a portion or all of their materials and have had some labor and overhead applied but that are not completed.

Indirect labor the labor of superintendents, foremen, millwrights, engineers, janitors, and others that contribute to production but do not work specifically on the manufactured products; therefore, labor that cannot be easily associated with specific units of product.

Indirect materials commodities, such as oil for machinery, that are used in production but that are not easily traced to specific units or batches of production; accounted for as factory overhead.

Manufacturing overhead a synonym for factory overhead. Also called factory burden.

Manufacturing statement a schedule showing the costs incurred to manufacture a product or products during a period.

Period costs costs that are not incurred as part of manufacturing operations and that are charged to expense in the periods they are incurred.

Product costs costs that are assigned to units of product and reported in the balance sheet as inventories and in the income statement as cost of goods sold; included are all manufacturing costs.

Raw materials commodities that are purchased for use in the manufacturing process, normally as direct materials. Occasionally used as indirect materials.

Schedule of the cost of goods manufactured a synonym for manufacturing statement.

Work in process a synonym for goods in process.

Questions for Class Discussion

1. What is the difference between a general accounting system for manufacturers and a cost accounting system?
2. What is the basic difference between a manufacturing company and a merchandising company?

3. Manufacturing costs consist of three elements. What are they?

4. Explain how the income statement of a manufacturing company differs from the income statement of a merchandising company.

5. What is the difference between direct materials and indirect materials?

6. What is the difference between raw materials and direct materials?

7. What is the difference between direct labor and indirect labor?

8. How is the cost of indirect labor charged to production?

9. Factory overhead costs include a variety of items. List several examples of factory overhead costs.

10. What is the difference between factory overhead and selling or administrative expenses?

11. If a general accounting system is used, when in the accounting cycle are the costs of raw material purchases, direct labor, and factory overhead allocated to Raw Materials Inventory, Goods in Process Inventory, Finished Goods Inventory, and cost of goods sold?

12. Name several accounts that are often found in the ledgers of both manufacturing and merchandising companies. Name several accounts that are found only in the ledgers of manufacturing companies.

13. What three new inventory accounts appear in the ledger of a manufacturing company?

14. How are the raw material inventories handled on the work sheet of a manufacturing company? How are the goods in process inventories handled? How are the finished goods inventories handled?

15. Which inventories of a manufacturing company receive the same work sheet treatment as the merchandise inventories of a merchandising company?

16. Which inventories of a manufacturing company appear on its manufacturing statement? Which appear on the income statement?

17. What accounts are summarized in the Manufacturing Summary account? What accounts are summarized in the Income Summary account?

18. What are the three manufacturing cost elements emphasized on the manufacturing statement?

19. What account balances are carried into the Manufacturing Statement columns of the manufacturing work sheet? What account balances are carried into the Income Statement columns? What account balances are carried into the Balance Sheet columns?

20. Why is the cost of goods manufactured entered in the Manufacturing Statement credit column of a work sheet and again in the Income Statement debit columns?

21. May prices paid a previous manufacturer for items of raw materials be used to determine the balance sheet value of the items in the raw materials inventory? Why? May such prices also be used to determine the balance sheet values of the goods in process and finished goods inventories? Why?

22. Standard Company used an overhead rate of 75% of direct labor cost to apply overhead to the items of its goods in process inventory. If

the manufacturing statement of the company showed total overhead costs of $138,000, how much direct labor did it show?

☐   **Class Exercises**   **Exercise 21-1**

Barnes Corporation began manufacturing operations this year and purchased on account $20,000 of raw materials during the year. These materials included paint that is applied to the units being produced as they are finished. During the year, $150 of the paint was used to repaint some of the tools used in the factory. Prepare general journal entries to record the purchase of raw materials and the use of paint to repaint tools.

Exercise 21-2

The following costs were incurred by a manufacturing company. Indicate which of these costs should be classified as product costs and which should be classified as period costs.

Sales salaries   Direct materials used
Small tools written off   Office salaries
Depreciation of factory building   State and federal income taxes
Bad debts expense   Insurance on factory workers
Interest on long-term debt   Repairs to machinery
Amortization of patents   Advertising

Exercise 21-3

After Edwards Corporation posted its adjusting entries on December 31, 198A, the general ledger included the following account balances. (Some accounts in the general ledger have not been listed.)

Sales	$792,000
Raw materials inventory, January 1, 198A	44,000
Goods in process inventory, January 1, 198A	50,600
Finished goods inventory, January 1, 198A	63,800
Raw material purchases	127,600
Direct labor	151,800
Factory supplies used	15,400
Indirect labor	37,400
Machinery repairs	6,600
Rent expense, factory building	55,000
Selling expenses, controlling	94,600
Administrative expenses, controlling	112,200

On December 31, 198A, the inventories of Edwards Corporation were determined to be:

Raw materials inventory	$39,600
Goods in process inventory	35,200
Finished goods inventory	59,400

Given the above information, prepare a manufacturing statement for Edwards Corporation.

Exercise 21-4

Use the information provided in Exercise 21-3 and prepare an income statement for Edwards Corporation.

Exercise 21-5

Use the information provided in Exercise 21-3 and prepare closing entries for Edwards Corporation.

Exercise 21-6

The following information was taken from the accounting records of Blay Company and Crawford Company.

	Blay Company	Crawford Company
Ending finished goods inventory	$ 300	$ 950
Direct labor.	1,500	2,400
Factory electricity	200	400
Ending raw materials inventory	350	450
Machinery repairs	200	400
Raw material purchases	1,700	2,200
Beginning goods in process inventory	500	850
Sales salaries.	600	900
Beginning finished goods inventory	500	700
Indirect labor	400	800
Depreciation on factory.	450	750
Beginning raw materials inventory	650	500
General and administrative expenses.	1,750	1,900
Factory supplies used	150	200
Ending goods in process inventory	550	650

Calculate the cost of goods manufactured and the cost of goods sold for each company.

Exercise 21-7

Goettsche Company's ending goods in process inventory included 600 units of product; its finished goods inventory included 1,400 units of product. Factory officials determined that goods in process included direct materials cost of $4.65 per unit and direct labor cost of $6.80. Finished goods units were estimated to have $4.65 of direct materials and $9.40 of direct labor. During the period, the company incurred $78,400 of direct labor and $58,800 of factory overhead. Factory overhead is assumed to be closely related to direct labor. Calculate the total cost of each ending inventory. Also calculate how much direct labor and how much factory overhead will be included in cost of goods sold.

Exercise 21-8

Froh Corporation's accounting system uses highly summarized controlling accounts. The following information for the year 198A was drawn from the company's accounting records:

Sales	$147,000
Raw material purchases	24,000
Direct labor	34,400
Factory overhead	28,000
Selling expenses, controlling	15,900
General and administrative expenses, controlling	14,500
State and federal income taxes	16,500
Raw materials inventory	4,400
Goods in process inventory	3,600
Finished goods inventory	5,900
Ending inventories:	
Raw materials	6,700
Goods in process	8,800
Finished goods	5,500

Prepare closing entries for the company.

Exercise 21-9

A company that uses the relation between overhead and direct labor costs to apply overhead to its goods in process and finished goods inventories incurred the following costs during a year: materials, $237,500; direct labor, $200,000; and factory overhead costs, $400,000. (a) Determine the company's overhead rate. (b) Under the assumption the company's $31,250 goods in process inventory had $7,500 of direct labor costs, determine the inventory's material costs. (c) Under the assumption the company's $42,500 finished goods inventory had $12,500 of material costs, determine the inventory's labor cost and overhead costs.

Exercise 21-10

The December 31 trial balance of DeShazo's Dock Company follows:

DeShazo's Dock Company
Trial Balance
December 31, 198A

Cash	$ 1,125	
Accounts receivable	1,275	
Allowance for doubtful accounts		$ 400
Raw materials inventory	475	
Goods in process inventory	1,025	
Finished goods inventory	625	
Factory supplies	825	
Prepaid factory insurance	875	
Factory machinery	5,400	
Accumulated depreciation, factory machinery		1,000
Common stock		3,750
Retained earnings		1,500
Sales		20,250
Raw material purchases	4,250	
Freight on raw materials	250	
Direct labor	2,750	
Indirect labor	850	
Factory utilities	1,450	
Machinery repairs	375	
Rent expense, factory	1,500	
Selling expenses, controlling	2,175	
Administrative expenses, controlling	1,675	
Totals	$26,900	$26,900

Additional information to be used in preparing a work sheet for 198A financial statements is as follows:

a. Ending inventories:
   Raw materials, $800.
   Goods in process, $1,325.
   Finished goods, $450.
   Factory supplies, $175.

b. Allowance for doubtful accounts should be increased by $550.

c. Expired factory insurance for the year is $625.

d. Depreciation of factory machinery amounted to $700.

e. Accrued payroll on December 31:
   Direct labor, $1,100.
   Indirect labor, $400.
   Office salaries, $275 (debit Administrative Expenses, controlling account).

Required

Prepare a work sheet for the year ended December 31, 198A.

Problems

Problem 21-1

Camcrete Company's work sheet prepared at the end of last year had the following items in its manufacturing statement columns:

	Manufacturing Statement	
	Debit	Credit
Raw materials inventory	36,900	40,500
Goods in process inventory	44,100	?
Raw material purchases	162,900	
Direct labor	270,000	
Indirect labor	106,800	
Factory utilities	50,700	
Machinery repairs	15,600	
Rent expense, factory	36,000	
Property taxes, machinery	9,600	
Expired factory insurance	7,800	
Factory supplies used	18,300	
Depreciation expense, machinery	45,900	
Amortization of patents	6,300	
	810,900	?
Cost of goods manufactured		?
	810,900	810,900

Camcrete Company's work sheet does not show the amount of the ending goods in process inventory or the cost of goods manufactured. However, the company makes a single product; and on December 31, at the end of last year, there were 1,500 units of goods in process with each unit containing an estimated $6.30 of materials and having had an estimated $9.00 of direct labor applied.

Required

1. Calculate the relation between direct labor and factory overhead costs and use this relation to place an accounting value on the ending goods in process inventory.

2. After placing a value on the ending goods in process inventory, prepare a manufacturing statement for the company.

3. Prepare entries to close the manufacturing accounts and to summarize their balances in the Manufacturing Summary account.

4. Prepare an entry to close the Manufacturing Summary account.

Problem 21-2

The following items appeared in the Manufacturing Statement and Income Statement columns of a work sheet prepared for Franco Corporation on December 31, 198A:

	Manufacturing Statement		Income Statement	
	Debit	Credit	Debit	Credit
Raw materials inventory	22,680	21,780		
Goods in process inventory	26,640	23,220		
Finished goods inventory			28,980	33,840
Sales.				650,700
Raw material purchases	106,200			
Discounts on raw material purchases		1,440		
Direct labor	162,000			
Indirect labor	24,840			
Factory supervision.	21,600			
Factory utilities.	33,120			
Machinery repairs	8,100			
Rent expense, factory.	12,960			
Property taxes, machinery	3,060			
Selling expenses, controlling.			55,440	
Administrative expenses, controlling.			52,020	
Expired factory insurance	4,320			
Factory supplies used.	10,980			
Depreciation expense, factory machinery . .	18,900			
Small tools written off	720			
Amortization of patents	4,500			
State and federal income taxes expense. . .			53,100	
	460,620	46,440		
Cost of goods manufactured		414,180	414,180	
	460,620	460,620	603,720	684,540
Net income			80,820	
			684,540	684,540

Required

1. From the information given prepare an income statement and a manufacturing statement for the company.

2. Prepare compound closing entries for the company.

Problem 21-3

Burkhalder Company began this year with the following inventories: raw materials, $27,600; goods in process, $30,900; and finished goods, $37,500. The company uses the relation between its overhead and direct labor costs to apply overhead to its inventories of goods in process and finished goods; and at the end of this year its inventories were assigned these costs:

	Raw Materials	Goods in Process	Finished Goods
Material costs.	$25,800	$ 8,400	$13,500
Direct labor costs	–0–	10,800	16,800
Overhead costs	–0–	?	21,000
Totals	$25,800	?	$51,300

And this additional information was available from the company's records:

Total factory overhead costs incurred during the year	$247,500
Cost of all goods manufactured during the year	595,200

Required

On the basis of the information given plus any data you can derive from it, prepare a manufacturing statement for Burkhalder Company.

Problem 21-4

The December 31, 198A, trial balance of Megan Manufacturing Company's ledger carried the following items:

Megan Manufacturing Company
Trial Balance
December 31, 198A

Cash	$ 16,150	
Accounts receivable	18,100	
Allowance for doubtful accounts		$ 100
Raw materials inventory	18,550	
Goods in process inventory	17,200	
Finished goods inventory	24,350	
Prepaid factory insurance	2,050	
Factory supplies	6,550	
Machinery	113,750	
Accumulated depreciation, machinery		39,200
Accounts payable		12,650
Common stock		50,000
Retained earnings		47,450
Sales		346,250
Raw material purchases	92,550	
Direct labor	79,750	
Indirect labor	18,300	
Factory utilities	6,800	
Machinery repairs	4,700	
Selling expenses, controlling	40,600	
Administrative expenses, controlling	36,250	
Totals	$495,650	$495,650

The following adjustments and inventory information was available at year-end:

a. Allowance for doubtful accounts to be increased to $850 (debit Administrative Expenses, controlling account).
b. An examination of policies showed $1,550 of factory insurance expired.
c. An inventory of factory supplies showed $4,850 of factory supplies used.
d. Estimated depreciation of factory machinery, $15,650.
e. Accrued direct labor, $250; and accrued indirect labor, $150.
f. Accrued state and federal income taxes payable amount to $18,750.
g. Year-end inventories:
   (1) Raw materials, $18,350.
   (2) Goods in process consisted of 800 units of product with each unit containing an estimated $7.30 of materials and having had an estimated $8 of direct labor applied.
   (3) Finished goods inventory consisted of 750 units of product with each unit containing an estimated $15 of materials and having had an estimated $12 of direct labor applied.

Required

1. Enter the trial balance on a work sheet form and make the adjustments from the information given. Then sort the items to the proper Manufacturing Statement, Income Statement, and Balance Sheet columns.
2. After the Direct Labor account and factory overhead cost accounts have been adjusted and carried into the Manufacturing Statement columns, determine the relation between direct labor and overhead costs and use this relation to determine the overhead applicable to each unit of goods in process and finished goods. Next, calculate the balance sheet values for these inventories, enter the inventory amounts on the work sheet, and complete the work sheet.
3. From the work sheet prepare a manufacturing statement and an income statement.
4. Prepare compound closing entries.

Problem 21-5

A trial balance of Daggler Company's ledger on December 31, 198A, the end of an annual accounting period, appeared as shown on page 775.

Additional information

a. Expired factory insurance, $1,200.
b. Factory supplies used, $2,950.
c. Depreciation of factory machinery, $5,100.
d. Small tools written off, $250.
e. Amortization of patents, $700.

f. Accrued wages payable:
  (1) Direct labor, $800.
  (2) Indirect labor, $350.
  (3) Factory supervision, $150.
g. Ending inventories:
  (1) Raw materials, $6,600.
  (2) Goods in process consisted of 500 units of product with each unit containing an estimated $2.75 of raw materials and having had an estimated $5 of direct labor applied.
  (3) Finished goods consisted of 400 units of product with each unit containing an estimated $6.50 of raw materials and having had an estimated $9 of direct labor applied.
h. Estimated state and federal income taxes payable, $15,000.

Daggler Company
Trial Balance
December 31, 198A

Cash	$ 7,400	
Raw materials inventory	6,850	
Goods in process inventory	6,250	
Finished goods inventory.	7,550	
Prepaid factory insurance	1,800	
Factory supplies	3,400	
Factory machinery	84,100	
Accumulated depreciation, factory machinery		$ 15,650
Small tools.	2,050	
Patents	3,350	
Common stock		50,000
Retained earnings.		8,350
Sales		185,000
Raw material purchases	31,000	
Discounts on raw material purchases		600
Direct labor	49,200	
Indirect labor.	6,050	
Factory supervision	5,850	
Factory utilities	8,950	
Machinery repairs.	2,100	
Rent expense, factory	3,000	
Property taxes, machinery	850	
Selling expenses, controlling	15,700	
Administrative expenses, controlling	14,150	
Totals	$259,600	$259,600

Required

1. Enter the trial balance on a work sheet form. Make the adjustments from the information given. Sort the items to the proper Manufacturing Statement, Income Statement, and Balance Sheet columns.

2. After the Direct Labor account and the factory overhead cost accounts have been adjusted and carried into the Manufacturing Statement columns, determine the relation between overhead costs and direct labor cost and use the relation to determine the amount of overhead applicable to each unit of goods in process and finished goods. After overhead applicable to each unit of goods in process and finished goods is determined, calculate the inventory values of the goods in process and finished goods inventories. Enter these inventory amounts on the work sheet and complete the work sheet.

3. From the work sheet prepare a manufacturing statement and an income statement.

4. Prepare closing entries.

□ **Alternate Problems**   **Problem 21-1A**

In Hurley Corporation's work sheet prepared at the end of last year, the Manufacturing Statement columns appeared as follows. The illustrated columns show the items as they appeared after all adjustments were completed but before the ending work in process inventory was calculated and entered and before the cost of goods manufactured was calculated.

Hurley Corporation makes a single product called Blacons. On December 31, at the end of last year, the goods in process inventory consisted of 1,250 units of Blacons with each unit containing an estimated $11.52 of direct materials and having had an estimated $28.80 of direct labor applied.

	Manufacturing Statement	
	Debit	Credit
Raw materials inventory	76,320	69,480
Goods in process inventory.	64,080	?
Raw material purchases	293,040	
Direct labor.	360,000	
Indirect labor	60,840	
Factory supervision	43,200	
Factory utilities	30,960	
Machinery repairs	22,680	
Rent expense, factory	25,920	
Property taxes, machinery	6,840	
Factory insurance expired	11,880	
Factory supplies used	26,640	
Depreciation expense, factory machinery	60,840	
Small tools written off	1,800	
	1,085,040	?
Cost of goods manufactured		?
	1,085,040	1,085,040

Required

1. Calculate the relation between direct labor and factory overhead costs and use this relation to determine the value of the ending goods in process inventory.

2. After placing a value on the ending goods in process inventory, determine the cost of goods manufactured.

3. Prepare a manufacturing statement for Hurley Corporation.

4. Prepare entries to close the manufacturing accounts and to summarize their balances in the Manufacturing Summary account.

5. Prepare an entry to close the Manufacturing Summary account.

Problem 21-2A

The following alphabetically arranged items were taken from the Manufacturing Statement and Income Statement columns of Intercomp Manufacturing Company's year-end work sheet:

Advertising	$ 5,400	Goods in process, December 31	$ 33,750
Depreciation, machinery	9,450	Finished goods, January 1	47,250
Depreciation, office equipment	2,250	Finished goods, December 31	37,800
Depreciation, selling equipment	2,700	Miscellaneous factory expenses	2,250
Direct labor	174,600	Office salaries	18,900
Factory supplies used	4,950	Raw material purchases	231,750
Factory utilities	9,000	Rent on factory building	21,600
Federal income taxes expense	36,450	Rent expense, office space	6,300
Freight on raw materials	6,750	Rent expense, selling space	7,200
Indirect labor	15,750	Repairs to machinery	8,100
Inventories:		Sales	810,450
Raw materials, January 1	44,100	Sales discounts	15,300
Raw materials, December 31	45,450	Sales salaries	78,750
Goods in process, January 1	36,900	Superintendence, factory	32,400

Required

Prepare an income statement and a manufacturing statement for the company.

Problem 21-3A

Heavy Products Company incurred a total of $651,600 of direct material, direct labor, and factory overhead costs in manufacturing its product last year. Of this amount, $280,800 represented factory overhead costs. The company began last year with the following inventories: raw materials, $25,200; goods in process, $43,500; and finished goods, $52,500. It applies overhead to its goods in process and finished goods inventories on the basis of the relation of overhead to direct labor costs; and at the end of last year, it assigned the following costs to its inventories:

	Raw Materials	Goods in Process	Finished Goods
Material costs	$27,600	$14,100	$17,250
Direct labor costs	–0–	14,400	17,400
Overhead costs	–0–	?	26,100
Totals	$27,600	$?	$60,750

Required

On the basis of the information given plus any information you can derive from it, prepare a manufacturing statement for Heavy Products Company.

Problem 21-4A

The December 31, 198A, trial balance of Iberg Corporation's ledger carried the following items:

Iberg Corporation
Trial Balance
December 31, 198A

Cash	$ 30,600	
Accounts receivable	37,900	
Allowance for doubtful accounts		$ 900
Raw materials inventory	47,500	
Goods in process inventory	21,200	
Finished goods inventory	25,400	
Prepaid factory insurance	7,600	
Factory supplies	11,600	
Machinery	222,000	
Accumulated depreciation, machinery		89,000
Accounts payable		41,500
Common stock		60,000
Retained earnings		68,200
Sales		678,700
Raw material purchases	175,000	
Direct labor	118,600	
Indirect labor	27,000	
Factory utilities	23,100	
Machinery repairs	7,300	
Selling expenses, controlling	87,400	
Administrative expenses, controlling	96,100	
Totals	$938,300	$938,300

The following adjustments and inventory information was available at year-end:

a. Allowance for doubtful accounts to be increased to $1,800 (debit Administrative Expenses, controlling account).
b. An examination of policies showed $5,000 of factory insurance expired.
c. An inventory of factory supplies showed $7,400 of factory supplies used.
d. Estimated depreciation of factory machinery, $31,600.
e. Accrued direct labor, $1,400; and accrued indirect labor, $600.
f. Accrued state and federal income taxes payable amount to $39,400.
g. Year-end inventories:
 (1) Raw materials, $36,700.
 (2) Goods in process consisted of 1,400 units of product with each unit containing an estimated $10 of materials and having had an estimated $8 of direct labor applied.
 (3) Finished goods inventory consisted of 1,800 units of product with each unit containing an estimated $16 of materials and having had an estimated $13 of direct labor applied.

Required

1. Enter the trial balance on a work sheet form and make the adjustments from the information given. Then sort the items to the proper Manufacturing Statement, Income Statement, and Balance Sheet columns.

2. After the Direct Labor account and factory overhead cost accounts have been adjusted and carried into the Manufacturing Statement columns, determine the relation between direct labor and overhead costs and use this relation to determine the overhead applicable to each unit of goods in process and finished goods. Next, calculate the balance sheet values for these inventories (rounded to the nearest whole dollar). Enter the inventory amounts on the work sheet and complete the work sheet.

3. From the work sheet prepare a manufacturing statement and an income statement.

4. Prepare compound closing entries.

Problem 21-5A

Newsome Manufacturing Company prepared the following trial balance at the end of its annual accounting period:

Newsome Manufacturing Company
Trial Balance
December 31, 108A

Cash	$ 26,250	
Raw materials inventory	19,950	
Goods in process inventory	22,950	
Finished goods inventory.	24,900	
Prepaid factory insurance	6,300	
Factory supplies	9,600	
Factory machinery	263,250	
Accumulated depreciation, factory machinery		$ 43,200
Small tools	5,550	
Patents	6,750	
Common stock		150,000
Retained earnings.		51,600
Sales		539,550
Raw material purchases	92,700	
Discounts on raw material purchases		1,500
Direct labor	133,650	
Indirect labor.	19,950	
Factory supervision	17,700	
Factory utilities	26,850	
Machinery repairs.	6,600	
Rent expense, factory	10,800	
Property taxes, machinery	1,200	
Selling expenses, controlling	47,100	
Administrative expenses, controlling	43,800	
Totals	$785,850	$785,850

Additional information

a. Expired factory insurance, $3,300.

b. Factory supplies used, $9,450.

c. Depreciation of factory machinery, $14,850.

d. Small tools written off, $1,050.

e. Amortization of patents, $1,950.

f. Accrued wages payable:
   (1) Direct labor, $1,350.
   (2) Indirect labor, $750.
   (3) Factory supervision, $300.

g. Ending inventories:
  (1) Raw materials, $19,200.
  (2) Goods in process consisted of 2,000 units of product with each
      unit containing an estimated $4.20 of direct materials and having
      had an estimated $3 of direct labor applied.
  (3) Finished goods consisted of 1,500 units of product with each unit
      containing an estimated $5.88 of direct materials and having an
      estimated $7.20 of direct labor applied.
h. Estimated state and federal income taxes expense, $43,500.

Required

1. Enter the trial balance on a work sheet form. Make the adjustments
   from the information given. Sort the items to the proper Manufacturing
   Statement, Income Statement, and Balance Sheet columns.

2. After the Direct Labor account and factory overhead cost accounts have
   been adjusted and carried into the Manufacturing Statement columns,
   determine the relation between direct labor and overhead costs and
   use this relation to determine the overhead applicable to each unit of
   goods in process and finished goods. After the amounts of overhead
   applicable to the units of goods in process and finished goods are
   determined, calculate the balance sheet values of these inventories, enter
   these inventory amounts on the work sheet, and complete the work
   sheet.

3. From the work sheet prepare a manufacturing statement and an income
   statement.

4. Prepare compound closing entries.

Provocative Problems

Provocative Problem 21-1 Intercontinental Tool Company

Intercontinental Tool Company has been in operation for three years,
manufacturing and selling a single product. Although sales have increased
materially each year, profits have increased only slightly. The company
president, Blake Jones, has asked you to analyze the situation and tell
him why. Mr. Jones is primarily a production man and knows little about
accounting. The company bookkeeper knows a debit from a credit, is an
excellent clerk, but has little accounting training.

The company's condensed income statements for the past three years
show:

	198A	198B	198C
Sales.	$225,000	$315,000	$360,000
Cost of goods sold:			
Finished goods inventory, January 1	$ –0–	$ 13,500	$ 40,500
Cost of goods manufactured.	148,500	230,400	252,450
Goods for sale.	$148,500	$243,900	$292,950
Finished goods inventory, December 31.	13,500	40,500	54,000
Cost of goods sold.	$135,000	$203,400	$238,950
Gross profit from sales	$ 90,000	$111,600	$121,050
Selling and administrative expenses	67,500	88,200	97,200
Net income	$ 22,500	$ 23,400	$ 23,850

Further investigation yields the following additional information:

a. The company sold 2,500 units of its product during the first year in business, 3,500 during the second year, and 4,000 during the third. All sales were priced at $90 per unit, and no discounts were granted.

b. There were 250 units in the finished goods inventory at the end of the first year, 750 at the end of the second, and 1,000 at the end of the third.

c. The units in the finished goods inventory were valued each year at 60% of their selling price, or at $54 per unit.

Required

Prepare a report for Mr. Jones that shows (a) the number of units of product manufactured each year, (b) the cost each year to manufacture a unit of product, and (c) the selling and administrative expenses per unit of product sold each year. Also, (d) prepare an income statement showing the correct net income each year, using a FIFO basis for pricing the finished goods inventory. And finally, (e) express an opinion as to why net income has not kept pace with the rising sales volume.

Provocative Problem 21-2   Trailers Unique

Several years ago Karen Tucker took over the operation of her family's trailer manufacturing company. The company previously specialized in manufacturing utility trailers, but recently it has turned more and more to building boat trailers to the specifications of its customers. The seasonality of this business means that shop activity is rather slow during October, November, and December.

Karen has tried to increase business during the slow months. However, most prospective customers who come to the business during these months are shoppers; and when Karen quotes a price for a boat trailer, they commonly decide the price is too high and walk out. Karen thinks the trouble arises from her application of a rule established by her father when he ran the business. The rule is that in pricing a job to a customer, "always set the price so as to make a 10% profit over and above all costs, and be sure that all costs are included."

Karen says that in pricing a job, the material and labor costs are easy to figure but that overhead is another thing. Her overhead consists of depreciation of building and machinery, manufacturing utilities, taxes, and so on, which in total run to $7,500 per month whether she builds any trailers or not. Furthermore, when she follows her father's rule, she has to charge more for a boat built during the slow months because the overhead is spread over fewer jobs. She readily admits that this seems to drive away business during the months she needs business most, but she finds it difficult to break her father's rule, for as she says, "Dad did all right in this business for many years."

Required

Explain with assumed figures to illustrate your point why Karen charges more for a boat made in December than for one built in May, a very busy month. Suggest how Karen might solve this pricing problem and still follow her father's rule.

Provocative Problem 21-3   Buffalo Production Company

On January 1, 198A, Buffalo Production Company had outstanding 54,000 shares of $10 par value common stock. The stock was issued at par. The assets and liabilities of the company on that date were as follows:

Cash.	$120,000
Accounts receivable	60,000
Raw materials inventory.	75,000
Goods in process inventory	90,000
Finished goods inventory	105,000
Plant and equipment, net	255,000
Accounts payable	60,000

During 198A, the company paid no dividends, although it earned a 198A net income (ignore income taxes) of $56,250. At year-end, the amounts of the company's accounts receivable, accounts payable, and common stock outstanding were the same as at the beginning of the year. However, its cash decreased by $11,250, its raw materials inventory increased by 40%, its goods in process inventory increased by 25%, and its finished goods inventory increased by one half during the year. The net amount of its plant and equipment decreased by $37,500 due to depreciation, chargeable four fifths to factory overhead costs and one fifth to general and administrative expenses. The year's direct labor costs were $150,000, and factory overhead costs excluding depreciation were 60% of that amount. Cost of goods sold was $375,000, and all sales were made at prices 50% above cost. Selling expenses were 14%, and general and administrative expenses excluding depreciation were 8% of sales.

Required

Based on the information given and on amounts you can derive therefrom, prepare a manufacturing work sheet for the company.

22   Cost Accounting, Job Order, and Process

After studying Chapter 22, you should be able to:

1. State the conditions under which job order cost accounting should be used and those under which process cost accounting should be used.

2. Describe how costs for individual jobs are accumulated on job cost sheets and how control accounts are charged with the total costs of all jobs.

3. Allocate overhead to jobs and distribute any over- or underapplied overhead.

4. Describe how costs are accumulated by departments under process costing.

5. Explain what an equivalent finished unit is and how equivalent finished units are used in calculating unit costs.

6. Prepare a process cost summary.

7. Define or explain the words and phrases listed in the chapter Glossary.

When a company uses a general manufacturing accounting system such as that described in the previous chapter, physical counts of inventories are required at the end of each accounting period in order to determine cost of goods manufactured. Furthermore, cost of goods manufactured as determined under such a system is the cost of all goods that were manufactured during the period; usually, no effort is made to determine unit costs. In contrast to a general manufacturing accounting system, a **cost accounting system** is based on perpetual inventories and emphasizes unit costs and the control of costs.

There are two common types of cost accounting systems: (1) job order cost systems and (2) process cost systems. However, of the two there are an infinite number of variations and combinations. A job order system is described first.

JOB ORDER COST ACCOUNTING

The type of cost accounting system used by a manufacturing company depends on the nature of its products and the manufacturing process necessary to produce the products. In some cases, each unit of product tends to have a unique design that requires the manufacturing process to focus on the production of that specific unit. Such products tend to be large, high-cost items. They often are manufactured especially for and to the specifications of each customer. When a unique product of this sort is ordered to be produced, it is called a **job.** Examples of such products may include a custom-designed yacht, a special-purpose machine, or a construction project of a contractor. Some jobs consist of a quantity of identical items, in which case they are called **job lots.** In this type of company, manufacturing costs are assembled in terms of jobs or job lots of product, and the system of accounting for manufacturing costs is called a **job order cost system.**

■ **The Purpose and General Design of a Job Order Cost System**

As previously stated, a job cost system differs from a general accounting system in that its primary objective is the determination of the cost of producing each job or job lot. A job cost system also differs in that all inventory accounts used in such a system are perpetual inventory accounts that control subsidiary ledgers. For example, in a job cost system, the purchase and use of all materials are recorded in a perpetual inventory account called Raw Materials. The Raw Materials account controls a subsidiary ledger having a separate ledger card (Illustration 22-1) for each different kind of material used. Likewise, in a job cost system, the Goods in Process and Finished Goods accounts are also perpetual inventory accounts controlling subsidiary ledgers.

■ **The Flow of Costs in a Job Order Cost System**

In addition to perpetual inventory controlling accounts, job cost accounting is also distinguished by the flow of manufacturing costs through the accounts. Costs flow from the Raw Materials, Factory Payroll, and Factory Overhead accounts into and through the Goods in Process and Finished

Illustration 22-1

RAW MATERIALS LEDGER CARD

Item _Whatsit clip_   Stock No. _C-347_   Location in Storeroom _Bin 137_

Maximum _400_   Minimum _150_   Number to Reorder _200_

	Received					Issued				Balance	
Date	Receiving Report No.	Units	Unit Price	Total Price	Requisition No.	Units	Unit Price	Total Price	Units	Unit Price	Total Price
3/1									180	1.00	180.00
3/5					4345	20	1.00	20.00	160	1.00	160.00
3/11					4416	10	1.00	10.00	150	1.00	150.00
3/12	C-114	200	1.00	200.00					350	1.00	350.00
3/25					4713	21	1.00	21.00	329	1.00	329.00

Goods accounts and on to the Cost of Goods Sold account. This flow is diagrammed in Illustration 22-2. An examination of the diagram will show that costs flow through the accounts in the same way direct materials, direct labor, and overhead are placed in production in the factory, are combined to become finished goods, and finally are sold.

Illustration 22-2 also shows the relationships between the controlling accounts and the subsidiary ledgers in a job cost system. In order to better understand the role played by each component of the system, students should refer back to Illustration 22-2 as they study the discussion of each component.

■ **Job Cost Sheets**

The heart of a job cost system is a subsidiary ledger of **job cost sheets** called a **Job Cost Ledger.** The cost sheets are used to accumulate costs by jobs. A separate cost sheet is used for each job.

Observe in Illustration 22-3 that a job cost sheet is designed to accumulate costs. Although this accumulation is discussed in more detail later, it may be summarized as follows. When a job is begun, information regarding the customer, job number, and job description is recorded on a blank cost sheet and the cost sheet is placed in the Job Cost Ledger. Identifying each job with a job number simplifies the process of charging direct materials, direct labor, and overhead to the job. As materials are required for the job, they are transferred from the materials storeroom and are used to complete the job. At the same time their cost is charged to the job in the Direct Materials column of the job's cost sheet. Labor used directly on the job is likewise charged to the job in the Direct Labor column; and when the job is finished, the amount of overhead applicable is entered in the Overhead Costs Applied column. After this, the cost totals are summarized and the job's total cost is determined.

Illustration 22-2   Cost Flows and Subsidiary Ledgers for a Job Cost System

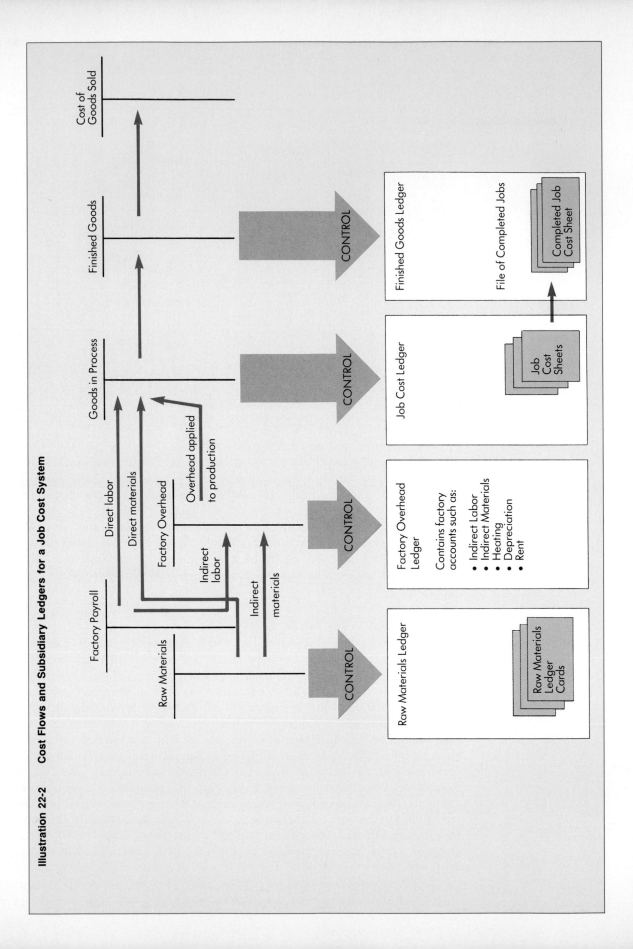

Illustration 22-3

JOB COST SHEET

Customer's Name _Cone Lumber Company_   Job No. _7452_

Address _Eugene, Oregon_

Job Description _10 H.P. electric motor to customer's specifications_

Date Promised _4/1_   Date Started _3/23_   Date Completed _3/29_

Date	Direct Materials Requisition No.	Amount	Direct Labor Time Ticket No.	Amount	Overhead Costs Applied Date	Rate	Amount
19-- Mar 23	4698	53.00	C-3122	12.00	3/20	150 per cent of the direct labor	$123.00
24			C-3478 C-3479	16.00 6.00			
25	4713	21.00	C-4002	16.00			
26			C-4015	10.00			
27			C-4032	12.00			
28			C-4044	10.00			
	Total	74.00	Total	82.00			

Summary of Costs

Materials _____ $ 74.00

Labor _____ 82.00

Overhead _____ 123.00

Total Cost of the Job _____ 279.00

Remarks: Completed and shipped 3/29

The Goods in Process Account

The job cost sheets in the Job Cost Ledger are controlled by the Goods in Process account, which is kept in the General Ledger. And, the Goods in Process account and its subsidiary ledger of cost sheets operate in the usual manner of controlling accounts and subsidiary ledgers. The direct materials, direct labor, and overhead costs debited to each individual job on its cost sheet must be debited to the Goods in Process account either as individual amounts or in totals. Likewise all credits to jobs on their cost sheets must be credited individually or in totals to the Goods in Process account.

In addition to being a controlling account, the Goods in Process account is a perpetual inventory account. At the beginning of a cost period, the cost of any unfinished jobs in process appears in the Goods in Process account as a debit balance. Throughout the cost period, direct materials, direct labor, and overhead are placed in production, and periodically their costs are debited to the account (note the last three debits in the Goods in Process account that follows). Also, throughout the period the cost of each job completed (the sum of the job's direct materials, direct labor, and overhead costs) is credited to the account as each job is finished. As a result, the account functions as a perpetual inventory account. After all entries are posted, the debit balance shows the cost of the unfinished jobs still in process. This current balance is obtained and maintained without having to take a physical count of inventory, except as an occasional means of confirming the account balance. For example, the following Goods in Process account shows a $12,785 March 31 ending inventory of unfinished jobs in process.

Goods in Process

Date		Explanation	Debit	Credit	Balance
Mar.	1	Balance, beginning inventory			2,850
	10	Job 7449 completed		7,920	(5,070)
	18	Job 7448 completed		9,655	(14,725)
	24	Job 7450 completed		8,316	(23,041)
	29	Job 7452 completed		279	(23,320)
	29	Job 7451 completed		6,295	(29,615)
	31	Direct materials used	17,150		(12,465)
	31	Direct labor applied	10,100		(2,365)
	31	Overhead applied	15,150		12,785

■ **Accounting for Materials under a Job Cost System**

Under a job cost system, all raw materials purchased are placed in a materials storeroom under the care of a storeroom keeper and are issued to the factory only in exchange for properly prepared **materials requisitions** (Illustration 22-4). The storeroom provides physical control over materials. The requisitions enhance the control and also provide a means of charging material costs to jobs or, in the case of indirect materials, to factory overhead costs. The use of requisitions is described in the next paragraphs.

Using Materials Requisitions

When a raw material is needed in the factory, a materials requisition is prepared and signed by a superintendent or other responsible person. The requisition identifies the material and shows the job number or overhead account to which it is to be charged and is given to the storeroom keeper in exchange for the material. The storeroom keeper collects the requisitions and then forwards them, in batches, to the accounting department.

Issuing units of material to the factory obviously reduces the amount of that particular material in the storeroom. Consequently, when a materials requisition reaches the accounting department, it is first recorded in the

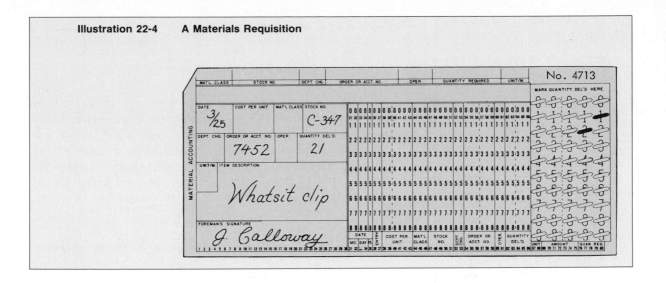

Illustration 22-4   A Materials Requisition

Issued column of the raw materials ledger card of the material issued. This reduces the number of units of that material shown to be on hand. Note the last entry in Illustration 22-1, which records the requisition of Illustration 22-4.

Charging the Cost of Materials to Jobs and to Overhead

Materials issued to the factory may be used on jobs or for some overhead task, such as machinery repairs. Consequently, after being entered in the Issued columns of the proper raw materials ledger cards, a batch of requisitions is sorted by jobs and overhead accounts and charged to the proper jobs and overhead accounts. Direct materials used on jobs are charged to the jobs in the Direct Materials columns of the job cost sheets. (Note the last entry in the Direct Materials column on the cost sheet of Illustration 22-3 where the requisition of Illustration 22-4 is recorded.) Raw materials used for overhead tasks are charged to the proper overhead accounts in the Factory Overhead Ledger. A company using a job cost system commonly has a Factory Overhead controlling account in its General Ledger that controls a subsidiary Factory Overhead Ledger having an account for each overhead cost, such as Factory Utilities or Machinery Repairs. Consequently, a requisition for light bulbs, for example, is charged to the Factory Utilities account in the subsidiary Factory Overhead Ledger.

Raw materials ledger cards, job cost sheets, and overhead cost accounts are all subsidiary ledger accounts controlled by accounts in the General Ledger. Consequently, in addition to the entries just described, entries must also be made in the controlling accounts. To make these entries, the requisitions charged to jobs and the requisitions charged to overhead accounts are accumulated until the end of a month or other cost period when they are separately totaled. If, for example, the requisitions charged to jobs during the month total $17,150 and those charged to overhead accounts total $320, an entry like the following is made:

Mar.	31	Goods in Process	17,150.00	
		Factory Overhead	320.00	
		Raw Materials.		17,470.00
		To record the materials used during March.		

The debit to Goods in Process in the illustrated entry is equal to the sum of the materials requisitions charged to jobs as detailed on the job cost sheets during March. The debit to Factory Overhead is equal to the sum of the requisitions charged to overhead accounts, and the credit to Raw Materials is equal to the sum of all requisitions entered in the Issued columns of the raw materials ledger cards during the month.

Accounting for Labor in a Job Cost System

Time clocks, clock cards, and a Payroll Register similar to those described in an earlier chapter are commonly used in factories to record the hours and cost of the direct and indirect labor provided by employees. Without the complications of payroll taxes, income taxes, and other deductions, the entry to pay the employees is as follows:

Mar.	7	Factory Payroll	2,900.00	
		Cash		2,900.00
		To record the factory payroll and pay the employees.		

This entry is repeated at the end of each pay period. Thus, at the end of a month or other cost period, the Factory Payroll account has a series of debits (see Illustration 22-6) like the debit of this entry. The sum of these debits is the total amount paid to employees for the direct and indirect labor during the month.

Gathering Information about Factory Labor Costs

The clock cards just mentioned are a record of hours worked each day by each employee, but they do not show how the employees spent their time or the specific jobs and overhead tasks on which they worked. Consequently, if the hours worked by each employee are to be charged to specific jobs and overhead accounts, another record called a **labor time ticket** must be prepared. Labor time tickets like the one shown in Illustration 22-5 describe how each employee's time was spent while at work.

The time ticket of Illustration 22-5 is a "pen-and-ink" ticket and is suitable for use in a plant in which only a small number of such tickets are prepared and recorded each day. In a plant in which many tickets are prepared, a time ticket that can be made into a punched card similar to Illustration 22-4 would be more suitable.

Labor time tickets serve as a basis for charging jobs and overhead accounts for an employee's wages. Throughout each day a labor time ticket is prepared each time an employee moves from one job or overhead task to another. The tickets may be prepared by the worker, the worker's supervi-

Illustration 22-5   A Labor Time Ticket

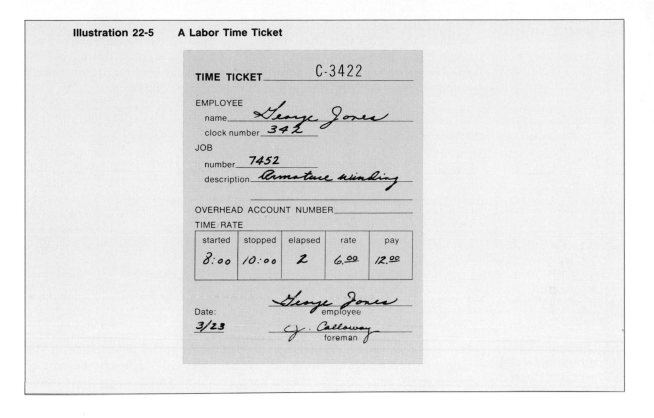

sor, or a clerk called a timekeeper. If the employee works on only one job all day, only one ticket is prepared. If more than one job is worked on, a separate ticket is made for each. At the end of the day all the tickets prepared that day are sent to the accounting department.

Charging Labor Costs to Jobs and to Overhead

In the accounting department, the direct labor time tickets are charged to jobs on the job cost sheets (see the first entry in the Labor column of Illustration 22-3 where the ticket of Illustration 22-5 is recorded), and the indirect labor tickets are charged to overhead accounts in the Factory Overhead Ledger. The tickets are than accumulated until the end of the cost period when they are separately totaled. If, for example, the direct labor tickets total $10,100 and the indirect labor tickets total $2,500, the following entry is made:

Mar.	31	Goods in Process	10,100.00	
		Factory Overhead	2,500.00	
		Factory Payroll		12,600.00
		To record the March time tickets.		

The first debit in the illustrated entry is the sum of all direct labor time tickets charged to jobs on the job cost sheets, and the second debit is the sum of all tickets charged to overhead accounts. The credit is the total of the month's labor time tickets, both direct and indirect. Notice in Illustration 22-6 that after this credit is posted, the Factory Payroll account has a $605 credit balance. This $605 is the accrued factory payroll payable at the month's end, and it is also the dollar amount of time tickets prepared and recorded during the last three days of March.

Illustration 22-6

Factory Payroll

Date		Explanation	Debit	Credit	Balance
Mar.	7	Weekly payroll payment	2,900		2,900
	14	Weekly payroll payment	2,950		5,850
	21	Weekly payroll payment	3,105		8,955
	28	Weekly payroll payment	3,040		11,995
	31	Labor cost summary		12,600	(605)

Accounting for Overhead in a Job Cost System

In a job cost system, if the cost of each job is to be determined at the time it is finished, it is necessary to associate with each job the cost of its materials, labor, and overhead. Requisitions and time tickets make possible a direct association of material and labor costs with jobs. However, overhead costs are incurred for the benefit of all jobs and cannot be related directly to any one job. Consequently, to associate overhead with jobs it is necessary to relate overhead to another variable, such as direct labor costs, and to apply overhead to jobs by means of a **predetermined overhead application rate.**

A predetermined overhead application rate based on direct labor cost is established before a cost period begins by (1) estimating the total overhead that will be incurred during the period; (2) estimating the cost of the direct labor that will be incurred during the period; then (3), calculating the ratio, expressed as a percentage, of the estimated overhead to the estimated direct labor cost. For example, if a cost accountant estimates that a factory will incur $180,000 of overhead during the next year and that $120,000 of direct labor will be applied to production during the year, these estimates are used to establish an overhead application rate of 150%, calculated as follows:

$$\frac{\text{Next year's estimated overhead costs, \$180,000}}{\text{Next year's estimated direct labor costs, \$120,000}} = 150\%$$

Charging Overhead to Jobs as They Are Finished

After a predetermined overhead application rate is established, it is used throughout the year to apply overhead to jobs as they are finished. Overhead is assigned to each job, and its cost is calculated as follows: (1) As each job is completed, the cost of its direct materials is determined by adding the amounts in the Direct Materials column of its cost sheet. Then

(2), the cost of its direct labor is determined by adding the amounts in the Direct Labor column. Next (3), the applicable overhead cost is calculated by multiplying the job's total direct labor cost by the predetermined overhead application rate and is entered in the Overhead Costs Applied column. Finally (4), the job's direct material, direct labor, and overhead costs are entered in the summary section of the cost sheet and totaled to determine the total cost of the job.

Charging Overhead to Ending Goods in Process

The predetermined overhead application rate is also used to assign overhead to any jobs still in process at the end of the cost period. Then, the total overhead assigned to all jobs during the period is recorded in the accounts with an entry like this:

Mar.	31	Goods in Process	15,150.00	
		Factory Overhead		15,150.00
		To record the overhead applied to jobs during March.		

The illustrated entry assumes that the overhead applied to all jobs during March totaled $15,150. After it is posted, the Factory Overhead account appears as in Illustration 22-7.

Illustration 22-7

Factory Overhead

Date		Explanation	PR	Debit	Credit	Balance
Mar.	31	Indirect materials	G24	320		320
	31	Indirect labor	G24	2,500		2,820
	31	Miscellaneous payments	D89	3,306		6,126
	31	Accrued and prepaid items	G24	9,056		15,182
	31	Applied			15,150	32

In the Factory Overhead account of Illustration 22-7, the actual overhead costs incurred during March are represented by four debits. The first two need no explanation; the third represents the many payments for such things as water, telephone, and so on; the fourth represents such things as depreciation, expired insurance, taxes, and so forth.

When overhead is applied to jobs on the basis of a predetermined overhead rate based upon direct labor costs, it is assumed that the overhead applicable to a particular job bears the same relation to the job's direct labor cost as the total estimated overhead of the factory bears to the total estimated direct labor costs. This assumption may not be proper in every case. However, when the ratio of overhead to direct labor cost is approximately the same for all jobs, an overhead rate based upon direct labor cost offers an easily calculated and fair basis for assigning overhead to jobs. In those cases in which the ratio of overhead to direct labor cost does not remain the same for all jobs, some other relationship must be used. Often overhead rates based upon the ratio of overhead to direct labor hours or overhead to machine-hours are used. However, a discussion of these alternative bases is reserved for a course in cost accounting.

■ Overapplied and Underapplied Overhead

When overhead is applied to jobs by means of an overhead application rate based on estimates, the Factory Overhead account seldom, if ever, has a zero balance. At times actual overhead incurred exceeds overhead applied, and at other times overhead applied exceeds actual overhead incurred. When the account has a debit balance (overhead incurred in excess of overhead applied), the balance is known as **underapplied overhead** (see Illustration 22-7); and when it has a credit balance (overhead applied in excess of overhead incurred), the balance is called **overapplied overhead.** Usually the balance is small and fluctuates from debit to credit throughout a year. However, any remaining balance in the account at the end of each year must be disposed of before a new accounting period begins.

If the year-end balance of the Factory Overhead account is material in amount, it is reasonable that it be disposed of by apportioning it among the goods still in process, the finished goods inventory, and cost of goods sold. This has the effect of restating the inventories and goods sold at "actual" cost. For example, assume that at the end of an accounting period, (1) a company's Overhead Costs account has a $1,000 debit balance (under-applied overhead) and (2) the company had charged the following amounts of overhead to jobs during the period: jobs still in process, $10,000; jobs finished but unsold, $20,000; and jobs finished and sold, $70,000. In such a situation, the following entry apportions the underapplied overhead fairly among the jobs worked on during the period:

Dec.	31	Goods in Process	100.00	
		Finished Goods	200.00	
		Cost of Goods Sold	700.00	
		Factory Overhead		1,000.00
		To clear the Factory Overhead account and charge the underapplied overhead to the work of the accounting period.		

When the amount of over- or underapplied overhead is immaterial, all of it is closed to Cost of Goods Sold under the assumption that the major share of these costs would be charged to this account anyway and any extra exactness gained from prorating would not be worth the extra record keeping involved.

■ Recording the Completion of a Job

When a job is completed, its cost is transferred from the Goods in Process account to the Finished Goods account. For example, the following entry transfers the cost of the job the cost sheet of which appears on page 787.

Mar.	29	Finished Goods	279.00	
		Goods in Process		279.00
		To transfer the cost of Job No. 7452 to Finished Goods.		

At the same time this entry is made, the completed job's cost sheet is removed from the Job Cost Ledger, marked "completed," and filed. This is in effect the equivalent of posting a credit to the Job Cost Ledger equal to the credit to the Goods in Process controlling account.

■ **Recording Cost of Goods Sold**

When a cost system is in use, the cost to manufacture a job or job lot of product is known as soon as the goods are finished. Consequently, when goods are sold, since their cost is known, the cost can be recorded at the time of sale. For example, if goods costing $279 are sold for $450, the cost of goods sold may be recorded at the time of sale as follows:

Mar.	29	Accounts Receivable—Cone Lumber Co. . . .	450.00	
		Cost of Goods Sold	279.00	
		Sales		450.00
		Finished Goods		279.00
		Sold for $450 goods costing $279.		

When cost of goods sold is recorded at the time of each sale, the balance of the Cost of Goods Sold account shows at the end of an accounting period the cost of goods sold during the period.

PROCESS COST ACCOUNTING

At the beginning of this chapter, we noted that the type of cost accounting system used by a manufacturing company depends on the nature of its products and the manufacturing process necessary to produce the products. When companies produce a large volume of standardized units that are manufactured on a more or less continuous basis, the units under production generally pass from one **process** or step in the manufacturing of a product to another. Each process or step usually is organized as a separate manufacturing department, and the focus of the manufacturing activity is on the series of processes through which units are passed. Companies of this type use a **process cost system** in which costs are assembled in terms of processes or manufacturing steps.

Process cost systems are found in companies that produce products such as cement, flour, automobiles, or television sets. In such companies, manufacturing costs are assembled by and assigned to each processing department. A record is kept of the number of units that pass through each department. Periodically, the costs assigned to each department are divided by the number of units produced to determine the average cost per unit. The efficiency of each department is measured by comparing planned and actual processing costs incurred in processing the units of product that flow through the department.

Cost Flows in a Process Cost System

When costs are assembled by departments in a process cost system, a separate goods in process account is used for the costs of each department. For example, assume a company makes a product from metal pieces that are cut to size and bent into shape in a cutting department. Then, the pieces are sent to an assembly department in which the pieces are bolted together to form the finished product. Such a company would collect costs in two goods in process accounts, one for each department, and costs would flow through the accounts as in Illustration 22-8.

Observe in Illustration 22-8 that direct materials, direct labor, and factory overhead costs are charged to each department's goods in process account. It is assumed that direct materials charged to the cutting department relate to metal used in that department. Direct materials charged to the assembly department consist of bolts, washers, and nuts. Also observe how costs are transferred from the cutting department to the assembly department and then to finished goods, just as the product is physically transferred in the manufacturing procedure. The costs transferred from the cutting department to the assembly department include all of the direct materials, direct labor, and factory overhead costs that were charged to the cutting department and assigned to units that completed that process. The costs transferred from the assembly department to finished goods include the costs that had first been transferred out of the cutting department plus the additional direct materials, direct labor, and factory overhead that were charged to the assembly department and assigned to finished units.

Charging Costs to Departments

Materials Costs

Companies using process cost systems often use materials requisitions just like they would under a job order cost system. However, some companies substitute a **materials consumption report** kept by the materials storeroom keeper. This report shows the materials issued to each department during a cost period and provides the information that is needed to prepare journal entries charging the cost of direct materials to the appropriate departments. If materials are used for maintenance or other types of factory-wide activities, the materials consumption report discloses that they should be charged to factory overhead.

Direct Labor Costs

In a process cost system, costs are assembled in terms of manufacturing processes. This differs from a job order cost system in which costs are assembled in terms of jobs or job lots. There is a related difference between the concepts of direct and indirect labor. In a process cost system, all costs that are easily identified with a particular department are direct costs of that department. For example, suppose a person works full time doing maintenance on the production machinery in the cutting department. In a process cost system, the cost of that person's labor is a direct cost of

Illustration 22-8   Cost Flows for a Process Cost System

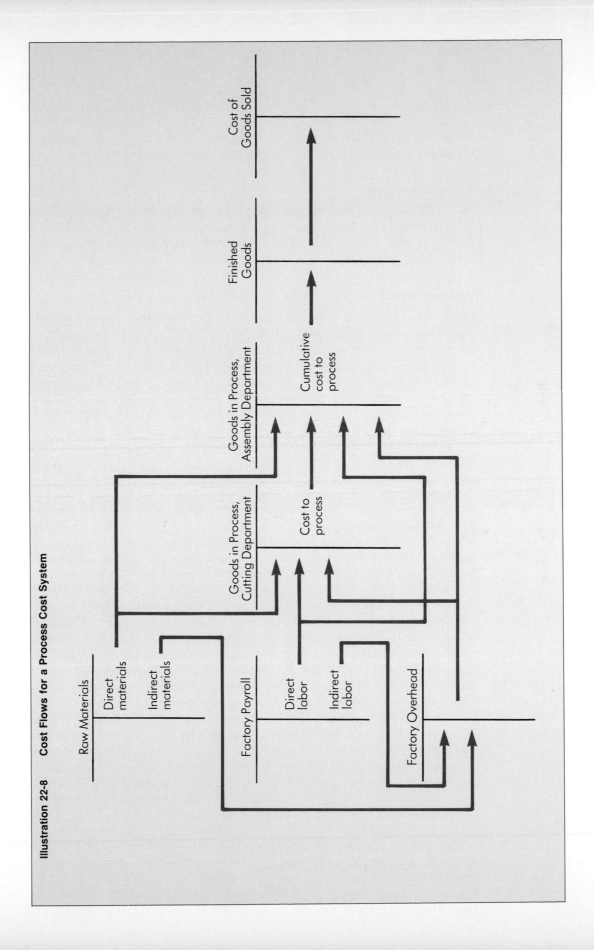

the cutting department; it would be treated as direct labor. But, if a job order cost system was in use, the cost of the maintenance person's labor would be indirect labor, since maintenance on production machinery is not easily associated with specific units of product or specific jobs.

Indirect Labor Costs

Not all labor is classified as direct labor in a process cost system. Indirect labor relates to persons whose work involves more than one department. Examples may include the labor of some maintenance workers, quality control inspectors, and overall plant supervisors.

Factory Overhead

In a process cost system, factory overhead includes all those manufacturing costs that are not easily traced to a specific department. These costs may be incurred for the benefit of all manufacturing departments and must be allocated to the departments on some reasonable basis. Like in job order cost systems, factory overhead costs are estimated prior to the beginning of the period and are expressed as a percentage of estimated total direct labor costs. Then, factory overhead is assigned to the departments by applying this predetermined overhead application rate to the actual direct labor cost incurred by each department.

■ Equivalent Finished Units

A basic objective of a process cost system is the determination of unit processing costs for direct materials, direct labor, and overhead in each processing department. This requires that (1) materials, labor, and overhead costs be accumulated for each department for a cost period of, say, a month; (2) a record be kept of the number of units processed in each department during the period; and then (3) costs be divided by units processed to determine unit costs. However, it should be observed that when a department begins and ends a cost period with partially processed units of product, the units completed in the department are not an accurate measure of the department's total production. When the production of the period includes completing units that were partially finished at the beginning of the period and also includes working on units that remain partially finished at the end of the period, the following question arises: How many units did the department produce during the period? In other words, how many units would have been produced if all activity in the department had been concentrated on units that were started this period and finished this period? The answer is the number of **equivalent finished units produced** by the department during the period. Thus, when a department's beginning and ending inventories include partially finished units, the department's production for the period must be measured in terms of **equivalent finished units produced.** Unit costs are then determined by dividing total costs by the number of equivalent finished units produced.

The idea of an equivalent finished unit is based on the idea that it takes the same amount of direct labor, for instance, to one-half finish each of two units of product as it takes to fully complete one, or it takes the same amount of labor to one-third finish each of three units as to complete one. Also, since a department may add direct materials to production at a different rate than it adds labor and overhead, separate measures of production are often required for direct materials and for direct labor and overhead. For example, a department may have added enough materials to produce 1,000 equivalent finished units, and during the same period, the department may have added enough labor and overhead to produce 900 equivalent finished units. The concept of equivalent finished units produced and the related calculations are discussed further in the Delta Processing Company illustration that follows.

Process Cost Accounting Illustrated

The process cost system of Delta Processing Company, a company manufacturing a nonprescription medicine called Noxall, is used to illustrate process cost accounting.

The procedure for manufacturing Noxall is as follows: Material A is finely ground in Delta Processing Company's grinding department. Then, it is transferred to the mixing department where Material B is added, and the two materials are thoroughly mixed. The mixing process results in the finished product, Noxall, which is transferred on completion to finished goods. All the Material A placed in process in the grinding department is placed in process at the beginning of the grinding process, but the Material B added in the mixing department is added evenly throughout its process. In other words, a product one-third mixed in the latter department has received one third of its Material B and a product three-fourths mixed has received three fourths. Direct labor and overhead are applied evenly throughout each department's process.

At the end of the April cost period, entries were made to charge direct materials, direct labor, and factory overhead to the departments. After those entries were posted, the company's two goods in process accounts appeared as follows:

Goods in Process, Grinding Department

Date		Explanation	Debit	Credit	Balance
Apr.	1	Beginning inventory			4,250
	30	Direct materials	9,900		14,150
	30	Direct labor	5,700		19,850
	30	Overhead	4,275		24,125

Goods in Process, Mixing Department

Date		Explanation	Debit	Credit	Balance
Apr.	1	Beginning inventory			3,785
	30	Direct materials	2,040		5,825
	30	Direct labor	4,080		9,905
	30	Overhead	1,020		10,925

The production reports prepared by the company's two department managers give the following information about inventories and goods started and finished in each department during the month:

	Grinding Department	Mixing Department
Units in the beginning inventories of goods in process	30,000	16,000
April 1 stage of completion of the beginning inventories of goods in process	⅓	¼
Units started in process and finished during period	70,000	85,000
Total units finished and transferred to next department or to finished goods	100,000	101,000
Units in the ending inventories of goods in process	20,000	15,000
Stage of completion of ending inventories of goods in process . . .	¼	⅓

Process Cost Summary

After receiving the production reports, the company's cost accountant prepared a process cost summary, Illustration 22-9, for the grinding department. A process cost summary is a report unique to a processing company. A separate report is prepared for each processing department and shows (1) the costs charged to the department, (2) the department's equivalent unit processing costs, and (3) the assignment of costs to the department's goods in process inventories and its goods started and finished.

Costs Charged to the Department   Observe in Illustration 22-9 that a process cost summary has three sections. In the first, headed Costs Charged to the Department, the costs charged to the department are summarized. Information for this section comes from the department's Goods in Process account. Compare the first section of Illustration 22-9 with the Goods in Process account of the grinding department shown on page 799.

Equivalent Unit Processing Costs   The second section of a process cost summary shows the calculation of equivalent unit processing costs. In this section, information concerning the units involved and fractional units applicable to the inventories comes from the production report prepared by the department manager. Information about the total costs of direct materials, direct labor, and overhead comes from the first section of the summary.

In the second section of Illustration 22-9, **note that there are two separate calculations of equivalent units produced.** Two calculations are required because direct labor and overhead are not applied to production at the same rate as direct materials are entered into production. As previously stated, all direct materials are added at the beginning of this department's process, and direct labor is applied evenly throughout the process. Hence, overhead also is applied evenly throughout the process. Consequently, the number of equivalent units produced for direct materials is not the same as the number of equivalent units produced for direct labor and overhead.

Observe in the calculation of equivalent finished units produced for direct materials that the beginning-of-month inventory is assigned no additional direct materials. In the grinding department, all materials are entered into production at the beginning of the process. The 30,000 beginning inventory units were begun during March and were one-third completed at the beginning of April. Consequently, these units received all their direct materials during March when their processing was first begun.

Illustration 22-9

Delta Processing Company
Process Cost Summary, Grinding Department
For Month Ended April 30, 198A

COSTS CHARGED TO THE DEPARTMENT:

Direct materials requisitioned.	$ 9,900
Direct labor charged	5,700
Overhead costs incurred (predetermined overhead rate is 75% of direct labor) . . .	4,275
Total processing costs	$19,875
Goods in process at the beginning of the month	4,250
Total costs to be accounted for.	$24,125

1 (left margin marker)

EQUIVALENT UNIT PROCESSING COSTS:

	Units Involved	Fraction of a Unit Added	Equivalent Units Added
Direct materials:			
Beginning inventory	30,000	–0–	–0–
Units started and finished	70,000	One	70,000
Ending inventory.	20,000	One	20,000
			90,000

2 (left margin marker)

Equivalent unit processing cost for direct materials: $9,900 ÷ 90,000 = $0.11

	Units Involved	Fraction of a Unit Added	Equivalent Units Added
Direct labor and overhead:			
Beginning inventory	30,000	⅔	20,000
Units started and finished	70,000	One	70,000
Ending inventory.	20,000	¼	5,000
			95,000

Equivalent unit processing cost for direct labor: $5,700 ÷ 95,000 = $0.06
Equivalent unit processing cost for overhead: $4,275 ÷ 95,000 = $0.045

ASSIGNMENT OF COSTS TO THE WORK OF THE DEPARTMENT:

Goods in process, one-third processed at the beginning of April:

Costs charged to the beginning inventory of goods in process during previous month	$4,250	
Direct materials added (all added during March).	–0–	
Direct labor applied (20,000 × $0.06)	1,200	
Overhead applied (20,000 × $0.045)	900	
Cost to process.		$ 6,350

3 (left margin marker)

Goods started and finished in the department during April:

Direct materials added (70,000 × $0.11)	$7,700	
Direct labor applied (70,000 × $0.06)	4,200	
Overhead applied (70,000 × $0.045)	3,150	
Cost to process.		15,050

Total cost of the goods processed in the department and transferred to the mixing department (100,000 units at $0.214 each)*	$21,400

Goods in process, one-fourth processed at the end of April:

Direct materials added (20,000 × $0.11)	$2,200	
Direct labor applied (5,000 × $0.06).	300	
Overhead applied (5,000 × $0.045)	225	
Cost to one-fourth process		2,725
Total costs accounted for		$24,125

* Note that the $0.214 is an average unit cost based on all 100,000 units finished. Other alternatives such as FIFO and LIFO are deferred to a more advanced course.

Note also how the $9,900 cost of the materials charged to the department in April is divided by 90,000 equivalent units produced to arrive at an $0.11 per equivalent unit cost for direct materials consumed in this department.

Now move on to the calculation of equivalent finished units for direct labor and overhead and note that the beginning inventory units were each assigned two thirds of a unit of direct labor and overhead. If these units were one-third completed on April 1, then two thirds of the work done on these units was done in April. Study this carefully. Do not make the common mistake of assigning only an additional one-third unit of direct labor and overhead when two thirds is required.

Before going further, observe that the essence of the equivalent units calculation for direct labor and overhead is that to do two thirds of the work on 30,000 units, all the work on 70,000 units, and one fourth the work on 20,000 units is the equivalent of completing all the work on 95,000 units. Consequently, the $5,700 of direct labor cost and $4,275 of overhead cost charged to the department are each divided by 95,000 to determine equivalent unit costs for direct labor and overhead.

Assignment of Costs to the Work of the Department When a department begins and ends a cost period with partially processed units of product, it is necessary to allocate the department's costs among the units that were in process in the department at the beginning of the period, the units started and finished during the period, and the ending inventory units. This division is necessary to determine the cost of the units completed in the department during the period; and the division and assignment of costs are shown in the third section of the process cost summary.

Notice in the third section of Illustration 22-9 how costs are assigned to the beginning inventory. The first amount assigned is the $4,250 beginning inventory costs. This amount represents the direct materials, direct labor, and overhead costs used to one-third complete the inventory during March, the previous cost period. Normally, the second charge to a beginning inventory is for additional direct materials assigned to it. However, in the grinding department no additional materials costs are assigned the beginning inventory because these units received all of their materials when their processing was first begun during the previous month. The second charge to the beginning inventory is for direct labor. The $1,200 portion of applicable labor costs is calculated by multiplying the number of equivalent finished units for labor used to complete the beginning inventory by the cost of an equivalent finished unit for labor (20,000 equivalent finished units at $0.06 each). The third charge to the beginning inventory is for overhead. The applicable $900 portion is determined by multiplying the equivalent finished units for labor or overhead used to complete the beginning inventory by the cost of an equivalent finished unit for overhead (20,000 × $0.045).

After costs are assigned to the beginning inventory, the procedures used in their assignment are repeated for the units started and finished. Then, the cost of the units completed and transferred to finished goods, in this case the cost of the 30,000 beginning inventory units plus the cost of the 70,000 units started and finished, is determined by adding the costs assigned to the two groups. In this situation, the total is $21,400 or $0.214 per unit ($21,400 ÷ 100,000 units = $0.214 per unit).

Before proceeding further, notice in the second section of the grinding department's process cost summary that the equivalent finished unit cost for direct materials is $0.11, for direct labor is $0.06, and for overhead is $0.045, a total of $0.215. Notice, however, in the third section of the summary that the unit cost of the 100,000 units finished and transferred is $0.214, which is less than $0.215. It is less because costs were less in the department during the previous month and the 30,000 beginning units were one-third processed at these lower costs.

Transferring Costs from One Department to the Next

A process cost summary is completed by assigning costs to the ending inventory. After the grinding department's process cost summary was completed, the accountant prepared the following entry to transfer from the grinding department to the mixing department the cost of the 100,000 units processed in the department and transferred during April. Information for the entry as to the cost of the units transferred was taken from the third section of Illustration 22-9.

Apr.	30	Goods in Process, Mixing Department	21,400.00	
		Goods in Process, Grinding Department		21,400.00
		To transfer the cost of the 100,000 units of product transferred to the mixing department.		

Posting this entry had the effect on the accounts shown in Illustration 22-10. Observe that the effect is one of transferring and advancing costs from one department to the next just as the product is physically transferred and advanced in the manufacturing procedure.

Illustration 22-10

Goods in Process, Grinding Department

Date		Explanation	Debit	Credit	Balance
Apr.	1	Beginning inventory			4,250
	30	Direct materials	9,900		14,150
	30	Direct labor	5,700		19,850
	30	Overhead	4,275		24,125
	30	Units to mixing department		21,400	2,725

Goods in Process, Mixing Department

Date		Explanation	Debit	Credit	Balance
Apr.	1	Beginning inventory			3,785
	30	Direct materials	2,040		5,825
	30	Direct labor	4,080		9,905
	30	Overhead	1,020		10,925
	30	Units from grinding department	21,400		32,325

Process Cost Summary—Mixing Department

After posting the entry transferring to the mixing department the grinding department costs of the units transferred, the cost accountant prepared a process cost summary for the mixing department. Information required in its preparation was taken from the mixing department's goods in process account and production report. This summary appeared as in Illustration 22-11.

Two points in Illustration 22-11 require special attention. The first is the calculation of equivalent finished units produced. Since the direct materials, direct labor, and overhead added in the mixing department are all added evenly throughout the process of this department, only a single equivalent unit calculation is required. This differs from the grinding department, the previous department, where two equivalent unit calculations were required. Two were required because direct materials were not placed in process at the same stage in the processing procedure as were direct labor and overhead.

The second point needing special attention in the mixing department cost summary is the method of handling the grinding department costs transferred to this department. During April, 100,000 units of product, with accumulated grinding department costs of $21,400, were transferred to the mixing department. Of these 100,000 units, 85,000 were started in process in the department, finished, and transferred to finished goods. The remaining 15,000 were still in process in the department at the end of the cost period.

Notice in the first section of Illustration 22-11 how the $21,400 of grinding department costs transferred to the mixing department are added to the other costs charged to the department. Compare the information in this first section with the mixing department's Goods in Process account as it is shown on page 799 and again in Illustration 22-10.

Notice again in the third section of the mixing department's process cost summary how the $21,400 of grinding department costs are apportioned between the 85,000 units started and finished and the 15,000 units still in process in the department. The 16,000 beginning goods in process units received none of this $21,400 charge because they were transferred from the grinding department during the previous month. Their grinding department costs are included in the $3,785 beginning inventory costs.

The third section of the mixing department's process cost summary shows that 101,000 units of product (16,000 beginning inventory units plus 85,000 started and finished) with accumulated costs of $28,765 were completed in the department during April and transferred to finished goods. The cost accountant used the entry below to transfer the accumulated cost of these 101,000 units from the mixing department's goods in process account to the Finished Goods account. Posting the entry had the effect shown in Illustration 22-12.

Apr.	30	Finished Goods.	28,765.00	
		Goods in Process, Mixing Department . .		28,765.00
		To transfer the accumulated grinding department and mixing department costs of the 101,000 units transferred to Finished Goods.		

Illustration 22-11

Delta Processing Company
Process Cost Summary, Mixing Department
For Month Ended April 30, 198A

COSTS CHARGED TO THE DEPARTMENT:

Direct materials requisitioned	$ 2,040
Direct labor charged.	4,080
Overhead costs incurred (predetermined overhead rate is 25% of direct labor).	1,020
Total processing costs	$ 7,140
Goods in process at the beginning of the month	3,785
Cost transferred from the grinding department (100,000 units at $0.214 each)	21,400
Total costs to be accounted for	$32,325

EQUIVALENT UNIT PROCESSING COSTS:

	Units Involved	Fraction of a Unit Added	Equivalent Units Added
Direct materials, direct labor, and overhead:			
Beginning inventory.	16,000	¾	12,000
Units started and finished	85,000	One	85,000
Ending inventory	15,000	⅓	5,000
Total equivalent units			102,000

Equivalent unit processing cost for direct materials: $2,040 ÷ 102,000 = $0.02
Equivalent unit processing cost for direct labor: $4,080 ÷ 102,000 = $0.04
Equivalent unit processing cost for overhead: $1,020 ÷ 102,000 = $0.01

ASSIGNMENT OF COSTS TO THE WORK OF THE DEPARTMENT:

Goods in process, one-fourth completed at the beginning of April:

Costs charged to the beginning inventory of goods in process during previous month	$ 3,785	
Direct materials added (12,000 × $0.02).	240	
Direct labor applied (12,000 × $0.04)	480	
Overhead applied (12,000 × $0.01)	120	
Cost to process.		$ 4,625

Goods started and finished in the department during April:

Costs in the grinding department (85,000 × $0.214)	$18,190	
Direct materials added (85,000 × $0.02)	1,700	
Direct labor applied (85,000 × $0.04)	3,400	
Overhead applied (85,000 × $0.01)	850	
Cost to process.		24,140
Total accumulated costs of goods transferred to finished goods (101,000 units at $0.2848)		$28,765

Goods in process, one-third processed at the end of April:

Costs in the grinding department (15,000 × $0.214)	$ 3,210	
Direct materials added (5,000 × $0.02)	100	
Direct labor applied (5,000 × $0.04).	200	
Overhead applied (5,000 × $0.01)	50	
Cost to one-third process		3,560
Total costs accounted for		$32,325

Illustration 22-12

Goods in Process, Mixing Department

Date		Explanation	Debit	Credit	Balance
Apr.	1	Beginning inventory			3,785
	30	Direct materials	2,040		5,825
	30	Direct labor	4,080		9,905
	30	Overhead	1,020		10,925
	30	Units from grinding department	21,400		32,325
	30	Units to finished goods		28,765	3,560

Finished Goods

Date		Explanation	Debit	Credit	Balance
Apr.	30	Units from mixing department	28,765		28,765

☐   **Glossary**

Cost accounting system an accounting system based on perpetual inventory records that is designed to emphasize the determination of unit costs and the control of costs.

Equivalent finished units a measure of production with respect to direct materials or direct labor (and overhead), expressed as the number of units that could have been manufactured from start to finish during a period given the amount of direct materials or direct labor (and overhead) used during the period.

Job a special production order of a unique product, often manufactured especially for and to the specifications of a customer.

Job Cost Ledger a subsidiary ledger to the Goods in Process account in which are kept the job cost sheets of unfinished jobs.

Job cost sheet a record of the costs incurred on a single job.

Job lot a job that consists of a quantity of identical items.

Job order cost system a system of accounting for manufacturing costs in which costs are assembled in terms of jobs or job lots.

Labor time ticket a record of how an employee's time at work was used; the record serves as the basis for charging jobs and overhead accounts for the employee's wages.

Materials consumption report a document, kept by the materials storeroom keeper as a substitute for materials requisitions, the purpose of which is to show the raw materials issued to each department during a cost period and to provide the information necessary to prepare journal entries charging materials costs to the appropriate accounts.

Materials requisition a document, given to the materials storeroom keeper in exchange for raw materials, that has the purpose of enhancing control over materials and providing a means of charging the cost of raw materials to jobs, or processing departments, or factory overhead; the document identifies the materials needed for a specific job, processing department, or purpose and the account to which the materials cost should be charged.

Overapplied overhead the amount by which overhead applied on the basis of a predetermined overhead application rate exceeds overhead actually incurred.

Predetermined overhead application rate a rate that is used to charge overhead cost to production; calculated by relating estimated overhead cost for a period to another variable such as estimated direct labor cost.

Process cost system a system of accounting for manufacturing costs in which costs are assembled in terms of processes or steps in manufacturing a product.

Underapplied overhead the amount by which actual overhead incurred exceeds the overhead applied to production, based on a predetermined application rate and evidenced by a debit balance in the Factory Overhead account at the end of the period.

☐ **Questions for Class Discussion**

1. What are the two primary types of cost accounting systems? Indicate which of the two would best fit the needs of a manufacturer who (*a*) produces special-purpose machines designed to fit the particular needs

of each customer, (b) produces electric generators in lots of 10, and (c) manufactures copper tubing.

2. What is the difference between a job and a job lot?

3. What accounts do raw materials costs flow through in a job order cost system?

4. Why are materials requisitions used?

5. A manufacturing company produces a single product by processing it first through a mixing department and next through a cutting department. What accounts do direct labor costs flow through in this company's process cost system?

6. What purpose is served by a job cost sheet?

7. What use is made of labor time tickets?

8. In a job order cost system, the Raw Materials account and the Goods in Process account each serve as a controlling account for a subsidiary ledger. What subsidiary ledgers do these accounts control?

9. How is the inventory of goods in process determined in a general accounting system like that described in Chapter 21? How may this inventory be determined in a job cost system?

10. What is a job cost sheet?

11. What is the name of the ledger containing the job cost sheets of the unfinished jobs in process? What account controls this ledger?

12. What business papers provide the information that is used to make the job cost sheet entries for (a) direct materials and (b) direct labor?

13. Refer to the job cost sheet of Illustration 22-3. How was the amount of overhead costs charged to this job determined?

14. How is a predetermined overhead application rate established? Why is such a predetermined rate used to charge overhead to jobs?

15. Why does a company using a job cost system normally have either overapplied or underapplied overhead at the end of each accounting period?

16. At the end of a cost period, the Overhead Costs controlling account has a debit balance. Does this represent overapplied or underapplied overhead?

17. What are the basic differences in the products and in the manufacturing procedures of a company to which a job cost system is applicable as opposed to a company to which a process cost system is applicable?

18. What is meant by the equivalent finished units produced with respect to direct labor?

19. What is the assumption on which the idea of an equivalent finished unit of, for instance, direct materials is based?

20. What is the production of a department measured in equivalent finished units if it began an accounting period with 8,000 units of product that were one-fourth completed at the beginning of the period, started and finished 50,000 units during the period, and ended the period with 6,000 units that were one-third processed at the period end?

21. The process cost summary of a department commonly has three sections. What is shown in each section?

| □ | **Class Exercises** | **Exercise 22-1** |

During the month of May, a company that uses a job cost system purchased raw materials for $12,000 cash, used $300 of raw materials as factory supplies, and entered $10,400 of raw materials into production as direct materials. Factory payroll incurred for the month (paid in cash) amounted to $15,000, of which $1,400 was classified as indirect labor. Prepare general journal entries to record these activities.

Exercise 22-2

A company that uses a job cost system provides the following information:

	May 31	June 30	During June
Raw materials inventory	$2,000	$8,000	
Goods in process	4,000	5,000	
Finished goods	8,000	7,000	
Raw materials purchased			$16,000
Factory payroll costs incurred			14,700
Overhead incurred (includes $500 of raw materials used as supplies and $700 of indirect labor)			8,700
Cost of goods sold			?

The company's predetermined overhead application rate is 60% of direct labor. Set up T-accounts like those in Illustration 22-2. Show the June flows of manufacturing costs in the company by entering the above information in the T-accounts and drawing arrows similar to those in Illustration 22-2. Leave any underapplied or overapplied overhead in the Factory Overhead account.

Exercise 22-3

Part 1. During December 198A, Turner Corporation's cost accountant established the company's 198B overhead application rate based on direct labor cost. In setting the rate, the cost accountant estimated the company would incur $450,000 of overhead costs during 198B, and it would apply $562,500 of direct labor to the products that would be manufactured during 198B. Determine the rate.

Part 2. During March 198B, Turner Corporation of Part 1 began and completed Job 212. Determine the job's cost under the assumption that on its completion the job's cost sheet showed the following materials and labor charged to it:

		Job Cost Sheet						

Customer's Name _____Barney Corp._____   Job No. ___212___
Job Description ___2.5 Watt Power Supply_____

	Direct Materials		**Direct Labor**		**Overhead Costs Applied**		
Date	**Requisition Number**	**Amount**	**Time-Ticket Number**	**Amount**	**Date**	**Rate**	**Amount**
Mar. 2	1340	890.00	2116	650.00			
4	1367	1,880.00	2117	900.00			
9	1389	740.00	2122	1,500.00			

Exercise 22-4

At the end of March, the job cost sheets of a company had been assigned the following costs:

	Job 14	Job 15	Job 16
Direct materials	$2,600	$9,200	$5,500
Direct labor	3,400	7,800	6,000
Overhead	3,740	8,580	6,600

Job 14 was started in production during February and had direct materials of $1,200, direct labor of $500, and overhead of $550 assigned to the job at the end of February. Jobs 14 and 15 were finished during March and Job 16 will be finished during April. Answer the following questions: (a) Assuming no raw materials costs were assigned to overhead during March, what amount of raw materials were requisitioned during March? (b) How much direct labor was incurred during March? (c) What is the predetermined overhead application rate? (d) What amount of cost was transferred to finished goods during March?

Exercise 22-5

In December 198A, a cost accountant for Oyster Company established the following overhead application rate for applying overhead to the jobs that would be completed during 198B:

$$\frac{\text{Estimated overhead costs, \$399,000}}{\text{Estimated direct labor costs, \$570,000}} = 70\%$$

At the end of 198B, the company's accounting records showed that $408,000 of overhead costs had actually been incurred during 198B and $600,000 of direct labor, distributed as follows, had been applied to jobs during the year.

Direct labor on jobs completed and sold . . .	$510,000
Direct labor on jobs completed and in the finished goods inventory	60,000
Direct labor on jobs still in process	30,000
	$600,000

Required

1. Set up a Factory Overhead T-account and enter on the proper sides the amounts of overhead costs incurred and applied. State whether overhead was overapplied or underapplied during the year.
2. Give the entry to close the Factory Overhead account and allocate its balance between jobs sold, jobs finished but unsold, and jobs in process.

Exercise 22-6

Fields Company uses a job cost system in which overhead is charged to jobs on the basis of direct labor cost. At the end of a year, the company's Goods in Process account showed the following:

Goods in Process			
Direct materials	272,000	To finished goods	656,600
Direct labor	192,000		
Overhead	240,000		

Required

1. Determine the overhead application rate used by the company under the assumption that the direct labor and overhead costs actually incurred were the same as the amounts estimated.

2. Determine the cost of direct labor and the cost of overhead charged to the one job in process at year-end under the assumption it had $17,700 of materials charged to it.

Exercise 22-7

A company's product is manufactured by processing it first through Department A and then through Department B. Information about manufacturing operations during January is as follows:

	Dept. A	Dept. B
Direct materials requisitioned by	$18,000	$ 4,000
Direct labor charged to	15,000	22,000
Predetermined overhead application rate.	80%	80%
Cost of goods transferred in from Department A		34,000
Cost of goods transferred out of Department B		52,000
Cost of goods sold		49,000

Based on the cost flows diagramed in Illustration 22-8, prepare general journal entries to record the January cost flows shown above.

Exercise 22-8

During a cost period, a department finished and transferred 44,800 units of product to finished goods, of which 12,800 were in process in the department at the beginning of the cost period and 32,000 were begun and completed during the period. The 12,800 beginning inventory units were three-fourths completed when the period began. In addition to the 44,800 units completed, 9,600 more units were in process in the department, one-half completed when the period ended.

Required

Calculate the equivalent units of product completed in the department during the cost period.

Exercise 22-9

Assume the department of Exercise 22-8 had $28,000 of direct labor charged to it during the cost period of the exercise and that direct labor is applied in the process of the department evenly through the process.

Required

Calculate the cost of an equivalent unit of labor in the department and the portion of the department's $28,000 labor cost that should be assigned to each of its inventories and to the units started and finished.

Exercise 22-10

A department completed and transferred to finished goods 57,600 units of product during a cost period. Of these units, 14,400 were in process and were one-third completed at the beginning of the period, and 43,200 units were begun and completed during the period. In addition to the 57,600 units completed, 12,000 more units were in process in the department, three-fifths processed at the period end.

Required

Calculate the equivalent units for direct materials added to the product processed in the department during the period under each of the following unrelated assumptions: (*a*) All direct materials added to the product of the department are added when the department's process is first begun. (*b*) The direct materials added to the product of the department are added evenly throughout the department's process. (*c*) One half the direct materials added in the department is added when the department's process is first begun, and the other half is added when the process is three-fourths completed.

Problems

Problem 22-1

A cost accountant for Nolte Company estimated before a year began that the company would incur during the year the direct labor cost of 24 persons working 2,000 hours each at an average rate of $8 per hour. The accountant also estimated that the following overhead costs would be incurred during the year:

Indirect labor	$ 50,400
Superintendence	38,400
Rent of factory building	23,040
Factory utilities	15,360
Insurance expense	10,880
Depreciation of machinery	77,440
Machinery repairs	9,600
Supplies expense	4,800
Miscellaneous factory expenses	4,320
Total	$234,240

At the end of the year for which the estimates were made, the cost records showed the company had actually incurred $232,960 of overhead costs and had completed and sold five jobs that had direct labor costs as follows: Job 406, $81,300; Job 407, $74,200; Job 408, $69,500; Job 409, $72,900; and Job 410, $79,700. In addition, Job 411 was in process at the period end and had been charged $8,000 of direct labor plus its share of overhead costs.

Required

   Under the assumption the company used a predetermined overhead application rate based on the foregoing overhead and direct labor estimates, determine: (*a*) the predetermined application rate used, (*b*) the total overhead applied to jobs during the year, and (*c*) the over- or underapplied overhead at year-end. (*d*) Under the further assumption that the company considered the amount of its over- or underapplied overhead to be immaterial, give the entry to close the Factory Overhead account.

Problem 22-2

A company completed the following transactions and activities, among others, during a cost period:

a. Purchased raw materials on account, $40,000.
b. Paid factory wages, $31,000.
c. Paid miscellaneous factory overhead costs, $2,000.
d. Materials requisitions were used during the cost period to charge direct materials to jobs. The requisitions were then accumulated until the end of the cost period at which time they were totaled and recorded with a general journal entry. (Instructions for this entry are given in Item *[j].*) An abstract of the requisitions showed the following direct materials charged to jobs. (Charge the direct materials to the jobs by making entries directly in the job T-accounts in the subsidiary Job Cost Ledger.)

Job 12	$ 6,500
Job 13	3,250
Job 14	7,000
Job 15	7,500
Job 16	1,500
Total	$25,750

e. Labor time tickets were used to charge jobs with direct labor. The tickets were then accumulated until the end of the cost period at which time they were totaled and recorded with a general journal entry. (Instructions for the entry are given in Item *k.*) An abstract of the tickets showed the following direct labor charged to jobs. (Charge the direct labor to the jobs by making entries directly in the job T-accounts in the Job Cost Ledger.)

Job 12	$ 6,000
Job 13	3,500
Job 14	6,500
Job 15	7,000
Job 16	1,000
Total	$24,000

f. Jobs 12, 14, and 15 were completed and transferred to finished goods. A predetermined overhead application rate, 150% of direct labor cost, was used to apply overhead to each job upon its completion. (Enter the overhead in the job T-accounts; mark the jobs "completed"; and make a general entry to transfer their costs to the Finished Goods account.)

g. Jobs 12 and 14 were sold on account for a total of $60,000.

h. At the end of the cost period, overhead was charged to the jobs in process at the rate of 150% of direct labor cost. (Enter the overhead in the job T-accounts.)

i. At the end of the cost period, a general journal entry was made to record: depreciation, factory building, $5,750; depreciation, machinery, $10,250; expired factory insurance, $1,500; and accrued factory taxes payable, $3,000.

j. Separated the materials requisitions into direct materials requisitions and indirect materials requisitions, totaled each kind, and made a general journal entry to record them. The requisition totals were:

Direct materials.	$25,750
Indirect materials	5,000
Total	$30,750

k. Separated the labor time tickets into direct labor time tickets and indirect labor time tickets, totaled each kind, and made a general journal entry to record them. The time ticket totals were:

Direct labor.	$24,000
Indirect labor	7,750
Total.	$31,750

l. Determined the total overhead assigned to all jobs and made a general journal entry to record the assignment.

Required

1. Open the following general ledger T-accounts: Raw Materials, Goods in Process, Finished Goods, Factory Payroll, Factory Overhead, and Cost of Goods Sold.

2. Open an additional T-account for each of the five jobs. Assume that each job's T-account is a job cost sheet in a subsidiary Job Cost Ledger.

3. Prepare general journal entries to record the applicable information of Items *a, b, c, f, g, i, j, k,* and *l.* Post the entry portions that affect the general ledger accounts opened.

4. Enter the applicable information of Items *d, e, f,* and *h* directly in the T-accounts that represent job cost sheets.

5. Present statistics to prove the balances of the Goods in Process and Finished Goods accounts.

6. List the general ledger accounts and describe what is represented by the balance of each.

Problem 22-3

If the working papers that accompany this text are not being used, omit this problem.

The Swea City Company manufactures to the special order of its customers a machine called a stargazer. On January 1, the company had an $8,920 raw materials inventory but no inventories of goods in process and finished goods. However, on that date it began Job 10, a stargazer for Looking Company, and Job 12, for Findit Company; and during the January cost period, it completed the following activities and transactions:

a. Recorded invoices for the purchase of raw materials on credit. The invoices and receiving reports carried this information:

Receiving Report No. 1, Material A, 50 units at $176 each.
Receiving Report No. 2, Material B, 60 units at $100 each.

(Record the invoices with a single general journal entry and post to the general ledger T-accounts, using the transaction letter to identify the amounts in the accounts. Enter the receiving report information on the proper raw materials ledger cards.)

b. Raw materials were requisitioned as follows:

Requisition No. 1, for Job 10, 25 units of Material A.
Requisition No. 2, for Job 10, 24 units of Material B.
Requisition No. 3, for Job 12, 20 units of Material A.
Requisition No. 4, for Job 12, 20 units of Material B.
Requisition No. 5, for 2 units of machinery lubricant.

(Enter the requisition amounts for direct materials on the raw materials ledger cards and on the job cost sheets. Enter the indirect materials amount on the proper raw materials ledger card and debit it to the Indirect Materials account in the subsidiary Factory Overhead Ledger. Assume the requisitions are accumulated until the end of the month and will be recorded with a general journal entry. Instructions for this entry follow in the problem.)

c. Received the following labor time tickets from the timekeeping department:

Time tickets Nos. 1 through 60 for direct labor on Job 10, $4,000.
Time tickets Nos. 61 through 100 for direct labor on Job 12, $3,200.
Time tickets Nos. 101 through 120 for machinery repairs, $1,500.

(Charge the direct labor time tickets to the proper jobs and charge the indirect labor time tickets to the Indirect Labor account in the subsidiary Factory Overhead Ledger. Assume the time tickets are accumulated until the end of the month for recording with a general journal entry.)

d. Made the following cash disbursements during the month:

Paid the month's factory payroll, $8,400.
Paid for miscellaneous overhead items totaling $4,000.

(Record the payments with general journal entries and post to the general ledger accounts. Enter the charge for miscellaneous overhead items in the subsidiary Factory Overhead Ledger.)

e. Finished Job 10 and transferred it to the finished goods warehouse.

(The company charges overhead to each job by means of a predetermined overhead application rate based on direct labor costs. The rate is 80%. (1) Enter the overhead charge on the cost sheet of Job 10. (2) Complete the cost summary section of the cost sheet. (3) Mark "Finished" on the cost sheet. (4) Prepare and post a general journal entry to record the job's completion and transfer to finished goods.)

f. Prepared and posted a general journal entry to record both the cost of goods sold and the sale of Job 10 to Looking Company, sale price $20,000.

g. At the end of the cost period, charged overhead to Job 12 based on the amount of direct labor applied to the job thus far. *(Enter the applicable amount of overhead on the job's cost sheet.)*

h. Totaled the requisitions for direct materials, totaled the requisitions for indirect materials, and made and posted a general journal entry to record them.

i. Totaled the direct labor time tickets, totaled the indirect labor time tickets, and made and posted a general journal entry to record them.

j. Determined the amount of overhead applied to jobs and made and posted a general journal entry to record it.

Required

1. Record the transactions as instructed in the narrative.
2. Complete the statements in the book of working papers by filling in the blanks.

Problem 22-4

In the mixing department of a manufacturing company, direct labor is added to the department's product evenly throughout its processing. During a cost period, 112,500 units of product were finished in this department and transferred to finished goods. Of these 112,500 units, 33,750 were in process at the beginning of the period and 78,750 were begun and completed during the period. The 33,750 beginning goods in process units were one-fifth completed when the period began. In addition to the foregoing units, 20,250 additional units were in process and were two-thirds completed at the period end.

Required

Under the assumption that $102,555 of direct labor was charged to the mixing department during the period, determine *(a)* the equivalent finished units produced with respect to direct labor applied to the department's product, *(b)* the cost of an equivalent finished unit for labor, and *(c)* the portion of the $102,555 that should be charged to the beginning inventory, the units started and finished, and the ending inventory.

Problem 22-5

The product of Tortolla Manufacturing Company is produced on a continuous basis in a single processing department in which direct materials, direct labor, and overhead are added to the product evenly throughout the manufacturing process.

At the end of the July 198A cost period, after the direct materials, direct labor, and overhead costs were charged to the Goods in Process account of the single processing department, the account appeared as follows:

Goods in Process		
July 1	Balance	13,620
31	Direct materials	53,250
31	Direct labor	119,280
31	Overhead	89,460
		275,610

During the cost period, the company finished and transferred to finished goods 54,000 units of the product, of which 6,750 were in process at the beginning of the period and 47,250 were begun and finished during the period. The 6,750 units that were in process were one-third processed when the period began. In addition to the foregoing units, 6,000 additional units were in process and were one-fourth completed at the end of the cost period.

Required

1. Prepare a process cost summary for the department.
2. Draft the general journal entry to transfer to Finished Goods the cost of the product finished in the department during the month.

Problem 22-6

Lowtech Production Company manufactures a simple product on a continuous basis in one department. All direct materials are added in the manufacturing process of this product when the process is first begun. Direct labor and overhead are added evenly throughout the process.

During the current June cost period, the company completed and transferred to finished goods 64,500 units of the product. These consisted of 7,500 units that were in process at the beginning of the period and 57,000 units begun and finished during the period. The 7,500 beginning goods in process units were complete as to direct materials and four-fifths complete as to direct labor and overhead when the period began. In addition to the foregoing units, 9,000 additional units were in process at the end of the period, complete as to direct materials and one-half complete as to direct labor and overhead.

Since the company has only one processing department, it has only one Goods in Process account. At the end of the period, after entries recording direct material, direct labor, and overhead had been posted, the account appeared as follows:

Goods in Process		
June 1 Balance	12,200	
30 Direct materials	62,700	
30 Direct labor	65,520	
30 Overhead	81,900	
	222,320	

Required

Prepare a process cost summary and the entry to transfer to Finished Goods the cost of the product completed in the department during June.

□ **Alternate Problems**   **Problem 22-1A**

Late in 198A, the cost accountant for Wimberly Company established the 198B overhead application rate by estimating that the company would assign 15 persons to direct labor tasks during 198B and that each person would work 2,000 hours at $9 per hour during the year. At the same time the accountant estimated that the company would incur the following amounts of overhead costs during 198B:

Indirect labor	$ 90,000
Factory building rent	54,000
Depreciation expense, machinery	67,500
Machinery repairs expense	13,500
Factory utilities	27,000
Factory supplies expense	4,500
Total.	$256,500

At the end of 198B, the accounting records showed the company had actually incurred $263,520 of overhead costs during the year while completing four jobs and beginning the fifth. The completed jobs were assigned overhead on completion, and the in-process job was assigned overhead at year-end. The jobs had the following direct labor costs:

Job No. 71 (sold and delivered)	$ 57,700
Job No. 72 (sold and delivered)	58,500
Job No. 73 (sold and delivered)	63,900
Job No. 74 (in finished goods inventory)	63,000
Job No. 75 (in process, unfinished)	31,400
Total	$274,500

Required

1. Determine the overhead application rate established by the cost accountant under the assumption it was based on direct labor cost.
2. Determine the total overhead applied to jobs during the year and the amount of over- or underapplied overhead at year-end.
3. Give the entry to dispose of the over- or underapplied overhead by prorating it between goods in process, finished goods inventory, and cost of goods sold.

Problem 22-2A

During its first cost period, King Company completed the following activities and transactions:

a. Purchased raw materials on account, $33,000.
b. Paid factory wages, $28,200.
c. Paid miscellaneous factory overhead costs, $4,500.
d. Materials requisitions were used during the cost period to charge direct materials to jobs. The requisitions were accumulated until the end of the cost period and then were totaled and recorded with a general journal entry. (Instructions for the entry are given in Item *j*.) An abstract of the requisitions showed the following direct materials charged to jobs. (Charge the materials to the jobs by making entries directly in the job T-accounts in the subsidiary Job Cost Ledger.)

Job 51	$ 6,000
Job 52	3,150
Job 53	5,850
Job 54	6,450
Job 55	1,200
Total	$22,650

e. Labor time tickets were used to charge jobs with direct labor. The tickets were accumulated until the end of the cost period and then were totaled and recorded with a general journal entry. (Instructions for the entry are given in Item *k.*) An abstract of the tickets showed the following direct labor charged to jobs. (Charge the direct labor to the jobs by making entries directly in the job T-accounts in the Job Cost Ledger.)

Job 51	$ 5,700
Job 52	3,300
Job 53	6,000
Job 54	5,400
Job 55	600
Total	$21,000

f. Jobs 51, 53, and 54 were completed and transferred to finished goods. A predetermined overhead application rate, 200% of direct labor cost, was used to apply overhead to each job upon its completion. (Enter the overhead in the job T-accounts; mark the jobs "completed"; and make a general journal entry to transfer their costs to the Finished Goods account.)

g. Jobs 51 and 54 were sold on account for a total of $62,400.

h. At the end of the cost period, charged overhead to the jobs in process, using the 200% of direct labor cost application rate. (Enter the overhead in the job T-accounts.)

i. Made a general journal entry at the end of the cost period to record depreciation on the factory building, $9,000; machinery depreciation, $10,050; expired factory insurance, $1,800; and accrued factory taxes payable, $2,800.

j. Separated the materials requisitions into direct materials requisitions and indirect materials requisitions, totaled each kind, and made a general journal entry to record them. The requisition totals were:

Direct materials	$22,650
Indirect materials	6,000
Total	$28,650

k. Separated the labor time tickets into direct labor time tickets and indirect labor time tickets, totaled each kind, and made a general journal entry to record them. The time ticket totals were:

Direct labor.	$21,000
Indirect labor	7,500
Total	$28,500

l. Determined the total overhead assigned to all jobs and made a general journal entry to record it.

Required

1. Open the following general ledger T-accounts: Raw Materials, Goods in Process, Finished Goods, Factory Payroll, Factory Overhead, and Cost of Goods Sold.

2. Open an additional T-account for each of the five jobs. Assume that each job's T-account is a job cost sheet in a subsidiary Job Cost Ledger.

3. Prepare general journal entries to record the applicable information of Items *a, b, c, f, g, i, j, k,* and *l.* Post the entry portions that affect the general ledger accounts opened.

4. Enter the applicable information of Items *d, e, f,* and *h* directly in the T-accounts that represent job cost sheets.

5. Present statistics to prove the balances of the Goods in Process and Finished Goods accounts.

6. List the general ledger accounts and describe what is represented by the balance of each.

Problem 22-3A

If the working papers that accompany this text are not being used, omit this problem.

The Waterloo Company manufactures to the special order of its customers a machine called a sifting tank. On January 1, the company had an $8,920 raw materials inventory but no inventories of goods in process and finished goods. However, on that date it began Job 10, a sifting tank for Looking Company, and Job 12, for Findit Company; and during the January cost period, it completed the following activities and transactions:

a. Recorded invoices for the purchase of raw materials on credit. The invoices and receiving reports carried this information:
   Receiving Report No. 5, Material A, 30 units at $176 each.
   Receiving Report No. 6, Material B, 36 units at $100 each.
   (Record the invoices with a single general journal entry and post to the general ledger T-accounts, using the transaction letter to identify the amounts in the accounts. Enter the receiving report information on the proper raw materials ledger cards.)

b. Raw materials were requisitioned as follows:
   Requisition No. 16, for Job 10, 15 units of Material A.
   Requisition No. 17, for Job 10, 14 units of Material B.
   Requisition No. 18, for Job 12, 12 units of Material A.
   Requisition No. 19, for Job 12, 10 units of Material B.
   Requisition No. 20, for 3 units of machinery lubricant.
   (Enter the requisition amounts for direct materials on the raw materials ledger cards and on the job cost sheets. Enter the indirect materials amount on the proper raw materials ledger card and debit it to the Indirect Materials account in the subsidiary Factory Overhead Ledger. Assume the requisitions are accumulated until the end of the month and will be recorded with a general journal entry. Instructions for this entry follow in the problem.)

c. Received the following labor time tickets from the timekeeping department:
   Time tickets Nos. 50 through 75 for direct labor on Job 10, $5,500.
   Time tickets Nos. 76 through 105 for direct labor on Job 12, $7,200.
   Time tickets Nos. 106 through 118 for machinery repairs, $1,200.
   (Charge the direct labor time tickets to the proper jobs and charge the indirect labor time tickets to the Indirect Labor account in the subsidiary Factory Overhead Ledger. Assume the time tickets are accumulated until the end of the month for recording with a general journal entry.)

d. Made the following cash disbursements during the month:

Paid the month's factory payroll, $11,900.

Paid for miscellaneous overhead items totaling $6,200.

(Record the payments with general journal entries and post to the general ledger accounts. Enter the charge for miscellaneous overhead items in the subsidiary Factory Overhead Ledger.)

e. Finished Job 10 and transferred it to the finished goods warehouse.

(The company charges overhead to each job by means of a predetermined overhead application rate based on direct labor costs. The rate is 70%. (1) Enter the overhead charge on the cost sheet of Job 10. (2) Complete the cost summary section of the cost sheet. (3) Mark "Finished" on the cost sheet. (4) Prepare and post a general journal entry to record the job's completion and transfer to finished goods.)

f. Prepared and posted a general journal entry to record both the cost of goods sold and the sale of Job 10 to Looking Company, sale price $32,000.

g. At the end of the cost period, charged overhead to Job 12 based on the amount of direct labor applied to the job thus far. *(Enter the applicable amount of overhead on the job's cost sheet.)*

h. Totaled the requisitions for direct materials, totaled the requisitions for indirect materials, and made and posted a general journal entry to record them.

i. Totaled the direct labor time tickets, totaled the indirect labor time tickets, and made and posted a general journal entry to record them.

j. Determined the amount of overhead applied to jobs and made and posted a general journal entry to record it.

Required

1. Record the transactions as instructed in the narrative.

2. Complete the statements in the book of working papers by filling in the blanks.

Problem 22-4A

The PAK Company is a one-department operation in which direct labor and overhead are added to the department's product evenly throughout the production process. In October, 52,500 units of product were transferred from the shop to finished goods inventory. Included in these 52,500 units were 20,000 units from the September 30 work in process inventory, at which time those units were one-fourth finished. In addition to the beginning inventory, 67,500 units were placed in process during October. On October 31, the units that remained in process were one-half complete. Total overhead costs incurred during October were $930,800.

Required

Determine *(a)* the equivalent finished units produced in October to be used in applying overhead costs to the product of the shop, *(b)* the overhead cost of an equivalent unit of production, and *(c)* the portion of October overhead cost that should be charged to completing the units in beginning inventory, to units started and finished during October, and to the ending inventory.

Problem 22-5A

Two operations, forming and finishing, are used in the manufacturing procedure of Florida Manufacturing Company. The procedure is begun in the forming department and completed in the finishing department.

At the beginning of the February cost period there were 6,250 units of product in the forming department that were three-fifths processed. These units were completed during the period and transferred to the finishing department. Also, the processing of 38,750 additional units was begun in the forming department during the period. Of these 38,750 units, 28,750 were finished and transferred to the finishing department. The remaining 10,000 units were in the department in a one-half processed state at the end of the period.

It is assumed that the direct materials, direct labor, and overhead applied in the forming department are applied evenly throughout the process of the department.

At the end of the cost period, after entries recording direct materials, direct labor, and overhead were posted, the company's Goods in Process, Forming Department account appeared as follows:

Goods in Process, Forming Department

Feb.	1	Balance	58,000
	28	Direct materials	185,600
	28	Direct labor	246,500
	28	Overhead	123,250
			613,350

Required

1. Prepare a process cost summary for the forming department.
2. Prepare the journal entry to transfer to the finishing department the cost of the goods completed in the forming department and transferred.

Problem 22-6A

The product of Albany Company is manufactured in one continuous process in which all direct materials are entered into production at the beginning of the process. Direct labor and overhead are applied evenly throughout the process.

Albany Company's Goods in Process account reflects the following charges during the month of November:

Beginning balance.	$ 38,400
Direct materials added to production	183,210
Direct labor charged to production.	137,560
Overhead charged to production	110,048

During November, the company completed the manufacture of 34,900 units of product. These included 5,700 units that had entered production the previous month, and on November 1 were complete as to direct materials and two-thirds complete as to direct labor and overhead. At the end of November, 10,200 units remained in process, completed as to direct materials and one-half complete as to direct labor and overhead.

Required

Prepare a process cost summary and the entry to transfer to Finished Goods the cost of the product completed during November.

Provocative Problems

Provocative Problem 22-1   The Barlow Corporation

The Barlow Corporation uses a job order cost system to account for manufacturing costs, and a number of its general ledger accounts with the January 1 balances and some January postings shown are shown below. The postings are incomplete. Commonly only the debit or credit of a journal entry appears in the accounts, with the offsetting debits and credits being omitted. Also, the amounts shown represent total postings for the month and no date appears. However, this additional information is available: (*a*) The company charges jobs with overhead on the basis of direct labor cost, using a 150% overhead application rate. (*b*) The $63,750 debit in the Factory Overhead account represents the sum of all overhead costs for January other than indirect materials and indirect labor. (*c*) The accrued factory payroll on January 31 was $11,250

Raw Materials			Factory Payroll			
Jan. 1 Bal. 41,250		45,000	71,250	Jan. 1 Bal.	7,500	
56,250						

Goods in Process			Cost of Goods Sold	
Jan. 1 Bal. 22,500		180,000		
Dir. mat. 37,500				
Dir. labor 60,000				

Finished Goods			Factory Overhead	
Jan. 1 Bal. 45,000		187,500	63,750	

Required

Copy the accounts on a sheet of paper, supply the missing debits and credits, and tie together the debits and credits of an entry with key letters. Answer these questions: (*a*) What was the January 31 balance of the Finished Goods account? (*b*) How many dollars of factory labor cost (direct plus indirect) were incurred during January? (*c*) What was the cost of the goods sold during January? (*d*) How much overhead was actually incurred during the month? (*e*) How much overhead was charged to jobs during the month? (*f*) Was overhead overapplied or underapplied during the month?

Provocative Problem 22-2   Pergamum Company

The production facility of the Pergamum Company was nearly destroyed on March 6, 198B, as a consequence of an explosion and fire in the plant. Assets lost in the blaze included all of the inventories. In addition, many of the accounting records were destroyed. In preparation for settlement with the insurance company, you are requested to estimate the amounts of raw materials, goods in process, and finished goods destroyed. Through your investigation, you determined that the company used a job order cost system, and you also obtained the following additional information:

a. The company's December 31, 198A, balance sheet showed the following inventory amounts: raw materials, $37,500; goods in process, $52,500; and finished goods, $60,000. The balance sheet also showed a $7,500 liability for accrued factory wages payable.

b. The overhead application rate used by the company was 70% of direct labor cost.

c. Goods costing $202,500 were sold and delivered to customers between January 1 and March 6, 198B.

d. Raw materials purchased between January 1 and March 6 amounted to $77,500, and $67,500 of direct and indirect materials were issued to the factory during the same period.

e. Factory wages totaling $87,500 were paid between January 1 and March 6, and there were $2,500 of accrued factory wages payable on the latter date.

f. The debits to the Factory Overhead account during the period before the fire totaled $52,500 of which $7,500 was for indirect materials and $12,500 was for indirect labor.

g. The cost of goods finished and transferred to finished goods inventory during the January 1 to March 6 period amounted to $190,000.

h. It was decided that the March 6 balance of the Overhead Costs account should be apportioned between goods in process, finished goods, and cost of goods sold. Between January 1 and March 6, the company had charged the following amounts of overhead to jobs: to jobs sold, $31,850; to jobs finished but unsold, $9,800; and to jobs still in process on March 6, $7,350.

Determine the March 6 inventories of raw materials, goods in process, and finished goods. (T-accounts may be helpful in organizing the data.)

Provocative Problem 22-3   Fence Company

The processing department of Fence Company began January 198A with 16,000 units in the goods in process inventory, each of which was 60% complete. During January, an additional 192,000 units were entered into the production process.

A total of 168,000 units were completed and transferred to finished goods. If January's equivalent finished units produced amounted to 169,600 units, how many units remained in process at the end of the month and what was their average stage of completion?

23 Accounting for the Segments and Departments of a Business; Responsibility Accounting

After studying Chapter 23, you should be able to:

1. Describe the segmental information disclosed in the financial reports of large companies having operations in several lines of business.

2. List the four basic issues faced by accountants in developing segmental information.

3. State the reasons for departmentalization of businesses.

4. Describe the types of expenses that should be allocated among departments, the bases for allocating such expenses, and the procedures involved in the allocation process.

5. Explain the differences between reports designed to measure the profitability of a department and reports that are used to evaluate the performance of a department manager.

6. Describe the problems associated with allocation of joint costs between departments.

7. Define or explain the words and phrases listed in the chapter Glossary.

In previous chapters, attention was focused on understanding financial statements and related accounting information for a **whole** business. This chapter shifts the attention to accounting for the "parts" or subunits of a business. This is normally called **segmental reporting** or **departmental accounting.** Information on the subunits of a business may be useful to (1) outsiders generally interested in an overall evaluation of the business and (2) internal managers responsible for planning and controlling the operations of the business.

The term **segmental reporting** is used most often in reference to published information for the use of outsiders; this information generally relates to a company's operations in different industries or geographical areas. Usually, the term **departmental accounting** relates to information on the subunits of a business that is prepared for the use of internal managers.

■ Reporting on Broad Business Segments

When a company is large and has operations in more than one type of business, outsiders may gain a better understanding of the overall business by examining information on each segment. For example, Illustration 23-1 shows segmental information provided in the annual report of The Southland Corporation.

Segmental Information to Be Disclosed

In Illustration 23-1, observe that the activities of the business are grouped into four major segments: the Stores Group, the Dairies Group, the Special Operations Group, and Gasoline Supply. Some additional activities do not fit into any of these major groups and are lumped into a category called Corporate. Note that five different items of information are presented for each segment. They are:

1. Revenues.
2. Operating profits (before interest and taxes).
3. Identifiable assets.
4. Capital expenditures.
5. Depreciation and amortization expense.

Large firms that operate in more than one industry are required to disclose these items of information on each industrial segment of the business. In addition, they may be required to report (1) a geographical distribution of sales and (2) sales to major customers.

Four Basic Issues in Segmental Reporting

Companies face four basic problems in developing segmental information. Detailed guidelines for dealing with these problems are provided by the FASB. While the study of these guidelines is too detailed for inclusion at this introductory level, students should be aware of each basic issue.

Identifying Significant Segments   The operations of a business may not be neatly organized in terms of segments that are important to financial statement readers. For purposes of segmental reporting, the business must be divided into enough segments to show the basic industries in which the business

Illustration 23-1

16.   Segment Information:

The Stores Group includes all convenience and grocery stores in the United States and Canada, as well as those activities (such as distribution and food preparation) which derive the majority of their revenues and operating profits from support of these stores. The Dairies Group includes milk and ice cream processing and distribution. The Special Operations Group includes the ice, chemical, Tidel and Chief Auto Parts divisions. Gasoline Supply includes gasoline storage facilities and gasoline wholesaling operations. Corporate items reflect income, expenses and assets not allocable to segments.

Intersegment sales are accounted for on a cost-plus-markup basis. Expenses directly identifiable with a segment and certain allocated income and expenses are used to determine operating profit by segment.

Amounts for 1981 and 1980 have been restated to reflect the retroactive application of SFAS No. 52. The effect was not material.

Segment information is as follows (000's omitted):

	1982	1981	1980
Revenues:			
Stores Group	$5,721,099	$5,144,087	$4,307,876
Dairies Group	584,422	568,560	534,699
Special Operations Group	165,154	140,904	122,645
Gasoline Supply	1,259,493	103,754	—
Corporate	9,031	7,725	8,864
	7,739,199	5,965,030	4,974,084
Intersegment revenues:			
Dairies Group	(229,833)	(198,329)	(175,251)
Special Operations Group	(13,745)	(14,069)	(16,228)
Gasoline Supply	(713,238)	(18,472)	—
Consolidated revenues	$6,782,383	$5,734,160	$4,782,605
Operating profits:			
Stores Group	$ 224,916	$ 219,887	$ 174,399
Dairies Group	12,457	13,333	15,325
Special Operations Group	(3,137)	(9,503)	(3,053)
Gasoline Supply	23,009	2,994	—
Consolidated operating profits	257,245	226,711	186,671
Interest expense	(48,735)	(47,587)	(46,337)
Corporate expense — net	(19,769)	(14,363)	(9,191)
Consolidated earnings before income taxes	$ 188,741	$ 164,761	$ 131,143
Identifiable assets (including capital leases) at December 31:			
Stores Group	$1,253,280	$1,216,037	$1,180,889
Dairies Group	114,799	120,313	116,051
Special Operations Group	97,122	96,463	95,617
Gasoline Supply	140,006	107,045	—
Corporate	237,377	132,313	103,685
Total identifiable assets	$1,842,584	$1,672,171	$1,496,242
Capital expenditures (excluding capital leases):			
Stores Group	$ 184,677	$ 150,301	$ 92,112
Dairies Group	15,966	14,213	9,656
Special Operations Group	11,164	11,462	10,712
Gasoline Supply	15,681	14,700	—
Corporate	109,800	33,215	2,030
	$ 337,288	$ 223,891	$ 114,510
Depreciation and amortization expense:			
Stores Group	$ 99,200	$ 85,009	$ 74,870
Dairies Group	8,648	7,930	7,474
Special Operations Group	5,327	4,538	4,488
Gasoline Supply	3,571	203	—
Corporate	4,955	3,151	3,015
	$ 121,701	$ 100,831	$ 89,847

operates. On the other hand, it should not be divided into so many segments that the information becomes confusing.

Transfer Pricing between Segments   Sometimes one or more segments of a business make sales of products or services to the other segments. These sales are eliminated when the overall statements for the business are prepared. However, sales between segments should not be eliminated when evaluating the performance of each segment. Sales between segments result in revenues to the selling segment and costs to the purchasing segment. The problem is to determine a fair price at which to report such sales, so that the profitability of both the selling segment and the purchasing segment are fairly measured.

Measuring Segmental Profitability Even if each segment operates as a highly independent unit, some expenses of the business will benefit more than one segment. Some of these **common expenses** can be allocated to the segments on a reasonable basis. Others may defy meaningful allocation. The accountant must first decide which expenses are to be allocated and which are to be left unallocated when measuring the profitability of each segment. For those expenses to be allocated, the accountant must then determine the most reasonable basis for allocation.

Identifying Segmental Assets Many assets are easily identified with specific segments because they are used solely by one segment or another. Other assets are shared by more than one segment. The accountant must determine reasonable bases for allocating shared assets to the segments that benefit from the assets.

■   **Departmental Accounting**

The previous discussion of segmental reporting related primarily to large businesses that have operations in more than one industry. However, students should not presume that accounting for the subunits of a business is limited to large companies with diverse operations. Businesses are divided into subunits or departments whenever they become too large to be effectively managed as a single unit.

Accounting for the departments of a business is characterized by two primary goals. One goal is to provide information that management can use in evaluating the profitability or cost effectiveness of each department. The second goal is to assign costs and expenses to the particular managers who are responsible for controlling those costs and expenses. In this way, the performance of managers can be evaluated in terms of their responsibilities. Thus, **departmental accounting** is closely related to what is called **responsibility accounting**.

Departmentalizing a Business

Most businesses are large and complex enough to require that they be divided into subunits or departments. When a business is departmentalized, a manager is usually placed in charge of each department. If the business grows even larger, each department may be further divided into smaller segments. Thus, a particular manager can be assigned responsibilities over the activities of a unit that is not too large for the manager to effectively oversee and control. Also, departments can be organized so that the specialized skills of each manager can be used most effectively.

Basis for Departmentalization

In a departmentalized business, there are two basic kinds of departments, **productive departments** and **service departments.** In a factory, the productive departments are those engaged directly in manufacturing operations. In a store, they are the departments making sales. Departmental divisions in a factory are commonly based on manufacturing processes employed or products or components manufactured. The divisions in a store are usually based on kinds of goods sold, with each selling or productive department being assigned the sale of one or more kinds of merchandise. In either type of business, the service departments, such as the general office, advertising, purchasing, payroll, and personnel departments, assist or perform services for the productive departments.

Information to Evaluate Departments

When a business is divided into departments, management must be able to find out how well each department is performing. Thus, it is necessary for the accounting system to supply information by departments as to resources expended and outputs achieved. This requires that revenue and expense information be measured and accumulated by departments. However, before going further it should be observed that such information is generally not made public, since it might be of considerable benefit to competitors. Rather, it is for the use of management in controlling operations, appraising performances, allocating resources, and in taking remedial actions. For example, if one of several departments is particularly profitable, perhaps it should be expanded. Or, if a department is showing poor results, information as to its revenues, costs, and expenses may point to a proper remedial action.

The information used to evaluate a department depends on whether the department is a **cost center** or a **profit center.** A cost center is a unit of the business that incurs costs (or expenses) but does not directly generate revenues. The productive departments of a factory and such service departments as the general office, advertising, and purchasing departments are cost centers. A profit center differs from a cost center in that it not only incurs costs but also generates revenues. The selling departments of a store are profit centers. In judging efficiencies in the two kinds of centers, managers of cost centers are judged on their ability to control costs and keep costs within a satisfactory range. Managers of profit centers, on the other hand, are judged on their ability to generate earnings, which are the excess of revenues over costs.

Securing Departmental Information

The methods used to gather information about the departments of a business vary from business to business. They often depend on the extent to which a company uses computers and modern cash registers.

Methods Used with Computerized Systems   Modern cash registers enable a merchandising company to accumulate information as to sales and sales returns by departments. Often, the registers transfer the information directly into the store's computer. This kind of system is capable of much more than accumulating sales information by departments. The cash registers will print all pertinent information on the sales ticket given to the customer, total the ticket, and initiate entries to record credit sales in the customer's account. Also, if the required information as to type of goods sold is keyed into the registers by means of code numbers, the computer can save and print out detailed daily departmental summaries of goods sold and remaining inventories of unsold goods.

Using Separate Accounts for Each Department Cash registers also enable a small store to determine daily totals for sales and sales returns by departments. However, since the registers often are not connected to a computer, the totals must be accumulated by some other method. Two methods are commonly used. A small store may provide separate Sales and Sales Returns accounts in its ledger for each of its departments or it may use analysis sheets. Either method may also be used to accumulate information as to purchases and purchases returns by departments.

If a store chooses to provide separate Sales, Sales Returns, Purchases, and Purchases Returns accounts in its ledger for each of its departments, it may also provide columns in its journals to record transactions by departments. Illustration 23-2 shows such a journal for recording sales by departments. The amounts to be debited to the customers' accounts are entered in the Accounts Receivable Debit column and are posted to these accounts each day. The column's total is debited to the Accounts Receivable controlling account at the end of the month. The departmental sales are entered in the last three columns and are posted as column totals at the end of the month.

Illustration 23-2

Sales Journal

Date		Account Debited	Invoice Number	P R	Accounts Receivable Debit	Departmental Sales		
						Dept. 1 Credit	Dept. 2 Credit	Dept. 3 Credit
Oct.	1	Walter Marshfield. .	737		145.00	90.00	55.00	. . .
	1	Thomas Higgins . .	738		85.00	. . .	40.00	45.00

Using Departmental Sales Analysis Sheets Separate departmental accounts are practical only for a store having a limited number of departments. In a store having more than a few departments, a more practical procedure is to use departmental sales analysis sheets.

When a store uses departmental sales analysis sheets, it provides only one undepartmentalized general ledger account for sales, another account for sales returns, another for purchases, and another for purchases returns; and it records its transactions and posts to these accounts as though it were not departmentalized. In addition to this, each day it also summarizes its transactions by departments and enters the summarized amounts on analysis sheets. For example, a company using analysis sheets, in addition to recording sales in its usual manner, will total each day's sales by departments and enter the daily totals on a sales analysis sheet like Illustration 23-3. As a result, at the end of a month or other period, the column totals of the analysis sheet show sales by departments, and the grand total of all the columns should equal the balance of the Sales account.

Illustration 23-3

Departmental Sales Analysis Sheet

Date		Men's Wear Dept.	Boys' Wear Dept.	Shoe Dept.	Leather Goods Dept.	Women's Wear Dept.
May	1	$357.15	$175.06	$115.00	$ 75.25	$427.18
	2	298.55	136.27	145.80	110.20	387.27

When a store uses departmental analysis sheets, it uses one analysis sheet to accumulate sales figures, another for sales returns, another for purchases, and still another for purchases returns. At the end of the period, the several analysis sheets show the store's sales, sales returns, purchases, and purchases returns by departments. If the store then takes inventories by departments, it can calculate gross profits by departments.

Accumulating information and arriving at a gross profit figure for each selling department in a departmentalized business is not too difficult, as the discussion thus far reveals. However, to go beyond this and arrive at useful departmental net income figures is not so easy. As a result, many companies make no effort to calculate more than gross profits by departments.

Allocating Expenses

If a business attempts to measure not only departmental gross profit but also departmental net income, special problems are confronted. They involve dividing the expenses of the business among the selling departments of the business.

Direct Expenses Do Not Require Allocation   Some expenses, called **direct expenses,** are easily traced to specific departments. The direct expenses of a department are easily traced to the department because they are incurred for the sole benefit of that department. For example, the salary of an employee who works in only one department is a direct expense of that department.

Note that the concept of direct expense is just like the concept of direct cost that was first introduced in Chapter 21. The term **direct cost** was used in reference to a manufacturing operation; all manufacturing costs are treated as product costs rather than as expenses. In departments that are not related to manufacturing, costs are charged to expense as they are incurred; hence the term **direct expense** is used.

Allocating Indirect Expenses The expenses of a business include both direct expenses and **indirect expenses.** Indirect expenses (like indirect costs) are incurred for the joint benefit of more than one department. For example, where two or more departments share a single building, the expenses of renting, heating, and lighting the building jointly benefit all of the departments in the building. Although such indirect expenses cannot be easily traced to a specific department, they must be allocated among the departments that benefited from the expenses. Each indirect expense should be allocated on a basis that fairly approximates the relative benefit received by each department. However, measuring the benefit each department receives from an indirect expense is often difficult. Even after a reasonable allocation basis is chosen, considerable doubt often exists regarding the proper share to be charged to each department.

To illustrate the allocation of an indirect expense, assume that a jewelry store purchases janitorial services from an outside firm. The jewelry store then allocates the cost among its three departments according to the floor space occupied. The cost of janitorial services for a short period is $280, and the amounts of floor space occupied are:

Jewelry department.	250 sq. ft.
Watch repair department	125
China and silver department	500
Total	875 sq. ft.

The calculations to allocate janitorial expense to the departments are:

$$\text{Jewelry department:} \quad \frac{250}{875} \times \$280 = \$80$$

$$\text{Watch repair department:} \quad \frac{125}{875} \times \$280 = \$40$$

$$\text{China and silver department:} \quad \frac{500}{875} \times \$280 = \$160$$

Do not forget that the concepts of **direct costs or expenses** and **indirect costs or expenses** can be usefully applied in a variety of situations. In general, direct costs or expenses are easily traced to or associated with a "cost object." In this chapter, the cost object of significance is the department. However, other cost objects may also be of interest. When we discussed general accounting systems for manufacturing operations (Chapter 21) and job order cost systems (Chapter 22), the cost object was a unit or batch of product. When we discussed process cost systems (Chapter 22), the cost object was a process or processing department.

Bases for Allocating Indirect Expenses

In the following paragraphs, bases for allocating some common indirect expenses are discussed. In the discussions, no hard-and-fast rules are given because several factors are often involved in an expense allocation and the relative importance of the factors varies from situation to situation.

As previously stated, indirect expenses are, by definition, subject to doubt as to how they should be allocated between departments. Judgment rather than hard-and-fast rules is required, and different accountants may not agree on the proper basis for allocating an indirect expense.

Wages and Salaries An employee's wages may be either a direct or an indirect expense. If an employee's time is spent all in one department, the employee's wages are a direct expense of the benefited department; but if an employee works in more than one department, the wages become an indirect expense to be allocated between or among the benefited departments. Normally, working time spent in each department is a fair basis for allocating wages.

A supervisory employee may supervise more than one department; and in such cases, the time spent in each department is usually a fair basis for allocating his or her salary. However, since a supervisory employee is frequently on the move from department to department, the time spent in each is often difficult to measure. Consequently, some companies allocate the salary of such an employee to his or her departments on the basis of the number of employees in each department. Others make the allocation on the basis of the supervised departments' sales. When a supervisor's salary is allocated on the basis of employees, it is assumed that he or she is supervising people and the time spent in each department is related to the number of employees in each. When the salary is allocated on the basis of sales, it is assumed that the time devoted to each department is related to the department's production.

Rent or Depreciation and Related Expenses of Buildings Rent expense is normally allocated to benefited departments on the basis of the amount and value of the floor space occupied by each. Furthermore, since all customers who enter a store must pass the departments by the entrance and only a fraction of these people go beyond the first floor, ground floor space is more valuable for retail purposes than is basement or upper floor space, and space near the entrance is more valuable than is space in an out-of-the-way corner. Yet, since there is no exact measure of the floor space values, all such values and the allocations of rent based on such values must depend on judgment. Fair allocations depend on the use of good judgment, statistics as to customer traffic patterns, and the opinions of experts who are familiar with current rental values. When a building is owned instead of being rented, expenses such as depreciation, taxes, and insurance on the building are allocated like rent expense.

Advertising When a store advertises a department's products, if the advertising is effective, people come into the store to buy the products. However, at the same time they also often buy other unadvertised products. Consequently, advertising benefits all departments, even those the products of which are not advertised. Thus, many stores treat advertising as an indirect expense and allocate it on the basis of sales. When advertising costs are allocated on a sales basis, a department producing $\frac{1}{10}$ of the total sales is charged with $\frac{1}{10}$ of the advertising cost; a department producing $\frac{1}{6}$ of the sales is charged with $\frac{1}{6}$.

Although in many stores advertising costs are allocated to departments on the basis of sales, in others each advertisement is analyzed and the cost of the column inches of newspaper space or minutes of TV or radio time devoted to the products of a department is charged to the department.

Depreciation of Equipment Depreciation on equipment used solely in one department is a direct expense of that department; and if detailed plant asset records are kept, the depreciation applicable to each department may be determined by examining the records. Where adequate records are not maintained, depreciation must be treated as an indirect expense and allocated to the departments on the basis of the value of the equipment in each. Where items of equipment are used by more than one department, the relative number of hours used is usually a fair basis of allocating depreciation costs by each department.

Heating and Lighting Expense Heating and lighting expense is usually allocated on the basis of floor space occupied under the assumption that the amount of heat and the number of lights, their wattage, and the extent of their use are uniform throughout the store. Should there be a material variation in lighting, however, further analysis and a separate allocation may be advisable.

Service Departments In order to manufacture products and make sales, the productive departments must have the services supplied by departments such as the general office, personnel, payroll, advertising, and purchasing departments. Such departments are called **service departments.** Since service departments do not produce revenues, they are evaluated as cost centers rather than as profit centers. Although each service department should be separately evaluated, the costs it incurs must also be allocated among the departments it services. Thus, the costs of service departments are, in effect, indirect expenses of the selling departments; and the allocation of service department costs to selling departments is required if net incomes of the selling departments are to be calculated. The following list shows commonly used bases for these allocations:

Departments	Commonly Used Expense Allocation Bases
General office department . . .	Number of employees in each department or sales.
Personnel department	Number of employees in each department.
Payroll department	Number of employees in each department.
Advertising department	Sales or amounts of advertising charged directly to each department.
Purchasing department	Dollar amounts of purchases or number of purchase invoices processed.
Cleaning and maintenance department	Square feet of floor space occupied.

Mechanics of Allocating Expenses

It would be difficult or impossible to analyze each indirect expense incurred and allocate and charge portions to several departmental expense accounts at the time of incurrence or payment. Consequently, expense amounts paid or incurred, both direct and indirect, are commonly accumulated in undepartmentalized expense accounts until the end of a period, when a **departmental expense allocation sheet** (see Illustration 23–4) is used to allocate and charge each expense to the benefited departments.

To prepare an expense allocation sheet, the names of the to-be-allocated expenses are entered in the sheet's first column along with the names of the service departments. Next, the bases of allocation are entered in the second column, and the expense amounts are entered in the third. Then, each expense is allocated according to the basis shown, and the allocated portions are entered in the departmental columns. After this, the departmental columns are totaled and the service department column totals are allocated in turn to the selling departments. Upon completion, the amounts in the departmental columns are available for preparing income statements showing net income by departments, as in Illustration 23-5.

■ **Departmental Contributions to Overhead**

Some people argue that departmental net incomes do not provide a fair basis for evaluating departmental performance. This is because the assumptions and somewhat arbitrary decisions involved in allocating the indirect expenses impact on the net income figures. The criticism of departmental net incomes is most likely heard in companies where indirect expenses represent a large portion of total expenses. Those who criticize departmental net income numbers usually suggest the substitution of what are known as **departmental contributions to overhead.** A department's contribution to overhead is the amount its revenues exceed its direct costs and expenses. Illustration 23-6 shows the departmental contributions to overhead for Beta Company.

Compare the performance of the appliance department as it is shown in Illustrations 23-5 and 23-6. Illustration 23-5 shows an absolute loss of $400 resulting from the department's operations. On the other hand, Illustration 23-6 shows a positive contribution to overhead of $9,500, which is 19.9% of sales. While this contribution is not as good as for the other departments, it appears much better than the $400 loss. Which is the better basis of evaluation? To resolve the matter, one must critically review the bases used for allocating the indirect expenses to departments. In the final analysis, answering the question is a matter of judgment.

■ **Eliminating the Unprofitable Department**

When a department's net income shows a loss or when its contribution to overhead appears very poor, management may consider the extreme action of eliminating the department. However, in considering this extreme action, neither the net income figure nor the contribution to overhead provides the best information on which to base a decision. Instead, consideration should be given to the department's **escapable expenses** and **inescapable expenses.** Escapable expenses are those that would be avoided if the department were eliminated; inescapable expenses are those that would continue even though the department were eliminated. For example, the management of Beta Company is considering whether to eliminate its appli-

Illustration 23-4

Beta Hardware Store
Departmental Expense Allocation Sheet
Year Ended December 31, 19—

Undepartmentalized Expense Accounts and Service Departments	Bases of Allocation	Expense Account Balance	Allocation of Expenses to Departments				
			General Office Dept.	Pur- chasing Dept.	Hard- ware Dept.	House- wares Dept.	Appli- ances Dept.
Salaries expense	Direct, payroll records	51,900	13,300	8,200	15,600	7,000	7,800
Rent expense.	Amount and value of space . .	12,000	500	500	6,000	1,400	3,600
Heating and lighting . . .	Floor space.	2,000	100	100	1,000	200	600
Advertising expense . . .	Sales	1,000	. . .	. . .	500	300	200
Depreciation, equipment . .	Direct, depreciation records . .	1,500	500	300	400	100	200
Supplies expense	Direct, requisitions	900	200	100	300	200	100
Insurance expense	Value of assets insured . . .	2,500	400	200	900	600	400
Total expenses by departments . .		71,800	15,000	9,400	24,700	9,800	12,900
Allocation of service department expenses:							
General office department . . .	Sales		15,000		7,500	4,500	3,000
Purchasing department	Purchase requisitions. . . .			9,400	3,900	3,400	2,100
Total expenses applicable to selling departments . . .		71,800			36,100	17,700	18,000

Illustration 23-5

Beta Hardware Store
Departmental Income Statement
Year Ended December 31, 19—

	Hardware Department	Housewares Department	Appliances Department	Combined
Sales	$119,500	$71,700	$47,800	$239,000
Cost of goods sold	73,800	43,800	30,200	147,800
Gross profit on sales	$ 45,700	$27,900	$17,600	$ 91,200
Gross profit percentages	38.2%	38.9%	36.8%	38.2%
Operating expenses:				
Salaries expense	$ 15,600	$ 7,000	$ 7,800	$ 30,400
Rent expense	6,000	1,400	3,600	11,000
Heating and lighting expense	1,000	200	600	1,800
Advertising expense	500	300	200	1,000
Depreciation expense, equipment	400	100	200	700
Supplies expense	300	200	100	600
Insurance expense	000	000	400	1,900
Share of general office department expenses	7,500	4,500	3,000	15,000
Share of purchasing department expenses	3,900	3,400	2,100	9,400
Total operating expenses	$ 36,100	$17,700	$18,000	$ 71,800
Net income (loss)	$ 9,600	$10,200	$ (400)	$ 19,400

ances department. An evaluation of the inescapable expenses and escapable expenses of the appliances department reveals the following:

	Escapable Expenses	Inescapable Expenses
Salaries expense	$ 7,800	
Rent expense		$3,600
Heating and lighting expense		600
Advertising expense	200	
Depreciation expense, equipment		200
Supplies expense	100	
Insurance expense (merchandise and equipment)	300	100
Share of office department expenses	2,200	800
Share of purchasing department expenses	1,000	1,100
Totals	$11,600	$6,400

If the appliances department is discontinued, its $6,400 of inescapable expenses will have to be borne by the remaining departments; thus, until the appliances department's annual loss exceeds $6,400, Beta Company is better off continuing the unprofitable department. In addition, another factor must be weighed when considering the elimination of an unprofitable department. Often, the existence of a department, even though unprofitable, contributes to the sales and profits of the other departments. In

Illustration 23-6

Beta Hardware Store
Income Statement Showing Departmental Contributions to Overhead
Year Ended December 31, 19—

	Hardware Department	Housewares Department	Appliances Department	Combined
Sales	$119,500	$71,700	$47,800	$239,000
Cost of goods sold	73,800	43,800	30,200	147,800
Gross profit on sales	$ 45,700	$27,900	$17,600	$ 91,200
Direct expenses:				
Salaries expense	$ 15,600	$ 7,000	$ 7,800	$ 30,400
Depreciation expense, equipment	400	100	200	700
Supplies expense.	300	200	100	600
Total direct expenses	$ 16,300	$ 7,300	$ 8,100	$ 31,700
Departmental contributions to overhead . . .	$ 29,400	$20,600	$ 9,500	$ 59,500
Contribution percentages	24.6%	28.7%	19.9%	24.9%
Indirect expenses:				
Rent expense				$ 11,000
Heating and lighting expense				1,800
Advertising expense.				1,000
Insurance expense				1,900
General office department expense				15,000
Purchasing department expense				9,400
Total indirect expenses				$ 40,100
Net income				$ 19,400

such a case, a department might be continued even when its losses exceed its inescapable expenses.

Controllable Costs and Expenses

Net income figures and contributions to overhead are used in judging departmental efficiencies, but is either a good index of how well a department manager has performed? The answer is that neither may be a good index. Since many expenses entering into the calculation of a department's net income or into its contribution to overhead may be beyond the control of the department's manager, neither net income nor contribution to overhead is the best means of judging how well the manager has performed. Instead, the performance of a manager should be evaluated in terms of **controllable costs and expenses.**

Controllable Costs or Expenses Are Different than Direct Costs or Expenses

What is the distinguishing characteristic of controllable costs and expenses? The critical factor is that the manager must have the power to determine or at least strongly influence the amounts to be expended. Controllable costs and expenses are not the same thing as direct costs and expenses. Direct costs and expenses are easily traced and therefore chargeable to a specific department, but the amounts expended may or may not be under the control of the department's manager. For example, a department manager often has little or no control over the amount of equipment assigned to the department and the resulting depreciation expense. Also, the manager has no control over his or her own salary. On the other hand, a department manager commonly has some control over the employees and the amount of work they do. Also, the manager normally has some control over supplies used in the department.

When controllable costs and expenses are used in judging a manager's efficiency, statistics are prepared showing the department's output and its controllable costs and expenses. The statistics of the current period are then compared with prior periods and with planned levels, and the manager's performance is judged.

Why a Cost Is Controllable or Uncontrollable

The concepts of **controllable costs** and **uncontrollable costs** must be defined with reference to a particular manager and within a definite time period. Without these two reference points, all costs are controllable; that is, **all costs are controllable at some level of management if the time period is long enough.** For example, a cost such as property insurance may not be controllable at the level of a department manager, but it is subject to control by the executive who is responsible for obtaining insurance coverage for the company. Likewise, the executive responsible for obtaining insurance coverage may not have any control over insurance expense resulting from insurance contracts presently in force. But when a contract expires, the executive is free to renegotiate and thus has control over the long run. Thus, it is recognized that all costs are subject to the control of some manager at some point in time. Revenues are likewise subject to the control of some manager.

■   **Responsibility Accounting**

The concept of controllable costs and expenses provides the basis for a system of responsibility accounting. In responsibility accounting, each manager is held responsible for the costs and expenses that fall under the manager's control. Prior to each period of activity, plans are developed that specify the expected costs or expenses under the control of each manager. Those plans are called **responsibility accounting budgets.** To secure the cooperation of each manager and to be sure that the budgets represent reasonable goals, each manager should be closely involved in the preparation of his or her budget.

The accounting system is then designed to accumulate costs and expenses so that timely reports can be made to each manager of the costs for which the manager is responsible. These reports (called **performance reports**) compare actual costs and expenses to the budgeted amounts. Managers use these reports to focus their attention on the specific areas in which actual costs exceed budgeted amounts. With this information in hand, they proceed to take corrective action.

Performance reports are also used to evaluate the effectiveness of each manager. The reports allow managers to be evaluated in terms of their ability to control costs and keep them within budgeted amounts. Importantly, managers are not held responsible for costs over which they have no control. Further consideration is given to performance reports in Chapter 26.

A responsibility accounting system must reflect the fact that control over costs and expenses applies to several levels of management. For example, consider the partial organization chart shown in Illustration 23-7. In Illustration 23-7, the lines connecting the various managerial positions represent lines of authority. Thus, while each department manager is responsible for the controllable costs and expenses incurred in his or her department, those same costs are subject to the general control of the plant manager. More generally, those costs are also subject to the control of the vice president of production, and of the president, and finally of the board of directors.

At the lowest levels of management, responsibilities and costs over which control is exercised are limited. Consequently, performance reports for this management level cover only those costs over which the department managers exercise control. Moving up the management hierarchy, responsi-

Illustration 23-7

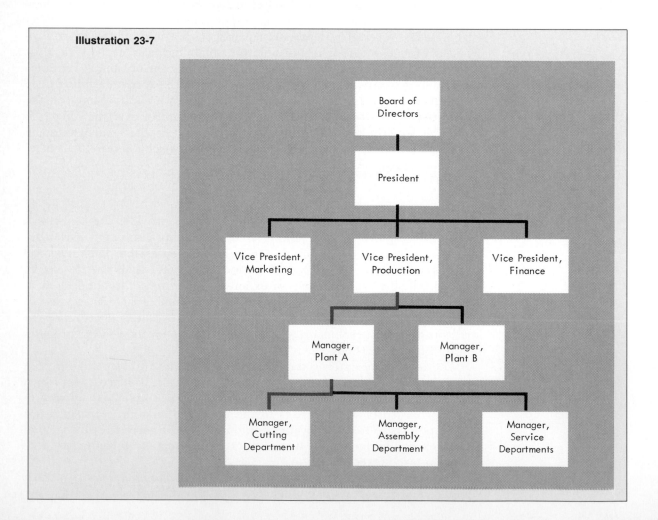

bilities and control broaden, and reports to higher level managers are broader and cover a wider range of costs. However, reports to higher level managers normally do not contain the details reported to their subordinates. Rather, the details reported to lower level managers are normally summarized on the reports to their superiors. The details are summarized for two reasons: (1) lower level managers are primarily responsible and (2) too many details can be confusing. If reports to higher level managers contain too much detail, they may draw attention away from the broad, more important issues confronting the company.

Illustration 23-8 shows summarized performance reports for three of the management levels depicted in Illustration 23-7. Observe in Illustration 23-8 how the costs under the control of the cutting department manager are totaled and included among the controllable costs of the plant manager. Similarly, the costs under the control of the plant manager are totaled and included among the controllable costs of the vice president of produc-

---

Illustration 23-8

Performance Reports

Vice President, Production

For the Month of July

Controllable Costs	Budgeted Amount	Actual Amount	Over (under) Budget
Salaries, plant managers	$ 80,000	$80,000	$ –0–
Quality control costs . . .	21,000	22,400	1,100
Office costs	29,500	28,800	(700)
Plant A	**276,700**	**279,500**	**2,800**
Plant B	390,000	380,600	(9,400)
Totals	$797,200	$791,300	$(5,900)

Manager, Plant A

For the Month of July

Controllable Costs	Budgeted Amount	Actual Amount	Over (under) Budget
Salaries, department managers . .	$ 75,000	$ 78,000	$ 3,000
Depreciation	10,600	10,600	–0–
Insurance	6,800	6,300	(500)
Cutting department	**79,600**	**79,900**	**300**
Assembly department	61,500	60,200	(1,300)
Service Department 1	24,300	24,700	400
Service Department 2	18,900	19,800	900
Totals	$276,700	$279,500	$ 2,800

Manager, Cutting Department

For the Month of July

Controllable Costs	Budgeted Amount	Actual Amount	Over (under) Budget
Raw materials	$ 26,500	$ 25,900	$ (600)
Direct labor	32,000	33,500	1,500
Indirect labor	7,200	7,000	(200)
Supplies	4,000	3,900	(100)
Other controllable costs	9,900	9,600	(300)
Totals	$ 79,600	$ 79,900	$ 300

tion. In this manner, a responsibility accounting system provides information that is relevant to the control responsibilities of each management level.

In conclusion, it should be said that the ability to produce vast amounts of raw data mechanically and electronically has far outstripped our ability to use the data. What is needed is the ability to select the data that is meaningful for planning and control. This is recognized in responsibility accounting, and every effort is made to get the right information to the right person at the right time, and the right person is the person who can control the cost or revenue.

Joint Costs

Joint costs are encountered in some manufacturing companies and are introduced here because they have much in common with indirect expenses. A **joint cost** is a cost incurred to secure two or more essentially different products. For example, a meat-packing company incurs a joint cost when it buys a pig from which it will get bacon, hams, shoulders, liver, heart, hide, pig feet, and a variety of other products. Likewise, a sawmill incurs joint costs when it buys a log and saws it into portions of Clears, Select Structurals, No. 1 Common, No. 2 Common, and other grades of lumber. In both cases, as with all joint costs, the problem is one of allocating the costs to the several joint products.

A joint cost may be, but is not commonly, allocated on some physical basis, such as the ratio of pounds, square feet, or gallons of each joint product to total pounds, square feet, or gallons of all joint products flowing from the cost. The reason this method is not commonly used is that the resulting cost allocations may be completely out of keeping with the market values of the joint products, and thus may cause certain of the products to sell at a profit while other products always show a loss. For example, a sawmill bought for $30,000 a number of logs that when sawed produced a million board feet of lumber in the grades and amounts shown in Illustration 23-9.

Illustration 23-9

Grade of Lumber	Production in Board Feet	Market Price per 1,000 Board Feet	Market Value of Production of Each Grade	Ratio of Market Value of Each Grade to Total
Structural.	100,000	$120	$12,000	12/50
No. 1 Common . . .	300,000	60	18,000	18/50
No. 2 Common . . .	400,000	40	16,000	16/50
No. 3 Common . . .	200,000	20	4,000	4/50
	1,000,000		$50,000	

Observe in Illustration 23-9 that the logs produced 200,000 board feet of No. 3 Common lumber and that this is two tenths of the total lumber produced from the logs. If the No. 3 lumber is assigned two tenths of the $30,000 cost of the logs, it will be assigned $6,000 of the cost ($30,000

× ²⁄₁₀ = $6,000); and since this lumber can be sold for only $4,000, the assignment will cause this grade to show a loss. As a result, as in this situation, **to avoid always showing a loss on one or more of the products flowing from a joint cost, such costs are commonly allocated to the joint products in the ratio of the market values of the joint products at the point of separation.**

The ratios of the market values of the joint products flowing from the $30,000 of log cost are shown in the last column of Illustration 23-9. If these ratios are used to allocate the $30,000 cost, the cost will be apportioned between the grades as follows:

Structural:	$30,000 × 12/50 =	$ 7,200
No. 1 Common:	$30,000 × 18/50 =	10,800
No. 2 Common:	$30,000 × 16/50 =	9,600
No. 3 Common:	$30,000 × 4/50 =	2,400
		$30,000

Observe that if the No. 3 Common is allocated a share of the $30,000 joint cost based on market values by grades, it is allocated $2,400 of the $30,000. Furthermore, when the $2,400 is subtracted from the grade's $4,000 market value, $1,600 remains to cover other after-separation costs and provide a profit.

□   **Glossary**   **Common expenses** those expenses of a business that benefit more than one segment of the business.

Controllable costs or expenses costs over which the manager has the power to determine or strongly influence amounts to be expended.

Cost center a unit of business that incurs costs or expenses but does not directly generate revenues; as a result, a unit the efficiency of which cannot be judged in terms of its ability to generate earnings.

Departmental accounting accounting for the "parts" or subunits of a business, especially relating to the development of subunit information for the use of internal managers.

Departmental contribution to overhead the amount by which a department's revenues exceed its direct costs and expenses.

Direct costs or expenses costs or expenses that are easily traced to or associated with a cost object; for example, the cost of materials that become part of a manufactured product, or labor cost that is used solely in one processing department of a manufacturer, or wages expense incurred solely for the benefit of a specific department of a merchandising company.

Direct expenses expenses that are easily associated with and assigned to a specific department.

Escapable expenses costs that would end with an unprofitable department's elimination.

Indirect costs or expenses costs or expenses that are not easily traced to a cost object such as a department; for example, costs incurred for the joint benefit of more than one department.

Indirect expenses expenses that are not easily associated with a specific department.

Inescapable expenses expenses that would continue even though a department were eliminated.

Joint cost a single cost incurred to secure two or more essentially different products.

Performance report a financial report that compares actual costs and expenses to the budgeted amounts.

Productive departments subunits of a business, the operations of which involve manufacturing or selling the goods or services of the business.

Profit center a unit of business that incurs costs and generates revenues, the efficiency of which therefore can be judged in terms of its ability to generate earnings.

Responsibility accounting an accounting system designed to accumulate controllable costs in timely reports to be given to each manager who is responsible for the costs, and also to be used in judging the performance of each manager.

Responsibility accounting budget a plan that specifies the expected costs and expenses falling under the control of a manager.

Segmental reporting providing information about the subunits of a business, especially published information about a company's operations in different industries or geographical areas.

Service departments departments that do not manufacture products or produce revenue but that supply other departments with essential services.

Uncontrollable cost a cost the amount of which a specific manager cannot control within a given period of time.

□ **Questions for Class Discussion**

1. What is the difference, if any, between segmental reporting and departmental accounting?

2. What are five items of segmental information about operations in different industries that may be required disclosures in the annual report of a company?

3. What are four basic issues confronted by the accountant in developing information on broad industrial segments?

4. Why does the existence of common expenses cause the accountant difficulty in preparing segmental reports?

5. Why are businesses divided into departments?

6. What are two primary goals of departmental accounting?

7. Is it possible to evaluate the profitability of a cost center? Why?

8. What is the difference between productive departments and service departments?

9. Name several examples of service departments.

10. Are service departments analyzed as cost centers or as profit centers? Why?

11. If a company with a computerized accounting system uses modern cash registers that are directly connected to its computer, is the company likely to require the use of departmental sales analysis sheets? Why?

12. How is a departmental sales analysis sheet used in determining sales by departments?

13. What is the difference between direct and indirect expenses?

14. In a merchandising company, what are the typical cost objects that serve as the basis for classifying expenses as direct or indirect?

15. Suggest a reasonable basis for allocating each of the following indirect expenses to departments: (*a*) salary of a supervisory employee, (*b*) rent, (*c*) heat, (*d*) electricity used in lighting, (*e*) janitorial services, (*f*) advertising, (*g*) expired insurance, and (*h*) taxes.

16. How is a departmental expense allocation sheet used in allocating indirect expenses to departments?

17. How reliable are the amounts shown as net incomes for the various departments of a store when indirect expenses are allocated to the departments?

18. How is a department's contribution to overhead measured?

19. As the terms are used in departmental accounting, what are (*a*) escapable expenses and (*b*) inescapable expenses?

20. What are controllable costs and expenses?

21. Why should a manager be closely involved in preparing his or her responsibility accounting budget?

22. In responsibility accounting, who is the right person to be given timely reports and statistics on a given cost?

23. What is a joint cost? How are joint costs normally allocated?

Class Exercises

Exercise 23-1

Twin Corporation has two business segments for which the following operating information is available:

	Segment A	Segment B
Sales to outside parties	$60,000	$80,000
Sales to segment B	?	
Purchases from segment A		?
Other expenses of each segment	45,000	30,000

The items that segment A sold to segment B were resold by B to outside parties. In reporting the intersegment sales, the manager of segment A argues that the sales to segment B should be priced at $30,000, which is approximately the same prices that would have been charged to outside parties. The segment B manager argues that segment B should be charged only $15,000, since segment B is a member of the Twin Corporation family. A price of $15,000 more than covers segment A's cost according to the segment B manager.

Present reports that show the sales, expenses, and income from operations of each segment assuming the intersegment sales are priced at (a) $30,000, and (b) $15,000. Then express each segment's income from operations as a percent of sales. Comment on the importance of the intersegment pricing decision in evaluating the performance of each segment. Which price do you think provides the best basis for evaluating the performance of each segment?

Exercise 23-2

A company rents for $250,000 per year all the space in a building, which is assigned to its departments as follows:

> Department 1: 1,600 square feet of first-floor space
> Department 2: 2,400 square feet of first-floor space
> Department 3: 1,000 square feet of second-floor space
> Department 4: 1,200 square feet of second-floor space
> Department 5: 1,800 square feet of second-floor space

The company allocates 70% of the total rent to the first floor and 30% to the second floor, and then allocates the rent of each floor to the departments on that floor on the basis of the space occupied. Determine the rent to be allocated to each department.

Exercise 23-3

A company rents for $240,000 per year all the space in a small building, and it occupies the space as follows:

Department X: 900 square feet of first-floor space
Department Y: 2,100 square feet of first-floor space
Department Z: 3,000 square feet of second-floor space

Determine the rent expense to be allocated to each department under the assumption that first-floor space rents for twice as much as second-floor space in the city in which this company is located.

Exercise 23-4

Darcy DeShazo works part-time in the appliances department and in the hardware department of Scarblows Department Store. Her work consists of waiting on customers who enter either department and also in straightening and rearranging merchandise in either department as needed after it has been shown to customers. The store allocates her $18,000 in annual wages to the two departments in which she works. Last year the division was based on a sample of the time DeShazo spent working in the two departments. To obtain the sample, observations were made on several days throughout the year of the manner in which DeShazo spent her time while at work. Following are the results of the observations:

Minutes spent on various activities:
  Selling in the appliances department   2,775
  Straightening and rearranging merchandise
    in the appliances department   525
  Selling in the hardware department.   2,120
  Straightening and rearranging merchandise
    in the hardware department   580
  Idle time spent waiting for a customer to
    enter one of the selling departments   375

Prepare a calculation to show the shares of the employee's wages that should be allocated to the departments.

Exercise 23-5

Blake Products has two service departments, the purchasing department and the advertising department, and two sales departments, sails and spars. During 198A, the departments had the following direct expenses: purchasing department, $5,700; advertising department, $4,200; sails department, $15,000; and spars department, $10,500. The departments occupy the following amounts of floor space: purchasing, 400; advertising, 300; sails, 800; and spars, 500. The sails department had three times as many dollars of sales during the year as did the spars department, and during the year the purchasing department processed twice as many purchase orders for the sails department as it did for the spars department.

Required

Prepare an expense allocation sheet for Blake Products on which the direct expenses are entered by departments, the year's $42,000 of rent expense is allocated to the departments on the basis of floor space occupied, advertising department expenses are allocated to the sales departments on the basis of sales, and purchasing department expenses are allocated on the basis of purchase orders processed.

Exercise 23-6

A company has five departments that are expected to have the following results of operations next year.

	Dept. 1	Dept. 2	Dept. 3	Dept. 4	Dept. 5
Sales.	$ 6,500	$ 9,400	$4,700	$ 7,900	$8,100
Expenses:					
Escapable.	$ 3,900	$ 9,800	$2,800	$ 8,600	$3,500
Inescapable	5,000	4,400	2,600	4,400	2,200
Total expenses	$ 8,900	$14,200	$5,400	$13,000	$5,700
Net income (loss)	$(2,400)	$ (4,800)	$ (700)	$ (5,100)	$2,400

Prepare a combined income statement for the company under each of the following conditions: (*a*) none of the departments are eliminated, (*b*) all of the unprofitable departments are eliminated, and (*c*) departments are only eliminated if the effect is to increase net income or reduce the net loss of the company.

Exercise 23-7

Robert Mayfield is the manager of the automobile service department of a large department store. A 198A income statement for the department included the following:

Revenues:		
Sales of services	$245,000	
Sales of parts	170,000	$415,000
Cost and expenses:		
Cost of parts sold	$ 78,000	
Wages (hourly)	145,000	
Salary of manager	28,000	
Payroll taxes	19,000	
Supplies.	38,000	
Depreciation of building	22,000	
Utilities	34,000	
Interest on long-term debt	17,000	
Income taxes allocated to department	11,000	
Total costs and expenses		392,000
Department net income		$ 23,000

Which of the income statement items do you think should be excluded from a report to be used in evaluating Mr. Mayfield's performance? State your reasons. If the exclusion of some items is questionable, list those items and explain why the exclusion is questionable.

Exercise 23-8

LeMaster Development Company has just completed a subdivision containing 40 building lots, of which 32 lots are for sale at $24,000 each and 8 are for sale at $48,000 each. The land for the subdivision cost $176,000, and the company spent $208,000 on street and utilities improvements. Assume that the land and improvement costs are to be assigned to the lots as joint costs and determine the share of the costs to assign to a lot in each price class.

Exercise 23-9

Dodge Packing Company purchases front quarters of beef and processes them into round steaks and hamburger. It then sells the round steaks for $2.80 per pound and sells the hamburger for $2.10 per pound. On average, 100 pounds of front quarter can be processed into 25 pounds of round steak and 50 pounds of hamburger.

Assume that 100 pounds of front quarter is purchased for $1 per pound. The 100 pounds is then processed into round steak and hamburger, which requires additional labor cost of $30. If 10 pounds of round steak are sold and 30 pounds of hamburger are sold, what cost of goods sold and ending inventory amounts should be reported?

Problems

Problem 23-1

Pressley Company occupies all the space in a two-story building, and it has an account in its ledger called Building Occupancy to which it charged the following during the past year:

Depreciation, building	$24,000
Interest, building mortgage	19,800
Taxes, building and land	7,400
Heating expenses	3,300
Lighting expense	4,300
Cleaning and maintenance	16,800
Total	$75,600

The building has 2,500 square feet of floor space on each of its two floors, a total of 5,000 square feet; and the bookkeeper divided the $75,600 by 5,000 and charged the selling departments on each floor with $15.12 of occupancy cost for each square foot of floor space occupied.

Mary Malone, the manager of a second-floor department occupying 1,200 square feet of floor space, saw the $15.12 per square foot, or $18,144 of occupancy cost, charged to her department and complained. She cited a recent real estate board study that showed average rental charges for similar space, including heat but not including lights, cleaning, and maintenance, as follows:

Ground-floor space	$18 per sq. ft.
Second-floor space	12 per sq. ft.

Required

Prepare a computation showing how much building occupancy cost you think should have been charged to Mary Malone's department last year.

Problem 23-2

Langley Company began its operations one year ago with two selling departments and one office department. The year's operating results are:

Langley Company
Departmental Income Statement
For the Year Ended December 31, 198A

	Dept. X	Dept. Y	Combined
Revenue from sales	$120,000	$75,000	$195,000
Cost of goods sold	78,000	45,000	123,000
Gross profit from sales.	$ 42,000	$30,000	$ 72,000
Direct expenses:			
Sales salaries.	$ 15,800	$ 9,000	$ 24,800
Advertising	1,400	1,000	2,400
Store supplies used	600	300	900
Depreciation of equipment	1,600	900	2,500
Total direct expenses	$ 19,400	$11,200	$ 30,600
Allocated expenses:			
Rent expense.	$ 7,200	$ 3,600	$ 10,800
Heating and lighting expense	1,800	900	2,700
Share of office department expenses. . . .	7,200	4,500	11,700
Total allocated expenses	$ 16,200	$ 9,000	$ 25,200
Total expenses	$ 35,600	$20,200	$ 55,800
Net income.	$ 6,400	$ 9,800	$ 16,200

The company plans to open a third selling department which it estimates will produce $45,000 in sales with a 35% gross profit margin and will require the following direct expenses: sales salaries, $6,800; advertising, $700; store supplies, $260; and depreciation of equipment, $500.

A year ago, when operations began, it was necessary to rent store space in excess of requirements. This extra space was assigned to and used by Departments X and Y during the year; but when the new Department Z is opened, it will take one fourth of the space presently assigned to Department X and one sixth of the space assigned to Department Y.

The company allocates its general office department expenses to its selling departments on the basis of sales, and it expects the new department to cause a $788 increase in general office department expenses.

The company expects Department Z to bring new customers into the store who in addition to buying goods in the new department will also buy sufficient merchandise in the two old departments to increase their sales by 5% each. And, although the old department's sales are expected to increase, their gross profit percentages are not expected to change. Likewise, their direct expenses, other than supplies, are not expected to change. The supplies used will increase in proportion to sales.

Required

Prepare a departmental income statement showing the company's expected operations with three selling departments. Round all amounts to the nearest whole dollar.

Problem 23-3

Cedar Company is considering the elimination of its unprofitable Department N. The company's income statement for last year appears as follows:

Cedar Company
Income Statement
For the Year Ended December 31, 19—

	Dept. M	Dept. N	Combined
Sales.	$216,000	$103,200	$319,200
Cost of goods sold	119,600	75,000	194,600
Gross margin on sales	$ 96,400	$ 28,200	$124,600
Operating expenses:			
Direct expenses:			
Advertising	$ 2,700	$ 1,980	$ 4,680
Store supplies used.	2,520	1,620	4,140
Depreciation of store equipment	2,180	1,320	3,500
Total direct expenses	$ 7,400	$ 4,920	$ 12,320
Allocated expenses:			
Sales salaries	$ 45,500	$ 27,300	$ 72,800
Rent expense	7,600	3,600	11,200
Bad debts expense.	820	680	1,500
Office salaries	13,650	8,190	21,840
Insurance expense	800	400	1,200
Miscellaneous office expenses	1,100	600	1,700
Total allocated expenses	$ 69,470	$ 40,770	$110,240
Total operating expenses	$ 76,870	$ 45,690	$122,560
Net income (loss)	$ 19,530	$ (17,490)	$ 2,040

If Department N is eliminated:

a. The company has one office worker who earns $420 per week or $21,840 per year and four salesclerks each of whom earns $350 per week or $18,200 per year. At present the salaries of two and one-half salesclerks are charged to Department M and one and one-half salesclerks to Department N. The sales salaries and office salaries presently assigned to Department N can be avoided if the department is eliminated. However, management is considering another plan, as follows. It is the opinion of management that two salesclerks may be dismissed if Department N is eliminated, leaving only two full-time clerks in Department M and making up the difference by assigning the office worker to part-time sales work in the department. It is felt that although the office worker has not devoted half of his time to the office work of Department N, if he devotes the same amount of time to selling in Department M during rush hours as he has to the office work of Department N, it will be sufficient to carry the load.

b. The lease on the store building is long term and cannot be changed; therefore, the space presently occupied by Department N will have to be used by and charged to Department M. Likewise, Department M will have to make whatever use of Department N's equipment it can, since the equipment has little or no sales value.

c. The elimination of Department N will eliminate the Department N advertising expense, losses from bad debts, and store supplies used. It will also eliminate 80% of the insurance expense allocated to the department (the portion on merchandise) and 25% of the miscellaneous office expenses presently allocated to Department N.

Required

1. List in separate columns the amounts of Department N's escapable and inescapable expenses.

2. Under the assumption that Department M's sales and gross profit will not be affected by the elimination of Department N, prepare an income statement showing what the company can expect to earn from the operation of Department M after Department N is eliminated. Assume that the plan of assigning part of the office worker's time to the sales force is used.

Problem 23-4

Darwin and Mary Summers own a farm that produces potatoes. Last year after preparing the following income statement, Darwin remarked to Mary that they should have fed the No. 3 potatoes to the pigs and thus avoided the loss from the sale of this grade.

Darwin and Mary Summers
Income from the Production and Sale of Potatoes
For the Year Ended December 31, 198A

| | Results by Grades | | | |
	No. 1	No. 2	No. 3	Combined
Sales by grades:				
No. 1, 150,000 lbs. @ $0.27 per lb. . .	$40,500			
No. 2, 250,000 lbs. @ $0.24 per lb. . .		$60,000		
No. 3, 100,000 lbs. @ $0.18 per lb. . .			$18,000	
Combined				$118,500
Costs:				
Land preparation, seed, planting, and cultivating @ $0.08532 per lb. . .	$12,798	$21,330	$ 8,532	$ 42,660
Harvesting, sorting, and grading @ $0.0711 per lb.	10,665	17,775	7,110	35,550
Marketing @ $0.0249 per lb.	3,735	6,225	2,490	12,450
Total costs	$27,198	$45,330	$18,132	$ 90,660
Net income (or loss)	$13,302	$14,670	$ (132)	$ 27,840

On the foregoing statement, Darwin and Mary divided their costs among the grades on a per pound basis. They did this because with the exception of marketing costs, their records did not show costs per grade. As to marketing costs, the records did show that $12,060 of the $12,450 was the cost of placing the No. 1 and No. 2 potatoes in bags and hauling them to the warehouse of the produce buyer. Bagging and hauling costs were the same for both grades. The remaining $390 of marketing costs was the cost of loading the No. 3 potatoes into trucks of a potato starch factory that bought these potatoes in bulk and picked them up at the farm.

Required

Prepare an income statement that will show better the results of producing and marketing the potatoes.

Problem 23-5

El Paso Company has three selling departments, A, B, and C, and two service departments, general office and purchasing. At the end of 198A, its bookkeeper brought together the following information for use in preparing the year-end statements:

	Dept. A	Dept. B	Dept. C
Sales	$190,800	$102,400	$146,800
Purchases	135,800	70,600	83,600
January 1 (beginning) inventory	24,600	17,000	20,400
December 31 (ending) inventory. . . .	29,000	18,800	14,600

El Paso Company treats salaries, supplies used, and depreciation as direct departmental expenses. The payroll, requisition, and plant asset records showed the following amounts of these expenses by departments:

	Salaries Expense	Supplies Used	Depreciation of Equipment
General office	$18,690	$ 470	$1,250
Purchasing department	12,320	390	750
Department A	20,720	770	1,700
Department B	11,020	430	900
Department C	16,280	590	1,000
	$79,030	$2,650	$5,600

The company incurred the following amounts of indirect expenses:

Rent expense.	$13,200
Advertising expense	11,000
Expired insurance	1,500
Heating and lighting expense	3,500
Janitorial expense.	4,200

El Paso Company allocates the foregoing expenses to its departments as follows:

a. Rent expense on the basis of the amount and value of floor space occupied. The general office and purchasing departments occupy space in the rear of the store that is not as valuable as space in the front; consequently, $1,200 of the total rent is allocated to these two departments in proportion to the space occupied by each. The remainder of the rent is divided between the selling departments in proportion to the space occupied. The five departments occupy these amounts of space: general office, 900 square feet; purchasing department, 600 square feet; Department A, 4,500 square feet; Department B, 2,250 square feet; and Department C, 2,250 square feet.

b. Advertising expense on the basis of sales.

c. Expired insurance on the basis of equipment book values. The book values of the equipment in the departments are: general office, $7,000; purchasing department, $4,000; Department A, $18,000; Department B, $10,000; and Department C, $11,000.

d. Heating and lighting and janitorial expenses on the basis of floor space occupied.

El Paso Company allocates its general office department expenses to its selling departments on the basis of sales, and it allocates purchasing department expenses on the basis of purchases.

Required

1. Prepare a departmental expense allocation sheet for the company.
2. Prepare a departmental income statement showing sales, costs of goods sold, expenses, and net incomes by departments and for the entire store.
3. Prepare a second departmental income statement showing departmental contributions to overhead and overall net income.

Problem 23-6

MPSI Company's Chicago plant is managed by Donna Jamison, who is responsible for all costs of the Chicago operation other than her own salary. The plant is divided into two production departments and an office department. The motor and the generator departments manufacture different products and have separate managers; the office department is managed by the plant manager. MPSI Company prepares a monthly budget for each of the production departments (motor and generator) and then accumulates costs in a manner that assigns all of the Chicago plant costs to the departments.

The department budgets and cost accumulations for the month of July were as follows:

	Budget		Actual Costs		
	Motor Dept.	Generator Dept.	Motor Dept.	Generator Dept.	Combined
Raw materials	$390,000	$280,000	$418,000	$287,000	$ 705,000
Wages	220,000	200,000	233,200	206,400	439,600
Salary—department manager	50,000	44,000	50,000	46,000	96,000
Supplies used	20,000	18,000	17,200	19,800	37,000
Depreciation of equipment.	12,000	10,000	12,000	11,600	23,600
Heating and lighting	40,000	20,000	50,000	25,000	75,000
Rent on building	48,000	24,000	48,000	24,000	72,000
Share of office department costs	82,000	82,000	77,600	77,600	155,200
	$862,000	$678,000	$906,000	$697,400	$1,603,400

Office department costs consisted of the following:

	Budget	Actual
Salary—plant manager	$84,000	$84,000
Other salaries	56,000	53,000
Other costs	24,000	18,200

Each department manager is responsible for the purchase and maintenance of equipment in the department. Heating and lighting cost and building rent are allocated to the production departments on the basis of relative space used by those departments.

Required

Prepare responsibility accounting performance reports on the managers of each production department and on the plant manager.

☐ Alternate Problems

Problem 23-1A

Pacific Super Store has in its ledger an account called Building Occupancy Costs to which it charged the following last year:

Building rent	$270,000
Lighting expense	10,000
Cleaning and maintenance	50,000
Total	$330,000

The store occupies all the space in a building having selling space on three levels—basement level, street level, and second-floor level. Each level has 8,000 square feet of selling space, a total of 24,000 square feet; and the bookkeeper divided the $330,000 of building occupancy cost by 24,000 and charged each selling department with $13.75 of building occupancy cost for each square foot of space occupied.

When Joe Froh, the manager of a basement-level department having 2,400 square feet of floor space, saw the $13.75 per square foot of building occupancy cost charged to his department, he complained. In this complaint, he cited a recent local real estate study that showed average charges for like space, including heat but not including lights and janitorial service, as follows:

Basement-level space	$ 8 per sq. ft.
Street-level space	24 per sq. ft.
Second-floor-level space	16 per sq. ft.

Required

Prepare a computation showing the amount of building occupancy cost you think should be charged to Joe Froh's department.

Problem 23-2A

The Nebraska Company began business last year with two selling departments and a general office department. It had the following results for the year:

Nebraska Company
Departmental Income Statement
For the Year Ended December 31, 198A

	Dept. 1	Dept. 2	Combined
Sales	$480,000	$240,000	$720,000
Cost of goods sold	336,000	144,000	480,000
Gross profit from sales	$144,000	$ 96,000	$240,000
Direct expenses:			
Sales salaries	$ 50,000	$ 28,800	$ 78,800
Advertising expense	4,500	3,000	7,500
Store supplies used	2,400	1,200	3,600
Depreciation of equipment	4,100	2,200	6,300
Total direct expenses	$ 61,000	$ 35,200	$ 96,200
Allocated expenses:			
Rent expense	$ 21,600	$ 14,400	$ 36,000
Heating and lighting expense	4,320	2,880	7,200
Share of office expenses	28,000	14,000	42,000
Total allocated expenses	$ 53,920	$ 31,280	$ 85,200
Total expenses	$114,920	$ 66,480	$181,400
Net income	$ 29,080	$ 29,520	$ 58,600

The company plans to add a third selling department which it estimates will produce $160,000 in sales with a 35% gross profit margin. The new department will require the following estimated direct expenses: sales salaries, $18,000; advertising expense, $1,800; store supplies, $1,000; and depreciation on equipment, $2,100.

When the company began its operations, it was necessary to rent a store room having selling space in excess of requirements. This extra space was assigned to and used by Departments 1 and 2 during the year, but when Department 3 is opened, it will take over one third the space assigned to Department 2. The space reductions are not expected to affect the operations or sales of the old departments.

The company allocates its general office department expenses to its selling departments on the basis of sales. It expects the new department to cause a $3,800 increase in general office department expenses.

The company expects the addition of Department 3 to bring new customers to the store who in addition to buying Department 3 merchandise will also do sufficient buying in the old departments to increase their sales by 5% each. It is not expected that the increase in sales in the old departments will affect their gross profit percentages nor any of their direct expenses other than supplies. It is expected the supplies used will increase in proportion to sales.

Required

Prepare a departmental income statement showing the company's expected operations with three departments.

Problem 23-3A

Bradgate Company is considering the elimination of its unprofitable Department B. The company's income statement for last year appears as follows:

Bradgate Company
Income Statement
For the Year Ended December 31, 19—

	Dept. A	Dept. B	Combined
Sales	$180,000	$ 80,000	$260,000
Cost of goods sold	88,000	62,000	150,000
Gross profit from sales	$ 92,000	$ 18,000	$110,000
Operating expenses:			
Direct expenses:			
Advertising.	$ 4,000	$ 1,800	$ 5,800
Store supplies used.	1,600	1,200	2,800
Depreciation of store equipment	3,000	1,500	4,500
Total direct expenses	$ 8,600	$ 4,500	$ 13,100
Allocated expenses:			
Sales salaries	$ 45,000	$ 9,000	$ 54,000
Rent expense	6,400	4,800	11,200
Bad debts expense	1,000	800	1,800
Office salaries	12,500	12,500	25,000
Insurance expense	1,500	500	2,000
Miscellaneous office expenses	1,100	400	1,500
Total allocated expenses.	$ 67,500	$ 28,000	$ 95,500
Total operating expenses	$ 76,100	$ 32,500	$108,600
Net income (loss).	$ 15,900	$(14,500)	$ 1,400

If Department B is eliminated:

a. The company has one office worker who earns $25,000 per year and three salesclerks each of whom earns $1,500 per month or $18,000 per year. At present the salaries of two and one-half salesclerks are charged to Department A and one-half salesclerk to Department B. The sales salaries presently assigned to Department B can be avoided if the department is eliminated and the office worker's salary could be reduced from full time to three-fourths time. However, management is considering another plan, as follows. It is the opinion of management that one salesclerk may be dismissed if Department B is eliminated, leaving only two full-time clerks in Department A and making up the difference by assigning the office worker to half-time sales work in the department. The office work could be squeezed into the remaining half-time.

b. The lease on the store building is long term and cannot be changed; therefore, the space presently occupied by Department B will have to be charged to Department A. Likewise, Department A will have to make whatever use of Department B's equipment it can, since the equipment has little or no sales value.

c. The elimination of Department B will eliminate the Department B advertising expense, losses from bad debts, and store supplies used. It will also eliminate 75% of the insurance expense allocated to the department (the portion on merchandise) and 50% of the miscellaneous office expenses presently allocated to Department B.

Required

1. List in separate columns the escapable and inescapable expenses associated with eliminating Department B.

2. Under the assumption that Department A's sales and gross profit will not be affected by the elimination of Department B, prepare an income statement showing what the company can expect to earn from the operation of Department A after Department B is eliminated. Assume that the plan of assigning part of the office worker's time to the sales force is used.

Problem 23-4A

Dan Post's business produced and sold a half million pounds of peaches last year, and he prepared the following statement to show the results:

Dan Post
Income from the Sale of Peaches
Year Ended December 31,198A

	Results by Grades			
	No. 1	**No. 2**	**No. 3**	**Combined**
Sales by grades:				
No. 1, 100,000 lbs. @ $0.44 per lb. . . .	$44,000			
No. 2, 100,000 lbs. @ $0.28 per lb. . . .		$28,000		
No. 3, 50,000 lbs. @ $0.16 per lb. . . .			$ 8,000	
Combined				$80,000
Costs:				
Tree pruning and orchard care @ $0.084 per lb.	$ 8,400	$ 8,400	$ 4,200	$21,000
Fruit picking, grading, and sorting @ $0.1008 per lb.	10,080	10,080	5,040	25,200
Marketing @ $0.0336 per lb.	3,360	3,360	1,680	8,400
Total costs	$21,840	$21,840	$10,920	$54,600
Net income (or loss).	$22,160	$ 6,160	$ (2,920)	$25,400

Upon completing the statement, Mr. Post thought a wise course of future action might be to leave the No. 3 peaches on the trees to fall off and be plowed under when the ground is cultivated between the trees, and thus avoid the loss from their sale. However, before doing so he consulted you.

When you examined the statement, you recognized that Mr. Post had divided all his costs by 250,000 and allocated them on a per pound basis. You asked him about the marketing costs and learned that $7,920 of the $8,400 was incurred in placing the No. 1 and No. 2 fruit in boxes and delivering them to the warehouse of the fruit buyer. The cost for this was the same for both grades. You also learned that the remaining $480 was for loading the No. 3 fruit on the trucks of a fruit juice manufacturer who bought this grade of fruit in bulk at the orchard for use in making fruit juice.

Required

Prepare an income statement that will reflect better the results of producing and marketing the peaches.

Problem 23-5A

Thomas Company carries on its operations with two service departments, the general office department and the purchasing department, and with three selling departments, 1, 2, and 3. At the end of its annual accounting period the company's accountant prepared the following adjusted trial balance:

Thomas Company
Adjusted Trial Balance
December 31, 198A

Cash	$ 15,750	
Merchandise inventory, Department 1	18,600	
Merchandise inventory, Department 2	36,400	
Merchandise inventory, Department 3	29,000	
Supplies	1,240	
Equipment	73,880	
Accumulated depreciation, equipment		$ 20,270
Helen Thomas, capital		145,850
Helen Thomas, withdrawals	18,000	
Sales, Department 1		104,800
Sales, Department 2		208,400
Sales, Department 3		136,800
Purchases, Department 1	68,800	
Purchases, Department 2	158,600	
Purchases, Department 3	83,400	
Salaries expense.	73,710	
Rent expense	15,000	
Advertising expense	11,250	
Expired insurance	1,000	
Heating and lighting expense	2,400	
Depreciation of equipment.	3,640	
Supplies used	2,250	
Janitorial services	3,200	
Totals	$616,120	$616,120

Required

1. Prepare a departmental expense allocation sheet for Thomas Company, using the following information:

   a. Thomas Company treats salaries, supplied used, and depreciation of equipment as direct departmental expenses. The payroll, requisition, and plant asset records show the following amounts of these expenses by departments:

	Salaries Expense	Supplies Used	Depreciation of Equipment
General office	$20,590	$ 290	$ 500
Purchasing department	14,080	260	440
Department 1	9,320	550	850
Department 2	16,640	630	1,230
Department 3	13,080	520	620
	$73,710	$2,250	$3,640

   b. The company treats the remainder of its expenses as indirect and allocates them as follows:

(1) Rent expense on the basis of the amount and value of floor space occupied. The general office occupies 600 square feet and the purchasing department occupies 400 square feet on a balcony at the rear of the store. This space is not as valuable as space on the main floor; therefore, the store allocates $1,000 of its rent to these two departments on the basis of space occupied and allocates the remainder to the selling departments on the basis of the main-floor space they occupy. The selling departments occupy main-floor space as follows: Department 1, 2,000 square feet; Department 2, 3,500 square feet; and Department 3, 1,500 square feet.

(2) Advertising expense on the basis of sales.

(3) Insurance expense on the basis of the book values of the equipment in the departments, which are: general office, $5,000; purchasing, $4,000; Department 1, $13,000; Department 2, $19,000; and Department 3, $9,000.

(4) Heating and lighting and janitorial services on the basis of floor space occupied.

c. The company allocates general office department expenses to the selling departments on the basis of sales, and it allocates purchasing department expenses on the basis of purchases.

2. Prepare a departmental income statement for the company showing sales, cost of goods sold, expenses, and net incomes by departments and for the entire store. The year-end inventories were Department 1, $23,200; Department 2, $46,800; and Department 3, $26,800.

3. Prepare a second income statement for the company showing departmental contributions to overhead and overall net income.

Problem 23-6A

Fiberbowl Inc.'s Boston plant is managed by George Awn, who is responsible for all costs of the Boston operation other than his own salary. The plant is divided into two production departments and an office department. The webbing and dalite departments manufacture different products and have separate managers; the office department is managed by the plant manager. Fiberbowl prepares a monthly budget for each of the production departments (webbing and dalite) and then accumulates costs in a manner that assigns all of the Boston plant costs to the departments.

The department budgets and cost accumulations for the month of April were as follows:

	Budget		Actual Costs		
	Webbing Dept.	Dalite Dept.	Webbing Dept.	Dalite Dept.	Combined
Raw materials	$345,000	$420,000	$335,250	$431,400	$ 766,650
Wages	252,000	297,000	260,850	289,350	550,200
Salary—department manager	39,000	42,000	41,250	42,000	83,250
Supplies used	11,250	12,000	14,400	13,800	28,200
Depreciation of equipment	21,000	15,000	21,000	16,500	37,500
Heating and lighting	24,000	36,000	29,160	43,740	72,900
Rent on building	15,000	22,500	15,000	22,500	37,500
Share of office department costs . . .	97,500	97,500	104,250	104,250	208,500
	$804,750	$942,000	$821,160	$963,540	$1,784,700

Office department costs consisted of the following:

	Budget	Actual
Salary—plant manager	$81,000	$81,000
Other salaries	90,000	93,000
Other costs	24,000	34,500

Each department manager is responsible for the purchase and maintenance of equipment in the department. Heating and lighting cost and building rent are allocated to the production departments on the basis of relative space used by those departments.

Required

Prepare responsibility accounting performance reports on the managers of each production department and on the plant manager.

Provocative Problems

Provocative Problem 23-1 The LTV Corporation

The LTV Corporation is a diversified operating company involved in steel, aerospace/defense and energy products. In its 1984 annual report, the company presented information on its business segments that included the following:

The results of operations, identifiable assets, capital expenditures and depreciation and amortization of LTV's three continuing business segments are outlined in the accompanying three year summary of segment information.

THREE YEAR SUMMARY BY BUSINESS SEGMENT (IN MILLIONS)

	Net Sales						Operating Income (Loss)		
	1984		1983		1982				
	To Unaffiliated Customers	Between Segments	To Unaffiliated Customers	Between Segments	To Unaffiliated Customers	Between Segments	1984	1983	1982
Segment									
Steel	$4,447.1	$ 74.4	$2,935.3	$ —	$2,797.6	$ 242.0	$(217.4)	$(200.2)	$(298.9)
Aerospace/Defense									
Aerospace Products	1,066.2	—	842.2	—	776.9	—	78.5	56.8	45.1
Special Government Vehicles	886.7	—	299.6	—	—	—	46.3	10.5	—
Energy Products	646.1	0.9	500.7	—	1,202.3	0.3	(73.1)	(56.9)	35.1
Intersegment eliminations	—	(75.3)	—	—	—	(242.3)	—	—	(18.7)
Total operations	$7,046.1	$ —	$4,577.8	$ —	$4,776.8	$ —	(165.7)	(189.8)	(237.4)
Interest expense and debt discount							(250.6)	(154.9)	(105.0)
Corporate income, net							10.7	92.9	72.9
Income (loss) before taxes — continuing operations							$(405.6)	$(251.8)	$(269.5)

	Identifiable Assets			Capital Expenditures(1)			Depreciation and Amortization		
	1984	1983	1982	1984	1983	1982	1984	1983	1982
Segment									
Steel	$5,429.3	$2,972.7	$2,615.4	$140.9	$230.4	$237.6	$166.9	$ 89.8	$ 83.7
Aerospace/Defense									
Aerospace Products	609.8	559.9	301.1	39.6	11.7	14.4	12.6	9.5	8.5
Special Government Vehicles	341.1	328.1	—	13.0	5.5	—	3.5	1.4	—
Energy Products	640.1	592.3	679.6	7.9	6.8	37.7	10.5	8.9	8.9
Corporate and other	69.3	(38.9)	317.9	4.1	0.3	0.4	0.5	0.5	0.4
Intersegment eliminations	(163.6)	(7.8)	(3.2)	—	—	—	—	—	—
Total continuing operations	6,926.0	4,406.3	3,910.8	$205.5	$254.7	$290.1	$194.0	$110.1	$101.5
Discontinued ocean shipping operations	—	—	112.4						
Total	$6,926.0	$4,406.3	$4,023.2						

(1) Does not include property, plant and equipment acquired as part of business acquisitions. See "BUSINESS ACQUISITIONS" note to financial statements.

Answer the following questions about the segmental information contained in the 1984 annual report of The LTV Corporation.

1. What are the industrial segments into which the operations of The LTV Corporation are divided?

2. What was the 1984 net sales of the Energy Products segment to (a) outside parties and (b) the other segments of The LTV Corporation?

3. Which segment earned the largest profit in 1984? Which resulted in the largest loss?

4. In which segment did The LTV Corporation have the largest investment of identifiable assets at the end of 1984?

5. What amount of net sales would you expect to have been presented on the 1984 income statement of The LTV Corporation?

6. The presentation of 1984 net sales shows a $75.3 million intersegment elimination. Why was this amount eliminated?

7. What amount of total assets would you expect to have been presented on the 1984 balance sheet of The LTV Corporation?

8. What possible explanation might you give for the $163.6 million intersegment elimination of identifiable assets?

Provocative Problem 23-2   R-E-D, A Real Estate Partnership

Terry Rich, Janet Ermine, and Tom Deal entered into a partnership for the purpose of developing and selling a plot of land currently owned by Rich. Ermine invested $260,000 cash in the partnership. Rich invested his land at its $300,000 fair market value, and Deal invested $40,000; and they agreed to share losses and gains equally. Deal was to provide the necessary real estate expertise to make the project a success. The partnership installed streets and water mains costing $300,000 and divided the land into 14 building lots. They priced Lots 1, 2, 3, and 4 for sale at $60,000 each; Lots 5, 6, 7, 8, 9, 10, 11, and 12 at $70,000 each; and Lots 13 and 14 at $80,000 each. The partners agreed that Deal could take Lot 13 at cost for his personal use. The remaining lots were sold, and the partnership dissolved. Determine the amount of partnership cash each partner should receive in the dissolution.

Provocative Problem 23-3   Solar-Drive Company

The Solar-Drive Company bookkeeper prepared the following income statement for May of the current year:

Solar-Drive Company
Income Statement for May 198A

	Solar Panels Department	Battery Department	Combined
Sales	$160,000	$240,000	$400,000
Cost of goods sold	114,400	171,600	286,000
Gross profit on sales	$ 45,600	$ 68,400	$114,000
Warehousing expenses	$ 11,800	$ 11,800	$ 23,600
Selling expenses	22,400	24,400	46,800
General and administrative expenses	6,100	6,100	12,200
Total expenses	$ 40,300	$ 42,300	$ 82,600
Net income	$ 5,300	$ 26,100	$ 31,400

The company is a wholesaler of solar panels and batteries and is organized on a departmental basis. However, the company manager does not feel that the bookkeeper's statement reflects the profit situation in the company's two selling departments and he has asked you to redraft it with any supporting schedules or comments you think desirable. Your investigation reveals the following:

1. The company sold 1,000 solar panels and 800 batteries during May. The bookkeeper allocated cost of goods sold between the two departments on an arbitrary basis. A battery actually costs the company twice as much as a solar panel.

2. A solar panel and a battery take approximately the same space for storage. However, because there are two styles of solar panels and three styles of batteries the company must carry a 50% greater inventory of batteries than of panels.

3. The company occupies its building on the following bases:

	Area of Space	Value of Space
Warehouse.	80%	60%
Solar panel sales office	5	10
Battery sales office	5	10
General office	10	20

4. Warehousing expenses for May consisted of the following:

Wages expense	$12,000
Depreciation of building	8,000
Heating and lighting expenses	2,000
Depreciation of warehouse equipment	1,600
Total	$23,600

The bookkeeper had charged all of the building's depreciation plus all of the heating and lighting expenses to warehousing expenses.

5. Selling expenses for May consisted of the following:

	Solar Panels Department	Battery Department
Sales salaries	$16,000	$18,000
Advertising	6,000	6,000
Depreciation of office equipment.	400	400
Totals	$22,400	$24,400

Sales salaries and depreciation were charged to the two departments on the basis of actual amounts incurred. Advertising was allocated by the bookkeeper. The company has an established advertising budget based on dollars of sales which it followed rather closely in May.

6. General and administrative expenses for May consisted of the following:

Salaries and wages	$11,200
Depreciation of office equipment	800
Miscellaneous office expenses	200
Total	$12,200

Provocative Problem 23-4   VCR Corporation

VCR Corporation wholesales high-quality camera/recorders that are designed for professional usage. Operations of the company during the past year resulted in the following:

	Standard	Deluxe
Units sold	300	100
Selling price per unit	$1,500	$2,000
Cost per unit	800	1,050
Sales commission per unit.	225	300
Indirect selling and administrative expenses	375	500

Indirect selling and administrative expenses totaled $162,500 and were allocated between the sales of Standard and Deluxe units on the basis of their relative sales volumes. The Standard model produced $450,000 of revenue, and the Deluxe model produced $200,000; thus, the Standard model was assigned 45/65 of the $162,500 of indirect expenses and the Deluxe model was assigned 20/65. After allocating the total indirect expenses to the two models, the indirect expenses per unit were determined by dividing the total by the number of units sold. Hence, the Standard model's cost per unit was $375 and the Deluxe model's cost per unit was $500.

Management of VCR Corporation is attempting to decide between three courses of action and asks you to evaluate which of the three courses is most desirable. The three alternatives are: (1) through advertising push the sales of the Standard model, (2) through advertising push the sales of the Deluxe model, or (3) do no additional advertising, in which case sales of each model will continue at present levels. The demand for camera/recorders is fairly stable, and an increase in the number of units of one model sold will cause an equally large decrease in unit sales of the other model. However, through the expenditure of $5,000 for advertising, the company can shift the sale of 50 units of the Standard model to the Deluxe model, or vice versa, depending upon which model receives the advertising attention. Should the company advertise; and if so, which model? Back your position with income statements.

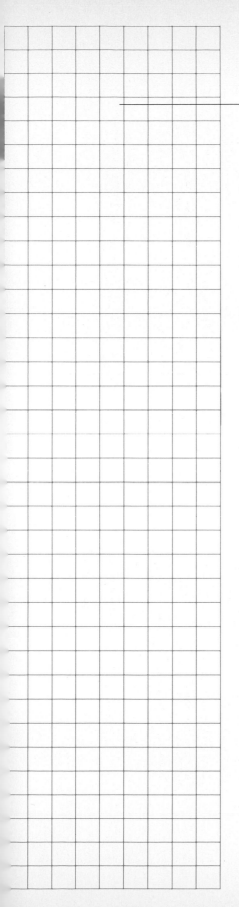

Part Eight

Planning and Controlling Business Operations

24 Cost-Volume-Profit Analysis

After studying Chapter 24, you should be able to:

1. Describe the different types of cost behavior experienced by a typical company.

2. State the assumptions that underlie cost-volume-profit analysis and explain how these assumptions restrict the usefulness of the information obtained from the analysis.

3. Prepare and interpret a scatter diagram of past costs and sales volume.

4. Calculate a break-even point for a single product company and graphically plot its costs and revenues.

5. Describe some extensions that may be added to the basic cost-volume-profit analysis of break-even point.

6. Calculate a composite sales unit for a multiproduct company and a break-even point for such a company.

7. Define or explain the words and phrases listed in the chapter Glossary.

Cost-volume-profit analysis is a means of predicting the effect of changes in costs and sales levels on the income of a business. In its simplest form, it involves the determination of the sales level at which a company neither earns a profit nor incurs a loss, or in other words, the point at which it breaks even. For this reason, cost-volume-profit analysis is often called **break-even analysis.** However the technique can be expanded to answer additional questions, such as: What sales volume is necessary to earn a desired net income? What net income will be earned if unit selling prices are reduced in order to increase sales volume? What net income will be earned if a new machine that will reduce unit labor costs is installed? What net income will be earned if we change the sales mix? When the technique is expanded to answer such additional questions, the descriptive phrase **cost-volume-profit analysis** is more appropriate than **break-even analysis.**

■ Cost Behavior

Conventional cost-volume-profit analyses require that costs be classified as either fixed or variable. Some costs are definitely fixed in nature. Others are strictly variable. But, when costs are examined, some are observed to be neither completely fixed nor completely variable.

Fixed Costs

A **fixed cost** remains unchanged in total amount over a wide range of production levels. For example, if the factory building is rented for, say, $1,000 per month, this cost remains the same whether the factory operates on a one-shift, two-shift, or an around-the-clock basis. Likewise, the cost is the same whether one hundred units of product are produced in a month, one thousand units are produced, or any other number up to the full production capacity of the plant. Note, however, that while the total amount of a fixed cost remains constant as the level of production changes, fixed costs per unit of product decrease as volume increases. For example, if rent is $1,000 per month and two units of product are produced in a month, the rent cost per unit is $500; but if production is increased to 10 units per month, rent cost per unit decreases to $100. Likewise it decreases to $2 per unit if production is increased to 500 units per month.

When production volume is plotted on a graph, units of product are shown on the horizontal axis and dollars of cost are shown on the vertical axis. Fixed costs are then expressed as a horizontal line, since the total amount of fixed costs remains constant at all levels of production. This is shown in the Illustration 24-1 graph where the fixed costs remain at $32,000 at all production levels up to 2,000 units of product.

Variable Costs

A **variable cost** changes in total amount as production volume changes. For example, the cost of the material that enters into a product is a variable cost. If material costing $20 is required in the production of one unit of product, total material costs are $20 if one unit of product is manufactured, $40 if two units are manufactured, $60 if three units are manufactured, and so on up for any number of units. In other words, the variable cost

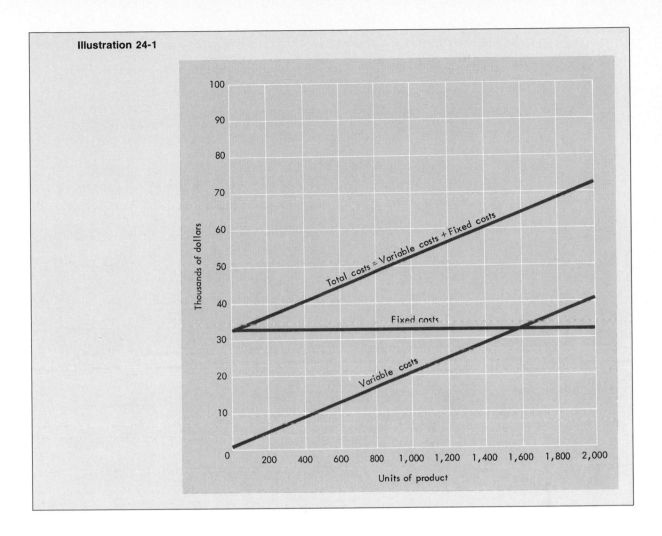

Illustration 24-1

per unit of production remains constant while the total amount of variable cost changes in direct proportion to changes in the level of production. Variable costs appear on a graph as a straight line with a positive slope; the line rises as the production volume increases, as in Illustration 24-1.

Semivariable Costs and Stair-Step Costs

All costs are not necessarily either fixed or variable. For example, some costs go up in steps. Consider the salaries of production supervisors. Supervisory salaries may be more or less fixed for any production volume from zero to the maximum that can be completed on a one-shift basis. Then, if an additional shift must be added to increase production, a whole new group of supervisors must be hired and supervisory salaries go up by a lump-sum amount. Total supervisor costs then remain fixed at this level until a third shift is added when they increase by another lump sum. Costs such as these are called **stair-step costs** and are shown graphically in Illustration 24-2.

In addition to stair-step costs, some costs may be semivariable or curvi-

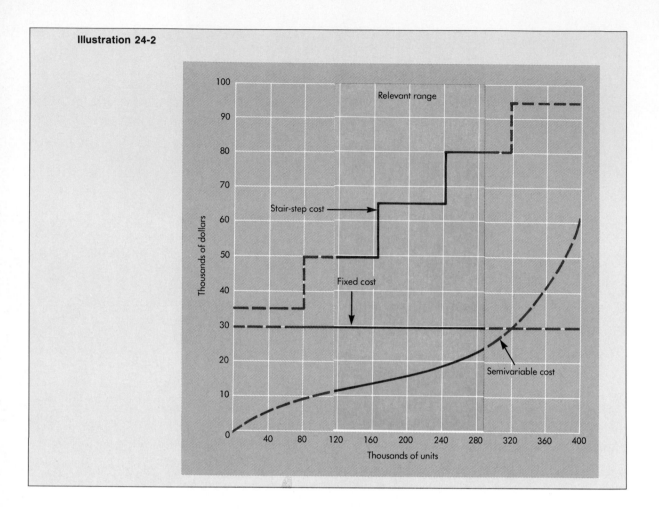

Illustration 24-2

linear in nature. **Semivariable costs** go up with volume increases, but when plotted on a graph, they must be plotted as a curved line (see Illustration 24-2). These costs change with production-level changes, but not proportionately.

For example, at low levels of production, the addition of more laborers may allow each laborer to specialize so that the whole crew becomes more efficient. Each new laborer increases the total cost, but the increased production more than compensates for the increased cost so that the cost per unit is reduced. Eventually, however, the addition of more laborers in a given plant may cause inefficiencies; laborers may begin to waste time bumping into each other. Thus, the addition of a new laborer may add some production, but the cost per unit increases.

Cost Assumptions

Conventional **cost-volume-profit analysis** is based on relationships that can be expressed as straight lines. Costs are assumed to be either fixed or variable. With the costs expressed as straight lines, the lines are then analyzed in order to answer a variety of questions. The reliability of the answers secured through application of the technique rests on three basic assumptions. If a cost-volume-profit analysis is to be reliable:

1. The per unit selling price must be constant. (The selling price per unit must remain the same regardless of production level.)
2. The costs classified as "variable" must, in fact, behave as variable costs; that is, the actual (variable) cost per unit of production must remain constant.
3. The costs classified as "fixed" must, in fact, remain constant over wide changes in the level of production.

When these assumptions are met, costs and revenues may be correctly represented by straight lines. However, the actual behavior of costs and revenues often is not completely consistent with these assumptions, and if the assumptions are violated by significant amounts, the results of cost-volume-profit analysis will not be reliable. Yet, there are at least two reasons why these assumptions tend to provide reliable analyses.

Aggregating Costs May Support Assumptions While individual variable costs may not act in a truly variable manner, the process of adding such costs together may offset such violations of the assumption. In other words, the assumption of variable behavior may be satisfied in respect to total variable costs even though it is violated in respect to individual variable costs. Similarly, the assumption that fixed costs remain constant may be satisfied for total fixed costs even though individual fixed costs may violate the assumption.

Relevant Range of Operations Another reason why the assumptions that revenues, variable costs, and fixed costs can be reasonably represented as straight lines is that the assumptions are only intended to apply over the **relevant range of operations.** The relevant range of operations, as plotted in Illustration 24-2, is the normal operating range for the business. It excludes the extremely high and low levels that are not apt to be encountered. Thus, a specific fixed cost is expected to be truly fixed only within the relevant range. It may be that beyond the limits of the relevant range, the fixed cost would not remain constant.

The previous discussion defined variable costs and fixed costs in terms of levels of production activity. However, in cost-volume-profit analysis, the level of activity is usually measured in terms of sales volume, whether stated as sales dollars or number of units sold. Thus, an additional assumption is frequently made that the level of production is the same as the level of sales, or if they are not the same, that the difference will not be enough to materially damage the reliability of the analysis.

It must also be recognized that cost-volume-profit analysis yields approximate answers to questions concerning the interrelations of costs, volume, and profits. So long as management understands that the answers provided are approximations, cost-volume-profit analysis can be a useful managerial tool.

Estimating Cost Behavior

The process of estimating the behavior of a company's costs requires judgment and, to the extent past data is available, a careful examination of past experience. Initially, the individual costs should be reviewed and classified as fixed or variable based on the accountant's understanding of how each cost is likely to behave. Some costs may be classified quite easily. For example, raw materials costs of a manufacturer or cost of goods sold of a merchandiser are undoubtedly variable costs. Similarly, a constant monthly rent expense or the monthly salaries of administrative personnel are clearly fixed costs.

Mixed Costs Although some costs are easily classified as variable or fixed, the behavior of other costs may be less obvious. For example, compensation to sales personnel might include a constant monthly salary plus a commission based on sales. A cost of this type is called a **mixed cost** (see Illustration 24-3). Instead of classifying a mixed cost as variable or fixed, it should be divided into its separate fixed and variable components so that each can be classified correctly.

Scatter Diagrams Classifying costs as fixed or variable should be based, to the extent possible, on an analysis of past experience. One helpful technique of analyzing past experience is to display past data on a **scatter diagram,** such as is shown in Illustration 24-4. In preparing a scatter diagram, volume in dollars or units is measured on the horizontal axis and cost is measured on the vertical axis. The cost and volume of each period are entered as a single point on the diagram.

Illustration 24-4 shows a scatter diagram of a company's total costs and sales for each of 12 months. Each point shows the total costs incurred and the sales volume during a given month. For example, in one month, sales amounted to $30,000 and total costs were $26,000. These results were entered on the diagram as the point labeled "A."

Estimated Line of Cost Behavior In Illustration 24-4, observe the **estimated line of cost behavior.** This line attempts to reflect the average relationship

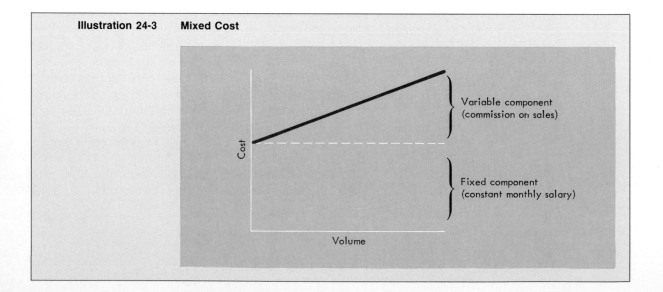

Illustration 24-3   Mixed Cost

Illustration 24-4

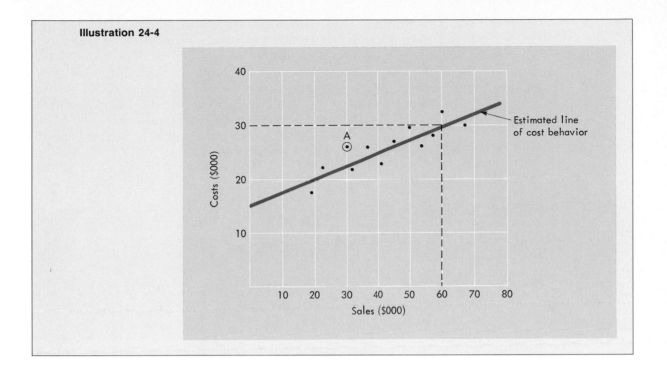

between total costs and sales volume. Several alternative methods can be used to derive this line.

A crude means of deriving this line is called the **high-low method.** To use this method, all that is required is to identify the two points in the diagram that represent the highest total cost and the lowest total cost. A line is then drawn between these two points. The most obvious deficiency in this approach is that it totally ignores all of the available cost and sales volume points except the highest and lowest.

Another, somewhat better approach is to visually inspect the scatter of points and draw a line through the scatter that appears to provide an average reflection of the relationship between costs and volume. For quick and rough analyses, this approach is often satisfactory.

More sophisticated methods of approximating cost behavior are also available. Among these, perhaps the most often used is the statistical method of **least-squares regression.** This method requires fairly extensive calculations but results in an approximation that can be described as a line that best fits the actual cost and sales volume experience of the company. The calculations for least-squares regressions are typically covered in statistics courses and are applied to accounting data in more advanced cost accounting courses.

Return to Illustration 24-4 and observe that the sales volume each month ranged from approximately $20,000 to $67,000. If the estimated line of cost behavior is extended too far beyond this range, it is likely to be an unreliable basis for predicting actual costs. Note, however, that the line has been extended downward to the point at which it intersects the horizontal axis ($15,000). This should be interpreted as follows: Assuming sales volume in the range of past operations ($20,000 to $67,000), the company's total costs apparently include fixed costs of approximately $15,000.

Variable costs per sales dollar are represented in Illustration 24-4 by the slope of the estimated line of cost behavior. The slope may be calculated by comparing any two points on the line. To estimate variable cost per sales dollar, the change in total cost between the two points is divided by the change in sales volume between the two points.

For example, in Illustration 24-4, two points could be selected and the variable cost per sales dollar calculated as follows:

	Sales	Cost
First point	$60,000	$30,000
Second point	–0–	15,000
Changes	$60,000	$15,000

$$\frac{\text{Change in cost}}{\text{Change in sales}} = \frac{\$15,000}{\$60,000} = \$0.25 \text{ of cost per sales dollar}$$

An analysis of past experience may allow the accountant to estimate total fixed costs and variable costs per unit of volume without making a detailed classification of each individual cost. However, the accountant will have greater confidence in the analysis if individual costs are classified and the results are tested against observations of past experience. In testing the classifications, scatter diagrams may be prepared for individual costs, total variable costs, total fixed costs, and total costs.

■ **Break-Even Point**

A company's **break-even point** is the sales level at which it neither earns a profit nor incurs a loss. It may be expressed either in units of product or in dollars of sales. To illustrate, assume that Alpha Company sells a single product for $100 per unit and incurs $70 of variable costs per unit sold. If the fixed costs involved in selling the product are $24,000, the company breaks even on the product as soon as it sells 800 units or as soon as sales volume reaches $80,000. This break-even point may be determined as follows:

1. Each unit sold at $100 recovers its $70 variable costs and contributes $30 toward the fixed costs.
2. The fixed costs are $24,000; consequently, 800 units ($24,000 ÷ $30 = 800) must be sold to pay the fixed costs.
3. And 800 units at $100 each produce an $80,000 sales volume.

The $30 amount by which the sales price exceeds variable costs per unit is this product's **contribution margin per unit.** In other words, the contribution margin per unit is the amount that the sale of one unit contributes toward recovery of the fixed costs and then toward a profit.

Also, the contribution margin of a product expressed as a percentage of its sales price is its **contribution rate.** For instance, the contribution rate of the $100 product of this illustration is 30% ($30 ÷ $100 = 30%).

With contribution margin and contribution rate defined, it is possible to set up the following formulas for calculating a break-even point in units and in dollars:

$$\text{Break-even point in units} = \frac{\text{Fixed costs}}{\text{Contribution margin per unit}}$$

$$\text{Break-even point in dollars} = \frac{\text{Fixed costs}}{\text{Contribution rate}}$$

Application of the second formula to figures for the product of this illustration gives this result:

$$\text{Break-even point in dollars} = \frac{\$24,000}{30\%} = \frac{\$24,000}{0.30} = \$80,000$$

Although the solution in the present example comes out evenly, a contribution rate should be carried out several decimal places to avoid minor rounding errors when calculating the break-even point in dollars. In solving the exercises and problems at the end of this chapter, for example, calculations of contribution rate should be carried to six decimal places unless the requirements state otherwise. Calculated either way, Alpha Company's break-even point may be verified with an income statement, as in Illustration 24-5. Observe in the illustration that revenue from sales exactly equals the sum of the fixed and variable costs at the break-even point. Recognizing this will prove helpful in understanding the material that follows in this chapter.

■ **Break-Even Graph**

A cost-volume-profit analysis may be shown graphically as in Illustration 24-6. When presented in this form, the graph is commonly called a break-even graph or break-even chart. On such a graph, the horizontal axis shows units sold and the vertical axis shows both dollars of sales and dollars of costs; costs and revenues are plotted as straight lines. The illustrated graph shows the break-even point of Alpha Company. A break-even graph is prepared as follows:

1. The line representing fixed costs is plotted at the fixed cost level. Note that it is a horizontal line, since the fixed costs are the same at all sales levels. Actually, the fixed costs line is not essential to the analysis;

Illustration 24-5

Alpha Company
Income Statement at the Break-Even Point

Sales (800 units @ $100 each)		$80,000
Costs:		
Fixed costs	$24,000	
Variable costs (800 units @ $70 each)	56,000	80,000
Net income		$ –0–

Illustration 24-6

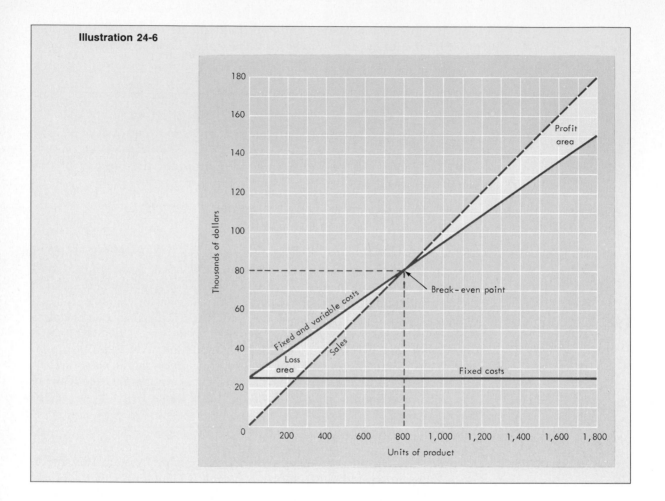

however, it contributes important information and is commonly plotted on a break-even chart.

2. Next, the sales line is projected from the point of zero units and zero dollars of sales to the point of maximum sales shown on the graph. In choosing the maximum number of units to be shown, a better graph results if the number chosen is such that it will cause the break-even point to appear near the center of the graph.

3. Next, the variable cost plus fixed cost line is plotted. Note that it begins at the fixed cost level and, as a result, shows total costs at all production levels. At the zero sales level, there are no variable costs, only fixed costs. However, at any level above zero sales, all the fixed costs are presented and so are the variable costs for that level. Also observe that the variable cost plus fixed cost line intersects the sales line at the break-even point. It intersects at this point because at the break-even point the revenue from sales exactly equals the sum of the fixed and variable costs, or in other words, the total costs.

In reading a break-even chart, the vertical distance between the sales line and the total cost line represents a loss to the left of the break-even point and a profit to the right of it. The amount of profit or loss at any given sales level can be determined from the graph by measuring the vertical distance between the sales line and the total cost line at the given level.

■ **Sales Required for a Desired Net Income**

A slight extension of the concept behind the break-even calculation will produce a formula that may be used in determining the sales level necessary to produce a desired net income. The formula is:

$$\text{Sales at desired income level} = \frac{\underset{\text{costs}}{\text{Fixed}} + \underset{\text{income}}{\text{Net}} + \underset{\text{taxes}}{\text{Income}}}{\text{Contribution rate}}$$

To illustrate the formula's use, assume that Alpha Company of the previous discussion, the company having $24,000 of fixed costs and a 30% contribution rate, has set a $20,000 after-tax income goal for itself. Assume further that in order to have a $20,000 net income, the company must earn $28,500 and pay $8,500 in income taxes. Under these assumptions, $175,000 of sales are necessary to produce a $20,000 net income. This is calculated as follows:

$$\text{Sales at desired income level} = \frac{\underset{\text{costs}}{\text{Fixed}} + \underset{\text{income}}{\text{Net}} + \underset{\text{taxes}}{\text{Income}}}{\text{Contribution rate}}$$

$$\text{Sales at desired income level} = \frac{\$24,000 + \$20,000 + \$8,500}{30\%}$$

$$\text{Sales at desired income level} = \frac{\$52,500}{30\%} = \$175,000$$

In the formula just given, the contribution rate was used as the divisor and the resulting answer was in dollars of sales. The contribution margin can also be used as the divisor; when it is, the resulting answer is in units of products.

■ **Margin of Safety**

The difference between a company's current sales and sales at its break-even point, when sales are above the break-even point, is known as its margin of safety. The **margin of safety** is the amount sales may decrease before the company will incur a loss. It may be expressed in units of product, dollars, or as a percentage of sales. For example, if current sales are $100,000 and the break-even point is $80,000, the margin of safety is $20,000, or 20% of sales, calculated as follows:

$$\frac{\text{Sales} - \text{Break-even sales}}{\text{Sales}} = \text{Margin of safety}$$

or

$$\frac{\$100,000 - \$80,000}{\$100,000} = 20\% \text{ margin of safety}$$

■ **Income from a Given Sales Level**

Cost-volume-profit analysis goes beyond break-even analysis and can be used to answer other questions. For example, what income will result from a given sales level? To understand the analysis used in answering this question, recall the factors that enter into the calculation of income. When expressed in equation form, they are:

$$\text{Sales} - (\text{Fixed costs} + \text{Variable costs}) = \text{Income}$$

or

$$\text{Income} = \text{Sales} - (\text{Fixed costs} + \text{Variable costs})$$

This equation may be used to calculate the income that will result at a given sales level. For example, assume that Alpha Company of the previous illustrations wishes to know what income will result if its sales level can be increased to $200,000. That would be 2,000 units of its product at $100 per unit. To determine the answer, recall that the variable costs per unit of this product are $70 and note that the $70 is 0.7 of the product's selling price. Consequently, variable costs for 2,000 units of the product are 0.7 of the selling price of these units, or $(0.7 \times \$200,000) = \$140,000$. Alpha Company's fixed costs are $24,000. Therefore, if these known factors are substituted in the equation for determining income, the equation will read:

$$\text{Income} = \$200,000 - [\$24,000 + (0.7 \times \$200,000)]$$
$$\text{Income} = \$200,000 - \$164,000$$
$$\text{Income} = \$36,000$$

The $36,000 is "before-tax" income; and as a result, if Alpha Company wishes to learn its after-tax income from the sale of 2,000 units of its product, it will have to apply the appropriate tax rates to the $36,000.

■ **Other Questions**

A company may wish to know what would happen to its break-even point if it reduced the selling price of its product in order to increase sales. Or it might wish to know what would happen if it installed a new machine that would increase its fixed costs but which would reduce variable costs. These are two of several possible questions involving changes in selling prices and costs. At first glance such changes seem to violate the basic assumptions on which cost-volume-profit analysis is based. But this is not true. A constant selling price, truly variable costs, and truly fixed costs are assumed to hold for any analysis involving the assumed price and costs. However, changes may be made, and if made, the new price and new costs are assumed to remain constant for the analyses involving that price and those costs. The fact that changes can be made in these factors is helpful for planning purposes because the effect of changes can be predicted before the changes are actually made.

To illustrate the effect of changes, assume that Alpha Company is considering the installation of a new machine that will increase the fixed costs of producing and selling its product from $24,000 to $30,000. However, the machine will reduce the variable costs from $70 per unit of product to $60. The selling price of the product will remain unchanged at $100, and the company wishes to know what its break-even point will be if the machine is installed. Examination of the costs shows that the installation will not only increase the company's fixed costs but it will also change the contribution margin and contribution rate of the company's product. The new contribution margin will be $40, that is, ($100 − $60) = $40, and the new contribution rate will be 40%, that is, ($40 ÷ $100) = 0.4 or 40%. Consequently, if the machine is installed, the company's new break-even point will be:

$$\text{Break-even point in dollars} = \frac{\$30,000}{0.4} = \$75,000$$

In addition to their use in determining Alpha Company's break-even point, the new fixed costs and the new contribution rate may be used to determine the sales level needed to earn a desired net income. They may also be used to determine the expected income at a given sales level, or to answer other questions the company will want to answer before installing the new machine.

■ **Multiproduct Break-Even Point**

The break-even point for a company selling a number of products can be determined by using a hypothetical unit made up of units of each of the company's products in their expected **sales mix.** Such a hypothetical unit is really a composite unit and is treated in all analyses as though it were a single product. To illustrate the use of such a hypothetical unit, assume that Beta Company sells three products, A, B, and C, and it wishes to calculate its break-even point. Unit selling prices for the three products are Product A, $5; Product B, $8; and Product C, $4. The sales mix or ratio in which the products are expected to be sold is 4:2:1, and the company's fixed costs are $48,000. Under these assumptions a composite unit selling price for the three products can be calculated as follows:

4 units of Product A @ $5 per unit =	$20
2 units of Product B @ $8 per unit =	16
1 unit of Product C @ $4 per unit =	4
Selling price of a composite unit . .	$40

Also, if the variable costs of selling the three products are Product A, $3.25; Product B, $4.50; and Product C, $2, the variable costs of a composite unit of the products are:

4 units of Product A @ $3.25 per unit =	$13
2 units of Product B @ $4.50 per unit =	9
1 unit of Product C @ $2.00 per unit =	2
Variable costs of a composite unit . .	$24

With the variable costs and selling price of a composite unit of the company's products calculated, the contribution margin for a composite unit may be determined by subtracting the variable costs of a composite unit from the selling price of such a unit, as follows:

$$\$40 - \$24 = \$16 \text{ contribution margin per composite unit}$$

The $16 contribution margin may then be used to determine the company's break-even point in composite units. The break-even point is:

$$\text{Break-even point in composite units} = \frac{\text{Fixed costs}}{\text{Composite contribution margin per unit}}$$

$$\text{Break-even point in composite units} = \frac{\$48,000}{\$16}$$

$$\text{Break-even point} = 3,000 \text{ composite units}$$

The company breaks even when it sells 3,000 composite units of its products. However, to determine the number of units of each product it must sell to break even, the number of units of each product in the composite unit must be multiplied by the number of composite units needed to break even, as follows:

Product A: 4 × 3,000 = 12,000 units
Product B: 2 × 3,000 =   6,000 units
Product C: 1 × 3,000 =   3,000 units

The accuracy of all these computations can be verified by preparing an income statement showing the company's revenues and costs at the break-even point. Such a statement is shown in Illustration 24-7.

A composite unit made up of units of each of a company's products in their expected sales mix may be used in answering a variety of cost-volume-

---

Illustration 24-7

Beta Company
Income Statement at the Break-Even Point

Sales:		
Product A (12,000 units @ $5)		$ 60,000
Product B (6,000 units @ $8)		48,000
Product C (3,000 units @ $4)		12,000
Total revenues		$120,000
Costs:		
Fixed costs	$48,000	
Variable costs:		
Product A (12,000 units @ $3.25) . . . $39,000		
Product B (6,000 units @ $4.50) 27,000		
Product C (3,000 units @ $2.00) 6,000		
Total variable costs	72,000	
Total costs		120,000
Net income		–0–

profit questions. In making all such analyses, it is assumed that the product mix remains constant at all sales levels just as the other factors entering into an analysis are assumed to be constant. Nevertheless, this does not prevent changes in the assumed sales mix in order to learn what would happen if the mix were changed. However, problems involving changes in the sales mix require a recomputation of the composite unit selling price and composite unit variable costs for each change in the mix.

■   **Evaluating the Results**

Cost-volume-profit analyses have their greatest use in predicting what will happen when changes are made in selling prices, product mix, and the various cost factors. However, in evaluating the results of such analyses, several points should be kept in mind. First, the analyses are used to predict future results. Therefore, the data used in the formulas and on the graphs are assumed or forecasted data. Consequently, the results of the analyses are no more reliable than the data used. Second, cost-volume-profit analyses as presented here are based on the assumptions that in any one analysis selling price will remain constant, fixed costs are truly fixed, and variable costs are truly variable. These assumptions do not always reflect reality. Therefore, at best the answers obtained through cost-volume-profit analyses are approximations. However, if this is recognized, cost-volume-profit analyses can be useful to management in making decisions.

The cost-volume-profit analyses presented in this chapter are based on the assumption that revenues and costs may be expressed as straight lines; and as pointed out, such an assumption does not always hold. Therefore, it should be noted that cost-volume-profit analyses based on curvilinear relationships are also possible. However, the use of curvilinear relationships requires rather sophisticated mathematics, and a discussion is deferred to a more advanced text.

Glossary

Break-even analysis a synonym for cost-volume-profit analysis.

Break-even point the sales level at which a company neither earns a profit nor incurs a loss.

Contribution margin per unit the dollar amount that the sale of one unit contributes toward the recovery of fixed costs and a profit.

Contribution rate the contribution margin per unit expressed as a percentage of sales price.

Cost-volume-profit analysis a method of predicting the effects of changes in costs and sales level on the income of a business.

Estimated line of cost behavior a line that attempts to reflect the average relationship between cost and volume.

Fixed cost a cost that remains unchanged in total amount over a wide range of production levels.

High-low method a crude technique for deriving an estimated line of cost behavior that connects the highest and lowest costs shown on a scatter diagram with a straight line.

Least-squares regression a sophisticated method of deriving an estimated line of cost behavior; the resulting estimate can be described as a line that best fits the actual cost and volume data of a company.

Margin of safety the amount by which a company's current sales exceed the sales necessary to break even.

Mixed cost a cost that includes two components, one of which is fixed and one of which is variable.

Relevant range of operations the normal operating range for the business, which excludes extremely high and low levels of production that are not apt to be encountered.

Sales mix the ratio in which a company's different products are sold.

Scatter diagram a graph used to display the relationship between costs and volume in which the cost and volume for each period is shown as a point on the diagram.

Semivariable cost a cost that changes with production volume but not in the same proportion.

Stair-step cost a cost that remains constant over a range of production, then increases by a lump sum if production is expanded beyond this range, then remains constant over another range of production increases, and so forth.

Variable cost a cost that changes in total amount proportionately with production level changes.

Questions for Class Discussion

1. Why is cost-volume-profit analysis used?
2. What is a fixed cost? Name two fixed costs.
3. When there are fixed costs in manufacturing a product and the number of units manufactured is increased, do fixed costs per unit increase or decrease? Why?
4. What is a variable cost? Name two variable costs.

5. If production and sales are increased from period 1 to period 2, what effect will the increase have upon variable costs per unit?

6. What is a semivariable cost?

7. The reliability of cost-volume-profit analysis rests upon three basic assumptions. What are they?

8. What two factors tend to make it possible to classify costs as either fixed or variable?

9. Why is the relevant range concept of significance in cost-volume-profit analysis?

10. What is a mixed cost? How should a mixed cost be classified for the purpose of cost-volume-profit analysis?

11. How are scatter diagrams used in the process of estimating the behavior of a company's costs?

12. What is the primary weakness of the high-low method of deriving an estimated line of cost behavior?

13. What is the break-even point in the sale of a product?

14. A company sells a product for $90 per unit. The variable costs of producing and selling the product are $54 per unit. What is the product's contribution margin per unit? What is its contribution rate?

15. If a straight line is begun at the fixed cost level on a break-even graph and the line rises at the variable cost rate, what does the line show?

16. When a break-even graph is prepared, why are the fixed costs plotted as a horizontal line?

17. Two similar companies each have sales of $100 and total costs of $80. A Company's total costs include $20 variable costs and $60 fixed costs. If B Company's total costs include $60 variable costs and $20 fixed costs, which company will profit most by an increase in sales?

18. What is a company's margin of safety?

19. What is meant by the sales mix of a company?

20. If a company produces and sells more than one product, the reliability of cost-volume-profit analysis depends on an additional assumption in regard to sales mix. What is that assumption?

Class Exercises

Exercise 24-1

The past experience of a company discloses the following information about a particular cost and sales volume:

Period	Sales	Cost
1	$22,000	$9,000
2	11,000	6,300
3	21,000	9,500
4	14,000	7,300
5	18,000	8,100
6	15,000	7,200

Prepare a scatter diagram of the cost and volume data, estimate the line of cost behavior, and decide whether the cost is a variable, fixed, or mixed cost.

Exercise 24-2

Given the following information about a particular cost and sales volume, prepare a scatter diagram of the cost and volume data, draw a line that appears to reflect the typical cost behavior, and decide whether the cost is a variable, semivariable, stair-step, fixed, or mixed cost.

Period	Sales	Cost
1	$ 5,000	$ 4,100
2	15,000	10,200
3	9,900	7,900
4	7,600	4,700
5	13,100	9,900
6	10,500	7,800

Exercise 24-3

Given the following information about a particular cost and sales volume, prepare a scatter diagram of the cost and volume data, draw a line that appears to reflect the typical cost behavior, and decide whether the cost is a variable, semivariable, stair-step, fixed, or mixed cost.

Period	Sales	Cost	Period	Sales	Cost
1	$ 7,500	$10,400	7	$16,500	$11,500
2	29,500	21,500	8	22,500	14,600
3	17,600	10,800	9	10,400	10,400
4	26,600	19,700	10	25,400	15,500
5	12,500	9,800	11	19,700	12,200
6	21,300	12,900	12	27,700	18,600

Exercise 24-4

Given the following information about a particular cost and sales volume, prepare a scatter diagram of the cost and volume data, draw a line that appears to reflect the typical cost behavior, and decide whether the cost is a variable, semivariable, stair-step, fixed, or mixed cost.

Period	Sales	Cost	Period	Sales	Cost
1	$ 7,800	$ 5,900	9	$27,600	$19,100
2	14,200	4,700	10	24,400	18,200
3	29,800	19,800	11	11,600	4,300
4	23,100	19,400	12	20,100	12,900
5	18,300	12,400	13	16,800	11,800
6	21,300	11,700	14	15,200	12,500
7	9,700	4,900	15	26,600	18,200
8	12,800	6,000			

Exercise 24-5

Brake Company manufactures a single product that it sells for $159 per unit. The variable costs of manufacturing the product are $123 per unit, and the annual fixed costs incurred in manufacturing it are $178,740. Calculate the company's (a) contribution margin, (b) contribution rate, (c) break-even point for the product in units, and (d) break-even point in dollars of sales. The calculation of contribution rate should be carried to six decimal places.

Exercise 24-6

Prepare an income statement for Brake Company's operations (Exercise 24-5) showing sales, fixed costs, and variable costs at the break-even point. Also, if Brake Company's fixed costs increased by $14,220, calculate the additional sales (in dollars) that would be necessary to break even.

Exercise 24-7

Assume that Brake Company of Exercise 24-5 wishes to earn a $54,000 annual after-tax income from the sale of its product, and that it must pay 50% of its income in state and federal income taxes. Calculate (a) the number of units of its product it must sell to earn a $54,000 after-tax income from the sale of the product and (b) the number of dollars of sales that are needed to earn a $54,000 after-tax income.

Exercise 24-8

The sales manager of Brake Company (Exercise 24-5) thinks that within two years annual sales of the company's product will reach 9,600 units while the price per unit will go up to $180. Variable costs are expected to increase only $15 per unit, and fixed costs are not expected to change. Calculate the company's (a) before-tax income from the sale of these units and (b) calculate its after-tax income from the sale of the units.

Exercise 24-9

A company sold 14,000 units of its product, producing $336,000 in sales. The before-tax income of the company was $45,000, and the contribution margin per unit was $5. Calculate (a) the total variable costs and (b) the total fixed costs of the company.

Exercise 24-10

In selling its product last period, a company incurred $130,000 of variable costs and $45,000 of fixed costs and earned a before-tax income of $20,000. Assuming the contribution margin per unit was $20, calculate (a) the number of units sold and (b) total dollar sales.

Exercise 24-11

In selling its product last period, a company incurred fixed costs of $48,000 and earned a before-tax income of $22,000. Assuming the company's contribution rate was 40%, calculate (a) total dollar sales and (b) total variable costs.

Exercise 24-12

Twin Company markets Products A and B which it sells in the ratio of three units of Product A at $10 per unit to four units of Product B at $40 per unit. The variable costs of marketing Product A are $6 per unit, and the variable costs for Product B are $26 per unit. The annual fixed costs for marketing both products are $166,600. Calculate (a) the selling price of a composite unit of these products, (b) the variable costs per composite unit, (c) the break-even point in composite units, and (d) the number of units of each product that will be sold at the break-even point.

Problems

Problem 24-1

Turnkey Company has collected the following monthly total cost and sales volume data related to its recent operations:

Period	Costs	Sales
1	$42,500	$56,000
2	45,000	60,000
3	25,000	20,000
4	36,000	56,000
5	37,500	36,000
6	42,500	60,000
7	27,500	32,000
8	40,000	48,000
9	35,000	44,000
10	37,500	40,000
11	30,000	24,000
12	42,500	68,000

Required

1. Design a diagram with sales volume marked off in $8,000 intervals on the horizontal axis and cost marked off in $5,000 intervals on the vertical axis. Record the cost and sales data of Turnkey Company as a scatter of points on the diagram.

2. Based on your visual inspection of the scatter diagram, draw an estimated line of cost behavior that appears to show the average relationship between cost and sales.

3. Based on the estimated line of cost behavior, estimate the amount of Turnkey Company's fixed costs.

4. Use the estimated line of cost behavior to approximate cost when sales volume is $16,000 and when sales volume is $64,000. Calculate an estimate of variable cost per sales dollar.

Problem 24-2

Portland Company manufactures a number of products, one of which, Product X, is produced and sold quite independently from the others and sells for $480 per unit. The fixed costs of manufacturing Product X are $84,000, and the variable costs are $330 per unit. In solving Requirements 1 (b) and 4 (below), the calculation of a contribution rate should be carried to four decimal places.

Required

1. Calculate the company's break-even point in the sale of Product X (a) in units and (b) in dollars of sales.

2. Prepare a break-even graph for Product X. Use 1,000 as the maximum number of units on your graph and 500 as the maximum number of dollars (in thousands).

3. Prepare an income statement showing sales, fixed costs, and variable costs for Product X at the break-even point.

4. Determine the sales volume in dollars that the company must achieve to earn a $21,600 after-tax (40% rate) income from the sale of Product X.

5. Determine the after-tax income the company will earn from a $408,000 sales level for Product X.

Problem 24-3

Cedar Falls Company sells one product. Last year the company sold 4,500 units and incurred a $5,500 loss, as shown in the following income statement.

Cedar Falls Company
Last Year's Income Statement

Sales		$112,500
Costs:		
Fixed	$28,000	
Variablo	90,000	118,000
Net loss		$ (5,500)

The production manager has pointed out that the variable costs can be reduced 25% by installing a machine that performs operations presently done by hand. However, the new machine will increase fixed costs by $10,000 annually.

Required

1. Calculate last year's dollar break-even point.
2. Calculate the dollar break-even point under the assumption the new machine is installed.
3. Prepare a break-even chart under the assumption the new machine is installed. Use 6,000 as the maximum number of units on your chart.
4. Prepare an income statement showing expected annual results with the new machine installed. Assume no change in the selling price, no change in the number of units sold, and a 50% income tax rate.
5. Calculate the sales level required to earn a $35,000 per year after-tax income with the new machine installed and no change in the selling price. Prepare an income statement showing the results at this sales level.

Problem 24-4

Last year Maynard Company earned an unsatisfactory 8.2% after-tax return on sales from the sale of 55,000 packages of its product, called Flasher 600. The company buys Flasher 600 in bulk and packages it for resale, at a price of $2.50 each. Following are last year's costs for the product:

Cost of bulk Flasher 600 (sufficient for 55,000 packages) . . .	$68,750
Packaging materials and other variable packaging costs . . .	13,750
Fixed costs	43,750
Income tax rate.	40%

It has been suggested that if the selling price of the product is reduced 10% and a change is made in its packaging, the number of units sold can be increased by 50%. The packaging change will increase packaging costs 30% per unit, but the 50% increase in sales volume will allow the company to take advantage of a quantity discount of 9% on the product's bulk purchase price. The packaging and volume changes will not affect fixed costs.

Required

1. Calculate the dollar break-even points for Flasher 600 at the $2.50 per unit sales price and at $2.25 per unit.
2. Prepare a break-even chart for the sale of the product at each price. Use 100,000 units as the upper limit of your charts.
3. Prepare a condensed comparative income statement showing the anticipated results of selling the product at $2.50 per unit and the estimated results of selling it at $2.25 per unit.

Problem 24-5

Double Company sells two products, A and B, which are produced and sold independently. Last year, the company sold 7,500 units of each of these products, earning $112,500 from the sale of each as the following condensed income statement shows:

	Product A	Product B
Sales	$900,000	$900,000
Costs:		
Fixed costs.	$150,000	$562,500
Variable costs	562,500	150,000
Total costs	$712,500	$712,500
Income before taxes.	$187,500	$187,500
Income taxes (40% rate). . .	75,000	75,000
Net income.	$112,500	$112,500

Required

1. Calculate the break-even point for each product in units.
2. Prepare a break-even graph for each product. Use 10,000 as the maximum number of units on each graph.
3. Prepare a condensed income statement showing in separate columns the net income the company will earn from the sale of each product under the assumption that without a change in selling prices, the number of units of each product sold declines to 5,625 units.
4. Prepare a second condensed income statement showing in separate columns the net income the company will earn if the number of units of each product increases 20%.

Problem 24-6

Atlanta Company manufactures and sells three products, X, Y, and Z. Product X sells for $21 per unit, Product Y sells for $14 per unit, and

Product Z sells for $6 per unit. Their sales mix is in the ratio of $2:3:6$, and the variable costs of manufacturing and selling the products have been: Product X, $12; Product Y, $9; and Product Z, $4. The fixed costs of manufacturing the three products are $108,000. A special material labeled 247 has been used in manufacturing both Products X and Y; however, a new material called 742 has just become available, and if it is substituted for material 247, it will reduce the variable cost of manufacturing Product X by $1.75 and Product Y by $0.50. However, fixed costs will go up to $118,000 because of special equipment needed to process material 742.

Required

1. Determine the company's break-even point in dollars and the number of units of each product sold at the break-even point under the assumption that material 247 is used in manufacturing Products X and Y. Show all pertinent calculations.

2. Determine the company's break-even point in dollars and the number of units of each product sold at the break-even point under the assumption that the new material 742 is used in manufacturing Products X and Y. Show all pertinent calculations.

□ Alternate Problems

Problem 24-1A

Entrepid Company has collected the following monthly total cost and sales volume data related to its recent operations:

Period		Costs	Sales
1	. . . .	$39,000	$67,000
2	. . . .	27,000	24,000
3	. . . .	46,000	72,000
4	. . . .	38,000	52,000
5	. . . .	46,000	81,000
6	. . . .	30,000	38,000
7	. . . .	41,000	48,000
8	. . . .	41,000	43,000
9	. . . .	46,000	67,000
10	. . . .	44,000	57,000
11	. . . .	33,000	28,000
12	. . . .	49,000	72,000

Required

1. Design a diagram with sales volume marked off in $8,000 intervals on the horizontal axis and cost marked off in $5,000 intervals on the vertical axis. Record the cost and sales data of Entrepid Company as a scatter of points on the diagram.

2. Based on your visual inspection of the scatter diagram, draw an estimated line of cost behavior that appears to show the average relationship between cost and sales.

3. Based on the estimated line of cost behavior, estimate the amount of Entrepid Company's fixed costs.

4. Use the estimated line of cost behavior to approximate cost when sales volume is $40,000 and when sales volume is $72,000. Calculate an estimate of variable cost per sales dollar.

Problem 24-2A

Among the products sold by The Thames Company is Product A, which is produced and sold independently from the other products of the company, and which sells for $250 per unit. The fixed costs of manufacturing and selling Product A are $26,000, and the variable costs are $120 per unit.

Required

1. Calculate the company's break-even point in the sale of Product A *(a)* in units and *(b)* in dollars of sales.
2. Prepare a break-even graph for Product A, using 400 as the maximum number of units on the graph.
3. Prepare an income statement showing sales, fixed costs, and variable costs for Product A at the break-even point.
4. Determine the sales volume in dollars required to achieve a $9,100 after-tax (30% rate) income from the sale of Product A.
5. Determine the after-tax income the company will earn from a $86,500 sales level for Product A.

Problem 24-3A

Hudson Company lost $1,500 last year in selling 1,800 units of its product as the following income statement shows:

Hudson Company
Income Statement for Last Year

Sales		$90,000
Costs:		
Fixed	$24,000	
Variable	67,500	91,500
Net loss		$ (1,500)

    The company management is convinced that if a new machine is installed, enough piece-rate labor and spoiled materials can be saved to reduce variable costs by 20%. However, the new machine will increase fixed costs by $4,400 annually.

Required

1. Calculate last year's dollar break-even point.
2. Calculate the dollar break-even point assuming the new machine is installed.
3. Prepare a break-even chart under the assumption the new machine is installed. Use 3,000 as the maximum number of units on your chart.
4. Prepare an income statement showing expected annual results with the new machine installed, no change in the product's price, and sales at last year's level. Assume a 30% income tax rate.
5. Calculate the sales level required to earn a $7,000 per year after-tax income with the new machine installed and no change in the product's selling price. Prepare an income statement showing the results at this sales level.

Problem 24-4A

Last year Marvel Company sold 17,500 units of its product at $20 per unit. To manufacture and sell the product required $85,000 of fixed manufacturing costs and $35,000 of fixed selling and administrative expenses. Last year's variable costs and expenses per unit were:

Material	$6.00
Direct labor (paid on a piece-rate basis)	5.00
Variable manufacturing overhead costs	0.55
Variable selling and administrative expenses	0.45

A new material has just come on the market that is cheaper than the old material and also easier to work with. If the new material is substituted for the material presently being used, material costs will be decreased by 40% ($2.40), and direct labor costs will be decreased by 32% ($1.60). The substitution will have no effect on the product's quality, but it will give the company a choice in pricing the product. (1) The company can maintain the present per unit price, sell the same number of units, and make a larger profit as a result of the substitution. Or (2) it can reduce the product's price $4 per unit to an amount equal to the material and labor savings and, because of the reduction, increase the number of units sold by 80%. If the latter choice is made, the fixed manufacturing overhead and fixed selling and administrative expenses will not change, and the remaining variable costs per unit will not change.

Required

1. Calculate the break-even point in dollars for each alternative.
2. Prepare a break-even chart for each. The company's production capacity is 40,000 units, and this should be used as the upper limit of your charts.
3. Prepare a comparative income statement showing sales, total fixed costs, and total variable costs and expenses, operating income, income taxes (40% rate), and net income for each alternative.

Problem 24-5A

Pairs Company has two essentially unrelated divisions, each of which produces a single product. The two products, D and E, are produced and sold independently. Coincidentally, each product sold last year at a price of $150, and 6,250 units of each product were sold.

Last year's income statements for the two products are as follows:

	Product D	Product E
Sales	$937,500	$937,500
Costs:		
Fixed costs	$500,000	$187,500
Variable costs	187,500	500,000
Total costs	$687,500	$687,500
Income before taxes	$250,000	$250,000
Income taxes (40% rate) . .	100,000	100,000
Net income	$150,000	$150,000

Required

1. Calculate the break-even point for each product in units.
2. Prepare a break-even graph for each product. Use 10,000 as the maximum number of units on each graph.
3. Prepare a condensed income statement showing in separate columns the net income the company will earn from the sale of each product under the assumption that without a change in selling prices, the number of units of each product sold declines to 4,167 units.
4. Prepare a second condensed income statement showing in separate columns the net income the company will earn if sales of each product increase to 8,000 units.

Problem 24-6A

Triple Company manufactures and sells three products, B, C, and D, which sell for $75 per unit, $50 per unit, and $40 per unit, respectively. Their sales mix is in the ratio of 2:5:8, and the variable costs of manufacturing and selling the products have been: Product B, $40; Product C, $34; and Product D, $25. Fixed manufacturing, selling, and administrative costs amount to $264,600.

The management of Triple Company is considering the purchase of a new machine that will be used in the manufacture of Products C and D. If the machine is purchased, fixed manufacturing costs will increase by $27,000. However, variable costs of Product C will decrease by $6 per unit, and variable costs of Product D will decrease by $3 per unit.

Required

1. Determine the company's break-even point in dollars and the number of units of each product sold at the break-even point assuming the new machine is not purchased. Show all necessary calculations.
2. Determine the company's break-even point in dollars and the number of units of each product sold at the break-even point assuming that the new machine is purchased. Show all pertinent calculations.

Provocative Problems

Provocative Problem 24-1   Chlor Corporation

Chlor Corporation produces a high-quality chemical called Pure-All for use in swimming pools. The company's plant produced at near capacity last year with the results shown in the following condensed income statement:

Sales (120,000 lbs.)	$240,000
Cost of goods manufactured and sold	
(fixed, $40,000; variable, $96,000) . .	136,000
Gross margin	$104,000
Selling and administrative expenses	
(fixed, $32,000; variable, $24,000) . .	56,000
Income before taxes	$ 48,000

Big Splash Company has offered Chlor a two-year contract whereby Big Splash will buy 80,000 pounds of Pure-All annually at $1.60 per pound for export sales. Delivery on the contract would require a plant addition that would double fixed manufacturing costs. The contract would not affect present selling and administrative expenses. Variable manufacturing costs per unit would be the same in the new plant as they have been in the old plant.

Required

Management is not certain it should enter into the contract and has asked for your opinion, including the following:

1. An estimated income statement for the first year following the plant addition, assuming no change in domestic sales.
2. A comparison of break-even sales levels before the plant addition and after the contract with Big Splash expires. Assume after-contract sales and expense levels, other than fixed manufacturing costs, will be at the same levels as last year.
3. A statement showing net income after the contract expiration but at sales and expense levels of last year, other than fixed manufacturing costs.

Provocative Problem 24-2 Image Corporation

Image Corporation manufactures and sells three products, called Attract, Prosper, and Strong. Last year's sales mix for the three products was in the ratio of 5:1:4, with combined sales of all products totaling 9,000 units. Attract sells for $60 per unit and has a 20% contribution rate. Prosper sells for $50 per unit and has a 30% contribution rate, and Strong sells for $45 per unit and has a 40% contribution rate. The fixed costs of manufacturing and selling the products amount to $72,600. The company estimates that combined sales of the three products will continue to be 9,000 total units next year. However, the sales manager is of the opinion that if the company's advertising and sales efforts are slanted further towards Prosper and Strong during the coming year, with no increases in the amounts of money expended, the sales mix of the three products can be changed to the ratio of 2:3:5.

Required

Should the company change its sales mix through advertising and sales efforts? What effect will the change have on the combined contribution rate of the three products? What effect will it have on the company's break-even point? Back your answers with figures. Calculations of contribution rate should be carried to seven decimal places.

Provocative Problem 24-3 Northeastern Company

Northeastern Company operated at near capacity during 198A, and a 25% annual increase in the demand for its product is expected in 198B. As a result, the company's management is trying to decide how to meet this demand. Two alternatives are being considered. The first calls for changes that will increase variable costs to 57.5% of the selling price of the company's product but will not change fixed costs. The second calls for a capital investment that will increase fixed costs 15% but will not affect variable costs.

Northeastern Company's income statement for 198A provided the following summarized information:

Sales		$640,000
Costs:		
Variable costs	$320,000	
Fixed costs	240,000	560,000
Income before taxes		$ 80,000

Required

Which alternative do you recommend? Back your recommendation with income statement information and any other data you consider relevant.

25 The Master Budget: A Formal Plan for the Business

After studying Chapter 25, you should be able to:

1. Explain the importance of budgeting.

2. Describe the specific benefits derived from budgeting.

3. List the sequence of steps required to prepare a master budget.

4. Prepare each budget in a master budget and explain the importance of each budget to the overall budgeting process.

5. Integrate the individual budgets into planned financial statements.

6. Define or explain the words and phrases listed in the chapter Glossary.

The process of managing a business consists of two basic elements: **planning and control.** If a business is to accomplish the variety of objectives expected of it, management must first carefully plan the activities and events the business should enter into and accomplish during future weeks, months, and years. Then, as the activities take place, they must be monitored and controlled so that actual events conform as closely as possible to the plan.

The management functions of planning and control are perhaps equally important to the long-run success of a business. Nevertheless, most business failures appear to result from inadequate planning. Countless pitfalls can be avoided if management carefully anticipates the future conditions within which the business will operate and prepares a detailed plan of the activities the business should pursue. Furthermore, the plans for future business activities should be formally organized and preserved. This process of planning future business actions and expressing those plans in a formal manner is called **budgeting.** Correspondingly, a **budget** is a formal statement of future plans. Since the economic or financial aspects of the business are primary matters of consideration, budgets are usually expressed in monetary terms.

■ The Master Budget

When the plan to be formalized is a comprehensive or overall plan for the business, the resulting budget is called a **master budget.** As an overall plan, the master budget should include specific plans for expected sales, the units of product to be produced, the materials or merchandise to be purchased, the expense payments to be made, the long-term assets to be purchased, and the amount of cash to be borrowed, if any. The planned activities of each subunit of the business should be separately organized and presented within the master budget. Thus, the master budget for a business consists of several sub-budgets, all of which articulate or join with each other to form the overall, coordinated plan for the business. As finally presented, the master budget typically includes sales, expense, production, equipment, and cash budgets. Also, the expected financial results of the planned activities may be expressed in terms of a planned income statement for the budget period and a planned balance sheet for the end of the budget period.

■ Benefits from Budgeting

All business managements engage in planning; some planning is absolutely necessary if business activities are to continue. However, a typical characteristic of poor management is sloppy or incomplete planning. But, if management plans carefully and formalizes its plans completely enough, that is, if management engages in a thorough budgeting process, it may expect to obtain the following benefits.

Budgeting Promotes Study, Research, and a Focus on the Future

When a business plans with sufficient care and detail to prepare a budget, the planning process usually involves thorough study and research. Not only should this result in the best conceivable plans but it should also instill in executives the habit of doing a reasonable amount of research and study before decisions are made. In short, budgeting tends to promote good decision-making processes. In addition, the items of interest to a budgetary investigation lie in the future. Thus, the attention of management is focused on future events and the associated opportunities available to the business. The pressures of daily operating problems naturally tend to take precedence over planning, thereby leaving the business without carefully thought-out objectives. Budgeting counteracts this tendency by formalizing the planning process; it makes planning an explicit responsibility of management.

Budgeting Provides a Basis for Evaluating Performance

The control function of management requires that performance be evaluated in light of some norms or objectives. On the basis of this evaluation, appropriate corrective actions can be implemented. In evaluating performance, there are two alternative norms or objectives against which actual performance can be compared: (1) past performance or (2) expected (budgeted) performance. Although past performance is sometimes used as the basis of comparison, budgeted performance is generally superior for determining whether actual performance is acceptable or in need of corrective action. Past performance fails to take into account all of the environmental changes that may impact on the performance level. For example, in the evaluation of sales performance, past sales occurred under economic conditions that may have been dramatically different from those that apply to the current sales effort. Economy-wide fluctuations, competitive shifts within the industry, new product line developments, increased or decreased advertising commitments, and so forth, all tend to invalidate comparisons between past performance and present performance. On the other hand, budgeted (anticipated) performance levels are developed after a research and study process that attempts to take such environmental factors into account. Thus, budgeting provides the benefit of a superior basis for evaluating performance and a more effective control mechanism.

Budgeting Is a Means of Coordinating Business Activities

Coordination requires that a business be operated as a whole rather than as a group of separate departments. When a budget plan is prepared, each department's objectives are determined in advance, and these objectives are coordinated. For example, the production department is budgeted to produce approximately the number of units the selling department can sell. The purchasing department is budgeted to buy raw materials on the basis of budgeted production; and the hiring activities of the personnel department are budgeted to take into account budgeted production levels. Obviously, the departments and activities of a business must be closely coordinated if the business operations are to be efficient and profitable. Budgeting provides this coordination.

Budgeting Is a Means of Communicating Plans and Instructions

In a very small business, adequate communication of business plans might be accomplished by direct contact between the employees. Frequent conversations could perhaps serve as the means of communicating management's plans for the business. However, oral conversations often leave ambiguities and potential confusion if not backed up by documents that clearly state the content of the plans. Further, businesses need not be very large before informal conversations become obviously inadequate. When a budget is prepared, the budget becomes a means of informing the organization not only of plans that have been approved by management but also of budgeted actions management wishes the organization to take during the budget period.

Budgeting Is a Source of Motivation

As previously mentioned, budgets provide the standards against which actual performance is evaluated. Because of this, the budget and the manner in which it is used can significantly affect the attitudes of those who are to be evaluated. If management is not careful, the budgeting process may have a negative impact on the attitudes of employees. Budgeted levels of performance must be realistic. Also, the personnel who will be evaluated in terms of a budget should be consulted and involved in preparing the budget. Finally, the subsequent evaluations of performance must not be given critically without offering the affected employees an opportunity to explain the reasons for performance failures. These three factors are important: (1) If the affected employees are consulted when the budget is prepared, (2) if obtainable objectives are budgeted, and (3) if the subsequent evaluations of performance are made fairly with opportunities provided to explain performance deficiencies, budgeting can be a strongly positive, motivating force in the organization. Budgeted performance levels can provide goals that individuals will attempt to attain or even exceed as they fulfill their responsibilities to the organization.

■ The Budget Committee

The task of preparing a budget should not be made the responsibility of any one department; and the budget definitely should not be handed down from above as the "final word." Rather, budget figures and budget estimates should be developed from "the bottom up." For example, the sales department should have a hand in preparing sales estimates. Similarly, the production department should have initial responsibility for preparing its own expense budget. Otherwise, production and salespeople may say the budget figures are meaningless because they were prepared by front office personnel who know little if anything of sales and production problems.

Although budget figures should be developed from "the bottom up," the preparation of a budget needs central guidance. This is commonly supplied by a budget committee of department heads or other high-level executives who are responsible for seeing that budget figures are realistic and coordinated. If a department submits budget figures that do not reflect proper performance, the figures should be returned to the department with the budget committee's comments. The originating department then either adjusts the figures or defends them. It should not change the figures just to please the committee, since it is important that all parties agree that the figures are reasonable and attainable.

■ **The Budget Period**

Budget periods normally coincide with accounting periods. This means that in most companies the budget period is one year in length. However, in addition to their annual budgets, many companies prepare long-range budgets that set forth major objectives for periods of 3 to 5 or 10 years in advance. These long-range budgets are particularly important in planning for major expenditures of capital to buy plant and equipment. Additionally, the financing of major capital projects, for example, by issuing bonds, by issuing stock, by retaining earnings, and so forth, can be anticipated and planned as a part of preparing long-range budgets.

Long-range budgets of 2, 3, 5, and 10 years should reflect the planned accomplishment of long-range objectives. Within this context, the annual master budget for a business reflects the objectives that have been adopted for the next year. The annual budget, however, is commonly broken down into quarterly or monthly budgets. Short-term budgets of a quarter or a month are useful yardsticks that allow management to evaluate actual performance and take corrective actions promptly. After the quarterly or monthly results are known, the actual performance is compared to the budgeted amounts in a report similar to that disclosed in Illustration 25-1.

Many businesses follow the practice of **continuous budgeting** and are said to prepare **rolling budgets.** As each monthly or quarterly budget period goes by, these firms revise their entire set of budgets, adding new monthly or quarterly sales, production, expense, equipment, and cash budgets to replace the ones that have elapsed. Thus, at any point in time, monthly or quarterly budgets are available for a full year in advance.

■ **Preparing the Master Budget**

As indicated in the previous discussion, the master budget consists of a number of budgets that collectively express the planned activities of the business. The number and arrangement of the budgets included in the master budget depend on the size and complexity of the business. However, a master budget typically includes:

1. Operating budgets.
    a. Sales budget.
    b. For merchandising companies: Merchandise purchases budget.
    c. For manufacturing companies:
        (1) Production budget (stating the number of units to be produced).
        (2) Manufacturing budget.
    d. Selling expense budget.
    e. General and administrative expense budget.
2. Capital expenditures budget, which includes the budgeted expenditures for new plant and equipment.
3. Financial budgets.
    a. Budgeted statement of cash receipts and disbursements, called the cash budget.
    b. Budgeted income statement.
    c. Budgeted balance sheet.

In addition to these budgets, numerous supporting calculations or schedules may be required.

Illustration 25-1

Consolidated Stores, Inc.
Income Statement with Variations from Budget
For Month Ended April 30, 19—

	Actual	Budget	Variations
Sales	$63,500	$60,000	$+3,500
Less: Sales returns and allowances	1,800	1,700	+100
Sales discounts	1,200	1,150	+50
Net sales	$60,500	$57,150	$+3,350
Cost of goods sold:			
Merchandise inventory, April 1, 19—	$42,000	$44,000	$−2,000
Purchases, net	39,100	38,000	+1,100
Freight-in	1,250	1,200	+50
Goods for sale	$82,350	$83,200	$ −850
Merchandise inventory, April 30, 19—	41,000	44,100	−3,100
Cost of goods sold	$41,350	$39,100	$+2,250
Gross profit	$19,150	$18,050	$+1,100
Operating expenses:			
Selling expenses:			
Sales salaries	$ 6,250	$ 6,000	$ +250
Advertising expense	900	800	+100
Store supplies used	550	500	+50
Depreciation of store equipment	1,600	1,600	
Total selling expenses	$ 9,300	$ 8,900	$ +400
General and administrative expenses:			
Office salaries	$ 2,000	$ 2,000	
Office supplies used	165	150	$ +15
Rent	1,100	1,100	
Expired insurance	200	200	
Depreciation of office equipment	100	100	
Total general and administrative expenses . . .	$ 3,565	$ 3,550	$ +15
Total operating expenses	$12,865	$12,450	$ +415
Income from operations	$ 6,285	$ 5,600	$ +685

Some of the budgets listed above cannot be prepared until other budgets on the list are first completed. For example, the merchandise purchases budget cannot be prepared until the sales budget is available, since the number of units to be purchased depends upon how many units are to be sold. As a consequence, preparation of the budgets within the master budget must follow a definite sequence, as follows:

First: The sales budget must be prepared first because the operating and financial budgets depend upon information provided by the sales budget.

Second: The remaining operating budgets are prepared next. For manufacturing companies, the production budget must be prepared prior to the manufacturing budget, since the number of units to be manufactured obviously affects the amounts of materials, direct labor, and overhead to be budgeted. Other than this, the budgets for manufacturing costs or merchandise costs, general and administrative expenses, and selling expenses may be prepared in any sequence.

Third: If capital expenditures are anticipated during the budget period, the capital expenditures budget is prepared next. This budget usually depends upon long-range sales forecasts more than it does upon the sales budget for the next year.

Fourth: Based upon the information provided in the above budgets, the budgeted statement of cash receipts and disbursements is prepared. If this budget discloses an imbalance between disbursements and planned receipts, the previous plans may have to be revised.

Fifth: The budgeted income statement is prepared next. If the plans contained in the master budget result in unsatisfactory profits, the entire master budget may be revised to incorporate any corrective measures available to the firm.

Sixth: The budgeted balance sheet for the end of the budget period is prepared last. An analysis of this statement may also lead to revisions in the previous budgets. For example, the budgeted balance sheet may disclose too much debt resulting from an overly ambitious capital expenditures budget, and revised plans may be necessary.

■ **Preparation of the Master Budget Illustrated**

The following sections explain the procedures involved in preparing the budgets that comprise the master budget. Northern Company, a wholesaler of a single product, provides an illustrative basis for the discussion. The September 30, 198A, balance sheet for Northern Company is presented in Illustration 25-2. The master budget for Northern Company is prepared on a monthly basis, with a budgeted balance sheet prepared for the end of each quarter. Also, a budgeted income statement is prepared for each quarter. In the following sections, Northern Company budgets are prepared for October, November, and December 198A.

Illustration 25-2

Northern Company
Balance Sheet
September 30, 198A

Cash	$ 20,000	Accounts payable	$ 58,200
Accounts receivable	42,000	Loan from bank	10,000
Inventory (9,000 units @ $6)	54,000	Accrued income taxes payable	
Equipment*	200,000	(due October 15, 198A)	20,000
Less accumulated		Common stock	150,000
depreciation	(36,000)	Retained earnings	41,800
Total	$280,000	Total	$280,000

* The equipment is being depreciated on a straight-line basis over 10 years. Estimated salvage value is $20,000.

Preparing a Sales Budget

The **sales budget** provides an estimate of goods to be sold and revenue to be derived from sales. It is the starting point in the budgeting procedure, since the plans of all departments are related to sales and expected revenue. The sales budget commonly grows from a reconciliation of forecasted business conditions, plant capacity, proposed selling expenses such as advertising, and estimates of sales. As to sales estimates, since people normally feel a greater responsibility for reaching goals they have had a hand in setting, the sales personnel of a company are often asked to submit, through the sales manager, estimates of sales for each territory and department. The final sales budget is then based on these estimates as reconciled for the forecasted business conditions, selling expenses, and so forth.

During September 198A, Northern Company sold 7,000 units of product at a price of $10 per unit. After obtaining the estimates of sales personnel and considering the economic conditions affecting the market for Northern Company's product, the sales budget (Illustration 25-3) is established for October, November, and December 198A. Since the purchasing department must base December 198A purchases on estimated sales for January 198B, the sales budget is expanded to include January 198B.

Observe in Illustration 25-3 that the sales budget is more detailed than simple projections of total sales; both unit sales and unit prices are forecasted. Some budgeting procedures are less detailed, expressing the budget only in terms of total sales volume. Also, many sales budgets are far more detailed than the one illustrated. The more detailed sales budgets may show units and unit prices for each of many different products, classified by salesperson and by territory or by department.

Illustration 25-3

Northern Company
Monthly Sales Budget
October 198A–January 198B

	Budgeted Unit Sales		Budgeted Unit Price		Budgeted Total Sales
September 198A (actual)	7,000	×	$10	=	$ 70,000
October 198A	10,000	×	10	=	100,000
November 198A	8,000	×	10	=	80,000
December 198A	14,000	×	10	=	140,000
January 198B	9,000	×	10	=	90,000

Preparing a Merchandise Purchases Budget

A variety of sophisticated techniques have been developed to assist management in making inventory purchase decisions. All of these techniques recognize that the number of units to be added to inventory depends upon the budgeted sales volume. Whether a company manufactures or purchases the product it sells, budgeted future sales volume is the primary factor to be considered in most inventory management decisions.

The amount of merchandise or materials to be purchased each month is determined as follows:

Budgeted sales for the month.	XXX
Add the budgeted end-of-month inventory	XXX
Required amount of available merchandise	XXX
Deduct the beginning-of-month inventory	(XXX)
Inventory to be purchased	XXX

The calculation may be made in either dollars or in units. If the calculation is in units and only one product is involved, the number of dollars of inventory to be purchased may be determined by multiplying units to be purchased by the cost per unit.

After considering the cost of maintaining an investment in inventory and the potential cost associated with a temporary inventory shortage, Northern Company has decided that the number of units in its inventory at the end of each month should equal 90% of the next month's sales. In other words, the inventory at the end of October should equal 90% of the budgeted November sales, the November ending inventory should equal 90% of the expected December sales, and so on. Also, the company's suppliers have indicated that the September 198A per unit cost of $6 can be expected to remain unchanged through January 198B. Based on these factors the company prepared the merchandise purchases budget of Illustration 25-4.

The calculations of Northern Company's merchandise purchases budget differ slightly from the basic calculation previously given in that the first lines are devoted to determining the desired end-of-month inventory. Also, budgeted sales are added to the desired end-of-month inventory instead of vice versa, and on the last lines the number of dollars of inventory to be purchased is determined by multiplying units to be purchased by the cost per unit.

It was previously mentioned that some budgeting procedures are designed to provide only the total dollars of budgeted sales. Likewise, the **merchandise purchases budget** may not state the number of units to be purchased, and may be expressed only in terms of the total cost of merchandise

Illustration 25-4

Northern Company
Merchandise Purchases Budget
October, November, and December 198A

	October	November	December
Next month's budgeted sales (in units)	8,000	14,000	9,000
Ratio of inventory to future sales	×90%	×90%	×90%
Desired end-of-month inventory	7,200	12,600	8,100
Budgeted sales for the month (in units)	10,000	8,000	14,000
Required units of available merchandise.	17,200	20,600	22,100
Deduct beginning-of-month inventory	(9,000)	(7,200)	(12,600)
Number of units to be purchased.	8,200	13,400	9,500
Budgeted cost per unit	×$6	×$6	×$6
Budgeted cost of merchandise purchases	$49,200	$80,400	$57,000

to be purchased. In such situations, it is assumed that there is a constant relationship between sales and cost of goods sold. For example, Northern Company expects that cost of goods sold will equal 60% of sales. (Note that the budgeted sales price is $10 and the budgeted unit cost is $6.) Thus, its cost of purchases can be budgeted in dollars on the basis of budgeted sales without requiring information on the number of units involved.

Preparing Production Budgets and Manufacturing Budgets

Since Northern Company does not manufacture the product it sells, its budget for acquiring goods to be sold is a merchandise purchases budget (Illustration 25-4). If Northern Company had been a manufacturing company, a production budget rather than a merchandise purchases budget would be required. In a **production budget,** the number of units to be produced each month is shown. For Northern Company such a budget would be very similar to a merchandise purchases budget. It would differ in that the number of units to be purchased each month (see Illustration 25-4) would be described as the number of units to be manufactured each month. Also, it would not show costs, since a production budget is always expressed entirely in terms of units of product and does not include budgeted production costs. Such costs are shown in the manufacturing budget, which is based on the production volume shown in the production budget.

A **manufacturing budget** shows the budgeted costs for raw materials, direct labor, and manufacturing overhead. In many manufacturing companies, the manufacturing budget is actually prepared in the form of three subbudgets: a raw materials purchases budget, a direct labor budget, and a manufacturing overhead budget. These budgets show the total budgeted cost of goods to be manufactured during the budget period.

Preparing a Selling Expense Budget

The responsibility for preparing a budget of selling expenses typically falls on the vice president of marketing or the equivalent sales manager. Although budgeted selling expenses should affect the expected amount of sales, the typical procedure is to prepare a sales budget first and then to budget selling expenses. Estimates of selling expenses are based on the tentative sales budget and upon the experience of previous periods adjusted for known changes. After the entire master budget is prepared on a tentative basis, it may be decided that the projected sales volume is inadequate. If so, subsequent adjustments in the sales budget would generally require that corresponding adjustments be made in the selling expense budget.

Northern Company's selling expenses consist of commissions paid to sales personnel and a $24,000 per year salary, paid on a monthly basis to the sales manager. Sales commissions amount to 10% of total sales and are paid during the month the sales are made. The selling expense budget for Northern Company is presented in Illustration 25-5.

Preparing a General and Administrative Expense Budget

General and administrative expenses usually are the responsibility of the office manager, who should therefore be charged with the task of preparing

Illustration 25-5

Northern Company
Selling Expense Budget
October, November, and December 198A

	October	November	December	Total
Budgeted sales	$100,000	$80,000	$140,000	$320,000
Sales commission percentage . .	×10%	×10%	×10%	×10%
Sales commissions	$ 10,000	$ 8,000	$ 14,000	$ 32,000
Salary for sales manager ($24,000/12 = $2,000 per month)	2,000	2,000	2,000	6,000
Total selling expenses.	$ 12,000	$10,000	$ 16,000	$ 38,000

the budget for these items. The amounts of some general and administrative expenses may depend upon budgeted sales volume. However, most of these expenses depend more upon other factors such as management policies, inflationary influences, and so forth, than they do upon monthly fluctuations in sales volume. Although interest expense and income tax expense are frequently classified as general and administrative expenses, they generally cannot be budgeted at this point in the budgeting sequence. Interest expense must await preparation of the cash budget, which determines the need for loans, if any. Income tax expense must await preparation of the budgeted income statement, at which time taxable income and income tax expense can be estimated.

General and administrative expenses for Northern Company include administrative salaries amounting to $54,000 per year and depreciation of $18,000 per year on equipment (see Illustration 25-2). The salaries are paid each month as they are earned. Illustration 25-6 shows the budget for these expenses.

Preparing a Capital Expenditures Budget

The **capital expenditures** or plant and equipment **budget** lists equipment to be scrapped and additional equipment to be purchased if the proposed production program is carried out. The purchase of additional equipment

Illustration 25-6

Northern Company
General and Administrative Expense Budget
October, November, and December 198A

	October	November	December	Total
Administrative salaries ($54,000/12 = $4,500)	$4,500	$4,500	$4,500	$13,500
Depreciation of equipment ($18,000/12 = $1,500)	1,500	1,500	1,500	4,500
	$6,000	$6,000	$6,000	$18,000

requires funds; and anticipating equipment additions in advance normally makes it easier to provide the funds. Also, at times, estimated production may exceed plant capacity. Budgeting makes it possible to anticipate this and either revise the production schedule or increase plant capacity. Planning plant and equipment purchases is called capital budgeting, and this is discussed in more detail in Chapter 27.

Northern Company does not anticipate any sales or retirements of equipment through December 198A. However, management plans to acquire additional equipment for $25,000 cash near the end of December 198A.

Preparing a Cash Budget

After tentative sales, merchandise purchases, expenses, and capital expenditures budgets have been developed, the **cash budget** is prepared. This budget is especially important; a company should have at all times enough cash to meet needs, but it should not hold too much cash. Too much cash is undesirable because it often cannot be profitably invested. A cash budget requires management to forecast cash receipts and disbursements, and usually results in better cash management. Also, it enables management to arrange well in advance for loans to cover any anticipated cash shortages.

In preparing the cash budget, anticipated receipts are added to the beginning cash balance and anticipated expenditures are deducted. If the resulting cash balance is inadequate, the required additional cash is provided in the budget through planned increases in loans.

Much of the information that is needed to prepare the cash budget can be obtained directly from the previously prepared operating and capital expenditures budgets. However, further investigation and additional calculations may be necessary to determine the amounts to be included.

Illustration 25-7 shows the cash budget for Northern Company. October's beginning cash balance was obtained from the September 30, 198A, balance sheet (Illustration 25-2).

Budgeted sales of Northern Company are shown in Illustration 25-3. An investigation of previous sales records indicates that 40% of Northern Company's sales are for cash. The remaining 60% are credit sales, and customers can be expected to pay for these sales in the month after the sales are made. Thus, the budgeted cash receipts from customers are calculated as follows:

	September	October	November	December
Sales	$70,000	$100,000	$80,000	$140,000
Credit sales percentage	×60%	×60%	×60%	×60%
Accounts receivable, end of month . .	$42,000	$ 60,000	$48,000	$ 84,000
Cash sales percentage		×40%	×40%	×40%
Cash sales		$ 40,000	$32,000	$ 56,000
Collections of accounts receivable . .		42,000	60,000	48,000
Total cash receipts		$ 82,000	$92,000	$104,000

Observe in the calculation that the October cash receipts consist of $40,000 from cash sales ($100,000 × 40%) plus the collection of $42,000 of accounts

Illustration 25-7

Northern Company
Cash Budget
October, November, and December 198A

	October	November	December
Beginning cash balance	$ 20,000	$ 20,000	$ 22,272
Cash receipts from customers.	82,000	92,000	104,000
Totals	$102,000	$112,000	$126,272
Cash disbursements:			
Payments for merchandise	$ 58,200	$ 49,200	$ 80,400
Sales commissions (Illustration 25-5)	10,000	8,000	14,000
Salaries: Sales (Illustration 25-5)	2,000	2,000	2,000
Administrative (Illustration 25-6) . .	4,500	4,500	4,500
Accrued income taxes payable	20,000		
Dividends ($150,000 × 0.02 = $3,000). . .		3,000	
Interest on loan from bank:			
$10,000 × 0.01 = $100	100		
$22,800 × 0.01 = $228		228	
Purchase of equipment.			25,000
Total cash disbursements.	$ 94,800	$ 66,928	$125,900
Balance	$ 7,200	$ 45,072	$ 372
Additional loan from bank	12,800		19,628
Repayment of loan from bank.		(22,800)	
Ending cash balance.	$ 20,000	$ 22,272	$ 20,000
Loan balance, end of month	$ 22,800	$ –0–	$ 19,628

receivable as calculated in the previous column. Also, note that each month's total cash receipts are listed on the second line of Illustration 25-7.

Northern Company's purchases of merchandise are entirely on account, and full payments are made regularly in the month following purchase. Thus, in Illustration 25-7, the cash disbursements for purchases are obtained from the September 30, 198A, balance sheet (Illustration 25-2), and from the merchandise purchases budget (Illustration 25-4), as follows:

September 30, accounts payable equal October payments	$58,200
October purchases equal November payments	49,200
November purchases equal December payments	80,400

Sales commissions and all salaries are paid monthly, and the budgeted cash disbursements for these items are obtained from the selling expense budget (Illustration 25-5) and the general and administrative expense budget (Illustration 25-6).

As indicated in the September 30, 198A, balance sheet (Illustration 25-2), accrued income taxes are paid in October. Estimated income tax expense for the quarter ending December 31 is 40% of net income and is due in January 198B.

Northern Company pays 2% quarterly cash dividends, and the November payment of $3,000 is the planned disbursement for this item. Also, Northern Company has an agreement with the bank whereby additional loans are granted at the end of each month if they are necessary to maintain a minimum cash balance of $20,000 at the end of the month. Interest is paid at the end of each month at the rate of 1% per month; and if the cash balance at the end of a month exceeds $20,000, the excess is used to repay the loans to the bank. Illustration 25-7 indicates that the $10,000 loan from the bank at the end of September was not sufficient to provide a $20,000 cash balance at the end of October, and as a result, the loan was increased by $12,800 at the end of October. The entire loan was repaid at the end of November, and $19,628 was again borrowed at the end of December.

Preparing a Budgeted Income Statement

One of the final steps in preparing a master budget is to summarize the effects of the various budgetary plans on the **budgeted income statement.** The necessary information to prepare a budgeted income statement is drawn primarily from the previously prepared budgets or from the investigations that were made in the process of preparing those budgets.

For many companies, the volume of information that must be summarized in the budgeted income statement and the budgeted balance sheet is so large that a work sheet must be used to accumulate all of the budgeted transactions and to classify them in terms of their impact on the income statement and/or on the balance sheet. However, the transactions and account balances of Northern Company are few in number, and the budgeted income statement (and balance sheet) can be prepared simply by inspecting the previously discussed budgets and recalling the information that was provided in the related discussions. Northern Company's budgeted income statement is shown in Illustration 25-8.

Illustration 25-8

Northern Company
Budgeted Income Statement
For Three Months Ended December 31, 198A

Sales (Illustration 25-3, 32,000 units @ $10)		$320,000
Cost of goods sold (32,000 units @ $6)		192,000
Gross profit		$128,000
Operating expenses:		
Sales commissions (Illustration 25-5)	$32,000	
Sales salaries (Illustration 25-5).	6,000	
Administrative salaries (Illustration 25-6)	13,500	
Depreciation on equipment (Illustration 25-6)	4,500	
Interest expense (Illustration 25-7)	328	(56,328)
Net income before income taxes		$ 71,672
Income tax expense ($71,672 × 40%)		(28,669)
Net income		$ 43,003

Preparing a Budgeted Balance Sheet

If a work sheet is used to prepare the budgeted income statement and **budgeted balance sheet,** the first two columns of the work sheet are used to list the estimated post-closing trial balance of the period prior to the budget period. Next, the budgeted transactions and adjustments are entered in the second pair of work sheet columns in the same manner as end-of-period adjustments are entered on an ordinary work sheet. For example, if the budget calls for sales on account of $250,000, the name of the Sales account is entered on the work sheet in the Account Titles column below the names of post-closing trial balance accounts; and then Sales is credited and Accounts Receivable is debited for $250,000 in the second pair of money columns. After all budgeted transactions and adjustments are entered on the work sheet, the estimated post-closing trial balance amounts in the first pair of money columns are combined with the budget amounts in the second pair of columns and are sorted to the proper Income Statement and Balance Sheet columns of the work sheet. Finally, the information in these columns is used to prepare the budgeted income statement and budgeted balance sheet.

As previously mentioned, the transactions and account balances of Northern Company are few in number, and its budgeted balance sheet, shown in Illustration 25-9, can be prepared simply by inspecting the previously prepared budgets and recalling the related discussions of those budgets.

Illustration 25-9

Northern Company
Budgeted Balance Sheet
December 31, 198A

Assets

Cash (Illustration 25-7)		$ 20,000
Accounts receivable (page 908)		84,000
Inventory (Illustration 25-4, 8,100 units @ $6)		48,600
Equipment (Illustrations 25-2 and 25-7)	$225,000	
Less accumulated depreciation (Illustrations		
25-2 and 25-6)	40,500	184,500
Total assets		$337,100

Liabilities and Stockholders' Equity

Liabilities:		
Accounts payable (Illustration 25-4)	$ 57,000	
Accrued income taxes payable (Illustration 25-8)	28,669	
Bank loan payable (Illustration 25-7)	19,628	$105,297
Stockholders' equity:		
Common stock (Illustration 25-2)	$150,000	
Retained earnings (see discussion)	81,803	231,803
Total liabilities and stockholders' equity		$337,100

Observe that the retained earnings balance in Illustration 25-9 is $81,803. This amount was determined as follows:

Retained earnings, September 30, 198A (Illustration 25-2)	$41,800
Net income for three months ended December 31, 198A (Illustration 25-8).	43,003
Total	$84,803
Dividends declared in November, 198A (Illustration 25-7)	(3,000)
Retained earnings, December 31, 198A	$81,803

☐   **Glossary**   **Budget** the formal statement of future plans, usually expressed in monetary terms.

Budgeted balance sheet a projected balance sheet estimated to result at the end of the future budgeting period if the activities projected in each of the related budgets actually occur.

Budgeted income statement a projected income statement that draws upon the estimates shown in all of the related revenue and expense budgets and shows the effects of the separate budgets on the income of the future budget period.

Budgeting the process of planning future business actions and expressing those plans in a formal manner.

Capital expenditures budget a listing of the plant and equipment to be purchased if the proposed production program is carried out. Also called the plant and equipment budget.

Cash budget a forecast of cash receipts and disbursements.

Continuous budgeting the practice of preparing budgets for each of several future periods and revising those budgets each period, adding a new budget each time so that budgets are always available for a given number of future periods.

Manufacturing budget a statement of the estimated costs for raw materials, direct labor, and manufacturing overhead associated with producing the number of units estimated in the production budget.

Master budget a comprehensive or overall plan for the business that typically includes budgets for sales, expenses, production, capital expenditures, cash, and also a planned income statement and balance sheet.

Merchandise purchases budget an estimate of the units and/or cost of merchandise to be purchased by a merchandising company.

Production budget an estimate of the number of units to be produced during a budget period, based on the budgeted sales for the period and the levels of inventory necessary to support future sales.

Rolling budgets a sequence of revised budgets that are prepared in the practice of continuous budgeting.

Sales budget an estimate of goods to be sold and revenue to be derived from sales; serves as the usual starting point in the budgeting procedure.

☐ **Questions for Class Discussion**

1. What are the two basic elements involved in managing a business?
2. What is a budget? What is a master budget?
3. What are the benefits from budgeting?
4. How does the process of budgeting tend to promote good decision making?
5. What are the two alternative norms or objectives against which actual performance is sometime compared and evaluated? Which of the two is generally superior?
6. How does budgeting contribute to the coordination of business activities?

7. If the managers of a business are able to communicate business plans to their employees through direct conversations, in what sense are budgets still useful in facilitating that communication?

8. Why should each department be asked to prepare or at least to participate in the preparation of its own budget estimates?

9. What are the duties of the budget committee?

10. What is the normal length of a master budget period? How far in advance are long-range budgets generally prepared?

11. What is meant by the terms *continuous budgeting* and *rolling budgets*?

12. What are the three primary types of budgets that make up the master budget?

13. In comparing merchandising companies and manufacturing companies, what differences show up in the operating budgets?

14. What is the sequence that is followed in preparing the set of budgets that collectively make up the master budget?

15. What is a sales budget? A selling expense budget? A capital expenditures budget?

16. What is the difference between a production budget and a manufacturing budget?

17. What is a cash budget? Why must it be prepared after the operating budgets and the capital expenditures budget?

Class Exercises

Exercise 25-1

The sales budget of Auto Stop's tires department calls for sales of $57,000 during October. The department expects to begin October with a $27,600 inventory and end the month with a $31,200 inventory. Its cost of goods sold averages 60% of sales.

Required

Prepare a merchandise purchases budget for the tires department showing the amount of goods to be purchased during October.

Exercise 25-2

Settle Company manufactures a product called Sorp. The company's management estimates there will be 19,800 units of Sorp in the March 31 finished goods inventory, that 44,100 units will be sold during the year's second quarter, that 52,500 units will be sold during the third quarter, and that 57,600 units will be sold during the fourth quarter. Management also believes the company should begin each quarter with units in the finished goods inventory equal to 30% of the next quarter's budgeted sales.

Required

Prepare a production budget showing the units of Sorp to be manufactured during the year's second quarter and third quarter.

Exercise 25-3

A company has budgeted the following cash receipts and cash disbursements from operations during the third quarter of 198A:

	Receipts	Disbursements
July	$215,000	$181,000
August.	102,000	219,900
September	186,000	134,000

According to a credit agreement with the bank, the company promises to maintain a minimum, end-of-month cash balance of $20,000. In return, the bank has agreed to provide the company the right to receive loans up to $150,000 with interest of 12% per year, paid monthly on the last day of the month. If the loan must be increased during the last 10 days of a month to provide enough cash to pay bills, interest will not begin to accrue until the end of the month.

The company is expected to have a cash balance of $20,000 and a loan balance of $10,000 on June 30, 198A.

Required

Prepare a monthly cash budget for the third quarter of 198A.

Exercise 25-4

Using the following information, prepare a cash budget showing expected cash receipts and disbursements for the month of April and the balance expected on April 30, 198A.

a. Beginning cash balance on April 1: $63,000.
b. Budgeted sales for April: $420,000; 40% are collected in the month of sale, 50% in the next month, 5% in the following month, and 5% are uncollectible.
c. Sales for March: $480,000.
d. Sales for February: $360,000.
e. Budgeted merchandise purchases for April: $270,000; 50% are paid in month of purchase; 50% are paid in the month following purchase.
f. Merchandise purchased in March: $180,000.
g. Budgeted cash disbursements for salaries in April: $120,000.
h. Depreciation expense in April: $6,000.
i. Other cash expenses budgeted for April: $30,000.
j. Budgeted taxes payable in April: $67,500.
k. Budgeted interest payable on bank loan in April: $4,500.

Exercise 25-5

Based on the information provided in Exercise 25-4 and the additional information that follows, prepare a budgeted income statement for the month of April and a budgeted balance sheet for April 30, 198A.

a. Cost of goods sold is 50% of sales.
b. The inventory at the end of March was $81,000.
c. Salaries payable on March 31 was $21,000 and is expected to be $12,000 on April 30.

d. The Equipment account shows a balance of $615,000. On March 31, Accumulated Depreciation had a balance of $157,500.

e. The $4,500 cash payment of interest represents the 1% monthly expense on a bank loan of $450,000.

f. Income taxes payable on March 31 amounted to $67,500, and the income tax rate applicable to the company is 40%.

g. The 5% of sales that prove to be uncollectible are debited to Bad Debts Expense and credited to Allowance for Doubtful Accounts during the month of sale. However, specific accounts that prove to be uncollectible are not written off until the second month after the sale, at which time all accounts not yet collected are so written off.

h. The only balance sheet accounts other than those implied by the previous discussion are Common Stock, which shows a balance of $150,000, and Retained Earnings, which showed a balance of $105,000 on March 31.

Exercise 25-6

A merchandising company prepared monthly budgets for the year 198A. The budgets called for a May 31 inventory of 15,000 units. The company follows a policy of beginning each month with merchandise inventory on hand equal to a specific percentage of the budgeted sales for the next month. Budgeted unit sales and merchandise purchases for selected months were as follows:

	Sales (in units)	Purchases (in units)
March	40,000	43,750
April	55,000	60,000
May	75,000	71,250

Based on the information given, reconstruct the merchandise purchases budget for March, April, and May. Also show your calculation of the budgeted relationship between beginning inventory and next month's sales.

Exercise 25-7

A merchandising company's cost of goods sold is consistently 60% of sales. The company plans to have a merchandise inventory at the start of each month that is 40% of the next month's cost of goods sold. All merchandise is purchased on credit and 30% of the purchases during a month are paid for during the same month. Another 50% is paid for during the month after purchase, and the remaining 20% is paid for during the second month after purchase. Calculate the expected cash payments to be made during March, given the following sales budget: January, $20,000; February, $30,000; March, $25,000; and April, $40,000.

Exercise 25-8

A company purchases its merchandise on credit and budgets its accounts payable balances and merchandise inventory balances to be as follows:

	Accounts Payable	Merchandise Inventory
January 31.	$15,000	$19,000
February 28	20,000	13,000
March 31	18,000	24,000
April 30	25,000	21,000

Cash payments of accounts payable during each month are expected to be: January, $47,000; February, $57,000; March, $42,000; and April, $66,000. Calculate the budgeted amounts of cost of goods sold for February, March, and April.

Exercise 25-9

A merchandising company budgets cost of goods sold to be 55% of sales and plans to purchase enough merchandise each month to provide a beginning inventory each month that is 30% of budgeted cost of goods sold for the month. All purchases are on credit, and 10% of the purchases in any month are paid for during the same month. Another 50% is paid during the first month after purchase, and the remaining 40% is paid in the second month after purchase. Calculate the budgeted amounts of accounts payable at the end of August and September given the following sales budget:

June.	$ 70,000
July	90,000
August.	60,000
September	80,000
October	100,000

Problems

Problem 25-1

Gadget Manufacturing Company manufactures a steel product called a Squeezer. Each Squeezer requires 8 pounds of steel and is produced in a single operation by a stamping process. The company's management estimates there will be 600 units of the product and 4 tons of steel on hand on June 30 of the current year, and that 3,400 units of the product will be sold during the year's third quarter. Management also believes that due to the possibility of a strike in the steel industry, the company should begin the fourth quarter with a 12-ton steel inventory and 1,000 finished Squeezers. Steel can be purchased for approximately $600 per ton ($0.30 per pound).

Required

  Prepare a third-quarter production budget and a third-quarter steel purchases budget for the company.

Problem 25-2

During the latter part of May, the owner of Kingsville Store approached the bank for a $40,000 loan to be made on July 1 and repaid 60 days thereafter with interest at 12%. The owner planned to increase the store's inventory by $40,000 during June and needed the loan to pay for the merchandise during July. The bank's loan officer was interested in Kingsville Store's ability to repay the loan and asked the owner to forecast the store's August 30 cash position.

On June 1, Kingsville Store was expected to have a $15,000 cash balance, $85,000 of accounts receivable, and $52,500 of accounts payable. Its budgeted sales, purchases, and cash expenditures for the following three months are as follows:

	June	July	August
Sales	$75,000	$82,500	$72,500
Merchandise purchases	86,500	45,000	42,500
Payroll.	7,500	7,500	7,500
Rent.	2,500	2,500	2,500
Other cash expenses	4,000	4,500	4,750
Repayment of bank loan			40,800

The budgeted June purchases include the inventory increase. All sales are on account; and past experience indicates 80% is collected in the month following the sale, 15% in the next month, 4% in the next, and the remainder is not collected. Application of this experience to the June 1 accounts receivable balance indicates $68,000 of the $85,000 will be collected during June, $12,750 during July, and $3,400 during August. All merchandise is paid for in the month following its purchase.

Required

Prepare cash budgets for June, July, and August 198A for Kingsville Store under the assumption the bank loan will be paid on August 30.

Problem 25-3

Easterdown Company has a cash balance of $28,800 on June 1, 198A. The product sold by the company sells for $25 per unit. Actual and projected sales are:

April, actual	$192,000
May, actual	144,000
June, estimated	240,000
July, estimated.	192,000
August, estimated	172,800

Experience has shown that 50% of the billings are collected in the month of sale, 30% in the second month, 15% in the third month, and 5% will prove to be uncollectible.

All purchases are payable within 15 days. Thus, approximately 50% of the purchases in a month are due and payable in the next month. The unit purchase cost is $18. Easterdown Company's management had established a policy of maintaining an end-of-month inventory of 250 units plus 50% of the next month's unit sales, and the June 1 inventory is consistent with this policy.

Selling and general administrative expenses (excluding depreciation) for the year amount to $432,000 and are distributed evenly throughout the year.

Required

Prepare a monthly cash budget for June and July, with supporting schedules showing cash receipts from collections of receivables and cash payments for merchandise purchases.

Problem 25-4

Covington Company buys merchandise at $17.40 per unit and sells it as $30 per unit. Sales personnel are paid a commission of 10% of sales. The September 198A income statement of Covington Company is as follows:

Covington Company
Income Statement
For September 198A

Sales	$300,000
Cost of goods sold	174,000
Gross profit	$126,000
Expenses:	
Sales commissions	$ 30,000
Advertising	18,000
Store rent	6,000
Administrative salaries	12,000
Depreciation expense	3,000
Other expenses	9,000
Total	$ 78,000
Net income	$ 48,000

The management of Covington Company expects the September results to be repeated during October, November, and December. However, certain changes are being considered. Management believes that if selling price is reduced to $27 and advertising expenses are increased by 50%, unit sales will increase at a rate of 10% each month during the last quarter of 198A. If these changes are made, merchandise will still be purchased at $17.40 per unit. Sales personnel will continue to earn a commission of 10%, and the remaining expenses will remain constant.

Required

Prepare a budgeted income statement that shows in three columns the planned results of operations for October, November, and December 198A, assuming the changes are implemented. Based on the budgeted income statement, decide whether management should make the changes.

Problem 25-5

During March 198A, the management of River Corporation prepared a budgeted balance sheet for March 31, 198A, which is presented below.

River Corporation
Budgeted Balance Sheet
For March 31, 198A

Cash	$ 30,000	Accounts payable	$ 50,000
Accounts receivable	93,750	Loan from bank	30,000
Inventory.	156,250	Taxes payable (due	
Equipment	375,000	June 15, 198A)	75,000
Accumulated depreciation . .	(37,500)	Common stock	312,500
		Retained earnings	150,000
Total	$617,500	Total	$617,500

In the process of preparing a master budget for April, May, and June 198A, the following information has been obtained:

a. The product sold by River Corporation is purchased for $10 per unit and resold for $15 per unit. Although the inventory level on March 31 (15,625 units) is smaller than desired, management has established a new inventory policy whereby the end-of-month inventory should be 80% of the next month's expected sales (in units). Budgeted unit sales are: April, 62,500; May, 56,250; June, 75,000; and July, 75,000.

b. Total sales each month are 50% for cash and 50% on account. Of the credit sales, 80% are collected in the first month after the sale and 20% in the second month after the sale. Similarly, 80% of the Accounts Receivable balance on March 31 should be collected during April and 20% should be collected in May.

c. Merchandise purchased by the company is paid for as follows: 70% in the month after purchase and 30% in the second month after purchase. Similarly, 70% of the Accounts Payable balance on March 31 will be paid during April, and 30% will be paid during May.

d. Sales commissions amounting to 10% of sales are paid each month. Additionally, the salary of the sales manager is $75,000 per year.

e. Repair expenses amount to $3,125 per month and are paid in cash. General and administrative salaries amount to $675,000 per year.

f. The equipment shown in the March 31, 198A, balance sheet was purchased one year ago. It is being depreciated over 10 years according to the straight-line method. Regarding new purchases of equipment, management has decided to take a full month's depreciation during the month the equipment is purchased, and to use straight-line depreciation over 10 years, assuming no salvage value. The company plans to purchase additional equipment worth $69,000 in April, $36,000 in May, and $90,000 in June.

g. The company plans to acquire some land in June at a cost of $625,000. The land will not require a cash outlay until the last day of June. Thus, if a bank loan is necessary, the first payment of interest will be due at the end of July.

h. River Corporation has an arrangement with the bank whereby additional loans are available as they are needed at a rate of 12% per year, paid monthly. If part or all of a loan is repaid during a month, the payment will be made on the last day of the month, along with any interest that is due. River Corporation has agreed to maintain an end-of-month cash balance of at least $30,000.

i. The income tax rate applicable to the company is 40%. However, tax
on the income for the second quarter of 198A will not be paid until
July.

Required

Prepare a master budget for the second quarter of 198A, with the
operating budgets, capital expenditures budget, and the cash budget
prepared on a monthly basis. The budgeted income statement should show
operations for the second quarter, and the budgeted balance sheet should
be prepared as of June 30, 198A. The operating budgets included in the
master budget should include a sales budget (showing both budgeted unit
sales and dollar sales), a merchandise purchases budget, a selling expense
budget, and a general and administrative expense budget. Round all
amounts to the nearest dollar.

□ **Alternate Problems**   **Problem 25-1A**

Tucker Corporation sells three products that it purchases in their finished
ready-for-sale state. The company's April 30 inventories are Product A,
19,500 units; Product B, 18,750 units; and Product C, 31,500 units. The
company's management is disturbed because each product's April 30
inventory is excessive in relation to immediately expected sales.
Consequently, management has set as a goal a month-end inventory for
each product that is equal to one half the following month's expected
sales. Expected sales in units for May, June, July, and August are as follows:

| | **Expected Sales in Units** | | | |
	May	**June**	**July**	**August**
Product A	25,000	23,000	25,000	19,000
Product B	14,000	14,000	17,000	18,000
Product C	30,000	27,000	26,000	29,000

Required

Prepare purchases budgets in units for the three products for May, June,
and July 198A.

Problem 25-2A

Bonzo Company expects to have a $17,400 cash balance on December
31, 198A. It also expects to have a $105,600 balance of accounts receivable
and $62,700 of accounts payable. Its budgeted sales, purchases, and cash
expenditures for the first three months of 198B are:

	January	**February**	**March**
Sales	$72,000	$54,000	$81,000
Purchases	42,000	51,900	54,000
Payroll	7,200	7,200	8,400
Rent	3,000	3,000	3,000
Other cash expenses	3,600	4,800	4,200
Purchase of store equipment	—	15,000	—
Payment of quarterly dividend	—	—	12,000

All sales are on account; and past experience indicates that 85% will be collected in the month following the sale, 10% in the next month, and 4% in the third month. Notwithstanding these expectations for future sales, an analysis of the December 31 accounts receivable balance indicates that $84,000 of the $105,600 balance will be collected in January, $15,600 in February, and $4,800 in March.

Purchases of merchandise on account are paid in the month following each purchase; likewise, the store equipment will be paid for in the month following its purchase.

Required

Prepare cash budgets for the months of January, February, and March 198B.

Problem 25-3A

The actual and projected monthly sales of Buster Company are as follows:

September 198A, actual	$384,000
October 198A, actual.	256,000
November 198A, estimated	304,000
December 198A, estimated	368,000
January 198B, estimated	336,000

Experience has shown that 40% of the sales are collected in the month of sale, 40% are collected in the first month after the sale, 18% in the second month after the sale, and 2% prove to be uncollectible.

Approximately one fourth of the merchandise purchased by Buster Company is paid for during the month of purchase. The remaining three fourths is paid in the following month. Buster Company pays $25 per unit of merchandise and subsequently sells the merchandise for $50 per unit. The company always plans to maintain an end-of-month inventory of 500 units plus 60% of the next month's unit sales, and the October 31, 198A, inventory is consistent with this policy.

In addition to cost of goods sold, Buster Company incurs other operating expenses (excluding depreciation) of $931,200 per year, and they are distributed evenly throughout the year. On October 31, 198A, the company has a cash balance of $64,000.

Required

Prepare a monthly cash budget for November and December, with supporting schedules showing cash receipts from collections of receivables and cash payments for merchandise purchases. Round all amounts to the nearest dollar.

Problem 25-4A

Dafney Company buys merchandise at $42 per unit and sells it at $75 per unit. Sales personnel are paid a commission of 8% of sales. The June 198A income statement of Dafney Company is as follows:

Dafney Company
Income Statement
For June 198A

Sales	$675,000
Cost of goods sold	378,000
Gross profit	$297,000

Expenses:

Sales commissions	$ 54,000
Advertising	48,000
Store rent	15,000
Administrative salaries	18,000
Depreciation expense	9,000
Other expenses	22,500
Total	$166,500
Net income	$130,500

The management of Dafney Company expects the June results to be repeated during July, August, and September. However, certain changes are being considered. Management believes that if selling price is reduced to $66 and advertising expenses are increased by 40%, unit sales will increase at a rate of 10% each month during the third quarter of 198A. If these changes are made, merchandise will still be purchased at $42 per unit. Sales personnel will continue to earn a commission of 8% (rounded to the nearest whole dollar), and the remaining expenses will remain constant.

Required

Prepare a budgeted income statement that shows in three columns the planned results of operations for July, August, and September 198A, assuming the changes are implemented. Based on the budgeted income statement, decide whether management should make the changes.

Problem 25-5A

Shortly before the end of 198A, Bailey Company's management prepared a budgeted balance sheet for December 31, 198A, as follows:

Bailey Corporation
Budgeted Balance Sheet
For December 31, 198A

Cash	$ 15,000	Accounts payable	$ 24,000
Accounts receivable	45,000	Loan from bank	15,000
Inventory	75,000	Taxes payable (due	
Equipment	180,000	March 15, 198A)	36,000
Accumulated depreciation	(18,000)	Common stock	150,000
		Retained earnings	72,000
Total	$297,000	Total	$297,000

In the process of preparing a master budget for January, February, and March 198B, the following information has been obtained:

a. The product sold by Bailey Company is purchased for $10 per unit and resold for $15 per unit. Although the inventory level on December 31, 198A (7,500 units), is smaller than desired, management has established a new inventory policy for 198B whereby the end-of-month inventory should be 80% of the next month's expected sales (in units). Budgeted unit sales are: January, 30,000; February, 27,000; March, 36,000; April, 36,000.

b. Total sales each month are 50% for cash and 50% on account. Of the credit sales, 80% are collected in the first month after the sale and 20% in the second month after the sale. Similarly, 80% of the Accounts Receivable balance on December 31, 198A, should be collected during January, and 20% should be collected in February.

c. Merchandise purchased by the company is paid for as follows: 70% in the month after purchase, and 30% in the second month after purchase. Similarly, 70% of the Accounts Payable balance on December 31, 198A, will be paid during January, and 30% will be paid during February.

d. Sales commissions amounting to 10% of sales are paid each month. Additionally, the salary of the sales manager is $36,000 per year.

e. Repair expenses amount to $1,500 per month and are paid in cash. General administrative salaries amount to $324,000 per year.

f. The equipment shown in the December 31, 198A, balance sheet was purchased one year ago. It is being depreciated over 10 years according to the straight-line method. Regarding new purchases of equipment, management has decided to take a full month's depreciation (rounded to the nearest dollar) during the month the equipment is purchased, and to use straight-line depreciation over 10 years, assuming no salvage value. The company plans to purchase additional equipment worth $30,000 in January, $15,000 in February, and $45,000 in March.

g. The company plans to acquire some land in March at a cost of $300,000. The land will not require a cash outlay until the last day of March. Thus, if a bank loan is necessary, the first payment of interest will be due at the end of April.

h. Bailey Company has an arrangement with the bank whereby additional loans are available as they are needed at a rate of 10% per year, paid monthly. If part or all of a loan is repaid during a month, the payment will be made on the last day of the month, along with any interest that is due. Bailey Company has agreed to maintain an end-of-month cash balance of at least $15,000.

i. The income tax rate applicable to the company is 40%. However, tax on the income for the second quarter of 198B will not be paid until April.

Required

Prepare a master budget for the first quarter of 198B, with the operating budgets, capital expenditures budget, and the cash budget prepared on a monthly basis. The budgeted income statement should show operations for the first quarter, and the budgeted balance sheet should be prepared as of March 31, 198B. The operating budgets included in the master budget should include a sales budget (showing both budgeted unit sales and dollar sales), a merchandise purchases budget, a selling expense budget, and a general and administrative expense budget. Round all amounts to the nearest dollar.

Provocative Problem 25-1 Mippsee Company

Mippsee Company produces a Product M that requires five pounds of Dilitate per unit of M. The owner of Mippsee Company is in the process of negotiating with the bank for the approval to make loans as they are needed by the company. One of the important items in their discussion has been the question of how much cash will be needed to pay for purchases of Dilitate. Mippsee Company purchases Dilitate on account, and the resulting payables are paid in cash as follows: 75% during the month after purchase and 25% during the second month after purchase. The company plans to manufacture enough units of M to maintain an end-of-month inventory of finished units equal to 80% of the next month's sales, and enough Dilitate is purchased each month to maintain an end-of-month inventory equal to 60% of the next month's production requirements. Budgeted sales (in units) are as follows: February, 8,000; March, 9,000; April, 10,500, and May, 12,000. On January 31, 198A, the following data are available: finished units of Product M on hand, 6,400; pounds of Dilitate on hand, 26,400; Accounts Payable, $180,000 due in February plus $40,000 due in March.

In recent months, the price of Dilitate has varied substantially, and the owner estimates that during the next few months the price could range from $5 to $10 per pound. You are asked to assist the owner by estimating the cash payments to be made in February, in March, and in April. In preparing your answer, you should prepare separate estimates based on a $5 price and a $10 price.

Provocative Problem 25-2 Howberg Corporation

The Howberg Corporation has budgeted the following monthly sales volumes: July, 20,000 units; August 6,000 units; September, 9,000 units; and October, 15,000 units. The company's policy is to maintain an end-of-month finished goods inventory equal to 2,000 units plus 25% of the next month's budgeted sales in units. Consistent with this policy, the July 1 inventory was 7,000 units.

An analysis of Howberg Corporation's manufacturing costs show the following:

Material cost per unit.	$24.40
Direct labor cost per unit	18.00
Fixed manufacturing overhead costs	36,000 per month
Variable manufacturing overhead costs	8.80 per unit manufactured

Required

Prepare production budgets and manufacturing budgets for the months of July, August, and September.

26   Flexible Budgets; Standard Costs

After studying Chapter 26, you should be able to:

1. State the deficiencies of fixed budgets.

2. Prepare flexible budgets and state their advantages.

3. State what standard costs represent, how they are determined, and how they are used in the evaluation process.

4. Calculate material, labor, and overhead variances, and state what each variance indicates about the performance of a company.

5. Explain the relevance of standard cost accounting to the management philosophy known as *management by exception*.

6. Define or explain the words and phrases listed in the chapter Glossary.

The development of a master plan for a business was discussed in Chapter 25. Consideration was also given to the importance of controlling subsequent operations. This function of control was recognized as one of the two basic functions of management. In order to control business operations, management must obtain information or feedback regarding how closely actual operations conform to the plans. To the extent possible, the comparison of actual performance with planned performance should direct management's attention toward the reasons why actual performance differs from planned performance. Flexible budgets and standard costs are important techniques that are used to help management determine why actual performance differs from the plan.

■ Fixed Budgets and Performance Reports

In preparing a master budget as discussed in Chapter 25, the initial step is to determine the expected sales volume for the budget period. All of the subsequent budget procedures are based on this specific estimate of sales volume. The amount of each budgeted cost is based on the assumption that a specific or fixed amount of sales will take place. When a budget is based on a single estimate of sales or production volume, the budget is called a **fixed** or **static budget**. In budgeting the total amount of each cost, a fixed budget gives no consideration to the possibility that the actual sales or production volume may be different from the fixed or budgeted amount.

If a company uses only fixed budgets, the comparison of actual performance with the budgeted performance is presented in a **performance report** such as that shown in Illustration 26-1.

The budgeted sales volume of Tampa Manufacturing Company is 10,000 units (see Illustration 26-1). Also, to simplify the discussion, production volume is assumed to equal sales volume; and no beginning or ending inventory is maintained by the company. In evaluating Tampa Manufacturing Company's operations, management should be interested in answering such questions as: Why is the actual income from operations $13,400 higher than the budgeted amount? Are the prices being paid for each expense item too high? Is the manufacturing department using too much direct material? Is it using too much direct labor? The performance report shown in Illustration 26-1 provides little help in answering questions such as these. Since the actual sales volume was 2,000 units higher than the budgeted amount, it may be assumed that this increase caused total dollar sales and many of the expenses to be higher. But other factors may have influenced the amount of income, and the fixed budget performance report fails to provide management much information beyond the fact that the sales volume was higher than budgeted.

FLEXIBLE BUDGETS

To help answer questions such as those mentioned above, many companies prepare **flexible** or **variable budgets**. In contrast to fixed budgets, which are based on one fixed amount of budgeted sales or production, flexible budgets recognize that different levels of activity should produce different amounts of cost.

Illustration 26-1

Tampa Manufacturing Company
Fixed Budget Performance Report
For Month Ended November 30, 198A

	Fixed Budget	Actual Performance	Variances
Sales: In units	10,000	12,000	
In dollars	$100,000	$125,000	$25,000 F
Cost of goods sold:			
Direct materials	$ 10,000	$ 13,000	$ 3,000 U
Direct labor	15,000	20,000	5,000 U
Overhead:			
Factory supplies	2,000	2,100	100 U
Utilities	3,000	4,000	1,000 U
Depreciation of machinery	8,000	8,000	—
Supervisory salaries	11,000	11,000	—
Selling expenses:			
Sales commissions	9,000	10,800	1,800 U
Shipping expenses	4,000	4,300	300 U
General and administrative expenses:			
Office supplies	5,000	5,200	200 U
Insurance expense	1,000	1,200	200 U
Depreciation of office equipment	7,000	7,000	—
Administrative salaries	13,000	13,000	—
Total expenses	$ 88,000	$ 99,600	$11,600 U
Income from operations	$ 12,000	$ 25,400	$13,400 F

F = Favorable variance; that is, compared to the budget, the actual cost or revenue contributes to a higher income.
U = Unfavorable variance; that is, compared to the budget, the actual cost or revenue contributes to a lower income.

Preparing a Flexible Budget

To prepare a flexible budget, each type of cost is examined to determine whether it should be classified as a variable cost or as a fixed cost. Recall from Chapter 24 that the total amount of a variable cost changes in direct proportion to a change in the level of activity. Thus, variable cost per unit of activity remains constant. On the other hand, the total amount of a fixed cost remains unchanged regardless of changes in the level of activity (within the relevant or normal operating range of activity).[1]

After each cost item is classified as variable or fixed, each variable cost is expressed as a constant amount of cost per unit of sales (or per sales dollar). Fixed costs are, of course, budgeted in terms of the total amount of each fixed cost that is expected regardless of the sales volume that may occur within the relevant range.

Illustration 26-2 shows how the fixed budget of Tampa Manufacturing Company is reformulated as a flexible budget. Compare the first column of Illustration 26-2 with the first column of Illustration 26-1. Notice that seven of the expenses have been reclassified as variable costs; the remaining

[1] In Chapter 24, it was recognized that some costs are neither strictly variable nor strictly fixed. However, in the present discussion, it is assumed that all costs can be reasonably classified as being either variable or fixed.

five expenses have been reclassified as fixed costs. This classification results from an investigation of each expense incurred by Tampa Manufacturing Company, and the classification should not be misunderstood. It does not mean that these particular expenses are always variable costs in every company. For example, Office Supplies Expense may frequently be a fixed cost, depending upon the nature of the company's operations. Nevertheless, Tampa Manufacturing Company's accountant investigated this item and concluded that the Office Supplies cost behaves as a variable cost.

Observe in Illustration 26-2 that the variable costs of Tampa Manufacturing Company are listed together, totaled, and subtracted from sales. As explained in Chapter 24, the difference between sales and variable costs is identified as the contribution margin. The budgeted amounts of fixed costs are then listed and totaled.

In Illustration 26-2, columns 2 and 3 show the flexible budget amounts that may be applied to any volume of sales that occurs. The last two columns merely illustrate what form the flexible budget takes when the budget amounts are applied to particular sales volumes.

Illustration 26-2

Tampa Manufacturing Company
Flexible Budget
For Month Ended November 30, 198A

	Fixed Budget	Flexible Budget Variable Cost per Unit	Flexible Budget Total Fixed Cost	Flexible Budget for Unit Sales of 12,000	Flexible Budget for Unit Sales of 14,000
Sales: In units	10,000			12,000	14,000
In dollars	$100,000	$10.00		$120,000	$140,000
Variable costs:					
Direct materials	$ 10,000	$ 1.00		$ 12,000	$ 14,000
Direct labor	15,000	1.50		18,000	21,000
Factory supplies	2,000	0.20		2,400	2,800
Utilities	3,000	0.30		3,600	4,200
Sales commissions	9,000	0.90		10,800	12,600
Shipping expenses	4,000	0.40		4,800	5,600
Office supplies	5,000	0.50		6,000	7,000
Total variable costs	$ 48,000	$ 4.80		$ 57,600	$ 67,200
Contribution margin	$ 52,000	$ 5.20		$ 62,400	$ 72,800
Fixed costs:					
Depreciation of machinery . .	$ 8,000		$ 8,000	$ 8,000	$ 8,000
Supervisory salaries	11,000		11,000	11,000	11,000
Insurance expense	1,000		1,000	1,000	1,000
Depreciation of office equipment	7,000		7,000	7,000	7,000
Administrative salaries	13,000		13,000	13,000	13,000
Total fixed costs	$ 40,000		$40,000	$ 40,000	$ 40,000
Income from operations	$ 12,000			$ 22,400	$ 32,800

Recall from Illustration 26-1 that Tampa Manufacturing Company's actual sales volume for November 198A was 12,000 units. This was 2,000 units more than the 10,000 units originally forecasted in the master budget. The effect of this sales increase on the income from operations can be determined by comparing the budget for 10,000 units with the budget for 12,000 units (see Illustration 26-2). At a sales volume of 12,000 units, the budgeted income from operations is $22,400, whereas the budget for sales of 10,000 units shows income from operations of $12,000. Thus, if sales volume is 12,000 rather than 10,000 units, management should expect income from operations to be higher by $10,400 ($22,400 − $12,000). In other words, the difference between the $25,400 actual income from operations (see Illustration 26-1) and the $12,000 income from operations shown on the master budget can be analyzed, as follows:

Actual income from operations (12,000 units)		$25,400
Income from operations on master budget (10,000 units) . .		12,000
Difference to be explained		$13,400
Income from operations:		
On the flexible budget for 12,000 units.	$22,400	
On the budget for 10,000 units	12,000	
Additional income caused by increase in sales volume . . .		(10,400)
Unexplained difference		$ 3,000

This $3,000 unexplained difference is the amount by which the actual income from operations exceeds budgeted income from operations as shown on the flexible budget for a sales volume of 12,000 units. As management seeks to determine what steps should be taken to control Tampa Manufacturing Company's operations, the next step is to determine what caused this $3,000 unexplained difference. Information to help answer this question is provided by a flexible budget performance report.

■ **Flexible Budget Performance Report**

A **flexible budget performance report** is designed to analyze the difference between actual performance and budgeted performance, where the budgeted amounts are based on the actual sales volume or level of activity. The report should direct management's attention toward those particular costs or revenues where actual performance has differed substantially from the budgeted amount.

The flexible budget performance report for Tampa Manufacturing Company is presented in Illustration 26-3.

Observe in Illustration 26-3 the $5,000 favorable variance in total dollar sales. Since the actual number of units sold amounted to 12,000 and the budget was also based on unit sales of 12,000, the $5,000 variance must have resulted entirely from a difference between the average price per unit and the budgeted price per unit. Further analysis of the $5,000 variance is as follows:

Average price per unit, actual	$125,000/12,000	= $10.42
Budgeted price per unit	$120,000/12,000	= 10.00
Favorable variance in price per unit . . .	$5,000/12,000	= $ 0.42

The variances in Illustration 26-3 direct management's attention toward the areas in which corrective action may be necessary to control Tampa Manufacturing Company's operations. In addition, students should recognize that each of the cost variances can be analyzed in a manner similar to the above discussion of sales. Each of the expenses can be thought of as involving the use of a given number of units of the expense item, and paying a specific price per unit. Following this approach, each of the cost variances shown in Illustration 26-3 might result in part from a difference between the actual price per unit and the budgeted price per unit (a price variance); and they may also result in part from a difference between the actual number of units used and the budgeted number of units to be used (a quantity variance). This line of reasoning, called variance analysis, is discussed more completely in the following section on standard costs.

Illustration 26-3

Tampa Manufacturing Company
Flexible Budget Performance Report
For Month Ended November 30, 198A

	Flexible Budget	Actual Performance	Variances
Sales (12,000 units).	$120,000	$125,000	$5,000 F
Variable costs:			
Direct materials	$ 12,000	$ 13,000	$1,000 U
Direct labor	18,000	20,000	2,000 U
Factory supplies	2,400	2,100	300 F
Utilities	3,600	4,000	400 U
Sales commissions	10,800	10,800	
Shipping expenses	4,800	4,300	500 F
Office supplies	6,000	5,200	800 F
Total variable costs	$ 57,600	$ 59,400	$1,800 U
Contribution margin	$ 62,400	$ 65,600	$3,200 F
Fixed costs:			
Depreciation of machinery	$ 8,000	$ 8,000	
Supervisory salaries	11,000	11,000	
Insurance expense	1,000	1,200	$ 200 U
Depreciation of office equipment . .	7,000	7,000	
Administrative salaries	13,000	13,000	
Total fixed costs	$ 40,000	$ 40,200	$ 200 U
Income from operations	$ 22,400	$ 25,400	$3,000 F

F = Favorable variance; that is, compared to the budget, the actual cost or revenue contributes to a higher income.
U = Unfavorable variance; that is, compared to the budget, the actual cost or revenue contributes to a lower income.

STANDARD COSTS

In Chapter 22, it was said that there are two basic types of manufacturing cost systems, job order and process, but a large number of variations of the two. A **standard cost system,** one based on **standard** or **budgeted costs,** is such a variation.

The costs of a job or a process as discussed in Chapter 22 were historical costs, historical in the sense that they had been incurred and were "history" by the time they were recorded. Such costs are useful; but to judge whether or not they are reasonable or what they should be, management needs a basis of comparison. Standard costs offer such a basis.

Standard costs are the costs that should be incurred under normal conditions in producing a given product or part or in performing a particular service. They are established by means of engineering and accounting studies made before the product is manufactured or the service performed. Once established, standard costs are used to judge the reasonableness of the actual costs incurred when the product or service is produced. Standard costs are also used to place responsibilities when actual costs vary from standard.

Accountants speak of **standard material cost, standard labor cost,** and **standard overhead cost;** and this terminology is used in this chapter. However, it should be observed that standard material, labor, and overhead costs are really budgeted direct material, direct labor, and overhead costs.

■ **Establishing Standard Costs**

Great care and the combined efforts of people in accounting, engineering, personnel administration, and other management areas are required to establish standard costs. Time and motion studies are made of each labor operation in a product's production or in performing a service. From these studies, management learns the best way to perform the operation and the standard labor time required under normal conditions for performance. Exhaustive investigations are commonly made of the quantity, grade, and cost of each material required; and machines and other productive equipment are subject to detailed studies in an effort to achieve maximum efficiencies and to learn what costs should be.

However, regardless of care exercised in establishing standard costs and in revising them as conditions change, actual costs incurred in producing a given product or service commonly vary from standard costs. When this occurs, the difference in total cost is likely to be a composite of several cost differences. For example, the quantity and/or the price of the material used may have varied from standard. Also, the labor time and/or the labor price may have varied. Likewise, overhead costs may have varied.

■ **Variances**

When actual costs vary from standard costs, the differences are called **cost variances.** Variances may be favorable or unfavorable. A favorable variance is one in which actual cost is below standard cost, and an unfavorable variance is one in which actual cost is above standard.

When variances occur, they are isolated and studied for possible remedial action and to place responsibilities. For example, assume the standard direct material cost for producing 2,000 units of Product A is $800, but material costing $840 was used in producing the units. The $40 variance may have resulted from paying a price higher than standard for the material. Or, a greater quantity of material than standard may have been used. Or, there may have been some combination of these causes. The price paid for a material is a purchasing department responsibility; consequently, if the variance was caused by a price greater than standard, responsibility rests with the purchasing department. On the other hand, since the production department is usually responsible for the amount of material used, if a quantity greater than standard was used, responsibility normally rests with the production department. However, if more than a standard amount of material was used because the material was of a grade below standard, causing more than a normal waste, responsibility is back on the purchasing department for buying a substandard grade.

Isolating Material and Labor Variances

As previously stated, when variances occur, they are isolated and studied for possible remedial action and to place responsibilities. For example, assume that XL Company has established the following standard costs per unit for its Product Z:

Direct materials (1 lb. per unit at $1 per lb.) . . .	$1.00
Direct labor (1 hr. per unit at $3 per hr.)	3.00
Overhead ($2 per standard direct labor hour) . . .	2.00
Total standard cost per unit	$6.00

Material Variances

Assume further that during May, XL Company completed 3,500 units of Product Z, using 3,600 pounds of direct materials costing $1.05 per pound or $3,780. Under these assumptions the actual and standard direct material costs for the 3,500 units are:

Actual cost: 3,600 lbs. @ $1.05 per lb.	$3,780
Standard cost: 3,500 lbs. @ $1 per lb.	3,500
Direct material cost variance (unfavorable)	$ 280

Observe that the actual direct material cost for these units is $280 above their standard cost. This unfavorable direct material cost variance may be isolated as to causes in the following manner:

QUANTITY VARIANCE:			
Actual units at the standard price	3,600 lbs. @ $1.00 =	$3,600	
Standard units at the standard price.	3,500 lbs. @ $1.00 =	3,500	
Variance (unfavorable).	100 lbs. @ $1.00 =		$100
PRICE VARIANCE:			
Actual units at the actual price	3,600 lbs. @ $1.05 =	$3,780	
Actual units at the standard price	3,600 lbs. @ $1.00 =	3,600	
Variance (unfavorable).	3,600 lbs. @ $0.05 =		180
Direct material cost variance (unfavorable) . . .			$280

The analysis shows that $100 of the excess direct material cost resulted from using 100 more pounds than standard, and $180 resulted from a unit purchase price that was $0.05 above standard. With this information management can go to the responsible individuals for explanations.

Labor Variances

Labor cost in manufacturing a given part or in performing a service depends on a composite of the number of hours worked (quantity) and the wage rate paid (price). Therefore, when the labor cost for a task varies from standard, it too may be analyzed into a **quantity variance** and a **price variance.**

For example, the direct labor standard for the 3,500 units of Product Z is one hour per unit, or 3,500 hours at $3 per hour. If 3,400 hours costing $3.10 per hour were used in completing the units, the actual and standard labor costs for these units are:

Actual cost: 3,400 hrs. @ $3.10 per hr. . .	$10,540
Standard cost: 3,500 hrs. @ $3.00 per hr. . .	10,500
Direct labor cost variance (unfavorable) . . .	$ 40

In this case, actual cost is only $40 over standard, but isolating the quantity and price variances involved reveals the following:

QUANTITY VARIANCE:
Standard hours at standard price	3,500 hrs. @ $3.00 = $10,500	
Actual hours at standard price.	3,400 hrs. @ $3.00 = 10,200	
Variance (favorable)	100 hrs. @ $3.00 =	$300

PRICE VARIANCE:
Actual hours at actual price	3,400 hrs. @ $3.10 = $10,540	
Actual hours at standard price.	3,400 hrs. @ $3.00 = 10,200	
Variance (unfavorable)	3,400 hrs. @ $0.10 =	340
Direct labor cost variance (unfavorable). . . .		$ 40

The analysis shows a favorable quantity variance of $300, which resulted from using 100 fewer direct labor hours than standard for the units produced. However, this favorable variance was more than offset by a wage rate that was $0.10 above standard.

When a factory or department has workers of various skill levels, it is the responsibility of the foreman or other supervisor to assign to each task a worker or workers of no higher skill level than is required to accomplish the task. In this case, an investigation could reveal that workers of a higher skill level were used in producing the 3,500 units of Product Z. Hence, fewer labor hours were required for the work. However, because the workers were of a higher skill level, the wage rate paid them was higher than standard.

■ **Charging Overhead to Production**

When standard costs are used, factory overhead is charged to production by means of a predetermined standard overhead rate. The rate may be based on the relationship between overhead and standard labor cost, standard labor hours, standard machine-hours, or some other measure of production. For example, XL Company charges its Product Z with $2 of overhead per standard direct labor hour; and since the direct labor standard for Product Z is one hour per unit, the 3,500 units manufactured in May were charged with $7,000 of overhead.

Before going on, recall that only 3,400 actual direct labor hours were used in producing these units. Then, note again that overhead is charged to the units, not on the basis of actual labor hours but on the basis of standard labor hours. Standard labor hours are used because the amount of overhead charged to these units should not be less than standard simply because less than the standard (normal) amount of labor was used in their production. In other words, overhead should not vary from normal simply because labor varied from normal.

■ **Establishing Overhead Standards**

A variable or flexible factory overhead budget is the starting point in establishing reasonable standards for overhead costs. A flexible budget is necessary because the actual production level may vary from the expected level; and when this happens, certain costs vary with production, but others remain fixed. This may be seen by examining XL Company's flexible budget shown in Illustration 26-4.

Observe in Illustration 26-4 that XL Company's flexible budget has been used to establish standard costs for four production levels ranging from 70% to 100% of capacity. When actual costs are known, they should be

Illustration 26-4

XL Company
Flexible Overhead Costs Budget
For Month Ended May 31, 198A

	Budget Amounts	Production Levels			
		70%	80%	90%	100%
Production in units	1 unit	3,500	4,000	4,500	5,000
Standard direct labor hours . . .		3,500	4,000	4,500	5,000
Budgeted factory overhead:					
Fixed costs:					
Building rent	$1,000	$1,000	$1,000	$1,000	$1,000
Depreciation, machinery . .	1,200	1,200	1,200	1,200	1,200
Supervisory salaries	1,800	1,800	1,800	1,800	1,800
Totals	$4,000	$4,000	$4,000	$4,000	$4,000
Variable costs:					
Indirect labor	$0.40	$1,400	$1,600	$1,800	$2,000
Indirect materials.	0.30	1,050	1,200	1,350	1,500
Power and lights.	0.20	700	800	900	1,000
Maintenance	0.10	350	400	450	500
Totals	$1.00	$3,500	$4,000	$4,500	$5,000
Total factory overhead		$7,500	$8,000	$8,500	$9,000

compared with the standards for the level actually achieved and not with the standards at some other level. For example, if the plant actually operated at 70% capacity during May, actual costs incurred should be compared with standard costs for the 70% level. Actual costs should not be compared with costs established for the 80% or 90% levels.

In setting overhead standards, after the flexible overhead budget is prepared, management must determine the expected operating level for the plant. This can be 100% of capacity, but it seldom is. Errors in scheduling work, breakdowns, and, perhaps, the inability of the sales force to sell all the product produced are factors that commonly reduce the operating level to some point below full capacity.

After the flexible budget is set up and the expected operating level is determined, overhead costs at the expected level are related to, for example, labor hours at this level to establish the standard overhead rate. The rate thus established is then used to apply overhead to production. For example, assume XL Company decided that 80% of capacity is the expected operating level for its plant. The company then would calculate a $2 per direct labor hour overhead rate by dividing the budgeted $8,000 of overhead costs at the 80% level by the 1,000 standard direct labor hours required to produce the product manufactured at this level.

■   **Overhead Variances**

As previously stated, when standard costs are used, overhead is applied to production on the basis of a predetermined overhead rate. Then, at the end of a cost period the difference between overhead applied and overhead actually incurred is analyzed and variances are calculated to determine what was responsible for the difference.

Overhead variances are computed in several ways. A common way divides the difference between overhead applied and overhead incurred into (1) the **volume variance** and (2) the **controllable variance.**

Volume Variance

The **volume variance** is the difference between **(1) the amount of overhead budgeted at the actual operating level achieved during the period and (2) the standard amount of overhead charged to production during the period.** For example, assume that during May, XL Company actually operated at 70% of capacity. It produced 3,500 units of Product Z, which were charged with overhead at the standard rate. Under this assumption the company's volume variance for May is:

VOLUME VARIANCE:	
Budgeted overhead at 70% of capacity	$7,500
Standard overhead charged to production (3,500 standard labor hours at the $2 per hour standard rate).	7,000
Variance (unfavorable)	$ 500

To understand why this volume variance occurred, reexamine the flexible budget of Illustration 26-4. Observe that at the 80% level the $2 per hour overhead rate may be subdivided into $1 per hour for fixed overhead and $1 per hour for variable overhead. Furthermore, at the 80% (normal) level, the $1 for fixed overhead exactly covers the fixed overhead. However, when this $2 rate is used for the 70% level, and again subdivided, the $1 for fixed overhead will not cover all the fixed overhead because $4,000 is required for fixed overhead and 3,500 hours at $1 per hour equals only $3,500. In other words, at this 70% level the $2 per hour standard overhead rate did not absorb all the overhead incurred; it was short by $500, the amount of the volume variance. Or again, the volume variance resulted simply because the plant did not reach the expected operating level.

An unfavorable volume variance tells management that the plant did not reach its normal operating level; and when such a variance is large, management should investigate the cause or causes. Machine breakdowns, failure to schedule an even flow of work, and a lack of sales orders are common causes. The first two may be corrected in the factory, but the third requires either more orders from the sales force or a downward adjustment of the operating level considered to be normal.

Controllable Variance

The **controllable variance** is the difference between **(1) overhead actually incurred and (2) the overhead budgeted at the operating level achieved.** For example, assume that XL Company incurred $7,650 of overhead during May. Since its plant operated at 70% of capacity during the month, its controllable overhead variance for May is:

CONTROLLABLE VARIANCE:
Actual overhead incurred.	$7,650
Overhead budgeted at operating level achieved . . .	7,500
Variance (unfavorable).	$ 150

The controllable overhead variance measures management's efficiency in adjusting controllable overhead costs (normally variable overhead) to the operating level achieved. In this case, management failed by $150 to maintain overhead costs at the amount budgeted for the 70% level.

The controllable overhead variance measures management's efficiency in adjusting overhead costs to the operating level achieved. However, an overhead variance report is a more effective means for showing just where management achieved or failed to achieve the budgeted expectations. Such a report for XL Company appears in Illustration 26-5 on the next page.

Combining the Volume and Controllable Variances

The volume and controllable variances may be combined to account for the difference between overhead actually incurred and overhead charged to production. For example, XL Company actually incurred $7,650 of overhead during May and charged $7,000 to production. Its overhead variances may be combined as follows to account for the difference:

VOLUME VARIANCE:		
Overhead budgeted at operating level achieved	$7,500	
Standard overhead charged to production (3,500 standard hours at $2 per hour)	7,000	
Variance (unfavorable)		$500
CONTROLLABLE VARIANCE:		
Actual overhead incurred	$7,650	
Overhead budgeted at operating level achieved	7,500	
Variance (unfavorable)		150
Excess of overhead incurred over overhead charged to production		$650

Controlling a Business through Standard Costs

Business operations are carried on by people, and control of a business is gained by controlling the actions of the people responsible for its revenues, costs, and expenses. When a budget is prepared and standard costs established, control is maintained by taking appropriate action when actual costs vary from standard or from the budget.

Reports like the ones shown in this chapter are a means of calling management's attention to these variations, and a review of the reports is essential to the successful operation of a budget program. However, in making the review, management should practice the control technique known as **management by exception.** Under this technique, management gives its attention only to the variances in which actual costs are significantly different from standard; it ignores the cost situations in which performance is satisfactory.

Illustration 26-5

XL Company
Factory Overhead Variance Report
For Month Ended May 31, 198A

VOLUME VARIANCE:

Normal production level	80%	of capacity.
Production level achieved	70%	of capacity.
Volume variance	$ 500 (unfavorable)	

CONTROLLABLE VARIANCE:

	Budget	Actual	Favorable	Unfavorable
Fixed overhead costs:				
Building rent	$1,000	$1,000		
Depreciation, machinery	1,200	1,200		
Supervisory salaries	1,800	1,800		
Total fixed costs	$4,000	$4,000		
Variable overhead costs:				
Indirect labor	$1,400	$1,525		$125
Indirect materials	1,050	1,025	$ 25	
Power and lights	700	750		50
Maintenance	350	350		
Total variable costs	$3,500	$3,650		
Total controllable variances			$ 25	$175
Net controllable variance (unfavorable) . .			150	
			$175	$175

In other words, management concentrates its attention on the exceptional or irregular situations and pays little or no attention to the normal.

Many companies develop standard costs and apply variance analysis only when dealing with manufacturing costs. In these companies, the master budget includes selling, general, and administrative expenses, but the subsequent process of controlling these expenses is not based upon the establishment of standard costs and variance analysis. However, other companies have recognized that standard costs and variance analysis may help control selling, general, and administrative expenses just as well as manufacturing costs. Students should understand that the previous discussions of material and labor cost variances can easily be adapted to many selling, general, and administrative expenses.

■ Standard Costs in the Accounts

Standard costs can be used solely in the preparation of management reports and need not be taken into the accounts. However, in most standard cost systems such costs are recorded in the accounts to facilitate both the record-keeping and the preparation of reports.

No effort will be made here to go into the record-keeping details of a standard cost system. This is reserved for a course in cost accounting. Nevertheless, when standard costs are taken into the accounts, entries like the following (the data for which are taken from the discussion of material variances on pages 934–935) may be used to enter standard costs into the Goods in Process account and to separately identify variances in variance accounts.

May	31	Goods in Process	3,500.00	
		Material Quantity Variance	100.00	
		Material Price Variance	180.00	
		Raw Materials		3,780.00
		To charge production with 3,600 pounds of direct material @ $1.05 per pound.		

Variances taken into the accounts are allowed to accumulate in the variance accounts until the end of an accounting period. If at that time the variance amounts are immaterial, they are closed directly to Cost of Goods Sold. However, if the amounts are material, they may be prorated between Goods in Process, Finished Goods, and Cost of Goods Sold.

□ **Glossary**	**Controllable variance** the difference between the overhead actually incurred and the overhead budgeted at the operating level achieved.

Controllable variance the difference between the overhead actually incurred and the overhead budgeted at the operating level achieved.

Cost variance the difference between the actual or incurred amount of a cost and the standard or budgeted amount of the cost.

Fixed budget a budget based on a single estimate of sales or production volume that gives no consideration to the possibility that the actual sales or production volume may differ from the assumed amount.

Flexible budget a budget that provides budgeted amounts for all levels of production within the relevant range.

Flexible budget performance report a report designed to analyze the difference between actual performance and budgeted performance, where the budgeted amounts are based on the actual sales volume or level of activity.

Management by exception a technique whereby management gives its attention to the variances in which actual costs are significantly different from standard costs and generally ignores the cost situations in which performance is satisfactory.

Performance report a financial report that compares actual cost and/or revenue performance with budgeted amounts and designates the differences between them as favorable or unfavorable variances.

Price variance a difference between actual and budgeted revenue or cost caused by the actual price per unit being different from the budgeted price per unit.

Quantity variance the difference between actual cost and budgeted cost that was caused by a difference between the actual number of units used and the number of units budgeted.

Standard costs the costs that should be incurred under normal conditions in producing a given product or part or in performing a particular service.

Static budget a synonym for fixed budget.

Variable budget a synonym for flexible budget.

Volume variance the difference between the amount of overhead budgeted at the actual operating level achieved during the period and the standard amount of overhead charged to production during the period.

□ **Questions for Class Discussion**

1. What is a *fixed* or *static* budget?
2. What limits the usefulness of fixed budget performance reports?
3. What is the essential difference between a fixed budget and a flexible budget?
4. What is the initial step in preparing a flexible budget?
5. Is there any sense in which a variable cost may be thought of as being constant in amount? Explain.
6. A particular type of cost may be classified as variable by one company and fixed by another company. Why might this be appropriate?
7. What is meant by contribution margin?
8. What is a flexible budget performance report designed to analyze?

9. In cost accounting, what is meant by a variance?

10. A cost variance often consists of a price variance and a quantity variance. What is a price variance? What is a quantity variance?

11. What is the purpose of a standard cost?

12. What department usually is responsible for a direct material price variance? What department generally is responsible for a direct material quantity variance?

13. What is a predetermined standard overhead rate?

14. In analyzing the overhead variance, what is meant by a volume variance?

15. Under what conditions is the overhead volume variance said to be favorable?

16. In analyzing the overhead variance, what is meant by a controllable variance?

17. If a company is budgeted to operate at 80% of capacity and actually operates at 84% of capacity, what effect will the 4% excess have on the controllable variance?

18. What is the relationship between standard costs, variance analysis, and management by exception?

19. If standard costs of manufacturing are recorded in the accounts, how are the manufacturing cost variances disposed of at the end of each accounting period?

☐ **Class Exercises**

Exercise 26-1

A company manufactures and sells small sailboats and normally operates eight hours a day, five days per week. On the basis of this general information, classify the following costs as fixed or variable. In those instances where further investigation might reverse your classification, comment on the possible reasons for treating the item in the opposite manner.

a. Electricity to run power tools.	h.	Sailcloth.
b. Repair expense on power tools.	i.	Teak wood for trim pieces.
c. Management salaries.	j.	Utilities (gas and water).
d. Bolts and screws.	k.	Fire insurance on property.
e. Shipping expenses.	l.	Sales commissions.
f. Paint.	m.	Office supplies.
g. Direct labor.	n.	Depreciation on power tools.
	o.	Fiberglass materials.

Exercise 26-2

Saxton Company's fixed budget for the third quarter of 198A is presented below. Recast the budget as a flexible budget and show the budgeted amounts for 19,200 units and 21,600 units of production.

Sales (20,400 units)		$ 428,400
Cost of goods sold:		
Direct materials	$79,560	
Direct labor	88,740	
Production supplies	12,240	
Depreciation	9,000	
Plant manager's salary	13,200	(202,740)
Gross profit		$ 225,660
Selling expenses:		
Sales commissions	$35,496	
Packaging expense	9,180	(44,676)
Administrative expenses:		
Administrative salaries	$18,000	
Insurance expense	4,560	
Office rent expense	15,000	
Executive salaries	30,000	(67,560)
Income from operations		$ 113,424

Exercise 26-3

Blevin Company's fixed budget performance report for last period appeared as follows:

	Fixed Budget	Actual Performance	Variance
Sales: In units	12,400	15,500	
In dollars	$99,200	$127,875	$28,675 F
Expenses	86,800	104,050	17,250 U
Income from operations	$12,400	$ 23,825	$11,425 F

The budgeted expenses of $86,800 included $62,000 of variable expenses; the remainder were fixed. Prepare an analysis of the variance in the income from operations that shows (1) how much of the variance resulted from operating at a level that was higher than budgeted, and (2) how much of the variance remains to be explained by other factors.

Exercise 26-4

Office Equipment Company has just completed 120 units of its finest executive desk using 18,200 board feet of lumber costing $27,664. The company's direct material standards for one unit of this desk are 145 board feet of lumber at $1.55 per board foot.

Required

Isolate the direct material variances incurred in manufacturing these desks.

Exercise 26-5

Office Equipment Company takes its standard costs into its cost records. As a result, in charging material costs to Goods in Process, it also records any variances in its accounts.

Required

1. Under the assumption that the direct materials used to manufacture the desks of Exercise 26-4 were charged to Goods in Process on November 17, give the entry to charge the direct materials and to take the variances into the accounts.

2. Under the further assumption that the direct material variances of Exercise 26-4 were the only variances of the accounting period and were considered immaterial, give the year-end entry to close the variance accounts.

Exercise 26-6

After carefully evaluating a company's production process, management decided to budget 0.8 hours of direct labor per unit of product, at an average cost of $8.50 per hour. During January, the company used 2,040 hours of direct labor at a total cost of $17,544 to produce 2,400 units of product. In February, the company used 2,090 hours of direct labor at a total cost of $17,347 to produce 2,750 units of product. Calculate the quantity variance, the price variance, and the direct labor cost variance for January and for February.

Exercise 26-7

During a recent period's manufacturing operations, a company's use of direct material resulted in a favorable price variance of $210. The actual price per pound of material was $3.10 while the standard price was $3.25. How many pounds of material were used during the period?

Exercise 26-8

Calculate an answer for each of the following independent cases:

a. A company's production for the period required standard direct material cost of $26,300. During the period, the direct material variances included a favorable price variance of $360 and an unfavorable quantity variance of $740. What was the total actual cost of direct materials incurred during the period?

b. During a period, a company had a favorable direct labor price variance of $325 and a favorable direct labor quantity variance of $890. Goods produced during the period required standard direct labor cost of $14,300. What was the total actual cost of direct labor incurred during the period?

c. During a period, a company reported an unfavorable overhead volume variance of $2,500 and a favorable overhead controllable variance of $600. Standard overhead charged to production during the period amounted to $9,700. What was the total actual overhead incurred during the period?

Exercise 26-9

A company normally operates at 70% of capacity, which requires 1,750 standard direct labor hours to produce 1,750 units of product per period.

At that level of production, its overhead budget includes $14,000 of fixed overhead plus $9,100 of variable overhead. Calculate the volume variance and the controllable variance if the company incurred $23,200 of overhead during a period in which it produced 1,500 units of product.

Exercise 26-10

A company has established the following standard costs for one unit of its product:

Direct material (1.5 gallons @ $4 per unit)	$ 6
Direct labor (2 hrs. @ $8 per hr.)	16
Factory overhead (2 hrs. @ $7 per hr.)	14
Standard cost	$36

The $7 per direct labor hour overhead rate is based on a normal 80% of capacity operating level and the following monthly flexible budget information:

	Operating Levels		
	75%	**80%**	**85%**
Budgeted production in units . .	11,250	12,000	12,750
Budget production in standard labor hours	22,500	24,000	25,500
Budgeted overhead:			
Fixed overhead	$84,000	$84,000	$84,000
Variable overhead	78,750	84,000	89,250

During the past month, the company operated at 75% of capacity and incurred the following overhead costs:

Fixed overhead costs	$ 84,000
Variable overhead costs	84,375
Total overhead costs	$168,375

Required

Isolate the overhead variances into a volume variance and a controllable variance.

Problems   **Problem 26-1**

Earhard Company's master (fixed) budget for 198A was based on an expected production and sales volume of 6,900 units and included the following operating items:

Earhard Company
Fixed Budget
For Year Ended December 31, 198A

Sales		$ 552,000
Cost of goods sold:		
Direct materials	$138,000	
Direct labor	82,800	
Machinery repairs (variable cost)	4,140	
Depreciation of plant	15,000	
Utilities (40% of which is a variable cost)	27,600	
Supervisory salaries	36,000	(303,540)
Gross profit		$ 248,460
Selling expenses:		
Packaging	$ 13,800	
Shipping	20,700	
Sales salary (an agreed-upon, annual salary) . . .	42,000	(76,500)
General and administrative expenses:		
Insurance expense	$ 9,000	
Salaries	63,000	
Rent expense	48,000	(120,000)
Income from operations		$ 51,960

Required

1. Prepare a flexible budget for the company and show detailed budgets for sales and production volumes of 6,300 units and 7,500 units.

2. A consultant to the company has suggested that developing business conditions in the area are reaching a crossroads, and that the impact of these events on the company could result in a sales volume of approximately 8,500 units. The president of Earhard Company is confident that this is within the relevant range of existing production capacity but is hesitant to estimate the impact of such a change on operating income. What would be the expected increase in operating income?

3. In the consultant's report, the possibility of unfavorable business events was also mentioned, in which case production and sales volume for 198A would likely fall to 6,000 units. What amount of income from operations should the president expect if these unfavorable events occur?

Problem 26-2

Refer to the discussion of Earhard Company in Problem 26-1. Earhard Company's actual statement of income from 198A operations is as follows:

Earhard Company
Statement of Income from Operations
For Year Ended December 31, 198A

Sales (7,500 units)		$ 570,000
Cost of goods sold:		
Direct materials	$135,000	
Direct labor.	93,000	
Machinery repairs	3,000	
Depreciation of plant	15,000	
Utilities (50% of which was a variable cost) . . .	33,120	
Supervisory salaries	35,100	(314,220)
Gross profit		$ 255,780
Selling expenses:		
Packaging	$ 13,500	
Shipping	23,700	
Sales salary	42,000	(79,200)
General and administrative expenses:		
Insurance expense	$ 9,300	
Salaries	64,500	
Rent expense.	48,000	(121,800)
Income from operations		$ 54,780

Required

1. Using the flexible budget you prepared for Problem 26-1, present a flexible budget performance report for 198A.

2. Explain the sales variance.

Problem 26-3

Holiday Manufacturing Company makes a single product for which it has established the following standard costs per unit:

Direct material (15 lbs. @ $1.40 per lb.) . . .	$21.00
Direct labor (3 hr. @ $12 per hr.).	36.00
Factory overhead (3 hr. @ $3.40 per hr.) . .	10.20
Total standard cost	$67.20

The $3.40 per direct labor hour overhead rate is based on a normal, 90% of capacity, operating level and the following flexible budget information:

	Operating Levels		
	80%	**90%**	**100%**
Production in units.	12,800	14,400	16,000
Standard direct labor hours . . .	38,400	43,200	48,000
Fixed factory overhead	$86,400	$86,400	$86,400
Variable factory overhead. . . .	$53,760	$60,480	$67,200

During March, the company operated at 80% of capacity, producing 12,800 units of product that were charged with the following standard costs:

Direct material (192,000 lbs. @ $1.40 per lb.)	$268,800
Direct labor (38,400 hrs. @ $12 per hr.)	460,800
Factory overhead costs (38,400 hrs. @ $3.40 per hr.) . . .	130,560
Total standard cost	$860,160

Actual costs incurred during March were:

Direct material (189,500 lbs.)	$274,775
Direct labor (39,200 hrs.).	462,560
Fixed factory overhead costs	86,600
Variable factory overhead costs . . .	52,224
Total actual costs	$876,159

Required

Isolate the direct material and direct labor variances into price and quantity variances and isolate the overhead variance into the volume and the controllable variance.

Problem 26-4

Tanner Company has established the following standard costs per unit for the product it manufactures:

Direct material (6 lbs. @ $5 per lb.) . . .	$30.00
Direct labor (2 hrs. @ $9 per hr.)	18.00
Overhead (2 hrs. @ $6.25 per hr.) . . .	12.50
Total standard cost	$60.50

The $6.25 per direct labor hour overhead rate is based on a normal, 85% of capacity, operating level and the following flexible budget information for one month's operations.

	Operating Levels		
	80%	85%	90%
Production in units	2,720	2,890	3,060
Standard direct labor hours	5,440	5,780	6,120
Budgeted factory overhead:			
Fixed costs:			
Rent of factory building	$ 7,000	$ 7,000	$ 7,000
Depreciation, machinery. . . .	4,850	4,850	4,850
Taxes and insurance	1,445	1,445	1,445
Supervisory salaries	5,490	5,490	5,490
Total fixed costs	$18,785	$18,785	$18,785
Variable costs:			
Indirect materials	$ 8,160	$ 8,670	$ 9,180
Indirect labor	2,720	2,890	3,060
Power	1,088	1,156	1,224
Maintenance.	4,352	4,624	4,896
Total variable costs	$16,320	$17,340	$18,360
Total factory overhead costs . . .	$35,105	$36,125	$37,145

During May 198A, the company operated at 90% of capacity, produced 3,060 units of product and incurred the following actual costs:

Direct material (16,830 lbs. @ $4.90 per lb.) . .		$ 82,467
Direct labor (6,732 hrs. @ $9 per hr.)		60,588
Overhead costs:		
Rent of factory building	$7,000	
Depreciation, machinery	4,850	
Taxes and insurance	1,600	
Supervisory salaries	6,000	
Indirect materials	9,486	
Indirect labor	3,672	
Power	1,377	
Maintenance	4,590	38,575
Total costs		$181,630

Required

1. Isolate the direct material and direct labor variances into quantity and price variances and isolate the overhead variance into the volume variance and the controllable variance.

2. Prepare a factory overhead variance report showing the volume and controllable variances.

Problem 26-5

Blizzard Company has established the following standard costs for one unit of its product:

Direct material (6 lbs. @ $1.50 per lb.) . . .	$ 9.00
Direct labor (1 hr. @ $10 per hr.)	10.00
Overhead (1 hr. @ $9.60 per hr.)	9.60
Total standard cost	$28.60

The $9.60 per direct labor hour overhead rate is based on a normal, 80% of capacity, operating level, and at this level the company's monthly output is 9,600 units. Following are the company's budgeted overhead costs at the 80% level for one month:

Blizzard Company
Budgeted Monthly Factory
Overhead at 80% Level

Fixed costs:		
Depreciation, building	$11,520	
Depreciation, machinery . . .	17,280	
Taxes and insurance	4,800	
Supervision	19,200	
Total fixed costs		$52,800
Variable costs:		
Indirect materials	$10,560	
Indirect labor	12,480	
Power	7,680	
Repairs and maintenance . . .	8,640	
Total variable costs		39,360
Total overhead costs		$92,160

During August 198A, the company operated at 70% of capacity and incurred the following actual costs:

Direct material (50,000 lbs.)	$ 71,500
Direct labor (8,550 hrs.)	89,775
Depreciation, building	11,520
Depreciation, machinery	17,280
Taxes and insurance	5,100
Supervision	20,000
Indirect materials	9,660
Indirect labor	12,600
Power	6,300
Repairs and maintenance	7,450
Total costs	$251,185

Required

1. Prepare a flexible overhead budget for the company showing the amount of each fixed and variable cost at the 70%, 80%, and 90% levels.

2. Isolate the material and labor variances into quantity and price variances and isolate the overhead variance into the volume variance and the controllable variance.

3. Prepare a factory overhead variance report showing the volume and controllable variances.

Alternate Problems

Problem 26-1A

In the process of preparing a master budget for 198A, Rather Company assumed a sales volume of 6,750 units. The resulting budgeted income statement included the following items that comprise income from operations:

Rather Company
Fixed Budget
For Year Ended December 31, 198A

Sales		$ 236,250
Cost of goods sold:		
Direct materials	$39,000	
Direct labor	31,200	
Factory supplies	3,100	
Depreciation of plant	5,800	
Utilities (of which $4,500 is a fixed cost)	8,800	
Salary of plant manager	28,500	(116,400)
Gross profit		$ 119,850
Selling expenses:		
Packaging	$17,500	
Sales commissions	18,500	
Shipping	10,600	
Salary of vice president—marketing	28,000	
Promotion (variable)	8,400	(83,000)
General and administrative expenses:		
Depreciation	$ 5,200	
Consultant's fees (annual retainer)	5,600	
Administrative salaries	25,500	(36,300)
Income from operations		$ 550

Required

1. Prepare a flexible budget for the company, showing specific budget columns for sales and production volumes of 7,500 units and 8,250 units. Round all unit costs to three decimal places.

2. What would be the expected increase in income from operations if sales and production volume were 8,775 units rather than 6,750 units?

3. Although the management of Rather Company believes that the master budget was a conservative estimate of sales and production volume, it is possible that the level of activity could fall to 5,670 units. What will be the effect on income from operations if this occurs?

Problem 26-2A

Refer to the discussion of Rather Company in Problem 26-1A. Rather Company's actual statement of income from 198A operations is as follows:

Rather Company
Statement of Income from Operations
For Year Ended December 31, 198A

Sales (7,500 units)		$ 273,750
Cost of goods sold:		
Direct materials	$42,900	
Direct labor	36,750	
Factory supplies	3,675	
Depreciation of plant	5,850	
Utilities (of which 50% is a fixed cost)	9,300	
Salary of plant manager	28,500	(126,975)
Gross profit		$ 146,775
Selling expenses:		
Packaging	$19,250	
Sales commissions	23,400	
Shipping	11,212	
Salary of vice president—marketing	27,000	
Promotion (variable)	11,600	(92,462)
General and administrative expenses:		
Depreciation	$ 5,200	
Consultant's fees	5,960	
Administrative salaries	25,000	(36,160)
Income from operations		$ 18,153

Required

1. Using the flexible budget you prepared for Problem 26-1A, present a flexible budget performance report for 198A.

2. Explain the sales variance.

Problem 26-3A

A company has established the following standard costs for one unit of its product:

Direct material (5 lbs. @ $1.50 per lb.)	$ 7.50
Direct labor (1.5 hrs. @ $8 per hr.)	12.00
Overhead (1.5 hrs. @ $5 per hr.)	7.50
Total standard cost	$27.00

The overhead rate of $5 per direct labor hour is based on a normal, 90% of capacity, operating level for the company's plant and the following flexible budget information for April 198A.

	Operating Levels		
	80%	90%	100%
Production in units	1,200	1,350	1,500
Direct labor hours	1,800	2,025	2,250
Fixed factory overhead . . .	$4,860	$4,860	$4,860
Variable factory overhead . .	$4,680	$5,265	$5,850

During April, the company operated at 80% of capacity, producing 1,200 units of product and incurring actual costs as follows:

Direct material (6,600 lbs. @ $1.60 per lb.) . . .	$10,560
Direct labor (1,720 hrs. @ $9.80 per hr.)	16,856
Fixed factory overhead costs	4,860
Variable factory overhead costs	4,550

Required

Isolate the direct material and direct labor variances into price and quantity variances, and isolate the overhead variance into the volume and the controllable variance.

Problem 26-4A

Richfield Company has established the following standard costs per unit for the product it manufactures:

Direct material (3 lbs. @ $2 per lb.)	$ 6.00
Direct labor (1 hr. @ $9 per hr.)	9.00
Overhead (1 hr. @ $7 per hr.)	7.00
Total standard cost	$22.00

The $7 per direct labor hour overhead rate is based on a normal, 80% of capacity, operating level and the flexible budget information for one month's operations shown at the top of the next page.

During August 198A, the company operated at 75% of capacity, produced 3,000 units of product, and incurred the following actual costs:

Direct material (8,860 lbs. @ $2.10 per lb.)		$18,606
Direct labor (3,120 hrs. @ $8.75 per hr.)		27,300
Overhead costs:		
Depreciation, building	$4,500	
Depreciation, machinery	3,600	
Taxes and insurance.	1,450	
Supervisory salaries	3,000	
Indirect materials	3,280	
Indirect labor	4,670	
Power	1,190	
Maintenance	360	22,050
Total costs		$67,956

	Operating Levels		
	75%	80%	85%
Production in units	3,000	3,200	3,400
Standard direct labor hours . . .	3,000	3,200	3,400
Budgeted factory overhead:			
Fixed costs:			
Depreciation, building	$ 4,500	$ 4,500	$ 4,500
Depreciation, machinery . . .	3,600	3,600	3,600
Taxes and insurance	1,220	1,220	1,220
Supervisory salaries	3,000	3,000	3,000
Total fixed costs	$12,320	$12,320	$12,320
Variable costs:			
Indirect materials	$ 3,000	$ 3,200	$ 3,400
Indirect labor	4,500	4,800	5,100
Power	1,350	1,440	1,530
Maintenance	600	640	680
Total variable costs	$ 9,450	$10,080	$10,710
Total factory overhead costs . .	$21,770	$22,400	$23,030

Required

1. Isolate the direct material and direct labor variances into price and quantity variances and isolate the overhead variance into the volume variance and the controllable variance.

2. Prepare a factory overhead variance report showing the volume and controllable variances.

Problem 26-5A

Patten Company has established the following standard costs for one unit of its product:

Direct material (2 lbs. @ $1.50 per lb.) . . . . $ 3.00
Direct labor (½ hr. @ $11 per hr.) 5.50
Overhead (½ hr. @ $6 per hr.) 3.00
Total standard cost $11.50

The $6 per direct labor hour overhead rate is based on a normal, 95% of capacity, operating level, and at this level the company's monthly output is 3,800 units. Following are the company's budgeted overhead costs at the 95% level for one month:

Patten Company
Budgeted Monthly Factory
Overhead at 95% Level

Fixed costs:

Depreciation, building	$2,400	
Depreciation, machinery	1,800	
Taxes and insurance	1,200	
Supervision	2,200	
Total fixed costs		$ 7,600

Variable costs:

Indirect materials	$1,330	
Indirect labor	1,140	
Power	760	
Repairs and maintenance	570	
Total variable costs		3,800
Total overhead costs		$11,400

During July of the current year, the company operated at 85% of capacity and incurred the following actual costs:

Direct material (7,050 lbs.)	$11,280
Direct labor (1,750 hrs.)	18,375
Depreciation, building	2,400
Depreciation, machinery	1,800
Taxes and insurance	1,150
Supervision	2,200
Indirect materials	1,200
Indirect labor	1,000
Power	750
Repairs and maintenance	400
Total costs	$40,555

Required

1. Prepare a flexible overhead budget for the company showing the amount of each fixed and variable cost at the 75%, 85%, and 95% levels.

2. Isolate the material and labor variances into quantity and price variances and isolate the overhead variance into the volume variance and the controllable variance.

3. Prepare a factory overhead variance report showing the volume and controllable variances.

Provocative Problems

Provocative Problem 26-1 Embassy Company

Embassy Company's management plans to sell artistic, plaster statues for $28 each. Each statue should require 2.5 pounds of a specially processed plaster that the company expects to purchase for $5 per pound. The statues ought to be produced at the rate of three statues per direct labor hour, and the company should be able to hire the needed laborers for $9 per hour. Each statue will be packaged in a cardboard container that weighs one pound, and the company will seek to buy cardboard for $0.50 per pound.

If actual sales and production volume range from 10,000 to 20,000 statues, the manager would expect the company to incur administrative and sales personnel salaries of $60,000, depreciation of $18,000, utilities expenses of $14,000, and insurance expense of $10,000.

In 198A, Embassy Company actually produced and sold 15,000 statues at $26 each. It used 38,600 pounds of plaster, purchased at $5.20 per pound. Laborers were paid $8.70 per hour and worked 4,800 hours to produce the statues. Cardboard was purchased for $0.54 per pound, and 14,550 pounds were used. All other expenses occurred as planned.

Although the above facts are all available to management, they have expressed considerable confusion over the matter of evaluating the operating performance of the company. They recognize that the actual operating income was different from the expected amount but are not able to sort out which items caused the change. They also expressed interest in learning the magnitude of the impact of price changes in specific items purchased by the company as well as any other factors that might be of help in evaluating the company's performance. Can you help management?

Provocative Problem 26-2   Tensil Products Company

Karen Tucker has been an employee of Tensil Products Company for nine years, the last seven of which she has worked in the molding department. Eight months ago she was made supervisor of the department, and since then has been able to end a long period of internal dissension, high employee turnover, and inefficient operation in the department. Under Karen's supervision, the department's production has increased, employee morale has improved, absenteeism has dropped, and for the past two months the department has regularly been beating its standard for the first time in years.

However, a few days ago Helen Martin, an employee in the department, suggested to Karen that the company install new controls on the department's machinery similar to those developed by a competitor. The controls would cost $12,000 installed and would have an eight-year life and no salvage value. They should increase production 10%, reduce maintenance costs $400 per year, and do away with the labor of one person.

Karen's answer to Helen was: "Forget it. We are doing OK now; we don't need the extra production; and besides, jobs are hard to find and if we have to let someone go, who'll it be?"

Do you think standard costs had anything to do with Karen's answer to Helen? Explain. Do you agree with Karen's answer? Should Karen be the person to make a decision such as this? How can a company be sure that suggestions such as Helen's are not lost in the chain of command?

Provocative Problem 26-3   Molenco Company

Molenco Company manufactures a product that has a seasonal demand and that cannot be stored for long periods; consequently, the number of units manufactured varies with the season. In accounting for costs, the company charges actual costs incurred to a Goods in Process account maintained for the product, which it closes at the end of each quarter to Finished Goods. At the end of last year, which was an average year, the following cost report was prepared for the company manager:

Molenco Company
Quarterly Report of Product Costs
Year Ended December 31, 198A

	First Quarter	Second Quarter	Third Quarter	Fourth Quarter
Direct materials	$ 15,600	$ 19,450	$ 7,850	$ 3,950
Direct labor	46,700	58,000	23,500	11,800
Fixed overhead costs.	21,000	21,000	21,000	21,000
Variable overhead costs	25,600	31,950	12,950	6,500
Total manufacturing costs	$108,900	$130,400	$65,300	$43,250
Production in units	10,000	12,500	5,000	2,500
Cost per unit	$ 10.890	$ 10.432	$13.060	$17.300

The manager has asked you to explain why unit costs for the product varied from a low of $10.432 in the second quarter to a high of $17.300 in the last quarter, and to suggest a better way to accumulate or allocate costs. The manager feels that the quarterly reports are needed for purposes of control, so attach to your explanation a schedule showing what last year's direct material, direct labor, and overhead costs per unit would have been had your suggestion or suggestions been followed for the year.

27 Capital Budgeting; Managerial Decisions

After studying Chapter 27, you should be able to:

1. Describe the impact of capital budgeting on the operations of a company.

2. Calculate a payback period on an investment and state the inherent limitations of this method.

3. Calculate a rate of return on an investment and state the assumptions on which this method is based.

4. Describe the information obtained by using the discounted cash flow method, the procedures involved in using this method, and the problems associated with its use.

5. Explain the effects of incremental costs on a decision to accept or reject additional business and on a decision whether to make or buy a given product.

6. State the meaning of sunk costs, out-of-pocket costs, and opportunity costs, and describe the importance of each type of cost to decisions such as to scrap or rebuild defective units or to sell a product as is or process it further.

7. Define or explain the words and phrases listed in the chapter Glossary.

A business decision involves choosing between two or more courses of action, and the best choice normally offers the highest return on the investment or the greatest cost savings. Business managers at times make decisions intuitively, without trying to measure systematically the advantages and disadvantages of each possible choice. Often they make intuitive decisions because they are unaware of any other way to choose; but sometimes the available information is so sketchy or unreliable that systematic measurement is useless. Also, intangible factors such as convenience, prestige, and public opinion are at times more important than the factors that can be reduced to a quantitative basis. Nevertheless, in many situations it is possible to reduce the anticipated consequences of alternative choices to a quantitative basis and measure them systematically. This chapter will examine several areas of decision making in which more or less systematic methods of analysis are available.

■ Capital Budgeting

Planning plant asset investments is called **capital budgeting.** The plans may involve new buildings, new machinery, or whole new projects. In all such cases, a fundamental objective of business firms is to earn a satisfactory return on the invested funds. Capital budgeting often requires some of the most crucial and difficult decisions faced by management. The decisions are difficult because they are commonly based on estimates projected well into a future that is at best uncertain. Capital budgeting decisions are crucial because (1) large sums of money are often involved; (2) funds are committed for long periods of time; and (3) once a decision is made and a project is begun, it may be difficult or impossible to reverse the effects of a poor decision.

Capital budgeting involves the preparation of cost and revenue estimates for all proposed projects, an examination of the merits of each, and a choice of those worthy of investment. It is a broad field, and the discussion of this chapter must be limited to three ways of comparing investment opportunities. They are the **payback period,** the **rate of return on average investment,** and **net present value.**

Payback Period

Generally, an investment in a machine or other plant asset will produce a **net cash flow,** and the **payback period** for the investment is the time required to recover the investment through this net cash flow. For example, assume that Murray Company is considering several capital investments. One investment involves the purchase of a machine to be used in manufacturing a new product. The machine will cost $16,000, have an eight-year service life, and no salvage value. The company estimates that 10,000 units of the machine's product will be sold each year, and the sales will result in $1,500 of after-tax net income, calculated as follows:

Annual sales of new product		$30,000
Deduct:		
Cost of materials, labor, and overhead other than depreciation on the new machine	$15,500	
Depreciation on the new machine	2,000	
Additional selling and administrative expenses	9,500	27,000
Annual before-tax income		$ 3,000
Income tax (assumed rate, 50%)		1,500
Annual after-tax net income from new product sales		$ 1,500

Through annual sales of 10,000 units of the new product, Murray Company expects to gain $30,000 of revenue and $1,500 of net income. The net income represents an inflow of assets that will be available to pay back the new machine's cost. Also, since depreciation expense does not involve a current outflow of assets or funds, the amount of the annual depreciation charge represents an additional inflow of assets that will be available to pay back the machine's cost. The $1,500 of net income plus the $2,000 depreciation charge total $3,500, and together are the **annual net cash flow** expected from the investment. Furthermore, this annual net cash flow will pay back the investment in the new machine in 4.6 years, calculated as follows:

$$\frac{\text{Cost of new machine, \$16,000}}{\text{Annual net cash flow, \$3,500}} = 4.6 \text{ years to recover investment}$$

The answer just given is 4.6 years. Actually, when $16,000 is divided by $3,500, the result is just a little over 4.57; but 4.6 years is close enough. Remember that the calculation is based on estimated net income and estimated depreciation; consequently, it is pointless to carry the answer to several decimal places.

Calculating Payback When Cash Flows Are Not Uniform The previous example assumed that net cash flows were $3,500 each and every year. However, the payback period can be calculated just as easily when cash flows vary from year to year. For example, assume an investment of $15,000 is expected to produce annual net cash flows as follows:

	Annual Net Cash Flows	Total Net Cash Flows
Year 1	$3,000	$ 3,000
Year 2	4,000	7,000
Year 3	5,000	12,000
Year 4	6,000	18,000

Total net cash flows are $12,000 at the end of year 3 and $18,000 at the end of year 4. Obviously, the payback period for the $15,000 investment is between three and four years. Of the $15,000 investment, $12,000 is paid back during the first three years. The remaining $3,000 that is paid back during year 4 amounts to one half or 0.5 of the $6,000 net cash flow for the entire year. Thus, the payback period is 3.5 years.

Evaluating Payback Period as a Method of Comparing Investments   In choosing between investment opportunities, a short payback period is desirable because (1) the sooner an investment is recovered the sooner the funds are available for other uses, and (2) a short payback period also means the invested funds are at risk for a shorter period of time. In other words, a short "bail-out period" improves the company's ability to respond if conditions change.

The payback period should never be the only consideration is evaluating investments because it ignores at least two important factors. First, it fails to reflect differences in the timing of net cash flows. In the previous example, the net cash flows in years 1, 2, and 3 were $3,000, $4,000, and $5,000. If they had been $5,000, $4,000, and $3,000 in years 1, 2, and 3, the payback period would still be 3.5 years.

Second, payback period ignores the length of time revenue will continue to be earned after the end of the payback period. For example, one investment may pay back its cost in 3 years and cease to produce revenue at that point, while a second investment may require 5 years to pay back its cost but will continue to produce income for another 15 years.

Rate of Return on Average Investment

The **rate of return on the average investment** in a machine is calculated by dividing the after-tax net income from the sale of the machine's product by the average investment in the machine.

Average Investment Assuming Revenues Are Spread Evenly throughout Year   In calculating the average investment, an assumption must be made as to the timing of the cost recovery from depreciation. If sales are earned evenly throughout the year, the cost recovery from depreciation may be assumed to occur at the middle of the year. Under these conditions, the average investment each year may be calculated as the average of the beginning-of-year book value and the end-of-year book value. If Murray Company's $16,000 machine is depreciated $2,000 each year, the average investment each year and the average investment over the life of the machine may be calculated as shown in Illustration 27-1.

More simply, the average investment may be calculated as:

$$\$16,000 \div 2 = \$8,000$$

Note that the above example is simplified by the fact that the machine has no salvage value. If the machine had a salvage value, the average investment would be calculated as (Original cost + Salvage value) ÷ 2.

After average investment is determined, the rate of return on average investment is calculated. As previously stated, this involves dividing the estimated annual after-tax net income from the sale of the machine's product by average investment. Since Murray Company expects an after-tax net income of $1,500, the expected rate of return is calculated as follows:

$$\$1,500 \div \$8,000 = 18\tfrac{3}{4}\% \text{ return on average investment}$$

Illustration 27-1

Year	Beginning-of-Year Book Value	Average Investment Each Year	
1 . . .	$16,000	$15,000	
2 . . .	14,000	13,000	
3 . . .	12,000	11,000	
4 . . .	10,000	9,000	$\dfrac{\$64,000}{8}$ = $8,000 average
5 . . .	8,000	7,000	investment over
6 . . .	6,000	5,000	life of machine
7 . . .	4,000	3,000	
8 . . .	2,000	1,000	
Totals . .	$72,000	$64,000	

Average Investment Assuming Revenues Are Received at Year-End In some investments, the revenue from the investment is not spread evenly over each year and may be received near the end of each year. If the revenue is expected to be received at the year's end, the cost recovery from depreciation also occurs at the year's end. Thus, the average investment each year is the beginning-of-year book value. Referring back to Illustration 27-1, these assumptions result in the following calculation of average investment:

$72,000 ÷ 8 = $9,000 average investment over life of investment

Instead of adding the beginning-of-year book values and averaging over eight years, a shorter way to the same answer is to average the book values of the machine's first and last years in this manner:

$16,000 book value at beginning of (and throughout) first year
  2,000 book value at beginning of (and throughout) last year
$18,000

$18,000 ÷ 2 = $9,000 average investment over life of investment

---

Note that if the machine had a salvage value, the book value at the beginning of (and throughout) the last year would be the salvage value plus the depreciation expense of the last year.

Evaluating the Return on Average Investment Given a $9,000 average investment, the return on investment is:

$1,500 ÷ $9,000 = $16\frac{2}{3}\%$ return on average investment

At this point the question naturally arises whether $16\frac{2}{3}\%$ or $18\frac{3}{4}\%$ are good rates of return. Obviously, $18\frac{3}{4}\%$ appears better than $16\frac{2}{3}\%$. However, even this may not be true. A project that is expected to yield $18\frac{3}{4}\%$ may be much riskier than another project having a $16\frac{2}{3}\%$ expected return. And, depending on other available investment alternatives, neither may be acceptable. In other words, a return is good or bad only when related to other returns and taking into consideration the differing riskiness of the alternatives. However, when average investment returns are used in comparing and deciding between capital investments, the one having the least risk, the shortest payback period, and the highest return for the longest time is usually the best.

Rate of return on average investment is easy to calculate and understand. As a result, it has long been used in selecting investment opportunities. However, its usefulness as a method of evaluating investments is limited when the net incomes are expected to vary. If the annual net income from an investment is expected to vary from year to year, the calculation of rate of return on average investment must be based on the average annual net income. Two investments with the same average annual net income may not be equally desirable because one is expected to have higher net incomes in the early years and lower net incomes in the later years. Rate of return on average investment fails to distinguish between these two investments. In such cases, a comparison of net present values generally offers a better means of selection.

An understanding of net present values requires an understanding of the concept of discounting. This concept was explained in Chapter 12, beginning on page 428. That explanation should be reviewed at this point by any student who does not fully understand it. An expanded explanation of discounting is presented in Appendix A, beginning on page 1023. The present value tables in Appendix A, on pages 1031 and 1033, may be used to solve some of the problems at the end of the present chapter.

Net Present Values

When a business invests in a new plant asset, it expects to secure from the investment a stream of future cash flows. Normally it will not invest unless the flows are sufficient to return the amount of the investment plus a satisfactory return on the investment. For example, assume that the cash flows from Murray Company's investment will be received at the end of each year. Will the investment in the machine return the amount of the investment plus a satisfactory return? If Murray Company considers a 10% compound annual return a satisfactory return on its capital investments, it can answer this question with the calculations of Illustration 27-2.

To secure the machine of Illustration 27-2, Murray Company must invest $16,000. However, from the sale of the machine's product it will recapture $2,000 of its investment each year in the form of depreciation; in addition, it will earn a $1,500 annual net income. In other words, the company will receive a $3,500 net cash flow from the investment each year for eight years. The first column of Illustration 27-2 indicates that the net cash flows of the first year are received one year hence, and so forth for subsequent years. This means that the net cash flows are received at the end of the year. To simplify the discussion of this chapter and the problems at the end of the chapter, the net cash flows of a company's operations are generally assumed to occur at the end of the year. More refined calculations are left for consideration in an advanced course.

The annual net cash flows, shown in the second column of Illustration 27-2, are multiplied by the amounts in the third column to determine their present values, which are shown in the last column. Observe that the total of these present values exceeds the amount of the required invest-

Illustration 27-2

Analysis of Proposed Investment in Machine

Years Hence	Net Cash Flows	Present Value of $1 at 10%	Present Value of Net Cash Flows
1	$3,500	0.9091	$ 3,181.85
2	3,500	0.8264	2,892.40
3	3,500	0.7513	2,629.55
4	3,500	0.6830	2,390.50
5	3,500	0.6209	2,173.15
6	3,500	0.5645	1,975.75
7	3,500	0.5132	1,796.20
8	3,500	0.4665	1,632.75
Total present value.			$18,672.15
Amount to be invested			16,000.00
Positive net present value.			$ 2,672.15

ment by $2,672.15. Consequently, if Murray Company considers a 10% compound return satisfactory, this machine will recover its required investment, plus a 10% compound return, and $2,672.15 in addition.

Generally, when the cash flows from an investment are discounted at a satisfactory rate and have a positive **net present value,** the investment is worthy of acceptance. Also, when several investment opportunities are being compared, and each requires the same investment and has the same risk, the one having the highest positive net present value is the best.

Shortening the Calculation

In Illustration 27-2, the present values of $1 at 10% for each of the eight years involved are shown. Each year's cash flow is multiplied by the present value of $1 at 10% for that year to determine its present value. Then, the present values of the eight cash flows are added to determine their total. This is one way to determine total present value. However, since in this case the cash flows are uniform, there are two shorter ways. One shorter way is to add the eight yearly present values of $1 at 10% and to multiply $3,500 by the total. Another even shorter way is based on Table A-3 on page 1033. Table A-3 shows the present value of $1 to be received periodically for a number of periods. In the case of the Murray Company machine, $3,500 is to be received annually for eight years. Consequently, to determine the present value of these annual receipts discounted at 10%, go down the 10% column of Table A-3 to the amount opposite eight periods. It is 5.3349. Therefore, the present value of the eight annual $3,500 receipts is $3,500 multiplied by 5.3349, or is $18,672.15.

Cash Flows Not Uniform

Net present value analysis has its greatest usefulness when cash flows are not uniform. For example, assume a company can choose one capital investment from among Projects A, B, and C. Each requires a $12,000 investment and will produce cash flows as follows:

Years Hence	Annual Cash Flows		
	Project A	Project B	Project C
1	$ 5,000	$ 8,000	$ 1,000
2	5,000	5,000	5,000
3	5,000	2,000	9,000
	$15,000	$15,000	$15,000

Note that all three projects produce the same total cash flow. However, the flows of Project A are uniform, those of Project B are greater in the earlier years, while those of Project C are greater in the later years. Consequently, when present values of the cash flows, discounted at 10%, are compared with the required investments, the statistics of Illustration 27-3 result.

Illustration 27-3

	Years Hence	Present Values of Cash Flows Discounted at 10%		
		Project A	Project B	Project C
	1	$ 4,545.50	$ 7,272.80	$ 909.10
	2	4,132.00	4,132.00	4,132.00
	3	3,756.50	1,502.60	6,761.70
Total present values		$12,434.00	$12,907.40	$11,802.80
Required investments		12,000.00	12,000.00	12,000.00
Net present values.		+$ 434.00	+$ 907.40	−$ 197.20

Note that an investment in project A has a $434.00 positive net present value; an investment in Project B has a $907.40 positive net present value; and an investment in Project C has a $197.20 negative net present value. Therefore, if a 10% return is required, an investment in Project C should be rejected, since the investment's net present value indicates it will not earn such a return. Furthermore, as between Projects A and B, other things being equal, Project B is the better investment, since its cash flows have the higher net present value. Although the present value numbers in Illustration 27-3 show dollars and cents, present values are always approximations. Hence, it would be appropriate to round such calculations to the nearest whole dollar.

Salvage Value and Accelerated Depreciation

The $16,000 machine of the Murray Company example was assumed to have no salvage value at the end of its useful life. Often a machine is expected to have a salvage value, and in such cases the expected salvage value is treated as an additional cash flow to be received in the last year of the machine's life.

Also, in the Murray Company example, depreciation was deducted on a straight-line basis; but in actual practice, an accelerated depreciation method is commonly used for tax purposes. Accelerated depreciation results in larger depreciation deductions in the early years of an asset's life and smaller deductions in the later years. This results in smaller income tax liabilities in the early years and larger ones in later years. However, this does not change the basic nature of a present value analysis. It only results in larger cash flows in the early years and smaller ones in later years, which normally make an investment more desirable.

Selecting the Earnings Rate

The selection of a satisfactory earnings rate for capital investments is always a matter for top-management decision. Formulas have been devised to aid management. But, in many companies, the choice of a satisfactory or required rate of return is largely subjective. Management simply decides that enough investment opportunities can be found that will earn, say, a 10% compound return; and this becomes the minimum below which the company refuses to make an investment of average risk.

Whatever the required rate, it is always higher than the rate at which money can be borrowed, since the return on a capital investment must include not only interest but also an additional allowance for risks involved. Therefore, when the rate at which money can be borrowed is around 10%, a required after-tax return of 15% may be acceptable in industrial companies, with a lower rate for public utilities and a higher rate for companies in which the risks are unusually high.

Replacing Plant Assets

In a dynamic economy, new and better machines are constantly coming on the market. As a result, the decision to replace an existing machine with a new and better machine is common. Often, the existing machine is in good condition and will produce the required product; but the new machine will do the job with a large savings in operating costs. In such a situation, management must decide whether the after-tax savings in operating costs justifies the investment.

The amount of after-tax savings from the replacement of an existing machine with a new machine is complicated by the fact that depreciation on the new machine for tax purposes is based on the book value of the old machine plus the cash given in the exchange. There can be other complications too. Consequently, a discussion of the replacement of plant assets is deferred to a more advanced course.

■   **Accepting Additional Business**

Costs obtained from a cost accounting system are average costs and also historical costs. They are useful in product pricing and in controlling operations. But, in a decision to accept an additional volume of business they are not necessarily the relevant costs. In such a decision, the relevant costs are the additional costs, commonly called the **incremental** or **differential costs.**

For example, a company operating at its normal capacity, which is 80%

of full capacity, has annually produced and sold approximately 100,000 units of product with the following results:

Sales (100,000 units @ $10).		$1,000,000
Direct materials (100,000 units @ $3.50).	$350,000	
Direct labor (100,000 units @ $2.20)	220,000	
Factory overhead (100,000 units @ $1.10).	110,000	
Selling expenses (100,000 units @ $1.40)	140,000	
Administrative expenses (100,000 units @ $0.80)	80,000	900,000
Operating income.		$ 100,000

The company's sales department reports it has an exporter who has offered to buy 10,000 units of product at $8.50 per unit. The sale to the exporter is several times larger than any previous sale made by the company; and since the units are being exported, the new business will have no effect on present business. Therefore, in order to determine whether the order should be accepted or rejected, management of the company asks that statistics be prepared to show the estimated net income or loss that would result from accepting the offer. It received the following figures based on the average costs previously given:

Sales (10,000 units @ $8.50)		$85,000
Direct materials (10,000 units @ $3.50).	$35,000	
Direct labor (10,000 units @ $2.20)	22,000	
Factory overhead (10,000 units @ $1.10).	11,000	
Selling expenses (10,000 units @ $1.40)	14,000	
Administrative expenses (10,000 units @ $0.80)	8,000	90,000
Operating loss		$ (5,000)

If a decision were based on these average costs, the new business would likely be rejected. However, in this situation, average costs are not relevant. The relevant costs are the added costs of accepting the new business. Consequently, before rejecting the order, the costs of the new business were examined more closely and the following additional information obtained: (1) Manufacturing 10,000 additional units of product would require direct materials and direct labor at $3.50 and $2.20 per unit just as with normal production. (2) However, the 10,000 units could be manufactured with factory overhead costs, in addition to those already incurred, of only $5,000 for power, packing, and handling labor. (3) Commissions and other selling expenses resulting from the sale would amount to $2,000 in addition to the selling expenses already incurred. And (4), $1,000 additional administrative expenses in the form of clerical work would be required if the order were accepted. Based on this added information, the statement of Illustration 27-4 showing the effect of the additional business on the company's normal business was prepared.

Illustration 27-4 shows that the additional business should be accepted. Present business should be charged with all present costs, and the additional

Illustration 27-4

	Present Business		Additional Business		Present plus the Additional Business	
Sales		$1,000,000		$85,000		$1,085,000
Direct materials	$350,000		$35,000		$385,000	
Direct labor	220,000		22,000		242,000	
Factory overhead	110,000		5,000		115,000	
Selling expenses	140,000		2,000		142,000	
Administrative expense . .	80,000		1,000		81,000	
Total		900,000		65,000		965,000
Operating income		$ 100,000		$20,000		$ 120,000

business should be charged only with its incremental or differential costs. When this is done, accepting the additional business at $8.50 per unit will apparently result in $20,000 additional income before taxes.

Incremental or differential costs always apply to a particular situation at a particular time. For example, adding units to a given production volume may or may not increase depreciation expense. If the additional units require the purchase of more machines, depreciation expense is increased. Likewise, if present machines are used but the additional units shorten their life, more depreciation expense results. However, if present machines are used and their depreciation depends more on the passage of time or obsolescence rather than on use, additional depreciation expense might not result from the added units of product.

■   **Buy or Make**

Incremental or differential costs are often a factor in a decision as to whether a given part or product should be bought or made. For example, a manufacturer has idle machines that can be used to manufacture one of the components (Part 417) of the company's product. This part is presently purchased at a $1.20 delivered cost per unit. The manufacturer estimates that to make Part 417 would cost $0.45 for direct materials, $0.50 for direct labor, and an amount of factory overhead. At this point a question arises as to how much overhead should be charged. If the normal overhead rate of the department in which the part would be manufactured is 100% of direct labor cost, and this amount is charged against Part 417, then the unit costs of making Part 417 would be $0.45 for direct materials, $0.50 for direct labor, and $0.50 for factory overhead, a total of $1.45. At this cost, the manufacturer would be better off to buy the part at $1.20 each.

However, on a short-run basis the manufacturer might be justified in ignoring the normal overhead rate and in charging Part 417 for only the additional overhead costs resulting from its manufacture. Among these additional overhead costs might be, for example, power to operate the machines that would otherwise be idle, depreciation on the machines if the part's manufacture resulted in additional depreciation, and any other overhead that would be added to that already incurred. Furthermore, if these added overhead items total less than $0.25 per unit, the manufacturer might be justified on a short-run basis in manufacturing the part. However, on a long-term basis, Part 417 should be charged a full share of all overhead.

Any amount of overhead less than $0.25 per unit results in a total cost for Part 417 that is less than the $1.20 per unit purchase price. Nevertheless, in making a final decision as to whether the part should be bought or made, the manufacturer should consider in addition to costs such things as quality, the reactions of customers and suppliers, and other intangible factors. When these additional factors are considered, small cost differences may become a minor factor.

Other Cost Concepts

Sunk costs, out-of-pocket costs, and opportunity costs are additional concepts that may be encountered in managerial decisions.

A **sunk cost** is a cost resulting from a past irrevocable decision, and is sunk in the sense that it cannot be avoided. As a result, sunk costs are irrelevant in decisions affecting the future.

An **out-of-pocket cost** is a cost requiring a current outlay of funds. Material costs, supplies, heat, and power are examples. Generally, out-of-pocket costs can be avoided; consequently, they are relevant in decisions affecting the future.

Costs as discussed thus far have been outlays or expenditures made to obtain some benefit, usually goods or services. However, the concept of cost can be expanded to include **opportunity costs;** these are potential benefits that are lost as a result of choosing an alternative course of action. For example, if a job that will pay a student $1,200 for working during the summer must be rejected in order to attend summer school, the $1,200 is an opportunity cost of attending summer school.

Opportunity costs are not entered in the accounting records; but they may be relevant in a decision involving rejected opportunities. For example, decisions to scrap or rebuild defective units of product commonly involve situations that evidence both sunk costs and opportunity costs.

Scrap or Rebuild Defective Units

Any costs incurred in manufacturing units of product that do not pass inspection are sunk costs and as such should not enter into a decision as to whether the units should be sold for scrap or be rebuilt to pass inspection. For example, a company has 10,000 defective units of product that cost $1 per unit to manufacture. The units can be sold as they are for $0.40 each, or they can be rebuilt for $0.80 per unit, after which they can be sold for their full price of $1.50 per unit. Should the company rebuild the units or should it sell them in their present form? The original manufacturing costs of $1 per unit are sunk costs and are irrelevant in the decision; so, based on the information given, the comparative returns from scrapping or rebuilding are:

	As Scrap	Rebuilt
Sales of defective units . . .	$4,000	$15,000
Less cost to rebuild		(8,000)
Net return	$4,000	$ 7,000

From the information given, it appears that rebuilding is the better decision. This is true if the rebuilding does not interfere with normal operations. However, suppose that to rebuild the defective units the company must forgo manufacturing 10,000 new units that will cost $1 per unit to manufacture and can be sold for $1.50 per unit. In this situation the comparative returns may be analyzed as follows:

	As Scrap	Rebuilt
Sale of defective units	$ 4,000	$15,000
Less cost to rebuild the defective units . . .		(8,000)
Sale of new units	15,000	
Less cost to manufacture the new units . . .	(10,000)	
Net return	$ 9,000	$ 7,000

If the defective units are sold without rebuilding, then the new units can also be manufactured and sold, with a $9,000 return from the sale of both the new and old units, as shown in the first column of the analysis. Obviously, this is better than forgoing the manufacture of the new units and rebuilding the defective units for a $7,000 net return.

The situation described here also may be analyzed on an opportunity cost basis as follows: If to rebuild the defective units the company must forgo manufacturing the new units, then the return on the sale of the new units is an opportunity cost of rebuilding the defective units. This opportunity cost is measured at $5,000 (revenue from sale of new units, $15,000, less their manufacturing costs, $10,000, equals the $5,000 benefit that will be sacrificed if the old units are rebuilt); and an opportunity cost analysis of the situation is as follows:

	As Scrap	Rebuilt
Sale of defective units.	$4,000	$15,000
Less cost to rebuild the defective units.		(8,000)
Less opportunity cost (return sacrificed by		
not manufacturing the new units)		(5,000)
Net return	$4,000	$ 2,000

Observe that it does not matter whether this or the previous analysis is made. Either way there is a $2,000 difference in favor of scrapping the defective units.

■ **Process or Sell**   Sunk costs, out-of-pocket costs, and opportunity costs are also encountered in a decision as to whether it is best to sell an intermediate product as it is or process it further and sell the product or products that result from the additional processing. For example, a company has 40,000 units of Product A that cost $0.75 per unit or a total of $30,000 to manufacture. The 40,000 units can be sold as they are for $50,000 or they can be processed further into Products X, Y, and Z at a cost of $2 per original Product

A unit. The additional processing will produce the following numbers of each product, which can be sold at the unit prices indicated:

Product X	10,000 units @ $3
Product Y	22,000 units @ $5
Product Z	6,000 units @ $1
Lost through spoilage . . .	2,000 units (no salvage value)
Total	40,000 units

The net advantage of processing the product further is $16,000, as shown in Illustration 27-5.

Illustration 27-5

Revenue from further processing:		
Product X, 10,000 units @ $3	$ 30,000	
Product Y, 22,000 units @ $5	110,000	
Product Z, 6,000 units @ $1	6,000	
Total revenue.		$146,000
Less:		
Additional processing costs, 40,000 units @ $2 . . .	$ 80,000	
Opportunity cost (revenue sacrificed by not		
selling the Product A units)	50,000	
Total		130,000
Net advantage of further processing		$ 16,000

Note that the revenue available through the sale of the Product A units is an opportunity cost of further processing these units. Also notice that the $30,000 cost of manufacturing the 40,000 units of Product A does not appear in the Illustration 27-5 analysis. This cost is present regardless of which alternative is chosen; therefore, it is irrelevant to the decision. However, the $30,000 does enter into a calculation of the net income from the alternatives. For example, if the company chooses to further process the Product A units, the gross return from the sale of Products X, Y, and Z may be calculated as follows:

Revenue from the sale of Products X, Y, and Z		$146,000
Less:		
Cost to manufacture the Product A units.	$30,000	
Cost to further process the Product A units	80,000	110,000
Gross return from the sale of Products X, Y, and Z . . .		$ 36,000

■ **Deciding the Sales Mix**

When a company sells a combination of products, ordinarily some of the products are more profitable than others, and normally management should concentrate its sales efforts on the more profitable products. However, if production facilities or other factors are limited, an increase in the production and sale of one product may require a reduction in the production and sale of another. In such a situation, management's job is to determine the most profitable combination or sales mix for the products and concentrate on selling the products in this combination.

To determine the best sales mix for its products, management must have information as to the contribution margin of each product, the facilities required to produce and sell each product, and any limitations on these facilities. For example, assume that a company produces and sells two products, A and B. The same machines are used to produce both products, and the products have the following selling prices and variable costs per units:

	Product A	Product B
Selling price.	$5.00	$7.50
Variable costs	3.50	5.50
Contribution margin. . . .	$1.50	$2.00

If the amount of production facilities required to produce each product is the same and there is an unlimited market for Product B, the company should devote all its facilities to Product B because of its larger contribution margin. However, the answer differs if the company's facilities are limited to, say, 100,000 machine-hours of production per month and one machine-hour is required to produce each unit of Product A but two machine-hours are required for each unit of Product B. Under these circumstances, if the market for Product A is unlimited, the company should devote all its production to this product because it produces $1.50 of contribution margin per machine-hour, while Product B produces only $1 per machine-hour.

Actually, when there are no market or other limitations, a company should devote all its efforts to its most profitable product. It is only when there is a market or other limitation on the sale of the most profitable product that a need for a sales mix arises. For example, if in this instance one machine-hour of production facilities are needed to produce each unit of Product A and 100,000 machine-hours are available, 100,000 units of the product can be produced. However, if only 80,000 units can be sold, the company has 20,000 machine-hours that can be devoted to the production of Product B, and 20,000 machine-hours will produce 10,000 units of Product B. Consequently, the company's most profitable sales mix under these assumptions is 80,000 units of Product A and 10,000 units of Product B.

☐   **Glossary**   **Capital budgeting** planning plant asset investments; involves the preparation of cost and revenue estimates for all proposed projects, an examination of the merits of each, and a choice of those worthy of investment.

Differential cost a synonym for incremental cost.

Net present value the value of an investment calculated by discounting the future cash flows from the investment at an interest rate that gives a satisfactory return on investment and then subtracting the present cost of the investment.

Incremental cost an additional cost resulting from a particular course of action.

Opportunity cost the benefit of one course of action that is lost or sacrificed as a result of choosing an alternative course of action.

Out-of-pocket cost a cost requiring a current outlay of funds.

Payback period the time required to recover the original cost of an investment through net cash flows from the investment.

Rate of return on average investment the annual, after-tax income from the sale of an asset's product divided by the average investment in the asset.

Sunk cost a cost incurred as a consequence of a past irrevocable decision and that, therefore, cannot be avoided; hence, irrelevant to decisions affecting the future.

☐ **Questions for Class Discussion**

1. What is capital budgeting? Why are capital budgeting decisions crucial to the business making the decisions?
2. What is the difference between comprehensive budgeting and capital budgeting?
3. A successful investment in a machine will produce a net cash flow. Of what does this consist?
4. If depreciation is an expense, explain why, when the sale of a machine's product produces a net income, the portion of the machine's cost recovered each year through the sale of its product includes both the net income from the product's sale and the year's depreciation on the machine.
5. Why is a short payback period on an investment desirable?
6. If two alternate investments have the same payback period, will the investments be equally desirable?
7. What is the average amount invested in a machine during its life if the machine costs $44,000 and has an estimated five-year life with an estimated $9,000 salvage value? Assume that annual revenues are received at the end of each year.
8. What is your answer to Question 7, assuming the annual revenues are received evenly throughout each year?
9. Is a 15% return on the average investment in a machine a good return?
10. Why is the present value of the expectation of receiving $100 a year hence less than $100? What is the present value of the expectation of receiving $100 one year hence, discounted at 12%?

11. Two investment alternatives are expected to generate annual cash flows for six years and, when discounted at 11%, have the same net present values. Based on this information, can you say with confidence that the two alternatives are equally desirable?

12. What is indicated when the present value of the net cash flows from an investment in a machine, discounted at 12%, exceeds the amount of the investment? What is indicated when the present value of the net cash flows, discounted at 12%, is less than the amount of the investment?

13. When two investment alternatives have the same total expected cash flows but differ in the timing of those flows, which method of evaluating those investments is superior: (a) rate of return on average investment or (b) net present values?

14. Why might the selection of accelerated depreciation for tax purposes make an investment more attractive than it would be if straight-line depreciation were used?

15. What are the differential costs of accepting an additional volume of business?

16. A company manufactures and sells in this country 250,000 units of product at $5 per unit. The product costs $3 per unit to manufacture. Can you describe a situation under which the company may be willing to sell an additional 25,000 units of the product abroad at $2.75 per unit?

17. What is the sunk cost? An out-of-pocket cost? An opportunity cost? Is an opportunity cost typically recorded in the accounting records?

18. Any costs that have been incurred in manufacturing a product are sunk costs. Why are such costs irrelevant in deciding whether to sell the product in its present condition or to make it into a new product through additional processing?

☐ **Class Exercises**   **Exercise 27-1**

Calculate the payback periods for each of the following independent investments:

a. A machine costs $22,000, has a $4,000 salvage value, is expected to last six years, and will generate net income of $5,000 per year after straight-line depreciation and after income taxes of 40%.

b. A product-packaging system is expected to cost $140,000 and have a useful life of 10 years. The system should save $43,500 (after taxes) each year, after deducting straight-line depreciation on the system. Estimated salvage value of the system is $15,000.

Exercise 27-2

A company is asked to advance $100,000 to an affiliate in return for which the company will receive cash payments as follows: During year 1, $30,000; during year 2, $25,000; during year 3, $35,000; during year 4, $40,000; during year 5, $50,000. The payments are spread evenly throughout each year. Calculate the payback period for the advance to the affiliate.

Exercise 27-3

A limousine can be purchased for $47,000 and used for six years to generate net incomes as follows: year 1, $9,000; year 2, $8,000; year 3, $6,000; year 4, $4,000; year 5, $3,000; and year 6, $3,000. In calculating the net incomes, sum-of-the-years'-digits depreciation on the limousine was deducted, based on a six-year life and a salvage value of $5,000. Present calculations to show the payback period for the limousine.

Exercise 27-4

Machine A cost $60,000 and has an estimated four-year life and no salvage value. Machine B cost $75,000 and has an estimated five-year life and a $12,500 salvage value. Calculate the average investment in each machine under the assumptions that the revenues from using the machine are received (a) uniformly throughout each year and (b) at the end of each year.

Exercise 27-5

A company is planning to purchase a machine and add a new product to its line. The machine will cost $120,000, have a four-year life, no salvage value, and will be depreciated on a straight-line basis. The company expects to sell 24,000 units of the machine's product each year. Production will occur throughout the year. However, the product is only marketable during the holiday season at the end of each year, and all sales will occur during the last 15 days of the year. Expected annual results are as follows:

Sales		$300,000
Costs:		
Materials, labor, and overhead excluding depreciation on the new machine	$156,000	
Depreciation on the new machine	30,000	
Selling and administrative expenses	90,000	276,000
Operating income		$ 24,000
Income taxes		12,000
Net income		$ 12,000

Required

Calculate (a) the payback period and (b) the return on the average investment in this machine.

Exercise 27-6

After evaluating the risk characteristics of the investment described in Exercise 27-5, the company concludes that it must earn at least a 12% compound return on the investment in the machine. Based on this decision, determine the total present value and net present value of the net cash flows from the machine the company is planning to buy.

Exercise 27-7

A company can invest in each of three projects, X, Y, and Z. Each project requires a $70,000 investment and will produce cash flows as follows:

Years	Annual Cash Flows		
Hence	Project X	Project Y	Project Z
1	$16,800	$28,000	$39,200
2	28,000	28,000	28,000
3	39,200	28,000	16,800
	$84,000	$84,000	$84,000

Required

Under the assumption the company requires a 10% compound return from its investments, determine in which of the projects it should invest.

Exercise 27-8

A company expects to sell 4,000 units of its product during the next period with the following results:

Sales		$26,000
Costs and expenses:		
Direct materials	$4,800	
Direct labor	5,600	
Factory overhead	2,800	
Selling expenses	3,000	
Administrative expenses . .	5,000	21,200
Net income		$ 4,800

The company has an opportunity to sell 1,500 additional units at a price of $5. The additional sales will not affect the regular sales but will have the following effects on costs. Costs per unit for direct materials and direct labor will be the same for the additional sales as they are for regular sales. Factory overhead will increase by 10%, selling expenses will be unchanged, and administrative expenses will increase by $1,000. Present calculations to show whether the company should accept the offer to sell the additional units.

Exercise 27-9

A company has 8,000 units of Product X that cost $4.40 per unit to manufacture. The 8,000 units can be sold for $66,000, or they can be further processed at a cost of $30,800 into Products Y and Z. The additional processing will produce 3,200 units of Product Y that can be sold for $8.80 each and 4,800 units of Product Z that can be sold for $9.90 each.

Required

Prepare an analysis to show whether the Product X units should be further processed.

Exercise 27-10

A company has a machine that can produce Product A at the rate of 2 units per hour or produce Product B at the rate of 3 units per hour.

The capacity of the machine is 3,800 hours per year. The products are sold to a single customer who has agreed to buy all of the company's production up to a maximum of 5,000 units of A and 7,000 units of B. Selling prices and variable costs per unit to produce the products are:

	Product A	Product B
Selling price.	$8.50	$6.00
Variable costs	5.00	4.00
Contribution margin. . .	$3.50	$2.00

Determine the most profitable sales mix for the company and calculate the contribution to fixed costs plus profits that will result from that sales mix.

Problems

Problem 27-1

A company is planning to add a new product to its line, the production of which will require new machinery that costs $157,500 and has a five-year life and no salvage value. This additional information is available:

Estimated annual sales of new product.	$525,000
Estimated costs:	
Direct materials.	105,000
Direct labor	140,000
Factory overhead excluding depreciation on new machinery.	133,000
Selling and administrative expenses	87,500
State and federal income taxes	50%

Required

Using straight-line depreciation, calculate (*a*) the payback period on the investment in new machinery, (*b*) the rate of return on the average investment, and (*c*) the net present value of the net cash flows discounted at 14%. In calculating the rate of return and the net present value, assume that all cash flows occur at the end of each year.

Problem 27-2

A company has an opportunity to invest in either of two projects. Project 1 requires an investment of $108,000 for new machinery having a five-year life and a $12,000 salvage value. Project 2 requires an investment of $92,400 for new machinery having a seven-year life and a $8,400 salvage value. The products of the projects differ; however, each will produce for the life of the machinery an annual profit of $7,200 after subtracting straight-line depreciation and taxes of 50%.

Required

1. Assuming the revenues are earned uniformly throughout each year, calculate the payback period and return on average investment for each project.

2. Now assume that the machines related to both projects have zero salvage values and that the expected annual profits after deducting depreciation and taxes of 50% are $6,720. Assume also that the annual cash flows from each project occur at year-end. Calculate the return on average investment and the net present value of the cash flows from each project, discounted at 10%.

Problem 27-3

Cut 'n Fix Company manufactures a small tool that it sells to wholesalers at $8 each. The company manufactures and sells approximately 50,000 of the tools each year, and a normal year's costs for the production and sale of this number of tools are as follows:

Direct materials	$ 75,000
Direct labor	62,500
Manufacturing overhead . . .	93,750
Selling expenses	37,500
Administrative expenses . . .	31,250
	$300,000

A mail-order company has offered to buy 5,000 of the tools at $5.50 each to be marketed under the mail-order company's trade name. If accepted, the order is not expected to affect sales through present channels.

A study of normal costs and their relation to the new business reveals the following: (a) Direct material costs are 100% variable. (b) The per unit direct labor costs for the additional units will be 50% greater than normal since their production will require overtime at time and one half. (c) Of a normal year's manufacturing overhead costs, two thirds will remain fixed at any production level from zero to 65,000 units, and one third will vary with volume. (d) There will be no additional selling costs if the new business is accepted. (e) Acceptance of the new business will increase administrative costs $4,000.

Required

Prepare a comparative income statement that shows (a) in one set of columns the operating results and operating income of a normal year, (b) in the second set of columns the operating results and income that may be expected from the new business, and (c) in the third set of columns the combined results from normal and the expected new business.

Problem 27-4

Benold Corporation is considering a project that requires a $300,000 investment in machinery having a six-year life and no salvage value. The project will produce $105,000 at the end of each year for six years, before deducting depreciation on the new machinery and income taxes of 50%.

For tax purposes, the company may choose between two alternative depreciation schedules, as follows:

Year	Straight-Line Depreciation Schedule	ACRS Depreciation Schedule
1 . .	$30,000	$45,000
2 . .	60,000	66,000
3 . .	60,000	63,000
4 . .	60,000	63,000
5 . .	60,000	63,000
6 . .	30,000	–0–

Required

1. Calculate the company's cash flow from the project for each of the six years with depreciation for tax purposes calculated according to (a) the straight-line depreciation schedule and (b) the ACRS depreciation schedule.

2. Calculate the net present value of the net cash flows discounted at 14% assuming the straight-line depreciation schedule is used.

3. Calculate the net present value of the net cash flows discounted at 14% assuming the ACRS depreciation schedule is used.

4. Explain why the ACRS depreciation method increases the net present value of this project.

Problem 27-5

Player Company's sales and costs for its two products last year were:

	Product A	Product B
Unit selling price	$60	$45
Variable costs per unit . . .	$36	$15
Fixed costs.	$180,000	$210,000
Units sold	12,000	13,500

Through sales effort the company can change its sales mix. However, sales of the two products are so interrelated that a percentage increase in the sales of one product causes an equal percentage decrease in the sales of the other, and vice versa.

Required

1. State which of its products the company should push, and why.

2. Prepare a columnar statement showing last year's sales, fixed costs, variable costs, and income before taxes for Product A in the first pair of columns, the results for Product B in the second set of columns, and the combined results for both products in the third set of columns.

3. Prepare a like statement for the two products under the assumption that the sales of Product A are increased 25%, with a resulting 25% decrease in the sales of Product B.

4. Prepare a third statement under the assumption that the sales of Product A are decreased 25%, with a resulting 25% increase in the sales of Product B.

☐ **Alternate Problems**   **Problem 27-1A**

A company is considering adding a new product to its line, of which it estimates it can sell 18,000 units annually at $23 per unit. To manufacture the product will require new machinery having an estimated five-year life, no salvage value, and costing $108,000. The new product will have a $9.60 per unit direct material cost and a $4.80 per unit direct labor cost. Manufacturing overhead chargeable to the new product, other than for depreciation on the new machinery, will be $59,400 annually. Also, $45,000 of additional selling and administrative expenses will be incurred annually in producing and selling the product, and state and federal income taxes will take 50% of the before-taxes profit.

Required

Using straight-line depreciation, calculate (*a*) the payback period on the investment in new machinery, (*b*) the rate of return on the average investment, and (*c*) the net present value of the net cash flows discounted at 12%. Assume that revenues are received at year-end.

Problem 27-2A

A company has the opportunity to invest in either of two projects. Project A requires an investment of $70,000 for new machinery having a seven-year life and no salvage value. Project B requires an investment of $75,000 for new machinery having a five-year life and no salvage value. Sales of the two projects will produce the following estimated annual results:

	Project A		Project B	
Sales		$162,500		$187,500
Costs:				
Direct materials.	$37,500		$45,000	
Direct labor	33,750		43,750	
Manufacturing overhead including depreciation on new machinery	47,500		55,000	
Selling and administrative expenses	31,250	150,000	31,250	175,000
Operating income.		$ 12,500		$ 12,500
State and federal income taxes . . .		6,250		6,250
Net income		$ 6,250		$ 6,250

Required

Calculate the payback period, the return on average investment, and the net present value of the net cash flows from each project discounted at 12%. State which project you think the better investment and why. Assume that revenues are received at year-end.

Problem 27-3A

Mobilheat Company annually sells at $10 per unit 30,000 units of its product. At the 30,000-unit production level the product costs $9 a unit to manufacture and sell, and at this level the company has the following costs and expenses:

Fixed manufacturing overhead costs.	$30,000
Fixed selling expenses	15,000
Fixed administrative expenses	18,000

Variable costs and expenses:	
Direct materials ($2 per unit)	60,000
Direct labor ($2.50 per unit)	75,000
Manufacturing overhead ($1.50 per unit) . . .	45,000
Selling expenses ($0.50 per unit)	15,000
Administrative expense ($0.40 per unit) . . .	12,000

All the units the company presently sells are sold in this country. However, recently an exporter has offered to buy 3,000 units of the product for sale abroad, but he will pay only $8.90 per unit, which is below the company's present $9 per unit manufacturing and selling costs.

Required

Prepare an income statement that shows (*a*) in one set of columns the revenue, costs, expenses, and income from selling 30,000 units of the product in this country; (*b*) in a second set of columns the additional revenue, costs, expenses, and income from selling 3,000 units to the exporter; and (*c*) in a third set of columns the combined results from both sources. (Assume that acceptance of the new business will not increase any of the company's fixed costs and expenses nor change any of the variable per unit costs and expenses.)

Problem 27-4A

Hudson Company is considering a project that requires a $216,000 investment in machinery having a six-year life and no salvage value. The project will produce $75,600 at the end of each year for six years, before deducting depreciation on the new machinery and income taxes of 50%.

For tax purposes, the company may choose between two alternative depreciation schedules, as follows:

Year	Straight-Line Depreciation Schedule	ACRS Depreciation Schedule
1 . .	$21,600	$32,400
2 . .	43,200	47,520
3 . .	43,200	45,360
4 . .	43,200	45,360
5 . .	43,200	45,360
6 . .	21,600	–0–

Required

1. Calculate the company's cash flow from the project for each of the six years with depreciation for tax purposes calculated according to (*a*) the straight-line depreciation schedule and (*b*) the ACRS depreciation schedule.
2. Calculate the net present value of the net cash flows discounted at 12% assuming the straight-line depreciation schedule is used.
3. Calculate the net present value of the net cash flows discounted at 12% assuming the ACRS depreciation schedule is used.

4. Explain why the ACRS depreciation method changes the net present value of this project.

Problem 27-5A

Beeville Corporation manufactures and sells a machine called a powerpac. Last year the company made and sold 350 powerpacs, with the following results:

Sales (350 units @ $450)		$157,500
Costs and expenses:		
Variable:		
Direct materials	$34,650	
Direct labor	28,350	
Factory overhead	23,625	
Selling and administrative expenses . . .	15,750	
Fixed:		
Factory overhead	23,750	
Selling and administrative expenses . . .	15,000	141,125
Income before taxes		$ 16,375

The city street department has asked for bids on 50 powerpacs almost identical to Beeville Corporation's machine, the only difference being a timer not presently installed on the Beeville Corporation powerpac. To install the timer would require the purchase of a new machine costing $750, plus $10 per powerpac for additional direct material and $6.50 per powerpac for additional direct labor. The new machine would have no further use after the completion of the street department contract, but it could be sold for $250. Sale of the additional units would not affect the company's fixed costs and expenses, but all variable costs and expenses, including variable selling and administrative expenses, would increase proportionately with the volume increase.

Required

1. List with their total the unit costs of the direct material, direct labor, and so forth, that would enter into the lowest unit price the company could bid on the special order without causing a reduction in income from normal business.
2. Under the assumption the company bid $400 per unit and was awarded the contract for the 50 special units, prepare an income statement showing (*a*) in one set of columns the revenues, costs, expenses, and income before taxes from present business; (*b*) in a second set of columns the revenue, costs, expenses, and income before taxes from the new business; and (*c*) in a third set of columns the combined results of both the old and new business.

Provocative Problems

Provocative Problem 27-1   Golead Corporation

Golead Corporation operates metal alloy producing plants, one of which is located at Rockport. The Rockport plant no longer produces a satisfactory profit due to its distance from raw material sources, relatively high electric power costs, and lack of modern machinery. Consequently, construction of a new plant to replace the Rockport plant is under consideration.

The new plant would be located close to a raw material source and near low-cost electric power, but its construction would necessitate abandonment of the Rockport plant. The company president favors the move; but several members of the board are not convinced the Rockport plant should be abandoned in view of the great loss that would result.

You have been asked to make recommendations concerning the proposed abandonment and construction of the new plant. Data developed during the course of your analysis include the following:

Loss from Abandoning the Rockport Plant The land, buildings, and machinery of the Rockport plant have a $2,850,000 book value. Very little of the machinery can be moved to the new plant. Most will have to be scrapped. Therefore, if the plant is abandoned, it is estimated that only $600,000 of the remaining investment in the plant can be recovered through the sale of its land and buildings, the sale of scrap, and by moving some of its machinery to the new plant. The remaining $2,250,000 will be lost.

Investment in the New Plant The new plant will cost $9,000,000, including the book value of any machinery moved from Rockport, and will have a 20-year life. It will also have double the 12,500-ton capacity of the Rockport plant, and it is estimated the 25,000 tons of metal alloy produced annually can be sold without a price reduction.

Comparative Production Costs A comparison of the production costs per ton at the old plant with the estimated costs at the new plant shows the following:

	Old Plant	New Plant
Raw material, labor, and plant costs (other than depreciation)	$450	$378
Depreciation	30	18
Total costs per ton	$480	$396

The higher per ton depreciation charge of the old plant results primarily from depreciation being allocated to fewer units of product.

Prepare a report analyzing the advantages and disadvantages of the move, including your recommendation. You may assume that the Rockport plant can continue to operate long enough to recover the remaining investment in the plant; however, due to the plant's high costs, operation will be at the break-even point. Furthermore, a shortage of skilled personnel would not allow the company to operate both the Rockport plant and the new plant. Present any pertinent analyses based on the data given.

Provocative Problem 27-2   Conset Corporation

Conset Corporation has operated at substantially less than its full plant capacity for several years, producing and selling an average of 16,250 units of its product annually and receiving a per unit price of $52. Its cost at this sales level are:

Direct materials	$266,500
Direct labor.	208,000
Manufacturing overhead:	
Variable	81,250
Fixed	40,000
Selling and administrative expenses:	
Variable	39,000
Fixed	80,000
Income taxes	50%

After searching for ways to utilize the plant capacity of the company more fully, management has begun to consider the possibility of processing the product beyond the present point at which it is sold. If the product is further processed, it can be sold for $60 per unit. Further processing will increase fixed manufacturing overhead by $16,500 annually, and it will increase variable manufacturing costs per unit as follows:

Direct materials	$0.84
Direct labor	0.76
Variable manufacturing overhead . . .	0.60
Total	$2.20

Selling the further processed product will not affect fixed selling and administrative expenses, but it will increase variable selling and administrative expenses by 25%. Further processing is not expected to either increase or decrease the number of units sold.

Should the company further process the product? Back your opinion with a simple calculation and also a comparative income statement showing present results and the estimated results with the product further processed.

Provocative Problem 27-3 Newark Corporation

Newark Corporation manufactures and sells a common piece of construction machinery, selling an average of 21,000 units of the machine each year. The company generally earns an after-tax (50% rate) net income of $256 per unit sold. Newark Corporation's production process involves assembling the several components of the machine, some of which are manufactured by the company and others of which are purchased from a variety of suppliers.

One of the components that has been manufactured by the company is a pump which is also available from other suppliers. Newark Corporation uses special equipment to make the pump, and the equipment has no alternative uses. The equipment has a $126,000 book value, a seven-year remaining life, and is depreciated at the rate of $18,000 per year. In addition to depreciation of the equipment, the costs to manufacture the pump are: direct materials, $32.00; direct labor, $25.60; and variable overhead, $6.40.

One of Newark's suppliers has recently offered the company a contract to purchase pumps from the supplier at a delivered cost of $68.16 per unit. If the company decides to purchase the pumps, the special equipment used to manufacture them can be sold for cash at its book value (no profit or loss), and the cash can be invested in other projects that will pay a

14% compound after-tax return, which is the return the company demands on all of its capital investments.

Should the company continue to manufacture the pump, or should it sell the special equipment and buy the pump? Back your answer with explanations and computations.

28   Tax Considerations in Business Decisions

After studying Chapter 28, you should be able to:

1. Explain the importance of tax planning.

2. Describe the steps an individual must go through to calculate his or her tax liability; and explain the difference between deductions to arrive at adjusted gross income, deductions from adjusted gross income, and tax credits.

3. Calculate the taxable income and net tax liability for an individual.

4. Define capital assets and describe the tax treatment for capital losses in comparison with ordinary (noncapital) losses.

5. Describe the differences between the calculations of taxable income and tax liability for corporations and for individuals.

6. Explain why income tax expenses shown in financial statements may differ from taxes actually payable.

7. Define or explain the terms and phrases listed in the chapter Glossary.

Perhaps the most common topic of conversation in the United States is taxes, especially federal income taxes. A large variety of individual and business decisions are influenced by income tax considerations. In studying this chapter, you should expect to gain an introductory understanding of the rules governing federal income taxes and some of the ways in which they can affect personal and business decisions.

■ Tax Planning

When taxpayers plan their affairs in such a way as to incur the smallest possible tax liability, they are engaged in **tax planning.** Many business deals can be designed in more than one alternative way. For example, equipment might be purchased for cash, purchased through borrowed money, or perhaps even leased from the owner. Tax planning involves evaluating each alternative in terms of the resulting tax liability and selecting the one alternative that will be most profitable.

Normally, tax planning requires that a tax-saving opportunity be recognized prior to the occurrence of the transaction. Although it is sometimes possible to take advantage of a previously overlooked tax saving, the common result of an overlooked opportunity is a lost opportunity, since the Internal Revenue Service usually deems the original action in a tax situation the final action for tax purposes.

Since effective tax planning requires an extensive knowledge of both tax laws and business procedures, it is not the purpose of this chapter to make expert tax planners out of you. Rather, the purpose is to make you aware of the merits of effective tax planning, recognizing that for complete and effective planning, the average student, business executive, or citizen should seek the advice of a certified public accountant, tax attorney, or other person qualified in tax matters.

■ Tax Evasion and Tax Avoidance

In any discussion of taxes, a clear distinction should be drawn between tax evasion and tax avoidance. **Tax evasion** is illegal and may result in heavy penalties, including prison sentences in some instances; but **tax avoidance** is a perfectly legal and profitable activity.

Taxes are avoided by preventing a tax liability from coming into existence. This may be accomplished by any legal means, for example, by the way in which a transaction is completed, or the manner in which a business is organized, or by a wise selection from among the options provided in the tax laws.

In contrast, tax evasion involves the fraudulent denial and concealment of an existing tax liability. For example, taxes are evaded if a taxpayer consciously fails to report taxable income, such as interest, dividends, tips, fees, or profits from the sale of stocks, bonds, and other assets. Taxes are also evaded when items not legally deductible from income are deducted. For example, taxes are evaded when the costs of operating the family automobile are deducted as a business expense, or when charitable contributions not allowed or not made are deducted. Tax evasion is illegal and should be scrupulously avoided.

■ **State and Municipal Income Taxes**

Most states and a number of cities levy income taxes, in most cases modeling their laws after the federal laws. However, other than noting the existence of such laws and that they increase the total tax burden and make tax planning even more important, the following discussion is limited to the federal income tax.

■ **History and Objectives of the Federal Income Tax**

Although the federal government first used an income tax during the War Between the States, the history of today's federal income tax dates from the 1913 ratification of the Sixteenth Amendment, which cleared away all questions as to the constitutionality of such a tax. Since its ratification, Congress has passed numerous revenue acts and other laws implementing the tax, placing the responsibility for their enforcement in the hands of the Treasury Department acting through the Internal Revenue Service. Collectively, the statutes dealing with taxation that have been adopted by Congress are called the **Internal Revenue Code.**

The original purpose of the federal income tax was to raise revenue. But, over the years this original goal has been expanded to include a variety of nonrevenue objectives. Examples of such objectives are:

1. To assist small businesses.
2. To encourage foreign trade.
3. To encourage exploration for oil and minerals.
4. To redistribute the national income.
5. To control inflation and deflation.
6. To stimulate business.
7. To attain full employment.
8. To support other social objectives.

When federal income taxes were first imposed in the United States, the tax rates were very low; in 1913, the maximum was 7%. As years passed, the rates were increased. For awhile, the maximum rate was in excess of 90%. Later, tax rates began to decline so that by 1986, the maximum rates were 46% for corporations and 50% for individuals. Tax rates have been reduced further with the passage of the Tax Reform Act of 1986. The new law reduces individual and corporation rates in 1987. And beginning in 1988, the law provides a maximum rate for individuals of 28% (33% in some circumstances) and a maximum rate for corporations of 34% (39% in some circumstances).

Two major thrusts of the 1986 legislation were to broaden the tax base, through the repeal of or reduction in many tax deductions, and to reduce tax rates. A third apparent objective was to make the tax more **neutral.** In other words, a goal was to reduce the number of instances in which one type of income or expenditure receives a more favorable tax treatment than does some other type of income or expenditure.

The 1986 legislation represents a dramatic change in the rules and likely will have a significant effect on investment and other business decisions. In lowering the rates, Congress expects that tax consequences will be less apt to dominate other economic considerations in decisions to make certain expenditures or investments. Nevertheless, despite the reduction in the tax rates, tax consequences will continue to be important factors in many decisions.

Changes in the Tax Law

Extensive changes in the tax laws have been enacted more and more frequently in recent years. During the period 1976 to 1986, major changes were enacted in 1976, 1978, 1981, 1982, 1984, and especially in 1986. Because of the changing nature of the tax laws, businesses find it difficult to plan, especially with respect to investments in long-term projects. A project that is expected to be very profitable, given present tax laws, may become less profitable or even unprofitable if Congress enacts unfavorable changes in the tax laws. And other investment opportunities that were rejected as unprofitable might prove to be very profitable if favorable changes in the tax laws are passed. In any event, businesses and individuals must recognize that many transactions entered into today have uncertain consequences because tax laws may be changed.

Despite the fact that tax laws change frequently, the basic concepts of taxation and the tax formula have remained fairly consistent over many decades. While the tax rates and the amount of certain deductions will likely differ in the future, the overall structure of the system is not likely to change greatly. Tax-free treatment for certain types of income and deductibility of certain expenditures will likely continue, although the items eligible for such treatment may vary to some extent over the years.

Synopsis of the Federal Income Tax

The following brief synopsis of the federal income tax is given at this point because it is necessary to know something about the federal income tax in order to appreciate its effect on business decisions.

Classes of Taxpayers

Federal income tax law recognizes three classes of taxpayers: individuals, corporations, and estates and trusts. Members of each class must file returns and pay taxes on taxable income.

A business operated as a single proprietorship or partnership is not treated as a separate taxable entity under the law. Rather, single proprietors must include the income from their businesses on their individual tax returns. A partnership must file an information return showing its net income and the distributive shares of the partners. Nevertheless, the partnership is not subject to tax. Instead, the partners are required to include their shares on their individual returns. In other words, the income of a single proprietorship or partnership, whether withdrawn from the business or not, is taxed as the individual income of the single proprietor or partners.

The treatment given to corporations under the law is different from that of proprietorships or partnerships. A business operated as a corporation must file a return and pay taxes on its taxable income. Also, if a corporation pays out in dividends some or all of its "after-tax income," its stockholders must report these dividends as income on their individual returns. A corporation cannot deduct dividends paid in calculating its taxa-

Illustration 28-1

Gross income.		$ xx,xxx
Less: Deductions to arrive at adjusted		
gross income		(xx,xxx)
Adjusted gross income		$ xx,xxx
Less: The greater of total itemized deductions		
or the standard deduction	$x,xxx	
Deduction for exemptions	x,xxx	(x,xxx)
Taxable income.		$ xx,xxx
Gross tax liability from tax rate schedule		$ xx,xxx
Less: Tax credits and prepayments		(xx,xxx)
Net tax payable (or refund)		$ xxx

ble income. Because of this, it is commonly claimed that corporation income is taxed twice, once to the corporation and again to its stockholders.

A discussion of the federal income tax as applied to estates and trusts is not necessary at this point and is deferred to a more advanced course.

The Individual Income Tax

The amount of federal income tax individuals must pay each year depends upon their gross incomes, deductions, exemptions, and tax credits. The typical calculation of the tax liability involves the sequence shown in Illustration 28-1.

To determine the federal income tax liability of an individual, the amounts of gross income, deductions, exemptions, tax credits (if any), and prepayments are listed on forms supplied by the federal government. Then, the appropriate calculations (additions, subtractions, and so forth) are performed in accordance with the instructions. The listing of the items on the forms is not precisely the same for all classes of taxpayers and does not always follow the general pattern shown in Illustration 28-1; however, the illustration does show the relation of the items and the basic mathematics required in completing the tax forms.

The items that appear on a tax return as gross income, adjusted gross income, deductions, exemptions, tax credits, and prepayments require additional description and explanation.

Gross Income Income tax law defines **gross income** as **all income from whatever source derived, unless expressly excluded from taxation by law.** Gross income therefore includes income from operating a business; gains from property sales, dividends, interest, rents, royalties; and compensation for services, such as salaries, wages, fees, commissions, bonuses, and tips. Actually, the answers to two questions are all that is required to determine whether an item should be included or excluded. The two questions are: (1) Is the item income? (2) Is it expressly excluded by law? If an item is income and not specifically excluded, it must be included.

Certain items are specifically excluded from gross income, for example, gifts, inheritances, scholarships up to the cost of tuition, fees, and course-related materials, social security benefits (unless the taxpayer has a relatively large amount of other income), veterans' benefits, workers' compensation insurance, and in most cases the proceeds of life insurance policies paid upon the death of the insured. Because these items are excluded from gross income, they are nontaxable.

Another item that generally is excluded from gross income is interest on the obligations of the states and their subdivisions. The Supreme Court has held that a federal income tax on such items would, in effect, amount to having the power to destroy these governmental units. Thus, a federal income tax on the interest from bonds or other obligations of states or their subdivisions would violate constitutional guarantees. With a few exceptions, interest from such items is therefore nontaxable.

Deductions to Arrive at Adjusted Gross Income These are generally deductions of a business nature. For example, **all ordinary and necessary expenses of a self-employed person in carrying on a business, trade, or profession are deductions to arrive at adjusted gross income.** To understand this, recognize that under income tax law, gross profit from sales (sales less cost of goods sold) is gross income to a merchant, and gross legal fees earned are gross income to a lawyer. Consequently, the merchant and the lawyer may each deduct all ordinary and necessary expenses of carrying on the business or profession, such as salaries, wages, rent, depreciation, supplies used, repairs, maintenance, insurance, taxes, interest, and so on.

Expenses of producing rent income are another category of deductions to arrive at adjusted gross income. Examples of such deductions include depreciation, repairs, real estate leases, and insurance expense related to the rent property.

Deductions from Adjusted Gross Income By legislative grace, an individual taxpayer is permitted certain deductions from adjusted gross income. These are of two kinds: (1) the greater of itemized personal expenses or the standard deduction, and (2) the deduction for exemptions.

The Standard Deduction Congress entitles all taxpayers to an automatic deduction of a set amount regardless of how they spend their money, on tax deductible expenditures or not. This deduction is known as the **standard deduction.** Taxpayers should elect to deduct the standard deduction if its amount exceeds their itemized deductions (described below). The amounts of the standard deduction are:

In 1987:
    $3,760 on a joint return,
    $1,880 on a separate return, and
    $2,540 on returns for all other taxpayers.
    Taxpayers who are age 65 or older or blind are, in 1987, entitled
    to the 1988 amounts.

In 1988:
    $5,000 on a joint return,
    $2,500 on a return for married taxpayers filing separately,
    $4,400 for taxpayers classified as heads of households, and
    $3,000 for other single taxpayers.

In addition to the above 1987 and 1988 amounts, taxpayers and their spouses (in the case of a joint return) are entitled to an additional standard deduction if they are age 65 or older or blind. On a joint return, the additional deduction is $600 per taxpayer per item. Thus, if both spouses are 65 or older and blind, they would receive additional standard deductions of $2,400 (4 × $600) plus the regular standard deduction of $5,000. For single taxpayers, the additional standard deductions are $750 per item instead of $600.

In years after 1988, the 1988 standard deduction amounts, including the additional $600 or $750 amounts, are indexed for inflation.

Itemized Personal Expenses Instead of choosing the standard deduction, taxpayers may itemize and deduct their allowable personal expenses. Obviously, taxpayers tend to elect whichever alternative results in the largest deduction. Itemized deductions commonly consist of certain personal interest expenses, state and local property and income taxes, charitable contributions, a casualty loss deduction, a medical expense deduction, a moving expense deduction, and miscellaneous itemized deductions.

The rules for **interest expense** deductions are somewhat detailed. In general, taxpayers may deduct interest on loans secured by up to two personal residences. However, the amount of such qualifying loans generally is limited to the original cost of the residences plus the cost of any improvements. Interest on money borrowed for investment purposes is deductible up to the amount of the taxpayer's net investment income. In general, consumer interest (for example, interest on car loans and credit cards) is nondeductible, subject to a phase-in rule allowing deduction of a portion of consumer interest through 1990.

Casualty losses are deductible only to the extent that each loss exceeds $100; then the resulting amounts are aggregated and deducted only to the extent they exceed 10% of adjusted gross income. The **medical expense deduction** consists of that portion of prescription drugs, doctor, dental, hospital, and medical insurance expenses in excess of 7.5% of the taxpayer's adjusted gross income.

Employees generally cannot deduct employment-related expenses from gross income to get adjusted gross income. However, **employees may claim itemized deductions for certain expenses incurred in connection with their employment (if paid by the employees).** These include transportation and travel expenses, expenses of an outside salesperson, and moving expenses. Employees who work in more than one place during a day may deduct transportation costs incurred in moving from one place of employment to another during the day. However, as a general rule they may not deduct the cost of commuting from home to the first place of employment or from the last place of employment to home. Travel expenses include, in addition to transportation expenses, the cost of lodging and 80% of the cost of meals while away from home overnight on employment-connected business.[1] Other employee business expenses include such things as telephone, stationery, and postage. Moving expenses are expenses incurred by employees (or self-employed individuals) in moving their place of residence upon being transferred by their employer or upon taking a new

---

[1] Self-employed taxpayers and corporations are also subject to the rule allowing a deduction for only 80% of the cost of meals.

job. Certain minimum requirements as to the distance moved and the length of employment in the new location must be met.

Unreimbursed employee business expenses (other than moving expenses) plus deductions such as tax return preparation fees and safe deposit box rent are referred to as **miscellaneous itemized deductions.** The total amount of miscellaneous itemized deductions is deductible only to the extent that it exceeds 2% of adjusted gross income. For example, if a taxpayer's adjusted gross income is $30,000, only his miscellaneous itemized deductions in excess of $600 can be included in the calculation of total itemized deductions.

Exemptions In additon to itemized deductions or the standard deduction, a taxpayer is allowed a second kind of deduction, called the deduction for exemptions. The amount of the exemption deduction will increase over the next few years. It is $1,900 for 1987, $1,950 for 1988, and $2,000 for 1989. For years after 1989, the $2,000 amount will be adjusted for inflation. High-income taxpayers lose the benefit of the exemption deduction beginning in 1988. A 5% surcharge implements the phase out of the deduction. A taxpayer is allowed one personal exemption for himself or herself. If a husband and wife file a joint return, each is a taxpayer and they may combine their exemptions. Taxpayers are also granted one exemption for each dependent.

To qualify as a dependent for whom an exemption may be claimed, the person must meet these tests: (1) be closely related to the taxpayer or have been a member of the taxpayer's household for the entire year; (2) have received over half his or her support from the taxpayer during the year; (3) if married, has not and will not file a joint return with his or her spouse; and (4) had gross income during the year of less than the amount of the personal exemption. An exception to the gross income test is granted if the person claimed as a dependent is a child of the taxpayer and under 19 years of age at the end of the tax year or was a full-time student in an educational institution during each of five months of the year. As a result of changes made by the 1986 law, a person (such as a child) who is claimed as a dependent on another taxpayer's return may not claim an exemption deduction for himself or herself on his or her own return.[2]

Observe in the discussion thus far that there are deductions to arrive at adjusted gross income and also deductions from adjusted gross income. Furthermore, it is important that each kind of deduction be subtracted at the proper point in the tax calculation because the allowable amounts of some deductions from adjusted gross income are determined by the amount of adjusted gross income.

Federal Income Tax Rates A person's tax liability is calculated by applying the appropriate tax rates to his or her taxable income. Illustration 28-2 shows the 1987 and 1988 rates for an unmarried person not qualifying as a head of household and for married persons filing a joint return or

---

[2] Under another rule of the 1986 law, the unearned income in excess of $1,000 of children younger than age 14 is taxed at their parent's top tax rate.

Illustration 28-2

For taxable years beginning in 1987—
Schedule X—Single Taxpayers

If taxable income is:	**The tax is:**
Not over $1,800	11% of taxable income
Over $ 1,800 but not over $16,800	$ 198 plus 15.0% of the excess over $ 1,800
Over $16,800 but not over $27,000	$ 2,448 plus 28.0% of the excess over $16,800
Over $27,000 but not over $54,000	$ 5,304 plus 35.0% of the excess over $27,000
Over $54,000	$14,754 plus 38.5% of the excess over $54,000

For taxable years beginning in 1987—
Schedule Y—Married Individuals Filing Joint Returns and Qualifying Widows and Widowers

If taxable income is:	**The tax is:**
Not over $3,000	11% of taxable income
Over $ 3,000 but not over $28,000	$ 330 plus 15.0% of the excess over $ 3,000
Over $28,000 but not over $45,000	$ 4,080 plus 28.0% of the excess over $28,000
Over $45,000 but not over $90,000	$ 8,840 plus 35.0% of the excess over $45,000
Over $90,000	$24,590 plus 38.5% of the excess over $90,000

For taxable years beginning in 1988—
Schedule X—Single Taxpayers

If taxable income is:	**The tax is:**
Not over $17,850	15% of taxable income
Over $17,850	$2,677.50 plus 28% of the excess over $17,850
(See note below)	

For taxable years beginning in 1988—
Schedule Y—Married Individuals Filing Joint Returns and Qualifying Widows and Widowers

If taxable income is:	**The tax is:**
Not over $29,750	15% of taxable income
Over $29,750	$4,462.50 plus 28% of the excess over $29,750
(See note below)	

Note: In addition to the tax computed under the above rate schedules for years beginning in 1988, higher income taxpayers incur additional taxes as follows:

1. Single taxpayers—a 5% tax on taxable income between $43,150 and $89,560
   Married taxpayers filing joint returns—a 5% tax on taxable income between
   $71,900 and $149,250

PLUS—

2. Single taxpayers—a 5% tax on taxable income in excess of $89,560
   Married taxpayers filing joint returns—a 5% tax on taxable income in
   excess of $149,250.

   However, the tax liability under this computation may not exceed a specified amount. The maximum in 1988 is $546 times the number of exemptions claimed on the tax return. For 1989 the maximum is $560 times the number of exemptions claimed. For later years, the amount is indexed for inflation.

---

qualifying widows or widowers. The Tax Rate Schedules shown in Illustration 28-2 are used by taxpayers who do not qualify to use simplified Tax Tables, which are discussed later in the chapter. To use the rate schedules of Illustration 28-2, a taxpayer reads down the left column of the appropriate schedule until arriving at the bracket of his or her taxable income. For example, if an unmarried taxpayer's 1988 taxable income is $27,850, the taxpayer reads down the column of Schedule X to the bracket "over

$17,850." The right column explains that the tax on $17,850 is $2,677.50, and the excess over $17,850 is taxed at 28%. Thus, the tax on $27,850 is $2,677.50 + (28% × $10,000) = $5,477.50.

Observe in Illustration 28-2 that, in general, the federal income tax rates are progressive in nature. By this is meant that each additional segment or bracket of taxable income is subject to a higher rate than the preceding segment or bracket. Beginning in 1988, however, the rates have a regressive feature for taxpayers with high amounts of taxable income. Such persons are subject to a 33% rate (28% regular rate plus a 5% additional rate) on a portion of their income. Eventually, if their income is high enough, it returns to being taxed at the 28% rate.

The 5% additional tax applicable to high-income taxpayers serves two functions. The first is to convert the 15% tax on the lowest level of income to a 28% tax. To illustrate the first function of the 5% additional tax, consider a single taxpayer in 1988. The 5% tax on a single taxpayer's taxable income between $43,150 and $89,560 recovers the tax savings from having the first $17,850 of taxable income taxed at 15%. For example, a single taxpayer with exactly $89,560 will pay a tax of $25,077 (or 15% of $17,850 + 28% of $71,710 + 5% of $46,410). As a result, this taxpayer's tax is exactly 28% of his $89,560 taxable income.

The second function of the 5% additional tax is to eliminate the tax savings that were generated by the deduction for personal exemptions. For single taxpayers, this is accomplished by the 5% tax on taxable income in excess of $89,560. Recall that, in 1988, the amount of the personal exemption for a single taxpayer is $1,950. Also, 28% of $1,950 = $546. Since the additional tax liability is limited to $546 times the number of exemptions claimed, the effect of this additional tax is to phase out the exemption deduction for high-income taxpayers.

To clarify the use of the rate schedules, assume that a single taxpayer has $250,000 of taxable income in 1988. The taxpayer claims only one exemption deduction. The taxpayer's tax liability would be calculated as follows:

15% × $17,850	$ 2,677.50
28% × ($250,000 − $17,850)	65,002.00
5% × ($89,560 − $43,150)	2,320.50
The lesser of:	
(a) 5% × ($250,000 − $89,560), or	
(b) $546 × 1 exemption.	546.00
Tax liability.	$70,546.00

Note that this taxpayer's **marginal tax rate** is 28%. The marginal tax rate is the rate that applies to the next dollar of income to be earned. By comparison, a single taxpayer with a taxable income between $43,150 and $89,560 has a marginal tax rate of 33%. Thus, at certain levels of taxable income the rate structure is said to have a regressive feature.

A husband and wife have a choice concerning rate schedules. They may combine their incomes and use the rate schedule shown for married individuals (Schedule Y) or they may each file a separate return using a rate schedule (not shown) that results in a tax for each somewhat in excess of that shown in Illustration 28-2 for single taxpayers. The phrase *qualifying widows and widowers* in the title of Schedule Y refers to surviving spouses who, if they are not remarried and if they have a dependent child, may continue to use Schedule Y for two tax years after the year of their spouse's death.

Also, a person who can qualify as a **head of household** may use a rate schedule (not shown) in which the rates fall between those for unmarried individuals and those for married couples filing jointly. Generally, a head of household is an unmarried or legally separated person who maintains a home in which his or her unmarried child or a qualifying dependent lives for over half the year.

The rate schedules shown in Illustration 28-2 for 1988 are to be indexed for inflation beginning in 1989. As a result, if a person's taxable income does not increase at a rate in excess of the consumer price index, that person will not be thrown into a higher tax bracket.

Tax Credits and Prepayments After an individual's gross income tax liability is computed from the appropriate tax rate schedule, the individual's tax credits, if any, and prepayments are deducted to determine the net tax liability. **Tax credits** represent direct, dollar-for-dollar reductions in the amount of tax liability; that is, a $100 tax credit reduces the tax liability by $100. By comparison, deductions (as discussed earlier) reduce the amount of taxable income, against which the appropriate tax rates are applied to determine the gross tax liability. Thus, a tax credit of $100 is more valuable to the taxpayer than a tax deduction of $100. Assuming a marginal tax rate of 28%, an additional tax deduction of $100 effectively reduces the tax liability by $28 ($100 $\times$ 28%), whereas a tax credit of $100 reduces the tax liability by $100.

Examples of tax credits include the following. A retired taxpayer with retirement income may receive a **credit for the elderly.** A taxpayer who has paid income taxes to a foreign government may be eligible for a **foreign tax credit.** Also, taxpayers with lower incomes may qualify for an **earned income credit.** The earned income credit, unlike the other tax credits, can generate a tax refund. Thus, it is similar to a negative income tax.

In addition to tax credits, any prepayments of tax are also deducted in order to determine the net tax liability. Most taxpayers have income taxes withheld from their salaries and wages. Other taxpayers have income that is not subject to withholding and on which they are required to estimate and pay the estimated amount of the tax on the income in advance installments. Both the income tax withholdings and the estimated tax paid in advance are examples of tax prepayments that are deducted in determining a taxpayer's net tax liability.

Special Tax Treatment of Capital Gains and Losses From a tax planning point of view, one of the most important features of our federal income tax laws in past years has been the special treatment given to capital gains and losses. The Internal Revenue Code defines a **capital asset** as any item of property except (*a*) inventories; (*b*) trade notes and accounts receivable;

(c) real property and depreciable property used in a trade or business; and (d) copyrights, letters, and similar property in the hands of the creator or his or her donee or certain other transferees. Common examples of capital assets held by individuals and subject to sale or exchange are stocks, bonds, and a personal residence.

A gain on the sale of a capital asset occurs when the proceeds of the sale exceed the **basis** of the asset sold, and a loss occurs when the asset's basis exceeds the proceeds. The basis of a purchased asset is generally its cost less any depreciation previously allowed or allowable for tax purposes.

In 1987, a distinction is made between short- and long-term **capital gains and losses.** Short-term gains and losses result when capital assets are held six months or less before being sold or exchanged, and long-term gains and losses result when such assets are held more than six months. The excess of net long-term capital gains over net short-term capital losses is included in taxable income. However, the tax on such gains is limited, in 1987, to a maximum rate of 28% even though the tax on other income may be as high as 38.5%. Beginning in 1988, long-term capital gains will be treated the same as any other type of income. As such they may be taxed at a rate as high as 33% (28% + 5%).

Although capital gains are treated just like other types of income beginning in 1988, the distinction between capital gains and losses and noncapital (or ordinary) gains and losses is still important because of limitations on deductions for capital losses. When an individual's capital losses exceed capital gains, the individual may deduct up to $3,000 of the excess losses ($1,500 for a married taxpayer filing a separate return) from ordinary income in the year of the loss. A carryover provision is available to allow deduction in subsequent years of losses that were in excess of the $3,000 or $1,500 limitations.

Remember that the definition of capital assets does not include real property and depreciable property used in a taxpayer's trade or business. When such properties are sold or exchanged, the excess of losses over gains is fully deductible in arriving at taxable income.

Tax Tables   As previously mentioned, not all taxpayers are required to use the Tax Rate Schedules such as those shown in Illustration 28-2. Instead, most individual taxpayers use simplified Tax Tables. The Tax Tables are constructed from the Tax Rate Schedules. Individuals who use the Tax Tables have to calculate their taxable income according to the formula of Illustration 28-1 and then search through the appropriate Tax Table to determine their gross income tax liability.

The Corporation Income Tax

For federal tax purposes, the taxable income of a corporation organized for profit is calculated in much the same way as the taxable income of an individual. However, there are important differences, five of which follow:

a. A corporation (but not an individual) may deduct from gross income the first 80% of dividends received from stock it owns in other domestic corporations. This, in effect, means that only 20% of such dividends are taxed. However, if two corporations qualify as affiliated corporations, which essentially means that one owns 80% or more of the other's stock, then 100% of the dividends received by the investor corporation from the investee corporation may be deducted. These rules provide relief from the triple taxation of dividends that would otherwise apply.

b. During 1987, the long-term capital gains of a corporation will be subject to a top tax rate of 34% in comparison with a top rate of 28% for individuals.

c. A corporation may only offset capital losses against capital gains; and if in any year the offset results in a net capital loss, the loss may not be deducted from other income. However, it may be carried back to the three preceding years and forward to the next five years and deducted from any capital gains of those years.

d. The standard deduction and the deduction for exemptions do not apply to a corporation, and a corporation does not have certain other deductions of an individual, such as that for personal medical expenses.

e. In addition, a different rate schedule applies to the taxable income of corporations. The corporate income tax rates for 1988 and later years are as follows:[3]

Amount of Taxable Income	Tax Rate
Portion from $0 to $50,000	15%
Portion over $50,000 to $75,000	25
Portion in excess of $75,000	34

In addition, if the corporation's taxable income exceeds $100,000, the corporation will incur an additional tax equal to the lesser of: (a) 5% of its taxable income in excess of $100,000, or (b) $11,750. Imposition of this additional tax results in recovering some, or all, of the tentative tax savings from having income taxed under the rate schedule at rates below 34%.

To illustrate the use of the corporate rate schedule, assume a corporation has taxable income of $130,000 in 1988. Its tax liability is calculated as follows:

15% × $50,000	$ 7,500
25% × $25,000	6,250
34% × $55,000	18,700
The lesser of:	
(a) 5% × ($130,000 − $100,000), or	
(b) $11,750	1,500
	$33,950

---

[3] The corporate rates shown for 1988 become effective on July 1, 1987. For taxable years that include any portion of the first half of 1987, the applicable rates are an average of the 1986 and 1988 rates.

■ **Tax Effects of Business Alternatives**

Alternative decisions commonly have different tax effects. Following are several examples illustrating this.

Form of Business Organization

The difference between individual and corporation tax rates commonly affects one of the basic decisions a business executive must make, which is to select the legal form the business should take. Should it be a single proprietorship, partnership, or corporation? The following factors influence the decision:

a. As previously stated, a corporation is a taxable entity. Its income is taxed at corporation rates, and any portion paid in dividends is taxed again as individual income to its stockholders. By comparison, the income of a single proprietorship or partnership, whether withdrawn or left in the business, is taxed as individual income of the proprietor or partners.

b. In addition, a corporation may pay reasonable amounts in salaries to stockholders who work for the corporation, and the sum of these salaries is a tax deductible expense in arriving at the corporation's taxable income. In a partnership or a single proprietorship, on the other hand, salaries of the partners or the proprietor are nothing more than allocations of income.

In arriving at a decision as to the legal form a business should take, a business executive, with the foregoing points in mind, must estimate the tax consequences of each form and select the best. For example, assume that Ralph Jones is choosing between the single proprietorship and corporate forms, and that he estimates the business will have annual gross sales of $250,000, with cost of goods sold and operating expenses, other than his own salary as manager, of $185,000. Assume further that $45,000 per year is a fair salary for managing such a business and that Mr. Jones plans to withdraw all profits from the business. Under these assumptions, the 1988 tax consequences of each alternative business form are calculated in Illustration 28-3.

Under the assumptions of Illustration 28-3, the smaller tax and the larger after-tax income will result from using the single proprietorship form. However, this may not be true in every case. For instance, if Mr. Jones has large amounts of income from other sources, he may find he would incur less tax if the business were organized as a corporation.

Furthermore, in the example just given it is assumed that all profits are withdrawn and none are left in the business for growth. This happens. However, growth is commonly financed through the retention of earnings; and when it is, the relative desirability of the two forms may change. This is because income retained in the business organized as a corporation is not taxed as individual income to its stockholders, but the income of a single proprietorship or partnership is so taxed, whether retained in the business or withdrawn.

For instance, if the business of Illustration 28-3 is organized as a single proprietorship, the tax burden of the owner remains the same whether he withdraws any of his profits or not. But, if organized as a corporation,

Illustration 28-3

	Proprietorship		Corporation	
Operating results under each form:				
Estimated sales.		$250,000		$250,000
Cost of goods sold and operating expenses				
other than owner-manager's salary	$185,000		$185,000	
Salary of owner-manager.	–0–	185,000	45,000	230,000
Before-tax income.		$ 65,000		$ 20,000
Corporation income tax at 15%		–0–		3,000
Net income.		$ 65,000		$ 17,000
Owner's after-tax income under each form:				
Single proprietorship net income		$ 65,000		
Corporation salary.				$ 45,000
Dividends				17,000
Total individual income.		$ 65,000		$ 62,000
Individual income tax (assuming a joint				
return with itemized deductions of $10,100				
and a deduction for exemptions				
of $3,900)		10,413		9,573
Owner's after-tax income.		$ 54,587		$ 52,427

and assuming all $17,000 of the earnings are retained in the business, the owner is required to pay individual income taxes on his $45,000 salary only. This would reduce his annual individual income tax from $9,573 shown in Illustration 28-3 to $4,813 and would reduce the total tax burden with the corporation form to $7,813 ($3,000 + $4,813), which is $2,600 less than the tax burden under the single proprietorship form.

The foregoing is by no means all of the picture. Other tax factors may be involved. For example, a corporation may incur an extra tax if it accumulates more than $250,000 of retained earnings and such accumulations are beyond the reasonable needs of the business. Also, under present laws a corporation may elect to be treated for tax purposes like a partnership, thus eliminating the corporate tax. Furthermore, in deciding the legal form a business should take, factors other than taxes are important. For example, lack of stockholder liability often is a strong reason for choosing the corporation form.

Method of Financing

When a business organized as a corporation is in need of additional financing, the owners may supply whatever funds the corporation needs by purchasing its stock. However, an overall tax advantage may often be gained if instead of purchasing stock, they supply the funds through long-term loans. Insofar as the owners are concerned, it makes no difference on their individual returns whether they report interest or dividends from the funds supplied. However, whether the corporation issues stock or floats a loan usually makes a big difference on its return. Interest on borrowed funds is a tax-deductible expense, but dividends are a distribution of earnings and have no effect on the corporation's taxes. Consequently, if owners lend the corporation funds rather than buy its stock, the total tax liability (their own plus their corporation's) will be reduced. In addition, the repayment of long-term debt always is considered to be a return of capital transaction. The redemption of stock, however, may result in the proceeds being treated as dividend income to the shareholders.

In making financial arrangements such as these, owners must be careful not to overreach themselves in attempting to maximize the interest deduction of their corporation. If they do so and thereby create what is called a *thin corporation,* one in which the owners have supplied an unreasonably small portion of capital through stock purchases, the Internal Revenue Service may disallow the interest deductions and require that such deductions be treated as dividends. Furthermore, repayments of "principal" may also be held to be taxable dividends.

Timing Transactions

The timing of transactions can be of major importance in tax planning. For example, taxpayers using the cash method of tax accounting instead of the accrual method have considerable flexibility in timing their income and deductions. Thus, if they anticipate that their tax rates will be lower during the next taxable year, it may be to their advantage to accelerate the payment of deductible expenditures into the current year and to postpone the receipt of income until early the next year. This planning tip presupposes that the taxpayer will not experience cash flow problems from such behavior.

Because of the flexibility the cash method affords with respect to timing, the 1986 law placed restrictions on the availability of the cash method. In general, corporations other than those that have elected to be treated much like partnerships cannot use the cash method. Exceptions apply, however, for farm businesses, personal service corporations (such as professional corporations), and corporations with average annual gross receipts of less than $5 million.

Forms in which Related Transactions Are Completed

The tax consequences of related transactions are often dependent upon the forms in which they are completed. For example, the sale of one property at a profit and the immediate purchase of another like property normally results in a taxable gain on the property sold, but an exchange of these properties may result in a tax-free exchange.

A tax-free exchange occurs when like kinds of property are exchanged for each other, or when one or more persons transfer property to a corporation and immediately thereafter are in control of the corporation. Control in such cases is interpreted as meaning that after the transfer the transferring persons (or person) must own at least 80% of the corporation's voting stock plus at least 80% of the total number of shares of all other classes of stock.

At first glance, it seems that it should be to anyone's advantage to take a tax-free exchange rather than to pay taxes, but this may not be so. For example, 10 years ago a corporation paid $50,000 for land located at the edge of the city. Today, due to booming growth, the land is well within the city and has a fair market value of $250,000. The land has been held as an investment and is without improvements. The corporation plans to move part of its operations to a suburb and has an opportunity to trade the city property for vacant suburban acreage on which it would build a factory. Should it make the trade? From a tax viewpoint the answer is probably yes—the company should make the tax-free exchange. That way, the company avoids having to pay a tax on the gain at the present time. From a present value standpoint, postponing the tax payment is important.

However, assume a different set of facts in which the suburban property to be purchased consists of land having a fair market value of $25,000 with a suitable factory building thereon valued at $225,000. Also, assume that the corporation experienced a $200,000 capital loss from selling stock held as an investment. The corporation had no other capital gains this year or in the past three years, nor does it expect to have any in the next five years (against which the capital loss might be offset).

If the corporation exchanges the city land for the suburban land and factory, it will receive no current benefit from its capital loss. On the other hand, if it sells the land, the $200,000 gain on the land sale can be exactly offset by the $200,000 loss on the stock sale. Then, the $250,000 cash proceeds can be used to buy the suburban land and factory. By purchasing the new factory, the corporation gains the right to deduct the building's $225,000 cost on a straight-line basis over the next 31½ years. On this set of facts, the corporation would likely choose a sale over a tax-free exchange.

Compensation of Employees

Businesses can compensate their employees in a variety of ways. One way, of course, is to compensate them solely with salary payments. Many employees prefer, however, to receive a smaller amount of salary and to receive their additional compensation in the form of noncash compensation on which they are not taxed. Congress frequently discusses narrowing the range of fringe benefits eligible for tax-free treatment. However, at present, several types of fringe benefits are received by employees tax free. For example, employers may pay premiums on group-term life or health insurance for employees; employers also may make payments to qualified retirement plans for employees. In all of these instances, the employees will not pay taxes on the value of such benefits received.

To illustrate the value of these forms of compensation, consider an employee-taxpayer who is in the 33% marginal tax bracket. The employee would need to receive $100 of before-tax compensation to pay a $67 life insurance premium from his or her own after-tax funds. But the employee can obtain the same benefit if the $67 premium is paid by the employer, in which case the employee would not pay tax on this $67 of noncash compensation. At the same time, the employer's before-tax cost of additional compensation is reduced from $100 to $67.

Accounting Basis and Procedures

With certain exceptions, the accounting basis and procedures used by taxpayers in keeping their records must also be used in computing taxable income. Generally, taxpayers keep their records on either a cash or an accrual basis (see page 91); but regardless of which they use, the basis and any procedures used must clearly reflect income and be consistently followed.

When inventories are a material factor in calculating income, taxpayers are required to use the accrual basis in calculating gross profit from sales. Also, plant assets cannot be expensed in the year of purchase but must be depreciated over the time periods specified in the tax laws (see Chapter 10). However, other than for gross profit from sales and depreciation, many taxpayers may use the cash basis in accounting for income and expenses. Furthermore, this is often an advantage, since under the cash basis, taxpayers can often shift expense payments and the receipt of items of revenue other than from the sale of merchandise from one accounting period to the next and thus increase or decrease taxable income.

An accrual-basis taxpayer cannot shift income from year to year by timing receipts and payments; however, somewhat of the same thing may be accomplished through a choice of accounting procedures. For example, recognition of income on a cash collection basis (see Chapter 1) commonly shifts income from one year to another. Likewise, a contractor may use the percentage-of-completion basis (Chapter 1) to shift construction income from one year to another and to level taxable income over a period of years.

Furthermore, any taxpayer may shift taxable income to future years through a choice of inventory and depreciation procedures. For example, during periods of rising prices, the LIFO inventory method results in charging higher costs for goods sold against current revenues and thus reduces taxable income and taxes. It may be argued that this only postpones taxes since in periods of declining prices the use of LIFO results in lower costs and higher taxes. However, the history of recent years has been one of rising prices; therefore, it may also be argued that LIFO will postpone taxes indefinitely.

Depreciation methods that result in higher depreciation charges in an asset's early years and lower charges in later years, such as the accelerated cost recovery system (ACRS), also postpone taxes. ACRS is also favorable because it generally allows taxpayers to recover the cost of a property over a period shorter than the asset's useful life. And while tax postponement is not as desirable as tax avoidance, postponement gives the taxpayer interest-free use of tax dollars until these dollars must be paid to the government.

Before turning to a new topic, it should be pointed out that the opportunities for tax planning described in these pages are only illustrative of those available. The wise business executive will seek help from a professional who specializes in tax consultation in order to take advantage of every tax-saving opportunity.

■ **Taxes and the Distortion of Net Income**

Financial statements for a business should be prepared in accordance with generally accepted accounting principles. Tax accounting, on the other hand, must be done in accordance with tax laws. As a consequence, income (before taxes) measured in accordance with generally accepted accounting principles is not always the same as income subject to state and federal income taxes. They may differ for two reasons. The first reason is that some items may be included in (or excluded from) the calculation of taxable income but be excluded from (or included in) net income according to generally accepted accounting principles. These items involve permanent differences between taxable income and income before taxes. For example, interest received on state and municipal bonds must be included in income on the financial statements of the company that owns the bonds. In contrast, such interest usually is not subject to tax and therefore is not included in taxable income.

The second reason why there may be a difference between taxable income and income before taxes on the financial statements involves temporary differences between tax procedures and financial statement procedures. In other words, a business may select different procedures for tax purposes and for financial statement purposes where the income effect of the difference between the procedures is temporary or a matter of timing. For example, unearned income such as rent collected in advance usually is taxable in the year of receipt. However, under the accrual basis of accounting such items are taken into income in the year earned regardless of when received. As another example, a business may apply straight-line depreciation over the estimated useful life of an asset for accounting purposes. At the same time, it may use the accelerated cost recovery system for tax purposes.[4]

When a corporation uses different procedures for tax and financial statement purposes and the difference between the procedures is temporary, a problem arises in measuring net income. The problem involves deciding how much income tax expense should be shown on the income statement. If the actual tax to be paid is shown as an expense, the amount of tax will appear inconsistent with the known tax rate. Consequently, generally accepted accounting principles require that income tax expense should be calculated so that distortions caused by temporary differences between tax accounting procedures and financial accounting procedures are avoided.[5]

To appreciate the problem involved here, assume that on January 1, 1988, a corporation purchased a light truck for $15,000, which will produce $50,000 dollars of revenue and $9,000 of income before depreciation and taxes in each of the succeeding six years. Assume further that the company plans to use straight-line depreciation in its records but the **accelerated cost recovery system (ACRS)** for tax purposes. The truck has a six-year useful life, no salvage value, and is included in the five-year class of property for tax purposes. Under ACRS, property in the five-year class is depreciated under the 200% declining-balance method, switching to straight line. Also, the half-year convention must be followed for tax purposes. (See pp. 368–370 in Chapter 10 for a review of ACRS depreciation.) Depreciation calculated by each method is as follows:

---

[4] While the tax rules for calculating taxable income are different from financial reporting rules used to calculate income before taxes, the two numbers are not completely independent, especially in 1987–89. To assure that all profitable corporations pay at least some tax in these years, some corporations may be required to pay an "alternative minimum tax." The base for this tax includes taxable income plus certain items that receive favorable treatment in the calculation of taxable income. In addition, the base includes one half of the amount by which the corporation's income for financial statement purposes is greater than its taxable income. Further consideration of the alternative minimum tax is beyond the introductory scope of this chapter.

[5] FASB, *Accounting Standards—Current Text* (Stamford, Conn., 1984), sec. I24.102. First published in *APB Opinion No. 11,* par. 29.

Year		ACRS	Straight Line
1	($15,000 × .2) =	$ 3,000	$ 2,500
2	($15,000 − $ 3,000) × .4 =	4,800	2,500
3	($15,000 − $ 7,800) × .4 =	2,880	2,500
4	($15,000 − $10,680) × .4 =	1,728	2,500
5	($15,000 − $12,408) × ⅔ =	1,728	2,500
6	($15,000 − $12,408) × ⅓ =	864	2,500
Totals . . .		$15,000	$15,000

And since the company uses the accelerated cost recovery system for tax purposes, it will be liable for $900 of income tax on the first year's income, $630 on the second, $918 on the third, $1,091 on the fourth, $1,091 on the fifth, and $1,220 on the sixth. The calculation of these taxes is shown in Illustration 28-4.

Furthermore, if the company were to deduct its actual tax liability each year in arriving at income to be reported to its stockholders, it would report the amount shown in Illustration 28-5. Observe in Illustration 28-5 the fluctuation in annual income after depreciation and taxes. Even though income before depreciation and income taxes is $9,000 each year and straight-line depreciation is $2,500 each year, the subtraction of the actual tax liability causes the remaining income to fluctuate. This fluctuation is generally thought to be a distortion of the final income figures.

If this company should report successive annual income figures of $5,600, $5,870, $5,582, $5,409, $5,409, and $5,280, some readers of the financial statements might be misled as to the company's earnings trend. Consequently, in cases such as this, generally accepted accounting principles require that income tax expense should be calculated so that the distortion caused by the postponement of taxes is removed from the income statement. In essence, the reporting requirement is as follows: When a procedure used in the accounting records and an alternative procedure used for tax purposes result in temporary differences in respect to expense recognition or revenue recognition, the tax expense deducted on the income statement should not be the actual tax liability, but the amount that would have resulted if the procedure used in the records had also been used in calculating the tax.

Illustration 28-4

Annual Income Taxes	Year 1	Year 2	Year 3	Year 4	Year 5	Year 6	Total
Income before depreciation and income taxes	$9,000	$9,000	$9,000	$9,000	$9,000	$9,000	$54,000
Depreciation for tax purposes (ACRS method)	3,000	4,800	2,880	1,728	1,728	864	15,000
Taxable income	$6,000	$4,200	$6,120	$7,272	$7,272	$8,136	$39,000
Annual income taxes (15% of taxable income)	$ 900	$ 630	$ 918	$1,091	$1,091	$1,220	$ 5,850

Illustration 28-5

Income after Deducting Actual Tax Liabilities	Year 1	Year 2	Year 3	Year 4	Year 5	Year 6	Total
Income before depreciation and income taxes	$9,000	$9,000	$9,000	$9,000	$9,000	$9,000	$54,000
Depreciation per books (straight-line method)	2,500	2,500	2,500	2,500	2,500	2,500	15,000
Income before taxes	$6,500	$6,500	$6,500	$6,500	$6,500	$6,500	$39,000
Income taxes (actual liability each year)	900	630	918	1,091	1,091	1,220	5,850
Remaining income	$5,600	$5,870	$5,582	$5,409	$5,409	$5,280	$33,150

Illustration 28-6

Net Income That Should Be Reported to Stockholders	Year 1	Year 2	Year 3	Year 4	Year 5	Year 6	Total
Income before depreciation and income taxes	$9,000	$9,000	$9,000	$9,000	$9,000	$9,000	$54,000
Depreciation per books (straight-line method)	2,500	2,500	2,500	2,500	2,500	2,500	15,000
Income before taxes	$6,500	$6,500	$6,500	$6,500	$6,500	$6,500	$39,000
Income taxes (amounts based on straight-line depreciation) . .	975	975	975	975	975	975	5,850
Remaining income	$5,525	$5,525	$5,525	$5,525	$5,525	$5,525	$33,150

If the foregoing is applied in this case, the corporation will report to its stockholders in each of the six years the amounts of income shown in Illustration 28-6.

In examining Illustration 28-6, recall that the company's tax liabilities are actually $900 in the first year, $630 in the second, $918 in the third, $1,091 in the fourth, $1,091 in the fifth, and $1,220 in the sixth, a total of $5,850. Then observe that when the expense associated with this $5,850 liability is spread evenly over the six years, the distortion of the annual net incomes due to the postponement of taxes is removed from the income statements.

■   **Entries for the Allocation of Taxes**

When income tax expenses are reported as in Illustration 28-6, the tax liability of each year and the deferred taxes are recorded with an adjusting entry. The adjusting entries for the six years of Illustration 28-6 and the entries in general journal form for the payment of the taxes (without explanations) are as follows:

Year 1	Income Taxes Expense	975.00	
	Income Taxes Payable		900.00
	Deferred Income Taxes		75.00
Year 1	Income Taxes Payable*	900.00	
	Cash		900.00
Year 2	Income Taxes Expense	975.00	
	Income Taxes Payable		630.00
	Deferred Income Taxes		345.00
Year 2	Income Taxes Payable*	630.00	
	Cash		630.00
Year 3	Income Taxes Expense	975.00	
	Income Taxes Payable		918.00
	Deferred Income Taxes		57.00
Year 3	Income Taxes Payable*	918.00	
	Cash		918.00
Year 4	Income Taxes Expense	975.00	
	Deferred Income Taxes	116.00	
	Income Taxes Payable		1,091.00
Year 4	Income Taxes Payable*	1,091.00	
	Cash		1,091.00
Year 5	Income Taxes Expense	975.00	
	Deferred Income Taxes	116.00	
	Income Taxes Payable		1,091.00
Year 5	Income Taxes Payable*	1,091.00	
	Cash		1,091.00
Year 6	Income Taxes Expense	975.00	
	Deferred Income Taxes	245.00	
	Income Taxes Payable		1,220.00
Year 6	Income Taxes Payable*	1,220.00	
	Cash		1,220.00

* To simplify the illustration, it is assumed here that the entire year's tax liability is paid at one time. However, as previously explained, corporations are usually required to pay estimated taxes on a quarterly basis.

In the entries, the $975 debited to Income Taxes Expense each year is the amount that is deducted on the income statement in reporting annual net income. Also, the amount credited to Income Taxes Payable each year is the actual tax liability of that year.

Observe in the entries that since the actual tax liability in each of the first three years is less than the amount debited to Income Taxes Expense, the difference is credited to **Deferred Income Taxes**. Then, note that in the last three years, since the actual liability each year is greater than the debit to Income Taxes Expense, the difference is debited to Deferred Income Taxes. Now observe in the following illustration of the company's

Deferred Income Taxes account that the debits and credits exactly balance each other out over the six-year period:

Deferred Income Taxes

Year	Explanation	Debit	Credit	Balance
1			75.00	75.00
2			345.00	420.00
3			57.00	477.00
4		116.00		361.00
5		116.00		245.00
6		245.00		–0–

At the end of years 1, 2, 3, 4, and 5, the credit balance in the Deferred Income Taxes account is reported in the balance sheet. As of this writing, the account is shown as a separate item between long-term liabilities and stockholders' equity. However, a proposal of the FASB (that may be issued in 1987) would require that the portion of the balance that will result in taxable amounts during the next year be reported as a current liability and the remaining portion be reported as a long-term liability.[6]

[6] FASB, "Accounting for Income Taxes," *Proposed Statement of Financial Accounting Standards No. 025* (Stamford, Conn., September 2, 1986), par. 21.

□   **Glossary**   **Accelerated cost recovery system (ACRS)** a unique, accelerated depreciation method prescribed in the tax law.

Adjusted gross income gross income minus ordinary and necessary expenses of carrying on a business, trade, or profession as a self-employed person.

Basis in general, the cost of a purchased asset less any depreciation previously allowed or allowable for tax purposes.

Capital asset any item of property except (1) inventories, (2) trade notes and accounts receivable, (3) real property and depreciable property used in a trade or business, and (4) copyrights or similar property.

Capital gain or loss the difference between the proceeds from the sale of a capital asset and the basis of the asset.

Deferred income taxes the difference between the income tax expense in the financial statements and the income taxes payable according to tax law, resulting from temporary differences between financial accounting and tax accounting with respect to expense or revenue recognition.

Earned income wages, professional fees, and certain compensation for personal services.

Gross income all income from whatever source derived, unless expressly excluded from taxation by law.

Head of household an unmarried or legally separated person who maintains for more than half the year a home in which lives his or her unmarried child or a qualifying dependent.

Internal Revenue Code collectively, the statutes dealing with taxation that have been adopted by Congress.

Marginal tax rate the rate that applies to the next dollar of income to be earned.

Standard deduction a deduction from adjusted gross income that an individual may claim as an alternative to itemizing his or her personal deductions.

Tax avoidance a legal means of preventing a tax liability from coming into existence.

Tax credit a direct, dollar-for-dollar, reduction in the amount of tax liability.

Tax evasion the fraudulent denial and concealment of an existing liability.

Tax planning evaluating the alternative ways in which business transactions can be structured in terms of the resulting tax liability and selecting the alternatives that will be most profitable.

□ **Questions for Class Discussion**

1. An individual expects to have $500 of income in a 28% bracket; consequently, which should be desirable to him: (a) a transaction that will reduce his income tax by $125, or (b) a transaction that will reduce an expense of his business by $150?

2. Why must a taxpayer normally take advantage of a tax-saving opportunity at the time it arises?

3. Distinguish between tax avoidance and tax evasion. Which is legal and desirable?

4. What constitutional amendment resolved the question of the constitutionality of the income tax?

5. What are some of the nonrevenue objectives of the federal income tax?

6. What questions must be answered in determining whether an item should be included or excluded from gross income for tax purposes?

7. Name several items that are not included in gross income for tax purposes.

8. What justification might be given for permitting a corporation to claim a tax deduction for a portion of its dividend income?

9. For tax purposes, define a capital asset.

10. What is the significance of defining capital assets separately from other types of assets?

11. An individual had capital asset transactions that resulted in nothing but losses. What tax treatment is given to these losses?

12. What preferential tax treatment, if any, do long-term capital gains receive in 1987? In 1988 and later years?

13. Why do tax planners try to have losses emerge as ordinary losses instead of as capital losses?

14. Why would an owner of an incorporated business prefer to be paid a salary by the corporation instead of having the money paid to him in the form of dividends?

15. Why might stockholders in a small corporation prefer to invest additional capital in the corporation through the purchase of long-term bonds from the corporation instead of through the purchase of additional shares of stock?

16. What are some ways that a corporation might provide tax-free compensation to its employees?

17. What does it mean when a corporation is said to be a "thin" corporation?

18. If a corporation is proven to be a thin corporation, what effect might this have on the Internal Revenue Service's treatment of the corporation's payment of interest and repayment of principal to the owners?

19. Why does the taxable income of a business commonly differ from its net income?

20. For financial accounting purposes, what is the importance of the distinction between permanent differences and temporary differences in income before taxes and taxable income?

□ **Class Exercises** In some of the Exercises and Problems that follow, the taxpayers would qualify to use the simplified Tax Tables (not provided in the book) rather than the Tax Rate Schedules. However, to restrict the length of the chapter and to facilitate student understanding of the underlying concepts, calculations of individual tax liability should be based on the Tax Rate Schedules shown in Illustration 28-2.

Exercise 28-1

List the letters of the following items and write after each either the word **included** or **excluded** to tell whether the item should be included in or excluded from gross income for federal income tax purposes.

a. Tips received while working as a waiter.
b. Cash inherited from a deceased parent.
c. Gain on the sale of a personal automobile bought and rebuilt.
d. Workers' compensation insurance received as the result of an accident while working on a part-time job.
e. A computer game having a $300 fair market value that was received as a door prize.
f. Dividends from stock received by an individual.
g. Gift of stock from wealthy aunt.
h. Scholarship received from a state university. The scholarship is for an amount substantially in excess of the cost of the tuition, fees, and course-related materials.

Exercise 28-2

Amy Searcy earned $42,000 during 1988 as an employee of a law firm. She is unmarried and furnishes more than half the support of her brother, a college student who lived in a dormitory and had no income. Amy had $8,100 of federal income tax and $3,154 of FICA tax withheld from her paychecks. She received $300 interest on a savings account and $90 in dividends from a corporation in which she owned stock. During the year, she paid $1,800 state income tax, $950 qualified interest on the mortgage on her personal residence, and gave her church $2,200. Show the calculation of Amy's taxable income in the manner outlined in Illustration 28-1. Then, using the rate schedule of Illustration 28-2, show the calculation of the net federal income tax payable or refund due Amy.

Exercise 28-3

The following cases involve single individuals who sold some capital assets during 1988. In each case, the person's only other income was a $50,000 salary. Each case is independent from the others. For each case, indicate the dollar amount of capital losses that will provide a tax benefit to the individual in 1988.

a. One asset was sold for a $10,000 capital gain, and another was sold for a $6,000 capital loss.
b. One asset was sold for a $10,000 capital gain, and another was sold for a $12,000 capital loss.
c. One asset was sold for a $10,000 capital gain, and another was sold for an $18,000 capital loss.

Exercise 28-4

Ralph Harrison, Doris Kelly, and Mike Dunn are unmarried and have three income tax exemptions each. None qualify as a head of household. In 1988, their adjusted gross incomes were: Harrison, $26,000; Kelly, $45,000;

and Dunn, $72,000. Their itemized deductions were: Harrison, $1,500; Kelly, $9,900; and Dunn, $14,300. Prepare calculations to show the taxable income of each person.

Exercise 28-5

Bob and Barbara Summers had $37,000 of adjusted gross income in 1988. They are 37 and 40 years old, respectively, and have two children ages 10 and 15. Their automobile having a fair value of $6,500 was stolen during 1988, and their insurance did not cover the loss. They donated $400 to the college from which they had both graduated and incurred the following expenses during the year: local property taxes, $1,200; qualified interest on home mortgage, $1,600; hospital insurance, $1,900; and uninsured doctor and dentist bills, $1,550. Prepare a calculation to show their taxable income on a joint return.

Exercise 28-6

On January 1, 1988, a machine was purchased for $120,000. It will be used eight years in research and development activities and then discarded with no salvage value. Straight-line depreciation is taken for financial statement purposes, and the accelerated cost recovery system (see Chapter 10) is used for tax purposes. The company earns $126,000 income before depreciation and taxes during 1988, and the machine is in the five-year class for tax purposes. Make the journal entry to record income tax expense and liability for 1988. For simplicity, assume a 30% tax rate on all taxable income.

Exercise 28-7

In 1988, Carl had salary income of $35,000 and itemized deductions of $11,670. Carl's sister Cory had the very same amounts of income and deductions. Carl is married and filed a joint return with his wife Emily, who had no income. Cory is single. Assume two personal exemption deductions are claimed on the joint return for Carl and Emily and one is claimed on Cory's return. Calculate the taxable income and gross tax liability to be reported on each return.

Exercise 28-8

In 1988, Peggy Porter, who is single, had adjusted gross income of $30,000 and was entitled to only one personal exemption deduction. Her activities and expenditures during the year included the items listed below. Determine her taxable income.

Charitable contributions	$2,000
Qualified interest paid on mortgage on personal residence	3,000
Repairs to personal residence	1,200
State income taxes paid	700
Medical expenses paid	4,200
Fire loss to kitchen of her residence	3,700
Cost of vacation to Bermuda	2,300

Exercise 28-9

Calculate the 1988 tax liability for each of the following corporations:

a. Motto Corporation sold two capital assets in 1988. Asset A was sold at a gain of $10,000. Asset B was sold at a loss of $12,000. Motto Corporation's taxable income exclusive of the above gains and losses was $102,000.

b. Calgram Corporation sold two capital assets in 1988. Asset A was sold at a gain of $14,000. Asset B was sold at a loss of $8,000. Calgram Corporation's taxable income exclusive of the above gains and losses was $240,000.

Exercise 28-10

Round-Up Corporation reported taxable income for 1988 of $3,000,000. Determine its tax liability. Might it be argued that the corporation is paying tax at a flat rate? Explain.

Exercise 28-11

Bill Phillips is single, age 69, and blind. What is the amount of the standard deduction he may claim on his 1988 return?

Problems

Problem 28-1

Paul and Joan Johnson are married and are also partners in New World Art, a profitable business that averages $500,000 annually in sales, with a 40% gross profit and $112,500 of operating expenses. The Johnsons file a joint tax return, have no dependents, but each year have $6,000 of itemized deductions and two exemptions. In the past, the Johnsons have withdrawn $37,500 annually from the business for personal living expenses plus sufficient additional cash to pay the income tax on their joint return.

Paul and Joan think they can save taxes by reorganizing their business into a corporation beginning with the 1988 tax year. If the corporation is organized, it will issue 1,000 shares of no-par stock, 500 to Paul and 500 to Joan. Also, $37,500 per year is a fair salary for managing such a business, and the corporation will pay that amount to Joan.

Required

1. Prepare a comparative income statement for the business showing its net income as a partnership and as a corporation.
2. Use the rate schedule of Illustration 28-2 and determine the amount of federal income taxes the Johnsons will pay for themselves on a joint return and for the business under each of the following assumptions: (a) the business remains a partnership; (b) the business is incorporated, pays Joan a $37,500 salary, but pays no dividends; and (c) the business is incorporated, pays Joan a $37,500 salary, and pays $25,000 in dividends, $12,500 to Joan and $12,500 to Paul.

Problem 28-2

Terry and Paula Higgin, husband and wife who file a joint return, own all the outstanding stock of Higgin Corporation. The corporation, which currently has taxable income in excess of $400,000, has an opportunity to expand. To do so, however, it will need $250,000 of additional capital. The Higgins have the $250,000 and can either lend this amount to the corporation at 10% interest or they can invest the $250,000 in the corporation by purchasing additional shares of previously unissued stock from the corporation. They calculate that with the additional $250,000 the corporation will earn additional income of $40,000 annually before interest on the loan, if made, and before income taxes. If they invest the additional $250,000 in the corporation by purchasing stock, the corporation will pay the Higgins additional dividends of $30,000 per year. But, if they lend the corporation the $250,000, they will receive $25,000 interest on the loan, plus additional dividends of only $5,000 each year.

Required

Determine whether the loan to the corporation or an investment in its stock is to the best interest of the Higgins. Assume that the decision is being made in 1988.

Problem 28-3

Linda Stewart owns all the outstanding stock of Superbond Company. The corporation is a small manufacturing company; however, over the years it has purchased and owns stocks costing $125,000 (present market value is much higher) which it holds as long-term investments. The corporation has seldom paid a dividend, but it does pay Ms. Stewart a $60,000 annual salary as president and manager. In 1988, the corporation earned $45,000, after its president's salary but before income taxes, consisting of $28,000 in manufacturing income and $17,000 in dividends on its long-term investments.

Ms. Stewart is unmarried and has no dependents. She had $11,450 of itemized deductions during 1988 plus a single exemption deduction. She had no income other than her corporation salary and $4,000 in interest from bank deposits.

Required

1. Prepare a comparative statement showing for 1988 the operating income, investment income, total income, share of the dividend income deducted, taxable income, and income tax of the corporation under the (a) and (b) assumptions which follow. (a) The corporation owns the investment stocks and had the operating income just described. (b) The corporation had the operating income described; but instead of owning the investment stock, over the years it paid dividends (none in 1988) and Ms. Stewart used them to buy the stocks in her own name rather than in the name of the corporation.
2. Calculate the amounts of individual income tax and corporation income tax incurred by Ms. Stewart and the corporation under the (a)

assumptions, and the amount that would have been incurred under the (b) assumptions. Also, calculate the amount of individual income tax Ms. Stewart would have incurred with the business organized as a single proprietorship and the stocks registered in Ms. Stewart's name. Under this last assumption remember that the corporation's operating income plus its president's salary equal the operating income of the single proprietorship. Use the rate schedule of Illustration 28-2 in all individual income tax calculations.

Problem 28-4

Dickens Corporation purchased a fleet of light trucks at a $210,000 total cost early in January 1988. It was estimated the trucks would have a six-year life, no salvage value at the end of that period, and would produce $105,000 of income before depreciation and income taxes during each of the six years. For tax purposes, the trucks are in the five-year class. The company uses straight-line depreciation in its accounting records but the accelerated cost recovery system for tax purposes.

Required

1. Prepare a schedule showing 1988, 1989, 1990, 1991, 1992, 1993, and total net income for the six years after deducting ACRS depreciation and income tax expense calculated as the actual income taxes paid. For simplicity, assume a 25% tax rate on all taxable income.
2. Prepare a second schedule showing each year's net income and the six-year total after deducting straight-line depreciation as recorded in the accounting records and income tax expense calculated as the actual income taxes paid.
3. Prepare a third schedule showing income to be reported to stockholders with straight-line depreciation and income tax expense calculated according to generally accepted accounting principles.
4. Set up a T-account for Deferred Income Taxes and show therein the entries that will result from recording income tax expense.

Problem 28-5

Mr. and Mrs. Gary DeShazo are both 48 years old and file a joint income tax return. They have two children, Darcy and Libby. Darcy is a student in high school, lives at home, and earned $930 from part-time jobs in 1988. Libby is 20 years old and a sophomore in college. She was a full-time student for two semesters in 1988; however, she did not go to summer school but drove a delivery truck and earned $2,600 during the summer, which was less than half what her parents paid during the year for her tuition, books, and other items of support. Darcy also received over half of her support from her parents.

  Mr. and Mrs. DeShazo had the following cash receipts and disbursements during 1988:

Cash Receipts

Mr. DeShazo:

Salary as manager of Shelter Island Marina ($42,000 gross pay less $7,980 federal income taxes, $3,154 FICA taxes, and $1,400 hospital and medical insurance premiums withheld)	$29,466
Dividends from stocks in domestic corporations	730
Interest on bonds of the city of Detroit	1,240

Mrs. DeShazo:

Rentals from a small house purchased in January 1987 (the house cost $110,000 and is depreciated on a straight-line basis over a period of 27.5 years)	6,600
Salary from part-time position ($12,000 gross pay less $1,250 federal income taxes and $901 FICA taxes)	9,849
Proceeds of insurance received on the death of an aunt	12,000

Cash Disbursements

Charitable contributions	3,800
Qualified interest on mortgage on family residence	4,950
Property taxes on family residence	2,200
Property taxes on rental house	880
Interest on morgage on rental house	1,300
Plumbing repairs at rental house	180
Insurance (one year) on rental house	370
Uninsured doctor and dental bills	1,900
Prescription drugs	450
Advance payments of estimated federal income tax on income not subject to withholding	600

Also, Mr. DeShazo had a $4,400 capital gain on shares of stock held five years.

Required

Follow the form of Illustration 28-1 and use the rate schedule of Illustration 28-2 to calculate the net federal income tax payable or refund for Mr. and Mrs. DeShazo.

☐ **Alternate Problems**   **Problem 28-1A**

Janet LeMaster has operated The Antique Store for a number of years with the following average annual results:

The Antique Store
Income Statement for an Average Year

Sales		$375,000
Cost of goods sold	$187,500	
Operating expenses	112,500	300,000
Net income		$ 75,000

Ms. LeMaster is unmarried and without dependents and has been operating The Antique Store as a single proprietorship. She has been withdrawing $50,000 each year to pay her personal living expenses, including $6,870 of charitable contributions, state and local income and property taxes, and other itemized deductions. She has no income other than from The Antique Store.

Required

1. Assume that Ms. LeMaster is considering the incorporation of her business beginning with the 1988 tax year and prepare a comparative income statement for the business showing its net income as a single proprietorship and as a corporation. Assume that if she incorporates, Ms. LeMaster will pay $50,000 per year to herself as a salary, which is a fair amount.

2. Use the rate schedule of Illustration 28-2 and determine the amount of federal income tax Ms. LeMaster will have to pay for herself and for her business under each of the following assumptions: *(a)* the business is not incorporated; *(b)* the business is incorporated, pays Ms. LeMaster a $50,000 annual salary as manager, but does not pay any dividends; and *(c)* the business is incorporated, pays Ms. LeMaster a $50,000 salary, and also pays her $8,000 in dividends.

Problem 28-2A

Diawon Corporation needs additional capital for a new investment that will cost $480,000 and will increase its earnings $96,000 annually before interest on the money used in the expansion, if borrowed, and before income taxes. The Dale family owns all the outstanding stock of Diawon Corporation and will supply the money to finance the investment, either investing an additional $480,000 in the corporation by purchasing its unissued stock or lending it $480,000 at 12% interest.

The corporation presently earns well in excess of $400,000 annually and pays $96,000 per year to the family in dividends. If the loan is made, the dividends will be reduced by an amount equal to the interest on the loan.

Required

Prepare an analysis showing whether it would be advantageous for the family to make the loan or to purchase the corporation's stock. Assume the decision is being made in 1988.

Problem 28-3A

Zane Downs, Jr., recently inherited the business of his father. The business, Tackle, Inc., is a small manufacturing corporation; however, a share of its assets, $80,000 at cost, consists of blue-chip investment stocks purchased over the years by the corporation from earnings. Zane's father was the sole owner of the corporation at his death, and before his death he had paid himself a $40,000 annual salary for a number of years as president and manager. Over the years, the corporation seldom paid a dividend but instead had invested any earnings not needed in the business in the blue-chip stocks previously mentioned. At the father's death the market value of these stocks far exceeded their cost.

Zane's mother is dead, and after Zane graduated from college, the father had no dependents. The father's tax return for the 1988 year (the year before his death) showed $44,000 of gross income, consisting of his $40,000 corporation salary plus $4,000 interest from real estate loans. It also showed $3,950 of itemized deductions plus a single exemption deduction. During the year before the father's death, the corporation had earned $60,000 from its manufacturing operations plus $15,000 in dividends from its investments, a total of $75,000 after the president's salary but before income taxes.

Required

1. Prepare a comparative statement showing for the year before the father's death the corporation's operating income, dividend income, total income, share of the dividend income deducted, taxable income, and income tax under the following (a) and (b) assumptions. (a) The corporation owns the investment stocks and had the operating income just described. (b) The corporation had the operating income described; but instead of owning the investment stocks, over the years it paid dividends (none last year), and Zane Downs, Sr., used the dividends to buy the stocks in his own name rather than in the corporation's name.

2. Calculate the amounts of individual income tax and corporation income tax incurred by Mr. Downs, Sr., and the corporation for the year before Mr. Downs' death under the foregoing (a) assumptions and the amount that would have been incurred under the (b) assumptions. Also calculate the amount of individual income tax Mr. Downs would have incurred with the business organized as a single proprietorship and the stocks registered in his own name. Under this last assumption, remember that the corporation's operating income plus the salary paid its president equal the operating income of the single proprietorship. Use the rate schedule of Illustration 28-2 in the individual income tax calculations.

Problem 28-4A

Cross Company completed the installation of new equipment in its plant at a $240,000 total cost on January 2, 1988. It was estimated that the equipment would have a six-year life, no salvage value, and that it would produce $90,000 of income during each of the six years, before depreciation and income taxes. The company uses straight-line depreciation in its accounting records and the accelerated cost recovery system (ACRS) for tax purposes. The machine falls in the five-year asset class for tax purposes.

Required

1. Prepare a schedule showing 1988, 1989, 1990, 1991, 1992, 1993, and total net income for the six years after deducting ACRS depreciation and actual taxes paid. Assume a 25% income tax rate on all taxable income.

2. Prepare a second schedule showing each year's net income and the six-year total after deducting straight-line depreciation as recorded in the accounting records and actual taxes paid.

3. Prepare a third schedule showing income to be reported to stockholders with straight-line depreciation and income tax expense calculated according to generally accepted accounting principles.

4. Set up a T-account for Deferred Income Taxes and show therein the entries that will result from recording income tax expense.

Problem 28-5A

Frank and Darlene Smith are both 45 years old, have three sons, and file a joint tax return. Their oldest son, Richard, is a junior high school student and earned $690 in 1988 working at odd jobs. The other two sons earned nothing during the year. Mr. and Mrs. Smith furnished over half of each son's support and had the following cash receipts and disbursements during 1988.

Cash Receipts

Salary to Frank Smith from his employer, a real estate developer, for which Frank is an outside salesman ($32,000 gross income less $3,200 federal income taxes withheld, $2,403 FICA taxes, and $900 hospital insurance premiums)	$25,497
Dividends from AT&T common stock (jointly owned)	1,900
Interest from savings account owned by Darlene Smith	2,300
Interest from municipal bonds issued by El Paso, Texas	3,400
Proceeds from sale of Chrysler common stock that had been acquired 26 months ago at a cost of $12,000 (jointly owned)	19,000

Cash Disbursements

Cost of Frank driving from home to business office and back	$ 850
Unreimbursed telephone costs to call customers	1,602
Unreimbursed cost of meals incurred in connection with business travel	1,500
Contributions to church	1,000
Local property taxes on residence	700
Qualified interest on home mortgage	3,250
Uninsured doctor and dentist bills	3,907
Donation to college from which Frank and Darlene graduated	2,000
Advance payment of federal income tax	300

Required

Follow the form of Illustration 28-1 and use the rate schedule of Illustration 28-2 to calculate for the Smiths the amount of federal income tax due or to be refunded.

□   **Provocative Problems**

Provocative Problem 28-1 Surprises Corporation

Robert Thompson and his wife own all the outstanding stock of Surprises Corporation, a company Robert organized several years ago and which is growing rapidly and needs additional capital. At the request of Robert, Kevin Sanger examined the following comparative income statement, which shows the corporation's net income for the past three years and which was prepared by its bookkeeper. Kevin expressed a tentative willingness to invest the required capital by purchasing a portion of the corporation's unissued stock.

Surprises Corporation
Comparative Income Statement
For the Years 198A, 198B, and 198C

	198A	198B	198C
Sales	$560,000	$640,000	$720,000
Costs and expenses other than depreciation and federal income taxes.	$360,000	$384,000	$416,000
Depreciation expense	72,000	80,000	88,000
Federal income taxes	44,800	60,800	73,600
Total costs and expenses	$476,800	$524,800	$577,600
Net income.	$ 83,200	$115,200	$142,400

Before making a final decision, Kevin asked permission for his own accountant to examine the accounting records of the corporation. Permission was granted, the examination was made, and the accountant prepared the following comparative income statement covering the same period of time.

Surprises Corporation
Comparative Income Statement
For the Years 198A, 198B, and 198C

	198A	198B	198C
Sales	$560,000	$640,000	$720,000
Costs and expenses other than depreciation and federal income taxes.	$360,000	$384,000	$416,000
Depreciation expense*	72,000	80,000	88,000
Total operating expenses.	$432,000	$464,000	$504,000
Income before federal income taxes	$128,000	$176,000	$216,000
Federal income taxes	51,200	70,400	86,400
Net income.	$ 76,800	$105,600	$129,600

* Under the accelerated cost recovery system, the corporation deducted $88,000 of depreciation expense on its 198A return, $104,000 on its 198B return, and $120,000 on its 198C return.

Robert Thompson was surprised at the difference in annual net incomes reported on the two statements and immediately called for an explanation from the accountant who set up the corporation's accounting system and who prepares the annual tax returns of the corporation and the Thompsons.

Explain why there is a difference between the net income figures on the two statements, and account for the difference in the net incomes. Prepare a statement that will explain the amounts shown on the corporation bookkeeper's statement. For simplicity, assume a 40% federal income tax rate on all taxable income.

Provocative Problem 28-2   City Delivery, Inc.

City Delivery, Inc., is planning to invest $30,000 in a light truck. The new truck will be purchased in January 1988 and is expected to have a six-year life with no salvage value. The bookkeeper for the company prepared the following statement showing the expected results from the services provided by the new truck. The statement calculates income after actual tax payments, assuming straight-line depreciation for tax purposes. The truck is in the five-year class. For simplicity, assume that the company must pay out 40% of its before-tax earnings in state and federal income taxes.

City Delivery, Inc.
Expected Results from Use of New Trucks

	1988	1989	1990	1991	1992	1993	Totals
Sales	$56,250	$56,250	$56,250	$56,250	$56,250	$56,250	$337,500
All costs other than depreciation and income taxes	37,500	37,500	37,500	37,500	37,500	37,500	225,000
Income before depreciation and income taxes	$18,750	$18,750	$18,750	$18,750	$18,750	$18,750	$112,500
Depreciation deduction	3,000	6,000	6,000	6,000	6,000	3,000	30,000
Taxable income	$15,750	$12,750	$12,750	$12,750	$12,750	$15,750	$ 82,500
Actual income tax liability	6,300	5,100	5,100	5,100	5,100	6,300	33,000
Remaining income	$ 9,450	$ 7,650	$ 7,650	$ 7,650	$ 7,650	$ 9,450	$ 49,500

When the company president examined this statement, he said he knew that regardless of how calculated, the company could charge off no more than $30,000 of depreciation on the new truck during its six-year life. Furthermore, he said he could see that this would result in $82,500 of taxable income for the six years, $33,000 of income taxes, and $49,500 of remaining income, regardless of how depreciation was calculated. Nevertheless, he continued to say that he had been talking to a friend on the golf course a few days back and the friend had tried to explain the tax advantage of using the accelerated cost recovery system. He said he did not understand all the friend had tried to tell him; and as a result he would like for you to prepare an additional statement that calculates income after actual tax payments but based on ACRS depreciation. He said he would also like a written explanation of the tax advantage the company would gain through the use of the accelerated cost recovery system, with a dollar estimate of the amount the company would gain in this case.

The president also expressed the belief that straight-line depreciation was the best method to use in financial statements. As a consequence, he wants you to explain the impact that ACRS depreciation for tax purposes will have on the income statements. Prepare the information for the president. (In making your estimate, assume the company can earn a 10% after-tax return, compounded annually, on any deferred taxes. Also, to simplify the problem, assume that the taxes must be paid the first day of January following their incurrence.)

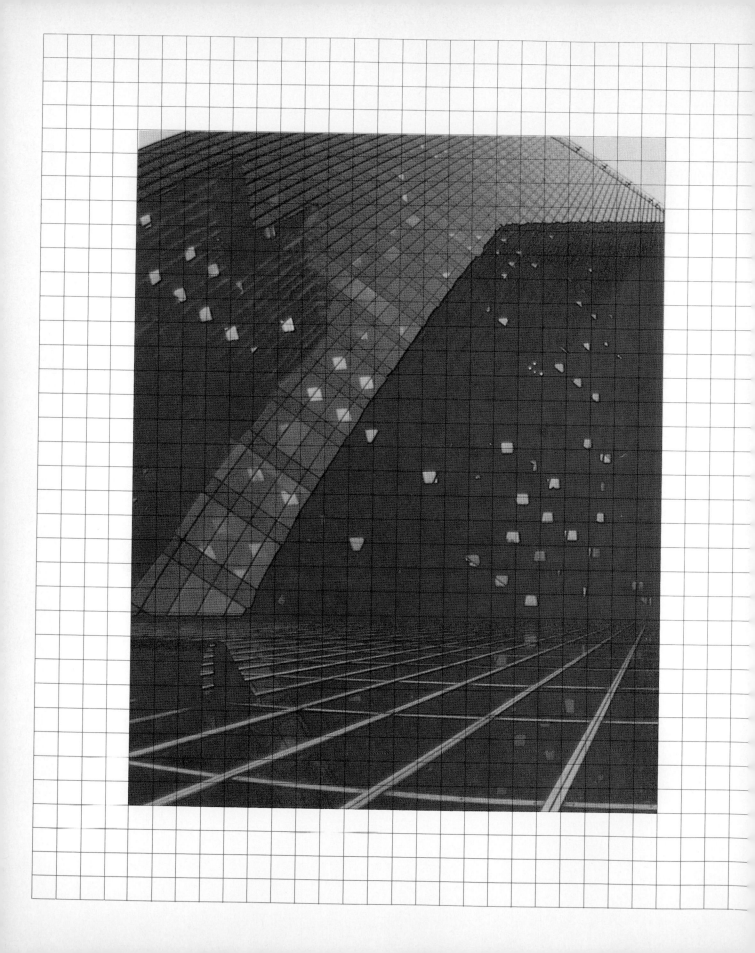

Present and Future Values:
An Expansion

The concept of present values was introduced in Chapter 12 and was applied to accounting problems in Chapters 12 and 17. This appendix is
designed to supplement the treatment of present values with additional
discussion, more complete tables, and additional homework exercises. The
appendix also includes the concept of future values.

■ **Present Value of a**
Single Amount

The present value of a single amount to be received or paid at some
future date may be expressed as:

$$p = \frac{f}{(1+i)^n} \tag{1}$$

where

p = present value
f = future value
i = rate of interest per period
n = number of periods

For example, assume $2.20 is to be received one period from now. This
amount will be received because a smaller amount ($2.00) was invested
now, for one period, at an interest rate of 10%. Using the formula:

$$p = \frac{f}{(1+i)^n} = \frac{\$2.20}{(1+.10)^1} = \$2.00$$

Alternatively, assume the present investment of $2.00 is to remain in-
vested for two periods at 10% and the future amount to be received is
$2.42. Using the formula:

$$p = \frac{f}{(1+i)^n} = \frac{\$2.42}{(1+.10)^2} = \$2.00$$

Note that n (the number of periods) need not be expressed in years.
Any period of time such as a day, a month, a quarter, or a year may be
used. However, whatever period is used, i (the interest rate) must be per
the same period. Thus, if a problem requires that n be expressed in months,
then an i of 1% means 1% per month. This means that each month,
1% of the invested amount at the beginning of the month is earned and
added to the investment. Another way of expressing this is to say that
interest is compounded monthly.

A present value table is designed to show present values for a variety
of i's (interest rates) and a variety of n's (number of periods). Throughout
the table, each present value is based on the assumption that f (the future
value) is 1.00. Since the future value is assumed to be 1, (in other words,
$f = 1$), the formula to construct a table of present values of a single future
amount is as follows:

Since $f = 1$,

$$p = \frac{f}{(1+i)^n} = \frac{1}{(1+i)^n}$$

A table of present values of a single future amount often is called a *present
value of 1* table. Table A-1 on page 1031 is such a table.

**Future Value of a
Single Amount**

The formula for the present value of a single amount may be manipulated to solve for the future value of a single amount. Thus, the formula presented above as (1) may be manipulated as follows:

$$p = \frac{f}{(1+i)^n} \qquad (1)$$

multiply both sides of the equation by $(1+i)^n$,

$$(1+i)^n \times p = (1+i)^n \times \frac{f}{(1+i)^n}$$

cancel the common terms in the numerator and denominator,

$$(1+i)^n \times p = \cancel{(1+i)^n} \times \frac{f}{\cancel{(1+i)^n}}$$

and the result is,

$$(1+i)^n \times p = f$$

or

$$f = p \times (1+i)^n \qquad (2)$$

For example, assume that $2.00 is to be invested for one period at an interest rate of 10%. The $2.00 amount will increase to a future value of $2.20. Using the formula:

$$f = p \times (1+i)^n = \$2.00 \times (1+.10)^1 = \$2.20$$

Alternatively, assume the present investment of $2.00 is to remain invested for three periods at 10%. The amount to be received three periods hence is $2.662 and is calculated with the formula as follows:

$$f = p \times (1+i)^n = \$2.00 \times (1+.10)^3 = \$2.662$$

A future value table is designed to show future values for a variety of i's (interest rates) and a variety of n's (number of periods). Throughout the table, each future value is based on the assumption that p (the present value) is 1.00. Since the present value is assumed to be 1 (in other words, $p = 1$), the formula to construct a table of future values of a single amount is as follows:

Since $p = 1$,

$$f = p(1+i)^n = (1+i)^n$$

A table of future values of a single amount is often called a *future value of 1* table. Table A-2 on page 1032 is such a table.

In Table A-2, look at the row where $n = 0$ and observe that, regardless of the interest rate, the future value is 1. When $n = 0$, the period of time over which interest is earned is zero. Hence, no interest is earned. The future value is calculated as of the date of the investment. Since the table assumes that the investment is 1, the "future value" on that date is also 1.

Students should also observe that a table showing the present values of 1 and a table showing the future values of 1 contain exactly the same information. Both tables are based on the same equation. That is,

$$p = \frac{f}{(1+i)^n}$$

is nothing more than a reformulation of

$$f = p(1+i)^n$$

Both tables reflect the same four variables, p, f, i, and n. Therefore, any problem that can be solved using one of the two tables can also be solved using the other table.

For example, suppose a person invests $100 for five years and expects to earn 12% per year. How much should the person receive five years hence?

To solve the problem using Table A-2, look in the table to find the future value of 1, five periods hence, compounded at 12%. In the table, $f = 1.7623$. Thus,

$$\$100 \times 1.7623 = \$176.23$$

To solve the problem using Table A-1, look in the table to find the present value of 1, 5 periods hence, discounted at 12%. In the table, where $n - 5$, and $i = 12\%$, $p = 0.5674$. Recall that $f - 1$ in the table. This relationship between present value and future value may be expressed as:

$$\frac{p}{f} = \frac{0.5674}{1}$$

This relationship between p and f is the same as in the problem where $100 is to be invested for five years. Thus,

$$\frac{0.5674}{1}$$

is the same as

$$\frac{\$100}{f}$$

$$\frac{0.5674}{1} = \frac{\$100}{f}$$

$$0.5674 \times f = \$100 \times 1$$

$$f = \frac{\$100}{0.5674} = \$176.24$$

The $0.01 difference between the two answers ($176.23 and $176.24) occurs only because the numbers in the tables were rounded.

■ **Present Value of an Annuity**   A series of equal payments is called an annuity. For example, if a person offers to make three annual payments of $100 each, the person is offering an annuity. The present value of an annuity is defined as the value of the payments one period prior to the first payment. Graphically, this may be presented as follows:

$$\overset{\circ}{\underset{p}{\rule{0pt}{0pt}}} \underset{\circ}{\overline{\quad\overset{\$100}{\rule{0pt}{0pt}}\quad}} \underset{\circ}{\overline{\quad\overset{\$100}{\rule{0pt}{0pt}}\quad}} \underset{\circ}{\overline{\quad\overset{\$100}{\rule{0pt}{0pt}}\quad}}$$

To calculate the present value of this annuity, one might calculate the present value of each payment and add them together. For example, assuming an interest rate of 18%, the calculation would be:

$$p = \frac{\$100}{(1+.18)^1} + \frac{\$100}{(1+.18)^2} + \frac{\$100}{(1+.18)^3} = \$217.43$$

Another way of calculating the present value of the annuity is to use Table A-1. The calculation appears as follows:

First payment: $p = \$100 \times 0.8475 = \$\ 84.75$
Second payment: $p = \$100 \times 0.7182 = \quad 71.82$
Third payment: $p = \$100 \times 0.6086 = \quad 60.86$
Total: $p = \$217.43$

Another way of using Table A-1 to solve the problem is to add the present values of three payments of 1 and multiply the answer times $100. Thus,

From Table A-1: $i = 18\%, n = 1, p = \ 0.8475$
$i = 18\%, n = 2, p = \ 0.7182$
$i = 18\%, n = 3, p = \ 0.6086$
2.1743
$2.1743 \times \$100 = \$217.43$

The easiest way to solve the problem is to use a table that shows the present values of a series of payments. That type of table often is called a *present value of an annuity of 1* table. Table A-3 on page 1033 is such a table. Look in Table A-3 on the row where $n = 3$ and $i = 18\%$ and observe that the present value is 2.1743. Stated in other words, an annuity of 1 for three periods, discounted at 18%, is 2.1743.

Although a formula is used to construct a table showing the present values of an annuity,[1] students should understand that the table can be constructed simply by adding together the amounts in a present value of 1 table (such as Table A-1). To check your understanding of this, examine Table A-1 and Table A-3 to confirm that the following numbers were drawn from those tables.

From Table A-1		From Table A-3	
$i = 8\%, n = 1$	0.9259	$i = 8\%, n = 1$	0.9259
$i = 8\%, n = 2$	0.8573		
$i = 8\%, n = 3$	0.7938		
$i = 8\%, n = 4$	0.7350		
Total	3.3120	$i = 8\%, n = 4$	3.3121

[1] The formula for a table showing the present values of an annuity of 1 is:

$$p = \frac{1 - \dfrac{1}{(1+i)^n}}{i}$$

The minor difference in the results (3.3120 and 3.3121) occurs only because the numbers in the tables have been rounded.

■ **Future Value of an Annuity**

An annuity was previously defined as any series of equal payments. Just as the present value of an annuity may be calculated, so may be the future value of an annuity. The future value of an annuity is defined as the value of the annuity on the date of the final payment. Consider the earlier example of a person who offers to make three annual payments of $100 each. Graphically, the points in time at which the present value and the future value are calculated may be shown as follows:

$$\underset{p}{\circ}\!\!-\!\!\!\underset{}{\overset{\$100}{\circ}}\!\!\!-\!\!\!\underset{}{\overset{\$100}{\circ}}\!\!\!-\!\!\!\underset{f}{\overset{\$100}{\circ}}$$

To calculate the future value of this annuity, one might calculate the future value of each payment and add them together. Assuming an interest rate of 18%, the calculation would be:

$$f = \$100(1 + .18)^2 + \$100(1 + .18)^1 + \$100(1 + .18)^0 = \$357.24$$

Another way of calculating the future value of the annuity is to use Table A-2. The calculation appears as follows:

First payment: $f = \$100 \times 1.3924 = \$139.24$
Second payment: $f = \$100 \times 1.1800 = 118.00$
Third payment: $f = \$100 \times 1.0000 = \underline{100.00}$
Total: $f = \underline{\underline{\$357.24}}$

In the calculations and the graph above, note that the first payment is made two periods prior to the point at which future value is determined. Therefore, for the first payment, $n = 2$. For the second payment, $n = 1$. Since the third payment occurs on the future value date, $n = 0$.

Instead of adding the future value of each payment, another approach is to add the future values of three payments of 1 and multiply the answer by $100. This approach appears as follows:

From Table A-2: $i = 18\%, n = 2, f = 1.3924$
$i = 18\%, n = 1, f = 1.1800$
$i = 18\%, n = 0, f = \underline{1.0000}$
$\overline{3.5724}$

$$3.5724 \times \$100 = \underline{\underline{\$357.24}}$$

The easiest way to solve the problem is to use a table that shows the future values of a series of payments. That type of table often is called a *future value of an annuity of 1* table. Table A-4 on page 1034 is such a table. Note in Table A-4 that when $n = 1$, the future values are equal to 1 ($f = 1$) for all rates of interest. When $n = 1$, the "annuity" consists of only one payment and the future value is determined on the date of the payment. Hence, the future value equals the payment.

Although a formula[2] is used to construct a table showing the future values of an annuity of 1, students should understand that the table can be constructed simply by adding together the amount in a future value of 1 table (such as Table A-2). To check your understanding of this, examine Table A-2 and Table A-4 to confirm that the following numbers were drawn from those tables.

From Table A-2		From Table A-4	
$i = 8\%$, $n = 0$	1.0000	$i = 8\%$, $n = 1$ . . .	1.0000
$i = 8\%$, $n = 1$	1.0800		
$i = 8\%$, $n = 2$	1.1664		
$i = 8\%$, $n = 3$	1.2597		
Total	4.5061	$i = 8\%$, $n = 4$ . . .	4.5061

Minor differences in the results may sometimes occur but only because the numbers in the tables have been rounded.

Observe that, in Table A-2, the future value is 1.0000 when $n = 0$. However, in Table A-4, the future value is 1.0000 when $n = 1$. Why is this true?

When $n = 0$ in Table A-2, the future value is determined on the same date as the single payment of 1 is made. The investment period over which interest is earned is zero ($n = 0$). However, Table A-4 is designed so that one payment is made each period. When $n = 2$, two payments are assumed, or when $n = 1$, one payment is assumed. And since future value is calculated as of the date of the last payment, future value = 1 when $n = 1$.

---

[2] The formula for a table showing the future values of an annuity of 1 is:

$$f = \frac{(1 + i)^n - 1}{i}$$

Table A-1   Present Value of 1 Due in *n* Periods

Periods	1.0%	1.5%	3.0%	4.0%	8.0%	10.0%	12.0%	14.0%	16.0%	18.0%	20.0%
1	0.9901	0.9852	0.9709	0.9615	0.9259	0.9091	0.8929	0.8772	0.8621	0.8475	0.8333
2	0.9803	0.9707	0.9426	0.9246	0.8573	0.8264	0.7972	0.7695	0.7432	0.7182	0.6944
3	0.9706	0.9563	0.9151	0.8890	0.7938	0.7513	0.7118	0.6750	0.6407	0.6086	0.5787
4	0.9610	0.9422	0.8885	0.8548	0.7350	0.6830	0.6355	0.5921	0.5523	0.5158	0.4823
5	0.9515	0.9283	0.8626	0.8219	0.6806	0.6209	0.5674	0.5194	0.4761	0.4371	0.4019
6	0.9420	0.9145	0.8375	0.7903	0.6302	0.5645	0.5066	0.4556	0.4104	0.3704	0.3349
7	0.9327	0.9010	0.8131	0.7599	0.5835	0.5132	0.4523	0.3996	0.3538	0.3139	0.2791
8	0.9235	0.8877	0.7894	0.7307	0.5403	0.4665	0.4039	0.3506	0.3050	0.2660	0.2326
9	0.9143	0.8746	0.7664	0.7026	0.5002	0.4241	0.3606	0.3075	0.2630	0.2255	0.1938
10	0.9053	0.8617	0.7441	0.6756	0.4632	0.3855	0.3220	0.2697	0.2267	0.1911	0.1615
11	0.8963	0.8489	0.7224	0.6496	0.4289	0.3505	0.2875	0.2366	0.1954	0.1619	0.1346
12	0.8874	0.8364	0.7014	0.6246	0.3971	0.3186	0.2567	0.2076	0.1685	0.1372	0.1122
13	0.8787	0.8240	0.6810	0.6006	0.3677	0.2897	0.2292	0.1821	0.1452	0.1163	0.0935
14	0.8700	0.8118	0.6611	0.5775	0.3405	0.2633	0.2046	0.1597	0.1252	0.0985	0.0779
15	0.8613	0.7999	0.6419	0.5553	0.3152	0.2394	0.1827	0.1401	0.1079	0.0835	0.0649
16	0.8528	0.7880	0.6232	0.5339	0.2919	0.2176	0.1631	0.1229	0.0930	0.0708	0.0541
17	0.8444	0.7764	0.6050	0.5134	0.2703	0.1978	0.1456	0.1078	0.0802	0.0600	0.0451
18	0.8360	0.7649	0.5874	0.4936	0.2502	0.1799	0.1300	0.0946	0.0691	0.0508	0.0376
19	0.8277	0.7536	0.5703	0.4746	0.2317	0.1635	0.1161	0.0829	0.0596	0.0431	0.0313
20	0.8195	0.7425	0.5537	0.4564	0.2145	0.1486	0.1037	0.0728	0.0514	0.0365	0.0261
21	0.8114	0.7315	0.5375	0.4388	0.1987	0.1351	0.0926	0.0638	0.0443	0.0309	0.0217
22	0.8034	0.7207	0.5219	0.4220	0.1839	0.1228	0.0826	0.0560	0.0382	0.0262	0.0181
23	0.7954	0.7100	0.5067	0.4057	0.1703	0.1117	0.0738	0.0491	0.0329	0.0222	0.0151
24	0.7876	0.6995	0.4919	0.3901	0.1577	0.1015	0.0659	0.0431	0.0284	0.0188	0.0126
25	0.7798	0.6892	0.4776	0.3751	0.1460	0.0923	0.0588	0.0378	0.0245	0.0160	0.0105
26	0.7720	0.6790	0.4637	0.3607	0.1352	0.0839	0.0525	0.0331	0.0211	0.0135	0.0087
27	0.7644	0.6690	0.4502	0.3468	0.1252	0.0763	0.0469	0.0291	0.0182	0.0115	0.0073
28	0.7568	0.6591	0.4371	0.3335	0.1159	0.0693	0.0419	0.0255	0.0157	0.0097	0.0061
29	0.7493	0.6494	0.4243	0.3207	0.1073	0.0630	0.0374	0.0224	0.0135	0.0082	0.0051
30	0.7419	0.6398	0.4120	0.3083	0.0994	0.0573	0.0334	0.0196	0.0116	0.0070	0.0042
31	0.7346	0.6303	0.4000	0.2965	0.0920	0.0521	0.0298	0.0172	0.0100	0.0059	0.0035
32	0.7273	0.6210	0.3883	0.2851	0.0852	0.0474	0.0266	0.0151	0.0087	0.0050	0.0029
33	0.7201	0.6118	0.3770	0.2741	0.0789	0.0431	0.0238	0.0132	0.0075	0.0042	0.0024
34	0.7130	0.6028	0.3660	0.2636	0.0730	0.0391	0.0212	0.0116	0.0064	0.0036	0.0020
35	0.7059	0.5939	0.3554	0.2534	0.0676	0.0356	0.0189	0.0102	0.0055	0.0030	0.0017
36	0.6989	0.5851	0.3450	0.2437	0.0626	0.0323	0.0169	0.0089	0.0048	0.0026	0.0014
37	0.6920	0.5764	0.3350	0.2343	0.0580	0.0294	0.0151	0.0078	0.0041	0.0022	0.0012
38	0.6852	0.5679	0.3252	0.2253	0.0537	0.0267	0.0135	0.0069	0.0036	0.0019	0.0010
39	0.6784	0.5595	0.3158	0.2166	0.0497	0.0243	0.0120	0.0060	0.0031	0.0016	0.0008
40	0.6717	0.5513	0.3066	0.2083	0.0460	0.0221	0.0107	0.0053	0.0026	0.0013	0.0007
41	0.6650	0.5431	0.2976	0.2003	0.0426	0.0201	0.0096	0.0046	0.0023	0.0011	0.0006
42	0.6584	0.5351	0.2890	0.1926	0.0395	0.0183	0.0086	0.0041	0.0020	0.0010	0.0005
43	0.6519	0.5272	0.2805	0.1852	0.0365	0.0166	0.0076	0.0036	0.0017	0.0008	0.0004
44	0.6454	0.5194	0.2724	0.1780	0.0338	0.0151	0.0068	0.0031	0.0015	0.0007	0.0003
45	0.6391	0.5117	0.2644	0.1712	0.0313	0.0137	0.0061	0.0027	0.0013	0.0006	0.0003
46	0.6327	0.5042	0.2567	0.1646	0.0290	0.0125	0.0054	0.0024	0.0011	0.0005	0.0002
47	0.6265	0.4967	0.2493	0.1583	0.0269	0.0113	0.0049	0.0021	0.0009	0.0004	0.0002
48	0.6203	0.4894	0.2420	0.1522	0.0249	0.0103	0.0043	0.0019	0.0008	0.0004	0.0002
49	0.6141	0.4821	0.2350	0.1463	0.0230	0.0094	0.0039	0.0016	0.0007	0.0003	0.0001
50	0.6080	0.4750	0.2281	0.1407	0.0213	0.0085	0.0035	0.0014	0.0006	0.0003	0.0001

Table A-2   Future Value of 1 Due in *n* Periods

Periods	1.0%	1.5%	3.0%	4.0%	8.0%	10.0%	12.0%	14.0%	16.0%	18.0%	20.0%
0	1.0000	1.0000	1.0000	1.0000	1.0000	1.0000	1.0000	1.0000	1.0000	1.0000	1.0000
1	1.0100	1.0150	1.0300	1.0400	1.0800	1.1000	1.1200	1.1400	1.1600	1.1800	1.2000
2	1.0201	1.0302	1.0609	1.0816	1.1664	1.2100	1.2544	1.2996	1.3456	1.3924	1.4400
3	1.0303	1.0457	1.0927	1.1249	1.2597	1.3310	1.4049	1.4815	1.5609	1.6430	1.7280
4	1.0406	1.0614	1.1255	1.1699	1.3605	1.4641	1.5735	1.6890	1.8106	1.9388	2.0736
5	1.0510	1.0773	1.1593	1.2167	1.4693	1.6105	1.7623	1.9254	2.1003	2.2878	2.4883
6	1.0615	1.0934	1.1941	1.2653	1.5869	1.7716	1.9738	2.1950	2.4364	2.6996	2.9860
7	1.0721	1.1098	1.2299	1.3159	1.7138	1.9487	2.2107	2.5023	2.8262	3.1855	3.5832
8	1.0829	1.1265	1.2668	1.3686	1.8509	2.1436	2.4760	2.8526	3.2784	3.7589	4.2998
9	1.0937	1.1434	1.3048	1.4233	1.9990	2.3579	2.7731	3.2519	3.8030	4.4355	5.1598
10	1.1046	1.1605	1.3439	1.4802	2.1589	2.5937	3.1058	3.7072	4.4114	5.2338	6.1917
11	1.1157	1.1779	1.3842	1.5395	2.3316	2.8531	3.4785	4.2262	5.1173	6.1759	7.4301
12	1.1264	1.1956	1.4258	1.6010	2.5182	3.1384	3.8960	4.8179	5.9360	7.2876	8.9161
13	1.1381	1.2136	1.4685	1.6651	2.7196	3.4523	4.3635	5.4924	6.8858	8.5994	10.6993
14	1.1495	1.2318	1.5126	1.7317	2.9372	3.7975	4.8871	6.2613	7.9875	10.1472	12.8392
15	1.1610	1.2502	1.5580	1.8009	3.1722	4.1772	5.4736	7.1379	9.2655	11.9737	15.4070
16	1.1726	1.2690	1.6047	1.8730	3.4259	4.5950	6.1304	8.1372	10.7480	14.1290	18.4884
17	1.1843	1.2880	1.6528	1.9479	3.7000	5.0545	6.8660	9.2765	12.4677	16.6722	22.1861
18	1.1961	1.3073	1.7024	2.0258	3.9960	5.5599	7.6900	10.5752	14.4625	19.6733	26.6233
19	1.2081	1.3270	1.7535	2.1068	4.3157	6.1159	8.6128	12.0557	16.7765	23.2144	31.9480
20	1.2202	1.3469	1.8061	2.1911	4.6610	6.7275	9.6463	13.7435	19.4608	27.3930	38.3376
21	1.2324	1.3671	1.8603	2.2788	5.0338	7.4002	10.8038	15.6676	22.5745	32.3238	46.0051
22	1.2447	1.3876	1.9161	2.3699	5.4365	8.1403	12.1003	17.8610	26.1864	38.1421	55.2061
23	1.2572	1.4084	1.9736	2.4647	5.8715	8.9543	13.5523	20.3616	30.3762	45.0076	66.2474
24	1.2697	1.4295	2.0328	2.5633	6.3412	9.8497	15.1786	23.2122	35.2364	53.1090	79.4968
25	1.2824	1.4509	2.0938	2.6658	6.8485	10.8347	17.0001	26.4619	40.8742	62.6686	95.3962
26	1.2953	1.4727	2.1566	2.7725	7.3964	11.9182	19.0401	30.1666	47.4141	73.9490	114.4755
27	1.3082	1.4948	2.2213	2.8834	7.9881	13.1100	21.3249	34.3899	55.0004	87.2598	137.3706
28	1.3213	1.5172	2.2879	2.9987	8.6271	14.4210	23.8839	39.2045	63.8004	102.9666	164.8447
29	1.3345	1.5400	2.3566	3.1187	9.3173	15.8631	26.7499	44.6931	74.0085	121.5005	197.8136
30	1.3478	1.5631	2.4273	3.2434	10.0627	17.4494	29.9599	50.9502	85.8499	143.3706	237.3763
31	1.3613	1.5865	2.5001	3.3731	10.8677	19.1943	33.5551	58.0832	99.5859	169.1774	284.8516
32	1.3749	1.6103	2.5751	3.5081	11.7371	21.1138	37.5817	66.2148	115.5196	199.6293	341.8219
33	1.3887	1.6345	2.6523	3.6484	12.6760	23.2252	42.0915	75.4849	134.0027	235.5625	410.1863
34	1.4026	1.6590	2.7319	3.7943	13.6901	25.5477	47.1425	86.0528	155.4432	277.9638	492.2235
35	1.4166	1.6839	2.8139	3.9461	14.7853	28.1024	52.7996	98.1002	180.3141	327.9973	590.6682
36	1.4308	1.7091	2.8983	4.1039	15.9682	30.9127	59.1356	111.8342	209.1643	387.0368	708.8019
37	1.4451	1.7348	2.9852	4.2681	17.2456	34.0039	66.2318	127.4910	242.6306	456.7034	850.5622
38	1.4595	1.7608	3.0748	4.4388	18.6253	37.4043	74.1797	145.3397	281.4515	528.9100	1020.6747
39	1.4741	1.7872	3.1670	4.6164	20.1153	41.1448	83.0812	165.6873	326.4838	635.9139	1224.8096
40	1.4889	1.8140	3.2620	4.8010	21.7245	45.2593	93.0510	188.8835	378.7212	750.3783	1469.7716
41	1.5083	1.8412	3.3599	4.9931	23.4625	49.7852	104.2171	215.3272	439.3165	885.4464	1763.7259
42	1.5188	1.8688	3.4607	5.1928	25.3395	54.7637	116.7231	245.4730	509.6072	1044.8268	2116.4711
43	1.5340	1.8969	3.5645	5.4005	27.3666	60.2401	130.7299	279.8392	591.1443	1232.8956	2539.7653
44	1.5493	1.9253	3.6715	5.6165	29.5560	66.2641	146.4175	319.0167	685.7274	1454.8168	3047.7183
45	1.5648	1.9542	3.7816	5.8412	31.9204	72.8905	163.9876	363.6791	795.4438	1716.6839	3657.2620
46	1.5805	1.9835	3.8950	6.0748	34.4741	80.1795	183.6661	414.5941	922.7148	2025.6870	4388.7144
47	1.5963	2.0133	4.0119	6.3178	37.2320	88.1975	205.7061	472.6373	1070.3492	2390.3106	5266.4573
48	1.6122	2.0435	4.1323	6.5705	40.2106	97.0172	230.3908	538.8065	1241.6051	2820.5665	6319.7487
49	1.6283	2.0741	4.2562	6.8333	43.4274	106.7190	258.0377	614.2395	1440.2619	3328.2685	7583.6985
50	1.6446	2.1052	4.3839	7.1067	46.9016	117.3909	289.0022	700.2330	1670.7038	3927.3569	9100.4382

Table A-3 Present Value of an Annuity of 1 per Period

Periods	1.0%	1.5%	3.0%	4.0%	8.0%	10.0%	12.0%	14.0%	16.0%	18.0%	20.0%
1	0.9901	0.9852	0.9709	0.9615	0.9259	0.9091	0.8929	0.8772	0.8621	0.8475	0.8333
2	1.9704	1.9559	1.9135	1.8861	1.7833	1.7355	1.6901	1.6467	1.6052	1.5656	1.5278
3	2.9410	2.9122	2.8286	2.7751	2.5771	2.4869	2.4018	2.3216	2.2459	2.1743	2.1065
4	3.9020	3.8544	3.7171	3.6299	3.3121	3.1699	3.0373	2.9137	2.7982	2.6901	2.5887
5	4.8534	4.7826	4.5797	4.4518	3.9927	3.7908	3.6048	3.4331	3.2743	3.1272	2.9906
6	5.7955	5.6972	5.4172	5.2421	4.6229	4.3553	4.1114	3.8887	3.6847	3.4976	3.3255
7	6.7282	6.5982	6.2303	6.0021	5.2064	4.8684	4.5638	4.2883	4.0386	3.8115	3.6046
8	7.6517	7.4859	7.0197	6.7327	5.7466	5.3349	4.9676	4.6389	4.3436	4.0776	3.8372
9	8.5660	8.3605	7.7861	7.4353	6.2469	5.7590	5.3282	4.9464	4.6065	4.3030	4.0310
10	9.4713	9.2222	8.5302	8.1109	6.7101	6.1446	5.6502	5.2161	4.8332	4.4941	4.1925
11	10.3676	10.0711	9.2526	8.7605	7.1390	6.4951	5.9377	5.4527	5.0286	4.6560	4.3271
12	11.2551	10.9075	9.9540	9.3851	7.5361	6.8137	6.1944	5.6603	5.1971	4.7932	4.4392
13	12.1337	11.7315	10.6350	9.9856	7.9038	7.1034	6.4235	5.8424	5.3423	4.9095	4.5327
14	13.0037	12.5434	11.2961	10.5631	8.2442	7.3667	6.6282	6.0021	5.4675	5.0081	4.6106
15	13.8651	13.3432	11.9379	11.1184	8.5595	7.6061	6.8109	6.1422	5.5755	5.0916	4.6755
16	14.7179	14.1313	12.5611	11.6523	8.8514	7.8237	6.9740	6.2651	5.6685	5.1624	4.7296
17	15.5623	14.9076	13.1661	12.1657	9.1216	8.0216	7.1196	6.3729	5.7487	5.2223	4.7746
18	16.3983	15.6726	13.7535	12.6593	9.3719	8.2014	7.2497	6.4674	5.8178	5.2732	4.8122
19	17.2260	16.4262	14.3238	13.1339	9.6036	8.3649	7.3658	6.5504	5.8775	5.3162	4.8435
20	18.0456	17.1686	14.8775	13.5903	9.8181	8.5136	7.4694	6.6231	5.9288	5.3527	4.8696
21	18.8570	17.9001	15.4150	14.0292	10.0168	8.6487	7.5620	6.6870	5.9731	5.3837	4.8913
22	19.6604	18.6208	15.9369	14.4511	10.2007	8.7715	7.6446	6.7429	6.0113	5.4099	4.9094
23	20.4558	19.3309	16.4436	14.8568	10.3711	8.8832	7.7184	6.7921	6.0442	5.4321	4.9245
24	21.2434	20.0304	16.9355	15.2470	10.5288	8.9847	7.7843	6.8351	6.0726	5.4509	4.9371
25	22.0232	20.7196	17.4131	15.6221	10.6748	9.0770	7.8431	6.8729	6.0971	5.4669	4.9476
26	22.7952	21.3986	17.8768	15.9828	10.8100	9.1609	7.8957	6.9061	6.1182	5.4804	4.9563
27	23.5596	22.0676	18.3270	16.3296	10.9352	9.2372	7.9426	6.9352	6.1364	5.4919	4.9636
28	24.3164	22.7267	18.7641	16.6631	11.0511	9.3066	7.9844	6.9607	6.1520	5.5016	4.9697
29	25.0658	23.3761	19.1885	16.9837	11.1584	9.3696	8.0218	6.9830	6.1656	5.5098	4.9747
30	25.8077	24.0158	19.6004	17.2920	11.2578	9.4269	8.0552	7.0027	6.1772	5.5168	4.9789
31	26.5423	24.6461	20.0004	17.5885	11.3498	9.4790	8.0850	7.0199	6.1872	5.5227	4.9824
32	27.2696	25.2671	20.3888	17.8736	11.4350	9.5264	8.1116	7.0350	6.1959	5.5277	4.9854
33	27.9897	25.8790	20.7658	18.1476	11.5139	9.5694	8.1354	7.0482	6.2034	5.5320	4.9878
34	28.7027	26.4817	21.1318	18.4112	11.5869	9.6086	8.1566	7.0599	6.2098	5.5356	4.9898
35	29.4086	27.0756	21.4872	18.6646	11.6546	9.6442	8.1755	7.0700	6.2153	5.5386	4.9915
36	30.1075	27.6607	21.8323	18.9083	11.7172	9.6765	8.1924	7.0790	6.2201	5.5412	4.9929
37	30.7995	28.2371	22.1672	19.1426	11.7752	9.7059	8.2075	7.0868	6.2242	5.5434	4.9941
38	31.4847	28.8051	22.4925	19.3679	11.8289	9.7327	8.2210	7.0937	6.2278	5.5452	4.9951
39	32.1630	29.3646	22.8082	19.5845	11.8786	9.7570	8.2330	7.0997	6.2309	5.5468	4.9959
40	32.8347	29.9158	23.1148	19.7928	11.9246	9.7791	8.2438	7.1050	6.2335	5.5482	4.9966
41	33.4997	30.4590	23.4124	19.9931	11.9672	9.7991	8.2534	7.1097	6.2358	5.5493	4.9972
42	34.1581	30.9941	23.7014	20.1856	12.0067	9.8174	8.2619	7.1138	6.2377	5.5502	4.9976
43	34.8100	31.5212	23.9819	20.3708	12.0432	9.8340	8.2696	7.1173	6.2394	5.5510	4.9980
44	35.4555	32.0406	24.2543	20.5488	12.0771	9.8491	8.2764	7.1205	6.2409	5.5517	4.9984
45	36.0945	32.5523	24.5187	20.7200	12.1084	9.8628	8.2825	7.1232	6.2421	5.5523	4.9986
46	36.7272	33.0565	24.7754	20.8847	12.1374	9.8753	8.2880	7.1256	6.2432	5.5528	4.9989
47	37.3537	33.5532	25.0247	21.0429	12.1643	9.8866	8.2928	7.1277	6.2442	5.5532	4.9991
48	37.9740	34.0426	25.2667	21.1951	12.1891	9.8969	8.2972	7.1296	6.2450	5.5536	4.9992
49	38.5881	34.5247	25.5017	21.3415	12.2122	9.9063	8.3010	7.1312	6.2457	5.5539	4.9993
50	39.1961	34.9997	25.7298	21.4822	12.2335	9.9148	8.3045	7.1327	6.2463	5.5541	4.9995

Table A-4   Future Value of an Annuity of 1 per Period

Periods	1.0%	1.5%	3.0%	4.0%	8.0%	10.0%	12.0%	14.0%	16.0%	18.0%	20.0%
1	1.0000	1.0000	1.0000	1.0000	1.0000	1.0000	1.0000	1.0000	1.0000	1.0000	1.0000
2	2.0100	2.0150	2.0300	2.0400	2.0800	2.1000	2.1200	2.1400	2.1600	2.1800	2.2000
3	3.0301	3.0452	3.0909	3.1216	3.2464	3.3100	3.3744	3.4396	3.5056	3.5724	3.6400
4	4.0604	4.0909	4.1836	4.2465	4.5061	4.6410	4.7793	4.9211	5.0665	5.2154	5.3680
5	5.1010	5.1523	5.3091	5.4163	5.8666	6.1051	6.3528	6.6101	6.8771	7.1542	7.4416
6	6.1520	6.2296	6.4684	6.6330	7.3359	7.7156	8.1152	8.5355	8.9775	9.4420	9.9299
7	7.2135	7.3230	7.6625	7.8983	8.9228	9.4872	10.0890	10.7305	11.4139	12.1415	12.9159
8	8.2857	8.4328	8.8923	9.2142	10.6366	11.4359	12.2997	13.2328	14.2401	15.3270	16.4991
9	9.3685	9.5593	10.1591	10.5828	12.4876	13.5795	14.7757	16.0853	17.5185	19.0859	20.7989
10	10.4622	10.7027	11.4639	12.0061	14.4866	15.9374	17.5487	19.3373	21.3215	23.5213	25.9587
11	11.5668	11.8633	12.8078	13.4864	16.6455	18.5312	20.6546	23.0445	25.7329	28.7551	32.1504
12	12.6825	13.0412	14.1920	15.0258	18.9771	21.3843	24.1331	27.2707	30.8502	34.9311	39.5805
13	13.8093	14.2368	15.6178	16.6268	21.4953	24.5227	28.0291	32.0887	36.7862	42.2187	48.4966
14	14.9474	15.4504	17.0863	18.2919	24.2149	27.9750	32.3926	37.5811	43.6720	50.8180	59.1959
15	16.0969	16.6821	18.5989	20.0236	27.1521	31.7725	37.2797	43.8424	51.6595	60.9653	72.0351
16	17.2579	17.9324	20.1569	21.8245	30.3243	35.9497	42.7533	50.9804	60.9250	72.9390	87.4421
17	18.4304	19.2014	21.7616	23.6975	33.7502	40.5447	48.8837	59.1176	71.6730	87.0680	105.9306
18	19.6147	20.4894	23.4144	25.6454	37.4502	45.5992	55.7497	68.3941	84.1407	103.7403	128.1167
19	20.8109	21.7967	25.1169	27.6712	41.4463	51.1591	63.4397	78.9692	98.6032	123.4135	154.7400
20	22.0190	23.1237	26.8704	29.7781	45.7620	57.2750	72.0524	91.0249	115.3797	146.6280	186.6880
21	23.2392	24.4705	28.6765	31.9692	50.4229	64.0025	81.6987	104.7684	134.8405	174.0210	225.0256
22	24.4716	25.8376	30.5368	34.2480	55.4568	71.4027	92.5026	120.4360	157.4150	206.3448	271.0307
23	25.7163	27.2251	32.4529	36.6179	60.8933	79.5430	104.6029	138.2970	183.6014	244.4868	326.2369
24	26.9735	28.6335	34.4265	39.0826	66.7648	88.4973	118.1552	158.6586	213.9776	289.4945	392.4842
25	28.2432	30.0630	36.4593	41.6459	73.1059	98.3471	133.3339	181.8708	249.2140	342.6035	471.9811
26	29.5256	31.5140	38.5530	44.3117	79.9544	109.1818	150.3339	208.3327	290.0883	405.2721	567.3773
27	30.8209	32.9867	40.7096	47.0842	87.3508	121.0999	169.3740	238.4993	337.5024	479.2211	681.8528
28	32.1291	34.4815	42.9309	49.9676	95.3388	134.2099	190.6989	272.8892	392.5028	566.4809	819.2233
29	33.4504	35.9987	45.2189	52.9663	103.9659	148.6309	214.5828	312.0937	456.3032	669.4475	984.0680
30	34.7849	37.5387	47.5754	56.0849	113.2832	164.4940	241.3327	356.7868	530.3117	790.9480	1181.8816
31	36.1327	39.1018	50.0027	59.3283	123.3459	181.9434	271.2926	407.7370	616.1616	934.3186	1419.2579
32	37.4941	40.6883	52.5028	62.7015	134.2135	201.1378	304.8477	465.8202	715.7475	1103.4960	1704.1095
33	38.8690	42.2986	55.0778	66.2095	145.9506	222.2515	342.4294	532.0350	831.2671	1303.1253	2045.9314
34	40.2577	43.9331	57.7302	69.8579	158.6267	245.4767	384.5210	607.5199	965.2698	1538.6878	2456.1176
35	41.6603	45.5921	60.4621	73.6522	172.3168	271.0244	431.6635	693.5727	1120.7130	1816.6516	2948.3411
36	43.0769	47.2760	63.2759	77.5983	187.1021	299.1268	484.4631	791.6729	1301.0270	2144.6489	3539.0094
37	44.5076	48.9851	66.1742	81.7022	203.0703	330.0395	543.5987	903.5071	1510.1914	2531.6857	4247.8112
38	45.9527	50.7199	69.1594	85.9703	220.3159	364.0434	609.8305	1030.9981	1752.8220	2988.3891	5098.3735
39	47.4123	52.4807	72.2342	90.4091	238.9412	401.4478	684.0102	1176.3378	2034.2735	3527.2992	6119.0482
40	48.8864	54.2679	75.4013	95.0255	259.0565	442.5926	767.0914	1342.0251	2360.7572	4163.2130	7343.8578
41	50.3752	56.0819	78.6633	99.8265	280.7810	487.8518	860.1424	1530.9086	2739.4784	4913.5914	8813.6294
42	51.8790	57.9231	82.0232	104.8196	304.2435	537.6370	964.3595	1746.2358	3178.7949	5799.0378	10577.3553
43	53.3978	59.7920	85.4839	110.0124	329.5830	592.4007	1081.0826	1991.7088	3688.4021	6843.8646	12693.8263
44	54.9318	61.6889	89.0484	115.4129	356.9496	652.6408	1211.8125	2271.5481	4279.5465	8076.7603	15233.5916
45	56.4811	63.6142	92.7199	121.0294	386.5056	718.9048	1358.2300	2590.5648	4965.2739	9531.5771	18281.3099
46	58.0459	65.5684	96.5015	126.8706	418.4261	791.7953	1522.2176	2954.2439	5760.7177	11248.2610	21938.5719
47	59.6263	67.5519	100.3965	132.9454	452.9002	871.9749	1705.8838	3368.8380	6683.4326	13273.9480	26327.2863
48	61.2226	69.5652	104.4084	139.2632	490.1322	960.1723	1911.5898	3841.4753	7753.7818	15664.2586	31593.7436
49	62.8348	71.6087	108.5406	145.8337	530.3427	1057.1896	2141.9806	4380.2819	8995.3869	18484.8251	37913.4923
50	64.4632	73.6828	112.7969	152.6671	573.7702	1163.9085	2400.0182	4994.5213	10435.6488	21813.0937	45497.1908

☐ **Exercises** **Exercise A-1**

X Company is considering an investment which, if paid for immediately, is expected to return $80,000, seven years hence. If X Company demands a 16 percent return, how much will X Company be willing to pay for this investment?

Exercise A-2

Y Company invested $20,000 in a project that is expected to earn a 14% rate of return. The earnings will be reinvested in the project each year until the entire investment is liquidated 15 years hence. What will be the cash proceeds when the project is liquidated?

Exercise A-3

Z Company is considering a contract that will return $10,000 annually at the end of each year for 18 years. If Z Company demands an annual return of 20% and pays for the investment immediately, how much should it be willing to pay?

Exercise A-4

James Smith is planning to begin an individual retirement program in which he will invest $2,000 annually at the end of each year. Mr. Smith plans to retire after making 45 annual investments in a program that earns a return of 8%. What will be the value of the program on the date of the last investment?

Exercise A-5

Mr. Blue has been offered the possiblity of investing $0.1486 for 20 years, after which he will be paid $1. What annual rate of interest will Mr. Blue earn? (Use Table A-1 to find the answer.)

Exercise A-6

Mr. White has been offered the possibility of investing $0.0245. The investment will earn 16% per year and will, at the end of the investment, return Mr. White $1. How many years must Mr. White wait to receive the $1? (Use Table A-1 to find the answer.)

Exercise A-7

Ms. North expects to invest $1 at 12% and, at the end of the investment, receive $15.1786. How many years will elapse before Ms. North receives the payment? (Use Table A-2 to find the answer.)

Exercise A-8

Ms. West expects to invest $1 for 15 years, after which she will receive $7.1379. What rate of interest will Ms. West earn? (Use Table A-2 to find the answer.)

Exercise A-9

Mr. Black expects an immediate investment of $5.8775 to return $1 annually for 19 years, the first payment to be received in one year. What rate of interest will Mr. Black earn? (Use Table A-3 to find the answer.)

Exercise A-10

Ms. Brown expects an investment of $7.3667 to return $1 annually for several years. If Ms. Brown is to earn a return of 10%, how many annual payments must she receive? (Use Table A-3 to find the answer.)

Exercise A-11

Mr. Dame expects to invest $1 annually for 30 years and have an accumulated value of $113.2832 on the date of the last investment. If this occurs, what rate of interest will Mr. Dame earn? (Use Table A-4 to find the answer.)

Exercise A-12

Ms. Jain expects to invest $1 annually in a fund that will earn 18%. How many annual investments must Ms. Jain make to accumulate $50.818 on the date of the last investment? (Use Table A-4 to find the answer.)

Exercise A-13

Kay Long financed a new automobile by paying $2,500 cash and agreeing to make 24 monthly payments of $400 each, the first payment to be made one month after the purchase. The loan was said to bear interest at an annual rate of 12%. What was the cost of the automobile?

Exercise A-14

Frank Thomas deposited $5,000 in a savings account that earns interest at an annual rate of 16%, compounded quarterly. The $5,000 plus earned interest must remain in the account three years before it can be withdrawn. How much money will be in the account at the end of three years?

Exercise A-15

Joan Johnson plans to have $100 withdrawn from her monthly paycheck and deposited in a savings account that earns 12% annually, compounded monthly. If Joan continues with her plan for two and a half years, how much will be accumulated in the account on the date of the last deposit?

Exercise A-16

X Company plans to issue 9%, 20-year, $500,000 par value bonds that pay interest semiannually on June 30 and December 31. The bonds are dated December 31, 198A, and are to be issued on that date. If the market rate of interest for the bonds is 8% on the date of issue, what will be the cash proceeds from the bond issue?

Exercise A-17

Fry Company has decided to establish a fund that will be used five years hence to replace an aging productive facility. The company makes an initial contribution of $100,000 to the fund and plans to make quarterly contributions of $25,000 beginning in three months. The fund is expected to earn 12%, compounded quarterly. What will be the value of the fund five years hence?

Exercise A-18

Jets Company expects to earn 14% on an investment that will return $100,000, 12 years hence. (Use Table A-2 to calculate the present value of the investment.)

Exercise A-19

Barth Company invests $100,000 at 16% for 10 years. Use Table A-1 to calculate the future value of the investment, 10 years hence.

CBS Inc. and Subsidiaries
1985 Financial Statements

FINANCIAL
STATEMENTS

**Management's Responsibility
for Financial Statements**

The consolidated financial statements presented on the following pages have been prepared by management in conformity with generally accepted accounting principles consistently applied. The reliability of the financial information, which includes amounts based on judgment, is the responsibility of management.

The Company uses systems and procedures for handling routine business activities that seek to prevent or detect unauthorized transactions. The Company's internal control system envisages a segregation of duties among the Company's personnel, a wide dissemination to these personnel of the Company's written policies and procedures, the use of formal approval authorities and the selection and training of qualified people. The design of internal control systems involves a balancing of estimated benefits against estimated costs. The system is monitored by an internal audit program. The scope and results of the internal audit function and the adequacy of the system of internal accounting controls are reviewed regularly by the Audit Committee of the Board of Directors.

Management believes that the Company's system provides reasonable assurance that assets are safeguarded against material loss and that the Company's financial records permit the preparation of financial statements that are fairly presented in accordance with generally accepted accounting principles.

**Report of Independent
Certified Public Accountants**

To the Shareholders of CBS Inc.:

We have examined the consolidated balance sheets of CBS Inc. and subsidiaries as of December 31, 1985, 1984 and 1983, and the related consolidated statements of income, retained earnings, additional paid-in capital and changes in financial position for the years then ended. Our examinations were made in accordance with generally accepted auditing standards and, accordingly, included such tests of the accounting records and such other auditing procedures as we considered necessary in the circumstances.

In our opinion, the financial statements referred to above present fairly the consolidated financial position of CBS Inc. and subsidiaries as of December 31, 1985, 1984 and 1983, and the results of their operations and the changes in their financial position for the years then ended, in conformity with generally accepted accounting principles applied on a consistent basis.

1251 Avenue of the Americas   COOPERS & LYBRAND
New York, New York 10020
February 12, 1986

CONSOLIDATED STATEMENTS
OF INCOME

(Dollars in millions, except per share amounts)

CBS Inc. and subsidiaries

| | Year ended December 31 | | |
	1985	1984	1983
Revenues:			
Net sales:			
Broadcasting	$2,777.8	$2,714.5	$2,380.2
Products	1,899.0	1,834.2	1,708.2
Interest and other income (note 23)	78.8	91.4	74.7
Total revenues	**4,755.6**	**4,640.1**	**4,163.1**
Expenses:			
Cost of sales:			
Broadcasting	2,082.7	1,988.1	1,816.6
Products	1,020.5	984.2	949.7
Selling, general and administrative expenses	1,192.2	1,073.8	983.0
Interest and other expenses (note 23)	117.1	50.1	54.5
Total expenses	**4,412.5**	**4,096.2**	**3,803.8**
Income from continuing operations before unusual items and income taxes	**343.1**	**543.9**	**359.3**
Unusual items (note 9)	11.2		
Income from continuing operations before income taxes	**354.3**	**543.9**	**359.3**
Income taxes (note 8)	151.7	245.5	158.7
Income from continuing operations	**202.6**	**298.4**	**200.6**
Discontinued operations, net of taxes (note 6):			
Gain from joint venture sale of stock	2.1		
Loss from operations	(56.5)	(59.5)	(13.4)
Loss on disposal	(120.8)	(43.1)	
Extraordinary credit, net of taxes (note 5):			
Gain on sale of land		16.6	
Net income	**$ 27.4**	**$ 212.4**	**$ 187.2**
Per share of common stock (note 1):			
Income from continuing operations	**$ 7.27**	**$ 10.04**	**$ 6.76**
Loss from discontinued operations	(6.46)	(3.45)	(.45)
Extraordinary credit		.56	
Net income	**$ .81**	**$ 7.15**	**$ 6.31**

See notes to consolidated financial statements

CONSOLIDATED BALANCE SHEETS
CBS Inc. and subsidiaries

ASSETS

	1985	December 31 1984	1983
Current assets:			
Cash and cash equivalents:			
Cash and cash items	$ 75.8	$ 14.0	$ 24.1
Short-term marketable securities, at cost plus			
accrued interest (approximates market)	44.3	265.6	18.7
	120.1	279.6	42.8
Notes and accounts receivable, less allowances for			
doubtful accounts, returns and discounts:			
1985, $155.9; 1984, $153.3; 1983, $146.9	785.0	849.8	829.6
Inventories (note 11)	173.3	290.5	295.3
Program rights and feature film productions	483.9	462.0	490.9
Recoverable income taxes	130.9		
Prepaid expenses	142.9	144.0	150.9
Total current assets	**1,836.1**	**2,025.9**	**1,809.5**
Property, plant and equipment:			
Land	27.6	31.4	45.0
Buildings	304.0	333.6	315.9
Machinery and equipment	620.4	596.9	573.4
Leasehold improvements	53.0	51.8	49.4
	1,005.0	1,013.7	983.7
Less accumulated depreciation	445.7	414.4	372.8
Net property, plant and equipment	**559.3**	**599.3**	**610.9**
Investments and other assets:			
Investments (notes 3, 4 and 12)	252.9	200.7	163.8
Excess of the cost over the fair value of net assets of			
businesses acquired, less amortization (note 3)	420.8	67.0	68.2
Other intangible assets (note 3)	70.9	25.7	30.4
Other program rights and feature film productions . . .	169.6	170.3	144.0
Other assets	199.1	172.9	163.0
Total investments and other assets	**1,113.3**	**636.6**	**569.4**
	$3,508.7	**$3,261.8**	**$2,989.8**

(Dollars in millions, except per share amounts)

LIABILITIES AND SHAREHOLDERS' EQUITY

| | December 31 | | |
	1985	1984	1983
Current liabilities:			
Accounts payable (note 13)	$ 228.9	$ 174.6	$ 172.2
Accrued royalties	240.6	252.5	230.1
Accrued salaries, wages and benefits	130.5	100.0	124.2
Liabilities for talent and program rights	278.7	253.2	247.4
Commercial paper	109.6		64.8
Other current debt (note 13)	167.9	15.7	10.7
Income taxes	14.6	37.4	88.4
Other	379.4	263.9	198.4
Total current liabilities	1,550.2	1,097.3	1,136.2
Long-term debt (note 13)	954.3	370.8	232.5
Other liabilities	173.8	146.8	110.1
Deferred income taxes	160.7	94.0	70.5
Common stock subject to redemption (note 17)	65.2		
Preference stock, Series B, par value $1.00 per share, subject to redemption (note 18)	123.2		
Shareholders' equity:			
Preference stock, Series A, par value $1.00 per share (note 19)		.1	.1
Common stock, par value $2.50 per share; authorized 100,000,000 shares; issued 24,334,678 shares (notes 17, 19 and 20)	59.8	76.6	76.6
Additional paid-in capital	226.9	286.4	286.6
Foreign currency fluctuations (note 21)	(7.2)	(68.2)	(51.4)
Retained earnings	251.4	1,309.3	1,181.7
	530.9	1,604.2	1,493.6
Less common stock in treasury, at cost: 885,997 shares in 1985; 924,028 shares in 1984 and 962,605 shares in 1983 (note 19)	49.6	51.3	53.1
Total shareholders' equity	481.3	1,552.9	1,440.5
	$3,508.7	$3,261.8	$2,989.8

See notes to consolidated financial statements

CONSOLIDATED STATEMENTS OF RETAINED EARNINGS AND ADDITIONAL PAID-IN CAPITAL
CBS Inc. and subsidiaries

(Dollars in millions, except per share amounts)

	Year ended December 31		
RETAINED EARNINGS	1985	1984	1983
Balance at beginning of year	$1,309.3	$1,181.7	$1,077.6
Net income	27.4	212.4	187.2
Less cash dividends:			
Common stock, $3.00 per share in 1985, $2.85 per share in 1984 and $2.80 per share in 1983 (dividend restrictions are contained in note 13)	(79.8)	(84.7)	(83.0)
Preference stock, Series A, $1.00 per share		(.1)	(.1)
Preference stock, Series B, $4.17 per share	(5.2)		
Accretion of preference stock, Series B (note 18)	(.1)		
Retirement of common stock repurchased (note 16)	(936.8)		
Reclassification to common stock subject to redemption (note 17)	(63.4)		
Balance at end of year	$ 251.4	$1,309.3	$1,181.7

ADDITIONAL PAID-IN CAPITAL			
Balance at beginning of year	$ 286.4	$ 286.6	$ 287.7
Retirement of common stock repurchased (note 16)	(58.3)		
Reclassification to common stock subject to redemption (note 17)	(4.0)		
Conversion of Series A preference stock	(.8)	(.3)	(.9)
Exercise of stock options	3.4	.1	
Miscellaneous, net	.2		(.2)
Balance at end of year	$ 226.9	$ 286.4	$ 286.6

See notes to consolidated financial statements

CONSOLIDATED STATEMENTS OF CHANGES IN FINANCIAL POSITION
CBS Inc. and subsidiaries

(Dollars in millions)

	Year ended December 31		
	1985	1984	1983
Funds provided by operations:			
Income from continuing operations	$ 202.6	$ 298.4	$ 200.6
Items not affecting funds:			
Depreciation and amortization	134.9	81.5	80.7
Deferred income taxes	57.5	10.6	2.6
Share of undistributed income in companies accounted for under the equity method	(16.2)	(22.1)	(3.8)
Funds provided by continuing operations	378.8	368.4	280.1
Funds provided by (used for) discontinued operations, excluding items not affecting funds . . .	(164.3)	(83.1)	4.0
Funds provided by net gain on sale of land		16.6	
	214.5	301.9	284.1
Net change in working capital excluding cash and debt	221.4	41.3	32.4
Dividends to shareholders	(85.0)	(84.8)	(83.1)
Funds provided by (used for) investment:			
(Increase) decrease in property, plant and equipment:			
Capital expenditures	(113.6)	(111.1)	(101.5)
Other[a]	82.5	56.2	51.1
Investments in joint ventures and other[b]	(36.0)	(15.9)	(22.9)
(Increase) decrease in excess of the cost over the fair value of net assets of businesses acquired[a] . .	(362.7)	(.3)	3.2
Increase in other net assets[a]	(100.3)	(13.9)	(95.4)
	(530.1)	(85.0)	(165.5)
Increase (decrease) due to:			
Issuance of Series B preference stock	123.2		
Retirement of repurchased common stock	(962.9)		
Foreign currency fluctuations and other changes . . .	14.1	(15.1)	.1
Increase (decrease) in cash and cash equivalents before financing activities	(1,004.8)	158.3	68.0
Funds provided by (used for) financing activities:			
Increase (decrease) in short-term debt	261.8	(59.8)	(47.6)
Increase (decrease) in long-term debt	583.5	138.3	(5.5)
	845.3	(78.5)	(53.1)
Net increase (decrease) in cash and cash equivalents	(159.5)	236.8	14.9
Cash and cash equivalents at beginning of year	279.6	42.8	27.9
Cash and cash equivalents at end of year	$ 120.1	$ 279.6	$ 42.8

[a] Excludes effect of depreciation and amortization, included above.
[b] Excludes undistributed income from equity investments, included above.

See notes to consolidated financial statements

NOTES TO CONSOLIDATED FINANCIAL STATEMENTS

1. Statement of Significant Accounting Policies

Principles of Consolidation. The consolidated financial statements include the accounts of the Company, its domestic subsidiaries and substantially all of its foreign subsidiaries. Those foreign subsidiaries that are not consolidated are not significant and are carried at cost. Investments in 20-50 percent owned companies are generally carried on the equity basis. Other investments are generally carried at cost. All significant intercompany transactions have been excluded from the consolidated financial statements. The financial statements of most foreign subsidiaries are as of a date one or two months prior to the date of the consolidated financial statements in order to be available for inclusion in the consolidation.

Revenue Recognition. The Company's practice is to record revenues from sales of products when shipped and services when performed. Allowances for estimated returns are provided based upon prior experience.

Income Taxes. The Company recognizes the tax effects of transactions in the year such transactions enter into the determination of net income regardless of when they are recognized for income tax purposes. Deferred income taxes are provided for accelerated tax depreciation, capitalization of interest and for other timing differences. Investment tax credits are applied as a reduction of the current tax provision.

Inventories. Inventories are stated at the lower of cost (principally based on average cost) or market value.

Programs for Television Broadcast. Costs incurred in connection with the production or purchase of programs to be broadcast on television within one year are classified as current assets, representing the principal portion of the balance sheet caption "Program rights and feature film productions." The noncurrent portion is included as a part of the balance sheet caption "Other program rights and feature film productions." The program costs are charged to expense as the respective programs are broadcast.

Property, Plant and Equipment. Land, buildings and equipment are stated at cost. Depreciation is computed principally using the straight-line method over the estimated useful lives of the assets. Major improvements to existing plant and equipment are capitalized. Expenditures for maintenance and repairs which do not extend the life of the assets are charged to expense as incurred. The cost of properties retired or otherwise disposed of and any related accumulated depreciation are generally removed from the accounts and the resulting gain or loss is reflected in income currently.

Intangibles. The excess of the cost over the fair value at the date of acquisition of net assets of businesses and investments acquired subsequent to October 31, 1970 is being amortized over a period of 40 years on a straight-line basis; amounts applicable to businesses and investments acquired on or prior to that date are not being amortized. The costs of other intangible assets are being amortized over their respective economic lives.

Income Per Share of Common Stock. Income from continuing operations and net income per share have been computed by dividing the applicable income amounts, after deducting dividend requirements on the Series A and Series B preference stock, by the weighted average number of common shares outstanding of 27,123,000 in 1985, 29,708,000 in 1984 and 29,665,000 in 1983.

2. Business Segment Information (Dollars in millions)

Segment information is included on pages 38 through 49 of this report. In 1985, the primary financial statements and related segment information were restated for the discontinuance of certain operations as described in note 6.

The Company's operations are segregated into the CBS/Broadcast, CBS/Records and CBS/Publishing Groups and Other. Other primarily consists of various smaller operations. Other revenues also include Corporate interest income and income from Joint Ventures. The Corporate and Other caption listed under Identifiable Assets and Capital Expenditures includes discontinued operations and all other amounts not assignable to the three groups.

Certain information is segregated between domestic and foreign operations. The Company's foreign operations are located principally in Europe, Latin America, Asia and Canada and essentially consist of the production, sale and distribution of recorded music, the publication of educational and medical books, and the sale of television programming and rights. Home office operations of international divisions are included in Foreign. Interest income and expense of foreign subsidiaries are included within the operating segments rather than in Corporate Interest, net.

Records Group operating profits include income from a 50 percent owned equity-basis investment in Japan. The related income for the years 1985-1981 were $9.2, $8.6, $9.3, $6.8 and $9.5, respectively.

During 1985, the Company reported an $11.2 net pretax gain in unusual items (note 9), which have not been included in segment operating profits. Had these items been included, operating profits for Broadcast, Records and Other would have been $13.2, $2.5 and $14.3 higher, respectively, while Publishing's would have been $18.8 lower.

3. Business Acquisitions (Dollars in millions, except per share amounts)

In January 1985, the Company acquired interests in four regional pay cable sports networks (SportsChannels), a producer of pay cable program services (Rainbow Services) and various management agreements for $53.3. In July 1985, the Company also acquired, for $3.7, an interest in a company which markets and distributes programming for the SportsChannels and Rainbow Services. These interests are accounted for on an equity basis. In October 1985, Rainbow Services settled a legal dispute with MGM/UA and Turner Broadcasting over the licensing of films from the MGM/UA film library. Under this agreement, Rainbow Services gave up rights to the films and received $50.0, which was distributed equally to the partners, net of certain legal expenses. The Company recorded a $2.9 post-tax gain on this transaction.

In February 1985, the Company acquired the Ziff-Davis Publishing Company's consumer magazines for $362.5 in cash and the assumption of the subscription liabilities related to the 12 magazines purchased.

In June 1985, the Company acquired a controlling 50 percent interest in Winterland Concessions Company (Winterland) for $7.0 and has therefore accounted for it as a consolidated subsidiary. The Company is also obligated to purchase the remaining 50 percent interest if Winterland's average annual pretax profits (subject to certain adjustments) for the three-year period ending May 31, 1988 exceeds $4.2. The price will be between $6.0 and $36.0, depending upon the level of profits achieved. Winterland is engaged in the design, printing and marketing of merchandise for the music and entertainment industries.

In July 1985, the Company purchased from Taft Broadcasting Company five radio stations in Dallas, Houston, Tampa (two) and Washington D.C. for a cash consideration of $107.5.

These acquisitions were accounted for by the purchase method and the results of operations from the acquisition dates are included in the accompanying financial statements. Had the above acquisitions occurred January 1, 1984, unaudited pro forma data for the years ended December 31, 1985 and 1984 would be as indicated below:

| | Year ended December 31 | |
	1985	1984
Total revenues	$4,803.7	$4,828.2
Income from continuing operations	$ 197.5	$ 247.0
Net income	$ 22.3	$ 161.0
Per share of common stock:		
Income from continuing operations	$ 7.09	$ 8.31
Net income	$ .63	$ 5.42

The pro forma results include adjustments primarily for imputed interest attributable to the financing of these acquisitions, amortization of goodwill and other tangible and intangible assets and estimated income taxes. The results, which are based on various assumptions, are not necessarily indicative of what would have occurred had these acquisitions occurred at the beginning of the respective periods, or the results which may occur in the future. Other smaller acquisitions were also consummated during the period. Had these occurred January 1, 1984, unaudited pro forma results of operations for 1984 and 1985 would not have been materially different.

4. Formation of Joint Ventures (Dollars in millions)

The joint ventures described below were formed during the period 1983-1985. All are accounted for on an equity basis.

The CBS/MTM Company—In December 1984, in a transaction that had no effect on income, The CBS/FOX Company, an equal partnership of the Company and a subsidiary (Fox) of The Twentieth Century-Fox Film Corporation, distributed its Studio Center property equally to the partners, who formed a separate equal partnership to operate the Studio. Concurrently with the formation of this partnership Fox transferred its interest in the partnership to its parent, who sold it to MTM Studios, Ltd. (MTM). CBS paid Fox $5.0 in settlement of certain related tax allocation liabilities, pursuant to The CBS/FOX Company partnership agreement. CBS and MTM each made $1.5 in cash equity contributions to the new partnership, The CBS/MTM Company. Any additional equity contributions will be made equally by the partners as required.

TRINTEX—In February 1984, the Company, IBM Corporation and Sears, Roebuck and Co. completed the formation of TRINTEX, an equal partnership to develop and market a commercial videotex service to persons with personal computers. Videotex is an interactive service that enables persons in homes and offices to call up a wide range of information, to send messages and to perform two-way transactions. The Company is not forecasting the equity contributions which it may make, but its obligation to make equity contributions is limited, by contract, to not more than $83.5. Through December 31, 1985 the Company has contributed $18.8.

CBS Catalogue Partnership—In January 1983, the Company acquired the music publishing business of United Artists Corporation and MGM/UA Entertainment Co., Inc. (MGM/UA) for a cash consideration of $67.8. This transaction also involved (i) a co-publishing arrangement with MGM/UA relating to music created for its motion picture and audio-visual productions over the next five years and (ii) a first negotiation right to distribute audio recordings of future MGM/UA movie soundtracks over the next five years. During 1983, the Company sold certain music publishing print rights and materials at a pretax gain of approximately $4.5, which was included in other income.

In September 1983, the Company completed the sale, at book value, of the music publishing business to the CBS Catalogue Partnership, a limited partnership in which CBS is the general partner and holds a 50 percent partnership interest. The partnership's acquisition of the business was funded by the sale to three institutional investors of $38.8 of notes and $13.9 of partnership interests, and by the sale to the Company of an equal partnership interest. The Company's investment in the limited partnership and its results are included in the CBS/Records Group segment.

5. Extraordinary Credit

During 1984, the Company sold the land immediately east of its headquarters for the construction of an office building. This sale resulted in a post-tax gain of $16.6 million ($.56 per share), recognized as an extraordinary credit in 1984. The post-tax gain was net of $7.5 million in income taxes. The Company retained a 17.5 percent interest as a joint developer in this project. In 1985, the Company's interest was sold as part of its asset disposition program (note 9).

6. Discontinued Operations (Dollars in millions)

On September 30, 1985, the Company decided to discontinue its toys, theatrical films (which includes the internal theatrical films unit, as well as the Company's equity basis investment in Tri-Star Pictures, Inc.) and home computer software (software) operations. In addition, during 1984 the Company discontinued its musical instruments and videodisc pressing operations. There were no discontinued operations in 1983.

Certain properties and assets of the toys operation and the Company's investment in Tri-Star Pictures, Inc. were sold during 1985. The sale of substantially all of the assets of the musical instruments operation was also completed in 1985.

Results of these discontinued operations through the date of discontinuance and including losses on disposal were:

	1985	Year ended December 31 1984	1983
Revenues:			
Videodisc pressing		$ 2.6	$ 19.8
Musical instruments		97.7	124.1
Toys	$103.2	267.5	218.1
Theatrical films	3.4	8.4	12.7
Software	2.1	8.9	2.3
Total	108.7	385.1	377.0
Losses from Operations, net of taxes:			
Videodisc pressing		2.8	2.8
Musical instruments		3.2	1.0
Toys	43.8	42.2	4.4
Theatrical films	8.2	7.0	3.8
Software	4.5	4.3	1.4
Total	56.5	59.5	13.4
Losses on Disposal, net of taxes:			
Videodisc pressing		12.2	
Musical instruments	8.8	30.3	
Toys	91.1		
Theatrical films	14.4		
Software	6.5		
Other		.6	
Total	120.8	43.1	
Gain from Joint Venture Sale of Stock, net of $1.0 in taxes:			
Theatrical films	2.1		
Total Losses, net of taxes:			
Videodisc pressing		15.0	2.8
Musical instruments	8.8	33.5	1.0
Toys	134.9	42.2	4.4
Theatrical films	20.5	7.0	3.8
Software	11.0	4.3	1.4
Other		.6	
Total	$175.2	$102.6	$ 13.4

Tax benefits applicable to losses from operations for years 1985 through 1983 were $60.4, $47.3 and $19.4, respectively, and to losses on disposal were $113.5 and $24.5 for 1985 and 1984, respectively. There were no discontinued operations in 1983.

Losses on disposal in 1985 include total anticipated net operating losses until final disposition for toys, theatrical films and software of $10.4, $3.1 and $1.2, respectively. Losses on disposal in 1984 included net operating losses until final disposition of $.4 for musical instruments.

At December 31, 1985, discontinued operations had current assets of $32.1, noncurrent assets of $54.9, current liabilities of $2.2 and noncurrent liabilities of $1.0.

7. Litigation

Various legal actions, governmental proceedings and other claims against the Company are pending or, with respect to certain claims, unasserted. The types of relief requested in pending matters include injunctions, damages (including, in some instances, treble damages) and revocation of the Company's broadcast licenses. While the Company cannot predict the results of any litigation, it believes that it has meritorious defenses to those actions, proceedings and claims (whether asserted or unasserted). The Company believes that the liability, if any, which may result from such litigation or unasserted claims will not have a materially adverse effect on its consolidated financial position.

8. Income Taxes (Dollars in millions)

The provision for income taxes consisted of the following:

	DOMESTIC			FOREIGN	TOTAL
	Federal	State and Local	Total		
1985					
Income from continuing operations before income taxes			$292.6	$61.7	$354.3
Income tax expense:					
Current	$ 62.3	$19.4	$ 81.7	$21.5	$103.2
Deferred	46.7*	3.2	49.9	7.6	57.5
Investment tax credits	(9.0)		(9.0)		(9.0)
	$100.0	$22.6	$122.6	$29.1	$151.7

> * Relates to tax benefit leases–$39.6; amortization of intangibles–$32.2; depreciation–$11.9; equity income in joint ventures–$(8.3); and other miscellaneous federal tax items–$(28.7).

	DOMESTIC			FOREIGN	TOTAL
	Federal	State and Local	Total		
1984					
Income from continuing operations before income taxes			$473.1	$70.8	$543.9
Income tax expense:					
Current	$171.4	$33.9	$205.3	$37.1	$242.4
Deferred	11.9*	1.1	13.0	(2.4)	10.6
Investment tax credits	(7.5)		(7.5)		(7.5)
	$175.8	$35.0	$210.8	$34.7	$245.5

> * Relates to tax benefit leases–$39.7; amortization of intangibles–$1.3; depreciation–$8.0; equity income in joint ventures–$(5.0); and other miscellaneous federal tax items–$(32.1).

	DOMESTIC			FOREIGN	TOTAL
	Federal	State and Local	Total		
1983					
Income from continuing operations before income taxes			$291.4	$67.9	$359.3
Income tax expense:					
Current	$106.7	$18.4	$125.1	$36.4	$161.5
Deferred	1.9*	3.2	5.1	(2.5)	2.6
Investment tax credits	(5.4)		(5.4)		(5.4)
	$103.2	$21.6	$124.8	$33.9	$158.7

> * Relates to tax benefit leases–$39.8; amortization of intangibles–$1.2; depreciation–$8.2; equity income in joint ventures–$0.0; and other miscellaneous federal tax items–$(47.3).

As of December 31, 1985, the Company had not provided income taxes for the remittance of undistributed earnings of foreign subsidiaries where the intention of the Company is to reinvest such earnings in operations of those subsidiaries. If such earnings, which approximated $110.2 at December 31, 1985, were to be remitted as dividends, the income taxes which would be incurred are estimated at $17.5.

A reconciliation between the Company's effective income tax rates and the statutory federal income tax rate as a percentage of income from continuing operations before income taxes is as follows:

| | Year ended December 31 | | |
	1985	1984	1983
Statutory federal income tax rate	46.0%	46.0%	46.0%
Increase (decrease) in rates resulting from:			
Equity income	(3.8)	(2.8)	(2.3)
Tax benefit leases	(.2)	(.3)	(.5)
Investment tax credits	(2.5)	(1.4)	(1.5)
Foreign subsidiaries income taxation	.2	.4	.7
State and local taxes	3.5	3.5	3.2
Other items, net	(.4)	(.3)	(1.4)
Effective income tax rates	42.8%	45.1%	44.2%

9. Unusual Items (Dollars in millions)

During 1985, the Company underwent a major recapitalization (note 16). It also successfully defended itself against a hostile tender offer. As a result, certain expenses were incurred and the Company instituted specific asset disposition and expense reduction programs designed to streamline its operations and reduce debt. The effect of these activities on 1985 income from continuing operations before taxes was a gain of $11.2, which has been included in Unusual Items in the Company's income statement. The components of the $11.2 are as follows:

Net gain on asset dispositions	$39.3
Repurchase of $50 million of 14 1/2%	
notes payable (note 13)	(8.9)
Special early retirement pension program	
(note 22)	(6.7)
Takeover defense expenses	(12.5)
	$11.2

Excluded from the net gain on asset dispositions are those dispositions classified as discontinued operations (note 6). The major dispositions included are the sale of an interest in a real estate joint venture, the disposition of various domestic and international publishing properties and the sale of a small cable television system.

10. Sale of KMOX-TV (Dollars in millions)

In December 1985, the Company entered into an agreement for the sale of KMOX-TV, its television station in St. Louis, Missouri, for a cash consideration of $122.5. Consummation of the transaction is subject to the approval of the Federal Communications Commission. If consummated, it is anticipated that this transaction will result in a material gain to the Company.

11. Inventories (Dollars in millions)

Inventories are summarized as follows:

| | December 31 | | |
	1985	1984	1983
Finished goods	$122.9	$175.5	$175.8
Work in process	6.8	35.9	40.3
Raw materials	39.6	73.8	75.4
Supplies	4.0	5.3	3.8
	$173.3	$290.5	$295.3

12. Investments (Dollars in millions)

Summarized financial information for 50 percent or less owned companies accounted for by the equity method and for unconsolidated subsidiaries is as follows:

	EQUITY BASIS INVESTMENTS (a)			UNCONSOLIDATED SUBSIDIARIES (b)		
	1985(c)	1984	1983	1985	1984	1983
As of December 31,						
Current Assets	$419.7	$421.5	$270.3	$11.7	$11.9	$10.9
Noncurrent Assets	475.1	351.7	294.7	5.5	8.7	6.8
Current Liabilities	(274.1)	(260.1)	(154.6)	(5.1)	(8.0)	(9.0)
Noncurrent Liabilities	(216.9)	(160.7)	(76.4)	(.2)	(.1)	
Net Assets	403.8	352.4	334.0	11.9	12.5	8.7
Company's Share of Net Assets	176.0	172.0	159.7	11.9	12.5	8.7
Investment Balance Included in Company's Consolidated Balance Sheet (d)	129.7	142.0	110.6	9.0	9.2	2.9
Year ended December 31,						
Revenues	662.2	601.4	398.2	18.1	19.6	17.2
Expenses	576.8	535.6	337.9	19.9	18.3	15.1
Pretax Income (Loss):						
Partnerships	33.9	21.3	18.7			
Corporations	51.5	44.5	41.6	(1.8)	1.3	2.1
Total	85.4	65.8	60.3	(1.8)	1.3	2.1
Net Income (Loss) (e):						
Corporations	26.2	16.9	18.6	(2.1)	.5	.9
Net Income Recognized by CBS	$ 29.4	$ 31.2	$ 17.4	$ —	$ —	$ .1

(a) The Company's share of net assets exceeds the investment balance on the Company's balance sheet primarily because contributed assets of certain investments were recorded on the books of the ventures at fair market value, which exceeded cost, as of the date contributed. (The difference is being amortized as an adjustment to income from the ventures over the estimated lives of the assets in the ventures.) Also, certain provisions for losses were established by the Company in 1985.

(b) The Company believes that restrictions on the repatriation of funds warrant accounting for these subsidiaries on a cost basis and recognizing income on a cash basis. Income is recognized as it is received in the form of dividends.

(c) The Company's equity interest in Tri-Star Pictures, Inc. was sold in 1985 (note 6).

(d) Notes receivable from the Twentieth Century-Fox Film Corporation relating to the formation of The CBS/FOX Company joint venture are excluded from the data in this schedule. The balances amounted to $37.0, $45.5 and $33.5 as of December 31, 1985, 1984 and 1983, respectively. Also excluded is a $75.0 note receivable from The CBS/FOX Company as of December 31, 1985. These notes are included in Investments in the Company's Consolidated Balance Sheets, as are various cost basis investments.

(e) Partnership net income is not available since it is calculated by the individual partners.

13. Long-Term Debt (Amounts in millions)

Long-term debt consisted of the following:

	1985	December 31 1984	1983
10 ⅞% senior notes due 1995	$699.9		
14½% notes due 1992	100.0	$150.0	$150.0
11⅜% notes due 1992	100.0	100.0	
10⅞% sterling notes due 1994	56.9	46.7	
7.85% debentures due 2001	38.9	41.0	41.5
5½% promissory notes due 1991		24.5	28.0
Medium-term notes	112.2		
Other notes and mortgages payable	6.4	15.1	18.7
Reclassified to current debt	(160.0)	(6.5)	(5.7)
	$954.3	$370.8	$232.5

During 1985, in connection with the Repurchase of Shares (note 16), the Company issued $699.9 of 10⅞ percent senior notes and redeemed all of the outstanding 5½ percent promissory notes. In January 1986, the Company repurchased $100.0 of these 10⅞ percent senior notes. The repurchased notes have been reclassified to Other Current Debt in the December 31, 1985 Consolidated Balance Sheet.

Also during 1985, the Company issued $112.2 of privately placed medium-term notes with various interest rates (approximating 10 percent) and maturities through September 30, 1988 and, in December, repurchased $50.0 of the 14½ percent notes for settlement in January 1986. The amount payable is excluded from the above table and classified as Accounts Payable in the December 31, 1985 Consolidated Balance Sheet.

In February 1986, the Company completed transactions whereby it repurchased 10 percent of the outstanding 10⅞ percent sterling notes and defeased the remaining 90 percent. The in-substance defeasance was accomplished through the purchase of £36.0 of United Kingdom Treasury Loan securities which, together with £1.0 in cash, were placed in an irrevocable trust established by the Company for the payment of all future interest and principal on these notes. The repurchased and defeased 10⅞ percent sterling notes have been reclassified to Other Current Debt in the December 31, 1985 Consolidated Balance Sheet.

Other Current Debt consists of the following at December 31, 1985:

Reclassified from long-term debt:	
10⅞% senior notes repurchased	$100.0
10⅞% sterling notes repurchased and defeased	56.9
Current portion of long-term debt	3.1
	160.0
Other	7.9
	$167.9

The terms of the various long-term notes are as follows:

The 10⅞ percent senior notes have a stated maturity of August 1, 1995. The notes, which were issued in connection with the Company's Repurchase of Shares (note 16), are redeemable in whole or in part, at the option of the Company, upon not less than 30 or more than 60 days notice, at any time after August 1, 1992, at 100 percent of their principal amount plus accrued and unpaid interest to the date fixed for redemption. In addition, the Company is prohibited from making cash dividend payments exceeding $150.0 plus 50 percent of consolidated net income (loss) of the Company between June 30, 1985 and the end of the most recent fiscal quarter. The amount available for dividends at December 31, 1985 is $80.2.

The 14½ percent notes are not redeemable prior to June 15, 1989. Thereafter, the notes may be redeemed, in whole or in part, at the option of the Company, at the principal amount thereof together with accrued interest to the date fixed for redemption.

The 11⅜ percent notes are not redeemable before December 20, 1990. Thereafter, the notes may be redeemed, in whole or in part, during the 12-month period beginning December 20, 1990, at a redemption price of 100.50 percent of their principal amount and at their principal amount on or after December 20, 1991, together in each case with accrued interest to the date fixed for redemption. However, if certain events occur involving U.S. taxes or U.S. information reporting requirements, the Company may redeem all the outstanding notes at par value plus accrued interest.

The 10⅞ percent sterling notes, denominated in British pounds, are not redeemable before December 20, 1992. Thereafter, the notes may be redeemed, in whole or in part, during the 12-month period beginning December 20, 1992, at a redemption price of 100.50 percent of their principal amount and at their principal amount on or after December 20, 1993, together in each case with accrued interest to the date fixed for redemption. However, if certain events occur involving U.S. taxes or U.S. information reporting requirements, the Company may redeem all the outstanding notes at par value plus accrued interest.

The 7.85 percent debentures are redeemable, in whole or in part, at the option of the Company, at a redemption price which declines from 103.45 percent of the principal amount during the 12-month period ending July 31, 1986 to 100 percent in 1996 and thereafter. The Company is required to make annual sinking fund deposits of $2.5 in cash or debentures. These deposits commenced on August 1, 1982.

The 5½ percent promissory notes due 1991 were redeemed in 1985.

The aggregate amounts of maturities of the Company's long-term debt for the five years subsequent to December 31, 1985 are as follows.

1986	$ 3.1
1987	56.4
1988	64.1
1989	3.5
1990	3.1
	$130.2

14. Lines of Credit (Dollars in millions)

As of December 31, 1985, the Company had available unused short and long-term credit facilities of $476.7 with a number of banks. Long-term credit agreements of $420.0 expire at various dates not later than November 8, 1990.

15. Leases and Commitments (Dollars in millions)

Rent expense, excluding payments of real estate taxes, insurance and other expenses required under some leases, amounted to $60.2 in 1985, $66.8 in 1984 and $65.6 in 1983. Minimum rental commitments under noncancelable leases at December 31, 1985 amounted to $189.7 payable as follows:

1986	$50.4	1989	$22.8
1987	$41.7	1990	$15.7
1988	$30.7	Thereafter	$28.4

The Company had no significant capital leases.

The Company routinely enters into commitments to purchase the rights to broadcast programs, including feature films and sports events, on television. These contracts permit the broadcast of such properties for various periods ending no later than September 30, 1995. The Company also enters into long-term contracts with recording artists and companies for the production and/or distribution of records and tapes. These contracts cover various periods through December 31, 1993. As of

December 31, 1985 the Company was committed to make payments under such broadcasting and recorded music contracts of $903.3 and $178.1, respectively.

16. Repurchase of Shares (Dollars in millions)

On August 1, 1985, the Company repurchased 6.365 million shares of its common stock for a consideration of $254.9 in cash and $699.9 in 10⅞ percent Senior Notes Due 1995 pursuant to the Offer to Purchase that was made by the Company on July 3, 1985. In addition, the costs associated with the repurchase of shares were $8.1. These shares were retired and the pro rata share of the individual components of Shareholders' Equity related to these shares has been removed from Shareholders' Equity as follows:

Common stock	$ (15.9)
Additional paid-in capital	(58.3)
Foreign currency fluctuations	48.1
Retained earnings	(936.8)
	$(962.9)

17. Common Stock Subject To Redemption

At the time of the Offer to Purchase, as described in note 16, William S. Paley, Founder Chairman, Chairman of the Executive Committee and a director of the Company, owned directly 1,548,091 shares of the Company's common stock, and certain members of his family, a related partnership and certain affiliated trusts (Related Persons) collectively owned 360,155 shares of common stock. Mr. Paley and the partnership entered into an agreement with the Company under which they agreed not to tender any shares owned by them pursuant to the Offer to Purchase. However, Mr. Paley and the Related Persons have the option to sell to the Company, subject to certain limitations, a maximum of 434,489 shares for $150 per share in cash (without interest). The option may not be exercised prior to August 1, 1988, except in the case of the earlier death of Mr. Paley, and will expire on August 1, 1995.

A reclassification to Common Stock Subject to Redemption has been made by the removal from Shareholders' Equity of the pro rata share of the individual components related to the shares covered by the option as follows:

	(In millions)
Common stock	$ (1.1)
Additional paid-in capital	(4.0)
Foreign currency fluctuations	3.3
Retained earnings	(63.4)
	$(65.2)

18. Redeemable Preference Stock

In July 1985, in connection with the Company's Repurchase of Shares (note 16), a series of $1 par value preference stock consisting initially of 1.25 million shares specifically authorized and designated as $10 Convertible Series B preference stock was issued. The net proceeds of the issuance were $123.1 million. The issue has an aggregate liquidation preference of $125 million. Each share is entitled to receive cumulative cash dividends at the rate of $10 per annum, payable in equal quarterly installments. Dividends commenced accruing on August 1, 1985. Additionally, each share of preference stock, which is subject to mandatory redemption on August 1, 1995, is convertible, at the option of the holder, into .6915 of a share of common stock. There were 864,375 common shares reserved for issuance upon conversion of these shares. Upon redemption or in the event of voluntary or involuntary liquidation, each shareholder will be entitled to $100 per share plus any accrued or unpaid dividends. The difference between the redemption value and the net proceeds from the issue is being amortized to retained earnings over 10 years. At December 31, 1985 there were 1.25 million shares of Series B preference stock outstanding.

19. Preference and Common Stock

The Company's certificate of incorporation provides authority for the issuance of 6 million shares of preference stock, $1 par value, and an initial series of preference stock consisting of 3.3 million shares has been specifically authorized and designated as Series A preference stock. In addition, 1.25 million shares have been specifically authorized, designated as Series B preference stock and issued (note 18).

Each share of Series A preference stock, which is redeemable at the Company's option, is convertible into .6886 of a share of common stock. Upon redemption or in the event of voluntary or involuntary liquidation, each shareholder will be entitled to $43.50 per share plus any accrued and unpaid dividends. The aggregate liquidation value at December 31, 1985 was $1.7 million. There were 26,185 common shares reserved for issuance upon conversion of Series A preference stock at December 31, 1985.

Changes in common and Series A preference stock during 1983, 1984 and 1985 were as follows:

| | COMMON | | | | PREFERENCE | |
| | Issued | | Treasury | | Series A | |
	Shares	Amount	Shares	Amount	Shares	Amount
			(In thousands)			
Balance, December 31, 1982	30,639	$76,597	997	$54,906	91	$91
Conversions of preference stock			(16)	(915)	(24)	(24)
Issuances under employee benefit plans			(18)	(868)	—	—
Balance, December 31, 1983	30,639	76,597	963	53,123	67	67
Conversions of preference stock			(6)	(335)	(8)	(8)
Issuances under employee benefit plans	3	7	(33)	(1,488)	—	—
Balance, December 31, 1984	30,642	76,604	924	51,300	59	59
Conversions of preference stock			(14)	(826)	(21)	(21)
Issuances under employee benefit plans	58	145	(24)	(916)		
Retirement of common stock repurchased (note 16)	(6,365)	(15,912)	—	—	—	—
Balance, December 31, 1985	24,335	60,837	886	49,558	38	38
Reclassification to common stock subject to redemption (note 17) . .		(1,086)	—	—	—	—
Balance, December 31, 1985, net of reclassification	24,335	$59,751	886	$49,558	38	$38

20. Stock Rights Plan

Under the terms of the Company's 1983 Stock Rights Plan (as amended), which is administered by a committee of the Board, certain key employees (including officers) of the Company may be granted non-qualified stock options at an exercise price not less than 100 percent of the closing market price of a share of common stock on the date of the grant. These are 10-year options which, unless accelerated under certain defined circumstances, become exercisable 25 percent per year effective one year following the date of the grant, and are coupled with alternative regular stock appreciation rights or alternative limited stock appreciation rights. (Limited stock appreciation rights will become exercisable only if certain defined changes in control or concentration of equity ownership of the Company occur.)

In addition, unless reduced in the discretion of the committee, dividend share credits will be credited to optionees on common stock dividend payment dates, in amounts equal to the number of outstanding options and previously credited dividend share credits times an amount not to exceed the dividend paid, divided by the fair market value of a share of common stock. The maximum number of shares for which options may be granted under the Plan, and dividend share credits credited, is 1.5 million.

Options granted under the Plan to purchase 169,155 shares of common stock were exercisable at December 31, 1985. The number of shares available for option grants and dividend share credits under the Plan were 746,253 shares, 936,233 shares and 1,167,675 shares at December 31, 1985, 1984 and 1983, respectively. During 1985, 1984 and 1983, $5.3 million, $1.0 million and $.3 million, respectively, was charged to income to cover the estimated cost of the Plan.

The following table summarizes the activity under the Plan during the years ended December 31, 1983, 1984 and 1985:

	OPTIONS					
	With Regular Stock Appreciation Rights		With Limited Stock Appreciation Rights			
	Common Shares	Exercise Price	Common Shares	Exercise Price		Dividend Share Credits
Granted..........	70,775	$ 56¼–$ 69⅝	265,450	$ 56¼–$ 69⅝		7,995
Cancelled	(2,400)	56¼– 65	(9,175)	56¼– 65		(320)
Outstanding– December 31, 1983	**68,375**	**56¼– 69⅝**	**256,275**	**56¼– 69⅝**		**7,675**
Granted..........	44,400	76¾	190,325	72 – 76¾		15,311
Exercised			(3,021)	56¼– 69⅝		(177)
Cancelled			(17,791)	56¼– 69⅝		(803)
Outstanding– December 31, 1984	**112,775**	**56¼– 76¾**	**425,788**	**56¼– 76¾**		**22,006**
Granted..........	42,975	108⅞– 118¾	182,299	108⅞– 118¾		11,432
Exercised	(4,838)	56¼– 69⅝	(60,640)	56¼– 76¾		(4,969)
Cancelled	(6,675)	56¼– 76¾	(39,090)	56¼– 118¾		(1,950)
Outstanding– December 31, 1985	**144,237**	**$ 56¼–$118¾**	**508,357**	**$ 56¼–$118¾**		**26,519**

21. Foreign Currency Translation (Dollars in millions)

The accounting for foreign currency translation conforms to Statement of Financial Accounting Standards No. 52. Generally, adjustments for currency exchange rate changes are excluded from net income for those fluctuations that do not impact cash flow.

Net income included foreign currency losses of $6.6, $8.3 and $15.9 for 1985, 1984 and 1983, respectively.

An analysis of the changes to the "Foreign currency fluctuations" component of Shareholders' Equity is as follows:

	Year ended December 31		
	1985	1984	1983
Balance at beginning of year	$(68.2)	$(51.4)	$(50.8)
Translation adjustments and gains and losses from certain hedges, net....................	.2	(16.8)	(.5)
Income taxes related to hedges included above	9.4		(.1)
Retirement of common stock repurchased (note 16)	48.1		
Reclassification to common stock subject to redemption (note 17).................	3.3		
Balance at end of year	$ (7.2)	$(68.2)	$(51.4)

22. Retirement Plans (Dollars in millions)

The Company and certain of its subsidiaries have several pension plans covering substantially all of their employees, including certain employees in foreign countries. The Company's general policy is to fund pension costs accrued to the extent the contributions will be tax deductible. Annual pension costs generally include only current service costs, since the Company's major domestic plans do not have any unfunded prior service cost. The total pension expenses were $26.4, $22.2 and $35.7 for 1985, 1984 and 1983, respectively.

During 1985, the Company made a special one-time offer to allow certain eligible employees to retire early with increased benefits. Acceptances of this offer resulted in an expense of $6.7 which was treated as an unusual item (note 9) in 1985.

A decrease of $16.2 in pension expense in 1984 was attributable to a change in the actuarial assumptions and method used in computing the pension cost of the Company's major domestic plan. In 1983, other changes reduced pension expense by $3.3.

A comparison of accumulated plan benefits and net assets available for the Company's domestic defined benefit plans is presented below:

	1985	January 1 1984	1983
Actuarial present value of accumulated plan benefits:			
Vested	$214.6	$189.3	$182.6
Nonvested	29.7	23.7	21.7
Total	$244.3	$213.0	$204.3
Net assets available for benefits	$471.1	$467.8	$397.6

The weighted average assumed rate of return used in determining the actuarial present value of accumulated plan benefits was 9 percent in 1985 and 1984 and 8.5 percent in 1983.

The Company's foreign pension plans are not required to report to certain governmental agencies pursuant to ERISA and generally do not determine the data as calculated and disclosed above. For those plans, the pension funds and balance sheet accruals exceed the actuarially computed values of vested benefits.

In addition to providing pension benefits, the Company and certain of its subsidiaries provide certain health care and life insurance benefits for retired employees. Substantially all of the Company's non-union employees, other than employees in foreign countries, may become eligible for these benefits when they retire from the Company. Also included are the Company's union employees, where covered by collective bargaining agreements which provide for such benefits. The estimated cost of such benefits is determined actuarially and accrued over the working lives of those employees expected to qualify for these benefits. Accrued costs are contributed to a trust fund annually and were $4.2, $5.6 and $3.2 for 1985, 1984 and 1983, respectively.

23. Additional Information (Dollars in millions)

"Interest and other income" includes interest income, principally from cash equivalents, of $23.5 in 1985, $26.6 in 1984 and $23.7 in 1983, royalty income and income from equity-basis investments (note 12). In 1984, the Company adopted a more preferable method with regard to the manner in which it allocated and amortized the difference between its cost and the higher aggregate fair market value of the assets contributed to The CBS/FOX Company joint venture. As a result, equity income for 1984 was increased $7.1 due to the cumulative adjustment of prior years' amortization. In addition, amortization for 1984 was $4.7 higher than under the previous method.

"Interest and other expenses" includes interest expense of $94.5 in 1985, $29.5 in 1984 and $34.9 in 1983. The total amount of interest cost for the years 1985, 1984 and 1983 was $106.9, $41.2 and $45.7, respectively, of which $12.4, $11.7 and $10.8, respectively, was capitalized as part of the cost of major investments in property, plant and equipment, made-for-television movies and mini-series.

In February 1985, the Company sold *Family Weekly*, a newspaper supplement, at a pretax loss of $4.0 ($2.2 post-tax).

OTHER FINANCIAL INFORMATION

CURRENT COST INFORMATION (Unaudited)

Current cost information is furnished in accordance with the requirements of the Financial Accounting Standards Board (FASB). This information, as explained in more detail below, reflects changes in price levels that were specific to the Company's inventories and property, plant and equipment. Prior years' amounts have been restated in accordance with the restatements of the primary financial statements. For purposes of this data, the redeemable common and preference stock have not been considered to be liabilities and have therefore been excluded from net assets. Adjustments to the current cost information to reflect the effects of general inflation are based on the U.S. Consumer Price Index (Urban).

The Company cautions that there are significant inherent limitations in using this information, for the following reasons:

1. The information is experimental and preparers and users of financial reports have not yet reached a consensus on its usefulness.

2. The disclosures are limited to selected categories of assets and costs and disregard other assets and costs.

3. The information involves the use of many estimates and judgments by management which may differ from the estimates and judgments of other companies.

4. The estimated current cost of property, plant and equipment represents a calculation of the estimated costs that would be incurred if all existing assets could be replaced at year-end. Actual replacement of productive capacity will take place over many years, and in some cases will be accomplished by improvements to existing assets.

Property, Plant and Equipment. The current cost of land was determined on the basis of tax-assessed values and management estimates. In general, the current cost of buildings was estimated by applying appropriate construction cost indices to the acquisition prices of the buildings. The current cost of the remaining components of property, plant and equipment was estimated by applying appropriate industry indices to the historical cost of such assets.

Depreciation expense was computed on the current cost bases of depreciable assets by using the same rates and lives as used in computing historical cost depreciation expense. The total amount of depreciation expense reported on a current cost basis is $99.3 million, compared to $67.6 million in the primary financial statements.

Inventories. The current costs of work in process and finished goods inventories were estimated principally on the basis of costs adjusted to reflect current material, labor and overhead costs. Raw materials and supplies inventories were valued principally at current vendor prices. Constant dollar calculations were used for current cost purposes with respect to motion picture films in accordance with FASB rules. These amounts are included within inventory for inflation accounting purposes. Cost of sales was adjusted to the current cost of inventories at the time of sale.

Income Taxes. As required, no adjustment has been made to the provision for income taxes. As a result, the effective tax rate on a current cost basis is 47.4 percent as compared to 42.8 percent in the primary financial statements.

Income From Continuing Operations. Income from continuing operations adjusted for changes in the Company's specific prices (current cost) of inventories and property, plant and equipment decreased $34.5 million from the historical amounts reported in the primary financial statements. This decrease was primarily attributable to the impact of general inflation.

Current Cost Increase. The inventories and property, plant and equipment held during 1985 increased $43.5 million in value on a current cost basis. Had current costs increased in accordance with the United States general price level, these values would have increased $35.2 million.

Net Monetary Position. The impact of inflation has generated a gain of $30.7 million from the "decline in purchasing power of net amounts owed." This increase is reflective of the increased borrowings in 1985.

Current Cost Trend Data. In 1985, revenues were up slightly on a historical basis over 1984's level but declined on a current cost basis. Income from continuing operations was down on both a historical and current cost basis by approximately one-third from 1984. The decline in net assets at year-end between 1985 and 1984 is due to the Company's recapitalization (note 16).

CONSOLIDATED STATEMENT OF INCOME ADJUSTED FOR CHANGING PRICES (Unaudited)
Year ended December 31, 1985

(Dollars in millions, except per share amounts)

	AS REPORTED IN THE PRIMARY STATEMENTS	ADJUSTED FOR CHANGES IN SPECIFIC PRICES (CURRENT COST)
Revenues:		
Net sales	$4,676.8	$4,676.8
Interest and other income	78.8	78.8
Total revenues	**4,755.6**	**4,755.6**
Expenses:		
Cost of sales	3,103.2	3,126.9
Selling, general and administrative expenses	1,192.2	1,201.6
Interest and other expenses	117.1	118.5
Total expenses	**4,412.5**	**4,447.0**
Income from continuing operations before unusual items and income taxes	**343.1**	**308.6**
Unusual items	11.2	11.2
Income from continuing operations before income taxes	**354.3**	**319.8**
Income taxes	151.7	151.7
Income from continuing operations	**$ 202.6**	**$ 168.1**
Income from continuing operations per common share	**$ 7.27**	**$ 6.00**
Additional Data:		
Gain from decline in purchasing power of net amounts owed		$ 30.7
Increase in specific prices (current cost) of inventories and property, plant and equipment held during the year		$ 43.5
Amount by which these prices would have increased if computed by reference to changes in the general price level		35.2
Excess of increase in specific prices over increase in general price level		$ 8.3
Net assets at year-end	$ 669.7	$ 977.0*

*The current cost of inventories, including motion picture films, and net property, plant and equipment was $206.9 and $836.6, respectively.

FIVE-YEAR COMPARISON OF SELECTED SUPPLEMENTARY FINANCIAL DATA ADJUSTED FOR GENERAL INFLATION (Unaudited)

(Stated in average 1985 dollars, in millions, except per share amounts)

	Year ended December 31				
	1985	**1984**	**1983**	**1982**	**1981**
Net sales and other operating revenues	$4,676.8	$4,709.4	$4,413.0	$4,152.5	$4,259.5
Current Cost Information:					
Income from continuing operations	168.1	256.7	183.8	104.7	176.4
Income from continuing operations per common share	6.00	8.64	6.20	3.73	6.32
Net assets at year-end	977.0	1,517.2	1,503.0	1,522.5	1,533.5
Foreign currency translation and parity adjustment	(8.4)	(39.9)	(30.8)	(26.3)	(13.8)
Amount that increase in general price level was higher (lower) than increase in specific prices of inventories and property, plant and equipment held during the year	(8.3)	10.4	30.0	9.2	93.1
Gain from decline in purchasing power of net amounts owed	30.7	19.4	23.5	14.3	30.5
Cash dividends declared per common share	3.00	2.95	3.02	3.12	3.31
Market price per common share at year-end	114.0	73.77	69.95	65.22	53.74
Average consumer price index	322.2	311.2	298.5	289.5	272.5

QUARTERLY RESULTS OF OPERATIONS *(Unaudited)

(Dollars in millions, except per share amounts)

The following is a tabulation of the quarterly results of operations for the years ended December 31, 1985 and 1984.

	1985	1984	1985	1984
	REVENUES		OPERATING PROFITS	
1st Quarter	$1,101.0	$1,108.9	$ 63.8	$ 91.4
2nd Quarter	1,189.6	1,124.7	203.6	188.3
3rd Quarter	1,117.7	1,075.8	95.8	123.5
4th Quarter	1,347.3	1,330.7	115.4	196.7
	$4,755.6	$4,640.1	$478.6	$599.9
	INCOME FROM CONTINUING OPERATIONS		NET INCOME (LOSS)	
1st Quarter	$ 26.5	$ 43.2	$ 16.8	$ 38.9
2nd Quarter	91.6	88.7	69.3	88.6
3rd Quarter	29.1	56.0	(114.1)	48.8
4th Quarter	55.4	110.5	55.4	36.1
	$202.6	$298.4	$ 27.4	$212.4
	INCOME FROM CONTINUING OPERATIONS PER COMMON SHARE		NET INCOME (LOSS) PER COMMON SHARE	
1st Quarter	$ .89	$ 1.46	$ .56	$1.31
2nd Quarter	3.08	2.98	2.33	2.98
3rd Quarter	1.06	1.88	(4.55)	1.64
4th Quarter	2.23	3.72	2.23	1.22
	$7.27	$10.04	$ .81	$7.15

The sum of 1985 quarterly per share data does not equal the full year amounts due to the repurchase of 6.365 million shares in the third quarter.

*Amounts have been revised for the reclassification of the operating results of the discontinued operations from continuing operations to discontinued operations (note 6). This reclassification had no impact on quarterly net income.

The differences between net income (loss) and income from continuing operations are attributable to the discontinued operations (note 6) and extraordinary credit (note 5).

The net loss for the third quarter of 1985 was due to losses on disposal and the operating results of the discontinued operations (note 6).

SHAREHOLDER REFERENCE INFORMATION

STOCK DATA

The principal market for CBS common stock is the New York Stock Exchange. In addition, it is traded on the Pacific Stock Exchange. There were approximately 19,400 holders of record of CBS common stock as of December 31, 1985. The following table indicates the quarterly high and low prices for CBS common stock as reported in the composite transactions quotations of consolidated trading for issues on the New York Stock Exchange during the past two years:

	1985	1984	1985	1984
Common Stock:	HIGH		LOW	
1st Quarter	$111¼	$72	$ 70⅞	$61½
2nd Quarter	122	80	98	68¼
3rd Quarter	125	87¾	105	76⅛
4th Quarter	126¼	82¾	107⅛	68⅞

DIVIDENDS

Cash dividends of $.75 per share on CBS common stock were paid in the fourth quarter of 1984 and quarterly throughout 1985. Quarterly cash dividends of $.70 were paid during the first three quarters of 1984. The Company is subject to certain restrictions on the payment of dividends on common stock as discussed in note 13.

Quarterly cash dividends of $.25 per share were paid on CBS Series A preference stock during 1985 and 1984. Cash dividends of $1.67 and $2.50 per share were paid on CBS Series B preference stock in the third quarter and fourth quarter of 1985, respectively.

Transfer Agent and Registrar
Morgan Guaranty Trust Company of New York
30 West Broadway
New York, New York 10015

Independent Certified Public Accountants
Coopers & Lybrand
1251 Avenue of the Americas
New York, New York 10020

Form 10-K Annual Report
The Form 10-K Annual Report for CBS to the Securities and Exchange Commission for the Company's 1985 fiscal year is available to shareholders.

This report contains certain financial information and, when appropriate, other matters concerning the Company which are required to be reported to the Commission including information on certain legal proceedings and reports of matters submitted to a vote of shareholders.

Shareholders who wish a copy of this report may obtain one, without charge, upon request to the CBS Investor Relations Department, 51 West 52 Street, New York, New York 10019.

Index